FOUNDATIONS *of*

TROPICAL FOREST

BIOLOGY

FOUNDATIONS

FOREST

Classic Papers with

Published in association with
THE ASSOCIATION FOR TROPICAL BIOLOGY

OF TROPICAL BIOLOGY

Commentaries

EDITORS

Robin L. Chazdon and T. C. Whitmore

THE UNIVERSITY OF CHICAGO PRESS
Chicago & London

ROBIN L. CHAZDON is a professor in the Department of Ecology and Evolutionary Biology at the University of Connecticut and a coeditor of *Tropical Forest Plant Ecophysiology.*   T. C. WHITMORE is an affiliated lecturer in the Department of Geography at the University of Cambridge and the author of seven books, including most recently *An Introduction to Tropical Rain Forests.*

The University of Chicago Press, Chicago 60637
The University of Chicago Press, Ltd., London
© 2002 by The University of Chicago
All rights reserved. Published 2002
Printed in The United States of America
11 10 09 08 07 06 05 04 03 02   5 4 3 2 1

ISBN (cloth): 0-226-10224-6
ISBN (paper): 0-226-10225-4

Library of Congress Cataloging-in-Publication Data

Foundations of tropical forest biology : classic papers with
    commentaries / editors, Robin L. Chazdon and T. C. Whitmore.
        p. cm.
    Includes bibliographical references (p.).
    ISBN 0-226-10244-6 (cloth : alk. paper—ISBN 0-226-10225-4 (alk.
paper)
    1. Forest ecology—Tropics.   2. Forests and forestry—Tropics.
I. Chazdon, Robin Lee, 1957–   II. Whitmore, T. C. (Timothy Charles)

QH84.5 .F68 2002
577.3'0913—dc21
                                                      2001005769

Contents

PART TWO

What Shaped Tropical Biotas as We See Them Today?
T. C. Whitmore   69

PART THREE

PART ELEVEN

Human Impact and Species Extinction
Rodolfo Dirzo and Robert W. Sussman   703

Preface

The idea for this book first took shape at a council meeting of the Association for Tropical Biology (ATB) in August 1998. I was completing my term as ATB president, and the publication of a book like this was one of several fund-raising issues on the table. This idea was initially inspired by the book *Foundations of Ecology* (Real and Brown 1991), an anthology of seminal works with commentaries written by authorities in the field. Our thinking was that a similar book could be developed that would generate funds for the Association for Tropical Biology while contributing a timely synthesis of pioneering research. The idea caught on, and soon I was busy assembling a group of collaborators. Tim Whitmore offered such valuable insights early on that I invited him to serve as a coeditor. It has been a rather smooth ride ever since, mostly due to Tim's editorial skills, extensive experience in the Far East, quick turnarounds, and seemingly limitless knowledge of tropical forest biology and historical events. John Kress, the executive director of ATB, has been highly supportive and enthusiastic throughout the entire process. We have arranged for all of the royalties generated from sales of *Foundations of Tropical Forest Biology* to be donated to ATB and earmarked for special programs, such as travel awards for international meetings.

Susan Abrams's enthusiasm and encouragement have been critical factors throughout. From the start, Susan was excited about this book, and she consistently supported our work at the University of Chicago Press. During those moments when coherence was lacking, or when fretting about delays threatened to disturb my slumber for one too many nights, Susan helped me to regain focus, recharge my batteries, and allay my worries. Jennifer Howard provided much logistical assistance throughout.

Tim and I thank the many individuals who came up with suggestions for reprinted papers and collaborators or who reviewed drafts of part introductions. The list is very long, but I particularly thank Kamal Bawa, Michael Breed, David Clark, Deborah Clark, Jack Ewel, James Mallet, Gordon Orians, Richard Primack, Jay Savage, and Andrew Sugden. Jonathan Coddington provided critical feedback during the initial development of the book. Eldridge Adams and Robert Colwell provided much-needed entomological assistance with several parts. Robert Colwell deserves special appreciation for reading over some drafts of part introductions and for participating in endless odd-hour discussions of tropical and nontropical topics. All of the contributors deserve much commendation for their thorough and authoritative work on the section introductions.

My family has been especially generous and patient during my periods of writing and editing. Dena and Isidore Hauser provided wonderful work space and quiet time during the big push to pull it all together. My children Rachel and Charlie Colwell, through their excitement and awe of the tropics, have given me hope that the next generation will continue to carry the torch for tropical biology.

Robin Chazdon
January 2001

Introduction

Robin L. Chazdon

This book begins with an explanation—and an apology. The original concept was to produce an anthology of classic and foundational works in the field of tropical biology, with an emphasis on tropical forests. Recognizing that all current work has historical precedents, conceptual origins, and methodological antecedents, we set ourselves the explicit goal of bringing these early works into sharp focus within the context of more recent ideas, research, and literature. Tropical biologists today follow a rich tradition of mentors, explorers, and groundbreakers. Here we celebrate these visionary people and their works, on whose foundation the edifice of tropical biology now rests.

A book like this must unavoidably have subjective biases and restrictions. We restricted our focus to terrestrial systems, with an emphasis on moist, wet, or seasonally wet tropical forests, known generally as tropical rain forests. We assembled an international editorial team of prominent researchers representing a range of fields, taxonomic expertise, and geographical experience. We labored to select the most appropriate works, making efforts to include a wide array of geographic regions. The selections that emerged as our consensus were grouped into parts, and introductory commentaries were written for each part to link the reprinted works with ideas and works that reflect the ebb and flow of current tropical biological research.

And now, the apology. Collections such as these invariably omit important works, people, and places. Here I respectfully borrow an apology from William Beebe, one of the world's most renowned tropical ornithologists. A prolific writer of natural history (Beebe 1918, 1921, 1925), Beebe also edited a highly readable anthology of what he considered to be the world's best natural history. In his preface to this anthology he wrote,

labors of an anthologist are and should be full of pleasure, but his reward is invariably lost in sarcastic if not acrimonious criticism both of omission and of commission. This, too, is as it should be, since the personal equation is so great. More than once I have been strongly tempted to base a decision on the toss of a coin, and I should have been wise to include several blank pages in each volume with an invitation to every reader to damn my selection and satisfy his personal convictions with his own choice. (Beebe 1944, ix)

We hope this book will serve as a springboard for the next generation of indefatigable biologists who will investigate, inventory, conserve, and restore the world's tropical forests and the unique diversity of life that dwells therein. We can take courage from a long tradition of achievement, enterprise, and synthesis. *Foundations of Tropical Forest Biology* provides a strong historical perspective; part 1 highlights the contributions and insights of naturalists and explorers dating back to the sixteenth century. Part 2 focuses on geological forces that have shaped the evolution and biogeography of tropical biotas. Ecological and evolutionary perspectives on the origin of tropical diversity are synthesized in part 3, the largest section of the book.

Parts 4 and 5 focus on species interactions in tropical forests. Part 4 emphasizes studies of the interactions between plants and their herbivores, seed predators, pathogens, pollinators, and frugivores, illustrating the ecological consequences of plant-animal interactions on community structure. With a more evolutionary perspective, part 5 examines studies of intricate coevolutionary relationships and specialized mutualistic interactions among plants and animals of tropical forests.

Parts 6, 7, and 8 discuss numerous studies of patterns of species richness and species distributions of arthropods, vertebrates, and plants, respectively. The emphasis in these sections is on description of patterns of species occurrence and associations. Forest dynamics and regeneration are the focus of selections in part 9, and ecosystem processes are discussed in part 10.

Parts 11 and 12 cover foundational works in the realm of conservation biology and tropical forest management. Part 11 focuses on selections dealing with human impact and extinction, whereas part 12 discusses sustainable use of tropical forests and their resources.

These twelve parts treat topics and themes that originated early in the development of tropical biology. Our purpose in identifying these thematic sections is not to represent a comprehensive overview of these topics, but rather to highlight important foundational works that influenced future research and ideas in tropical biology as well as in the encompassing fields of ecology and evolutionary biology. In this regard, this volume is similar to a compilation of papers edited by Carl F. Jordan (1981), which lacked the detailed commentaries. A few papers appear both in this book and in Jordan's.

Newer, more technologically advanced disciplines, such as physiological ecology, canopy biology, and molecular ecology have been deliberately excluded from this volume, although the antecedents are all here, between the lines. Also excluded are nonterrestrial subjects, such as estuarine biology, coral reef biology, tropical marine biology, aquatic biology, and tropical fish biology.

Tropical Biology and Tropical Biologists

It is far easier to define tropical biologists than to define tropical biology. Tropical biology is, simply, what biologists choose to study in the tropics, be it arthropods, birds, plants, mammals, herps, species interactions, behavior, populations, communities, or ecosystems. Tropical biology is about the world's tropical regions, about understanding the evolutionary and ecological processes in the tropics that generate such bewildering diversity of life on earth, and about understanding the functioning of the world's living systems. In a thought-provoking paper, Michael Robinson (1978) raised the question of whether or not "tropical biology" is a phenomenologically distinct subject. He argued that the biology of organisms in rich tropical environments may, in fact, be qualitatively distinct, owing to the extreme complexity of interspecific interactions among tropical organisms. In Robinson's view (also see Robinson 1992), the preeminence of biotic interactions defines the unique feature of tropical biology. Whatever the subject of study within tropical biology, interspecific interactions are ever-present elements. Yet many have questioned whether evolutionary or ecological processes in the tropics are qualitatively or quantitatively distinct from those in other climatic regions of the world. These questions justifiably permeate most of the sections of this book, and are specifically addressed in part 3.

In the preface to his book, Jordan (1981) proposed that higher species richness and higher process rates set tropical ecosystems apart from temperate ecosystems. He linked foundational studies of species richness in the tropics to key insights that contributed to the development of the field of ecology. Moreover, these studies stimulated the development of evolutionary theory and fostered the growth of applied fields, such as tropical forest management, agroforestry, and agricultural ecology. *Foundations of Tropical Forest Biology* provides ample evidence in support of Jordan's proposition.

The Legacy of Colonial Empires

Not surprisingly, the legacy of tropical biology has followed the forces of geopolitical history. As discussed in part 1, European colonial empires dominated the development of scientific knowledge in the world's tropical regions through the nineteenth century (see also Whitmore 1993). This history is still much in evidence today, although Europe no longer dominates the world scene. In 1999, the largest group of first authors of articles published in *Biotropica*, the journal of the Association for Tropical Biology, were North Americans, followed by South Americans and Europeans

(Braker 2000). These trends parallel scientific publication trends worldwide; a recent study found that 70 percent of all scientific papers published from 1991 to 1998 were written by authors from western Europe and North America (Gálvez et al. 2000). The tendency for British field biologists to conduct research and collecting expeditions in the African and Asian tropics continues to this day, whereas North Americans tend to focus on Central and South America. These trends are reflected in the two leading international journals of tropical biology. *Biotropica* is biased toward Neotropical studies, whereas the *Journal of Tropical Ecology* is biased toward Paleotropical studies. Educational and research infrastructures are rapidly developing and maturing in tropical countries (Gálvez et al. 2000), and tropical nations are justly reclaiming patrimony over genetic resources and natural wealth. These positive changes are ushering in a new era of tropical biological research and applications, driven increasingly by the needs of tropical nations and their peoples.

The world is shrinking and the reach of tropical biology now knows no geographical bounds. International projects such as those spawned by the International Biological Program (IBP), UNESCO's Man in the Biosphere (MAB) program, large-scale and long-term biotic inventories, monitoring projects, and comparative descriptive and experimental studies in tropical forest regions throughout the globe constitute major research efforts today (Dallmeier and Comiskey 1998, 1999; Gentry 1990b).

Defining Moments in Tropical Biology

The publication of Paul Richards's textbook *The Tropical Rain Forest* in 1952 was a defining moment in tropical biology (Richards 1952). Whitmore (1993) views this landmark book as the culmination of the "colonial" phase of tropical forest study. This volume, based on three periods of a few months of study in Guyana, Sarawak, and Nigeria, galvanized interest in tropical forest biology and ecology throughout the world. The first edition was reprinted six times, and a second edition was published in 1996

(Richards 1996). Although both editions have a decidedly botanical orientation, the second, in particular, is an essential resource for any tropical biology student. A few more textbooks focusing on tropical rain forests have appeared within the last twenty years, providing authoritative general resources for students and practitioners (Jacobs 1988; Leigh 1999; Longman and Jenik 1987; Mabberly 1992; Whitmore 1984b, 1998).

The first organization dedicated specifically to the study of tropical nature was the Bombay Natural History Society, founded in 1883. In 1909 the East African Natural History Society was formed in Nairobi, Kenya, and the Malaysian Nature Society was founded in 1940. It wasn't until the second half of the twentieth century, however, that academic tropical biologists began to form professional societies, organize international symposia, publish journals, manage field stations, and offer international field courses in the tropics. The International Society for Tropical Ecology was founded in India in 1956, and the society began publishing a journal, *Tropical Ecology,* in 1960. Several international symposia have also been organized by the society (Misra and Gopal 1968). In 1961, Paul Richards, while president of the British Ecological Society, spearheaded the effort to form its Tropical Ecology Group, which became the society's first specialist group. This action resulted in a large influx of new members (Sheail 1987). Meanwhile, across the Atlantic, the Association for Tropical Biology was formed in 1963 to promote research and to foster the exchange of ideas, primarily among North American biologists working in tropical environments.

Educational and research consortia focusing on tropical biology began to develop at about the same time as these professional societies. In 1960, a conference sponsored by the U.S. National Science Foundation was held in Miami to examine the status of teaching and research on tropical plants. The conference led to a series of recommendations to enhance teaching and research in the tropics (National Research Council 1960), and stimulated the design of a field course, Fundamentals of Tropical Biology, taught in Costa Rica in 1961 (Stone 1988). In 1963 the Organization for Tropical Studies was founded as a consortium of educational and research institutions dedicated to biological training, research, and service in the tropics and began offering graduate-level field courses in Latin America (Stone 1988). The Tropical Biological Association followed a similar path in Europe, with field courses in Africa beginning in 1994. Intensive field courses, in both the Old and New World tropics are training a new generation of biologists from tropical and nontropical countries who are future leaders in education, research, and resource management in their home countries. The next generation of tropical biology field courses will likely involve visits to multiple continents.

The last forty years have seen a proliferation of specialty journals in tropical biology and tropical ecology. These include *Tropical Ecology, Biotropica, Ecotropica, Revista de Biología Tropical, Journal of Tropical Forest Science, Journal of Tropical Ecology, Tropics,* and *Tropical Ecology Letters.* The latter two journals reflect major tropical research contributions by Japanese ecologists. As always, research papers in tropical biology are published in an exceedingly wide array of journals, in many subject areas, and in many languages.

The 1970s ushered in a new era of tropical biology. The term "tropical rain forest" became commonplace, appearing on bookstore shelves, in the nightly news, and in daily newspapers. The tide of attention that focused on deforestation and its consequences in the tropics as well as other global environmental concerns stimulated governmental and nongovernmental action (Myers 1980) and development of new research and conservation programs and helped trigger the first United Nations Conference on the Environment in Stockholm in 1972. Twenty years later, at the second United Nations Conference on Environment and Development in Rio de Janeiro, the UN Conventions on Biological Diversity and on Climate Change were drafted.

This chain of events led to the veritable explosion of research and ideas in tropical biology during the late twentieth century. Worldwide concerns about tropical deforestation, species extinction, and global climate change continue to stimulate international interest in tropical biological diversity, conservation, and restoration. Large-scale, multitaxa biodiversity inventories are being conducted in several tropical countries, including Costa Rica, Mexico, Brazil, and Australia. In 1999, the first international conference on ecological restoration in the tropics was held in Puerto Rico (Holl and Kappelle 1999). It is now widely recognized that tropical organisms, their interactions, and their ecosystems are essential subjects of ecological and evolutionary inquiry. These developments signal that the field of tropical biology has now come of age. The papers reprinted in this book, along with the introductory commentaries, give us an ample opportunity to look back as well as to look forward. We still have much to do.

1 Tropical Naturalists of the Sixteenth through Nineteenth Centuries

Robin L. Chazdon and the Earl of Cranbrook

An earnest desire to visit a tropical country, to behold the luxuriance of animal and vegetable life said to exist there, and to see with my own eyes all those wonders which I had so much delighted to read of in the narratives of travellers, were the motives that induced me to break through the trammel of business, and the ties of home, and start for some far land where endless summer reigns.

—A. R. Wallace, *A Narrative of Travels on the Amazon and Rio Negro* (London: Ward, Lock and Co., 1889)

The story of tropical biology begins with naturalists—explorers with a keen curiosity, an eye for variation, and a passion for collecting. Cartographers, missionaries, collectors, and chroniclers set out from their home bases in Europe to discover new worlds and to document the riches they discovered. These trailblazers brought home a new vision that changed the world in countless ways. Their many published works still speak to us today. In this part we highlight works of these pioneering tropical biologists, some of whom never lived to see their major works in print.

Naturalists of the Early Colonial Period

Sixteenth- and seventeenth-century missionaries and explorers laid the groundwork for later scientific expeditions by beginning the process of documenting the biological riches of tropical regions of the New and Old Worlds (von Hagen 1951). Gonzalo Fernández de Oviedo y Valdés spent thirty-four years in the New World as a colonial administrator and royal chronicler to King Ferdinand of Spain. Oviedo's famous *Sumario de la natural história de las Indias* was published in 1526 in Spanish, English, and French. José de Acosta, a Jesuit priest sent to Peru as a missionary, published *História natural y moral de las Indias* in 1590. This treatise on native life, medical flora, and diseases of the New World enjoyed phenomenal success in Europe. Early in the seventeenth century, the Dutch prince Maurice von Nassau-Siesgen traveled to Recife, Brazil, with fellow European naturalists and collected many botanical and zoological treasures, surpassing anything done earlier in the Americas. These collections were studied by Georg Marcgrave and Willem Piso, the first European scientists to study the flora and fauna of Brazil (F. Ortiz-Crespo, personal communication).

Compared to other centuries, however, the

Alexander von Humboldt (standing) and Aimé Bonpland with their collections from the Orinoco region. (Engraving by O. Roth)

seventeenth was a "sterile century" for natural history in the Hispanic world—not a word was published during this time of inquisitions, prohibitions, and exclusivism (von Hagen 1951). Elsewhere in Europe, however, the lamp of curiosity burned as brightly as before. As natural sciences developed alongside advances in medical understanding, the seafaring nations of northwestern Europe extended ever further into the tropical world, in exploration for trade and discovery for its own sake. The coasts of Africa, India, Ceylon, the East Indies, and beyond were visited and trading outposts established. The Dutch had strong interests in botany. Their universities were equipped with botanical gardens and heated houses to cultivate tender tropical plants (Burkill 1965).

The Dutch East India Company set its capital at Batavia on Java, in the early part of the seventeenth century, and its officer Georg Everard Rumpf (Latinized as Rumphius) was soon settled further east in Amboina in the Moluccas. In 1662, Rumphius set out to make a systematic study of the flora, fauna, and geology of Amboina and arranged a leave of absence to devote himself full time to natural history endeavors (Sirks 1945). Disaster struck in 1670, when he went blind. Four years later, he lost his wife and youngest daughter in a violent earthquake. As if these disasters weren't enough, his books, collections, and manuscripts were destroyed by fire in 1687, and then the manuscript of his major work, *Amboinsche Kruidboek* (also known as *Herbarium Amboinense*), was lost at sea (although a copy survived). This and his other great work, *Amboinsche Rariteitkamer*, were published posthumously. In this monumental work, Rumpf describes and illustrates the organisms of the seas surrounding Ambon Bay, as well as minerals and rare concretions taken from animals and plants. An English translation is now available for the first time, under the title *The Ambonese Curiosity Cabinet* (Rumpf 1999). Yet, in his lifetime, through his specimens and correspondence, descriptions, and anecdotes of the natural history of this tropical region, Rumphius became known to the world of scholars and educated

people generally. His floristic descriptions laid the foundations for a knowledge of the vegetation of Amboina and other islands of the Malay Archipelago. Moreover, as a precursor of the binary nomenclature of Linnaeus, he developed a system for naming crustaceans based on two names, a generic name followed by an adjectival one to describe the species (Sirks 1945). Heinrich van Rheede tot Draakestein (1636–1691), the governor of the Dutch possessions in Malabar, is also well known for the collections and descriptions of plants of the Malabar Coast in his monumental work *Hortus Malabaricus*, which was heavily dependent on local knowledge (Went and Went 1945, Burkill 1965, Larsen 1989).

The expansion of the British East India Company in India and beyond similarly engendered a flood of returning specimens, stories, and surveys of the natural history of South Asia. In Britain, 1628 saw the publication of the first compendious bird book in English, Francis Willughby's *Ornithology*. The book was compiled by the famous botanist John Ray (1678), who drew on the variety of written sources available to him, covering familiar native species as well as exotics from unknown parts of the world.

The Enlightenment turned things around in the eighteenth century; international collaborative ventures blossomed. Louis XIV asked King Philip V of Spain for permission to send a scientific expedition to Quito, Ecuador. The French scientist Charles Marie de La Condamine joined with Pedro Vicente Maldonado, a renowned cartographer born in Riobamba, to explore the Esmeraldas forest and to undertake the first scientific descent of the Amazon. La Condamine's expeditions led to the first botanical description of rubber, chemical tests on curare poison, and the first collections of quinine plants (von Hagen 1951). Accompanying the expedition was the French botanist Joseph de Jussieu, who spent thirty-five years collecting in Ecuador. In 1749, Jussieu sent specimens of coca back to Paris, but later suffered a terrible loss when boxes of his specimens were stolen by a thief who mistook them for precious commercial merchandise (Acosta-Solis 1968). La

Condamine's account, *Relation abrégée d'un voyage fait dans l'intérieur de l'Amérique méridionale,* published in 1745, stimulated an entire century of Spanish exploration in South America.

The Influence of Linnaeus

The stability that Carl von Linnaeus brought to systematics in the mid-eighteenth century inspired a new emphasis on identification and classification of species. Botanical discoveries abounded when the Spaniard Jose Celestino Mutis traveled to New Granada (now Colombia) in 1760 as a physician to the viceroy. Accompanying Mutis was Pehr Löfling, a favorite pupil of Linnaeus, who died before he could write about his experiences (von Hagen 1951). Mutis organized a botanical expedition and trained many native South American naturalists, while maintaining correspondence with Linnaeus (Mutis 1760–90). His thirteen-volume *Flora Bogota* was never entirely finished. Over a hundred boxes of botanical specimens, 6,840 drawings of plants, and four thousand pages of manuscript still reside in the Spanish national archives (von Hagen 1951). Since 1988 eighteen volumes of the "Mutis Flora" have been published (Castroviejo 1989). Also remaining in the Spanish archives are many collections and writings of Hipólito Ruiz and José Pavón, who collected during a 1777–1778 expedition to Chile and Peru. Many of their collections fell victim to fire, a grounded ship, and lack of funds (von Hagen 1951). Padre Juan de Velasco, born in Ecuador in 1727, published a four-volume work on the natural history of Ecuador (Velasco 1789, Acosta-Solis 1968). Alexandre Rodrigues Ferreira from Bahia, Brazil, led a scientific pilgrimage along the Amazon and elsewhere in Brazil, collecting thousands of well-preserved and carefully labeled specimens. Ferreira's discoveries were documented in his book *Viagem Filosófica* (1783–1792). His specimens, including many Neotropical monkeys and marmosets, were sent to Lisbon, where they were later plundered by Napoleon's troops and brought to the Paris Natural History Museum (F. Ortiz-Crespo, personal communication).

Eighteenth-century British naval expeditions left more than a legacy of naval charts. In 1768, Captain James Cook set out in the *Endeavour* to Tahiti to observe the transit of Venus (Raby 1997). On board were two naturalists, Joseph Banks and Douglas Solander, a pupil of Linnaeus. Banks later became president of the Royal Society for forty-two years and helped found the Royal Botanic Gardens at Kew. The new map of the world, based on Cook's voyages, testified to the treasury of newly discovered plants—Point Solander and Cape Banks define the extreme points of Botany Bay on the New South Wales coast (Raby 1997). The African Association was formed in 1788 to promote exploration and provided a focus for a series of British-sponsored expeditions in the late eighteenth century (Raby 1997). Banks was one of the founders and Baron Alexander von Humboldt signed on as a member. Banks helped to arrange the African voyage of Mungo Park to visit Timbuktu and the Niger River in 1795. This and subsequent expeditions produced few contributions to natural history of equatorial Africa, however. It wasn't until the late nineteenth and early twentieth centuries that scientific exploration in equatorial Africa yielded biological riches (Worthington 1938).

The influence of Linnaeus spread quickly to the Indian subcontinent, where botanical collecting and cultivation blossomed during the eighteenth century. In 1778, the Dutch East India Company contracted Johann Gerhard Koenig, a protégé of Linnaeus, as a naturalist, to make trips to Siam and the Malay Peninsula for the purpose of tracing the origins of spices and medicinal plants (Burkill 1965). Koenig was the first of a long succession of botanists and naturalists who worked out of Madras, including William Roxburgh and ending in 1828 with Robert Wight. Koenig first traveled to Madras in 1768 to join other Danish missionaries at their Royal Danish Mission at Tranquebar. The Madras botanists did much to promote botanical exploration in India (Burkill 1965). Their botanical legacy includes Roxburgh's three-volume *Flora Indica* (published posthumously in 1820–24) and Wight and Arnott's

Prodromus Florae Peninsulae Indiae Orientalis (1834).

The Legacy of Alexander von Humboldt

While a student at the University of Göttingen, Alexander von Humboldt (1769–1859) met Georg Forster, who had been with Captain Cook on his second voyage and published an account of the expedition. The two traveled together in 1790 to France and England, where Humboldt became influenced by Forster's experience in scientific traveling and writing (Nicholson 1995). In 1798, Humboldt met Aimé Goujaud Bonpland, a physician and amateur botanist, in Paris, where they had both been invited to join a French expedition around the world. The venture was cancelled and the two traveled to Spain, where they found the Spanish ministers eager to support their proposal for a scientific expedition to Spanish America.

Humboldt has probably exerted more influence than any other tropical naturalist. His five years of exploration in South and Central America from 1799 to 1804 produced a rich scientific harvest. He and Bonpland traversed ten thousand kilometers on foot and by canoe, collecting twelve thousand plant specimens—three thousand of which were new species. They doubled the number of plant species known in the Western Hemisphere (Raby 1997). Their *Voyage aux Régions équinoxiales* occupies thirty volumes and cost Humboldt his entire fortune to publish (Stearn 1968). Although Humboldt attributed all thirty volumes to Bonpland and himself, Bonpland authored only one of the volumes (Wilson 1995). The first English translation of this work was published between 1814 and 1829 in five volumes under the title *Personal Narrative of Travels to the Equinoctial Regions of the New Continent during the years 1799–1804.* Humboldt's *Essai sur la geographie des plants* (1805) firmly established plant geography as a scientific discipline. To Humboldt we also owe the concepts of plant associations, life forms, and isotherms (Stearn 1968). In the words of the young Simón Bolí-

var, "Baron Humboldt did more for the Americas than all the conquistadores" (Wilson 1995, xxxix).

Perhaps the most lasting legacy of Humboldt is the spark that he ignited in the next generation, creating a wave of European biological exploration. The mid-nineteenth century witnessed a new breed of explorer-naturalists, "scientific entrepreneurs," many of whom were not subsidized by family wealth or government sponsorship. Charles Darwin, one of the last independently wealthy amateur naturalists, spent five years exploring South America as an unpaid naturalist aboard the *Beagle* (Desmond and Moore 1991, Desmond 1994). On board he carried a copy of Humboldt and Bonpland's *Personal Narrative,* a gift from J. S. Henslow, his Cambridge professor of botany. From Santa Cruz in 1832, Darwin wrote in a letter to Henslow,

Here I first saw a Tropical forest in all its sublime grandeur. Nothing, but the reality can give any idea, how wonderful, how magnificent the scene is. . . . I never experienced such intense delight. I formerly admired Humboldt, I now almost adore him; he alone gives any notion of the feelings which are raised in the mind on first entering the Tropics. (Wilson 1995, Raby 1997, 19)

In his old age, Alfred Russel Wallace wrote that *Personal Narrative* was "the first book that gave me a desire to visit the tropics" (Stearn 1968, 122).

It is therefore fitting to begin this volume of key papers with Humboldt's words. A brief selection from volume 3 of his *Personal Narrative* describes his overall impression of tropical climates and scenery. A second selection from volume 5 discusses intriguing global patterns of plant distribution. Here, Humboldt is grappling with the notion that climate alone cannot explain the unique geographic distribution of certain plant groups. Reading these selections provides a sense of Humboldt's eloquent synthesis of scientific observation and poetry. If you have the opportunity to read the entire work, you will not waste a moment of your time. There is still plenty of inspiration lurking within these yellowed pages. A considerably less flowery (but abridged) translation of Humboldt's *Personal Narrative* by Jason Wilson was published in 1995.

Early Nineteenth-Century and Victorian Naturalists

The Amazon attracted the greatest concentration of Victorian naturalists. Historian Peter Raby (1997) writes, "The great triumvirate of Amazon naturalists, Bates, Wallace, and Spruce, followed in Humboldt's footsteps—literally, in the case of Wallace and Spruce—as they quartered the forest of the Amazon basin and the Andean foothills" (13–14). Alfred Russel Wallace and Henry Walter Bates were inspired to travel to South America after reading Darwin's *Voyage of the Beagle* (1839) and especially William Henry Edwards's *A Voyage up the River Amazon* (1847), as well as *Personal Narrative*. In 1848 Wallace and Bates set sail for Pará, present day Belém. Wallace was to spend four years and Bates eleven years in the Amazon Basin. Lacking university education, they were eager, self-taught collectors of meager means who supported their travels by selling specimens to dealers in London.

While in the Amazon, Bates collected 14,712 species, 14,000 of them insects. No fewer than eight thousand of the species he collected were new to science. He spent four and a half years in the Upper Amazon at his headquarters on the mouth of the Rio Tefé, collecting and making observations on insects. On his return to Britain he published *The Naturalist on the River Amazons* in 1862. This book depicts Bates's experiences in the Amazon in vivid detail, highlighting his passion for collecting, classification, and behavioral studies. We reprint a description of army ants that illustrates his keen powers of observation and biological insight, as well as his engaging writing style. Bates became the secretary of the Royal Geographical Society in London and came to be best known for his studies of mimicry in insects (see part 5). Before Darwin's *Origin of Species* was published, Bates wrote, "Nature writes,

as on a tablet, the story of the modification of species" (Bates 1864, 413).

Wallace combined the mind of a scientific inquirer with the enthusiasm of a collector (Raby 1997, Knapp 1999). He worked out the theory of natural selection independently from Darwin, writing to Bates as early as 1848, "I should like to take some one family to study thoroughly, principally with a view to the origin of species. By that means I am strongly of opinion that some definite results might be arrived at" (Beddall 1969, 3). Wallace explored extensively up the Rio Negro, penetrating further up the Uaupés River than any previous European traveler (Raby 1997, Knapp 1999). After four years of enthusiastic collecting, his health failing from malaria and intestinal difficulties, Wallace boarded the steamer *Helen* to return to England. Here he met tragedy when the ship caught fire and his entire collection (including a large assortment of live animals) went up in flames. Fortunately, Wallace was rescued, as were one parrot and his journal notes from the beginning and end of his trip. Three days after returning to England, Wallace attended a meeting of the Royal Entomological Society, his ankles so swollen that he could scarcely stand up (Raby 1997). Within one year, he published *A Narrative of Travels on the Amazon and Rio Negro* (1853). He had not lost his zeal for exploration and promptly began preparations for his next journey, this time to the Malay Archipelago under the sponsorship of the Council of the Royal Geographical Society. Wallace was no longer an amateur naturalist—he was now a recognized scientist and professional collector.

Wallace spent eight years in the Malay Archipelago, collecting 125,660 specimens of animals, of which 88,200 were Coleoptera. He wrote *On the Law Which Has Regulated the Introduction of New Species* in 1855 while in Sarawak. This monumental work, Wallace's first attempt at conceptual biology, is relatively poorly known, yet it is one of the historical landmarks of evolutionary biology (Quammen 1996). Here we reprint the first nine pages. In 1858, while in Ternate in the Moluccas recovering from an attack of malaria, Wallace sent an outline of his theory (*On the Tendency of Varieties to Depart Indefinitely from the Original Type*) to Darwin, which precipitated the long-delayed publication of Darwin's book *On the Origin of Species* (Beddall 1969, Desmond and Moore 1991, Quammen 1996, Raby 1997). He recorded his discoveries in *The Malay Archipelago* (1869) and *Island Life* (1880). *Tropical Nature*, published much later (1895), firmly established Wallace's founding role in tropical biology. The section of *Tropical Nature* reprinted here, "Concluding Remarks on Tropical Vegetation," highlights observations that stimulated research in tropical forests for over a hundred years. These observations include latitudinal gradients of diversity at the species level and higher taxonomic levels, the diversity of higher life forms in the tropics, spacing and low density of tropical tree species, niche partitioning of plant species, climatic stability and uniformity, recruitment limitation, and stochastic events that prevent competitive exclusion and monopolization of resources (see parts 3 and 9).

Throughout his time in the East, Wallace kept in correspondence with Bates (still in Amazonia), Darwin, and Richard Spruce, who was then collecting plants in the Andes. Spruce, another self-taught naturalist of humble origins, did for tropical botany what Bates and Wallace did for tropical entomology. In his first eighteen months on the lower Amazon he collected over eleven hundred species of plants. During his fifteen years in South America he amassed over thirty thousand specimens, more than seven thousand species. Although his abiding interest was in cryptogamic botany, Spruce opened up the Amazon to modern botany. His dedication to collecting is well illustrated by the following remark that he made while sitting on the upper deck of the two-deck steamer *Monarca* on the Solimões River in the Upper Amazon. Surveying the vegetation whizzing by, he laments, "There goes a new *Dipteryx*, there goes a new *Qualea*—there goes a new 'Lord knows what.' I could no longer bear the sight, and covering my face with my hands, I resigned myself to the sorrowful reflection that I must

leave all these fine things to waste their sweetness on the jungle air" (von Hagen 1945, 277). Spruce did leave some fine things for future botanists to discover. He returned to England in 1864 and headed straight to the Royal Botanic Gardens at Kew to identify his many collections. Spruce died in 1893, before his major work was published. Following his death, Wallace, a close friend for more than fifty years, took on the task of editing a two-volume collection of his botanical papers, letters, journals, and geographical articles entitled *Notes of a Botanist on the Amazon and Andes* (Spruce 1908). This collection is a landmark publication that might well have achieved the greatness of *Voyage of the Beagle* had Spruce himself published it (von Hagen 1945).

South America was not the only New World frontier for Victorian naturalists. In 1868, Thomas Belt traveled to Nicaragua to be superintendent of the mining operations of the Chontales Gold-Mining Company. He remained there until 1872 and began to write *The Naturalist in Nicaragua* on the voyage home. Darwin considered his book, published in 1874, to be "the best of all natural history journals which have ever been published." A geologist by training, Belt was a keen observer of nature and recorded many details referred to later by Wallace and others. Although less known than that of Bates, Wallace, or Spruce, Belt's work has made significant contributions to tropical biology. He was the first to document the intricate association between the bull's horn acacia and the *Pseudomyrmex* ants that inhabit the thorns (part 5). We reprint in this part a selection from *The Naturalist in Nicaragua*, in which Belt describes the feeding and nesting behavior of leaf-cutting ants and proposes the novel idea that these ants cultivate an edible fungus using leaf fragments as substrate.

At the height of European colonial rule, national policies dictated the establishment of state repositories in major European cities and smaller republics. Natural history exploration became part of a political strategy for colonial development. Intensive rivalries developed among European powers for collecting and classifying the natural wealth of tropical Asia. Thomas Stamford Raffles, an administrator of the British East India company (and founder of Singapore) drafted the zoological catalogue of his Sumatran collections (1821) in a hurried race to beat his colleagues Diard and Duvaucel, who were intent on sending material to Paris. The Dutch set the pace in Indonesia, establishing the Natuurkundige Commissie voor Nederlandsch-Indie in 1820 specifically to investigate the natural history of regions under Dutch administration. Under the general editorship of C. J. Temminck, the *Verhandelingen over de Natuurlijk Geschiedenis der Nederlandsche Overzeesche Bezittinger* (1839–1845) was a landmark publication. The botanic garden at Buitenzorg (Bogor), Java was founded by the Dutch colonial government in 1817.

Nineteenth century explorers and naturalists fanned out to other remote tropical regions of the globe. In 1807, Nathaniel Wallich (originally named Nathan Wulff), a young Danish surgeon and pupil of Martin Vahl, went to practice medicine in Serampore, a Danish settlement near Calcutta (Larsen 1989). Wallich eventually became superintendent of the botanic garden in Calcutta. During a leave from 1828 to 1832, he traveled to Britain, transporting his massive plant collection, consisting of twenty tons of dried specimens and twenty tons of living plants (Larsen 1989). There he gathered together a number of botanists, George Bentham among them, to sort through and catalogue the material. With the assistance of many botanists, Wallich published the three-volume *Plantae Asiaticae Rariores*.

Botanical exploration in India continued through the work of dedicated British botanists. Joseph Hooker landed a position as the ship's assistant surgeon and botanist on the *Erebus* in 1839. After seeing much of the Southern Hemisphere he yearned to visit the tropics and made his way to Calcutta and the Himalayas (Raby 1997). Hooker was a superb plant collector and exported many live specimens back to Kew. Hooker became director of Kew and later went on to publish the *Flora of British India* (the last volume was published in 1887) with

contributions from many other botanists. Another of Darwin's compatriots, Thomas Henry Huxley, sailed on the *HMS Rattlesnake* in 1846 as the ship's assistant surgeon to survey the Great Barrier Reef, east coast of Australia, and eastern New Guinea (Desmond 1994). In the *Diary of the Voyage of the Rattlesnake*, Huxley's scientific studies focused on marine life, jellyfish in particular.

Odoardo Beccari, an Italian botanist, spent two and a half years in Sarawak (1865–68), where he collected over four thousand specimens, including many fertile samples obtained by tree climbers (Cranbrook 1986). He made later trips to Ethiopia and New Guinea, collecting extensively. His book, *Nelle Foreste di Borneo* was published in Florence in 1902 and in English translation as *Wanderings in the Great Forests of Borneo* in 1904. Beccari later became the world's foremost authority on palms and has been widely recognized for the quality and diversity of his collections, which also included marine algae, dipterocarps, beetles, orangutans, and two hundred Papuan human skulls. Beccari is known for making outstanding, complete botanical specimens with both flowers and fruit. Many specimens were accompanied by copious notes, descriptions, and splendid drawings (Pichi Sermolli and Steenis 1983). His account of Bornean forests is a vivid record of the diversity of tropical plant life (Cranbrook 1986).

Among vertebrate natural history subjects, birds led the way. T. T. C. Jerdon was employed as a surgeon general in the Madras Army, but he apparently spent much of his time on his natural history interests, which encompassed all vertebrates. In 1862 he published *The Birds of India* and in 1867 *The Mammals of India; a Natural History of all the Animals Known to Inhabit Continental India*. Both were landmark publications. During this same period, Henry Forbes from Scotland traveled throughout the Malay Archipelago, having been inspired by the publication of Wallace's *The Malay Archipelago* in 1869. Forbes focused primarily on birds, butterflies, and beetles and, like Wallace, was fascinated by the native peoples he encountered, their physical appearance, dress, behavior, and languages. His account of his travels, *A Naturalist's Wanderings in the Eastern Archipelago* (1885) abounds with detailed descriptions and species lists. Witnessing the disappearance of much of Java's original forest, Forbes's words resonate today: "Our children's children will search in vain in their travels for the old forest trees of which they have read in the books of their grandfathers; and to make their acquaintance, they will have to content themselves with what they can glean from the treasured specimens in various herbaria, which will then be the only remains of the extinct vegetable races" (Forbes 1885, 132).

Nineteenth-century exploration in equatorial Africa continued where Mungo Park and others had left off with the travels of Paul Du Chaillu in Gabon. Du Chaillu, a French-American blend of hunter, naturalist, explorer, and journalist, traveled thirteen thousand kilometers in Gabon, amassing over two thousand bird collections (which he sold to the British Museum), including sixty new species and two hundred quadrupeds with eighty skeletons. His *Explorations and Adventures in Equatorial Africa* (1861) offered a systematic account of various species of apes that he encountered. Mary Kingsley, one of the few Victorian women to pursue a life as a field naturalist, set out from Britain to gather fish specimens in West Africa in the 1880s (Gates 1998). She was inspired by Wallace's writings and heard the call "Go and learn your tropics" (Kingsley 1897, 1; see also Raby 1997, Gates 1998). Kingsley returned to Britain with sixty-five species of fish, three new to science. Her book *Travels in West Africa* (1887) is an authoritative account of her collection of reptiles and fishes in the swamps of West Africa.

Marianne North (1830–90), a botanical artist, also from Britain, traveled widely throughout the tropics, in search of botanical subjects and contributing a wealth of observations. During an era of large-scale, ruthless plant collecting, North was a nonintrusive collector who made many lasting contributions. With her own funds, she established the North Gallery of botanical paintings in 1882 at Kew. Her book

Recollections of a Happy Life (1894) was published posthumously and enjoyed great popularity. For Kingsley and North, travel writing became scientific narrative, making their science accessible to a broader audience of women, children, and working people (Gates 1998).

Building on Humboldt's lead, the pace of European botanical exploration in the New World tropics accelerated during the nineteenth-century. Karl von Martius, professor of botany at Munich, explored Brazil with Johann Baptist von Spix from 1819 and wrote pioneering books on South American plants, including *Flora Brasiliensis* (1829–1833). Johannes Eugenius Bülow Warming from Denmark embarked for Brazil in 1863 at the age of twenty-four and stayed for three years. He studied botany under von Martius at Munich in 1868. In Brazil, Warming avidly collected specimens and began studying vegetation. These efforts culminated thirty years later in the ecological classic *Lagoa Santa* (1892) (Goodland 1975). Warming's research combined systematics, morphology, and biogeography. He is best known for writing the first textbook of plant ecology, *Plantesamfund* (1895) and is considered by some to be the founder of tropical ecology (Larsen 1989). So fundamental was this work that pioneering British ecologist Sir Arthur Tansley acknowledged that upon reading Warming's textbook in 1898 he was converted from anatomy to ecology (Goodland 1975).

The late nineteenth century produced several other tropical botanical masterpieces. Most influential were works by Engler (1892), Haberlandt (1893), and Schimper (1898) that became part of the foundations of modern botany and plant ecology. Andreas Franz Wilhelm Schimper was a well-traveled botanist, having visited tropical forests in Java, the Antilles, Venezuela, and Brazil. His detailed descriptions of plant structure and tropical vegetation are without compare. He is well known for his original studies of epiphytes (Schimper 1884, 1888). Here we include one selection from the English translation (1903) of Schimper's book *Pflanzengeographie auf physiologischer Grundlage* (1898), in which he describes the functioning and classification of epiphytes. One of the most enduring and important contributions of this book was to create the framework of tropical vegetation formations that remains the basis for our modern forest classifications.

Concluding Remarks

During the twentieth century, tropical biology advanced well beyond the hunting-and-gathering stage. Naming and collecting species now had a higher purpose—there were theories to test, ecological problems to solve, and evolutionary puzzle pieces to assemble. What was once the literal new ground for early explorers became the conceptual new ground for tropical biologists.

The world of tropical biology was opened up by outsiders—naturalists of European origins. For tropical naturalists of the sixteenth through nineteenth centuries, their origins in the world *outside* the tropics strongly shaped their views of tropical nature. But their exposure to the world *inside* the tropics profoundly influenced the development of modern biological science. Great naturalists created the foundations of tropical biology. But it was the grandeur and magnificence of the tropical world that inspired the work of these great naturalists and continues to inspire tropical biologists today.

Reprinted Selections

Alexander von Humboldt, von and A. Bonpland. 1814–21. *Personal Narrative of Travels to the Equinoctial Regions of the New Continent, during the years 1799–1804.* Translated by Helen Maria Williams, 3:35–37; 5:180–83. 5 vols. London: Longman, Hurst, Rees, Orme, and Brown

Henry Walter Bates. 1864. *The Naturalist on the River Amazons,* 412–26. John Murray, London. Reprinted by the University of California Press, Berkeley, 1962

Thomas Belt. 1874. *The Naturalist in Nicaragua,* 71–84. John Murray, London. Reprinted by the University of Chicago Press, 1985

A. R. Wallace. 1895. "On the law which has regulated the introduction of new species," and "Concluding remarks on tropical vegetation." In *Natural Selection and Tropical Nature,* 3–11, 267–69. London: Macmillan

A. F. W. Schimper. 1903. "Epiphytes." In *Plant-Geography upon a Physiological Basis.* Translated by W. R. Fischer; edited by P. Groom and I. B. Balfour, 197–201. Oxford: Clarendon Press

Personal Narrative of Travels to the Equinoctial Regions of the New Continent, during the Years 1799–1804

A. von Humboldt and A. Bonpland

35

which are easily forded. We observed, that the cecropia, which by the disposition of it's branches, and it's slender trunk, resembles the port of the palm tree, is covered with leaves more or less silvery, in proportion as the soil is dry or moist. We saw some plants of it, the leaf of which was on both sides entirely green *. The roots of these trees are hid under tufts of dorstenia, which flourishes only in humid and shady places. In the midst of the forest, on the banks of the Rio Cedeno, as well as on the southern declivity of the Cocollar, we find, in their wild state, papaw trees, and orange trees with large and sweet fruit. These are probably the remains of some *conucos*, or Indian plantations; for in those countries the orange tree cannot be counted among the indigenous plants, any more than the banana tree, the papaw tree, maize, cassava, and so many other useful plants, with the true country of which we are unacquainted, though they have accompanied man in his migrations from the remotest times.

When a traveller newly arrived from Europe penetrates for the first time into the forests of South America, nature presents herself to him under an unexpected aspect. The objects that

perez, with a habitation that is called *Pie de la Cuesta*; the Rio St. Juan; &c.

* Is not the cecropia concolor of Willdenouw a variety of the cecropia peltata?

36

surround him recall but feebly those pictures,
which celebrated writers have traced on the
banks of the Missisippi, in Florida, and in other
temperate regions of the new world. He feels
at every step, that he is not on the confines,
but in the centre of the torrid zone : not in one
of the West India islands, but on a vast continent, where every thing is gigantic, the mountains, the rivers, and the mass of vegetation.
If he feel strongly the beauty of picturesque
scenery, he can scarcely define the various emotions, which crowd upon his mind ; he can
scarcely distinguish what most excites his admiration, the deep silence of those solitudes,
the individual beauty and contrast of forms, or
that vigour and freshness of vegetable life, which
characterize the climate of the tropics. It
might be said that the earth, overloaded with
plants, does not allow them space enough to
unfold themselves. The trunks of the trees are
every where concealed under a thick carpet of
verdure ; and if we carefully transplanted the
orchideæ, the pipers, and the pothos, which a
single courbaril, or American fig-tree* nourishes,
we should cover a vast extent of ground. By
this singular assemblage, the forests, as well as
the flanks of the rocks and mountains, enlarge
the domains of organic nature. The same

---

* Ficus gigantea.

37

lianas as creep on the ground, reach the tops of the trees, and pass from one to another at the height of more than a hundred feet. Thus by a continual interlacing of parasite plants, the botanist is often led to confound the flowers, the fruits, and leaves, which belong to different species.

We walked for some hours under the shade of these arcades, that scarcely admit a glimpse of the sky; which appeared to me of an indigo blue, so much the deeper as the green of the equinoctial plants is generally of a stronger hue, with somewhat of a brownish tint. A great fern tree *, very different from the polypodium arboreum of the West Indies, rose above masses of scattered rocks. In this place we were struck for the first time with the sight of those nests in the shape of bottles, or small pockets, which are suspended to the branches of the lowest trees, and which attest the admirable industry of the orioles, that mingle their warblings with the hoarse cries of the parrots and the macaws. These last, so well known for their vivid colours, fly only in pairs, while the real parrots wander about in flocks of several hundreds. A man must have lived in those climates, particularly in the hot valleys of the Andes, to conceive how these birds sometimes drown with their voice

* Perhaps our aspidium caducum.

180

the cultivation of which Mr. Mutis introduced
at Mariquita* are however less aromatic than
the cinnamon of Ceylon, and would still be so,
even if dried and prepared by similar processes.

Every hemisphere produces plants of a different species ; and it is not by the diversity of climates that we can attempt to explain, why equinoctial Africa has no laurineæ, and the New World no heaths ; why the calceolariæ are found only in the southern hemisphere ; why the birds of the continent of India glow with colours less splendid than the birds of the hot parts of America ; finally, why the tiger is peculiar to Asia, and the ornithorhincus to New-Holland. In the vegetable as well as in the animal kingdom, the causes of the distribution of the species are among the number of mysteries, which natural philosophy cannot reach. This science is not 'occupied in the investigation of the origin of beings, but of the laws according to which they are distributed on the globe. It examines the things that are, the coexistence of vegetable and animal forms in each latitude, at different heights, and at different degrees of temperature ; it studies the relations under which particular organizations are more vigorously developed, multiplied, or modified ; but it approaches not problems, the solution of which is impossible,

* A town of New Grenada, west of Honda.

181

since they touch the origin, the first existence
of a germe of life. We may add, that the attempts which have been made, to explain the
distribution of various species on the globe by
the sole influence of climate, date at a period
when physical geography was still in it's infancy ;
when, recurring incessantly to pretended contrasts between the two worlds, it was imagined,
that the whole of Africa and of America resembled the deserts of Egypt and the marshes of
Cayenne. At present, when men judge of the
state of things not from one type arbitrarily chosen, but from positive knowledge, it is ascertained, that the two continents in their immense extent contain countries that are altogether analogous. There are regions of America
as barren and burning as the interior of Africa.
The islands that produce the spices of India are
scarcely remarkable for their dryness ; and it is
not on account of the humidity of the climate,
as it has been affirmed in recent works, that
the New Continent is deprived of those fine
species of laurineæ and myristicæ, which are
found united in one little corner of the Earth in
the Archipelago of India. For some years past
the real cinnamon has been cultivated with
success in several parts of the New Continent ;
and a zone that produces the coumarouna*, the

* The Tonga bean, coumarouna odora of Aublet.

182

vanilla, the pucheri, the pine-apple, the myrtus pimenta, the balsam of tolu, the myroxylon peruvianum, the crotons, the citrosmas, the pejoa*, the *incienso* of the Silla of Caraccas†, the *quereme*‡, the pancratium, and so many majestic liliaceous plants, cannot be considered as destitute of aromatics. Besides, a dry air favors the development of the aromatic, or exciting properties, only in certain species of plants. The most cruel poisons are produced in the most humid zone of America; and it is precisely under the influence of the long rains of the tropics, that the American pimento, capsicum baccatum§, the fruit of which is often as caustic and fiery as Indian pepper, vegetates best. From the whole of these considerations it follows, 1st, that the New Continent possesses spices, aromatics, and very active vegetable poisons, that are peculiar to itself, differing specifically from those of the ancient world; 2dly, that the primitive distribution of species in the torrid zone cannot be explained by the influence of cli-

---

* Gaultheria odorata.

† Trixis neriifolia. See vol. iii, p. 500. (Baillieria neriifolia, *Nov. Gen.*, vol. iv, p. 227.)

‡ Thibaudia quereme. (*Nov. Gen.*, vol. iii, p. 274.)

§ Mr. Robert Brown, in his important researches on the origin of the cultivated plants of equinoctial Africa, considers the genus capsicum as belonging exclusively to the New Continent. (*Botany of Congo*, 1818, p. 52.)

183

mate solely, or by the distribution of temperature, which we observe in the present state of
our planet; but that this difference of climates
leads us to perceive, why a given type of organization develops itself more vigorously in such
or such local circumstances.   We can conceive,
that a small number of the families of plants,
for instance the musaceæ and the palms, cannot belong to very cold regions, on account of
their internal structure, and the importance of
certain organs*; but we cannot explain why
no one of the family of melastomas vegetates
north of the parallel of thirty degrees, or why
no rose-tree belongs to the southern hemisphere.   Analogy of climates is often found in
the two continents, without identity of productions.

The Rio Vichada (Bichada), which has a
small *raudal* at it's confluence with the Oroo-
noko, appeared to me, next to the Meta and the
Guaviare, to be the most considerable river
coming from the west.   During the last forty
years no European has navigated the Vichada.
I could learn nothing of it's sources; they rise,
I believe, with those of the Tomo, in the plains
that extend to the south of Casimena.   It appears to me at least not to be doubtful, that the
most ancient missions were founded on the

* The *frondes*, so important from their size, would not
resist vigorous cold.

PAPER 2

The Naturalist on the River Amazons

H. W. Bates

some of them swinging on the loops and cables of woody lianas, and all croaking and fluttering their wings like so many furies. If I had had a long stick in my hand I could have knocked several of them over. After killing the wounded one I began to prepare for obtaining more specimens and punishing the viragos for their boldness; but the screaming of their companion having ceased, they remounted the trees, and before I could reload, every one of them had disappeared.

Insects.—Upwards of 7000 species of insects were found in the neighbourhood of Ega. I must confine myself in this place to a few remarks on the order Lepidoptera, and on the ants, several kinds of which, found chiefly on the Upper Amazons, exhibit the most extraordinary instincts.

I found about 550 distinct species of butterflies at Ega. Those who know a little of Entomology will be able to form some idea of the riches of the place in this department, when I mention that eighteen species of true Papilio (the swallow-tail genus) were found within ten minutes' walk of my house. No fact could speak more plainly for the surpassing exuberance of the vegetation, the varied nature of the land, the perennial warmth and humidity of the climate. But no description can convey an adequate notion of the beauty and diversity in form and colour of this class of insects in the neighbourhood of Ega. I paid especial attention to them, having found that this tribe was better adapted than almost any other group of animals or plants to furnish facts in illustration of the modifications which all species undergo in nature, under changed local conditions. This accidental superiority is owing partly to the simplicity and distinctness of the specific characters of the insects, and partly to the facility with which very copious series of specimens can be collected and placed side by side for comparison. The distinctness of the specific characters is due probably to the fact that all the superficial signs of change in the organisation are exaggerated, and made unusually plain by affecting the framework, shape, and colour of the wings, which, as many anatomists believe, are magnified extensions of the skin around the breathing orifices of the thorax of the insects. These expansions are clothed with minute feathers or scales, coloured in regular patterns, which vary in accordance with the slightest change in the conditions to which the species are

exposed. It may be said, therefore, that on these expanded membranes Nature writes, as on a tablet, the story of the modifications of species, so truly do all changes of the organisation register themselves thereon. Moreover, the same colour-patterns of the wings generally show, with great regularity, the degrees of blood-relationship of the species. As the laws of Nature must be the same for all beings, the conclusions furnished by this group of insects must be applicable to the whole organic world; therefore, the study of butterflies—creatures selected as the types of airiness and frivolity—instead of being despised, will some day be valued as one of the most important branches of Biological science.

Before proceeding to describe the ants, a few remarks may be made on the singular cases and cocoons woven by the caterpillars of certain moths found at Ega. The first that may be mentioned is one of the most beautiful examples of insect workmanship I ever saw. It is a cocoon, about the size of a sparrow's egg, woven by a caterpillar in broad meshes of either buff or rose-coloured silk, and is frequently seen in the narrow alleys of the forest, suspended from the extreme tip of an outstanding leaf by a strong silken thread five or six inches in length. It forms a very conspicuous object, hanging thus in

Suspended cocoon of Moth.

mid-air. The glossy threads with which it is knitted are stout, and the structure is therefore not liable to be torn by the beaks of insectivorous birds, whilst its pendulous position makes it doubly secure against their attacks, the apparatus giving way when they peck at it. There is a small orifice at each end of the egg-shaped bag, to admit of the escape of the moth when it changes from the little chrysalis which sleeps tranquilly in its airy cage. The moth is of a dull slaty colour, and belongs to the Lithosiide group of the silk-worm family (Bombycidæ). When the caterpillar begins its work, it lets itself down from the tip of the leaf which it has chosen, by

Sack-bearing Caterpillar (Saccophora).

spinning a thread of silk, the thickness of which it slowly increases as it descends. Having given the proper length to the cord, it proceeds to weave its elegant bag, placing itself in the centre and spinning rings of silk at regular intervals, connecting them at the same time by means of cross threads; so that the whole, when finished, forms a loose web, with quadrangular meshes of nearly equal size throughout. The task occupies about four days: when finished, the enclosed caterpillar becomes sluggish, its skin shrivels and cracks, and there then remains a motionless chrysalis of narrow shape, leaning against the sides of its silken cage.

Many other kinds are found at Ega belonging to the same cocoon-weaving family, some of which differ from the rest in their caterpillars possessing the art of fabricating cases with fragments of wood or leaves, in which they live secure from all enemies whilst they are feeding and growing. I saw many species of these; some of them knitted together, with fine silken threads, small bits of stick, and so made tubes similar to those of caddice-worms; others (Saccophora) chose leaves for the same purpose, forming with them an elongated bag open at both ends, and having the inside lined with a thick web. The tubes of full-grown caterpillars of Saccophora are two inches in length, and it is at this stage of growth that I have generally seen them. They feed on the leaves of Melastomæ, and as, in crawling, the weight of so large a dwelling would be greater than the contained caterpillar could sustain, the insect attaches the case by one or more threads to the leaves or twigs near which it is feeding.

Foraging Ants.—Many confused statements have been published in books of travel, and copied in Natural History works, regarding these ants, which appear to have been confounded with the Saüba, a sketch of whose habits has been given in the first chapter of this work. The Saüba is a vegetable feeder, and does not attack other animals; the accounts that have been published regarding carnivorous ants which hunt in vast armies, exciting terror wherever they go, apply only to the Ecitons, or foraging ants, a totally different group of this tribe of insects. The Ecitons are called Tauóca by the Indians, who are always on the look-out for their armies when they traverse the forest, so as to avoid being attacked. I met with ten distinct species of them, nearly all of which have a different system of marching; eight were new to science when I sent them to England. Some are found commonly in every part of the country, and one is peculiar to the open campos of Santarem ; but, as nearly all the species are found together at Ega, where the forest swarmed with their armies, I have left an account of the habits of the whole genus for this part of my narrative. The Ecitons resemble, in their habits, the Driver ants of Tropical Africa ; but they have no close relationship with them in structure, and indeed belong to quite another sub-group of the ant-tribe.

Like many other ants, the communities of Ecitons are composed, besides males and females, of two classes of workers, a large-headed (worker-major) and a small-headed (worker-minor) class ; the large-heads have, in some species, greatly lengthened jaws, the small-heads have jaws always of the ordinary shape ; but the two classes are not sharply-defined in structure and function, except in two of the species. There is, in all of them a little difference amongst the workers regarding the size of the head ; but in some species this is not sufficient to cause a separation into classes, with division of labour ; in others the jaws are so monstrously lengthened in the worker-majors, that they are incapacitated from taking part in the labours which the worker-minors perform ; and again, in others the difference is so great that the distinction of classes becomes complete, one acting the part of soldiers, and the other that of workers. The peculiar feature in the habits of the Eciton genus is their hunting for prey in regular bodies, or armies. It is this which chiefly distinguishes them from the genus of common red stinging-ants, several species of which inhabit England, whose habit is to search for food in the usual irregular manner. All the Ecitons hunt in large organised bodies ; but almost every species has its own special manner of hunting.

Eciton rapax.—One of the foragers, Eciton rapax, the giant of its genus, whose worker-majors are half-an-inch in length, hunts in single file through the forest. There is no division into classes amongst its workers, although the difference in size is very great, some being scarcely one-half the length of others. The head and jaws, however, are always of the same shape, and a gradation in size is presented from the largest to the smallest, so that all are able to take part in the common labours of the colony. The chief employment of the species seems to be plundering the nests of a large and defenceless ant of another genus (Formica), whose mangled bodies I have often seen in their possession, as they were marching away. The armies of Eciton rapax are never very numerous.

Eciton legionis.—Another species, E. legionis, agrees with E. rapax in having workers not rigidly divisible into two classes; but it is much smaller in size, not differing greatly, in this respect, from our common English red ant (Myrmica rubra), which it also resembles in colour. The Eciton legionis lives in open places, and was seen only on the sandy campos of Santarem. The movement of its hosts were, therefore, much more easy to observe than those of all other kinds, which inhabit solely the densest thickets; its sting and bite, also, were less formidable than those of other species. The armies of E. legionis consist of many thousands of individuals, and move in rather broad columns. They are just as quick to break line, on being disturbed, and attack hurriedly and furiously any intruding object, as the other Ecitons. The species is not a common one, and I seldom had good opportunities of watching its habits. The first time I saw an army, was one evening near sunset. The column consisted of two trains of ants, moving in opposite directions; one train empty-handed, the other laden with the mangled remains of insects, chiefly larvæ and pupæ of other ants. I had no difficulty in tracing the line to the spot from which they were conveying their booty: this was a low thicket; the Ecitons were moving rapidly about a heap of dead leaves; but as the short tropical twilight was deepening rapidly, and I had no wish to be benighted on the lonely campos, I deferred further examination until the next day.

On the following morning, no trace of ants could be found near the place where I had seen them the preceding day, nor were there signs of insects of any description in the thicket; but at the distance of eighty or one hundred yards, I came upon the same army, engaged, evidently, on a razzia of a similar kind to that of the previous evening; but requiring other resources of their instinct, owing to the nature of the ground. They were eagerly occupied, on the face of an inclined bank of light earth, in excavating mines, whence, from a depth of eight or ten inches, they were extracting the bodies of a bulky species of ant, of the genus Formica. It was curious to see them crowding round the orifices of the mines, some assisting their comrades to lift out the bodies of the Formicæ, and others tearing them in pieces, on account of their weight being too great for a single Eciton; a number of carriers seizing each a fragment, and carrying it off down the slope. On digging into the earth with a small trowel near the entrances of the mines, I found the nests of the Formicæ, with grubs and cocoons, which the Ecitons were thus invading, at a depth of about eight inches from the surface. The eager freebooters rushed in as fast as I excavated, and seized the ants in my fingers as I picked them out, so that I had some difficulty in rescuing a few entire for specimens. In digging the numerous mines to get at their prey, the little Ecitons seemed to be divided into parties, one set excavating, and another set carrying away the grains of earth. When the shafts became rather deep, the mining parties had to climb up the sides each time they wished to cast out a pellet of earth; but their work was lightened for them by comrades, who stationed themselves at the mouth of the shaft, and relieved them of their burthens, carrying the particles, with an appearance of foresight which quite staggered me, a sufficient distance from the edge of the hole to prevent them from rolling in again. All the work seemed thus to be performed by intelligent co-operation amongst the host of eager little creatures; but still there was not a rigid division of labour, for some of them, whose proceedings I watched, acted at one time as carriers of pellets, and at another as miners, and all shortly afterwards assumed the office of conveyors of the spoil.

In about two hours, all the nests of Formicæ were rifled, though not completely, of their contents, and I turned towards the army of Ecitons, which were carrying away the mutilated remains. For some distance there were many separate lines of them moving along the slope of the bank; but a short distance off, these all converged, and then formed one close and broad column, which continued for some sixty or seventy yards, and terminated at one of those large termitariums or hillocks of white ants which are constructed of cemented material as hard as stone. The broad and compact column of ants moved up the steep sides of the hillock in a continued stream; many, which had hitherto trotted along empty-handed, now turned to assist their comrades with their heavy loads, and the whole descended into a spacious gallery or mine, opening on the top of the termitarium. I did not try to reach the nest, which I supposed to lie at the bottom of the broad mine, and therefore in the middle of the base of the stony hillock.

Eciton drepanophora.—The commonest species of foraging ants are the Eciton hamata and E. drepanophora, two kinds which resemble each other so closely that it requires attentive

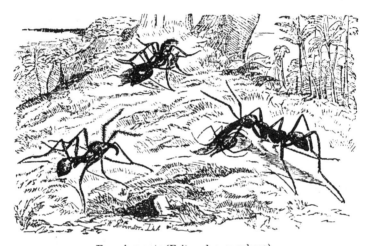

Foraging ants (Eciton drepanophora).

examination to distinguish them; yet their armies never inter-mingle, although moving in the same woods and often crossing each other's tracks. The two classes of workers look, at first sight, quite distinct, on account of the wonderful amount of difference between the largest individuals of the one, and the smallest of the other. There are dwarfs not more than one-fifth of an inch in length, with small heads and jaws, and giants half an inch in length with monstrously enlarged head and jaws, all belonging to the same brood. There is not, how-ever, a distinct separation of classes, individuals existing which connect together the two extremes. These Ecitons are seen in the pathways of the forest at all places on the banks of the Amazons, travelling in dense columns of countless thousands. One or other of them is sure to be met with in a woodland

ramble, and it is to them, probably, that the stories we read
in books on South America apply, of ants clearing houses
of vermin, although I heard of no instance of their entering
houses, their ravages being confined to the thickest parts of the
forest.

When the pedestrian falls in with a train of these ants, the
first signal given him is a twittering and restless movement of
small flocks of plain-coloured birds (ant-thrushes) in the jungle.
If this be disregarded until he advances a few steps farther, he
is sure to fall into trouble, and find himself suddenly attacked
by numbers of the ferocious little creatures. They swarm up
his legs with incredible rapidity, each one driving his pincer-
like jaws into his skin, and with the purchase thus obtained,
doubling in its tail, and stinging with all its might. There is
no course left but to run for it; if he is accompanied by natives
they will be sure to give the alarm, crying "Tauóca!" and
scampering at full speed to the other end of the column of ants.
The tenacious insects who have secured themselves to his legs
then have to be plucked off one by one, a task which is generally not accomplished without pulling them in twain, and
leaving heads and jaws sticking in the wounds.

The errand of the vast ant-armies is plunder, as in the case
of Eciton legionis; but from their moving always amongst
dense thickets, their proceedings are not so easy to observe as
in that species. Wherever they move, the whole animal world
is set in commotion, and every creature tries to get out of their
way. But it is especially the various tribes of wingless insects
that have cause for fear, such as heavy-bodied spiders, ants of
other species, maggots, caterpillars, larvæ of cockroaches and
so forth, all of which live under fallen leaves, or in decaying
wood. The Ecitons do not mount very high on trees, and
therefore the nestlings of birds are not much incommoded by
them. The mode of operation of these armies, which I ascertained only after long-continued observation, is as follows. The
main column, from four to six deep, moves forward in a given
direction, clearing the ground of all animal matter dead or
alive, and throwing off here and there, a thinner column to
forage for a short time on the flanks of the main army, and re-
enter it again after their task is accomplished. If some very

rich place be encountered anywhere near the line of march, for example, a mass of rotten wood abounding in insect larvæ, a delay takes place, and a very strong force of ants is concentrated upon it. The excited creatures search every cranny and tear in pieces all the large grubs they drag to light. It is curious to see them attack wasps' nests, which are sometimes built on low shrubs. They gnaw away the papery covering to get at the larvæ, pupæ, and newly-hatched wasps, and cut everything to tatters, regardless of the infuriated owners which are flying about them. In bearing off their spoil in fragments, the pieces are apportioned to the carriers with some degree of regard to fairness of load: the dwarfs taking the smallest pieces, and the strongest fellows with small heads the heaviest portions. Sometimes two ants join together in carrying one piece, but the worker-majors, with their unwieldy and distorted jaws, are incapacitated from taking any part in the labour. The armies never march far on a beaten path, but seem to prefer the entangled thickets where it is seldom possible to follow them. I have traced an army sometimes for half a mile or more, but was never able to find one that had finished its day's course and returned to its hive. Indeed, I never met with a hive; whenever the Ecitons were seen, they were always on the march.

I thought one day, at Villa Nova, that I had come upon a migratory horde of this indefatigable ant. The place was a tract of open ground near the river side, just outside the edge of the forest, and surrounded by rocks and shrubbery. A dense column of Ecitons was seen extending from the rocks on one side of the little haven, traversing the open space, and ascending the opposite declivity. The length of the procession was from sixty to seventy yards, and yet neither van nor rear was visible. All were moving in one and the same direction, except a few individuals on the outside of the column, which were running rearward, trotting along for a short distance, and then turning again to follow the same course as the main body. But these rearward movements were going on continually from one end to the other of the line, and there was every appearance of there being a means of keeping up a common understanding amongst all the members of the army, for the retrograding ants stopped very often for a moment to touch one or other of their onward-moving comrades with their antennæ; a proceeding which has been noticed in other ants, and supposed to be their mode of conveying intelligence. When I interfered with the column or abstracted an individual from it, news of the disturbance was very quickly communicated to a distance of several yards towards the rear, and the column at that point commenced retreating. All the small-headed workers carried in their jaws a little cluster of white maggots, which I thought, at the time, might be young larvæ of their own colony, but afterwards found reason to conclude were the grubs of some other species whose nests they had been plundering, the procession being most likely not a migration, but a column on a marauding expedition.

The position of the large-headed individuals in the marching column was rather curious. There was one of these extraordinary fellows to about a score of the smaller class; none of them carried anything in their mouths, but all trotted along empty-handed and outside the column, at pretty regular intervals from each other, like subaltern officers in a marching regiment of soldiers. It was easy to be tolerably exact in this observation, for their shining white heads made them very conspicuous amongst the rest, bobbing up and down as the column passed over the inequalities of the road. I did not see them change their position, or take any notice of their small-headed comrades marching in the column, and when I disturbed the line, they did not prance forth or show fight so eagerly as the others. These large-headed members of the community have been considered by some authors as a soldier class, like the similarly-armed caste in Termites; but I found no proof of this, at least in the present species, as they always seemed to be rather less pugnacious than the worker-minors, and their distorted jaws disabled them from fastening on a plane surface like the skin of an attacking animal. I am inclined, however, to think that they may act, in a less direct way, as protectors of the community, namely, as indigestible morsels to the flocks of ant-thrushes which follow the marching columns of these Ecitons, and are the most formidable enemies of the species. It is possible that the hooked and twisted jaws of the large-headed class may be effective weapons of annoyance when in the gizzards or stomachs of these birds, but I unfortunately omitted to ascertain whether this was really the fact.

The life of these Ecitons is not all work, for I frequently saw them very leisurely employed in a way that looked like recreation. When this happened, the place was always a sunny nook in the forest. The main column of the army and the branch columns, at these times, were in their ordinary relative positions; but, instead of pressing forward eagerly, and plundering right and left, they seemed to have been all smitten with a sudden fit of laziness. Some were walking slowly about, others were brushing their antennæ with their fore-feet; but the drollest sight was their cleaning one another. Here and there an ant was seen stretching forth first one leg and then another, to be brushed or washed by one or more of its comrades, who performed the task by passing the limb between the jaws and the tongue, finishing by giving the antennæ a friendly wipe. It was a curious spectacle, and one well calculated to increase one's amazement at the similarity between the instinctive actions of ants and the acts of rational beings, a similarity which must have been brought about by two different processes of development of the primary qualities of mind. The actions of these ants looked like simple indulgence in idle amusement. Have these little creatures, then, an excess of energy beyond what is required for labours absolutely necessary to the welfare of their species, and do they thus expend it in mere sportiveness, like young lambs or kittens, or in idle whims like rational beings? It is probable that these hours of relaxation and cleaning may be indispensable to the effective performance of their harder labours, but whilst looking at them, the conclusion that the ants were engaged merely in play was irresistible.

Eciton prædator.—This is a small dark-reddish species, very similar to the common red stinging-ant of England. It differs from all other Ecitons in its habit of hunting, not in columns, but in dense phalanxes consisting of myriads of individuals, and was first met with at Ega, where it is very common. Nothing in insect movements is more striking than the rapid march of these large and compact bodies. Wherever they pass all the rest of the animal world is thrown into a state of alarm.

They stream along the ground and climb to the summits of all the lower trees, searching every leaf to its apex, and whenever they encounter a mass of decaying vegetable matter, where booty is plentiful, they concentrate, like other Ecitons, all their forces upon it, the dense phalanx of shining and quickly-moving bodies, as it spreads over the surface, looking like a flood of dark-red liquid. They soon penetrate every part of the confused heap, and then, gathering together again in marching order, onward they move. All soft-bodied and inactive insects fall an easy prey to them, and, like other Ecitons, they tear their victims in pieces for facility of carriage. A phalanx of this species, when passing over a tract of smooth ground, occupies a space of from four to six square yards; on examining the ants closely they are seen to move, not altogether in one straightforward direction, but in variously-spreading contiguous columns, now separating a little from the general mass, now re-uniting with it. The margins of the phalanx spread out at times like a cloud of skirmishers from the flanks of an army. I was never able to find the hive of this species.

Blind Ecitons.—I will now give a short account of the blind species of Eciton. None of the foregoing kinds have eyes of the facetted or compound structure such as are usual in insects, and which ordinary ants (Formica) are furnished with, but all are provided with organs of vision composed each of a single lens. Connecting them with the utterly blind species of the genus, is a very stout-limbed Eciton, the E. crassicornis, whose eyes are sunk in rather deep sockets. This ant goes on foraging expeditions like the rest of its tribe, and attacks even the nests of other stinging species (Myrmica), but it avoids the light, moving always in concealment under leaves and fallen branches. When its columns have to cross a cleared space, the ants construct a temporary covered way with granules of earth, arched over, and holding together mechanically; under this the procession passes in secret, the indefatigable creatures repairing their arcade as fast as breaches are made in it.

Next in order comes the Eciton vastator, which has no eyes, although the collapsed sockets are plainly visible; and, lastly, the Eciton erratica, in which both sockets and eyes have disappeared, leaving only a faint ring to mark the place where they are usually situated. The armies of E. vastator and E. erratica move, as far as I could learn, wholly under covered. roads, the ants constructing them gradually but rapidly as they advance. The column of foragers pushes forward step by step, under the protection of these covered passages, through the thickets, and on reaching a rotting log, or other promising hunting-ground, pour into the crevices in search of booty. I have traced their arcades, occasionally, for a distance of one or two hundred yards; the grains of earth are taken from the

Foraging ants (Eciton erratica) constructing a covered road—Soldiers sallying out on being disturbed.

soil over which the column is passing, and are fitted together without cement. It is this last-mentioned feature that distinguishes them from the similar covered roads made by Termites, who use their glutinous saliva to cement the grains together. The blind Ecitons, working in numbers, build up simultaneously the sides of their convex arcades, and contrive, in a surprising manner, to approximate them and fit in the key-stones without letting the loose uncemented structure fall to pieces. There was a very clear division of labour between the two classes of neuters in these blind species. The large-headed class, although not possessing monstrously-lengthened jaws like the worker-majors in E. hamata and E. drepanophora, are rigidly defined in structure from the small-headed class, and act as soldiers, defending the working community (like soldier Termites) against all comers.   Whenever I made a breach in one of their covered ways, all the ants underneath were set in commotion, but the worker-miners remained behind to repair the damage, whilst the large-heads issued forth in a most menacing manner, rearing their heads and snapping their jaws with an expression of the fiercest rage and defiance.

PAPER 3

The Naturalist in Nicaragua
T. Belt

productions of one country on the soil of some distant one,
study the mutual relations of plants and animals, they
will find that in the case of many plants it is important
that the insects specially adapted for the fertilisation of
their flowers should be introduced with them. Thus, if
the insect or bird that assists in the fertilisation of the
vanilla could be introduced into and would live in India,
the growers of that plant would be relieved of much
trouble, and it might be thoroughly naturalised. Judging from my experience, it would be useless to attempt
the acclimature of the scarlet-runner bean in Chontales
unless the humble-bee were also introduced.

Caterpillars, plant-lice, bugs, and insect pests of all
kinds were numerous, and did much harm to my garden;
but the greatest plague of all were the leaf-cutting ants,
and I had to wage a continual warfare against them.
During this contest I gained much information regarding their habits, and was successful in checking their
ravages, and I shall occupy the remainder of this
chapter with an account of them.

LEAF-CUTTING ANTS.—Nearly all travellers in tropical
America have described the ravages of the leaf-cutting
ants (*Œcodoma*); their crowded, well-worn paths through
the forests, their ceaseless pertinacity in the spoliation
of the trees—more particularly of introduced species—
which are stripped bare and ragged, with the midribs
and a few jagged points of the leaves only left. Many a
young plantation of orange, mango, and lemon trees has
been destroyed by them. Again and again have I been
told in Nicaragua, when inquiring why no fruit-trees
were grown at particular places, " It is no use planting

them ; the ants eat them up." The first acquaintance a stranger generally makes with them is on encountering their paths on the outskirts of the forest crowded with the ants ; one lot carrying off the pieces of leaves, each piece about the size of a sixpence, and held up vertically between the jaws of the ant ; another lot hurrying along in an opposite direction empty-handed, but eager to get loaded with their leafy burdens. If he follows this last division, it will lead him to some young trees or shrubs, up which the ants mount ; and then each one, stationing itself on the edge of a leaf, commences to make a circular cut, with its scissor-like jaws, from the edge, its hinder feet being the centre on which it turns. When the piece is nearly cut off, it is still stationed upon it, and it looks as though it would fall to the ground with it ; but, on being finally detached, the ant is generally found to have hold of the leaf with one foot, and soon righting itself, and arranging its burden to its satisfaction, it sets off at once on its return. Following it again, it is seen to join a throng of others, each laden like itself, and, without a moment's delay, it hurries along the well-worn path. As it proceeds, other paths, each thronged with busy workers, come in from the sides, until the main road often gets to be seven or eight inches broad, and more thronged than the streets of the city of London.

After travelling for some hundreds of yards, often for more than half a mile, the formicarium is reached. It consists of low, wide mounds of brown, clayey-looking earth, above and immediately around which the bushes have been killed by their buds and leaves having been persistently bitten off as they attempted to grow after their first defoliation. Under high trees in the thick forest the ants do not make their nests, because, I believe, the ventilation of their underground galleries, about which they are very particular, would be interfered with, and perhaps to avoid the drip from the trees. It is on the outskirts of the forest, or around clearings, or near wide roads that let in the sun, that these formicariums are generally found. Numerous round tunnels, varying from half an inch to seven or eight inches in diameter, lead down through the mounds of earth; and many more, from some distance around, also lead underneath them. At some of the holes on the mounds ants will be seen busily at work, bringing up little pellets of earth from below, and casting them down on the ever-increasing mound, so that its surface is nearly always fresh and new-looking.

Standing near the mounds, one sees from every point of the compass ant-paths leading to them, all thronged with the busy workers carrying their leafy burdens. As far as the eye can distinguish their tiny forms, troops upon troops of leaves are moving up towards the central point, and disappearing down the numerous tunnelled passages. The outgoing, empty - handed hosts are partly concealed amongst the bulky burdens of the incomers, and can only be distinguished by looking closely amongst them. The ceaseless, toiling hosts impress one with their power, and one asks—What forests can stand before such invaders? How is it that vegetation is not eaten off the face of the earth? Surely nowhere but in the tropics, where the recuperative powers of nature are immense and ever active, could such devastation be withstood.

Further acquaintance with the subject will teach the

inquirer that, just as many insects are preserved by being distasteful to insectivorous birds, so very many of the forest trees are protected from the ravages of the ants by their leaves either being distasteful to them, or unfitted for the purpose for which they are required, whilst some have special means of defence against their attacks. None of the indigenous trees appear so suitable for them as the introduced ones. Through long ages the trees and the ants of tropical America have been modified together. Varieties of plants that arose unsuitable for the ants have had an immense advantage over others that were more suitable; and thus through time every indigenous tree that has survived in the great struggle has done so because it has had originally, or has acquired, some protection against the great destroyer. The leaf-cutting ants are confined to tropical America; and we can easily understand that trees and vegetables introduced from foreign lands where these ants are unknown could not have acquired, excepting accidentally, and without any reference to the ants, any protection against their attacks, and now they are most eagerly sought by them. Amongst introduced trees, some species of even the same genus are more acceptable than others. Thus, in the orange tribe, the lime (*Citrus lemonum*) is less liked than the other species; it is the only one that I ever found growing really wild in Central America: and I have sometimes thought that even in the short time since the lime was first introduced, about three hundred years ago, a wild variety may have arisen, less subject to the attacks of the ants than the cultivated variety; for in many parts I saw them growing wild, and apparently not touched. The orange (*Citrus aurantium*) and the citron (*Citrus medi-cus*), on the other hand, are only found where they have been planted and protected by man ; and, were he to give up their cultivation, the only species that would ultimately withstand the attacks of the ants, and obtain a permanent footing in Central America, would be the lime.   The reason why the lime is not so subject to the attacks of the ants is unknown ; and the fact that it is so is another instance of how little we know why one species of a particular genus should prevail over another nearly similar form.   A little more or less acridity, or a slight chemical difference in the composition of the tissues of a leaf, so small that it is inappreciable to our senses, may be sufficient to ensure the preservation or the destruction of a species throughout an entire continent.

The ravages of this ant are so great that it may not be without interest for me to enter upon some details respecting the means I took to protect my own garden against their attacks, especially as the continual warfare I waged against them for more than four years made me acquainted with much of their wonderful economy.

In June 1869, very soon after the formation of my garden, the leaf-cutting ants came down upon it, and at once commenced denuding the young bananas, orange and mango trees of their leaves.   I followed up the paths of the invading hosts to their nest, which was about one hundred yards distant, close to the edge of the forest. The nest was not a very large one, the low mound of earth covering it being about four yards in diameter. At first I tried to stop the holes up, but fresh ones were immediately opened out : I then dug down below the mound, and laid bare the chambers beneath, filled with ant-food and young ants in every stage of growth; but I soon found that the underground ramifications extended so far, and to so great a depth, while the ants were continually at work making fresh excavations, that it would be an immense task to eradicate them by such means; and notwithstanding all the digging I had done the first day, I found them the next as busily at work as ever at my garden, which they were rapidly defoliating. At this stage, our medical officer, Dr. J. H. Simpson,* came to my assistance, and suggested pouring carbolic acid, mixed with water, down their burrows. The suggestion proved a most valuable one. We had a quantity of common brown carbolic acid, about a pint of which I mixed with four buckets of water, and, after stirring it well about, poured it down the burrows; I could hear it rumbling down to the lowest depths of the formicarium four or five feet from the surface. The effect was all that I could have wished: the marauding parties were at once drawn off from my garden to meet the new danger at home. The whole formicarium was disorganised. Big fellows came stalking up from the cavernous regions below, only to descend again in the utmost perplexity.

Next day I found them busily employed bringing up the ant-food from the old burrows, and carrying it to a new one a few yards distant; and here I first noticed a wonderful instance of their reasoning powers. Between the old burrows and the new one was a steep slope.

---

* This gentleman, beloved by all who knew him, of rare talent, and with every prospect of a prosperous career before him, died at Jamaica from hydrophobia, between two and three months after being bitten by a small dog that had not itself shown any symptoms of that disease.

Instead of descending this with their burdens, they cast them down on the top of the slope, whence they rolled down to the bottom, where another relay of labourers picked them up and carried them to the new burrow. It was amusing to watch the ants hurrying out with bundles of food, dropping them over the slope, and rushing back immediately for more. They also brought out great numbers of dead ants that the fumes of the carbolic acid had killed. A few days afterwards, when I visited the locality again, I found both the old burrows and the new one entirely deserted, and I thought they had died off; but subsequent events convinced me that the survivors had only moved away to a greater distance.

It was fully twelve months before my garden was again invaded. I had then a number of rose-trees and also cabbages growing, which the ants seemed to prefer to everything else. The rose-trees were soon defoliated, and great havoc was made amongst the cabbages. I followed them to their nest, and found it about two hundred yards from the one of the year before. I poured down the burrows, as before, several buckets of water with carbolic acid. The water is required to carry the acid down to the lowest chambers. The ants, as before, were at once withdrawn from my garden; and two days afterwards, on visiting the place, I found all the survivors at work on one track that led directly to the old nest of the year before, where they were busily employed making fresh excavations. Many were bringing along pieces of the ant-food from the old to the new nests; others carried the undeveloped white pupæ and larvæ. It was a wholesale and entire migration; and the next day the formicarium down which I had last poured the carbolic acid was entirely deserted. I afterwards found that when much disturbed, and many of the ants destroyed, the survivors migrate to a new locality. I do not doubt that some of the leading minds in this formicarium recollected the nest of the year before, and directed the migration to it.

Don Francisco Velasquez informed me, in 1870, that he had a powder which made the ants mad, so that they bit and destroyed each other. He gave me a little of it, and it proved to be corrosive sublimate. I made several trials of it, and found it most efficacious in turning a large column of the ants. A little of it sprinkled across one of their paths in dry weather has a most surprising effect. As soon as one of the ants touches the white powder, it commences to run about wildly, and to attack any other ant it comes across. In a couple of hours, round balls of the ants will be found all biting each other; and numerous individuals will be seen bitten completely in two, whilst others have lost some of their legs or antennæ. News of the commotion is carried to the formicarium, and huge fellows, measuring three-quarters of an inch in length, that only come out of the nest during a migration or an attack on the nest or one of the working columns, are seen stalking down with a determined air, as if they would soon right matters. As soon, however, as they have touched the sublimate, all their stateliness leaves them: they rush about; their legs are seized hold of by some of the smaller ants already affected by the poison; and they themselves begin to bite, and in a short time become the centres of fresh balls of rabid ants. The sublimate can only be used effectively in dry weather. At Colon I found the Americans using coal tar, which they spread across their paths when any of them led to their gardens. I was also told that the Indians prevent them from ascending young trees by tying thick wisps of grass, with the sharp points downwards, round the stems. The ants cannot pass through the wisp, and do not find out how to surmount it, getting confused amongst the numberless blades, all leading downwards. I mention these different plans of meeting and frustrating the attacks of the ants at some length, as they are one of the greatest scourges of tropical America, and it has been too readily supposed that their attacks cannot be warded off. I myself was enabled, by using some of the means mentioned above, to cultivate successfully trees and vegetables of which the ants were extremely fond.

Notwithstanding that these ants are so common throughout tropical America, and have excited the attention of nearly every traveller, there still remains much doubt as to the use to which the leaves are put. Some naturalists have supposed that they use them directly as food ; others, that they roof their underground nests with them. I believe the real use they make of them is as a manure, on which grows a minute species of fungus, on which they feed ;—that they are, in reality, mushroom growers and eaters. This explanation is so extraordinary and unexpected, that I may be permitted to enter somewhat at length on the facts that led me to adopt it. When I first began my warfare against the ants that attacked my garden, I dug down deeply into some of their nests. In our mining operations we also, on two occasions, carried our excavations from below up through very large formicariums, so that

all their underground workings were exposed to observation. I found their nests below to consist of numerous
rounded chambers, about as large as a man's head,
connected together by tunnelled passages leading from
one chamber to another. Notwithstanding that many
columns of the ants were continually carrying in the cut
leaves, I could never find any quantity of these in the
burrows, and it was evident that they were used up
in some way immediately they were brought in. The
chambers were always about three parts filled with a

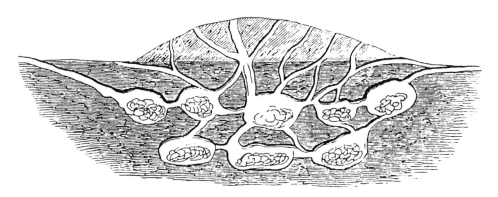

NEST OF LEAF-CUTTING ANT.

speckled, brown, flocculent, spongy-looking mass of a
light and loosely connected substance. Throughout these
masses were numerous ants belonging to the smallest
division of the workers, which do not engage in leaf-
carrying. Along with them were pupæ and larvæ, not
gathered together, but dispersed, apparently irregularly,
throughout the flocculent mass. This mass, which I
have called the ant-food, proved, on examination, to
be composed of minutely subdivided pieces of leaves,
withered to a brown colour, and overgrown and lightly
connected together by a minute white fungus that rami-

fied in every direction throughout it. I not only found this fungus in every chamber I opened, but also in the chambers of the nest of a distinct species that generally comes out only in the night-time, often entering houses and carrying off various farinaceous substances, and which does not make mounds above its nests, but long, winding passages, terminating in chambers similar to the common species, and always, like them, three parts filled with flocculent masses of fungus-covered vegetable matter, amongst which are the ant-nurses and imma-ture ants. When a nest is disturbed, and the masses of ant-food spread about, the ants are in great concern to carry every morsel of it under shelter again; and some-times, when I had dug into a nest, I found the next day all the earth thrown out filled with little pits that the ants had dug into it to get out the covered up food. When they migrate from one part to another, they also carry with them all the ant-food from their old habita-tions. That they do not eat the leaves themselves I con-vinced myself; for I found near the tenanted chambers, deserted ones filled with the refuse particles of leaves that had been exhausted as manure for the fungus, and were now left, and served as food for larvæ of *Staphy-linidæ* and other beetles.*

These ants do not confine themselves to leaves, but also carry off any vegetable substance that they find suitable for growing the fungus on. They are very partial to the inside white rind of oranges, and I have

---

* This theory that the leaf-cutting ants feed on a fungus which they cultivate has been confirmed by Mr. Fritz Müllar, who had arrived at it independently in Brazil. His observations on this and various other habits of insects are contained in a letter to Mr. Charles Darwin, pub-lished in *Nature* of June 11, 1874.

also seen them cutting up and carrying off the flowers of certain shrubs, the leaves of which they neglected. They are particular about the ventilation of their underground chambers, and have numerous holes leading up to the surface from them. These they open out or close up, apparently to keep up a regular degree of temperature below. The great care they take that the pieces of leaves they carry into the nest should be neither too dry nor too damp, is also consistent with the idea that the object is the growth of a fungus that requires particular conditions of temperature and moisture to ensure its vigorous growth. If a sudden shower should come on, the ants do not carry the wet pieces into the burrows, but throw them down near the entrances. Should the weather clear up again, these pieces are picked up when nearly dried, and taken inside; should the rain, however, continue, they get sodden down into the ground, and are left there. On the contrary, in dry and hot weather, when the leaves would get dried up before they could be conveyed to the nest, the ants, when in exposed situations, do not go out at all during the hot hours, but bring in their leafy burdens in the cool of the day and during the night. As soon as the pieces of leaves are carried in they must be cut up by the small class of workers into little pieces. I have never seen the smallest class of ants carrying in leaves; their duties appear to be inside, cutting them up into smaller fragments, and nursing the immature ants. I have, however, seen them running out along the paths with the others; but instead of helping to carry in the burdens, they climb on the top of the pieces which are being carried along by the middle-sized workers, and so get a ride home again. It is very probable that they take a run out merely for air and exercise. The largest class of what are called workers are, I believe, the directors and protectors of the others. They are never seen out of the nest, excepting on particular occasions, such as the migrations of the ants, and when one of the working columns or nests is attacked; they then come stalking up, and attack the enemy with their strong jaws. Sometimes, when digging into the burrows, one of these giants has unperceived climbed up my dress, and the first intimation of his presence has been the burying of his jaws in my neck, from which he would not fail to draw the blood. The stately observant way in which they stalk about, and their great size, compared with the others, always impressed me with the idea that in their bulky heads lay the brains that directed the community in its various duties. Many of their actions, such as that I have mentioned of two relays of workmen carrying out the ant-food, can scarcely be blind instinct. Some of the ants make mistakes, and carry in unsuitable leaves. Thus grass is nearly always rejected by them, yet I have seen some ants, perhaps young ones, carrying in leaves of grass. After a while these pieces were invariably brought out again and thrown away. I can imagine a young ant getting a severe earwigging from one of the major-domos for its stupidity.

I shall conclude this long account of the leaf-cutting ants with an instance of their reasoning powers. A nest was made near one of our tramways, and to get to the trees the ants had to cross the rails, over which the waggons were continually passing and repassing. Every time they came along a number of ants were crushed to death. They persevered in crossing for several days, but at last set to work and tunnelled underneath each rail. One day, when the waggons were not running, I stopped up the tunnels with stones; but although great numbers carrying leaves were thus cut off from the nest, they would not cross the rails, but set to work making fresh tunnels underneath them. Apparently an order had gone forth, or a general understanding been come to, that the rails were not to be crossed.

These ants do not appear to have many enemies, though I sometimes found holes burrowed into their nests, probably by the small armadillo. I once saw a minute parasitic fly hovering over a column of ants, near a nest, and every now and then darting down and attaching an egg to one entering. Large, horned beetles (*Cœlosis biloba*) and a species of Staphylinus are found in the nests, but probably their larvæ live on the rotten leaves, after the ants have done with them.

PAPER 4

Natural Selection and Tropical Nature
A. R. Wallace

I

ON THE LAW WHICH HAS REGULATED THE INTRODUCTION OF NEW SPECIES [1]

Geographical Distribution dependent on Geologic Changes

EVERY naturalist who has directed his attention to the subject of the geographical distribution of animals and plants must have been interested in the singular facts which it presents. Many of these facts are quite different from what would have been anticipated, and have hitherto been considered as highly curious, but quite inexplicable. None of the explanations attempted from the time of Linnæus are now considered at all satisfactory; none of them have given a cause sufficient to account for the facts known at the time, or comprehensive enough to include all the new facts which have since been, and are daily being, added. Of late years, however, a great light has been thrown upon the subject by geological investigations, which have shown that the present state of the earth and of the organisms now inhabiting it is but the last stage of a long and uninterrupted series of changes which it has undergone, and consequently, that to endeavour to explain and account for its present condition without any reference to those changes (as has frequently been done) must lead to very imperfect and erroneous conclusions.

The facts proved by geology are briefly these: That

---

[1] This article, written at Sarawak in February 1855 and published in the *Annals and Magazine of Natural History*, September 1855, was intended to show that some form of evolution of one species from another was needed in order to explain the various classes of facts here indicated; but at that time no means had been suggested by which the actual change of species could have been brought about.

during an immense but unknown period the surface of the
earth has undergone successive changes; land has sunk beneath the ocean, while fresh land has risen up from it;
mountain chains have been elevated; islands have been
formed into continents, and continents submerged till they
have become islands; and these changes have taken place,
not once merely, but perhaps hundreds, perhaps thousands of
times.— That all these operations have been more or less
continuous but unequal in their progress, and during the
whole series the organic life of the earth has undergone a
corresponding alteration.   This alteration also has been
gradual, but complete; after a certain interval not a single
species existing which had lived at the commencement of the
period.   This complete renewal of the forms of life also
appears to have occurred several times.—That from the last
of the geological epochs to the present or historical epoch,
the change of organic life has been gradual: the first appearance of animals now existing can in many cases be traced,
their numbers gradually increasing in the more recent formations, while other species continually die out and disappear,
so that the present condition of the organic world is clearly
derived by a natural process of gradual extinction and creation of species from that of the latest geological periods.
We may therefore safely infer a like gradation and natural
sequence from one geological epoch to another.

Now, taking this as a fair statement of the results of
geological inquiry, we see that the present geographical distribution of life upon the earth must be the result of all the
previous changes, both of the surface of the earth itself and
of its inhabitants.   Many causes, no doubt, have operated of
which we must ever remain in ignorance, and we may, therefore, expect to find many details very difficult of explanation,
and in attempting to give one, must allow ourselves to call
into our service geological changes which it is highly probable
may have occurred, though we have no direct evidence of
their individual operation.

The great increase of our knowledge within the last twenty
years, both of the present and past history of the organic
world, has accumulated a body of facts which should afford
a sufficient foundation for a comprehensive law embracing and

explaining them all, and giving a direction to new researches. It is about ten years since the idea of such a law suggested itself to the writer of this essay, and he has since taken every opportunity of testing it by all the newly-ascertained facts with which he has become acquainted, or has been able to observe himself. These have all served to convince him of the correctness of his hypothesis. Fully to enter into such a subject would occupy much space, and it is only in consequence of some views having been lately promulgated, he believes, in a wrong direction, that he now ventures to present his ideas to the public, with only such obvious illustrations of the arguments and results as occur to him in a place far removed from all means of reference and exact information.

A Law deduced from well-known Geographical and Geological Facts

The following propositions in Organic Geography and Geology give the main facts on which the hypothesis is founded.

GEOGRAPHY

1. Large groups, such as classes and orders, are generally spread over the whole earth, while smaller ones, such as families and genera, are frequently confined to one portion, often to a very limited district.

2. In widely distributed families the genera are often limited in range ; in widely distributed genera well-marked groups of species are peculiar to each geographical district.

3. When a group is confined to one district, and is rich in species, it is almost invariably the case that the most closely allied species are found in the same locality or in closely adjoining localities, and that therefore the natural sequence of the species by affinity is also geographical.

4. In countries of a similar climate, but separated by a wide sea or lofty mountains, the families, genera, and species of the one are often represented by closely allied families, genera, and species peculiar to the other.

GEOLOGY

5. The distribution of the organic world in time is very similar to its present distribution in space.

6. Most of the larger and some small groups extend through several geological periods.

7. In each period, however, there are peculiar groups, found nowhere else, and extending through one or several formations.

8. Species of one genus, or genera of one family occurring in the same geological time, are more closely allied than those separated in time.

9. As, generally, in geography no species or genus occurs in two very distant localities without being also found in intermediate places, so in geology the life of a species or genus has not been interrupted. In other words, no group or species has come into existence twice.

10. The following law may be deduced from these facts: *Every species has come into existence coincident both in space and time with a pre-existing closely allied species.*

This law agrees with, explains, and illustrates all the facts connected with the following branches of the subject: 1st, The system of natural affinities. 2d, The distribution of animals and plants in space. 3d, The same in time, including all the phenomena of representative groups, and those which Professor Forbes supposed to manifest polarity. 4th, The phenomena of rudimentary organs. We will briefly endeavour to show its bearing upon each of these.

The Form of a true system of Classification determined by this Law

If the law above enunciated be true, it follows that the natural series of affinities will also represent the order in which the several species came into existence, each one having had for its immediate antitype a closely allied species existing at the time of its origin. It is evidently possible that two or three distinct species may have had a common antitype, and that each of these may again have become the antitypes from which other closely allied species were created. The effect of this would be, that so long as each species has had but one new species formed on its model, the line of affinities will be simple, and may be represented by placing the several species in direct succession in a straight line. But if two or more species have been independently formed on the plan of a common antitype, then the series of affinities will be compound, and can only be represented by a forked or many-branched line.   Now, all attempts at a Natural classification and arrangement of organic beings show that both these plans have obtained in creation.   Sometimes the series of affinities can be well represented for a space by a direct progression from species to species or from group to group, but it is generally found impossible so to continue.   There constantly occur two or more modifications of an organ or modifications of two distinct organs, leading us on to two distinct series of species, which at length differ so much from each other as to form distinct genera or families.   These are the parallel series or representative groups of naturalists, and they often occur in different countries, or are found fossil in different formations.   They are said to have an analogy to each other when they are so far removed from their common antitype as to differ in many important points of structure, while they still preserve a family resemblance.   We thus see how difficult it is to determine in every case whether a given relation is an analogy or an affinity, for it is evident that as we go back along the parallel or divergent series, towards the common antitype, the analogy which existed between the two groups becomes an affinity.   We are also made aware of the difficulty of arriving at a true classification, even in a small and perfect group ; in the actual state of nature it is almost impossible, the species being so numerous and the modifications of form and structure so varied, arising probably from the immense number of species which have served as antitypes for the existing species, and thus produced a complicated branching of the lines of affinity, as intricate as the twigs of a gnarled oak or the vascular system of the human body.   Again, if we consider that we have only fragments of this vast system, the stem and main branches being represented by extinct species of which we have no knowledge, while a vast mass of limbs and boughs and minute twigs and scattered leaves is what we have to place in order, so as to determine the true position which each originally occupied with regard to the others, the whole difficulty of the true Natural System of classification becomes apparent to us.

We shall thus find ourselves obliged to reject all those

systems of classification which arrange species or groups in circles, as well as those which fix a definite number for the divisions of each group.   The latter class have been very generally rejected by naturalists, as contrary to nature, notwithstanding the ability with which they have been advocated; but the circular system of affinities seems to have obtained a deeper hold, many eminent naturalists having to some extent adopted it.   We have, however, never been able to find a case in which the circle has been closed by a direct and close affinity.   In most cases a palpable analogy has been substituted, in others the affinity is very obscure or altogether doubtful.   The complicated branching of the lines of affinities in extensive groups must also afford great facilities for giving a show of probability to any such purely artificial arrangements.   Their death-blow was given by the admirable paper of the lamented Mr. Strickland, published in the *Annals of Natural History*, in which he so clearly showed the true synthetical method of discovering the Natural System.

Geographical Distribution of Organisms

If we now consider the geographical distribution of animals and plants upon the earth, we shall find all the facts beautifully in accordance with, and readily explained by, the present hypothesis.   A country having species, genera, and whole families peculiar to it, will be the necessary result of its having been isolated for a long period, sufficient for many series of species to have been created on the type of pre-existing ones, which, as well as many of the earlier-formed species, have become extinct, and thus made the groups appear isolated.   If in any case the antitype had an extensive range, two or more groups of species might have been formed, each varying from it in a different manner, and thus producing several representative or analogous groups.   The Sylviadæ of Europe and the Sylvicolidæ of North America, the Heliconidæ of South America and the Euplœas of the East, the group of Trogons inhabiting Asia and that peculiar to South America, are examples that may be accounted for in this manner.

Such phenomena as are exhibited by the Galapagos Islands, which contain little groups of plants and animals peculiar to themselves, but most nearly allied to those of South America, have not hitherto received any, even a conjectural explanation. The Galapagos are a volcanic group of high antiquity, and have probably never been more closely connected with the continent than they are at present. They must have been first peopled, like other newly-formed islands, by the action of winds and currents, and at a period sufficiently remote to have had the original species die out, and the modified prototypes only remain. In the same way we can account for the separate islands having each their peculiar species, either on the supposition that the same original emigration peopled the whole of the islands with the same species from which differently modified prototypes were created, or that the islands were successively peopled from each other, but that new species have been created in each on the plan of the pre-existing ones. St. Helena is a similar case of a very ancient island having obtained an entirely peculiar, though limited, flora. On the other hand, no example is known of an island which can be proved geologically to be of very recent origin (late in the Tertiary, for instance), and yet possesses generic or family groups, or even many species peculiar to itself.

When a range of mountains has attained a great elevation, and has so remained during a long geological period, the species of the two sides at and near their bases will be often very different, representative species of some genera occurring, and even whole genera being peculiar to one side only, as is remarkably seen in the case of the Andes and Rocky Mountains. A similar phenomenon occurs when an island has been separated from a continent at a very early period. The shallow sea between the Peninsula of Malacca, Java, Sumatra, and Borneo was probably a continent or large island at an early epoch, and may have become submerged as the volcanic ranges of Java and Sumatra were elevated ; the organic results we see in the very considerable number of species of animals common to some or all of these countries, while at the same time a number of closely allied representative species exist peculiar to each, showing that a considerable period has elapsed since their separation. The facts of geographical distribution and of geology may thus mutually explain each other in doubtful cases, should the principles here advocated be clearly established,

In all those cases in which an island has been separated from a continent, or raised by volcanic or coralline action from the sea, or in which a mountain-chain has been elevated in a recent geological epoch, the phenomena of peculiar groups or even of single representative species will not exist. Our own island is an example of this, its separation from the continent being geologically very recent, and we have consequently scarcely a species which is peculiar to it; while the Alpine range, one of the most recent mountain elevations, separates faunas and floras which scarcely differ more than may be due to climate and latitude alone.

The series of facts alluded to in Proposition (3), of closely allied species in rich groups being found geographically near each other, is most striking and important. Mr. Lovell Reeve has well exemplified it in his able and interesting paper on the Distribution of the Bulimi. It is also seen in the Humming-birds and Toucans, little groups of two or three closely allied species being often found in the same or closely adjoining districts, as we have had the good fortune of personally verifying. Fishes give evidence of a similar kind : each great river has its peculiar genera, and in more extensive genera its groups of closely allied species. But it is the same throughout Nature ; every class and order of animals will contribute similar facts. Hitherto no attempt has been made to explain these singular phenomena, or to show how they have arisen. Why are the genera of Palms and of Orchids in almost every case confined to one hemisphere? Why are the closely allied species of brown-backed Trogons all found in the East, and the green-backed in the West? Why are the Macaws and the Cockatoos similarly restricted ? Insects furnish a countless number of analogous examples— the Goliathi of Africa, the Ornithopteræ of the Indian Islands, the Heliconidæ of South America, the Danaidæ of the East, and in all the most closely allied species found in geographical proximity. The question forces itself upon every thinking mind, Why are these things so ? They could not be as they are had no law regulated their creation and dispersion. The law here enunciated not merely explains but necessitates the facts we see to exist, while the vast and long - continued geological changes of the earth readily account for the exceptions and apparent discrepancies that here and there occur. The writer's object in putting forward his views in the present imperfect manner is to submit them to the test of other minds, and to be made aware of all the facts supposed to be inconsistent with them. As his hypothesis is one which claims acceptance solely as explaining and connecting facts which exist in nature, he expects facts alone to be brought to disprove it, not à *priori* arguments against its probability.

Geological Distribution of the Forms of Life

The phenomena of geological distribution are exactly analogous to those of geography. Closely allied species are found associated in the same beds, and the change from species to species appears to have been as gradual in time as in space. Geology, however, furnishes us with positive proof of the extinction and production of species, though it does not inform us how either has taken place. The extinction of species, however, offers but little difficulty, and the *modus operandi* has been well illustrated by Sir C. Lyell in his admirable *Principles*. Geological changes, however gradual, must occasionally have modified external conditions to such an extent as to have rendered the existence of certain species impossible. The extinction would in most cases be effected by a gradual dying-out, but in some instances there might have been a sudden destruction of a species of limited range. To discover how the extinct species have from time to time been replaced by new ones down to the very latest geological period, is the most difficult, and at the same time the most interesting problem in the natural history of the earth. The present inquiry, which seeks to eliminate from known facts a law which has determined, to a certain degree, what species could and did appear at a given epoch, may, it is hoped, be considered as one step in the right direction towards a complete solution of it.

High Organisation of very ancient Animals consistent with this Law

Much discussion has of late years taken place on the question whether the succession of life upon the globe has

the numbers of suitable insects are totally inadequate to the
fertilisation of the countless millions of forest trees over such
vast areas as the equatorial zone presents, and that, in consequence, a large proportion of the species have become
adapted either for self-fertilisation, or for cross-fertilisation by
the agency of the wind. Were there not some such limitation as this, we should expect that the continued struggle for
existence among the plants of the tropical forests would have
led to the acquisition, by a much larger proportion of them,
of so valuable a character as bright-coloured flowers, this
being almost a necessary preliminary to a participation in the
benefits which have been proved to arise from cross-fertilisation by insect agency.

Concluding Remarks on Tropical Vegetation

In concluding this general sketch of the aspects of tropical
vegetation, we will attempt briefly to summarise its main
features. The primeval forests of the equatorial zone are
grand and overwhelming by their vastness, and by the display
of a force of development and vigour of growth rarely or
never witnessed in temperate climates. Among their best
distinguishing features are the variety of forms and species
which everywhere meet and grow side by side, and the extent
to which parasites, epiphytes, and creepers fill up every available station with peculiar modes of life. If the traveller
notices a particular species and wishes to find more like it, he
may often turn his eyes in vain in every direction. Trees of
varied forms, dimensions, and colours are around him, but he
rarely sees any one of them repeated. Time after time he
goes towards a tree which looks like the one he seeks, but
a closer examination proves it to be distinct. He may at
length, perhaps, meet with a second specimen half a mile off,
or may fail altogether, till on another occasion he stumbles
on one by accident.

The absence of the gregarious or social habit, so general in
the forests of extra-tropical countries, is probably dependent
on the extreme equability and permanence of the climate.
Atmospheric conditions are much more important to the
growth of plants than any others. Their severest struggle
for existence is against climate. As we approach towards

regions of polar cold or desert aridity the variety of groups and species regularly diminishes; more and more are unable to sustain the extreme climatal conditions, till at last we find only a few specially organised forms which are able to maintain their existence. In the extreme north, pine or birch trees—in the desert, a few palms and prickly shrubs or aromatic herbs—alone survive. In the equable equatorial zone there is no such struggle against climate. Every form of vegetation has become alike adapted to its genial heat and ample moisture, which has probably changed little even throughout geological periods; and the never ceasing struggle for existence between the various species in the same area has resulted in a nice balance of organic forces, which gives the advantage, now to one, now to another species, and prevents any one type of vegetation from monopolising territory to the exclusion of the rest. The same general causes have led to the filling up of every place in nature with some specially adapted form. Thus we find a forest of smaller trees adapted to grow in the shade of greater trees. Thus we find every tree supporting numerous other forms of vegetation, and some so crowded with epiphytes of various kinds that their forks and horizontal branches are veritable gardens. Creeping ferns and arums run up the smoothest trunks; an immense variety of climbers hang in tangled masses from the branches and mount over the highest tree-tops. Orchids, bromelias, arums, and ferns grow from every boss and crevice, and cover the fallen and decaying trunks with a graceful drapery. Even these parasites have their own parasitical growth, their leaves often supporting an abundance of minute creeping mosses and hepaticæ. But the uniformity of climate which has led to this rich luxuriance and endless variety of vegetation is also the cause of a monotony that in time becomes oppressive. To quote the words of Mr. Belt: "Unknown are the autumn tints, the bright browns and yellows of English woods; much less the crimsons, purples, and yellows of Canada, where the dying foliage rivals, nay excels, the expiring dolphin in splendour. Unknown the cold sleep of winter; unknown the lovely awakening of vegetation at the first gentle touch of spring. A ceaseless round of ever-active life weaves the fairest scenery of the tropics into one monotonous whole, of which the component parts exhibit in detail untold variety and beauty." [1]

To the student of nature the vegetation of the tropics will ever be of surpassing interest, whether for the variety of forms and structures which it presents, for the boundless energy with which the life of plants is therein manifested, or for the help which it gives us in our search after the laws which have determined the production of such infinitely varied organisms. When, for the first time, the traveller wanders in these primeval forests, he can scarcely fail to experience sensations of awe, akin to those excited by the trackless ocean or the alpine snowfields. There is a vastness, a solemnity, a gloom, a sense of solitude and of human insignificance, which for a time overwhelm him ; and it is only when the novelty of these feelings have passed away that he is able to turn his attention to the separate constituents that combine to produce these emotions, and examine the varied and beautiful forms of life which, in inexhaustible profusion, are spread around him.

[1] *The Naturalist in Nicaragua*, p. 58.

PAPER 5

Plant-Geography upon a Physiological Basis
A. F. W. Schimper

are unfavourable to the production of long axes[1]. The guild therefore inhabits an enormous area, although it is very unequally distributed. In by far the majority of cases, lianes are inhabitants of the tropics and of a few neighbouring lands with a tropical climate, such as Southern Brazil and South Florida. According to an estimate, which H. Schenck considers as probably too low, about ten-elevenths or over ninety per cent. of the lianes are tropical. Even in the tropics the distribution of lianes is very unequal; most of the long woody forms only appear in damp rain-forests and monsoon-forests[2], whilst dry woodlands and savannahs produce hardly any but thin-stemmed and chiefly herbaceous forms.

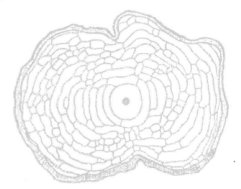

Fig. 110. Transverse section of stem of *Securidaca lanceolata*, St.-Hil. Natural size. After H. Schenck.

Outside the tropics, lianes occur chiefly in temperate rain-forests in Southern Japan, New Zealand, Southern Chili, more rarely and in less variety in very damp summer-forests[3] in Central Japan, Atlantic and Central North America, without showing anything like such variety as in the tropics.

2. EPIPHYTES[4].

Epiphytes are plants that germinate on other plants and grow without obtaining nutriment at the cost of the substance of their host. In this they differ from true parasites, with which they are often confounded.

Their mode of life makes the acquisition of the necessary nourishment a matter of difficulty, but starvation is not the chief danger to which they are exposed. Epiphytes, attached as they are to the surface of other plants, are more exposed to the danger of drought, and they are consequently confined to regions where long persistent drought is unknown, except when they have the faculty of existing in a desiccated condition, a power which is possessed by many mosses and lichens, but which appears to be altogether wanting in ferns and phanerogams, in spite of the ability of a few species to withstand very considerable loss of water. The epiphytic guild therefore exhibits, according to the nature of the climate, an inequality in systematic composition and in diversity and luxuriance of growth.

Districts where a drying up of the plants owing to scarcity of water is

[1] See Part III, Sects. III and IV.
[2] See Part III, Sect. II.
[3] See Part III, Sect. I, Chap. III.
[4] Schimper, op. cit.

impossible are confined to the tropics. The rain-forests of the tropics are always moist. This is much less true of rain-forests of the warmer temperate zones and not at all true of the summer-forests of higher latitudes, for the cold of winter there constitutes a period of physiological drought, which, even with the heaviest atmospheric precipitation, is more opposed to the supply of water than great dryness when united with heat. Under heat and dryness transpiration is indeed much greater, but the absorption of water is not hindered and the nightly dew is of direct advantage to the superficial roots of the epiphytes, whereas under temperate conditions there is no supply of water to be set against its loss by epiphytes, for the frozen or at any rate very cold exposed roots transpire, but absorb nothing.

Corresponding to these conditions of life, the vast majority of epiphytes belong to tropical rain-forests. Only there do they luxuriantly cover stems, branches, and frequently even the leaves of trees, and often themselves attain the dimensions of trees. In districts with markedly dry seasons, and on the isolated trees of savannahs, epiphytes are either completely wanting, or rare and represented by relatively few forms. Such forms as are found are emigrants from the rain-forests, and their presence is always a sign that the dry season is not long, or, as in the monsoon-forests, is accompanied by copious dew.

The origin of the guild of epiphytes in tropical forests may have come about in the following way. Many terrestrial plants living in the forest are able to settle and grow on rough fissured stems, in the forks of boughs, and on other spots where humus collects. This happens in the tropics in the case of many Solanaceae, Melastomaceae, and ferns. From such accidental epiphytes true epiphytes were derived, since many of these plants owed their existence to this faculty, which secured for them a safe retreat outside the seat of conflict. The competition on the trees was limited to few species, because the faculty of existing as an epiphyte demands certain definite and by no means common characters. Obviously, for instance, only such plants germinate on trees as are provided with seeds capable of dispersal not only in a horizontal, but also in a vertical direction, and the latter demands adaptations to arboreal animals and to the wind. Moreover, the seeds must be very small, so that they can enter narrow crevices, and in the case of dispersal by the wind they must be extremely light, because vertical wind-currents are weak in the forest. The seeds of epiphytes actually fulfil all these conditions; they are always small, and either surrounded by succulent envelopes, as in Aroideae, many Bromeliaceae, Rubiaceae, Melastomaceae, Ficus, Cactaceae, and Gesneraceae, or they are extremely light, even like powder, as for instance the spores of ferns, the seeds of orchids, or they are provided, in spite of their very small dimensions, with a most suitable parachute, as in Rhododendron, many Bromeliaceae,

Asclepiadaceae, Gesneraceae, and Rubiaceae.   Moreover, from the first all plants that produce many lateral roots and require relatively little water gain an advantage.   Hence the number of species that could emigrate to trees was relatively small, and victory over competitors was dependent on conditions other than those prevailing on the ground.

In those species which no longer grew on the ground and therefore could persist as epiphytes only, those characters were naturally selected that were specially suited for existence on trees; they have been adapted to this. Especially was every characteristic that enabled an epiphyte to advance upwards towards the light preserved and further developed.   In the first place, in this relation protective means against the loss of water are in question, for every step on the way from the base to the summit of a tree brings with it not only more light but also greater dryness.   Epiphytes growing at the base of trees in a rain-forest are hygrophilous, those that occur on the highest branches are xerophilous.   The whole matter gives the impression of a gradual ascent from the deep shade into the sunlight, from the damp cool air of the interior of the forest to the dry heat of the top of the forest.

Xerophilous sun-loving epiphytes of the summits of trees, although they represent the descendants of hygrophilous shade-bearing plants, are able to desert the rain-forest.   Thanks to their changed characters they are able to inhabit quite open country.   Thus they emigrated from the rain-forests, and colonized regions with markedly dry seasons, especially monsoon-forests, savannahs, and savannah-forests.   A limit was set to their success only where the drought lasted several months without being interrupted regularly by heavy falls of dew; yet there they were able to settle permanently on the banks of rivers and lakes.   The winter cold more completely arrested the emigration of tropical epiphytes.   Only few species endowed with specially strong powers of resisting drought and cold, such as Tillandsia usneoides and Polypodium incanum in North America, were able to advance into districts with cold winters.

The tropical rain-forests have been by far the most important sources of origin of the epiphytic guild, and their productions have penetrated far into the warm temperate zones of North America, Argentina, Japan, and Australia.   We also find, however, in the temperate zones two limited autochthonous sources of origin of higher epiphytes, namely, in the comparatively inextensive temperate rain-forests of Southern Chili and of New Zealand.   Here real temperate higher epiphytes have sprung from temperate phanerogams and ferns.

Outside this region, as autochthonous epiphytes, we find only small Algae, lichens, and mosses, that is to say, plants that, owing to their faculty of existing for months in a dry condition, can resist even the desiccating effects of prolonged winter cold.   But even they are found richly developed

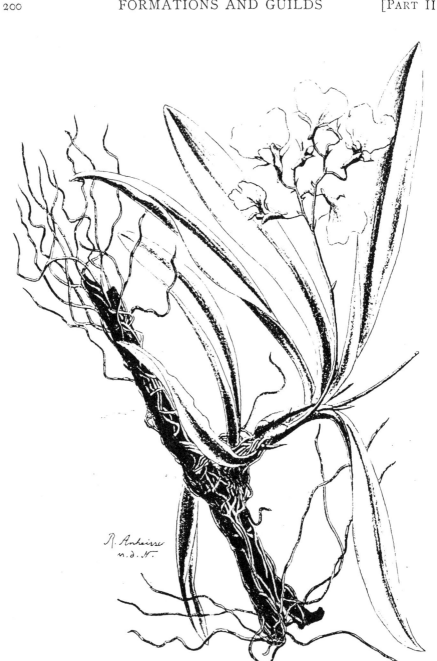

FIG. III. Ionopsis sp. An epiphytic orchid on an orange branch. Blumenau, Southern Brazil. Natural size.

only in damp districts, especially in a cloudy climate, or near stretches of water. As in the tropics, so also in temperate regions, terrestrial plants may be found growing accidentally in the hollows of old trees; they occur however only in places where considerable masses of soil facilitate the development of true subterranean roots, and they cannot in any way be considered as epiphytes.

The varied contrivances by means of which higher epiphytes have become adapted to their mode of life are so closely connected with the conditions of existence in rain-forests and are so characteristic of the latter, that they and the forests should be discussed together. It may now merely be stated that they chiefly belong to the ferns and orchids (Fig. 111), and in America specially to the Bromeliaceae.

3. SAPROPHYTES.

Saprophytes constitute a group of plants that dispense with chlorophyll and are therefore dependent on organic nutriment. They obtain this nutriment from dead vegetable and animal substances, and in a more or less decomposed condition according to the particular species.

The vast majority of saprophytes belong to the Bacteria, Myxomycetes, and Fungi; the remainder are phanerogams. There are no other classes of plants represented among them. In accordance with their mode of nutrition, all saprophytes, except perhaps bacteria, must be derived from green assimilating plants. Among phanerogams, numerous transitions still exist between purely inorganic and purely organic methods of nutrition. The first stage is denoted by the appearance of the mycorhiza, by means of which phanerogams and ferns were first enabled to utilize the organic constituents of humus. Increasing dependence on the fungus of the mycorhiza, whose rôle has been transformed from that of a mere supplier of nitrogen to that of a universal provider, has led through numerous intermediate stages to the purely saprophytic mode of life. The saprophytic habit has conferred on the plants which possess it the power of occupying stations where, on account of insufficient illumination, green plants can exist feebly or not at all. Like halophytes and epiphytes, saprophytes are also fugitives from the struggle for existence.

Despite the wide distribution of mycorhiza only a relatively small number of phanerogams, belonging to a few families, have adopted the purely saprophytic mode of life. The majority of these are monocotyledons and chiefly orchids, but the small family of Burmanniaceae is chiefly saprophytic, and that of Triuridaceae exclusively so. Among dicotyledonous plants only Gentianaceae and Monotropeae possess saprophytic species.

The change in the mode of nutrition causes a change in the structure and oecology of the plant. Chlorophyll having become useless is suppressed or transformed into other brown, yellow, or brick-red pigments apparently allied to chlorophyll, and these give to saprophytes a vivid

2

What Shaped Tropical Biotas as We See Them Today?

T. C. Whitmore

Two great series of events have provided the background against which today's plants and animals evolved and came to form the arrays of flora and fauna that occupy different parts of the contemporary world. These are, first, continental movements driven by ocean floor spreading and the development of new land as island arcs and, second, the major fluctuations in climate epitomized by, but by no means confined to, the Ice Ages of the Pleistocene.

The main story was clear by about 1980 and is well encapsulated in rather few key publications. Since then there has been refinement, although some details remain controversial and continue to be debated.

Plate Tectonics

The late 1960s saw a revolution in the earth sciences with the discovery of plate tectonics (Hallam 1973), built on earlier notions of continental drift dating back to early in the century, plus the discovery of ocean floor spreading, which provided a plausible and demonstrable mechanism for continental movement. The geographical ranges of many plant and animal groups had long previously persuaded biogeographers that there must have been contact between different continents; they had proposed such mechanisms as long-distance dispersal (e.g., Darlington 1957), previous land bridges (e.g., Steenis 1962), and, indeed, continental drift, which geologists at that time would not countenance as they thought no big enough force existed.

Flowering plant fossils become frequent in the early Cretaceous about the time Gondwana was beginning to break up into separate continents (Smith and Briden 1977). Botanists were quick to use plate tectonics to interpret the evolution and spread of flowering plants from an origin in west Gondwana. This picture is well described by Raven and Axelrod (1974); a key section of their paper is reprinted here.

Developments in plate tectonics since then have been, in essence, clarifications of details of the broad overall picture. A difficult problem facing geoscientists for a long while was how to determine whether certain land masses had been above or below sea level, a problem largely resolved by Smith, Smith, and Funnell (1994). Plate tectonics illuminated two long-standing biogeographical debates, one concerning the Malay Archipelago, the other concerning the Americas.

Wallace's line. The eastern tropics from Assam to Fiji have a particularly complex plate tec-

The "king" and the "twelve wired" birds of paradise. From Wallace (1869)

tonic history, involving collision of Gond-wanan frag-ments with Laurasia during the mid-Tertiary. First, India drifted north to dock with Laurasia, bearing with it Gondwanan biota. Second, further east, the Gondwanan fragment comprising Australia and attendant islands to its north collided with the southeastern extremity of Laurasia somewhere east of present-day Borneo, again bringing Gondwanan and Laurasian biotas into contact. Wallace's line, running between Bali and Lombok then north up through the Makassar Strait, had been discovered in the late nineteenth century by Alfred Russel Wallace and is one of the strongest zoogeographical boundaries on earth (see part 1). Plate tectonics showed its origin. Gondwanan and Laurasian faunas brought into proximity by drift have scarcely mixed.

The geological and biological implications of plate tectonics in the Malay Archipelago were explored in two volumes of essays (Whitmore 1981, 1987), but many loose ends remained. The geological history is extremely intricate. It involves much more than a single collision and is still being unravelled (Hall and Blundell 1996; Hall and Holloway 1998; Morley 2000). Many distributions can now be related to particular paleogeographical features (Hall and Holloway 1998). Wallace's line is weaker for plants than animals; this, it is now believed, is because the eastern part of the archipelago was colonized by Laurasian plants originating from southwest Sulawesi, a piece of Laurasia east of Wallace's line that became separated from Borneo when the Makassar Strait opened up (Morley 2000).

The great American biotic interchange. The Central American isthmus also has a complex geological history. The intermittent existence of connections between North and South America has led to intermingling of North and South American floras and faunas, with subsequent further evolution and extinction. This is exemplified particularly dramatically by mammals. Their investigation was pioneered by Simpson (1950) before the discovery of plate tectonics, summed up by him (Simpson 1980)

and then comprehensively reviewed by Stehli and Webb (1985), part of whose introduction is reprinted here. Krishtalka (1986) gave a brief, lively overview, and Webb (1991) gave a further update. The main interchange three million years ago was preceded by a lesser episode between eight and nine million years ago. Perhaps the most remarkable aspect of the great interchange was the massive extinction of the original South American mammals. About half the modern genera there gained a foothold from the north and evolved in less than three million years (Hallam 1994).

Palaeoclimates

The world's climate fluctuated greatly throughout the Tertiary and then during a series of Ice Ages through the Quaternary. A vast amount of evidence, much of it from interpretation of unpublished oil company stratigraphical analyses, has now accumulated. These cryptic data are reviewed and synthesized by Morley (2000), who has reconstructed the waxing and waning of tropical forests, driven by the series of climatic pulsations, since the first diversification of flowering plants in the early Cretaceous (c. 120 Ma). The Tertiary (since 65 Ma) has also seen the rise, diversification and spread of mammals. Flowering plants rose to dominance during the Cenomanian (96–92 Ma) and created tropical moist forests that are believed to have been of lower stature than those of today.

Morley's reconstruction is that tropical forests and their component megathermal species originally developed in three parallel belts separated by the subtropical high-pressure zones. The northern belt encompassed moist mid latitudes of Europe and North America, the central belt was equatorial, and the southern belt centered on southern South America and eastern Gondwana. These belts are characterized by Bombacaceae, palms, and Proteaceae, among other plant families. The giant meteor that hit earth at the end of the Cretaceous (65 Ma) was followed by the evolution during the Tertiary of new lineages of megathermal plants, which created multistoried tropical rain forests. Mammals, which had first appeared in the Jurassic, diversified in the Tertiary and filled niches left empty by the demise of the dinosaurs or newly created in the evolving forests. Fruit- and seed-eating arboreal species evolved and became dispersers of the big seeds of many closed-canopy trees. There was a phase of very warm climate at c. 54 Ma (late Paleocene, early Eocene), unequaled since, during which the rain forest belts extended poleward; the northern belt covered much of Europe and North America, the southern much of Australia, New Zealand, and southern South America. Severe cooling and drying at 36 Ma (end of the Eocene) led to the dramatic contraction of tropical rain forests. Both the northern and southern belts disappeared. The climate then ameliorated and allowed expansion, but several Ice Ages during the past 2 Ma (Pleistocene) led again to severe contraction of rain forests, yet again to expand in the past 10 Ka (the Holocene). The extent today, until recent human desecration, was as extensive as at any time during the past two million years.

Continental movements and creation of island arcs, simultaneous with these massive changes in climate, provided the stimulus for migration of the evolving flora and fauna until it arrived at the configurations seen today.

Today, the Holocene, we live at the height of an interglacial, albeit slightly cooler than the one at 54 Ma. During Ice Ages the tropics have become cooler, more seasonal, and drier. Sea level has dropped by as much as 160 meters. Tropical mountain vegetation belts have been depressed and glaciers have formed on the highest mountains. Some of the best direct evidence for these climatic changes is provided by the pollen record, and this is best preserved in peat deposits, which are mainly montane. The longest and most detailed such record comes from Colombia and extends back to the Pliocene. Van der Hammen (1974), reprinted here, reviewed historic changes to vegetation and climate in South America, centered on the very long Colombian record that he had himself analyzed earlier. Similar fluctuations in climate and vegetation were discovered from analysis of African and Asian montane peats.

Flenley (1979) put together the pantropical picture.

Once it was realized that lowland tropical rain forest climates have been less extensive in the past, Pleistocene climate changes proved useful in helping to explain present-day ranges. Amazonian birds show curious ranges within what today is a vast area of fairly uniform perhumid climate and rain forest. Haffer (1969), reprinted here, argued that these ranges show the existence of Pleistocene refugia to which the birds retreated when the rain forests were reduced to 'islands' in a 'sea' of savanna at Ice Age maxima. This idea quickly caught on and distribution patterns of numerous other groups were similarly and sometimes enthusiastically interpreted (e.g., Vuilleumier 1971; Prance 1982; Whitmore and Prance 1987). Pleistocene refugia have also been invoked to explain biogeographic patterns in Africa (Mayr and O'Hara 1986; Maley 1996), which had been well described for birds by Moreau (1966) and for plants by White (1983).

In tropical South America, subsequent research has led to more refined views and a serious questioning of whether climatic desiccation has been sufficient to explain present-day ranges (Colinvaux 1987; Bush 1994). The idea may have been pushed too far. As one instance, some purported refugia for angiosperms seem simply to reflect intensity of collecting, for example in the vicinity of Manaus (Nelson et al. 1990). It is now accepted that rain forests may have been reduced in area, but that seasonal forests rather than savanna came to expand (Mayle, Burbridge, and Killeen 2000). Further, many species had evolved before the Quaternary, and their present-day distributions reflect a long series of climatic fluctuations extending back into the Tertiary. The debate continues on the causes of patchiness of Amazonian biota, specifically the very real existence (at least in some taxa) of rich and poor regions (see for example Haffer 1997, Tuomisto and Ruokolainen 1997, and Nores 1999).

Climatic fluctuation is more generally accepted as the explanation for the small regions of very high species richness and endemism embedded within the tropical moist forests of Africa. However, Africa has long been regarded as the odd man out in its floristic poverty compared to Asia and America (Richards 1973; see also part 8). Greater desiccation is invoked, coupled to continental uplift during the Tertiary, which resulted in a paucity of low-elevation humid refugia during epochs of cold climate (Morley 2000).

Conclusion

The distribution patterns today of tropical plants, animals, and forests reflect a long history of fluctuations of climate and continually changing geography resulting from plate tectonics (both continental movements and the emergence of island arcs). Evolution has taken place in this milieu of movement and fluctuating climate. The Quaternary is just the last chapter of a long story. It is now appreciated that tropical rain forests and their component plants and animals have experienced massive reduction in area several times during their evolution. The difference between past contractions and deforestation today is that reduction is now occur-

ring faster than on any previous occasion and is accompanied by fragmentation, so that migration is not possible (part 11). The historical record does, however, show that today's other big impact, rapidly warming climate, does have several past equals, and that global climate is still cooler than at the Paleocene-Eocene boundary fifty-four million years ago.

Reprinted Selections

T. van der Hammen. 1974. The Pleistocene changes of vegetation and climate in tropical South America. *Journal of Biogeography* 1:3–26. Reprinted with the permission of Blackwell Science

J. Haffer. 1969. Speciation in Amazonian forest birds. *Science* 165:131–37

P. H. Raven and D. I. Axelrod. 1974. Angiosperm biogeography and past continental movements. *Annals of the Missouri Botanic Garden* 61:539–61, 637–57

F. G. Stehli and D. S. Webb. 1985 A kaleidoscope of plates, faunal and floral dispersals, and sea level changes. In *The Great American Biotic Interchange*, ed. F. G. Stehli and S. D. Webb, 3–6, 8–16. New York: Plenum Press

Journal of Biogeography (1974) **1**, 3–26

The Pleistocene changes of vegetation and climate in tropical South America

T. VAN DER HAMMEN

Hugo de Vries Laboratorium, Afdeling Palynologie, University of Amsterdam, Netherlands

Abstract

Palynological studies in the Northern Andes have shown a gradual upheaval of the Cordillera during the Late Pliocene and the creation of the high montane environment. A long sequence of glacial and interglacial periods has been recorded from the Pleistocene. The successive appearance of new taxa, by evolutionary adaptation from the local neotropical flora and from elements immigrated from the holarctic and austral-antarctic floral regions, can be followed step by step. For the Last Glacial to Holocene sequence the contemporaneity of the changes of temperature with those recorded from the northern temperate latitudes could be proved by ^{14}C dating. During the coldest part of the Last Glacial the tree line descended to c. 2000 m altitude, i.e. 1200–1500 m lower than where it lies today. During the period from c. 21,000 to c. 13,000 B.P. the climate was, moreover, much drier. Even taking the greater aridity into account, the lowering of the temperature during the coldest part of the Last Glacial may have been 6–7° C or more. The lowering of the temperature in the tropical lowlands during glacial times may have been c. 3°C. The temperature gradient must, therefore, have been steeper than it is today.

In the coastal lowlands of Guyana and Surinam glacial-interglacial eustatic movements of sea level have been recorded. Pollen diagrams show in this area a considerable extension of savannas during glacial periods with low sea levels.

In the inland savannas of the Llanos Orientales of Colombia and the Rupununi savanna of Guyana, several periods of grass-savanna and of savanna-woodland alternate during the Late Pleistocene and the Holocene; lower and higher lake levels corroborate

the conclusions that these are caused by changes in the effective precipitation. One of the driest periods in the Rupununi seems to correspond to the time immediately before c. 13,000 B.P.

Pollen data from a series of samples from Rondonia, in the southern part of the Amazon basin, have shown that in that area grass-savannas replaced the tropical forest during a certain interval of Pleistocene age.

From the above it appears that in considerable parts of the South American tropics a much drier climate prevailed during certain parts of the Pleistocene. A major dry period seems to have occurred during the later part of the Last Glacial, when the glaciers in the northern latitudes and in the Andes were reaching their maximum extension. These changes of climate and vegetation are of considerable importance for the explanation of speciation patterns and the recent distribution of plant and animal taxa.

Introduction

It has been known for a considerable length of time that the Pleistocene glacials and interglacials changed repeatedly and greatly the face of the earth in the northern and temperate latitudes. This happened during at least the last two million years. It caused extinction, speciation and profound changes in the geographical distribution of plants and animals.

It is only rather recently that we learned that the so-called stable tropics, likewise, became subjected to drastic changes in climates which were apparently contemporaneous with those in the northern hemisphere.

In the last 15 years a considerable amount of data relevant to these changes in northern South America has become available, especially from the Northern Andes, but also from the tropical lowlands. I will try to present here the broad outlines of these results, which are mainly based on pollen analyses, and partly still unpublished.

Figure 1 shows the distribution of the three major

4   *T. van der Hammen*

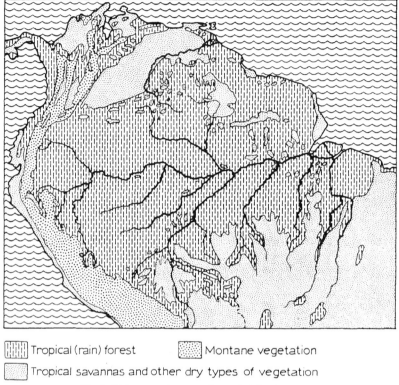

Tropical (rain) forest   Montane vegetation

Tropical savannas and other dry types of vegetation

Fig. 1. Major vegetation types in tropical South America.

'formations' of vegetation in tropical South America: the montane vegetation, tropical forest, and tropical savannas with other relatively dry types of vegetation. I shall deal with the history of the montane Andean vegetation, of the coastal vegetation, and of the savannas and tropical forest of the inland in this order. At the end I shall give some general conclusions and make comparisons with other tropical areas.

The Northern Andes

The present vegetation belts (Fig. 2)

The Eastern Cordillera of the Northern Andes rise from tropical lowlands, where rain forests, savannas, or xerophytic vegetation types dominate. To the NE of this Cordillera lies the savanna area of the Llanos Orientales and the Orinoco, to the SE the

rain forest. West of the Cordillera lies the Magdalena valley, the northern part of which bears rain forest and the southern part tropical xerophytic vegetation.

In the Eastern Cordillera the tropical belt extends from these lowlands to approximately 1000 m. At about this altitude several tropical taxa, such as the Bombacaceae, disappear, whereas several other ones are restricted to this belt or to a part of it (*e.g. Byrsonima, Iriartea, Mauritia* and *Spathiphyllum*).

The next altitudinal zone is that of the Subandean Forest, between *c.* 1000 and *c.* 2300 (–2500) m. Such genera as *Acalypha, Alchornea* and *Cecropia,* good pollen producers, are of frequent occurrence in this zone and do not extend beyond its upper limit. The same holds for many Palmae, *Hieronima, Ficus* and Malpighiaceae.

From 2300 (–2500) to 3200–3500 m the Andean Forest belt is present. In this belt forests of *Weinmannia* sp. div. and *Quercus* dominate. *Alnus, Myrica, Styloceras, Podocarpus, Clusia, Rapanea, Juglans,*

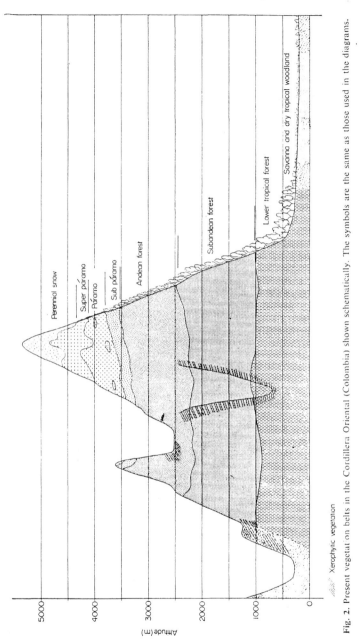

Fig. 2. Present vegetation belts in the Cordillera Oriental (Colombia) shown schematically. The symbols are the same as those used in the diagrams.

6   *T. van der Hammen*

Ilex, and *Hedyosmum* etc. are frequently present, although most of these genera are not restricted in their distribution to this belt.

The next higher belt is that of the high Andean dwarf forest and shrub formations, and the Subpáramo. It may be developed as a rather irregular belt, especially at its upper limit. Patches of this type of forest or shrub may be found at altitudes of up to 4000 m and over. The forest trees of the genera *Weinmannia* and *Quercus* are absent and the commonest woody taxa are various Compositae and Ericaceae, *Polylepis*, *Aragoa*, *Hypericum* etc. Some species of *Espeletia* may be present.

The proper Páramo belt extends from *c.* 3500 m up to 4000–4200 m. Open Andean grasslands may, however, be found from 3200 to 3300 m in the Subpáramo zone, patches of forest and ·shrub occurring in the higher grasslands at altitudes of up to 4000 m and over. Bogs and mires may be frequent. Apart from grasses and some sedges, the most characteristic elements are species of *Espeletia*. Amongst the herbs *Gentiana*, *Halenia*, *Valeriana*, *Bartschia*, *Geranium*, *Plantago*, *Ranunculus* and *Paepalanthus* may be mentioned.

The Super Páramo belt extends from 4000 to 4200 m upwards. Frost action on the soil is common here and the vegetation cover is incomplete to very scanty. *Espeletia* is mostly lacking. Characteristic elements are e.g. *Draba* sp. div. and *Senecio niveoaureus*. The proper nival zone, practically devoid of vegetation, extends from 4500 to 4800 m, or locally from somewhat higher altitudes upwards. The highest areas extending to *c.* 5500 m may be covered by snow and ice.

The ecological grouping of pollen types for the pollen diagrams

In order to make the pollen diagrams presented here easier to understand for non-palynologists, we have redrawn them as cumulative diagrams showing the percentage variation in time of ecological groups of pollen grains. These groups are the following.

(1) Pollen from taxa common in the Páramo (dominating elements Gramineae).
(2) Pollen from taxa common in the highest zone of the Andean Forest and shrub, or the Subpáramo, respectively.
(3) Pollen from elements common in both the Andean and Subandean Forest.
(4) Pollen from elements of the Subandean Forest.

(5) Pollen from elements common in the tropical forest.

Although these types of diagrams give, generally speaking, a very clear picture of the changing vegetation, it will be clear that for a correct interpretation one must take into account both the present-day relation between vegetation and pollen rain in the area and the altitudinal range and ecology of the individual taxa.

The Pliocene, the upheaval of the Andes, and the early montane vegetation types (*Figs 3 and 4*)

At the beginning of the Pliocene the area of the Eastern Cordillera lay mainly in the tropical belt. Folding had already taken place, so that hill ridges and low mountains, probably not exceeding 1000 m, were present. Rather extensive lowlands extended in broad synclinal basins, where fluvial and lacustrine sedimentation took place. This is proved by the pollen diagram of the lower part of the Tilatá formation (Fig. 3, lower part), which diagram shows a complete dominance of tropical elements. The middle part of the Tilatá formation of later Pliocene age provided pollen diagrams showing an uplift of the basins in which sedimentation continued during this later stage of the Pliocene (Fig. 3, middle part). The specific content shows that the dominating Subandean–Andean pollen group represents elements of the Subandean Forest, indicating an altitude of sedimentation of *c.* 1500 m and *c.* 2300 m respectively. When this elevation was reached, open high Andean vegetation, somehow comparable with the recent Páramo, must have been developed already on nearby higher mountains. During the Pliocene, *Hedyosmum*, and later *Myrica*, appeared for the first time. Sediments of the uppermost part of the formation already show a dominance of the primitive Páramo (Fig. 3), although its present elevation is in the lower part of the Andean Forest belt. This means that the climate was considerably colder than it is today, and this part of the diagram must represent already a very early Pleistocene glacial, possibly of an age of some 2 million years.

There are clear indications that at this time the Andean Forest belt was not yet fully developed; it may have been narrower because the process of adaptation to the new biotopes had only just begun. Important taxa nowadays frequent in this belt, such as *Quercus* and *Alnus*, were absent at that time. Similarly, the primitive Páramo vegetation is still

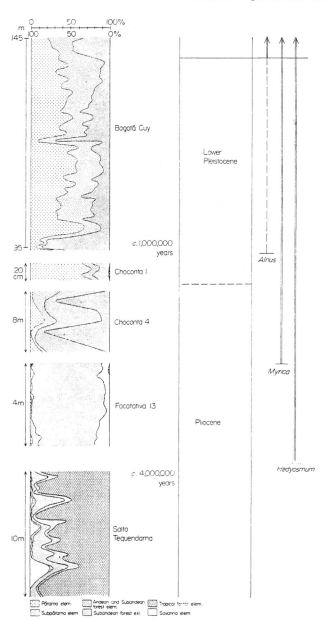

Fig. 3. Pollen diagrams from the Pliocene and Lower Pleistocene of the high plain of Bogotá (Colombia), demonstrating the uplift of the area and the Early Pleistocene glacials and interglacials.

very poor in species. Apart from the dominant grasses, the earliest elements of this vegetation include *Polylepis, Aragoa, Hypericum, Miconia,* Umbelliferae (*Borreria, Jussiaea, Polygonum*), *Valeri-* *ana, Plantago,* Ranunculaceae, *Myriophyllum* and *Jamesonia.* Some of these elements were derived from the local flora, whereas other ones must have been derived from founder species which arrived at the

8   *T. van der Hammen*

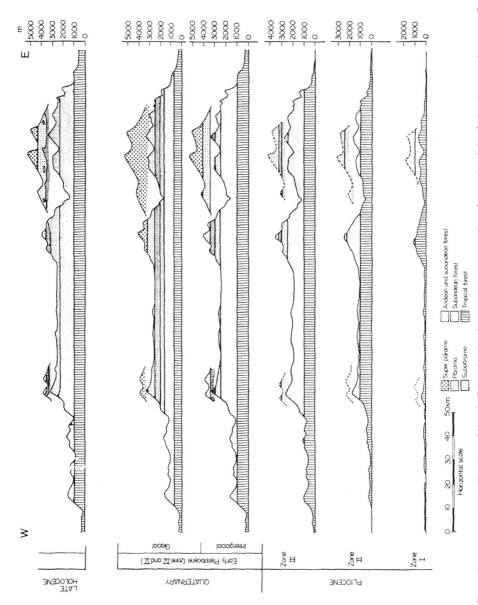

Fig. 4. Sections through the Cordillera Oriental (Colombia) showing tentative reconstruction of vegetation belts during the successive stages of uplift and during an early Pleistocene interglacial and glacial. The uppermost section shows the present situation. The main section is east–west at the latitude of Bogotá. The small sections above each section are from higher areas farther to the north.

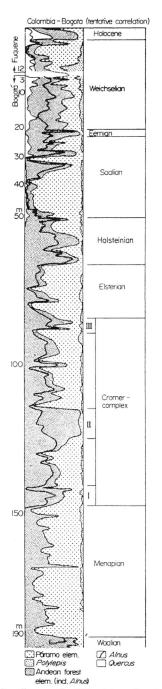

Colombia – Bogota (tentative correlation)

Holocene	
Weichselian	
Eemian	
Saalian	
Holsteinian	
Elsterian	
III	
Cromer – complex	
II	
I	
Menapian	
Waalian	

☐ Páramo elem.
▨ Polylepis
☐ Andean forest elem. (incl. Alnus)
▨ Alnus
☐ Quercus

Fig. 5. Pollen diagram of c. 200 m lake sediments from the high plain of Bogotá (section CUY); the uppermost part is from Fuquene. The European chronostratigraphic names are only tentatively used.

Pleistocene vegetation and climate changes 9

newly created 'islands' of Páramo by long-distance dispersal. The chances of such founders arriving and establishing themselves were certainly increased by the formation of the isthmus of Pánama and by the considerable enlargement of the Páramo islands (and the enlargement and displacement of their areas of origin in the Holarctic and Antarctic floral areas).

In Fig. 4 the successive upheaval of the Cordillera and the creation of vegetation belts is shown diagrammatically (for further details, see Van der Hammen, Werner & van Dommelen, 1973).

The Lower and Middle Pleistocene sequence (Fig. 3, upper part and Fig. 5)

At the beginning of the Pleistocene, the principal upheaval of the area had ceased. Several hundreds of metres of lake sediments were deposited during the Pleistocene in the basin of the high plain of Bogotá (altitude c. 2580 m), providing us with a unique, very long and continuous palynological record of the changing vegetation and climate.

During the Lower Pleistocene several conspicuous, recurrent changes of the vegetation cover from Andean Forest to open Páramo (and *vice versa*) took place (Fig. 3, upper part; Fig. 4, upper part; and Fig. 5, lower part). They were caused by the changes of climate from glacial to interglacial or the other way around, resulting in a downward and upward displacement of vegetation zones. At the same time at least the upper vegetation belts were gradually enriched by new taxa. In the Páramo belt *Geranium* and *Lycopodium* appear and somewhat later *Gunnera*, *Gentiana corymbosa* and *Lysipomia* sp. In the Andean Forest belt there appeared *Styloceras*, and somewhat later *Juglans* and Urticaceae. It seems as if *Alnus* appeared for the first time on the eastern slopes of the Eastern Cordillera during the later part of the Lower Pleistocene.

Our conclusion that the climate prevailing during the Early Pleistocene glacials was really much colder than it is today at the same elevation, is corroborated by the occurrence of simultaneous depositions of solifluction and fluvioglacial sediments.

At the beginning of the Middle Pleistocene (Fig. 5, middle part) *Alnus* immigrated into the high plains. It had apparently become adapted to the ecological conditions of the Andean Forest belt and suddenly started to become a quantitatively important element (at least on wetter soil types).

The gradual enrichment of the flora continued

10   *T. van der Hammen*

(see Van der Hammen & Gonzalez, 1964), while the rhythm of glacial–interglacial displacement of vegetation belts continued likewise and resulted in the development of Páramo vegetation and Andean Forest on the mountain slopes surrounding the high plain, respectively.

Towards the end of the Middle Pleistocene *Quercus* made its first appearance in the Eastern Cordillera, as is manifest from the pollen diagrams of the *penultimate interglacial* (age: approximately 250,000 years ago). During the penultimate glacial it increases in quantitative importance, apparently becoming progressively adapted to the environmental conditions prevailing in the higher parts of the Andean Forest belt (Fig. 5; see also Van der Hammen *et al.*, 1973).

The Upper Pleistocene: the last interglacial–glacial cycle

The Upper Pleistocene of the 'Sabana de Bogotá' (altitude *c.* 2580 m) was studied in greater detail (Van der Hammen & Gonzalez, 1960a). The terminal stage of the penultimate glacial period apparently was very cold and dry; the pollen diagram (Fig. 5) suggests the absolute dominance of open grass-páramo with such high-páramo species as *Malvastrum acaule*. Virtually no trace of forest elements remains.

During the next and last interglacial that probably started about 130,000 years ago, the area around the high plain is forested once more; the frequency of some of the elements from the uppermost Subandean Forest seems to indicate that the climate became even slightly warmer than it is at the present time.

The first part of the Last Glacial (the 'Early Glacial'), with a much wetter climate, shows several interstadials and stadials comparable to those of the northern temperate latitudes. During the forest phases of this Early Glacial, *Quercus* becomes a much more dominant element than before.

The following Pleniglacial was much colder and Páramo vegetation dominated. Elements of the uppermost forest and shrub and Subpáramo became more important during some of the minor 'interstadials' of the Middle Pleniglacial. The coldest phase of the Last Glacial started approximately 26,000 years ago. Around that time the Pleistocene lake of the 'Sabana de Bogotá' had dried up (see Fig. 5). Sedimentation continued, however, in the lake of Fuquene on the next high plain (also at *c.* 2580 m), to the north of the plain of Bogotá,

where we can follow the history until the present.

The pollen diagram from Laguna de Fuquene (Fig. 6; Van Geel & Van der Hammen, 1973) provides a fine and complete record of the vegetational history of the last 32,000 years. The results are summarized in Fig. 7. From the pollen diagram we may deduce that fluctuations in the temperature and in humidity occurred. The first kind of fluctuation can be estimated by means of the displacement of vegetation belts, and the second can be deduced from the extension and retraction of the marshy zone of the hydrosere reflected in the pollen diagram. Approximately 30,000 years ago *Polylepis* scrub dominated completely in the area, its occurrence indicating conditions slightly above the limit of the proper Andean Forest. Shortly afterwards the climate became progressively colder so that open Páramo vegetation started to dominate.

About 21,000 years ago the climate became extremely cold and dry. The water in the lake dropped to a very low level and extreme Páramo conditions prevailed. This lasted till the beginning of the Late Glacial, 13,000 years ago. *The lowering of vegetation belts during this* period was of the order of 1200–1500 m. Taking the influence of aridity into account, the average annual temperature during this very cold Upper Pleniglacial may have been something like 8°C (and at least 6°C to 7°C) lower than it is today, and the annual precipitation may have been as low as 100–400 mm, which is less than half of the present value. We shall see presently that a lowering of the tree line by about 1500 m is confirmed by the pollen diagram from the Laguna de Pedro Palo at an elevation of 2000 m. At the same time (during the Upper Pleniglacial) the mountain glaciers extended downwards to an altitude of approximately 3000 m.

The Late Glacial and the Holocene

At present a considerable number of pollen diagrams covering the last 13,000 years have been drawn up from sediments in lakes situated at elevations between 2000 and 4000 m.

About 14,000–13,000 years ago the climate started to become less severe. This Late Glacial period lasted till approximately 10,000 years ago and exhibited several minor climatic fluctuations that could be correlated, by means of ^{14}C dating, with those of the northern temperate latitudes, and also with the climatic sequence in, e.g. tropical Africa.

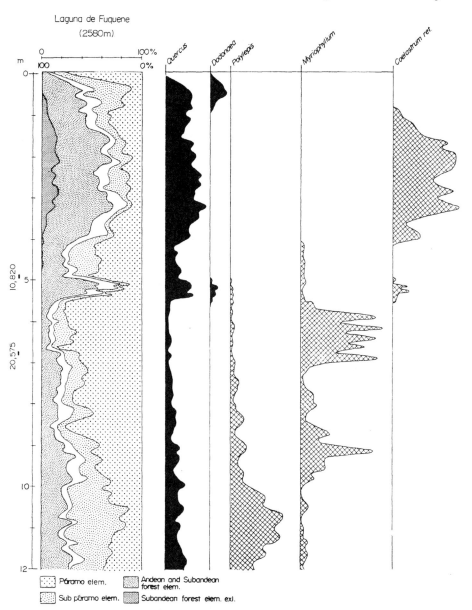

Fig. 6. Pollen diagram from Laguna de Fuquene, Cordillera Oriental, Colombia (adapted from Van Geel & Van der Hammen, 1973). The white area represents the percentage of *Alnus*.

In Fuquene (Figs 6 and 7) a major interstadial, the Guantiva interstadial, is represented. It lasted until *c.* 11,000 B.P. and was followed by the El Abra stadial that lasted until approximately 10,000–9500 years ago, the beginning of the Holocene. During the Guantiva interstadial the area was forested. *Dodonaea*, a pioneer of bare soil, was abundant and the composition of the forest seems to indicate that

12   *T. van der Hammen*

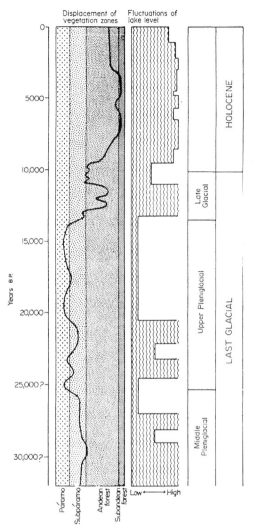

Fig. 7. Displacement of vegetation zones and fluctuations of lake level, Laguna de Fuquene (see diagram Fig. 6). (Adapted from Van Geel & Van der Hammen, 1973.)

the temperature was not much lower than it is at the present time. The incidence of the alga *Coelastrum reticulatum* corroborates this conclusion. During the El Abra stadial there was a considerable cooling of the climate, so that the site was near the forest limit. A striking fact is the sudden rising of the lake level at the beginning of the Guantiva interstadial, which indicates a much wetter climate than before. After a minor lowering of the water table

during the El Abra stadial, the water in the lake again rose to a slightly higher level than today by the beginning of the Holocene.

In the higher mountains the glaciers had retreated with fluctuations since their maximum extension at about 20,000 B.P. During the Guantiva interstadial they had retreated to altitudes above 4000 m to descend again to *c.* 3900 m during the El Abra stadial.

During the Holocene the climate in the Fuquene area became even warmer than it is today during the 'hypsothermal'. Elements from the uppermost Subandean Forest (*Cecropia*, *Acalypha*) could even grow in the area at altitudes several hundreds of metres above their present upper limit of occurrence. It seems, therefore, as if the annual temperature was about 2°C higher than today. The forest elements in question disappeared again about 3000 years ago when the temperature fell again to the present-day average.

An example of the succession at higher elevation is provided by the diagram from Páramo de Palacio (*c.* 3500 m), NE of Bogotá (Fig. 8) (see Van der Hammen & Gonzalez, 1960b). The site lies at 200–300 m above the present-day limit of the *Weinmannia* forest. The Late Glacial clayey sediments, deposited after the retraction of the glaciers from the lake area, show fluctuations in the pollen diagram similar to those noted in the Late Glacial of Fuquene. During the Guantiva interstadial the forest limit seems to have been even slightly higher than where it lies today, although the composition of this forest seems to be somewhat different from the present, with Urticaceae being much more frequent. During the El Abra stadial the forest limit descended again, but during the Holocene hypsothermal this limit lay at an altitude several hundreds of metres higher than the present one, and the area around the lake must have been forested. At about 3000 years ago a lowering of the forest limit took place which persists until today.

Another Late Glacial–Holocene sequence is represented in a pollen diagram from the El Abra valley in the high plain of Bogotá (Fig. 9) (compare Schreve-Brinkman & Van der Hammen, in preparation). The diagram starts with lake sediments (see the curve of the alga *Botryococcus*) of Guantiva interstadial age; the climate was wet and *Alnus* carr must have been abundant in the area. The latest part of this interstadial is dated here as 11,200 B.P. The climate became drier at the beginning of the El Abra stadial and the local lake became a marsh. The

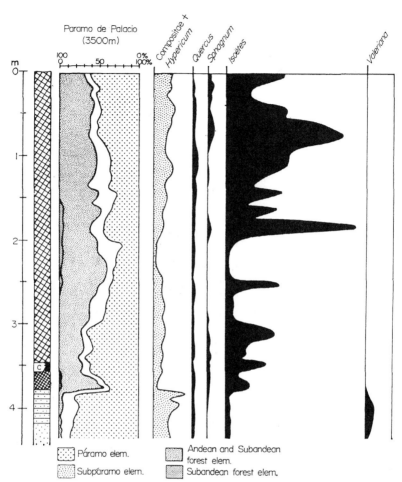

Fig. 8. Pollen diagram of the Late Glacial and Holocene from Páramo de Palacio (Cordillera Oriental, Colombia). (Adapted from Van der Hammen & Gonzalez, 1960b.) The stratigraphical column indicates from top to bottom: detritus gyttja, volcanic ash, detritus gyttja, sandy clay and clayey sand. In this diagram certain elements of the Subpáramo group (*Hypericum*, Compositae) were not included in the pollen total. The white area represents the percentage of *Alnus*.

vegetation in the area became dominated by low forest and grassland, the presence of Cactaceae corroborating the palynological indications pointing to a relatively dry climate. During the Holocene forest vegetation dominated.

From the area of Páramo de Guantiva in the western part of the Cordillera Oriental, two pollen diagrams are presented to show the influence of local climatic conditions (Van der Hammen, 1962; Van der Hammen & Gonzalez, 1965). Figure 10 shows these conditions in an E–W transect. The western slopes of the mountains fall off steeply to much more

low-lying areas and have a much wetter climate, the upper limit of the oak forest lying at *c.* 3500 m. Behind these mountains is shown a flat area at *c.* 3300 m that lies in rain shadow and supports only small patches of forest. The pollen diagram from this drier area (Fig. 11) shows in its lower part a dated Late Glacial with the Guantiva interstadial. The climate was apparently much wetter during the interstadial and a much larger area was under forest than today. Trees disappeared from the area by the beginning of the cooler and drier El Abra stadial. When at the beginning of the Holocene the climate

14   *T. van der Hammen*

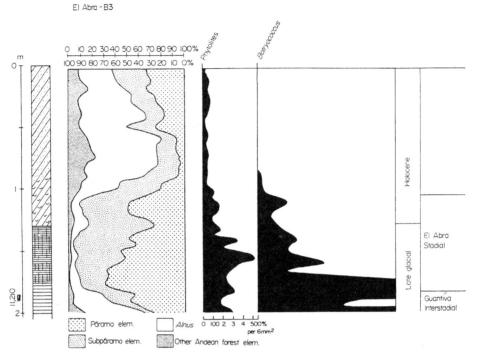

Fig. 9. Pollen diagram of the Late Glacial and Holocene from El Abra (Sabana de Bogotá). The stratigraphical column indicates from top to bottom: dark partly sandy soil, black humic clay and grey lake clay. (Adapted from Schreve-Brinkman & Van der Hammen, in preparation.)

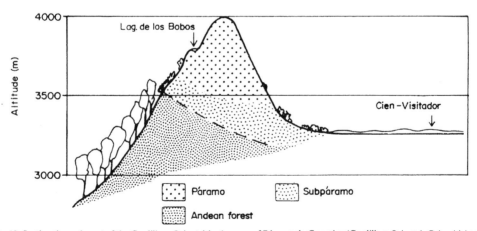

Fig. 10. Section through part of the Cordillera Oriental in the area of Páramo de Guantiva (Cordillera Oriental, Colombia); the localities of the diagrams of Figs 11 and 12 are indicated.

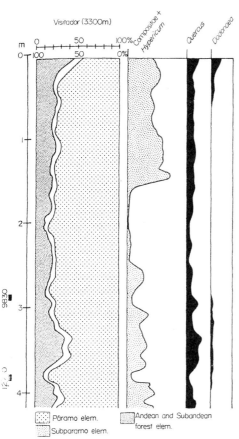

Fig. 11. Pollen diagram from the Late Glacial and Holocene of Cienaga del Visitador (see Fig. 10). The elements of the Subpáramo group Compositae and *Hypericum* are not included in the pollen total. The white area represents the percentage of *Alnus* in the pollen total. (Adapted from Van der Hammen & Gonzalez, 1965.)

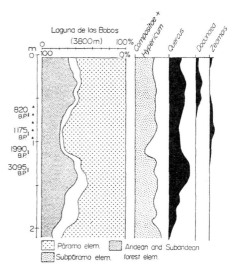

Fig. 12. Pollen diagram from the Late Holocene of Laguna de Los Bobos (see Fig. 10). The elements of the Subpáramo group Compositae and *Hypericum* are not included in the pollen total. The white area represents the percentage of *Alnus* in the pollen total. (Adapted from Van der Hammen, 1962.)

became warmer again, the area did not become reforested, apparently because of the low amount of precipitation.

The pollen diagram from a small lake on the western slopes of these mountains show the conditions on the western wet slopes during the late Holocene (Figs 10 and 12). Even at an elevation of 3800 m the percentage of forest elements is much higher here than at the former site. A cooling is recorded at *c*. 3000 years ago.

From a lake (Laguna de Pedro Palo, W of the Sabana de Bogotá) at *c*. 2000 m, a most elucidating diagram of the Late Glacial was obtained (Fig. 13; Sieswerda, in preparation). The site is in the upper

part of the Andean Forest belt. Sedimentation started in the early Late Glacial or Late Pleniglacial. The area subsequently became covered with open grassland vegetation, and the forest limit must clearly have lain below 2000 m. The presence of grains of *Isoetes* and of *Myriophyllum* (and of other, non-aquatic, herbs), which taxa are today mainly found above 3000 m corroborates the conclusion that this open vegetation resembled Páramo vegetation very much, so that the timber line must have been at least 1300 (probably 1500) m lower than today. Some 12,000 years ago the area became invaded by Andean Forest, and towards the end of the Guantiva interstadial by Subandean Forest.

Conclusions (*Figs* 14–16)

The tropical-montane, northern Andean climatic belts came into being during the Late Pliocene upheaval of the Cordillera. These newly created belts gradually became populated by processes of evolutionary adaptation of elements from the local Neotropical flora and by the arrival of elements which immigrated from the Holarctic and Antarctic floral areas. This process continued during the entire Pleistocene. In the Andean Forest belt local elements are frequent, but *Weinmannia* originally

16   *T. van der Hammen*

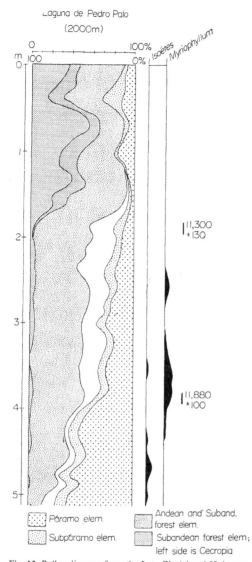

Fig. 13. Pollen diagram from the Late Glacial and Holocene of Laguna de Pedro Palo (Cordillera Oriental, Colombia). (Adapted from Sieswerda, in preparation.) The white area represents the percentage of *Alnus* in the pollen total.

came from the south and *Myrica, Alnus* and *Quercus* from the north.

In the transitional and Subpáramo forest and scrub local genera are still abundant, but elements from more remote areas gradually became more frequent to reach their highest frequencies of occurrence in open Páramo vegetation (*Gentiana,*

Bartschia, Valerians, Draba, Hypericum, Berberis etc. from the Holarctic; *Muehlenbeckia, Acaena, Azorella* etc. from the Antarctic). The most characteristic Páramo genus, *Espeletia*, is of local Andean origin, however, and other endemics are, e.g. *Aciachne, Distichia, Puya* and *Rhizocephalum*.

The Pleistocene shows a sequence of several glacials and interglacials comparable with those of the northern hemisphere and the contemporaneity of the changes of temperature could be substantiated for the last 50,000 years, i.e. for the period within the reach of reliable ^{14}C dating.

The depression of the Andean Forest limit (presently between *c.* 3200 and 3500 m) was of the order of 1200–1500 m. Although this limit must have been as irregular as it is today owing to local climatic and micro-climatic conditions, it seems as if a probable average value of 2000 m for its altitudinal position during periods of maximum glaciation can be considered to be established. Under extreme arid conditions the lowermost limit of dry Páramo vegetation in the Eastern Cordillera today is at 3000 m. If such conditions prevailed during the Upper Pleniglacial, we still have to accept a lowering of temperature of 6–7°C to explain the total depression of the altitudinal forest limit.

During the coldest period of the Last Glacial (Upper Pleniglacial), the climate on the high plains was much drier than today, and for the areas of Fuquene the annual precipitation may have been less than half that at present. As we shall see presently, the temperature in the tropical lowlands during glacial time may only have been about 3°C lower than today; this means that the temperature gradient in the Northern Andes was much steeper than it is at present.

During glacial time the surface area occupied by Páramo vegetation was a multiple of its present extension; many now isolated 'islands' were in former times linked together. The Páramos of Cocuy and Sumapaz formed then part of a large and continuous area of Páramo that covered the entire central portion of the Cordillera Oriental. The Superpáramos of these two areas were never in direct contact with one another, however. This seems to be reflected in the relatively high degree of endemism, especially in the Superpáramo of the Sierra Nevada del Cocuy.

The distribution patterns in the Northern Andes may be partly explained by long-distance dispersal, partly by the erstwhile continuity of areas of Páramo during glacial times. Conditions for immigration by

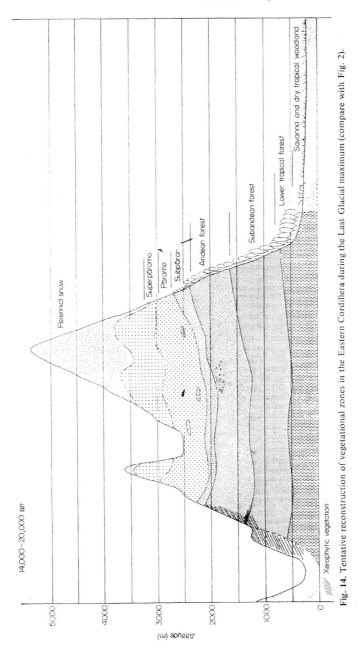

Fig. 14. Tentative reconstruction of vegetational zones in the Eastern Cordillera during the Last Glacial maximum (compare with Fig. 2).

18   *T. van der Hammen*

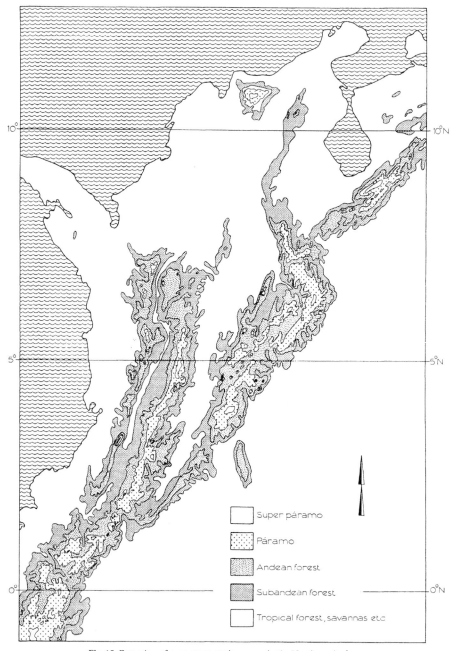

Fig. 15. Extension of present vegetation zones in the Northern Andes.

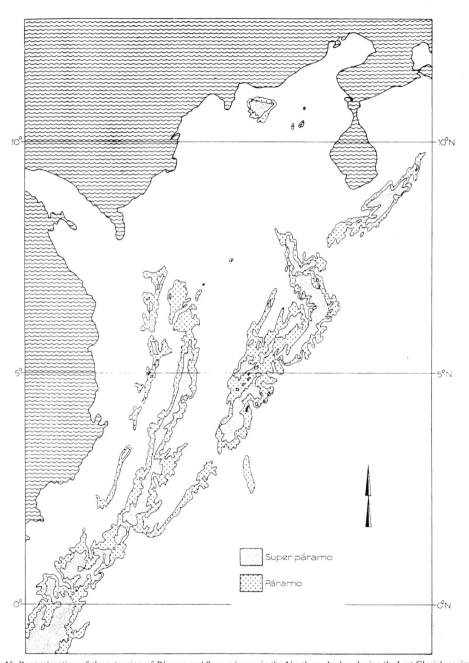

Fig. 16. Reconstruction of the extension of Páramo and Superpáramo in the Northern Andes, during the Last Glacial maximum. The area indicated as Superpáramo was partly occupied by glaciers. Compare with Fig. 15.

20   *T. van der Hammen*

long-distance dispersal (or from one 'island' to another) were certainly much more favourable for elements of the high Andean vegetation groups during glacial times. Speciation of both the local and the alien elements must have been stimulated by the successive periods of separation and union of populations.

The coastal lowlands

A diagrammatic transect of the vegetation zones along the Caribbean coast of Guyana and Surinam is shown in Fig. 17. Along the estuaries and the muddy shores of the seas and lagoons mangrove forest is found. Often the outermost zone is formed by *Rhizophora*, *Avicennia* forest following behind it on still periodically inundated soil. Behind the mangrove belt there is an alternation of somewhat more elevated former beach ridges and more low-lying swampy areas. The ridges are covered with a type of forest characteristic of drier soils; while the swamps sustain open herbaceous vegetation or swamp forest. Common elements in the open swamps are, e.g. *Cyperus*, *Typha* and *Acnida*; in the swamp forest such arborescent taxa as *Symphonia*, *Ilex*, *Virola* and *Tabebuia* abound, and palms may locally be very abundant. Farther inland, the relatively dry Wallaba forest, or more humid tropical forests, are found. Where edaphic conditions are extreme (e.g. on the 'White sands') the vegetation tends to become savanna-like, but true savannas are only found much farther in the interior, e.g. in the Rupununi and Sipaliwini.

A 30 m section from a bore hole in the sediments of the coastal plain near Georgetown, Guyana, provided a pollen diagram (Fig. 18) that shows something of the history of this area during the last interglacial, the Last Glacial and the Holocene (Van der Hammen, 1963). The cumulative diagram shows the variation in time of the percentages of four ecological groups. The first two groups (left) are elements of the mangrove forest (*Avicennia* and *Rhizophora*, respectively). The next groups are forest elements and grass-savanna elements. For a good understanding it must be pointed out that *Avicennia* is a poor pollen producer and that its pollen is not widely dispersed, so that an appreciable pollen percentage is only found inside the *Avicennia* belt. *Rhizophora*, on the other hand, produces much more pollen that is easily transported seawards, so that a very high percentage is found not only inside the mangrove belt, *in situ*, but also in marine sediments on the shelf lying to seawards of this belt.

The lower part of the diagram, with a ^{14}C date of > 45,000 B.P., indicates that at the time of deposition the site was within the mangrove belt. There follows an extension of swamp forest elements and the sea seems to have retired; the site then apparently lay behind the coast line. Mangrove elements disappear completely from the diagram in the next phase, open grass-savanna elements becoming completely dominant and the sediment showing clear signs of soil formation. The site is now well above sea level. This situation lasts until the beginning of the Holocene, when the area gradually becomes invaded by the sea. First the *Avicennia* belt passed along the site (c. 8600 B.P.) and subsequently *Rhizophora* dominated completely; the presence of micro-foraminifera in this part of the section indicates that at that time the coast line proper lay farther inland than today. The later Holocene part of the diagram shows that the coast line moved northwards again and *Avicennia* forest, swamp forest and open swamps were frequent in the Georgetown area. The very last pollen spectra of the diagram show

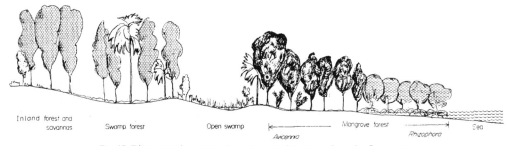

Fig. 17. Diagrammatic transect through vegetation zones along the Guyana coast.

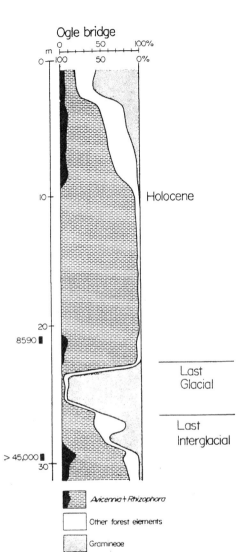

Ogle bridge

Holocene

Last
Glacial

Last
Interglacial

Avicennia + Rhizophora

Other forest elements

Gramineae

Fig. 18. Pollen diagram from Ogle Bridge, near Georgetown, Guyana. (Adapted from Van der Hammen, 1963).

show that in Quaternary sediments from the coastal plain the type of sequence as recorded from near Georgetown, is repeated many times and most probably reflects the sequence of Quaternary glacial–interglacial eustatic movements of the sea level. An example is given of a 120 m bore hole section from Surinam (Fig. 19). The Pleistocene (or Plio-Pleistocene, respectively) age of the series can be deduced from the presence of a number of taxa such as *Alnus*. Although *Byrsonima* occurs locally in the late Holocene part of the sections, the overall composition of the spectra indicates that at that time in this area extensive grass-savannas were not developed. On the other hand, many of the recorded older, low sea level sites are similar to that from the Last Glacial in Georgetown. They show a dominance of grass-savanna with *Byrsonima* and *Curatella*. Therefore, we have to conclude that the available data all point to the erstwhile dominance of real savanna vegetation in the present coastal area of Guyana and Surinam during glacial times, or at least during a part of each glacial time. Although the influence of edaphic factors cannot be ruled out, it seems as if the dominance of grass-savannas over so large an area cannot be explained by edaphic factors alone and requires the existence, at times, of a zone with a 'savanna-climate', i.e. with a lower annual precipitation, and/or more pronounced dry and wet seasons than at present.

The vegetational succession during an eustatic climatic cycle (see Wijmstra, 1971) is schematically indicated in Fig. 20 as being *Rhizophora* → *Avicennia* → Palm swamp forest → grass-savanna with *Byrsonima* and *Curatella* shrub, or *vice versa*.

The inland savannas

A number of pollen diagrams are available from lakes in the savannas of the Llanos Orientales of Colombia and the Rupununi savannas in Guyana (Wijmstra & Van der Hammen, 1966). Most of these are from the Holocene but one reaches back to the last glacial. We present here two of the more informative diagrams (Fig. 21), which show the variation in time of the percentage of pollen grains of three groups: forest elements; savanna woodland and shrub (*Byrsonima* and *Curatella*); and open savanna (Gramineae, Cyperaceae and other savanna herbs).

The first diagram is from Laguna de Agua Sucia, south of San Martin and not far from the Ariari

the present situation and the influence of man on the recent vegetation.

It is evident that the diagram not only reflects the glacial/interglacial eustatic fluctuations of sea level, but also shows that grass-savanna dominated in the area during at least a part of the last glacial.

Deep bore holes from Surinam and Guyana (Wijmstra, 1969, 1971; Van der Hammen, 1963)

22   *T. van der Hammen*

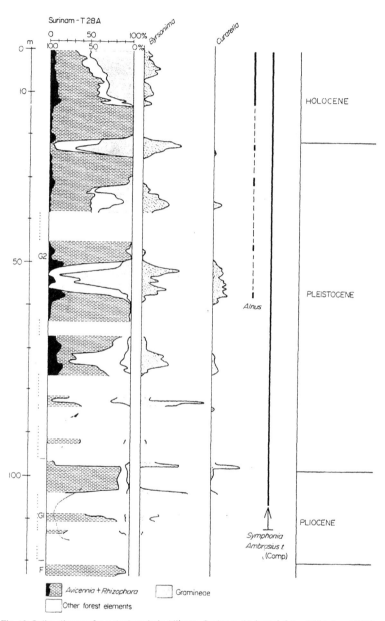

Fig. 19. Pollen diagram from the bore hole Alliance, Surinam. (Adapted from Wijmstra, 1969.)

river in the Colombian Llanos Orientales. Nowadays the area is dominated by grass-savanna with some swamp forest or gallery forests in low-lying places and in the Ariari valley proper.

Two layers of peat, intercalated in the lake sediments, represent low lake levels and were dated at *c.* 4000 and *c.* 2200 years B.P. The lower part of the diagram, dating from possibly *c.* 6000–5000 to

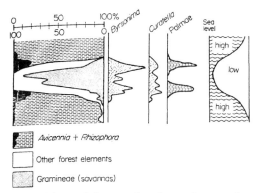

Fig. 20. Scheme of the succession of vegetation types (as reflected in the pollen diagram) during an interglacial–glacial–interglacial cycle in the present coastal plain of Guyana–Surinam. (Adapted from Wijmstra, 1971.)

c. 4000 years ago, shows a complete dominance of grass-savanna; it seems that the lake became seasonally desiccated. After *c.* 3800 B.P. the lake level rose and open water remained in the lake all the year round. At the same time *Byrsonima* woodland invaded the open savanna and became dominant. There is also an increase of the other forest elements. All these facts point, generally speaking, to a wetter climate. Open savanna subsequently increased gradually until about 2200 B.P. when the formation of peat indicates a very low lake level again; and at this time *Mauritia* swamp forests invaded part of the area of the lake. A little later the lake level rose again and a final sharp increase of grass-savanna elements can only be interpreted as being the effect of human influence (especially burning). From the data provided by this diagram we may conclude that, during the Holocene, changes in the rates of precipitation (annual total, and/or seasonal distribution) took place, which resulted in appreciable changes in the proportion of savanna in respect of savanna-woodland. A major period of open savanna, apparently drier than today, lasted from about 6000–5000 B.P. to *c.* 3800 B.P.

The second diagram of Fig. 21 is from Lake Moreiru in' the Rupununi savannas of Guyana. [14]C analyses of *c.* 7300 and *c.* 6000 B.P. date the upper part of the diagram. The lower part of the diagram shows approximately equal proportions of savanna woodland and open savanna, followed by a major extension of open savanna coinciding with a very low lake level. When the lake level rises again, the area around the lake is completely invaded by

Byrsonima woodland, so that virtually no open grass-savanna is left. The age of the lower limit of this woodland period was not established directly. If we use the sedimentation rate between 7300 B.P. and the present, the age would be *c.* 13,000 B.P., but if we use the rate between *c.* 7300 and 6000 B.P., the age would be *c.* 10,000 B.P. There seems, however, to be no doubt that the sediments below that limit (at *c.* 340 cm) are from the later part of the Last Glacial period. Towards the end of the above-mentioned savanna woodland period, open savanna increases again to dominate around 7300 B.P. Then follows a minor increase of *Byrsonima*, followed by an increase of open savanna, the lower part of which is dated *c.* 6000 B.P. Later, there is a slight final increase of trees. If the calculated date of *c.* 13,000 B.P. is correct, this implies that the extreme grass-savanna period immediately before it, associated with very low lake levels, would be of Upper Pleniglacial age, and also that the effective precipitation was low, probably lower than today, especially when we take into consideration that the temperature was most probably lower. The previous period must have been wetter and the subsequent period, corresponding with the Late Glacial and possibly the Early Holocene, much wetter than today. This would mean that the curve for the effective precipitation, corresponding with the lower part of the diagram, is apparently in phase with that from Lake Fuquene in the Andes (see Fig. 6). I think that this is the most likely interpretation of the diagram.*

There is no doubt that we urgently need more sections and more ^{14}C datings. However, the available data prove the existence of drier and wetter phases in the Holocene and in the Late Pleistocene and are highly suggestive of a very dry period in the Upper Pleniglacial and a wet period in the Late Glacial.

The Amazon basin

There has been a considerable amount of discussion concerning the possible occurrence during the Pleistocene of considerably drier climates in the

---

* Even if we accept the date of 10,000 instead of 13,000 B.P., we would have to conclude that the period corresponding in time with the El Abra stadial was dry, preceded by a wetter period (like the Guantiva interstadial) and followed by a wetter period corresponding with the Early Holocene. This also suggests that these changes seem to be in phase with those of Fuquene.

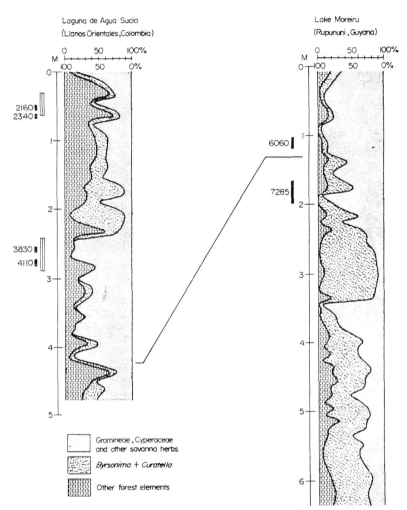

Fig. 21. Pollen diagrams (from the Late Pleistocene and Holocene) from areas at present covered with savanna vegetation (Llanos Orientales, Colombia; Rupununi, Guyana). (Adapted from Wijmstra & Van der Hammen, 1966.)

Amazon basin. Geomorphologists have repeatedly adduced arguments to prove this theory. Considerable support for this point of view has also come from biogeographers (e.g. Haffer, 1969 and Simpson, 1971). Recently some palynological data became available that strongly favour the idea of the former existence of savannas in areas at present covered with tropical forest (Van der Hammen, 1972). The samples providing the evidence hail from Rondonia (Brazil) in the southern part of the Amazon basin.

The general diagram presented here (Fig. 22) is composed of two sections from the same area. The

uppermost part corresponds with 2 m of recent sediments of a river, and the lower part (representing *c*. 13 m of sediments) is from the bottom of a small valley. The cumulative diagram shows the variation in time of the percentages of three groups of pollen grains: those belonging to trees from the humid tropical forest; those belonging to *Mauritia* (mainly occurring in swamp forest); and those belonging to open grass-savanna (Gramineae, *Cuphea* and a few other herbs).

The lower section shows in its lower part a darker type of humic clay and the pollen of humid tropical

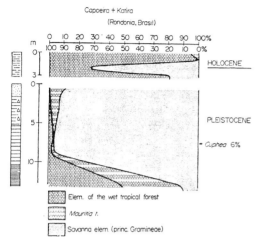

Fig. 22. Pollen diagrams from Capoeira and Katira, Rondonia Brazil.

and swamp forest dominates. In the upper part of the lower section the clays are of a lighter colour and show intercalations of reddish and sandy material, apparently correlating with slope deposits washed down from the sides of the valley during a period of instability (information provided by, e.g. J. Wiersma, who collected the samples). This part of the section shows a complete dominance of open savanna elements (mainly grasses, but also herbs like *Cuphea*).

In the upper section of recent river valley sediments, elements of the humid tropical forest are completely dominating in the upper part. Here again we can see that in the lower portion savanna elements are much more abundant.

The Holocene age of the uppermost recent sediments seems to be certain; their pollen content is entirely in agreement with the present situation. The age of the lower part of these river-valley sediments might be still Holocene or Late Glacial. Although we do not know the exact age of the other sections, it is clear that they represent Quaternary sediments from an earlier phase. We cannot yet be certain that they represent, e.g. the Last Glacial, but the data presented here show, without reasonable doubt, that there were periods during the Pleistocene when savannas locally replaced part of the forest. As we will see below there are reasons to suppose that those periods correspond with the periods of maximum glaciation in the northern hemisphere and the Andes.

General conclusions

The highest zones of tropical montane South America (the Northern Andes) during the Quarternary exhibited changes in the average annual temperature contemporaneous with those of the northern temperate latitudes. For the Last Glacial the maximal decrease of temperature was estimated at at least 6–7°C. The upper limit of the Andean Forest proper was lowered to an elevation of *c.* 2000 m (today's position: 3200–3500 m). In the Last Glacial an extremely dry period coincides with the period of maximum glaciation (*c.* 21,000–13,000 B.P.) The glacial climate before that time was wetter. The Late Glacial Guantiva interstadial (in time corresponding with the European Bølling and Allerød) was wet, the El Abra stadial (corresponding mainly with the Younger Dryas time) was again drier. It seems as if a major part of the Last Glacial (between *c.* 90,000 and 21,000 B.P.) had a climate with a higher effective precipitation than the Holocene. During the period 21,000–*c.* 13,000 B.P. the effective precipitation was much lower than during the Holocene, however.

No temperature data for the Last Glacial can as yet be deduced from pollen diagrams of the tropical lowlands. From deep-sea sediments in the Caribbean, however, a decrease of temperature of the superficial waters of 2–3°C has been calculated (corrected O^{16}/O^{18} data and data on foraminiferal assemblages; oral information by John Imbrie). As at present the temperature of superficial sea water in the Caribbean seems to correspond approximately with the average annual temperature, it seems reasonable to accept now a lowering of *c.* 3°C for the tropical lowlands of northern South America. If we remember that this cipher was at least 6–7°C in the higher Andes, the altitudinal temperature gradient must have been much steeper during glacial time than it is now.

The changes of vegetation registered in diagrams from the tropical lowlands are changes from forest or woodland to savanna and *vice versa*. They can be explained by changes in effective precipitation. During at least a part of the Last Glacial, savannas existed in the coastal lowlands of Guyana, and the climate was favourable for the development of dry savanna in the Rupununi area. A period of savanna vegetation is also recorded in an area in the southern part of the Amazon basin. The fact that there are clear indications in northern South America of a dry period between *c.* 21,000 and 13,000 B.P. (and such a period is also known from many places in Africa) renders it probable that in many parts of the

26 *T. van der Hammen*

tropics this was the case and, furthermore, that such dry periods, or at least part of them, may well correspond with the periods of maximum extension of glaciation in northern latitudes. Many parts of the world (but not all, the S.W. United States of America forming one of the exceptions) seem to have had a drier climate during that period.

The repeated lowering of the tree line in the Andes led to direct connections between groups of Páramo islands and the possibility of exchange of species. In interglacial times populations were isolated again and conditions for speciation through isolation were favourable. Immigration by founder species from abroad, according to the island model as proposed by Simpson (1973), must have had a much greater chance during glacial time, when Páramo 'islands' joined up and were much larger and nearer to each other.

The repeated extension in the tropical lowlands of savanna vegetation (and locally perhaps of more xerophytic types of vegetation) in areas that now support forest vegetation (or a savanna vegetation, respectively), may have led to an exchange of savanna (and possibly of xerophytic) species from e.g. the north to the south (or *vice versa*) through the Amazon basin, and from the east to the west (or *vice versa*) along the Caribbean coast. It may also have led to the formation of forest refuges, temporarily separating populations of forest animals and plants and leading to speciation in isolation. Much more pollen-analytical work in the tropical lowlands is needed before the extent of these phenomena can be ascertained. The preliminary results are at any rate very promising.

References

HAFFER, J. (1969) Speciation in Amazonian forest birds. *Science, N.Y.* **165**, 131–137.

SCHREVE-BRINKMAN, E.J. & VAN DER HAMMEN, T. In preparation. Palynology, stratigraphy and paleoecology of the El Abra valley.

SIESWERDA, R. In preparation. Late Glacial and Holocene vegetation history of Laguna de Pedro Palo.

SIMPSON, B. (1971) Pleistocene changes in the fauna and flora of South America. *Science, N.Y.* **173**, 771–780.

SIMPSON, B. (1973) Pleistocene speciation in the mountains of tropical South America. *First Int. Congr. Syst. Ecol. Biol., Boulder*, mimeographed manuscript of lecture.

VAN DER HAMMEN, T. (1962) Palinologia de la region de 'Laguna de los Bobos'. *Revta Acad. colomb. Cienc. exact. fis. nat.* **11**, No. 44.

VAN DER HAMMEN, T. (1963) A palynological study of the Quaternary of British Guiana. *Leid. geol. Meded.* **29**, 125–180.

VAN DER HAMMEN, T. (1972) Changes in vegetation and climate in the Amazon basin and surrounding areas during the Pleistocene. *Geologie mijnb.* **51**, 641–643.

VAN DER HAMMEN, T. & GONZALEZ, E. (1960a) Upper Pleistocene and Holocene climate and vegetation of the 'Sabana de Bogotá' (Colombia, South America). *Leid. geol. Meded.* **25**, 126–315.

VAN DER HAMMEN, T. & GONZALEZ, E. (1960b) Holocene and Late Glacial climate and vegetation of Páramo de Palacio (Eastern Cordillera, Colombia, South America). *Geologie mijnb.* **39**, 737–746'

VAN DER HAMMEN, T. & GONZALEZ, E. (1964) A pollen diagram from the Quaternary of the Sabena de Bogotá (Colombia) and its significance for the geology of the Northern Andes. *Geologie mijnb.* **43**, 113–117.

VAN DER HAMMEN, T. & GONZALEZ, E. (1965) Late Glacial and Holocene pollen diagram from 'Ceinaga del Visitador' (dept Boyacá, Colombia). *Leid. geol. Meded.* **32**, 193–201.

VAN DER HAMMEN, T., WERNER, J.H. & VAN DOMMELEN, H. (1973) Palynological record of the upheaval of the Northern Andes: a study of the Pliocene and Lower Quaternary of the Colombian Eastern Cordillera and the early evolution of its high-andean biota. *Palaeogeog. Palaeoclim. Palaeoecol* **16**, 1–24.

VAN DER HAMMEN, T., WIJMSTRA, T. A. & ZAGWIJN, W.H. (1971) The floral record of the Late Cenozoic of Europe. In: *The Late Cenozoic of Glacial Ages* (Ed. by K.K. Turekian). Yale University Press, New Haven and London.

VAN GEEL, B. & VAN DER HAMMEN, T. (1973) Upper Quaternary vegetational and climatic sequence of the Fuquene area (Eastern Cordillera, Colombia). *Palaeogeog. Palaeoclim. Palaeoecol.* **14**, 9–92.

WIJMSTRA, T.A. (1969) Palynology of the Alliance Well. *Geologie mijnb.* **48**, 125–133.

WIJMSTRA, T.A. (1971) *The palynology of the Guyana coastal basin.* Dissertation, University of Amsterdam.

WIJMSTRA, T.A. & VAN DER HAMMEN, T. (1966) Palynological data on the history of tropical savannas in Northern South America. *Leid. geol. Meded.* **38**, 71–90.

11 July 1969, Volume 165, Number 3889

SCIENCE

Speciation in Amazonian Forest Birds

Most species probably originated in forest refuges during dry climatic periods.

Jürgen Haffer

The richest forest fauna of the world is found in the tropical lowlands of central South America. This fauna inhabits the vast Amazonian forests from the base of the Andes in the west to the Atlantic coast in the east, and its range extends far to the north and south of the Amazon valley onto the Guianan and Brazilian shields, respectively (Fig. 1). Here I propose a historical explanation of the immense variety of the Amazonian forest bird fauna, postulating that, during several dry climatic periods of the Pleistocene and post-Pleistocene, the Amazonian forest was divided into a number of smaller forests which were isolated from each other by tracts of open, nonforest vegetation. The remaining forests served as "refuge areas" for numerous populations of forest animals, which deviated from one another during periods of geographic isolation. The isolated forests were again united during humid climatic periods when the intervening open country became once more forest-covered, permitting the refuge-area populations to extend their ranges. This rupturing and rejoining of the various forests in Amazonia probably was repeated several times during the Quaternary and led to a rapid differentiation of the Amazonian forest fauna in geologically very recent times.

This interpretation should be considered merely a working model based on a number of inferences. It may, however, serve for testing the distribution pattern of various groups of organisms. Much more concrete information on the climatic and vegetational history of Amazonia, as well as on the population structure and species relationships of Amazonian birds and other animals, is needed if one is to reconstruct the actual course of species formation in particular areas or in certain families.

Climatic Fluctuations during the Quaternary

The worldwide climatic fluctuations of the Pleistocene and post-Pleistocene severely influenced environmental conditions in the tropics. In the mountains, altitudinal temperature zones and life zones were repeatedly compressed and expanded vertically during cold and warm periods, respectively (1). At the same time the lowlands probably remained "tropical," but humid and dry climatic periods caused vast changes in the distribution of forest and nonforest vegetation. The present continuity of the Amazonian forest seems to be a rather recent and temporary stage in the vegetational history of South America (2). Geomorphological observations in southern Venezuela (3), lower Amazonia (4), central Brazil (5), and eastern Peru (6) indicate that, during

the Quaternary, arid climatic conditions repeatedly prevailed over large parts of Amazonia. During these periods dense forests probably survived in a number of rather small, humid pockets (7). Palynological studies in northern South America (8) also revealed repeated vegetational changes over large areas during the Pleistocene and post-Pleistocene. The absolute ages of the various humid and arid climatic phases, in particular the age of the last severe arid period, are not yet known. Moreover, correlation of the warm-dry and cool-humid periods of the low-latitude lowlands with the glacial and interglacial periods of the temperate regions remains a matter of controversy.

The immense importance of the Quaternary climatic fluctuations for the latest differentiation of tropical faunas has been recognized for some time (9). Stresemann and Grote (10) long ago emphasized the significance of humid and dry periods for the history of the fauna of central Africa and the East Indies. The extent of vegetational changes in Africa has been amply demonstrated in recent years by detailed palynologic studies (11). Moreau (12) analyzed the differentiation of African bird faunas in the light of the geological and climatic history of the African continent, in a very convincing interpretation. Similar zoogeographic analyses have been published on the bird faunas of Australia (13), Tasmania (14), and parts of the Old World tropics (15). But the significance of Quaternary climatic fluctuations for the differentiation of the forest faunas of tropical South America has hitherto received little attention.

Reconstruction of Forest Refuges in Amazonia

On the basis of the theory of geographic speciation (16) let us assume that most or all Amazonian forest species originated from small populations which were isolated from their parent population and deviated by selection and chance. Most of this differentiation probably took place in re-

The author is research geologist in the Field Research Laboratory of Mobil Research and Development Corporation, Dallas, Texas. He worked for several years in South America prior to his assignment in the United States.

stricted refuge areas. Thus our main problem becomes the reconstruction of the probable geographic location of the forest refuges. I have used the following criteria for a first tentative approach to this problem: (i) current inequalities of annual rainfall in Amazonia, and (ii) current distribution patterns of Amazonian birds, particularly members of superspecies.

Current rainfall maxima. Rainfall is not evenly distributed over the Ama-zonian lowlands (*17, 18*). There are three main centers of rainfall (Fig. 2) which receive over 2500 millimeters of rain per year. These areas usually are humid throughout the year, having no *pronounced* dry season. The largest of these rainfall centers comprises upper Amazonia from the Río Juruá and the upper Río Orinoco west to the base of the Andes, where the annual rainfall increases to 4000 to 5000 millimeters. The second of the three centers is the Madeira–upper Río Tapajós re-gion, which is separated from upper Amazonia by a somewhat drier cor-ridor between the Negro, Purús, and Juruá rivers. The third center com-prises the southern Guianas and the area extending southeastward to the mouth of the Amazon. The very humid regions of western and central Ama-zonia are separated from the rainfall center near the Atlantic coast by a comparatively dry transverse zone ex-tending in a northwest-southeast direc-tion and crossing the lower Amazon around Óbidos and Santarém. Al-though most of this region is forested, numerous isolated savannas are found here. This comparatively dry belt has a very dry season, and the total annual rainfall is less than 2000 or even 1500 millimeters per year. This zone connects the open plains of central Venezuela with the unforested region of central and northeastern Brazil. The relatively dry areas north and south of the humid upper Amazonian lowlands extend their influence near the base of the Andes far to the southwest and northwest, respectively. In Fig. 2 this is obvious from the conspicuous southwestward bulging of the isohyets in eastern Colombia and from the characteristic course of the 2000-millimeter isohyet near the Andes in eastern Peru [where rather dry forests are found from Bolivia northwest to the middle Río Ucayali and Huallaga valleys (*19*)]. The foothill regions of the Andes in eastern Colombia and southeastern Peru and Bolivia represent narrow ex-tensions of humid Amazonia which receive 2000 to 5000 millimeters of rain per year. In these regions the air is forced to rise, and it loses its moisture in the form of mist and frequent rain.

Reinke (*18*) has given a detailed climatologic interpretation of this rain-fall pattern and has discussed the signif-icance of the Andes and of the moun-tains in the interior of the Guianas for the location of current rainfall maxima.

Fig. 1 (above left). Distribution of humid tropical lowland forests in central and northern South America. Forests surround-ing savanna regions are mostly semi-deciduous. (Black areas) Andes moun-tains above 1000 meters. [Adapted from Hueck (*38*), Haffer (*39*), Aubréville (*40*), and Denevan (*41*)]

Fig. 2 (bottom left). Total annual rainfall (in millimeters) in northern and central South America. (Large dots) Weather stations; (black area) Andes mountains above 1000 meters. [Adapted from Reinke (*18*)]

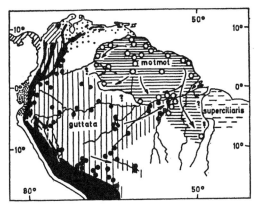 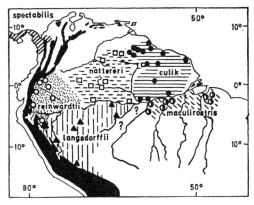

Fig. 3 (left). Distribution of the chachalaca, the *Ortalis motmot* superspecies, in Amazonia. Additional species occur north and south of the area shown. The trans-Andean forms are (stippled area) *O. erythroptera*, (hatched area) *O. garrula*, and (sparsely dotted area) *O. ruficauda*. [Adapted from Vaurie (*42*)] Fig. 4 (right). Distribution of a toucan, the *Selenidera maculirostris* superspecies, in Amazonia. Additional isolated populations of *S. maculirostris* occur in eastern Brazil. Hybridization between *S reinwardtii* and *S. langsdorffii* is known in northeastern Perú.

During arid periods the effective humidity in Amazonia was reduced by a reduction in rainfall or by a rise in temperature and an increase in evaporation, or by both. I assume that, during dry phases, rainfall in the areas of current rainfall maxima remained high enough to permit the continued growth of forests, while the forest probably disappeared from the intervening areas of lower rainfall. Since the major orographic features that cause the current inequalities in rainfall in Amazonia were present during most of the Pleistocene, possibly the basic rainfall pattern was fairly constant, though probably not entirely so, during the various climatic periods. For this reason I suggest that the main Amazonian forest refuges of arid climatic periods coincided with the present centers of high rainfall.

Current distribution patterns of Amazonian birds. Important indirect evidence concerning the possible geographic location of former forest refuges may also be obtained from the present distribution of localized Amazonian animal species, which apparently never extended their ranges far beyond their center of survival or area of origin. For Amazonian birds I distinguish the following "centers of distribution": (i) upper Amazonia from the base of the Andes east to the Río Negro and the Río Madeira; (ii) the Guianas west to the Río Negro and south to the Amazon; and (iii) lower Amazonia south of the Amazon from the lower Río Tapajós east to the Atlantic coast. Each of these areas is characterized by many distinc-

tive and morphologically rather isolated bird species which do not range beyond the *approximate* limits indicated above. An additional "center of distribution" is the region between the Río Madeira and the upper Río Tapajós, where several endemic species occur. The foothills of the Peruvian Andes and forests of the upper Río Negro–Río Orinoco region represent other such centers.

A number of Amazonian forest birds of particular zoogeographic interest form allopatric (that is, mutually excluding) species assemblages which are designated superspecies (*16*). Members of different superspecies often have similar distributions. Many are restricted to the Guianas and adjacent territories, to parts of upper Amazonia, or to various portions of the lowlands south of the Amazon. Numerous examples could be cited from the Cracidae (*20*), the toucans, the antbirds, the cotingas, the manakins, and others. The distribution of two superspecies is shown in Figs. 3 and 4. The component species of the Amazonian superspecies probably originated in forest refuges from a common ancestor whose range was split into a number of isolated portions during arid periods. By comparing the ranges of localized forms we may derive important clues concerning the former location of refuge areas.

Location of forest refuges. Using the above indirect evidence derived from rainfall inequalities and from patterns of avian distribution, I have reconstructed and named the probable geographic location of various Quaternary forest

refuges in the lowlands of tropical South America (Fig. 5). The postulated refuges west of the Andes are as follows.

Chocó refuge, which comprised the central Pacific lowlands of Colombia (*21*).

Nechí refuge, on the northern slope and the foreland of the central and western Andes of Colombia (*21*).

Catatumbo refuge, on the eastern slope and base of the Serranía de Perijá (*21*).

There are six postulated refuges east of the Andes, as follows.

Napo refuge, which comprised mainly the lowlands of eastern Ecuador from the Andes to the Marañón River. This may have been the largest and ecologically most varied forest refuge for a great number of Amazonian forest animals. It is named after the Río Napo in eastern Ecuador (*22*).

East Peruvian refuges. Several isolated lowland forests probably existed along the eastern base of the Peruvian Andes and, farther east, on the low mountains between the Río Ucayali and the Juruá-Purús drainage (*23*).

Madeira-Tapajós refuge, which comprised the lowlands between the middle Río Madeira and the upper Río Tapajós (*24*).

Imerí refuge—a small area around the Sierra Imerí and Cerro Neblina between the headwaters of the Río Orinoco and the upper Río Negro (*25*).

Guiana refuge, on the northern slope and foreland of the mountains of Guyana, Surinam, and Cayenne (*26*).

Belém refuge, in the region south of

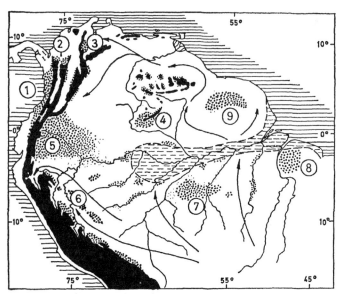

Fig. 5. Presumed forest refuges in central and northern South America during warm-dry climatic periods of the Pleistocene. The arrows indicate northward-advancing nonforest faunas of central Brazil. (1) Chocó refuge; (2) Nechí refuge; (3) Catatumbo refuge; (4) Imerí refuge; (5) Napo refuge; (6) East Peruvian refuges; (7) Madeira-Tapajós refuge; (8) Belém refuge; (9) Guiana refuge; (hatched area) interglacial Amazonian embayment (sea level raised by about 50 meters); (black areas) elevations above 1000 meters.

the mouth of the Amazon and west to the lower Río Tocantins (27).

There were probably additional smaller forests along the major river courses of Amazonia, on the slopes of isolated mountains, and in the extensive lowlands between the upper Río Madeira and the Marañón River. Even when palynological field data from Amazonia become available it will remain difficult to map the distribution of forest and nonforest vegetation at any given time under the constantly changing climatic conditions of the Pleistocene. The table mountains of southern Venezuela are today located in the dry transverse zone of Amazonia and may have supported no tropical, but only subtropical, forests on the higher slopes during arid climatic phases. These may have served as refuges for the montane forest fauna of the highlands of Southern Venezuela.

Since climatic fluctuations were much more pronounced during the Pleistocene than in post-Pleistocene time, it seems possible that the rupturing of the Amazonian forest was most marked during the arid periods of the Pleistocene. During the post-Pleistocene merely a separation of an upper Amazonian forest from lower Amazonian forests

may have resulted from the disappearance of forest growth in the dry transverse zone through the Obidos-Santarém region.

During these arid periods many nonforest animals of central Brazil probably advanced across the lower Amazon to reach the upper Río Branco valley and the nonforest regions of central Venezuela and eastern Colombia (28). Many relict populations of nonforest bird species still inhabit the isolated remnants of savannas and campos found in the forests on both sides of the lower Amazon (29). Nonforest regions probably also extended during dry periods northwestward from central Brazil and eastern Bolivia, near the Andes, through the Ucayali-Huallaga valleys, to connect with the arid upper Marañón valley. A number of Brazilian bird species even crossed the Andes, probably in the area of the low Porcula Pass west of the upper Marañón River, to reach the arid Pacific lowlands of Peru and southwestern Ecuador (28). Without palynological data from eastern Peru we have no means of knowing during which dry phase (or phases) of the Quaternary the postulated connection of the upper Marañón fauna and the Brazilian

nonforest fauna may have been established.

During humid periods the Amazonian forest probably was repeatedly connected with the forests of southeastern Brazil over the now unforested tableland of central Brazil. The connecting forests may not have been very extensive, but they probably made possible the exchange of numerous plants and animals *(30, 31)*. Remnants of these forests are still preserved in small humid pockets and are inhabited by isolated populations of Amazonian animals.

Secondary Contact Zones

Upon the return of humid climatic conditions many forest refuge populations followed the expanding forests and often came in contact with sister populations of neighboring or even far-distant refuges. Because of variation in the rate of differentiation of different animal species, the populations that came in contact reached many different levels in the speciation process. Basically, we may distinguish the following situations.

1) Geographic overlap. The speciation process was completed during the period of geographic isolation—that is, the allies had attained reproductive isolation as well as ecologic compatibility. This resulted in sympatry and a more or less extensive overlap of the ranges occupied.

2) Geographic exclusion. The speciation process was not fully completed. Although reproductively isolated (and therefore treated taxonomically as species) the allies remained ecologically incompatible. This situation led to mutual exclusion presumably as a result of ecologic competition without hybridization along the zone of contact *(31a)*.

3) Hybridization. The speciation process was not completed and the allies hybridized along the zone of contact. Hybridization may occur along a rather narrow belt, indicating that a certain degree of incompatibility of the gene pools had been reached before contact was established in ecologically more or less uniform continuous forests *(32)*. Hybridization over a broad zone may lead to the more or less complete fusion of the populations in contact.

The zones of presumably secondary contact of Amazonian forest birds are in areas between the postulated forest refuges—for example, north and south of the middle Amazon River and in the Huallaga-Ucayali region of eastern

Peru (Fig. 6). A number of representative bird species doubtless met along broad rivers, such as the Amazon or its large tributaries, which separate their ranges today. In these cases, expansion of the allies' range beyond the rivers appears to be inhibited by competition or by swamping of the occasional colonists which manage to get across the watercourse (*33*). A few forms were able to build up small populations on the opposite river bank. Most bird species eventually crossed the rivers in the course of extending their ranges, provided the opposite bank was not occupied by a close relative or, if it was, provided the two allies had acquired complete ecologic compatibility. Few species seem to be definitely halted solely by the river courses of Amazonia, especially a number of birds inhabiting the dark forest interior. However, many such bird species as well as arboreal and small terrestrial mammals probably surrounded the broad portions of the rivers by crossing the latter in the narrow middle and upper parts, in this way often extending their ranges far beyond the areas of origin or survival; again, provided they did not meet ecologically competing close relatives which extended their ranges from other refuge areas. Interspecific competition seems to be very important in limiting the range of numerous forest birds in tropical South America.

In summarizing, the rivers probably are not a causal factor of avian speciation in Amazonia (except perhaps in a few cases), but merely modified, or occasionally limited, the dispersal of forest bird species after the latter had originated in forest refuges during dry climatic periods.

Conclusion and Summary

The Tertiary forest fauna of central South America inhabited comparatively restricted forests along marginal portions of the Guianan and Brazilian shields. Although several species of the present Amazonian forest bird fauna may represent direct descendants of Tertiary forms, most or all species seem to have undergone considerable evolutionary change during the Pleistocene. Several factors, in combination, probably caused this rather recent faunal differentiation in Amazonia: (i) the great expansion of dense forests onto the fully emerging Amazonian basin and into the lowlands around the rising

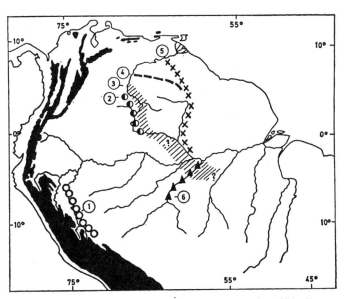

Fig. 6. Location of some secondary contact zones of Amazonian forest birds. (1, open circles) *Pipra chloromeros–P. rubrocapilla* and *Gymnopithys lunulata–G. salvini*; (2, half-solid circles) *Ortalis guttata–O. motmot* and *Gymnopithys leucaspis–G. rufigula*; (3, hatched area) *Ramphastos vitellinus culminatus–R. v. vitellinus*, north of the Amazon, and *R. v. culminatus–R. v. ariel*, south of the Amazon (this hybrid belt probably extends in a southeasterly direction beyond the Tapajós and Xingú rivers); (4, dashed line) *Pteroglossus pluricinctus–P. aracari*; (5, crosses) *Celeus grammicus–C. undatus* and *Tyranneutes stolzmanni–T. virescens*; (6, triangles) *Pteroglossus flavirostris mariae–P. bitorquatus*; (black areas) Andes mountains above 1000 meters.

northern Andes, at the end of the Tertiary; (ii) the repeated contraction and expansion of the forests as a result of climatic fluctuations during the Quaternary, leading to repeated isolation and rejoining of forest animal populations; (iii) the increased rate of extinction of animal forms. Because the populations of many tropical forest animals are small, a reduction in the size of their habitat must have drastically increased the chances of extinction of a number of forms, either within the forest refuges or through competition with newly evolved forms from other refuges upon the return of humid conditions.

Possibly the Amazonian forest fauna was not nearly so rich and diversified in the upper Tertiary as it is at present, mainly because of intensified speciation in the greatly enlarged forests and because of the fluctuating climate of the Pleistocene. This evolutionary boom may have been comparable to that of the montane fauna of the Andes during the Quaternary.

On the basis of evidence discussed by Moreau (*12*), it appears possible that, under favorable circumstances, the

speciation process in birds may be completed in 20,000 to 30,000 years or less, particularly in the tropics, where birds generally seem to occupy smaller niches than they do in cooler and less stable climates. This estimate refers mainly, though not exclusively, to passerine birds with a high reproductive rate and evolutionary potential. Under the same conditions speciation may take longer in larger birds, perhaps requiring on the order of a hundred thousand to several hundred thousand years. Factors such as the size of the refuge population and the degree of isolation of course influence the rate of speciation considerably. The above estimates are highly speculative, and the error involved may be very substantial. However, if the order of magnitude is at least approximately correct, it indicates that the Tertiary ancestors of present Amazonian birds may have speciated *repeatedly* during the Quaternary, and that many connecting links may have disappeared due to extinction. A similar assumption may also apply to the insect (*34*), amphibian, reptile (*35*), and mammal faunas (*36*) of Amazonia. Some of the more strongly differentiated species probably originated in early Pleistocene refuges, while most other species and semi-species may date back to the late Pleistocene or, in the case of the latter, to the post-Pleistocene only. In view of the length of the Tertiary period (60 million years), during which the Amazonian fauna probably evolved rather slowly under quite uniform environmental conditions, the Quaternary faunal differentiation in tropical South America during the last 1 to 2 million years is, geologically speaking, very "recent" and occurred rather "rapidly."

It follows from the foregoing discussion that the Quaternary history of tropical faunas was basically quite similar to that of the faunas of higher latitudes (37). In the temperate regions, as well as in the tropics, climatic fluctuations caused pronounced changes in the vegetation cover and led to the isolation of comparatively small populations in refuge areas. The presumably smaller niche size (and lower population density) of tropical relative to temperate-zone forest animals and the correspondingly higher rate of speciation in the tropics under conditions of large-scale climatic fluctuations may explain the rapid differentiation of tropical forest faunas during the Pleistocene.

References and Notes

1. During cold and warm periods the vertical temperature gradient probably was increased and decreased, respectively, relative to the present gradient (a change of approximately 0.5°C per 100-meter difference in elevation); see J. Haffer [*Amer. Museum Novitates No. 2294* (1967)] for details pertaining to South America. The repeated vertical displacement of the temperature zones led to frequent interruptions and rejoining of the animal populations along the mountain slopes, thereby causing a rapid differentiation of the montane faunas during the Pleistocene.
2. The main uplift of the Andes mountains did not take place until the upper Pliocene and lower Pleistocene [R. W. R. Rutland, J. E. Guest, R. L. Grasty, *Nature* 208, 677 (1965); J. Haffer, *J. Ornithol.* 109, 67 (1968)]. The rise of the Andes caused the climate to be very humid along the eastern base and foreland of the mountains. This was partly responsible for the vast expansion of dense forests onto the fully emerging Amazonian lowlands and northward and southward along the base of the rising Andes to Colombia and Bolivia, respectively. During the Tertiary, prior to the Andean uplift and the emergence of the Amazonian lowlands, forests probably had a rather restricted distribution along rivers and marginal lowlands of the elevated land areas north and south of the present Amazon valley.
3. H. F. Garner, *Rev. Geomorphol. Dynamique* 2, 54 (1966); *Sci. American* 216, 84 (1967).
4. A. N. Ab'Saber, *Bol. Soc. Brasileira Geol.* 6, 41 (1957); *Notic. Geomorfol.* 1, 24 (1958); A. Barbosa, *ibid.*, p. 87.
5. A. Cailleux and J. Tricart, *Compt. Rend. Soc. Biogeograph.* 293, 7 (1957); J. J. Bigarella and G. O. de Andrade, *Geol. Soc. Amer. Spec. Paper 84* (1965), p. 433; M. M. Cole, *Geograph. J.* 126, 166 (1960).
6. H. F. Garner, *Bull. Geol. Soc. Amer.* 70, 1870 (1959).

7. The shrinkage of the humid lowland forests probably was more pronounced than it is shown to be on hypothetical vegetation maps by J. Hester [*Amer. Naturalist* 100, 383 (1966)] and T. C. Patterson and E. P. Lanning [*Bol. Soc. Geograf. Lima* 86, 8 (1967)]. The sweeping interpretation of Pleistocene vegetational changes in Amazonia by A. Aubréville [*Adansonia* 2, 16 (1962)] appears to be unacceptable in view of the fact that climatic changes occurred simultaneously in the Northern and Southern hemispheres.
8. T. van der Hammen and E. Gonzalez, *Leidse Geol. Mededel.* 25, 261 (1960); T. A. Wijmstra and T. van der Hammen, *ibid.* 38, 71 (1966); T. A. Wijmstra, *ibid.* 39, 261 (1967). Additional evidence of climatic fluctuations is available from currently arid western Peru; see E. P. Lanning, *Sci. Amer.* 213, 68 (1965); *Peru before the Incas* (Prentice-Hall, Englewood, N.J., 1967).
9. P. J. Darlington, *Zoogeography* (Wiley, New York, 1957), pp. 586–88; E. Mayr, *Animal Species and Evolution* (Harvard Univ. Press, Cambridge, 1963), p. 372.
10. E. Stresemann and H. Grote, *Trans Intern. Congr. Ornithol. 6th, Copenhagen, 1926* (1929), p. 358; E. Stresemann, *J. Ornithol.* 87, 409 (1939).
11. R. E. Moreau, *Proc. Zool. Soc. London* 141, 395 (1963); E. M. van Zinderen Bakker, Ed., *Palaeoecology of Africa and of the Surrounding Islands and Antarctica* (Balkema, Cape Town, 1967), vols. 2 and 3.
12. R. E. Moreau, *The Bird Faunas of Africa and Its Islands* (Academic Press, New York, 1966).
13. A. Keast, *Bull. Museum Comp. Zool.* 123, 305 (1961).
14. M. G. Ridpath and R. E. Moreau, *Ibis* 108, 348 (1966).
15. P. Hall, *Bull. Brit. Museum Zool.* 10, 105 (1963).
16. E. Mayr, *Systematics and the Origin of Species* (Columbia Univ. Press, New York, 1942); *Animal Species and Evolution* (Harvard Univ. Press, Cambridge, 1963).
17. K. Knoch, in *Handbuch der Klimatologie*, H. Köppen and C. Geiger, Eds. (Borntraeger, Berlin, 1930), vol. 2, pp. 68–95; M. Velloso, in *Geografia do Brasil*, A. Teixeira, Ed. (Rio de Janeiro, 1959), vol. 1, pp. 61–111.
18. R. Reinke, "Das Klima Amazoniens," dissertation, University of Tübingen (1962).
19. J. A. Tosi, *Inst. Interamer. Cienc. Agr. OEA, Bol. Tec. No. 5* (1960), with ecological map of Peru.
20. C. Vaurie, *Bull. Amer. Museum Nat. Hist.* 138, 131 (1968).
21. J. Haffer [*Amer. Museum Novitates No. 2294* (1967); *Auk* 84, 343 (1967)] has given details on this refuge as well as data on southern Central America.
22. Bird species which may have originated in this refuge include *Mitu salvini*, *Nothocrax urumutum*, *Gymnopithys leucaspis*, *Grallaria (Thamnocharis) dignissima*, *Metopothrix aurantiacus*, *Ancistrops strigilatus*, *Porphyrolaema porphyrolaema*, *Heterocercus aurantiivertex*, and *Todirostrum capitale*.
23. Bird species which may have originated in these refuges include *Pithys castanea*, *Gymnopithys lunulata* and *G. salvini*, *Formicarius rufifrons*, *Grallaria (Thamnocharis) eludens*, *Conioptilon mcilhennyi*, *Pipra chloromeros*, *Todirostrum albifacies*, and *Rhegmatorhina melanosticta*.
24. Bird species which may have originated in this refuge include *Neomorphus squamiger*, *Pyrrhura rhodogaster*, *Dendrocolaptes hoffmannsi*, *Myrmotherula sclateri*, *Rhegmatorhina hoffmannsi*, *Phlegopsis (Skutchia) borbae*, ?*Heterocercus linteatus*, *Pipra nattereri*, *Pipra vilasboasi* (isolated forest east of the Tapajós river), *Todirostrum senex*, and *Idioptilon aenigma*.
25. Bird species which may have originated in this refuge include *Mitu tomentosa*, *Selenidera nattereri*, *Herpsilochmus dorsimaculatus*, *Myrmotherula ambigua*, *Myrmeciza disjuncta*, *Myrmeciza pelzelni*, *Percnostola caurensis*, *Rhegmatorhina cristata*, *Pipra cornuta*, *Heterocercus flavivertex*, and *Cyanocorax heilprini*.
26. Bird species which may have originated in this refuge include *Ortalis motmot*, *Brotogeris chrysopterus*, *Pionopsitta caica*, *Pteroglossus aracari*, *Pteroglossus viridis*, *Selenidera culik*, *Ramphastos t. tucanus*, *R. v. vitellinus*, *Celeus undatus*, *Hylexetastes perrotii*, *Myrmotherula guttata*, *M. gutturalis*,

Gymnopithys rufigula, *Xipholaena punicea*, *Iodopleura fusca*, *Pachyramphus surinamensis*, *Haematoderus militaris*, *Perissocephalus tricolor*, *Pipra serena*, *Tyranneutes virescens*, *Microcochlearius josephinae*, *Phylloscartes virescens*, *Euphonia cayennensis*, and *Phaethornis malaris*.
27. Bird species which may have originated in this refuge include *Ortalis superciliaris*, *Pyrrhura perlata*, *Xipholaena lamellipennis*, *Selenidera gouldi*, *Ramphastos vitellinus ariel*, ?*Pteroglossus bitorquatus*, *Pipra iris*, and *Gymnostinops bifasciatus*.
28. J Haffer, *Hornero* (Buenos Aires) 10, 315 (1967).
29. This historic interpretation of the occurrence of nonforest birds in lower Amazonia contrasts with the earlier explanation given by E. Snethlage [*Bol. Museu Goeldi* 6, 226 (1910); *J. Ornithol.* 61, 469 (1913); *ibid.* 78, 58 (1930)], who assumed that the nonforest birds reached their present stations by following the river valleys. The following facts strongly support the interpretation of a natural rather than a secondary (man-made) origin of the isolated savannas of lower Amazonia. (i) The soil of the savannas is a bleached sand (podzol type) in contrast to the lateritic brown loamy soil of the forests. The forest soil could not have been replaced completely by podzol in the short period since the supposed artificial clearing by man [H. Sioli, *Erdkunde* 10, 100 (1956)]. (ii) The flora of the isolated campos is decidedly nonhylean and is similar to that of the *cerrado* of central Brazil [A. Ducke and G. A. Black, *Anais Acad. Brasil. Cienc.* 25, 1 (1953); *Bol. Tec. Inst. Agr. Norte Belém* 29, 50 (1955); K. Hueck, *Die Wälder Südamerikas* (Fischer, Stuttgart, 1966), pp. 18, 21, 23]. (iii) The fauna of the isolated campos must be comparatively old, as a number of endemic forms are present. Examples are the mockingbird, *Mimus s. saturninus*; the grassland finch, *Coryphaspiza melanotis marajoara*; and the snakes *Bothrops marajoensis* and *Crotalus durissus marajoensis*, the latter being restricted to Isla Marajó [P. Müller, *Die Herpetofauna der Insel von São Sebastião (Brasilien)* (Saarbrücker Zeitung, Saarbrücken, 1968), pp. 60–61].
30. L. Smith, *U.S. Nat. Museum Contrib. U.S. Nat. Herbarium* 35, 222 (1962); P. Müller, *Die Herpetofauna der Insel von São Sebastião (Brasilien)* (Saarbrücker Zeitung, Saarbrücken, 1968), pp. 60–61.
31. P. E. Vanzolini, *Arquiv. Zool. (São Paulo)* 17, 105 (1968).
31a. Several examples of this interesting situation have been discussed by J. Haffer [*Amer. Museum Novitates No. 2294* (1967); *Auk* 84, 343 (1967)] and by C. Vaurie (20).
32. This situation is probably much more common among Amazonian animals than is recognized. Examples are found among toucans and other forest birds.
33. According to this view the rivers merely keep the representative species (which originated in distant forest refuges) geographically separated. By contrast, H. Sick [*Atas Simp. Biota Amazônica* (1967), vol. 5, p. 517] recently postulated that the ancestors of many Amazonian forest birds "must have lived at a time when the area was not yet divided by large rivers as it is today." He assumed that the rivers later acted as effective barriers and caused the differentiation of the representative species on opposite banks. The effect of the river barriers may be restricted to variation at the subspecies level.
34. M. G. Emsley, *Zoologica* 50, 244 (1965). Contrary to Emsley's views, I believe that the differentiation of the *Heliconius* butterfly species may be related to the Quaternary climatic history of tropical South America rather than to the Tertiary paleogeographic history of this region.
35. E. E. Williams and P. E. Vanzolini, *Papéis Avulsos Dept. Zool. (São Paulo)* 19, 203 (1963); ———, in *Simp. sobre o Cerrado* (Univ. of São Paulo, São Paulo, 1963), p. 307; ———, *Atlas Simp. Biota Amazônica* (1967), vol. 5, p. 85; P. Müller, *Die Herpetofauna der Insel von São Sebastião (Brasilien)* (Saarbrücker Zeitung, Saarbrücken, 1968). These authors emphasized the importance of vegetational changes in Amazonia for the most recent differentiation of the neotropical reptile fauna. Direct evidence of a rapid rate of speciation in Brazilian reptiles

has been discussed recently by P. E. Vanzolini and A. N. Ab'Saber, *Papéis Avulsos Dept. Zool. (São Paulo)* **21**, 205 (1968).

36. P. Hershkovitz, *Proc. U.S. Nat. Museum* **98**, 323 (1949); *ibid.* **103**, 465 (1954); in *Ectoparasites of Panamá*, R. L. Wenzel and V. J. Tipton, Eds. (Field Museum of Natural History, Chicago, 1966), pp. 725–751; *Evolution* **22**, 556 (1968). The distributional history of the monkeys, tapirs, and rodents discussed in these articles may well be interpreted on the basis of Quaternary climatic and vegetational changes, many species probably having originated during the Pleistocene. B. Patterson and R. Pascual [*Quart. Rev. Biol.* **43**, 440 (1968)] also assumed that a rapid differentiation at the species level, in some cases to the generic level, took place in South American mammals, particularly the rodents, during the Pleistocene.

37. G. de Lattin [*Grundriss der Zoogeographie* (Fischer, Stuttgart, 1967), pp. 327–329] summarized the Pleistocene history of the north temperate faunas.

38. K. Hueck, *Die Wälder Südamerikas* (Fischer, Stuttgart, 1966).

39. J. Haffer, *Amer. Museum Novitates No. 2294* (1967); *Auk* **84**, 343 (1967).

40. A. Aubréville, *Etude écologique des principales formations végétales du Brasil et contribution à la connaissance des forets de l'Amazonie brésilienne* (Centre Technique Forestier Tropicale, Nogent-sur-Marne, France, 1961), pp. 1–265.

41. W. M. Denevan, *Ibero Americana* **48**, 7 (1966).

42. I am grateful to Professor Ernst Mayr, Harvard University, for many helpful suggestions concerning the manuscript of this article. I also thank Eugene Eisenmann, American Museum of Natural History, New York, and Dr. François Vuilleumier, University of Massachusetts, Boston, for critical remarks on an earlier version.

Angiosperm Biogeography and Past Continental Movements[1]

PETER H. RAVEN[2] AND DANIEL I. AXELROD[3]

The isolation of land areas by sea-floor spreading, the uplift of new cordilleras, the emergence of new archipelagos and the disappearance of old ones, and the shifting positions of (some) land-masses have both created and destroyed environments to which biota have responded. In this sense, changing physical environments governed by plate tectonics have had a major role in evolutionary history. Plate tectonic theory thus provides a more reliable basis for analyzing changes in land-sea relations and changes in climates, and hence for interpreting problems of evolution and distribution, than has been available earlier. The reappraisal of the nature of the earth's crust by plate tectonic theory does not require any modifications of previously established major principles of evolution. However, it does demand that we recognize certain new principles of biogeography (McKenna, 1973). Lands may be rafted across latitudinal belts of climate which may lead to *a*) widespread impoverishment of the biota (India), *b*) new opportunities for change (arid flora of Australia), or *c*) lead even to the total decimation of a rich biota (Antarctica). Since moving plates may carry ancient biota

[1] Acknowledgments.—We are grateful to the following colleagues who have provided useful information or critical commentary about this paper: W. R. Anderson, S. Archangelsky, C. C. Black, B. G. Briggs, J. P. M. Brenan, G. J. Brenner, J. E. Case, M. E. J. Chandler, E. H. Colbert, J. Cracraft, T. Croat, A. Cronquist, A. T. Cross, W. G. D'Arcy, T. Delevoryas, G. Dengo, D. L. Dilcher, J. A. Doyle, R. Estes, A. Gentry, P. Goldblatt, A. Graham, P. S. Green, W. Hamilton, R. M. Harley, F. N. Hepper, L. J. Hickey, J. A. Holman, R. A. Howard, L. A. S. Johnson, R. E. Jones, J. P. Kennett, B. E. Koch, B. Malfait, M. C. McKenna, H. E. Moore, Jr., V. M. Page, B. Patterson, R. M. Polhill, J. Savage, T. R. Soderstrom, G. L. Stebbins, R. F. Thorne, S. Tomb, B. L. Turner, J. H. Wahlert, J. K. Weissel, and J. A. Wolfe. Although no one of them would agree, in all probability, with everything we have to say here, their counsel has been of great importance in formulating our concepts and hypotheses.

We are grateful for the support, individually received, of varied grants from the National Science Foundation which have provided us with a background sufficiently diverse and complementary to have aided immeasurably in the present study. Carla Lange has provided expert and efficient bibliographical help during all aspects of the preparation of the paper.

[2] Washington University and Missouri Botanical Garden, 2315 Tower Grove Avenue, St. Louis, Missouri 63110.

[3] Department of Botany, University of California, Davis, California 95616.

ANN. MISSOURI BOT. GARD. 61: 539–673. 1974.

540 ANNALS OF THE MISSOURI BOTANICAL GARDEN [VOL. 61

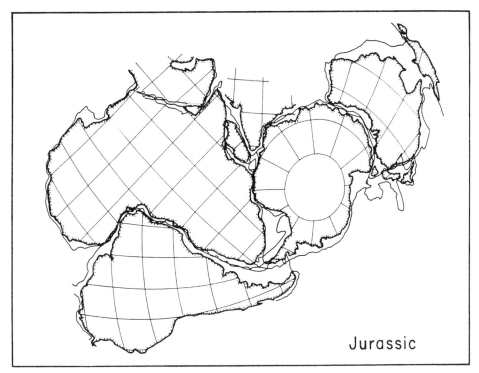

FIGURE 1. Fit of the Gondwana continents during the Jurassic, prior to breakup (after Smith & Hallam, 1970).

far from the area in which they lived, reconstructions of ancient biotic zones and climates must take cognizance of such changes

In the present paper, we examine the distributions of flowering plants, present and past, and attempt to interpret them in the light of newly available geological evidence. Although the field is vast, and we have been unable to provide a comprehensive survey of the available facts, we believe that an overview of angiosperm distributions in the light of geological history as now suggested by plate tectonic theory will be useful in suggesting new hypotheses and new directions for future research.

First, we shall review geological evidence as it pertains to certain areas that we believe were of prime importance to the evolution of flowering plants. Second, we shall review our current state of knowledge about the biogeography and history of the vertebrates of South America, critical for understanding the possibilities for migration between South America and other continents prior to the Miocene. Third, we shall attempt to interpret, insofar as possible, the timing of evolutionary radiation in the angiosperms so as to ascertain relative ages for some of the taxa. Fourth, we shall review the present distributions of the orders, families, and some infrafamilial groups of angiosperms, with selected references to the paleobotanical literature where we believe these to be useful. Fifth, we shall outline the broad patterns of angiosperm migration in the past, and interpret

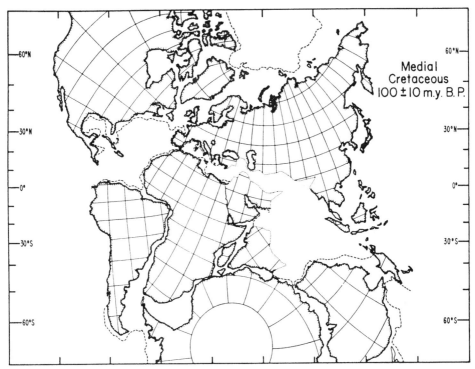

FIGURE 2. Relative positions of Laurasia and Gondwanaland in the medial Cretaceous ($\sim$ 100 $\pm$ 10 m.y. BP) (from Smith, Briden & Drewry, 1973). Note that the connection between South America and Antarctica was linear, having been deformed to make the Scotia Arc since the Cretaceous (Dalziel *et al.*, 1973).

the relationships between these patterns and the age of the respective taxa. Finally, we shall address ourselves to the question of the place of origin of the angiosperms in the light of this knowledge.

GEOLOGICAL BACKGROUND

OPENING OF THE INDIAN OCEAN

We start with a Jurassic Gondwanaland configuration like that presented by Smith and Hallam (1970; Fig. 1) or Tarling (1972). The formation of the Indian Ocean began with the rotation of Africa (with India) away from South America and the movement of Antarctica (with Australia) into a more polar position. The opening of the South Atlantic, reviewed below, began 125–130 m.y. BP. Sediments recently drilled from the ocean floor west of Australia indicate that the eastern Indian Ocean is about 150 m.y. old (Heirtzler *et al.*, 1973, footnote 13). If India was ever immediately adjacent to Australia, it separated at this time and moved westward for 80 m.y. As reviewed below, India certainly remained connected to Madagascar and Africa until at least 100 m.y. BP. Current evidence does not indicate with any degree of certainty the time of separation of Africa-Madagascar-India from Antarctica. However, in view of the configuration of the Indian Ocean 75 m.y. BP (Laughton *et al.*, 1973; Fig. 3), more or

542   ANNALS OF THE MISSOURI BOTANICAL GARDEN   [VOL. 61

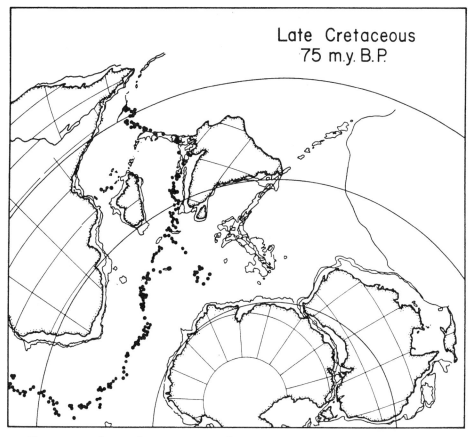

FIGURE 3. Relations between East and West Gondwanaland in the Late Cretaceous (∼ 75 m.y. BP), according to McKenzie and Sclater (1971).

less direct migration between Africa and Australia *via* East Antarctica was possible into mid-Cretaceous time (Fig. 2, Smith *et al.*, 1973; see also Jones, 1972). Even if the land masses were somewhat more separated at that time, plant migration would have been easy *via* volcanic islands on mid-ocean ridges. Epicontinental seas apparently had spread around the southern and eastern coast of Africa to Madagascar by the earliest Cretaceous (Dingle, 1973), but Madagascar and India were still attached and formed a more or less continuous bridge to Antarctica and Australia into the mid-Cretaceous (Fig. 2). The initial rifting of Africa from South America, at about the start of the Cretaceous, presumably sets a limit for the earliest date for the separation of Africa-Madagascar-India from East Antarctica. See Addendum, Sclater and Fisher (1974).

Madagascar has not moved significantly relative to mainland Africa (Green, 1972; Kent, 1972), and evidently has been separated from it for as much as 100 m.y. (Simpson *et al.*, 1972; see also references summarized in McKenna, 1973). Thus many of the plants and animals of Madagascar apparently reached it across a water barrier after the mid-Cretaceous, as hypothesized by Darlington (1957).

On the other hand, the presence of sauropods in the Upper Cretaceous of Madagascar, with the genus *Laplatasaurus* reported in India and Madagascar in addition to South America, and the presence of carnosaurs also in the Upper Cretaceous of Madagascar (Charig, 1973) negates Simpson's (1973) view that Madagascar has been separated from the mainland of Africa since the Permian. A modern review of the sauropods would be highly desirable. It is possible, as reviewed by Cracraft (1973c) that India and Madagascar remained joined longer than Madagascar and Africa.

Another event of biogeographic significance is the separation of New Zealand and New Caledonia from Australia, 80 m.y. BP (summary in Raven & Axelrod, 1972). Evidently the entire Campbell Plateau region, including New Caledonia and New Zealand, had reached approximately its present position by Paleocene time, and only subsequently did Australia begin to separate from Antarctica (Houtz et al., 1973; Hayes & Ringis, 1973). Normal oceanic crust began to form between the Australian and Antarctic continents about 55 m.y. BP (Weissel & Hayes, 1972; Kennett et al., 1972), with the separation of the continental margins of Australia and Antarctica taking place 49 m.y. BP (McGowran, 1973). More or less direct migration through the Tasmanian area may have been possible for perhaps another 10 m.y., especially since the South Tasman Rise is now known to be continental (Houtz et al., 1973; Kennett et al., 1973). Present features along the Scotia Arc developed from a linear Late Cretaceous trend (Anonymous, 1972; Adie, 1972; Dalziel et al., 1973), though the initial break between the Antarctic Peninsula and Tierra del Fuego, if they were ever joined (Katz, 1973), probably occurred before the Late Cretaceous (Dalziel et al., 1973). The water around Antarctica was cool temperate by Late Oligocene time (Hayes et al., 1973), and glaciation in Antarctica is now known to have begun at least 20 m.y. BP (Hayes et al., 1973), if not earlier, with a major increase in the icecap to continental extent about 4–5 m.y. BP. There may also have been episodes of glaciation in Paleogene time (Margolis & Kennett, 1971; Denton, Armstrong & Stuiver, 1971: 271–278). More or less direct migration *via* Antarctica between Australia and South America may have continued well into the Oligocene, and was certainly possible in Eocene time (Raven & Axelrod, 1972).

It is unlikely that any portion of Southeast Asia or Indonesia was once a part of Gondwanaland and moved north, since paleontological and geological evidence contradicts such a pattern of drift (Tarling, 1972; Audley-Charles et al., 1972; Stauffer & Gobbett, 1972; Ridd, 1972; Griffiths & Burrett, 1973). Not until mid-Miocene time was the migration of Asian plants and animals into Australasia relatively direct (Raven & Axelrod, 1972; Audley-Charles et al., 1972).

India, which commenced its northward motion about 100 m.y. BP, now appears to have collided with Asia by the Middle Eocene (Powell & Conaghan, 1973), and there are mammal faunas of obviously Laurasian character in the Lower Upper Eocene of the Murree Hills (Ranga Rao, 1971, 1972). The extensive crustal shortening and fracturing of the region, as well as the upthrust of the Himalayas, belongs to the second phase of development of the region, commencing in the Miocene and reaching its strongest phase in Plio-Pleistocene time (Gansser, 1964, 1966; Laughton et al., 1973; McKenzie & Sclater, 1973; Powell &

Conaghan, 1973). The presumed Lower Eocene Deccan Intertrappean floras reviewed by Lakhanpal (1970) may represent mixtures of groups that have come from the north (such as, perhaps, Datiscaceae) with those that were derived from the south, and the flora of peninsular India was progressively enriched from mid-Tertiary time onward with northern, predominantly tropical groups of angiosperms, such as Dipterocarpaceae (Axelrod, 1971).

To summarize for the lands around and east of the Indian Ocean, the following estimates are the last dates at which more or less direct migration may have been possible: 1) between West Gondwanaland and Australia, 110 ± 10 m.y. BP; 2) between Africa and Madagascar, about 100 m.y. BP; 3) between Australia-Antarctica and New Zealand or New Caledonia, 80 m.y. BP; 4) between Australia and South America *via* Antarctica, 45 m.y. BP. Direct communication between West Gondwanaland and India may have ceased about 100 m.y. BP, and direct communication between India and Asia was initiated about 45 m.y. BP.

CONNECTIONS OF AFRICA WITH OTHER CONTINENTS

The Atlantic Ocean began to open with the rotation of Africa and South America away from North America in the Early Jurassic (180 m.y. BP; Dietz & Holden, 1970; Pitman, Talwani & Heirtzler, 1971; Pitman & Talwani, 1972; Phillips & Forsyth, 1972; Walper & Rowett, 1972; Dewey *et al.*, 1973). Prior to this, Africa was also broadly connected with southwestern Europe (Smith, 1971). Beginning 148 m.y. BP and continuing until 80 m.y. ago, Africa rotated counterclockwise relative to Europe (Dewey *et al.*, 1973). During the interval 80–53 m.y. BP Africa continued its counterclockwise motion but also moved westward relative to Europe, with compressive components indicating connections until 63 m.y. BP, following which relative motion was almost entirely east-west strikeslip (Dewey *et al.*, 1973). In the Early Paleocene, Africa and Europe were connected *via* Spain. Africa may also have been connected broadly with Asia through Arabia at this time (Cooke, 1972). From the Early Paleocene (63 m.y. BP) into the Upper Eocene (53 m.y. BP), Africa and Europe seem to have become more widely separated (Dewey *et al.*, 1973, figs. 16–17), with convergence resulting in direct connection some 17 m.y. ago (Cooke, 1972; Hallam, 1973a; Dewey *et al.*, 1973). Following reestablishment of direct connections between Africa and Eurasia, many northern groups of plants and animals reached Africa, and many African taxa—for example, proboscideans and catarrhine primates—entered Eurasia.

RELATIONS WITHIN LAURASIA

As recently summarized by McKenna (1973), the European Plate (including Greenland) began to separate from the North American Plate in the Late Cretaceous (~ 81 m.y. BP; Laughton, 1971; Smith, 1971; Heirtzler, 1973), with spreading rapid until the Late Eocene and still continuing. Both the North American Mid-Continent Seaway and the Asian Turgai Strait divided the Laurasian landmass, and the Bering Strait was at a higher paleolatitude (~ 75°N) than at present. By 50 m.y. BP, direct migration was still possible across the North Atlantic, and the North American Mid-Continent Seaway had disappeared by 60 m.y. BP. Since the Bering Strait was at a higher latitude, migration between Eurasia and North America across the North Atlantic was probably the main route of communication between these landmasses. Direct overland migration across the North Atlantic was possible for land vertebrates until 49 m.y. BP (McKenna, 1972), but cool temperate conifer-hardwood forests continued to occupy Iceland during the Neogene, providing an interrupted pathway between America and Europe into the early Quaternary (Schwarzbach & Pflug, 1957). Migration *via* the Bering Straits became relatively more important for land vertebrates as the North Atlantic widened and as the latitude of the Bering Straits decreased.

RELATIONS OF SOUTH AMERICA WITH AFRICA

In the South Atlantic, separation seems to have commenced 125–130 m.y. BP (Maxwell *et al.*, 1970b; Wright, 1971; Francheteau & Le Pichon, 1972; Mascle & Phillips, 1972; Phillips & Forsyth, 1972; Heirtzler, 1973; Francheteau, 1973; Anonymous, 1973; Larson & Ladd, 1973). The final marine connection associated with the spreading apart of Africa and South America took place slightly less than 100 m.y. BP (Reyment, 1969, 1972; Reyment & Tait, 1972; Douglas *et al.*, 1973), with the continents remaining in near contact along strike-slip faults until at least 90 m.y. BP (Le Pichon & Hayes, 1971; Grant, 1971, 1972), when northeast Brazil (Sergipe) and Africa (Gabon) were separated by only a narrow strait. At the close of the Cretaceous, about 800 km probably separated Africa and South America at their closest points. However, they were still linked by numerous islands which existed along the Mid-Atlantic Ridge and its flanks at that time (*e.g.* see Klerkx & de Paepe, 1971; Addendum: Anonymous, 1974).

RELATIONS BETWEEN NORTH AND SOUTH AMERICA

Relationships between the American continents during the Cretaceous Period are of great biogeographic interest. Many extant groups of organisms originated and expanded greatly during this period, and the opportunities they had for migration between the Americas have long been a subject of discussion.

North and South America have converged at least from the mid-Cretaceous to the early Cenozoic (Dietz & Holden, 1970; Freeland & Dietz, 1971; Malfait & Dinkelman, 1972). In the following remarks, however, they will be considered to have remained in their present positions, which represents a minimum estimate of distance, and therefore of ease of migration.

During most of the Cretaceous, about 3,000 km seems to have separated the southern continental margin of North America (in Oaxaca) from the continental margin of South America (the Guyana Shield; Fig. 4; Dengo, 1973). This exceeds the present distance (about 2,500 km) between Freetown, Sierra Leone, and Recife, Brazil. South America was joined to Africa until somewhat less than 100 m.y. BP, while North America was moving to the northwest; therefore, 3,000 km must be a minimum distance even if North and South America were still moving apart (*cf.* Freeland & Dietz, 1971), at least for the Early Cretaceous.

It is well established that the entire Atlantic and Gulf Coastal Plain, including Florida, was submerged in the Late Jurassic and continued to receive sediment

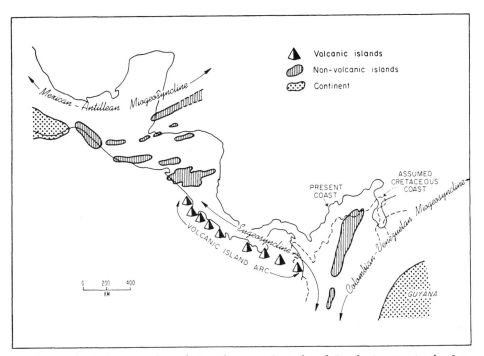

FIGURE 4. Paleogeographic relations between Central and South America in the Late Cretaceous (after Dengo, 1973).

from the Appalachians during Cretaceous and most of Tertiary time (King, 1951; Rodgers, 1970). By the Late Jurassic the distance between land at the southeastern margin of the Appalachians and the small islands along the chain of the Greater Antilles, probably was at least 1,000 km. This diminished only in the Oligocene when portions of the Coastal Plain, including Florida, began to emerge for the first time since the Jurassic (Cooke, 1945; James, 1961; Wilhelm & Ewing, 1972).

In the Late Cretaceous (Fig. 4), scattered and perhaps large continental islands were in the region of Nuclear Central America, including the Maya Mountains of Belize (Dengo & Bohnenberger, 1969) and the northern Cordillera Central in Colombia, itself probably an island. They were linked by scattered, small volcanic islands at the present site of southern Central America (Fig. 4). There also may have been a chain of scattered volcanic islands along the Greater Antilles and Lesser Antilles, leading to the continental margin of South America.

In evaluating whether this interrupted arc was an important dispersal path between North and South America, the distribution of land to the north must be borne in mind. As noted above, the southeastern margin of the Appalachians comprised the southeasternmost exposed land in North America throughout Cretaceous and Paleocene time and was separated by some 1,200 km of ocean from the volcanic islands of the Greater Antilles. The portion of North America nearest the Greater Antilles might have been an island near Honduras, itself a minimum of 650 km from Jamaica and Cuba. Apart from sea-drift moving northward, scattered small islands in the Bahaman area would have enabled some long-distance migration *via* island stepping stones.

A general period of uplift at the close of the Cretaceous resulted in Nuclear Central America and the northern Andes somewhat approaching their modern configuration. From then until the start of the Miocene, migration between North and South America would have been *via* volcanic islands spanning some 1,300 km between northern Nicaragua and northern Colombia. Following the Late Eocene uplift of Yucatán, and the Oligocene uplift of the southern Atlantic Coastal Plain, interrupted migration could have occurred between North and South America *via* the West Indies. On geological grounds, this has not been as important at any time as has migration *via* Central America, and it has never been more direct than it is at present. Uplift of southern Central America that commenced in the Miocene, and continuing volcanism, gradually led to the union of North and South America about 5.7 m.y. BP.

Since the final separation of South America and Africa took place about 100 m.y. BP, and the present distance between them is about 2,500 km, it can be calculated that in the Early Eocene, South America was about equally distant from Africa and North America. Earlier, opportunities for immigration from Africa were greater; later, the connection with and possibility for immigration to North America became more direct.

The Caribbean and its Borderlands.—The geologic history of this region is exceedingly complicated and not well understood, yet it seems desirable to present a general digest of events there so that some of the historical relations of biota in the region can be evaluated more accurately.

The Caribbean Sea and Gulf of Mexico formed during the period 180–105 m.y. BP as North America moved away from South America and Africa (Freeland & Dietz, 1971, 1972; Malfait & Dinkelman, 1972; Phillips & Forsyth, 1972; Walper & Rowett, 1972). Caribbean crust probably formed *in situ*, and not as an extension of the older Pacific crust (Phillips & Forsyth, 1972; Kesler, 1973). Freeland and Dietz (1972) indicate that the formation of the Caribbean Sea began about 135 m.y. BP. By the end of the Early Cretaceous, it had opened to its maximum extent, with North and South America farther apart than at present (Freeland & Dietz, 1971, fig. 6; Malfait & Dinkelman, 1972, fig. 1; Phillips & Forsyth, 1972). The Caribbean then began to close slowly as South America moved northward relative to North America, reaching a climax in the Middle Eocene, and marked by major tectonism on both its northern and southern margins (Freeland & Dietz, 1972; Mattson, 1972).

In the region of the Greater Antilles, small islands were in the area of Cuba by the Late Jurassic (Khudoley & Meyerhoff, 1971, fig. 22). The Cayman Ridge, extending westward from the Sierra Maestra of Cuba towards Guatemala, exhibits a geology that suggests it may have been land in Paleocene to Lower Eocene time (Heezen, Dreyfus & Catalano, 1973), this then facilitating migration to Cuba and indirectly the other Antilles. The Bahamas seem to have been subsiding since initiation of drift between Africa and North America (Dietz *et al.*, 1970a, 1971; Sheridan, 1971). Most existing islands east or south of Cuba are no older than Upper Cretaceous. Their origin probably resulted from intense crustal movements beginning in Late Aptian or Early Albian times, perhaps contemporary with the initial rifting of South America from Africa. By the Late Turonian, a chain of small- to medium-sized volcanic islands was in the area of the Greater Antilles and Lesser Antilles (*e.g.* Proto-Hispaniola, Bracey & Vogt, 1970; Puerto Rico, Mattson, 1973). However, most of the islands in both chains attained their present size and outlines only in the late Neogene.

Jamaica formed in the Early Cretaceous as a series of small volcanic islands that were uplifted substantially in the latest Cretaceous (Robinson & Lewis, 1971). However, no part of Jamaica seems to have been above sea level between Middle Eocene and the early Middle Miocene (Robinson & Lewis, 1971). This means that all of the plants and animals on Jamaica were derived by long-distance overseas dispersal since then. In this light, it is noteworthy that Jamaica has only 4 endemic genera and 784 endemic species of angiosperms (Adams, 1972), or about 27% of the native flora. By contrast, Cuba, which has not been submerged, has 41 endemic genera and about 50% endemic species (Liogier, 1962), and Hispaniola, which is younger than Cuba but has also not been submerged, has 26 endemic genera and about 33% endemic species (Howard, 1973).

In the Late Cretaceous, the Sierra Madre Occidental of Mexico was elevated and marine transgression limited to the area from Veracruz north. There was elevated land and mountains south to the present area of Oaxaca (*cf.* Malfait & Dinkelman, 1972, fig. 1; Kesler, 1973), which does not seem to have reoriented significantly relative to the mainland of Mexico since Precambian time (Kesler & Heath, 1970).

Nuclear Central America is a Paleozoic orogenic belt extending from the Isthmus of Tehuantepec to northeastern Nicaragua (Kesler, 1971), and possibly Cuba (MacGillavry, 1970). Lateral faulting in the region does not suggest great displacement during Tertiary time (Kesler, 1971; G. Dengo, personal communication). However, some paleomagnetic evidence suggests approximately 1,000 km of northeastward displacement of Jamaica since Aptian and Albian time (Steinhauser *et al.*, 1972). Clearly, the geologic history of the region is still far from completely understood. The area from southern Mexico to northeastern Nicaragua, the Nicaraguan bank, and possibly Cuba was uplifted in the Late Cretaceous and subsequently to form what has probably remained a peninsula from Mexico to northern Nicaragua (Mills *et al.*, 1967; Dengo, 1973). The portions of Nuclear Central America that were land before the latest Cretaceous are established only for certain areas, *e.g.* the Maya Mountains of Belize (Hall & Bateson, 1972) and Honduras (Mills *et al.*, 1967). A large portion of Yucatán may have been emergent in Late Eocene time (G. Dengo, personal communication), establishing essentially the modern configuration between Cuba and Central America.

Southern Central America, extending from central Nicaragua south to the Atrato lowland in Colombia, has an oceanic basement of Senonian age overlain by younger sedimentary and volcanic rocks (Dengo, 1969). The earliest deformation is latest Cretaceous, but major uplift occurred only in Late Miocene and Pliocene times. Scattered volcanic islands existed prior to the Oligocene

(Dengo, 1967, 1968, 1969; Case, 1973), but there was no substantial land area (McBirney & Williams, 1965; Malfait & Dinkelman, 1972).

At the start of the Cretaceous, a broad zone of northern Venezuela (Bell, 1971) and much of Colombia (Schuchert, 1935; Liddle, 1946; Jenks, 1956) was subsea. Alvarez (1971) has shown that the Guajira Peninsula of Colombia was receiving sediment from a landmass to the north, perhaps at the present site of the Nicaraguan Rise. In latest Cretaceous time, the Cordillera Central of Colombia (Campbell & Bürgl, 1965; Alvarez, 1971; Anderson, 1972) and the Cordillera de la Costa of Venezuela (Bell, 1971), together with Trinidad (Barr & Saunders, 1971), emerged above the sea, the latter a large island or group of small ones (Liddle, 1946). There is evidence a landmass of considerable size, "París," extending from Aruba to Tobago and even Barbados, was uplifted in early Tertiary time and resulted in deposition of thick sediments to the south (Schuchert, 1935; Edgar, Ewing & Hennison, 1971). The Cordillera Oriental was elevated in late Neogene time, and reached its full height during the Pleistocene (summary in Alvarez, 1971), giving the land area of northwestern South America its present configurations. The complex history of the Sierra Nevada de Santa Marta has been treated by Tschanz *et al.* (1974).

From the Early Oligocene onward, volcanic islands along the present axis of Central America gradually coalesced into continuous land. About 10–12 m.y. ago there was evidently an intermittent land connection to Panama from the north (Whitmore & Stewart, 1965; Malfait & Dinkelman, 1972), which finally coalesced to join North and South America about 5.7 m.y. BP (Simpson, 1950; Kaneps, 1970; Haffer, 1970; Graham, 1972a; Emiliani, *et al.*, 1972).

Summary.—Judging from the geology of the region, and the relative motions of the plates, South America was more accessible to immigration from Africa than from North America until after the Early Eocene. Subsequently, more and more insular connections with North America were established, culminating with a direct land connection only 5.7 m.y. BP. Clearly, the history of South American biota has been one of evolution in isolation of an initial West Gondwanaland stock shared with Africa. To South America have come many cool temperate Australasian plants and animals, essentially overland until the Eo-Oligocene, and by overseas long-distance dispersal subsequently. South America contributed increasingly to the flora of tropical and subtropical North America during the Tertiary, it received immigrants from temperate North America only as the Cordillera rose in the late Neogene, at which time it also contributed montane tropical taxa to Central America.

SUMMARY OF PLATE TECTONIC EVENTS

The following events have had great importance for the patterns of evolution and distribution of organisms: (1) Direct migration last possible between North America, Europe, and Africa, 180 m.y. BP. (2) Direct migration last possible between West Gondwanaland (Africa + South America) and Australasia for warm-temperate and subtropical plants and animals, 100 ± 10 m.y. BP. (3) Direct migration between Africa and Madagascar, and probably also India, last possible, about 100 m.y. BP (possibly more recent; evidence ambiguous). (4)

Overland direct migration last possible between South America and Africa, nearly 100 m.y. BP. (5) Direct migration between Australia and New Caledonia–New Zealand, 80 m.y. BP. (6) Last direct connection between Africa and Eurasia prior to the Miocene, ~ 63 m.y. BP. (7) Direct migration possible across the North Atlantic for plants throughout the Tertiary, but for land animals until 49 m.y. BP, when the Bering Straits became more and more important as a migration route. (8) South America equally distant from North America and from Africa, ~ 50 m.y. BP. (9) India abuts against Asia, ~ 45 m.y. BP. (10) More or less direct migration possible between South America and Australia *via* Antarctica until approximately 38 m.y. BP. (11) Reestablishment of direct connection between Africa and Eurasia, 17 m.y. BP. (12) More or less direct migration first possible between Asia and Australasia *via* New Guinea, ~ 15 m.y. BP. (13) Direct land connection between North and South America, 5.7 m.y. We shall now proceed to consider existing and past patterns of distribution among vertebrates and flowering plants in relation to these events.

BIOGEOGRAPHY OF SOUTH AMERICAN VERTEBRATES

Although we shall devote our attention chiefly to vascular plants, we shall first review the present state of understanding of vertebrate history in South America. We do this for precisely the same reasons that the entomologist Darlington (1957) selected the vertebrates as the primary material for his volume on zoogeography. Vertebrates, both Recent and fossil, are better known than any other group; the patterns of distribution that they display should parallel those found in other groups of organisms, and it should be simpler to look among the vertebrates for solutions to many outstanding problems that are evident in the distribution of other organisms. Furthermore, the basic hypotheses and the amount of evidence that were utilized in Darlington's (1957) synthesis are now so out of date it is necessary to review the facts again in a more modern context. Our remarks supplement the reviews presented by Cracraft (1973b, 1973c).

In preparing the present paper, we have consulted a number of treatments of invertebrates and cryptogams, such as those presented in the two volumes on biogeography and ecology in South America (Fittkau *et al.*, 1968, 1969), and find their patterns of distribution to accord, in general, with those of the vertebrates and vascular plants upon which we shall focus here. A particularly elegant analysis of an exactly parallel pattern has been presented by Edmunds (1972) for the mayflies, and Schlinger (1974) has recently provided interesting new information on the insects associated with *Nothofagus*.

We shall now analyze the paleobiogeography of each of the groups of vertebrates in turn.

FISHES

The dominant freshwater fishes of Africa and South America are characoids and siluroids, both derived from ancestral forms that dispersed directly between these continents when they were united (Myers, 1966; Roberts, 1973, Fig. 1, 3). In South America, the characoids gave rise to the endemic gymnotids, and in Africa cyprinoids subsequently entered from the north (Gosline, 1972), probably at least in part in Neogene time. There are thus no gymnotids in Africa and no cyprinoids in South America. The non-ostariophysan primary freshwater fish families of South America, Lepidosirenidae, Osteoglossidae, and Nandidae, are all shared with Africa. No primary freshwater fishes of North American origin extend south of Lago Nicaragua, and none has reached South America (Myers, 1966), contrary to the elaborate scheme proposed by Darlington (1957). The dominant cichlids and poeciliids of Central America are secondary freshwater fishes that disperse across saltwater barriers. The cichlids probably were derived from South American forms, whereas the poeciliids may have been derived from North American cyprinoids. Both evidently have been radiating in Central America through most of Neogene time. No primary freshwater fish from South America reached Central America until these lands were connected, about 5.7 m.y. BP. Subsequently, a few genera of characoids extended their range north into Mexico, and one (*Astyanax*) reached the Rio Grande (Myers, 1966). The evidence from the distribution of freshwater fishes is in full accord with our present understanding of the relationships between Africa, South America, and North America.

AMPHIBIANS

Caecilians, recently reported from the Late Paleocene of Brazil (Estes & Wake, 1972), almost certainly dispersed overland between South America and Africa in the Cretaceous or earlier, and also spread between Africa and Asia. Salamanders are a Laurasian group, with plethodontids having reached South America from North America after the establishment of a direct land connection between them in the late Neogene.

Frogs may have originated in Gondwanaland, though the suggestion must remain speculative (Laurent, 1972; Estes & Reig, 1973: 48; Reig, 1973). At any rate, South America together with Africa (= West Gondwanaland) has clearly been the primary area from which most, if not all, modern lines of anurans have been derived (Savage, 1973). Pipidae almost certainly dispersed directly between Africa and South America. They are known from the Late Cretaceous of both regions, and from the Early Cretaceous of Israel (Laurent, 1972; Estes & Reig, 1973). Bufonidae (including Atelopidae) may also have done so (Cracraft, 1973b). Since *Heleophryne* of southern Africa is a leptodactylid (Lynch, 1971), it seems reasonable that the group dispersed directly between South America and Africa prior to their separation, and also across Antarctica to Australia (Darlington, 1957: 166; Lynch, 1971). However, Cracraft (1973b) points out that relationships with the Northern Hemisphere pelobatids and phylogenetic lines within the leptodactylids must be understood better before definite conclusions can be drawn.

Savage (1973) contends that one of the genera of Leptodactylidae (*Eleutherodactylus*) reached North America prior to the Pliocene. Savage (personal communication) has pointed out that *Eleutherodactylus* sens. lat. is an excellent candidate for overwater dispersal, with an encapsulated, land-laid egg, like the widely distributed ranid *Cornufer* (*Platymantis*), which has reached Fiji. There are approximately a hundred species of *Eleutherodactylus* in the West

Indies, and at least three derivative endemic genera—*Sminthillus, Syrrhophus,* and *Tomodactylus*—are north of South America.

Leiopelmidae, known as fossils in the Mesozoic of South America (Estes & Reig, 1973), occur today only in northwestern North America and New Zealand. Dispersal to New Zealand need not be explained *via* Antarctic connections. Since this group is known from the Early Jurassic, it may have spread directly between any of the continents (see Fig. 1), and may have arrived in North America much earlier than suggested by Estes and Reig (1973: 47).

Hyla is evidently a South American derivative of leptodactylid stock (Savage, 1973: 414). The Central American hylids are derived from South America, whereas the Nearctic hylids are more closely related to Eurasian taxa (Duellman, 1970). The recent record of *Hyla* from the Early Oligocene of Saskatchewan (Holman, 1969, 1972) implies sweepstakes dispersal from South to North America at least that early, whereas contemporary Central American hylids evidently came later. Although *Hyla,* using some current concepts, would seem to have migrated from South America to Australia directly (Raven & Axelrod, 1972), Tyler (1971) and Savage (1973: 356) have recently allied Australasian forms currently referred to *Hyla* to leptodactylids. This implies their independent derivation from other leptodactylids in Australia.

Bufo, first known from the Paleocene of Brazil (Estes & Reig, 1973), also seems to have been derived from leptodactylid stock in South America (Blair, 1972), spreading by sweepstakes dispersal to North America (Blair, 1972, Fig. 18-1). The presence of fossil bufonids in the Eocene of Europe (R. Estes, personal communication) implies their arrival in North America at least that early, even though the first fossils are from the Lower Miocene. The ancestors of the African groups, which are distinctive, might have arrived by rafting in the Paleocene across a much narrower South Atlantic (*cf.* Laurent, 1972), as we shall discuss below for primates and caviomorph rodents. Blair (1972) has emphasized the similarity between *Bufo* species in Africa and South America. *Rana* reached South America very recently, *via* North America from Eurasia (Darlington, 1957: 170).

To summarize, caecilians and several groups of anurans seem clearly to have migrated overland between South America and Africa in the Cretaceous. *Hyla* probably reached North America from South America by the Early Oligocene at least, and a number of other groups were exchanged between these two continents in the Miocene and more recently. There is no evidence that any amphibians passed directly between North and South America between Lower Jurassic and Early Oligocene times, although the presence of bufonids in the Eocene of Europe suggests that they may have done so.

REPTILES

The four families of dinosaurs recorded from the Upper Cretaceous of South America all occur in North America, and only one has been recorded definitely from Africa (Charig, 1973). These relationships have been used to argue that migration between North and South America must have been relatively direct at that time, and that migration between South America and Africa very indirect

(Colbert, 1952; Darlington, 1957; Charig, 1973). Of these four families, however, one is doubtful in South America and a second has been doubtfully recorded from Madagascar. Ceratopsidae, abundant in North America, are known in South America only from a single fragment of a lower jaw from the Upper Cretaceous of Argentina, which is very doubtfully assigned to this family (Colbert, 1948). Hadrosaurs, abundant in North America at the same time, have not been found in the Southern Hemisphere. Finally, at the generic level, as among the nearly cosmopolitan sauropods, there is as strong an indication of connection between South America, Africa/Madagascar, and India as between East Asia and North America (Charig, 1973).

This analysis of dinosaur distribution, therefore, does not support the notion of direct migration between North and South America in the Mesozoic, which agrees with the known positions of Africa and South America in Early Cretaceous time. There is, however, ample evidence of links between South America, Africa, India, and Madagascar, probably until Upper Cretaceous (Charig, 1973; Colbert, 1973). Cetiosaurinae are known from the Jurassic of Australia, Coeluridae (Charig, 1973), Megalosauridae (Colbert & Merrilees, 1967), and Iguanodontidae (E. H. Colbert, personal communication) from the Early Cretaceous. The presence of these large dinosaurs certainly indicates terrestrial connections between Australia and other parts of the World at that time (Colbert, 1973). However, all of these families existed in the Jurassic, and they might have arrived in Australia prior to the close of that period.

Among the turtles (Simpson, 1943), the pelomedusids evidently dispersed between South America and Africa when these were linked or close to one another, and fossils are known from both regions, as well as from the Northern Hemisphere (Darlington, 1957). Land tortoises (Testudininae) and Chelydridae may have reached South America from North America in the Miocene or more recently, and the Emydinae, basically a northern group, probably did the same. Most other groups are basically northern or southern. Before the arrival of the predominant northern groups of turtles in South America in Neogene time, there were meiolaniids and chelyids, both of which may have reached Australia *via* Antarctica (Raven & Axelrod, 1972). There is no evidence for dispersal of turtles between North and South America prior to Miocene time.

Of the lizards, Iguanidae first appear in the fossil record in the Upper Cretaceous of Brazil (Estes & Price, 1973). The diversity of Paleocene iguanids there suggests that the evolution of the family took place primarily in South America (Tihen, 1964; Estes, 1970). They appear in North America, which they probably reached by sweepstakes dispersal, in the Eocene. The presence of two relict genera on Madagascar suggests that iguanids passed from South America to Africa-Madagascar in the Cretaceous (Estes & Price, 1973). The occurrence of a third endemic genus on Fiji and Tonga seems to be related to long-distance trans-Pacific dispersal, presumably *via* archipelagos, since it is closely related to the American genus *Iguana* (R. Estes, personal communication).

Gekkonidae probably also dispersed more or less directly between South America and Africa during the Cretaceous (Cracraft, 1973*b*). Teiidae seem to have been in both North and South America in the Late Cretaceous (Estes, 1970) and probably spread to North America by sweepstakes dispersal at that time.

However, the only Recent teiid north of Mexico, *Cnemidophorus*, which undoubtedly came from South America, first appears in the North American fossil record in the Early or Middle Miocene (Estes, 1963; Estes & Tihen, 1964; Tihen, 1964). For Amphisbaenidae, now known chiefly from South America and Africa, the Paleocene fossil record in Eurasia and North America suggests a route from Africa to Europe and then to North America. Summarizing, teiids seem to have reached North America from South America by sweepstakes dispersal in the Upper Cretaceous, iguanids in the Eocene, and many other groups of lizards in the Miocene and subsequently.

Aniliid and boid snakes extend back to the Late Cretaceous (Estes, Berberian & Mesozoely, 1969; Estes, 1970), and more primitive snakes are in the Early Cretaceous (Hoffstetter, 1959). The boa *Madtsoia*, if correctly identified, is known from the Upper Cretaceous of Madagascar and the Paleocene-Eocene of Patagonia (Del Corro, 1968). Hence, some boids and possibly other primitive snakes dispersed more or less directly between Africa and South America. Tertiary boids known from North America may have arrived *via* Europe, and snakes must have reached Eurasia prior to the Early Paleocene. Colubroid snakes, which have diversified in the main Eurasian landmass (Rabb & Marx, 1973), reached South America from North America in the Miocene (Hoffstetter, 1967), and have undergone extensive radiation there subsequently. Their diversity in South America in itself seems to be insufficient evidence to postulate an antiquity there greater than the Miocene, contrary to the arguments of Raab and Marx (1973). The early evolution of tropical American colubroid stocks may have taken place in southern North America (= Central America), where Savage (1966) has demonstrated the presence of a substantial endemic element, presumably of some antiquity, among the reptiles. As for Australasia, it is unlikely that any snakes, except possibly seasnakes, reached the area prior to the Miocene, because the Australian snake fauna consists of groups not known to have been in existence prior to the Tertiary.

MAMMALS

As summarized by Clemens (1968, 1970), marsupials are known from the Albian (> 110 m.y. BP; but see Cox, 1973) to the Early Miocene of North America, the Early Eocene to Miocene of Europe, and are also reported from the Upper Cretaceous of Peru (Grambast *et al.*, 1967; Sigé, 1971). They have persisted to the present in South America, and *Didelphis* colonized North America in the Pleistocene, subsequent to the formation of a land connection, reestablishing marsupials in the north after an absence of some 20 m.y. The predominantly southern distribution of marsupials renders it probable that they originated in West Gondwanaland, dispersing directly to Australia (Raven & Axelrod, 1972; Keast, 1972; Cox, 1973). Didelphoids had reached North America by the Upper Cretaceous and were in Europe at least by the Early Eocene. Fossil marsupials are not known from Africa but may be expected there. They spread between North and South America either by sweepstakes dispersal (more likely if they were spreading near the end of the Cretaceous) or *via* Africa and Europe (which can only be confirmed if and when fossil marsupials are discovered in the Cretaceous of Africa and Europe; Cox, 1970; Fooden, 1972). If the Mongolian

Deltatherium proves to be a marsupial (Butler & Kielan-Jaworowska, 1973), the group would then be demonstrated to have been present in Eurasia in Santonian-Campanian time.

Monotremes, like dinosaurs, presumably reached Australasia overland *via* India in the Lower Cretaceous or even Jurassic. Although inferential and some direct evidence suggests the presence of prototherians (monotremes), metatherians (marsupials), and eutherians (placentals) in West Gondwanaland before the separation of Africa and South America, eutherians do not appear to have been in the region early enough for direct migration to Australasia, as discussed below.

One family of notoungulates, Arctostylopidae, is known only from the Upper Paleocene of Mongolia and the Upper Paleocene and Lower Eocene of North America (Simpson, 1945; M. C. McKenna, personal communication). Since other families of the group are exclusively South American, and it seems most likely that notoungulates ancestral to Arctostylopidae reached North America by sweepstakes dispersal from South America by the close of the Paleocene, thence *via* the Bering Straits to Asia. However, an indirect route from West Gondwanaland *via* Eurasia to North America is not precluded.

How the condylarths passed between North and South America is unknown (Kurtén, 1973). The group is not known from African fossils and presents an enigma comparable with that of the marsupials.

Darlington (1957), following Simpson (1945), places the Metacheiromyidae with the edentates, and says that the nearly complete skeletons of *Metacheiromys* are "among the most important of all fossil mammals," because they show that "early in the Tertiary, edentates were in North America, from where they may have reached South America" (Darlington, 1957: 383). Emry (1970) has since shown that the Metacheiromyidae are not edentates but members of the Pholidota. The edentates are therefore an exclusively austral group that spread to North America in the Pliocene.

Among other groups of mammals, caviomorph rodents and platyrrhine primates appear in the fossil record of South America in the Early Oligocene (Patterson & Pascual, 1972). Perhaps the ancestors of both groups arrived by rafting and island-hopping from Africa (Hoffstetter, 1972): in the Early Oligocene South America appears to have been about equally distant from North America and from Africa. Since a platyrrhine primate reached Jamaica in the Pliocene or Pleistocene over a water barrier of about 600 km, perhaps a gap of about twice that distance from Africa to South America was crossed in the Eocene. Hystricomorphous and hystricognathous rodents are known from the Eocene of Europe and North America (Wahlert, 1973), and there is one additional recent record of a hystricognathous rodent from the Eocene of North America (Wood, 1972). Otherwise, living hystricomorphous rodents occur in Eurasia (Old World porcupines only), Africa, and South America, with a Pleistocene invasion of North America by one group of New World porcupines, *Coenodon*. The New World hystricomorphous rodents, almost entirely South American, are all caviomorphs, a group that does not occur in the Old World. The known Eocene North American hystricomorphous and hystricognathous rodents clearly are not ancestral to the caviomorphs (Wood, 1972; Wahlert, 1973, and personal communication), and presumably evolved in North America from a mammalian fauna that was shared with Europe. Thus the derivation of the caviomorph rodents in South America may have been from ancestral forms that arrived from Africa, as mentioned above, and hystricomorph rodents provide no evidence for direct migration between North and South America until the Late Pliocene. The same is true for platyrrhine primates, which seem to have reached Central America and the West Indies only in Pliocene time, and subsequently.

Marsupials and condylarths might have dispersed between North and South America in the Cretaceous (Keast, 1972), but the evidence is not strong and the assumption is based mainly upon contemporary geography. The extensive exchange of mammalian faunas between North and South America which began about 5 m.y. BP is, of course, well established (Simpson, 1947a; Patterson & Pascual, 1972; Savage, 1973). However, there is no evidence for an earlier "intense exchange of land mammals" (Darlington, 1957: 365), and none would be expected from the geological history of Middle America. Before the extinct *Cyonasua* group of extinct procyonids arrived in South America in the Middle Pliocene, Arctostylopidae provide the only convincing case for direct dispersal between North and South America, although marsupials and condylarths might also have crossed the gap between these two continents. These facts argue compellingly for the absence of any direct, or even relatively direct, connection for mammals between North and South America until latest Neogene time.

It appears probable that the original mammalian stocks of South America (condylarth-ungulates and edentates) were derived from an Early Cretaceous mammal fauna shared with Africa (Hoffstetter, 1972). Unfortunately, nothing is known about the Cretaceous mammals of Africa, and we have only fragmentary knowledge about those in the South American Cretaceous. The earliest known African Tertiary mammals, from the Late Eocene, are highly endemic and all proboscideans (Coryndon & Savage, 1973; Cooke, 1973).

BIRDS

Although birds disperse readily across many sorts of barriers and have a poor fossil record, their patterns of distribution accord with those of other groups (Darlington, 1957; Cracraft, 1973*b*, *c*). Cracraft (1973*b*, *c*) has suggested that such families as Struthionidae, Musophagidae, Coliidae, Pteroclididae, Columbidae, Psittacidae, and Eurylaimidae and indeed such orders as Columbiformes, Galliformes, Psittaciformes, and Cuculiformes, may have radiated from West Gondwanaland, and the ratites as a whole may also have done so (Raven & Axelrod, 1972; Cracraft, 1973*c*). A number of important Oriental and otherwise cosmopolitan families of birds, such as Psittacidae and Columbidae, are especially well developed in Australasia. South America is a rich center of diversity for the latter two families and many others which apparently diversified there during the Late Cretaceous and Tertiary.

The absence of living or fossil ratite birds in North America and the presence of a distinctive tropical North American (including Central American) bird fauna, perhaps including such families as Motmotidae, Todidae, Cracidae, Trochilidae, and Thraupidae (Mayr, 1946, 1964; Bond, 1948; Cracraft, 1973*c*),

1974]   RAVEN & AXELROD—ANGIOSPERM BIOGEOGRAPHY   557

reemphasize the wide separation of North and South America in Paleogene times. In attempting to minimize this relationship, Darlington (1957: 279–287) confused the issue by assuming that Central America was an island lying between North and South America.

Although no confirmation is possible on the basis of present fossil evidence, the primary radiation of the birds as a group may well have taken place in West Gondwanaland, with migration to the Northern Hemisphere from Africa to Europe by the Late Jurassic. Judging from the pattern found in many other groups and discussed later in this paper, numerous phylogenetic lines became extinct in Africa after its separation from South America, and this, together with its ready access to Eurasia, may account for the low degree of endemism in Africa noted by Cracraft (1973b), as may the impact of spreading aridity (see p. 608).

Summary.—Direct dispersal between Africa and South America prior to Santonian time (80–85 m.y. BP) is evident for many tropical groups which basically have a West Gondwanaland pattern of distribution. These include characoid and siluroid primary freshwater fishes, as well as the fish families Lepidosirenidae, Osteoglossidae, and Nandidae; caecilians and at least two families of anurans, Pipidae and Leptodactylidae; pelomedusid turtles; iguanid and amphisbaenid lizards; boid snakes; several groups of dinosaurs; and ratite birds. It is probable that the condylarth-ungulate and edentate stocks of South America were derived from a Cretaceous mammal fauna shared with Africa, and that the primary radiation of anurans, birds, marsupials, snakes, and lizards also took place on this large tropical landmass.

Direct migration between Africa and Eurasia was possible at various times during the Cretaceous and Paleocene, and direct migration between Europe and North America was easily possible for vertebrates until the Early Eocene (~ 49 m.y. BP). However, it is uncertain whether such animals as marsupials, amphisbaenid lizards, boid snakes, and various dinosaurs passed between North and South America *via* Africa and Europe, or directly. A better understanding of the fossil record, and a clarification of the affinities of extinct members of these groups, may lead to the solution of this problem for at least some of the groups. At any rate, present evidence suggests that the following groups of vertebrates probably did pass *via* sweepstakes dispersal between North and South America by the times indicated: (1) teiid lizards, Late Cretaceous; (2) arctostylopid mammals, Upper Paleocene; (3) the genus *Bufo* and iguanid lizards, Eocene; (4) the frog genus *Hyla*, Early Oligocene. Marsupials and condylarths may have dispersed between the two continents in the Cretaceous, but otherwise the five groups mentioned above constitute the only likely instances of dispersal by land vertebrates between North and South America in Cretaceous and Paleogene times.

Considering the rich and varied vertebrate faunas of North and South America, the small amount of interchange certainly accords with the geological evidence that suggests a very wide separation of the Americas in Cretaceous and Paleogene time. In the Miocene and subsequently, interchange between the two continents of the Western Hemisphere accelerated and led eventually to the development of a Latin American fauna. The rich and endemic flora and fauna of South

558   ANNALS OF THE MISSOURI BOTANICAL GARDEN   [VOL. 61

America, however, evolved principally during its period of isolation from both Africa and North America, a span of some 70 m.y. between the Santonian (Upper Cretaceous) and the late Neogene. West Gondwanaland, a large landmass lying in tropical latitudes and more or less united until about 90 m.y. BP, seems to have been the primary seat of evolution and radiation of many groups of plants and animals, with intermittent migration to the north *via* Africa; a cool temperate connection to Australasia until about 45 m.y. BP; and an increasingly effective direct interchange between South America and North America during approximately the last 10 m.y.

THE BIOGEOGRAPHY OF ANGIOSPERMS

In the light of the geological evidence reviewed above, and the patterns of evolution and migration that can be seen among living and fossil vertebrates, we shall now review the patterns of distribution among the flowering plants. In order to establish the relevance of certain dates to the history of the groups concerned, we shall first briefly review what is known about the timing of major differentiation among the angiosperms.

THE AGE OF THE ANGIOSPERMS

Although the group might be considerably older, and have existed in low numbers (Axelrod, 1952b, 1970), undoubted monosulcate angiosperm pollen is first known from the Barremian of England, Maryland, and Argentina (Couper, 1964; Archangelsky & Gamero 1967; Kuprainova, 1967; Kemp, 1968; Doyle, 1969; Muller, 1970; Brenner, 1974; Wolfe *et al.*, 1975). Such pollen is characteristic of the Annonales ("woody Ranales") and Nymphaeales among the dicots and of the monocots, which were definitely distinct by Aptian time (Samylina, 1968; J. A. Doyle, 1973). Tricolpate pollen, characteristic of all dicots other than Annonales and Nymphaeales, is first reported from the Hauterivian to Barremian of the U.S.S.R. (Bolchovitina, 1953; Pokrovskaya, 1964; Voronova, 1966); these records have not been reconfirmed, as far as we are aware, in the more recent literature. It is next recorded from Barremian-Aptian beds in the Northern Negev of Israel (Brenner, 1974), and from the Aptian of Brazil (Muller, 1966; Brenner, 1974), the U.S.S.R. (Yedemskaya, 1960; Panova, 1964; Voronova, 1966; Khlonova, 1971; Orlova-Turchina, 1971; Papulov, 1971), and the U.S.A. (Hedlund & Norris, 1968; J. A. Doyle, personal communication). The information available at present is indecisive about the place of origin of plants with tricolpate pollen (Jones & Kremp, 1973; R. E. Jones, personal communication). An origin in tropical West Gondwanaland, attractive on ecological grounds, would be consistent with these data (Brenner, 1974). Tricolpate pollen does not appear in the record in Arctic North America until Cenomanian time, this certainly being in accordance with

→

FIGURE 5. Geological time scale since the Jurassic. The ages of most of the Epoch/Stage boundaries are correct to within 1–2 million years, as judged from radiometric dates. Some authorities (Berggren, 1972; Kaneps, 1970; Van Couvering & Miller, 1971) have shown that the Miocene-Pliocene boundary in the *marine* section may be as young as 5.5 m.y.; see dotted line). For Cretaceous time see Addendum: Baldwin *et al.* (1974). Neoc. = Neocomian.

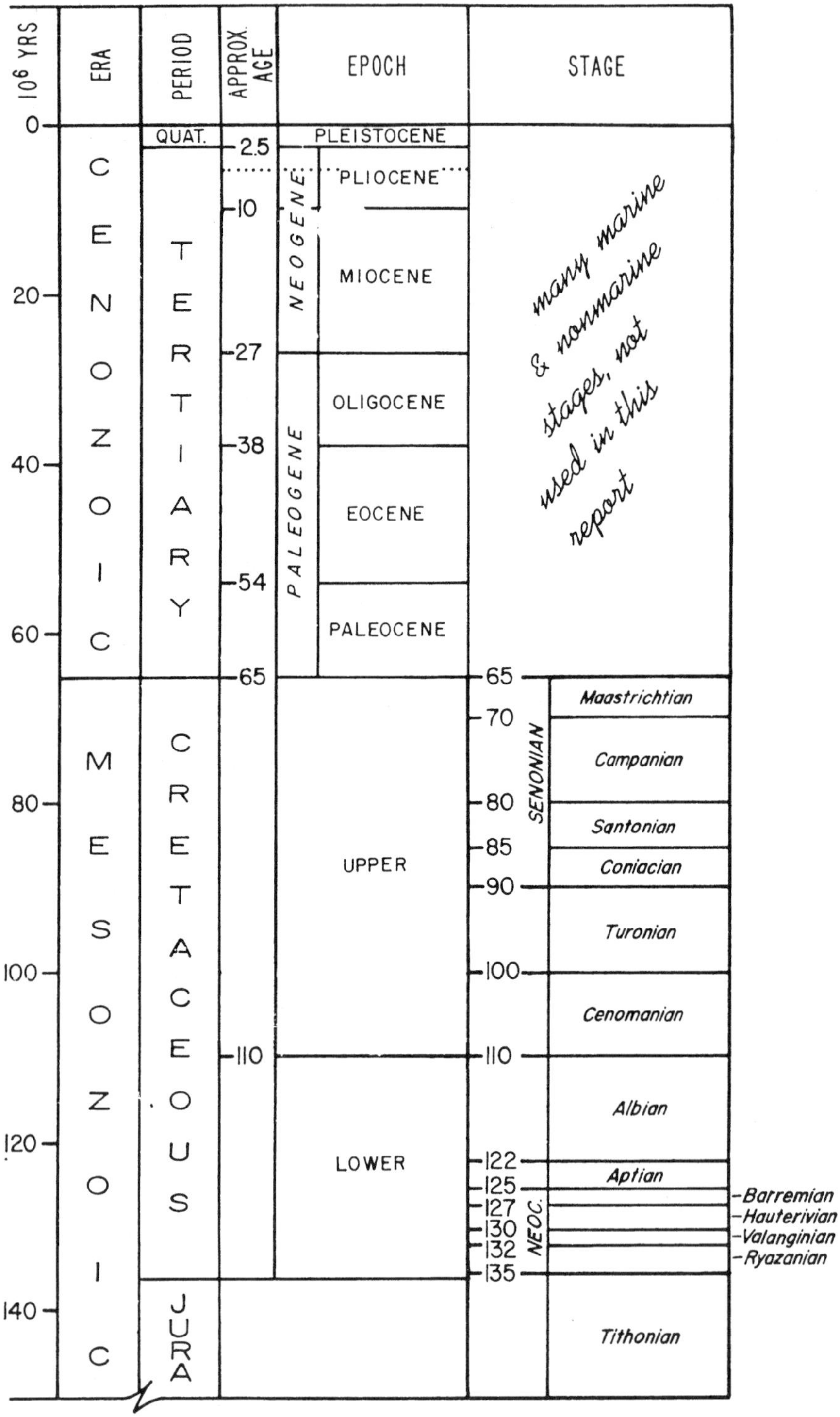

10⁶ YRS
ERA
PERIOD
APPROX. AGE
EPOCH
STAGE
0
20
40
60
80
100
120
140
CENOZOIC
MESOZOIC
QUAT.
TERTIARY
CRETACEOUS
JURA
2.5
10
27
38
54
65
110
PLEISTOCENE
PLIOCENE
MIOCENE
NEOGENE
OLIGOCENE
EOCENE
PALEOCENE
PALEOGENE
UPPER
LOWER
many marine & nonmarine stages, not used in this report
65
70
80
85
90
100
110
122
125
127
130
132
135
SENONIAN
NEOC.
Maastrichtian
Campanian
Santonian
Coniacian
Turonian
Cenomanian
Albian
Aptian
Barremian
Hauterivian
Valanginian
Ryazanian
Tithonian

the notion of a northward migration of early angiosperms from middle latitudes (Hughes, 1961, 1973; Doyle, 1969; Brenner, 1974), as suggested earlier on the basis of megafossil evidence by Axelrod (1959). See Hopkins (1974) in Addendum.

Among the few putative pre-Aptian megafossil records of angiosperms is *Onoana*, from the Hauterivian of northern California (Chandler & Axelrod, 1961), which is very likely a gynospermous seed (Wolfe *et al.*, 1975; M. E. J. Chandler, personal communication).

Chandler (1958) recorded a structure of uncertain affinity that she regarded as an angiosperm fruit from the Valanginian of France, but the specimen has not been traced since World War II and its identity is uncertain (M. E. J. Chandler, personal communication). Various pre-Campanian palmlike leaves such as the Jurassic *Propalmophyllum* and the Triassic *Sanmiguelia* are not now generally regarded as palms (Read & Hickey, 1972; Scott *et al.*, 1972; Moore, 1973; Doyle, 1973). An example of a pre-Cretaceous fossil which exhibits certain angiosperm-like tendencies (reduction in seed size, pappus-like parachute) is Upper Jurassic *Problematospermum* (Krassilov, 1973).

There are few suggestions of Aptian (122–125 m.y. BP) angiosperm diversity in the available record. Krassilov (1967, 1973) has assigned fruits from the Aptian of Primorye in the Far East of the U.S.S.R. to *Onoana*, but his description "probably many seeded, and spiny" (1973: 172) suggests they represent a very different taxon. Krassilov simply interprets it as a primitive angiosperm and apparently associates with it Upper Cretaceous staminate heads with pollen of the *Tricolpopollenites* type which is not recorded before the basal Albian.

By Upper Albian time (110–113 m.y. BP), diverse angiospermous floras existed, as shown for the Potomac Group (Wolfe *et al.*, 1975); the Dakota flora, that from the Cheyenne Sandstone (Lesquereux, 1891; Berry, 1922; most, if not all, of the generic determinations are incorrect); and other contemporary floras. Small tricolpate pollen with a psilate or finely reticulate sculpturing becomes abundant in the Middle Albian at many widely scattered localities at middle latitudes (Brenner, 1974), but was already widespread by Aptian time, as we have seen. On present evidence, it appears reasonable that primitive members of the Annonales and of one or more groups of monocotyledons were in existence by Neocomian time, at the latest. The tricolpate pollen which appears in the record in the Aptian may be compared with that characteristic of some modern families, but the picture is blurred (Doyle, 1969; Muller, 1970). In any event, such groups as Annonales, Theales, Berberidales, and Hamamelidales, or their immediate precursors, as well as some monocots (see also Samylina, 1968: 216; Doyle, 1973), might logically be considered to have existed before the close of the Lower Cretaceous and possibly considerably earlier.

Although more diversity appears in the pollen record in the Cenomanian, it is in general not until the Turonian and Senonian that angiosperm pollen becomes more abundant than the spores of ferns and the pollen of gymnosperms, with a concomitant great increase in angiosperm diversity. The number of modern angiosperm families recorded for the Cenomanian has apparently been greatly exaggerated by superficial comparisons of leaves and fruits with those of modern taxa (Penny, 1969; Muller, 1970). By Maastrichtian time, however, a number of modern genera and families were definitely present (Muller, 1970; Wolfe *et al.*, 1975; Wolfe, 1974). These include *Nypa* (Arecaceae), *Ctenolophon* (Linaceae), Proteaceae, Myrtaceae, *Ilex* (Aquifoliaceae), Poaceae, Sapotaceae, *Nothofagus* (Fagaceae), *Pachysandra* or *Sarcococca* (Buxaceae; Srivastava, 1972), *Ascarina* (Chloranthaceae), *Anacolasia* (Olacaceae), *Alnus* (Betulaceae), *Guarea* (Meliaceae; Graham, 1962), and *Symplocos* (Symplocaceae), as judged by very strict criteria (Muller, 1970). It is reasonable to infer the existence of some modern families by Turonian time (90–100 m.y. BP) and at least several orders in the Cenomanian, with some even earlier. By the Paleocene, *Alyxia* (Apocynaceae), *Betula* (Betulaceae), *Barringtonia* (Lecythidaceae), *Brownlowia* (Tiliaceae), *Bombax* (Bombacaceae), *Crudia* (Caesalpinaceae), and *Liquidambar* (Hamamelidaceae) were in existence, as were very many other living genera (*e.g.* see Brown, 1962).

This pattern of appearance of angiosperms in the lowland record suggests that the primitive members of several extant orders and perhaps even a few families were already in existence by the close of the Early Cretaceous, 110 m.y. BP. Many more were in existence when essentially direct interchange was still possible between Africa and South America, 90 m.y. BP, and a great many by the Paleocene when these two continents were only about 800 km apart and linked by numerous volcanic islands. Most modern angiosperm families were in existence before the connection between Africa and Eurasia was severed in the Paleocene, about 63 m.y. BP. All but the most recently derived families had originated when direct migration between Australia and South America was still possible, ~ 45 m.y. BP, although this path was used only by cool-temperate organisms. Many of the ancient angiosperms and animals of Australasia presumably did not come by this temperate pathway from South America prior to the Cenomanian, but directly from West Gondwanaland *via* India and Antarctica (see Fig. 2). Similarly, the ancient tropical and subtropical flora and fauna of South America was shared with Africa, and has been enriched only in the later Neogene and more recently with temperate North American taxa in ever-increasing numbers. It now remains to consider the patterns of distribution seen among living angiosperms in the light of these deductions.

Review of Existing Groups

We have had no opportunity to investigate the great majority of angiosperm orders in detail, but offer the following comments, arranged according to the system of Thorne (1968), to illustrate the major patterns that do exist in the group. In the following notes, we have used especially *Die Natürlichen Pflanzenfamilien* (Engler & Prantl, 1887–1915) and *Das Pflanzenreich* (Engler, 1900–1953), Airy Shaw (1966), and Hutchinson (1959). The following more local works have also been very useful: Burbidge (1963), Standley (1920–1926), Muñoz Pizarro (1966), Thorne (1965), Guillaumin *et al.* (1965), and Hillebrand (1888).

No extensive effort has been made to review the paleobotanical literature, especially since the identification of Cretaceous and Paleogene angiosperms with modern forms presents so many difficult problems. We do, however, mention a few records when they appear to be of special interest in relation to the distribution of patterns being discussed. In this connection, the bibliography assembled a lowland flora of northern Australia–New Guinea which, although part of the Australian plate, has been populated almost exclusively by tropical taxa derived from the Asian tropics *via* the intervening islands. Also, the cordilleras of southern North America and of South America have been populated largely by temperate taxa derived from North America, as have the mountains of New Guinea by temperate Australasian taxa. During the latest Cenozoic there has been trans-tropic migration in each hemisphere, with a transfer of taxa from the colder boreal to austral areas.

Both in Australasia and in Africa remnants of the ancient flora have persisted on offshore islands separated from the mainland by seafloor spreading in the Upper Cretaceous and subsequently. The increasing isolation of these islands and their highly equable, oceanic climates have made them excellent sites for survival of ancient taxa.

It is amply clear that a restudy of the known Cretaceous and Paleogene floras of Africa–South America is a research project of highest priority. Previously described fossil floras should be intensively recollected, utilizing earth-moving equipment to secure adequate samples wherever possible. The taxa must be compared with those in the American, Malaysian, Australasian and African tropics and border areas, so that past links between these regions may be established wherever possible. The results should dispel at least some of our uncertainty about the early history of tropical floras, and of the angiosperms themselves.

LITERATURE CITED

ABDALLAH, M. S. 1967. The Resedaceae. A taxonomical revision of the family. Meded. Landbouwhoogeschool 67(8).

ABDEL-MONEM, A., N. D. WATKINS & P. W. GAST. 1972. Potassium-argon ages, volcanic stratigraphy, and geomagnetic polarity history of the Canary Islands: Tenerife, La Palma, and Hierro. Amer. Jour. Sci. 272: 805–825.

ADAMS, C. D. 1972. Flowering Plants of Jamaica. Univ. of the West Indies, Mona, Jamaica. 848 pp.

ADIE, R. J. (editor). 1972. Antarctic Geology and Geophysics. Universitetsforlaget, Oslo. 876 pp.

AIRY SHAW, H. K. 1966. J. C. Willis. A Dictionary of Flowering Plants and Ferns. Cambridge Univ. Press, Cambridge. xxii + 1214 + liii pp. Ed. 7.

ALAIN, HERMANO (E. E. LIOGIER). 1958. La flora de Cuba: Sus principales caracteristicas (y) su origen probable. Revista Soc. Cubana Bot. 15: 36–96.

ALLARD, G. O. & V. J. HURST. 1969. Brazil-Gabon geologic link supports continental drift. Science 163: 528–533.

ALLEN, C. K. 1945. Studies in the Lauraceae, VI. Preliminary survey of the Mexican and Central American species. Jour. Arnold Arbor. 26: 280–434.

ALVAREZ, W. 1971. Fragmented Andean belt of northern Colombia. Mem. Geol. Soc. Amer. 130: 77–96.

ANDERSON, T. A. 1972. Paleogene nonmarine Gualanday Group, Neiva Basin, Colombia, and regional development of the Colombian Andes. Bull. Geol. Soc. Amer. 83: 2423–2438.

ANONYMOUS. 1972. Scotia axis confirmed. Nature 240: 14–15.

———. 1973. Pacific drilling dates Atlantic opening. Science News 104: 278.

———. 1974. Sahara's far-flung dust dims Atlantic sunlight. Science News 105: 38–39.

ARCHANGELSKY, S. & J. C. GAMERRO. 1967. Spore and pollen types of the Lower Cretaceous in Patagonia (Argentina). Rev. Palaeobot. Palynol. 1: 211–217.

AUBRÉVILLE, A. 1970. La flore tropicale Tertiare du Sahara. Adansonia, n.s. 10: 9–14.

———. 1971. La Flore Saharo-Lybienne tropicale d'après Paul Louvet. Adansonia, n.s. 11: 583–592.

———. 1973. Géophylétique florale des Sapotacées. Compt. Rend. Hebd. Séances Acad. Sci. 276: 2641–2644.

638 ANNALS OF THE MISSOURI BOTANICAL GARDEN [VOL. 61

AUDLEY-CHARLES, M. G., D. J. CARTER & J. S. MILSOM. 1972. Tectonic development of eastern Indonesia in relation to Gondwanaland dispersal. Nature Phys. Sci. 239: 36–39.

AXELROD, D. I. 1939. A Miocene flora from the western border of the Mohave Desert. Carnegie Inst. Washington Publ. 516: 1–129.

———. 1948. Climate and evolution in western North America during Middle Pliocene time. Evolution 2: 127–144.

———. 1950. Evolution of desert vegetation. Carnegie Inst. Washington Publ. 590: 215–306.

———. 1952a. Variables affecting the probabilities of dispersal in geologic time. Bull. Amer. Mus. Nat. Hist. 99: 177–188.

———. 1952b. A theory of angiosperm evolution. Evolution 6: 29–60.

———. 1958. Evolution of the Madro-Tertiary Geoflora. Bot. Rev. 24: 433–509.

———. 1959. Poleward migration of early angiosperm flora. Science 130: 203–207.

———. 1960. The evolution of flowering plants. Pp. 227–307, in S. Tax (editor), "Evolution after Darwin. Vol. 1, The Evolution of Life." Univ. of Chicago Press.

———. 1966. A method of determining the altitudes of Tertiary floras. Paleobotanist 14: 144–171.

———. 1967. Drought, diastrophism and quantum evolution. Evolution 21: 201–209.

———. 1970. Mesozoic paleogeography and early angiosperm history. Bot. Rev. 36: 277–319.

———. 1971 [1974]. Plate tectonics in relation to the history of the angiosperm flora of India. Birbal Sahni Inst. Paleobot. Spec. Publ. 1: 5–18.

———. 1972a. Ocean-floor spreading in relation to ecosystematic problems. Univ. Arkansas Mus. Occas. Paper 4: 15–76.

———. 1972b. Edaphic aridity as a factor in angiosperm evolution. Amer. Naturalist 106: 311–320.

———. 1972c. Plate tectonics and problems of angiosperm history. XVII Internat. Zool. Congr., Thème 1. Biogéographie et liasons intercontinentales au cours du Mésozoïque. 16 pp.

———. 1973. History of the Mediterranean ecosystem in California. Pp. 255–277, in H. Mooney & F. di Castri (editors), "Ecological Studies, vol. 7. Mediterranean Type Ecosystems." Springer Verlag, Berlin and New York.

——— & P. H. RAVEN. 1972. Evolutionary biology viewed from plate tectonic theory. Pp. 218–236, in J. A. Behnke (editor), "Challenging Biological Problems. Directions toward their Solution." Oxford Univ. Press, New York.

AYENSU, E. S. 1972. Dioscoreales. In C. R. Metcalfe (editor), "Anatomy of the Monocotyledons VI." Oxford Univ. Press. 184 pp.

———. 1973. Phytogeography and evolution of the Velloziaceae. Pp. 105–119, in B. J. Meggers, A. S. Ayensu & W. D. Duckworth (editors), "Tropical Forest Ecosystems in Africa and South America: A Comparative Review." Smithsonian Institution Press, Washington, D.C.

BAKER, B. H., P. A. MOHR & L. A. J. WILLIAMS. 1972. Geology of the eastern rift system of Africa. Geol. Soc. Amer. Spec. Paper 136: 1–67.

BAKER, H. G. 1973. Evolutionary relationships between flowering plants and animals in American and African tropical forests. Pp. 145–159, in B. J. Meggers, E. S. Ayensu & W. D. Duckworth (editors), "Tropical Forest Ecosystems in Africa and South America: A Comparative Review." Smithsonian Institution Press, Washington, D.C.

BANWAR, S. C. 1966. Morphological and anatomical studies on the genus *Lyonothamnus*. Univ. California, Berkeley, Ph.D. Dissertation, Botany. University Microfilms, Ann Arbor, Michigan. 66–8267.

BARBOUR, M. G. 1969. Patterns of genetic similarity between *Larrea divaricata* of North and South America. Amer. Midl. Naturalist 81: 54–67.

BARLOW, B. A. & D. WIENS. 1971. The cytogeography of the loranthaceous mistletoes. Taxon 20: 291–312.

BARR, K. W. & J. B. SAUNDERS. 1971. An outline of the geology of Trinidad. Pp. 2–12, in J. F. Tomblin (editor), "Field Guides to the Geology of Trinidad." Internat. Field Institute. Guidebook to the Caribbean Island-Arc System. Amer. Geol. Institute.

BATESON, J. H. 1972. New interpretation of geology of Maya Mountains, British Honduras. Bull. Amer. Assoc. Petrol. Geol. 56: 956–963.

BECKER, H. F. 1969. Fossil plants of the Tertiary Beaverhead Basin in Southwestern Montana. Palaeontographica B 127: 1–142, *pl. 1–44*.

BELL, J. 1971. Tectonic evolution of the central part of the Venezuelan Coast Ranges. Mem. Geol. Soc. Amer. 130: 107–118.

BERGGREN, W. A. 1972. A Cenozoic time scale—some implications for regional geology and biogeography. Lethaia 5: 195–215.

BERRY, E. W. 1916. The Lower Eocene floras of southeastern North America. U. S. Geol. Surv. Prof. Pap. 91: 1–481.

———. 1922. The flora of the Cheyenne Sandstone in Kansas. U. S. Geol. Surv. Prof. Paper 127-I: 199–225.

———. 1924. The Middle and Upper Eocene floras of southeastern North America. U. S. Geol. Surv. Prof. Pap. 92: 1–206.

———. 1937. Tertiary floras of eastern North America. Bot. Rev. 3: 31–46.

———. 1938. Tertiary flora from the Río Pichileufu, Argentina. Geol. Soc. Amer. Spec. Pap. 12: 1–149.

BEUSEKOM, C. F. VAN. 1971. Revision of *Meliosma* (Sabiaceae), section *Lorenzanea* excepted, living and fossil, geography and phylogeny. Blumea 19: 355–529.

BEWS, J. W. 1927. Studies in the ecological evolution of angiosperms. New Phytologist Reprint 16.

BIGARELLA, J. J. & G. O. DE ANDRADE. 1965. Contribution to the study of the Brazilian Quaternary. Special Paper Geol. Soc. Amer. 84: 433–451.

BLAIR, W. F. (editor). 1972. Evolution in the Genus *Bufo*. Univ. Texas Press, Austin. 459 pp.

BLAKE, S. T. 1972. *Idiospermum* (Idiospermaceae), a new genus and family for *Calycanthus australiensis*. Contr. Queensl. Herb. 12: 1–12.

BOGERT, C. M. 1953a. Body temperatures of the tuatara under natural conditions. Zoologica 38: 63–64.

———. 1953b. The tuatara. Sci. Monthly 76: 163–170.

BOLKHOVITINA, N. A. 1953. Sporovo-pyl'tsevaya kharakteristika melovykh otlozheniy Nizhnesyrdar'inskogo podnyatiya (Severo-vostochnoye Priaral'ye). Dokl. Akad. Nauk SSSR 152(2): 392–395.

BONATI, E. & S. GARTNER, JR. 1973. Caribbean climate during Pleistocene ice ages. Nature 244: 563–565.

BOND, J. 1948. Origin of the bird fauna of the West Indies. Wilson Bull. 60: 207–229.

BOWDEN, J., P. H. GREGORY & C. G. JOHNSON. 1971. Possible wind transport of coffee leaf rust across the Atlantic Ocean. Nature 229: 500–501.

BRACEY, D. R. & P. R. VOGT. 1970. Plate tectonics in the Hispaniola area. Bull. Geol. Soc. Amer. 81: 2855–2860.

BRAMWELL, D. 1972. Endemism in the flora of the Canary Islands. Pp. 141–159, in D. H. Valentine (editor), "Taxonomy, Phytogeography, and Evolution." Academic Press, London and New York.

BRATTSTROM, B. H. 1963. A preliminary view of the thermal requirements of amphibians. Ecology 44: 238–255.

BRENAN, J. P. M. 1966. The classification of Commelinaceae. Jour. Linn. Soc. Bot. 59: 349–370.

BRENNER, G. J. 1974. Middle Cretaceous floral provinces and early migrations of angiosperms. In C. B. Beck (editor), "Origin and Early Evolution of Angiosperms." (In press.)

BROWN, R. W. 1946. Walnuts from the Late Tertiary of Ecuador. Amer. Jour. Sci. 244: 554–556.

———. 1959. Some paleobotanical problematica. Jour. Paleontol. 33: 120–124, *pl. 23*.

———. 1962. Paleocene flora of the Rocky Mountains and Great Plains. U. S. Geol. Surv. Prof. Paper 375: 1–119, *pl. 1–69*.

BURBIDGE, N. T. 1963. Dictionary of Australian Plant Genera. Angus & Robertson Ltd., Sydney. xviii + 345 pp.

BURGER, D. 1968. Relationships of palynology to stratigraphy in the Lower Cretaceous of the Surat Basin in Queensland. Bur. Miner. Res. Geol. Geophys. Rec. 125 (Queensland).

BUTLER, P. M. & Z. KIELAN-JAWOROWSKA. 1973. Is *Deltatherium* a marsupial? Nature 245: 105–106.

BUXBAUM, F. 1969. Die Entwicklungswege der Kakteen in Südamerika. Monogr. Biol. 19: 583–623.

CAMP, W. H. 1947. Distribution patterns in modern plants and the problems of ancient dispersals. Ecol. Monogr. 17: 159–183.

————. 1952. Phytophyletic patterns on land bordering the South Atlantic basin. Bull. Amer. Mus. Nat. Hist. 99(3): 205–216.

CAMPBELL, C. J. & H. BÜRGL. 1965. Section through the Eastern Cordillera of Colombia, South America. Bull. Geol. Soc. Amer. 76: 567–590.

CAPOURON, R. 1963. Contributions à l'étude de la flore de Madagascar. XI. Présence à Madagascar d'un représentant du genre *Macadamia* F.v.M. (Protéacées). Adansonia n.s. 3: 370–373.

CARLQUIST, S. 1966. Anatomy of Rapateaceae—roots and stems. Phytomorphology 16: 17–38.

CAROLIN, R. C. 1960. The structures involved in the presentation of pollen to visiting insects in the order Campanulales. Proc. Linn. Soc. New South Wales 85: 166–177.

CASE, J. E. 1973. Geophysical data on Central American land bridge. Mexico City, July, 1973. Amer. Assoc. Adv. Sci.

CHANDLER, M. E. J. 1954. Some upper Cretaceous and Eocene fruits from Egypt. Bull. Brit. Mus. (Nat. Hist.), Geol. 2: 147–187.

————. 1958. Angiosperm fruits from the Lower Cretaceous of France and Lower Eocene (London Clay) of Germany. Ann. Mag. Nat. Hist., ser. 13. 1: 354–358.

————. 1964. The lower Tertiary floras of southern England. IV. A summary and survey of findings in the light of recent botanical observations. Bull. British Museum (Nat. Hist.), Geol. 12: 1–151, *pl. 1–4.*

———— & D. I. AXELROD. 1961. An early Cretaceous (Hauterivian) angiosperm fruit from California. Amer. Jour. Sci. 259: 441–446.

CHANEY, R. W. 1936. Plant distribution as a guide to age determination. Jour. Washington Acad. Sci. 26: 313–324.

CHARIG, A. J. 1973. Jurassic and Cretaceous dinosaurs. Pp. 339–352, *in* A. Hallam (editor), "Atlas of Palaeobiogeography." Elsevier Scientific Publicating Co., Amsterdam.

CHEVALIER, A. 1947. La famille des Huaceae et ses affinités. Rev. Int. Bot. App. Agric. Trop. 27: 26–29.

CHMURA, C. A. 1973. Upper Cretaceous (Campanian-Maastrichtian) angiosperm pollen *from the western San Joaquin Valley, California, U.S.A.* Palaeontographica B. 141: 89–171.

CLEMENS, W. A. 1968. Origin and early evolution of marsupials. Evolution 22: 1–18.

————. 1970. Mesozoic mammalian evolution. Annual Rev. Ecol. Syst. 1: 357–390.

COETZEE, J. A. 1967. Pollen analytical studies in east and southern Africa. *In* E. M. van Zinderen Bakker (editor), "Palaeoecology of Africa." 3: 1–146. A. A. Balkema, Cape Town.

COLBERT, E. H. 1948. Evolution of the horned dinosaurs. Evolution 2: 145–163.

————. 1952. The Mesozoic tetrapods of South America. Bull. Amer. Mus. Nat. Hist. 99: 237–249.

————. 1971. Tetrapods and continents. Quart. Rev. Biol. 46: 250–269.

————. 1973. Continental drift and the distributions of fossil reptiles. *In* D. H. Tarling & S. K. Runcorn (editors), "Implications of Continental Drift to the Earth Sciences." Vol. 1: 395–412. Academic Press, London and New York.

———— & D. MERRILESS. 1967. Cretaceous dinosaur footprints from Western Australia. Jour. Roy. Soc. West. Australia 50: 21–25.

COLINVAUX, P. A. 1972. Climate and the Galapagos Islands. Nature 240: 17–20.

COOKE, C. W. 1945. Geology of Florida. Florida Geol. Surv. Bull. 29.

COOKE, H. B. S. 1972. The fossil mammal fauna of Africa. Pp. 89–139, *in* A. Keast, F. C. Erk & B. Glass (editors), "Evolution, Mammals, and Southern Continents." State Univ. New York Press, Albany.

CORYNDON, S. C. & R. J. G. SAVAGE. 1973. The origin and affinities of African mammal faunas. *In* N. F. Hughes (editor), "Organisms and Continents through Time." Palaentol. Assoc. London, Spec. Pap. Palaeontol. 12: 121–135.

COUPER, R. A. 1953. Upper Mesozoic and Cainozoic spores and pollen grains from New Zealand. New Zeal. Geol. Surv. Paleontol. Bull. 22: 1–77, *9 pl.*

————. 1960. New Zealand Mesozoic and Cainozoic plant microfossils. New Zeal. Geol. Surv. Palaeont. Bull. 32: 1–87, *pl. 1–12.*

————. 1964. Spore-pollen correlation of the Cretaceous rocks of the Northern and Southern Hemispheres. Soc. Econ. Paleont. Mineral. Spec. Publ. 11: 131–142.

COX, C. B. 1970. Migrating marsupials and drifting continents. Nature 266: 767–770.

————. 1973. Systematics and plate tectonics in the spread of marsupials. *In* N. F. Hughes (editor), "Organisms and Continents through Time." Palaeontol. Assoc. London, Spec. Pap. Palaeontol. 12: 113–119.

CRACRAFT, J. 1973a. Mesozoic dispersal of terrestrial faunas around the southern end of the world. XVII Congr. Internat. Zool., Theme No. 1. Biogéographie et liaisons intercontinentales au cours du Mésozoïque.

———. 1973b. Vertebrate evolution and biogeography in the Old World tropics: Implications of continental drift and palaeoclimatology. In D. H. Tarling & S. K. Runcorn (editors), "Implications of Continental Drift to the Earth Sciences." Vol. 1: 373–393. Academic Press, London and New York.

———. 1973c. Continental drift, paleoclimatology, and evolution and biogeography of birds. Jour. Zool. London 179: 455–545.

CRANWELL, L. C. 1963. Nothofagus: living and fossil. Pp. 387–400, in L. J. Gressitt (editor), "Pacific Basin Biogeography: a Symposium." Univ. Hawaii Press, Honolulu.

———, H. J. HARRINGTON & I. G. SPEDEN. 1960. Lower Tertiary microfossils from McMurdo Sound, Antarctica. Nature 186: 700–702.

CRONQUIST, A. 1968. The Evolution and Classification of Flowering Plants. Thomas Nelson and Sons, Ltd., London. xi + 396 pp.

CUTLER, D. F. 1972. Vicarious species of Restionaceae in Africa, Australia and South America. Pp. 73–83, in D. H. Valentine (editor), "Taxonomy, Phytogeography, and Evolution." Academic Press, London and New York.

DAGHLIAN, C. P. & D. L. DILCHER. 1971. Philodendron leaves from Eocene sediments in Tennessee. Proc. Indiana Acad. Sci. 80: 95–96.

DAHLGREN, R. & V. S. RAO. 1971. The genus Oftia Adans. and its systematic position. Bot. Not. 124: 451–472.

DALRYMPLE, G. B., E. A. SILVER & E. D. JACKSON. 1973. Origin of the Hawaiian Islands. Amer. Sci. 61: 294–308.

DALZIEL, I. W. D., W. LOWRIE, R. KLINGFIELD & N. C. OPDYKE. 1973. Palaeomagnetic data from the southernmost Andes and the Arctandes. In D. H. Tarling & S. K. Runcorn (editors), "Implications of Continental Drift to the Earth Sciences." Vol. 1: 87–101. Academic Press, London and New York.

DAMUTH, J. E. & R. W. FAIRBRIDGE. 1970. Equatorial Atlantic deep-sea arkosic sands and ice-age aridity in tropical South America. Bull. Geol. Soc. Amer. 81: 189–206.

D'ARCY, W. G. & R. C. KEATING. 1973. The affinities of Lithophytum: A transfer from Solanaceae to Verbenaceae. Brittonia 25: 213–225.

DARLINGTON, P. J., JR. 1938. The origin of the fauna of the Greater Antilles, with discussion of dispersal of animals over water and through the air. Quart. Rev. Biol. 13: 274–300.

———. 1957. Zoogeography: The Geographical Distribution of Animals. John Wiley & Sons, Inc. xi + 675 pp.

———. 1965. Biogeography of the Southern End of the World. Harvard Univ. Press, Cambridge, Mass. x + 236 pp.

DEJARDIN, J., J.-L. GUILLAUMET & G. MANGENOT. 1973. Contribution à la connaissance de l'élément non endémique de la flore malgache (végétaux vasculaires). Candollea 28: 325–391.

DEL CORRO, G. 1968. La presencia de Madtsoa Simpson (Boidae) en el Eocene de Patagonia y en el Cretacio de Madagascar y algunos ejemplos de distribución disjuncta. Comm. Mus. Argent. Cíen. Nat. "Bernardino Rivadavia" Paleo. 1: 21–26.

DENGO, G. 1967. Geological structure of Central America. Studies in Tropical Oceanography 5: 56–73. Univ. Miami.

———. 1968. Estructura geológica, historia tectónica y morfológia de América Central. Centro Regional de Ayuda Técnica, A.I.D., México. 50 pp.

———. 1969. Problems of tectonic relations between Central America and the Caribbean. Trans. Gulf Assoc. Geol. 19: 311–320.

———. 1973. Estructura geológica, historia tectónica y morfológia de América Central. Ed. 2. Centro Regional de Ayuda Técnica, A.I.D., México. 52 pp.

——— & O. BOHNENBERGER. 1969. Structural development of northern Central America. Mem. Amer. Assoc. Petrol. Geol. 11: 203–220.

DENTON, G. H., R. L. ARMSTRONG & M. STUIVER. 1971. The late Cenozoic glacial history of Antarctica. Pp. 267–306, in K. K. Turekian (editor), "The Late Cenozoic Glacial Ages." Yale Univ. Press, New Haven.

DEPAPE, G. 1922. Recherches sur la flore Pliocène de la Vallée du Rhone. Ann. Sci. Nat. Bot., sér. 4. 10: 73–265.

Dewey, J. F., W. C. Pitman III, W. B. F. Ryan & J. Bonin. 1973. Plate tectonics and the evolution of the Alpine system. Bull. Geol. Soc. Amer. 84: 3137–3180.

Dickison, W. C. 1967a. Comparative morphological studies in Dilleniaceae, I. Wood anatomy. Jour. Arnold Arbor. 48: 1–29.

———. 1967b. Comparative morphological studies in Dilleniaceae, II. The pollen. Jour. Arnold Arbor. 48: 231–240.

Dietz, R. S. & J. C. Holden. 1970. Reconstruction of Pangaea: breakup and dispersion of continents, Permian to present. Jour. Geophys. Res. 75: 4939–4956.

——— & W. P. Sproll. 1970. East Canary Islands as a microcontinent within the Africa-North America continental drift fit. Nature 226: 1043–1044.

———, J. C. Holden & W. P. Sproll. 1970a. Geotectonic evolution and subsidence of Bahama platform. Bull. Geol. Soc. Amer. 81: 1915–1928.

———, ——— & ———. 1970b. Geotectonic evolution and subsidence of Bahama platform: Reply. Bull. Geol. Soc. Amer. 82: 811–814.

Dilcher, D. L. 1963. Cuticular analysis of Eocene leaves of *Ocotea obtusifolia*. Amer. Jour. Bot. 50: 1–8.

———. 1973a. A paleoclimatic interpretation of the Eocene floras of southeastern North America. Pp. 39–59, *in* A. Graham (editor), "Vegetation and Vegetational History of Northern Latin America." Elsevier Scientific Publ. Co., Amsterdam.

———. 1973b. A revision of the Eocene flora of southeastern North America. Paleobotanist 20: 7–18.

——— & G. E. Dolph. 1970. Fossil leaves of *Dendropanax* from Eocene sediments of southeastern North America. Amer. Jour. Bot. 57: 153–160.

Dingle, R. V. 1972. Reply to Jones (1972). Nature Phys. Sci. 235: 60.

———. 1973. Mesozoic paleogeography of the southern Cape, South America. Palaeogeogr. Palaeoclimatol. Palaeoecol. 13: 203–213.

Dolianiti, E. 1955. Frutos de *Nipa* no Paleoceno de Pernambuco, Brazil. Min. Agr., Dept. Nac. Prod. Min., Div. Geol. Min. Bol. 158: 1–36.

Dorofeev, P. I. 1963. Tretichnyye flory Zapodnoy Sibiri [Tertiary floras of western Siberia]. Bot. Inst. Komarov. Akad. Wiss. 316 pp.

Douglas, R. G., M. Moullade & A. E. M. Nairn. 1973. Causes and consequences of drift in the South Atlantic. *In* D. H. Tarling & S. K. Runcorn (editors), "Implications of Continental Drift to the Earth Sciences." Vol. 1: 517–537. Academic Press, London and New York.

Doyle, J. A. 1969. Cretaceous angiosperm pollen of the Atlantic coastal plain and its evolutionary significance. Jour. Arnold Arbor. 50: 1–35.

———. 1973. Fossil evidence on early evolution of the monocotyledons. Quart. Rev. Biol. 48: 399–413.

——— & L. J. Hickey. 1972. Coordinated evolution in Potomac Group angiosperm pollen and leaves. (Abstract.) Amer. Jour. Bot. 59: 660.

Duellman, W. E. 1970. The hylid frogs of Middle America. Mongr. Mus. Nat. Hist. Univ. Kansas. 2. 753 pp.

Edgar, N. T., J. T. Ewing & J. Hennion. 1971. Seismic refraction and reflection in Caribbean Sea. Amer. Assoc. Petrol. Geol. Bull. 55: 833–870.

Edmunds, G. F., Jr. 1972. Biogeography and evolution of Ephemeroptera. Annual Rev. Entom. 17: 21–42.

Ehrendorfer, F., F. Kerndl, E. Habeler & W. Sauer. 1968. Chromosome numbers and evolution in primitive angiosperms. Taxon 17: 337–353.

Emiliani, C. 1971. The amplitude of Pleistocene climatic cycles at low latitudes and the isotopic composition of glacial ice. Pp. 183–197, *in* K. K. Turekian (editor), "The Late Cenozoic Glacial Ages." Yale Univ. Press, New Haven.

———, S. Gaertner & B. Lidz. 1972. Neogene sedimentation on the Blake Plateau and the emergence of the Central American isthmus. Palaeogeogr. Palaeoclimatol. Palaeoecol. 11: 1–10.

Emry, R. J. 1970. A North American Oligocene pangolin and other additions to the Pholidota. Bull. Amer. Mus. Nat. Hist. 142: 455–510.

Engler, A. (editor). 1900–1953. Das Pflanzenreich. Pruess. Akademie der Wissenschaften, Berlin. No. 1–107.

———. 1905. Über floristische Verwandschaft zwischen dem tropischen Africa und Amerika, sowie über die Annahme eins versunkenen brasilianischen-äthiopischen Kontinents. Sitzsungsber. Köngl. Pruess. Akad. Wiss. Phys. Math. Kl. 6: 179–231.

————. 1915. Über herkunft, alter und verbreitung extremer xerothermer Pflanzen. Sitzungsber. Köngl. Pruess. Akad. Wiss. Phys. Math. Kl. 6: 180–231.

———— & K. A. E. PRANTL (editors). 1887–1915. Die natürlichen Pflanzenfamilien. Berlin.

ERNST, W. F. 1972. Floral morphology and systematics of *Lamourouxia* (Scrophulariaceae: Rhinanthoideae). Smithsonian Contr. Bot. 6: 1–63.

ESTES, R. 1963. Early Miocene salamanders and lizards from Florida. Quart. Jour. Florida Acad. Sci. 26: 234–256.

————. 1970. Origin of the Recent North American lower vertebrate fauna: An inquiry into the fossil record. Forma et Functio 3: 139–163.

———— & L. I. PRICE. 1973. Iguanid lizard from the Upper Cretaceous of Brazil. Science 180: 748–751.

———— & O. A. REIG. 1973. The early fossil record of frogs. A review of the evidence. Pp. 11–63, *in* J. L. Vial (editor), "Evolutionary Biology of the Anurans." Univ. Missouri Press, Columbia.

———— & J. TIHEN. 1964. Lower vertebrates from the Valentine Formation of Nebraska. Amer. Midl. Naturalist 72: 453–472.

———— & M. H. WAKE. 1972. The first fossil record of caecilian amphibians. Nature 239: 228–231.

————, P. BERBERIAN & C. MESZOELY. 1969. Lower vertebrates from the late Cretaceous Hell Creek Formation, McCone County, Montana. Mus. Comp. Zool. Harvard Univ. Breviora 337: 1–33.

EXELL, A. W. & C. A. STACE. 1966. Revision of the Combretaceae. Boll. Soc. Brot. 2. 40: 5–25.

———— & ————. 1972. Patterns of distribution in Combretaceae. Pp. 307–323, *in* D. H. Valentine (editor), "Taxonomy, Phytogeography, and Evolution." Academic Press, London and New York.

EYDE, R. H. 1966. Systematic anatomy of the flower and fruit of *Corokia*. Amer. Jour. Bot. 53: 833–847.

————. 1968. Flowers, fruits, and phylogeny of Alangiaceae. Jour. Arnold Arbor. 49: 167–192.

————. 1972*a*. Note on geologic history of flowering plants. Brittonia 24: 111–116.

————. 1972*b*. Pollen of *Alangium*: Toward a more satisfactory synthesis. Taxon 21: 471–477.

————. 1975. Floral anatomy and the bases of angiosperm phylogeny. Ann. Missouri Bot. Gard. 62: (in press).

FAIRBRIDGE, R. W. 1953. The Sahul Shelf, northern Australia: its structure and geological relations. Jour. Roy. Soc. West. Australia 37: 1–33.

FITTKAU, E. J., J. ILLIES, H. KLINGE, G. W. SCHWABE & H. SIOLI (editors). 1968. Biogeography and Ecology in South America. Volume 1. Monogr. Biol. 18: i–xvi, 1–447.

————, ————, ————, ———— & ———— (editors). 1969. Biogeography and Ecology in South America. Volume 2. Monogr. Biol. 19: i–xi, 449–946.

FLEMING, C. A. 1962. New Zealand biogeography. A paleontologist's approach. Tuatara 10: 53–108.

————. 1963. Paleontology and southern biogeography. Pp. 369–385, *in* J. L. Gressitt (editor), "Pacific Basin Biogeography." Bishop Museum Press, Honolulu.

FOODEN, J. 1972. Breakup of Pangaea and isolation of relict mammals in Australia, South America, and Madagascar. Science 175: 894–898.

FOSBERG, F. R. 1948. Derivation of the flora of the Hawaiian Islands. *In* E. C. Zimmerman, "Insects of Hawaii." 1: 107–119. Univ. Hawaii Press, Honolulu.

FRANCHETEAU, J. 1973. Plate tectonic model of the opening of the Atlantic Ocean south of the Azores. *In* D. H. Tarling & S. K. Runcorn (editors), "Implications of Continental Drift to the Earth Sciences." Vol. 1: 197–202. Academic Press, London and New York.

———— & X. LE PICHON. 1972. Marginal fracture zones as structural framework of continental margins in South Atlantic Ocean. Bull. Amer. Assoc. Petrol. Geol. 56: 991–1007.

FREAKE, J. R. 1966. A summary of results obtained during the 2nd W. African Micropaleontological Colloquium. Second W. African Micropal. Colloquium Proc. (Ibadan), p. 269.

FREELAND, G. L. & R. S. DIETZ. 1971. Plate tectonic evolution of Caribbean-Gulf of Mexico region. Nature 232: 20–23.

————. 1972. Plate tectonics in the Caribbean: a reply. Nature 235: 156–157.

FRENGUELLI, J. 1943. Restos de *Casuarina* en el Mioceno de El Mirador, Patagonia austral. La Plata Univ. Nac. Mus. Not. Paleont. 8(58): 349–354.

————. 1953. Restos del género *"Eucalyptus"* en el Mioceno del Neuquén. Not. Mus. La Plata 16: 210–213.

FRYXELL, P. A. 1969. The genus *Cienfuegosia* Cav. (Malvaceae). Ann. Missouri Bot. Gard. 56: 179–250.

GANSSER, A. 1964. Geology of the Himalayas. Interscience, London. xv + 289 pp.

————. 1966. The Indian Ocean and the Himalayas. A geological interpretation. Eclog. Geol. Helvet. 59: 831–848.

GARDNER, J. V. 1973. Eastern equatorial Atlantic: sea-surface temperature and circulation response to global climatic changes during the past 200,000 years. Geol. Soc. Amer. Abstr. Prog. 1973 Meetings, Dallas, p. 629.

GASKIN, D. E. 1972. Reappraisal of the New Zealand Mesozoic with respect to sea-floor spreading and modern tectonic plate theory. XVII Congr. Internat. Zool., Thème 1, Biogéographie et Liaisons inter-continentales au cours du Mésozoïque. 23 pp.

GEESINK, R. 1972. A new species of *Langsdorffia* from New Guinea (Balanophoraceae). Acta Bot. Neerl. 21: 102–106.

GERMERAAD, J. H., C. A. HOPPING & J. MULLER. 1968. Palynology of Tertiary sediments from tropical areas. Rev. Palaeobot. Palynol. 6: 189–348.

GERTH, H. 1941. Die Tertiärfloren des südlichen Südamerika und die angebliche Verlagerung des Südpols während einer Periode. Geol. Rundschau 32: 321–336.

GOLDBLATT, P. 1971. Cytological and morphological studies in the southern African Iridaceae. Jour. South Afr. Bot. 37: 317–460.

GOOD, R. D'O. 1964. The Geography of Flowering Plants. Wiley, New York. Ed. 3.

GORBUNOV, M. G. 1962. Description of Tertiary plants of western Siberia. Trudy Sib. Nauchn.-Issl. Inst. Geol., Geogr. Min. Ser. 22: 327–360, *pls. 66–76.* [in Russian.]

GOSLINE, W. A. 1972. A reexamination of the similarities between the freshwater fishes of Africa and South America. XVII Congr. Internat. Zool., Thème 1. Biogéographie et liaisons inter-continentales au cours du Mésozoïque. 12 pp.

GRAHAM, A. 1962. *Ficus ceratops* Knowlton and its affinities with the living genus *Guarea*. Jour. Paleontol. 36: 521–523, *pl. 90.*

————. 1972a. Some aspects of Tertiary vegetational history about the Caribbean Basin. Mem. Symp. I Congr. Latinoamer. Bot., pp. 97–117.

———— (editor). 1972b. Floristics and Paleofloristics of Asia and Eastern North America. Elsevier Publ. Co., Amsterdam. xii + 278 pp.

————. 1973a. History of the arborescent temperate element in the northern Latin American biota. Pp. 302–314, *in* A. Graham (editor), "Vegetation and Vegetational History of Northern Latin America." Elsevier Scientific Publ. Co., Amsterdam.

————. 1973b. Literature on vegetational history in Latin America. Pp. 315–360, *in* A. Graham (editor), "Vegetation and Vegetational History of Northern Latin America." Elsevier Scientific Publ. Co., Amsterdam.

———— & D. J. JARZEN. 1969. Studies in Neotropical paleobotany. I. The Oligocene communities of Puerto Rico. Ann. Missouri Bot. Gard. 56: 308–357.

———— & S. GRAHAM. 1971. The geologic history of Lythraceae. Brittonia 23: 335–346.

GRAMBAST, L., M. MARTÍNEZ, M. MATTAUER & L. THALER. 1967. *Perutherium altiplanense* nov. gen., nov. sp., premier mammifère Mésozoïque d'Amérique du Sud. Compt. Rend. Hebd. Séances Acad. Sci. 264: 707–710.

GRANT, N. K. 1971. South Atlantic, Benue Trough, and Gulf of Guinea Cretaceous triple junction. Bull. Geol. Soc. Amer. 82: 2295–2298.

————. 1972. Comments on paper by X. Le Pichon and D. E. Hayes, "Marginal offsets, fracture zones, and the early opening of the south Atlantic." Jour. Geophys. Res. 77: 3171–3173.

GRANT, V. 1959. Natural History of the Phlox Family. Vol. 1. Systematic Botany. Martinus Nijhoff, The Hague. xv + 280 pp.

GREEN, A. G. 1972. Seafloor spreading in the Mozambique Channel. Nature Phys. Sci. 236: 19–32.

GROOT, J. J. & C. R. GROOT. 1964. Quaternary stratigraphy of sediments of the Argentine basin—a palynological investigation. Trans. New York Acad. Sci., ser. 2. 26: 881–886.

———— & ————. 1966. Pollen spectra from deep-sea sediments as indicators of climatic changes in southern South America. Marine Geol. 4: 525–537.

GREEN, P. S. 1969. Notes on Melanesian plants: II. Old World *Heliconia* (Musaceae). Kew Bull. 23: 471–478.

GRIFFITHS, J. & C. BURRETT. 1973. Were South-east Asia and Indonesia parts of Gondwanaland? Nature Phys. Sci. 245: 92–93.

GUILLAUMET, J.-L. 1972. Les variations du genre *Rhipsalis* (Cactacées) à Madagascar. Adansonia, sér. 2. 12: 433–445.

GUILLAUMIN, A., R. F. THORNE & R. VIROT. 1965. Vascular plants collected by R. F. Thorne in New Caledonia in 1959. Univ. Iowa Stud. Nat. Hist. 20(7): 15–65.

HAFFER, J. 1969. Speciation in Amazonian forest birds. Science 165: 131–137.

———. 1970. Geologic-climatic history and zoogeographic significance of the Uraba region in northwestern Colombia. Caldasia 10: 603–636.

HALFFTER, G. 1964. Las regiones Neárctica y Neotropical desde el punto de vista de su entomofauna. Anais do Segundo Congresso Latino-Americano de Zoologia, São Paulo. 1: 51–61.

———. 1972. Éléments anciens de l'entomofauna Néotropicale: ses implications biogéographiques. XVII Congr. Internat. Zool., Thème 1. Biogéographie et Liaisons intercontinentales au cours du Mésozoïque. 40 pp.

HALL, I. H. S. & J. H. BATESON. 1972. Late Paleozoic lavas in Maya Mountains, British Honduras, and their possible regional significance. Bull. Amer. Assoc. Petrol. Geol. 56: 956–963.

HALLAM, A. 1973*a*. Distributional patterns in contemporary terrestrial and marine animals. *In* N. F. Hughes (editor), "Organisms and Continents through Time." Palaeontol. Assoc. London, Spec. Pap. Palaeontol. 12: 93–105.

———. 1973*b*. Provinciality, diversity and extinction of Mesozoic marine invertebrates in relation to plate movements. *In* D. H. Tarling & S. K. Runcorn (editors), "Implications of Continental Drift to the Earth Sciences." Vol. 1: 287–294.

HAMMEN, T. VAN DER. 1957. Climatic periodicity and evolution of South American Maastrichtian and Tertiary floras (A study based on pollen analysis in Colombia). Colombia Inst. Geol. Nac. Bol. Geol. 5: 49–91.

———. 1963. A palynological study on the Quaternary of British Guiana. Leidse Geol. Meded. 29: 125–180.

———. 1972. Historia de la vegetación y el medio ambiente del Norte Sudamérica. Mem. Symp. I Congr. Latino-Amer. Bot. 119–134.

——— & C. GARCÍA DE MUTÍS. 1966. The Paleocene pollen flora of Colombia. Leidse Geol. Meded. 35: 105–116.

HAMILTON, A. C. 1972. An interpretation of pollen diagrams from highland Uganda. *In* E. M. van Zinderen Bakker (editor), "Palaeoecology of Africa." 7: 45–149. A. A. Balkema, Capetown.

HANSEN, B. 1972. The genus *Balanophora* J. R. and G. Forster. A taxonomic monograph. Dansk Bot. Ark. 28: 1–188, *pl. 1–8*.

HARA, H. 1972. Corresponding taxa in North America, Japan and the Himalayas. Pp. 61–72, *in* D. H. Valentine (editor), "Taxonomy, Phytogeography and Evolution." Academic Press, London and New York.

HARLAND, W. B. & E. H. FRANCIS (editors). 1971. The Phanerozoic time scale: a supplement. Geol. Soc. London Spec. Publ. 5. 356 pp.

———, A. G. SMITH & B. WILCOCK (editors). 1964. The Phanerozoic time scale. Quart. Jour. Geol. Soc. London: 120s (supplement). 458 pp.

HARRIS, W. K. 1965. Basal Tertiary microfloras from the Princetown area, Victoria, Australia. Palaeontographica B. 115: 75–106.

HAYES, D. E. & J. RINGIS. 1973. Seafloor spreading in the Tasman Sea. Nature 243: 454–458.

——— ET AL. 1973. Leg 28 deep-sea drilling in the southern ocean. Geotimes 18(6): 19–24.

HAWKES, J. G. & P. M. SMITH. 1965. Continental drift and the age of angiosperm genera. Nature 207: 48–50.

HEDLUND, R. W. & G. NORRIS. 1968. Spores and pollen grains from Fredricksburgian (Albian) strata, Marshall County, Oklahoma. Pollen & spores 10: 129–159.

HEEZEN, B. C., M. DREYFUS & R. CATALANO. 1973. The Cayman Ridge. Geol. Soc. Amer. Abstr. Prog. 1973 Meetings, Dallas, p. 705.

HEINE, H. 1963. Boraginaceae. Fl. West. Trop. Africa 2: 317–325.

HEINRICH, B. & P. H. RAVEN. 1972. Energetics and pollination ecology. Science 176: 597–602.

HEIRTZLER, J. R. 1973. The evolution of the North Atlantic Ocean. *In* D. H. Tarling & S. K. Runcorn (editors), "Implications of Continental Drift to the Earth Sciences." Vol. 1: 191–196. Academic Press, London and New York.

——— ET AL. 1973. Age of the floor of the eastern Indian Ocean. Science 180: 952–954.

HEPPER, F. N. 1963. Styracaceae. Fl. West. Trop. Africa 2: 33–34.

———. 1965. Preliminary account of the phytogeographical affinities of the flora of West Tropical Africa. Webbia 19: 593–617.

———. 1968. The occurrence of *Ternstroemia* (Theaceae) in West Africa. Kew Bull. 21: 429–431.

HICKEY, L. J. 1974.– The stratigraphy and paleobotany of the Golden Valley Formation (Early Tertiary) of western North Dakota. Mem. Geol. Soc. Amer. (in press).

——— & J. A. DOYLE. 1972. Fossil evidence on evolution of angiosperm leaf venation. (Abstract.) Amer. Jour. Bot. 59: 661.

HILLEBRAND, W. 1888. Flora of the Hawaiian Islands. Reprinted by Hafner Publ. Co., New York and London, 1965. xcvi + 673 pp.

HOEKEN-KLINKENBERG, P. M. 1964. A palynological investigation of some Upper Cretaceous sediments in Nigeria. Pollen Spores 6: 209–231.

HOFFSTETTER, R. 1959. Un serpent terrestre dans le Crétacé inferieur du Sahara. Bull. Soc. Géol. France, sér. 7. 1: 897–902.

———. 1967. Observations additionelles sur les serpents du Miocéne de Colombie et rectification concernant la date d'arrivée des colubridés en Amérique du Sud. Comp. Rend. Sommaire Séances Soc. Géol. France 1967: 209–210.

———. 1972. Relationships, origins, and history of the ceboid monkeys and caviomorph rodents: a modern reinterpretation. Evol. Biol. 6: 323–347.

HOLLICK, A. 1924. A late Tertiary flora from Bahia, Brazil. Johns Hopkins Univ. Stud. Geol. 5: 1–136.

HOLMAN, J. 1969. Lower Oligocene amphibians from Saskatchewan. Quart. Jour. Florida Acad. Sci. 31: 273–289.

———. 1972. Herpetofauna of the Calf Creek local fauna (Lower Oligocene: Cypress Hills Formation) of Saskatchewan. Canad. Jour. Earth Sci. 9: 1612–1631.

HOOKER, J. D. 1853. Botany of the Antarctic Voyage of H. M. Discovery ships "Erebus" and "Terror" in the years 1831–43. Vol. 2: Flora Novae-Zelandiae. Pt. 1, Introductory Essay.

HOUTZ, R. E. ET AL. 1973. Geophysical results DSDP Leg 29: New Zealand, Tasmania, and magnetic quiet zone. Lamont-Doherty Geol. Observatory Contr. 1983.

HOWARD, R. A. 1973. The vegetation of the Antilles. Pp. 1–38, *in* A. Graham (editor), "Vegetation and Vegetational History of Northern Latin America." Elsevier Scientific Publ. Co., Amsterdam.

HUBER, H. 1969. Die Samenmerkmale und Verwantschaftsverhältnisse der Liliifloren. Mitt. Bot. München 8: 219–538.

HUGHES, N. F. 1961. Fossil evidence and angiosperm ancestry. Sci. Progr. 49: 84–102.

——— (editor). 1973. Organisms and Continents through Time. Palaeontol. Assoc. London, Spec. Pap. Palaeontol. 12: i–vi, 1–334.

HUNTER, G. E. 1966. Revision of Mexican and Central American *Saurauia* (Dilleniaceae). Ann. Missouri Bot. Gard. 53: 47–89.

HUNZIKER, J. H., R. A. PALACIOS, A. G. DE VALESI & L. POGGIO. 1972. Evolución en el género *Larrea*. Res. I Congr. Latino-Amer. Bot., p. 191–192.

———, ———, ——— & ———. 1973. Species disjunctions in *Larrea*: Evidence from morphology, cytogenetics, phenolic compounds, and seed albumins. Ann. Missouri Bot. Gard. 59: 224–233.

HURD, P. D. 1972. Evolutionary relationships between bees and *Larrea*. Origin & Structure of Ecosystems Newsletter 2(3): 38–41.

———, E. G. LINSLEY & T. W. WHITAKER. 1971. Squash and gourd bees (*Peponapis, Xenoglossa*) and the origin of the cultivated *Cucurbita*. Evolution 25: 218–234.

HUTCHINSON, J. 1959. The Families of Flowering Plants. Ed. 2. Vols. 1 and 2. Clarendon Press, Oxford.

ILTIS, H. H. 1967. Studies in the Capparidaceae, XI: *Cleome afrospina*, an African endemic with Neotropical affinities. Amer. Jour. Bot. 54: 953–962.

JACOBS, C., H. BÜRGL & D. L. CONLEY. 1963. Backbone of Columbia. Mem. Amer. Assoc. Petrol. Geol. 2: 62–72.

JAMES, C. W. 1961. Endemism in Florida. Brittonia 13: 225–244.

JARDINE, N. & D. McKENZIE. 1972. Continental drift and the dispersal and evolution of organisms. Nature 235: 20–24.

JEFFREY, C. 1962. Notes on Cucurbitaceae, including a proposed new classification of the family. Kew Bull. 15: 337–371.

JENKINS, D. G. 1971. New Zealand Cenozoic planktonic Foraminifera. New Zealand Geol. Surv. Palaeontol. Bull. 42.

JENKS, W. F. (editor). 1956. Handbook of South American geology. Mem. Geol. Soc. Amer. 65: i–xix, 1–378.

JOHNSON, C. C. & J. BOWDEN. 1973. Problems related to the transoceanic transport of insects, especially between the Amazon and Congo areas. Pp. 207–222, in B. J. Meggers, E. S. Ayensu & W. D. Duckworth (editors), "Tropical Forest Ecosystems in Africa and South America: A Comparative Review." Smithsonian Inst. Press, Washington, D.C.

JOHNSON, L. A. S. 1957. A review of the family Oleaceae. Contr. New South Wales Natl. Herb. 2: 395–418.

———— & B. G. BRIGGS. 1963. Evolution in the Proteaceae. Austral. Jour. Bot. 11: 21–61.

JONES, J. G. 1972. Significance of Upper Jurassic sediments in the Knysna Outlier (Cape Province). Nature Phys. Sci. 235: 59–60.

JONES, K. & C. JOPLING. 1972. Chromosomes and the classification of the Commelinaceae. Bot. Jour. Linn. Soc. 65: 129–162, 2 pl.

JONES, R. E. & G. O. W. KREMP. 1973. The earliest distribution of tricolpate angiospermous pollen. Jour. Arizona Acad. Sci. 8, Proceed. Suppl. 44–45.

KANEPS, A. G. 1970. Late Neogene Biostratigraphy (Planktonic Foraminifera), Biogeography and Depositional History. Columbia Univ., New York.

KATZ, H. R. 1973. Contrasts in tectonic evolution of orogenic belts in the south-east Pacific. Jour. Roy. Soc. New Zealand 3: 333–362.

KEAST, A. 1972. Continental drift and the evolution of the biota on southern continents. Pp. 23–87, in A. Keast, F. C. Erk & B. Glass (editors), "Evolution, Mammals, and Southern Continents." State Univ. New York Press, Albany.

————. 1973. Contemporary biotas and the separation sequence of the southern continents. In D. H. Tarling & S. K. Runcorn (editors), "Implications of Continental Drift to the Earth Sciences." Vol. 1: 309–343. Academic Press, London and New York.

————, F. C. ERK & B. GLASS (editors). 1972. Evolution, Mammals, and Southern Continents. State Univ. New York Press, Albany.

KEMP, E. M. 1968. Probable angiosperm pollen from British Barremian to Albian strata. Palaeontol. 11(3): 421–434.

KENDALL, R. L. 1969. An ecological history of the Lake Victoria basin. Ecol. Monogr. 39: 121–176.

KENNETT, J. P. ET AL. 1972. Australian-Antarctic continental drift, palaeocirculation changes and Oligocene deep-sea erosion. Nature Phys. Sci. 239: 51–55.

————. 1973. Deep-sea drilling in the roaring 40s. Geotimes 18(7): 14–17.

KENT, P. E. 1972. Mesozoic history of the east coast of Africa. Nature 238:147–148.

KESLER, S. E. 1971. Nature of ancestral orogenic zone in Nuclear Central America. Bull. Amer. Assoc. Petrol. Geol. 55: 2116–2129.

————. 1973. Basement rock structural trends in southern Mexico. Bull. Geol. Soc. Amer. 84: 1059–1064.

———— & S. A. HEATH. 1970. Structural trends in the southernmost North American Precambrian, Oaxaca, Mexico. Bull. Geol. Soc. Amer. 81: 2471–2476.

KHLONOVA, A. F. 1971. Palynological characteristics of Cretaceous layers in Siberia and the Far East. Akedemiya Nauk SSSR Sibirskoye Otdeleniye, Trudy Instituta Geologii i Geofiziki 138: 52–156. [In Russian.]

KHUDOLEY, K. M. & A. A. MEYERHOFF. 1971. Paleogeography and geological history of Greater Antilles. Mem. Geol. Soc. Amer. 129: i–xv, 1–199.

KING, P. B. 1951. The Tectonics of Middle North America. Princeton Univ. Press, Princeton, N.J. xix + 203 pp.

KLERKX, J. & P. DE PAEPE. 1971. Cape Verde Islands: Evidence for a Mesozoic oceanic ridge. Nature Phys. Sci. 233: 117–118.

KOCH, B. E. 1972. Fossil picrodendroid fruit from the upper Danain of Nugssauq, West Greenland. Meddel. Grønland 193(3): 1–33.

KOPP, L. E. 1966. A taxonomic revision of the genus Persea in the Western Hemisphere (Persea-Lauraceae). Mem. New York Bot. Gard. 14: 1–120.

648   ANNALS OF THE MISSOURI BOTANICAL GARDEN   [VOL. 61]

KORNAŚ, J. 1972. Corresponding taxa and their ecological background in the forests of temperate Eurasia and North America. Pp. 37–59, in D. H. Valentine (editor), "Taxonomy, Phytogeography, and Evolution." Academic Press, London and New York.

KOSTERMANS, A. J. G. H. 1952. A historical survey of the Lauraceae. Jour. Sci. Res. (Indonesia) 1: 83–95, 113–127, 141–159.

————. 1964. Bibliographia Lauracearum. Ministry of National Research, Bogor, Indonesia. 1450 pp.

KRASSILOV, V. 1967. Early Cretaceous Flora of South Primorye and its Bearing on the Stratigraphy. Nauka Publ. House, Moscow. 248 pp. [In Russian.]

————. 1973. Mesozoic plants and the problem of angiosperm ancestry. Lethaia 6: 163–178.

KRUTZSCH, W. 1967. Der Florenwechsel im Alttertiär Mitteleuropas auf Grund von sporenpaläontologischen Untersuchungen. Ahh. Zentr. Geol. Inst. 10: 17–37.

KUPRAINOVA, L. A. 1967. Palynological data for the history of the Chloranthaceae. Pollen & Spores 9: 95–100.

KURTÉN, B. 1973. Early Tertiary land mammals. Pp. 437–442, in A. Hallam (editor), "Atlas of Palaeobiogeography." Elsevier Scientific Publishing Co., Amsterdam.

LAKHANPAL, R. N. 1970. Tertiary floras of India and their bearing on the historical geology of the region. Taxon 19: 675–694.

LANGE, R. T. 1970. The Maslin Bay flora, South Australia. 2. The assemblage of fossils. Neues Jahrb. Geol. Paläont., Monatsh. 8: 486–490.

LANGENHEIM, J. H. 1964. Present status of botanical studies of ambers. Bot. Mus. Leafl. 20: 225–287.

————. 1972. Botanical origin of fossil resin and its relation to forest history in northeastern Angola. Publ. Cult. Comp. Diam. Angola 85: 13–36.

————. 1973. Leguminous resin-producing trees in Africa and South America. Pp. 89–104, in B. J. Meggers, E. S. Ayensu & W. D. Duckworth (editors), "Tropical Forest Ecosystems in Africa and South America; A Comparative Review." Smithsonian Inst. Press, Washington, D.C.

————, B. L. HACKNER & A. BARTLETT. 1967. Mangrove pollen at the depositional site of Oligo-Miocene amber from Chiapas, Mexico. Bot. Mus. Leafl. 21: 289–324.

LARSON, R. L. & J. W. LADD. 1973. Evidence for the opening of the South Atlantic in the Early Cretaceous. Nature 246: 209–212.

LAUGHTON, A. S. 1971. South Labrador Sea and the evolution of the North Atlantic. Nature 232: 612–617.

————, D. P. McKENZIE & J. G. SCLATER. 1973. The structure and evolution of the Indian Ocean. In D. H. Tarling & S. K. Runcorn (editors), "Implication of Continental Drift to the Earth Sciences." Vol. 1: 203–212. Academic Press, London and New York.

LAURENT, F. 1972. La distribution des amphibiens et les translations continentales. 17th Internat. Zool. Congr., Monte Carlo. Thème 1, Biogéographie et liaisons inter-continentales au cours du Mésozoïque, 16 pp. + 4 figs.

LEFFINGWELL, H. A. 1966. Palynology of the Lance (Late Cretaceous) and Fort Union (Paleocene) formations of the Type Lance Area, Wyoming. Geol. Soc. Amer. Spec. Pap. 127: 1–64.

LEOPOLD, E. B. 1969. Late Cenozoic palynology. Pp. 377–438, in R. H. Tschudy & R. A. Scott (editors), "Aspects of Palynology." Wiley-Interscience, New York.

———— & H. D. MacGINITIE. 1972. Development and affinities of Tertiary floras in the Rocky Mountains. Pp. 147–200, in A. Graham (editor), "Floristics and Paleofloristics of Asia and Eastern North America." Elsevier Publ. Co., Amsterdam.

LE PICHON, X. & D. E. HAYES. 1971. Marginal offsets, fracture zones, and the early opening of the South Atlantic. Jour. Geophys. Res. 76: 6283–6292.

LEROY, J.-F. 1949. De la morphologie florale et de la classification des Myricaceae. Compt. Rend. Hebd. Séances Acad. Sci. 229: 1162–1163.

LESQUEREUX, L. 1891. The Flora of the Dakota Group. U. S. Geol. Surv. Monogr. 17: 1–398, pl. i–lxvi.

LIDDLE, R. A. 1946. The Geology of Venezuela and Trinidad. Ed. 2. Paleontological Research Institution, Ithaca, N.Y. xlvii + 890 pp.

LILLEGRAVEN, J. A. 1969. Latest Cretaceous mammals of upper part of Edmonton Formation of Alberta, Canada, and review of marsupial-placental dichotomy in mammalian evolution. Paleont. Contr. Univ. Kansas 50: 1–122.

LIOGIER, E. E. (HERMANO ALAIN). 1962. Flora de Cuba. Vol. 5. Editorial Universitaria, Universidad de Puerto Rico, Río Piedras.

LIVINGSTONE, D. A. 1967. Post-glacial vegetation of the Ruzenwori Mountains in equatorial Africa. Ecol. Monogr. 37: 25–52.

———. 1968. A 22,000 year pollen record from Zambia. Geol. Soc. Amer. Spec. Paper 121: 177–178.

———. 1971. Speculations on the climatic history of mankind. Amer. Sci. 59: 332–337.

LLOYD, J. J. 1963. Tectonic history of the south Central-American orogen. Mem. Amer. Assoc. Petrol. Geol. 2: 88–100.

LOWE-McCONNELL, R. H. (editor). 1969. Speciation in tropical environments. Biol. Jour. Linn. Soc. 1: 1–246 (Also published by Academic Press).

LOWRY, J. B. 1973. Rhabdothamnus solandri: Some phytochemical results. New Zealand Jour. Bot. 11: 555–560.

LOZANO CONTRERAS, G. 1972. Contribución al conocimiento de las Magnoliaceae de Colombia. Res. I Congr. Latino-Amer. Bot., p. 191–192.

LYNCH, J. D. 1971. Evolutionary relationships, osteology, and zoogeography of leptodactylid frogs. Univ. Kansas Mus. Nat. Hist. Misc. Publ. 53: 1–238.

McBIRNEY, A. R. & H. WILLIAMS. 1965. Volcanic history of Nicaragua. Univ. Calif. Publ. Geol. Sci. 55: 1–65, pls. 1–3.

McCLURE, F. A. 1973. Genera of bamboos native to the New World (Gramineae: Bambusoideae). Smithsonian Contr. Bot. 9: i–xi, 1–148. [Edited by T. R. Soderstrom.]

MacGILLAVRY, H. J. 1970. Geological history of the Caribbean. Koninkl. Nederl. Akad. Wetensch Proc. B. 73: 64–96.

MacGINITIE, H. D. 1937. The flora of the Weaverville beds of Trinity County, California. Carnegie Inst. Wash. Publ. 465: 83–151.

———. 1941. A Middle Eocene flora from the central Sierra Nevada. Carnegie Inst. Wash. Publ. 534: 1–178.

———. 1969. The Eocene Green River flora of northwestern Colorado and northeastern Utah. Univ. Calif. Publ. Geol. 83: 1–140, 31 pl.

McGOWRAN, B. 1973. Rifting and drift of Australia and the migration of mammals. Science 180: 759–761.

McKENNA, M. C. 1972. Was Europe connected directly to North America prior to the Middle Eocene? Evol. Biol. 6: 179–189.

———. 1973. Sweepstakes, filters, corridors, Noah's Arks, and beached Viking funeral ships in paleogeography. Pp. 291–304, in D. H. Tarling & S. K. Runcorn (editors), Implications of Continental Drift to the Earth Sciences." Academic Press, London and New York.

McKENZIE, D. P. & J. G. SCLATER. 1973. The evolution of the Indian Ocean. Sci. Amer. 228(5): 62–72.

McWHAE, J. R. H., P. E. PLAYFORD, A. W. LINDNER, B. F. GLENISTER & B. E. BALME. 1958. The stratigraphy of Western Australia. Jour. Geol. Soc. Australia 4(2): 1–161.

MABESOONE, J. M. & I. M. TINOCO. 1973. Palaeoecology of the Aptian Santana Formation (Northeastern Brazil). Palaeogeogr. Palaeoclimatol. Palaeoecol. 14: 97–118.

MABRY, T., A. TAYLOR & B. L. TURNER. 1963. The betacyanins and their distribution. Phytochemistry 2: 61.

MAGUIRE, B. 1971. On the flora of the Guyana Highland. Pp. 63–78, in W. L. Stern (editor), "Adaptive Aspects of Insular Evolution." Washington State Univ. Press, Pullman.

MALFAIT, B. T. & M. G. DINKELMAN. 1972. Circum-Caribbean tectonic and igneous activity and the evolution of the Caribbean plate. Bull. Geol. Soc. Amer. 83: 251–272.

MARGOLIS, S. V. & J. P. KENNETT. 1971. Cenozoic paleoglacial history of Antarctica recorded in Subantarctic deepsea cores. Amer. Jour. Sci. 271: 1–36.

MARTIN, P. G. 1972. Marsupial biogeography in relation to continental drift. XVII Congr. Internat. Zool., Thème 1. Biogéographie et liaisons inter-continentales au cours du Mésozoïque.

MASCLE, J. & J. D. PHILLIPS. 1972. Magnetic smooth zones in the South Atlantic. Nature 240: 80–84.

MATHIAS, M. E. & L. CONSTANCE. 1965. A revision of the genus Bowlesia and its relatives. Univ. Calif. Publ. Bot. 38: 1–73.

MATTSON, P. H. 1972. Plate tectonics in the Caribbean. Nature 235: 155–156.

———. 1973. Middle Cretaceous nappe structures in Puerto Rican ophiolites and their relation to the tectonic history of the Greater Antilles. Bull. Geol. Soc. Amer. 84: 21–38.

650   ANNALS OF THE MISSOURI BOTANICAL GARDEN   [VOL. 61

MAXWELL, A. E., R. P. VON HERZEN, J. E. ANDREWS, R. E. BOYCE, E. D. MILOW, K. HSU, S. F. PERCIVAL & T. SAITO. 1970a. Initial Reports of the Deep Sea Drillings Project. Vol. III. Washington, U. S. Govt. Printing Office. 806 pp.

———. 1970b. Deep sea drilling in the South Atlantic. Science 168: 1047–1059.

MAYR, E. 1944. Timor and the colonization of Australia by birds. Emu 44: 113–130.

———. 1946. History of the North American bird fauna. Wilson Bull. 58: 1–41.

———. 1964. Inferences concerning the Tertiary American bird faunas. Proc. Natl. Acad. Sci. 51: 280–288.

———. 1969. Bird speciation in the tropics. Biol. Jour. Linn. Soc. 1: 1–17.

MEIJER, W. 1972. The genus *Axinandra*—Melastomataceae: A missing link in Myrtales. Ceylon Jour. Sci. (Biol. Sci.) 10: 72–74, 2 pl.

MENÉNDEZ, C. A. 1969. Die fossilen Floren Südamerikas. Monogr. Biol. 19: 519–561.

———. 1972. Estudios paleobotánicos en la Argentina, avances, problemas y perspectivas. Mem. Symp. I Congr. Latino-Amer. Bot., p. 61–97.

MEYERHOFF, A. A. 1973. Diapirlike features offshore Honduras: Implications regarding tectonic evolution of Cayman Trough and Central America: Discussion. Bull. Geol. Soc. Amer. 84: 2147–2152.

——— & H. A. MEYERHOFF. 1972. Continental drift, IV: The Caribbean "Plate." Jour. Geol. 80: 34–60.

MILDENHALL, D. C. & W. F. HARRIS. 1971. Status of *Haloragacidites* (al. *Triorites*) *harrisi* (Couper) Harris comb. nov. and *Haloragacidites trioratus* Couper, 1953. New Zealand Jour. Bot. 9: 297–306.

MILLS, R. A., K. E. HUGH, D. E. FERAY & H. C. SWOLFS. 1967. Mesozoic stratigraphy of Honduras. Bull. Amer. Assoc. Petrol. Geol. 51: 1711–1786.

MINDELMISS, F. A., P. F. RAWSON & G. NEWALL (editors). 1971. Faunal Provinces in Space and Time. Geol. Jour. Special Issue 4. Seel House Press, London.

MOORE, D. M. 1972. Connections between cool temperate floras, with particular reference to southern South America. Pp. 115–138, *in* D. H. Valentine (editor), "Taxonomy, Phytogeography, and Evolution." Academic Press, London and New York.

MOORE, H. E., JR. 1973a. Palms in the tropical forest ecosystems of Africa and South America. Pp. 63–88, *in* B. J. Meggers, E. S. Ayensu & W. D. Duckworth (editors), "Tropical Forest Ecosystems in Africa and South America: A Comparative Review." Smithsonian Institution Press, Washington, D.C.

———. 1973b. The major groups of palms and their distribution. Gentes Herb. 11: 27–140.

MORLEY, B. 1972. The distribution and variation of some gesneriads on Caribbean Islands. Pp. 239–257, *in* D. H. Valentine (editor), "Taxonomy, Phytogeography, and Evolution." Academic Press, London and New York.

MUDREY, M. G., JR., S. B. TREVES, P. R. KYLE & L. D. McGINNIS. 1973. Frozen jigsaw puzzle: First bedrock coring in Antarctica. Geotimes 18(11): 14–17.

MÜLLER, H. 1966. Palynological investigations of Cretaceous sediments in northeastern Brazil. Pp. 123–136, *in* "Proc. 2nd West African Micropaleontological Colloquium, Ibadan." Leiden.

MULLER, J. 1968. Palynology of the Pedawan and Plateau sandstone formations (Cretaceous-Eocene) in Sarawak, Malaysia. Micropaleontology 14(1): 1–37.

———. 1970. Palynological evidence on early differentiation of angiosperms. Biol. Rev. 45: 417–450.

MUÑOZ PIZARRO, C. 1966. Sinopsis de la Flora Chilena. Ed. 2. Univ. Chile. 500 pp.

MYERS, G. S. 1966. Derivation of the freshwater fish fauna of Central America. Copeia 1966: 766–773.

NEWBERRY, J. 1896. Flora of the Amboy clays. Monogr. U. S. Geol. Surv. 26.

NIEDENZU, F. 1928. Malpighiaceae. *In* A. Engler (editor), "Das Pflanzenreich." IV. 141: 1–870.

ORLOVA-TURCHINA, G. A. 1971. Lower Cretaceous palynostratigraphy of the Crimea (Abstract). Third Internat. Palynol. Conference, Novosibirsk, USSR, Sect. 5.

PAGE, V. M. 1970. Angiosperm wood from the Upper Cretaceous of central California, III. Amer. Jour. Bot. 57: 1139–1144.

PAPULOV, G. N. 1971. Change of floras at the Early-Late Cretaceous boundary of the Urals as revealed by palynological evidence (Abstract). Third Internat. Palynol. Conference, Novosibirsk, USSR, Sect. 5.

PATTERSON, B. & R. PASCUAL. 1972. The fossil mammal fauna of South America. Pp. 247–309, *in* A. Keast, F. C. Erk & B. Glass (editors), "Evolution, Mammals, and Southern Continents." State Univ. New York Press, Albany.

PAULIAN, R. 1972. La position de Madagascar dans le double probleme du peuplement animal et des translations continentales. XVII Contr. Internat. Zool., Thème 1. Biogéographie et liaisons inter-continentales au cours du Mésozoïque. 23 pp.

PENNY, J. S. 1969. Late Cretaceous and Early Tertiary palynology. Pp. 331–376, *in* R. H. Tschudy & R. A. Scott (editors), "Aspects of Palynology." Wiley-Interscience, New York.

PETRIELLA, B. 1972. Estudio de maderas pertificadas del Terciario Inferior del area central de Chubut (Cerro Bororo). Revista Mus. La Plata, n.s. 6: 159–254, *pls. 1–8*.

PFEIFER, H. W. 1966. Revision of the North and Central American hexandrous species of *Aristolochia* (Aristolochiaceae). Ann. Missouri Bot. Gard. 53: 115–196.

———. 1970. A taxonomic revision of the pentandrous species of *Aristolochia*. Univ. Connecticut Publ. Series. 134 pp.

PHILIPSON, W. R. 1967. *Griselinia* Forst. fil.—Anomaly or link. New Zealand Jour. Bot. 5: 134–165.

PHILLIPS, J. D. & D. FORSYTH. 1972. Plate tectonics, paleomagnetism, and the opening of the Atlantic. Bull. Geol. Soc. Amer. 83: 1579–1600.

PINET, P. R. 1972. Diapirlike features offshore Honduras: Implications regarding tectonic evolution of Cayman Trough and Central America. Bull. Geol. Soc. Amer. 83: 1911–1921.

PITMAN, W. C., III & M. TALWANI. 1972. Sea-floor spreading in the North Atlantic. Bull. Geol. Soc. Amer. 83: 619–646.

———, M. TALWANI & J. R. HEIRTZLER. 1971. Age of the North Atlantic Ocean from magnetic anomales. Earth Planet. Sci. Letters 11: 195–200.

PLUMSTEAD, E. P. 1962. Fossil floras of Antarctica. Trans-Antarctic Exped., 1955–1958. Sci. Rept. 9. 154 pp.

POKROVSKAYA, I. A. 1964. Lower Cretaceous spore-pollen complexes of the Western Siberian Lowland. Atlas of Lower Cretaceous Spore-Pollen Complexes of Some Regions of the USSR. All-Union Sci. Res., Geol. Inst. (VSEGEI), n. s., 124: 82–101. [In Russian.]

PORTER, D. M. 1974. Disjunct distributions in the New World Zygophyllaceae. Taxon 23: 339–346.

POWELL, C. McA. & P. J. CONAGHAN. 1973. Plate tectonics and the Himalayas. Earth Planet. Sci. Newsl. 20: 1–12.

PRAKASH, U. 1972. Paleoenvironmental analysis of Indian Tertiary floras. Geophytology 2: 178–205.

PRANCE, G. T. 1968. *Maranthes* (Chrysobalanaceae), a new generic record for America. Brittonia 20: 203–204.

PRELL, W. 1973. Evidence for Sargasso Sea-like conditions in the Colombia Basin, Caribbean Sea, during glacial periods. Geol. Soc. Amer. Abstr. Prog. 1973 Meetings, Dallas, p. 771.

PURI, G. S. 1965. Some plant microfossils from Nigeria. Proc. Central Afr. Sci. Medical Congr., Lusaka (Northern Rhodesia), 1963, pp. 391–404.

RABB, G. B. & H. MARX. 1973. Major ecological and geographic patterns in the evolution of colubroid snakes. Evolution 27: 69–83.

RANGA RAO, A. 1971. New mammals from Murree (Kalakot Zone) of the Himalayan foot hills near Kalakot, Jammu & Kashmir State, India. Jour. Geol. Soc. India 12: 125–134.

———. 1972. Further studies on the vertebrate fauna of Kalakot, India. Directorate of Geology Oil & Natural Gas Commission Dehra Dun India Spec. Paper 1: 1–22, *4 pl.*

RAO, V. S. & R. DAHLGREN. 1969. The floral anatomy and relationships of Oliniaceae. Bot. Not. 122: 160–171.

RAUH, W. 1973. Über die Zonierung and Differenzierung der Vegetation Madagaskars. Tropische und subtropische Pflanzenwelt 1: 1–146. Akad. Wissensch. Lit. Mainz.

RAVEN, P. H. 1963. Amphitropical relations in the flora of North and South America. Quart. Rev. Biol. 29: 151–177.

———. 1971. The relationship between 'mediterranean' floras. Pp. 119–134, *in* P. H. Davis, P. C. Harper & I. C. Hedge (editors), "Plant Life of South-west Asia." Bot. Soc. Edinburgh.

———. 1973a. Plant species disjunctions: A summary. Ann. Missouri Bot. Garden 59: 234–246.

652   ANNALS OF THE MISSOURI BOTANICAL GARDEN   [VOL. 61

————. 1973*b*. The origin of the alpine and subalpine floras of New Zealand. New Zealand Jour. Bot. 11: 177–200.

————. 1975. Cytology and the bases of angiosperm phylogeny. Ann. Missouri Bot. Gard. 62: (in press).

———— & D. I. AXELROD. 1972. Plate tectonics and Australasian paleobiogeography. Science 176: 1379–1386.

———— & D. W. KYHOS. 1965. New evidence concerning the original basic chromosome number of angiosperms. Evolution 19: 244–248.

READ, R. W. & L. J. HICKEY. 1972. A revised classification of fossil palm and palm-like leaves. Taxon 21: 129–137.

REID, E. M. & M. E. J. CHANDLER. 1933. The London Clay Flora. British Museum (Natural History), London. 561 pp.

REIG, O. A. 1973. Discussion. Pp. 204–206, *in* J. L. Vial (editor), "Evolutionary Biology of the Anurans." Univ. Missouri Press, Columbia.

REYMENT, R. A. 1969. Ammonite biostratigraphy, continental drift and oscillatory transgressions. Nature 224: 137–140.

————. 1972. The age of the Niger Delta (West Africa). 24th Internat. Geol. Congr., sect. 6: 11–13.

———— & E. A. TAIT. 1972. Biostratigraphical data of the early history of the South Atlantic Ocean. Trans. Roy. Soc. London 264: 55–95.

RICHARDS, P. W. 1973. Africa, the "odd man out." Pp. 21–26, *in* B. J. Meggers, E. S. Ayensu & W. D. Duckworth (editors), "Tropical Forest Ecosystems in Africa and South America: A Comparative Review." Smithsonian Institution Press, Washington, D.C.

RIDD, M. F. 1972. Southeast Asia a part of Gondwanaland?: Reply. Nature Phys. Sci. 240: 140.

ROBERTS, T. R. 1973. Ecology of fishes in the Amazon and Congo Basins. Pp. 239–254, *in* B. J. Meggers, E. S. Ayensu & W. D. Duckworth (editors), "Tropical Forest Ecosystems in Africa and South America: A Comparative Review." Smithsonian Institution Press, Washington, D.C.

ROBINSON, E. & J. F. LEWIS. 1971. Field guide to aspects of the geology of Jamaica. *In* Internat. Field Institute Guidebook to the Caribbean Island-Arc System, pp. 2–39 (Jamaica Section). Amer. Geol. Inst.

RODGERS, J. 1970. The Tectonics of the Appalachians. Wiley-Interscience, New York. xii + 271 pp.

ROMERO, E. J. 1968. *Palmoxylon patagonicum* n. sp., del Terciaro Inferior de la Provincia de Chubut, Argentina. Ameghiniana 5: 417–432.

————. 1970. *Ulminium atlanticum* n. sp. tronco petrificado de Lauraceae del Eocene de Bahía Solano, Chubut, Argentina. Ameghiniana 7: 205–224.

RONA, R. A. & A. J. NALWALK. 1970. Post-early Pliocene unconformity on Fuerteventura, Canary Islands. Bull. Geol. Soc. Amer. 81: 2117–2122.

RÜFFLE, L. 1965. Monimiaceen-Blätter im älteren Senon von Mitteleuropa. Geologie 14: 78–105.

RZEDOWSKI, J. 1962. Contribuciones a la fitogeografía florística e história de México. Bol. Soc. Bot. Méx. 27: 52–65.

————. 1964. Relaciones geográficas y posibles orígenes de la flore de México. Bol. Soc. Bot. Méx. 29: 121–177.

————. 1972. Contribuciones a la fitogeografía florística e histórica de México. II. Afinidades geográficas de la flora fanerogámica de deferentes regiones de la República mexicana. Anal. Esc. Nac. Ci. Biol. 19: 45–48.

————. 1973. Geographical relationships of the flora of Mexican dry régions. Pp. 61–72, *in* A. Graham (editor), "Vegetation and Vegetational History of Northern Latin America." Elsevier Scientific Publ. Co., Amsterdam.

SAHNI, B. & K. R. SURANGE. 1953. On the structure and affinities of *Cyclanthodendron sahnii* (Rode) Sahni & Surange from the Deccan Intertrappean Series. Paleobotanist 2: 93–100.

SAMYLINA, V. A. 1968. Early Cretaceous angiosperms of the Soviet Union based on leaf and fruit remains. Jour. Linn. Soc. Bot. 61: 207–216.

SAUER, E. G. F. & P. ROTHE. 1972. Ratite eggshells from Lanzarote, Canary Islands. Science 176: 43–45.

SAUER, J. 1969. Oceanic islands and biogeographical theory: A review. Geogr. Rev. 59: 582–593.

SAVAGE, J. M. 1966. The origins and history of the Central American herpetofauna. Copeia 1966: 719–766.

———. 1973. The geographic distribution of frogs: Patterns and predictions. Pp. 351–445, *in* J. L. Vial (editor), "Evolutionary Biology of the Anurans." Univ. Missouri Press, Columbia.

———. 1974. The Isthmian link and the evolution of Neotropical mammals. Contrib. Sci. Nat. Hist. Mus. Los Angeles County 260: 1–51.

SCHALKE, H. J. W. G. 1973. The Upper Quaternary of the Cape Flats area (Cape Province, South Africa). Scripta Geol. 15: 1–57, 8 appendices.

SCHLINGER, E. I. 1974. Continental drift, *Nothofagus* and some ecologically associated insects. Annual Rev. Entom. 19: 323–343.

SCHMID, R. & M. J. SCHMID. 1973. Fossils attributed to the Orchidaceae. Amer. Orchid Soc. Bull., Jan. 1973: 17–27.

SCHODDE, R. 1970. Two new suprageneric taxa in the Monimiaceae alliance. Taxon 19: 324–328.

SCHUCHERT, C. 1935. Historical Geology of the Antillean-Caribbean Region. John Wiley & Sons, Inc. xxvi + 811 pp.

SCHUSTER, R. M. 1972. Continental movements, "Wallace's line" and Indomalayan-Australasian dispersal of land plants: Some eclectic concepts. Bot. Rev. 38: 3–886.

SCHWARZBACH, M. & H. D. PFLUG. 1957. Das Klima des zungeren Tertiars in Island. Neues Jahrb. Geol. Paläontol., Abh. 104: 279–298.

SCOTT, J. A. 1972. Biogeography of Antillean butterflies. Biotropica 4: 32–45.

SCOTT, R. A. 1954. Fossil fruits and seeds from the Eocene Clarno formation of Oregon. Palaentographica 96B: 66–97.

——— & E. S. BARGHOORN. 1957. *Phytocrene microcarpa*—a new species of Icacinaceae based on Cretaceous fruits from Kreischerville, New York. Paleobotanist 6: 25–28.

———, P. L. WILLIAMS, L. C. CRAIG, E. S. BARGHOORN, L. J. HICKEY & H. D. MACGINITIE. 1972. "Pre-Cretaceous" angiosperms from Utah: Evidence for Tertiary age of the palm woods and roots. Amer. Jour. Bot. 59: 886–896.

SELLING, O. H. 1947. Aponogetonaceae in the Cretaceous of South America. Bot. Tidskr. 41: 182.

SEWARD, A. C. 1941. Plant life through the ages. Cambridge Univ. Press. 2nd ed. 607 pp.

SHARP, A. J. 1966. Some aspects of Mexican phytogeography. Ciencia 24: 229–232.

SHERIDAN, R. E. 1971. Geotectonic evolution and subsidence of Bahama platform: Discussion. Bull. Geol. Soc. Amer. 82: 807–810.

SIGÉ, M. B. 1971. Les Didelphoidea de Laguna Umayo (formation Vilquechico, Crétacé superieur, Pérou) et le peuplement marsupial d'Amérique du Sud. Compt. Rend. Hebd. Séances Acad. Sci. 273: 2479–2481.

SILVER, E. A. ET AL. 1972. USGS-IDOE Leg 4 Venezuelan borderland. Geotimes May 1972: 19–21.

SIMPSON, E. ET AL. 1972. Leg 25 DSPS. Western Indian Ocean. Geotimes Nov. 1972: 21–24.

SIMPSON, G. G. 1943. Turtles and the origin of the fauna of Latin America. Amer. Jour. Sci. 241: 413–429.

———. 1945. The principles of classification and a classification of the mammals. Bull. Amer. Mus. Nat. Hist. 85: 1–350.

———. 1947a. Holarctic mammalian faunas and continental relationships during the Cenozoic. Bull. Geol. Soc. Amer. 58: 613–688.

———. 1947b. Evolution, interchange, resemblance of the North American and Eurasian Cenozoic mammalian faunas. Evolution 1: 218–220.

———. 1950. History of the fauna of Latin America. Amer. Sci. 38: 361–389.

———. 1951. History of the fauna of Latin America. Pp. 369–408, *in* G. A. Gaitsell (editor), "Science in Progress." (7th Ser.) Yale Univ. Press, New Haven, Conn.

———. 1952. Probabilities of dispersal in geologic time. Bull. Amer. Mus. Nat. Hist. 99: 163–176.

———. 1956. Zoogeography of the West Indian land mammals. Amer. Mus. Novit. 1759: 1–28.

———. 1969. South American mammals. *In* E. J. Fittkau *et al.* (editor), "Biogeography and Ecology in South America." Monogr. Biol. 19: 879–909.

————. 1973. (Review of:) Biogeography and Ecology in Madagascar. R. Battistini and G. Richard-Vindard (Eds.). Monogr. Biol. 21. Science 180: 1163–1164.

SLEUMER, H. 1967. Monographia Clethracearum. Bot. Jahrb. Syst. 87: 36–175.

SMITH, A. C. 1963. Summary discussion on plant distribution patterns in the tropical Pacific. Pp. 247–249, in J. L. Gressitt (editor), Pacific Basin Biogeography." Bishop Museum Press, Honolulu.

————. 1967. The presence of primitive angiosperms in the Amazon Basin and its significance in indication migrational routes. Atas Simpos. Biota Amaz. 4: 37–59.

————. 1970. The Pacific as a key to flowering plant history. Univ. Hawaii, Harold L. Lyon Arboretum Lecture 1. 26 pp.

————. 1973. Angiosperm evolution and relationship of the floras of Africa and America. Pp. 49–61, in B. J. Meggers, A. S. Ayensu & W. D. Duckworth (editors), "Tropical Forest Ecosystems in Africa and South America: A Comparative review." Smithsonian Inst. Press, Washington, D.C.

SMITH, A. G. 1971. Alpine deformation and the oceanic areas of the Tethys, Mediterranean, and Atlantic. Bull. Geol. Soc. Amer. 82: 2039–2070.

———— & A. HALLAM. 1970. The fit of the southern continents. Nature 225: 139–144.

————, J. C. BRIDEN & G. E. DREWRY. 1973. Phanerozoic world maps. In N. F. Hughes (editor), "Organisms and Continents through Time." Palaeontol. Assn. London, Spec. Paper Palaeontol. 12: 1–43.

SMITH, L. S. 1958. New Species of and notes on Queensland plants—III. Proc. Roy. Soc. Queensland 69: 43–51.

SOLBRIG, O. T. 1972. New approaches to the study of disjunctions with special emphasis on the American amphitropical desert disjunctions. Pp. 85–100, in D. H. Valentine (editor), "Taxonomy, Phytogeography, and Evolution." Academic Press, London and New York.

————. 1973. The floristic disjunctions between the "Monte" in Argentina and the "Sonoran Desert" in Mexico and the United States. Ann. Missouri Bot. Gard. 59: 218–223.

SRIVASTAVA, S. K. 1970. Pollen biostratigraphy and paleoecology of the Edmonton formation (Maestrichtian), Alberta, Canada. Palaeogeogr. Palaeoclimatol. Palaeoecol. 7: 221–276.

————. 1972. Pollen genus *Erdtmanipollis* Krutzsch 1962. Pollen & Spores 14: 309–322.

STANDLEY, P. C. 1920–26. Trees and shrubs of Mexico. Contr. U. S. Natl. Herb. 23: i–vii, 1–1721.

STAUFFER, P. H. & D. J. GOBBETT. 1972. Southeast Asia a part of Gondwanaland? Nature Phys. Sci. 240: 139–140.

STEARN, W. T. 1971. A survey of the tropical genera *Oplonia* and *Psilanthele* (Acanthaceae). Bull. Brit. Mus. (Nat. Hist.), Bot. 4: 259–323.

STEBBINS, G. L. 1950. Variation and Evolution in Plants. Columbia Univ. Press, New York. 643 pp.

————. 1952. Aridity as a stimulus to evolution. Amer. Naturalist 86: 33–44.

————. 1972. Ecological distribution of centers of major adaptive radiation in angiosperms. Pp. 7–34, in D. H. Valentine (editor), "Taxonomy, Phytogeography, and Evolution." Academic Press, London and New York.

STEENIS, C. G. G. J. VAN. 1962. The land-bridge theory in botany. Blumea 11: 235–542.

————. 1972. *Nothofagus*, key genus to plant ge"rophy. Pp. 275–288, in D. H. Valentine (editor), "Taxonomy, Phytogeography, and Evolution." Academic Press, London and New York.

STEINHAUSER, P., S. A. VINCENZ, S. N. DASGUPTA. 1972. Paleamagnetism of some Lower Cretaceous lavas on Jamaica. Amer. Geophys. Union Trans. 53: 356–357.

STEVENS, P. F. 1970. *Agauria* and *Agarista*: An example of tropical transatlantic affinity. Notes Roy. Bot. Gard. Edinburgh 30: 341–359.

STEYERMARK, J. A. 1932. A revision of the genus *Menodora*. Ann. Missouri Bot. Gard. 19: 87–176, *pl. 1–11.*

STIRTON, R. A. 1950. Late Cenozoic avenues of dispersal for terrestrial animals between North America and South America. Abstr. Bull. Geol. Soc. Amer. 61: 1541–1542.

SZAFER, W. 1958. Nowa flora Eocenska in Tatrach. Kwart. Geol. Warsaw 2: 173–176.

TAKHTAJAN, A. 1957. On the origin of the temperate flora of Eurasia. Bot. Žurn. (Moscow & Leningrad) 42: 935–953. [In Russian, with English summary.]

————. 1969. Flowering Plants, Origin and Dispersal. Transl. by C. Jeffrey. Smithsonian Inst. Press, Washington, D.C. 310 pp.

TARLING, D. H. 1971. Gondwanaland, palaeomagnetism and continental drift. Nature 229: 17–21, 71.

——. 1972. Another Gondwanaland. Nature 238: 92–93.

THOMPSON, P. R. & T. SAITO. 1973. Equatorial Pacific climatic fluctuations during the last 500,000 years. Geol. Soc. Amer. Abstr. Prog. 1973 Meetings, Dallas, pp. 840–841.

THORNE, R. F. 1965. Floristic relationships of New Caledonia. Univ. Iowa Stud. Nat. Hist. 20(7): 1–14.

——. 1968. Synopsis of a putatively phylogenetic classification of the flowering plants. Aliso 4: 57–66.

——. 1973a. Major disjunctions in the geographical ranges of seed plants. Quart. Rev. Biol. 47: 365–411.

——. 1973b. Floristic relationships between tropical Africa and tropical America. Pp. 27–47, in B. J. Meggers, E. S. Ayensu & W. D. Duckworth (editors), "Tropical Forest Ecosystems in Africa and South America: A Comparative Review." Smithsonian Inst. Press, Washington D.C.

——. 1973c. Inclusion of the Apiaceae (Umbelliferae) in the Araliaceae. Notes Roy. Bot. Gard. Edinburgh 32: 161–165.

TIHEN, J. 1964. Tertiary changes in the herpetofaunas of temperate North America. Senckenberg. Biol. 45: 265–279.

TOMLINSON, P. B. 1966. Anatomical data in the classification of Commelinaceae. Jour. Linn. Soc. Bot. 59: 371–395.

TRALAU, H. 1964. The genus Nypa van Wurmb. Kungl. Svenska Vetenskapsakad. Handl. ser. 4. 10: 1–29.

TRAVERSE, A. 1955. Pollen analysis of the Brandon lignite of Vermont. U. S. Bur. Mines, Rept. of Investig. 5151. 107 pp.

TRIVEDI, B. S. & C. L. VERMA. 1972. Occurrence of Heliconites mohgaonensis gen. et sp. nov. from the Early Eocene and Deccan Intertrappean Series, M. P., India. Paleontographica B. 139: 73–82.

TSCHANZ, C. M., R. F. MARVIN, J. CRUZ B., H. H. MEHNERT & G. T. CEBULA. 1974. Geologic evolution of the Sierra Nevada de Santa Marta, northeastern Colombia. Bull. Geol. Soc. Amer. 85: 273–284.

TSCHUDY, B. D. 1970. Palynology of the Cretaceous-Tertiary boundary in the Rocky Mountain and Mississippi embayment regions. Geol. Soc. Amer. Spec. Paper 127: 65–111.

——. 1971. Two new fossil pollen genera from Upper Campanian (Cretaceous) rocks of Montana. U. S. Geol. Surv. Prof. Paper 750-B: 53–61.

TURNER, B. L. 1973. Chemosystematic data: Their use in the study of disjunctions. Ann. Missouri Bot. Gard. 59: 152–164.

TYLER, M. J. 1971. Phylogenetic relationships of certain Neotropical toads with the description of a new genus (Anura: Bufonidae). Los Angeles County Mus. Contr. Sci. 216: 1–40.

UCHUPI, E., J. D. MILLIMAN, B. P. LUYENDKY, C. O. BOWIN & K. W. EMERY. 1971. Structure and origin of southeastern Bahamas. Bull. Amer. Assoc. Petrol. Geol. 55: 687–704.

VAN COUVERING, J. A. & J. A. MILLER. 1971. Late Miocene marine and non-marine time scale in Europe. Nature 230: 559–563.

VANZOLINI, P. E. 1970. Zoologia sistemática, geografia e a origem das espécies. Instituto de Geografia, Univ. São Paulo, Série Teses e Monografias 3: 1–56.

—— & E. E. WILLIAMS. 1970. South American anoles: The geographical differentiation and evolution of the Anolis chrysolepis species group (Sauria, Iguanidae). Arq. Zool. São Paulo 19: 1–298.

VENKATO RAO, O. 1971. Proteaceae. Botanical Monograph No. 6, Council of Scientific and Industrial Research, New Delhi.

VERDCOURT, B. 1958. Remarks on the classification of the Rubiaceae. Bull. Jard. Bot. Bruxelles 28: 209–290.

VESTER, H. 1940. Die Areale und areal Typen der Angiospermen-Familien. Bot. Archiv. 40: 203–275, 295–356, 530–577.

VORONOVA, M. A. 1966. Subdivision of Lower Cretaceous deposits in the northwestern part of the Dnieper-Donets depression on the ground of spore-pollen analysis. Pp. 80–86, in "The Importance of Palynologic Analysis for the Stratigraphic and Paleofloristic Investigations." Acad. Sci. USSR, Moscow. For the Second Internat. Palynol. Conf., Utrecht. [In Russian with English summary.]

VUILLEUMIER, B. S. 1971. Pleistocene changes in the flora and fauna of South America. Science 173: 771–780.

WAHLERT, J. H. 1973. *Protoptychus*, a hystricomorphous rodent from the Late Eocene of North America. Mus. Comp. Zool. Harvard Univ. Breviora 419: 1–14.

WALKER, J. W. 1971. Pollen morphology, phytogeography, and phylogeny of the Annonaceae. Contr. Gray Herb. 202: 3–130.

———. 1972. Chromosome numbers, phylogeny, phytogeography of the Annonaceae and their bearing on the (original) basic chromosome number of angiosperms. Taxon 21: 57–65.

WALPER, J.L. & C. L. Roᵥᴇᴅᴛ. 1972. Plate tectonics and the origin of the Caribbean Sea and the Gulf of Mexico. Gulf Coast Assoc. Geol. Soc. Trans. 22: 105–116.

WEBSTER, P. J. & N. A. STRETEN. 1973. Aspects of late Quaternary climate in tropical Australasia. *In* D. Walker (editor), "Bridge and Barrier. The Natural and Cultural History of Torres Strait." Res. Pac. Stud., Dept. Biogeogr. Geomorph. Publ. BG/3: 39–60. Australian Nat. Univ. Press, Canberra.

WEEKS, L. A., R. K. LATTIMORE, R. N. HARBISON, B. G. BASSINGER & G. F. MERRILL. 1971. Structural relations among Lesser Antilles, Venezuela, and Trinidad-Tobago. Bull. Amer. Assoc. Petrol. Geol. 55: 1741–1752.

WEISSEL, J. K. & D. E. HAYES. 1972. Magnetic anomalies in the southeast Indian Ocean. Antarct. Res. Serv. 19: 165–196, 1 map.

WERGER, M. J. A. 1973. Las disyunciones anfitrópicas en las floras xerofíticas norte y sudamericanas. Darwiniana 18: 9–18.

WHITE, C. T. 1936. Contribution to the Queensland flora, no. 5. Proc. Roy Soc. Queensland 47: 51–84.

WHITMORE, F. C., JR. & R. H. STEWART. 1965. Miocene mammals and Central American seaways. Science 148: 180–185.

WIENS, D. & B. A. BARLOW. 1971. The cytogeography and relationships of the viscaceous and eremolepidaceous mistletoes. Taxon 20: 313–332.

WIJMSTRA, R. A. & T. VAN DER HAMMEN. 1966. Palynological data on the history of tropical savannas in northern South America. Leidse. Geol. Meded. 38: 71–90.

WILD, H. 1968. Phytogeography in South Central Africa. Kirkia 6: 197–222.

WILDE, W. J. J. O. DE. 1972. The indigenous Old World passifloras. Blumea 20: 227–250.

WILHELM, O. & M. EWING. 1972. Geology and history of the Gulf of Mexico. Bull. Geol. Soc. Amer. 83: 575–600.

WILLIAMS, C. A. & D. McKENZIE. 1971. The evolution of the north-east Atlantic. Nature 232: 168–173.

WOLFE, J. A. 1962. A Miocene pollen sequence from the Cascade range of northern Oregon. U. S. Geol. Surv. Prof. Paper 450C: 81–84.

———. 1972. An interpretation of Alaskan Tertiary floras. Pp. 201–233, *in* A. Graham (editor), "Floristics and Paleofloristics of Asia and Eastern North America." Elsevier Publ. Co., Amsterdam.

———. 1974. Fossil forms of Amentiferae. Brittonia 25: 334–335.

——— & H. M. PAKISER. 1971. Stratigraphic interpretations of some Cretaceous microfossil floras of the Middle Atlantic States. U. S. Geol. Surv. Prof. Paper 750B: 35–47.

———, J. A. DOYLE, V. M. PAGE & L. J. HICKEY. 1975. The bases of angiosperm phylogeny: fossil evidence. Ann. Missouri Bot. Gard. 62: (in press).

WOOD, A. E. 1972. An Eocene hystricognathous rodent from Texas: *Its significance in interpretations of continental drift*. Science 175: 1250–1251.

WOOD, C. E., JR. 1973. Morphology and phytogeography: The classical approach to the study of disjunctions. Ann. Missouri Bot. Gard. 59: 107–124.

WRIGHT, J. B. 1968. South Atlantic continental drift and the Benue Trough. Tectonophysics 6: 301–310.

———. 1971. Comments on "Timing of break-up of the continents round the Atlantic as determined by Paleomagnetism" by E. E. Larson and L. La Fontain, Earth and Planetary Science Letters 8 (1970) 341–344. Earth Planet. Sci. Lett. 10: 271–272.

YEDEMSKAYA, A. L. 1960. Sporovo-pyl'tsevyye kompleksy iz aptskikh i al'bskikh otlozheniy vostochnoy chasti severnogo Kavkaza. Byul. Mosk. O-va. Isp. Prirody, Otd. Geol. 35(6): 110–115.

ZIMMERMAN, E. C. 1963. Pacific Basin biogeography. A summary discussion. Pp. 477–481, in J. L. Gressitt (editor), "Pacific Basin Biogeography." Bishop Museum Press, Honolulu.

ZINDEREN BAKKER SR., E. M. VAN. 1972. Late Quaternary lacustrine phases in the southern Sahara and east Africa. In E. M. van Zinderen Bakker (editor), "Palaeoecology of Africa." 6: 15–27. A. A. Balkema, Cape Town.

———— & J. A. COTZEE. 1972. A reappraisal of late Quaternary climatic evidence from tropical Africa. In E. M. van Zinderen Bakker (editor), "Palaeoecology of Africa." 7: 151–181. A. A. Balkema, Cape Town.

Chapter 1

A Kaleidoscope of Plates, Faunal and Floral Dispersals, and Sea Level Changes

FRANCIS G. STEHLI and S. DAVID WEBB

1. Introduction

Complex problems seem to have a way of becoming increasingly complex as we learn more, recognize new variables, and appreciate the labyrinthine nature of interactions. When we learn to deal with them as large-scale systems, however, models can be posited and tested, and it becomes possible to move from an observational-analytical approach to one allowing a certain degree of experimentation.

Experimentation in systems containing a large historical component is difficult. A well-designed and controlled experiment leading to a unique answer is almost never possible. Instead, one must proceed through an "if . . . then" approach, in which consideration of the interaction of elements in the system under study leads to a model that allows a question to be posed and an answer sought; i.e., an experiment can be performed.

FRANCIS G. STEHLI • College of Geosciences, University of Oklahoma, Norman, Oklahoma 73019.   S. DAVID WEBB • Florida State Museum, University of Florida, Gainesville, Florida 32611.

The large-scale system under consideration in this volume is the cause, nature, timing, and biotic result of the changing degrees of isolation between North and South America. New observations, concepts, and experimental techniques have provided a wealth of data to be used in studying this system and bring us to the threshold of experiment. No field of study moving so rapidly or advancing in so many directions can ever be wholly or even comprehensively reviewed, but this volume summarizes advances in as many aspects of this complex system as possible. We hope that in doing so it stimulates the design of experiments that will test models, help to discriminate among them, and lead eventually to resolution of the fascinating geobiologic problem posed by the interrelationship of North and South America.

The outlines of the question have been drawn together by distinguished scientists in both biology and geology. Perceptive and pioneering syntheses have led to step function increases in our understanding. From the perspective of geology, Schuchert (1935) had a profound effect when he drew together most of the available geologic information on the complex and dynamic region that lies between North and South America, synthesized its geology, and produced a treatise entitled *Historical Geology of the Antillean–Caribbean Region*. This remarkable work did much to guide thinking about the region, call attention to problems requiring research, and stimulate actual research through the vast area with which it dealt. The synthesis reflects the dominant tectonic concept of the time—the permanency of continents and ocean basins. By this hypothesis the Central American land bridge that now connects North and South America was thought to have resulted from vertical uplift and volcanic upbuilding *in situ*. Because continents and ocean basins were thought to be permanent features, it followed that, unless erosion or metamorphism had destroyed the record, it remained to be deciphered. Thus, one could look forward eventually to a reasonably complete understanding of the historical geology of the Antillean–Caribbean region.

By the early 1960s the concept of sea-floor spreading was providing a new vehicle for consideration of tectonics and new perspectives on historical geology and the long-term availability of a geologic record in the oceans. Large-scale horizontal transport of crustal blocks seemed not only possible but likely and pervasive. Volume changes due to heating or cooling of large thicknesses of crustal rock seemed to provide a mechanism for understanding vertical motions, especially in the ocean basins. Hope that a near-perfect record of geological history lay sequestered in the ocean's depths was shattered by the discovery that there was virtually no old ocean crust because subduction destroyed it within 200 million years and commonly much less. As one demonstration of the reality of sea-floor spreading followed another, it became clear that the crust was far more dynamic than previously thought, that horizontal movements on a vast scale had occurred, that large and systematic changes in crustal elevation with respect to sea level were obligate handmaidens of sea-floor spreading, that the geologic record of the oceans was systematically destroyed and, in short, that paleogeography was a far more complex subject than had been realized.

It became apparent that all aspects of historical geology required new assessment and that Schuchert's *Historical Geology of the Antillean–Caribbean Region* was no exception. In fact, the tectonic dynamism of the area and its pivotal position in the alteration of land connections between North and South America and marine connections between the Atlantic and Pacific made it a subject of extraordinary interest and complexity. As the subject became the focus of increased attention, it also benefited from a wealth of new data provided by vigorous oceanographic exploration, improved geophysical and geochemical tools and interpretations, much basic and essential geological mapping, and the reinterpretation of much geology on land.

From the perspective of continental biogeography, Matthew (1915) and Simpson (1940, 1950) produced the classic studies. Their syntheses not only organized vertebrate paleontological data from all land masses but also produced many of the principles and methods of paleobiogeography that worked for half a century. The great service of their studies was to frame vertebrate biogeographic problems in a way that demonstrated the efficacy of the historical approach and that clearly showed what vast and dramatic changes had taken place in past faunal and floral distributions.

Our increased understanding of crustal behavior complicated not only the study of paleogeography but also that of paleobiogeography and, indeed, the entire synthesis of fields included in historical geology in the broadest sense. Such disciplines as paleo-oceanography, paleoecology, and paleoclimatology all had to be newly integrated into a far more dynamic geobiologic system.

New understanding of crustal dynamics, drawn largely from the oceans, began to complicate biogeography in the decade of the 1960s. It became clear that the mobility of land and sea, even within the Cenozoic Era, could play as important a role as the mobility of organisms. If spreading rates on mid-ocean ridges were on the order of a few centimenters per year, then crustal segments once adjacent could be separated by a whole ocean within half the Cenozoic Era. To account for a disjunct distribution of land and fresh-water species between two land masses, one could as well consider a tectonic dispersal as a biological one. Clearly, the geological processes to be considered in biogeography operated on a grander scale and at a more rapid tempo than was conceivable before the 1960s.

In the case of interamerican biotic interchanges, the entire record and its interpretation were reopened by the new crustal dynamics. Were the classic principles still applicable? The answer was neither a simple yes nor a no; more complex answers were needed. Collections of greater diversity, especially in micropaleontological specimens, of greater geographic coverage, and of finer chronostratigraphic resolution were required to test and refine the more dynamic new historical geology.

A great deal remains to be learned about the Antillean-Caribbean region, but so much has been discovered, and it has so profoundly affected our understanding of the fascinating interplay between North American and South American biotas, the interaction between the Atlantic and the Pacific, and the kaleidoscopic rearrangements of crustal blocks in the region that the subject deserves renewed consideration. We know now that much of the older record of what has happened, at least as it was recorded in the oceans, is lost to us, but new techniques allow us to decipher with increasing clarity the more recent history of this extraordinary region. The chances for improved understanding of this involved problem seem better than ever since it is increasingly viewed as a complexly interacting system.

2. The Importance of Refined Chronology in Correlating Events in Plate Tectonics and Organic Evolution

The most important advances in geology may be those that permit more refined correlations between diverse events in various places. When a newly refined chronology is applied to questions about interamerican biotic dispersals or the physical relationships between the Pacific and the Caribbean Sea, it allows the broad picture to assume a clearer focus; at the same time, it permits greater understanding of specific facets of the problem. The greater temporal resolution of events that has accompanied the painstaking integration of biostratigraphy, geochronology, and magnetic reversals has strikingly refined our perception of the lengths of time involved and of the temporal placement of discrete events. Success in this critical aspect of the problem has come about through refinements in the measurement of isotope ratios used in the K–Ar technique of geochronology and through improved understanding of sampling requirements for reliable geochronology. Detailed understanding of the sequence and temporal distribution of magnetic reversal events has provided a broadly applicable means of correlation, particularly on the sea floor, in volcanic rocks exposed on land, and increasingly, as cryogenic magnetometry is used, in sedimentary rocks as well. Much greater attention to detailed sampling for fossils and precise stratigraphy have resulted in greatly enhanced precision in biostratigraphy (e.g. Tedford, 1970). K–Ar geochronology, magnetic stratigraphy, and detailed biostratigraphy have been united into a broadly applicable temporal framework having the strengths of both the relative and absolute time scales. An accurate, precise, and broadly applicable chronology is one of the essentials in organizing the wealth of data available so that it can be treated systematically. The outlines of such a chronology seem now to be at hand.

3. Paleomagnetic Data

Paleomagnetic data have contributed importantly to chronology by virtue of the increasingly well-known sequence of polarity reversals. They have contributed with equal impact to tectonics, as a means to constrain the position of crustal blocks in space and time. Measurement of the magnetic field recorded in ancient rocks can indicate rotational and latitudinal movements but is insensitive to longitudinal motions unless independent constraining evidence is at hand. Improvements in the "magnetic cleaning" of fossil magnetic fields to remove secondary overlays have resulted in increasingly refined suites of data and an increasing ability to resolve movement of crustal blocks.

In the tectonically complex area around the Caribbean, paleomagnetic data have contributed importantly to our understanding of the former position of itinerant crustal blocks, the paths through which they moved, and the timing of their arrival at a place where they became sutured to some other element of continental crust. They also have helped to define the place through time of the massive North American and South American land masses that have surrounded the much smaller Caribbean, like the jaws of a vise—sometimes closing, sometimes relaxing—to influence tectonic events in the area of interest to us here.

4. New Depth in Our Knowledge of the Sea

A second area of major importance and great significance to the whole question of links between South America and neighboring land masses has been an enormous increase in our knowledge of the sea floor. The greatest advances have come through marine geophysics and have involved accurate and close-spaced soundings, reflection and refraction seismology, gravity, magnetics, and heat flow. Verification of many of the conclusions drawn from geophysical surveys, together with a great deal of additional information, has come through the Deep-Sea Drilling Program (DSDP). The result of this combination of geophysical hypothesis and test by the drill has been the general acceptance of the theory of plate tectonics as a unifying concept, which integrates many formerly disparate observations regarding the topography and structure of the sea floor.

Once thought to be more or less featureless, the sea floor has been shown to be topographically complex. Even the vast, almost flat abyssal plains are now known to result from a sedimentary cover consisting largely of turbidites that conceal a complex underlying topography. Deep-sea trenches, with their large, negative gravity anomalies, are the loci of subduction where one crustal plate descends below another. Mid-ocean ridges are the surface expression of spreading centers. Submarine plateaus may be crustal fragments broken off during sea-floor spreading, while sea mounts are likely to be submarine volcanoes. Passive continental margins may be partly structural but often are constructional and fre-

5.2. Subducting Margins

To satisfy the geometric constraints of an earth of constant diameter, the addition of new crustal material along a spreading ridge must somehow be compensated by equivalent crustal shortening or by crustal destruction at some other place. Normally, this occurs at the margin opposite the generating edge where a neighboring plate is impinged upon. A common response when two plate margins collide in this way is for one plate to underthrust the other, a process that has become known as subduction. During subduction the descending plate moves downward across the increasing thermal gradient normally encountered with increasing depth and may reach a region where the ambient temperature results in partial melting, or mantle rocks trapped between the surface plate and the subducting plate may be at temperatures that allow melting. When this happens, molten rock moves upward and produces intrusive plutonic rock bodies within the overlying crust and frequently builds volcanoes and associated extrusive volcanic piles at the surface. Volcanoes and other evidences of volcanism are frequent in the Caribbean region due to subduction of the Cocos and Atlantic Plates beneath the Caribbean Plate. Volcanism at the surface in such regions can build the crust above sea level to provide new islands or even land connections.

Volcanoes are only one common accompaniment of subduction. Seismic activity is another and most areas of active subduction are subject to frequent earthquakes as the two impacting plates interact and the crust adjusts to the accompanying stresses. Adjustment along faults may result in vertical or horizontal movement or in a combination of both. If stress is relieved along a particular zone of weakness over a long period of time, then the effect may be profound. When movement is primarily vertical, great crustal dislocation may occur, but topographic effects are often minimized by rapid erosion of the uplifted block and equally rapid sedimentation on the surface of the downthrown block. On the other hand, if movement is mainly horizontal, great lateral displacement of crustal blocks with concomitant geographic changes may occur. This may be the case where Honduras on land and the Nicaragua Rise to the east on the Caribbean sea floor may be displaced along the Motagua–Polochic Fault Zone and the Cayman Trench.

Deep-sea trenches are another common feature of subduction zones. In addition to linear regions at abyssal depths, deep-sea trenches commonly exhibit large negative gravity anomalies due to mass deficiency. The deficiencies are caused partly by the water-filled topographic depression and are dynamically maintained by subduction. Doubling the thickness of the crust as one plate subducts below another and becomes warmer can produce isostatic effects, causing surficial rocks to float higher with the development of new land or the increased elevation of extant land. This process can create land bridges and allow migration of a terrestrial biota, or it can reduce a migration corridor to a filter bridge by imposing inimical high land areas. It may be through some process such as this that the last element in the present day land bridge between the two Americas was added when a strip of rocks having the characteristics of ocean crust was elevated above sea level in the Panama segment of the land bridge.

6. The New Historical Biogeography

In such a dynamic physical world the possibilities for passive geologic transportation of organisms between different land masses or oceans over long intervals of time become impressive. No longer is it taken for granted that organisms disperse in a short-term manner either by active dispersal or by such passive present agents as winds or currents. Now it is at least as plausible that they or even their fossil remains were transported by long-term geodynamic processes. Indeed, some recent biogeographers maintain that plate tectonics alone accounts for virtually all organismic distribution patterns (Nelson and Rosen, 1981). The variety of modes by which organisms may have dispersed in the past renders modern biogeography an exciting and very demanding historical science (Brown and Gibson, 1983). As Nelson states (in Nelson and Rosen, 1981, p. 525), biogeography is "a 19th century science that . . . has become interesting once again."

In the classic view (Simpson, 1950), the dispersal route of a species from one land mass to another is assigned to one of three categories graded according to the difficulty of the passage. The most probable and least difficult route is a corridor: an essentially continuous band of congenial habitat by which many ecologically compatible species might extend their ranges. The Great American Biotic Interchange itself is a classic example in which the major Plio-Pleistocene isthmian connection between North and South America provided for a broad two-way movement of fauna and flora.

The second, somewhat less probable kind of dispersal route is a filter bridge in which a moderately severe ecological barrier or a moderately broad physical barrier blocks dispersal of many species. A modest number of species still can pass, usually in reciprocal fashion. An example of a filter bridge that compares nicely with the preceding one of a corridor is the late Miocene relationship between the American continents where a few species of land mammals were able to cross the narrowing Bolivar Trough in each direction.

The third, least probable route is the sweepstakes (or waif) dispersal across a very wide, usually physical barrier. Only extremely vagile or durable organisms can make such crossings and then rarely. Of course, these three categories are somewhat arbitrary divisions of a stochastic spectrum that might be defined somewhat differently by biogeographers studying different groups of organisms.

The new biogeography continues to utilize these concepts while reading into them a more dynamic history. They are now supplemented explicitly by various plate-mediated modes of transportation. The most obvious such case arises when a land mass rifts apart and the biota at all taxonomic levels begins separate evolutionary histories; such separations fall under the rubric (quite current among modern biogeographers) of "vicariance." McKenna (1972, 1973) named and distinguished two mechanisms by which plates, once adrift, could transport terrestrial biota: if the plate conveys living biota from one landmass to another, then it is labeled a "Noah's Ark," whereas if it redistributes fossil biota between continents it is a "Viking Funeral Ship." Unlike corridors and filter bridges, Noah's Arks and Viking Funeral Ships conduct biota in one direction only, namely, from the plate's origin to its destination.

The last 100 million years of interamerican history probably include case histories of all five mechanisms for biotic dispersal or transport. It is a major challenge to the historical biogeographer to demonstrate which species were subject to which mechanisms in the course of their histories.

6.1. An Outline of South American Biogeographic History

The history of South America's biotic contacts illustrates most (if not all) of the biogeographic concepts of dispersal and transport. (See Table I) The changing configurations of the earth's crust are seen as the 1st-order control over which dispersal modes are most likely through that history. Second-order environmental changes such as sea-level fluctuations and climatic shifts also govern the probability that one or another mode of dispersal will prevail.

Commencing in the Mesozoic Era, South America was broadly connected with the other southern continents and India by a system of corridors, as indicated by the broad floral and faunal resemblances throughout Gondwanaland. The most dramatic confirma-

Table I.   Outline of South America's Biogeographic History

Time interval	Years ago $\times$ 10^6	Continent in proximity	Biogeographic nature of terrestrial contact
Late Pliocene to Recent	0–3	North America	Corridor
Late Miocene	7–9	North America	Filter bridge
Medial Oligocene	34–38	North America	Noah's Ark (to South America)
Medial Paleocene	58–61	North America	Filter bridge
Late Cretaceous	70–75	North America	Filter bridge
Medial Cretaceous	90–110	Antarctica Australia	Vicariance and waif dispersal
Early Cretaceous	120–140	Gondwanaland including Africa	Vicariance and corridor

tion of Gondwanan biotic continuity comes from Antartica, which, as predicted, finally yielded abundant evidence of a reptile and amphibian fauna closely related to that of South Africa and India. Indeed, the species of *Lystrosaurus* from Coalsack Bluff were identical to those from the rich faunal sequence from the Karroo Desert of South Africa (Colbert, 1971). South America and the other Gondwanaland fragments still support many important disjuncts from that great Mesozoic biota, including Proteaceae and other archaic flowering plants, midges and many other insect taxa, parastacoid crayfishes, osteoglossids and other fresh-water fishes, pipids and other amphibians, amphisbaenids and other lizards, and ratites and many suboscines among the birds.

The, during the mid-Cretaceous, South America separated from Africa. A tenuous connection was maintained between South America and Australia via Antartica, and a strong case has been made for late Cretaceous contiguity between western Gondwanan marsupial mammals, ratite birds, and among higher plants such as *Nothofagus* and austral gymnosperms (Tedford, 1974, Raven and Axelrod, 1975; Cracraft, 1973). It would be difficult to distinguish, at such a long time perspective, between simple separation of common stocks by rifting and subsequent waif dispersal across moderate gaps; perhaps the simpler interpretation of passive vicariant splitting is preferable in such cases. On the other hand, discovery of the late Eocene marsupial *Antarctodolops* on Seymour Island, representing a distinctive and highly derived group of frugivores previously known only in South America, is more probably the result of waif dispersal across a moderate water gap (Woodburne and Zinsmeister, 1984).

The first evidence of a terrestrial biotic connection between North and South America arises in the latest Cretaceous and earliest Cenozoic. The most diverse and detailed evidence involves three families of marsupials shared between the Americas in the latest Cretaceous and the Paleocene (e.g., Marshall et al., 1983). Tedford (1974) presented two lines of evidence suggesting that the direction of dispersal in this case was from South America to North America: first, the presumably very ancient marsupial connection with Australia tends to place the group's origin in the southern hemisphere; second, the marsupials have their greatest early taxonomic diversity in the Paleocene of South America. The same arguments support northward dispersal of the notoungulates, if the late Cretaceous specimens from Peru and Bolivia represent the same group of ungulates as the Paleocene forms in Asia (but see Cifelli, Chapter 9, this volume). Not all of this presumed set of dispersals appear to have moved northward, however; this is an important point because otherwise a Noah's Ark might be postulated. Among mammals, there is at least weak phylogenetic distributional evidence that edentates and uintathere-xenungulates distributed from north to south (McKenna, 1980; Simpson, 1980). Other groups, including caimanoid and hadrosaurine archosaurs, teiid lizards, aniliid, boid and possibly xeno-dontine snakes (Bonaparte, 1984; Cadle, 1984; Duellman, 1979; Estes and Baez, Chapter 6, this volume), as well as diverse nonmarine mollusks (Parodiz, 1969) and angiospermous plants (Raven and Axelrod, 1975) probably filtered both northward and southward. Presumably their route was by island-arc stepping stones across the Caribbean region. Possibly the eastern half of North America (Euramerica) with its extensive Bahaman peninsula was then the more likely area of embarcation (and disembarcation).

After the very early Cenozoic, South America produces a substantial record (at least for land mammals) indicating (by negative evidence) complete isolation until the late Oligocene. At that time, an important set of arrivals includes the hystricognath rodents, the ceboid primates, the *Geochelone (Chelonoides)* tortoises and probably the phyllostomatoid bats. It should be added that the earliest records of most of these groups (in the Deseadan) was preceded by a hiatus that may represent most of the Oligocene and that, when they appear, the South American rodents already had diversified to at least seven families (Wood, Chapter 10, this volume). The unique feature of this set of interamerican dispersals is that it appears to have moved from north to south only: no reciprocal dispersals of South American taxa have been recognized in North America. It is also notable that the nearest tortoise record (in time and space) is *Geochelone (Chelonoides)* from the Oligocene of Costa Rica. In the western Caribbean, the impingement of the Cocos Plate was then producing extensive volcanism and for the first time had closed off deep-water circulation from the Pacific. Thus, there is *prima facie* evidence for proposing that the Oligocene immigrants to South America were conveyed across the Caribbean by a Noah's Ark.

The later Cenozoic interamerican biotic events can be divided into two final episodes. The principle event is the "Great American Biotic Interchange": an episode involving reciprocal passage of numerous land and freshwater taxa between the Americas via the isthmian corridor about 3 million years ago. This major event was preceded by a lesser episode in which a few taxa reciprocally crossed a filter bridge between 8 and 9 million years ago. These latest biogeographic episodes conform well to Simpson's earlier characterizations and still serve well as the "type examples" of a filter bridge and a corridor, respectively.

6.2. The Central American Paradox

Central America has played a crucial, but often enigmatic, role in interamerican history. Emplacement of the isthmian link some 3 million years ago was, of course, the essential geological event that triggered the Great American Interchange. That narrow tropical link almost surely mediated any late Cenozoic continuities in either terrestrial or freshwater organisms between North America and South America. Prior to that time, Central America was predominantly—indeed to judge from the Miocene fossil mammals, wholly—an adjunct of North America, separated widely from South America by the Bolivar Trough. The historical paradox is that the modern biota of Central America (as judged by virtually all biogeographers, beginning with Wallace [1876]), has much stronger affinities with the biota of South America than with that of North America. Simpson (1950) noted the near coincidence between the biogeographic realm known as "Neotropica" and the cultural realm known as "Latin America." How in geobiological history did this shift of allegiance on the part of Central America come about? How did it come about merely within the duration of the Pleistocene?

The strong surge of outstanding work in tropical American ecology, as reflected for example in the rich volumes of Janzen (1983) and Leigh et al. (1982), promises a realistic resolution to the question of what environmental changes might have produced such rapid biological changes. The persistent influence of Pleistocene history in modern neotropical biotas has been well documented in the refugia of the Amazon Basin (e.g. Haffer, 1974). Such 2nd-order geological effects were surely at work in Central America as well.

6.3. Rates of Evolution and Biotic Turnover

The long period of isolation and of near-isolation of the South American biota render it a particularly interesting "laboratory" for the study of macroevolutionary processes. By selecting appropriate taxa and analyzing their history during appropriate intervals, evolutionary biologists can perform some magnificent experiments. Of special interest is the early history of a successful new immigrant group such as the cricetid rodents.

Koopman (1964) recognized the South American radiation of cricetid rodents, from a few genera in the late Pliocene to some 60 at present, as an exemplary unfolding of "a basal group." Another interesting case study would be to compare the hystricognath rodent radiation that began in South America before the Deseadan with the cricetid explosion just noted. Comparing diversification rates of allochthons with diversification rates of related autochthons also provides a "controlled experiment" of considerable theoretical interest.

Similar timed experiments with multiple subjects exist in the marine realm. The rates and modes of divergence between geminate marine species of the Caribbean and the Pacific may be analyzed in two sets: (1) deep-water Tethyan forms that separated with the Oligocene shallowing episode; and (2) late Cenozoic forms including planktonics that were divided by late Pliocene closure of the Panama portal. For both sets, useful replicate studies of known-age samples may be made.

The number of species or higher taxa recorded at various stages in various parts of the New World provide an exceedingly valuable data set for species-equilibrium studies. Such studies, originally developed by MacArthur and Wilson (1967) in analyses of modern island biotas, are of surpassing interest in a dynamic system of changing biogeographic areas. The changing trajectory of the American continents from complete isolation through partial communication to complete connection offers a magnificent experiment in species equilibria and diversity control insofar as the chronostratigraphic framework (discussed above) and paleontological record warrant it (e.g., Marshall *et al.*, 1982).

7. What Is Land, What Is Sea—Fluctuating Sea Levels

From the perspective of a terrestrial creature, a connection between two continental masses is of little value unless it happens to be above sea level. However, sea level is a sometime thing, able to make or break land connections without the direct imposition of local tectonic deformation. The best attainable record of temporal variation in sea level is, thus, of much interest in the matter of development and persistence of a land connection between the two Americas.

The increasing development of a quantitative time scale in geology has helped to clarify some of the questions related to sea level change. For many years, it was thought that the Pleistocene glaciation began about 1 million years ago and that sea-level changes related to it were a rather new phenomenon. It is now known that in Antartica glaciation is as much as 15 million years old, while the massive exchange of North and South American faunas began near 3 million years ago. Therefore, it appears that glacially induced eustatic sea level changes may well have exercised an effect on the timing of the final emergence of a land connection (Cronin *et al.*, 1981). Much of the evidence for Tertiary glaciation has come from study of samples taken in the DSDP, which revealed fluctuations in water temperatures in the oceans and the presence of ice-rafted debris. The deep seas have also yielded a more detailed record of Pleistocene climate than was available on land and have shown many more than the four glacial-interglacial episodes developed from classical Pleistocene stratigraphy on land.

While a detailed understanding of the chronology of Pleistocene and pre-Pleistocene glacial events is of great importance in the history of land connections and many other aspects of historical geology, much work remains to be done in perfecting it. Much of the difficulty presently experienced is the result of the disparate half-lives of the radioactive parents in the two most applicable geochronologic techniques. Radiocarbon (^{14}C) dating has revolutionized the chronology of the late Pleistocene but is limited by its short half-life to use with the interval younger than about 40,000 years (perhaps 60,000 or 70,000 years with the new mass-charge separation techniques). The K-Ar technique suffers from the long half-life of ^{40}K, which requires extreme precision of measurement if the method is to be applied to material younger than about 500,000 years. This gap is being steadily narrowed and may eventually disappear, but it is not yet gone.

For the earlier glacial cycles we still suffer from a lack of materials in deep-sea sediments to which the K-Ar technique can be reliably applied and from the rarity of undisturbed cores of sea-floor materials. The application of the K-Ar method to new material is continuing, and improved understanding of the conditions and crystal structures in which argon is retained is being gained. New deep-sea coring techniques have begun to yield essentially undisturbed cores up to 100 m long, which should allow the piecing together of a long and detailed history of glacial events. Studies of ^{18}O/^{16}O ratios in such well-dated and complete cores should provide a detailed record of the relative amplitude of glacial events. However, a record for the period around 3 million years ago is not yet available in sufficient detail, to allow us to assess the contribution of glacially controlled sea level fluctuations to our problem.

Sea-floor spreading with a concomitant heating and cooling of large volumes of rock beneath the sea, has the potential to change the volume of the ocean basins and so produce eustatic sea-level changes. A sea-level curve developed by Vail et al. (1977), based on a combination of stratigraphic information and assumptions about correlations with geophysical data, attempts to summarize relative sea-level stands through time. As yet, there seems to be neither general consensus as to the utility of this curve nor as to the total amplitude of sea-level fluctuations. Thus, while this line of inquiry is important in terms of episodes of communication or isolation between South America and neighboring continents, more work seems required before it can be applied with any rigor.

8. Change in Climates

Even if a land connection were to exist between the Americas, it is conceivable that inimical conditions along it or in the provenance regions at either end could force it to function as a filter bridge rather than as a corridor. Consideration of climate, therefore, is important both before and after establishment of a connection. Climatic data comes from a variety of sources, and the development of an integrated paleoclimatic model is in itself an exceedingly complex problem. Computer modeling of Cretaceous climates, such as is now in progress using the NCAR Global Climate Model, suggests what may ultimately become possible as more data and clearer understanding are achieved. The existence of clear evidence of mountain glaciation along the continental divide in Guatemala suggests that simply extending present-day conditions back in time will not suffice to allow a real understanding of the physical nature of the link between the two Americas or of its effect on biotic interchange.

The late Cenozoic record of land mammals in the Americas indicates that the isthmian corridor strongly favored reciprocal transmission of savanna-adapted forms during the late Pliocene and early Pleistocene (Webb, 1978). By the late Pleistocene, however, as in the recent, open-country taxa were excluded from the isthmian region, which was given over to tropical rainforest and transmitted mainly arboreal taxa. This pattern, which is a weak and indirect reflection of the regional ecology, appears to have a much longer duration than the glacial-interglacial cycle.

Much remains to be learned of climate across this critical isthmian link over the last 3 million years and before. Much remains also to be learned of the response of plants to such climatic conditions as may have prevailed and of their ability to support or deny access to various potential, herbivorous immigrants.

9. Time Perspective

The long and complex history featured in this volume requires the reader, as well as the authors, to pay particular attention to changing time perspectives. In earth history, more ancient time units are generally less finely divided and their records less completely recorded than are more recent intervals. A corollary observation is that evolutionary processes observed at a greater remove in time appear to occur more slowly than such processes observed more proximately. This effect has been extensively documented by Gingerich (1983), and he has concluded that evolutionary rates are inversely related to the time interval over which they are measured. Gingerich's Law must be factored into any comparisons between different paleontological intervals or with any biological studies that transcend the narrow time perspective of our brief sway.

A similar problem in paleoperspective is the perennial contest between gradualism and catastrophism. Do the processes of earth history and life history proceed in a smooth manner or do they follow an erratic path? In evolutionary studies must we abandon such stately metaphors as "time's arrow" and substitute saltations and random walks? Such questions are explored in diverse ways (e.g., Berggren and Van Couvering, 1984). In general, one senses a rising tide of neocatastrophism in geobiological perspectives. The improving systems of physical, chemical, and biological methods of measuring time in ancient environments will continue to provide relevant sets of real data with which the rates of earth and life history processes may be measured.

The present volume views geobiological transactions between the Americas in diverse perspectives. We believe that is a strength. We also believe that the diverse views presented by geologists and biologists working at various scales all strengthen one another.

Apparent contradictions in the conclusions derived from distinct methodologies will serve as valuable directions for further study; apparently different modes, rates, or directions of processes will either yield useful indications of different modalities or remind researchers that different scales yield different perspectives. There was only one true history of the Great American Biotic Interchange, yet no single discipline can fully reveal it. This volume may well raise more problems than it resolves, but we are proud of the diversity and energy it brings to the quest for that true history.

The time perspectives encompassed by the contributions to this book span at least six orders of magnitude. We have taken the time perspective as the most fundamental means of organizing views. This introductory section includes several views that seek to cover broad topics spanning the last 100 million years. Then, several chapters focus mainly on events that occurred during the transition from the Mesozoic to the Cenozoic about 60–100 million years ago. A third section emphasizes mid-Cenozoic events, roughly 30 million years ago. Events of the Great American Biotic Interchange itself, which took place during the last few million years of the late Cenozoic, make up the fourth section. Finally, a sampling of contributions from the Recent, with the richest perspective of all, constitutes the fifth and final section of this volume about interamerican history.

References

Berggren, W. A., and Van Couvering, J. A. (eds.), 1984, *Catastrophes and Earth History: The new Uniformitarianism*, Princeton University Press, Princeton.

Bonaparte, J. F., 1984, Nuevas pruebas de la conexión física entre Sudamérica y Norteamérica en el Cretácico tardio (Campaniano), Actas III Congr. Arg. Paleontol. y Bioestraet., 6–10 Sept., 1982, pp. 141–149.

Brown, J. H., and Gibson, A. C., 1983, *Biogeography*, C. V. Mosby, St. Louis.

Cadle, J. E., 1985, The Neotropical Colubrid snake fauna (Serpentes: Colubridae): Lineage components and biogeography, *Syst. Zool.* (in press).

Colbert, E. H., 1971, Tetrapods and continents, *Q. Rev. Biol.* **46:**250–269.

Cracraft, J., 1973, Continental drift, paleoclimatology, and the evolution and biogeographphy of birds, *J. Zool.* **169:**455–545.

Cronin, T. M., Szabo, B. J., Ager, T. A., Hazel, V. E., and Owens, J. P., 1981, Quaternary climates and sea levels of the U. S. Atlantic Coastal Plain, *Science* **211:**233–240.

Duellman, W. E. (ed.), 1979, *The South American Herpetofauna: Its Origin, Evolution and Dispersal, Mus. Nat. Hist. Univ. Kansas Lawrence Monogr.* **7:**1–485.

Gingerich, P. D., 1983, Rates of evolution: Effects of time and temporal scaling, *Science* **222:**159–161.

Haffer, J., 1974, Avian speciation in tropical South America with a systematic survey of the Toucans (Ramphastidae) and Jacomars (Galbulidae), *Publ. Nuttall Ornithol. Club* **14:**1–390.

Janzen, D. H. (ed.), 1983, *Costa Rican Natural History*, University of Chicago Press, Chicago.

Koopman, K., 1964, Review: "Evolution of Neotropical Cricetine Rodents" by P. Hershkovitz, *Am. Midl. Nat.* **71:**255–256.

Leigh, E. G., Rand, A. S., and Windsor, D. M., (eds.), 1982, *The ecology of a Tropical forest: Seasonal Rhythms and Long-Term Changes*, Smithsonian Institute Press, Washington, DC.

MacArthur, A. H., and Wilson, E. O., 1967, *The Theory of Island Biogeography*, Princeton Univ. Popul. Biol. Int. Monogr., 1–203. Princeton University Press, New Jersey.

Marshall, L. G., Webb, S. D., Sepkoski, J., Jr., and Raup, D. M., 1982, *Science* **215:**1351–1357.

Marshall, L. G., Muizon, C. de, and Sige, B., 1983, Late Cretaceous mammals (Marsupialia) from Bolivia, *Geobios* **16:**739–745.

Matthew, W. D., 1915, Climate and evolution, *Ann. NY Acad. Sci.* **24:**171–318.

McKenna, M. C., 1972, Possible biological consequences of plate tectonics, *Bioscience* **22:**519–525.

McKenna, M. C., 1973, Sweepstakes, filters, corridors, Noah's Arks, and beached viking funeral ships in palaeogeography, in: *Implications of Continental Drift to the Earth Sciences*, Volume 1 (D. H. Tarling and S. K. Runcorn, eds.), Academic Press, London, pp. 295–308.

McKenna, M. C., 1980, Early history and biogeography of South America's extinct land mammals, in: *Evolutionary Biology of the New World Monkeys and Continental Drift*, (R. L. Ciochon and A. B. Chiarelli, eds.), Plenum Press, New York, pp. 43–77.

Nelson, G., and Rosen, D. E. (ed.), 1981, *Vicariance Biogeography: A Critique*, Columbia University Press, New York.

Parodiz, J. J., 1969, The Tertiary non-marine Molluska of South America, *Ann. Carnegie Mus.* **40:**1–242.

Raven, P. H., and Axelrod, D. I., 1975, History of the flora and fauna of Latin America, *Am. Sci.* **63:**420–429.

Schuchert, C., 1935, *Historical Geology of the Antillean—Caribbean Region*, John Wiley and Sons, New York, 811 pp.

Simpson, G., 1940, Review of the mammal-bearing Tertiary of South America, *Proc. Am. Philos. Soc.* **83:**649–709.

Simpson, G., 1950, History of the fauna of Latin America, in: *Science in Progress*, 7th ser. (G. Baitsell, ed.), Yale University Press, New Haven.

Simpson, G., 1980, *Splendid Isolation: The Curious History of South American Mammals*, Yale University Press, New Haven, 266 pp.

Tedford, R., 1970, Principles and practices of mammalian geochronology in North America, in: *Proceedings of the North American Paleontological Convention* (E. Yoghelson, ed.), Allen Press, Lawrence, pp. 666–703.

Tedford, R., 1974, Marsupials and the new paleogeography, in: *Paleogeographic Provinces and Provinciality* (C. A. Ross, ed.), Society of Economic Paleontologists and Minerologists Special Publication No. 21, pp. 109–126.

Vail, P. R., Mitchum, R. M., Todd, R. G., Widmier, J. M., *et al.*, 1977, Seismic stratigraphy and global changes in sea level, in: *Stratigraphic Interpretation of Seismic Data*, (C. E. Payton, ed.), American Association of Petroleum Geologists Memoir No. 26, pp. 49–212.

Wallace, A. R., 1876, *The Geographic Distribution of Animals*, reprinted 1962, Hafner Publishing, New York, Vol. 1, 503 pp., Vol. 2, 607 pp.

Webb, S. D., 1978, A history of savanna vertebrates in the New World, Part II: South America and the great interchange, *Ann. Rev. Ecol. Syst.* **9**:393–426.

Woodburne, M. O., and Zinsmeister, W. J., 1984, The first land mammal from Antartica and its biogeographic implications, *J. Paleontol.* **58**(4):913–948.

3

Ecological and Evolutionary Perspectives on the Origins of Tropical Diversity

Douglas W. Schemske

How can we explain the extraordinary biological diversity of tropical regions? Few questions have generated such interest, yet we still struggle to find the answers. One of the greatest obstacles is that a single mechanism is unlikely to provide both a necessary and sufficient explanation. Most of the hypotheses put forth to explain tropical diversity are purely ecological and therefore do not identify the causal mechanisms responsible for diversity gradients. For example, energy is one of the best predictors of diversity (Currie 1991; Gaston 2000), yet the energy hypothesis fails to identify how or why new species originate in productive sites. As Currie (1991, 46) asked: "Why doesn't a small number of species monopolize the available energy?" Similarly, competition and predation may contribute to the maintenance of species, but it is unclear how such ecological mechanisms would influence speciation.

The distinction between ecological and evolutionary hypotheses put forth to explain tropical diversity is made clear by Rohde (1992, 516):

[T]here is evidence that, under certain conditions, increased competition, mutualism, predation and biotic spatial heterogeneity are associated with increased diversity. However, with regard to increased species richness in the tropics, the main problem is

not to demonstrate such an association but to answer the question of the origin of the greater numbers of competitors, predators, or organisms.

Thus, a complete explanation for the rich diversity of tropical regions must include evolutionary mechanisms. As stated by Dobzhansky (1950, 209): "Since the animals and plants which exist in the world are products of the evolutionary development of living matter, any differences between tropical and temperate organisms must be the outcome of differences in evolutionary patterns."

Here I review the major ideas concerning the origins of tropical diversity, with the goal of linking ecological and evolutionary perspectives. First, I discuss the papers reprinted in this part, illustrating their individual contributions and their relationship to a general theory of tropical diversity. I then provide a review of the evidence and explanations for latitudinal diversity gradients, a discussion of the mechanisms that may contribute to the origin and maintenance of diverse communities, and recommendations for future research directions.

The papers reprinted in this part span a period of nearly three decades. Dobzhansky's 1950 classic "Evolution in the tropics" provided the first modern empirical evidence of latitudinal

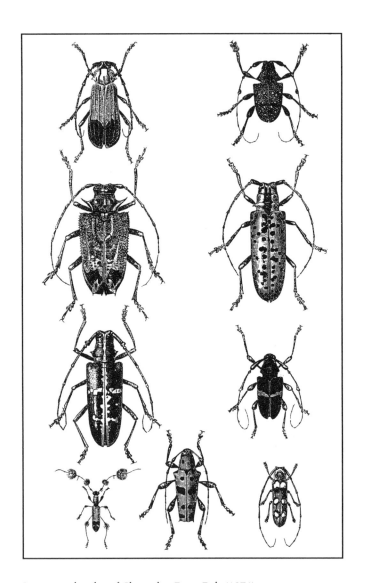

Longicorn beetles of Chontales. From Belt (1874)

diversity gradients, as well as the first evolutionary explanation for high tropical diversity (although Wallace [part 1] anticipated many of Dobzhansky's ideas). Dobzhansky suggested that organisms in temperate regions face a severe, variable climate, and that this results in the evolution of a few generalized species, able to cope with a wide range of abiotic challenges. In comparison, he proposed that tropical climates are relatively benign, and far more predictable. Thus natural selection in the tropics is governed more by biotic interactions, which results in the evolution of increased specialization and greater species diversity (see part 4 for further discussion of biotic interactions).

Fischer (1960) expanded Dobzhansky's evidence for latitudinal gradients in species diversity, including new support from marine systems. Although Fischer is widely cited as the source of the "time" hypothesis, which states that all communities will diversify with time (Brown and Lomolino 1998; Pianka 1966; Rohde 1992), this was only part of his explanation for high tropical diversity; he also proposed that the favorable climate in tropical regions facilitates biotic interactions, and that this will cause higher rates of diversification. While this view is similar to that of Dobzhansky (1950) in its emphasis on species interactions, Fischer seems to be the first to suggest that speciation in the tropics is faster than in temperate regions. Connell and Orias (1964) further develop the notion that the speciation rate could be higher in the tropics due to positive feedback mechanisms linking stability of the physical environment, increased productivity, larger population sizes, and greater opportunities for reproductive isolation and adaptive specialization.

Dobzhansky (1950) and Fischer (1960) each maintained that natural selection via strong biotic interactions was the major evolutionary mechanism in the tropics. Fedorov (1966) took quite the opposite view, suggesting instead that the low population densities of most tropical species would cause random genetic drift to prevail over natural election. Furthermore, he proposed that changes in just a few genes could result in dramatic differences in morphology

and presented this as an alternative to Corner's Durian theory for the evolution of tropical trees (Corner 1949, 1954). Fedorov's discussion of the genetic basis of species differences is still current today, as new genetic techniques are being used to address this fundamental problem (Schemske and Bradshaw 1999).

Pianka (1966) provided the first summary of explanations for latitudinal diversity gradients, recognizing six different hypotheses. This influential paper provided a template for studying the origins and maintenance of diversity in natural communities and thus contributed to the emerging field of community ecology. He brought clarity to a number of important issues in the debate, e.g., the need to identify the appropriate geographic scale for comparison of diversity patterns and the assumption of community equilibrium shared by most ecological hypotheses. Furthermore, he cautioned that finding a correlation between species richness and one or more ecological variables is not evidence of a causal relationship and called for the development of experimental approaches to the problem. The classic experimental work by Paine (1966) on the role of keystone predators in the maintenance of prey species diversity is a good example of the shift in emphasis that was taking place at this time.

Janzen (1967) explored the role of climatic variability in the evolution of physiological limits to species distributions. He predicted that the greater climatic stability of tropical regions should result in selection for narrow ecological tolerances. By contrast, organisms in temperate regions face drastic temporal variation in the physical environment, which results in the evolution of broad tolerances. He concluded that "barriers involving gradients in temperature or rainfall are more effective in preventing dispersal in the tropics" (Janzen 1967, 244), hence the title of the paper: "Why mountain passes are higher in the tropics." Although Janzen clearly stated that his paper was not intended as an explanation for tropical diversity, he provides a mechanistic explanation for Dobzhansky's suggestion that climatic uniformity in the tropics contributes to diversification. Moreover,

Janzen echoes Fischer's suggestion that diversity is positively reinforcing, when he suggests that "increased biotic fidelity leads to further biotic fidelity" (Janzen 1967, 245).

R. H. MacArthur was one of the main proponents of a geographical approach to the study of species diversity. MacArthur (1969) described the distinction between local and global diversity and used data on the geographic pattern of bird species to conclude that for samples of comparable area, tropical habitats are richer than temperate ones. He suggested that high diversity in the tropics is a consequence of the greater role for species interactions, illustrating the mechanism by way of analogy: "the tropical environment is not like a box that will hold only so many eggs; rather it is like a balloon which resists further invasion proportionally to its present contents but which can always hold a little bit more if necessary" (MacArthur 1969, 26). MacArthur (1969) also presented a verbal model to explain the lognormal distribution of Preston (1948), based upon the geometric properties of the niche. This is a simple yet elegant description of the relationship between the number of niche dimensions and population density that bears further investigation.

Connell (1978) challenged the conventional wisdom that communities such as tropical rain forests consist of highly specialized, coevolved assemblages that persist at an equilibrium state. Instead, he proposed that diverse communities rarely attain an equilibrium and that disturbances such as windstorms or floods create new habitats where competitively inferior species find refuge, thereby maintaining diversity. This nonequilibrium hypothesis stands in marked contrast to the views of Dobzhanksy (1950) and MacArthur (1969) that competition is the driving force in specialization and that tropical diversity results from successively finer partitioning of limited resources. Connell suggested that tropical trees have very general resource requirements, and that "it is highly unlikely that these can be partitioned finely enough to allow 100 or more species of trees to be packed, at equilibrium, on a single hectare" (Connell 1978, 1309). This view set the stage for an entirely new approach to the study of tropical diversity, with greater emphasis on the role of chance and disturbance and less emphasis on competitive interactions (Hubbell 1979). Predation and pest-herbivore pressure were also viewed by Gillett (1962); Janzen (1970), and Connell (1971) as important mechanisms for the evolution and maintenance of species diversity (see part 4).

For further reading on the subject of organismal diversity, there are a number of excellent contributions, including Huston (1979), Ricklefs and Schluter (1993), Rosenzweig (1995), Gaston (1996), and Leigh (1999).

Latitudinal Diversity Gradients

Patterns. Since the early explorations by Wallace (1878; see part 1), biologists have recognized that the species richness of many groups of plants and animals increases as one approaches equatorial regions. Dobzhansky (1950, 212) provided a vivid illustration of this from his own travels: "In the forested belt of western Siberia one may ride for hundreds of miles through birch forest interrupted only by some meadows and bogs. . . . By contrast tropical forests, even those growing on so perfect a plain as that stretching on either side of the Amazon, contain a multitude of species, often with no single species being clearly dominant." He concluded, "There can be no doubt that, for most groups of organisms, tropical environments support a greater diversity of species than do temperate- or cold-zone environments" (214). Subsequent studies support this view (Darlington 1959; Fischer 1960; Simpson 1964; Cook 1969; Kiester 1971; Stevens 1989; Kaufman and Willig 1998), as do recent reviews of the literature (Stevens 1989; Huston 1994; Rosenzweig 1995; Gaston 1996). Although the peak in species richness is not always located at the equator (Roy et al. 1998), and the pattern of diversity on a local scale is often disrupted by altitudinal and climatic factors (Gaston 2000), the latitudinal gradient in species richness is a fact (Rosenzweig 1995).

To gain some perspective on the scope of

latitudinal diversity gradients, consider forest trees and arthropods. These two groups of organisms process much of the energy in terrestrial communities in both temperate and tropical regions, and therefore should reflect communitywide diversity patterns. Leigh (1999, appendix 8.1) summarized data on the density and species composition of forest communities in a number of geographic regions. Tree diversity increases sharply as one moves toward the equator, with 32 species in the most diverse temperate locality, and 88, 108, and 307 species in tropical forests located in Mexico, Costa Rica, and Ecuador, respectively (for more on species diversity, see part 8). In Manu National Park (Peru), Pitman et al. (1999) found 825 tree species on a total of 21 forest plots comprising an area of approximately 36 hectares. By comparison, there are only 620 tree species in all of North America (Currie and Paquin 1987). Erwin (1982) estimated that the total arthropod diversity of the tropics is 27 million species, as compared with 3 million species in temperate regions (see the discussion of Erwin 1982 in part 6).

Studies of tree and arthropod diversity reveal that tropical habitats possess an order of magnitude more species than their temperate counterparts. This is consistent with the exponential increase in species richness observed in equatorial regions for bats, termites, coastal fishes, amphibians, and reptiles (but not quadrapedal mammals; Rosenzweig 1995, 25–28). To say the tropics are simply more diverse than temperate regions is therefore a gross understatement—they are remarkably so.

Ecological hypotheses. Some three decades after Pianka (1966) first listed the hypotheses proposed to explain latitudinal diversity gradients, tabulating the explanations for the pattern has become nearly as complicated as the problem itself. Palmer (1994) lists 120 plausible hypotheses, although he notes that these are not mutually exclusive. Rohde (1992) grouped related hypotheses together, giving a total of twenty-eight. Givnish (1999) listed nine hypotheses for latitudinal gradients in tree species

diversity, with seven proposed to explain the maintenance of high tropical diversity and two to explain its origin. Brown and Lomolino (1998, table 15.2) summarized the current literature, and identified six explanations for geographic patterns of species diversity. Their list has extensive overlap with that first presented by Pianka (1966), and includes: (1) productivity, (2) harshness, (3) climatic stability, (4) habitat heterogeneity, (5) interspecific interactions, and (6) historical perturbation. Considered as a whole, these mechanisms predict high diversity in productive habitats that have a benign, stable climate, a diverse physical environment, abundant biotic interactions, and long periods of time without major climatic or geologic disturbances.

Area has been proposed as a specific cause of tropical diversity, based on the observation that tropical habitats taken together comprise more area than other geographic regions (Terborgh 1973; Rosenzweig 1995; Rosenzweig and Sandlin 1997). However, temperate and tropical regions of comparable size differ in diversity (MacArthur 1969), and large high-latitude regions such as Eurasia have far fewer species than smaller tropical regions (Rohde 1997, 1998). Gaston (2000) observed that the area of ecoclimatic zones does not vary systematically with latitude, so the area hypothesis cannot be a general explanation for latitudinal diversity gradients.

Stevens (1989) suggested an explanation for latitudinal gradients in species richness based upon observations that species range size increases with latitude for some taxa, a pattern he termed Rapoport's rule. He proposed that organisms living at high latitudes face greater temporal variation in climate and that this results in selection favoring wide climatic tolerances. In contrast, tropical organisms encounter a much more limited range of environmental variation, and are therefore not expected to evolve the same degree of climatic tolerance as temperate species. As a result, Stevens (1989, 246) suggested that "individual organisms of high latitudes are less restricted in their habitat use; their distribution thus shows greater latitudinal extent than that of species in low latitudes." Furthermore, he suggested that the narrow tolerance of tropical species results in greater spatial heterogeneity in their population dynamics. The greater diversity of tropical regions is caused by the constant migration of species from their optimal habitats and into marginal ones, "prolonging the coexistence of species whose traits would otherwise lead to competitive exclusion" (Stevens 1989, 251). Stevens believed that migration coupled with narrow tolerances thus produces a community of higher diversity. The mechanism is similar to the rescue effect proposed by Brown and Kodric-Brown (1977), in which a high immigration rate for competitively inferior species prevents their extinction.

Although Stevens's hypothesis has stimulated much useful discussion and increased interest in patterns of range size, further work has failed to support the generality of Rapoport's rule and has cast doubt on the mechanisms that Stevens proposed (see Gaston, Blackburn, and Spicer 1998 and Rohde 1992).

Energy appears to be the single best predictor of species richness. Currie and his colleagues (Currie and Paquin 1987; Currie 1991) find that the species richness of trees, birds, mammals, amphibians, and reptiles is most highly correlated with either actual (trees) or potential (vertebrates) evapotranspiration. Each of these measures provides an estimate of productivity. Rohde (1992) and Gaston (2000) cite numerous similar findings for other groups, but caution that the relationship between diversity and energy is not always straightforward (see also Huston 1994; Rosenzweig 1995). Latham and Ricklefs (1993) found that energy, as measured by actual evapotranspiration, did not explain tree species richness in a model that included the effect of region (temperate vs. tropical), suggesting that other factors, e.g., history, may be more important (Ricklefs, Latham, and Qian 1999; see also part 2). Moreover, Tilman and Pacala (1993) report that within geographic regions, plant species diversity is highest in relatively unproductive habitats.

As suggested by MacArthur (1972, 183), "The knowledge that two habitats differ in their total productivity is not sufficient information to allow us to predict whether one will have more or fewer species." Srivastava and Lawton (1998) review four hypotheses proposed to explain the correlation between productivity and species diversity. Productive sites may have more species because: (1) there is increased opportunity for specialization, (2) populations can recover faster from disturbance, (3) addition of a higher trophic level reduces population sizes and competition, and (4) population density is higher, resulting in a lower risk of extinction. The last, sometimes called the more-individuals hypothesis, was first proposed by Wright (1983), and has received the most attention. Srivastava and Lawton (1998) found that it failed to explain the species richness of treehole insect communities, while Kaspari, O'Donnell, and Kercher (2000) found that it provided a good explanation for gradients in ant diversity. Contrary to the more-individuals hypothesis, plant density decreases with increasing productivity (Tilman and Pacala 1993), so the mechanism responsible for the observed correlation between productivity and species richness in plants (Currie and Paquin 1987) has not yet been identified.

Are tropical communities at an equilibrium species richness? As discussed previously, most ecological explanations for latitudinal diversity gradients assume that communities are at their equilibrium, i.e., they are saturated with species. For example, the area hypothesis of community diversity suggests that the number of species at equilibrium represents the point at which the rate of immigration of new species is balanced by the rate of loss from species extinctions (MacArthur and Wilson 1963). By this reasoning, perturbations away from the equilibrium are temporary and result in only a temporary a drop in species richness. Connell (1978) proposed instead that species richness is enhanced following perturbations that move communities away from their equilibrium. Specifically, he suggested that when disturbance is frequent or extreme, only colonizing species survive, while at low levels of disturbance, only the most competitive species survive. Diversity is highest at intermediate levels of disturbance, where the loss of species by competitive exclusion is matched by the production of newly disturbed sites for colonization. Although there is considerable evidence in support of the intermediate-disturbance hypothesis within geographic regions (Petraitis, Latham, and Niesenbaum 1989), it seems doubtful that it can explain the latitudinal diversity gradients observed in such a broad range of aquatic and terrestrial organisms (see part 8). To do so would require the existence of a consistent latitudinal pattern of disturbance independent of other ecological processes.

Evolutionary hypotheses. While literally thousands of papers have investigated the ecological processes that contribute to high tropical diversity, far less effort has been invested in addressing its origins. Dobzhansky (1950) looked to evolutionary biology for an explanation, asking: "How does life in tropical environments influence the evolutionary potentialities of the inhabitants?" (210). It is both surprising and disappointing that we have made so little progress on this question. Dobzhansky (1950), Fischer (1960), and Fedorov (1966) remain the primary sources of ideas.

Dobzhansky (1950) provided few specifics in support of his hypothesis that the greater importance of biotic interactions in the tropics was the cause of latitudinal diversity gradients. In contrast, Fischer (1960) posed a number of testable evolutionary hypotheses. For example, he proposed that speciation is affected by genetic variation and generation time, and concluded that neither of these features varies in a consistent manner with climate, so they cannot explain the latitudinal gradient in species richness. In addition, he suggested that the variety of edaphic and microclimatologic features is no greater in the tropics (but see Baker 1970), so edaphic specialization is not a distinct feature of tropical communities. He concluded that the tropics have had a longer history without major climatic disturbance than have temperate regions, so there has been more time for speciation, a view supported by Baker (1970) for plant communities. Fischer also proposed that, owing to species interactions, the curve of species richness through time "would rise somewhat faster in the tropics than in the temperate latitudes, and would rise slowest in the polar regions" (1960, 77). Furthermore, Fischer proposed that in the climatically stable tropics, specialized organisms provide new, adaptive opportunities for further biotic specialization and speciation, an evolutionary feedback mechanism in which diversity begets diversity. Connell and Orias (1964) later proposed that positive feedback mechanisms leading to ever-increasing diversity in the tropics are countered by negative feedback mechanisms resulting from overspecialization.

Fedorov's (1966) hypothesis that low population density increases the importance of genetic drift in the tropics has not been tested, nor has his hypothesis that many morphological differences between tropical species are due to the fixation of major genes by genetic drift. His proposed mechanism for nonadaptive speciation by genetic drift is circular, as it postulates high diversity as the cause of low density, not the other way around. His prediction that self-pollination prevails in tropical forest trees owing to their low density has been refuted by numerous studies that demonstrate that tropical trees are primarily outcrossing, even those at low density (Ashton 1969; Bawa 1974; Nason and Hamrick 1997; Nason, Herre, and Hamrick 1998). Moreover, many tree species, even in hyperdiverse lowland rain forests, do not occur at low density (Ashton 1969; Pitman et al. 1999; see also part 8).

Rohde (1992) proposed that latitudinal gradients in species richness are due to the greater "effective" evolutionary speed in the tropics, owing to shorter generation times, higher mutation rates, and the acceleration of selection caused by faster physiological processes at high temperatures. Evidence that these features are more important in the tropics is weak or nonexistent.

Null hypotheses. Colwell and Hurtt (1994) used null models with no assumptions about environmental gradients to generate latitudinal gradients in species richness produced by constraints on the placement of species ranges within geographic boundaries. The mid-domain effect is defined as "the increasing overlap of species ranges towards the centre of a shared geographic domain due to geometric boundary constraints in relation to the distribution of species' range sizes and midpoints" (Colwell and Lees 2000, 72). This effect results from constraints that species with small geographic ranges may have their midpoints near a geographic boundary, whereas species with broader geographic ranges must have range midpoints nearer the center of the domain. Thus, ranges are more likely to overlap near the center of the domain. Taylor and Gaines (1999) showed that a model based only on Rapoport's rule generates a latitudinal gradient of species richness with the highest diversity at the poles, opposite to the pattern observed. More complex models that include Rapoport's rule, the rescue effect, and competition produce the correct diversity gradient, but only under restrictive and perhaps unrealistic assumptions (Taylor and Gaines 1999).

Evolution of Tropical Diversity

Modes of speciation. Although the mechanisms of speciation have been debated for decades, the prevailing view is that geographic isolation is the first step toward speciation (Mayr 1963). This allopatric model proposes that populations evolve reproductive isolation as a result of ecological and genetic differences that accumulate during the period of geographic isolation. The alternative is that reproductive isolation evolves in partial or complete sympatry due to direct selection for ecological specialization and assortative mating. Based upon phylogenetic and geographic data for different groups of animals, Barraclough and Vogler (2000) show that sister taxa are allopatric at the earliest stage of divergence, a result consistent with the allopatric model of speciation.

Periodic climatic catastrophes such as a killing frost or an extended cold period are major selective agents in the temperate zone. Although the timing of these events may be somewhat unpredictable, in terms of the probability of their occurrence they are an inevitable. Selection in these predictably adverse conditions will therefore operate with considerable precision. The optimal phenotype for a given population in the temperate zone is best characterized as a fixed target, varying far more in time than in space. Even geographically isolated populations in temperate regions should experience qualitatively similar selective pressures, and will tend to evolve similar adaptations to cope with the climatic stress.

There is no evidence to suggest that temperate and tropical communities differ in mode of speciation (Mayr 1969; Ashton 1969). Gentry (1989) proposed that fine-scale habitat specialization in tropical plant populations gives rise to the parapatric distributions commonly observed in closely related species. He described this process as "essentially sympatric" speciation, yet geographic isolation is the critical first step even in this model of divergence. Although there are too few data to make a definitive conclusion at this point, it is clear that geographic isolation is often a critical phase in the speciation of temperate and tropical organisms. I therefore assume for the remainder of this discussion that allopatric speciation is the major mode of speciation.

The challenge is to determine how the selective forces experienced by organisms in tropical habitats might differ from those in temperate habitats, and how such differences might cause geographic variation in the opportunity for evolutionary diversification. We can then identify three steps in the evolution of tropical diversity: (1) the geographic isolation of populations, (2) divergence leading to the evolution of reproductive isolation in allopatry, and (3) coexistence in sympatry following the breakdown of geographic barriers. I will discuss each of these in turn, providing evidence where it is available, and suggestions for further research.

Geographic isolation. In a recent review of paleobotanical studies, Graham (1997) concludes that there were three major biogeographic regions in the Neotropics, each experiencing a somewhat different variety and magnitude of environmental changes (see also part 2). Fluctuating temperatures were of primary importance in the northern regions of Central America, while volcanism predominated in southern Central America, and fluctuating water levels caused by sea-level changes characterized the Amazon basin. Current evidence suggests that in the past two million years there have been eighteen to twenty major glacial advances, and many more smaller ones, and that the present environment of the Amazon basin has persisted for only the last twelve thousand years. The fluctuating water levels resulted in numerous, small refuges throughout the Amazon, and in the "alternating separation and convergence of populations" in Central America (Graham 1997, 146). Bush (1994) proposed that the high diversity and endemism in Amazonia was a consequence of population fragmentation that resulted from a variety of climatic factors. We can conclude that there has been considerable opportunity for the geographic isolation of tropical populations (see also Vrba et al. 1995). In addition, the environmental changes in the tropics are less severe than those in the temperate zone, so isolated tropical populations may face a lower risk of extinction (Fischer 1960). However, it is not clear whether the opportunity for geographic isolation is substantially greater in tropical than in temperate regions.

Mechanisms of divergence in allopatry. Dobzhansky (1950) and Corner (1949, 1954) were among the first to suggest that biotic interactions play a fundamental role in the evolution of tropical diversity. With the exception of Fedorov (1966), virtually everyone who has considered the problem of tropical diversity has concluded that natural selection due to biotic interactions plays a greater role in the evolution of tropical organisms than in that of their temperate counterparts. What then are the consequences of biotic interactions for speciation?

Populations in the tropics should experience a much wider variety of selective forces, owing to the greater importance of biotic interactions and to the stochasticity in community composition that follows geographic isolation (see part 4). Assuming that competition, predation, parasitism, and mutualism are more important in the tropics than in temperate environments, then it also follows that the composition of interacting species within isolated populations will have a greater effect on the form and magnitude of selection there. Consider the typical tropical tree species, which utilizes one or more animals to pollinate its flowers and to disperse its seeds, and which encounters a variety of insect herbivores and fungal pathogens at different stages in its life history. As its populations become geographically isolated, the composition of interacting species will differ among isolates as a result of stochastic processes. Once populations are isolated, demographic stochasticity within isolates contributes further to the spatial variation in the assemblage of interacting species. As a consequence of these two sources of stochasticity, the selective pressures experienced by each population will differ unpredictably, and each will evolve a somewhat different set of adaptations to its local biotic community. The optimum phenotype in tropical regions thus differs among populations and is analogous to a moving target, where each episode of geographic isolation results in a new set of biotic selective pressures. Thompson (1994) has also suggested that geographic variation in ecological interactions can contribute to speciation.

Thus, the rate and magnitude of population divergence during episodes of geographic isolation may be higher in tropical regions owing to the increased importance of stochastic, coevolutionary interactions (see part 5). We may also suspect that the magnitude of community stochasticity increases with diversity, such that diversification contributes to greater opportunities for further speciation. Assuming a finite environment, each new species added to a community harvests some of the resources used by other species; thus average species density will decline with diversity (MacArthur 1969; Tilman and Pacala 1993). Thus, where coevolutionary diversification is the primary mode of speciation, diversity becomes positively reinforcing. Fischer (1960), Connell and Orias (1964), and Ashton (1969) all proposed that biotic interactions under favorable conditions would cause a cascade of increasing diversity over time.

Differences proposed in the nature of selection in temperate and tropical regions leads to the prediction that the genetic basis of adaptations should also differ. Fisher (1930) proposed that adaptation is due to the fixation of many genes with small individual effects, based on the assumption that mutations with large effects move a population farther from, rather than closer to, its phenotypic optimum (Fisher 1930). This micromutationist view of "adaptive geometry" (Barton 1998) has had widespread support, but was challenged recently by Orr (1998), who suggested that mutations of large effect can often be beneficial during the early stages of adaptation as populations move toward their optimum phenotype. If adaptation in temperate regions is toward a fixed optimum, we should expect a higher frequency of adaptive traits controlled by mutations of small effect than in tropical regions, where stochastic coevolution ensures that populations are often some distance from their optimum phenotype. Although there is mounting evidence for a role of large-effect mutations in the evolution of adaptations (Orr 1998; Schemske and Bradshaw 1999), the data are insufficient at present to compare the genetic basis of adaptation in temperate and tropical systems.

Species coexistence. Speciation is complete when populations that were once geographically isolated maintain separate gene pools in sympatry. To explain the evolution of tropical diversity thus requires a mechanism to promote coexistence (MacArthur 1969; Stevens 1989). It is doubtful that the latitudinal gradient in species richness is due primarily to differences between temperate and tropical regions in the mechanisms of coexistence. The simplest theoretical explanation is that the prob-

ability of species coexistence in sympatry is proportional to the degree of ecological differentiation achieved during the period of geographic isolation (MacArthur and Levins 1967). The spatially variable composition of interacting species in isolated tropical populations should facilitate the evolution of divergent ecological adaptations, leading to a higher likelihood that populations will have evolved sufficient differences to permit coexistence. In comparison, the greater importance of predictable, large-scale climatic events in temperate regions should cause geographically isolated populations to follow similar adaptive trajectories, thus reducing the probability of coexistence in sympatry.

A number of environmental and demographic features may influence the limiting similarity required for coexistence (Abrams 1983; May and MacArthur 1972), so tropical and temperate regions may impose different thresholds for coexistence. The greater climatic stability of tropical regions suggests that tropical species could coexist with smaller ecological differences than temperate species, a view consistent with the suggestion that tropical organisms have narrower niches (Ashton 1969; MacArthur 1969). Biotic interactions in the tropics have been proposed as a cause of specialization (Dobzhansky 1950; Fischer 1960; Ashton 1969; MacArthur 1969), but the mechanisms are poorly understood. Biotic interactions may increase the number of niche dimensions. As an example, consider the pollination and seed dispersal characteristics of temperate and tropical trees (see part 4). The former are typically wind pollinated and often have wind-dispersed propagules, while the latter, with few exceptions, are both pollinated and dispersed by animals. These two additional dimensions to the niche of tropical species greatly increase the number of possible niches, and the degree of specialization. Following MacArthur (1969), the niche utilization of an organism can be estimated as the product of the proportional availabilities of resources for all niche axes. Assuming resource competition, the fraction of the community with suitable resources will decrease as the number of niche dimensions increases (MacArthur 1969).

Each additional niche axis results in a geometric increase in the number of possible niches, and this may result in greater niche specialization and higher species diversity (see part 7).

Nonequilibrium mechanisms may also contribute to species coexistence in tropical regions, as discussed earlier (Connell 1978; Hubbell 1979; Huston 1979). For example, periodic disturbance can reduce the likelihood of competitive exclusion, thereby effectively increasing the diversity of species with similar ecological niches. High pest pressure in tropical wet climates may also promote high plant diversity and coexistence of competitively equivalent species (Gillett 1962; Janzen 1970; Connell 1971; see part 4 for further discussion). The lower amplitude of climatic stresses in tropical environments may facilitate these nonequilibrium modes of species coexistence.

Conclusion

We still do not have an adequate explanation for the evolution of species-rich tropical communities. To address this problem will require new information from both temperate and tropical communities concerning: (1) the mechanisms of speciation, (2) the genetic basis of adaptation, and (3) the ecology of species coexistence. The recent revolution in molecular genetic techniques holds great promise for future studies in the tropics, particularly with respect to the development of species-level phylogenies that will aid our understanding of character evolution. These advances should finally allow empirical estimates of diversification rates, to address the question first posed by Fischer (1960): Is speciation faster in the tropics? Recent evidence from birds suggests that it is (Ricklefs, Latham, and Qian 1999), but more data are needed.

With the decline of tropical communities throughout the world, there is an urgent need to catalogue its diversity and to understand its origins. As Baker (1970, 110) suggested: "When we have a more complete picture of the evolution of organism diversity in the tropics, we shall be in a better position to conserve it." The first explorers (see part 1) described a tropical landscape different from any that remains today. We should leave no less to the explorers of tomorrow.

Reprinted Selections

T. Dobzhansky. 1950. Evolution in the tropics. *American Scientist* 38:209–221

A. G. Fischer. 1960. Latitudinal variation in organic diversity. *Evolution* 14:64–81

A. A. Fedorov. 1966. The structure of the tropical rain forest and speciation in the humid tropics. *Journal of Ecology* 54:1–11

E. R. Pianka. 1966. Latitudinal gradients in species diversity: A review of concepts. *American Naturalist* 100: 33–46

D. H. Janzen. 1967. Why mountain passes are higher in the tropics. *American Naturalist* 101:233–249

R. H. MacArthur. 1969. Patterns of communities in the tropics. *Biological Journal of the Linnean Society* 1:19–30

J. H. Connell. 1978. Diversity in tropical rain forests and coral reefs. *Science* 199:1302–1310

AMERICAN SCIENTIST

SPRING ISSUE APRIL 1950

EVOLUTION IN THE TROPICS

By THEODOSIUS DOBZHANSKY

Columbia University

BECOMING acquainted with tropical nature is, before all else, a great esthetic experience. Plants and animals of temperate lands seem to us somehow easy to live with, and this is not only because many of them are long familiar. Their style is for the most part subdued, delicate, often almost inhibited. Many of them are subtly beautiful; others are plain; few are flamboyant. In contrast, tropical life seems to have flung all restraints to the winds. It is exuberant, luxurious, flashy, often even gaudy, full of daring and abandon, but first and foremost enormously tense and powerful. Watching the curved, arched, contorted, spirally wound, and triumphantly vertical stems and trunks of trees and lianas in forests of Rio Negro and the Amazon, it often occurred to me that modern art has missed a most bountiful source of inspiration. The variety of lines and forms in tropical forests surely exceeds what all surrealists together have been able to dream of, and many of these lines and forms are endowed with dynamism and with biological meaningfulness that are lacking, so far as I am able to perceive, in the creations exhibited in museums of modern art.

Tropical rainforest impresses even a casual observer by the enormity of the mass of protoplasm arising from its soil. The foliage of the trees makes a green canopy high above the ground. Lianas, epiphytes, relatively scarce undergrowth of low trees and shrubs, and, finally, many fungi and algae form several layers of vegetational cover. Of course, tropical lands are not all overgrown with impenetrable forests and not all teeming with strange-looking beasts. One of the most perfect deserts in the world lies between the equator and the Tropic of Capricorn, in Peru and northern Chile. Large areas of the Amazon and Orinoco watersheds, both south and north of the equator, are savannas, some of them curiously akin to southern Arizona and Sonora in type of landscape. But regardless of the mass of living matter per unit area, tropical life is impressive in its endless variety and exuberance.

Since the animals and plants which exist in the world are products of the evolutionary development of living matter, any differences between tropical and temperate organisms must be the outcome of differences in evolutionary patterns. What causes have brought about

the greater richness and variety of the tropical faunas and floras, compared to faunas and floras of temperate and, especially, of cold lands?
How does life in tropical environments influence the evolutionary
potentialities of the inhabitants? Should the tropical zone be regarded
as an evolutionary cradle of new types of organization which sends
out migrants to colonize the extratropical world? Or do the tropics
serve as sanctuary for evolutionary old age where organisms that were
widespread in the geological past survive as relics? These and related
problems have never been approached from the standpoint of modern
conceptions of the mechanism of evolutionary process. Temperate
faunas and floras, and species domesticated by or associated with man,
have supplied, up to now, practically all the material for studies on
population genetics and genetical ecology.

Classical theories of evolution fall into two broad groups. Some
assume that evolutionary changes are autogenetic, i.e., directed somehow from within the organism. Others look for environmental agencies
that bring forth evolutionary changes. Although two eminent French
biologists, Cuénot and Vandel, have recently espoused autogenesis,
autogenetic theories have so far proved sterile as guides in scientific
inquiry. Ascribing arbitrary powers to imaginary forces with fancy
names like "perfecting urge," "combining ability," "telefinalism," etc.,
does not go beyond circular reasoning.

Environmentalist theories stem from Lamarck and from Darwin.
Lamarck and psycholamarckists saw in exertion to master the environment the principal source of change in animals. Induction of changes
in the body and the germ cells by direct action of physical agencies
is the basis of mechanolamarckism. The organism is molded by
external factors. A blend of psycholamarckist and mechanolamarckist
notions, the latter borrowed chiefly from Herbert Spencer, has been
offered by Lysenko as "progressive," "Michurinist," and "Marxist"
biology. Advances of genetics have made Lamarckist theories untenable.
There is not only no experimental verification of the basic assumptions
of Lamarckism, but the known facts about the mechanics of transmission of heredity make these assumptions, to say the least, far-fetched.

Important developments and many changes have taken place in
Darwinism since the publication of *The Origin of Species* in 1859. The
essentials of the modern view are that the mutation process furnishes
the raw materials of evolution; that the sexual process, of which Men-
delian segregation is a corollary, produces countless gene patterns; that
the possessors of some gene patterns have greater fitness than the possessors of other patterns, in available environments; that natural selection
increases the frequency of the superior, and fails to perpetuate the adaptively inferior, gene patterns; and that groups of gene combinations of
proved adaptive worth become segregated into closed genetic systems
called species.

The role of environment in evolution is more subtle than was realized
in the past. The organism does not suffer passively changes produced

Evolution in the Tropics   211

by external agents. In the production of mutations, environment acts as a trigger mechanism, but it is, of course, decisive in natural selection. However, natural selection does not "change" the organism; it merely provides the opportunity for the organism to react to changes in the environment by adaptive transformations. The reactions may or may

Fig. 1. Interior of equatorial rainforest near Belem, Brazil. The "terra firme" association. (Courtesy of Mr. Otto Penner, of the Instituto Agronomico do Norte, Belem do Pará.)

not occur, depending upon the availability of genetic materials supplied by the mutation and recombination processes.

Diversity of Species in the Tropics

Gause pointed out in 1934 that two or more species with similar ways of life can not coexist indefinitely in the same habitat, because one of them will inevitably prove more efficient than the others and will crowd out and eliminate its competitors. This "Gause principle" is a fruitful working hypothesis in studies on evolutionary patterns in tropical and temperate climates. The diversity of organisms which live in a given territory is a function of the variety of available habitats. The richer and more diversified the environment becomes, the greater should be the multiformity of the inhabitants. And vice versa: diversity of the inhabitants signifies that the environment is rich in adaptive opportunities.

Now, the greater diversity of living beings found in the tropical compared to the temperate and cold zones is the outstanding difference which strikes the observer. This is most apparent when tropical and temperate forests are compared. In temperate and cold countries, the forest which grows on a given type of terrain usually consists of masses of individuals of a few, or even of a single, species of tree, with only an admixture of some less common tree species and a limited assortment of shrubs and grasses in the undergrowth. The vernacular as well as the scientific designation of the temperate forest associations usually refers to these dominant species ("pine forest," "oak woodland," etc.). The forests of northern plains may, in fact, be monotonously uniform. In the forested belt of western Siberia one may ride for hundreds of miles through birch forests interrupted only by some meadows and bogs. Mountain forests are usually more diversified than those of the plains. Yet in the splendid forest of the Transition Zone of Sierra Nevada of California one rarely finds more than half a dozen tree species growing together. By contrast tropical forests, even those growing on so perfect a plain as that stretching on either side of the Amazon, contain a multitude of species, often with no single species being clearly dominant. Dr. G. Black, of the Instituto Agronomico do Norte in Belem, Brazil, made, in cooperation with Dr. Pavan and the writer, counts of individuals and species of trees 10 or more centimeters in diameter at chest height on one-hectare plots (100 × 100 meters) near Belem. On such a plot in a periodically inundated (igapó) forest 60 species were found among 564 trees. The numbers of species represented by various numbers of individuals on this plot were as follows:

Individuals	1	2	3	4	5	6	7	8	9
Species	22	9	7	2	2	2	4	2	1
Individuals	10	14	15	16	21	29	33	41	241
Species	1	1	1	1	1	1	1	1	1

The commonest species was the assaí palm (*Euterpe oleracea*), of

Evolution in the Tropics   213

which 241 individuals were found in the hectare plot, but as many as 22 species were represented by single individuals. On a plot of similar size, only a mile away but on higher ground (terra firma), 87 species were found among 423 trees. The numbers of individuals per species were as follows:

Individuals	1	2	3	4	5	6	7	9	12	17	20	25	37	49
Species	33	15	15	3	4	2	3	4	1	2	1	1	2	1

Here the commonest species was represented by only 49 individuals and as many as 33 species were found as single individuals. This high frequency of species represented by single individuals means that if

Fig. 2. The wet ground ("igapo") forest near Belem, Brazil. (Courtesy of Mr. Otto Penner, of the Instituto Agronomico do Norte, Belem do Pará.)

we had studied other hectare plots contiguous to the one actually examined, many new species would have been found. It is probable that each of the plant associations which we have sampled in the vicinity of Belem contains many more than 100 tree species, and, incidentally, only a few species occur in both associations. Similar results were obtained by Davis and Richards in the forests of British Guiana and by Beard in Trinidad.

The numbers of breeding species of birds recorded in the literature for territories in various latitudes, from arctic North America to equatorial Brazil, are as follows (data kindly supplied by Dr. E. Mayr):

Territory	Number of Species	Authority
Greenland	56	F. Salomonsen
Peninsular Labrador	81	H. S. Peters

214   *American Scientist*

Newfoundland	118	H. S. Peters
New York	195	K. C. Parkes
Florida	143	S. A. Grimes
Guatemala	469	L. Griscom
Panama	1100	L. Griscom
Colombia	1395	R. M. de Schauensee
Venezuela	1148	W. H. Phelps, Jr.
Lower Amazonia	738	L. Griscom

The numbers of recorded species of snakes are as follows (data obtained through the courtesy of Dr. C. M. Bogert):

Territory	*Number of Species*	*Authority*
Canada	22	Mills
United States	126	Steineger and Barbour
Mexico	293	Taylor and Smith
Brazil	210	Amaral

The progressive increase in diversity of species from the Arctic toward the equator is apparent in general, even though there are irregularities in this increase, resulting from such factors as how the different territories compare in size, how uniform or varied they are ecologically and topographically, and how intensively their faunas have been studied. There can be no doubt that, for most groups of organisms, tropical environments support a greater diversity of species than do temperate- or cold-zone environments.

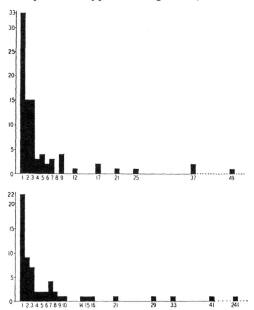

FIG. 3. Numbers of species of trees (ordinates) represented by different numbers of individuals (abscissae) on 1-hectare (100 × 100 meters) plots of equatorial rainforest near Belem, Brazil. "Terra firme" association (above) and "igapo" association (below). Only trees 10 or more cm. at chest height counted. (*Data of Black, Dobzhansky, and Pavan.*)

In order to survive and to leave progeny, every organism must be adapted to its physical and biotic environments. The former includes temperature, rainfall, soil, and other physical variables, while the latter is composed of all the organisms that live in the same neighborhood. A diversified biotic environment influences the evolutionary patterns of the inhabitants in several ways. The greater the diversity of inhabitants in a territory, the more adaptive opportunities exist in it. A tropical forest with its numerous tree species supports many species of insects, each feeding on a single or on several species of plants. On the other hand, the greater the number of competing species in a territory, the fewer become the habitats open for occupancy by each of these species. In the absence of competition a species tends to fill all the habitats that it can make use of; abundant opportunity favors adaptive versatility. When competing species are present, each of them is forced to withdraw to those habitats for which it is best adapted and in which it has a net advantage in survival. The presence of many competitors, in biological evolution as well as in human affairs, can be met most successfully by specialization. The diversity of habitats and the diversity of inhabitants which are so characteristic of tropical environments are conflicting forces, the interaction of which will determine the evolutionary fates of tropical organisms.

Chromosomal Polymorphism in Drosophila

Adaptive versatility is most easily attained by a species' becoming adaptively polymorphic, i.e., consisting of two or more types, each possessing high fitness in a certain range of environments. One of the most highly polymorphic species in existence is _Homo sapiens,_ and it is this diversity of human nature which has engendered cultural growth and has permitted man to draw his existence from all sorts of environments all over the world. Now, the adaptive polymorphism of the human species is conditioned, on the cultural level, chiefly by the ability to become trained and educated to perform different activities. In species other than man, adaptive polymorphism is attained chiefly through genetic diversification—formation of a group of genetically different types with different habitat preferences.

In _Drosophila_ flies, organisms best suited for this type of study, adaptive polymorphism takes its chief form in diversification of chromosome structure. In some American and European species of these flies, natural populations are mixtures of several interbreeding chromosome types which differ in so-called inverted sections. These chromosomal types have been shown, both observationally and experimentally, to have different environmental optima. The situation in tropical species has been studied in various bioclimatic regions in Brazil by a group consisting of Drs. A. Brito da Cunha, A. Dreyfus, C. Pavan, and E. N. Pereira of the University of São Paulo, A. G. L. Cavalcanti and C. Malogolowkin of the University of Rio de Janeiro, A. R. Cordeiro of the University of Rio Grande do Sul, M. Wedel of the University of Buenos Aires, H. Burla of the University of Zürich, N. P. Dobzhansky, and the writer. During the school year 1948-1949, the work of this group was supported by grants from the University of São Paulo, the Rockefeller Foundation, and the Carnegie Institution of Washington.

The commonest species in Brazil is _Drosophila willistoni._ It is also the adaptively most versatile species, since it has been found in every one of the 35 localities in various bioclimatic regions of Brazil in which collection was made. Significantly enough, this species, taken as a whole, shows not only the greatest chromosomal polymorphism among Brazilian species but the greatest so far known anywhere. The species *Drosophila nebulosa* and *Drosophila paulistorum* are also very common, but somewhat more specialized than *Drosophila willistoni*. *Drosophila nebulosa* is at its best in the savanna environments where dry seasons alternate with rainy ones, and *Drosophila paulistorum*, conversely, in superhumid tropical climates. The species are rich in chromosomal polymorphism, but not so rich as *Drosophila willistoni* in this respect. We have also examined some less common and biotically more specialized species, all of which showed much less or no chromosomal polymorphism.

The comparison of chromosomal polymorphism in *Drosophila willistoni* in different bioclimatic zones of Brazil proved to be even more interesting. The greatest diversity is found in those parts of the valleys of the Amazon and its tributaries where *Drosophila willistoni* is the dominant species. The exuberant rainforests and savannas of the Amazon basin are remarkable in the rich diversity of their floras and faunas; furthermore, the Amazon basin appears to be the geographical center of the distribution of the species under consideration, where it has captured the greatest variety of habitats. Yet, wherever in this region *Drosophila willistoni* surrenders its dominance to competing species, the chromosomal polymorphism is sharply reduced. This has been found to happen in the forested zone of the territory of Rio Branco, near Belem, in the state of Pará, and in the savanna of Marajó Island. In the first and the second of the regions named, *Drosophila paulistorum,* and in the third region, *Drosophila tropicalis,* reduce *Drosophila willistoni* to the status of a relatively rare species. In the peculiar desert-like region of northeastern Brazil, called "caatingas," *Drosophila willistoni* reaches its limit of environmental tolerance; *Drosophila nebulosa* seems to be the only species which still flourishes in this highly rigorous environment. The chromosomal variability of *Drosophila willistoni* is much reduced on the caatingas. It is also reduced in southern Brazil where *Drosophila willistoni* approaches the southern limit of its distribution, and is, presumably, losing its grip on the habitats.

Any organism which lives in a temperate or a cold climate is exposed at different periods of its life cycle or in different generations to sharply different environments. The evolutionary implications of nature's annually recurrent drama of life, death, and resurrection have not been sufficiently appreciated. In order to survive and reproduce, any species must be at least tolerably well adapted to every one of the environments which it regularly meets. No matter how favored a strain may be in summer, it will be eliminated if it is unable to survive winters, and vice versa. Faced with the need of being adapted to diverse environments, the organism may be unable to attain maximum efficiency in any one of them. Changeable environments put the highest premium on versatility rather than on perfection in adaptation.

Evolution in the Tropics 217

Adaptive Versatility in the Tropics

The widespread opinion that seasonal changes are absent in the tropics is a misapprehension. Seasonal variations in temperature and in duration and intensity of sunlight are, of course, smaller in the tropical than in the extratropical zones. However, the limiting factor for life in the tropics is often water rather than temperature. Some tropical climates, for example those of the caatingas of northeastern Brazil, have variations of such an intensity in the availability of water that plants and animals pass through yearly cycles of dry and wet environments which entail biotic changes probably no less serious than those brought about by the alternation of winter and summer in temperate lands. Absence of drastic seasonal changes in tropical environments is evidently a relative matter. In Belem, at the opening of the Amazon Valley to the Atlantic Ocean, the mean temperature of the warmest month, 26.2° C., is only 1.3° C. higher than that of the coolest month, and the highest temperature ever recorded, 35.1° C., is only 16.6° C. higher than the all-time low, which was 18.5° C. The wettest month has 458 mm. of precipitation, and the driest has 86 mm., which is still sufficient to prevent the vegetation from suffering from drought.

It might seem that the inhabitants of the relatively invariant tropical climates should be free from the necessity of being genetically adapted to a multitude of environments, and hence that evolution in the tropics would tend toward perfection and specialization, rather than to adaptive versatility. This is not the case, however. The climate of Espirito Santo Island, in the tropical Pacific, is seasonally one of the most constant in the world as far as temperature and humidity are concerned. Nevertheless, Baker and Harrison found that native plants have definite flowering and fruiting seasons, and animals have cycles of breeding activity in this climate. Our observations in Brazil show that populations of *Drosophila* flies undergo expansions or contractions from month to month, as well as changes in the relative abundance of different species. The magnitude and speed of these changes are quite comparable to those which occur in California, for example, or in the eastern part of the United States. Such pulsations have been observed even in the rainforests of Belem, about 1½° latitude south of the equator. They are caused mainly by seasonal variations in the availability of different kinds of fruits which are preferred by different species of *Drosophila*. Despite the apparent climatic uniformity, the biotic environment of tropical rainforests is by no means constant in time.

This writer observed several years ago that certain populations of the fly *Drosophila pseudoobscura* which live in the mountains of California undergo seasonal changes in the relative frequencies of chromosomal types. Dubinin and Sidorov found similar changes in the Russian *Drosophila funebris*. What happens is that some of the chromosomal types of these flies possess highest adaptive values in summer, and other types in winter or in spring environments. Natural selection augments the frequency of favorable types and reduces the frequency of unfavorable types. The populations thus ⸌react to changes in their environment by adaptive modifications. This is one of the rare occasions when evolutionary changes taking place in nature under the

FIG. 4. Giant trees and lianas in the "terra firme" rainforest near Belem. (Courtesy of Mr. Otto Penner, of the Instituto Agronomico do Norte, Belem do Pará.)

influence of natural selection can actually be observed in the process of happening. We may add that some of these changes have also been

Evolution in the Tropics   219

reproduced in laboratory experiments in which artificial populations of the species concerned were kept in special "population cages."

We have observed populations of *Drosophila willistoni* in three localities in southern Brazil for approximately one year. One of the localities, situated in the coastal rainforests south of São Paulo, has a rather uniform superhumid tropical climate. Periodic sampling of these populations has disclosed alterations in the incidence of chromosomal types similar in character to those observed in California and in Russian fly species. Adaptive alterations which keep living species attuned to their changing environments occur in tropical as well as in temperate-zone organisms. This constant evolutionary turmoil, so to speak, precludes evolutionary stagnation and rigidity of the adaptive structure of tropical and of temperate species equally.

It is nevertheless true that tropical environments are more constant than temperate ones, in a geological sense. Major portions of the present temperate and cold zones of the globe underwent drastic climatic and biotic changes owing to the Pleistocene glaciation. The present floras and faunas of the territories that were covered by Pleistocene ice are composed almost entirely of newcomers. The territories adjacent to the glaciated areas have passed through more or less radical climatic upheavals. Although the bioclimatic history of the tropical continents is still very little known, it is fair to say that their environments suffered less change.

The repeated expansions and contractions of the continental ice sheets, and the alternation of arid and pluvial climates in broad belts of land bordering on the ice, made large territories rather suddenly (in the geological sense) available for occupation by species that could evolve the necessary adaptations in the shortest possible time. This has not simply increased the rates of evolution, but often has favored types of changes which can be characterized collectively as evolutionary opportunisms. Such changes have the effect of conferring on the organism a temporary adaptive advantage at the price of loss or limitation of evolutionary plasticity for further change. Here belong the various forms of deterioration of sexuality observed in so many species of temperate- and cold-zone floras. An apomictic or an asexual species, with an unbalanced chromosome number and a heterosis preserved by loss of normal meiotic behavior of the chromosomes, may be highly successsful for a time but its evolutionary possibilities in the future are more limited than those of sexual and cross-fertilizing relatives. Polyploidy is also a form of evolutionary opportunism in so far as it produces at least a temporary loss of genetic variability. Although some plant species native in the tropics have also become stranded in these evolutionary blind alleys, the incidence of such species is higher in and near the regions which were glaciated.

Evolutionary Importance of Biotic Environment

The contradictory epithets of "El Dorado" and "Green Hell," so often used in descriptions of tropical lands, really epitomize the two aspects of tropical environments. The process of adaptation for life in temperate and especially in cold zones consists, for man as well as for other organisms, primarily in coping with the physical environment and in securing food. Not so in the tropics. Here little protection against winter cold and inclement weather is needed. In the rainforests, the amount of moisture is sufficient at any time to prevent the inhabitants from suffering from desiccation. Relatively little effort is necessary for man to secure food, and it seems that the amount of food is less often a limiting factor for the growth of populations of tropical animals than it is in the extratropical zones. But the biological environment in the tropics is likely to be harsh and exacting. Man must beware that his blood does not become infected with malarial plasmodia, his intestines with hookworms, and his skin with a variety of parasites always ready to pounce on him and rob him of his vitality if not of life itself. The tremendous intensity of the competition for space among plants in tropical forests can be felt even by a casual observer. The apparent scarcity, concealment, and shyness of most tropical animals attest to the same fact of extremely keen competition among the inhabitants.

Now, the processes of natural selection which arise from encounters between living things and physical forces in their environment are different from those which stem from competition within a complex community of organisms. The struggle for existence in habitats in which harsh physical conditions are the limiting factors is likely to have a rather passive character as far as the organism is concerned. Physical factors, such as excessive cold or drought, often destroy great masses of living beings, the destruction being largely fortuitous with respect to the individual traits of the victims and the survivors, except for traits directly involved in resistance to the particular factors. As pointed out by Schmalhausen, indiscriminate destruction is countered chiefly by development of increased fertility and acceleration of development and reproduction, and does not lead to important evolutionary advances. Physically harsh environments, such as arctic tundras or high alpine zones of mountain ranges, are inhabited by few species of organisms. The success of these species in colonizing such environments is due simply to the ability to withstand low temperatures or to develop and reproduce during the short growing season.

Where physical conditions are easy, interrelationships between competing and symbiotic species become the paramount adaptive problem. The fact that physically mild environments are as a rule inhabited by many species makes these interrelationships very complex. This is probably the case in most tropical communities. The effectiveness of natural selection is by no means proportional to the severity of the struggle for existence, as has so often been implied, especially by some early Darwinists. On the contrary, selection is most effective when, instead of more or less random destruction of masses of organisms, the survival and elimination acquire a differential character. Individuals that survive and reproduce are mostly those that possess combinations of

Evolution in the Tropics   221

traits which make them attuned to the manifold reciprocal dependences in the organic community. Natural selection becomes a creative process which may lead to emergence of new modes of life and of more advanced types of organization.

The role of environment in evolution may best be described by stating that the environment provides "challenges" to which the organisms "respond" by adaptive changes. The words "challenge" and "response" are borrowed from Arnold Toynbee's analysis of human cultural evolution, although not necessarily with the philosophical implications given to the terms by this author. Tropical environments provide more evolutionary challenges than do the environments of temperate and cold lands. Furthermore, the challenges of the latter arise largely from physical agencies, to which organisms respond by relatively simple physiological modifications and, often, by escaping into evolutionary blind alleys. The challenges of tropical environments stem chiefly from the intricate mutual relationships among the inhabitants. These challenges require creative responses, analogous to inventions on the human level. Such creative responses constitute progressive evolution.

REFERENCES

1. ANONYMOUS. Normais Climatologicas. Serviço da Meteorologia, Ministerio da Agricultura. Rio de Janeiro, 1941.
2. BAKER, J. R. The seasons in a tropical forest. Part 7. *Jour. Linn. Soc. London 41*, 248-258, 1947.
3. BEARD, J. S. The natural vegetation of Trinidad. *Oxford Forestry Mem. 20*, 1-155, 1946.
4. BLACK, G. A., DOBZHANSKY, TH., and PAVAN, C. Some attempts to estimate the species diversity and population density of trees in Brazilian forests. *Bot. Gaz.*, 1950. (In press.)
5. DA CUNHA, A. B., BURLA, H., and DOBZHANSKY, TH. Adaptive chromosomal polymorphism in *Drosophila willistoni. Evolution*, 1950. (In press.)
6. DAVIS, T. A. V., and RICHARDS, P. W. The vegetation of Moraballi Creek, British Guiana. *J. Ecol. 22*, 106-155, 1934.
7. DOBZHANSKY, TH. Observations and experiments on natural selection in *Drosophila. Proc. 8 Internat. Cong. Genetics, Hereditas Suppl.*, 210-224, 1949.
8. DOBZHANSKY, TH., and PAVAN, C. Local and seasonal variations in relative frequencies of species of *Drosophila* in Brazil. *Jour. Animal. Ecol.*, 1950. (In press.)
9. DUBININ, N. P., and TINIAKOV, G. G. Inversion gradients and natural selection in ecological races of *Drosophila funebris. Genetics 31*, 537-545, 1946.
10. GAUSE, G. F. The struggle for existence. Baltimore, 1934.
11. LACK, D. Darwin's finches. Cambridge, 1947.
12. PATTERSON, J. T. The Drosophilidae of the Southwest. *Univ. Texas Publ. 4313*, 7-216, 1943.
13. SCHMALHAUSEN, I. I. Factors of evolution. Philadelphia, 1949.
14. STEBBINS, G. L. Variation and evolution in plants, New York, 1950. (In press.)
15. TOYNBEE, A. J. A study of history. New York and London, 1947.
16. VANDEL, A. L'homme et l'évolution. Paris, 1949.
17. VAVILOV, N. I. Studies on the origin of cultivated plants. Leningrad, 1926.

LATITUDINAL VARIATIONS IN ORGANIC DIVERSITY

ALFRED G. FISCHER

Princeton University, Princeton, N. J.

Received July 1, 1959

"Animal life is, on the whole, far more abundant and varied within the tropics than in any other part of the globe, and a great number of peculiar groups are found there which never extend into temperate regions. Endless eccentricities of form and extreme richness of color are its most prominent features, and these are manifested in the highest degree in those equatorial lands where the vegetation acquires its greatest beauty and its fullest development." Thus wrote A. R. Wallace (1878). His remarks apply equally to the vegetable and animal kingdoms, to the terrestrial realm and to at least the surficial parts of the oceans. Surely this correlation of floral and faunal diversity with latitude is one of the most imposing biogeographic features on earth. On the one hand, its existence poses large-scale problems in evolution. On the other, it offers a potential tool to the geologist-paleontologist who attempts to wring patterns of earth history out of the fossil record.

The following pages serve to review some previously known latitudinal gradients in organic diversity, to describe quantitatively gradients in molluscan diversity along North American shores, and to inquire into the origin of these patterns.

SOME EXAMPLES OF DIVERSITY GRADIENTS

Terrestrial gradients

The overwhelming variety of trees in tropical rain forests has impressed northern travellers, from the early navigators on, and offers a striking contrast to the solid stands of timber to be found in the austral and boreal regions. This floral diversity gradient is widely recognized by botanists.

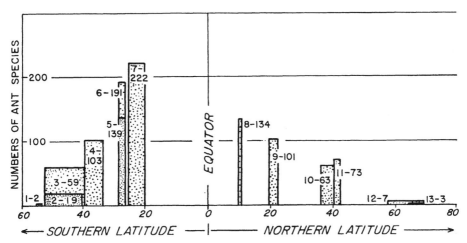

FIG. 1. Northern and southern diversity gradients in ants. 1—Tierra del Fuego; 2—Patagonia, humid western side; 3—Patagonia, as a whole; 4—Buenos Aires, Argentina; 5—Tucuman, Arg.; 6—Missiones, Arg.; 7—Sao Paulo, Brazil; 8—Trinidad; 9—Cuba; 10—Utah, USA; 11—Iowa, USA; 12—Alaska as a whole; 13—Alaska, arctic part. After Kusnezov (1957).

EVOLUTION 14: 64–81. March, 1960

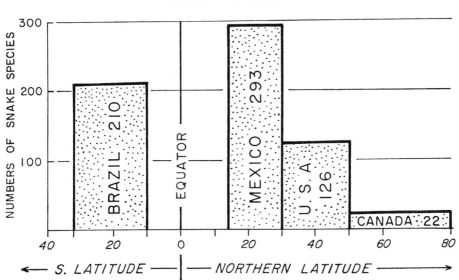

Fɪɢ. 2. Diversity gradient in American snakes. After Dobzhansky (1950, credited to Bogert).

Kusnezov (1957) compared ant diversity in areas of different latitudes, and his findings for the Americas are summarized in figure 1. In a stimulating paper dealing with the general problem of tropical diversity, Dobzhansky (1950) published figures on diversity gradients in American snakes (fig. 2) and birds (fig. 3). Distribution of snake species within Argentina follows a striking di-

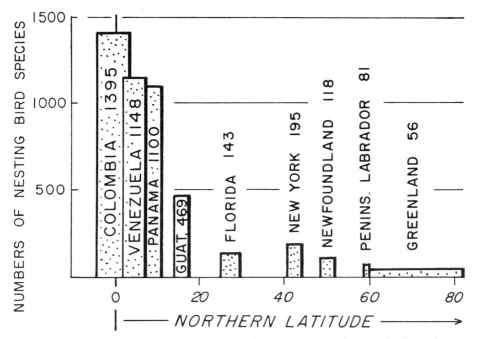

Fɪɢ. 3. Diversity gradient in nesting birds, from equator to Greenland. Data from Dobzhansky (1950, credited to Mayr).

66   ALFRED G. FISCHER

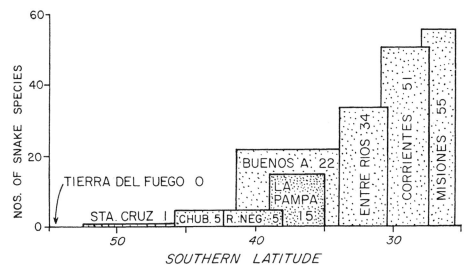

FIG. 4.   Diversity gradient shown by numbers of snake species reported from the various provinces of Argentina.   Data from Série (1936).

versity gradient described by Série (1936) (fig. 4). Bourlière (1957) shows comparisons of animal diversity between France and Barro Colorado Island in Panama.

Darlington (1957) does not deal with this problem as such, but points out repeatedly that amphibians, reptiles, birds and mammals are more diversified in the tropics than in higher latitudes; while the abundant figures provided by him are not readily plotted in diversity gradients, they illustrate the general principle.

Marine gradients

Any beachcomber who strays from northern shores into the tropics is im-

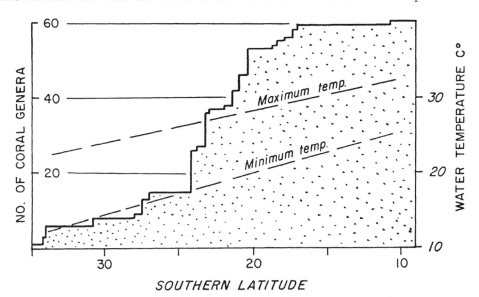

FIG. 5.   Diversity gradient of coral genera along great Barrier Reef of Australia, after Wells (1956).

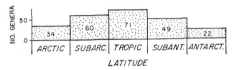

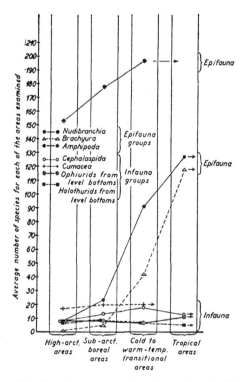

Fig. 6. Specific and generic diversity gradients in tunicates. After Hartmeyer (1909).

pressed with the greater variety of shells cast up on the shores there. Among general text and reference books the phenomenon has been noted, among others, in Hesse (1924) and Hesse, Allee, and Schmidt (1937). as well as by Thorson (1957).

Few if any groups of animals illustrate the principle more vividly than do the corals, with their bewildering variety of reef-building types in suitable tropical habitats, contrasted with a handful of solitary or at best bank-forming species in cold waters. Wells (1956) has studied the distribution of coral genera along the Great Barrier Reef of Australia, and his findings are summarized in figure 5. Some 60 genera of corals coexist in the northern part of this great reef belt, around lat. 9° S. and from this maximum the number dwindles to a single genus at the south end (35° S).

Hartmeyer (1919) illustrated similar diversity gradients in tunicates (fig. 6). Thorson (1952, 1957) shows similar gradients for amphipods, nudibranchs, and crabs (fig. 7), and Brodskij (1959) has illustrated the same principle in pelagic calanid crustaceans of the surficial water masses (fig. 8).

On the other hand. Thorson has shown that such gradients are not universal. As shown in figure 7, they are not exhibited by such burrowing groups as soft-bottom ophiuroids, holothuroids, cephalaspids and cumacids. These groups show little diversity anywhere. This difference between epifaunal or pelagic and infaunal

animals is particularly well shown by Thorson's comparison of prosobranch gastropods (fig. 9). Taking prosobranchs as a whole, and comparing areas of equal size, tropical faunas show approximately five times as many prosobranch species as do arctic ones. Throughout this range, the great majority of prosobranchs is epifaunal. However, the prosobranch family Naticidae is largely restricted to infaunal soft-bottom dwellers. and the naticids show only slightly more diversity in the tropics than in high latitudes.

Some groups of organisms are more diverse in the temperate latitudes than in the tropics. This appears to be true for certain groups of algae. No actual figures on diversity are available to me, but from Tilden (1937) one would gather that

Fig. 7. Average number of species of different groups of bottom invertebrates from equal-sized coastal areas in different latitudes. Only depths from the shore to 300 m have been regarded, and all pelagic and parasitic species have been neglected. From Thorson (1952 and 1957).

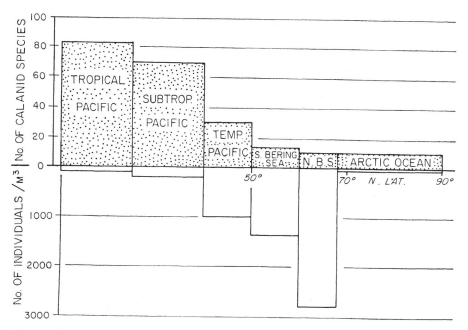

FIG. 8. Diversity gradient in calanids (pelagic crustacea) from the upper 50 meters. Abundance of individuals per cubic meter (lower graph) shows a strikingly divergent pattern. After Brodskij (1959).

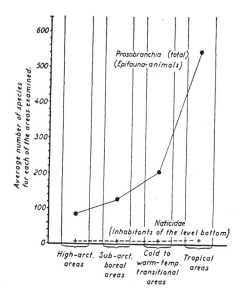

FIG. 9. Average number of prosobranch species from equally large coastal areas in different latitudes. Whereas the prosobranchs as a whole, a mainly epifaunal group, show a striking diversity gradient, the family Naticidae, mainly infaunal, does not. From Thorson (1952 and 1957).

whereas the green and the bluegreen algae are most diversely developed in the tropics, the red algae and kelps reach their acmes in the temperate zones.

Surely many similar examples of distribution, showing no correlation of diversity and latitude, or even "reversed" gradients from high diversity in temperate latitudes to little diversity in the tropics, could be found in various branches of the plant and animal kingdoms. They appear to be, however, no more than exceptions which prove the rule.

THE RELATION OF GRADIENTS TO CLIMATE

Within the tropical belt, similar gradients mark the passage from hot lowlands into cold and variable mountain areas, from the humid rainforest into deserts, from the warm shallow waters into the frigid ocean depths, and from normal warm-water areas into belts of cold upwelling. It is evident that diversity gradients are related to gradients in environmental factors—temperature, humidity, etc., whether developed on a regional or on a local scale.

On land we speak of the combinations of such physical factors as *weather,* and of the long-period weather patterns as *climate.* These concepts apply equally well to the underwater world, where there are both uniform and seasonal climates, and where, like on land, weather fluctuations may be gradual or catastrophic. Temperatures change, the place of winds is taken by waves and currents, and instead of moisture fluctuations there are changes in salinity (with rather similar physiologic effects). Suspended particles take the place of cloud cover in limiting penetration of solar energy, and excessive sedimentation replaces dust storms and ash falls. We may therefore extend the familiar terms to the world of water, and may speak of *atmospheric weather and climate* on the one hand, and *hydrospheric weather and climate* on the other. Hedgpeth (1957) speaks of *hydrographic* climate in this sense, but to me the adjective *hydrospheric* seems more apt and more consistent.

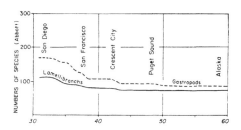

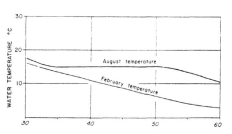

FIG. 11. Comparison of molluscan diversity and marine climate along west coast of Canada and United States. Data from Abbott (1954) and Sverdrup *et al.* (1942).

From a regional standpoint, temperature is the main factor in the climatic control of marine plant and animal distribution. This matter has been considered by Hutchins (1947) and is reviewed by Hedgpeth (1957b). The individuals which compose a population or a species can exist only within certain temperature limits; and within this viability range, there lies a further restricted temperature range outside of which reproduction is impossible.

The diversity gradients which have been observed lend themselves to the following generalization or rule:

The diversity of biotas, on land and in the sea, is greatest in climates of relatively high and constant temperatures, such as those found over much of the tropics, and decreases progressively into the fluctuating and the cold climates normally associated with the higher latitudes.

MOLLUSCAN FAUNAS ALONG THE COASTS OF NORTH AMERICA

Climatic gradients. The east and west coasts of North America show distinct climatic gradients in respect to tempera-

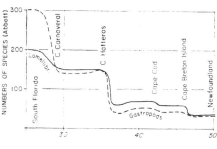

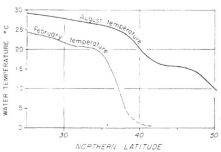

FIG. 10. Comparison of molluscan diversity and marine climate along east coast of Canada and United States. Data from Abbott (1954) and Sverdrup *et al.* (1942).

ture, as illustrated in figures 10–11. Along the east coast this gradient is a very sharp one, for here the climatic differences to be expected as an expression of latitude are reinforced by oceanic circulation, which brings tropical waters northward to Cape Hatteras and arctic waters south to Cape Cod. On the West Coast, the opposite situation prevails; here the gradient is a very gentle one, for the circulation modifies the gradient to be expected from latitudinal differences: the northern part of the coastline is warmed by the Alaska current, while the southern shores are cooled by the upwelling California current.

Data desirable. A study relating the diversity patterns of marine organisms to climatic gradients such as these should ideally be based on data which include:

(1) reasonably detailed and evenly distributed systematic treatment of the chosen group along the entire belt studied, so that monographic highs resulting from patchy collecting or overzealous taxonomic splitting are avoided.

(2) restriction to shallow waters, so as to exclude the deeper forms which are under the influence of climates somewhat different from those expressed by the surface isotherms.

(3) accurate data on the geographic ranges of the species or genera chosen as the units of study.

Data used. The full measure of such information probably is not available for any group of organisms along the North American shoreline; yet, for many groups existing data are probably sufficient for a rough approximation which serves to delineate the basic pattern.

Abbott's *American Seashells* (1954) offers a source for such a compilation on mollusks. This magnificent volume, primarily a guide to shallow-water shells, deals with some 1,500 of the more than 6,000 species of mollusks described to date from North American waters. It provides range data. In emphasizing the shallow-water forms, it largely avoids species belonging to deep-water climates. In excluding the rare forms, it avoids the pit-

falls of poorly known ranges and monographic highs. The intense activity of shell collectors in Florida has perhaps introduced some bias, but probably not enough to distort the pattern seriously. Though many ranges given extend on into the Caribbean Island arc and into Mexican waters, Abbott's selection in these outlying regions may not be as representative of the actual fauna as it is off the U. S. and Canadian coasts, and therefore the compilations here made do not extend beyond the tip of Florida and the Coronado Islands. All in all, Abbott's selection within these limits appears to be an adequate index to molluscan diversity, and therefore worth the effort of compilation and presentation.

Results. Figures 10–15 show the diversity gradients in mollusks along the East and West Coast of North America, as compiled from Abbott. Snails and clams are considered separately. Among the snails, the naked forms, pelagic species and pyramidellids were not included. No

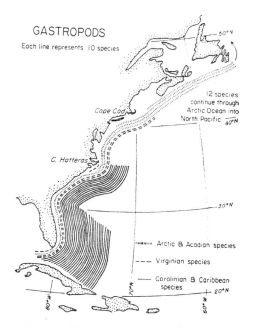

FIG. 12. Diversity gradient of gastropods along eastern coast of United States and Canada. Each line stands for ten species. Data from Abbott (1954).

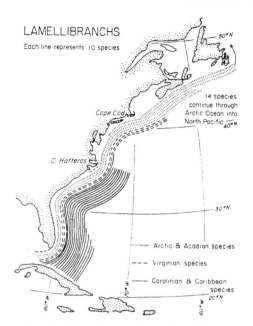

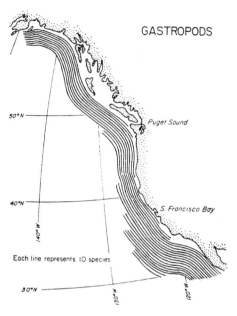

FIG. 13. Diversity gradient of lamellibranchs along eastern coast of United States and Canada. Each line stands for ten species. Data from Abbott (1954).

FIG. 14. Diversity gradient in gastropods along west coast of Canada and United States. Each line stands for ten species. Data from Abbott (1954).

compilations were made for the Amphineura, Scaphopoda and Cephalopoda.

The patterns found lend themselves to the following generalizations:

(1) Each case conforms to the rule of correlation between biotic diversity and climate.

(2) The gastropods (mainly epifaunal) illustrate this rule better than the lamellibranchs (which include large numbers of burrowers).

(3) There appears to be no particularly close correlation of the numbers of species with the pattern of seasonal high (August) temperatures, nor with that of seasonally low (February) temperatures, nor with a mean between these: All of these may have some effect, and in addition, the amount of seasonal variation appears to be important, for both graphs show a marked rise in the number of species associated with a convergence of August and February temperatures. No doubt other climatic factors not plotted are of importance; regions strongly influenced

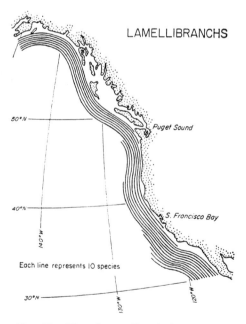

FIG. 15. Diversity gradient in lamellibranchs along west coast of Canada and United States. Each line stands for ten species. Data from Abbott (1954).

72   ALFRED G. FISCHER

by currents are particularly subject to annual or occasional temperature changes of great magnitude and short duration, which would not find expression on normal isotherm maps, and which must have a catastrophic effect upon marine life (see below).

Origin of Diversity Gradients

Biogeographic patterns are the results of two closely interwoven processes: the evolution of organisms, and the evolution of their habitats. Both of these are time-rate problems: Organisms, climates, and the landscape itself are ceaselessly fluctuating, and the extent to which the status quo is altered depends (1) on the direction in which they change, (2) the rate at which they change, and (3) the time-span under consideration.

A model of biotic evolution

Let us consider the change of a fauna by means of a simple model, figure 16. A given fauna, F-1, occupies a certain area at a certain time. It contains 15 species (if you prefer, 150, or 1,500). Some millions of years later the same area is occupied by fauna F-2, numbering 20 species 6 of which are in common with F-1. Figure 16 shows graphically how the change has taken place: Of the original 15 species, 4 were exterminated without having left descendants; 6 survived unchanged; 12 are newly evolved species, of which we may arbitrarily consider 5 to be direct lineal descendants of a similar

number of species in F-1, and 7 to be "side-branches"; and 2 immigrated from other regions. It is evident that the difference between F-1 and F-2 depends (1) on the rates at which species are evolved, exterminated, and immigrated, and (2) on the duration of the timespan between F-1 and F-2.

Using this model, we may now inquire into the factors which bring about the addition and subtraction of species, and the ways in which these changes may be influenced by climate. In this inquiry, we shall neglect the immigration factor, to concentrate on (1) *speciation*, the addition of species to a biota by evolutionary processes, and (2) *extinction*.

Speciation

Addition of new species (other than immigrants) to a biota is dependent on two factors: (a) the evolutionary potential of existing species, as determined by mutation rates and other factors to be reviewed below, and (b) the rate at which mutants will be selected—something which might be termed environmental receptivity.

Evolutionary potential

The evolutionary potential of any one species would seem to depend on two factors: its genetic variability, and the length of its generations.

Genetic variability involves a number of more or less distinct qualities. One of these is the mutation rate, which may be defined as the ratio of mutant to normal

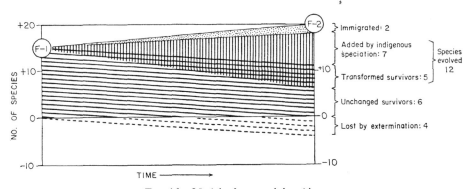

Fig. 16. Model of an evolving biota.

offspring. One might expect this to be related to the complexity of the genetic mechanism—surely the more elaborate the system, the greater the chances for mishaps, alterations and modifications within it—i.e., the greater the chance for mutations. Another is the extent to which mutations are retained and perpetuated within the population gene pool; this factor, also, may be dependent largely upon the complexity of the genetic system. Population size is a third factor: Just as the corner grocery store lacks variety as compared with a supermarket, so very small populations lack genetic variety (and therefore evolutionary potential) as compared with larger ones.

None of these factors appear to bear any relation to climate, and we may therefore incline to discount them as sources of diversity gradients related to climate.

A special aspect of population size, worth a short digression, is the number of offspring produced. Offhand one might think that an organism capable of producing some millions of young per year (such as the oyster) would enjoy a considerable advantage in evolutionary potential over the much less prolific cephalopods, or over certain mammals reproducing at less than one millionth that rate. But this apparent advantage is largely spurious: the production of vast numbers of progeny in oysters is the price paid by a benthonic animal for a defenseless pelagic larval stage, during which the vast majority of the offspring are destroyed in a nonselective fashion. This subject has been discussed by Thorson (1952), who has shown that at the height of the oyster breeding season a single medium-sized *Mytilus* will strain 100,000 oyster larvae in a period of 24 hours. Only a minute fraction of the oyster offspring ever reaches the stage which mutations or gene combinations for a modified filter system or circulatory system can be tested.

Generation length is another factor in evolutionary potential, since the generation is the unit link in the history of any life strain, and new mutants and new gene combinations arise from one to the next. Simpson (1953, pp. 129–132) admits this, but on empirical evidence concludes that the genetic evolutionary potential of organisms is but rarely approached by actual evolutionary sequences. He contrasts the slow evolution of short-generation opossums with the rapid evolution of long-generation elephants, but admits that shortness of generation may be a factor in the rapid evolution of pathogenic bacteria. The development of DDT resistance in certain insects may be another example of rapid evolution facilitated by shortness of generations.

The question which here concerns us is the problem of variations in generation-length with environment: obviously, if species in general mature more rapidly in the tropics than in the higher latitudes, then tropical generations will succeed each other more rapidly; and this might then endow tropical organisms with a somewhat greater evolutionary potential. But observations on maturation rates and generation length show that there is no simple relation between these factors and environment (or latitude). On the one hand, the metabolism of some species seems to vary directly with temperature: Bourlière (1957) points out that the butterfly *Danaus chrysippus* matures in one year in North America and in 23 days in the Philippines, and the beetle *Crioceris asperagi* matures in Germany in one year, whereas *C. subpolita* matures in Java in 25–31 days. Thorson (1952) has reviewed this subject for marine organisms. Some observations on *Ostrea, Mytilus,* and *Balanus* show amazingly high maturation rates in the tropics. *Hydroides norvegica* becomes sexually mature 9 days after attachment in Madras, 4 months after attachment in England.

On the other hand, many species and genera appear to be "temperature-adapted," i.e. their tropical representatives and their cold-water forms live at the same rates, and show no significant variation in maturation rate and generation length. Thorson lists observations to this effect on *Littorina,* decapod crustacea, and echinoids. Furthermore, contrary to widespread opinion, many tropical plants and animals do not reproduce continuously, but have definite breeding periods. Bünning (1956) has pointed out that these may be very long—the sexual reproductive cycle of bamboos, for example, is measured in decades. Nor are the tropical mammals characterized by unusually rapid succession of generations. At this stage, then, it appears that *evolutionary advantage of tropical over high-latitude organisms due to different generation length is at best a minor factor.*

Environmental receptivity

Ecologic niches. A given physical environment provides a variety of possible ways for organisms to make a living, and the organisms themselves greatly multiply the number of these *ecologic niches,* in which properly adapted species can prosper and procreate.

Some workers believe that the main cause for differences in diversity lies in the number of ecological niches available. Thus Bourlière (1957), in writing about animals, states: "It is, however, in the abundance and variety of suitable habitats that one must seek the principle cause of richness of tropical faunas. The environments in which they live is in fact infinitely more diverse than that of temperate latitudes, and many of the habitats of the warm regions have no counterpart in other parts of the world."

The development of major physiographic characters — mountain ranges, alluvial plains etc.—occurs in temperate as well as in tropical regions; certainly there is in the tropics no more diversity of landforms than in other parts of the earth. The related edaphic and microclimatologic features show, if anything, a greater variety within temperate landscapes than within tropical ones: a case in point is the great variety of soil types in the north-temperate regions. Another is the uniform distribution of solar energy in the tropics in contrast to its directional character in the

higher latitudes: in the tropics the sun alternately shines from the north and south, as anyone there who tries to grow plants on the "sunny" or the "shady" side of the house will find out in the course of the year. Hence, the striking vegetation contrasts between the north and south flanks of hills, which we tend to take for granted, are not to be found in lower latitudes. Even the change in seasons increases the number of physical niches.

Among the various ecological features of the tropics, it is the organic ones which provide such a rich range of habitats, as discussed by Bünning (1956). Bourlière, in illustrating the richness of tropical environments, cites the variety of animal habitats provided by that most complex of all plant associations, the tropical rainforest. But this accounts neither for the astonishing diversity of tropical plant life, nor for the marine animal diversity gradients which are not associated with such highly organized plant communities.

Differences in selection. Since Darwin's time, the process of selection, resulting from the struggle for survival, has been considered to be one of the main springs of the evolutionary process. And, since biotic diversity is the result of evolution, we may well ask whether differences in the manner of natural selection may partly account for biotas of different diversity.

Schmalhausen (1949) and Dobzhansky, (1950) among others, believe that this is the case.

The size to which a given population may grow depends on its rate of reproduction, and on the pattern according to which individuals are killed off (I use the term pattern rather than rate, for the rate may vary from one stage of life history to another). The nature of the survivors will determine the course of evolution. Two things are therefore of great importance: (1) the selectivity (as opposed to randomness) of killing (or, survival); (2) the direction or directions in which variation is encouraged and accepted by the environment.

Selective factors may be divided arbitrarily into two groups: organic and in-organic. Both operate everywhere. At all places, some organisms die because of inclement weather; and others die because of lack of food, or because they are eaten by others, or because they fall prey to disease. But the relative balance between these two sets of factors varies from place to place.

Darwin, Schmalhausen (1949) and Dobzhansky (1950) all call attention to one aspect of this matter: In the high latitudes, one is struck by the havoc wrought among organisms by the physical environment: the changing seasons, and the thereon superimposed catastrophes of weather take a large toll. And, as these investigators have pointed out, the selection accomplished by winter storms, summer droughts etc. is rather crude: mainly such disasters result in random killing of large numbers of individuals. To be sure, organic selective factors are also at work here, since individuals compete with each other, prey and are preyed upon, and succumb to parasites and diseases. And these factors appear to be more selective, in that they involve intense individual competition, and put a premium on individual excellence. But the point is that *much of the killing in high latitudes is done by the less selective inorganic forces.*

In the tropics, on the other hand, the physical environment is more benign to most organisms, and the highly selective interorganic struggle for existence is more apparent. The struggle of plants for light in the rain forest, and the shyness of tropical mammals are dramatic expressions thereof. Dobzhansky believes that this difference may be an important factor in the differential evolution of high-latitude versus tropical biotas.

But the matter is really somewhat more involved than this. The extensive random killing in the high latitudes is largely offset by higher rates of reproduction (Schmalhausen, 1949). And the competition between organisms in the tropics is so apparent because of such a large number of species present. As in the case of the ecologic niches, we are in danger of circular reasoning: is the diversity of tropical biotas due to more intense competition, or is the more intense competition an outcome of the more diverse biota?

One thing appears fairly clear, although it seems not to have been emphasized: In a biota lacking diversity, a great deal of the competition is between members of the same species. This effect is intensified if these species produce vast numbers of progeny, as many of the high-latitude plants and animals do. *In the high latitudes, organic selection results to a great extent from competition of an individual with other members of his species; in the tropics, it tends to be much more a competition of one individual against the members of other species.* This difference must have some effects on the patterns of evolution; to some extent it is a result rather than a cause of differences in diversity, but in part it is linked to the numbers of offspring, and may therefore have had some effect in the differentiation of high-latitude and tropical faunas and floras.

There is, however, a much more direct difference in selection: the tropical temperatures (continental and shallow-water) are nearer the mid-point of the temperature range which protoplasm can endure than are the high-latitude temperatures. Furthermore, the tropical temperatures show less seasonal variation (as has already been mentioned). As a result, tropical conditions permit a wider range of physiologic and structural variation than do high-latitude conditions, which seasonally approach the lower limits at which life can be maintained, and at other times may range into temperatures comparable to those of the tropics. Thus *the tropical environment is receptive to wider latitudes of physiologic variation— to a wider range of mutations—than is the temperate and polar environment.* And this, it seems to me, may be one of the most important factors in the equation which has produced the biogeographic pattern under discussion.

Extinction

In our model (fig. 16) the diversity of F-2 is determined not only by the rate at which species are added, but also by the rate at which they have disappeared. They vanished in two ways: by evolving into new species, and by becoming exterminated. In a way these two modes of disappearance are more alike than their separation on the model would suggest, inasmuch as the transformation of one species into another (a into b) involves the preferred killing-off of individuals of type a. For practical purposes here we may, however, restrict our attention to the outright eradication of species without descendants.

The question is: how does extinction vary with climate; and do old species survive more readily in the tropics than in the higher latitudes?

Extinction of a species can be a sudden process, as demonstrated by the passenger pigeon. On the other hand extinction of a species or a larger taxon can be a very gradual kind of process. This may involve the gradual restriction of members to a smaller and smaller area, where the form may persist (and may be very prominent) for some time as a relict. Or it may come about by the gradual thinning of population density throughout its range, until the spacing between individuals interferes with reproduction.

The mixed and diffuse population patterns of the tropical rainforest and the low density of given species populations suggest that in the tropics extinction may come about chiefly as a result of this gradual dilution. The patchy population patterns and the prevalence of relict population in the higher latitudes suggest that here the relict pattern dominates. In the former case continued organic competition is likely to strike the final blow: relict patches, on the other hand, are particularly vulnerable to the accidents of weather mentioned before. Which extinction mechanism is the more efficient, and what role, if any, such differences have played in the

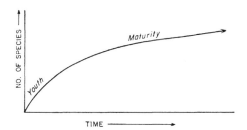

FIG. 17.   The curve of biotic maturity.

development of diversity gradients, under conditions of constant climate, remains to be seen.

The time factor and biotic maturity

So far we have considered only relative rates of speciation and extinction as related to climate. We have not and shall not here deal with absolute rates. Neither have we considered (1) relative changes in rates through time, and (2) the evolution of habitats through time.

The maturity model

Again, let us refer to a model, figure 17, simple at the expense of being somewhat remote from reality. We assume a given physical setting without organic inhabitants, and then introduce a limited number of immigrants to start a biota. Most of us would surely agree that in this kind of a setting the availability of many unfilled ecologic niches would lead to a rapid evolution of species and a corresponding diversification of the biota: the diversity curve rises in a steep gradient. To some degree this is a self-generating process: as plants evolve in a first approximation to fill all of the available physical niches, they provide the basis for a first wave of animal evolution. Secondary refinement will lead to the evolution of many species more closely adapted to specific subniches, and these will largely replace their more generalized ancestors; and so the process may go on, almost *ad infinitum.* From the simple dependence of plant on soil, air, sunlight and water, and of animals on plants, there will arise commensalism and symbiosis of plant-with-plant, animal-with-plant, animal-with-animal, and even 3-way relationships. At this level of complexity we reach the stage shown by tropical coral reefs and rain forests. By now the curve of diversity increase has probably flattened out, as the rate of extinction of old species approaches the rate at which new ones are evolved, but I see no reason why the rise could not continue even beyond the richest biotas existing today.

We may speak of the different parts of this curve as youthful and mature, and accordingly of *degree of biotic maturity*.

From what has gone before, we may conclude that such a curve would rise somewhat faster in the tropics than in the temperate latitudes, and would rise slowest in the polar regions (fig. 18). Yet, the basic patterns should remain the same: evolution within each may be expected to lead from simple biotas to more and more diversified ones, as a result of increasingly specialized adaptation and of more elaborate interrelations with other organisms.

We now face two possibilities: either the biotas of the major climatic belts we have discussed have been evolving for the same length of time, and the differences in their diversity are simply a result of different rates of diversification (slope of the maturity curve) as shown in figure 18. Or the time factor itself is involved as well: some biotas have attained higher diversification (maturity) because they have been evolving steadily over greater periods of time; others are truly immature,

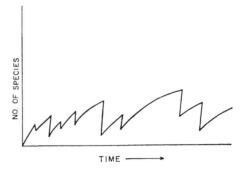

FIG. 19. History of organic diversity in an area subjected to climatic fluctuations during geologic time.

having originated much later or having been set back by periodic decimations (fig. 19). So long as we know so little of the quantitative aspects of evolution, the biotic patterns alone are not likely to give us a definitive answer to this question.

Climates through geologic time

If there is any one theme which runs through the geological record, it is that of ceaseless change.

Given a spheroidal globe, rotating on an inclined axis and circling the sun in a certain orbit, we may be sure that the solar energy received in the equatorial regions was always markedly greater than that received at the poles, and that the reception of this energy at the equator varied but little through the year, whereas it was subjected to seasonal variations in the polar areas. But beyond these basic invariables there lies a host of variable factors. Some of these are known to have operated, others are at the present stage of knowledge no more than possibilities and probabilities.

The variation is in the rate and pattern of redistribution of this energy. The rising of air in the tropical belt, its descent at the horse latitudes and in the polar regions, and the turbulent mixing in between greatly affect weather and climate —as does to a lesser extent the circulation of water in the oceans. Both are to a very large extent governed by the distribution of land and sea. This distribution is less

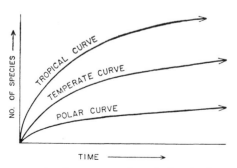

FIG. 18. Comparison of tropical and other maturity curves.

important in the tropical belt, which has probably always extended over a mixture of land and sea in which the sea was dominant, than it is in the small polar regions, which have at times been dominantly continental, at others dominantly marine.

Land areas have their surface layer heated quickly to comparatively high temperatures by incident sunlight. Downward conduction of heat is slow, but loss to the atmosphere is rapid, and thus little of the energy becomes stored. As a result we experience the extremes of "continental climates." In water covered areas, the solar energy is only partly absorbed at the surface, and heats deeper layers as well. Partly because of this, partly because of the much greater specific heat of water, and partly because of convection, the water mass stores the solar energy at lower temperatures and in a form which is gradually released to the atmosphere. As a result we speak of the ameliorating climatic effects of water bodies. In oceanic areas water circulation itself introduces an additional ameliorating factor, which tends to keep the circum-polar oceans warmer in winter than the circum-polar landmasses.

Four polar models. To visualize possible climatic extremes we may consider four situations; (1) a pole in the midst of an oceanic area; (2) a pole in the midst of a large continental area; (3) a pole in a limited continental area surrounded by seas (the present South Pole); and (4) a pole in a sea surrounded by continental areas (the present North Pole).

In the first model, the polar regions would be of moderate temperature in summer and in winter, maintained during the latter from the vast thermal reservoir of the oceans. A polar climate with extensive ice, such as we know today, would not exist. Neither would there be the giant struggle of the polar and the equatorial air masses, which stamps the present "temperate" region with their catastrophic character. Instead, the temperate regions around this polar ocean area might show climates like those of

present-day New Zealand, Tasmania, and coastal Alaska.

Model 2 would provide the opposite extreme. The polar landmass would be subject to extensive heating in the summer and to extremely frigid winter weather. Great polar air masses would make extensive inroads into the subtropical fringe during the winter. The "temperate" areas would thus be even less temperate than those we know. Ice sheets might accumulate in the central area, but the summer heat and lack of moisture would make widespread glaciation improbable.

Models 3 and 4 are available for study. In model 3, the polar landmass is utterly frigid, but the surrounding oceanic belt (famous for its violent storms) takes the brunt of the atmospheric mixing, and beyond them lies a truly temperate zone, protected from the catastrophic inroads of polar air masses.

In model 4, the polar ocean helps to ameliorate the climatic extremes of the polar area and adjacent regions, but provides a source of moisture which encourages the development of glaciers, and may thus cause a widespread development of what we normally think of as polar conditions. The history of the northern hemisphere during the last million years bears witness to this.

The history of the polar regions. Present polar and near-polar continental areas have in the past been widely covered by seas, just as have other continental regions. The existence of these seas is recorded in the form of marine sedimentary rocks. Thus we need no further proof that extensive changes of land and sea have taken place in the polar regions, and that profound climatic effects must have been felt in the polar and temperate regions.

But, beyond this, different lines of evidence suggest strongly that the poles and the earth's crust have shifted with respect to each other. The fossil record shows biotic patterns difficult to reconcile with the present geographic grid: for example, the lower Paleozoic faunas of South

America are very limited in variety (immature?), while exceedingly rich faunas and coral reefs thrived from central North America to the Arctic and to Scandinavia. The patterns of ancient glaciations, while still far from well understood, are also difficult to reconcile with the present pole positions. Remanent magnetism in sediments and lava flows offers a possible clue to pole positions of the past, and work to date suggests extensive polar shifting.

Such polar wandering might have come about either by shifting of the earth's crust over the underlying "mantle." or by displacement of the globe as a whole relative to its axis of rotation, or by extensive displacements of oceans and continents relative to each other and to the earth's axis. The work on remanent magnetism and the current discoveries of extensive wrench faulting in the earth's crust offer support for such theories.

Conclusions. It is concluded from this that widespread climatic changes have been a normal feature of earth evolution. The broad tropical belt, with its mixture of lands and seas, has probably been the most constant feature of the earth, although its position may have shifted. Polar climates of the present type have probably existed at some times and not at others. The temperate zones have undergone severe changes involving great expansions and contractions (as during the Pleistocene), changes from truly temperate to rigorous and subject to seasonal catastrophes, and possibly extensive shifting over the globe.

From these considerations it appears probable that the tropical marine and continental biotas of today are the products of a long and relatively undisturbed evolutionary history, and are truly mature, while the polar and temperate biotas have experienced a turbulent history of mass extinctions and gradual re-evolution. At times they have been more mature than at present. The great Tertiary mammalian faunas of North America, and the rich marine fauna of the East Coast Miocene, may be examples of comparatively mature

faunas adjusted to a truly temperate climate in the temperate zone. They were decimated by the more rigorous and catastrophic climates which may have had their beginnings in the Pliocene and reached their climax in the Pleistocene glacial stages. Our present North American temperate biotas probably represent a mixture of polar types and the most hardy survivors of the pre-Pleistocene temperate biotas, undergoing rapid evolution in a comparatively immature stage of the curve (fig. 17). This evolutionary surge is not likely to be carried very far: So long as the North Pole remains in the Arctic Ocean, a kind of self-induced oscillation involving freezing and thawing of the arctic seas, waxing and waning of ice caps, and rise and fall of sea level (Ewing and Donn 1956, 1958) may continue to bring alternate glacial advances and retreats, and may effectively prevent the northern temperate biotas from becoming mature.

Local diversity gradients

We may now return to glance at the local climatic diversity gradients, only mentioned above. The tropical rain forest and the warm tropical sea are normal and enduring features of the tropical belt. Mountain ranges, rainshadow deserts and areas of cold upwelling are geologically transient phenomena; their biotas are either lately evolved in place, or have been subjected to drastic migrations in the not-too-distant geologic past. They are therefore immature as compared to the normal tropical biotas.

GENERAL CONCLUSIONS

The diversity of biotas, on land and in the sea, is greatest in climates of relatively high and constant temperatures, such as those found over much of the tropics, and decreases progressively into the fluctuating and the cold climates associated with the higher latitudes. It is proposed that this pattern results largely from the following causes:

80   ALFRED G. FISCHER

(1) Biotas in the warm, humid tropics are likely to evolve and diversify more rapidly than those in the higher latitudes, mainly because of a more constant (favorable) normal environment, and relative freedom from climatic disasters.

(2) Biotic diversity is a product of evolution, and is therefore dependent upon the length of time through which a given biota has developed in an uninterrupted fashion. The low-level tropics represent that part of the globe which has been least affected by climatic fluctuations. Such factors as marine transgressions and regressions in the polar regions, possible polar wandering, and oscillations of glacial polar conditions have caused extensive fluctuations in polar and "temperate" climates, and have thereby profoundly disturbed the normal course of evolutionary diversification. The tropical coral reef and rainforest biotas are considered as examples of mature biotic evolution, whereas the biotas of the regions covered by Pleistocene ice sheets are prime examples of "immature" relicts of the more mature temperate Tertiary faunas and floras. We thus return to A. R. Wallace's words (1878): "The equatorial zone, in short, exhibits to us the result of a comparatively continuous and unchecked development of organic forms; while in the temperate regions there have been a series of periodical checks and extinctions of a more or less disastrous nature, necessitating the commencement of the work of development in certain lines over and over again. In the one, evolution has had a fair chance; in the other, it has had countless difficulties thrown in its way. The equatorial regions are then, as regards their past and present life history, a more ancient world than that represented by the temperate zones, a world in which the laws which have governed the progressive development of life have operated with comparatively little check for countless ages, and have resulted in those wonderful eccentricities of structure, of function, and of instinct—that rich variety of colour, and that nicely balanced harmony of relations

which delight and astonish us in the animal productions of all tropical countries."

ACKNOWLEDGEMENTS

This paper grew out of a discussion with Professor Erling Dorf, who wished for material to illustrate latitudinal diversity gradients in his classes. To him, to Professors G. L. Jepsen, F. B. Van Houten and C. S. Pittendrigh, and to Mr. W. Zimmerman I am indebted for stimulating discussions, and for help with the literature and manuscript.

LITERATURE CITED

ABBOTT, P. T. 1954. American Seashells. Van Nostrand, New York, xiv + 541 pp.

AUBERT DE LA RÜE, E., F. BOURLIÈRE AND J. P. HARROY. 1957. The Tropics. Knopf, New York, 208 pp.

BOURLIÈRE, F. 1957. See AUBERT DE LA RÜE et al.

BRODSKIJ, A. K. 1959. Leben in der Tiefe des Polarbeckens. Naturwissenschaftliche Rundschau, **12**: 52–56.

BÜNNING, E. 1956. Der tropische Regenwald. Verständliche Wissenschaft, vol. 56. Springer, Berlin-Göttingen-Heidelberg, 118 pp.

DARLINGTON, P. J. 1957. Zoogeography. John Wiley & Sons, New York, 675 pp.

DOBZHANSKY, T. 1950. Evolution in the tropics. Amer. Scientist, **38**: 208–221.

EWING, M., AND W. L. DONN. 1956. A theory of ice ages. Science, **123**: 1061–1066.

————. 1958. A theory of ice ages. II. Science, **125**: 1159–1162.

HARTMEYER, R. 1911. Tunicata, ch. XVII, Die geographische Verbreitung. In *Bronn's Klassen und Ordnungen des Tier-Reichs,* III, Suppl.: 1498–1726.

HEDGPETH, J. W. 1957 a. Classification of marine environments. In *Treatise on Marine Ecology and Paleoncology* (ed. Ladd), Geol. Soc. Amer. Mem. 67, chap. 1.

————. 1957 b. Marine biogeography. Ibid, pp. 359–382.

HESSE, R. 1924. Tiergeographie auf ökologischer Grundlage. Fischer, Jena, xii + 613 pp.

————, W. C. ALLEE, AND K. P. SCHMIDT. 1937. Ecological Animal Geography. John Wiley & Sons, New York, xiv + 597 pp.

HUTCHINS, L. W. 1947. The bases for temperature zonation in geographical distribution. Ecological Monogr. **17**: 325–335.

KUSNEZOV, M. 1957. Numbers of species of ants in faunae of different latitudes. EVOLUTION, **11**: 298–299.

SCHMALHAUSEN, I. I.   1949.   Factors in Evolution. Blakiston, Philadelphia, 327 pp.

SÉRIE, P. 1936. Distribucion geográfica de los ofidios argentinos. Obra cincuentenario Museo de la Plata, **2**: 33–61.

SVERDRUP, H. U., M. W. JOHNSON, AND R. H. FLEMING. 1942. The Oceans. Prentice-Hall, New York, 1087 pp.

THORSON, G. 1952. Zur jetzigen Lage der marinen Bodentier-Ökologie. Verh. de Deutsch. Zool. Ges. 1951. Zool. Anzeiger Supplbd. **16**: 276–327.

——. 1957. Bottom communities (sublittoral or shallow shelf). In *Treatise on Marine Ecology and Paleoecology* (ed. Ladd). Geol. Soc. Amer. Mem. **67**: 461–534.

TILDEN, J. E. 1937. The Algae and Their Life Relations. Milford, London, 550 pp.

WALLACE, A. R. 1878. Tropical Nature and Others Essays. MacMillan, London & New York. xiii + 356 pp.

WELLS, J. W. 1955. A survey of the distribution of reef coral genera in the Great Barrier Reef region. Reports of the Great Barrier Reef Committee, IV, pt. 2: 21–29.

THE STRUCTURE OF THE TROPICAL RAIN FOREST AND SPECIATION IN THE HUMID TROPICS*

By AN. A. FEDOROV

Botanical Institute, Academy of Sciences of the U.S.S.R., Leningrad

In the course of investigations into the distribution of plants of the Temperate and Cold Zones of the Northern Hemisphere it was long ago established that taxonomically close, and therefore closely allied, species of plants, do not as a rule occupy the same area, but are most usually geographically isolated from one another, the areas of these species being either distant from each other, or adjacent, or arranged as a kind of mosaic consisting of intermingled contiguous areas. Vicarism is also a related phenomenon, studied and described particularly thoroughly by Vierhapper (1919).

The wide distribution of the phenomenon of geographical isolation in the Holarctic even served as a basis for a special morphologico-geographical method in plant taxonomy the authors of which were Kerner (1865, 1869) and von Wettstein (1896, 1898) in Austria, and almost at the same time Bunge (1872), Korshinsky (1892) and Komarov (1908) in Russia.

It was also established that the isolation of closely allied species may be not only geographical, but ecological as well, as when such species are found in different habitats within one area.

It is important to point out that both the geographical and the ecological types of isolation characteristic of holarctic plant species are good illustrations of the principle of incompatibility of closely allied species under the same environmental conditions, ensuing from Darwin's theory of natural selection. However, an entirely different situation with respect to the distribution of closely allied species was discovered in the course of investigations of the flora and vegetation of humid tropics, in particular, of the Tropical Rain forest.

So far as I know, Richards (1945) was the first to note that a great number of closely allied species occur side by side within the same community of a tropical rain forest. Van Steenis (1957) made the same point more explicitly. Sukachev (1958) was the next to observe this phenomenon, which suggested an absence of isolation between closely allied species in tropical forest. He concluded that 'it is of prime importance for the understanding of the process of speciation in nature'. Naturally, during my observations in the tropics of China (Fedorov 1957) and subsequently in Ceylon (Fedorov 1961) and Indonesia my attention was also arrested by the remarkable fact of the existence of uninterrupted series of closely allied species in tropical rain forest and in the humid tropics in general. Takhtajan (1957) generalized this phenomenon, pointing out the existence, in the humid tropics, of continuous series not only of allied species, but also of taxa of higher ranks, such as genera and families. However, no explanation of this phenomenon has so far been found, as was also noted by van Steenis (1957), one of the most eminent authorities on the flora of the tropics. It is possible that we are now on the way to explaining this phenomenon. In this connection let us draw attention to some basic relevant facts, using as our first example the family Dipterocarpaceae which is typical of the tropics of Asia and extends to Madagascar and Africa. From the work of

* Presented at the Xth International Botanical Congress, Edinburgh, August 1964.

2   *Tropical rain forest structure and speciation*

many botanists, particularly of Foxworthy (1911, 1927, 1932, 1938), van Slooten (1926–32), and Symington (1941), we know that not only the large genera of this family, containing many species, such as *Dipterocarpus*, *Shorea* and *Hopea*, but in fact almost all the other genera, including those which are oligotypic, e.g. *Dryobalanops*, and monotypic (*Upuna*) comparatively seldom transgress in their distribution the limits of the tropical rain forest. The numbers of species belonging to the main genera of Dipterocarpaceae are very indicative: *Shorea* comprises about 167 species, *Hopea* about 100, *Dipterocarpus* about 80, *Vatica* about 87, *Balanocarpus* about 20, *Anisoptera* about 14, *Doona* (Ceylon) about 12.*

There are many other tropical families, in which the overwhelming majority of species are represented in the tropical rain forest community. These are: Annonaceae (particularly the genera *Mitrephora* with 25, and *Polyalthia* with 70), Burseraceae (particularly *Protium* with 60 in South America), Bombacaceae (*Bombax* 60, *Durio* 27), Caesalpiniaceae (*Bauhinia* 250, *Cynometra* 40, *Dialium* 20), Combretaceae (*Combretum* 350, *Terminalia* 120), Clusiaceae (*Calophyllum* 80, *Garcinia* 200, *Mammea* 26), Elaeocarpaceae (*Elaeocarpus* 90, *Sloanea* 45), Lauraceae (*Actinodaphne* 128, *Beilschmiedia* 236, *Cryptocarya* 318, *Endiandra* 95, *Litsea* 474, *Neolitsea* 93, *Ocotea* 697, *Persea* 240, *Phoebe* 174), Lecythidaceae (*Eschweilera* 80, *Lecythis* 45), Meliaceae (*Aglaia* 125, *Dysoxylum* 140), Mimosaceae (*Abarema* 44, *Albizzia* 50, *Piptadenia* 45, *Pithecolobium* 60, *Parkia* 20), Myristicaceae (*Knema* 40, *Myristica* 85), Moraceae (*Artocarpus* 60, *Ficus* over 900), Myrtaceae (*Eugenia* 750, *Syzygium* 140), Sapindaceae (*Allophyllus* 120, *Nephelium* 25), Sapotaceae (*Mimusops* 65, *Palaquium* 65, *Sideroxylon* 100).

Some genera of these families comprising especially large numbers of species are of particular interest. For instance, according to Corner (1958), the genus *Ficus* within the limits of Asia and Australasia contains 900 species most of which are encountered in the tropical rain forest, the strangling figs (that become independent trees after having passed the epiphytic stage) often reaching the upper canopy of the forest and sometimes attaining large numbers per unit area. Corner, a specialist in this genus, is justified in his opinion that its significance for the knowledge of the plant world in the Eastern tropics is quite as important as that of the family Dipterocarpaceae.

The above-mentioned numbers of species of the large genera belonging to the typical tropical families are certainly understated, except for the quite exact data for Lauraceae taken from the most recent work of Kostermans (1957). All the other data were taken mainly from Willis's *Dictionary* (1931), an excellent book, but rather out of date. There is no doubt that for many genera the actual numbers of species are about twice as high.

In mountain rain forests a great diversity of species having the character of a complete series of species is observed in the genera of Ericaceae (particularly in *Rhododendron*), Fagaceae, Magnoliaceae, Lauraceae, Symplocaceae, Theaceae and of some other families. The family Fagaceae includes several allied genera, each of which contains a large number of species. These genera are: *Castanopsis*, *Cyclobalanopsis*, *Lithocarpus*, *Pasania*, *Quercus* (s. str.). In the uper part of the forest belt of the tropical mountains there also occur all the other genera of Fagaceae, except *Castanea* (s. str.), viz. *Fagus*, a monotypic genus *Trigonobalanus* (northern Thailand to Celebes) and an oligotypic genus *Nothofagus* (New Guinea, more widespread farther south in the Antarctic Region).

---

* At present intensive studies of the family Dipterocarpaceae are in progress. Every year numerous descriptions of new species are published. A multitude of new species have been described for British Borneo alone by Ashton (1962) and the taxonomy of the family is being made more precise (Ashton 1963).

AN. A. FEDOROV   3

The fact that the species belonging to the above-mentioned families and genera form not merely random groups or mixtures, but natural series and other groups of affinity, can be seen from the analysis of the above-mentioned family Dipterocarpaceae.

Unfortunately, as yet there is no completely elaborated system for this family, as is the case in fact for many other extremely important tropical families of plants. Taxa of a rank lower than section, i.e. of such a rank as series, have almost never been described; however, should such a genus as *Shorea* be considered at the level of section, it would be found that in the tropical rain forest of the Malay Peninsula alone this genus is represented by almost all its sections, viz. Shorea, Anthoshorea, Richetioides, Brachyptera, Mutica (Symington 1941).* More or less the same holds true also for such genera as *Dipterocarpus, Hopea, Vatica* and others. Thus it is perfectly obvious that (as reflected in the system) the genera of the family Dipterocarpaceae and other tropical families are concentrated in the tropical rain forest as a multitude of clearly allied species, grouped into various series and other groups of allied taxa up to the rank of the family, which, as it has already been mentioned, is itself almost entirely confined in its distribution to the limits of the tropical rain forest.

It might appear possible to assume that all the multitude of allied species of the genus *Shorea* and of the other genera of Dipterocarpaceae is distributed in a tropical rain forest among different strata and synusiae, and that previously developed ecological isolation provides the possibility of the co-existence of several closely allied species within the same area without being isolated geographically. In fact, however, only a small proportion of species is isolated in this way. An overwhelming majority of species of, for instance, the above-mentioned genus *Shorea*, are found within the same stratum, in this particular instance in the upper storey (stratum A, according to the terminology of Richards, 1952) or even above this stratum, among 'outstanding' or emergent trees.

Therefore it must be assumed that a great number of closely allied species can co-exist side by side in the tropical rain forest because there had been established some special kind of isolation, each species being confined to a corresponding niche, and most species from their very origin forming populations which were very small, but stable with respect to the numbers of constituent individuals.

Symington (1941), who studied the Dipterocarpaceae of the Malay Peninsula in detail, obtained some evidence from which the following principles of distribution of species belonging to the genera *Dipterocarpus, Hopea, Shorea* and *Vatica* in the tropical rain forests of this part of south-eastern Asia can be inferred: (1) a certain proportion of species, particularly some of those endemic in the Malay Peninsula, occur only in a few localities, (2) an appreciable number of species, both endemic and more widespread, occur as small groups of individuals, as it were in isolated dots, (3) some species are characteristic of mountain ridges or, on the contrary, of patches of lowlands; many species are dispersed all over the forest area in the Peninsula. However, they form no perceptible accumulations and the density of their populations never exceeds one or two individuals per acre (0·4 ha). It might be concluded that both partly geographical and partly ecological isolation are observed here. However, the nature of this phenomenon is different. Even if both these types of isolation do exist, it still cannot be imagined that scores and hundreds of species belonging to the genera of Dipterocarpaceae, characteristic of the tropical rain forest of the Malay Peninsula, are distributed in such a way as to indicate that there was a special niche for each of them within the same plant community. For such a tremendous number of species of Dipterocarpaceae (156 species belong to ten

* The names of the sections of *Shorea* have been amended as in Ashton (1963).

4   *Tropical rain forest structure and speciation*

genera) it is impossible to assume the existence of such a great diversity of physico-geographical and ecological conditions within the area of so small a patch of land as the Malay Peninsula. Although it is frequently alleged that a tropical rain forest is 'a conglomerate of habitats', nevertheless, so far as large, or even gigantic, trees are concerned, such as most species of Dipterocarpaceae are, the diversity of habitats for them is confined to one or two upper strata of the forest. On the contrary, it would be more appropriate to call to mind in this connection the smoothness, uniformity and ubiquitous 'paradisiacal' optimality of environment for the growth and development of trees in the tropical rain forest.

Several taxonomically close species of such genera as *Shorea* or *Dipterocarpus* can be found on practically any standard sample area in a tropical rain forest of any region of south-eastern Asia where Dipterocarp forests are widespread; however, the population density of each of these species usually does not exceed one or two individuals per acre (0·4 ha). In other words, the fact of geographical compatibility of distribution areas of closely allied species is beyond doubt. The compatibility of distribution areas of many species of Dipterocarpaceae becomes particularly obvious from the numbers of these species in but one forest type, the Lowland Dipterocarp Forest that is characteristic of the Malay Peninsula from sea level up to an altitude of only 1000 ft (300 m). In this forest there are 59 species of *Shorea*, 31 species of *Dipterocarpus*, 35 species of *Hopea*, 22 species of *Vatica* and 9 species of *Anisoptera*. The genus *Shorea* is represented here by four sections: (1) Shorea, (2) Anthoshorea, (3) Richetioides, and (4) Mutica and Brachyptera, comprising 13, 13, 10 and 23 species respectively.

An essential characteristic feature of the interesting phenomenon of coincidence of distribution areas and habitats of a large number of closely allied species in the tropical rain forest, without any geographical or ecological isolation between these species, has thus been established. This feature is the very low value of the population density, usually not exceeding one or two individuals per acre (0·4 ha).

Therefore, for the further elucidation of the problem studied it is necessary to take into consideration the available data on the numbers of species for the tropical rain forest.

The works of Dobzhansky and his colleagues (Black *et al.* 1950; Pires *et al.* 1953) are of particular interest in this respect. Working in the Amazonian rain forest, these investigators made counts of trees with trunks over 10 cm in diameter in three 1 ha (100 × 100 m) plots in the vicinity of Tefé, State of Amazonas, in a tropical rain forest of the type called 'terra firme', and later in the forest of the 'Igapo' type near Belém, State of Pará. In these three plots 50, 87 and 79 tree species were represented by 564, 423 and 230 individuals respectively.

It was shown by analysis of the data obtained that only about half of the total number of species can be recorded in this way, since most rare, or even merely uncommon, species are usually missing in the plots. For most species present in such plots in the Amazonian tropical rain forest the population density does not exceed one individual per hectare, there being observed an inverse relationship between the number of species and the numbers of individuals. Thus, 22–35 species present in a plot are represented by not more than one individual per hectare, and only one or two species have a population density attaining 40–50 and even up to 200 or still more individuals per hectare. The transition between these numbers in both directions is quite gradual, the series of the number of species being, as it were, balanced by the inversely progressing series of the numbers of individuals.

AN. A. FEDOROV   5

Dobzhansky and his colleagues arrived at the conclusion that 'the population density of a half or more of the tree species . . . is likely to be less than one individual per hectare. This is a low population density by the standards of temperate zone forests. It is probable that at least some of the rare species of trees are cross-pollinated. Provided that the distribution of pollen by insects and by wind is about equally efficient in tropical and temperate zone forest, the reproductive communities in tropical species of trees will contain on the average fewer individuals than reproductive communities in temperate zone species. If so, the genetically effective population sizes in many tropical species are likely to be limited. This would have a profound influence on their evolutionary patterns' (Black *et al.* 1950, p. 425).

Having resumed, after a 3 years' interval, their investigations in an Amazonian forest, Dobzhansky and his colleagues (Pires *et al.* 1953) chose an experimental plot in 'a luxuriant and virgin terra firme forest' also in the state of Pará, but in another locality, near the village of Tres de Outubro, between Castanhal and the River Guama. This plot had an area of 3·5 ha and was divided into smaller sections for the sake of accurateness of tree counts. In this study also, the general character of the results established earlier remained unchanged, but the actual numbers observed were somewhat different. It is remarkable that even with a larger plot size about seventy species known for the forest studies were missing from the plot. Thus the minimal area is apparently so large in a tropical rain forest that it cannot be covered even by the largest possible plot which would permit precise investigations and accurate counts.

Most of the recent data obtained by studies of the number of species and the abundance of individuals in tropical rain forests are summarized in the book by Cain & Castro (1959).

Only a small number of species in the tropical rain forest can attain a relatively large population density. Usually these are species occupying the lower strata, but occasionally the same phenomenon is observed also among the species of the uppermost storey (stratum A). Such instances were described by Richards (1952) for the forests of British Guiana (the forests with separate dominance of *Eperua falcata, Mora excelsa, M. gonggrijpii, Ocotea rodiaei*). Monodominance is known in tropical rain forests of Central Africa, Ceylon and of some other regions of the tropics. I was lucky to find a tropical rain forest with dominance of *Dipterocarpus retusus* on Sumbawa Island in Indonesia. Another forest I have visited, belonging to this type of monodominant community, is the famous Tjibodas forest on the slopes of the volcano Gedeh in Java. The dominant species here is *Altingia excelsa*: this forest, however, belongs to a somewhat different type of montane rain forest.

For all that, a pure, one-species canopy is almost never observed in the tropical rain forest and the dominant species never suppresses any other tree species of the forest. The general floristic composition always remains very diverse and rich, containing an immense multitude of species in any one part of the forest.

Dominant tree species most frequently also form relatively small patches or consociations. In other words, not only rare species, but dominant species too, usually form small populations.

Thus the main principles underlying the numbers of species and the abundance of individuals within species in a tropical rain forest are clear: the number of species per unit area is extremely large, but all the species are represented by sparse populations and the population density of most species is, as a rule, extremely low.

Another remarkable feature of the tropical rain forest, having a direct bearing on the

6   *Tropical rain forest structure and speciation*

problem considered in this study, is the absence of climatic seasons* and the consequent irregular rhythm of flowering and fructification of most tree species. Many species of trees flower very seldom, sometimes only once in 5 or even 10 years, each time possibly at a different season of the year, with almost no relation to any particular season. Coincidence in the time of flowering is rare not only in any two or more closely allied species, but also in different individuals of the same species. If the extremely small population density of most tree species be taken into consideration, it must be assumed that the possibilities for cross-pollination are so scanty in the tropical rain forest that self-pollination presumably prevails here.

What might be the result of such a combination of circumstances as the small size and isolation of populations, the extremely low population density and the difficulty of cross-pollination? Apparently these conditions are favourable for the development of auto-matic genetic processes such as genetic drift.

In botanical literature the great significance of this phenomenon for speciation and even for the rapid origin of differences distinguishing higher taxa was pointed out by Takhtajan (1961). It was by the favourable combined effect of the genetic drift and natural selection that he tried to explain the mystery of the origin of the angiosperms. An attempt will be made here to apply the concept of genetic drift to the problem considered in this paper, the problem of speciation in the tropical rain forest.

As is generally known, the probability of the meeting of genetically identical gametes is higher in small populations; this results in homozygous forms appearing with increasing frequence and accumulating. The elimination of deleterious genes and the accumulation of beneficial genes by natural selection increases. Alongside this the role of chance in the accumulation of separate genotypes also becomes more important. The frequency of mutant genes or the 'saturation with mutations' in small populations is very high and may increase with increasing numbers in these populations.

It is interesting that Dubinin (1940), one of the authors of the theory of genetic drift, a long time ago advanced a suggestion about an important significance of these 'genetico-automatic processes' for speciation in the tropics. He wrote: 'It is quite possible that the relatively small size of the populations of tropical organisms provides the conditions for the rapid initiation of new races and species by means of the accumulation both of adaptive characters and of diverse indifferent characters fixed by means of genetico-automatic processes.'

Thus considerable genetic differences may accumulate in separate small populations of any tree species of the tropical rain forest, differences that as a consequence of the fortuitous and rare exchanges of genes owing to the above-mentioned difficulty of cross-pollination, may become a source of still greater and more rapid shifts towards speciation.

In short, in the tropical rain forest there exist conditions favourable for the relatively rapid origin of species by means of genetic drift, which explains why many genera in this community have very large numbers of closely allied species, not exhibiting in their distribution any ecological or geographical isolation. In consequence of the low popula-ation density and partial, though considerable, biotic isolation due to the limited possibi-lities of cross-pollination, they all co-exist here *in loco natali*, side by side, without any mutual supersession.

* Certainly there are some partly seasonal rhythms of vegetation in certain tree species in the Equatorial Zone of the Tropics. This seasonal character of rhythms increases towards the northern and the southern limits of the Tropical Zone and becomes quite distinct by 20° N and S. See Aubréville (1949), Foggie (1947) and also the present author (Fedorov 1958). Nevertheless in the Equatorial Zone rhythms of leaf change, flowering and fructification not synchronous with seasons obviously prevail over seasonal phenomena.

AN. A. FEDOROV   7

Thus a tropical rain forest becomes gradually flooded with a multitude of small new populations, of complete series of closely allied species originated within it and possessing various characters that are, however, neither beneficial, nor deleterious under the given conditions and play no significant part in adaptive evolution. However, as the distribution areas of these species expand or in consequence of climatic and other physico-geographical changes, some of the morphological changes initiated in the species that had originated by means of genetic drift may subsequently acquire considerable adaptive significance.

It was shown by studies in the size of leaf-blade in tree species of the Amazonian rain forest, carried out by Cain *et al.* (1956), that the prevailing type of leaf is the mesophyll about 15 cm long and about 8 cm wide. Apparently the trees with such leaves are best adapted to the conditions of the tropical rain forest. But alongside these there are also some tree species with leaves of the microphyll type and some with leaves of the macro- and megaphyll type. Nevertheless these leaf characters have no distinct adaptive significance in the tropics, as is the case in fact with many other specific distinguishing features. Evidently there are many such species in the tropical rain forest, particularly among closely allied species of the same genus, that differ in characters that are perfectly indifferent, though clearly distinct. But this is exactly the manifestation of the genetic drift, in the course of which natural selection does not eliminate indifferent mutations and their distribution takes place purely at random.

Let us assume that mutations appear inducing increased branching. Under conditions in which genetic drift prevails over natural selection these would very rapidly lead to splitting up of large boughs into small branches, which in its turn would involve a whole series of new morphological changes, possibly even if there were no new genetical reconstructions. The splitting of branches would inevitably lead to a considerable reduction in the size of leaves, flowers, fruits and other organs borne on ramified shoots. Megaphyll and macrophyll leaves might be reduced in size to mesophyll and microphyll respectively. It is interesting to note that flowers and fruits may retain their large size while leaves are reduced in size if the progenitor species was already characterized by cauliflory. Cauliflorous flowers and fruits are not affected by the splitting up of branches. This, by the way, is one of the many remarkable conclusions drawn by Corner (1949, 1954) from his Durian theory.

The existence in the tropical rain forest of series of species developing in the direction of splitting up of branches, determined by the mutation process under the conditions of the genetic drift, becomes evident from an examination of the species composition of such genera as *Dipterocarpus* or *Shorea*, or even only of their species growing in the forests of the Malay Peninsula. In most of these species there is a conspicuous correlation between the leaf and fruit size. Species having large leaves have, as a rule, large fruits, and vice versa, small-leaved species are small-fruited. Thus there are several scores of species of *Dipterocarpus* having leaves and fruits varying in length from 20 to 30 cm and from 3 to 5 cm respectively. Especially large fruits and leaves are found in *Dipterocarpus retusus*, *D. cornutus*, while the smallest are those of *D. semivestitus* and *D. verrucosus*.

The hypothesis proposed is open to criticisms based on the existence of many interspecific differences (besides those involving the ratios of leaf, flower and fruit size) between certain closely allied species of some sections of *Dipterocarpus* or *Shorea* (or in fact any other tropical genus comprising a multitude of species). How can such differences be explained from the positions of this hypothesis? It appears most probable to me that the origin of at least some of these new characters might be also explained in this way.

Let us assume that in some macrophyllous species with sparse pubescence a mutation occurs that causes the splitting of branches. Let us further assume that another species exists similar to the original one, but with small leaves and dense pubescence (which actually is frequently the case). The appearance of such a species is quite natural. Although the particular mutation that causes a more intense branching and a smaller leaf size does not affect directly the shape of hairs or the character of pubescence, the density of the pubescence will increase considerably, simply in consequence of the morphogenesis peculiar to the leaves of the new species. Since the area of the leaf-blade surface diminishes, the hairs grow closer to one another and the pubescence becomes dense. Thus, wide qualitative interspecific differences involving various plant parts may arise in the progenies of mutant parents not as the direct results of the corresponding mutations, but rather as the sequel to the consequent changes in the morphogenesis. Various deviations in the morphogenesis alone appear to be responsible for the most diverse changes of shape (contours) of leaves (or any other organs), of the venation, etc., if the mutation involves the processes governing the growth rates of different plant parts. This appears to be the mechanism of the initiation and development of a large number of specific characters of no selective advantage for the plant. Similarly mutations affecting other characters besides branching obviously entail swarms of morphological changes giving rise to distinct specific features of most various kinds in the newly originating forms of plants.

It was as early as the thirties that Koltzoff (1936) and Snell (1931) pointed out that there is no need to assume that a large number of mutations are necessary for any drastic morphological change. A very considerable phenotypic effect may be attained by means of quite slight changes in the genotype. Thus, according to the view of Koltzoff (1936) and shared by Takhtajan (1964), neoteny was the way of initiation as separate forms, of certain taxa, even of some high-rank taxa, although no more than a single mutation might have served to initiate this process.

At this point we inevitably approach a very important new problem which is not only of purely morphological and ecologic-geographical significance, but also particularly important for the the evolution of forms of the taxonomical rank of species in the tropical rain forest.

It becomes obvious that this significance is by no means the same in the tropics as in the Cold or Temperate Zone. If we abstract ourselves from the taxonomic rank of a species, however firmly the latter be established morphologically for tropical species, then, as compared to the species of the non-tropical zones, the tropical species representing any series of closely allied forms may be regarded as a single disintegrating species, as it were *in statu nascendi,* there being no geographical distribution of the different newly initiating species among different areas. In other words, a very widespread concept of the accelerated course of speciation under extreme or adverse environmental conditions, e.g. in the mountains, is in disagreement with the observations in the tropics. It is, under the optimum conditions of the humid tropics, apparently inhabited by the most ancient representatives of the plant kingdom, that the actual centre of speciation is located, the most cogent evidence for this being the immense number of species and, at the same time, the obviously primordial small numbers of individuals of each.

The extremely low population density of most tree species of the tropical rain forest affects in the first place competition between the constituents of the forest canopy.

No competitive relations ever develop within the populations of most species, except in some rare cases when a species forms more or less dense associations, and there is no elimination of individuals within populations such as would ensue from the overpopulation of any area by individuals of the same species. But undoubtedly there is violent competition for light and space among the representatives of a great many different genera and families forming the strata of forest, particularly the stratum A. The integrating effect of natural selection is very pronounced here, the result being that among the trees of any particular stratum the species belonging to quite different genera and families are very difficult to distinguish from one another, even for the experienced botanist, so much are their characters levelled down by biological convergence.

SUMMARY AND CONCLUSIONS

On the basis of all that has been said above, the following conclusions may be drawn:

1. The floristic composition of the tropical rain forest is remarkable in containing complete, uninterrupted series of taxa, particularly of species connected by indubitable affinity. Further, many entire plant families (with all their genera and species) and many very large genera are frequently confined within the limits of such a community, e.g. Dipterocarpaceae in the tropics of Asia, the rich genera of Lecythidaceae in South America, etc.

2. Besides this, it has been established by many investigators that most plant species (especially trees) of the tropical rain forest are characterized by very small numbers of individuals, being represented by populations with very low densities (one, two or three individuals per hectare). The lowest population density is characteristic both of the stratum of the 'outstanding' or emergent trees and of the uppermost storey situated below it. The highest population density is observed in the lower strata; here also, however, it is seldom found that a certain species prevails over the others; as a rule the species composition here is also mixed.

3. Occasional instances of the dominance of a certain species in the upper storey (stratum A) do not break the general principle, viz. the existence of a very large number of tree species always represented by small populations in any part of the tropical rain forest.

4. Small size of populations of tree species, low population density and partial, though considerable, biotic isolation between populations and even between separate individuals, associated with the absence of seasonal rhythm and extreme irregularity of flowering and the consequent difficulty of cross-pollination—all these factors create favourable conditions for the process of speciation in which the role of genetic drift prevails over that of natural selection. Under such conditions mutant genes accumulate in populations and contribute to the relatively rapid origin of series of closely allied species, differing considerably from one another morphologically but possessing many 'indifferent' characters.

5. Theoretically it might be assumed that the origin of a series of closely allied species was the result of only a few mutations causing changes directly in a relatively small number of characters, but leading indirectly, through the consequent changes in morphogenesis involving different plant organs, to changes in many other characters. Thus, a single mutation responsible for the intensification of branching leads, by means of the changes in the morphogenesis, to a more or less pronounced decrease in the size of leaves, flowers and fruits growing on branching shoots. Accordingly the shape and

10   *Tropical rain forest structure and speciation*

venation of leaves, the density of pubescence, etc., can be changed. The shape of the flower, the fruit and of the other organs can be changed in a similar way.

6. It may be concluded that in the tropical rain forest, in the absence of any considerable disturbances, there is no intraspecific competition and no species is ever superseded by other species closely allied to it. The only existing competition is between ecologically similar representatives of various families and genera which because of biological convergence, are externally hardly distinguishable.

REFERENCES

Ashton, P. S. (1962). Some new Dipterocarpaceae from Borneo. *Gdns' Bull., Singapore*, **19**, 253–319.

Ashton, P. S. (1963). Taxonomic notes on Bornean Dipterocarpaceae. *Gdns' Bull., Singapore*, **20**, 229–84.

Aubréville, A. (1949). *Climats, Forêts et Désertification de l'Afrique Tropicale*. Paris.

Black, G. A., Dobzhansky, Th. & Pavan, C. (1950). Some attempts to estimate species diversity and population density of trees in Amazonian forests. *Bot. Gaz.* **111**, 413–25.

Bunge, A. (1872). Die Gattung *Acantholimon*. *Zap. imp. Akad. Nauk*, Ser. 7, **18**,

Cain, S. A. & Castro, G. M. de O. (1959). *Manual of Vegetation Analysis*. New York.

Cain, S. A., Castro, G. M. de O., Pires, J. M. & de Silva, N. T. (1956). Application of some phytosociological techniques to Brazilian Rain forest. *Am. J. Bot.* **43**, 911–41.

Corner, E. J. H. (1949). The Durian Theory of the origin of the modern tree. *Ann. Bot.* N.S. **13**, 367–414.

Corner, E. J. H. (1954). The evolution of the tropical forest. In: *Evolution as a Process* (Ed. J. Huxley, A. C. Hardy and E. B. Ford). London.

Corner, E. J. H. (1958). An introduction to the distribution of *Ficus*. *Reinwardtia*, **4**, 15–45.

Dubinin, N. P. (1940). Darwinism and genetics of populations. (Russian). *Usp. sovrem. Biol.* **13**, 257.

Fedorov, An. A. (1957). The flora of south-western China and its significance to the knowledge of the plant-world of Eurasia. (Russian). *Komarov. Chten.* **10**, 20–50.

Fedorov, An. A. (1958). The tropical rain forest of China. (Russian with English summary). *Bot. Zh. SSSR*, **43**, 1385–408.

Fedorov, An. A. (1960). The Dipterocarp equatorial rain forest of Ceylon. (Russian with English summary). *Trudy mosk. Obshch. ispyt. Prir.* **3**, 306–32.

Fedorov, An. A. (1961). Preface to the Russian translation of P. W. Richards's *The Tropical Rain Forest*. Moscow.

Fedorov, An. A. (1964). Structure of a tropical rain forest and speciation in the humid tropics. (Abstract). *Abstracts Xth int. bot. Congr.*, p. 518.

Foggie, A. (1947). Some ecological observations on a tropical forest type in the Gold Coast. *J. Ecol.* **34**, 88–106.

Foxworthy, F. W. (1911). Philippine Dipterocarpaceae. *Philip. J. Sci.* **6**, 67.

Foxworthy, F. W. (1927). Commerical timber trees of the Malay Penninsula. *Malay. Forest Rec.* **3**.

Foxworthy, F. W. (1932). Dipterocarpaceae of the Malay Penninsula. *Malay. Forest Rec.* **10**.

Kerner, A. (1865). Gute und schlechte Arten. *Öst bot. Z.* **15**.

Kerner, A. (1869). *Die Abhängigkeit der Pflanzengestalt von Klima und Boden*. Innsbruck.

Koltzoff, N. K. (1936). *The Organisation of the Cell*. (Russian). Moscow and Leningrad.

Komarov, V. L. (1908). *Prolegomena ad floras Chinae necnon Mongoliae*. (Russian and Latin). *Trudy imp. S-peterb. bot. Sada*, **29**, 1–2.

Korshinsky, S. I. (1892). *Flora of the East of European Russia in its Taxonomical and Geographical Connections*. (Russian). Tomsk.

Kostermans, A. J. G. H. (1957). Lauraceae. *Reinwardtia*, **4**, 193–256.

Pires, J. M., Dobzhansky, Th. & Black, G. A. (1953). An estimate of the number of species of trees in an Amazonian forest community. *Bot. Gaz.* **114**, 467–77.

Richards, P. W. (1945). The floristic composition of primary tropical rain forest. *Biol. Rev.* **20**, 1–13.

Richards, P. W. (1952). *The Tropical Rain Forest*. Cambridge.

Slooten, D. F. van (1926–32). The Dipterocarpaceae of the Dutch East Indies. I–VI. *Bull. Jard. bot. Buitenz.* Ser. 3; **8**, 1–17, 263–352, 370–80; **9**, 67–137; **10**, 393–400; **12**, 1–45.

Slooten, D. F. van (1961). Sertulum Dipterocarpacearum Malayensium. VII. *Reinwardtia*, **5**, 457–79.

Snell, G. D. (1931). Inheritance in the house mouse, the linkage relation of short-ear, hairless and naked. *Genetics, Princeton*, **16**, 42–74.

Steenis, C. G. G. J. van (1957). Specific and infraspecific delimitation. In: *Flora Malesian*, Ser. 1, Vol. 5, pp. clxvii–ccxxxiv.

Sukachev, V. N. (1958). On the tropical forests of China. *Vest. Akad. Nauk SSSR*, **5**, 106–13.

AN. A. FEDOROV 11

Symington, C. F. (1938a). Notes on Malayan Dipterocarpaceae. IV. *Gdns' Bull. Straits Settl.* **9**, 321, 353.
Symington, C. F. (1938b). Notes on Malayan Dipterocarpaceae. VI. *J. Malayan Brch R. Asiat. Soc.* **19**, 139–68.
Symington, C. F. (1941). Foresters' manual of Dipterocarps. *Malay. Forest Rec.* **16**.
Takhtajan, A. L. (1957). On the origin of the temperate flora of Eurasia. (Russian with English summary). *Bot. Zh. SSSR*, **42**, 1635–52.
Takhtajan, A. L. (1961). *The Origin of Angiosperms.* (Russian). Moscow.
Takhtajan, A. L. (1964). *The Principles of the Evolutionary Morphology of Angiosperms.* (Russian). Moscow and Leningrad.
Vierhapper, F. (1919). Ueber echten und falschen Vikarismus. *Öst. bot. Z.* **68**.
Wettstein, R. von (1896). Die europaeischen Arten der Gattung *Gentiana*, sect. Endotricha. *Denkschr. Akad. Wiss., Wien, natp.-nat. Kl.* **64**.
Wettstein, R. von (1898). *Grundzüge der geographisch-morphologischen Methode der Pflanzensystematik.* Jena.
Willis, J. C. (1931). *A Dictionary of the Flowering Plants and Ferns*, 6th edn. Cambridge.

(*Received 28 January* 1965)

Vol. 100, No. 910   The American Naturalist   January–February, 1966

LATITUDINAL GRADIENTS IN SPECIES DIVERSITY:
A REVIEW OF CONCEPTS

Eric R. Pianka

Department of Zoology, University of Washington, Seattle, Washington*

INTRODUCTION: DIVERSITY INDICES

The simplest index of diversity is the total number of species, usually of a specific taxon under investigation, inhabiting a particular area. Since this index does not take into account differing abundances of species, divergent communities may show similar "diversities." Because of this, more sophisticated measures have been proposed which weight the contributions of species according to their relative abundances. As early as 1922 Gleason described and discussed the now well known "species-area" curve (Gleason, 1922, 1925). Later, Fisher, Corbet, and Williams (1943) proposed an index, alpha, discussed in detail by C. B. Williams (1964), which can be shown to approximate Gleason's "exponential ratio" (H. S. Horn, personal communication). Margalef (1958) has also used a modification of this index "d," in phytoplankton diversity studies, as well as several other indices (Margalef, 1957). The most recent, and currently widely used diversity index, is the information theory measure, H, derived by Shannon (1948). This index, $-\Sigma p_i \log p_i$, in which p_i represents the proportion of the total in the i-th category, has been used to quantify the "dispersion" of the distribution of entities with no ordered sequence, such as species in a community, alphabetic letters on a page, etc. Unfortunately, there has as yet been little discussion of the application of statistical procedures to this quantity. However, even without statistical embellishments, H has been a useful and productive tool (Crowell, 1961, 1962; MacArthur, 1955, 1964; MacArthur and MacArthur, 1961; Margalef, 1957, 1958; Paine, 1963; and Patten, 1962).

The choice of the index used in any particular investigation depends on several factors, especially the difficulty of appraisal of species abundances, but also on the degree to which relative abundances shift during the period of study, and for many purposes the simplest index, the number of species present, may be the most useful measure of local or regional diversity. This index weights rare and common species equally, and is the logical measure of diversity in situations with many rare, but regular, species (such as desert lizard faunas, Pianka, in preparation).

THE PROBLEM: SPECIES DIVERSITY GRADIENTS

Latitudinal gradients in species diversity have been recognized for nearly a century, but only recently have some of these polar-equatorial

*Present address: Department of Biology, Princeton University, P.O. Box 704, Princeton, New Jersey.

trends been discussed in any detail (Darlington, 1959; Fischer, 1960; Simpson, 1964; Terent'ev, 1963). A few groups, such as the marine infauna (Thorson, 1957), and some fresh water invertebrates and phytoplankton appear not to follow this pattern, but many plant and animal taxa display latitudinal gradients. A phenomenon as widespread as this may have a general explanation, knowledge of which would be of considerable utility in making predictions about the operation of natural selection upon community organization. Because of the global scope of the problem, however, it has usually been impossible for a single worker to study a complete species diversity gradient.

Approaches to the study of diversity gradients have so far been mainly of two types, the method of gross geographic lumping with comparison of total species lists for a group (Simpson, 1964; Terent'ev, 1963), and the approach by synecological studies on a smaller scale, comparing the diversity of a taxon through many different habitats (MacArthur and MacArthur, 1961; MacArthur, 1964, and in press). Terent'ev and Simpson used the number of species as indices of diversity, and MacArthur and MacArthur used Shannon's information theory formula to calculate indices of faunal and environmental diversity. Simpson (1964) points out that diversity gradients indicated by the method of gross geographic lumping have two components, one due to the number of habitats sampled by a given quadrate (and thus to the topographic relief) and another component due to ecological changes of some kind. Low latitude regions have more kinds of habitats, (i.e., Costa Rica has a whole range of habitats from low altitude tropical to middle altitude temperate to high altitude boreal habitats; whereas regions of higher latitude progressively lose some of these habitats) and therefore the presence of more species there is neither surprising nor theoretically very interesting. The question of basic ecological interest is that of the second component of diversity—namely, what are the factors that allow ecological co-existence of more species at low latitudes? Ecological data relating to species diversity gradients are scant, and no one has yet attempted the logical step of merging the synecological with an autecological approach.

Despite the handicap of insufficient ecological data, or perhaps because of it, theorization and speculation as to the possible causes of diversity gradients has been frequent and varied (Connell and Orias, 1964; Darlington, 1957, 1959; Dobzhansky, 1950; Dunbar, 1960; Fischer, 1960; Hutchinson, 1959; Klopfer, 1959, 1962; Klopfer and MacArthur, 1960, 1961; MacArthur, 1964, and in press; Paine, in press; and C. B. Williams, 1964). These efforts have produced six more or less distinct hypotheses: (a) the time theory, (b) the theory of spatial heterogeneity, (c) the competition hypothesis, (d) the predation hypothesis, (e) the theory of climatic stability, and (f) the productivity hypothesis. It is instructive to consider each of these hypotheses separately, attempting to suggest possible tests and observations for each, even though only one pair represent mutually exclusive alternatives, and thus several of the proposed mechanisms of control of diversity could be operating simultaneously in a given situation.

In the following discussion, ecological and evolutionary saturation are defined as the ecological and evolutionary upper limits to the number of species supported by a given habitat. The assumption of ecological saturation is implicit in ecological studies of species diversity gradients, an assumption without which the study of such gradients must be made in terms of the history of the area. There is reasonable evidence that the majority of habitats are ecologically saturated (Elton, 1958; MacArthur, in press).

The time theory

Proposed chiefly by zoogeographers and paleontologists, the theory of the "history of geological disturbances" assumes that all communities tend to diversify in time, and that older communities therefore have more species than younger ones. (The evidence behind this assumption is scanty, and the assumption may or may not be valid.) Temperate regions are considered to be impoverished due to recent glaciations and other disturbances (Fischer, 1960). It is useful to distinguish between ecological and evolutionary processes as subcategories of the theory. Ecological processes would be applicable to those circumstances where a species exists which can fill a particular position in the environment; but this species has not yet had time enough to disperse into the relatively newly opened habitat space. Evolutionary processes apply to longer time spans, to those cases where a newly opened habitat is not yet utilized, but will be occupied given time enough for speciation and the evolution of an appropriate organism.

Tests of the ecological and evolutionary time theories are by necessity indirect, but several authors have suggested possibilities for assessing the importance of evolutionary time as a control of species diversity. Simpson (1964) has argued that the warm temperate regions have had a long undisturbed history (from the Eocene to the present), long enough to become both ecologically and evolutionarily saturated, and that since there are fewer species in this zone than there are in the tropics, other factors must be invoked to explain the difference between tropical and temperate diversities. Beyond this, he reasons that if the time theory were correct, the steepest gradient in species diversities should occur in the recently glaciated temperate zone. Since, for North American mammals, at least, this zone shows a fairly flat diversity profile, there is some evidence against the evolutionary time theory. Simpson (1964) emphasizes that temperate zones have probably been in existence as long as have tropical ones. Newell (1962) stresses that temperate areas at intermediate latitudes were probably not eliminated during the glacial periods, but were simply shifted laterally along with their floras and faunas, and that, if this is the case, they have had as long a time to adapt as have the non-glaciated areas. R. H. MacArthur (personal communication) has suggested that possibilities exist for a test of the effects of glaciation, by comparisons of areas in the glaciated north temperate with their non-glaciated southern temperate counterparts. However, the evolutionary time theory is not readily amenable to conclusive tests, and will probably remain more or less unevaluated for some time.

The evidence relating to the ecological time theory, summarized in detail by Elton (1958), and discussed by Deevey (1949), indicates that most continental habitats are ecologically saturated. Only in those cases where barriers to dispersal are pronounced can the ecological time theory be of importance in determining species diversity. Islands have sometimes been considered cases of historical accident in which maximal utilization of the biotope is often achieved by pronounced behavioral modifications of those species which have managed to inhabit them (Crowell, 1961, 1962; Lack, 1947). More recently, several theories for equilibrium in insular zoogeography have been proposed, and data given which shows strong dependence ·of species composition on island size, distance from "source" areas, and time available for colonization (Hamilton, Barth, and Rubinoff, 1964; MacArthur and Wilson, 1963; Preston, 1962). These papers indicate that predictable patterns of species diversity occur even on islands, and further lessen the probable importance of the ecological time theory.

The theory of spatial heterogeneity

Proponents of this hypothesis claim that there might be a general increase in environmental complexity as one proceeds towards the tropics. The more heterogeneous and complex the physical environment becomes, the more complex and diverse the plant and animal communities supported by that environment. Again it is useful to distinguish two subcategories of this theory, one on a macro-, the other on a micro- scale. The first is the factor Simpson (1964) calls topographic relief, discussed in more detail by Miller (1958). The factor of topographic relief is especially interesting in the study of speciation, and has been much discussed in books and symposia on that subject (Blair, 1961; Mayr, 1942, 1957, 1963). The component of total diversity due to topographic relief has been mentioned earlier in this paper.

In contrast to topographic relief, micro-spatial heterogeneity is on a local scale, with the size of the environmental elements corresponding roughly to the size of the organisms populating the region. Elements of the environmental complex in this class might be soil particle size, rocks and boulders, karst topography, or if one is considering the animals in a habitat, the pattern and complexity of the vegetation. Environmental heterogeneity of the micro-spatial type has been little studied by zoologists, and is more interesting to the ecologist than to the student of speciation (considerations of sympatric speciation processes will, however, involve micro-spatial attributes of the environment). It should be noted here that in the only study which relates species diversity of a taxon to environmental diversity in a quantitative way, the environmental diversity is of the micro-spatial type (MacArthur and MacArthur, 1961; MacArthur, 1964). These authors demonstrate that foliage height diversity is a good predictor of bird species diversity, and that knowledge of plant species diversity does not improve the estimate. Further tests of the theory of environmental complexity will probably follow similar lines, although it would be useful to consider alternative ways of examining this hypothesis.

Spatial heterogeneity has several shortcomings when applied to the explanation of global diversity patterns. The component of total diversity due to topographic relief and number of habitats (macro-spatial heterogeneity) certainly increases towards the tropics, but does not offer an explanation for diversity gradients within a given habitat-type. Vegetative spatial heterogeneity is clearly dependent on other factors and explanation of animal species diversity in terms of vegetative complexity at best puts the question of the control of diversity back to the control of vegetative diversity. Since there is no reason to suppose that micro-spatial heterogeneity of the physical environment changes with latitude, the theory of micro-spatial heterogeneity seems to explain only local diversity. Ultimately, resolution into independent variables will require consideration of non-biotic factors such as climate which change more or less continuously from pole to pole (see section on the climatic stability hypothesis).

The competition hypothesis

Advocated by Dobzhansky (1950) and C. B. Williams (1964), this idea is that natural selection in the temperate zones is controlled mainly by the exigencies of the physical environment, whereas biological competition becomes a more important component of evolution in the tropics. Because of this there is greater restriction to food types and habitat requirements in the tropics, and more species can co-exist in the unit habitat space. Competition for resources is *keener* and niches 'smaller' in more diverse communities. Dobzhansky emphasizes that natural selection takes a different course in the tropics, because catastrophic indiscriminant mortality factors (density-independent), such as drought and cold, seldom occur there. He notes that catastrophic mortality usually causes selection for increased fecundity and/or accelerated development and reproduction, rather than selection for competitive ability and interactions with other species. Dobzhansky predicts that tropical species will be more highly evolved and possess finer adaptations than will temperate species, due to their more directed mortality and the increased importance of competitive interactions. No statement has been given as to exactly why competition might be more important in the tropics, but the hypothesis is testable in its present form.

Because the predation hypothesis predicts very nearly the opposite mechanisms of control of diversity than does the competition hypothesis, I will briefly outline the predation hypothesis before proceeding with discussion. These two hypotheses are almost mutually exclusive alternatives, and the same tests, by and large, apply to both.

The predation hypothesis

It has been claimed that there are more predators (and/or parasites) in the tropics, and that these hold down individual prey populations enough to lower the level of competition between and among them (Paine, in press). This lowered level of competition then allows the addition and co-existence of new intermediate prey types, which in turn support new predators in the system, etc. The mechanism can apply to both evolutionary and dispersal additions of new species into the community. Paine (1966) argues that the upper limits on the process are set by productivity factors, which will here be considered separately.

According to this hypothesis, competition among prey organisms is *less* intense in the tropics than in temperate areas. Thus, a test between these two hypotheses is possible, provided that the intensity of competition can be measured. Several approaches to the quantification of competition might find application here (Connell, 1961a, 1961b; Elton, 1946; Kohn, 1959; MacArthur, 1958; Moreau, 1948). Also, if the predation hypothesis holds, community structure should shift along a diversity gradient, with an increase in the proportion of predatory species as the communities become more diverse. Evidence for such a shift in trophic structure along a diversity gradient is given by Grice and Hart (1962). These authors present data showing that the proportion of predatory species in the marine zooplankton increases along a latitudinal diversity gradient. A similar shift in community structure accompanies a terrestrial species diversity gradient in the deserts of western North America (Pianka, in preparation). Fryer (1959, 1965) has argued that predation enhances migration and speciation, thereby resulting in increased species diversity, in some African lake fishes. As will be pointed out in a later section, demonstration that species have either finer or more overlapping habitat requirements in the tropics could be used to support three of the six hypotheses, and is therefore not a powerful distinguishing tool.

The theory of climatic stability

According to this hypothesis, restated by Klopfer (1959), regions with stable climates allow the evolution of finer specializations and adaptations than do areas with more erratic climatic regimes, because of the relative constancy of resources. This also results in "smaller niches" and more species occupying the unit habitat space. Another way of stating this principle in terms of the organism, rather than the environment, is that, in order to persist and successfully exploit an environment, a species must have behavioral flexibility which is roughly inversely proportional to the predictability of the environment (J. Verner, personal communication). In recent years the theory of climatic stability has become a favorite for explaining the generality of latitudinal gradients in species diversity, but has as yet remained untested. Rainfall and temperature can be shown to vary less in the tropics than in temperate zones, but rigorous correlation with faunal diversity, let alone demonstration of causal connection, has not yet been possible. It should be realized that climatic factors could well determine directly floral and/or vegetative complexity, while being only indirectly related to the faunal diversity of the area.

Evidence that tropical species have more restricted habitat requirements than temperate species would support the competition hypothesis, the predation hypothesis, and the theory of climatic stability. Klopfer and Mac-

Arthur (1960) have attempted to test the hypothesis that "niches" are "smaller" in the tropics by comparing the proportion of passerine birds to non-passerines along a latitudinal gradient. Their thesis is that the non-passerines, possessing a more stereotyped behavior, are better adapted to exploit the more constant tropical environment than are the passerines, whose more plastic behavior allows them to inhabit less predictable habitats. Klopfer (in press, in preparation) has compared the degree of behavioral stereotypy in temperate and tropical birds, and tentatively concludes that "while tropical species are in fact 'stereotyped,' this is more likely an effect rather than a cause of their greater diversity."

An interesting variation on this theme is that of increased "niche overlap" in more diverse communities (Klopfer and MacArthur, 1961). Klopfer and MacArthur attempted to test this idea by comparing the ratios of bill lengths in congeners among several sympatric bird species in Panama and Costa Rica. Simpson (1964) notes that this ratio may come as close to 1.00 in temperate birds as it did in Klopfer and MacArthur's tropical species, but fails to realize that morphological character displacement is expected only in species occupying the same space (Brown and Wilson, 1956; Hutchinson, 1959; Klopfer and MacArthur, 1961; MacArthur, in press). Ratios of culmen lengths may often approach unity in species such as *Dendroica* which clearly divide up the biotope space (MacArthur, 1958), and thus demonstrate behavioral, rather than morphological character displacement. However, it is apparent that even if the comparison were valid, the test would not distinguish between "smaller niches" and increased "niche overlap" (C. C. Smith, personal communication). It is difficult to devise tests which will distinguish between these alternatives, and perhaps none can be suggested until "niche" has been operationally defined. Use of some of the dimensions of Hutchinson's (1957) multidimensional niche may allow partial testing between these alternatives, as in the work of Kohn (1959) on *Conus* in Hawaii.

Increased overlap in selected dimensions of the niche can imply either increased, decreased, or constant competition; the first if the overlapping resources are in short supply, the second if the overlapping resources are so abundant that sharing of them is only slightly detrimental to each species, and the third if independent environmental factors (such as more predictable production) allow increased sharing of the same amount of resource. Hence, because data supporting the niche overlap idea has ambiguous competitive interpretations, it does not distinguish between three (or four) hypotheses either.

Tests distinguishing between the theory of climatic stability and the competition hypothesis are especially difficult to devise, as there is considerable overlap between the two, and indeed, they are usually mixed when either is suggested. This similarity makes it all the more important to evaluate the importance of each, and in keeping with the rest of this paper they will be considered separately and at least two possible distinguishing tests suggested.

According to the theory of climatic stability, a unit of habitat will support the same number of individuals in the tropics and temperate regions, but since each of the species may be rarer (without becoming extinct) in the tropics, there can be more of them. The competition hypothesis implies that more individuals occupy the same habitat space, or else competition would not be increased. Considering a fixed areal dimension as a unit of habitat, abundance data from the tropics generally suggest that the number of individuals is relatively similar from temperate to tropics and therefore support the theory of climatic stability (Klopfer and MacArthur, 1960; Skutch, 1954). Another way in which these two theories might be separated is by examining the intensity of competition occurring along an increasing diversity gradient; if the level of competition remained constant, or decreased along the gradient, the prediction of an increased proportion of predatory species could be used to separate the predation hypothesis from the theory of climatic stability.

The productivity hypothesis

The most recent and most complete statement of this hypothesis is that of Connell and Orias (1964). They blend this hypothesis with the theory of climatic stability, distinguishing between the energetic cost of maintenance and the energy left for growth and reproduction. Their synthesis also includes aspects of the theory of spatial heterogeneity, and reasonably explains latitudinal trends in diversity, but the productivity hypothesis will be considered here in its "pure" form.

The productivity hypothesis states that greater production results in greater diversity, everything else being equal. Since it is patently impossible to hold everything else equal, the hypothesis can only be tested in crude or indirect ways. Experimental manipulation of nutrient levels in freshwater lakes, for instance, might provide a possible test. Such enrichments have often been made, both intentionally and accidentally (sewage), and quantitative data have been taken on the response of the biota. The data needed for calculating diversities probably exist, and it would be interesting to see such calculations performed. Qualitative indications are that enrichment usually causes an impoverished fauna (Patrick, 1949; L. G. Williams, 1964).

If productivity were of overwhelming importance in the regulation of species diversity, one would expect a correlation despite uncontrolled extraneous variables. Only one such correlation is known to me (Patten, Mulford, and Warinner, 1963), and in fact there may often be an inverse relation between species diversity and abundance or standing crop (which should usually be positively correlated with production) (Hohn, 1961; Hulburt, 1963; Yount, 1956; L. G. Williams, 1964; and my own observations on desert lizards). Those who would claim that the above studies are on nonequilibrium populations and thus not applicable to the problem at hand, would do well to search for data from "equilibrium" conditions which are relevant to the productivity hypothesis.

A common modification of the productivity hypothesis which has been claimed to be of importance in regulating species diversity is the notion of increased temporal heterogeneity in the tropics. The main argument is that the longer season of tropical regions allows the component species to partition the environment temporally as well as spatially, thereby permitting the coexistence of more species (MacArthur, in press). This notion has been rephrased by Paine (in press) who argues that the "stability of primary production" is a major determinant of the species diversity of a community. Paine integrates the predation hypothesis with this idea to form a sort of synergistic system controlling diversity. This hypothesis is also a blend of the stability and productivity theories, but in this case, the mixing suggests new observations, and a new mechanism of control of diversity than does either hypothesis alone. The mechanism for the regulation of species diversity by stability of primary production may be similar to the mechanism suggested for climatic stability, except that in this case, plants may buffer climatic variability by utilizing their own homeostatic adaptations and storage capacities to increase the stability of primary production.

These notions can be tested by analyses, such as that of MacArthur (1964), of the length of breeding seasons, but there are other ways of examining them as well. Thus, comparisons of the division of the day (or night) and season into discrete activity periods by different animal species might elucidate latitudinal trends. Another possible angle of approach is by means of the "stability of primary production," which can be measured directly and examined for latitudinal trends. Unfortunately, there are all too few reliable measures of primary production, let alone the variability in this quantity, and at this point it is difficult to assess the stability of primary production along a latitudinal gradient. The necessary data are simple enough in theory, but in practice a single determination of primary productivity is tedious (especially in terrestrial habitats). An indirect possibility for testing the hypothesis exists, however, for arid regions, where primary productivity is strongly positively correlated with precipitation (Pearson, 1965; Walter, 1939, 1955, 1962). In this environment, the amount and variability of precipitation can be used to estimate the amount and variability of primary production. Preliminary analysis of weather and lizard data for the deserts of western North America shows no correlation with either the average amount or the variability of rainfall and the number of lizard species (Pianka, in preparation).

Since clutch size is closely related to these ideas of increased temporal heterogeneity and stability of primary production, it may be profitably considered here. The fact of reduced clutch size in tropical birds (Skutch, 1954) has been discussed as a possible factor allowing the coexistence of more species in the tropics (MacArthur, in press). MacArthur argues that by lowering its clutch size, a species reduces its total energy requirements and is therefore able to survive in less productive areas which were formerly marginal habitats. He reasons that such reductions in total energy requirements will also allow the existence of more species, when the total amount of energy available is held constant. Apart from the problems of population replacement raised by these theoretical arguments, there are other reasons for doubting the importance of reduced clutch size as a determinant of increased tropical diversity. For instance, it is highly possible that tropical habitats never achieve food densities as high as those usual further north, because of their greater species diversity and the fact that most of the breeding birds do not migrate. In contrast, great blooms of production characterize the temperate regions, and most of the breeding birds are migrants. Thus it may be energetically impossible for tropical birds to raise as many young as can be supported in the more productive northern areas (that is, more productive on a short term basis, during the short growing season) (Orians, personal communication). Support of this notion comes from the large territory sizes of many tropical bird species (Skutch, 1954), which suggests that food may be scarce. If this is indeed the case, the smaller clutches of tropical birds would be a result, rather than a cause of, the greater diversity in the tropics. These criticisms of the reduced clutch size hypothesis are, however, in themselves largely theoretical, and it will be worthwhile to examine clutch sizes of other taxa along various diversity gradients. Clutch sizes of desert lizards vary latitudinally, but whether or not the largest clutches are from the south depends on the species concerned (Pianka, in preparation).

CONCLUSIONS

Obviously, there is room for considerable overlap between these different hypotheses, and several may be acting in concert or in series in any particular situation. Because of the preliminary state of knowledge on the subject of species diversity, for the sake of clarity, and in order to suggest tests of the various hypotheses, it is useful first to consider and assess each of the components of control of diversity in isolation, before attempting various mixtures. Once the relative importance of each factor has been assessed for many different diversity gradients, an attempt may be made to merge them. In general, the compounding of hypotheses is to be avoided, unless such blending suggests new tests not applicable to the isolated theories. As more and more parameters are included, the more complex hypothesis tends to "answer" all cases and becomes less and less testable and useful.

A fact often overlooked is that most of the hypotheses can be either supported or rejected by appropriate observations on a limited scale; any species diversity gradient might be a suitable study system. If the broader geographical gradients are found to be qualitatively different from local diversity patterns, this in itself would be interesting, and understanding the difference would ultimately require thorough knowledge of the control of local species diversity.

Finally, since ecologists can seldom structure their experiments except by their choice of observations and measurements, the natural system usually sets the bounds within which they must work. The basic technique of descriptive science is correlation, and it is well to keep in mind that correlation does not necessarily mean causation. This is especially true in the study of latitudinal gradients in species diversity, where many different factors vary along the gradient in a fashion similar to the taxon studied, and spurious correlations may be frequent. For these reasons all significant correlations must be carefully examined and attempts made to understand the mechanisms and causal connections (if any) between variates. Unambiguous demonstration of causality can only be attained by experimental manipulation of the independent variables in the system.

SUMMARY

The six major hypotheses of the control of species diversity are restated, examined, and some possible tests suggested. Although several of these mechanisms could be operating simultaneously, it is instructive to consider them separately, as this can serve to clarify our thinking, as well as assist in the choice of the best test situations for future examination.

ACKNOWLEDGMENTS

Many fruitful discussions preceded this effort, particularly those with H. S. Horn, G. H. Orians, R. T. Paine, and C. C. Smith. Drs. A. J. Kohn, R. H. MacArthur, G. H. Orians, and R. T. Paine have read the manuscript and made many valuable suggestions. I wish to acknowledge J. F. Waters for translating Terent'ev's paper. The work was supported by the National Institutes of Health, predoctoral fellowship number 5-F1-GM-16,447-01 to -03.

LITERATURE CITED

Blair, W. F. [Editor]. 1961. Vertebrate speciation. Univ. Texas Press, Austin, Texas.

Brown, W. L., Jr., and E. O. Wilson. 1956. Character displacement. Syst. Zool. 5: 49–64.

Connell, J. H. 1961a. Effects of competition, predation by *Thais lapillus*, and other factors on natural populations of the barnacle *Balanus balanoides*. Ecol. Monogr. 31: 61–106.

———. 1961b. The influence of interspecific competition and other factors on the distribution of the barnacle *Chthamalus stellatus*. Ecology 42(4): 710–723.

Connell, J. H., and E. Orias. 1964. The ecological regulation of species diversity. Amer. Natur. 98: 399–414.

Crowell, K. 1961. The effects of reduced competition in birds. Proc. Nat. Acad. Sci. 47: 240–243.

———. 1962. Reduced interspecific competition among the birds of Bermuda. Ecology 43: 75–88.

Darlington, P. J., Jr. 1957. Zoogeography; the geographical distribution of animals. John Wiley & Sons, Inc., New York and London.

———. 1959. Area, climate, and evolution. Evolution 13: 488–510.

Deevey, E. S., Jr. 1949. Biogeography of the Pleistocene. Bull. Geol. Soc. Amer. 60: 1315–1416.

Dobzhansky, T. 1950. Evolution in the tropics. Amer. Sci. 38: 209–221.

44   THE AMERICAN NATURALIST

Dunbar, M. J. 1960. The evolution of stability in marine environments. Natural selection at the level of the ecosystem. Amer. Natur. 94: 129–136.

Elton, C. S. 1946. Competition and the structure of ecological communities. J. Anim. Ecol. 15: 54–68.

———. 1958. The ecology of invasions by animals and plants. Meuthen, London.

Fischer, A. G. 1960. Latitudinal variation in organic diversity. Evolution 14: 64–81.

Fisher, R. A., A. S. Corbet, and C. B. Williams. 1943. The relation between the number of species and the number of individuals in a random sample of an animal population. J. Anim. Ecol. 12: 42–58.

Fryer, G. 1959. Some aspects of evolution in Lake Nyasa. Evolution 13: 440–451.

———. 1965. Predation and its effects on migration and speciation in African fishes: A comment. Proc. Zool. Soc. London 144: 301–322.

Gleason, H. A. 1922. On the relation between species and area. Ecology 3: 158–162.

———. 1925. Species and area. Ecology 6: 66–74.

Grice, G. D., and A. D. Hart. 1962. The abundance, seasonal occurrence and distribution of the epizooplankton between New York and Bermuda. Ecol. Monogr. 32: 287–309.

Hamilton, T. H., R. H. Barth, Jr., and I. Rubinoff. 1964. The environmental control of insular variation in bird species abundance. Proc. Nat. Acad. Sci. 52: 132–140.

Hohn, M. H. 1961. The relationship between species diversity and population density in diatom populations from Silver Springs, Florida. Trans. Amer. Microscop. Soc. 80: 140–165.

Hulburt, E. M. 1963. The diversity of phytoplanktonic populations in oceanic, coastal, and esturine regions. J. Marine Res. 21: 81–93.

Hutchinson, G. E. 1957. Concluding remarks. Cold Spring Harbor Symp. Quant. Biol. 22: 415–427.

———. 1959. Homage to Santa Rosalia, or why are there so many kinds of animals? Amer. Natur. 93: 145–159.

Klopfer, P. H. 1959. Environmental determinants of faunal diversity. Amer. Natur. 93: 337–342.

———. 1962. Behavioral aspects of ecology. Prentice-Hall, Englewood Cliffs, N. J.

Klopfer, P. H., and R. H. MacArthur. 1960. Niche size and faunal diversity. Amer. Natur. 94: 293–300.

———. 1961. On the causes of tropical species diversity: niche overlap. Amer. Natur. 95: 223–226.

Kohn, A. J. 1959. The ecology of *Conus* in Hawaii. Ecol. Monogr. 29: 47–90.

Lack, D. 1947. Darwin's finches. Cambridge Univ. Press, Cambridge, England. Reprinted 1961 by Harper and Brothers, New York.

MacArthur, R. H. 1955. Fluctuations of animal populations, and a measure of community stability. Ecology 36: 553–536.

———. 1958. Population ecology of some warblers of north-eastern coniferous forests. Ecology 39: 599–619.

SPECIES DIVERSITY GRADIENTS   45

————. 1964. Environmental factors affecting bird species diversity. Amer. Natur. 98: 387-398.

————. 1965. Patterns of species diversity. Biol. Rev. (In press).

MacArthur, R. H., and J. W. MacArthur. 1961. On bird species diversity. Ecology 42: 594-598.

MacArthur, R. H., and E. O. Wilson. 1963. An equilibrium theory of insular zoogeography. Evolution 17: 373-387.

Margalef, D. R. 1957. Information theory in ecology. Gen. Syst. 3: 37-71. Reprinted 1958.

————. 1958. Temporal succession and spatial heterogeneity in phytoplankton. *In* Perspectives in marine biology. A. Buzzati-Traverso [ed.], Univ. California Press, Berkeley.

Mayr, E. 1942. Systematics and the origin of species. Columbia Univ. Press, New York. Reprinted 1964 by Dover Publications, Inc., New York.

————. 1957. [*Editor*], The species problem. Amer. Ass. Advance. Sci., Publ. No. 50.

————. 1963. Animal species and evolution. The Belknap Press of Harvard Univ. Press, Cambridge, Mass.

Miller, A. H. 1958. Ecologic factors that accelerate formation of races and species in terrestrial vertebrates. Evolution 10: 262-277.

Moreau, R. E. 1948. Ecological isolation in a rich tropical avifauna. J. Anim. Ecol. 17: 113-126.

Newell, N. D. 1962. Paleontological gaps and geochronology. J. Paleontol. 36: 592-610.

Paine, R. T. 1963. Trophic relationships of eight sympatric predatory gastropods. Ecology 44: 63-73.

————. 1966. Food web complexity and species diversity. Amer. Natur. 100: 65-75.

Patrick, Ruth. 1949. A proposed biological measure of stream conditions, based on a survey of the Conestoga Basin, Lancaster County, Pennsylvania. Proc. Acad. of Natur. Sci. Philadelphia 101: 277-341.

Patten, B. C. 1962. Species diversity in net phytoplankton of Raritan Bay. J. Marine Res. 20: 57-75.

Patten, B. C., R. A. Mulford, and J. E. Warinner. 1963. An annual phytoplankton cycle in the lower Chesapeake Bay. Chesapeake Sci. 4: 1-20.

Pearson, L. C. 1965. Primary production in grazed and ungrazed desert communities of eastern Idaho. Ecology 46(3); 278-286.

Preston, F. W. 1962. The canonical distribution of commonness and rarity. Part I: Ecology 43: 185-215. Part II: Ecology 43: 410-431.

Schoener, T. W. 1965. The evolution of bill size differences among sympatric congeneric species of birds. Evolution 19: 189-213.

Shannon, C. E. 1948. The mathematical theory of communication. *In* C. E. Shannon and W. Weaver, The mathematical theory of communication. Univ. Illinois Press, Urbana.

Simpson, G. G. 1964. Species density of North American recent mammals. Syst. Zool. 13: 57-73.

Skutch, A. F. 1954. Life histories of Central American birds. Vols. I and II. Cooper Ornithological Society Pacific Coast Avifauna Numbers 31 and 34.

Terent'ev, P. V. 1963. Opyt primeneniya analiza variansy k kachestvennomu bogatstvu fauny nazemnykh pozvonochnyk. Vestnik Leningradsk Univ. Ser. Biol. 18(21: 4); 19–26. English abstract in Biol. Abstr. 80822 (45).

Thorson, G. 1957. Bottom Communities (sublittoral or shallow shelf). In H. S. Ladd [ed.], Treatise on marine ecology and paleoecology. Geol. Soc. Amer. Mem. 67: 461–534.

Walter, H. 1939. Grasland, Savanne und Busch der arideren Teile Afikas in ihrer ökologischen Bedingtheit. Jahrbucher für wissenschaftliche Botanik 87: 750–860.

———. 1955. Le facteur eau dans les regiones arides et sa signification pour l'organisation de la vegetation dans les contrees sub-tropicales, p. 27–39. In Colloques Internationaux du Centre National de la Recherche Scientifique, Vol. 59; Les Divisions Ecologiques du Monde. Centre National de la Recherche Scientifique, Paris. 236 p.

———. 1962. Die Vegetation der Erde in ökologischer Betrachtung. Veb Gustav Fischer Verlag Jena. Jena, Germany.

Williams, C. B. 1964. Patterns in the balance of nature. Academic Press, New York and London.

Williams, L. G. 1964. Possible relationships between plankton-diatom species numbers and water-quality estimates. Ecology 45: 809–823.

Yount, J. L. 1956. Factors that control species numbers in Silver Springs, Florida. Limnol. Oceanogr. 1: 286–295.

Vol. 101, No. 919   The American Naturalist   May–June, 1967

WHY MOUNTAIN PASSES ARE HIGHER IN THE TROPICS*

DANIEL H. JANZEN

Department of Entomology, The University of Kansas, Lawrence

INTRODUCTION

This paper is designed to draw attention to the relation between tropical climatic uniformity at a given site and the effectiveness of topographic barriers adjacent to the site in preventing movements of plants and animals. This is not an attempt to explain tropical species diversity (see Pianka, 1966, for a review of this subject), but rather to discuss a factor that should be considered in any discussion of the relation between topographic and climatic diversity, and population isolation. Simpson (1964) states that "Small population ranges and numerous barriers against the spread and sympatry of related populations would therefore tend to increase density of species in a region as a whole. It will be suggested below that this is a factor in the increase of species densities in regions of high topographic relief. I do not, however, know of any evidence that it is more general or more effective in the tropics." I believe that the climatic regimes discussed below, and the reactions of organisms to them, indicate that topographic barriers may be more effective in the tropics. Mountain barriers and their temperature gradients in Central America, as contrasted to those in North America, are used as examples; but it is believed that the central idea equally applies to other tropical areas, types of barriers, and physical parameters.

There are three thoughts central to the argument to be developed: (1) in respect to temperature, it is the temperature gradient across a mountain range which determines its effectiveness as a barrier, rather than the absolute height; (2) in Central America, terrestrial temperature regimes are generally more uniform than North American ones, and differ in their patterns of overlap across geographic barriers; and (3) it can be assumed that animals and plants are evolutionarily adapted to, and/or have the ability to acclimate to, the temperatures normally encountered in their temporal and geographic habitat (or microhabitat).

MOUNTAIN TEMPERATURE GRADIENTS

Animals and plants encounter a mountain barrier as, among other things, different temperature regime from that to which they are acclimated or evolutionarily adapted. In general, and granting other environmental factors to be similar, this different temperature regime could occur as a band across a flat plain and still be just as impassable. The problem is the usual one of

*Contribution No. 1337 of the Department of Entomology, University of Kansas, Lawrence, Kansas. This paper is a by-product of National Science Foundation Grant No. GB-5206.

how much overlap there is between the temperature regime at the top of the pass and the valley below. This overlap bears two major considerations: (1) the number of hours, days, or months when the temperatures on the pass are similar to those in the valley, and (2) the amount of time and degree to which the organism can withstand temperatures different from those in the valley while it is crossing the pass. The outcomes of such crossings are theoretically measurable at all levels, from the single individual which establishes a new population but is never joined by further immigrating members, to varying rates of individual organism flow (sometimes resulting in gene flow); there will be some level where the overlap is so great that for a given population the barrier no longer exists. However, for some other population with less ability to withstand previously unexperienced temperatures, the same region may be an absolute barrier.

CLIMATIC UNIFORMITY AND OVERLAP

There are areas of great temperature stability in temperate North America (e.g., coastal bays backed by low mountain ranges such as the area of San Francisco Bay, California), and areas of large temperature fluctuation in Central America (e.g., areas of well marked dry and wet seasons, and under the influence of cold air masses off the Caribbean during the northern winter, e.g., Veracruz, Mexico). However, contrast of weather records from a Central American country with those of any state in the United States will quickly show that, in general, the Central American temperature regime at a given site is more uniform on a monthly and daily basis at any altitude of distance from the seas than that of a geographically comparable site in the United States (Fig. 1; representative monthly means of the daily means, maxima and minima, for six sites in Costa Rica and in the United States). It is clear from Fig. 1 that from site to site there may be large differences in monthly temperatures; but at a given site, relative uniformity is the rule in a representative tropical country such as Costa Rica.

In respect to the impassability of mountain barriers, and intimately related to the relative uniformity of temperature regimes, the amount of overlap between the weather regime at the top of the pass and the valley below is of utmost importance; the more overlap, the less of a temperature barrier the mountain presents, and the greater the difference between monthly mean maxima and minima in the two adjacent regimes, the more overlap there is likely to be. Six representative overlap patterns in the United States and Costa Rica are exemplified in Fig. 1. For Costa Rica, the weather records were extracted from the Annuario Meteorologico for 1961 and 1964. For the United States, they were taken from U.S. Department of Commerce Weather Bureau reports (1959) and Marr (1961). Both sets were chosen on the basis of availability of maxima and minima weather data, and their position on altitudinal transects. In Fig. 1, patterns of overlap are presented from virtually no overlap (a: Costa Rica—Palmar Sur to Villa Mills, 16 to 3096 meters; d: Colorado—Grand Junction to the top of the front range behind Boulder, 1616 to 4100 meters), to high containment of the mountaintop regime within that of the valley below (c: Costa Rica—Palmar Sur to San Isidro del General, 16 to 703 meters; f: California—Fresno to Bishop, 110 to 1369 meters).

The form of the Costa Rican temperature regimes and their overlaps in Fig. 1 is clearly not the same as that of the United States' regimes. The following traits of these representative patterns are of importance to organisms living in one regime and confronted with the problem of moving through the other temperature regime to get to another area, or merely into the other regime for short-term activities.

1. The temperate regimes involve much greater changes over the year than the tropical, in respect to monthly values, and daily values (not shown in the figures, but clear from weather records).

2. The variation in difference between the monthly mean maxima and minima, across the change of seasons, is greater in the temperate examples than the tropical ones.

3. The time of maximum difference between the monthly mean maxima and minima is the summer (growing season) in the temperate examples and is the dry season (dormancy season) in the tropical examples.

4. The absolute differences between monthly mean maxima and minima are greater in the temperate examples during the summer than in the tropical examples during the rainy season.

5. The greatest amount of overlap between temperature regimes occurs during the growing season in the temperate examples but during the dry season in the tropical examples.

It is hypothesized that the amount of overlap between two temperature adjacent regimes should be greater in the temperate region than in the tropics, for any given elevational difference between the sites of the two adjacent regimes, because of the greater distances between the extremes for the temperate regimes as contrasted to tropical. To test this, overlap values between the temperature regimes of 15 pairs of sites in Costa Rica and 15 pairs of sites in the continental United States (Appendix) were calculated by the following formula:

$$\text{overlap value} = \sum_{i=1}^{12} \frac{d_i}{\sqrt{R_{1i} R_{2i}}}$$

where d_i is the amount (in degrees) of one regime that is included within the other, for the ith month. If one regime is not included within the other, d_i is considered negative and has the value of the number of degrees separating the regimes. R_{1i} is the difference in degrees between the monthly mean maximum and minimum for the ith month of the higher elevational regime and R_{2i} is the equivalent value for the lower elevational regime. Overlap is being considered in units of the geometric mean between R_{1i} and R_{2i}; hence it is the *relative* overlap, called hereafter simply "overlap." The overlap value has the property that if the monthly mean maxima of the higher elevation regime are equal to the monthly mean minima of the lower elevation regime for all 12 months, the overlap value is zero (a case intermediate

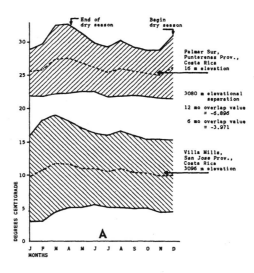

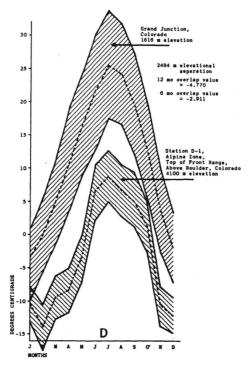

FIG. 1. Representative temperature regimes of three tropical (A, B, C) sites and three temperate (D, E, F) sites. Each graph figures two regimes. The dotted lines trace the monthly temperature means; in all cases the mean of the lower elevation regime is above that of the higher elevation mean. Solid lines trace the monthly means of daily maxima and minima; in all cases the two lower solid lines in each

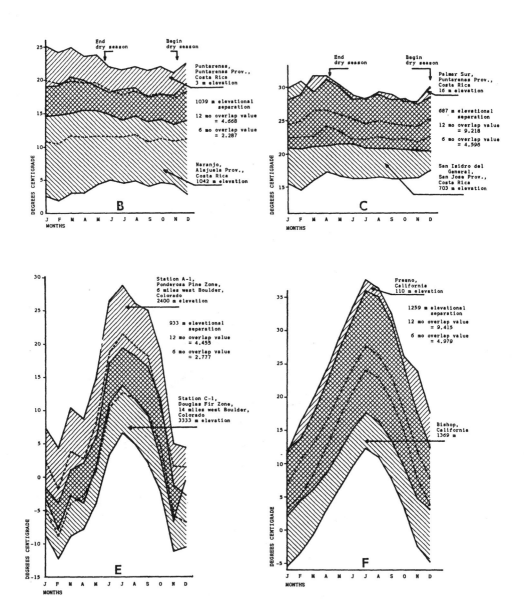

graph represent the monthly mean minima of the two regimes, with the lowermost
representing the higher elevation site. Overlap between temperature regimes of adjacent sites is portrayed by cross-hatching, and increases from A and D to C and F.
All graphs are to the same scale.

between that exemplified in Fig. 1a and 1b). As overlap increases, the overlap value increases to a value of 12 at the point where the two temperature regimes are congruent. Complete inclusion of one regime in the other does not guarantee maximal overlap (e.g., Fig. 1c, 1f). There is no lower limit to negative overlap values (e.g., Fig. 1a, 1d) as elevational separation between two regimes become progressively greater.

It is clear that the amount of overlap between the temperature regime of the valley bottom and the temperature regime on the mountainside above, at a specific geographic area, is primarily a function of the distance in elevation between the two weather stations. Thus the overlap between a pair of adjacent regimes in the tropics can only be compared with a temperate example of overlap where the elevational separation is similar in the two geographic areas. In Fig. 2 and 3, overlap values for each of the 30 pairs of adjacent regimes in Appendix A are plotted against the amount of elevational difference between the regimes of each pair. In Fig. 2, the overlap values are calculated for the entire 12 months of the year, while in Fig. 3, they are calculated for the six months of the growing season in the temperate examples (April through September) and for the first six months of the rainy season in the Costa Rican examples (May through October). Ideally, all 30 elevational transects should have been chosen from areas of similar rainfall patterns, but these weather data are not available.

From examination of these scattergrams and their regression lines, a number of statements have been generated that have a bearing on the effectiveness of temperature barriers in restricting the movements of organisms.

1. The overlap values of all 30 pairs of regimes for both 12 and 6 month periods, show an apparently linear relation of decreasing overlap with increasing elevational separation between the lowland and highland temperature regimes. It is this relation that leads to the classical feeling that effectiveness of mountain barriers is roughly related to their height.

2. The 12 month regression line (line I) for the Costa Rican sites has the steepest slope of the three lines in Fig. 2, but is not significantly different in slope from the 12 month regression line (line II) for all the United States' sites (line I, $b = -149$; line II, $b = -114$, $t_{26 d.f.} = 1.084$). However, the t value is high enough to suspect a relation that is obscured by the small sample size and high variance. If line I and line II are really representative of two different populations, as they appear to be following the manipulation described under 3 below, then it can be said that the overlap values demonstrated across the tropical elevational separations are less than those of the temperate examples, and become proportionally less as the elevational separation becomes less.

3. When the regression lines for the six months values are compared (Fig. 3) their slopes are highly significantly different (line IV, $b = -299$; line V, $b = -208$; $t_{26 d.f.} = 3.1531$) indicating that there are two separate populations of overlap values. This indicates that there is more dissimilarity between the overlaps of the Costa Rican paired regimes and the overlaps of the United States' paired regimes during the growing season than during the dormancy

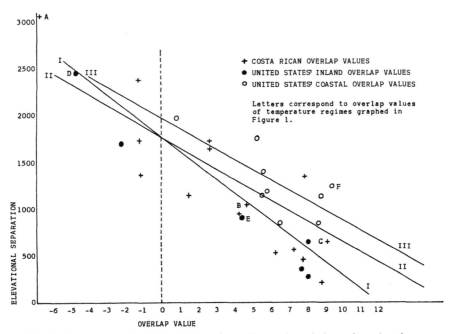

FIG. 2. Regression of overlap values for a 12-month period on elevational separation between the pair of temperature regimes for which the overlap value was calculated. Line I is that for 15 Costa Rican sites, line II is that for 15 United States' sites, and line III is that for the nine coastal sites included within the sites for line II.

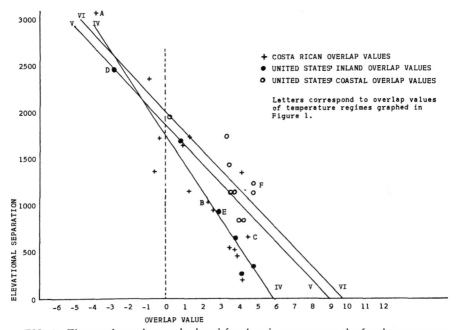

FIG. 3. The overlap values calculated for the six summer months for the temperate regimes (April through September) and the first six months of the rainy season for the tropical regimes (May through November). Line IV, Costa Rican sites; V, all United States sites; VI, nine U. S. coastal sites.

season. However, it should be noted that the removal of the winter months from the temperate data removes in absolute value much more of the variation in overlap from month to month than does the removal of the dry season months from the Costa Rican data.

4. If the six continental United States' records are removed, to make the relation to oceans more equivalent between the United States and Costa Rican sites, the 12 month regression line (line II) moves up the overlap scale to become line III (overlap value changes from 5.22 to 6.31), but lines II and III remain parallel (line II, $b = -114$; line III, $b = -110$; $t_{20 d.f.} = 0.1948$). The six-month regression line also moves following this manipulation but to a lesser extent (mean overlap changes from 3.335 to 3.650). From the distribution of the midcontinental United States' points in Fig. 2 and 3, it can be seen that, in respect to overlap for a given elevational separation, the Costa Rican sites have more in common with the midcontinental United States' sites than with the coastal ones. In other words, maximal differences between tropical and temperate overlaps are recorded when coastal areas of the United States are compared with Costa Rican transects. It should be emphasized at this point that virtually all of the Costa Rican records are coastal in the sense that no point in the country is more than about 125 miles from an ocean. In retrospect, it would seem advisable to remove this major source of variation in later comparisons of this type.

5. The variation of overlap value is great for any given elevational separation, and a given overlap value may be representative of a wide range of elevational separations in both the Costa Rican and United States data. In Fig. 3, based on six-month values, the variation in overlap for a given elevational separation is reduced. To compare any two barriers involving an elevational separation, it is clear from this that the actual amount of overlap between the upper and lower temperature regimes should be determined, since the same elevational separation on two different mountain ranges can yield quite different overlap values.

6. There is no obvious trend in change of amount of variation in overlap value along the various regression lines. For example, at an elevational separation of approximately 1700 m, the overlap values range from -2.25 to 5.40, and at 1150 m, they range from 1.50 to 8.75 (Fig. 2). This, coupled with the apparent linearity of the data, indicates that at one latitude the overlaps between temperature regimes lying at sea level and 500 m elevation should have about the same mean values and the same variances as overlaps between temperature regimes at 500 m and at 1000 m.

7. There is a point where the Costa Rican and United States' regression lines intersect (Fig. 2, zero overlap, 1780 m elevational separation; Fig. 3, -1.2 overlap, 2100 m elevational separation), and, thus, for these elevational separations, the overlap for the paired regimes are the same in the tropical and temperate example. It is notable that this point of overlap equality is at a larger elevational separation when the six-month records are considered. This indicates that the Costa Rican and United States' overlap values are even more dissimilar during the growing seasons.

8. The temperate and tropical regression lines become increasingly divergent as the elevational separation becomes less; the smaller the elevational separation, the greater will be the difference between a temperate and a tropical overlap value calculated for a pair of adjacent temperature regimes. It is not possible to compare the regression lines (I and II, IV and V) on the basis of population means since the slopes of the lines are not similar. However, in both Fig. 2 and 3, the temperate regression lines are above the Costa Rican lines, indicating that the more "tropical" the physical environment pattern, the more important are the smaller topographic features.

While there is great variation around the regression lines in Fig. 2 and 3, a major part of this variation could be removed if many weather records were available for a specific set of slopes of a major mountain range in Costa Rica, and another in the United States, both with similar exposures to an ocean and similar precipitation regimes. This statement is based on the observation that in the few cases where a long elevational transect could be broken up into component temperature regimes and an overlap value calculated between each pair of regimes, the points yield a straight line with almost no deviation from the line (e.g., Costa Rica: the overlaps of Puntarenas-Esparta, Puntarenas-Naranjo, Puntarenas-San Jose, Esparta-San Jose, and Naranjo-San Jose form a very straight line). A second source of variation, implied in the preceding paragraph, is that the points from different precipitation regimes tend to form different lines; but within a given regime, the points form very straight lines.

The minimum of the valley and the maximum on the pass do not occur at the same time during the 24 hour cycle. Thus it is that at any one point in time there is probably little or no overlap between two temperature regimes separated by more than 500 m. However, an organism is present for long periods of time and thus is subjected to all the temperature levels in its habitat. Thus the overlap as graphed in Fig. 1 and quantified in Fig. 2 and 3 is a measure of the amount of similarity between the temperature regimes experienced by an organism living in the valley bottom and then moving up and over the pass. If all the overlap patterns had the same shape as those of Costa Rica, the tropical and temperate values could be compared without qualification (as in Fig. 2). However, the manipulation used in Fig. 3 is in part justified by the fact that major periods of animal and plant activity are during the northern summer and tropical rainy season, and a purpose of this paper is to illustrate the relation between overlap and activities of organisms.

ACCLIMATION AND EVOLUTIONARY ADAPTATION

Throughout this discussion it is assumed that an organism is less likely to evolve mechanisms to survive at a given temperature if that temperature falls outside of the temperature regime of the organism's habitat than if it falls within it.

Allee et al. (1949, p. 538-539) in summarizing Payne's studies of cold hardiness in insects, has stated this in the following manner: "(1) degree of cold hardiness was [positively] correlated with seasonal periodicity of temperature, and (2) that degree of cold hardiness in a series of species, from a variety of habitats in terrestrial communities, was [positively] correlated with the normal seasonal fluctuation of temperature in that community or habitat in which a particular species was normally resident.'' In other words, the larger the usual variation around the mean environmental values, the higher the probability that an organism will survive a given deviation from that mean; this should apply to daily, as well as seasonal, predictability of deviations. This relation has been indicated in another manner by DuRant and Fox (1966) when discussing the effect of soil moisture on soil arthropods. Those in soil of consistently lower moisture content were more sensitive to small changes in soil moisture content than those in soils of consistently higher moisture content; i.e., the reaction of an organism to a change in the environment is dependent upon the relative as well as absolute values of that change.

It is reasonable to expect that an organism living within the relatively uniform tropical temperature regimes depicted in Fig. 1 (a, b, c) will more probably be acclimated and evolutionarily adapted to a narrower absolute range of temperatures than one which lives within the more highly fluctuating temperature ranges depicted in Fig. 1 (d, e, f). ''Fluctuation'' as used above applies to the variation in the monthly means across the 12-month period, the changes in the difference between the monthly means of the daily maxima and minima, and the variation in maxima and minima from day to day. This should be true even if the organism is in a resting stage during some part of the year and thus, by regulating its activity, it places itself in a more uniform environment during major activity periods. It seems likely that there will be residual ability to withstand temperatures outside of the usual habitat values at the times of activity, as physiological ''by-products'' of the mechanisms that allow survival during the times of inactivity.

The relation between relative uniformity of the normal habitat and the dispersal ability of the organism is well shown with weed or fugitive species of both plants and animals. These organisms customarily live in disturbed sites and have many mechanisms for survival under the physical extremes present at these places. While they have evolved great dispersal ability as a necessary part of the strategy of living in the temporary habitat of disturbed sites, mechanisms for living in this variable habitat are of obvious value in crossing the various temperature, etc., regimes necessary to find further disturbed sites.

Assuming the same amount of overlap between the temperature regimes of a valley bottom, and the pass above, at a tropical and at a temperate site with equal elevational separation, it is proposed that a tropical organism from the valley bottom is less likely to get over the pass than is a temperate organism, because the tropical organism has a higher probability of encountering temperatures to which it is neither acclimated nor evolutionarily adapted than does the temperate organism. In addition to the monthly changes exemplified in Fig. 1, this is due to the central fact that in the Costa Rican temperature regimes, for example, if the monthly mean maxima and minima are 28 and 19 C, respectively, the standard deviation of each of these means is normally less than 2 C, while the standard deviation of a similar pair of values for the United States' records in Fig. 2 and 3 would be 4 to 5 C.

However, as has been shown with the six-months values (Fig. 3) and indicated with the 12-month values (Fig. 2) for a given elevational difference in Costa Rica and in the United States, there is likely to be more overlap between the temperate adjacent temperature regimes than the tropical ones. In this case, the tropical organism has even less chance than the temperate one of getting over a pass.

This is why it is postulated that mountains are higher in the tropics figuratively speaking; they are harder to get over because, for a given elevational separation, the probability is lower in the tropics that a given temperature found at the higher elevation will fall within the temperature regime of the lower elevation than is the case in the temperate area. For example, an insect living in the forest around Puerto Viejo, Costa Rica (83 m elev.) is subjected to an annual absolute range of about 37 to 17 C; if the insect lives anywhere other than the upper surface of the canopy, the range is reduced by the insulating value of the vegetation. To move up to and over the adjacent pass at Vara Blanca, Costa Rica (1804 m elev.) it must pass through an area that is rarely, if ever, over 22 C but ranges down to 8 C (a similar regime is depicted in Fig. 1b). An insect living around Sacramento, California (8 m elev.) is subjected to an annual range of at least 46 to −9 C. To cross the Sierra Nevada at Blue Canyon, California (1760 m elev.), it must pass through an area that experiences annual ranges of about 31 to 8 C (a similar regime is depicted in Fig. 1e). The 12-month overlap value calculated for the Puerto Viejo–Vara Blanca transect is 2.648 and that for the Sacramento–Blue Canyon transect is 5.358. During the summer months, the temperature regime at Blue Canyon is almost completely contained within that of Sacramento. Thus the temperate elevational separation of 1758 m should not be nearly as inimical to animal movements as the tropical elevational spread of 1721 m.

DISCUSSION

The relation between the climatic uniformity of a habitat and the ability of the organisms living in that habitat to cross adjacent areas with different climatic regimes may indicate a general concept. In respect to temperature, valleys may figuratively be deeper to an organism living on the ridge top in the tropics than in a temperate area. In respect to rainfall patterns, one would expect the following situation. An organism living in an area with a uniform water supply (ground water or rainfall) should have more difficulty in crossing an adjacent desert than would an organism living in an area with a six-month dry season. Seasonal swamp inhabitants should be able to cross rivers more readily than those organisms which always live on the dry ground around the swamp. In other words, the greater the fluctuation of the environment in the habitat of the organism, the higher the probability that it will not encounter an unbearable combination of events in the adjacent different habitat that it is attempting to cross. Since the tropics are in general more uniform in relation to temperature, and often in respect to rainfall patterns, for a given habitat or site, it is expected that barriers involving gradients in temperature or rainfall are more effective in preventing dispersal in the tropics.

It is clear that the "tropics" are not a single phenomenon. Classical tropical climates and vegetation are at the intersections of the high ends of gradients of uniform solar energy and capture rainfall patterns. The classical tropical image is destroyed as one moves into seasonality in rainfall pattern and temperature, upward into colder elevations, laterally into areas of uniform dryness, or into areas of increased unpredictability in the absolute values and pattern of the physical environment. Thus it is that overlaps between temperature regimes in the tropics and temperate zones cannot be precisely compared, and the effect of rainfall patterns on temperature regimes is associated with much of the variation seen in Fig. 2 and 3.

Even if the "significant differences" in overlap values in Costa Rica and the United States are not truly representative of tropical and temperate temperature regime overlaps, the amount of overlap between a temperature regime at the pass and the temperature regime in the valley below are characteristcis of valley-mountain systems that should be considered in discussions of mountains as barriers between populations. Secondly, there is so much variation in the overlap value for a given elevational separation along both temperate and tropical transects that each pair of transects should be regarded as a special case in specific studies of barriers.

Since overlap values are not the same throughout the year over a specific elevational separation at a specific site, the evolutionary timing of the dispersal phases of organisms that use immigration across barriers as a strategy may be associated with the periods of greatest overlap. On the other hand, if segregation of populations is of selective value, as may well be the case if the dispersal forms are also the sexual forms, timing of production of dispersal forms may "move" away from the time of greatest overlap through evolutionary selection. In other words, if it is detrimental to the population to mate with other sexuals "coming over the mountain," then this can be avoided by production of sexuals at a time when other sexuals are not coming over the mountain (group selection is not being invoked here).

It is not intended that the idea of greater effectiveness of tropical barriers as compared with temperate ones of equal absolute magnitude be offered as an explanation of tropical species diversity. However, it is my intent to emphasize the concept that greater sensitivity to change is promoted by less frequent contact with that change.

With a few notable exceptions (e.g., Schulz' 1960 analysis of dry seasons in Suriname), investigators in tropical areas have generally ignored the problem that the usefulness of a given unit of scale in portraying constancy, variation, and variance, is directly related to the organism's sensitivity to the part of the environment being measured; while we are intuitively satisfied with monthly values in understanding the four temperate seasons, it is clear that monthly values are hardly adequate in a tropical area such as Costa Rica where eight seasons are customarily recognized (from the beginning of the rainy season: invierno, veranielo, canicula, invierno, temporales, chubascos, verano fresco, and verano caliente). That eight seasons are recognized in a supposedly more uniform climate underscores the topic of this paper. While the seasonal and daily variations in Costa Rica are smaller than those of most areas in the United States, they are simultaneously much more predictable; thus, the behavioral and developmental patterns of populations are more easily, in an evolutionary sense, associated with them than they are with unpredictable changes of equal magnitude. However, it is to be expected that more precise fitting of population activities to more predictable environmental conditions should lead to less ability to tolerate the different conditions encountered outside of the usual temporal and spatial habitat. This leads directly to the idea that the more predictable the environment, the smaller the change in that environment needs to be to serve as an immediate or long-term barrier to dispersal. This should be important in understanding the higher fidelity of tropical animals and plants to spatial and to temporal habitats which are set off by apparently minor differences in physical conditions (as compared with temperate habitats). This fidelity is experienced by anyone collecting in tropical areas, and has been documented (e.g., MacArthur, Recher, and Cody [1966] and included references, Janzen and Schoener [1967]). Such fidelity is obviously an important element of the structure of communities; and it is proposed that the increase in predictability of the physical and biotic environment, as one progresses from classical temperate environmental regimes to tropical ones, is causally related in a positive manner to the increase in species' fidelity to their habitats across the same progression. Further, this is a mutually reinforcing system whereby increased biotic fidelity leads to further biotic fidelity through the medium of interdependency of members of the same food chain.

ACKNOWLEDGMENTS

This paper was first written while teaching in the course entitled "Fundamentals of tropical biology: an ecological approach" under the auspices of the Organization for Tropical Studies during the summer of 1965 in Costa Rica. I am greatly indebted to L. Wolf and N. Scott for inspiring discussions on the subject. Student and faculty members of the Fundamentals courses in 1965 and 1966 have greatly assisted in criticism of the manuscript. F. J. Rohlf assisted in numerical treatment of the temperature data. The following persons have read the manuscript and contributed considerably by their comments: D. Johnston, J. Eagleman, and G. Orians.

LITERATURE CITED

Allee, W. C., A. E Emerson, O. Park, T. Park, and K. P. Schmidt. 1949. Principles of animal ecology. Saunders Co., Philadelphia. 837 p.

Annuario Meteorologico. 1961. Servicio Meteorologico Nacional, Seccion Climatologia. San Jose, Costa Rica. 43 p.

———. 1964. Servicio Meteorologico Nacional, Seccion Climatologia. San Jose, Costa Rica. 61 p.

DuRant, J. A., and R. C. Fox. 1966. Some arthropods of the forest floor in pine and hardwood forests in the South Carolina Piedmont region. Ann. Entomol. Soc. Amer. 59:202–207.

Janzen, D. H., and T. W. Schoener. 1967. Differences in insect abundance and diversity between wetter and drier sites during a tropical dry season. Ecology (in press).

MacArthur, R. H., H. Recher, and M. Cody. 1966. On the relation between habitat selection and species diversity. Amer. Natur. 100:319–332.

Marr, J. W. 1961. Ecosystems of the east slope of the Front Range in Colorado. University of Colorado Studies, Series in Biology No. 8, Univ. Colorado Press. 134 p.

Pianka, E. R. 1966. Latitudinal gradients in species diversity: a review of concepts. Amer. Natur. 100:33–46.

Schulz, J. P. 1960. Ecological studies on rain forest in northern Suriname. Verhandelingen der Koniklijke Nederlandse Akademie van Weten-schappen, Afd. Natuurkunde 53(1):1–267.

Simpson, G. G. 1964. Species density of North American recent mammals. Syst. Zool. 13:57–73.

U.S. Department of Commerce Weather Bureau. 1959. Climates of the States; Colorado (1959), California (1959), Oregon (1960), New Hampshire (1959), Idaho (1959), Nevada (1960). U.S. Government Printing Office.

APPENDIX

Localities of pairs of temperature regimes from which overlap values were calculated

Locality	Elevation of site (m)	Degrees N Latitude	Elevational separation	12 month overlap value	6 month overlap value
United States:					
(1) Sacramento, California	8	38° 35'	1173 m	5.712	3.774
Mount Shasta, California	1181	41° 19'			
(2) Los Angeles, California	100	34° 03'	1406 m	5.462	3.547
Sandburg, California	1506	34° 45'			
(3) Eureka, California	14	40° 48'	1167 m	5.616	3.528
Mount Shasta, California	1181	41° 19'			
(4) Roseburg, Oregon	168	43° 14'	1107 m	8.862	4.806
Sexton Summit, Oregon	1275	42° 37'			
(5) Fresno, California	110	36° 46'	1259 m	9.415	4.979
Bishop, California	1369	37° 22'			
(6) Sacramento, California	8	38° 35'	1752 m	5.358	3.460
Blue Canyon, California	1760	39° 17'			
(7) Pendleton, Oregon	497	45° 41'	853 m	6.662	4.300
Meacham, Oregon	1350	45° 30'			
(8) Concord, New Hampshire	113	43° 12'	1974 m	0.982	0.238
Mount Washington Observatory, New Hampshire	2087	44° 16'			
(9) Medford, Oregon	437	42° 22'	838 m	8.735	4.215
Sexton Summit, Oregon	1275	42° 37'			
(10) Las Vegas, Nevada	721	36° 05'	648 m	8.038	3.703
Bishop, California	1369	37° 22'			
(11) Reno, Nevada	1466	39° 30'	294 m	8.308	4.123
Blue Canyon, California	1760	39° 17'			
(12) Boise, Idaho	944	43° 34'	367 m	7.771	4.818
Idaho Falls, Idaho	1311	43° 32'			

APPENDIX (*Continued*)

Locality	Elevation of site (m)	Degrees N Latitude	Elevational separation	12 month overlap value	6 month overlap value
(13) Station A-1, Ponderosa Pine Zone, 6 miles west of Boulder, Colorado	2400	40°	1700 m	−2.291	−0.935
Alpine Zone, Top of Front Range above Boulder, Colorado	4100	40°			
(14) Grand Junction, Colorado	1616	39° 07'	2484 m	−4.770	−2.469
Station D-1, Alpine Zone, Top of Front Range above Boulder, Colorado	4100	40°			
(15) Station A-1, Ponderosa Pine Zone, 6 miles west of Boulder, Colorado	2400	40°	933 m	4.453	2.777
Station C-1, Douglas Fir Zone, 14 miles west of Boulder, Colorado	3333	40°			
Costa Rica:					
(16) Cairo, Limon Prov.	94	10° 07'	1341 m	7.717	4.027
Cartago, Cartago Prov.	1435	9° 40'			
(17) Palmar Sur, Puntarenas Prov.	16	8° 57'	3080 m	−6.896	−3.971
Villa Mills, Puntarenas Prov.	3096	9° 34'			
(18) Puntarenas, Puntarenas Prov.	3	9° 58'	205 m	8.779	4.192
Esparta, Puntarenas Prov.	208	9° 59'			
(19) Palmar Sur, Puntarenas Prov.	16	8° 57'	687 m	9.218	4.596
San Isidro del General, San Jose Prov.	703	9° 22'			
(20) Cartago, Cartago Prov.	1435	9° 40'	1661 m	2.656	0.969
Villa Mills, San Jose Prov.	3096	9° 34'			
(21) Esparta, Puntarenas Prov.	208	9° 59'	964 m	4.292	2.655
San Jose, San Jose Prov.	1172	9° 56'			
(22) Puerto Viejo, Heredia Prov.	89	10° 26'	1715 m	2.648	1.090
Vara Blanca, Heredia Prov.	1814	10° 10'			
(23) Canas, Guanacaste Prov.	45	10° 25'	517 m	6.291	3.689
Tilaran, Guanacaste Prov.	562	10° 28'			

APPENDIX (*Continued*)

(24) Quebrada Azul, Alajuela Prov. Tilaran, Guanacaste Prov.	83 562	10° 24' 10° 28'	479 m	7.895	3.900
(25) Quebrada Azul, Alajuela Prov. Villa Quesada, Alajuela Prov.	83 656	10° 24' 10° 17'	567 m	7.366	3.511
(26) Puntarenas, Puntarenas Prov. Naranjo, Alajuela Prov.	3 1042	9° 58' 10° 06'	1039 m	4.668	2.287
(27) Quebrada Azul, Alajuela Prov. Vara Blanca, Heredia Prov.	83 1814	10° 24' 10° 10'	1731 m	−1.016	−0.351
(28) Puntarenas, Puntarenas Prov. San Jose, San Jose Prov.	3 1172	9° 58' 9° 56'	1169 m	1.513	1.179
(29) Puntarenas, Puntarenas Prov. Monteverde, Puntarenas Prov.	3 1380	9° 58' 10° 20'	1377 m	−1.147	−0.590
(30) San Isidro del General, San Jose Prov. Villa Mills, San Jose Prov.	703 3096	9° 22' 9° 34'	2393 m	−1.162	−0.987

Biol. J. Linn. Soc., **1**, pp. 19–30. With 5 figures

April 1969

Patterns of communities in the tropics

ROBERT H. MacARTHUR

Department of Biology, Princeton University, Princeton, New Jersey, U.S.A.

Tropical countries have many times more species of most taxa than temperate ones, and small areas in the tropics have a smaller multiple of the number of species of small temperate areas. Where many species are present, abundances tend to be more equal and geographic distributions more spotty. Most tropical environments are less seasonal and more productive, and the dry areas and mountains which are relatively more seasonal and less productive have fewer species. The species which have reached offshore islands are often much commoner there and occupy expanded habitats.

To account for these relations, the following general hypothesis seems necessary: species interactions are important and the tropics have a head start on speciation. The head start, or greater rate, allows extra species to pile up in the tropics, but because of the importance of competition, no single area becomes as greatly enriched. Rather, faunal differences between areas increase. The lesser excess of tropical species in small areas is largely due to greater productivity and reduced seasonality which make marginal ways of life profitable. With more overlap in resources, the closely packed tropical species have more uniform abundances and the coexistence of these species is more precarious, causing the spotty geographic distributions.

Neither the species diversity of the food supply nor the longer breeding season (supposedly allowing staggered nesting seasons with an early shift and a later shift) is relevant to bird species diversity.

CONTENTS

INTRODUCTION

The wet tropical lowland environment is different from that in temperate regions, and in this tropical environment plant and animal communities exhibit various extreme patterns. As is well known, there are more species of most taxa in the tropics. Coupled with this, there are, in the tropics, lower birth rates, greater infant mortality (at least in birds), more uniform relative abundances (i.e., less 'dominance'), more spotty geographic distributions and, probably, greater annual productivity. Any hypothesis which can simultaneously relate all of these features of tropical biogeography must be treated with respect.

At least four hypotheses have been seriously put forth to account for the great species diversity in the tropics. (See Pianka, 1966, for an interesting but different review.)

(1) The tropics have offered more opportunities for speciation in the past, and these species have been slow in adapting to climates with a winter (Fischer, 1960). This can be completed in two ways:

20   ROBERT H. MACARTHUR

(*a*) Time is still short and the numbers of species are still increasing.

(*b*) There is a balance between new species entering and old ones vanishing.

(2) The tropics have more predation, parasitism and disease, putting a lower ceiling on the abundance of any given species and thus allowing more species to fit in. A sort of obverse of this theory says that moderate predation intensity not only allows more species but is necessary for their persistence, possibly because some species can be resource limited and other new ones predator limited. Paine (1966) has impressive empirical evidence for intertidal communities.

(3) In the more uniform tropical climates, competitors can be packed closer together (MacArthur & Levins, 1967) and, forthermore, the competition reduces the intrinsic rate of natural increase r^* and colonizing species will have a decreased chance of succeeding (MacArthur & Wilson, 1967).

(4) In the more productive tropical environments, what were marginally scarce resources become adequate and new species will occupy these new 'niches'. This is presumably what Odum, Cantlon & Kornicker (1960) had in mind, and Connell & Orias (1964) have added that there may be a feedback with more species causing more stability which in turn allows yet more species.

Now elementary events often have single clearcut explanations, but statistical events like species diversity often have complex and multiple explanations. Hence there is no reason that the validity of any of the explanations need preclude any of the others. In fact, I believe all of the proposals are partly right, if incomplete. The first explanation, which is essentially historical, allowing a future increase in the numbers of species, seems inconsistent with the others which predict a saturation with species, but even these can be mixed. Not only could some taxa have historical explanations while others have ecological, but also, the total fauna of a country could continue to grow as in hypothesis (1*a*), while the local biota of any subdivision might have reached saturation.

In what follows, I examine these ideas more carefully.

THE TROPICAL ENVIRONMENT

At first I planned a careful statistical analysis of the stability of tropical climates but this is more ambiguous than I had imagined and I now prefer a sort of bioassay of it.

The trees in temperate regions show marked annual growth rings because growth nearly ceases in the winter, but trees at least in wet tropical forests show less conspicuous growth rings, doubtless because the trees regard the climate as much less seasonal. Tropical birds of one species or another nest nearly the whole year round and individual species have longer nesting seasons indicating that their insect food regards the climate as much less seasonal, and no bird breeding in Colombia (de Schauensee, 1964) or Surinam (Haverschmidt, 1968), for instance, leaves to avoid an off season, so the birds seem to regard the climate as less seasonal.

For these reasons, and in spite of the importance and variability of tropical dry seasons, I believe the tropical environment must be regarded as more uniform than the temperate one.

---

* r is the intrinsic rate of natural increase defined by $\dfrac{1}{N}\dfrac{dN}{dt}$ where N is the population size.

That the lowland tropics are more productive is harder to demonstrate but equally important. Rosenzweig (1968) has shown that actual evapotranspiration (the total evaporation plus transpiration which equals the precipitation minus the percolation and run-off) is closely correlated with net production, and evapotranspiration is surely greater in the tropical lowlands (Holdridge, 1967). Winter, which for many organisms is critical, is surely less productive in the temperate zone. The upper Amazon, where Patrick (1966) found no increase over temperate rivers in diatoms or invertebrates, was not more productive and has great seasonal variability in depth so the greater productivity is not perfectly correlated with low latitude.

Other organisms of course form an important part of the tropical environment which we can therefore conclude is more diverse (at least in numbers of species). The tropical environment is also more diverse in other biological ways. For instance bird food not only comes in a large range of sizes (Schoener & Janzen, 1968) but also in more perennially available forms (e.g. fruit at all seasons).

It is often claimed that the tropical environments are actually structurally more complex. This is surely true from the viewpoint of some animals, and epiphytes in particular offer many new opportunities, but it is not so clear that the environment is more structured for trees, or for the animals in savanna country.

COMMUNITY PROPERTIES IN THE TROPICS

As mentioned in the introduction, several correlated changes occur in the tropics. The first is increase in numbers of species. Fischer's article (1960) documents many cases of this and I add another as shown in Fig. 1. Only freshwater invertebrates and diatoms (Patrick, 1966) seem to fail to increase in diversity in the tropics. (See Table 1.)

Table 1. Comparison of species numbers of major groups of organisms found in hard water with numbers found in temperate zone rivers and streams in the U.S.A. (After Patrick, 1966)

	Río Tulumayo	Quebrada de Puente Perez	Ottawa River 1955–1956	Potomac River
Algae	73*	62	69	103
Protozoa	33	40	47	68
Lower invertebrates†	5	6	8–15	27
Insects	104	78	51–64	104
Fish	26	22	17–28	28

* These numbers represent established numbers of taxa and do not include taxa represented by less than six specimens.
† Excluding Rotifers.

These patterns describe the numbers of species in large areas of many amalgamated habitats. In many ways the local pattern is more interesting, if harder to study. Consider these two hypothetical alternatives: in the first, tropical country A has ten times the number of species of temperate country B (of equal area), and each component 10 acres of A also has ten times as many species. In this case, the 'explanation' of the tropical diversity is local—if we can explain the increase in 10 acres, there is nothing further to account for. In the second alternative, country A still has ten times the number of species B has but now the component 10 acres of A and B have equal numbers of species. Here the explanation is global, not local—the tropical increase has nothing to do with events within the 10-acre plots and instead has to do with the magnitude of

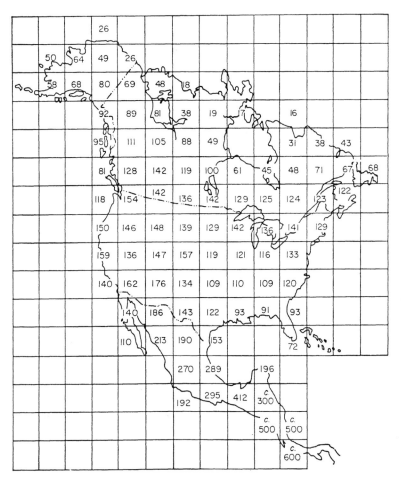

Figure 1. The numbers of breeding land bird species in different parts of North America, from various sources. (After MacArthur & Wilson, 1967.)

faunal differences between habitats. To detect the difference between these alternatives, plotting logarithms of the numbers of species is useful because than a constant vertical distance between curves indicates the top one is a constant multiple of the bottom one. In Fig. 2, I attempt to construct careful species-area curves for breeding land birds of various tropical and temperate new world areas ('land' birds are those which appear in the lists from 'pigeons' onwards). In each case I have tried to use nested lists—the birds of the smaller area are a subset of those of the larger area. Notice first that 5 acres of woodland in southern Vermont support about the same fraction of the birds in 6 square miles as do 5 acres on Barro Colorado Island in Panama of the total 6 square miles.

Thus no new causes of tropical diversity appear in that area increase. Rather, even small Panama censuses have the same multiple (about 2·5) of Vermont ones as do 6 square miles. Second, notice that the tropical curve rises faster at the far right, for areas greater than 6 square miles. This surely means that tropical bird species have subdivided the topography of the country into more parts, each species occupying a smaller range. Notice that because the graph is logarithmic, this accounts for most of the extra tropical diversity. Thus, Ecuador has seven times as many species as New England while Barro Colorado has only two and a half times as many as a similar area of southern Vermont.

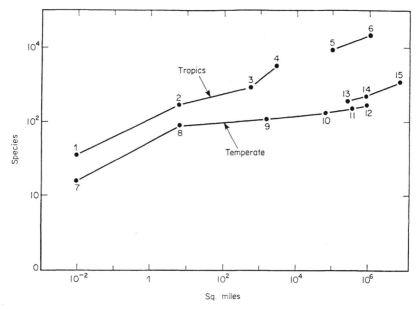

FIGURE 2. The number of breeding land bird species plotted against the area in square miles for tropical and temperate areas. 1, Five-acre census on Barro Colorado Is. (MacArthur, Recher & Cody, 1966). 2, Barro Colorado Island (six sq. miles) (Eisenmann, 1952). 3, Panama Canal Zone (Eisenmann & Loftin, 1967). 4, Republic of Panama (Eisenmann, 1955). 5, Ecuador (de Schauensee, 1966). 6, Columbia plus Ecuador plus Peru (de Schauensee, 1966). 7, Five-acre Vermont census (MacArthur & MacArthur, 1961). 8, Six sq. miles in southern Vermont (unpublished data). 9, Southern Vermont. 10, New England. 11, Northeastern U.S. and adjacent Canada. 12, Eastern U.S. and Canada. 13, Texas. 14, Western U.S. 15, North America (North of Mexico).
The points for western United States indicate the effect of greater topographic diversity.

This topographic subdivision is fairly clearcut, but the local increase is more puzzling: how do even 5 acres of Panama forest support two and a half times more species than 5 acres of Vermont forest? One more bit of evidence is relevant here: this local increase is largely in number of genera. Thus Barro Colorado has 175 species and 121 genera while the 6 square miles in Vermont have 80 species and 65 genera. The ratio of species is 175:80, i.e. 2·18 while the ratio of genera is 121:65, i.e. 1·86 which is nearly as great. Although genera are slightly arbitrary, I think this clearly means there is an increase in bird structural diversity in the tropics. Orians (in press) has some very interesting tables showing just which new ways of harvesting foods actually appear in the tropics. I shall discuss this later. The density of species is of course not uniform in the tropics.

Highlands and dry areas generally have fewer species than low wet areas. Holdridge (1967) in his figure 3 shows how tree diversity (designated by number of species, tree height, basal area and stem numbers) varies, generally decreasing with lowered temperatures (i.e. altitude in the tropics) and reduced rainfall. Although the data are less complete, numbers of bird species show the same general features. Seasonality is much greater in dry areas and slightly greater in high ones (Atlas Estadistico de Costa Rica, 1953) and the productivity as indicated by annual evapotranspiration is greater in low than high and in wet than dry areas. It is an informative exercise to explain why montane areas in the tropics should have temperate species diversities (although tropical clutch sizes).

One more feature of tropical species diversity needs to be pointed out here. It is not simply related to the species diversity of food. This is obvious for plants, whose food does not come in species. For insects, which eat the trees, there may be a correlation, but probably the number of insect species is more closely correlated with the number of plant genera than the number of plant species. Arthur Shapiro (pers. comm.) has found a correlation between plant genera and butterfly species, but I am not aware of an analysis for other insects. Particular species are sometimes associated with particular plant species, but the number of bird species is not usually associated with the number of plant species. In fact, forests of a single tree species will have as many bird species as others if they have a many-layer aspect due to trees of varied ages present. (MacArthur & MacArthur (1961) for temperate U.S.; Orians (pers. comm.) for tropics.)

Tropical naturalists have long been aware that nesting mortality rates were high in the tropics. The only case I know of a single species whose nesting mortality rates in tropics and temperate zone are known is the red-winged blackbird (*Agelaius phoeniceus*) which nests from Costa Rica to Canada. Dr Gordon Orians has kindly supplied me with data on its mortality in Costa Rica (his own data) and the State of Washington much nearer its northern terminus (data of Celia R. Haigh). These appear in the following table set up for 2×2 X^2 test:

	Costa Rica	Washington
Nest fledging at least one young	20	225
Nests fledging no young	73	274
Total nests	93	499

This is highly significant, so nest mortality rates are indeed higher in the tropics for this and probably most other species. It is well known that clutch sizes are lower in the tropics, but less well known that they are not only low in lowlands but also in highlands (Skutch, 1967). Thus, although tropical mountain species diversity is like the temperate, the clutch sizes are tropical. The highland regions have lower production but probably not much greater seasonality. They also have a more disturbed history, for warm interglacial periods probably eliminated some temperate species from the tops of the mountains.

The relative abundance pattern is particularly interesting because it seems to be well correlated with the number of species present. That is, wherever there are few species—whether in the temperate or on a remote tropical island or, perhaps, on tropical mountains—there are greater extremes of commonness and rarity. Grant (1966) has observed this for island birds, Patrick (see Fig. 3) for diatoms, E. MacArthur for trees, and Joel

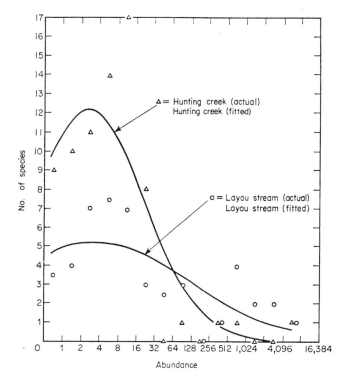

FIGURE 3. Truncated lognormal curves for diatom communities calculated by Patrick according to the method of Preston. Hunting Creek is in Maryland, U.S.A., while Layou Stream is on the island of Dominica in the Lesser Antilles. Notice that on Dominica, where fewer species are present, the standard deviation of the fitted curve is much greater. (After MacArthur & Wilson, 1967.)

Sohn (pers. comm.) for coral reef fish. That these results are not artifacts of sampling is most easily seen by presenting data as in Fig. 3. and estimating the value of the variance of the fitted truncated normal curve (Patrick, Hohn & Wallace, 1954, give the maximum likelihood equations and a graphical solution). The fitted σ^2 is a function of the topographic diversity of the area sampled and hence increases with area, but for fixed areas should be quite independent of adequacy of sample. On fitting truncated lognormal distributions to bird censuses from tropical and temperate and island homogeneous forest areas, I have obtained mean σ^2 values of $1\cdot861 \pm 0\cdot233$ for the temperate, $0\cdot972 \pm 0\cdot157$ for the low tropics and $3\cdot871 \pm 1\cdot437$ for islands. This is merely a documentation of what plant geographers have long known: there is usually less 'dominance' in the tropics.

Finally, the spotty geographic distribution of tropical species is harder to prove, since it can be claimed that further search will reveal the species in what are now regarded as gaps in their distributions. I believe this is not the major explanation and that tropical species do often have disjunct distributions. These are usually called relict distributions in temperate regions, but I believe their prevalence in the tropics reflects a very different cause.

AN HYPOTHESIS TO ACCOUNT FOR THESE PROPERTIES

The simplest—in fact the only—hypothesis I know which can account for all of these properties of tropical communities is that species interactions are important; both competition and predation influence species existence and abundance. The alternative, with which I cannot account for these data, is that species live their lives independently of one another. But if interactions are important the explanation proceeds easily and all of the hypotheses mentioned in the introduction can be amalgamated.

According to this hypothesis the tropical environment is not like a box that will hold only so many eggs; rather it is more like a balloon which resists further invasion proportionally to its present contents but which can always hold a little bit more if necessary. Furthermore its contents always try to escape to regions of lower pressure. Again, according to this hypothesis, if there is a global equilibrium in species diversity, it is achieved by a balance between speciation and immigration on the one hand and extinction and emigration on the other. If the tropical inflow of species were greater, or its outflow were less, then it would equilibrate with more species (Fig. 4).

Next notice that, in theory at least, there is a duality between predator and prey. In the classical predator-prey equations the symbols for predator and prey can be interchanged with only the values of the constants being altered. This leads to the conclusion that if 'Two prey-limited predators cannot coexist in a fine-grained environment containing one prey' is a valid statement, then so is 'Two predator-limited prey cannot coexist in a fine-grained environment containing one predator.' Among two predators, one must be more efficient on a single resource, and among two prey one must be more efficient at avoiding a single predator. Superficially, this seems to mean there must be equal numbers of predator and prey species, but this is a naive oversimplification. Rather there must be equal numbers of predator species and the resources on which they depend. A resource can be just part of a species (fallen leaves or fruit, for instance) or it can be several species which are harvested interchangeably (the plankton caught by a whale, for instance). Hence there should be only a rough correlation between numbers of species in different trophic levels. But they do grow 'hand in hand'. In what follows, I picture resource-limited predators, but everything should apply to predator limited prey and especially to species simultaneously limited by both resources and predators.

Now consider, as species B, C and D in Fig. 5, several species living their lives quite independently. Their abundances will be governed largely by the carrying capacity of the environment. I find it easiest to picture birds in which the abundances may be determined by amounts of resources. One species may require insect food of a particular (*a*) size, (*b*) height in the trees and stability of perch, (*c*) degree of mobility, and (*d*) lying in a habitat of particular layer structure. These four (and there are doubtless some more) requirements are independent; that is, all must be satisfied simultaneously. This means the proportion of resource which is suitable is roughly the product of the proportions independently satisfying the four requirements. Thus the abundances of the species will be determined as the distribution of a product of independent random variables. Now the logarithm of a product of independent random variables is the sum of the logarithms of the random variables, which is a sum of different independent random variables. Such sums become normally distributed, according to the central

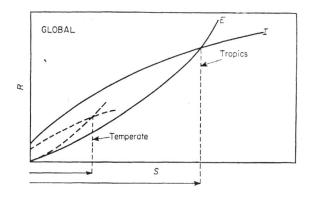

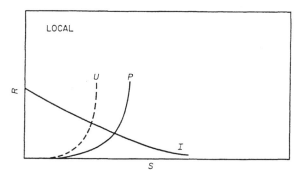

FIGURE 4. R is the rate of extinction plus emigration (curve E) and immigration plus speciation (curve I). On a global level, lower extinction and higher speciation rates will cause a higher equilibrium as shown for the solid lines supposedly representing the tropics. The dotted curves represent the temperate and the arrows show how the numbers of species (S) grow in each area. If history is important the numbers will not be at equilibrium but only part way along the arrows.

In the local graph the rate, I, of immigration falls as the number of species increases because competition can act at this level. U and P are the extinction rates in unproductive and productive environments, respectively.

limit theorem, and hence the logarithm of the product is similarly distributed. (For a more exact distribution, see Feller, 1966, chapter I, section 8.) This means the abundances are lognormally distributed, which is the pattern Preston (1948) found to fit the data and which we have used here (Fig. 3). As speciation adds more species, as in Fig. 5, many have difficulty in establishing a colony, and they become crowded in. The species marked with arrows in the figure, and which are too tightly crowded in, actually become eliminated by competition (MacArthur & Levins, 1967) except in habitats which happen to have an excess of those species' favoured resources. These species will tend to have very spotty distributions. Eventually, as enough species are tried in the area, it will become fairly uniformly packed with species and two features then become apparent. First, the relative abundances become much more uniform as the species overlap to this extent and share the common and rare resources. (The overlapping species act as a sort of smoothing device, smoothing the irregularities in abundance; when packed even tighter, relative abundances again become uneven, this time due to competition.) Second, with further speciation, additional species find it difficult to enter our area, although there may be some substitutions. The new species

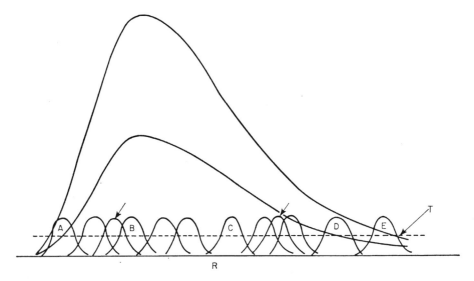

FIGURE 5. The utilization efficiency of various species (small bell-shaped curves) is plotted against a spectrum of resources, R, in a hypothetical community. The high curves indicated densities of the resources in productive and unproductive environments and T is the threshold density necessary for species to maintain their populations. See text for further details.

more easily persist by further subdivision of the geography of the country into small ranges. These two properties are of course exactly what were documented in the last section, and competition would tend to confine species to smaller horizontal layers in the forest as has been documented by MacArthur, Recher & Cody (1966). Within each area there are marginal niches which cannot at present support a species, but which could with an increase in resource production. These are species A, D and E in the figure. In the more productive tropics these species would be present, usually representing new genera, and would constitute part of the increase in species diversity which was found even within a habitat. And there will be more cases of large, medium and small relatives subdividing the food by size. Offshore islands, with fewer species of competitors and predators will, according to our hypothesis, be released to expand their niches. This surely happens (Wetmore, 1957; Grant, 1966; MacArthur & Wilson, 1967). Recher (pers. comm.) has actually shown that Australian habitats of the same layer structure as North American ones contain the same diversity of breeding birds, giving further evidence that there is a global equilibrium of species, in birds at least.

The reduced seasonality in the tropics would have two effects. Like a chain which is as strong as its weakest link, the predators can plausibly be commoner where no season is difficult. Also selection will tend to favour small clutch sizes since only these parents can feed their young successfully, whereas in varying climates there is a great spring bloom of food, which allows the parents with large clutches to outproduce those with small and gives these species a greater opportunity to recolonize each spring. And the increased predation reduces the optimal clutch size by causing disproportionately heavy mortality in large clutches. The increased predation influences the species diversity by reducing the food competition. Since the predation rate is empirically (and theoretically) greater in the tropics with their low seasonality, and since predators tend to focus their attention on common prey, the competition is eased and more species can coexist. Thus, plausibly, a greater historical accumulation of species in an area where production is greater and seasonality is less should, coupled with the effects of competition and predation, produce all of the characteristics of tropical communities. The arguments can be made mathematical, which serves to prove that all of the necessary ingredients are included. (See MacArthur, 1968; MacArthur & Wilson, 1967; MacArthur & Levins, 1967; Levins, 1968 for these mathematics.)

ACKNOWLEDGEMENTS

I have discussed most of these ideas profitably with Richard Levins, Henry Horn and Steven Fretwell, and with Gordon Orians who has kindly supplied me with some data from his forthcoming paper on bird species diversity in Costa Rica. I have also been privileged to see Terborgh and Weske's important account of habitat selection and species diversity in Peruvian birds.

REFERENCES

ATLAS ESTADISTICO DE COSTA RICA, 1953. Casa Grafica Ltda. San José.
CONNELL, J. & ORIAS, E., 1964. The ecological regulation of species diversity. *Am. Nat.* **98**: 399–414.
EISENMANN, E., 1952. Annotated list of birds of Barro Colorado Island, Panama Canal Zone. *Smithson. Misc. Colls*, **117**, No. 5.
EISENMANN, E., 1955. The species of Middle American birds. *Trans. Linn. Soc. N.Y.* **7**, 1–128.
EISENMANN, E. & LOFTIN, H., 1967. *Field check list of the birds of the Panama Canal Zone Area.* Fla. Audubon Society. Maitland, Fla.
FELLER, W., 1966. *An introduction to probability theory and its applications*, **II**. New York: Wiley.
FISCHER, A. G., 1960. Latitudinal gradients in organic diversity. *Evolution*, **14**: 64–68.
GRANT, P., 1966. The density of land birds on the Tres Marías Islands in Mexico. *Can. J. Zool.* **44**, 1023–1030.
HAVERSCHMIDT, F., 1968. *Birds of Surinam.* Edinburgh: Oliver & Boyd.
HOLDRIDGE, L. R., 1967. *Life zone ecology.* Tropical Science Center. San Jose, Costa Rica.
LEVINS, R., 1968. *Evolution in changing environments.* Princeton: Princeton University Press.
MACARTHUR, E. W., 1953. Unpublished thesis. Smith College, Northampton, Mass.
MACARTHUR, R. H., 1968. *The theory of the niche.* In Lewoutin, R. C. (ed.), *Population Biology and Evolution.* Syracuse University Press.
MACARTHUR, R. H. & LEVINS, R., 1967. The limiting similarity, convergence and divergence of coexisting species. *Am. Nat.* **101**: 377–385.
MACARTHUR, R. & MACARTHUR, J. W., 1961. On bird species diversity. *Ecology*, **42**: 594–598.
MACARTHUR, R., RECHER, H. & CODY, M. L., 1966. On the relation between habitat selection and species diversity. *Am. Nat.* **100**: 319–327.
MACARTHUR, R. & WILSON, E. O., 1967. *The theory of island biogeography.* Princeton: Princeton Univ. Press.
ODUM, H. T., CANTLON, J. & KORNICKER, L. S., 1960. An organizational hierarchy postulate. *Ecology*, **41**: 395–399.
ORIANS, G. (in press). The number of bird species in some Costa Rican Forests.

30   ROBERT H. MACARTHUR

PAINE, R. T., 1966. Food web complexity and species diversity. *Am. Nat.* **100**: 65–67.

PATRICK, R., HOHN, M. & WALLACE, J., 1954. A new method for determining the pattern of the diatom flora. *Notul. Nat.* **259**: 1–12.

PATRICK, R. *et al.* The Catherwood Foundation Peruvian-Amazon Expedition. Limnological Studies. *Monogr. Acad. nat. Sci. Philad.* **14**: 1–495.

PIANKA, E., 1966. Latitudinal gradients in species diversity: a review of concepts. *Am. Nat.* **100**: 33–46.

PRESTON. F. W., 1948. The commonness, and rarity, of species. *Ecology*, **29**: 254–283.

ROSENZWEIG, M., 1968. Net primary productivity of terrestrial communities: prediction from climatological data. *Am. Nat.* **102**: 67–74.

SCHAUENSEE, R. M. DE, 1964. *The birds of Columbia.* Narberth, Pa. Livingston Pub. Co.

SCHAUENSEE, R. M. DE, 1966. *The species of birds of South America.* Narberth Pa.: Livingston Pub Co.

SCHOENER, T. & JANZEN, D., 1968. Notes on environmental determinants of tropical vs. temperate insect size patterns. *Am. Nat.* **102**: 207–224.

SKUTCH, A., 1967. Life histories of Central American highland birds. *Publs Nuttall Orn. Club*, No. 7.

WETMORE, A., 1957. The birds of Isla Coiba, Panama. *Smithson. Misc. Colls*, **134**, No. 9.

Diversity in Tropical Rain Forests and Coral Reefs

High diversity of trees and corals is maintained only in a nonequilibrium state.

Joseph H. Connell

The great variety of species in local areas of tropical rain forests and coral reefs is legendary. Until recently, the usual explanation began with the assumption that the species composition of such assemblages is maintained near equilibrium (*1*). The question thus became: "how is high diversity maintained near equilibrium?" One recent answer for tropical bird communities is given as follows: "The working hypothesis is that, through diffuse competition, the component species of a community are selected, and coadjusted in their niches and abundances, so as to fit with each other and to resist invaders" (*2*). In this view, the species composition of tropical communities is a consequence of past and present interspecific competition, resulting in each species occupying the habitat or resource on which it is the most effective competitor. Without perturbation this species composition persists; after perturbation it is restored to the original state (*3*).

In recent years it has become clear that the frequency of natural disturbance and the rate of environmental change are often much faster than the rates of recovery from perturbations. In particular, competitive elimination of the less efficient or less well adapted species is not the inexorable and predictable process we once thought it was. Instead, other forces, often abrupt and unpredictable, set back, deflect, or slow the process of return to equilibrium (*4*). If such forces are the norm, we may question the usefulness of the application of equilibrium theory to much of community ecology.

In this article I examine several hypotheses concerning one aspect of community structure, that is, species richness or diversity (*5*). I first explore the view that communities seldom or never reach an equilibrium state, and that high diversity is a consequence of continually changing conditions. Then I discuss the opposing view that, once a community recovers from a severe perturbation, high diversity is maintained in the equilibrium state by various mechanisms.

Here I apply these hypotheses to organisms such as plants or sessile animals that occupy most of the surface of the land or the firm substrates in aquatic habitats. I consider two tropical communities, rain forests and coral reefs, concentrating on the organisms that determine much of the structure, in these cases, trees and corals. Whether my arguments apply to the mobile species, such as insects, birds, fish, and crabs, that use these structures as shelter or food, or to nontropical regions, remains to be seen. I deal only with variations in diversity within local areas, not with large-scale geographical gradients such as tropical to temperate differences. While the hypotheses I present may help explain them, such gradients are just as likely to be produced by mechanisms not covered in the present article (*6*).

Various hypotheses have been proposed to explain how local diversity is produced or maintained (or both). I have reduced the number to six, which fall into two general categories:

Summary. The commonly observed high diversity of trees in tropical rain forests and corals on tropical reefs is a nonequilibrium state which, if not disturbed further, will progress toward a low-diversity equilibrium community. This may not happen if gradual changes in climate favor different species. If equilibrium is reached, a lesser degree of diversity may be sustained by niche diversification or by a compensatory mortality that favors inferior competitors. However, tropical forests and reefs are subject to severe disturbances often enough that equilibrium may never be attained.

Joseph H. Connell is a professor of biology at the University of California, Santa Barbara 93106.

1) The species composition of communities is seldom in a state of equilibrium. High diversity is maintained only when the species composition is continually changing. (i) Diversity is higher when disturbances are intermediate on the scales of frequency and intensity (the "intermediate disturbance" hypothesis). (ii) Species are approximately equal in ability to colonize, exclude invaders, and resist environmental vicissitudes. Local diversity depends only on the number of species available in the geographical area and the local population density (the "equal chance" hypothesis). (iii) Gradual environmental changes, that alter the ranking of competitive abilities, occur at a rate high enough so that the process of competitive elimination is seldom if ever completed (the "gradual change" hypothesis).

2) The species composition of communities is usually in a state of equilibrium; after a disturbance it recovers to that state. High diversity is then maintained without continual changes in species composition. (iv) At equilibrium each species is competitively superior in exploiting a particular subdivision of the habitat. Diversity is a function of the total range of habitats and of the degree of specialization of the species to parts of that range (the "niche diversification" hypothesis). (v) At equilibrium, each species uses interference mechanisms which cause it to win over some competitors but lose to others (the "circular networks" hypothesis). (vi) Mortality from causes unrelated to the competitive interaction falls heaviest on whichever species ranks highest in competitive ability (the "compensatory mortality" hypothesis).

Nonequilibrium Hypotheses

The intermediate disturbance hypothesis. Organisms are killed or badly damaged in all communities by disturbances that happen at various scales of frequency and intensity. Trees are killed or broken in tropical rain forests by windstorms, landslips, lightning strikes, plagues of insects, and so on; corals are destroyed by agents such as storm waves, freshwater floods, sediments, or herds of predators. This hypothesis suggests that the highest diversity is maintained at intermediate scales of disturbance (Fig. 1).

The best evidence comes from studies of ecological succession. Soon after a severe disturbance, propagules (for example, seeds, spores, larvae) of a few species arrive in the open space. Diver-

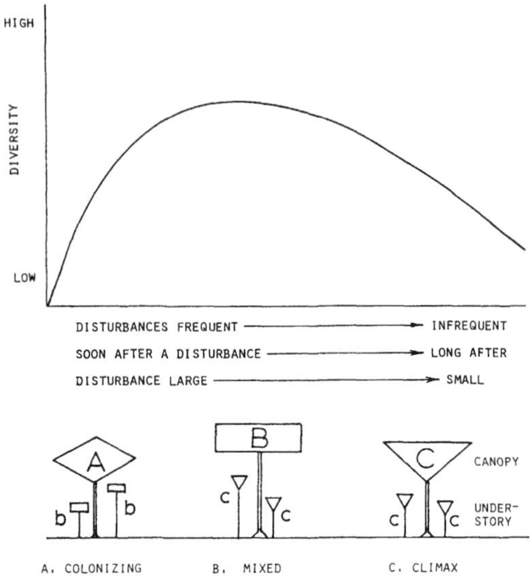

Fig. 1. The "intermediate disturbance" hypothesis. The patterns in species composition of adults and young proposed by Eggeling (8) for the different successional stages of the Budongo forest are shown diagrammatically at the bottom.

sity is low because the time for colonization is short; only those few species that both happen to be producing propagules and are within dispersal range will colonize. If disturbances continue to happen frequently, the community will consist of only those few species capable of quickly reaching maturity.

As the interval between disturbances increases, diversity will also increase, because more time is available for the invasion of more species. New species with lower powers of dispersal and slower growth, that were excluded by more frequent disturbances, can now reach maturity. As the frequency declines further and the interludes between catastrophes lengthen, diversity will decline, for one of two reasons. First, the competitor that is either the most efficient in exploiting limited resources or the most effective in interfering with other species (or both) will eliminate the rest. Second, even if all species were equal in competitive ability, the one that is most resistant to damage or to death caused by physical extremes or natural enemies will eventually fill much of the space. This process rests on the assumption that once a site is held by any occupant, it blocks all further invasion until it is damaged or killed. Thus it competitively excludes all potential invaders, which are by assumption incapable of competitively eliminating it (7).

Thus, diversity will decline during long interludes between disturbances unless other mechanisms, such as those given in the other hypotheses below, intervene to maintain diversity. Disturbances interrupt and set back the pro-

cess of competitive elimination, or remove occupants that are competitively excluding further invaders. Thus, they keep local assemblages in a nonequilibrium state, although large geographic areas may be stable in the sense that species are gained or lost at an imperceptible rate.

Evidence that this model applies to tropical rain forests comes from several sources. Eggeling (8) classified different parts of the Budongo forest of Uganda into three stages: colonizing, mixed, and climax stands. Using observations made many years apart, he showed that the colonizing forest was spreading into neighboring grassland. In these colonizing stands the canopy was dominated by a few species (class A in Fig. 1), but the juveniles (class B in Fig. 1) were of entirely different species. Adults of the class B species occurred elsewhere as canopy trees in mixed stands of many species. In these mixed stands, the juveniles were also mainly of different species (class C, Fig. 1), those with even greater shade tolerance. Adults of class C species occurred in the canopy of other climax stands where a few species dominated (mainly ironwood, *Cynometra alexandrei*, which comprised 75 to 90 percent of the canopy trees). However, in these stands, the understory was composed mainly of juveniles of the canopy species. Thus, an assemblage of self-replacing species (that is, a climax community of low diversity) had been achieved. This is not a special case; the Budongo forest is the largest rain forest in Uganda, and one-quarter of it is dominated by ironwood. Later and more ex-

Table 1. Mortality of young trees (between 0.2 and 6.1 meters tall) in relation to their abundance for two rain forests in Queensland. Not all species had enough young trees to analyze; only those whose adults were capable of reaching the canopy and that had at least six young trees are included. The mortality rate between 1965 and 1974 was plotted against the original numbers mapped in 1965; the least-squares regression slope and correlation coefficient are shown.

Site	Number of species	Regression of mortality (%) on abundance	
		Slope	r*
Tropical, North Queensland, 16°S	49	0.039	0.217
Subtropical, South Queensland, 26°S	46	0.002	0

*Neither correlation coefficient is significantly different from zero at $P < .05$

tensive surveys (9) showed that the proportion so dominated in other forests in Uganda is even higher and have confirmed that, where *Cynometra* dominates the canopy, its juveniles also dominate the understory.

Another excellent example is the work of Jones (10) in Nigeria. In this diverse tropical forest, many of the larger trees, aged about 200 years, were dying. They probably became established in abandoned fields in the first half of the 18th century, a time when the countryside was depopulated by the collapse of the Benin civilization. These trees had few offspring; most regeneration was by other species, shade-tolerant and of moderate stature. This mixed forest was in fact an "old secondary" forest that had invaded after agricultural disturbances. It was in about the same state as Eggeling's mixed forest in Uganda. In both Nigeria and Uganda, high diversity was found in a nonequilibrium intermediate stage in the forest succession.

In many studies of forest dynamics, the abundance of juvenile stages constitutes the evidence as to whether a species is expected to increase or to die out. Such inferences are of course open to the criticism that, if the mortality rate of juveniles increases with their abundance, it is not necessarily a good indicator of more successful recruitment. I tested this for young trees in two rain forest plots in Queensland that several colleagues and I have been studying since 1963 (11). Over a 9-year period, mortality showed no correlation with abundance (Table 1). Thus, it seems safe to assume that species which now have many offspring will be more abundant in the next generation of adult trees as compared to those species which now have few offspring.

In most of the mixed, highly diverse stands of tropical rain forests that have been studied, some species are represented by many large trees with few or no offspring, whereas others have a superabundance of offspring (8, 10–12). (Of course, many species are so rare as

adults that one would not expect to find many offspring.) My interpretation of this finding is that these mixed tropical forests represent a nonequilibrium intermediate stage in a succession after a disturbance, in which some species populations are decreasing whereas others are increasing. Since mixed rain forests are common in the tropics, this hypothesis suggests that disturbance is frequent enough to maintain much of the region in the nonequilibrium state.

If this is so, tropical forests dominated by a single canopy species that has abundant offspring in the understory must not have been disturbed for several generations. Such forests, similar to the ironwood climax of Eggeling (8), also occur commonly elsewhere in Africa as well as in tropical America and Southeast Asia (13). Two lines of evidence indicate that they have been less frequently disturbed than have mixed forests. First, the only papers that I have found in which the incidence of storms was described in relation to single-dominant forests state that destructive storms "never occur" in these regions (8, 14). Second, many of these forests are unlikely to have been disturbed by man, because they lie on poor soils, in swamps or along creek margins, on steep stony slopes, or on highly leached white sands (12, 15). All of these are soils that the farmers of shifting cultivation in forests avoid since they produce very poor crops (12). Such agriculture is confined mainly to the well-drained good soils, and these are the soils where the mixed diverse forests exist. Thus, mixed forests occur in the places most likely to have been disturbed by man, whereas single-dominant forests occur in those least likely to have been disturbed.

Since single-dominant forests often (though not always) lie on poor soils, it has usually been assumed that this is because only a few species have evolved adaptations to tolerate them (12, 15). However, the difference between forests on good soils and those on poor soils lies in the dominance of a single species in

the canopy rather than in the total number of species. Thus, in comparing plots in rain forests in Guyana, the commonest species constituted 16 percent of the large trees (more than 41 centimeters in diameter) on good soils and 67 percent on poor soils (leached white sands), yet the number of species of trees more than 20 centimeters in diameter was 55 and 49, respectively [table 27 in (12)]. Thus, a large number of moderate- to large-sized tree species occupy poor soils, even though only a few are common. The best evidence that single-species dominance is not necessarily due to poor soils is the example of the Budongo forest. Here, various forest stands, ranging from ones of mixed high diversity to those with single-species dominance, each occur on similar soils. Single-species dominance seems to be explained more satisfactorily by the absence of disturbance rather than by poor soil quality.

On coral reefs, the relation between disturbance and diversity is similar to that in tropical forests. At Heron Island, Queensland, the highest number of species of corals occurs on the crests and outer slopes that are exposed to damaging storms. Since I began studying this reef in 1962, two hurricanes have passed close to it, one in 1967 and one in 1972. Each destroyed much coral on the crest and outer slopes but failed to damage another slope protected by an adjacent reef. The disturbed areas have been recolonized by many species after each hurricane, but colonization has not been so dense that competitive exclusion has yet begun to reduce the diversity (Fig. 2A). Other workers on corals have witnessed the same phenomenon; disturbances caused both by the physical environment and by predation remove corals and then recolonization by many species follows (16, 17).

In contrast, in permanently marked quadrats observed over several years without disturbance at Heron Island, I found that competitive elimination of neighboring colonies was a regular feature, either by one colony overshadowing or overgrowing another, or by direct aggressive interactions (18). Here competition is by interference, rather than by more efficient exploitation of resources. On one region of the south outer slope, protected from storm disturbance by an adjacent reef, huge old colonies of a few species of "staghorn" corals occupy most of the surface (Fig. 2B). Since these are able to overshadow neighbors (18) at a height sufficient to be out of reach of the mesenteric filaments used as defenses (19), I infer that such staghorns have in fact competitively eliminated many neighbors during their growth. Here competitive elimination has apparently gone to completion, with a consequent reduction in local diversity. A similar situation has been described for Hawaii (*16*) and for the Pacific coast of Panama (*17*).

The discussion so far has concerned mainly the frequency of disturbance. However, the same reasoning applies to variations in intensity and area perturbed; diversity is highest when disturbances are intermediate in intensity or size, and lower when disturbances are at either extreme. For example, if a disturbance kills all organisms over a very large area, recolonization in the center comes only from propagules that can travel relatively great distances and that can then become established in open, exposed conditions. Species with such propagules are a small subset of the total pool of species, so diversity is low. In contrast, in very small openings, mobility is less advantageous: the ability to become established and grow in the presence of resident competitors and natural enemies is critical. In addition, recolonizing propagules are more likely to come from adults adjacent to the small opening. Therefore, colonizers will again be a small subset of the available pool of species, and diversity will tend to be low. When disturbances create intermediate-sized openings, both types of species can colonize and the diversity should be higher than at either extreme.

Not only the size, but also the intensity of disturbances makes a difference. If the disturbance was less intense so that some residents were damaged and not killed, in a large area recolonization would come both from propagules and from regeneration of survivors, so that diversity would be greater than was the case when all residents were killed and colonization came only from new propagules.

Direct evidence linking diversity with variations in intensity and total area of disturbance in tropical communities is meager. However, there is evidence that the processes described above do occur. For example, a 40-kilometer-wide swath of reef in Belize was heavily damaged by a hurricane in 1961, with lesser damage on both sides. Four years later, in the middle of the swath, new colonies of a few species were present, but the only significant frame-building corals, mainly *Acropora palmata*, were the survivors of the original storm (*20*). Ten years later many of the new colonies were of this species. In contrast, in the zone of lesser damage, colonies and broken fragments of many species had survived the storm

and had regenerated quickly so that recovery was complete.

Likewise, in rain forests, the size and intensity of a disturbance influences the process of recolonization. In a long-term study of a small experimental opening made in a Queensland rain forest, the most successful colonists after 12 years were either stump sprouts from survivors of the initial bulldozing or seedlings that came from adult trees at the edge of the clearing (*21*). Farther from the forest edge, in a much larger clearing, only species with great powers of seed dispersal had colonized (*22*).

It has recently been suggested (*23*) that in a nonequilibrium situation, any conditions that increase the population growth rates of a community of competitors should result in decreased diversity (since faster growth produces faster competitive displacement). In places with a lower rate of competitive elimination, there is also a greater chance for interruption by further disturbances. This "rate of competitive displacement" hypothesis is an extension of the intermediate disturbance hypothesis and should be true, other things being equal. How relevant it is for explaining differences in local diversity remains to be seen. However, present evidence from tropical communities does not support it. Forests on extreme soils (such as

leached white sands, heavy silt, or steep stony slopes) that have slower growth rates than those on less extreme soils have either few species or strong single-species dominance (*24*). Likewise, coral diversity shows little correlation with growth rates. Coral diversity varies with increasing depth, sometimes decreasing, sometimes increasing, or sometimes being greatest at intermediate depths. Coral growth rates tend to be faster at intermediate depths (*24*). Thus, among neither tropical rain forest trees nor corals is there a consistent correlation of diversity and growth rates, as predicted by the hypothesis.

In summary, variations in diversity between local stands of these tropical communities are more likely to be due to differences in the degree of past disturbances than to differences in the rate of competitive displacement during recovery from the disturbances. The high diversities observed in tropical rain forest trees and in corals on reefs appear to be a consequence of disturbances intermediate in the scales of frequency and intensity.

The equal chance hypothesis. In contrast to the previous model, let us assume that all species are equal in their abilities to colonize empty spaces, hold them against invaders, and survive the vicissitudes of physical extremes and natu-

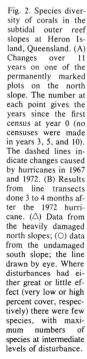

Fig. 2. Species diversity of corals in the subtidal outer reef slopes at Heron Island, Queensland. (A) Changes over 11 years on one of the permanently marked plots on the north slope. The number at each point gives the years since the first census at year 0 (no censuses were made in years 3, 5, and 10). The dashed lines indicate changes caused by hurricanes in 1967 and 1972. (B) Results from line transects done 3 to 4 months after the 1972 hurricane. (△) Data from the heavily damaged north slopes; (○) data from the undamaged south slope; the line drawn by eye. Where disturbances had either great or little effect (very low or high percent cover, respectively) there were few species, with maximum numbers of species at intermediate levels of disturbance.

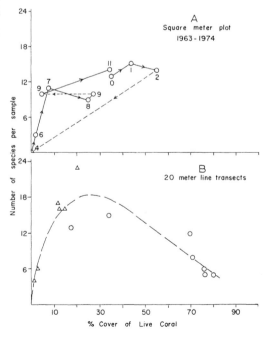

ral enemies. Then local diversity would simply be a function of the number of species available and the local population densities. The species composition at any site would be unpredictable, depending upon the history of chance colonization.

What conditions would produce this? First, for all species the number of young (such as larvae and seeds) invading empty places must be independent of the number produced by the parent population. Otherwise, any species that increased its production of offspring per parent would progressively increase at the expense of those with lesser production. Second, any occupant must be able to hold its place against invaders until it is damaged or killed. Otherwise, any species that evolved the ability to oust an occupant would also progressively increase. Last, all species must be equal in ability to resist physical extremes and natural enemies. Otherwise, the most resistant species will gradually increase, as was discussed in the previous hypothesis.

Do communities exist that satisfy these conditions? Sale (25) has proposed that certain guilds of coral reef fish do. He assumes that, as with many temperate fish, recruitment to newly vacated sites is independent of the stock of eggs released into the plankton. One must probably assume that the fecundity and mortality of all species are equal. The juveniles grow quickly after they colonize to vacant places, and thus they are able to hold their territory against further invasion by smaller juveniles of any species from the plankton. Space is limiting, as judged from the rapid colonization of vacated sites. Since the juvenile fish seem to be generalists in the use of food and space, Sale suggests that local diversity would be a function of chance colonization from the available pool of species. Clearly, the initial assumption of independence of stock and recruitment is critical and needs to be tested for these tropical fish.

Likewise, for rain forest trees, Aubreville (26) has suggested that many species have such similar ecological requirements that it would be impossible to predict which subset would occur together on a site. He based this suggestion on the observation that some of the commoner large trees on his study plot in the Ivory Coast had few or no offspring on the plot. He inferred that their offspring must be elsewhere, so that the species composition of the forest would continually shift in space and time. While this might be so, his original observation of few offspring could be explained if the

forest was an old secondary one, similar to Jones' (10) in Nigeria.

Other characteristics of trees and corals do not satisfy the requirements of the equal chance hypothesis. For example, dispersal of propagules of many trees and corals is quite restricted so that local recruitment of juveniles may not be as independent of local production of propagules as it apparently is in some fish populations. Likewise, species differ in fecundity, competitive ability, and resistance to environmental stresses, and the differences often result in predictable patterns of species distribution along environmental gradients (27). Therefore, it seems unlikely that either rain forest trees or corals conform to the equal chance hypothesis.

The gradual change hypothesis. This model was suggested by Hutchinson (28) to explain why many species coexist in phytoplankton assemblages. Seasonal changes in, for example, temperature and light, occur in a lake, and different species are assumed to be competitively superior at different times. It is postulated that no species has time to eliminate others before its ability to win in competition is reduced below that of another species by changes in the environment.

Climates change on all time scales from seasonal to annual to millennial and longer, and hence, this hypothesis may apply to organisms with any length of generation. With long-lived organisms such as trees or corals, gradual changes in climate over several hundred years represent the same scale as seasons do to a phytoplankton community. Drier periods producing a savanna vegetation in regions now covered with rain forest occurred about 3000 and 11,000 years ago in the Amazon basin; similar changes occurred in Africa and Australia (29). As Livingston (30) pointed out, "Climates change and vegetational adjustments are not rare and isolated events, they are the norm." As climates changed, marine transgressions shifted and altered coral reef environments (31).

Whether such gradual transitions would also produce the highly intermingled diverse assemblages seen in present forests and reefs depends on the rate of competitive elimination compared to the rate of environmental change. If the time required for one tree species to eliminate another in competition is much shorter than the time taken for an environmental change that reversed their positions in the hierarchy, they would not coexist. Therefore, very slow changes would not maintain diversity, but higher rates might do so.

Equilibrium Hypotheses

The niche diversification hypothesis. The key point in this model is the degree of specialization to subdivisions of the habitat. For a given range of habitat variation, more species can be packed in the more they are specialized. The question is: Are the species so often observed living in diverse local assemblages sufficiently specialized to coexist at equilibrium? Some ecologists believe that motile animals have reached the required degree of specialization, particularly if different aspects of habitat subdivision are considered (32). The different aspects such as food, habitat space, and time of activity are called "niche axes."

Specialization along niche axes does not seem to have evolved to this extent in plants and in sessile aquatic animals such as corals. For long-lived organisms there exists no regular temporal variation to which they could have specialized. Plants in general have not specialized along the food niche axis. They all have similar basic resource requirements (such as light, water, carbon dioxide, and mineral nutrients). Niche subdivisions are made on degrees of tolerance to different quantities of these resources. As a consequence, plants subdivide space along gradients of quantitative variations in light, water, and nutrients. These variations are often associated with variations in elevation, slope, aspect, soil type, understory position, and so on. Exceptions to this idea are marine algae that have adapted to the qualitative changes in wavelength of light at different depths. General observations and some statistical analyses (12, 15, 33) have revealed associations between sets of species and certain subdivisions of the habitat in tropical rain forests, for example, to broad variations in soil properties (such as parent material, drainage, and tip-up mounds and hollows at the roots of fallen trees), and topography (ridges, steep slopes, creek margins, and so on). Other analyses have shown little association between species and local soil types (15, p. 188). As was discussed earlier, plants are also specialized according to differences in habitats caused by variations in the frequency and intensity of disturbance. The aftermath of a disturbance presents a new local environment in which species with different traits are at an advantage. It has been suggested that tropical trees may have subdivided this niche axis finely (34); at present there is little direct evidence to support this view. It seems unlikely that tropical trees are so highly specialized to such small differences in the local physical environment that more than 100 species of trees could coexist at equilibrium on a single hectare of rain forest. In fact, the forests closest to equilibrium are those dominated by a single tree species, as was discussed earlier.

Corals seem as general in their requirements as trees; for example, although some of their energy comes from feeding on zooplankton, much comes from photosynthesis by their symbiotic zooxanthellae, which consist of a single species in all coral species studied to date, although several different strains detected by electrophoresis show some degree of specificity (*35*). It has been suggested (*36*) that corals have differentiated along the food niche axis between the extremes of autotrophy and heterotrophy. However, in shallow water where both light and species diversity is high, this differentiation could promote the coexistence of several species on the same space only if they were stratified vertically, autotrophs above, heterotrophs in the understory. Yet the layering observed thus far has not revealed specialized "shade" species adapted for life in the understory. Corals have been seen beneath open-branched species such as the Caribbean *Acropora cervicornis* (*37*) but, to my knowledge, never beneath close-branched species. One might expect that hetertrophy would be advantageous where light is reduced by deeper water. Yet there is evidence that a predominantly autotrophic coral was able, over a day's time, to meet its energy requirements down to a water depth of 25 meters (*38*). Thus, the proposed niche differentiation along the food axis has apparently contributed little to coexistence, and corals seem very generalized in their use of resources. On the habitat niche axis, corals are also generalized. Although some species are confined to certain zones, most corals have broad ranges of distribution with respect to depth and location on reefs, which indicates little precise specialization in habitat (*39*). Thus, like rain forest trees, corals do not seem to have specialized to the degree required to maintain the observed high diversities at equilibrium.

The circular networks hypothesis. This model suggests that, instead of the linear and transitive hierarchy (A eliminates B, B eliminates C, implying A eliminates C) presumed in the other hypotheses, the competitive hierarchy is circular (A > B > C, but C eliminates A directly). This hypothesis was first applied to sessile invertebrates living beneath ledges on coral reefs (*40*). Since it seems unlikely that the same competitive

mechanism could apply throughout such circular interactions, the reverse pathway acting against the highest ranked species is likely to be a different mechanism. For example, if species A and B overshadow the species below them in the hierarchy, but C poisons A, the network is biologically more plausible. A difficulty arises if the interactions are not exactly balanced: if A eliminated B first, then C, no longer reduced by B, would quickly eliminate A. However, if the species in this network competed only in pairs, none would be eliminated.

I tested this hypothesis (*18*) for interactions between adjacent coral colonies on a permanently marked plot (12 species, 55 colonies, 82 interactions observed over 9 years) and found no circular pathways, even though two mechanisms, overshadowing and direct extracoelenteric digestion, were acting. It is more likely that these networks would operate between more distantly related organisms. The original observations involved different phyla of invertebrates (*40*).

Among trees of the rain forest this hypothesis has not been examined. Shading, root competition, and allelopathy are different mechanisms, so that some circular networks might be possible. However, trees may also be too similar for this to maintain diversity.

The compensatory mortality hypothesis. If mortality falls most heavily on whichever species is ranked highest in competitive ability, or, if they are all of approximately equal rank and it falls heaviest on whichever species is commonest (that is, mortality is frequency-dependent), competitive elimination may be prevented indefinitely. In tropical forests, if herbivores attack and kill seeds or seedlings of common species more frequently and to a greater extent than they attack those of less common or rare species competitive elimination could be prevented. For example, if herbivores attack the offspring of a species more heavily nearer than farther from the parent tree, that species would probably not be able to form a single-species grove (*41*). This possibility has been tested by either observations or field experiments and rejected for four out of five species of seeds of rain forest trees and vines, but not rejected for seedlings in two other species (*41, 42*). In the analysis reported in Table 1, the mortality of seedlings or saplings did not increase significantly with their abundance. Thus, mortality of young trees is not generally frequency-dependent. Destruction of trees by elephants also does not seem to be compensatory. In Ugandan rain forests it has

been observed (*43*) that elephants preferentially destroy young of the fast-growing early and middle succession trees, leaving the young of the late succession ironwood alone, thus hastening progression toward the low-diversity forest. Therefore, contrary to my own earlier work on this aspect (*41*), I feel that while compensatory mortality may occur in some instances it does not seem to be a generally important factor in maintaining the high diversity of mixed tropical rain forests.

Watt's (*44*) "cyclic succession" is probably an example of this mechanism. The dominant species does not replace itself; other species intervene before the dominant becomes reestablished. This process has never, to my knowledge, been demonstrated in the tropics, but there seems no reason not to expect it to happen there.

In coral reefs, some predation does not act in a frequency-dependent fashion. An earlier claim (*45*) that the starfish *Acanthaster planci* might act in this way has now been demonstrated to be in error. Studies in Hawaii and Panama (*46*) indicate that the starfish attacks rarer species preferentially, which would reduce diversity. Studies in a much more diverse coral community on Saipan (*47*) suggest that *Acanthaster* might eliminate certain preferred species, although no data were given which indicated whether these were the common or rare species. In Panama, evidence indicates that other types of predators may possibly act in a compensatory manner, increasing diversity (*17, 46*).

In my studies of corals I found that the physical environment can inflict mortality in a manner that compensates for the competitive advantage of branching species that overshadow others. I measured the mortality of corals over a 4-year period that included a hurricane at Heron Island in Queensland (*18*). As described above, I had ranked these species in competitive ability by observing dynamic interactions over a period of 9 years on permanent quadrats. On the part of the reef crest that was badly damaged by the hurricane, the mortality of those species of corals that ranked high in the competitive hierarchy was much greater than those that ranked low. In contrast, the high-ranked species on an undamaged part of the reef crest had a lower mortality than low-ranked species, over the same period. The reason for the difference was that the high-ranked corals were branching species observed to grow above their neighbors, overshadowing and thus killing them. However, these branching species were more heavily damaged in the storms. Thus, species of corals that ordinarily win in competition suffer proportionately more from storm damage, compensating for their advantage.

In certain situations, diversity, instead of decreasing with high coral cover (Fig. 2), increases. This occurs on the very shallow reef crests at Heron Island and is due to compensatory mortality. The larger colonies that are spreading horizontally and eliminating their neighbors tend to die in the center, where they have grown up above the low tide level. This provides open spaces in which new species can colonize. Thus, on the reef crest no species is capable of monopolizing the space, in contrast to the slope situations shown in Fig. 2B.

High diversity at high cover has also been found in the Caribbean, and it was proposed that a balance in competitive abilities exists at equilibrium (48). Last, it occurred in the deepest samples at Eilat, Red Sea (49). Although no explanation was suggested for this last-mentioned instance, it and the Caribbean one could be explained by the intermediate disturbance hypothesis. In both cases, the slope is steep where diversity is highest. In such places, small-scale disturbances occur by slumping of coral blocks (17, 46). The deep corals at Eilat are very small (more than 100 colonies in some 10-meter line transects), which might indicate that they are recent colonists after local disturbances.

Tests of the Hypotheses

Hypotheses are made to be tested, and, in ecology, field experiments are often an excellent way to do so (50). The intermediate disturbance hypothesis can be tested in various ways. It will be necessary to verify that the sequence observed by Eggeling (8) also occurs in other rain forests. Probably the best way to do this would be to examine gaps of various sizes within forests dominated by a single species. In very small openings the shade-tolerant offspring of the dominant should grow and survive better than other species, whereas in larger openings, juveniles of less shade-tolerant species should perform better. To estimate the probability of replacement, one would need to measure the abundance and sizes of each species having juveniles in the light gap, and if possible their rates of growth and mortality. Even better than such observations are experimental transplants into different-sized light gaps of seedlings of species whose adults live in mixed and in

single-dominant stands. These experiments would test the prediction that the species of the single-dominant stands will be more successful in small openings near the parent tree, whereas those of mixed stands will be more successful in larger openings. The alternative hypothesis, that single-dominant stands are due to poor soils, could be tested by experimentally improving soils (by draining, for example, or by fertilizing) and then planting seedlings of species that do or do not live in poor soils, in these plots and in unmodified control plots.

Tests of the equal chance hypothesis involve determining whether recruitment is (i) independent of adult stock, and (ii) equal among the different species. This is a difficult problem if propagules are distributed widely. In addition, equality in ability to resist invaders, extremes of the physical environment, and natural enemies must be established. Sale (25) has made a start on this in his experiments with coral reef fish.

The hypothesis of continual change is difficult to test because of the impracticality of determining the fate of organisms as long-lived as trees or corals. Pollen records in lake sediments are seldom precise enough to distinguish species, although genera are often identifiable.

Attempts to test the niche-diversification hypothesis are sometimes made by postulating how the different species could divide up resources and then seeing whether the coexisting species overlap significantly in their use of resources. The degree of overlap is sometimes judged indirectly by the range of variation in those aspects of morphology associated with resource use, such as root depth in plants, or degree of branching and polyp size in corals. However, these indirect measures are open to the criticism that the particular resource chosen (or the structure used to indicate it) may not be the one for which the species are competing. Another criticism is that competition may not be taking place through superior efficiency in exploiting resources, but by superior ability in interfering with competitors. Until a precise definition of the range of resources of each species is specified, this hypothesis will remain untestable.

The circular networks hypothesis might be tested either by observing as many interactions as possible, or better, by transplanting individuals into mixed and single-species groups. Since circular networks are apparently rare, many replicate observations must be made if such a network is found. For example, if a single set of observations indicated that

$(A > B > C > A)$, further observations might uncover an instance where $(A > C)$, indicating "equal chance," which I found in observing coral interactions (18).

The compensatory mortality hypothesis can be tested in various ways. Observations of density and mortality before and after storms or predator attacks would reveal whether highly ranked species suffered greater mortality (18). Experiments in which seeds were placed both near and far from adult trees, or in both dense clumps and sparsely, have been done with several species of tropical trees (41, 42). Observations on the mortality of naturally occurring seedlings and on experimental plantings both near and far from adults have also been made (11). In addition, I have used cages to exclude insects and larger herbivores from seeds and seedlings, using opensided cages as controls. The purpose was to establish whether natural enemies act in a compensatory way. The experiments done so far should be regarded as pilot ones, since they were done with few replicates on a few species. More experiments need to be done before the role of compensatory mortality can be established.

Conclusion

This article discusses two opposing views of the organization of assemblages of competing species such as tropical trees or corals. One is that stability usually prevails and, when a community is disturbed, it quickly returns to the original state. Natural selection fits and adjusts species into this ordered system. Therefore, ecological communities are highly organized, biologically accommodated, coevolved species assemblages in which efficiency is maximized, life history strategies are optimized, populations are regulated, and species composition is stabilized. Tropical rain forests and coral reefs are generally regarded as the epitomes of such ordered systems. The last three hypotheses presented in this article detail the mechanisms that may maintain these systems.

In the contrasting view, equilibrium is seldom attained: disruptions are so common that species assemblages seldom reach an ordered state. Communities of competing species are not highly organized by coevolution into systems in which optimal strategies produce highly efficient associations whose species composition is stabilized. The first three hypotheses represent this view.

My argument is that the assemblages

of those organisms which determine the basic physical structure of two tropical communities (rain forest trees and corals) conform more closely to the non-equilibrium model. For these organisms, resource requirements are very general: inorganic substances (water, carbon dioxide, minerals) plus light and space, and, for corals, some zooplankton. It is highly unlikely that these can be partitioned finely enough to allow 100 or more species of trees to be packed, at equilibrium, on a single hectare (12). Instead, if competition is allowed to proceed unchecked, a few species eliminate the rest. The existence of high local diversity in the face of such overlap in resource requirements is a problem only if one assumes equilibrium conditions. Discard the assumption and the problem vanishes.

Although I have presented these ideas as separate hypotheses, they are not mutually exclusive. Within a local area, there are usually enough variations in habitats and resources to enable several species to coexist at equilibrium as a result of niche differentiation. In addition, a certain amount of compensatory mortality probably occurs, as some evidence from rain forests indicates (41, 42). In special circumstances, circular networks might also increase diversity. Thus, a certain amount of local diversity would exist under equilibrium conditions.

However, climates do change gradually, which probably results in changes in the competitive hierarchy. On a shorter time scale, disturbances frequently interrupt the competitive process. These variations prevent most communities from ever reaching equilibrium. In certain special cases, species may be so alike in their competitive abilities and life history characteristics that diversity is maintained by chance replacements.

Thus, all six hypotheses may contribute to maintaining high diversity. My contention is that the relative importance of each is very different. Rather than staying at or near equilibrium, most local assemblages change, either as a result of frequent disturbances or as a result of more gradual climatic changes. The changes maintain diversity by preventing the elimination of inferior competitors. Without gradual climatic change or sudden disturbances, equilibrium may be reached; diversity will then be maintained by the processes described in the hypotheses of niche diversification, of circular networks, and of compensatory mortality, but at a much lower level than is usually observed in diverse tropical forests and in coral reefs.

Although tropical rain forests and cor-

al reefs require disturbances to maintain high species diversity, it is important to emphasize that adaptation to these natural disturbances developed over a long evolutionary period. In contrast, some perturbations caused by man are of a qualitatively new sort to which these organisms are not necessarily adapted. In particular, the large-scale removal of tropical forests with consequent soil destruction (51), or massive pollution by biocides, heavy metals, or oil, are qualitatively new kinds of disturbances, against which organisms usually have not yet evolved defenses. Tropical communities are diverse, thus species populations are usually smaller than those in temperate latitudes, which increases the chances that such new disturbances will cause many species extinctions.

References and Notes

1. Equilibrium of species composition is usually defined as follows: (i) if perturbed away from the existing state (equilibrium point or stable limit cycle), the species composition would return to it; (ii) without further perturbations, it persists in the existing state. A perturbation is usually regarded as a marked change: death and replacement of single trees or coral colonies would not qualify.
2. J. Diamond, in *Ecology and Evolution of Communities*, M. L. Cody and J. Diamond, Eds. (Belknap, Cambridge, Mass., 1975), p. 343.
3. For discussions on ecological stability, natural balance, and related topics, see F. E. Clements, *Carnegie Inst. Wash. Publ.* **242**, 1 (1916); A. J. Nicholson, *J. Anim. Ecol.* **2**, 132 (1933); L. B. Slobodkin, *Growth and Regulation of Animal Populations* (Holt, Rinehart and Winston, New York, 1961), p. 46; R. M. May, *Stability and Complexity in Model Ecosystems* (Princeton Univ. Press, Princeton, N.J., 1973); R. M. May, Ed., *Theoretical Ecology* (Saunders, Philadelphia, 1976), pp. 158–162.
4. For discussions of nonequilibrium communities, see H. A. Gleason [*Bull. Torrey Bot. Club* **43**, 463 (1917)] and H. G. Andrewartha and L. C. Birch [*The Distribution and Abundance of Animals* (Univ. of Chicago Press, Chicago, 1954), pp. 648–665]. The case for the importance of catastrophes in keeping forests away from an equilibrium state is discussed in several of the subsequent references. See also J. D. Henry and J. M. A. Swan, *Ecology* **55**, 772 (1974); H. E. Wright and M. L. Heinselman, *Quat. Res.* (*N.Y.*) **3**, 319 (1973). For corals, see D. W. Stoddart [in *Applied Coastal Geomorphology*, J. A. Steers, Ed. (Macmillan, New York, 1971), pp. 155–197; *Nature (London)* **239**, 51 (1972)]. The case for catastrophes on a geological scale is convincingly presented by C. Vita-Finzi [*Recent Earth History* (Wiley, New York, 1973)] and D. V. Ager [*The Nature of the Stratigraphical Record* (Wiley, New York, 1973)].
5. It has been suggested that the term diversity be restricted to measures that include the relative abundance of species. However, since species number is certainly an indicator of diversity in the common usage of the word and since it is almost always closely correlated with indices based on relative abundance (16), I use the number of species as a measure of diversity.
6. R. W. Osman and R. B. Whitlatch, *Paleobiology*, in press.
7. A recent summary of various models of ecological succession is given by J. H. Connell and R. O. Slatyer [*Am. Nat.* **111**, 1119 (1977)].
8. W. J. Eggeling, *J. Ecol.* **34**, 20 (1947).
9. Later surveys are summarized by I. Langdale-Brown, H. A. Osmaston, and J. G. Wilson [*The Vegetation of Uganda and Its Bearing on Land-Use* (Government of Uganda, Kampala, 1964)]; they point out that in certain smaller forests in Uganda, the ironwood occurs in pure stands mainly on poorer soils. However, this is not the case in the Budongo forest, by far the most extensive in Uganda.
10. E. W. Jones, *J. Ecol.* **44**, 83 (1956).
11. J. H. Connell, J. G. Tracey, L. J. Webb, in preparation.

12. P. W. Richards, *The Tropical Rain Forest* (Cambridge Univ. Press, Cambridge, 1952).
13. Forests dominated by single species are common in northern South America; examples are species of *Mora*, *Eperua*, *Ocotea*, *Dicymbe*, *Dimorphandra*, *Aspidosperma*, and *Peltogyne*. In Africa, the dominants are species of *Macrolobium*, *Cynometra*, *Berlinia*, *Brachystegia*, *Tessmannia*, and *Parinari*. In Southeast Asia, they are species of *Eusideroxylon*, *Dryobalanops*, *Shorea*, and *Diospyros*. It is important to distinguish climax stands from colonizing forests that are also often dominated by a single canopy species that, in contrast, has few or no offspring in the understory (Fig. 1).
14. T. A. W. Davis, *J. Ecol.* **29**, 1 (1941).
15. T. C. Whitmore, *Tropical Rain Forests of the Far East* (Clarendon, Oxford, 1975).
16. R. W. Grigg and J. E. Maragos, *Ecology* **55**, 387 (1974); Y. Loya, *ibid.* **57**, 278 (1976).
17. P. W. Glynn, R. H. Stewart, J. E. McCosker, *Geol. Rundsch.* **61**, 483 (1972).
18. J. H. Connell, in *Coelenterate Ecology and Behavior*, G. O. Mackie, Ed. (Plenum, New York, 1976), pp. 51–58.
19. J. Lang, *Bull. Mar. Sci.* **23**, 260 (1973).
20. D. R. Stoddart, in *Proceedings of the Second International Coral Reef Symposium*, P. Mather, Ed. (Great Barrier Reef Committee, Brisbane, Australia, 1974), vol. 2, p. 473.
21. L. J. Webb, J. G. Tracey, W. T. Williams, *J. Ecol.* **60**, 675 (1972).
22. M. Hopkins, thesis, University of Queensland, Brisbane, Australia (1976).
23. M. Huston, *Am. Nat.*, in press.
24. For variations in tropical tree diversity and growth rates, see (12) and D. H. Janzen, *Biotropica* **6**, 69 (1974). Coral diversity may either increase or decrease with depth or be highest at intermediate depths. See J. W. Wells, *U.S. Geol. Surv. Prof. Pap.* **260**, 385 (1954); D. R. Stoddart, *Biol. Rev.* **44**, 433 (1969); J. E. Maragos, *Pac. Sci.* **28**, 257 (1974); T. F. Dana, thesis, University of California at San Diego (1975); Y. Loya, *Mar. Biol.* **13**, 100 (1972); T. J. Done, in *Proceedings of the Third International Coral Reef Symposium*, D. L. Taylor, Ed. (Univ. of Miami, Fla., 1977), vol. 1, p. 9. Growth of corals has been found to be greater at intermediate depths: see P. H. Baker and J. N. Weber, *Earth Planet. Sci. Lett.* **27**, 57 (1975); S. Neudecker, in *Proceedings of the Third International Coral Reef Symposium*, D. L. Taylor, Ed. (Univ. of Miami, Fla., 1977), vol. 1, p. 317.
25. P. Sale, *Am. Nat.* **111**, 337 (1977).
26. A. Aubreville, *Ann. Acad. Sci. Colon. Paris* **9**, 1 (1938).
27. R. H. Whittaker, *Taxon* **21**, 213 (1972).
28. G. E. Hutchinson, *Am. Nat.* **75**, 406 (1941); *ibid.* **95**, 137 (1961).
29. J. Haffer, *Science* **165**, 131 (1969); B. S. Vuilleumier, *ibid.* **173**, 771 (1971); A. Kearst, R. L. Crocker, C. S. Christian, *Biogeography and Ecology in Australia Monogr. Biol.* **8** (1959).
30. D. A. Livingstone, *Ann. Rev. Ecol. Syst.* **6**, 249 (1975).
31. D. R. Stoddart, *Symp. Zool. Soc. London* **28**, 3 (1971); J. G. Tracey and H. S. Ladd, in *Proceedings of the Second International Coral Reef Symposium*, P. Mather, Ed. (Great Barrier Reef Committee, Brisbane, Australia, 1974), vol. 2, p. 537; D. Hopley, in *ibid.*, p. 551.
32. T. W. Schoener, *Science* **185**, 27 (1974).
33. W. T. Williams, G. N. Lance, L. J. Webb, J. G. Tracey, J. H. Connell, *J. Ecol.* **57**, 635 (1969); M. P. Austin, P. S. Ashton, P. Grieg-Smith, *ibid.* **60**, 305 (1972).
34. R. Ricklefs, *Am. Nat.* **111**, 376 (1977).
35. D. A. Schoenberg and R. K. Trench, in *Coelenterate Ecology and Behavior*, G. O. Mackie, Ed. (Plenum, New York, 1976), pp. 423–432.
36. R. K. Trench, *Helgol. Wiss. Meeres* **26**, 174 (1974); J. W. Porter, *Am. Nat.* **110**, 731 (1976).
37. J. Lang, personal communication.
38. D. S. Wethey and J. W. Porter, in *Coelenterate Ecology and Behavior*, G. O. Mackie, Ed. (Plenum, New York, 1976), pp. 59–66.
39. T. F. Goreau, *Ecology* **40**, 67 (1959). See also (17) and (24).
40. J. B. C. Jackson and L. Buss, *Proc. Natl. Acad. Sci. U.S.A.* **72**, 5160 (1975); M. Gilpin, *Am. Nat.* **109**, 51 (1975).
41. D. H. Janzen, *Am. Nat.* **14**, 501 (1970); J. H. Connell, in *Dynamics of Populations*, P. J. den Boer and G. R. Gradwell, Eds. (PUDOC, Wageningen, 1970), pp. 298–312. This mechanism could also produce the mosaic pattern envisaged by Aubreville (26).
42. D. H. Janzen, *Ecology* **53**, 258 (1972); D. E. Wilson and D. H. Janzen, *ibid.*, p. 955; D. H. Janzen, *ibid.* p. 350.
43. R. M. Laws, I. S. C. Parker, R. O. B. John-

stone, *Elephants and Their Habitats* (Clarendon, Oxford, 1975).
44. A. S. Watt, *J. Ecol.* **35**, 1 (1947).
45. J. Porter, *Am. Nat.* **106**, 487 (1972).
46. J. M. Branham, S. A. Reed, J. H. Bailey, J. Caperon, *Science* **172**, 1155 (1971); P. W. Glynn, *Environ. Conserv.* **1**, 295 (1974); *Ecol. Monogr.* **46**, 431 (1976).
47. T. E. Goreau, J. C. Lang, E. A. Graham, P. D. Goreau, *Bull. Mar. Sci.* **22**, 113 (1972).
48. J. W. Porter, *Science* **186**, 543 (1974): "There appears to be a balance of abilities divided among the Caribbean corals such that no one species is competitively superior in acquiring and holding space. The effect of this balance of competitive abilities is to retard, even in high-density situations, the rapid competitive exclusion that takes place on undisturbed eastern Pacific reefs" (p. 544); L. A. Maguire and J. W. Porter, *Ecol. Modelling* **3**, 249 (1977).
49. Y. Loya, *Mar. Biol.* **13**, 100 (1972).
50. J. H. Connell, in *Experimental Marine Biology*, R. Mariscal, Ed. (Academic Press, New York, 1974), pp. 21–54.
51. A. Gómez-Pompa, C. Vázquez-Yanes, S. Guevara, *Science* **177**, 762 (1972).

52. I thank the following for critical discussions and readings of earlier drafts: J. Chesson, P. Chesson, J. Dixon, M. Fawcett, L. Fox, S. Holbrook, J. Kastendiek, A. Kuris, D. Landenberger, B. Mahall, P. Mather, J. Melack, W. Murdoch, A. Oaten, C. Onuf, R. Osman, D. Potts, P. Regal, S. Rothstein, W. Schlesinger, S. Schroeter, A. Sih, W. Sousa, R. Trench, R. Warner, G. Wellington, and two anonymous reviewers. Supported by NSF grants GB-3667, GB-6678, GB-23432, and DEB-73-01357, and by fellowships from the J. S. Guggenheim Memorial Foundation.

4

Plant–Animal Interactions and Community Structure

Bette A. Loiselle and Rodolfo Dirzo

Tropical forests are celebrated for their complex species interactions. In this part we focus on interactions between plants and their herbivores, seed predators, pathogens, pollinators, and frugivores. These ecological interactions have played a critical role in shaping the structure and organization of tropical plant and animal communities. Part 5 follows with a related focus on the coevolution of plants and animals in the tropics, emphasizing the evolutionary implications of highly specialized interactions.

Because the strength of species interactions can vary over space and time, understanding their ecological impacts on individuals, populations, and communities is a challenging prospect. Further, such interactions often involve only a subset of processes that affect individual fitness (e.g., pollination, seed removal). Evaluating the ultimate impacts of these interactions requires integrating across processes to quantify relative importance to individual fitness and then scaling up to examine effects on population and community parameters. Unfortunately, unprecedented rates of habitat alteration in the tropics during the past few decades (see part 11) have resulted in disruptions of a number of these species interactions (e.g., see Janzen 1970 [paper 17]; Stiles 1975 [paper 20];

Curran et al. 1999). These alterations have hampered our ability to unravel the complexities and ultimate importance of plant–animal interactions in tropical forests. Ironically, the role of some animals in forest ecosystems may become more evident when their abundance is reduced or when they are locally eradicated (Dirzo and Miranda 1991).

An underlying theme of the four items appearing in this part is the effect of animals on the maintenance of tropical plant diversity. Janzen (1970; paper 17) sought to understand how so many tree species can be packed into a tropical forest, and citing Paine's (1966) classic work, he considered how ecological forces can prevent "single species from monopolizing some important, limiting, requisite" (502, quoting Paine). Coley (1980; paper 18) examined differential susceptibility of tropical tree species to herbivores in relation to leaf age and plant life history patterns. Stiles (1975) examined how behavior and energy requirements of hummingbirds can influence phenology and flowering characteristics of *Heliconia* plants in the New World tropics, whereas van der Pijl (1972; paper 19) described adaptations and diversification of fruiting structures in response to major suites of fruit-feeding animals. Here we emphasize significant findings of the four selected

Hummingbirds. From Belt (1874)

contributions, highlight influential related studies that followed, and finally attempt to identify key directions that emerged from these studies of species interactions in tropical wet forest ecosystems.

Herbivores and Tree Spacing

The potential importance of "pests" in influencing population abundance and species richness was first discussed by J. B. Gillett (1962). He offered an explanation as to why species that appeared to be well adapted to their environments were infrequently encountered in nature. Gillett (1962) wrote: "Here is the answer to the mystery. Pest pressure is the inevitable, ubiquitous factor in evolution which makes for an apparently pointless multiplicity of species in all areas in which it has time to operate" (40). Gillett hoped to stimulate discussion and research with this new idea, and he clearly succeeded. In developing the theories presented in his 1970 paper (paper 17), Janzen cited observations by Gillett (1962) and others that demonstrated high levels of seed predation by a number of specialized insects.

Janzen (1970) provided a theoretical framework for understanding the effects of natural enemies on tree species richness, density, and dispersion in lowland tropical forests. He proposed that juvenile mortality is disproportionately high close to parent plants due to distance- and density-dependent predation by host-specific agents and by facultative seed or seedling predators. Consequently, adult recruitment occurs at distances away from other adults and spacing between adult trees is more regularly distributed than one would expect based on initial seed shadows (see also Schupp 1992). Janzen hypothesized that such density-dependent predation lowers local density and provides open habitat for additional species, thus promoting high tree species diversity and low density in tropical forests.

Shortly after publication of Janzen's (1970) work, Connell (1971) also predicted disproportionate juvenile mortality under adult trees due to the presence of herbivores that normally feed on adults. Connell and Janzen independently reached similar conclusions regarding the impact of herbivores on tree species diversity and dispersion. They both anticipated that effects of host-specific predators and pathogens on maintenance of tree species diversity would be greatest in tropical wet forests, where these animals are most abundant. This model, now known as the Janzen-Connell model, stimulated considerable theoretical and empirical work, although as Janzen (1970) predicted, testing this important theory has been problematic.

Three general features about tropical rain forests underlie the hypotheses proposed by Janzen (1970) and Connell (1971). These are: (1) high number of tree species, (2) low adult tree densities, and (3) spacing patterns that are more regular than one would predict based on seed shadows. The first two are well-known, long-established features of these forests (see parts 1 and 8), whereas the third was based on Janzen's own observations in Central and South America, discussions with foresters and with Joseph Connell regarding Australian rain forests. The Janzen-Connell model does not universally apply to tropical forests. For example, Whitmore (1975) pointed out that in some dipterocarps the fallen fruits are less heavily attacked near the parent tree. The universality of regular spacing patterns of tropical trees has also come under question. Hubbell (1979, 1980) challenged the Janzen-Connell model on the basis that tree species in a tropical dry forest showed clumped rather than uniform spacing. Hubbell (1979) proposed that densities of seeds and seedlings are highest below parent trees due to larger concentrations of seeds near rather than far from parents, despite greater risk of mortality. Condit et al. (2000) examined spatial patterns of tree distribution in six plots (25–52 ha in size) in five tropical countries, and reported that most tree species have aggregated spatial patterns (see also Lieberman and Lieberman 1994). Their observation that aggregation is weaker in larger-diameter classes, however, is compatible with the view that density-dependent mortality factors, such as herbivores and plant diseases, play a role in reducing aggregation. Dispersal limitation and seed shadows also influence aggregation patterns in tree populations. In the two Malaysian plots, dipterocarps with poorly dispersed winged seeds were strikingly more aggregated than nondipterocarps (Condit et al. 2000).

Clark and Clark (1984) argued that uniform spacing is not a prediction of the Janzen-Connell model (see also Becker et al. 1985). The survival pattern of juveniles over time, rather than the spacing among and between juveniles and adults, must be addressed in testing the theory (Clark and Clark 1984; Becker et al. 1985; Hammond and Brown 1998). By following cohorts of *Platypodium elegans* in Panama, Augspurger (1983a, 1983b) found evidence for both density- and distance-dependent mortality in juveniles. In the same forest, *Ocotea whitei* saplings closer to conspecific adults were more likely to be infected and die from a canker disease (Gilbert, Hubbell, and Foster 1994). Survival of *Dipteryx panamensis* juveniles in a Costa Rican wet forest, however, was found to be related to density-dependent factors, but not distance-dependent ones (Clark and Clark 1984). In two rain forests of Queensland, Australia, Connell, Tracey, and Webb (1984) found evidence for density-dependent mortality for most seedling species, but found little evidence for distance-dependent mortality. They also found some evidence for increased success of rare species, although this pattern did not hold across all age classes or spatial scales. Recent findings from the fifty-hectare plot on Barro Colorado Island, Panama, also point to strong density-dependent effects on sixty-seven of the eighty-four most common species (Wills et al. 1997). Working in a Bornean rain forest, Webb and Peart (1999) found strong evidence for density-dependent seedling mortality. Harms et al. (2000) demonstrated pervasive effects of density on seedling recruitment and diversity on Barro Colorado Island. Host-pathogen interactions appear to play an important role in explaining such recruitment patterns and maintaining tropical tree diversity (Wills et al. 1997; Harms et al. 2000). It is important to note, however, that spatial variation in resource availability can also influence spatial patterns of recruitent and mature tree distribution (Vandermeer 1977; Howe, Schupp, and Westley 1985; Sork 1987; Schupp 1992; also see part 9). In both *Platypodium* and *Dipteryx*, seedling survival is higher in tree fall gaps than beneath a closed canopy (Augspurger 1983a, 1983b; Clark and Clark 1984).

Patterns of seed dispersal are directly relevant to the impact of herbivores on tree spacing. Within the frugivory–seed dispersal literature, the Janzen-Connell model became known as the escape advantage of seed dispersal (Howe and Smallwood 1982). Escape, in this new sense, meant escape from not only seed and seedling predators or pathogens, but also escape from intraspecific competition. Although not mutually exclusive, other hypothesized advantages of seed dispersal were termed colonization and directed-dispersal advantages (see Howe and Smallwood 1982). Howe's extensive work with frugivory and seed dispersal in the nutmeg *Virola surinamensis* (e.g., Howe and Vande Kerckhove 1981; Howe 1983; Howe, Schupp, and Westley 1985) has become a classic example of the escape advantage of seed dispersal and the relative ineffectiveness of certain seed dispersers (see part 5). *Virola* seeds that fall or are dropped by frugivores near or underneath the parent crown suffered nearly 100 percent mortality due to a host-specific weevil in the genus *Conotrachelus*, whereas those dispersed only thirty meters from the crown edge had a fortyfold survival advantage (Howe, Schupp, and Westley 1985). Thus, dispersal even a short distance away from the parent plant greatly enhanced probabilities of sapling recruitment in *Virola*, as predicted by the Janzen-Connell model. In some cases, such as the directed dispersal of *Ocotea endresiana* fruits by bellbirds in a tropical cloud forest, seeds are deposited preferentially in sites that favor seedling survival (Wenny and Levey 1998).

Disparities among studies are not surprising, given the variety of plant species and sites where the model has been tested, as well as the diversity of mortality agents (e.g., pathogens, invertebrates, vertebrates). Studies involving invertebrate predators tend to support the

Janzen-Connell model regardless of locality (e.g., Janzen et al. 1976; Hart 1995; Lott et al. 1995), whereas those involving vertebrates do not (Kitajima and Augspurger 1989; Terborgh et al. 1993; Hart 1995; Notman, Gorchov, and Cornejo 1996; see also Hammond and Brown 1998). Differences in response among vertebrate and invertebrate seed predators most likely are due to the degree of specialization; greater specialization leads to a tighter relationship between predators and prey (Hammond and Brown 1998).

Our best insight into the importance of natural enemies for maintenance of tropical tree diversity may come from examining exceptions—that is, tropical forests that are dominated by a few species, such as *Shorea albida* forests in Sarawak (Anderson 1961) or *Mora excelsa* forests in Trinidad (Beard 1946) (see also Connell and Lowman 1989 and discussion in part 8). Hartshorn (1972) proposed that the dominance of *Pentaclethra macroloba* in lowland forests of northeast Costa Rica may result from its apparently strong defense mechanisms against seed predators (see also Janzen 1974a).

In the three decades since Janzen published his seminal paper, a growing number of long-term monitoring plots have been established around the world to measure tree diversity and demography (Condit 1995, 1997). These plots have provided and will continue to provide invaluable comparative data to test hypotheses relating to the importance of species interactions in the maintenance of tropical tree diversity (Lieberman and Lieberman 1994; Condit et al. 2000; see also parts 3 and 8).

Herbivory and Plant Defense

In the 1970s Feeny (1976) and Rhoades and Cates (1976) developed the theory of plant apparency to explain the evolution of defense mechanisms in plants. According to this theory, plants that are poorly defended rely on escape from their specialist herbivores. Coley (1980, 1982, 1983) studied the interactions between herbivores and plants for pioneer and "persistent" plant species, and young and mature

leaves, on Barro Colorado Island. She examined whether persistent plants or mature leaves, which are more predictable (i.e., apparent) resources with greater risk of discovery by herbivores, invest more in quantitative defenses than pioneer plants or young leaves, as predicted by apparency theory (Feeny 1976; Rhoades and Cates 1976). In a landmark paper reprinted here, Coley (1980; paper 18) demonstrated that life history and leaf age were, indeed, strong predictors of herbivory damage to leaves of 235 saplings, representing eleven pioneer and sixteen persistent tree species (see part 9 for a discussion of tree life history groups). Coley's community-based study of herbivory patterns opened the way to examining how plant growth and allocation traits influence herbivory rates in the context of tropical tree life history and regeneration modes. Mean grazing rate on mature leaves of pioneer species was an order of magnitude greater than that on mature leaves of persistent (slow-growing, mature forest) species, and in both groups of species, young leaves were more heavily grazed than mature leaves (Coley 1980). Thus, pioneer species do not demonstrate a greater ability to escape discovery by herbivores as predicted by the apparency hypothesis. On the contrary, these fast-growing species exhibit high rates of leaf removal by herbivores.

Coley's results suggested that mature leaves of persistent species have greater quantitative herbivore defenses than those of pioneer species, which was later confirmed by a study of forty-six canopy tree species at the same site (Coley 1983). Based on these findings, Coley (1983) and Coley, Bryant, and Chapin (1985) proposed the resource availability hypothesis, which defines a trade-off in plant growth and defense. According to this hypothesis, plants growing in high-quality (high-resource) environments should invest less in quantitative herbivore defense than plants growing in resource-limited environments. This hypothesis directly links plant growth traits with patterns of herbivory and defense allocation within and among tropical forest species. A key contribution of this work is the view that herbivore defense competes with plant growth for limited plant resources.

The resource availability hypothesis matched not only community-level patterns of plant defense allocation in Neotropical forests, but also in those found in Cameroon (McKey et al. 1978) and boreal habitats (Bryant and Kuropat 1980; Bryant, Chapin, and Klein 1983). Moreover, Coley (1983) suggested that while specialists were more likely to be the main herbivores on pioneers, generalists were likely to be primarily responsible for feeding on persistent species. Although Coley (1983) downplayed the importance of genotypic or phenotypic variation in plant defenses, Marquis (1984) demonstrated differential susceptibility to herbivores among genotypes of *Piper arieianum*, suggesting that this species is currently under selection to reduce herbivory damage, which has long-term reproductive costs to small- and medium-sized plants.

In a recent review Coley and Barone (1996) analyzed the available knowledge on herbivory in tropical ecosystems, highlighting some critical gaps in our knowledge and suggesting promising directions for future research in this topic. Among the many insights that emerge from this review, we would like to emphasize two critical aspects. First, most of our understanding of tropical herbivory is based on studies on tropical moist and wet forests. Knowledge on tropical dry forests is still very limited (see Dirzo and Dominguez 1985). Studies are badly needed in these forests if we are to understand the patterns and role of herbivory in the tropics. Second, the scarce available evidence indicates that the natural enemies (predators and parasitoids) of phytophagous insects play a critical role in determining the patterns of herbivory in tropical forests. These higher-order trophic interactions clearly warrant further investigation.

Frugivory and Seed Dispersal

Fruits found in tropical forests vary markedly in size, color, texture, number of seeds, seed size, and nutrition. Yet fruits eaten by particular groups of animals (e.g., ungulates, ants, bats,

birds) are often characterized by a syndrome of particular features (Ridley 1930; van der Pijl 1972; Gautier-Hion et al. 1985; Moermond and Denslow 1985; see also part 5). For example, fruits dispersed by bats in both Old and New World tropics are characterized by drab color, musty or rancid odor, and exposed position, such as outside the foliage or along the trunk (van der Pijl 1972). In some cases, these shared characteristics are the apparent result of natural selection as described by van der Pijl (1972), in paper 19. Substantially different nutritional rewards are found in "mammal" and "bird" fruits (e.g., Howe and Westley 1988); these differences presumably reflect largely different energetic needs of the primary consumers.

Although evolutionary history and phylogenetic inertia may constrain selection on fruit and seed characters (e.g., Mazer and Wheelwright 1993; Jordano 1995a), fruit and seed characters vary greatly within plant families (van der Pijl 1972). For example, closely related species of trees in the Sapotaceae show adaptations for seed dispersal by fish in flooded forest and dispersal by arboreal vertebrates in upland forests of Amazonia (Vásquez 1997). Further, adaptation to local seed disperser communities is evident among closely related species, or even the same species among sites. For example, Keeler-Wolf (1988) found that fruit and seed morphology of three species of trees reflected local seed disperser and predator communities in Trinidad and Tobago.

As van der Pijl (1972) noted, syndromes are not absolute and many fruits are eaten by both birds and mammals. Moreover, plants may have developed later modifications of their diaspores to attract "latecomers," such as ants, as seed dispersers (van der Pijl 1972). Structures found within some fruits of the Melastomataceae may provide an example of adaptations by plants to promote seed dispersal by two different taxa. Many fruits in the Melastomataceae produce multiseeded berries adapted for dispersal by birds. Byrne and Levey (1993) found that in some melastome species, minute seeds, defecated unharmed by birds, contained a small elaisome. In an experiment, ants preferentially selected seeds with the elaisome over seeds with their elaisome removed. Seeds were discarded by the ants after removing the elaisome back at the nest. These seeds thus appear to be adapted for primary dispersal by birds and secondary dispersal by ants. The latter is considered to be a derived feature (van der Pijl 1972).

The existence of recognizable dispersal syndromes implies that certain groups of animals are more effective seed dispersers than others. Moreover, as mentioned above, particular plant species can have a suite of fruit consumers that include mammals, birds, reptiles, fish, and ants. For example, *Virola* fruits in the nutmeg family (Myristicaceae) fit the classic bird dispersal syndrome by having a bright red, lipid-rich aril. On Barro Colorado Island in Panama, the most efficient dispersers of *Virola* were two large birds —the chestnut-mandibled toucan *(Ramphastos swainsonii)* and crested guan *(Penelope purpurascens)*—whereas spider monkeys *(Ateles geoffroyi)* were extremely inefficient in that they dropped many more seeds that they ingested (Howe 1980; Howe and Vande Kerckhove 1981). In contrast to Panama, in lowland forests of Manu National Park, Peru, spider monkeys *(Ateles paniscus)* provide much higher efficiency as seed dispersers than do birds for *Virola* (S. Russo, unpublished data; J. Terborgh, personal comm.). Therefore, fruit syndromes only provide suggestions regarding the key interactors in a system and the selective forces from which a group of plants has had to contend (Howe and Westley 1988).

Dispersal and pollination syndromes also provide insight regarding the types of plant–animal interactions likely to be present within a community. The predominance of certain syndromes changes along elevational and latitudinal gradients, as well as among geographic regions (Fleming, Breitwisch, and Whitesides 1987; Bawa 1990). Although in some cases it is probable that fruit and floral characters were derived prior to the evolution of present-day frugivores and pollinators, one can draw generalizations about the ecological structure of pre-

sent-day communities by examining the proportional distribution of plants among the various syndromes. For example, fruits adapted for dispersal by primates are much more evident in primate-rich forests of Amazonia than in the relatively primate-poor forests of Central America and Mexico (Terborgh 1983; Howe and Westley 1988). Similarly, African forests have many more fruits adapted for dispersal by large terrestrial mammals and arboreal seed predators than do South American forests (Emmons 1980; Gautier-Hion et al. 1985).

Plant-Pollinator Interactions

The dispersion patterns of plants, regardless of the causes, have important consequences for the foraging strategies of pollinators. Stiles and collaborators (see, e.g., Stiles and Wolf 1970; Wolf, Hainsworth, and Stiles 1972) set the stage for detailed studies of pollinator-plant interactions in the tropics using the framework of Heinrich and Raven (1972), based on energetics. These studies were important because they demonstrated important links between the foraging strategies of hummingbirds and plant characteristics such as morphology, energy rewards, life history, plant population abundance, phenology, and dispersion.

In paper 20, using hummingbirds and giant herbs in the genus *Heliconia*, Stiles (1975) clearly demonstrates that understanding plant-pollinator interactions requires looking beyond the "morphological fit" between corollas and hummingbird bills. Stiles (1975) developed a framework for examining evolutionary links between pollinator behavior, flowering strategies, floral morphology, and flowering phenology. Energetic requirements of hummingbirds and plant strategies and floral morphology that reflect resource availability, including accessibility of nectar resources, provide the basis for this framework.

Hummingbirds employ two strategies while exploiting *Heliconia* flowers—traplining and territoriality. Traplining hummingbirds tend to be hermits (phaethornine) with long curved bills, whereas territorial hummingbirds tend to be nonhermits with shorter straight bills. *Heli-*

conia species also employ two different floral strategies that appear adapted for pollination by either territorial or traplining hummingbirds. *Heliconia* differ in the amount of energy available to hummingbirds, the time over which this energetic award is available, and the accessibility of the reward. Higher amounts of readily accessible nectar favor territoriality, while smaller amounts of inaccessible nectar favor traplining. Stiles (1975) pointed out, however, that there must be enough nectar to be worth revisiting plants along a trapline, but not enough to be worth defending (cf. Heinrich and Raven 1972).

In the *Heliconia* system, plant strategies largely reflect local environmental conditions (Stiles 1975). Plants growing in high light environments produce many flowers that tend to be self-compatible. By contrast, *Heliconia* species that occur in resource-poor environments, such as deeply shaded forest understory, tend to occur at low densities and produce few flowers. The former is adapted for pollination by territorial hummingbirds, while the latter by traplining hummingbirds. For *Heliconia* species that occur at low densities and produce few flowers, selection for simultaneous periods of flower production may operate. Synchrony in blooming effectively increases nectar (energy) availability to traplining hummingbirds within the forest and increases the likelihood that individual plants would be visited along a trapline route. Thus, the energetic framework may also provide an explanation for why two closely related species might "risk" potential gamete wastage through hybridization (Stiles 1975).

Selection for pollinator specificity and divergence in phenological patterns as a mechanism to inhibit interspecific pollen transfer, may also have promoted diversification, or at least been important in maintaining species diversity in *Heliconia*. Nectar content and volume found among *Heliconia* species differ between the two types of hummingbird pollinators. Moreover, Baker and Baker (1983) suggest that pollinator specificity is related to

chemical composition of nectar. Among most hermit-pollinated *Heliconia* species, sequential and nonoverlapping peaks in flowering may be a response to competition for pollinators and a mechanism to reduce interspecific pollen transfer (Stiles 1975, 1977). Gentry (1974) also suggested that divergence in flowering phenology within Bignoniaceae was probably a response to sharing a limited set of pollinators (see also Frankie, Baker, and Opler 1973). In this family, the majority of pollinators are large and medium-sized bees. Gentry (1974) argued that selection to enhance pollination success has resulted in seasonal diversification in flowering time rather than in morphological differentiation. Similar to *Heliconia*, some Bignoniaceae produce a few flowers daily over an extended period and attract traplining euglossine bees (Janzen 1971; Gentry 1974). Several of these species overlap in flowering period. Yet factors other than competition for pollinators and selection against interspecific pollen transfer may also influence flowering phenology (see also Snow 1965; Medway 1972b; Opler, Frankie, and Baker 1976; Augspurger 1982). For example, a number of dipterocarps that flower sequentially in Malaysia mature their fruits simultaneously (Ashton 1988; Ashton, Givnish, and Appanah 1988). Asynchronous flowering is probably a mechanism to increase pollination success, while simultaneous mast fruiting likely serves to satiate predators and permits some seeds to escape seed predation (Ashton, Givnish, and Appanah 1988). Curran et al. (1999) document the combined effects of El Niño and logging of forests in West Kalimantan on dipterocarp seed production, seed predation, and seedling recruitment.

Mobile Links and Keystone Interactions

Tropical forests are characterized by high diversity and complex trophic relationships (see parts 3, 5, and 7). However, not all species have the same effects on communities—"there are little players and big players, and the biggest players of all are the keystone species" (Wilson 1992, 164). Certain species, keystone species, are strong "interactors" with a disproportionate impact on the system (Gilbert 1980). Terborgh (1986) identified certain keystone plants in Manu National Park. During periods of fruit scarcity, these species (figs, certain nectar providers, and palms), which represent less than 1 percent of the total plant species, are responsible for sustaining the entire frugivore community. Large predators, such as jaguars and pumas in tropical America, and large herbivores, such as elephants in Africa, also are keystone species because of their important impacts on prey abundance and vegetation structure, respectively (Wilson 1992). Other important interactors in tropical forests have been called mobile links, defined as "animals that are significant factors in the persistence of several plant species, which, in turn, support otherwise separate food webs" (Gilbert 1980, 19). Phaethornine hummingbirds and euglossine bees exemplify mobile links because they pollinate plant species across vertical strata and different habitats. Frugivorous bats also likely should be considered mobile links as they move seeds long distances, often across habitats and among oceanic islands. The identification of keystone species and mobile links is important to assess impacts on a large number of species and species interactions (Gilbert 1980). Habitat loss has resulted in numerous opportunities to study the loss of keystone species and mobile links from tropical forest communities (e.g., see Cox et al. 1991 and Renner 1998). Few studies have actually quantified impacts of local extinction, but dramatic and often disturbing results have been found. For example, defaunation of medium and large mammalian herbivores seems to be related to dramatic modifications of the understory plant community, including a reduction of species diversity (Dirzo and Miranda 1991; see also part 11).

Conclusion

Species interactions in tropical forests have undoubtedly played a major evolutionary and ecological role in the maintenance of tropical diversity. The Janzen-Connell model provided a framework for investigating how natural enemies might influence spatial patterns of tree recruitment and promote diversity through opening space for occupation of new species. These ideas triggered many empirical studies and contributed to development of theories on both herbivory and seed dispersal. Coley's (1980, 1983) studies of herbivory rates in relation to leaf age and plant life history further elucidate linkages between herbivores and the evolution of plant traits, including production of defensive compounds. Stiles (1975) and van der Pijl (1972) address mechanisms of species coexistence in tropical forests based on interactions between plants, pollinators, and frugivores. Further understanding of ecological and genetic consequences of plant–animal interactions requires studies that explicitly link animal behavior to fitness parameters of plants. Moreover, understanding the evolutionary impact of animal behavior will require selection experiments. Advances in technology (molecular tools, radiotelemetry, etc.) greatly enhance the kinds of questions we can now ask, although we need to describe the system and identify the actors before applying these tools. An aspect that has been almost entirely ignored is that of the interactions of different functional groups of animals such as herbivores, pollinators, and dispersal agents and the impact of such multiple interactions on plant ecology and evolution. With the exception of some isolated examples (e.g., Horvitz and Schemske 1984) and some ongoing studies, virtually no information exists, for example, on how herbivores affect the interactions of plants with their pollinators and dispersal agents in tropical ecosystems.

Another critical line of research is that of the disruption of ecological interactions between plants and animals by current patterns of land use, particularly deforestation and forest fragmentation. When concerns about tropical forest loss were just beginning to receive attention, Janzen (1970) and Stiles (1975) both warned about effects of habitat alteration by humans on species interactions. Stiles (1975) reported on the apparent breakdown of habitat isolation mechanisms as formerly isolated *Heliconia* species now came into contact. Janzen (1970) spoke of the potential of invasive species to achieve high abundances in disturbed tropical ecosystems, as they are, at least temporarily, free of natural enemies (see also Gillett 1962). The complexity of species interactions in tropical ecosystems is profound (see, e.g., Horvitz and Schemske 1984). The principal actors change geographically and the strength of interactions changes temporally and spatially as a result, or even in spite of, natural and newly created disturbances (see parts 3 and 9). Understanding the ecological and evolutionary impact of species interactions, especially those occurring among actors that are long lived, will require long-term perspectives and development of realistic models.

Reprinted Selections

D. H. Janzen. 1970. Herbivores and the number of tree species in tropical forests. *American Naturalist* 104:501–28

P. D. Coley. 1980. Effects of leaf age and plant life history patterns on herbivory. *Nature* 284:545–46

L. van der Pijl. 1972. *Principles of Dispersal in Higher Plants,* 40–52. 2d ed. New York: Springer-Verlag

F. G. Stiles. 1975. Ecology, flowering phenology, and hummingbird pollination of some Costa Rican *Heliconia* species. *Ecology* 56:285–301

THE
AMERICAN NATURALIST

| Vol. 104, No. 940 | The American Naturalist | November–December 1970 |

HERBIVORES AND THE NUMBER OF TREE SPECIES IN TROPICAL FORESTS

Daniel H. Janzen

Department of Biology, University of Chicago

Wet lowland tropical forests characteristically have many tree species and low density of adults of each species compared with temperate-zone forests in habitats of similar areal extent, topographic diversity, and edaphic complexity (Black, Dobzhansky, and Pavan 1950; Richards 1952; Poore 1968; Ashton 1969). Despite reports that adults of some species of lowland tropical trees show clumped distributions (Poore 1968; Ashton 1969), I believe that a third generalization is possible about tropical tree species as contrasted with temperate ones: for most species of lowland tropical trees, adults do not produce new adults in their immediate vicinity (where most seeds fall). Because of this, most adults of a given tree species appear to be more regularly distributed than if the probability of a new adult appearing at a point in the forest were proportional to the number of seeds arriving at that point. This generalization is based on my observations in Central and South American mainland forests, on discussions with foresters familiar with these forests, on discussions with J. H. Connell about Australian rain forests, and on data given in the papers cited above.

I believe that these three traits—many tree species, low density of each species, and more regular distribution of adults than expected—are largely the result of two processes common to most forests: (1) the number of seeds of a given species arriving at a point in the forest usually declines with distance from the parent tree(s) and varies as the size of the viable seed crop(s) at the time of dispersal, and (2) the adult tree and its seeds and seedlings are the food source for many host-specific plant parasites and predators. The negative effect of these animals on population recruitment by the adult tree declines with increasing distance of the juvenile trees from their parent and from other adult trees. A simple model summarizes these two processes (fig. 1). It will lead us to examine the effects of different kinds of plant predators on juveniles, ecological distance between parents, dispersal agents, environmental predictability and severity—among other factors—on the number of tree species in a habitat, their den-

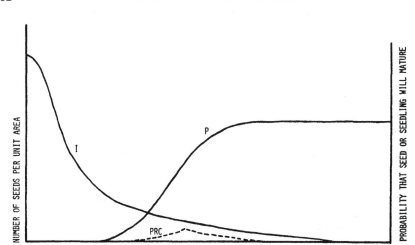

FIG. 1.—A model showing the probability of maturation of a seed or seedling at a point as a function of (1) seed-crop size, (2) type of dispersal agents, (3) distance from parent tree, and (4) the activity of seed and seedling predators. With increasing distance from the parent, the number of seeds per unit area (*I*) declines rapidly, but the probability (*P*) that a dispersed seed or seedling will be missed by the host-specific seed and seedling predators, before maturing, increases. The product of the *I* and *P* curves yields a population recruitment curve (*PRC*) with a peak at the distance from the parent where a new adult is most likely to appear; the area under this curve represents the likelihood that the adult will reproduce at all, when summed over all seed crops in the life of the adult tree. In most habitats, *P* will never approach 1, due to nonspecific predation and competition by other plants independent of distance from the parent. The curves in this and the following figures are not precise quantifications of empirical observations or theoretical considerations, but are intended to illustrate general relationships only.

sities, and their spatial juxtaposition. Almost none of the many hypotheses generated by this examination can be tested with data currently available in the literature. While I am at present testing some of these in Central American forests, they are all offered here in the hope of stimulating others to examine them as well.

It is my intention in studies of tropical species diversity to shift the emphasis away from the utilization and manipulation of diverse resources to generate a diverse consumer community (Are niches narrower in the tropics?), and toward an examination of the ability of the consumer community to generate and maintain a diverse resource base. Thus I am not so much concerned with Where did all the tropical tree species come from? (as Haffer [1969] has asked for birds), as I am in raising the question How do you pack so many into a forest? In short, this study is an extension to the plant community of Paine's (1966) suggestion that "local animal species diversity is related to the number of predators in the system and their efficiency in preventing single species from monopolizing some important, limiting, requisite" (see Spight 1967; Murdoch 1969, for elaborations of this statement). The same concept was applied by Barbehenn (1969) to the interactions of tropical mammals with their predators and parasites, and by Lowe-McConnell (1969) to tropical fishes. MacArthur (1969) has generalized the system for vertebrates that prey on other animals in tropical communities.

This paper presents a major problem in terminology. Words, such as "carnivore," "graminivore," "herbivore," "frugivore," and "sanguivore," designate clearly the type of host or prey of an animal. The terms, "predator" and "parasite," describe the effect of the animal on its host or prey. Unfortunately, both "predator" and "parasite" have conventionally been used as synonyms for "carnivore" and "sanguivore," thereby excluding those animals that feed on plants. However, "plant parasite" is appearing in the literature to denote animals or plants that feed on a plant but do not kill it. Similarly, I wish to use "seed predator" or "seedling predator" to cover those animals that eat entire plants, or at least eat enough so that the plant dies immediately. The act of a fox seeking out and eating mice differs in no significant way from a lygaeid bug seeking out and eating seeds, or a paca seeking out and eating seedlings. Words, such as "herbivore," "frugivore," or "graminivore," are inadequate substitutes for "seed predator" or "seedling predator" since they do not tell the fate of the juvenile plants.

HOST SPECIFICITY

The degree of host-specificity displayed by the seed and seedling predators strongly influences the model in figure 1. Without host-specificity, the P curve in figure 1 would be horizontal, offspring would more likely mature close to their parents, and regulation of tree density by seed predators would depend on the distance between seed-bearing trees of any species serving as foci for these predators. All tree species would be affected by physical environmental conditions favoring certain plant predators, and it is unlikely that these would make any particular tree species very rare or extinct. That the vast majority of insects that prey on seeds (of various ages) are host-specific in tropical communities must be inferred from three sources (the literature is sterile on the subject):

1. From 1963 to 1970, I have reared insects from the seeds of better than 300 lowland Central American plant species. Almost without exception, a given insect species reproduces on only a small subset (one to three species) of the hundreds of potential host species available in the habitat. This is not negated by the observation that some of these insects have different hosts at different times of the year or in different habitats, and may feed on a wide variety of water and food sources (e.g., *Dysdercus fasciatus* bugs feeding on dead insects [Janzen 1970c]) that do not result in egg production (e.g., Sweet 1964).

2. Detailed studies of the life histories of insects that prey on fruits and seeds of forest and orchard trees in the United States suggest strong host-

504   THE AMERICAN NATURALIST

specificity, both in terms of field censuses and the specific behavior of the insects themselves (e.g., Bush 1969; Schaefer 1962, 1963; and a voluminous forestry literature). However (and this is where temperate forests appear to differ from tropical ones), many of these are complexes of species, such as acorn weevils (*Curculio* spp.) on oaks (*Quercus* spp.), that feed on all members of a genus in a habitat and therefore will not necessarily result in extreme rarity of any of the prey species, unless all are made rare. Such complexes are also present in tropical forests, but do not appear to constitute as large a population of the total herbivore complex as in temperate forests. However, even if host specificity were no greater in the tropics than in temperate zones, it is clearly high enough in both areas to allow for a model such as that in figure 1.

3. While there are many cases of strong host specificity by predators on seeds and fruits (e.g., Janzen 1970a, 1970b, 1970c, 1971), examples of the opposite case are rare among insects in nature. This statement is not negated by the long host list that may be compiled for some insects by a study such as Prevett's (1967) or with a catalogue such as the new edition of Costa Lima's (1967–68) catalogue of insects that live on Brazilian plants, where host records are summed across many habitats, seasons, and geographic areas. In the latter reference, no distinction is made between insects reproducing on a plant or those merely feeding on it. For the purposes of this paper, a species of insect will be considered to be host-specific if most of its population feeds on one (or very few) species of seed or seedling in a habitat undisturbed by man.

Seed-eating vertebrates may show comparatively little host-specificity but, as will be discussed later, may be facultatively host-specific and thus can be included in the model in some cases.

SEED DISPERSAL

Seed dispersal to sites near parents is affected by two different groups of predators on dispersed juveniles, the distance-responsive and density-responsive predators. The probability that a juvenile plant will be eaten by a *distance-responsive* predator is primarily a function of the ecological distance between that juvenile and adult trees of the same species. Distance-responsive predators are commonly parasites on the adults, but predators on seedlings. This is because seedlings cannot withstand the loss of leaves and shoot tips to the degree that adult trees can. The probability that a juvenile plant will be eaten by a *density-responsive* predator is primarily a function of the ecological distance between that juvenile and other juveniles. Density-responsive predators rely primarily on the presence of one juvenile to survive long enough to find another or to be stimulated to search hard to find another. Any given species of predator can belong to both categories, but in general the activities of herbivores can be profitably viewed with this dichotomy in mind.

Seed Immigration and Distance-responsive Predators

Intensities and patterns of seed shadows cast by parent trees are functions of seed crop size, seed predation before dispersal, and characteristics of the dispersal agents. From figure 2, it is obvious that increasing the predation on seeds before dispersal (i.e., lowering I, the number of seeds dispersed per unit area) may (1) reduce immigration proportionately more, far from the parent than close to it, and therefore reduce the distance of new adults from their parents if juvenile trees are not subject to predation; (2) reduce the number of seeds that escape the distance-responsive herbivore because they fall sufficiently far from their parent; hence the probability that the adult will reproduce at all during its lifetime is lowered, as is the population density of adults in the habitat; and (3) reduce the likelihood that the tree species in question will competitively displace other tree species or reduce their population densities.

The similar immigration curves in figure 2 are only one of several possible sets that could result from lowering the size of the viable seed crop. If the seeds are killed after they are nearly mature, and therefore imbedded in an intact fruit, they may not be distinguished from viable

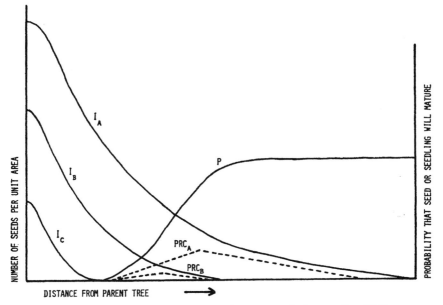

FIG. 2.—The effects of increased predispersal predation on the PRC curve when the predators are distance-responsive. The seed crop of I_B is about one-half of that of I_A, and the seed crop of I_C is about one-ninth that of I_A. This figure should be contrasted with figure 3, where a reduction in seed crop affects the PRC curve quite differently when the predators act in a density-responsive manner.

ones by the dispersal agent. Thus immigration curves produced by pre-dispersal seed mortabilty (e.g., fig. 2, curve I_C) are of similar form but lower than those of an intact crop (e.g., fig. 2, curve I_A). But if a potential dispersal agent selects and discards viable seeds at the parent tree (e.g., capuchin monkeys feeding on *Apeiba* fruits [Oppenheimer 1968]), the immigration curves may become steeper as seed destruction increases. On the other hand, if seed predation is early in the development of the fruit, and only fruits with viable seeds mature, then the immigration curves flatten out and accentuate the distance between new adult trees. This is because the reduced amount of fruit will result in a lower proportion of the total crop being ignored by satiated dispersal agents, and therefore falling to the ground beneath the parent tree. However, very small seed crops are often ignored by dispersal agents, leading to extreme truncation of the immigration curve at the right tail.

The most important predators on immature and mature seeds before dispersal are insects such as bruchid (Hinckley 1961; Wickens 1969; Prevett 1967; Parnell 1966; Janzen 1969a, 1970a), curculionid (e.g., De-Leon 1941; Janzen 1970b; Barger and Davidson 1967), and scolytid beetles (e.g., Shaefer 1962, 1963), lygaeid and pyrrhocorid bugs (e.g., Myers 1927; Yonke and Medler 1968; Eyles 1964; Janzen 1970c), Lepidoptera larvae (e.g., Breedlove and Ehrlich 1968; Hardwick 1966; Janzen 1970a; Coyne 1968; Dumbleton 1963), aphids (e.g., Phillips 1926b), and fly larvae (e.g., Pipkin, Rodriquez, and Leon 1966; Gillett 1962; Brncic 1966; Knab and Yothers 1914), birds such as parrots, and mammals, such as squirrels and monkeys (e.g., Smythe 1970; Smith 1968; Struhsaker 1967; Oppenheimer and Lang 1969). Insects are generally obligatorily host-specific, while vertebrates may be facultatively host-specific (for a given short time, they concentrate their foraging on or under the seed-breeding tree, but are not restricted to this species). A conservative estimate, based on large seed crop collections by Gordon Frankie and myself in Central America, is that at least 80% of the woody plants in lowland forest have mild to severe predispersal predation on reproductive parts by obligatorily or faculta-tively host-specific animals.

Any factor that increases the ability of these seed predators to move between seed crops in time or space, and to eat seeds more rapidly once there, will generally increase the number of tree species that can coexist in a given habitat (following the argument presented in an earlier section). Such a process would not result when the number of new adult trees produced by a parent is independent of the number of viable seeds dispersed. Such systems are not easy to imagine when the absolute number of surviving seeds is small. While the distance between new adults and their parents will be reduced by predispersal seed mortality (e.g., figs. 2, 3), two other processes would increase this distance. First, seed and seedling predators acting after dispersal are likely to prey more heavily on juveniles near the parent or near other juveniles (see later section). Second, any pair of exceptionally close adult trees will mutually contribute

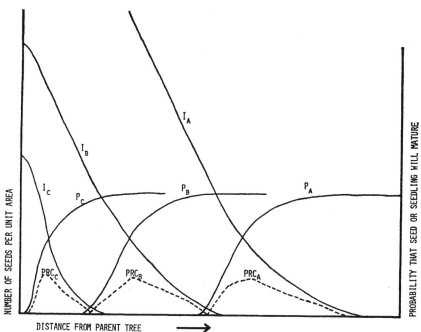

Fig. 3.—The effects of increased predispersal seed predation (progression from I_A to I_C) on the PRC curve when the predators are density-responsive. The PRC_C curve is slightly less peaked than would be the case if the density-responsive predators were identical for all three I curves; I have assumed that some density-responsive predators would be completely absent for the small I_C curve because there are not enough seeds or seedlings to attract them in the first place.

seed-crop predators, each greatly lowering the other's chances of reproducing at all, and lowering the probability of a third adult appearing at the same site.

There are two important characteristics of the dispersal agents. First, the faster they remove the seeds, the greater the survival of the seed crop that was subject to predispersal mortality. For example, in many legumes dispersed by birds and mammals, the second generation of bruchids in the seed crop kills virtually all seeds not yet dispersed (e.g., Janzen 1969a, 1970a).

Second, a large, but less intense, seed shadow can increase the distance between new adults and the parent. As used here, the intensity of a seed shadow is measured by the number of seeds falling per unit area and the size of a seed shadow is measured by the area over which the seeds are dispersed. My observations of dispersal around tropical forest trees, and the numerous anecdotes in Ridley's (1930) compendium of tropical seed dispersal systems, indicate that considerable variation in shape of immigration curves is possible (fig. 4). For example, the negative exponential (I_A) in figure 4 may be produced by wind dispersal (rare in tropical forest habitats but more common in dry areas [Smythe 1970; Croat 1970; Ridley

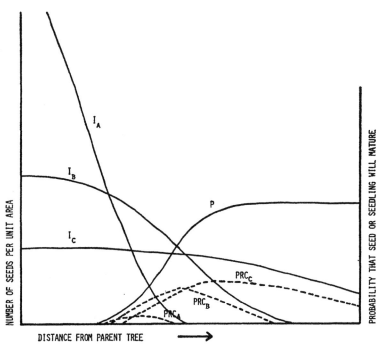

FIG. 4—The effects of different dispersal agents on the *PEC* curve when the predators are distance-responsive (see fig. 5 for the same effects associated with density-responsive predators). Each of the three *I* curves is generated by a viable seed crop of approximately the same size. For further explanation, see text.

1930]) or secondary dispersal by large mammals (e.g., *Persea*, Lauraceae; *Carapa*, Meliaceae) after the seeds have fallen. When water, steep topography, or seasonal winds are involved, the seed shadow is probably greatly skewed in one direction. Curve I_B may be associated with birds and rodents with short seed retention time (e.g., regurgitation of lauraceous fruits by trogons, toucans, and cotingas, and scatter-hording [Smythe 1970; Morris 1962] by rodents such as agoutis and agouchis). Curves of type I_C may be produced by vertebrates such as birds, bats and terrestrial mammals with long seed retention in the intestine, and by burs that stick to feathers and fur.

Thus dispersal agents may be responsible for the survival of a given tree species in a habitat that greatly favors the seed predators. In the progression from I_A to I_C there is (1) an increase in distance between new adults but at a decreasing rate, (2) an increase in seed survival (since for the present the P curve is held constant) which may lead to more adults surviving, (3) an increase in skewness of the PRC curve, leading to greater variation in adult tree dispersion and density, and higher rates of invasion of unoccupied habitats.

It is important to notice, however, that a major change in dispersal, as between the I_B and I_C curves, has relatively little influence on the height or location of the peak of the *PRC* curve.

If we add the complication that some dispersal agents are also major seed predators (e.g., agoutis [Smythe 1970]), it becomes apparent that the tremendous variety of fruit shapes, sizes, flavors, hardnesses, toxicities, and other traits are all probably highly adapted to taking advantage of those aspects of the dispersal agents that will yield an optimal seed shadow, counteracting the predispersal seed predators and the postdispersal predators discussed below.

A major constraint on the ways the adult may enhance seed escape is that dispersal must also get the seed to areas in the habitat where competitive and nutrient conditions are optimal for seedlings, a so-called safe site (Harper et al. 1961). While seed size is a major factor in determining the percentage of predation on a seed crop, it also influences strongly the suitability of a particular site for seedling survival. As seed size (or seed protection) decreases and seed number therefore increases (possibly leading to an increase in absolute numbers of surviving seeds through predator satiation [Janzen 1969a]), the number of safe sites in the habitat automatically decreases at an undetermined rate. Safe sites may disappear faster than new seeds are produced through reduction in seed size, and therefore this means of predator escape may yield no real increase in adult plant density. This complication does not, however, modify the interaction between the seed predators and the dispersal agents for any given regime of safe sites, edaphic heterogeneities, successional stages, and so forth.

Seed Dispersal and Density-responsive Predators

When the size of the seed crop is increased over evolutionary time, in the face of density-responsive predators on seeds and seedlings (e.g., fig. 3), the peak of the *PRC* curve moves rapidly outward. This and associated modifications of the *PRC* curve result in (1) only a slight increase in rate of new adult tree production for a large increase in viable seed crop size, (2) increased distance between newly appearing adults, and (3) a new equilibrium density lower than, or the same as, before the increase in seed crop size.

As conditions become more favorable for seed predation before dispersal, a given set of density-responsive predators will be less able to bring about wide spacing of new adults than distance-responsive seed and seedling predators (fig. 2). Also, density-responsive predators will not reduce the tree's total chance of reproducing to the degree that distance responsive predators can when predispersal predation is increased.

When seed shadows resulting from different sets of seed dispersal agents are compared against a background of density-responsive predators on juveniles (fig. 5), the *PRC* curves are dramatically different. As with the distance-responsive predator complex, the *PRC* is shifted outward with the progression of I_A to I_C, but unlike figure 4, it remains high. In general, it appears that the density-responsive predators will allow higher densities of adult trees in response to a change in the dispersal agents than is the

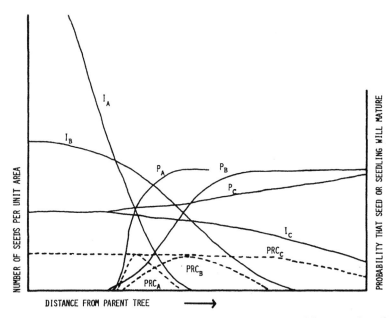

FIG. 5.—The effects of different dispersal agents on the *PRC* curve when the predators are density-responsive. A shift in the patterns of dispersal agents has a very marked effect on the shape of the *PRC* curves (in contrast with the effects of the distance-responsive seed predators depicted in fig. 4).

case with the distance-responsive predators. Curve I_C also shows that some dispersal agents can minimize the distance between new adults, if they lower sufficiently the seed density near the adult.

As mentioned previously, many predators on seeds and seedlings may act in either a distance- or density-responsive manner, depending (among other factors) on season, availability of alternate foods, and relative density of juvenile plants. When the immigration curve is viewed against the total array of predators, the actual outcome will depend on the relative proportions of these two types of predation activity. Enough data are not yet available to predict these proportions for various habitats.

PREDATION ON DISPERSED JUVENILES

Distance-responsive Predators

Once the juvenile trees have been dispersed, any factor increasing the effective distance to which the distance-responsive seed and seedling predators search will augment the distance between new adults and hence lower the density of new adults (fig. 6). An increase in the distance of effective searching may have a variety of causes, such as: (1) change in the search behavior of the predators, (2) increase in the size of the population of parasites (which act as predators to juveniles) feeding on the parent tree, (3) increased proximity of parent trees which may be due to increased

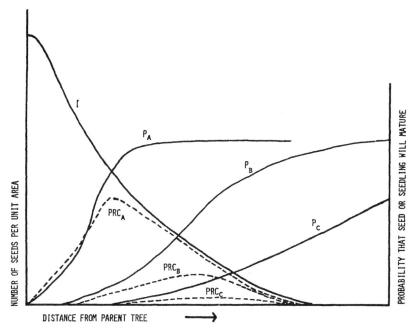

FIG. 6.—The impact of increasing the effective distance at which distance-responsive predators can act on a seed crop of fixed size. Were curve P_A simply to be shifted to the right, rather than changing in slope as well (as shown in curves P_B and P_C), the PRC_A curve would become lower and shift to the right, but would retain its sharp peak.

competitive ability or other factors, and (4) decreased synchrony of parent and offspring vegetative growth cycles, etc.

As implied earlier, the distance-responsive predators are primarily insects that fed on the canopy of the parent. For example, the crown on a mature woody vine, *Dioclea megacarpa*, in lowland deciduous forests in Costa Rica harbors a large population of apparently host-specific erebine noctuid larvae that feed on shoot tips. They harvest as much as 50% of the new branch ends. There is a steady but slow rain of these caterpillars on the forest floor; most return to the crown or wander off to pupate. However, they will feed on any intact shoot tip of a seedling of *D. megacarpa* they encounter. The young plant has sufficient reserves to produce about three main axes; further decapitation kills the seedling (the previous decapitations slowed its development, which probably would also be fatal over a longer period). For this reason, there is no survival of seedlings directly under the parent. But seedlings more than about 5 m from the edge of the parent's crown show only slight damage from these caterpillars (Janzen 1971). The well-known ability of the larvae of the shoot-tip borer *Hypsipyla grandella* to prevent plantation plantings of *Cedrela mexicana* (Meliaceae) on Caribbean islands (e.g., Beard 1942; Holdridge 1943; Cater 1945) is a similar case, and this moth is likely responsible for the wide spacing of adults of this lumber tree in natural forests in Central America.

Rodents may use the parent tree as "flags" indicating the presence of juveniles, and therefore function as distant-responsive predators. For example, in evergreen primary forest on the Osa Peninsula in southwestern Costa Rica, the large and winged seeds of *Huberodendron allenii* (Bombacaceae) are heavily preyed upon by numerous rodents on the forest floor. Any seed placed near the base of the parent, sterile or fertile, is invariably eaten within two nights. Seeds placed more than 50 m from adult *H. allenii* are found much more slowly, some lasting at least 7 days.

Host-specific fungi with resistant spores may also serve as distance-responsive predators (lethal parasites) since they do not wander off in search of more food as the seedling population is decimated. Even fungi without resistant spores may act in this fashion, if remnants of the seedling crop persist from year to year.

Distance-responsive predators may be very effective at producing wide spacing and low density of new adults near old parents, but they should be ineffective at far distances, compared with density-responsive predators. The danger of a "flag" or reservoir of predators in the crown of the parent tree declines rapidly with distance from the parent since the distance-responsive predators do not leave it to search for seeds or seedlings. Second, local patches of juveniles, resulting from overlap or concentration of the seed shadow far from a parent, are less likely to be located by distance-responsive predators than by density-responsive ones. This should be especially important for tree species in early succession. Some environments favor continual parasitism on the adult plant (e.g., tropical wet forest); habitats in these environments should have many widely spaced tree species. While this effect may be magnified for some tree species in seasonal habitats where deciduousness of adults can result in host-specific insects searching for more succulent juveniles, in general, seasonality probably allows more escape closer to the parent.

The three different dispersal distributions in figure 4 are differentially influenced by an increase in predation range by distance-responsive predators. This is shown in figure 7, where changing the survival probability curves from curve P_A to P_B (1) makes I_0 the dispersal curve that yields the highest peak rather than I_A as before, (2) increases the spread between peaks in the *PRC* curves, and (3) lowers the peaks of the *PRC* curves.

For a given predation range, figure 7 illustrates that changes in the dispersal agents can dramatically alter the location and size of the *PRC* curve.

Density-responsive Predators

The density-responsive predators should be much superior to distance-responsive ones at causing new adults to appear far from their parent (e.g., figure 3), since the distance-responsive predators do not search past a distance that is representative of some yearly average seed density. No matter how large the seed crop in a given year, or how far the seed from a

HERBIVORES AND TROPICAL FOREST DIVERSITY   513

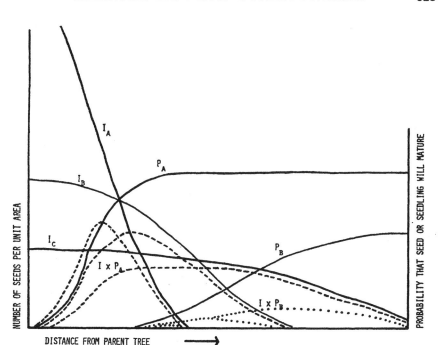

FIG. 7.—The effect of increasing the range of operation of the distance-responsive predators on the different I curves produced by different types of dispersal agents. As more of the seed is dispersed further from the parent (I_A to I_C) the PEC curve generated by the P_A curve is lowered slowly and broadened rapidly. For distance-responsive predators that act at far distances (P_B), however, the same change of I_A to I_C results in an increase in the height of the PEC curve and no gross change in its general shape.

parent, density-responsive predators will pursue seeds and seedlings until their density is so low that search is no longer profitable. This group comprises numerous insects that are host-specific on dispersed seeds and seedlings, and facultatively host-specific mammals and insects. As Phillips (1924) said when describing the reproductive biology of African *Ocotea*, "Aggregation is responsible for very few seedlings [surviving]. This is probably on account of the prevalence of pathogenic fungi and destructive insects in the neighborhood of a large accumulation of fruits." Numerous forest-floor mammals may subsist almost entirely on fallen seeds and fruits at certain times (e.g., peccaries, agoutis, pacas, coatis, deer, rats, etc.) and they tend to concentrate on the fruit under a particular tree (e.g., Kaufman 1962). That they will wander off when full, but return later, creates nearly the same effect as though they were obligatorily host-specific to that tree species. Incidentally, this heavy predation (e.g., African wild pigs killing most, but not all, of the capsules of *Platylophus* they ingest [Phillips 1925]) should not be allowed to obscure the extremely important roles these same mammals play in dispersing undigested or unopened seeds away from the parent (e.g., Phillips 1926a; Smythe 1970). This seed predation is one of the costs the plant pays for dispersal. Fungal, bacterial, and viral diseases can also be density-responsive predators, whether airborne or insect-borne. As Fournier and Salas (1967) found, the disease may enter at the point of insect damage, though it is not clear to what degree such diseases are host-specific. Even if not host-specific in the strict sense, they may yield a local epidemic because many hosts are available in the concentration of seedlings around a parent.

It is obvious that the change in dispersal agents from I_A to I_C in figure 5 can yield a major increase in the distance of new adults from parents, in the face of a given set of density-responsive predators. However, the shallower the dispersal curve, the more seeds will fall past a distance representing critical density for continued predation. As more seeds escape in this manner, the new adults should build up near the parent to the point where seed shadow overlap around parents makes the seed and seedling density as high with a I_C dispersal curve as with I_A or I_B curves (fig. 5). However, the better the conditions for searching by predators on seeds and seedlings, and the more time they have available to search, the less effective a flattening of the dispersal curve will be as a means of escape from them.

THE SYSTEM AS A WHOLE

Population Recruitment Surface

The adults of any tree species produce a total seed shadow that may be represented as a gently undulating surface with tall peaks of various shapes centered on the reproductive adults and occasional low rises where seed shadows overlap or dispersal agents concentrate owing to habitat heterogeneity (fig. 8). The general height of the entire surface, and the height of the peaks around the parents, will be a function of the efficiency of the dispersal agents, of the predispersal seed predators, and of the parents' productivity.

The distance- and density-responsive predators should produce an undulating probability surface for survival of the seeds. Depressions in this surface, ranging from large pits to shallow basins, should be centered on fertile adults of the tree species in question. The diameters and depths of basins will vary with the proximity of other fertile adults and the suitability of the habitat to survival of the predators while they are on the parent, or moving between juveniles. There may also be shallow basins representing increased survival wherever there are low rises in the total seed shadow.

Multiplying these two surfaces together yields a population recruitment surface (its cross-section is the *PRC* of figs. 1–7) which will generally be very low and flat, but also has low "crater rims" ringing the parents and slight rises in areas of multiple seed shadow overlap far from the parents (fig. 9). In determining the impact of any specific seed or seedling predator, dispersal agent, or rise in parental productivity on the population recruitment surface, we must consider that a specific change will often

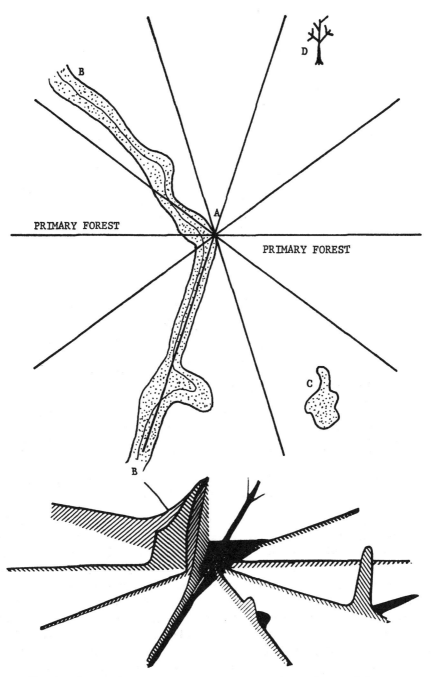

Fig. 8.—Hypothetical complex seed shadow (below) based on seed frequency plotted against distance from the parent for ten radial sectors around the parent at *A* (map shown above). It is assumed that there is only one parent of this species in the general area, and, for example, that the large seed crop is dispersed by birds living in early stages of primary plant succession. Environmental heterogeneity is represented by the river and accompanying narrow strip of primary succession (*B*: stippled), the small patch of primary succession where a large tree was windthrown (*C*), and the large dead tree emergent over the primary forest canopy where birds moving between vegetation in early stages of succession might rest (*D*).

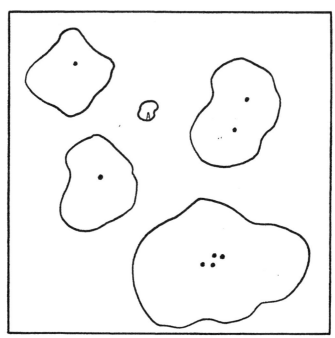

Fig. 9.—Vertical view of the population recruitment surface for a tree species with reproductive adults represented by solid dots. Heavy rings surrounding the adults represent the areas in the habitat where new trees are most likely to appear. The area inside a ring is very unlikely to produce another adult and is thus available to other species of trees, irrespective of the competitive ability of adults or seedlings of the first tree species. The area outside the rings is variably prone to production of new adults, depending on the dispersal agents. Area A represents a local rise in the population recruitment surface due to seed shadow overlap of the four uppermost trees.

yield a compensatory change in another aspect of the surface. For example, an evolutionary change that doubles seed number and thereby enhances predispersal predator satiation (Janzen 1969a), will result in smaller seeds and perhaps more effective dispersal. On the other hand, as mentioned earlier, it may also reduce the number of safe sites in the habitat, lower the number of surviving seedlings, and finally bring about no change in total adult density. Likewise, the evolution of a costly chemical defense of seeds may result in fewer seeds (provided that there is no concomitant increase in parental productivity), which may produce no net change in total juvenile survival to adulthood per parent (although the part of the habitat where these juveniles survive may be changed). The only safe prediction appears to be that conditions favoring the seed and seedling predators are likely to lower the density of reproducing adults of a given species and increase the distance of newly produced adults from their parents.

General Predictions

The general model described in figures 1–7, and the resultant population recruitment surface described above, generate several hypotheses that can be tested by field experimentation or observations. If these hypotheses are found to be generally false for any particular habitat, we must depend on competition, interference, and edaphic interactions to explain the low density of most tree species, high number of tree species, and wide spacing of adult trees in that habitat, be it tropical or temperate.

1. If seeds are placed or planted at various distances from a parent tree at low density (to avoid density-responsive predators), their survival to the well-developed sapling stage should increase with distance from the parent. The mortality agents should be predators on seeds and seedlings. Such observations should be possible on naturally dispersed seeds as well.

2. The percentage of seed mortality on a parent tree should be inversely correlated with its distance to other fertile adults of the same species (in this and previous years). In considering tests of this hypothesis, the distance between seed crops may also be measured in units of time (see example of *Hymenaea courbaril* below). This hypothesis is most relevant for predators that move directly from one seed crop to the next.

3. Where historical accident has produced various densities of reproducing adults of a given species, the average seed mortality on these parents should be an inverse function of the density of reproducing adults. This hypothesis is most relevant to predators that first spread out over the general habitat from an old seed crop, and subsequently find a seed crop.

4. If seeds or seedlings are placed in small patches of various densities in the usual seedling habitat, the survival of any one juvenile should be an inverse function of the number of juveniles in its group.

5. If we categorize the adults of the tree species in an area as either regularly spaced, distributed at random, or clumped, the regularly spaced species should show the best agreement with the first and fourth of these hypotheses.

Problems in Testing the Hypotheses

There are sampling problems as well as problems brought on by alternative population recruitment strategies available to the tree. Some problems are discussed below, primarily to emphasize the complexity of the interaction system being analyzed.

Sampling problems are the biggest impediment at present. The predators must be identified, but are extremely difficult to observe in action. In the case of *Dioclea megacarpa* mentioned previously, an entire crop of 58 seedlings can be killed by 16 "caterpillar-hours" spread over a 4-month period; a caterpillar is on a seedling only 0.6% of the time. A rodent pauses only a few seconds to pick up a seed from the forest floor. Since postdispersal

518   THE AMERICAN NATURALIST

predators exist by harvesting from a small population of small plants with little ability for self-repair, they must have low population densities at most places at most times. If seed or seedling densities are artificially increased to speed up an experiment, there may be a concentration of facultatively host-specific predators that normally feed on other, more abundant, species. Many parasites may have a synergistic effect with predators; for example, Homoptera feeding on phloem of shoot tips may have no direct effect, yet may weaken the plant to later or simultaneous microbial or insect attack. Also, just as Connell (1961) found barnacles weakened by competition to be more susceptible to natural catastrophes, a seedling weakened by mild parasitism by an insect is likely to be an inferior competitor when compared with undamaged sibs (Bullock 1967).

In contemporary tropical communities, usually lightly to heavily disturbed by European types of agriculture, the absence of many dispersal agents and superabundance of others may yield highly unadaptive seed shadows and dispersal timing (e.g., the heavy mortality of undispersed *Cassia grandis* seeds by bruchid beetles where the natural vertebrate dispersal agents have been hunted out [Janzen 1970*a*]). The seed and seedling predators are likely to be affected in the same manner, in addition to the direct destruction of seeds and seedling by humans. Introduced plants often serve as alternate or superior hosts. This results in very different patterns of survival of the predators than is the case in natural forests, at times when their native host plant is nonproductive or seedlings are missing. For example, the introduction of a cotton field into a habitat grossly changes the population structure of the wild cotton-stainer bugs (*Dysdercus* spp.) which are dependent on Malvales for reproduction (Bebbington and Allen 1936; Janzen 1970*c*). Selective logging, extremely common in the tropics, directly changes the density and distribution of adult trees, rendering examination of the population dynamics of adult trees nearly impossible.

Alternative population recruitment strategies, habitat heterogeneity, and differential competitive ability of the seedlings must also be considered when testing these hypotheses.

Allelopathic systems may have two very different effects. Webb, Tracey, and Haydock (1967) have shown that the roots of adult *Grevillea robusta* trees release a compound that kills their own seedlings in Australian rain forests, leading to wide spacing of adults. While this behavior cannot lead to spacing of new adults much past the root territory of the parent tree, it certainly will affect the postdispersal predators. Incidentally, this allelopathy may also serve as an effective escape mechanism from a very effective predispersal seed predator that has great difficulty moving between adults. On the other hand, the "allelopathic" activity of ants on ant-plants in killing other plants around the parent tree often aids in producing local pure stands of *Cecropia,* swollen-thorn acacias, *Tachigalia,* etc. (Janzen 1969*b*).

While geometric distance may be adequate for first approximations to the ecological distance between parent trees, such units are clearly inadequate for specific cases. Two trees 300 m apart along a dry ridge top are clearly not the same ecological distance from each other as they are from a tree 300 m away in the adjacent riparian bottom lands. An individual tree that regularly has a small seed crop may have much less influence on local seed predation than one much farther away that always has a large crop. Alternate host trees may provide enough food to maintain the metabolism of the predator during its dispersal, but not enough for its reproduction. Such trees may greatly shorten the ecological distance between two hosts. Edaphic conditions between two reproductive adults may prevent any maturation of seedlings, but seedlings surviving on seed reserves and some environmental resources may provide a continuous area between adult trees of habitat suitable for the predators.

Parents may compete more with their own seedlings than with those of other trees. Challinor (1968) has shown that different species of temperate forest trees produce differential shortages of inorganic nutrients under their canopies, and it is well known that nutrient requirements vary with the species of tree. This may also be the case in tropical forests to the degree that these trees depend on inorganic nutrients not tied up in the tree-leaf-mycorrhiza-root-tree cycle. However, just as with allelopathy, the negative effect of this competition on seedlings would not extend past the root territory of the individual adult, and might well be counterbalanced by the advantage to the seedling of having its own specific mycorrhizae (Went and Stark 1968) present at the time of germination. Further, the ions required by an insolated reproducing adult may be quite different from those required by a shaded seedling. Finally, I know of no evidence that the shade cast by a parent tree is likely to be more inimical to the growth of its own seedlings than to those of other trees.

Perhaps, the most difficult problem in examining this system is the escape through time by juveniles. Tropical forest trees have a reputation of fruiting at intervals of two or more years (e.g., Ashton 1969; Richards 1952; Janzen 1670b), as do many temperate trees (e.g. Salisbury 1942; Smith 1968; Sharp 1958; Sharp and Sprague 1967). This behavior may yield larger seed crops at greater ecological separation in time, and less predictable time intervals, than is the case with annual fruiting. However, the freedom from predators that may result from this behavior is bought at the cost of the adult not placing seeds in the habitat during many years of its life. Infrequent seed setting is therefore most likely where suitable habitat for seedling survival (in the physiological sense) is not in short supply or erratically available (unless, of course, a dormant seed or stunted seedling can survive until a site becomes available). In short, missing seed crops imply that the geometric distance between parents is not the main relevant variable determining the impact of predators on the presence of a tree species in the habitat. For example, individuals of *Hymenaea courbaril* (Leguminosae) fruit every 3–5 years in Costa Rica, and thus achieve moderate escape from the seed predator *Rhinochenus stigma* (Curculionidae). This behavior means that to the weevil, trees of *H. courbaril* are three to five times as sparse as would be indicated by the total density of adult trees. Where this curculionid weevil is absent (El Salvador north through southern Mexico, and in Puerto Rico), the tree usually fruits every year (Janzen 1970*b*). It is of interest in this connection that the dipterocarp forests of southeast Asia are well known for both clumped distributions of many species and long intervals between fruiting periods which are sometimes synchronized (Richards 1952; Federov 1968; Ashton 1969). They suffer very heavy seed predation (Ashton 1969), but by seed predators that are most likely generalists feeding on one or more genera of trees.

Since male trees do not bear seed crops, dioecious trees (more common in tropical than in temperate forests [Ashton 1969]) must likewise be censused with caution. For example, dioecious palms in the genus *Scheelea* suffer more than 90% seed predation by the bruchid, *Caryobruchus buscki,* in some Costa Rican forests (Janzen, unpublished). To the bruchid, the density of adult palms is only half that recorded by an observer who does not recognize that only female trees bear seeds. It is tempting to hypothesize that if the palm were hermaphroditic or monoecious, its equilibrium density of adult palms would be considerably lower than at present.

The discussion so far has focused on relatively host-specific predators, but some animals show relatively little response to changes in the density of juveniles of a given species. These animals have the same effect on population structure as a slight lowering of the total seed crop, except where they happen to be locally abundant (for reasons other than the seed crop). Predators of intermediate host-specificity may have an extremely confusing influence on field experiments. If one species of major predator is host-specific on two tree species that fruit slightly out of phase with each other, the first to fruit will have a more negative effect on seed survival of the second than vice versa. When censusing the adult and juvenile trees to evaluate natural experiments, all the prey species of the predator must be recorded.

DISCUSSION

Had biologists generally followed the brief introductory comments in Ridley's (1930) compendium of tropical seed dispersal, the body of the present paper might have been written many years ago.

In almost every plant the greatest number of its seeds fall too near the mother plant to be successful, and soon perish. Only the seeds which are removed to a distance are those that reproduce the species. Where too many plants of one species are grown together, they are apt to be attacked by some pest, insect, or fungus. It is largely due to this . . . that one-plant associations are prevented and nullified by better means for dispersal of the seeds. When plants are too close together, disease can spread from one to the other, and can become fatal to all. Where plants of one kind are separated by those of other kinds, the pest, even if present, cannot spread, and itself will die out, or at least become negligible.

Gillett (1962) and Bullock (1967) reemphasized this. Their brief papers emphasized that (1) previously unoccupied habitats are very important in the production of new populations because an invading species often leaves its predator and pest parasite population behind, allowing it to enter a new habitat more readily than a resident species can expand its population to use the same resources; and (2) that insect attack should strongly affect a seedling's competitive abilities. Van de Pijl (1969) followed with the statement that "dense stands of any species are thinned out by pests, the vacant places becoming occupied by other species," but did not develop the idea further.

These papers, and the plant-herbivore interactions hypothesized here, all point in one direction: as conditions become more favorable for the seed and seedling predators in a habitat (for example, in moving from moist temperate to moist tropical forests), that habitat will support more species of trees because no one species can become common enough to competively oust most of the others. The obvious corollary is that as the number of species of trees in a habitat increases, interspecific competitive ability of seedlings and saplings declines in proportional importance in determining the apportionment of the total biomass among those present. This is not to say that interspecific competition is unimportant in tropical forests; a tree may persist in the face of very heavy predation if the occasional surviving seedling is a very superior competitor, and a tree with very light predation may be a very poor competitor yet survive by repeated trials at establishment. Where the tree is free from predation on juveniles (for some or all of its reproductive life) and a superior competitor as well, we can expect to find conditions closer to those of the few-species stands characteristic of temperate forests. The single-species stands in tropical mangrove swamps are excellent examples of this. Numerous seed samples of the large and very abundant seeds or undispersed seedlings of red mangrove (*Rhizophora mangle*), black mangrove (*Avicennia nitida*), mangle pinuela (*Pelliciera rhizophora*), and white mangrove (*Laguncularia racemosa*) in Costa Rica have failed to reveal host-specific seed predators. The seeds are probably high in tannin content as are the vegetative parts of the plants from these four widely separated families (e.g., Allen 1956). To exist in such pure stands and bear seeds almost continually, the plants must have extremely good chemical defenses against insects. Despite the successional nature of the mangrove community, mangrove seeds or seedlings cannot even escape in space since an earlier sere than any given stage of mangrove succession is usually present within a few meters as the mangrove forest advances into the estuary.

A word of caution is in order regarding the spacing influence of seed and seedling predators on new adult trees, as supplementary to the effect of predators on the density of the adult tree population. Ashton (1969) and Poore (1968) have recently stressed that the trees of many species of southeast Asian rain forests are distributed with various amounts of contagion, but their figures do not distinguish between reproductive and sterile adult-sized individuals, or between males and females. In some cases, subadults are not distinguished from adults. Secondly, if the location of all members (seeds, saplings, adults) of the population of a given species of tree are recorded over a short period of time including a period of reproduction, I predict that their data will show that adults are not nearly so clumped as the total population (over all age classes). Nevertheless, it must be recognized that even a forest with all species having clumped distributions would have its equilibrium number of tree species greatly increased by a large complex of host-specific predators on juvenile plants.

The comments in this paper apply directly to other organisms where the survival of a juvenile to maturity requires the death of a long-lived adult at the same point in space, and where the juveniles are very susceptible to predation. Sessile marine invertebrates (Paine 1966) and ant colonies fall in this category. As Connell (1961, 1963) stresses, regular spacing of the adults of these types of organisms is generally attributed to strong intraspecific interference through a third agent, the predator.

Relative freedom from predation, and therefore a low number of tree species in the forest, may come about in at least three major ways.

1. Both Southwood (1961) and Gillet (1962) have emphasized that invading plant species may leave their predators and parasites behind. If my observations of Puerto Rican forests are representative (the situation on Hawaii is apparently similar [W. H. Hatheway, personal communication]), tree population structures on tropical islands differ strikingly from those on adjacent mainlands. Here, trees such as *Trophis* (Moraceae), have extremely dense stands of seedlings and saplings under the canopy of the parent; these forests lack the native rodents and large terrestrial birds (e.g., *Tinamus, Crypturellus, Crax*) that thoroughly remove *Trophis* seeds from under the parent in Costa Rican lowland forests. Puerto Rican forests have many fewer species of adult trees per unit area than do mainland Central American areas of similar weather regime. My cursory plot censuses in Puerto Rico indicated a structure much more similar to hardwood forests in the southeastern United States than to Central America, in that seedlings and saplings of the canopy member trees are very common in the vicinity of putative parents.

In the second growth vegetation in Puerto Rico, a similar case is presented by *Leucaena glauca*, a mimosaceous shrub that loses upward of 90% of its seed crop to bruchid beetle predation in central America, and occurs there as a scattered adult with rare seedlings. In Puerto Rico, no bruchids attack this species, virtually every seed is viable, the adults are surrounded by dense stands of seedlings and intermediate-aged juveniles, and are extremely common.

2. In predation-rich habitats, newness to the habitat may be an adequate defense mechanism for some species for a period of time. The critical point, however, is not so much that the previous predators were left behind, but that the new ones cannot deal with the chemical defenses of the seeds and seedlings, or lack the behavioral traits to attempt such attacks. This is unlikely to be a permanent condition, but when it lasts for a long time, it may

result in a very common tree species. One example is provided by ferns; they are notorious for being extremely free from insect attack both as juveniles and adults (which can only be for chemical reasons), and for occurring in large pure stands in tropical forests. Another is the tree *Pentaclethra macroloba*. A mimosaceous legume, it is extremely abundant in the wet lowland forests of northeastern Costa Rica. Mimosaceous legumes with finely divided leaves are generally very rare in tropical lowland evergreen forests and *P. macroloba* has likely left behind a major set of predators and parasites, if it came originally from the deciduous forests where mimosaceous legumes are very abundant. The large seeds, produced virtually throughout the year by the population, are preyed upon only very slightly by squirrels before dispersal, and by terrestrial rodents after dispersal. Its seeds and seedlings have only very slight predation by insects, when compared to other forest trees, and the insects involved appear to be general foragers. When a hole opens in the forest canopy, the chance of there being a seedling of *P. macroloba* below it is much greater than for any other single species in the forest. I predict that the introduction of an insect host-specific on *P. macroloba* seeds would both reduce the population of adults dramatically and allow either invasion of other species, or expansion of the adult populations of resident species. This latter event is unlikely, however, since pressure from predators, rather than competition with *P. macroloba*, is probably holding their populations down.

The *Pentaclethra* example stresses the importance of the invaded habitat having different predators from the habitat of origin. It should be much harder for a legume to invade a habitat rich in species attacked by bruchids than one in which bruchids are rare. A corollary of this is that a resident species may prevent the invasion of a closely related species, by serving as the source of a predator that finds seeds of the invader to be suitable prey (Janzen 1970a). To become established, the invading tree may have to exist at an even lower density than in its native habitat. Federov (1966) has recently stressed the sympatric existence of congeners as characteristic of tropical forests (although sympatry of congeners is certainly characteristic of temperate forests, too). In the light of the activity of the predators, this is easily understood. First, the density of congeners is held low enough so that they have no chance of directly competitively excluding each other. Second, they must be species that either do not share major seed and seedling predators, or can survive at the lower densities that will be produced by a predator that treats both as one species.

The minimal density at which a tree population can exist is of great importance for understanding how many tree species can ultimately be packed into a forest habitat. The major deterrent to low density of adults appears to be reduction in outcrossing. Several authors have concluded that self-pollination is probably the rule in tropical rain forest trees (Baker 1959; Corner 1954; Richards 1952, 1969). There are numerous pollinators in tropical forests with the ability to provide outcrossing at long interplant distances (Ashton 1969; Janzen 1968, unpublished). Second, contrary to popular belief, there is a major reason why outcrossing is of utmost importance in the relatively uniform climate of tropical forests. In more stringent and unpredictable climates, the physical climate is the major challenge (aside from intertree competition, a problem in all forests), and in great part can be met through vegetative plasticity as well as through genetic change. Most important, a genotype optimal for weather conditions now is most likely to be optimal or nearly optimal for a considerable number of generations (at least until the weather changes). However, the challenge of a seed or seedling predator can be met only through behavioral or chemical changes, the success of which cannot be monitored directly by the parent. Such change can be brought about by genetic change alone. The new challenge of a predator capable of breaching the current chemical defenses of the adult or its seeds may occur abruptly at any time, and will greatly lower the fitness of the current tree biochemical phenotype. In other words, the more favorable the physical environment to the predators, the more frequently in evolutionary time the chemical defenses of the plant will have to be modified through genetic change if the plant is to persist in the community, and therefore the more important will be outcrossing. Van Steenis's (1969) recent suggestion that extinction of trees ''is a common feature in tropical rain forest'' and Ashton's (1969) comment that interspecific tree hybrids do extremely poorly in rain forest thus take on new meaning.

3. Temporal heterogeneity and unpredictability of the physical environment may both lead to freedom from predation on juvenile trees at certain times. This is best reflected in the low number of tree species in temperate forests. Weather changes of a regular type are indirectly responsible for regular large fluctuations in insects that prey upon seeds and seedlings. To the degree that an adult tree can produce juvenile plants when the population of its predators is low, the juveniles will have only intertree competition and edaphic conditions to deal with (a major challenge irrespective of intraspecific seed and seedling proximity). While a tropical tree may put a new crop of seeds into the habitat once a year (similar to temperate trees), the predators may have as many as 12 months in the year to search for food, in contrast with the considerably shorter period in temperate forests or strongly seasonal tropical ones. The occasional unpredictably hard seasons for predators (e.g., Barrett 1931; Parnell 1966) may result in a wave of juveniles of a tree species passing through the habitat, especially if it is coupled with a very large crop of seeds (Smith 1968). This again leads to conditions in which adult tree community composition is primarily a function of the competitive ability of the seedlings and saplings, allowing a few competitively superior tree species to dominate the community.

SUMMARY

A high number of tree species, low density of adults of each species, and long distances between conspecific adults are characteristic of many lowland tropical forest habitats. I propose that these three traits, in large part, are the result of the action of predators on seeds and seedlings. A model is presented that allows detailed examination of the effect of different predators, dispersal agents, seed-crop sizes, etc. on these three traits. In short, any event that increases the efficiency of the predators at eating seeds and seedlings of a given tree species may lead to a reduction in population density of the adults of that species and/or to increased distance between new adults and their parents. Either event will lead to more space in the habitat for other species of trees, and therefore higher total number of tree species, provided seed sources are available over evolutionary time. As one moves from the wet lowland tropics to the dry tropics or temperate zones, the seed and seedling predators in a habitat are hypothesized to be progressively less efficient at keeping one or a few tree species from monopolizing the habitat through competitive superiority. This lowered efficiency of the predators is brought about by the increased severity and unpredictability of the physical environment, which in turn leads to regular or erratic escape of large seed or seedling cohorts from the predators.

ACKNOWLEDGMENTS

This study was supported by NSF grants GB-5206, GB-7819, and GB-7805, and the teaching program of the Organization for Tropical Studies. The manuscript has profited greatly through discussions with the staff and students in that organization. Special thanks are due to H. G. Baker, A. Bradshaw, R. K. Colwell, J. H. Connell, W. H. Hatheway, E. Leigh, R. Levins, R. C. Lewontin, M. Lloyd, C. D. Michener, G. H. Orians, N. J. Scott, N. Smythe, R. R. Sokal, and J. H. Vandermeer.

LITERATURE CITED

Allen, P. H. 1956. The rain forests of Golfo Dulce. Univ. Florida Press, Gainesville. 417 pp.

Ashton, P. S. 1969. Speciation among tropical forest trees: some deductions in the light of recent evidence. Biol. J. Linnean Soc. London 1:155–196.

Baker, H. G. 1959. Reproductive methods as factors in speciation in flowering plants. Cold Spring Harbor Symp. Quant. Biol. 24:177–191.

Barbehenn, K. R. 1969. Host-parasite relationships and species diversity in mammals: a hypothesis. Biotropica 1:29–35.

Barger, J. H., and R. H. Davidson. 1967. A life history study of the ash seed weevils, *Thysanocnemis bischoffi* Blatchley and *T. helvole* Leconte. Ohio J. Sci. 67:123–127.

Barrett, L. I. 1931. Influence of forest litter on the germination and early survival of chestnut oak, *Quercus montana* Willd. Ecology 12:476–484.

Beard, J. S. 1942. Summary of silvicultural experience with *Cedrela mexicana* Roem., in Trinidad. Caribbean Forest. 3:91–102.

Bebbington, A. G., and W. Allen. 1936. The food-cycle of *Dysdercus fasciatus* in acacia savannah in Northern Rhodesia. Bull. Entomol. Res. 27:237–249.

Black, G. A., T. Dobzhansky, and C. Pavan. 1950. Some attempts to estimate species diversity and population density of trees in Amazonian forests. Bot. Gaz. 111:413–425.

526   THE AMERICAN NATURALIST

Breedlove, D. E., and P. R. Ehrlich. 1968. Plant-herbivore coevolution in lupines and lycaenids. Science 162:671–672.

Brncic, D. 1966. Ecological and cytogenetic studies of *Drosophila flavopilosa*, neotropical species living in *Cestrum* flowers. Evolution 20:16–29.

Bullock, J. A. 1967. The insect factor in plant ecology. J. Indian Bot. Soc. 46:323–330.

Bush, G. L. 1969. Mating behavior, host specificity, and the ecological significance of sibling species in frugivorous flies of the genus *Rhagoletis* (Diptera—Tephritidae). Amer. Natur. 103:669–672.

Cater, J. C. 1945. The silviculture of *Cedrela mexicana*. Caribbean Forest. 6:89–113.

Challinor, D. 1968. Alteration of surface soil characteristics by four tree species. Ecology 49:286–290.

Connell, J. H. 1961. Effects of competition, predation by *Thais lapillus*, and other factors on natural populations of the barnacle *Balanus balanoides*. Ecol. Monogr. 31:61–104.

———. 1963. Territorial behavior and dispersion in some marine invertebrates. Jap. Soc. Population Ecol. 5:87–101.

Corner, E. J. H. 1954. The evolution of tropical forests. *In* J. Huxley, A. C. Hardy, and E. B. Ford [ed.], Evolution as a process. 2d ed. Humanities, New York. 367 pp.

Costa Lima, A. M. 1967–1968. Quarto catalogo dos insectos que vivem nas plantas do Brasil, seus parasitos e predadores. Pts. 1 and 2. D'Araujo e Silva et al. [ed.] Dept. Def. Insp. Agro., Minist. Agric., Rio de Janeiro. 2215 p. total.

Coyne, J. F. 1968. *Laspeyresia ingens*, a seed worm infesting cones of longleaf pine. Ann. Entomol. Soc. Amer. 61:1116–1122.

Croat, T. 1970. Seasonal flowering behavior in Central Panama. Ann. Mississippi Bot. Gardens (in press).

DeLeon, D. 1941. Some observations on forest entomology in Puerto Rico. Caribbean Forest. 2:160–163.

Dumbleton, L. J. 1963. The biology and control of *Coleophora* spp. (Lepidoptera—Coleophoridae) on white clover. New Zealand J. Agr. Res. 6:277–292.

Eyles, A. C. 1964. Feeding habits of some Rhyparochrominae (Heteroptera: Lygaeidae) with particular reference to the value of natural foods. *Roy. Entomol. Soc. London, Trans.* 116:89–114.

Federov, A. A. 1966. The structure of the tropical rain forest and speciation in the humid tropics. J. Ecol. 54:1–11.

Fournier, L. A., and S. Salas. 1967. Tabla de vida el primer año de la población de *Dipterodendron costaricense* Radlk. Turrialba 17:348–350.

Gillett, J. B. 1962. Pest pressure, an underestimated factor in evolution. Systematics Association Pub. No. 4. Pp. 37–46.

Haffer, J. 1969. Speciation in Amazonian forest birds. Science 165:131–137.

Hardwick, D. F. 1966. The life history of *Schinia niveicosta* (Noctiudae). J. Lepidoptera 20:29–33.

Harper, J. L., J. N. Clatworthy, I. H. McNaughton, and G. R. Sagar. 1961. The evolution and ecology of closely related species living in the same area. Evolution 15:209–227.

Hinckley, A. D. 1961. Comparative ecology of two beetles established in Hawaii: an anthribid, *Araecerus levipennis*, and a bruchid, *Mimosestes sallaei*. Ecology 42:526–532.

Holdridge, L. R. 1943. Comments on the silviculture of *Cedrela*. Carribbean Forest. 4:77–80.

Janzen, D. H. 1968. Reproductive behavior in the Passifloraceae and some of its pollinators in Central America. Behavior 32:33–48.

———. 1969a. Seed-eaters versus seed size, number, toxicity and dispersal. Evolution 23:1–27.

———. 1969b. Allelopathy by myrmecophytes: the ant *Azteca* as an allelopathic agent of *Cecropia*. Ecology 50:147–153.

HERBIVORES AND TROPICAL FOREST DIVERSITY   527

————. 1970a. *Cassia grandis* L. beans and their escape from predators: a study in tropical predator satiation. Ecology (in press).

————. 1970b. Escape in time by *Hymenaea courbaril* (Leguminosae from *Rhinochenus stigma* (Curculionidae). Ecology (submitted for publication).

————. 1970c. Escape of *Sterculia apetala* seeds from *Dysdercus fasciatus* bugs in tropical deciduous forest. Ecology (in press).

————. 1971. Predator escape in time and space by juveniles of the vine, *Dioclea megacarpa*, in tropical forests. Amer. Natur. (in press).

Kaufman, J. H. 1962. Ecological and social behavior of the coati *Nasau nasau* on Barro Colorado Island, Panama. Univ. of Calif. Pub. Zool. 60:95–222.

Knab, F., and W. W. Yothers. 1914. Papaya fruit fly. J. Agr. Res. 2:447–453.

Lowe-McConnell, R. H. 1969. Speciation in tropical freshwater fishes. Biol. J. Linnean Soc. London 1:50–75.

MacArthur, R. H. 1969. Patterns of communities in the tropics. Biol. J. Linnean Soc. London 1:19–30.

Morris, D. 1962. The behavior of green acouchi (*Myoprocta pratti*) with special reference to scatter-hoarding. Zool. Soc. London, Proc. 139:701–732.

Murdoch, W. W. 1969. Switching in general predators: experiments on predator specificity and stability of prey populations. Ecol. Monogr. 39:335–354.

Myers, J. G. 1927. Ethological observations on some Pyrrocoridae of Cuba. Ann. Entomol. Soc. Amer. 20:279–300.

Oppenheimer, J. R. 1968. Behavior and ecology of the white-faced monkey, *Cebus capucinus*, on Barro Colorado Island, C.Z. Ph.D. thesis. Univ. Michigan, Ann Arbor.

Oppenheimer, J. R., and G. E. Lang. 1969. *Cebus* monkey: effect on branching of *Gustavia* trees. Science 165:187–188.

Paine, R. T. 1966. Food web complex and species diversity. Amer. Natur. 100:65–75.

Parnell, J. R. 1966. Observations on the population fluctuations and life histories of the beetles *Bruchidius ater* (Bruchidae) and *Apion fuscirostre* (Curculionidae) on broom (*Sarothamnus scoparius*). J. Amer. Ecol. 35:157–188.

Phillips, J. F. V. 1924. The biology, ecology, and sylviculture of ''stinkwood'', *Ocotea bullata* E. Mey: introductory studies. South Afr. J. Sci. 21:275–292.

————. 1925. *Platylophus trifoliatus* D. Don: a contribution to its ecology. South Afr. J. Sci. 22:144–160.

————. 1926a. General biology of the flowers, fruits, and young regeneration of the more important species of the Kenyan forests. South Afr. J. Sci. 23:366–417.

————. 1926b. Biology of the flowers, fruits, and young regeneration of *Olinia cymosa* Thub. Ecology 7:338–350.

Pipkin, S. B., R. L. Rodriquez, and J. Leon. 1966. Plant host specificity among flower-feeding neotropical *Drosophila* (Diptera: Drosophilidae). Amer. Natur. 100:135–156.

Poore, M. E. D. 1968. Studies in Malaysian rainforest. I. The forest on Triassic sediments in Jengka Forest Reserve. J. Ecol. 56:143–196.

Prevett, P. F. 1967. Notes on the biology, food plants and distribution of Nigerian Bruchidae (Coleoptera), with particular reference to the northern region. Bull. Entomol. Soc. Nigeria 1:3–6.

Richards, P. W. 1952. The tropical rainforest. Cambridge Univ. Press, New York. 450 p.

————. 1969. Speciation in the tropical rainforest and the concept of the niche. Biol. J. Linnean Soc. London 1:149–153.

Ridley, H. N. 1930. The dispersal of plants throughout the world. L. Reeve & Co., Ashfort, England. 744 p.

Salisbury, E. J. 1942. The reproductive capacity of plants. Bell, London. 244 p.

Schaefer, C. H. 1962. Life history of *Conophthorus radiatae* (Coleoptera: Scolytidae) and its principal parasite, *Cephalonomia utahensis* (Hymenoptera: Bethylidae). Ann. Entomol. Soc. Amer. 55:569–577.

528   THE AMERICAN NATURALIST

Schaefer, C. H. 1963. Factors affecting the distribution of the Monterey pine cone beetle
    (*Conophthorus radiatae* Hopkins) in central California. Hilgardia 34:79–103.
Sharp, W. M. 1958. Evaluating mast yields in the oaks. Pennsylvania State Univ. Agr.
    Exp. Sta. Bull. 635:1–22.
Sharp, W. M., and V. G. Sprague. 1967. Flowering and fruiting in the white oaks.
    Pistillate flowering, acorn development, weather, and yields. Ecology 48:243–
    251.
Smith, C. C. 1968. The adaptive nature of social organization in the genus of tree
    squirrels, *Tamiasciurus*. Ecol. Monogr. 38:31–63.
Smythe, N. 1970. Relationships between fruiting seasons and seed dispersal methods
    in a neotropical forest. Amer. Natur. 104:25–35.
Southwood, T. R. E. 1961. The number of species of insects associated with various
    trees. J. Anim. Ecol. 30:1–8.
Spight, T. M. 1967. Species diversity: a comment on the role of the predator. Amer.
    Natur. 101:467–474.
Struhsaker, T. T. 1967. Ecology of vervet monkeys (*Cercopithecus aethiops*) in the
    Masai-Amboseli Game Reserve, Kenya. Ecology 48:891–904.
Sweet, M. 1964. The biology and ecology of the Rhyparochrominae of New England
    (Heteroptera: Lygaeidae). Entomol. Amer. 43:1–124; 44:1–201.
Van der Pijl, L. 1969. Evolutionary action of tropical animals on the reproduction of
    plants. Biol. J. Linnean Soc. London 1:85, 96.
Van Steenis, C. G. G. J. 1969. Plant speciation in Malasia, with special reference to
    the theory of non-adaptive saltatory evolution. Biol. J. Linnean Soc. London
    1:97–133.
Webb, L. J., J. G. Tracey, and K. P. Haydock. 1967. A factor toxic to seedlings of the
    same species associated with living roots of the non-gregarious subtropical rain
    forest tree *Grevillea robusta*. J. Appl. Ecol. 4:13–25.
Went, F. W., and N. Stark. 1968. Mycorrhiza. Bioscience 18:1035–1038.
Wickens, G. E. 1969. A study of *Acacia albida* Del. (Mimosoideae). Kew Bull. 23:181–
    202.
Yonke, T. R., and J. T. Medler. 1968. Biologies of three species of *Alydus* in Wisconsin.
    Ann. Entomol. Soc. Amer. 61:526–531.

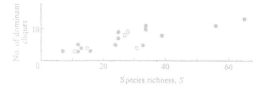

Fig. 3 The number of dominant cliques plotted against species richness S for the 24 community food web versions compiled by Cohen[5].

both slopes are negative and significantly different from zero (Student's t-test, $P = 0.0036$ for $(SC_3)^{-1/2}$, $P = 0.0006$ for $(SC_5)^{-1/2}$). The significance of this, at least within May's framework[7], is that unless average interaction strength tends to decrease with increasing S, systems with larger S will be closer to the critical value $\bar{i}(SC)^{1/2} = 1$ which marks the transition to instability; one expects that such systems would be more fragile in the sense of susceptibility to external perturbations.

Most ecologists would probably expect a decrease in C as S increases, on the basis that ecosystems tend to be organised into relatively small 'guilds' of species, with most interactions taking place within guilds[2,6-9]. This idea can be made precise and tested as follows. Define a 'clique' as a set of species with the property that every pair of species in the set has some food resource in common, and define a dominant clique as a clique which is contained in no other clique[5,10]. These dominant cliques may appropriately be regarded as 'guilds'. In Fig. 3 the number of dominant cliques is plotted against species richness S for the 24 Cohen community web versions. The number of dominant cliques increases with S, although perhaps not as rapidly as one might have expected.

This work was carried out at the Institut für Theoretische Physik der Universität Bern, Switzerland. I thank my friends and colleagues in Bern for their support.

Received 5 November 1979; accepted 13 February 1980.

1. Gardner, M. R. & Ashby, W. R. *Nature* **228**, 784 (1970).
2. May, R. M. *Stability and Complexity in Model Ecosystems* (Princeton University Press, 1974).
3. Hahn, W. *Stability of Motion* (Springer, Berlin, 1967).
4. Rejmánek, M. & Stary, P. *Nature* **280**, 311–313 (1979).
5. Cohen, J. E. *Food Webs and Niche Space* (Princeton University Press, 1978).
6. May, R. M. *Nature* **238**, 413–414 (1972).
7. McNaughton, S. J. *Nature* **274**, 251–253, 279, 351–352 (1979).
8. Harris, J. R. W. *Nature* **279**, 350–351 (1979).
9. Lawton, J. H. & Rallison, S. P. *Nature* **279**, 151 (1979).
10. Fulkerson, D. R. & Gross, O. A. *Pacif. J. Math.* **15**(3), 835–855 (1965).

Effects of leaf age and plant life history patterns on herbivory

Phyllis D. Coley

Committee on Evolutionary Biology, University of Chicago, Chicago, Illinois 60637

Current theories on plant–herbivore interactions suggest that plant species of different successional status and leaves of various ages differ in their degree of ephemerality and predictability to herbivores, and will therefore exhibit different antiherbivore characteristics[1-6]. Old leaves and leaves of mature forest plants are expected to be better defended than ephemeral young leaves and leaves of early successional plants. These predicted patterns of plant defence and the resultant patterns of insect grazing are not well documented for natural communities. Field studies have shown that mammalian herbivores in a tropical forest prefer young leaves[7] and that insect grazing in a temperate forest is heaviest on the young leaves[8]. Laboratory studies have shown that late successional species[9-12] or plants with certain chemical defences[13-17] are less palatable for generalist herbivores. Laboratory results depend, however, on the particular herbivore tested, and may not accurately predict rates of herbivory in natural systems. Here I report on rates of herbivory on young and mature leaves from tree species with different life history patterns. Grazing rates (% leaf area eaten per day) on mature leaves of fast growing, shade-intolerant species (pioneers) were an order of magnitude greater than those on slow growing, shade-tolerant species (persistents). Young leaves in both groups of species suffered significantly greater grazing damage than mature leaves.

For this study, tree species were classified into two groups, pioneers or persistents. Persistent species tolerate shade as seedlings and saplings, whereas pioneer species are unable to survive in the shade[18-23]. Pioneer species may differ from persistent ones in antiherbivore characteristics because of these differences in their life history patterns. Persistent species grow slowly for long periods of time in the understory before a light gap opens above them, and thus they may be a more predictable resource for herbivores and may be expected to possess costly and effective defences. Mature leaves may be tough and contain substances that reduce digestibility, such as tannins and resins[1-4,24,25]. In contrast, saplings of pioneer species may invest in metabolically less expensive toxic chemicals and instead rely primarily on escaping herbivory through fast growth and a patchy occurrence in light gaps[1-4]. Young expanding leaves of both types of plants are a nutritious[5,26,27] and ephemeral resource, and presumably are not heavily defended by chemicals, especially not substances that reduce digestibility (refs 1–6 but see 7, 28). Synchronous flushing of young leaves by individuals or populations could lead to temporal escape as well as satiation of herbivores[5,29,30].

Rates of insect grazing were evaluated for 235 saplings (1–2 m high) of 11 pioneer and 16 persistent species growing in 13 light gaps in the semideciduous forest of Barro Colorado Island, Panama[31]. These 27 species of canopy trees were chosen because both adults and saplings were abundant. I measured total leaf area and area of holes made by herbivores of 1,745 marked young and old leaves at 2-week intervals for three months at the beginning of the rainy season (April–July 1977). Young leaves were measured from the time they emerged from the bud until they were fully expanded and had mature characteristics. Grazing rates were expressed as the percentage of the entire leaf area eaten per day which controls for leaf area in expanding young leaves (see Table 1 for a description of rate measures).

The data on grazing rates (Table 1) suggest that there is a strong relationship of both life history patterns and leaf age with grazing by herbivores. For 23 of the 27 species, there is no overlap between the distributions of pioneer and persistent species in the mean grazing values on mature leaves. There is an order of magnitude difference between the mean grazing rate on mature persistent leaves and that on either mature leaves of pioneers or young leaves of persistents. There is a smaller but significant difference ($P < 0.01$) between the grazing rates on young and mature pioneer leaves. There is no significant difference between the grazing rates on young leaves of pioneer and persistent species.

These results support predictions of current hypotheses[1-4] which propose that investment in antiherbivore defences will reflect the degree of predictability of each plant or plant part as a resource for herbivores. Low rates of grazing on mature persistent leaves suggest that they are well defended from herbivores, possibly by digestibility reducing substances[3]. High rates of herbivory on young leaves and pioneer plants suggest that if escape in time or space is operating, it is apparently not so

0028-0836/80/150545—02$01.00

Table 1 Grazing rates (% leaf area eaten per day) on young and mature leaves of pioneer and persistent species

Persistent species*	Mature leaves	Young leaves
Faramea occidentalis	0.002	0.069
Virola sebifera	0.002	0.108
Prioria copaifera	0.002	0.014
Swartzia simplex	0.003	2.504
Simarouba amara	0.003	0.026
Trichilia cipo	0.003	0.522
Poulsenia armata	0.004	0.027
Desmopsis panamensis	0.004	0.783
Tachigalia versicolor	0.005	0.775
Tetragastris panamensis	0.005	1.477
Protium tenuifolium	0.008	0.928
Hirtella triandra	0.042	0.120
Quararibea asterolepis	0.114	0.316
Alseis blackiana	0.136	0.096
Zanthoxylum panamense	0.136	0.701
Cupania sylvatica	0.311	1.151
Mean†	0.041^{abc}	0.631^{c}
Standard error‡	0.024	0.151
No. of species	16	16
No. of plants	120	115
No. of leaves	452	509

Pioneer species	Mature leaves	Young leaves
Didymopanax morototoni	0.007	0.001
Croton bilbergianus	0.025	0.310
Zanthoxylum belizense	0.081	0.624
Spondias radlkoferi	0.186	1.492
Miconia argentea	0.189	0.509
Ochroma pyramidale	0.191	0.178
Alchornea costaricensis	0.210	0.818
Luehea seemannii	0.456	1.108
Cecropia insignis	0.797	0.111
Trema micrantha	1.071	0.053
Cecropia obtusifolia	2.267	1.299
Mean†	0.466^{ab}	0.663^{a}
Standard error‡	0.162	0.161
No. of species	11	11
No. of plants	102	105
No. of leaves	386	398

Grazing rates for each leaf were computed as $100 \times$ (change in hole area)/((total leaf area) × (no. of days between observations)). Significant distortion in the percentage of leaf area eaten does not occur during leaf expansion. Holes of known diameter were punched in 209 young leaves of five pioneer species (*Cecropia insignis, Croton bilbergianus, Miconia argentea, Trema micrantha* and *Zanthoxylum belizense*) and five persistent species (*Desmopsis panamensis, Protium tenuifolium, Trichilia cipo, Virola sebifera* and *Zanthoxylum panamense*). A regression of the percentage change in hole area against the percentage change in total leaf area over time gave a slope not significantly different from 1 ($P < 0.05$, $r^2 = 0.88$ around $\beta = 1$).
*Species are ordered by grazing rates on mature leaves.
†Values followed by the same letter are significantly different, $P < 0.01$ for *a* and $P < 0.001$ for *b* and *c*. Significance levels were determined by a nested 2-way ANOVA considering leaves as replicates on a transformation of the data: ln(1,000 × rate + 1). Although the data were not normally distributed (as a result of many zero values), ANOVA seemed the most appropriate statistical method. The results were not changed when leaves with values of zero damage were excluded. Similar results were obtained when a new rate was calculated by averaging the actual leaf and hole areas per plant rather than the percentage eaten. This second rate of herbivory was computed as: $(\Sigma_i$ change in hole area) $\times n_i)/((\Sigma_i$ leaf area) $\times (\Sigma_i$ no. of observation days)), where *i* is the *i*th plant and *n* the number of leaves. This measure of grazing is less sensitive to the contribution by young leaves that were completely eaten.
‡Standard error of the species means.

effective in reducing losses to herbivores. The magnitude of the differences in grazing rates that I observed emphasises the range of susceptibility to herbivores that exists in natural communities and the presumed variety and effectiveness of different anti-herbivore characteristics.

I thank D. P. Janos, E. G. Leigh, D. McCauley and M. J. Wade for helpful comments, P. McCullog for assistance with statistics, N. Brokaw for field advice and R. B. Foster for encouragement and assistance. The support of a Smithsonian Predoctoral Fellowship and a grant from the Hinds Fund of the University of Chicago are gratefully acknowledged.

Received 15 August 1979; accepted 7 February 1980.

1. Cates, R. G. & Rhoades, D. F. *Biochem. Syst. Ecol.* **5**, 185–193 (1977).
2. Feeny, P. P. in *Coevolution of Animals and Plants* (eds Gilbert, L. E. & Raven, P. H.) 3–19 (University of Texas Press, Austin, 1975); in *Biochemical Interaction Between Plants and Insects* (eds Wallace, J. W. & Mansell, R. L.) 1–40 (Plenum, New York, 1976).
3. Rhoades, D. F. & Cates, R. G. in *Biochemical Interaction Between Plants and Insects* (eds Wallace, J. W. & Mansell, R. L.) 168–213 (Plenum, New York, 1976).
4. Rhoades, D. F. in *Herbivores: Their Interrelationships with Plant Secondary Constituents* (eds Rosenthal, G. A. & Janzen, D. H.) 3–54 (Academic, New York, 1979).
5. Feeny, P. P. *Ecology* **51**, 565–581 (1970).
6. Dement, W. A. & Mooney, H. A. *Oecologia* **15**, 65–76 (1974).
7. Milton, K. *Am. Nat.* **114**, 362–378 (1979).
8. Reichle, D. E., Goldstein, R. A., Van Hook, R. I. & Dodson, G. J. *Ecology* **54**, 1076–1084 (1973).
9. Cates, R. G. & Orians, G. H. *Ecology* **56**, 410–418 (1975).
10. Freeland, W. J. & Winter, J. W. *J. chem. Ecol.* **1**, 439–455 (1975).
11. Grime, J. P., MacPherson-Stewart, S. F. & Dearman, R. S. *J. Ecol.* **56**, 405–420 (1968).
12. Otte, D. *Oecologia* **18**, 129–144 (1975).
13. Bernays, E. A. & Chapman, R. F. *Ecol. Ent.* **2**, 1–18 (1977).
14. Cooper-Driver, G. A. & Swain, T. *Nature* **260**, 604 (1976).
15. Cates, R. G. *Ecology* **56**, 391–400 (1975).
16. Feeny, P. P. *J. Insect Phys.* **14**, 805–817 (1968).
17. Jones, D. A. in *Phytochemical Ecology* (ed. Harborne, J. B.) 103–124 (Academic, New York, 1972).
18. Hartshorn, G. S. in *Tropical Trees as Living Systems* (eds Tomlinson, P. B. & Zimmerman, M. H.) 617–638 (Cambridge University Press, Cambridge, Mass. 1978).
19. Abreville, A. in *World Vegetation Types* (ed. Eyre, S. R.) 41–55 (Columbia University Press, New York, 1971).
20. Whitmore, T. C. *Tropical Rain Forests of the Far East* (Clarendon, Oxford, 1975); in *Tropical Trees as Living Systems* (eds Tomlinson, P. B. & Zimmerman, M. H.) 639–655 (Cambridge University Press, 1978).
21. Bray, J. R. *Ecology* **37**, 598–600 (1956).
22. Schulz, J. P. *Verh. K. Ned. Akad. Wet. Afd. natuurkd Tweed. Reeks.* **53**, 1–367 (1960).
23. van Steenis, C. G. G. J. *Proc. Kandy Symp. on Study of Trop. Veg.* 159–163 (UNESCO, Paris, 1956).
24. McKey, D. *Science* **202**, 61–64 (1978).
25. Oates, J. F., Swain, T. & Zantovska, J. *Biochem. Syst. Ecol.* **5**, 317–321 (1977).
26. Dixon, A. F. G. in *Animal Populations in Relation to Their Food Resources* (ed. Watson, A.) 271–287 (Br. Ecol. Soc., London 1970).
27. Oelberg, K. J. *Range Mgmt* **9**, 220–225 (1956).
28. Rhoades, D. F. *Biochem. Syst. Ecol.* **5**, 281–290 (1977); *The Biology and Chemistry of the Creosotebush in New World Deserts* (eds Mabry, T. Hunziker, J. & DiFeo, D. R.) 135–175 (Dowden, Hutchinson and Ross, Stroudsburg, 1977).
29. Janzen, D. H. *Ecology* **52**, 964–979 (1971).
30. McKey, D. *Am. Nat.* **108**, 305–320 (1974).
31. Knight, D. H. *Ecol. Monogr.* **45**, 259–284 (1975).

Female mimicry in male bluegill sunfish— a genetic polymorphism?

Wallace J. Dominey

Field of Neurobiology and Behavior, Cornell University, Ithaca, New York 14850

When male reproductive success depends on male–male competition and aggression, individuals which are at a competitive disadvantage sometimes adopt an entirely different constellation of reproductive behaviours. When such alternative reproductive patterns are practised opportunistically, as when a defeated territorial male adopts a parasitic role, or as part of a developmental sequence, as when younger males are satellites, they can be considered to be part of a single lifetime reproductive strategy. In contrast, when alternatives are available but individuals practise only a single reproductive option throughout their lifetime, the possibility of a genetic polymorphism can be considered. Such genetically mediated alternative reproductive strategies have been hypothesised[1], but the ontogeny of supposed alternative reproductive strategies is seldom known[2]. This letter describes two reproductive patterns in bluegill sunfish (*Lepomis macrochirus*), a nesting male strategy and a female mimic strategy, and demonstrates that an individual male does not practise both reproductive strategies.

40   Ecological Dispersal Classes, Established on the Basis of the Dispersing Agents

typical mammal-fruits. SERNANDER (1927) called this way of dispersal "gliro-chory" (glires = rodents).

BURKART (1943) quoted data on the chinchilla, which can only exist in the wild where *Balsamodendron brevifolium* (Leguminosae)grows. It stores and eats the fruits (algarobillas). The important contribution of HUBER (1910) contains the solution of the riddle as to how *Bertholletia excelsa*, the Brazil nut, is dispersed and regenerates in nature. Its woody capsules with internal arilloid pulp around the seeds can be opened by man only with the aid of an axe. Large rodents (agoutis, *Dasyprocta*) can open them, eat the pulp and bury the seeds as a reserve. Some *Lecythis* species there and some palms (such as *Attalea funifera*) have the same bond with these animals.

The diaspores can be large as the transport is stomatochorous (in the mouth).

3. Accidental Endozoochory

Browsing animals can swallow diaspores together with the foliage and partly evacuate them intact. In ruminants, this dispersal can hardly be separated from directed, intentional gathering of adapted diaspores. Many investigations have concerned the diaspores in the dung of vegetarian mammals, including hares. They were often carried out to explain the mass-infestation with weeds after dunging. Amaranthaceae, Chenopodiaceae, *Ranunculus, Urtica*, many grasses, and also leguminous herbs (like *Trifolium* species) with small pods and hard seeds can withstand digestion to some extent. For percentages of survival I refer to RIDLEY (p. 336—341) and the tables in MÜLLER (1955, p. 88—92). This is not the occasion to discuss in detail the agricultural effect, but one archaeological effect may be mentioned. Seeds of *Chenopodium album* were found in prehistoric dwellings in such masses that some investigators considered it to be an ancient food plant. MÜLLER (1959) made it clear that the layers found consisted of animal dung.

We also pass over here the effect which passing through animals has on germination; later on, we shall see that seedling development is often accelerated. Many agriculturalists prefer such "animal-treated" seed for sowing. In South Africa, eating of leguminous pods by antelopes has been seen not only to produce faster germination but also to prevent attack by insects, which damage uneaten seeds for the larger part. Perharps digestion eliminates mainly the already damaged seeds. JANZEN (1969 b, 1970) found a large difference in infection by Bruchids between seeds on the ground and in droppings, as well as between seeds underneath the mother plant and those transported some distance from it.

4. Adaptive Endozoochory

Mimetic deceit (which, in the case of mammals, would have to be by means of smell) cannot be expected. The rest of the chapter can, therefore, be devoted to the intentional intake of diaspores by various mammals, all with different ethology. The general syndrome of diaspores adapted to dispersal by mammals has much in common with that of ornithochores, mentioned before. In some points it deviates, according to the different ethology and sense physiology of the agents. Mammals have a sense of smell, possess teeth, masticate much better, are mostly larger, rarely lead an arboreal life, and are mostly night-feeders that are colour blind. The corresponding differential characteristics of diaspores eaten by mammals are: possession of a hard skin, which offers no impediment; a more evident protection of the seed proper against mechanical destruction, the protection often being assisted or replaced by the presence in the seed of toxic or bitter substances; a smell favourable for attraction; non-essentiality of colour; large size in a number of cases. Just as in earlier reptile-fruits, the demands of accessibility are more stringent than in bird-fruits, and dropping may be continued. For a good relation with flying mammals (bats), special requirements are evident, as will be shown later. This syndrome again represents a maximum. It is, just as in ecological flower classes, partly positive (attracting legitimate visitors) and partly negative (excluding others).

In Northern regions so few original mammalian dispersers survive, and so many edible fruits are introductions, that it is difficult to reconstruct the original relations. The influence of ungulates on fruits remained small after glaciation, when grass was present in sufficient quantities. In fruitless periods, migration or a switch in menu was not as easy as it was for birds. Fruit-bats stayed away entirely after glaciation, as did flower-birds. Some rodents managed to survive in the habitat or reconquered it by storing dry diaspores of the advancing plants. The natural role of martens, jackals and hedgehogs has largely to be surmised. Wild boars represent the villains of the piece, although in South America the peccary is beneficial to the low-growing, fragrant ananas. We have to speculate on the inclusion in our classification system, as mammal-fruits, of the following items: medlars *(Mespilus)*, melons, peaches, apples, pears, prunes, cucumbers, etc. — fruits which have, morover, been grossly modified by cultivation. The sweet-smelling green quince *(Cydonia)* is a typical mammal-fruit. Bears had and have a modest role as eaters of berries, also as consumers of larger fruits.

The tropics offer a rich and permanent table for fructivores such as monkeys, civet cats, bats, ungulates, bears, etc. The fruits and the animals reflect each other's characteristics there. In contrast to other handbooks (Europe-centered), the one by ULBRICH (1928) tries to bring this out for tropical fruits.

Ungulates. Tropical ruminants and elephants eat all kinds of vegetable matter that agree with their taste. Elephants mix fruit in their herbage and in Africa even follow the fruiting of preferred trees, e. g., *Dumoria heckeli,* with large seeds. The tree is said to be distributed along the trails. The very large kernels (13 cm) of the palm *Borassus flabellifer* have also been found sprouting in the dung, together with those of *Hyphaene* and *Adansonia* and the many leguminous pods discussed below. For details see PHILIPPS (1926), BURTT (1929) and GUILLAUMET (1967). In Asia, *Durio* and *Mangifera* seeds have been found sprouting in the dung.

Ruminants in African savannah regions rely to a considerable extent on fruits. Antelopes can digest rather woody fruits such as those of *Adansonia*. LEISTNER (1967) gives some details on their specific behaviour. The springbok *(Antidorcas)* is a grazer and browser, the gemsbok *(Oryx)* and the eland *(Taurotragus)* eat more fruit. GWYNNE and BELL (1968) pointed to the Thomson gazelle *(Gazella)* as a fruit-eater, in contrast to the gnu *(Connochaetes)* and the topi *(Damaliscus)*. Many Leguminosae, especially *Acacia* species, specialize in this way of dispersal, offering leathery, nutritive pods, sometimes keeping them on the tree, but mostly dropping them immediately at maturity. The fruits are often classified incorrectly as dry. A special adaptive point is the extreme hardness of the smooth seeds, resistant to strong molars, as is evident in *Tamarindus, Dichrostachys, Acacia* and those *Cassia* species with hard, indehiscent pods of the type of *C. fistula*. *Acacia arabica* and *A. horrida* are mentioned as pioneers in grassland, spread by ruminants (also goats). Some of those trees, including species of *Prosopis, Ceratonia,* and *Samanea,* are even cultivated for their fruits in diverse parts of the world; in South America, they are used as cattle fodder under the general name of algarobba (properly *Ceratonia*). In North America, *Lespedeza stricta* (Papilionideae) was spread by cattle in this way. Indian deer also eat large fallen fruits, disgorging the hard parts during rumination (TROUP, 1921).

Bats and Chiropterochory. The writer has published a monograph on the subject (1957 b), of which the following is an abstract. In tropical Asia and Africa, the old group of Macrochiroptera (fundamentally fruit-eaters) has a large influence. In America, fruit-eaters developed later independently and incompletely among Microchiroptera in some of the Phyllostomidae, viz., separately in the subfamilies Stenoderminae, Phyllonycterinae and Glossophaginae.

As experience with expatriate fruits teaches, the attractiveness of bat-fruits is international, obviously depending on some general preference in bats. The taste and consistency can vary between hard-sour and soft-sweet, but otherwise a syndrome of general characteristics can easily be recognized, in accordance with the ethology and sense physiology of the bats. Fruit-bats are nocturnal and colour blind, have a keen sense of smell, and have, apparently, an innate preference for "stale", musty odours like the one their own glands produce. Rarely (in the case of small-seeded *Ficus* and *Piper* species) do they ingest seeds or kernels, mostly consuming just the juice after intense chewing. After transport to a suitable place, the remnants are regurgitated, sometimes at the roosting places. The distance is not large, rarely exceeding 200 m. The larger species *(Pteropus)* can transport heavy mangoes, but other species have lower limits for loads. Fruit-bats have particular difficulty in flying through dense foliage, as their sonar-apparatus is weakly developed, at least in Asiatic, non-cavedwelling species.

The fruit-syndrome is, accordingly (see Table 1): drab colour, musty odour reminding one of fermentation and rancid substances (butyric acid), possibly large size with possession of large seeds, permanent attachment with exposure outside the foliage. The latter position can (as in bat-flowers, described in FAEGRI and VAN DER PIJL, 1966) be realized by a curious reorganization of the tree-structure, resulting in, e. g., an open structure of the canopy (pagoda structure, as in *Terminalia catappa),* projecting stalks, long stalks hanging underneath the canopy (flagellicarpy), or placement on the main trunk (caulicarpy, as in species of *Lansium, Ficus* and *Artocarpus).*

The occurrence of fleshy fruits with a caulicarpous position struck many early observers in the tropics. This was explained by them in many ways, none of which can be accepted, but the connection with bats for either pollination or dispersal is a satisfactory explanation. Entire reorganization of the crown of the female trees is conspicuous in the bat-dispersed species *Chlorophora excelsa* (Moraceae), as described by Eggeling (1955) and Osmaston (1965). A possible relation between darkness and odour production should be studied.

Table 1. Comparative Syndrome of Chiropterochory

fruit-bats	bat-fruits
nocturnal visits	exposed position, rarely nocturnal odour
vision limited, colour-blind	drab colour, rarely whitish
good sense of smell, with preference for fermentation odour	musty, sourish, rancid odour
rather large	diaspore may be large
blunt molars press out juice; gut simple, short, providing low body weight	weakly protected, juicy diaspore, juice easily digested
seeds. and pulp mostly expectorated	hard parts may be large
weak sonar system, visit impracticable inside foliage	diaspore exposed outside dense crown (flagelli-, caulicarpy)

A long list of cases can be found in my paper (1957 b) and a few in Kuhl-mann and Kühn (1947). Some cases deserve comment here from the viewpoint of human consumption. In contrast to temperate table fruits, those in the tropics rarely *(Capsicum)* represent gaudy ornithochores, being instead mostly large and drab with a smell to which one has to become accustomed. Instances are species of *Artocarpus, Achras* and *Psidium* and wild types of *Mangifera.*

Another link with man is that "ghost trees" in international folklore are visited at night by crying bats; their visits serve either pollination or seed dispersal.

The families most popular with the bats are: Palmae (including the date palm) in which caulicarpy is organizational, Moraceae (including *Antiaris toxicaria* and many *Ficus* species), Chrysobalanaceae, Annonaceae, Sapotaceae, Anacardiaceae. The first indication was given by Huber (1910). The few caulicarpous Leguminosae (among others, species of *Cordyla, Cynometra, Detarium, Inocarpus* and *Angylocalyx)* are mostly chiropterochorous. *Andira inermis* is even called "morceguiera" in Brazil and "andira" is an Indian native name for

44   Ecological Dispersal Classes, Established on the Basis of the Dispersing Agents

bat. The sole caulicarpous plant of temperate Europe *(Ceratonia)* is natural on
the northern limit of African fruit-bats; its fruits, containing butyric acid, are
eaten by them in time of need. In case of need, bats switch to leaves and to bird-
fruits.

Fig. 12. Mango fruits *(Mangifera indica)* dangling by weight underneath the foliage

With regard to the evolutionary development among the flowering plants,
the following can be stated: bat-fruits appear already in some Ranales, are
dominant in caulicarpous and flagellicarpous *Ficus* species (including the sycomore near the northern limit of fruit-bats), and also occur in advanced groups
on one level with and alternating with ornithochorous and other fruits. In the
Bignoniaceae, bat-flowers seem primary, probably having induced (by the
development of a special position and special odoriferous substances) the incidental switch to bat-fruits. The reverse may have happened elsewhere.

We can also review the evolution with regard to complexity of diaspores. Bat
dispersal of nude seeds has been found in the gymnosperm *Cycas rumphii,* where
it is not typical and is thus possibly a regressive overlapping. In *Cephalo-
taxus* the aromatic, pineapple-like fragance of the seed may also indicate reptile
connections, especially in those cases where it is dropped. In the leguminous
plant *Swartzia prouacensis,* the seed itself, still in the arilloid phase of exposed
seeds, has developed a bond with bats, whereas other species employing the same
device are ornithochorous. Its chiropterochorous adaptations consist of a fairly
large seed, a drab white arilloid, a brown pod and a most curious funicle of up

to 3 m length, so that we may speak of flagellispermy (see Fig. 13). The smell and the occurrence of bat visits to it deserve investigation in Guyana. The same applies to the long-funicled seeds of *Lecythis usitata* that are, indeed, collected by bats. For the arillate but short-funicled *Lecythis zabucajo* (sapucaya nut), the

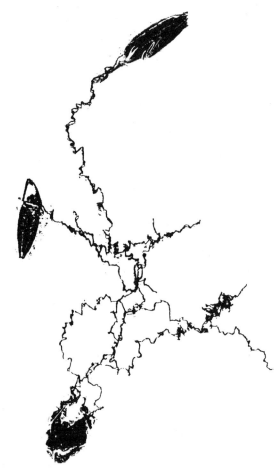

Fig. 13. *Swartzia prouacensis*. Dehisced valves of pod with seed taken out, the funicle still showing its folded condition inside the pod. Herbarium specimen attached with tape. (Photo NATAN)

picking out of the seeds from the hard fruit-boxes and their dispersal by bats have been described by GREENHALL (1965). He records that the odour of the arilloid suggests that its tissue is rotting. Some *Inga* species will probably have to be included, standing at the point of divergence from reptiles towards birds and bats. Closed sarcotesta fruits *(Lansium, Baccaurea)* are as frequent in the list as higher pericarp fruits.

46   Ecological Dispersal Classes, Established on the Basis of the Dispersing Agents

Regarding plant geography, I pointed (1957 b) to the concurrence of the limits of certain plants (such as *Spondias dulcis*) with those of fruit-bats in the Pacific, reflecting, perhaps, ancient land connections, as only *Pteropus*, the flying fox, can fly tens of kilometers. Bats contributed to the recolonization of Krakatau (DOCTERS VAN LEEUWEN, 1936). In Australia, *Pteropus* has recently spread southwards, outside the tropics, following fruit cultivation but switching to new, unadapted species of plants.

It is synecologically important that some fruit-bats, especially in Africa, migrate to neighbouring regions with a different crop. A number of more or less simultaneously fruiting species can therefore form one food association, as well as a number of subsequently fruiting species in one and the same community where bats can have a permanent base. The latter situation has been shown to exist also for flower-bats (FAEGRI and VAN DER PIJL, 1966).

Some plant species are bound to bats in a double sense, for pollination and dispersal; e. g., the wild bananas and *Sonneratia alba*. The hanging position is favourable to both processes. SIMMONDS (1959) reported that dense stands of *Musa* seedlings may be the result of the presence of a bat-colony in a tree.

Primates. Monkeys and apes are latecomers, taking advantage of ecological opportunities that open up incidentally, and forming incidental connections. They are mostly destructive, eating everything edible, ripe or unripe, also buds and leaves, soft- or hard-skinned fruits; they may or may not be instrumental in dispersal. They are not colour blind and rely more on visual perception than other mammals do. Some externally hard fruits with internal, soft arilloids suit them better than they do birds. The wild mangosteens *(Garcinia)* possessing such a structure are indeed eaten by monkeys. In a cultivated form, they are eaten by man as the monkey's successor in invading the environment. Because of the absence of a bat-smell, they are even popular with newly arrived Europeans. *Mammea* is somewhat of an American counterpart. Many fruits of Euphorbiaceae, Sapindaceae, Rubiaceae *(Gardenia)*, Loganiaceae *(Strychnos)*, Sterculiaceae *(Theobroma)* and Rutaceae *(Citrus)* are of this type.

The most curious fruit of this ecological group (armoured fruits) is the large, spiny durian *(Durio zibethinus)*. Its internal arilloid is preferred above everything else in Indonesia by orang utans, rhinos, tapirs, bears, elephants and man as successors to reptiles (see p. 22). The opening of fallen fruits requires skill and force. The smell is overwhelming, but not of the bat-type. Mechanically, the seeds are unprotected, but on the other hand they are toxic when raw. Even elephants defecate them undamaged. The arillode contains oil so that even panthers join in the battle for the fruit. Smaller-fruited sister species are ornithochorous (with dehiscing and coloured fruit), demonstrating the divergence from the reptile phase.

Various Mammals. STOPP (1958 b) discussed the geocarpy of *Cucumis humifructus*, apparently occurring together with other cases of geocarpy in desertlike regions in Africa. The position has, however, not the character of atelochory, as in the cases described in Chapter VI (see p. 80), and the fruit is large und juicy.

STOPP doubted the dispersal by aardvarks *(Orycteropus),* near whose tunnels the plants are found. MEEUSE (1958) brought good arguments in support of the idea that the animal eats the fruit for its water and buries its dung with the seeds near its nest. Otherwise the seeds germinate badly.

The role of tapirs in Amazonia is discussed in the works of HUBER (1910) and KUHLMANN (1947). To mention a curious case reported, they bury seeds of *Araucaria angustifolia,* so that thickets of it arise on the spot.

Civet cats *(Paradoxurus)* in Indonesia consume all kinds of fruit. They have the pleasant habit of defecating on fixed open spots, so that I could review the complete yearly menu. The data are lost, but the curious impression remains that such a small animal is able to eat the large palm fruits of *Arenga saccharifera* and defecate the large kernels. The animals can climb trees. BARTELS (1964) published a list of seeds dispersed by *Paradoxurus hermaphroditus* in Java.

I pointed out for *Durio* that large carnivores consider its oily fruit just as attractive as herbivores do (compare carnivorous birds and the fruits of the oil palm, *Elaeis).* Another oily fruit, the avocado *(Persea gratissima),* is sought after by wild cats and jaguars in America after being dropped. The seeds are too large to pass through birds.

We badly need information on the relations between diaspores and kangaroos in Australia. The absence of ruminants may give an interesting background to the form of *Acacia* fruits there, as it does to the relative scarceness of spiny plants on this continent.

G. Ants and Myrmecochory

Ants are latecomers in history, so that they do not play a fundamental role; the adaptations to them in diaspores have been built on top of, and utilize, older structures. SERNANDER (1906) and BERG (1954) proved that their temperate cases were of preglacial origin, but pointed also to the importance of ant dispersal for late speciation. On the other hand, ants evoke to an amazing degree responses and reorganizations in diaspores, often with such a strong and fast transference of function that closely related species use different organs for attracting ants.

An old objection to the concept that selective forces in the environment are creative is that ecological selection follows physiological causation. One might first ask whether the origin of a mutation is physiological causation and further what an induced physiological modification can offer to selection. The genetic steering by selection is causal to physiology.

The older literature has been covered in a review by UPHOF (1942). This shows the paucity of relations between plant diaspores and the (much older) termites, which are obviously purely destructive.

One group of ants, composed of the Mediterranean and North American harvester ants *(Messor, Atta, Tetramorium* and *Pheidole),* is also dyszoochorous. They carry the most varied materials to the nest, sort them out, store the edible parts and consume these after fermentation. The dispersal effect is small. Experiments with truly myrmecochorous seeds are necessary to study their resistance to harvester ants. Few are found in the "granaries". In rare cases (? abandoned nests) the collected seeds sprout, as reported for *Anogeissus leiocarpus* (Combretaceae) in nests of *Messor barbatus* in Senegal. This perhaps concerns as yet untreated seeds in provisional, superficial granaries.

Among really dispersing vegetarian ants, diverse genera sometimes collect unspecialized berries but mainly specialized diaspores, eating the (always white) edible part, the so-called elaiosome (oil body). This soft part got its name because

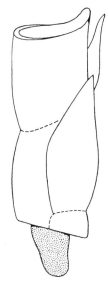

it usually contains drops of an oily substance. The rest of the diaspore, often hard and smooth and apparently difficult to destroy, is buried in nest-tunnels or in fissures. BRESINSKY (1963) demonstrated that broadly inserted elaiosomes are separated from the seed proper by special tissues, thick-walled and containing crystals. One might remark, that the distance of transport is small, but more than just transport is involved; there is often also fixation in a suitable spot, thus precision dispersal. Reduction in the number of seeds produced by the plant is a consequence.

For the root-parasites involved here, such as species of *Melampyrum, Pedicularis, Mystropetalon* and *Thesium*, burial is important. It is curious that of *Lathraea* seeds not only the ballistic ones but also those of the myrmecochorous *L. squamaria,* are larger and less numerous than they are in comparable parasites, such as *Orobanche.*

Fig. 14. Diaspore of the grass *Rottboelia exaltata* consisting of two spikelets of one internodium of the spike. Elaiosome from the medulla stippled

In simple cases, the fleshy testa itself contains edible material in a diffuse form. This *"Puschkinia-type"* embraces, among others, *Allium ursinum, Tozzia alpina, Cyclamen* and *Ornithogalum* species.

Diffuse drops of oil are present also in the seed coat of some ant-epiphytes such as *Myrmecodia,* but in some of them the connection is still more vague, as just an adhering piece of the infructescence suffices *(Procris laevigata* in Java).

In most cases, a specialized elaiosome is present. My experience in Java is that the ants in question react to it like lightning; elsewhere they may act with more hesitation. At an early date, I began to doubt that oil could be the attractive factor — this on the basis of experiments with just oil. Some volatile component must be present, probably in the oil, and is rapidly perceived. The lipoid often impregnates the tender outer cell walls. BRESINSKY determined that the attractant is an unsaturated free fatty acid, absent in nonmyrmecochorous appendages of the seed and not always connected with visible oildrops (as in *Melica* glumes). It is probably ricinolic acid with an oxy group which, in pure form also, attracts ants strongly, although its volatility is not great. It leads to the consumption of the inner protein, lipoid, starch and vitamins (B_1 and C were found by BRESINSKY; these vitamins also occur in the ant-bodies of myrmecotrophic plants).

SERNANDER's large monograph (1906) on European examples led to the distinction of several types of ant diaspores, often fruits. I shall not sum them up, as RIDLEY and UPHOF did, because ever more types are found in temperate regions as well as in the tropics. Here are some more European examples of seeds, in which a caruncle is often the basis of the elaiosome: *Helleborus* species, *Scilla bifolia, Galanthus nivalis, Chelidonium majus,* and species of *Euphorbia, Moehringia, Ulex, Viola, Primula, Sarothamnus* and *Arenaria;* in *Hepatica triloba* and species of *Anemone, Ranunculus* and *Lamium,* fruits are involved.

Most of the plants mentioned belong to the herbaceous spring flora in northern forests. In drier Mediterranean regions, *Melica* species developed new elaiosomes at the base of the spikelet; *Centaurea* species and other Compositae at the base of the achene — a process accompanied by loss of the pappus. The more tropical instances which I shall mention do not grow in dense forest; this is true even for a few of the ant-epiphytes.

The refinement of the appeal to ants (looking for mere physiological causation leaves us in the dark) is demonstrated by cases where an elaiosome is formed from very special organs. In *Primula acaulis* and some species of *Melampyrum* and *Veronica,* it arises from a swelling of the funicle; in *Pedicularis sylvatica* from a protruding endosperm-haustorium (BERG, 1954). BRESINSKY described the precise ontogeny of many elaiosomes, finding in species of *Melampyrum* and *Lathraea* that they arise from a separate part of the endosperm. In American *Nemophila* species, the elaiosome is the "cucullus" known for many Hydrophyllaceae. This is the outer layer of the testa with large, living and densely filled cells, a layer which becomes detached and is sloughed off by the placenta. BRESINSKY diagnosed changes in dispersal, also into myrmecochory, as important factors in speciation, demonstrated especially for *Anchuseae.* On the other hand VALENTINE (1966) pointed out that in *Primula* species that are not closely related, convergent myrmecochory can mask the essential differences.

What interests us here especially is that specific modifications of the plant as a whole occur, bringing the seeds into the life-sphere of the ants, perhaps also protecting the tender elaiosomes against desiccation and loss of volatile components by delay in shedding. Sometimes it is rapid disintegration of the spike (in grasses), sometimes disintegration of the fruit into irregular fragments (some Hydrophyllaceae, some species of *Trillium, Asarum europaeum* and *Datura fastuosa*). Often the modification consists of early detachment of the seeds or the wilting of non-sclerenchymatous flower (fruit) stalks, the presence of turned-down capsules *(Cyclamen, Scoliopus),* acauly, or even reorganization of the flowering axis, as described for species of the myrmecochore *Roscoea.* NORDHAGEN (1932) has described this process for the latter genus, a member of the Zingiberaceae from the Himalayas. Like SERNANDER, he and BERG (1958, 1959)

50   Ecological Dispersal Classes, Established on the Basis of the Dispersing Agents

pointed to such changes in dispersal as influencing the plant as early as the flower-ing phase, and even as necessitating adjustment for pollination (see p. 16).

When no special presentation occurs, the offering of postfloral nectar *(Melam-pyrum pratense)* or extrafloral nectar *(Turnera)* can lead the ants up to the dia-spores.

BERG (1958) has studied some American examples in this respect, adding in 1966 a review of other cases of myrmecochory known there, for example, *Uvu-laria grandiflora, Sanguinaria canadensis* and *Asarum canadense.* In the true pericarp berries of liliaceous *Trillium* species, he found a retrograde changeover to the sarcotesta as an elaiosome. The berries were suited to birds, but the sustained pulpiness of the seeds allowed them to form elaiosomes as well. I refer to this, as an analogy to the forest plants mentioned for Europe, because the change to myrmecochory in certain species was accompanied by a change in habitat; viz., from open field to forest. BERG proposed a revised taxonomy of the genus [later also of *Scoliopus* and other relatives of *Paris* and still later (1969) of *Dicentra*] on the basis of dispersal ecology. A reminder of what has been happening in the plant kingdom through the ages!

CROSBY (in HAWKES, 1966) found a reproductive disadvantage in the myr-mecochorous primrose *(Primula acaulis* or *P. veris acaulis),* which seeds in woody areas. He compared it to the non-myrmecochorous erect cowslip *(P. veris* or *P. veris officinalis* or *P. officinalis),* which grows in pastures. The precision of ant dispersal was nullified by poor establishment of the seedlings. We might remark that the latter factor is usually not considered under reproductive capa-city, and might also ask whether he investigated each species in its optimal hab-itat, also in regard to ants. Later, BERG (1966) added for California *Dendro-mecon,* the tree-poppy. This is interesting as it concerns a treelike shrub and a chaparral plant. Usually elaiosomes dry out quickly in a dry atmosphere.

In the tropics scattered cases have been found, which in this textbook will be dealt with collectively since they were often published in poorly accessible sources (cf. VAN DER PIJL, 1955 b). Berries of *Asparagus asparagoides* are com-parable to those of *Trillium.* In Malaysia, many grasses in dry regions have a disintegrating spike with a part of the medulla adhering to the units as an elaio-some (see *Rottboelia* in Fig. 14). Other examples include *Lochnera rosea, Cleome ciliata, Sterculia alexandri, Endonema retzioides, Desmodium gyroides, Cyana-strum cardifolium, Turnera ulmifolia, Datura fastuosa, Coluria* spp., *Mystro-petalon* (a parasite infecting its host underground). In some of these, parts of the placenta adhere as an elaiosome, in *Clerodendron incisum* a placental part of the pericarp, usually serving for ornithochory in the genus. *Sebastiana* in Argentina is treelike, with the combination of an explosive mechanism and the euphor-biaceous caruncle as elaiosome. Some Cyclanthaceae *(Ludovia, Cyclanthus)* may be suspected of being myrmecochorous too, and among the Papilionideae and Euphorbiaceae there are many representatives with beetle-like seeds (e. g. *Acalypha),* also in some Cactaceae *(Blassfeldia).*

A special group of myrmecochores is formed by the ant-epiphytes of the tropics. They live in the "ant gardens" on trees or provide nesting places themselves in hollows. ULE (1905) described the situation for Amazonia. Some of those Araceae and Bromeliaceae there have weakly myrmecochorous, berrylike fruits.

Fig. 15. Ant garden in Java with plant and seedlings of *Hoya lacunosa*

In Java, DOCTERS VAN LEEUWEN (1929) found true myrmecochory in those ant-epiphytes [species of *Hoya* (see Fig. 15), *Dischidia*, *Aeschynanthus*] which have oil in primarily anemochorous seed-hairs; also, there live in the nests some orchids with oil drops in the testa. The famous "living ant nests" of *Myrmecodia* have near ant dispersal (although distant ornithochory is more important) and offer postfloral nectar to their inhabitants. DOCTERS VAN LEEUWEN found that even some hollow-stemmed inhabited ferns had switched to myrmecochory by the

52   Ecological Dispersal Classes, Established on the Basis of the Dispersing Agents

formation of oil drops in the sporangium walls — unchanged through aeons, but now modified under the influence of ants.

When speaking about ants in general it is necessary, even when one leaves carnivores aside, to point out that finer specificity exists, especially in guests of ant-epiphytes.

References

Bartels, E. 1964. On Paradoxuus hermaphroditus. *Beaufortia* 10:193–201.

Berg, R. Y. 1954. Development and dispersal of the seed of Pedicularis silvatica. *Nytt Mag Bot* 2:1060.

———. 1958. Seed dispersal, morphology and phylogeny of trillium. *Skr Norske Vid-Akad Oslo (Math-nat Kl)* 1958 (1).

———. 1959. Seed dispersal, morphology and taxonomic position of Scoliopus, Liliaceae. *Skr Norske Vid-Akad Oslo (Mat-nat Kl)*, no. 4.

———. 1966. Seed dispersal of Dendromecon: Its ecologic, evolutionary and taxonomic significance. *Amer J Bot* 53:61–73.

———. 1969. Adaptation and evolution in Dicentra (Fumariaceae) with special reference to seed, fruit and dispersal mechanism. *Nytt Mag Bot* 16:49–75.

Bresinsky, A. 1963. Dau, Entwicklungsgeschichte und Inhaltsstoffe der elaiosomen. *Biblioth Botan* 126. Stuttgart.

Burtt, R. B. 1929. A record of fruits and seeds dispersed by mammals and birds from the Singida district of Tanganyika territory. *J Ecol* 17:351–55.

Docters van Leeuwen, W. M. 1929. Kurze Mitteilung über Ameisen-Epiphyten aus Java. *Ber Dtsch Bot Ges* 47:90–99.

———. 1936. *Krakatau*. Leiden: Brill.

Eggeling, W. J. 1955. The relationship between crown form and sex in Chlorophora excelsa. *Emp For Rev* 34:294.

Faegri, K., and L. van der Pijl. 1966. *Principles of pollination ecology*. Oxford: Pergamon (2d edition 1971).

Greenhall, A. M. 1965. Sapucaia nut dispersal by the greater spear-nosed bats in Trinidad. *Caribb J Sci* 5:167–71.

Guillaumet, J. L. 1967. Recherches sur la végétation et la flore de la région du Bas-Cavally (Côte d'Ivoire). *Mém* no. 20, O.R.S.T.O.M.

Gwynne, M. D., and R. V. V. Bell. 1968. Selection of vegetation components by grazing Ungulates in the Serengeti National Park. *Nature* 220:139.

Hawkes, J. G., ed. 1966. Reproductive biology and taxonomy of vascular plants. *Symposium B. S. B. I.* Oxford: Pergamon.

Huber, J. 1910. Mattas e madeiros amazonicas. *Bol Mus Goeldi* 6:91–225.

Kuhlmann, M., and E. Kühn. 1947. A flora do distrito de Ibiti. *Publçoes Inst Bot Secr Agric*. São Paulo.

Leistner, O. A. 1967. The plant ecology of the Southern Kalahari. *Bot Survey S-Africa*. Mem. no 38.

Meeuse, A. J. D. 1958. A possible case of interdependence between a mammal and a higher plant. *Arch Neerl Zoöl* 13:314–18.

Nordhagen, R. 1932. Zur Morphologie und Verbreitungsbiologie der Gattung Roscoea. *Bergens Mus Arbok 1932*. N.R. no. 4.

Osmaston, H. A. 1965. Pollen and seed dispersal in Chlorophora and Parkia. *Commonw Forestry Rev* 44:97–105.

Philipps, J. F. V. 1926. General biology of the flowers, fruits and young regeneration of the important species of the Knyska forests. *S Afr J Sci* 33:366–417.

Pijl, L. van der. 1955. Some remarks on myrmecophytes. *Phytomorphology* 5:190–200.

———. 1957. The dispersal of plants by bats. *Acta bot Neerl* 6:291–315.

Ridley, H. N. 1930. *The dispersal of plants throughout the world*. Ashford: Reeve.

Sernander, R. 1906. *Entwurf einer Monographie der europäischen Myrmekochoren*. Uppsala: Sv. Vet. Ak. Handl.

Simmonds, N. W. 1959. Experiments on the germination of banana seeds. *Trop Agric* 36:259.

Stopp, K. 1958. Die verbreitungshemmenden Einrichtungen in der Südafrikanischen Flora. *Botan Studien* 8. Jena.

Troup, R. S. 1921. *The sylviculture of Indian trees*. Oxford.

Ulbrich, E. 1928. *Biologie der Früchte und Samen (Karpobiologie)*. Berlin: Springer.

Ule, E. 1905. Wechselbeziehungen zwischen Ameisen und Pflanzen *Flora*. 94:491–97.

Uphof, J. C. Th. 1942. Ecological relations of plants with ants and termites. *Bot Rev* 8:563–98.

Valentine, D. A. 1966. The experimental taxonomy of some Primula species. *Trans Proc B Soc Edinburgh* 40.

Ecology (1975) **56**: pp. 285–301

ECOLOGY, FLOWERING PHENOLOGY, AND
HUMMINGBIRD POLLINATION OF SOME COSTA RICAN
HELICONIA SPECIES[1]

F. Gary Stiles[2]

*Departamento de Biología, Universidad de Costa Rica, Ciudad Universitaria
"Rodrigo Facio", Costa Rica*

Abstract. Nine hummingbird-pollinated species of *Heliconia* occur together at Finca La Selva, in the wet Caribbean lowlands of Costa Rica. In forest habitats, *Heliconia* clumps (clones) are typically small; in more open areas, many clumps attain large size. This probably reflects differences in light intensity and degree of vegetative competition in these habitats.

Nine species of hummingbirds regularly visit *Heliconia* flowers at La Selva. The four hermits are nonterritorial, traplining foragers with long, curved bills. Non-hermits frequently hold territories at *Heliconia* clumps, and have short, straight bills. Pollination by hermits tends to produce more cross-pollination; territorial hummingbirds increase self-pollination. Different *Heliconia* species appear to be specialized for pollination by either hermits or non-hermits, largely through components of the caloric phenotype: amount and timing of nectar production, rate of inflorescence and flower production, and morphological parameters that affect the energetic efficiency of nectar-harvesting hummingbirds. Habitat may influence pollination systems through its effects on clump size and thus on the number of flowers a clump can have at any one time. Ultimately, specialization for hermits or non-hermits may depend on the degree of self-compatibility of the different *Heliconia* species.

Hermit-pollinated *Heliconia* mostly show sequential and nonoverlapping flowering peaks, probably resulting from competition for pollinators and/or selection against hybridization. Two hermit-pollinated species bloom simultaneously, thereby inducing the birds to utilize an otherwise little-used microhabitat. *Heliconia* species pollinated by non-hermits bloom in the early to middle rainy season, and are mostly separated by habitat.

Isolating mechanisms among sympatric *Heliconia* species involve both spatial and temporal patterns of partitioning available pollinators. Floral parameters include mechanical (different site of pollen deposition on the bird) and ethological (caloric and visual factors affecting flower choice) mechanisms. Selection for pollinator specificity may result in convergence of blooming peaks, provided that other isolating mechanisms are present. Human activity has broken down some habitat barriers by producing large areas of second growth.

Key words: Community interactions; competition; Heliconia; *hummingbirds*; *phenology*; *pollination*; *resource partitioning*; *tropical rainforest*; *tropical seasonality*.

INTRODUCTION

When sympatric plant species flower simultaneously, they may have to compete for pollinators. Levin and Anderson (1970) argued that under such circumstances, if the plants differ only in relative abundance, there will be strong selection against the rarer species, leading to its elimination from the community or to its divergence from the more abundant species in some aspect of floral phenology. In fact, it is probably very unusual to find in nature simultaneously flowering species that are identical in floral phenology; an array of species differing in various parameters seems more likely. If these species are also closely related taxonomically, not only competition for pollinators but also means of reducing hybridization and promoting pollinator specificity must be considered. This paper deals with an array of sympatric plant species in the genus

Heliconia L. (Musaceae) that share a common group of pollinators, the hummingbirds. In particular, I shall focus on what Heinrich and Raven (1972) have called the "caloric phenotype" of the plants: the amount and concentration of nectar secreted, the morphological parameters that affect harvesting of this nectar by the birds, and the ecological factors influencing the rate and timing of flowering.

The "platanillos" or "wild plantains" of the genus *Heliconia* are moderate-to-large-sized herbs (Table 1) with banana-like leaves. They propagate vegetatively by rhizomes, and some species readily form large clones or "clumps." In its 2nd yr or later, each individual plant in a clump produces an inflorescence composed of several to many showy bracts, each of which encloses several flowers. This inflorescence opens, bract by bract, over a period of days or weeks; flowering usually starts in the older bracts before the inflorescence has fully opened. In all species examined so far, each flower lasts only 1 day. The flowers are tubular, of varying length and curvature (Fig. 1). Further discussion of the morphology of

---

[1] Manuscript received 23 January 1973; accepted 1 July 1974.

[2] Address reprint requests to: 76B Hardy Lane, Whispering Pines, North Carolina 28389 USA.

286   F. GARY STILES   Ecology, Vol. 56, No. 2

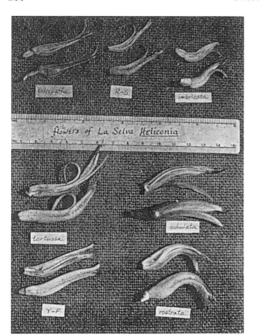

Fig. 1. Flowers of seven species of La Selva *Heliconia*. Name changes in this paper are as follows: "*rostrata*" = *pogonantha*, "*subulata*" = H-3, "Y-F" = H-16, "R-S" = H-17, "*tortuosa*" = H-18.

Heliconia inflorescences and flowers is given by Smith (1966).

The genus *Heliconia* is represented in Costa Rica by some 35 species, distributed mainly in the humid life zones of lower and middle altitudes (Stiles, *unpubl. data*). Unfortunately, the taxonomy and nomenclature of *Heliconia* are currently in a chaotic state, and I am unable to assign definite names to several of the taxa discussed here. Rather than complicate matters further, I shall refer to these species by taxon numbers, as used in a revision of the genus in Costa Rica currently in progress

(Daniels and Stiles, *unpubl. data*). (The species called "*acuminata*" by Linhart (1973) is referred to here as H-3; Linhart's "*tortuosa*" is here called H-18. The proper name for the species called "*rostrata*" by Wolf et al. (1972) is *pogonantha*).

STUDY AREA

This study was done at Finca La Selva, in the Sarapiquí lowlands of northeastern Costa Rica. The topography, climate, and flora of La Selva have been described by Holdridge et al. (1971), and the avifauna has been studied by Slud (1960). I completed most of my research between February 1971 and October 1972, but have also made observations during August and September 1968, July and August 1969, and March, April, and July 1970. Monthly temperature and rainfall for the months of this study, as well as longterm averages (1963–71) are given in Fig. 2.

The major part of La Selva is covered by virgin forest. However, most *Heliconia* species cannot tolerate deep shade, and are found only at breaks in the forest canopy. The smallest and most ephemeral light gaps result from tree falls, are seldom over 20–30 m in diameter, and are usually closed (at least to *Heliconia*) within a very few years by rapid growth of woody plants. Somewhat larger and more permanent light gaps may occur along forest streams, and at numerous small, open swamps that form in poorly drained pockets where there is standing water all year. The largest and most permanent natural light gaps in tropical forest occur along the larger streams and rivers, where periodic inundations and unstable substrates may keep extensive areas free of trees.

Manmade breaks in the forest canopy are frequently larger and more permanent than natural ones and can greatly increase the available second-growth and forest-edge habitat, thereby altering drastically the distribution and abundance of some *Heliconia*. At La Selva fairly extensive tracts of second growth

TABLE 1. Gross morphology and coloration of plants and inflorescences of La Selva *Heliconia*

Species	Plant height (m)	Aspect of inflorescence	Length of inflorescence (rachis) in cm	Color of branch bracts	Color of flowers
H. wagneriana	2½–4	erect	40–60	red, bordered with white and green	green
H. imbricata	3–6	erect	30–60	red	pale green
H. latispatha	2–5	erect	35–60	orange or red and yellow	green or yellow and green
H. mariae	6–10	pendant	45–85	red	pink
H. pogonantha	4–8	pendant	60–150	red and yellow	yellow
H-17	1½–4	erect	25–60	red, with yellow rachis	yellow
H-3	2–5	erect	6–12	red	yellow with red-orange base
H-18	½–2	erect	20–30	red	yellow
H-16	1–2½	erect	7–12	yellow	pale yellow

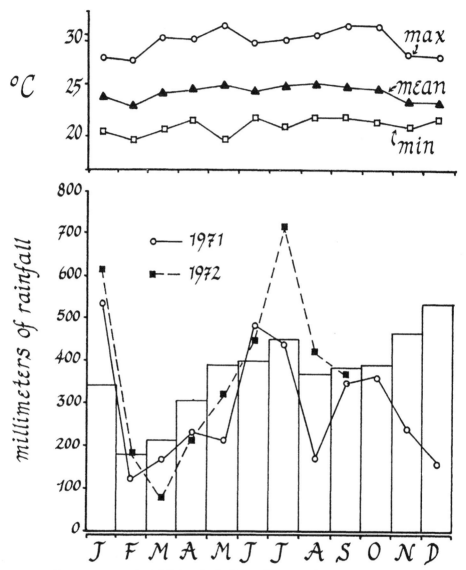

Fig. 2. Monthly temperature and rainfall data for La Selva. Upper graph: mean daily temperatures, October 1969–August 1971. Lower graph: mean monthly rainfall for 1963–71 (bar graphs), and monthly rainfall during the period of this study.

of various ages occur in several areas. Since the time of Slud's (1960) study, the only major changes in the habitat at La Selva have probably been the abandonment of cacao and banana plantations and the invasion of these by second-growth plants, and the continued growth of areas that were previously in pasture or second growth. There has also been sufficient deforestation in the surrounding areas that La Selva is now a peninsula of forest projecting into

a sea of pastures and cultivated land. A large, continuous expanse of forest still exists to the south, towards the Cordillera Central.

METHODS AND MATERIALS

I assessed distribution and relative abundance of *Heliconia* in different habitats at La Selva by counting clumps of the various species along 10 census routes during March 1972. Clumps were classified

288   F. GARY STILES   Ecology, Vol. 56, No. 2

TABLE 2.   Abundance of *Heliconia* clumps and plants along census routes at La Selva, March 1972

Census route	1	2	3	4	5	6	7	8	9	10
Approximate length (m)	2250	500	750	500	600	800	850	1850	1900	600
Habitat	forest	small forest stream	larger forest stream	open forest swamp	old second growth	old second growth	over grown cacao	shaded river-bank	open river-bank	young second growth
Species										
H. wagneriana										
No. clumps	0	0	0	0	23	1	12	11	15	24
No. plants	0	0	0	0	168	3	117	114	312	486
Plants/100 m	0	0	0	0	28.0	0.4	13.8	6.2	16.4	81.1
H. imbricata										
No. clumps	0	0	2	7	92	29	70	25	12	6
No. plants	0	0	6	39	1353	453	720	570	216	132
Plants/100 m	0	0	0.8	7.8	225.8	56.7	84.8	30.8	11.4	22.0
H. latispatha										
No. clumps	0	0	0	0	19	4	17	28	25	22
No. plants	0	0	0	0	211	21	207	434	694	502
Plants/100 m	0	0	0	0	35.2	2.6	24.4	23.5	36.5	88.7
H. mariae										
No. clumps	0	0	0	0	2	0	0	0	0	0
No. plants	0	0	0	0	60	0	0	0	0	0
Plants/100 m	0	0	0	0	10.0	0	0	0	0	0
H. pogonantha										
No. clumps	5	3	24	14	0	103	9	3	0	6
No. plants	24	18	207	96	0	1375	45	18	0	63
Plants/100 m	1.1	3.6	27.6	19.2	0	197.0	5.3	1.0	0	10.5
H-17										
No. clumps	12	45	13	7	0	0	0	0	0	0
No. plants	90	351	93	29	0	0	0	0	0	0
Plants/100 m	4.0	70.2	12.4	5.8	0	0	0	0	0	0
H-3										
No. clumps	5	12	40	66	5	5	6	11	4	0
No. plants	33	54	330	822	51	60	63	180	48	0
Plants/100 m	1.5	10.8	44.0	164.4	8.5	7.5	7.4	9.7	2.5	0
H-18										
No. clumps	41	29	15	4	2	14	0	0	0	0
No. plants	321	150	90	12	6	149	0	0	0	0
Plants/100 m	14.3	30.0	12.1	2.4	1.0	18.6	0	0	0	0
H-16										
No. clumps	20	2	1	0	0	2	0	0	0	0
No. plants	69	6	3	0	0	6	0	0	0	0
Plants/100 m	3.1	1.2	0.4	0	0	0.8	0	0	0	0
Total plants/100 m	24.0	115.8	97.3	199.6	308.5	283.6	135.7	71.2	66.8	202.3
Total no. of species	5	5	6	5	6	7	5	5	4	4

as small (1–5 plants), medium (6–20), large (20–50), or very large (50 plus). The census routes and habitats are listed in Table 2, in order of increasing openness. The routes were chosen because they provide a fairly representative selection of the habitats available for *Heliconia* and associated hummingbirds in the Sarapiquí region. Routes 8 and 9 were censused from a boat; all others were covered on foot.

The numbers of bracts per mature inflorescences and number of flowers produced per bract, were counted for all *Heliconia* species at La Selva. For

the commoner species I made daily checks of several inflorescences to determine the rate and sequence of flower opening. For each species, total corolla length and effective corolla length (the approximate minimum distance between the entrance to the corolla tube and nectar chamber) were measured.

For a quantitative evaluation of blooming seasonality, I counted the number of inflorescences and fresh flowers on 10 census clumps of each *Heliconia* at approximately monthly intervals. (For the very uncommon *H. mariae* only two census clumps were used.) I classified the age and flowering status of

TABLE 3. Bill morphology, body weights, and preferred habitats of hummingbirds that regularly visit *Heliconia* flowers at La Selva

Hummingbird species	Body weight (g)[a]	Bill length (mm)[a, b]	Bill curvature	Preferred habitat
Hermits				
Eutoxeres aquila	10.5	36.7[c]	very strongly decurved	forest, forest edge, old second growth
Phaethornis superciliosus	6.0	40.8	moderately decurved	forest, forest edge, old second growth
Threnetes ruckeri	5.8	33.2	slightly decurved	forest, forest edge, old second growth
Glaucis hirsuta	5.4	33.0	,,	young or old second growth, forest edge
Non-hermits				
Chalybura urochrysia	6.6	26.4	straight	forest, forest edge, old second growth
Thalurania furcata	4.3	23.5	,,	forest, forest edge, old second growth
Amazilia tzacatl	5.3	24.8	,,	young or old second growth
Amazilia amabilis	4.0	22.1	,,	old second growth, forest edge
Florisuga mellivora	7.0	23.4	,,	forest, forest edge, second growth

[a] Mean, $N = 10$; for sexually dimorphic species, 5 of each sex used.
[b] Length of total culmen (Stiles 1973).
[c] Measured along the arc of the culmen.

each inflorescence by a 7-stage system. The stages ranged from 0: inflorescence just appearing, no flowers, through 6: inflorescence old, dying or dead. In addition, a few inflorescences of most species were marked as they appeared, and were checked at shorter intervals to determine more precisely the duration of each age and flowering stage.

Since nectar is the resource in *Heliconia* flowers that is exploited by hummingbirds, nectar production was examined in some detail. Nectar was collected with fine calibrated capillary tubes (25, 50, or 100-μl Drummond "Microcaps"). In most *Heliconia*, the long and/or curved corolla tube prevented direct access to the nectar chamber by the capillary tube, and the flowers had to be picked and dissected to extract nectar. Flowers were bagged before they opened, either at dawn or on the preceding evening. Groups of 10 or more flowers were then sampled at regular intervals through the day; differences in mean nectar content could be used to estimate nectar production during each sample period.

I obtained nectar concentrations by measuring the refractive indices of the nectars with a temperature-compensated hand refractometer (National Instrument Co., Baltimore). Nectar of most flowers, including those of *Heliconia*, is essentially an aqueous solution of sucrose, fructose, and glucose in varying proportions (Percival 1961). These three sugars contain about an equal number of calories per gram. The 12-carbon sugar sucrose has a refractive index and a molecular weight twice those of the 6-carbon sugars glucose and fructose. Thus 1 mol of the former contains the same number of carbon atoms, yields about the same number of calories, and has the same refractive index as 2 mol of glucose or fructose. One can therefore express nectar concentrations in terms of an equivalent sucrose concentration, and calories per mol of nectar can be easily

calculated. (1 μl of 1.0 molar sucrose = 1.35 cal). Given such details of flowering phenology as amount of nectar per flower, number of flowers per inflorescence or per clump, one can quickly calculate calories per flower, and can view spatial or seasonal blooming patterns on a caloric basis.

Data on hummingbird utilization of *Heliconia* were gathered on three censuses, commencing at 0600, 1000, and 1400 h during 1 day in April, August, and October 1971 and January 1972, for each of three routes. This combination of census routes and times of year allowed me to observe all the La Selva *Heliconia* in good bloom. In addition, I conducted two or three all-morning watches (usually 0500–1100 or 1130 h) at clumps of each species of *Heliconia*. During these observations I recorded each instance of foraging or territoriality at *Heliconia*, and the species of hummingbird involved. A hummingbird was considered to be territorial if it remained in the immediate vicinity of a clump (or several adjacent clumps) of *Heliconia* for at least 1 h and if during this time it fed at the clump and attempted to prevent other hummingbirds from doing so by threatening or attacking them (Wolf 1969, Stiles and Wolf 1970). Observations of hummingbirds feeding at *Heliconia* flowers were made through 10-power binoculars, and sites of pollen deposition on the bird were noted. Hummingbirds were also captured by mist-netting in or near feeding areas and examined for presence of *Heliconia* pollen on bills or plumage. Weights (to the nearest 0.1 g) and bill measurements (total culmen, to nearest 0.5 mm) were also taken on mist-netted birds (Table 3).

RESULTS

Ecology of the plants

Eight species of *Heliconia* occur commonly at La Selva. A ninth species, *H. mariae*, is known

290   F. GARY STILES   Ecology, Vol. 56, No. 2

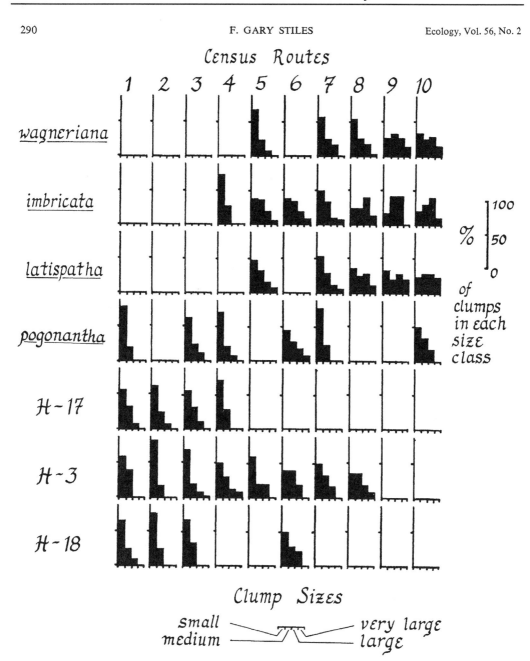

FIG. 3. Percentage distribution of *Heliconia* clumps in four size categories along census routes at La Selva. size classes are: small, 1–5 plants; medium, 6–20 plants; large, 20–50 plants; very large, over 50 plants. Sma clumps are preponderate in forested habitats, and larger clumps in more open habitats. Census routes arrangec order of increasingly open habitats.

FIG. 4. Seasonality of inflorescence and flower production of La Selva *Heliconia* species. Flower counts expre as % of maximum number of flowers recorded on 10 census clumps of each species (except only 2 clump: *mariae*) during the given blooming season (or during the entire study period for continuously blooming species). florescence counts are numbers of young (sta. 0–1), profusely flowering (sta. 3), and mostly fruiting (sta. 5) florescences recorded on censuses.

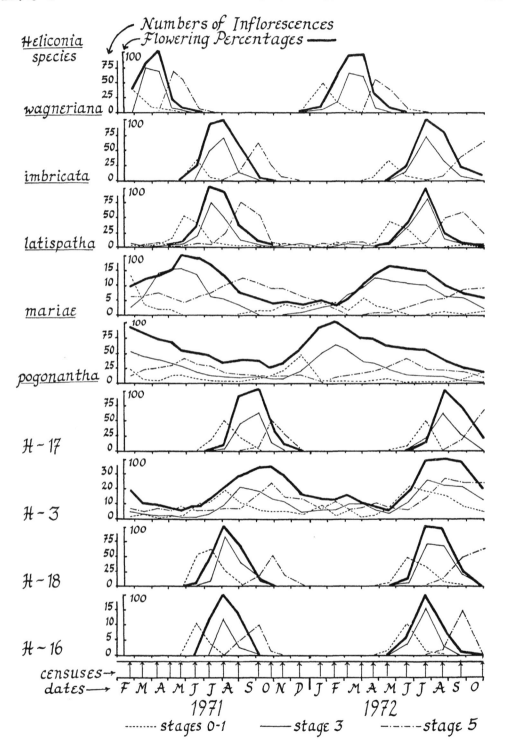

only from two large clumps on the Point. The morphological characteristics of the plants and inflorescences of these species are summarized in Table 1. As a group, *Heliconia* are least abundant in virgin forest and most abundant in second growth. Along forest streams and especially open swamps, *Heliconia* may be several times more abundant than inside the forest itself (Table 2). In these essentially natural habitats, the overall abundance of *Heliconia* appears to parallel relative size and permanence of the associated light gaps in the forest canopy. The highest densities of *Heliconia* occur in second growth. Old second growth (the East Boundary and the Point) supports the highest number of species, young open second growth (as at Puerto Viejo and along the Río Sarapiquí) the fewest.

Three groups of *Heliconia* species can be roughly distinguished at La Selva: highly shade-tolerant species found regularly within virgin forest; species requiring high light intensities and occurring only in the most open habitats; and species tolerating a wide range of light intensities and found in a variety of habitats. Light intensity is not the only environmental gradient important in *Heliconia* distribution: temperature, moisture, slope, and soil type are doubtless important, at least to some species (Sheffy, *unpubl. data*). However, none of these factors appears able to produce the relatively clearcut breakdown of species given by light intensity, at least among La Selva *Heliconia*.

The forest-based *Heliconia* at La Selva are H-16, H-17, and H-18. Of these, only H-18 is found to any extent in older second growth, where a canopy of small trees is fairly well developed. It is possible that at least H-18 could do well in full sunlight, but cannot stand the vegetative competition of other second-growth plants, especially the vines and shrubs of young second growth. Within the forest, H-17 and H-18 are usually found at small-to-moderate-sized light gaps. H-16 is a relatively uncommon species found scattered through the forest, often at no discernible light gap. As a group, forest *Heliconia* tend to occur in small clumps (Fig. 3), reflecting the relatively small, short-lived light gaps of these habitats: these *Heliconia* may not have enough time to attain large clump size before their light gap is closed.

True inhabitants of young, very open second growth are *H. wagneriana*, *H. latispatha*, and, perhaps to a lesser extent, *H. imbricata*. Only the last-named occurs in essentially forested country, and then only at the largest and most persistent of light gaps. The *Heliconia* of this group were, before widespread deforestation, probably restricted to open riverbanks or (*imbricata*) sunny forest streams and swamps. All of these species reproduce vegetatively very rapidly and within a short time will form large

clumps. Indeed large clumps are if anything more common than small ones in young second growth (Fig. 4) probably because many of the small clumps are overwhelmed by vines and other second-growth plants; only large clumps can long persist under such conditions.

Heliconia pogonantha and H-3 appear to tolerate a wide range of light conditions and occur in a diverse array of habitats: moderate to fairly deep shade along forest streams, at moderate-sized light gaps in forest (as at the small swamps in poorly drained glens), second growth of various ages, and open swamps. *Heliconia mariae* probably belongs in this group also, since in other areas I have found it common in similarly diverse habitats.

Both within and between species clump size tends to be larger in more open habitats. In forest habitats, no more than 20% of the clumps of any species are large or very large, whereas in young open second growth 40% to 50% of the clumps of most species are large to very large (Fig. 3).

Flowering phenology

All *Heliconia* species at La Selva have a pronounced seasonal peak of flowering and production of inflorescences (Fig. 4). Species that bloom year-round are *pogonantha*, with a peak in the early dry season (cf. Fig. 2); *mariae*, with a peak in the late dry or early wet season; and H-3, with its peak in the middle to late rainy season. Although a few *latispatha* inflorescences could be found in virtually every month at La Selva, the species as a whole shows a sharply defined peak in the early rainy season. Species having short, entirely discrete blooming seasons are *wagneriana* in the dry season and *imbricata*, H-16, H-17, and H-18 in the rainy season. For the *Heliconia* community generally, the rainy season is the peak of flowering, when up to 8 species are blooming compared to at most 4 (or 5 including *latispatha*) in the dry season. The time lags between high counts of preflowering (stages 0–1), profusely flowering (stage 3), and mostly fruiting (stage 5) inflorescences appear to be fairly constant within species (Fig. 4). This permits an estimate of the average lifetime of an individual inflorescence of each species. Such estimates range from 2 to 3 months in H-3 and H-17 to 6 months or more in *pogonantha* and *mariae* (Table 4).

For most *Heliconia* a high rate of flower production (short interval between flowers per bract), a small number of fertile bracts per inflorescence, and a short inflorescence life seem to go together (Table 4) and to be correlated with a short, discrete blooming season (Fig. 4). A given inflorescence of most species produces some 100 to 300 flowers in a lifetime of 2–4 mo. Highest rates of flower production

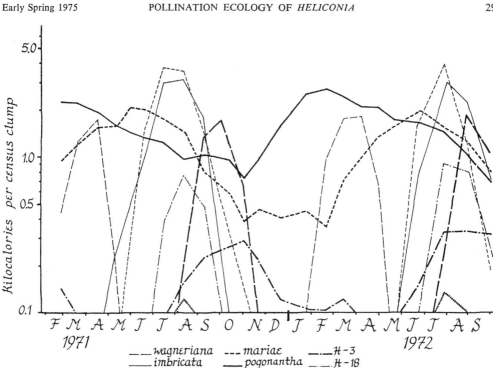

Fig. 5. Mean number of kcal available in flower nectar per census clump on monthly flower counts, as derived from the caloric equivalents per flower given in Table 5.

occur in *latispatha*, H-17, and *imbricata*. The larger number of bracts of *imbricata*, and the greater number of flowers per bract in *latispatha* and H-17, result in a fairly similar daily production of flowers per stage 3 inflorescence. Lower daily flower production per inflorescence is seen in H-3, H-16, and H-18 because of their smaller number of fertile bracts per inflorescence.

Heliconia mariae and *pogonantha* show a different pattern in several respects. These species combine a large number of bracts with low flowering rates and long inflorescence life. Their inflorescences are thus considerably more massive than those of other species; it seems likely that the pendant habit evolved in connection with the problem of supporting a large, heavy inflorescence. In these species, in-

TABLE 4.   Inflorescence and flower production of La Selva *Heliconia*

Species	% of plants with inflorescences		No. fertile bracts per inflorescence[a]	No. flowers per fertile bract	Total no. flowers per inflorescence	No. days between flowers in a given bract[b]	Length of blooming period of inflorescence (mo)	No. flowers per stage 3 inflorescence[a]
	1971	1972						
H. wagneriana	59.8	58.4	13.2 (8–17)	ca. 20	ca. 250	2 (2–5)	ca. 3	3.3 (1–6)
H. imbricata	51.5	52.6	22.8 (18–32)	ca. 10	ca. 225	2 (1–5)	ca. 4	4.2 (2–8)
H. latispatha	48.8	53.7	14.3 (12–17)	ca. 20	ca. 275	2 (1–4)	3–4	5.0 (2–9)
H. mariae	43.4	38.5	59.5 (44–72)	ca. 15	ca. 900	6 (4–9)	6–7	4.3 (2–8)
H. pogonantha	43.2	44.7	34.6 (16–53)	ca. 20	ca. 750	5 (3–8)	5–7	3.3 (1–7)
H-17	36.9	49.8	12.2 (6–15)	15–20	ca. 200	2 (1–4)	ca. 3	1971: 1.7 (0–7)
								1972: 4.1 (1–8)
H-3	24.6	27.8	6.0 (4–9)	10–20	ca. 80	3 (2–5)	2–3	1.0 (0–3)
H-18	35.1	37.1	8.8 (7–10)	ca. 15	ca. 135	3 (2–6)	ca. 3	1.4 (0–3)
H-16	34.3	36.8	5.7 (3–7)	ca. 20	ca. 110	3 (2–5)	ca. 3	1.3 (0–3)

[a] Mean and range, $N = 10$.
[b] Mode and approximate range for a bract in the middle of the inflorescence.

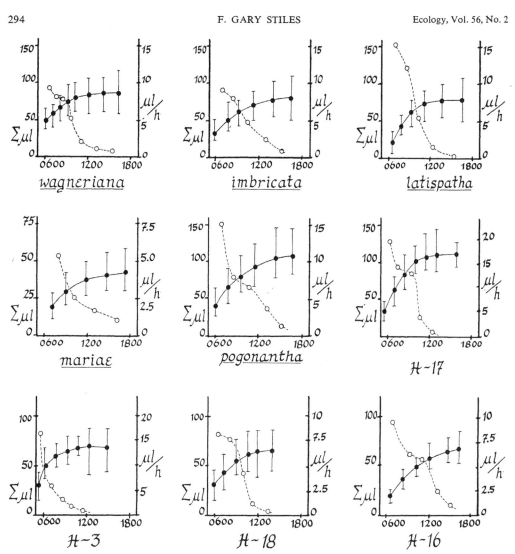

FIG. 6.   Daily pattern of nectar secretion of flowers of La Selva *Heliconia*. $\Sigma\mu l$ = solid circles = total microliters of nectar in bagged flowers sampled at different times of day (mean and range); $\mu l/h$ = open circles = average hourly rate of nectar production between samples.

florescences are mostly produced in a relatively short time; the long life of the inflorescence is largely responsible for the long blooming season. H-3, the other species that blooms year-round, relies on relatively continuous production of small, short-lived inflorescences.

The "percentage of plants with inflorescences" (Table 4) is that proportion of plants present at the start of a blooming season (or period of peak bloom for those species flowering year-round) which actually produced inflorescences during that season (or peak of blooming). Since the individual *Heliconia* plants usually flower in their 2nd yr, a given clump will, during any one season, contain a high proportion of nonblooming plants. Unfortunately, I did not record age of plants during the censuses but only counted numbers of plants. The highest percentages of plants with inflorescences occurs in those species of open areas with short blooming seasons: *wagneriana*, *imbricata*, and *latispatha*. Lower percentages are observed in some forest species with short blooming seasons. Of those species blooming year-round, *pogonantha* and *mariae* have intermediate inflorescence-to-plant percentages, while that of H-3 is much lower.

Several species showed differences in the timing of

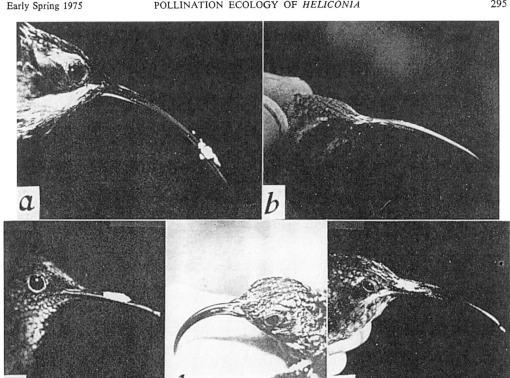

FIG. 7. Deposition sites of pollen of different *Heliconia* species on certain hummingbirds: (a) *H. imbricata* pollen on *Phaethornis superciliosus*, (b) H-18 (forehead, base of maxilla) and H-17 (side of maxilla) pollen on *Phaethornis superciliosus*, (c) *H. imbricata* pollen on *Thalurania furcata*, (d) *H. pogonantha* pollen on *Eutoxeres aquila*, (e) *H. pogonantha* pollen on *Glaucis hirsuta*.

flower and inflorescence production between two successive blooming seasons (Fig. 4). In particular, several species that reach their peak of flowering in the rainy season did so earlier in 1972 than in 1971; this was most pronounced in species that bloomed later in the season in 1971. Thus, *H. imbricata*, H-16, and H-18 reached peak bloom in late July 1972, compared to middle to late August 1971; H-17 peaked in August 1972 and October 1971; and H-3 in August 1972 and late October 1971. *Heliconia mariae* showed less synchrony in production of inflorescences, and less flowering in 1972 than in 1971, but as only two clumps are involved the data are not entirely equatable with data for other species. *Heliconia wagneriana* and *latispatha* attained peak bloom at about the same time in both years, and for *pogonantha* insufficient data are available to compare two successive flowering peaks.

The only species to show pronounced year-to-year variations in other aspects of flowering phenology was H-17. In 1971 relatively few plants produced inflorescences, and many inflorescences produced few or no flowers (Table 4). However, in 1972 this species flowered much more normally for the genus.

Nectar production

Amount, concentration, and caloric content of the nectars of La Selva *Heliconia* flowers are presented in Table 5. This information makes it possible to express the blooming season data (Fig. 4) in caloric terms (Fig. 5). The *Heliconia* species making the largest amounts of calories per clump available to hummingbirds over the longest period are *mariae* and *pogonantha*, although the relative caloric production of *mariae* is probably somewhat overestimated since both of the available clumps are large (Table 2). The caloric outputs of these species are approached or exceeded seasonally by those of *wagneriana*, H-17, and especially *imbricata* and *latispatha*. H-3, H-16, and H-18 nectars make available considerably fewer calories, even at their respective peaks of bloom.

To better understand these data from the birds' point of view, consider that the daily energy require-

TABLE 5. Caloric parameters of the nectars of La Selva *Heliconia* flowers

Species	Approx. daily nectar secretion per flower (μl)	Nectar concentration (M sucrose)[a]	Calories per flower per day (1M sucrose = 1.35 kcal/ml)
H. wagneriana	90	0.95 (0.92–1.00)	0.116
H. imbricata	85	0.65 (0.57–0.73)	0.077
H. latispatha	75	0.90 (0.86–0.93)	0.091
H. mariae	45	0.79 (0.74–0.83)	0.048
H-2	115	0.95 (0.85–1.06)	0.141
H-17	110	0.75 (0.65–0.82)	0.111
H-3	70	0.75 (0.63–0.81)	0.071
H-18	65	1.02 (0.98–1.06)	0.090
H-16	70	0.80 (0.66–0.91)	0.076

[a] Mean and range; N between 5 and 8.

ments of 4- to 6-g hummingbirds are on the order of 6–12 kcal (cf. Stiles 1971, Wolf and Hainsworth 1971). Large clumps of most La Selva *Heliconia* may contain 3 or 4 times more calories than the mean values for 10 census clumps of various sizes given in Fig. 5. Therefore, most or all of a hummingbird's daily energy needs could be supplied by a single clump of *H. wagneriana, imbricata, latispatha, pogonantha,* and H-17, but not H-3, H-16, or H-18.

The daily pattern of nectar production of all La Selva *Heliconia* is similar: very high nectar production in the early morning (with a considerable amount already available when the flowers open at dawn), then a rapid decline to low levels by midday (Fig. 6). The timing of the decline varies somewhat between species, and some show a pronounced "shoulder" of fairly high nectar production around

midmorning (e.g., *wagneriana,* H-16, H-17). There is considerable variation in amount of nectar available at any given time of day. Nectar production can be affected by many factors, including insolation and other microclimatic factors, and the nutritional status of the plants themselves (Huber 1956, Shuel 1966).

Floral morphology and hummingbird visitation

Nine species of hummingbirds are frequent visitors to, and pollinators of, at least one species of *Heliconia* at La Selva. These hummingbirds fall into two groups: the hermits, with long curved bills, and non-hermits, with shorter straight bills (Table 3, Fig. 7). Flowers of La Selva *Heliconia* also divide into two groups, corresponding to the difference in bill morphology between hermits and non-hermits: long and/or curved corollas (effective corolla length 33 mm or more), and short and/or straight corollas (effective length 32 mm or less) (Table 6). The correspondence is even closer if one bears in mind that the tongue can be extended up to 10 mm beyond the tip of the bill in even the smaller species considered here. Thus, on morphological grounds, La Selva *Heliconia* can be divided into "hermit flowers" and "nonhermit flowers."

This division is supported by the observed patterns of hummingbird foraging (Table 7). All five of the species with long, curved corollas (*wagneriana, pogonantha,* H-3, H-16, H-18) are visited to a significantly greater extent by hermits. Three of the four species with short and/or straight corollas (*imbricata, latispatha,* H-17) show a significant majority of visitation by non-hermits. Both bird groups foraged at *mariae,* but data from only two

TABLE 6. Morphology and pollen deposition of flowers of La Selva *Heliconia*

Species	Total corolla length (mm)	Effective corolla length (mm)	Corolla curvature	Site of pollen deposition on Hermits	Site of pollen deposition on Non-hermits
H. wagneriana	65 (59–68)[a]	48 (41–52)[a]	slight to moderate	forehead, crown	not visited
H. imbricata	27 (25–28)	21 (19–23)	slight to moderate	distal ½ to ¼ of maxilla	distal ½ of maxilla
H. latispatha	45 (43–48)	32 (29–34)	nearly straight	½ to ⅔ of way up bill from tip	basal ½ of mandible, chin
H. mariae	28 (25–31)	22 (20–25)	very slight	middle ½ of maxilla	basal ½ of mandible
H. pogonantha	41 (37–44)	33 (30–35)	fairly strong	basal ½ of maxilla, forehead	forehead, crown
H-17	38 (35–40)	28 (25–31)	straight with kink at base	distal ½ to ⅔ of bill	basal ½ of mandible, chin
H-3	53 (50–56)	41 (38–44)	slight	crown, forehead, base of maxilla	not visited
H-18	52 (40–61)	44 (38–50)	slight to moderate	crown, forehead, base of maxilla	not visited
H-16	48 (45–50)	40 (36–45)	slight	chin, base of bill	not visited

[a] Mean and range, $N = 10$.

TABLE 7. Records of hummingbird foraging and territoriality at different *Heliconia* species[a]

| | Hummingbird species (as listed in Table 3) | | | | | | | | | Foraging | | |
| | Hermits | | | | Non-hermits | | | | | Total: Hermits | Total: Non-hermits | $\chi^{2\,b}$ |
Species	E. a.	P. s.	T. r.	G. h.	C. u.	T. f.	A. t.	A. a.	F. m.			
H. wagneriana	0,0	36,2*	3,0	10,1*	0,0	0,0	2,0	0,0	0,0	49	2	43.3**
H. imbricata	0,0	22,0	11,0	12,0	59,41	83,76	40,36	25,2*	27,4	45	235	128.8**
H. latispatha	0,0	7,0	1,0	10,0	20,3	35,13	67,42	16,1	7,1	18	145	98.9**
H. mariae	0,0	2,0	5,0	6,1*	0,0	8,3	9,3	1,0	0,0	13	18	0.84
H. pogonantha	20,3*	73,3*	16,0	70,1*	61,34	24,7	12,2	5,0	3,0	179	105	19.3**
H-17	0,0	14,0	3,0	1,0	23,6	43,16	0,0	0,0	0,0	18	68	29.1**
H-3	0,0	27,0	1,0	14,0	2,0	1,0	1,0	0,0	0,0	42	4	31.4**
H-18	0,0	50,4*	3,0	10,0	1,0	0,0	1,0	0,0	0,0	63	2	57.4**
H-16	0,0	21,1*	2,0	0,0	0,0	0,0	0,0	0,0	0,0	23	0	23.0**

[a] First figure of each pair = foraging records; second figure = records of territoriality. Territoriality figures with an asterisk denotes instances of short-term aggressiveness, rather than true territoriality (see text).
[b] Null hypothesis states equal visitation by hermits and non-hermits. All values with double asterisk are highly significant ($P < .01$).

isolated clumps may not be properly representative for the species. Non-hermits also hold territories much more frequently at *Heliconia* with short, straight corollas (Table 7). Hermits seldom hold flower-centered territories, and even then these territories are inconsistently defended and are generally at flowers not used by non-hermits. The major exception appears to be at *pogonantha*, where *Chalybura* feeds and holds territories fairly regularly.

In addition to the length and curvature of a flower, its orientation in the bract is important in determining the position a hummingbird must take to feed. This in turn will determine where on the bird pollen from a given *Heliconia* species will be deposited (Table 6, Fig. 7). The flowers in Fig. 1 are shown in their normal orientations within their respective bracts. It is evident that hummingbirds with long, slightly to moderately downcurved bills should have no trouble reaching the nectar in flowers of *pogonantha*, H-3, and H-16. The length and curvature of a flower of H-18 also seem ideal for a hermit, but its orientation forces the bird to rotate its head more than 90 degrees in the vertical plane to insert its downcurved bill (the flower of *wagneriana* is similar in this respect). The pollen of these "hermit" flowers is always carried at the base of the bill or on the head of the bird. The straight-flowered *Heliconia* (*latispatha*, H-17) may be entered easily by straight-billed hummingbirds near the point where the epaxial petal diverges from the corolla tube (Fig. 1). The bird's bill is then above the anthers, and pollen is deposited on its mandible and chin. The flowers of *imbricata* and *mariae* are somewhat curved, but the path to the nectar is relatively short and straight, allowing easy access by straight-billed birds; pollen is deposited on the bills. The flowers of H-3 and *imbricata* are unusual in that they are rotated 180 degrees relative to flowers of other *Heliconia* with erect inflorescences (*latispatha*, H-16,

H-17, H-18). The epaxial petal thus diverges from the corolla tube downwards, as it does in pendant species (*pogonantha* in Fig. 1). This results in pollen being placed on the dorsal side of the bill or head of the bird, compared to the ventral side for *latispatha*, H-16 and H-17. *H. wagneriana* and H-18 accomplish this by in effect rotating the bird rather than the flower.

DISCUSSION

Adaptations for territorial vs. traplining pollinators

Evidence from both floral morphology and hummingbird foraging suggests a dichotomy within the genus *Heliconia* between hermit and nonhermit flowers (Linhart 1973); this may also occur in other groups of hummingbird-pollinated flowers (Snow and Snow 1972). One major behavioral difference between hermits and non-hermits is that the latter frequently hold territories at *Heliconia*, whereas hermits do so only rarely and inconsistently. The energetic feasibility of territoriality for the bird depends on the balance between the energy gained through exclusive or preferential access to the nectar, and the energy expenditures of foraging and defense (Brown 1964, Stiles and Wolf 1970, Wolf et al. 1972). An alternative feeding strategy is "traplining" (Janzen 1971 and *pers. comm.*), which consists of birds traveling between clumps of flowers, presumably following a regular route and visiting the clumps in a particular sequence. All the evidence to date indicates that it is the main strategy of flower exploitation employed by hermit hummingbirds (Stiles and Wolf, *unpubl. data*, Snow and Snow 1972). From the bird's point of view, the flower sources along a trapline must supply enough nectar to be worth revisiting, but not enough to be worth defending (cf. Heinrich and Raven 1972).

Various aspects of flowering phenology favor territorial or nonterritorial hummingirds: the amount

298 F. GARY STILES Ecology, Vol. 56, No. 2

of energy available, the time over which it is available, and its accessibility. The total amount of nectar available in a *Heliconia* clump can vary with size of clump, degree of synchrony of flowering of different plants, rate of flower production per inflorescence, and rate of nectar production per flower. A copious, concentrated, and/or easily accessible nectar may favor territoriality; smaller amounts of dilute, inaccessible nectar, traplining. Nectar concentration can also affect forager size, since relatively dilute nectars can be exploited somewhat more efficiently by small hummingbirds than by large ones, other things being equal (Wolf et al. 1972).

Heliconia imbricata, H. latispatha, and H-17 appear preeminently adapted to pollination by territorial hummingbirds. They frequently grow in large clumps and show both highly synchronous flowering and a high rate of flower production (Table 4). At peak bloom, a clump can produce sufficient nectar to satisfy most or all of a hummingbird's daily energy requirement (Fig. 5). The corollas of these species are short and/or straight, and daily nectar production is fairly high. *Heliconia imbricata* produces a relatively dilute nectar and therefore fewer calories per flower, which might favor the smaller *Thalurania furcata* over the larger *Chalybura urochrysia* and *Amazilia tzacatl* (Tables 3, 7). The nectar of these three *Heliconia* species is also accessible to hermits, which may regularly visit small, isolated, undefended clumps and less frequently try to poach from larger, defended clumps. Were it not for the territoriality of the non-hermits, hermit utilization of these *Heliconia* might well be considerably greater.

Specialization for hermit pollination is shown by H-3, H-16, and H-18 not only in their corolla morphology (Fig. 3), but in their caloric phenology as well. Not even at peak bloom does an average clump of these species contain enough calories of nectar to satisfy a bird's nectar requirements (Fig. 5); thus they favor traplining hummingbirds (cf. Heinrich and Raven 1972). This is achieved through low rates of flower production per inflorescence, and generally small clump size (H-16, H-18) or lack of synchrony of flowering of different plants in a clump (H-3). Daily nectar production of these species is low (H-18) to moderate (H-3, H-16); nectar concentration is moderate (H-3, H-16) to high (H-18), perhaps reflecting the moderate to large size of the hermits themselves (Table 3). By contrast, the specialization for hermit pollination of *wagneriana* appears to be exclusively in its corolla, much the longest of any La Selva *Heliconia* (Table 6). This species often occurs in large clumps, shows synchronous flowering, has a moderate rate of flower production per inflorescence, and secretes a large amount of nectar per flower.

Heliconia pogonantha appears to be primarily hermit-pollinated, at least in forest habitats where it nearly always occurs in small, scattered clumps. Under these conditions, its high nectar production, fairly high flower production per inflorescence, and moderate degree of synchrony of blooming of different plants (if only because individual inflorescences are so long-lived) generally do not result in a concentration of resource great enough to support territorial hummingbirds. Its nectar-rich, strongly curved flowers may reflect specialization for pollination by the large *Eutoxeres aquila,* the only hummingbird to visit exclusively only one species of *Heliconia* (Table 7). However, in second growth, dense populations with many large clumps may occur. *Chalybura urochrysia* is the most frequent territorial species at *pogonantha* under these conditions; perhaps its somewhat longer bill (Table 3) enables it to negotiate the corolla better than can other territorial species. Thus, to some extent the frequent utilization of *pogonantha* by *Chalybura* (Table 7) may reflect human disturbance.

On the other hand *H. mariae* may be adapted for pollination by small territorial hummingbirds like *Thalurania.* The long-lived inflorescences (thus considerable synchrony of flowering), the high rate of flower production per inflorescence, and the short, relatively straight corolla all favor territorial hummingbirds, while the very low nectar production per flower and fairly dilute nectar may favor smaller species. I have found relatively dense populations of *mariae* in northeastern Nicaragua and along the Caribbean coast of Costa Rica being visited mostly by territorial *Thalurania.* At La Selva, it is only near the peak of blooming that the two isolated clumps produce enough nectar to support territorial hummingbirds (Fig. 5). At other times, *mariae* is visited largely by hermits.

Linhart (1973) has shown that hummingbird territoriality can greatly decrease pollen flow to and from the defended clump. Since a *Heliconia* clump is a single individual genetically, this amounts to increasing self-pollination at the expense of cross-pollination, which may be disadvantageous if the *Heliconia* is self-incompatible to any great extent (cf. Levin and Kerster 1971). For a relatively self-compatible *Heliconia,* having a territorial bird in residence may increase the probability that every flower in the clump will be visited, especially if the hummingbird can keep track of which flowers in its territory it has visited most recently, and visit other flowers on its next feeding flight. I have evidence that at least some hummingbirds can do this. Hence, if a self-compatible *Heliconia* has a territorial hummingbird the result can conceivably be a higher fruit set. The degree of self-compatibility of a *Heliconia* species may thus select for phenology favoring territorial or nonterritorial hummingbirds. No data are yet available on the relative degree of self-compatibility of La Selva *Heliconia*.

Light gaps and pollination systems

The size and permanence of the light gap required by a *Heliconia* species may directly affect the pattern of vegetative growth and clump formation. This in turn can have pronounced effects in flowering phenology, and may restrict the possibilities of specialization for pollination by territorial or traplining hummingbirds. The severe vegetative competition in young second growth probably favors rapid attainment of large clump size in *H. wageneriana*, *imbricata*, and *latispatha*. A high reproductive rate and self-compatibility are also frequently selected for in plants of early successional habitats (Baker 1961). In *Heliconia* this amounts to selection for pollination by territorial hummingbirds, such as occurs in *H. imbricata* and *latispatha*. Hermit pollination in *H. wageneriana* may reflect a lack of self-compatibility in that species. With territorial species effectively excluded by corolla morphology, simultaneous flowering may not be disadvantageous and may make the individual clumps easier for hermits to locate. The main evolutionary risk run by a self-incompatible *wageneriana* would then be the development of a territorial hermit.

Under the forest canopy, low light intensity may make it difficult for a species like H-16 to photosynthesize the metabolic reserves necessary for flowering. I have repeatedly observed whole clumps going through two blooming seasons without flowering. Some plants may never flower, but simply continue photosynthesis until the clump has accumulated enough reserves to permit one of its plants to put out an inflorescence. In H-16, energy may be sufficiently limiting that allocation of reserves to vegetative growth or flowering would be mutually exclusive; hermit pollination is probably obligatory, since a clump can never put out enough nectar to attract a territorial hummingbird. The one forest-based *Heliconia* that does support territorial hummingbirds, H-17, is dependent upon light gaps where presumably enough energy is available to permit both vegetative growth and profuse flowering. In this respect, H-17 probably resembles the second-growth species mentioned in the preceding paragraph. H-18 is intermediate: at very small light-gaps, clumps are small and relatively few plants flower; at larger light-gaps, or in second growth, larger clumps with a high proportion of plants that flower are the rule.

Given the energetic problems of producing large amounts of flowers inside the forest, it may be no coincidence that H-16 and H-18 bloom simultaneously (Fig. 4). The main effect of this may be to increase the overall level of nectar resources there, so that hermits may more frequently extend their foraging routes through the forest itself; at other times of the year, their major flyways are along stream courses or other large breaks in the forest canopy. Perhaps the uncommon H-16 is in effect making its own clumps more accessible by converging in blooming seasonality with the common H-18. Heinrich and Raven (1972) noted that simultaneous blooming effectively decreases, in a caloric sense, the distance between clumps.

Isolating mechanisms

Since the La Selva *Heliconia* are presumably closely related, selection against hybridization and consequent gamete wastage may be expected. Such selection could occur at the level of the plant population, or that of the flower itself. The former would act to reduce the temporal and spatial overlap in flowering between species (Levin and Anderson 1970). With the exception of H-16 and H-18, the hermit-pollinated *Heliconia* of La Selva show a pattern of sequential and nonoverlapping peaks of flowering (Fig. 4). Among the *Heliconia* pollinated by non-hermits at La Selva, the major divergence has been spatial rather than temporal. H-17 occupies the most shaded habitats, *imbricata* habitats of intermediate light intensities, and *latispatha* the most open areas, often in full sun. A corresponding difference in habitat preference occurs in the hummingbirds, which may have resulted in a partitioning of pollinators. The main visitor to *latispatha* is *Amazilia tzacatl*, which also prefers very open habitats; *imbricata* and H-17 are visited mostly by the shade-loving *Chalybura* and *Thalurania*. Appreciable habitat overlap occurs only between *latispatha* and *imbricata*, and then mainly in second growth (Table 2); these are also the sites where *imbricata* is most visited by *Amazilia*, and *latispatha* by *Thalurania* and *Chalybura*. Human influences have probably caused a breakdown in habitat isolating mechanisms, and these are the only two La Selva *Heliconia* that hybridize to any extent. These hybrids are over 99% sterile, and selection against interspecific pollinations should be strong. The out-of-season flowering of *H. latispatha* (Fig. 4) may represent the early stages of selection for a divergence in blooming seasons between *latispatha* and *imbricata*.

Floral isolating mechanisms may be either mechanical (morphological specializations that impede interspecific pollen transfer) and/or ethological (adaptations that increase specificity of flower choice by pollinators) (Levin 1971 and included references). Among La Selva *Heliconia*, mechanical isolation is probably accomplished by deposition of pollen of different species in different places on a given type of hummingbird (Table 6; Fig. 7). The flowers of H-16 and H-18 may reduce or eliminate interspecific pollen transfer in this manner, and the same kind of difference is seen between *latispatha* and *imbricata*. In the latter case, this difference is apparently insufficient to prevent hybridization when other isolating mechanisms break down. The species most similar in site of pollen deposition are isolated, at least in part, by habitat (*latispatha* and H-17, *wagneriana* and *pogonantha*) or blooming season (*wagneriana*, *pogonantha*, and H-3).

Ethological isolating mechanisms are essentially visual and caloric. Visual mechanisms include all the various difference in color, form, and aspect of the inflorescences of different *Heliconia* (Table 1). At the level of the individual forager these factors probably do increase flower specificity. For example, in several instances where two or three *Thalurania* or *Chalybura* individuals held territories at adjacent or interdigitating clumps of *H. latispatha* and *imbricata*, the territorial boundaries always followed precisely the border between the two *Heliconia* species. One *latispatha* inflorescence that projected well into an *imbricata* clump was used and defended by the bird occupying the adjacent *latispatha* clump, rather than the one that held the *imbricata*.

The caloric parameters that may serve as ethological isolating mechanisms include all those factors affecting the ability of different hummingbirds to extract nectar from different *Heliconia*: the length and curvature of the corolla, and the amount and concentration of the nectar. Differences in foraging efficiency of several hummingbirds at different *Heliconia* flowers have been demonstrated (Wolf et al. 1972), and these often correspond to differences in flower choice (e.g., *Thalurania* vs. *Phaethornis* at *imbricata* and *pogonantha*: Table 7).

Competition vs. partitioning of pollinators

Linhart (1973) suggested that the dichotomy between hermit and nonhermit flowers in *Heliconia* may reduce competition for food among the birds, as well as competition for pollinators by the plants. However, with many hummingbirds and few flowers, severe food competition among the birds will coincide with little competition for pollinators among the plants; with many flowers and few hummingbirds, the reverse should occur. Thus the two types of competition may be inversely related, depending on the relative numbers of birds and flowers. At different times and in different habitats, both situations may occur in the La Selva hummingbird-*Heliconia* community.

Competition for pollinators should tend to produce

sequential nonoverlapping blooming seasons (Levin and Anderson 1970); the effect might be difficult to separate from that of selection against interspecific gene flow. Thus, the divergence in blooming seasons among hermit-pollinated *Heliconia* at La Selva could be in part a result of competition for pollinators. A comparable situation, also ascribed to competition, occurs in bat-pollinated plants of both Old and New World tropics (Allen 1939, van der Pijl 1956, Baker 1963, Salas 1973, P. Opler, *pers. comm.*). The overall effect is to provide the large, long-lived bats with a year-round food supply that may help to maintain their residence in the community (Baker 1963). The hermits are the only La Selva hummingbirds that are highly dependent on *Heliconia* flowers at all times of year. Only during the early wet season do the non-Hermits seem to depend on *Heliconia*; at other times of year, other flowers are used.

If the number of potential pollinators is large in relation to the amount of *Heliconia* available, then competition for pollinators may be less important than partitioning of pollinators. Caloric parameters can provide a means of effecting pollinator specificity if several species of hummingbirds and *Heliconia* are simultaneously present. For the hummingbirds, flower specificity should be most advantageous when overall nectar availability is greatest (Wolf et al. 1972, Emlen 1966). Selection for pollinator specificity therefore could result in convergence of blooming peaks between sympatric *Heliconia*. This may have occurred in *imbricata* and *latispatha* since *Thalurania* is more efficient at extracting nectar from *imbricata*, *Amazilia tzacatl* from *latispatha* (Wolf et al. 1972). In this case, pollinator specificity was probably reinforced originally by habitat selection.

Other sources of selection affecting flowering phenology

Some aspects of flowering phenology may reflect selective pressures arising from sources other than pollination biology. For instance, it appears that temporal partitioning of pollinators by *Heliconia* could be greatly enhanced if different species secreted nectar at more divergent times of day. That the flowers of all La Selva *Heliconia* (and indeed, of all hummingbird-pollinated flowers of wet lowland tropics I have seen) are only half-day flowers may be the result of selection by flower-destroying animals. By late morning, open *Heliconia* flowers are being attacked by insects (*Trigona*, bees, weevils, syrphid fly larvae, ants, etc.) and such birds as tanagers (e.g., *Ramphocelus*) and icterids (*Cacicus*). These animals eat the nectar, often damaging the flower itself, including the ovary. Therefore, exposing a nectar-rich flower for too many hours may well heighten the chances of discovery by destructive animals. Early morning is probably the best time of day for a flower to expose large amounts of nectar, since the nectar supply can be safely built up at night; most of the dystrophic animals mentioned are diurnal.

Selection arising from fruiting and seed dispersal mechanisms may also influence flowering phenology. For instance, Snow (1965) postulates that the staggered fruiting seasons of Trinidad melastomes is a result of competition for avian dispersal agents (manakins and tanagers). Actually, competition for both pollinators (hermits) and dispersers (chiefly manakins) could occur simultaneously, with both tending toward divergence of reproductive seasons in *Heliconia*.

It should be evident that the adaptation between plant and pollinator in the hummingbird-*Heliconia* system is indeed complex, involving much more than just the morphological fit between corolla and bill. Moreover, as Heinrich and Raven (1972) point out, it is the plant as a whole that is being selected, and its flowering phenology must be seen in the context of selection for other attributes as well.

ACKNOWLEDGMENTS

The bulk of this study was done while I held a Chapman-Naumberg postdoctoral fellowship from the American Museum of Natural History; I also received support from NSF grants GB-7611 and GB-19200 to Larry L. Wolf. The Organization for Tropical Studies provided logistical support at La Selva. Weather data for La Selva were collected and made available by Rafael Chavarría and Gary Hartshorn. The June 1972 *Heliconia* blooming census was conducted by Paul Opler. F. R. Hainsworth suggested the use of the refractometer for measuring nectar concentrations. R. J. Quigley prepared the photographs of hummingbirds and flowers. G. S. Daniels provided help with nomenclature. For helpful discussion and comments on the manuscript, I thank R. and B. Carroll, R. Colwell, B. Heinrich, P. Opler, D. Janzen, G. Orians, and an anonymous reviewer. The task of deciphering and typing the manuscript was done by Joanna Barnes and Kay García. Finally, I thank especially Larry L. Wolf, for help and stimulating discussion in the field and out.

LITERATURE CITED

Allen, G. M. 1939. Bats. Harvard Univ. Press, Cambridge. 368 p.

Baker, H. G. 1961. Reproductive methods as factors in speciation in flowering plants. Symp. Soc. Exp. Biol. **7**:114–143.

———. 1963. Evolutionary mechanisms in pollination biology. Science **139**:877–883.

Brown, J. L. 1964. The evolution of diversity in avian territorial systems. Wilson Bull. **76**:160–169.

Emlen, J. M. 1966. The role of time and energy in food preferences. Am. Nat. **100**:611–617.

Heinrich, B., and P. H. Raven. 1972. Energetics and pollination ecology. Science **176**:597–603.

Holdridge, L. R., W. C. Grenke, W. H. Hatheway, T. Liang, and J. A. Tosi Jr. 1971. Forest environments in tropical life zones: A pilot study. Pergamon Press, Oxford. 747 p.

Huber, H. 1956. Die Abhängigkeit der Nektarsekretion von Temperatur, Luft- und Bodenfeuchtigkeit. Planta **48**:47–49.

Janzen, D. H. 1971. Euglossine bees as long-distance pollinators. Science **171**:203–205.

Levin, D. A. 1971. The origin of reproductive isolating mechanisms in flowering plants. Taxon **20**:91–113.

Levin, D. A., and W. W. Anderson. 1970. Competition for pollinators between simultaneously flowering species. Am. Nat. **104**:345–354.

Levin, D. A., and H. W. Kerster. 1971. Neighborhood structure in plants under diverse reproductive methods. Am. Nat. **104**:345–354.

Linhart, Y. B. 1973. Ecological and behavioral determinants of pollen dispersal in hummingbird-pollinated *Heliconia*. Am. Nat. **107**:511–523.

Percival, M. 1961. Types of nectar in angiosperms. New Phytol. **60**:235–281.

Salas D., S. 1973. Una bromeliácea costarricense polinizada por murciélagos. Brenesia **2**:5–10.

Shuel, R. W. 1966. The influence of external factors on nectar production. Am. Bee J. **107**:54–56.

Slud, P. 1960. The birds of Finca "La Selva," Costa Rica: A tropical wet forest locality. Bull. Am. Mus. Nat. Hist. **121**:49–148.

Smith, R. R. 1966. A taxonomic revision of the genus *Heliconia* in Central America. Ph.D. Dissertation. Univ. Florida, Gainesville.

Snow, B. K., and D. W. Snow. 1972. Feeding niches of hummingbirds in a Trinidad valley. J. Anim. Ecol. **41**:471–485.

Snow, D. W. 1965. A possible selective factor in the evolution of fruiting seasons in a tropical forest. Oikos **15**:274–281.

Stiles, F. G. 1971. Time, energy and territoriality of the Anna Hummingbird (*Calypte anna*). Science **171**: 818–821.

———. 1973. Food supply and the annual cycle of the Anna Hummingbird. Univ. Calif. Publ. Zool. **97**: 1–116.

Stiles, F. G., and L. L. Wolf. 1970. Hummingbird territoriality at a tropical flowering tree. Auk **87**: 465–492.

van der Pijl, L. 1956. Remarks on bat pollination in the genera *Freycinetia*, *Haplophragma*, and *Duabanga*, and on chiropterophily in general. Acta Bot. Neerl. **5**:135–144.

Wolf, L. L. 1969. Female territoriality in a tropical hummingbird. Auk **86**:490–504.

Wolf, L. L., and F. R. Hainsworth. 1971. Time and energy budgets of territorial hummingbirds. Ecology **51**:980–988.

Wolf, L. L., F. R. Hainsworth, and F. G. Stiles. 1972. Energetics of foraging: Rate and efficiency of nectar extraction by hummingbirds. Science **176**:1351–1352.

5 Coevolution

Robert J. Marquis and Rodolfo Dirzo

Although the *term* coevolution is of relatively recent origin (Ehrlich and Raven 1964), recognition that organisms might undergo the *process* of coevolution (reciprocal evolutionary impacts between unrelated species: Janzen 1980) came a century before. Such reciprocal evolutionary impact was initially inferred based on natural history—that is, careful observations of the behavior, morphology, resource use, and timing of activity of the organisms involved. Benefits to the participants were deduced from observation, while the degree of evolutionary impact was suggested by comparison to closely related species not found in a similar interaction. Finally, the level of specialization was inferred based on the number of species participating in the interactions, both locally and regionally.

Many of the early ideas on the nature of coevolution came from studies of tropical organisms. In this part, we examine studies that address evolutionary implications of highly specialized interactions (see part 4 for a discussion of the role of ecological interactions in shaping the structure and organization of tropical plant and animal communities). The papers reprinted here either provided the bases for hypotheses of coevolution in a particular system (Bates 1862 [paper 21]; Belt 1874 [paper 22];

Snow 1971 [paper 25]) or contributed significantly to the further understanding of a previously recognized coevolutionary relationship (Galil and Eisikowitch 1968 [paper 23]; Dodson et al. 1969 [paper 24]). All of these studies are steeped in natural history, some of it exquisite in detail and clarity. Bates's (1862) paper led to the development of the general theory of mimicry, of which a special case involves coevolution between the model and the mimic. Belt's (1874) description of bull's horn acacia–ant interactions serves as a cornerstone for our understanding of coevolutionary interactions between ants and plants. The papers by Galil and Eisikowitch (1968) and Dodson et al. (1969) clarify the interactions between pollinators and angiosperms for two systems in which a high degree of specialization has evolved. Finally, Snow (1971) proposed that the relationships between frugivorous birds and plants that produce fleshy fruits could be viewed as coevolutionary. Tropical systems continue to be the focus of much research into the nature of coevolutionary relationships, including limits on specialization (Futuyma and Slatkin 1983), geographic variation in interaction participants and the strength of those interactions (Thompson 1994), the costs and benefits of the associations (Yu and Davidson 1997), and phylogenetic

The red Bird of Paradise (*Paradisea rubra*). From Wallace (1869)

approaches for describing patterns of cospeciation (Becerra 1997; Farrell 1998).

Mimicry among Butterflies

Henry Bates spent eleven years in the Amazon Basin, making natural history observations and collecting specimens of plants and animals (paper 21). His collections revealed that various local forms or species of *Leptalis* butterflies (now *Dismorphia*, family Pieridae) match very precisely the color patterns of the wings of the local species of *Ithomia* (Ithomiinae, family Nymphalidae) (Bates 1862). In nature, when alive, the two taxa are exceedingly difficult to tell apart, but when collected it is obvious that they are unrelated, based on characteristics other than wing shape and color. The latter are much more common than the former, outnumbering them by as much as 1000 to 1. Why should the Pieridae don the dress of the Ithomiinae?

Bates's explanation launched the field of mimicry. Drawing upon his observations in the Amazon and in England, personal communications from other naturalists, including Alfred Russel Wallace, and his reading of Darwin's *Origin of Species*, he concluded that the matching of color pattern is an adaptation in *Leptalis* shaped by natural selection. He presumed that in mimicking the color pattern of *Ithomia* species, *Leptalis* gains protection from predators who otherwise mistake the *Leptalis* species for members of the genus *Ithomia*. Bates concluded that the *Ithomia*, in contrast to their imitators, must be chemically protected, for "they show every sign of flourishing existence, although of slow flight, feeble structure, unfurnished with apparent means of defence, and living in places which are incessantly haunted by swarms of insectivorous birds" (499). Mimicry of a relatively common, distasteful model by an edible but rare species has since become known as Batesian mimicry.

Strictly speaking, classical Batesian mimicry, in which the mimic is in much lower abundance than the model, should not lead to reciprocal evolutionary effects between model and mimic. This is because the mimic is too low in abundance to influence predation rates and ef-

fect selection on its model. However, as more and more examples of such mimicry have been examined, it has become clear that mimicry complexes form a continuum in both relative abundance and difference in edibility for the species involved (Gilbert 1983). At one end of the continuum lies Batesian mimicry, as described by Bates (1862), in which one species is the mimic and the other is the model. At the other end lies Müllerian mimicry (Müller 1879), in which two or more distasteful species are of relative equal abundance and share a mutualistic, or mutually beneficial, relationship. Müllerian mimics are thought to coevolve toward a similar color pattern (Gilbert 1983). Coevolution, however, can also potentially occur in Batesian mimicry. As the Batesian mimic becomes more abundant, the model will be under selection to be less like its mimic, either in subtle shifts in color pattern or in phenology or habitat use (Gilbert 1983). Shifts by the model to be less like the mimic will in turn select for reciprocal changes in the mimic to track the model, thus resulting in coevolution. In a Batesian system in Africa involving *Danaus chrysippus* and its mimic *Hypolimnas misippus*, predation rate on the model increases with the relative abundance of the nontoxic mimic (Smith 1979). Such increased predation as the Batesian mimic becomes more common may help explain polymorphisms seen in some Batesian models, such as African *Acraea* and *Danaus*, and *Heliconius* in the Neotropics (Brown and Benson 1974). Variation in color pattern may allow escape from increasing predation. Explanation of the existence of such polymorphisms, and the role of coevolution in producing them, is an active area of discussion (Turner 1984; Joron and Mallet 1998; Mallet and Joron 1999).

That visual predators, in this case birds, select for color patterns based on similarity to a known toxic model has been demonstrated decidedly, albeit in a temperate system (Sternberg, Waldbauer, and Jeffords 1977; see also Benson 1972). Heliconid butterflies are now known to be involved in both Batesian and Müllerian mimicry systems. For example, the Müllerian mimics *H. erato* and *H. melpomene* exhibit parallel race formation in which local variants mimic each other (Eltringham 1916). When local variants of each species hybridize, insectivorous birds prey disproportionately on novel color patterns in these hybrids (Mallet and Barton 1989). Further, mtDNA phylogenetic analysis of these two species reveal that they do not share similar evolutionary histories, and parallel race formation has not arisen from parallel cladogenesis (Brower 1996). That is, local populations of the two species have coevolved, but cladogenesis in one species has not caused cladogenesis in the other species, as originally proposed by Turner (1982) and Sheppard et al. (1985). Gilbert (1983), Turner (1984), Thompson (1994), and Joron and Mallet (1998) discuss the coevolutionary issues surrounding Batesian and Müllerian mimicry systems. Many of the untested assumptions underlying previous explanations of the evolution of mimicry complexes are challenged by the existence of more than one mimicry complex or "mimicry ring" within one location and the occurrence of adjacent mimicry rings that differ in color patterns (Mallet and Joron 1999).

Ant-Plant Interactions

In the case of mimicry among butterflies, coevolution occurs within members of the same trophic level. Coevolution can also occur across trophic levels, a case in point being interactions between ants and plants. These interactions reach their highest diversity and the highest degree of specialization in tropical habitats. For example, as many as 90 percent of the trees of Amazonian Peru may have some relationship with protective ants (Foster, in Schupp and Feener 1991). Benefits to plants include protection against herbivores, nutrient supplementation, seed dispersal (see van der Pijl 1972 [paper 19]), pollination, and killing of plant competitors. Benefits to the ants include shelter, food, or both.

Thomas Belt (1874 [paper 3]) was the first to describe an interaction between ants that provide protection against herbivores and the plants they inhabit. In this publication, he describes the stinging and aggressive behavior of the ant *Pseudomyrma (Pseudomyrmex) bicolor* on *Acacia sphaerocephala* in Nicaragua. He inferred from these behavioral observations that the ants protect the tree from browsing mammals and herbivorous insects, including leaf-cutting ants. The plant houses the ants in hollow thorns, and provides food in the form of nectar from extrafloral nectaries and yellow food bodies (now called Beltian bodies) made at the tips of new leaflets. In inferring a protective role for the ants, Belt founded the so-called protectionist school of ant-plant interactions, which holds that the interaction is a mutualistic one in which plants provide reward in return for protection.

Belt also described plants (in this case, Melastomataceae) that house ants but do not provide reward directly (ants instead gain food from the honeydew of Homoptera, which they cultivate within plant shelters), and plants that provide reward through extrafloral nectaries (*Passiflora*) but do not house ants. Thus, he recognized from the start that ants and plants vary greatly in the nature of the potential benefits and degree of symbiosis. Forbes (1888) also made early descriptions of ant-Homopteran interactions.

Descriptions of other protective ant-plant associations quickly followed in the footsteps of Belt, including other New World associations as well as ants and acacia in the Old World. Wheeler (1910) reviewed this early work and Hocking (1970) described ant-acacia studies in Africa. Keller (1892) concluded that hollow thorns on *Acacia fistulosa* in Africa are adaptations whose function is to house protective ants. Brown (1960), drawing upon biogeographic evidence, hypothesized that browsing pressure has led to the evolution myrmecophytism in acacia. In Australia, where browsing mammals are absent, no myrmecophytic acacia species occur and most are spineless. In contrast, myrmecophytic acacia and browsers are abundant both in Africa and in the New World. An unstated underlying assumption is that herbivorous insects that attack acacia are abundant in all three tropical regions.

In a landmark study, Janzen (1966) was the first to demonstrate unequivocally a protective function by ants against herbivores, in this case for *Pseudomyrmex ferruginea* on *Acacia cornigea* in Mexico. By experimentally excluding ants, he found that plants without their colonies were heavily attacked by insect herbivores. Strangely, no one has yet tested the effect of ant presence against browsing mammals in ant-acacia systems. Since this initial study, numerous others have experimentally tested the impact of ants on plant fitness, both in symbioses where ants are housed on plants and where ants only visit plants for extrafloral nectar (Bronstein 1994). In many cases, ants provide both protection (by reducing damage) and benefit (by increasing plant fitness), but to varying degrees (de la Fuente and Marquis 1999). Again, despite the early proposal that ant-attracting traits evolved to protect plants against herbivorous mammals, the ability of ants to reduce attack by browsing mammals apparently has not been tested. Benefits to the ant partner remain almost universally untested (Cushman and Beattie 1991; Morales and Heithaus 1998).

Our current view of evolution in protective ant-plant systems was presaged by Belt's descriptions. Most would agree that certain plant species have evolved traits to attract aggressive ant species. Plants that have evolved extrafloral nectaries alone have probably done so in response to protection offered by a general ant community. More specialized relationships have developed much less frequently. One of these is the *Pseudomyrmex-Acacia* system first described by Belt. Janzen (1966) listed specific traits in both partners that he proposed were derived as a result of their coevolutionary interaction. Ward (1991), in his phylogeny of pseudomyrmecine ants, found that obligate symbiosis has evolved at least twelve times in this clade. Multiple unrelated ant species have evolved the ability to colonize the same species of acacia as well as other plant species, but some ant species remain specialized to a single host plant. Why some ant species remain specialized to a single host plant and others do not remains

unclear. *Leonardoxa africana*, a small leguminous tree from equatorial Africa, also has been shown to have an obligate relationship with *Petalomyrmex phylax* ants that inhabit swollen internodes and aggressively attack leaf herbivores (McKey 1984).

In Asia, a few species of the large genus of pioneer trees *Macaranga* are inhabited by ants. This association and the benefits to both partners have recently been thoroughly investigated (Fiala et al. 1989; Fiala et al. 1994). The ants commonly occupy hollowed-out twig tips and extract sap using Homoptera, and the *Macaranga* produces small starch bodies on its stipules and extrafloral nectaries. The ants have been observed to keep the tree clear of vine tendrils and of potentially leaf-eating insects.

Not all ant-plant symbioses involve protection. Ants can also provide a critical source of nutrients for epiphytic plants that inhabit nutrient-poor sites. The epiphyte genera *Myrmecodia* and *Hydnophytum* (Rubiaceae) of southeast Asia and northern Australia provide well-studied examples of nutritional myrmecophytes (Huxley 1978). The enlarged tuber of this epiphytic shrub contains large empty chambers where ants keep their brood and deposit refuse. Adventitious roots grow into these chambers (Huxley 1978) and absorb nutrients from the ant refuse (Treseder, Davidson, and Ehleringer 1995). In Sarawak, Malaysia, these species, along with other epiphytic species, *Phymatodes sinuosa* (Polypodiaceae) and *Dischidia rafflesiana* (Asclepiadaceae), grow in nutrient-poor, white sand soils and are all provided nutrients by the ants *Iridomyrmex myrmedodiae* (Janzen 1974b). Many epiphytic myrmecophytes are also myrmecochorous, with elaiosome-bearing seeds that are dispersed by ants in the canopy (Kleinfeldt 1978).

Pollination in *Ficus* by Fig Wasps

Much more specialized interactions have evolved among the 750 or so species of figs (*Ficus*) and their fig wasp pollinators (Agaonidae). Almost every fig species is pollinated by a single wasp species that pollinates nothing else (Wiebes 1979; Janzen 1979; but see Michaloud, Carrière, and Kobbi 1996). Three other systems have been described in which a specialized and highly coevolved relationship has developed between pollinator and plant, and in which the pollinator is a seed consumer. These are first, the relationship between the yucca and the yucca moth (Riley 1892; Pellmyr et al. 1996); second, that between the globeflower *Trollius europaeus* and three interacting species of *Chiastocheta* flies (Pellmyr 1989); and third, that of the cactus *Lophocereus schotii* and its pollinator, the senita moth *Upiga virescens* (Holland and Fleming 1999). Unlike almost all other pollinator-plant interactions, the pollinating insects come to their respective hosts to parasitize flowers rather than gather a nectar and/or pollen reward. In all but *Chiastocheta,* the insects also actively pollinate those flowers. In the case of figs, female wasps upon leaving one nearly mature fig carry pollen to the next fig, where they then actively pollinate some flowers and parasitize others. What is usually not appreciated is that nonpollinating wasp species also parasitize figs, and parasitoids attack both pollinating and nonpollinating wasp species. Galil and Eisikowitch, in a paper reprinted here (1968; paper 23), describe the reproductive behavior of *Ficus sycomorus* in Kenya, and the associated biology of the wasp species that oviposit in female flowers. This publication signaled a change in emphasis in studies of fig wasp interactions from mainly taxonomic to ecological issues. In particular, Galil and Eisikowitch emphasized how the nonpollinating species disrupt the potentially beneficial impact of the true pollinator. They recognized that the benefit to the plant (that is, the number of ovaries fertilized resulting in seeds) and to the pollinating wasp (successful production of offspring) is dependent on the level of intervention by nonpollinating and parasitizing species (see also West et al. 1996). The more interlopers involved, the less benefit gained by either mutualist, thus reducing their mutual selective impact on each other and the potential for coevolution. Whether such interlopers are involved is considered to be a major factor determining the degree of specialization (Pellmyr

and Thompson 1996; Holland and Fleming 1999).

Cospeciation, and a resulting congruence in phylogenies between coevolving species, is one possible but not necessary outcome of coevolution. Molecular phylogenies of the interactants in the fig systems are suggesting that there is a high degree of congruence not only between the figs and their fig wasp pollinators (Herre et al. 1996) but also between wasp pollinators and nonpollinating wasps (Machado et al. 1996).

To maintain a population of pollinating wasps, a population of figs must flower continuously, though individual trees may flower asynchronously. As a result, figs are a source of food for vertebrate frugivores year-round and thus act as a keystone resource for that community. Supporting evidence for this scenario comes from the Neotropics (Terborgh 1986) and Malaysia (Lambert 1991), but not from Africa (Gautier-Hion and Michaloud 1989). Current research in fig–fig wasp interactions focuses on the evolution of sex ratios in pollinating wasps (Herre 1985), interactions among mutualist and nonmutualist wasp species (West et al. 1996), the evolution of flowering phenology and sexual system in the figs (e.g., Spencer, Weiblen, and Flick 1996; Smith and Bronstein 1996), and the potential impact of current land-use patterns on fig population maintenance (Bronstein et al. 1990; Khadari et al. 1995; Nason, Herre, and Hamrick 1996). From the fig's point of view, emphasis on the impact of the various interactions has been on female fitness, while implications for male fitness have been overlooked.

Orchid Pollination by Euglossine Bees

Unlike the fig–fig wasp example, Neotropical orchids pollinated by bees of the tribe Euglossini (euglossine or golden bees) are often visited by one to a few pollinating species, and these bees visit a number of orchid species (Roubik and Ackerman 1987). Male bees are attracted to scents produced by orchid flowers, which they collect on hairs located on the pads of their forefeet. A series of papers describe both behavioral and morphological natural history of the bees and the chemical and behavioral natural history of the plants (Dodson et al. 1969 [paper 24]; Dressler 1968; Dodson 1975; and others reported therein). Dodson et al. (1969) established the components of a coevolutionary process between these plants and their euglossine pollinators. They discovered that different bee species, and in some cases different individuals within bee species, are attracted to different combinations of fragrances. In turn, each orchid species produces its own unique array of fragrances. Thus, slight changes in the fragrance profile can potentially lead to reproductive isolation and perhaps sympatric speciation within the orchid clade. Changes in morphology of the flower can reinforce isolation by placement of the pollinia on a different portion of the bee's body, but morphological change is not necessary for reproductive isolation to occur if a change in the fragrance profile that attracts a different set of bees has already taken place.

Euglossine bees have evolved specialized pads for collecting the fragrances, which they then pack into special sacs on the tibia of the hind legs. These fragrances may then be transformed into pheromones via secretion from the mandibular glands. The pheromones are used to attract other male bees to form groups called leks to attract females. In Panama, on Barro Colorado Island, there is a large group of euglossine bees that do not visit orchids, or visit them so infrequently that they do not carry orchid pollinia (Roubik and Ackerman 1987). Instead they must gather fragrances from rotting wood, leaves, and fruits, as well as flowers of other plant species (Roubik and Ackerman 1987). Furthermore, both male and female bees gather nectar as a food source from non-euglossine-pollinated plants. Euglossine-pollinated orchids are dependent on the bees for pollination (Dressler 1981). The bees, on the other hand, at least on Barro Colorado Island, are not dependent on the orchids. Thus, contrary to Dodson's initial proposal (Dodson 1975), preliminary evidence from one site suggests that the plants probably do not effect evolution in the bees, and therefore coevolution is not occurring.

The view that coevolutionary relationships could be extended to include frugivorous birds and the plants whose seeds they disperse was proposed by Snow (1971; paper 25). He based his proposal on four observations. First, he speculated that dispersal by animals was probably ancestral to dispersal by wind (see also Corner 1954), and therefore there has been the potential for interactions over long evolutionary time. Second, seeds of arillate fruits are passed unharmed, and sometimes have increased germinability, following passage through vertebrate guts. Third, fruits dispersed by birds can be characterized by a set of common characteristics (a "syndrome" suggesting convergent evolution on the part of the plants): they are conspicuous, accessible, and brightly colored. Fourth, the diet of certain bird species, mostly confined to tropical forests, consists almost entirely of fruit, and the plant species whose seeds are dispersed by these birds produce fruit rewards that are high in protein, fats, and carbohydrates. These apparent specializations in both the birds and plants suggested reciprocal evolutionary effects. In addition to morphological and nutritional factors, Snow also proposed that nonoverlapping but sequential fruiting times among plant species may have been selected for by fruiting birds in order to minimize competition (see also Snow 1965).

Snow's paper (see also Doctors van Leeuwen 1954, Corner 1954, Snow 1965, Morton 1973, and McKey 1975) led to a spate of research that has increased our understanding of the nature of vertebrate disperser–plant interactions. Snow himself was vague about the mutual benefits of the relationship. The benefits for the frugivorous bird (or vertebrate frugivore in general) are obvious: food, sometimes of very high quality, that is relatively abundant, and "easily obtained" compared to insects. Snow did not explore the benefits to the plant other than to imply that dispersal away from the parent plant is beneficial. Howe and Estabrook (1977) proposed a graphical model of how plants may or may not compete for the services of frugivorous bird species, depending on crop size and whether the birds were "specialist" dispersers vs. "opportunists" (harkening back to a dichotomy implied by Snow and expanded on by McKey 1975). Coevolution was mediated by intraspecific competition for dispersal. The proposed benefit to the plant was that dispersal leads to escape from seed predators (Janzen 1970 [paper 17]; Connell 1971; see also part 4). The nature of dispersal quality was further elaborated by Howe and Smallwood (1982).

Studies show that plants are often visited by a large number of fruit-eating species that vary greatly in the number of seeds they disperse, the dispersal distance, and whether those seeds are deposited in clumps or singly, or to safe sites. All have been shown to affect subsequent survival. For example, following visits to fruiting plants, bellbirds fly predictably to perches in canopy gaps, where they defecate seeds. Seed survival at these perches was higher than that for randomly dispersed seeds because there is reduced mortality by pathogens in light gaps (Wenny and Levey 1998). Findings from one system in particular, *Virola surinamensis* and its coterie of dispersers, indicate that certain disperser species have the capability to select for plant traits (summarized in Howe 1986; see also part 4). However, all bird species studied to date visit many different plant species not only in their lifetime but within a single day, thus reducing the potential selective impact of the plant on the frugivore. Unlike plant-pollinator interactions, coevolution between seed dispersers and plants is likely further constrained by the fact that birds receive the reward before they provide the service and thus the reward cannot be withheld if the service is not provided (Wheelwright and Orians 1982). Considering that research in tropical and extratropical regions (e.g., Herrera 1984; Jordano 1995b) has seriously challenged the coevolutionary interpretation for plant-frugivore interactions, the relevance of Snow's work was to prompt a plethora of studies in this field that have significantly contributed to our understanding of vertebrate-plant interactions. Future clarification of the benefits of fruit consumption hinges on the ability to develop techniques to follow the fates of individual seeds.

Conclusion

Highly specific, one-to-one coevolution is rare in nature, although as these papers show, such interactions can occur (e.g., fig–fig wasp interactions). A contributory cause to preventing specialization is that spatial and temporal variation in species interactions are common, if not ubiquitous (e.g., Schemske and Horvitz 1984). Although most species interact with a multitude of other species, pairwise coevolution is still possible, depending on the nature of the interactions. Criteria have been established for distinguishing diffuse from pairwise coevolution (Rausher 1992; Hougen-Eitzman and Rausher 1994), and statistical and experimental methods have been developed to investigate patterns of multiple-species interactions (Simms 1990; Iwao and Rausher 1997; Juenger and Bergelson 1998).

Diffuse interactions within food webs may also contribute to the maintenance of community diversity (e.g., Gilbert 1975), where multiple species are less susceptible to collapse by the loss of any one species. In contrast, loss of an interacting member of a pair of species may mean the loss of its partner and all dependent species. Although species may have a long list of partners at different times of the year, temporal scarcity of resources may, at times, force specialization. Such times of scarcity may make food webs particularly vulnerable to the loss of a single member of a coevolutionary web. Figs, fig wasps, and other fig-dependent frugivores (Terborgh 1986; Lambert 1991), and the frugivorous masked tityra, *Casearia corymbosa* fruits, and other associated frugivores (Howe 1977) are two suggested examples. Because of the sheer diversity of unstudied systems, future work on tropical systems has much to offer in terms of increasing our understanding of the conditions under which specialization is favored, and the consequences of such specialization for the maintenance of biotic diversity, both with and without habitat alteration. Both microevolutionary and macroevolutionary approaches will be valuable. The former can be used to define the consequences of interactions for fitness of the interacting species (Horvitz and Schemske 1995), while the latter can provide insight into the history of interactions to determine if that history is consistent with a coevolutionary scenario (e.g., Armbruster 1997).

Reprinted Selections

Henry Walter Bates. 1862. Contributions to an insect fauna of the Amazon Valley. Lepidoptera: Heliconidae. *Transactions of the Linnean Society of London* 23: 502–4, 506–15, 564–66, plates LV, LVI

Thomas Belt. 1874. *The Naturalist in Nicaragua*, 217–30. John Murray, London. Reprinted by the University of Chicago Press, 1985

J. Galil and D. Eiskowitch. 1968. On the pollination ecology of *Ficus sycomorus* in East Africa. *Ecology* 49:259–69

C. H. Dodson, R. L. Dressler, H. G. Hills, R. M. Adams and N. H. Williams. 1969. Biologically active compounds in orchid fragrances. *Science* 164:1243–49

D. W. Snow. 1971. Evolutionary aspects of fruit-eating by birds. *Ibis* 113:194–202. Reproduced with the kind permission of the British Ornithologists' Union

Contributions to an Insect Fauna of the Amazon Valley.
Lepidoptera: Helicanidae
Henry Walter Bates

strict reference to the *geographical relations* of their varieties. Many closet naturalists, who receive disconnectedly the different varieties in any group, treat them all as independent species: by such a proceeding, it is no wonder that they have faith in the absolute distinctness and immutability of species.

The sexes in the *Heliconidæ* very rarely differ in colours. Secondary sexual characters of another description occur, however, very generally in the Danaoid group. The males, in all the genera but two (*Lycorea* and *Ituna*) of this section, are furnished with a pencil or fringe of long hairs near the costal edge of the hind wings on the upper surface. It sometimes arises from the bottom of a shallow horny cup situated between the costal and subcostal nervures; the hairs are long, soft, and adpressed. I was unable to discover any use in this structure; it seemed not to be under the control of the insect. There is no movement in flight, or position in repose, peculiar to the male sex, which might require an instrument to hold the wings together—a function which the position of the hairs, in the place where the fore wing overlaps the hind wing, suggests to the mind. I believe the appendage must be considered as an outgrowth of the male organization, which is not in this case applied to any especial purpose: it may be taken to be of the same nature as the pencil of hairs on the breast of the male Turkey. Growths of one kind or other, on the surface of the wings, peculiar to the male sex, are frequent in Butterflies: in *Danais* the males have a small horny excrescence on the disk of the hind wings, which, considering the near relationship proved to exist between the two groups, I take to be homologically the same as the pencil of hairs in the *Danaoid Heliconidæ*. In the genus *Pavonia*, belonging to the family *Brassolidæ*, the males in some species have a fringe of hairs near the abdominal border; in others, a long pencil of the same on the disk; and, again, in others, instead of these appendages, a thickened plate on the inner margin of the hind wings.

The most interesting part of the natural history of the *Heliconidæ* is the mimetic analogies of which a great many of the species are the objects. Mimetic analogies, it is scarcely necessary to observe, are resemblances in external appearance, shape, and colours between members of widely distinct families: an idea of what is meant may be formed by supposing a Pigeon to exist with the general figure and plumage of a Hawk. Most modern authors who have written on the group have mentioned the striking instances of this kind of resemblances exhibited with reference to the *Heliconidæ*; but no attempt has been made to describe them fully, nor to explain them. I will give a short account of the leading facts, and then mention some circumstances which seem to throw light on their true nature and origin.

A large number of the species are accompanied in the districts they inhabit by other species which counterfeit them in the way described. The imitators belong to the following groups:—*Papilio*, *Pieris*, *Euterpe*, and *Leptalis* (fam. *Papilionidæ*), *Protogonius* (*Nymphalidæ*), *Ithomeis* (*Erycinidæ*), *Castnia* (*Castniadæ*), *Dioptis*, *Pericopis*, *Hyelosia*, and other genera (*Bombycidæ* Moths)*. I conclude that the *Heliconidæ* are the *objects imitated*, because they all have the same family facies, whilst the analogous species are dissimilar to their nearest allies—perverted, as it were, to produce the resemblance, from

* The accompanying Table, in which a number of the most striking of these are arranged in parallel columns, will give some idea of the extent to which this system of imitation prevails.

OF THE AMAZON VALLEY. 503

SPECIFIC MIMETIC ANALOGIES IN THE LEPIDOPTERA OF TROPICAL AMERICA, ESPECIALLY BETWEEN THE DOMINANT FAMILY HELICONIDÆ AND DIFFERENT OTHER FAMILIES.

Danaoid Heliconidæ.	Acræoid Heliconidæ.	Acræidæ.	Papilioninæ.	Pierinæ.	Erycinidæ.	Castniadæ.	Bombycidæ.
Lycorea Atergatis			Papilio Zagreus*	Euterpe Eurytele*.			Pericopis angulata.
Methona Psidii { Ituna Phenarete* / I. Ilione* }				Leptalis Orise*		Castnia Linus*	P. sp.
Dircenna Epidero							Hyelosia Tiresia.
Tithorea Bonplandii	Heliconius Hecuba.*						
Melinæa Egina	H. Sylvana.						
M. Pardalis	H. Pardalinus*.						
M. Lucifer	H. Aurora.						
M. Messatis	H. Ismenius.						
M. (?) Hezia	H. Zuleika.						
M. Mnasias*—Ceratinia Ninonia.							
M. Mneme	H. Numata.			L. Egaina*.			
Mechanitis Egaënsis	H. Eucoma, var.			L. Astyoche*.			
M. Nesæa—Napeogenes Xanthone*.	H. Ethra.						
M. Lysimnia	H. Eucrate.						
Callithomia Alexirhoë* — Ceratinia Ninonia.							
Ithomia Flora { I. Cymo / Napeogenes Ithra* }				L. Theonoë*	Ithomeis satellites*		Dioptis Cyma.
I. Phono							D. diaphana.
I. Illinissa } Napeogenes Ercilla* / and allies				L. Lysinoë, var.*	I. aurantiaca*.		D. Æliana.
I. Chrysodonia } N. Corena* / and allies				L. Erythroë* var. of Theonoë.	I. mimica*		D. sp.*
I. Ilerdina				L. Leuconoë* var. of Theonoë.			Dioptis I- } Perico- / lordina* } pis, sp.*
Ceratinia Fluonia.				L. Melania* var. of Theonoë.	I. Heliconina*		Dioptis, sp.*
Ithomia Onega				L. Argochloë*. var. of Theonoë.			Dioptis Onegra.
I. Virginia				L. Eunolia.			
I. Primula—Napeogenes Pharo.				L. Siloë*			
I. Euritæa—N. sulphurina.							
I. Eurimedia	Eueides Lampeto*		P. Pausanius*.		Stalachtis Calliope		Pericopis, sp.*
I. Celenia—Napeogenes Tolosa.	Heliconius Thelxiope						P. Isso*.
Ceratinia villula—N. Apulia.	H. Clytia { Eueides / Eanes*. }					C. Acreoides*.	
	H. Vesta { Eueides / E. Thales. }	Acræa Thalia.	P. Zacynthus ♀ / P. Æneas and allies } ♀ / P. Bolivar ♀	L. Acreoides*. / Euterpe Tereas.			
				Leptalis Lysinoë* var. of Theonoë.	Ithomeissta- } Stalachtis / lachtina* } Duvalii.	C. sp.*	Pericopis turbida*.

* Those species marked * have been ascertained beyond all doubt to be very much fewer in individuals than the species which they mimic.

the normal facies of the genus or family to which they severally belong*. The resemblance is so close, that it is only after long practice that the true can be distinguished from the counterfeit, when on the wing in their native forests. I was never able to distinguish the *Leptalides* from the species they imitated, although they belong to a family totally different in structure and metamorphosis from the *Heliconidæ*, without examining them closely after capture. They fly in the same parts of the forest, and generally in company with the species they mimic.

I have already given an account of the local modifications to which the *Heliconidæ* are subject. It is a most curious circumstance, that corresponding races or species of counterfeiting groups accompany these local forms. In some cases I found proof that such species are modified from place to place to suit the peculiar forms of *Heliconidæ* there stationed. As this is an important point, and one which throws light on the origin of mimetic species, I must ask the reader's careful attention to the details, referring to the plates.

Plate LV. fig. 1 *a* (*Ithomia Flora*) and fig. 1 (*Leptalis Theonöe*) represent a Heliconide and its imitator, both of which inhabit the banks of the Cuparí, a river belonging to the Amazon system, in 55° W. long. Neither of these is found on the Upper Amazons (60° to 70° W. long.), where I made the remaining part of my observations on these insects. At Ega, on this upper river, in 65° W. long., two species of *Ithomia* occurred, which I consider to be local varieties or races of *I. Flora*, namely, *I. Onega* (Pl. LV. fig. 2 *a*) and *I. Illinissa* (Pl. LV. fig. 6 *a*). It is immaterial to the question in hand whether these be considered absolutely distinct species or races; the *Leptalis* which was found in their company was the form called *L. Lysinöe* (Pl. LV. fig. 3), with its admitted varieties (figs. 4, 5, 6, and 8). Only one of these varieties of *Leptalis* mimics an *Ithomia*; this is our fig. 6, which evidently counterfeits *Ithomia Illinissa* (fig. 6 *a*). The prevailing form of *Leptalis*, the *L. Lysinöe* (fig. 3), has no resemblance to any *Ithomia* of Ega, but is, when flying, a wonderful imitation of the *Stalachtis Duvalii* (Pl. LV. fig. 3 *a*), a common insect belonging to a genus (family *Erycinidæ*) equally flourishing and abundant in individuals with the members of the family *Heliconidæ*. I think there will be no doubt in the mind of any one that the Ega *Leptalides* are local varieties of the Cuparí *L. Theonöe* (fig. 1), when all the connecting links between them are studied in the figures given on our two plates. It is highly probable, therefore, that this species has been by some means modified with especial reference to the changed *Ithomiæ*, or other insects, of the locality. The varieties, figs. 4, 5, and 8, were excessively rare: they have the appearance of *sports*, and show how variable the species has been in this district.

The same takes place at St. Paulo, in 69° W. long. Here we find the *Ithomiæ* again changed. Neither the *I. Flora* of the Cuparí and Lower Amazons nor the *I. Illinissa* of Ega occurs; but the second Ega species, *I. Onega*, inhabits the district, and several other species not found in other places, amongst them *I. Ilerdina* (Pl. LVI. fig. 4 *a*), *I. Chrysodonia* (Pl. LVI. fig. 3 *a*), and *I. Virginia* (Pl. LVI. fig. 6 *a*). The prevailing species of

---

* This may be seen from the figures given of *Leptalis*,—fig. 5, Pl. LVI. being *L. Nehemia*, a species exhibiting the usual form of the family *Pieridæ*, to which the genus *Leptalis* belongs; whilst all the other *Leptalides* figured are mimetic species, totally unlike, as far as facies is concerned, this normal form.

the connecting links have not all been found, they may be called species : the word is of little importance. The habits of all are the same. When I had collected only two or three of the most distinct, I considered them separate species ; but intermediate forms successively occurred, every capture tending to link the whole more closely together. The explanation that the whole are the result of hybridization from a few originally distinct species cannot at all apply in this case, because the distinct forms whose inter-crossing would be required to produce the hybrids are confined to districts situated many hundred miles apart.

None of these *Leptalides* have been found in any other district or country than those inhabited by the *Ithomiæ* which they counterfeit. A species very closely allied to *L. Lysinoë*, var. *Argochloë* (Pl. LVI. fig. 6), has been received from Mexico (*L. Antherize*) ; but an *Ithomia*, of nearly the same colours (*I. Nero*) also inhabits Mexico. Many other species of *Leptalis*, of much larger size than the one here discussed, also mimic *Heliconidæ*, the objects of imitation not being *Ithomiæ*, but other genera of the family. Two of these are figured on Pl. LVI. *L. Orise* (Pl. LVI. fig. 8) is a remarkably exact counterfeit of *Methona Psidii* (fig. 8 *a*), the resemblance being carried to minutiæ, such as the colour of the antennæ and the spotting of the abdomen. *L. Amphione*, var. *Egaëna* (Pl. LVI. fig. 7), is very curious, as being a satellite of *Mechanitis Polymnia*, var. *Egaënsis* (fig. 7 *a*), both peculiar to the district of Ega,—the typical *L. Amphione* being found at Surinam, in company with the typical *M. Polymnia*, which it resembles—local varieties or sister species of *Leptalis Amphione* accompanying local varieties of *Mechanitis Polymnia* in other parts of tropical America.

Several species of *Dioptis*, a genus of Moths, and *Ithomeis*, a genus of *Erycinidæ*, also accompany these species or distinct local forms of *Ithomia*. A few of the Moths are figured on Pl. LV. figs. 10, 11, 12, 13. The imitations may not appear very exact from the figures ; but when the insects are seen on the wing in their native woods, they deceive the most experienced eye.

A similar series of mimetic analogies occurs in the Old World, between the Asiatic and African *Danaidæ*, or representatives of the *Heliconidæ*, and species of other families of Butterflies and Moths. No instance is known in these families of a tropical species of one hemisphere counterfeiting a form belonging to the other. A most remarkable case of mimicry has been recorded by Mr. Trimen[*] in a *Papilio* of Southern Africa, *P. Cenea*, whose male wears to deception the livery of one species of *Danais*, namely, *D. Echeria*, whilst the female resembles a quite different one, *D. Chrysippus*,—both African. Mimetic analogies, however, are not confined to the Lepidoptera ; most orders of insects supply them ; but they are displayed only by certain families. Many instances are known where parasitic Bees and two-winged Flies mimic in dress various industrious or nest-building Bees, at whose expense they live in the manner of the Cuckoo. I found on the banks of the Amazons many of these Cuckoo Bees and Flies, which all wore the livery of working Bees peculiar to the country.

The instances of this kind of analogy most familiar to European entomologists are those of the European species of *Trochilium* (a genus of Moths), which strangely mimic various

---

[*] 'Rhopalocera Africæ Australis,' p. 21. Cape Town.

Bees, Wasps, and other Hymenopterous and Dipterous insects. The parallelism between these several forms and their geographical relations have not yet, I believe, been investigated. The resemblances seem to be more closely specific in tropical countries than in Europe; and I think it likely that the counterfeits in high latitudes may not always be found in company with their models. It is possible the geographical relations between the species concerned may have been disturbed by the great climatal and geological changes which have occurred in this part of the world since the date when they first came into existence.

Not only, however, are *Heliconidæ* the objects selected for imitation; some of them are themselves the imitators; in other words, they counterfeit each other, and this to a considerable extent. Species belonging to distinct genera have been confounded, owing to their being almost identical in colours and markings; in fact, many of them can scarcely be distinguished except by their generic characters. It is a most strange circumstance connected with this family, that its two sections, or subfamilies, have been mingled together by all authors, owing to the very close resemblance of many of their species. Analogies between the two subfamilies have been mistaken for affinities. It is sometimes difficult to understand in these cases which is the imitator and which the imitated. We have, however, generally a sure test in the one set exhibiting a departure from the normal style of colouring of their congeners, whilst the other are conformable to their generic types. The species of *Napeogenes* are, by this criterion, evidently all imitators of *Ithomiæ*; they are also rare insects, like the *Leptalides*. The mimetic species of *Heliconius* must be, for the same reason, imitators.

These imitative resemblances, of which hundreds of instances could be cited, are full of interest, and fill us with the greater astonishment the closer we investigate them; for some show a minute and palpably intentional likeness which is perfectly staggering. I have found that those features of the portrait are most attended to by nature which produce the most effective deception when the insects are seen in nature. The faithfulness of the resemblance, in many cases, is not so striking when they are seen in the cabinet. Although I had daily practice in insect-collecting for many years, and was always on my guard, I was constantly being deceived by them when in the woods. It may be asked, why are mimetic analogies so numerous and amazingly exact in insects, whilst so rare and vague in the higher animals*? The only answer that I can suggest is, that insects have perhaps attained a higher degree of specialization, after their type, than most other classes: this seems to be shown by the perfection of their adaptive structures and instincts. Their being more numerous and striking in tropical than in temperate countries is perhaps attributable to the more active competitive life, and the more rapid succession of their generations, in hot than in cold countries.

It is not difficult to divine the meaning or final cause of these analogies. When we

---

* Two instances of mimicry in birds, quite as wonderful as those between *Leptalis* and *Ithomia*, have just been communicated to me by my old travelling companion, Mr. A. R. Wallace. He has observed two species of *Oriolidæ* (perverted from the normal facies of the family) attendant on two species of *Meliphagidæ*, and mimicking them in the most curiously minute way in colours and in general figure. The associated pairs inhabit separate islands, as follows :—
—I. Bourou, *Mimeta (Oriolidæ) Bouroënsis*, *Tropidorhynchus (Meliphagidæ)*, n. sp. ; I. Ceram, *Mimeta Forstini*, *Tropidorhynchus subcarinatus*.

see a species of Moth which frequents flowers in the daytime wearing the appearance of a Wasp, we feel compelled to infer that the imitation is intended to protect the otherwise defenceless insect by deceiving insectivorous animals, which persecute the Moth, but avoid the Wasp. May not the Heliconide dress serve the same purpose to the *Leptalis*? Is it not probable, seeing the excessive abundance of the one species and the fewness of individuals of the other, that the Heliconide is free from the persecution to which the *Leptalis* is subjected?

I think it clear that the mutual resemblance in this and other cases cannot be entirely due to similarity of habits or the coincident adaptation of the two analogues to similar physical conditions. This is a very abstruse part of our subject; for I think the facts of similar variation in two already nearly allied forms do sometimes show that they have been affected in a similar way by physical conditions. A great number of insects are modified in one direction by a seaside habitat. I found, also, the general colours of many widely different species affected in a uniform way in the interior of the South American continent. But this does not produce the specific imitation of one species by another; it only prepares the way for it.

It is perhaps true that the causes (to be discussed presently) which produce a close or mimetic analogy cannot operate on forms which have not already a general resemblance, owing to similarity of habits, external conditions, or accidental coincidence. Species or groups which have this kind of resemblance to each other have been called by Dr. Collingwood recurrent animal forms. The English Bee-Moths owe the narrow and pointed shapes of their wings, which already approximate them to Bees, to their blood-relationship to the Hawk-Moth family. Their Bee-like size, form, and flight doubtless arise from their Bee-like habits. A close specific analogy between any one of these and a Bee, such as exists between the insects discussed in this memoir, could scarcely be due to an accidental resemblance like that between the Hawk-Moth and a Bee, or to similarity of habits. It would mean an adaptation of the Moth with especial reference to the Bee.

I believe, therefore, that the specific mimetic analogies exhibited in connexion with the *Heliconidæ* are adaptations—phenomena of precisely the same nature as those in which insects and other beings are assimilated in superficial appearance to the vegetable or inorganic substance on which, or amongst which, they live. The likeness of a Beetle or a Lizard to the bark of the tree on which it crawls cannot be explained as an identical result produced by a common cause acting on the tree and the animal.

Some of the imitations by insects of inanimate and living objects are very singular, and may be mentioned in this place. Many caterpillars of Moths, but sometimes the cases only which are manufactured and inhabited by the caterpillars, have a most deceptive likeness to dry twigs and other objects. Moths themselves very frequently resemble the bark on which they are found, or have wings coloured and veined like the fallen leaves on which they lie motionless. The accidental general resemblance between the shape of Moths' wings and leaves here gives nature the ground-work for much mimetic analogy. It has been pointed out by Rössler * that the Buff-tip Moth, when at rest, is intended to represent a broken piece of lichen-covered branch,

* In an article on resemblances between insects and vegetable substances (Wiener Entomol. Monatschrift, 1861,

—the coloured tips of these wings, when they are closed, resembling a section of the wood. Other Moths are deceptively like the excrement of birds on leaves. I met with a species of Phytophagous Beetle (*Chlamys pilula*) on the Amazons, which was undistinguishable by the eye from the dung of Caterpillars on foliage. These two latter cases of imitation should be carefully considered by those who would be inclined to think that the object of mimetic analogies in nature was simply variety, beauty, or ornament: nevertheless these are certainly attendants on the phenomena; some South-American *Cassidæ* resemble glittering drops of dew on the tips of leaves, owing to their burnished pearly gold colour. Some species of Longicorn Coleoptera (*Onychocerus scorpio* and *concentricus*) have precisely the colour and sculpture of the bark of the particular species of tree on which each is found. It is remarkable that other species of the same small group of *Longicornes* (*Phacellocera Buquetii*, *Cyclopeplus Batesii*) counterfeit, not inanimate objects, like their near kindred just cited, but other insects, in the same way as the *Leptalides* do the *Heliconidæ*.

Amongst the living objects mimicked by insects are the predacious species from which it is the interest of the mimickers to be concealed. Thus, the species of *Scaphura* (a genus of Crickets) in South America resemble in a wonderful manner different Sand Wasps of large size, which are constantly on the search for Crickets to provision their nests with. Another pretty Cricket, which I observed, was a good imitation of a Tiger Beetle *, and was always found on trees frequented by the Beetles (*Odontocheilæ*). There are endless instances of predacious insects being disguised by having similar shapes and colours to those of their prey; many Spiders are thus endowed: but some hunting Spiders mimic flower-buds, and station themselves motionless in the axils of leaves and other parts of plants to wait for their victims.

The most extraordinary instance of imitation I ever met with was that of a very large Caterpillar, which stretched itself from amidst the foliage of a tree which I was one day examining, and startled me by its resemblance to a small Snake. The first three segments behind the head were dilatable at the will of the insect, and had on each side a large black pupillated spot, which resembled the eye of the reptile : it was a poisonous or viperine species mimicked, and not an innocuous or colubrine Snake ; this was proved by the imitation of keeled scales on the crown, which was produced by the recumbent feet, as the Caterpillar threw itself backwards. The Rev. Joseph Greene, to whom I gave a description, supposes the insect to have belonged to the family *Notodontidæ*, many of which have the habit of thus bending themselves. I carried off the Caterpillar, and alarmed every one in the village where I was then living, to whom I showed it. It unfortunately died before reaching the adult state.

p. 164). The author enumerates many very singular cases of mimicry ; he also states his belief that the mimicry is intended to protect the insects from their enemies.

There is an interesting note, by the Rev. Joseph Greene, in the 'Zoologist,' 1856, p. 5073, on the autumn and winter Moths of England, whose colours are shown by the author to be adapted to the prevailing tints of nature in the season in which the species appear.

* A remarkable instance of deceptive analogy relating to a Cricket and a species of *Cicindela* is described by Westwood in Trans. Lin. Soc. vol. xviii. p. 419. In this memoir, Mr. Westwood has enumerated many curious cases of mimetic analogy.

I think it will be conceded that all these various kinds of imitative resemblances belong to the same class of phenomena, and are subject to the same explanation. The fact of one species mimicking an inanimate object, and another of an allied genus a living insect of another family, sufficiently proves this. I do not see how they differ from the adaptations of organs or instincts to the functions or objects they relate to. All are adaptations, either of the whole outward dress or of special parts, having in view the welfare of the creatures that possess them.

Every species in nature may be looked upon as maintaining its existence by virtue of some endowment enabling it to withstand the host of adverse circumstances by which it is surrounded. The means are of endless diversity. Some are provided with special organs of offence, others have passive means of holding their own in the battle of life. Great fecundity is generally of much avail, added to capabilities, active or passive, of wide dispersion; so that when the species is extirpated in one part of its area of distribution, the place is refilled by migration of individuals from another part. A great number have means of concealment from their enemies, of one sort or other. Many are enabled to escape extermination, or obtain subsistence, by disguises of various kinds: amongst these must be reckoned the adaptive resemblance of an otherwise defenceless species to one whose flourishing race shows that it enjoys peculiar advantages.

What advantages the *Heliconidæ* possess to make them so flourishing a group, and consequently the objects of so much mimetic resemblance, it is not easy to discover. There is nothing apparent in their structure or habits which could render them safe from persecution by the numerous insectivorous animals which are constantly on the watch in the same parts of the forest which they inhabit. It is probable they are unpalatable to insect enemies. Some of them (*Lycorea, Ituna*) have exsertible glands near the anus, which are protruded when the insects are roughly handled; it is well known that similar organs in other families (*Carabidæ, Staphylinidæ*) secrete fetid liquids or gases, and serve as a protection to the species. I have noticed also that recently killed specimens of Danaoid *Heliconidæ*, when set out to dry, were always less subject than other insects to be devoured by vermin. They have all a peculiar smell*. I never saw the flocks of slow-flying *Heliconidæ* in the woods persecuted by birds or Dragon-flies, to which they would have been easy prey; nor, when at rest on leaves, did they appear to be molested by Lizards or the predacious Flies of the family *Asilidæ*, which were very often seen pouncing on Butterflies of other families. If they owe their flourishing existence to this cause, it would be intelligible why the *Leptalidæ*, whose scanty number of individuals reveals a less protected condition, should be disguised in their dress, and thus share their immunity.

This explanation, however, would not apply to the imitation of Danaoid *Heliconidæ* by other species of the same subfamily. Moreover, there are several genera of other groups (*e. g.*, *Heliconius, Papilio*) which contain mimetic species side by side with species that are the objects of mimicry by members of other families, as will be seen by reference to the Table at p. 503. There is no reason to conclude that some of these possess the peculiar means of defence of the Danaoid *Heliconidæ*, whilst their near kindred are de-

* Mr. Wallace tells me the *Euplœa* of the Eastern Archipelago have also this peculiar smell.

prived of them. It is not unreasonable to suppose that some species are taken by insectivorous animals, whilst others flying in company with them are avoided. I could not, from their excessive scarcity, ascertain on the spot that the *Leptalides* were thus picked out. I noticed, however, that other genera of their family (*Pieridæ*) were much persecuted. We have proof, in the case of Sand-Wasps, which provision their nests with insects, that a single species is very generally selected out of numbers, even of the same genus, existing in the same locality. I was quite convinced in the case of *Cerceris binodis* of South America, which destroys numbers of a *Megalostomis* (family *Clythridæ*), that the great rarity of the Beetle was owing to its serving as prey to the *Cerceris*. We cannot point out all the conditions of life of each species concerned in these mimetic analogies. All that we can say is, that some species show, by their great abundance in the adult state, that during this period, before they propagate their kind, they enjoy by some means immunity from effective persecution, and that it is therefore an advantage to others not so fortunate, and otherwise unprovided for, if they are so like as to be mistaken for them.

The process by which a mimetic analogy is brought about in nature is a problem which involves that of the origin of all species and all adaptations. What I have previously said regarding the variation of species, and the segregation of local races from variations, the change of species of *Heliconidæ* from one locality to another, and the probable vital necessity of their counterfeits which accompany them keeping to the exact imitation in each locality, has prepared the way to the explanation I have to give. In the cases of local variation of the *Heliconidæ*, there was nothing, as before remarked, very apparent in the conditions of the localities to show why one or more of the varieties should prevail in each over their kindred varieties. There was nothing to show plainly that any cause of the formation of local varieties existed, other than the direct action of physical conditions on the individuals, although this might be seen to be clearly incompetent to explain the occurrence of several varieties of the same species in one locality. We could only conclude, from the way in which the varieties occur in nature, as described in the case of *Mechanitis Polymnia*, that the local conditions favoured the increase of one or more varieties in a district at the expense of the others—the selected ones being different in different districts. What these conditions were, or have been, was not revealed by the facts. With the mimetic species *Leptalis Theonoë* the case is different. We see here a similar segregation of local forms to that of *Mechanitis Polymnia*; but we believe we know the conditions of life of the species, and find that they vary from one locality to another. The existence of the species, in each locality, is seen to depend on its form and colours, or *dress*, being assimilated to those of the *Ithomiæ* of the same district, which *Ithomiæ* are changed from place to place, such assimilation being apparently its only means of escaping extermination by insectivorous animals. Thus we have here the reason why local races are formed out of the natural variations of a species : the question then remains, how is this brought about ?

The explanation of this seems to be quite clear on the theory of natural selection, as recently expounded by Mr. Darwin in the 'Origin of Species.' The local varieties or races cannot be supposed to have been formed by the direct action of physical conditions on the individuals, because, in limited districts where these conditions are the same, the most widely contrasted varieties are found existing together, and it is inexplicable how they could have produced the nice adaptations which these diverse varieties exhibit. All the varieties figured on Pl. LV. figs. 2, 7, 9, and on Pl. LVI. figs. 1, 2, 3, 4, 6, are found at St. Paulo, within a mile of each other, in the same humid forest. Neither can these adapted races, as before remarked, have originated in one generation by *sports* or a single act of variation in each case. It is clear, therefore, that some other active principle must be here at work to draw out, as it were, steadily in certain directions the suitable variations which arise, generation after generation, until forms have resulted which, like our races of *Leptalis Theonoë*, are considerably different from their parent as well as their sister forms. This principle can be no other than natural selection, the selecting agents being insectivorous animals, which gradually destroy those sports or varieties that are not sufficiently like *Ithomiæ* to deceive them. It would seem as though our *Leptalis* naturally produced simple varieties of a nature to resemble *Ithomiæ*; it is not always so, as is proved by many of them figured in the places above quoted. There is some general resemblance, it is true; and this is not purely accidental; for it is quite natural that the parent *Leptalis* should produce offspring varying in the direction of *Ithomiæ*, being itself similar to an *Ithomia*, and having inherited the property of varying in this manner through a long line of ancestors. We cannot ascertain, in this case, whether changed physical conditions have had any effect, quantitative or qualitative, on the variability of the species after migrating to a new district. At any rate, the existing varieties of our *Leptalis* show that the variations of *Leptalis* and *Ithomia* are not quite coincident, and that the agency of natural selection is required to bring the slowly forming race of one to resemble the other. I do not forget that at each step of selection the forms of *Leptalis* must have had sufficient resemblance to an *Ithomia* to lead to their preservation, or, at least, to prevent their complete extinction: as, however, the two analogues so much resemble each other at the commencement of the process, these steps would not be numerous. In many cases of mimetic resemblance, the mimicry is not so exact as in the *Leptalides*. This would show either that the imitator has only inherited its form from remote ancestors who were actively persecuted, the persecution having ceased during the career of its immediate ancestors; or it would show that the persecutor is not keen or rigid in its selection; a moderate degree of resemblance suffices to deceive it, and therefore the process halts at that point. I leave out of consideration all resemblances which can only be accidental, or which are resemblances of affinity.

If a mimetic species varies, some of its varieties must be more and some less faithful imitations of the object mimicked. According, therefore, to the closeness of its persecution by enemies, who seek the imitator, but avoid the imitated, will be its tendency to become an exact counterfeit,—the less perfect degrees of resemblance being, generation after generation, eliminated, and only the others left to propagate their kind. The actual state of *Leptalis Theonoë* is not the same in all of its three districts. A few varieties, or *sports*, are seen at Ega (65° W. long.) and St. Paulo (69° W. long.), namely, those figured Pl. LV. figs. 4, 5, 7, 8, and 9, which have an indeterminate resemblance. On the Cuparí

(55° W. long.) the resemblance is perfect (Pl. LV. fig. 1); and this is the only form of the *Leptalis* known in the locality. The varieties figured Pl. LVI. figs. 1, 2, 3, show different degrees of resemblance to *Ithomia Chrysodonia* (fig. 3 *a*); these, therefore, exhibit the selection in process. Thus, although we are unable to watch the process of formation of a new race as it occurs in time, we can see it, as it were, at one glance, by tracing the changes a species is simultaneously undergoing in different parts of the area of its distribution.

The fact of one of the forms of *Leptalis Theonoë*, namely *L. Lysinoë*, mimicking at Ega, not an *Ithomia*, but a flourishing species of another quite distinct family (*Stalachtis Duvalii*), shows that the object of the mimetic tendencies of the species is simply disguise, and that, the simple individual differences in that locality being originally in the direction, not of an *Ithomia*, but of another object equally well answering the purpose, selection operated in the direction of that other object. This point is well illustrated by the species of a small group of Longicorn Beetles already cited, some of which mimic a piece of bark, and others insects of another family—and by hunting Spiders, many of which wear the form of insects, and many that of inanimate objects amongst which they seek their prey.

When the persecution of a variable local form of our *Leptalis* is close or long continued, the indeterminate variations naturally become extinct; nothing then remains in that locality but the one exact counterfeit, whose exactness, it must be added, is henceforward kept up to the mark by the insect pairing necessarily with its exact counterpart, or breeding *in and in*. This is the condition of *Leptalis Theonoë* (Pl. LV. fig. 1) in its district; and it is the condition of all those numerous species of different orders which now appear fixed and distinct. When (as happens at St. Paulo, where a greater abundance of individuals and species, both of *Ithomia* and *Leptalis*, exists than in the locality of the last-named) many species have been in course of formation out of the varieties of one only, occasional intercrossing may have taken place; this would retard the process of segregation of the species, and, in fact, aid in producing the state of things (varieties and half-formed species) which I have already described as there existing.

In what way our *Leptalis* originally acquired the general form and colours of *Ithomiæ* I must leave undiscussed. We may conclude (if we are to reason at all from existing facts) that, as the antecedent forms of our races of *Leptalis* which are still undergoing change were themselves similar to *Ithomiæ*, the form has been inherited through a long line of ancestors, which have been more or less subjected to similar conditions. The instance of one of our forms leaving the *Ithomiæ* to mimic a species of another family may show us how a new line of mimetic analogy and gradual modification may have been originally opened.

Such, I conceive, is the only way in which the origin of mimetic species can be explained. I believe the case offers a most beautiful proof of the truth of the theory of natural selection. It also shows that a new adaptation, or the formation of a new species, is not effected by great and sudden change, but by numerous small steps of natural variation and selection. Some of the mutual resemblances of the *Heliconidæ* already mentioned seem not to be due to the adaptation of the one to the other, but rather, as they have a real affinity, the genera to which they belong being throughout very similar in colours and markings, and all equally flourishing, to the similar adaptation of all to the same local, probably inorganic, conditions. The selecting agent, which acts in each locality by destroying the variations unsuitable to the locality, would not in these cases be the same as in *Leptalis* ; it may act, for anything we know, on the larvæ; in other respects, however, the same law of nature appears, namely, the selection of one or more distinct varieties by the elimination of intermediate gradations *. The conditions of life of these creatures are different in each locality where one or more separate local forms prevail, and those conditions are the selecting agents. With regard to the *Leptalides*, I believe we may be said to know these conditions. To exist at all in a given locality, our *Leptalis Theonoë* must wear a certain dress, and those of its varieties which do not come up to the mark are rigidly sacrificed. Our three sets of *Leptalides* may be compared to a variable flowering plant in the hands of a number of floriculturists, whose aims are different, each requiring a different colour of flower, and attaining his end by " roguing " or destroying all variations which depart from the standard.

It may be remarked that a mimetic species need not always be a rare one, although this is very generally the case; it may be highly prolific, or its persecution may be intermitted when the disguise is complete.

The operation of selecting agents, gradually and steadily bringing about the deceptive resemblance of a species to some other definite object, produces the impression of there being some innate principle in species which causes an advance of organization in a special direction. It seems as though the proper variation always arose in the species, and the mimicry were a predestined goal. This suggested the only other explanations that I have heard of, namely, that there may be an innate tendency in the organization to become modified in a given direction—or that the parent insect, being powerfully affected by the desire of concealment from the enemies of its race, may transmit peculiarities to its offspring that help it to become modified, and thus, in the course of many generations, the species becomes gradually assimilated to other forms or objects. On examination, however, these explanations are found to be untenable, and the appearances which suggest them illusory. Those who earnestly desire a rational explanation, must, I think, arrive at the conclusion that these apparently miraculous, but always

---

* Some of the close resemblances amongst the *Heliconidæ* themselves seem to be kept up by their varying in a precisely similar way. There is a very singular instance in three species of three different genera, *Melinæa*, *Mechanitis* (*Mothone*), and *Heliconius*, which are all, in East Peru, orange and black in colour, and in New Granada orange, black, and yellow. This seems to be a case of coincident, simple variation ; for if three forms are quite alike in colours, it is conceivable that they may vary alike when placed under new conditions by migration. Our *Leptalides* have been shown not to vary precisely like their models ; and therefore the case just quoted does not throw any difficulty in the way of the explanation I have given ; but it is a very extraordinary one.

I have not thought it necessary to mention cases of close resemblances in insects which are only accidental, or which are explicable by the blood-relationship or affinity existing between the species which display them. Some orders of insects contain an almost infinite variety of forms, and it will not be wonderful, therefore, if species here and there be found to resemble each other, although inhabiting opposite parts of the earth, and belonging to widely different families. Such analogies are accidental, and can have nothing at all to do with the evidently intentional system of resemblances, carried on from place to place, which I have discussed. Some cosmopolitan families present very similar species in all parts of the earth ; it can scarcely be necessary to say that close resemblances between New and Old World forms in these cases are resemblances of affinity, and not mimetic analogies.

beautiful and wonderful, mimetic resemblances, and therefore probably every other kind of adaptation in beings, are brought about by agencies similar to those we have here discussed.

HELICONIDÆ.

I have mentioned, in a note at p. 496, that I should follow the example of Dr. Felder in separating the Danaoid *Heliconidæ* from the remainder of the family, and combining them with the *Danaïdæ*. I shall, however, consider these groups as sub-families, instead of families. The modifications in the classification thus introduced will be seen by the following synopsis of the section Rhopalocera.

Order LEPIDOPTERA.

Section RHOPALOCERA.

Family 1. HESPERIDÆ. Six perfect legs in ♂ ♀; hind tibiæ, with few exceptions, having two pair of spurs. *Larva inhabiting a rolled-up leaf; pupa secured by many threads, or enclosed in a slight cocoon.* (These characters approximate the family to the Moths, or Heterocera).

Family 2. PAPILIONIDÆ. Six perfect legs in ♂ ♀. Wing-cells (at least, of the hind wings) closed by perfect tubular nervules. Hind tibiæ with one pair of spurs. Pupa secured by the tail and a girdle across the middle in an upright position. (The *Papiliones* have a leaf-like appendage to the fore tibiæ, as pointed out recently by Dr. Adolf Speyer; the character approximates the family to the Hesperidæ and Moths.)

Family 3. LYCÆNIDÆ. Six perfect legs in ♀; four in ♂; the fore tarsi wanting the tarsal claws, but densely spined beneath. Wing-cells (except in *Eumæus*) not closed by perfect nervules. Pupa secured by the tail and a girdle across the middle.

Family 4. ERYCINIDÆ. Six perfect legs in ♀; four in ♂; the fore tarsi consisting only of one or two joints, and spineless.

    Subfam. 1. ERYCININÆ. Pupa recumbent, flattened beneath, secured by the tail and a girdle across the middle.

    Subfam. 2. STALACHTINÆ. Pupa not flattened beneath, secured rigidly by the tail in an inclined position, without girdle.

    Subfam. 3. LIBYTHÆINÆ. Pupa suspended freely by the tail.

Family 5. NYMPHALIDÆ. Fore legs imperfect in both sexes; in the ♀ wanting the tarsal claws; in the ♂ the fore tarsi aborted, consisting of one or two joints. Pupa suspended freely by the tail.

    a. Lower disco-cellular nervule, especially of the hind wing, more or less atrophied.

    Subfam. 1. NYMPHALINÆ (*Nymphalidæ, Ageronidæ, Eurytelidæ,* and *Morphidæ,* part, of authors).

    b. Lower disco-cellular nervule perfect.

    Subfam. 2. HELICONINÆ.

    Subfam. 3. ACRÆINÆ.

    Subfam. 4. BRASSOLINÆ.

    Subfam. 5. SATYRINÆ.

    Subfam. 6. DANAÏNÆ.

The *Danaoid Heliconidæ,* as before mentioned, are considered to stand at the head of

564   MR. H. W. BATES ON THE HELICONIDE LEPIDOPTERA

8. EUEIDES ALIPHERA, Godart.

Papilio Aliphera, Godt. Encyclopédie Méthodique, t. ix. p. 246.

A widely distributed species, being found over nearly the whole of tropical America. It seems to be constant throughout. I met with it at St. Paulo.

Subfamily ACRÆINÆ.

Genus ACRÆA, Fabricius.

1. ACRÆA THALIA, Linnæus.

Papilio Thalia, Linn. Syst. Nat. ii. 757, n. 57.

———— ————, Cramer, Pap. Exot. t. 246. f. A.

I took (at Pará) only one individual of this sole species of *Acræa* found in the Amazon region.

EXPLANATION OF THE PLATES.

The Plates are designed to show a few examples out of a great number of mimetic analogies between various Lepidopterous insects and the Heliconidæ. The insects figured belong to four families, very widely dissimilar in structure and metamorphosis: *Leptalis* (fam. Pieridæ), *Dioptis* (Bombycidæ, Moths), *Stalachtis* (fam. Erycinidæ), *Ithomia, Mechanitis, Methona* (fam. Heliconidæ). The figures also illustrate the process of the origination of a mimetic species through variation and natural selection. Reasons have been given (p. 504 *et seq.*) for considering the species of *Leptalis* and *Dioptis,* amongst others, as having been adapted by this process to the species of *Stalachtis* and the genera of Heliconidæ—the colours being brought into exact resemblance by the *successive* preservation of such naturally arising variations as tended more and more to resemble. One species only, *Leptalis Theonoë,* furnishes a good example of the process, it being one which, by a rare chance, shows in its existing varieties the process in different stages of completion. The figures indicated by a simple numeral represent the *adapted* forms; those marked *a,* the species to which they are adapted.

PLATE LV.

Fig. 1*. *Leptalis Theonoë* (Hewitson).—Inhabits Cuparí, 55° W. long.

Fig. 1 *a. Ithomia Flora* (Cramer).—Inhabits Cuparí, 55° W. long.; also the mouth of the Amazons and Surinam.

> Neither of these forms is found further westward on the Upper Amazons, where the following allied species and varieties alone occur.

Fig. 2. *Leptalis Theonoë,* var. *Melanoë.*—St. Paulo, Upper Amazons, 69° W. long.

Fig. 2 *a. Ithomia Onega* (Hewitson).—Upper Amazons, from 58° to 70° W. long.

---

* The specimen of *L. Theonoë* in the British Museum collection, which served Mr. Hewitson for his figure of the species, is very much larger than the one figured in this Plate. But the *Leptalides* are apt to vary very much in size.

Fig. 3. *Leptalis Theonoë*, var. *Lysinoë* (Hewitson. Described by this author as a distinct species. The white fore part of the hind wing is merely a sexual character, and is hidden by the fore wing in the natural position of the wings).—Ega, Upper Amazons, 65° W. long.

Fig. 3 a. *Stalachtis Phædusa*, var. *Duvalii* (Perty).—Ega, Upper Amazons, 65° W. long.

The resemblance between these two is very great, when flying in their native woods. The *Leptalis* is quite unlike any *Ithomia* found in the whole region, and is supposed to have been adapted to the *Stalachtis*, because its original variations were in the direction of *Stalachtis*, and this disguise equally well served the purpose of preservation with that of an *Ithomia*.

Fig. 4. *Leptalis Theonoë*, var.—Ega. Described by Hewitson as a variety of *L. Lysinoë*, Exot. Butt. *Leptalis*, fig. 13.

Fig. 5. *Leptalis Theonoë*, var.—Ega.

Fig. 6. *Leptalis Theonoë*, var.—Ega. This has considerable resemblance to *Ithomia Illinissa*, fig. 6 a.

Fig. 7. *Leptalis Theonoë*, var.—St. Paulo.

Fig. 8. *Leptalis Theonoë*, var.—Ega.

Fig. 9. *Leptalis Theonoë*, var.—St. Paulo.

These six varieties occurred only in single or very few examples : they imitate (with the exception of fig. 6) no other insect, and are supposed to be either simple variations (*sports*) or remnants of the steps of modification which have led to the various complete adaptations in the two districts where they are found. In any case (since it is impossible to suppose that each is an unmodified descendant of a parent originally created, in the usual sense of the term) they may be taken as affording proof of the variability of the species in several divergent directions, tending towards resemblance to *Ithomiæ*.

Fig. 6 a. *Ithomia Illinissa* (Hewits.).—Ega.

Fig. 10. *Dioptis Æliana* (n. sp. or var.?), deceptively like, when flying, *Ithomia Ælia*, a small species near akin to *I. Illinissa*, and found in company with it at Ega.

Fig. 11. *Dioptis Ilerdina* (n. sp. or var.?). Closely resembles, when flying, *Ithomia Ilerdina* (Pl. LVI. fig. 4 a), and found in company with it at St. Paulo.

Fig. 12. *Dioptis Onega* (n. sp. or var.?). Closely resembles, when flying, *Ithomia Onega* (Pl. LV. fig. 2 a), and flies in company with it at St. Paulo.

Fig. 13. *Dioptis Cyma* (Doubleday). Closely resembles *Ithomia Cymo*, a species similar to *I. Flora* (fig. 1 a of the present Plate), and flies in company with it at Pará.

PLATE LVI.

Fig. 1. *Leptalis Theonoë*, var. *Erythroë*.—St. Paulo, 69° W. long.

Fig. 2. *Leptalis Theonoë*, var. *Erythroë*.—St. Paulo.

Fig. 3. *Leptalis Theonoë*, var. *Erythroë*.—St. Paulo.

Fig. 3 a. *Ithomia Orolina*, var. *Chrysodonia*.—St. Paulo.

The linking variations between *L. Erythroë* and *Theonoë* can be traced through the varieties 8, 5, and 6 of the preceding Plate. The substitution of red for white in the fore wings is seen to be a simple variation. Some traces of the narrowing of the red margin of the hind wing are also seen. The imitation of *Ithomia* is not nearly so close as it is in the cases of figs. 1 and 2 of the preceding and fig. 4 of the present Plate, but there is a considerable approximation, giving the appearance of a striving after a correct imitation. The selection of individuals having the most faithful likeness is here either not rigid or we see the formation of an exact mimetic analogue in process.

Fig. 4. *Leptalis Theonoë*, var. *Leuconoë*.—St. Paulo.

Fig. 4 a. *Ithomia Ilerdina* (Hewitson).—St. Paulo.

This *Leptalis* appears at first sight an absolutely distinct species, but it is plainly a modification whose adaptation is complete. As to the fore wings, the vacillating nature of the colours is seen in figs. 4, 6, and 8 of Plate LV. in the clearest manner. The hind wings appear very peculiar, on account of the milky colour; but this is shown to arise by variation in *Ithomiæ*, which exhibit all the grades of variation from dusky to white nervures and ground of the hind wing.

Fig. 5. *Leptalis Nehemia* (of authors).—New Granada and S. Brazil.

Figured to show the normal form of the family (*Pieridæ*, called in England " Garden White " Butterflies) to which *Leptalis* belongs. The contrast in form and colours points to the conclusion that all the other forms of *Leptalis* are perverted from the usual facies of the family by long-continued process of adaptation to the Heliconidæ, in whose company (each species with its Heliconian model) they are solely found.

Fig. 6. *Leptalis Theonoë*, var. *Argochloë*.—St. Paulo.

Fig. 6 a. *Ithomia Virginia* (Hewits.).—St. Paulo.

The links of modification may be traced also with respect to this apparently distinct *Leptalis*. The shape of the spot of the fore wing is seen to be very variable in figs. 1, 2, 3 of this Plate, and in 9 and 4 of Plate LV.

Fig. 7. *Leptalis Amphione*, var. *Egaëna*.—Ega.

Fig. 7 a. *Mechanitis Polymnia*, var. *Egaënsis*.—Ega.

Fig. 8. *Leptalis Orise* (Boisduval).—Cuparí, 55° W. long.; also Cayenne.

Fig. 8 a. *Methona Psidii* (Linnæus).—Cuparí; also Cayenne.

ERRATUM.

At p. 515, after the characters of Family 2. PAPILIONIDÆ, insert
Subfam. 1. PAPILIONINÆ.
Subfam. 2. PIERINÆ.

Trans. Linn. Soc Vol. XXIII Tab.

Trans. Linn. Soc. Vol. XXIII Ia

The Naturalist in Nicaragua
Thomas Belt

room, found it consisted only of coffee and two small cakes called "roskears" for each of us; and we were told they had nothing else to offer us. So, munching our dry roskears, we mumbled over them as long as we could, and did not waste a crumb, wondering how our host got so fat on such fare. We were as hungry when we finished as when we began, and soon laid down on our hard couches to forget our hunger in sleep.

We started off early the next morning, as we were within a few leagues of the town of Matagalpa, and knew when we got there we should obtain plenty of provisions. About a league before arriving at Matagalpa there is a high range, with perpendicular cliffs near the summit. Rito told us that near the base of these cliffs there was a carving of a bull, and that the place was enchanted. I had heard in other parts stories of bulls being engraved or painted on rocks, but was very doubtful about their being true, as, up to the advent of the Spaniards, the Indians of Central America had never seen any cattle; and since the conquest they appear to have entirely given up their ancient practice of carving on stone, whilst the Spaniards and half-breeds have not learnt the art; so that I have never seen a single carving in the central departments that could be ascribed to a later period than the Spanish conquest.

Tired and hungry though we were, I was determined to put this story to the test; so Velasquez and I climbed up to the cliffs, and searched all round them, but could find no carving. At one place there was a large black stain on the cliff, produced by the trickling down of water from above, and I afterwards learnt that this stain at a distance somewhat resembled a bull, and a little imagination completed the likeness. The lady of the house where we stayed at Matagalpa assured us she had seen it, and that everything appertaining to a bull was there. This she insisted on with a minuteness of detail rather embarrassing to a fastidious auditor.

Clambering down the rocks, we reached our horse and mule, and started off again, passing over dry weedy hills. One low tree, very characteristic of the dry savannahs, I have only incidentally mentioned before.

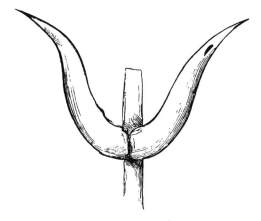

THE BULL S-HORN THORN.

It is a species of acacia, belonging to the section *Gummiferæ*, with bi-pinnate leaves, growing to a height of fifteen or twenty feet. The branches and trunk are covered with strong curved spines, set in pairs, from which it receives the name of the bull's-horn thorn, they having a very strong resemblance to the horns of that quadruped. These thorns are hollow, and are tenanted by ants, that make a small hole for their entrance and exit near one end of the thorn, and also

burrow through the partition that separates the two
horns ; so that the one entrance serves for both.   Here
they rear their young, and in the wet season every one
of the thorns is tenanted ; and hundreds of ants are to
be seen running about, especially over the young leaves.
If one of these be touched, or a branch shaken, the little
ants (*Pseudomyrma bicolor*, Guer.) swarm out from the
hollow thorns, and attack the aggressor with jaws and
sting.   They sting severely, raising a little white lump
that does not disappear in less than twenty-four hours.

These ants form a most efficient standing army for
the plant, which prevents not only the mammalia from
browsing on the leaves, but delivers it from the attacks
of a much more dangerous enemy—the leaf-cutting
ants.   For these services the ants are not only securely
housed by the plant, but are provided with a bountiful
supply of food, and to secure their attendance at the
right time and place, the food is so arranged and distributed as to effect that object with wonderful perfection.   The leaves are bi-pinnate.   At the base of each
pair of leaflets, on the mid-rib, is a crater-formed gland,
which, when the leaves are young, secretes a honey-
like liquid.   Of this the ants are very fond ; and they
are constantly running about from one gland to another
to sip up the honey as it is secreted.   But this is not
all ; there is a still more wonderful provision of more
solid food.   At the end of each of the small divisions
of the compound leaflet there is, when the leaf first
unfolds, a little yellow fruit-like body united by a point
at its base to the end of the pinnule.   Examined
through a microscope, this little appendage looks like
a golden pear.   When the leaf first unfolds, the little

pears are not quite ripe, and the ants are continually employed going from one to another, examining them. When an ant finds one sufficiently advanced, it bites the small point of attachment; then, bending down the fruit-like body, it breaks it off and bears it away in triumph to the nest. All the fruit-like bodies do not ripen at once, but successively, so that the ants are kept about the young leaf for some time after it unfolds. Thus the young leaf is always guarded by the ants; and no caterpillar or larger animal could attempt to injure them without being attacked by the little warriors. The fruit-like bodies are about one-twelfth of an inch long, and are about one-third of the size of the ants; so that an ant carrying one away is as heavily laden as a man bearing a large bunch of plantains. I think these facts show that the ants are really kept by the acacia as a standing army, to protect its leaves from the attacks of herbivorous mammals and insects.

The bull's-horn thorn does not grow at the mines in the forest, nor are the small ants attending on them found there. They seem specially adapted for the tree, and I have seen them nowhere else. Besides the *Pseudomyrma*, I found another ant that lives on these acacias; it is a small black species of *Crematogaster*, whose habits appear to be rather different from those of *Pseudomyrma*. It makes the holes of entrance to the thorns near the centre of one of each pair, and not near the end, like the *Pseudomyrma;* and it is not so active as that species. It is also rather scarce; but when it does occur, it occupies the whole tree, to the exclusion of the other. The glands on the acacia are also frequented by a small species of wasp (*Polybia occidentalis*). I sowed the seeds of the acacia in my garden, and reared some young plants. Ants of many kinds were numerous; but none of them took to the thorns for shelter, nor the glands and fruit-like bodies for food; for, as I have already mentioned, the species that attend on the thorns are not found in the forest. The leaf-cutting ants attacked the young plants, and defoliated them, but I have never seen any of the trees out on the savannahs that are guarded by the *Pseudo-myrma* touched by them, and have no doubt the acacia is protected from them by its little warriors. The thorns, when they are first developed, are soft, and filled with a sweetish, pulpy substance; so that the ant, when it makes an entrance into them, finds its new house full of food. It hollows this out, leaving only the hardened shell of the thorn. Strange to say, this treatment seems to favour the development of the thorn, as it increases in size, bulging out towards the base; whilst in my plants that were not touched by the ants, the thorns turned yellow and dried up into dead but persistent prickles. I am not sure, however, that this may not have been due to the habitat of the plant not suiting it.

These ants seem at first sight to lead the happiest of existences. Protected by their stings, they fear no foe. Habitations full of food are provided for them to commence housekeeping with, and cups of nectar and luscious fruits await them every day. But there is a reverse to the picture. In the dry season on the plains, the acacias cease to grow. No young leaves are produced, and the old glands do not secrete honey. Then want and hunger overtake the ants that have revelled in luxury all the wet season ; many of the thorns are depopulated, and only a few ants live through the season of scarcity. As soon, however, as the first rains set in, the trees throw out numerous vigorous shoots, and the ants multiply again with astonishing rapidity.

Both in Brazil and Nicaragua I paid much attention to the relation between the presence of honey-secreting glands on plants, and the protection the latter secured by the attendance of ants attracted by the honey. I found many plants so protected ; the glands being specially developed on the young leaves, and on the sepals of the flowers. Besides the bull's-horn acacias, I, however, only met with two other genera of plants that furnished the ants with houses, namely the *Cecropiæ* and some of the *Melastomæ*. I have no doubt that there are many others. The stem of the Cecropia, or trumpet-tree, is hollow, and divided into cells by partitions that extend across the interior of the hollow trunk. The ants gain access by making a hole from the outside, and then burrow through the partitions, thus getting the run of the whole stem. They do not obtain their food directly from the tree, but keep brown scale-insects (*Coccidæ*) in the cells, which suck the juices from the tree, and secrete a honey-like fluid that exudes from a pore on the back, and is lapped up by the ants. In one cell eggs will be found, in another grubs, and in a third pupæ, all lying loosely. In another cell, by itself, a queen ant will be found, surrounded by walls made of a brown waxy-looking substance, along with about a dozen *Coccidæ* to supply her with food. I suppose the eggs are removed as soon as laid,

for I never found any along with the queen-ant. If
the tree be shaken, the ants rush out in myriads, and
search about for the molester. This case is not like
the last one, where the tree has provided food and
shelter for the ants, but rather one where the ant has
taken possession of the tree, and brought with it the
Coccidæ; but I believe that its presence must be beneficial. I have cut into some dozens of the Cecropia trees,

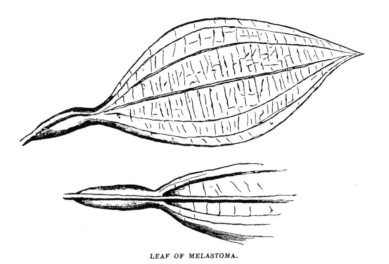

LEAF OF MELASTOMA.

and never could find one that was not tenanted by ants.
I noticed three different species, all, as far as I know,
confined to the *Cecropiæ*, and all farming scale-insects.
As in the bull's-horn thorn, there is never more than
one species of ant on the same tree.

In some species of *Melastomæ* there is a direct provision of houses for the ants. In each leaf, at the base
of the laminæ, the petiole, or stalk, is furnished with a

couple of pouches, divided from each other by the mid-rib, as shown in the figure. Into each of these pouches there is an entrance from the lower side of the leaf. I noticed them first in Northern Brazil, in the province of Maranham; and afterwards at Pará. Every pouch was occupied by a nest of small black ants, and if the leaf was shaken ever so little, they would rush out and scour all over it in search of the aggressor. I must have tested some hundreds of leaves, and never shook one without the ants coming out, excepting on one sickly-looking plant at Pará. In many of the pouches I noticed the eggs and young ants, and in some I saw a few dark-coloured *Coccidæ* or aphides; but my attention had not been at that time directed to the latter as supplying the ants with food, and I did not examine a sufficient number of pouches to determine whether they were constant occupants of the nests or not. My subsequent experience with the Cecropia trees would lead me to expect that they were. If so, we have an instance of two insects and a plant living together, and all benefiting by the companionship. The leaves of the plant are guarded by the ants, the ants are provided with houses by the plant, and food by the *Coccidæ* or aphides, and the latter are effectually protected by the ants in their common habitation.

Amongst the numerous plants that do not provide houses, but attract ants to their leaves and flower-buds by means of glands secreting a honey-like liquid, are many epiphytal orchids, and I think all the species of *Passiflora*. I had the common red passion-flower growing over the front of my verandah, where it was continually under my notice. It had honey-secreting glands on its young leaves and on the sepals of the flower-buds. For two years I noticed that the glands were constantly attended by a small ant (*Pheidole*), and, night and day, every young leaf and every flower-bud had a few on them. They did not sting, but attacked and bit my finger when I touched the plant. I have no doubt that the primary object of these honey-glands is to attract the ants, and keep them about the most tender and vulnerable parts of the plant, to prevent them being injured; and I further believe that one of the principal enemies that they serve to guard against in tropical America is the leaf-cutting ant, as I have observed that the latter are very much afraid of the small black ants.

On the third year after I had noticed the attendance of the ants on my passion-flower, I found that the glands were not so well looked after as before, and soon discovered that a number of scale-insects had established themselves on the stems, and that the ants had in a great measure transferred their attentions to them. An ant would stand over a scale-insect and stroke it alternately on each side with its antennæ, whereupon every now and then a clear drop of honey would exude from a pore on the back of the latter and be imbibed by the ant. Here it was clear that the scale-insect was competing successfully with the leaves and sepals for the attendance and protection of the ants, and was successful either through the fluid it furnished being more attractive or more abundant.* I have, from these facts, been led to the conclusion that the use of honey-secreting glands in plants is to attract insects that will protect

---

* I have since observed ants attending scale-insects on a large plant of *Passiflora macrocarpa* in the palm-house at Kew.

the flower-buds and leaves from being injured by herbivorous insects and mammals, but I do not mean to infer that this is the use of all glands, for many of the small appendicular bodies, called "glands" by botanists, do not secrete honey. The common dog-rose of England is furnished with glands on the stipules, and in other species they are more numerous, until in the wild *Rosa villosa* of the northern counties the leaves are thickly edged, and the fruit and sepals covered with stalked glands. I have only observed the wild roses in the north of England, and there I have never seen insects attending the glands. These glands, however, do not secrete honey, but a dark, resinous, sticky liquid, that probably is useful by being distasteful to both insects and mammals.

If the facts I have described are sufficient to show that some plants are benefited by supplying ants with honey from glands on their leaves and flower-buds, I shall not have much difficulty in proving that many plant-lice, scale-insects, and leaf-hoppers, that also attract ants by furnishing them with honey-like food, are similarly benefited. The aphides are the principal ant-cows of Europe. In the tropics their place is taken in a great measure by species of *Coccidæ* and genera of *Homoptera*, such as *Membracis* and its allies. My pine-apples were greatly subject to the attacks of a small, soft-bodied, brown coccus, that was always guarded by a little, black, stinging ant (*Solenopsis*). This ant took great care of the scale-insects, and attacked savagely any one interfering with them, as I often found to my cost, when trying to clear my pines, by being stung severely by them. Not content with watching over their cattle, the ants brought up grains of damp earth, and built domed galleries over them, in which, under the vigilant guard of their savage little attendants, the scale-insects must, I think, have been secure from the attacks of all enemies.

Many of the leaf-hoppers—species, I think, of *Membracis*—were attended by ants. These leaf-hoppers live in little clusters on shoots of plants and beneath leaves, in which are hoppers in every stage of development —eggs, larvæ, and adults. I believe it is only the soft-bodied larvæ that exude honey. It would take a volume to describe the various species, and I shall confine my remarks to one whose habits I was able to observe with some minuteness. The papaw trees growing in my garden were infested by a small brown species of *Membracis*—one of the leaf-hoppers—that laid its eggs in a cottony-like nest by the side of the ribs on the under part of the leaves. The hopper would stand covering the nest until the young were hatched. These were little soft-bodied dark-coloured insects, looking like aphides, but more robust, and with the hind segments turned up. From the end of these the little larvæ exuded drops of honey, and were assiduously attended by small ants belonging to two species of the genus *Pheidole,* one of them being the same as I have already described as attending the glands on the passion-flower. One tree would be attended by one species, another by the other ; and I never saw the two species on the same tree. A third ant, however—a species of *Hypoclinea—* which I have mentioned before as a cowardly species, whose nests were despoiled by the *Ecitons,* frequented all the trees, and whenever it found any young hoppers unattended, it would relieve them of their honey, but would scamper away on the approach of any of the *Pheidole*. The latter do not sting, but they attack and bite the hand if the young hoppers are interfered with. These leaf-hoppers are, when young, so soft-bodied and sluggish in their movements, and there are so many enemies ready to prey upon them, that I imagine that in the tropics many species would be exterminated if it were not for the protection of the ants.

Similarly as, on the savannahs, I had observed a wasp attending the honey-glands of the bull's-horn acacia along with the ants, so at Santo Domingo another wasp, belonging to quite a different genus (*Nectarina*), attended some of the clusters of frog-hoppers, and for the possession of others a constant skirmishing was going on. The wasp stroked the young hoppers, and sipped up the honey when it was exuded, just like the ants. When an ant came up to a cluster of leaf-hoppers attended by a wasp, the latter would not attempt to grapple with its rival on the leaf, but would fly off and hover over the ant; then when its little foe was well exposed, it would dart at it and strike it to the ground. The action was so quick that I could not determine whether it struck with its fore-feet or its jaws, but I think it was with the feet. I often saw a wasp trying to clear a leaf from ants that were already in full possession of a cluster of leaf-hoppers. It would sometimes have to strike three or four times at an ant before it made it quit its hold and fall. At other times one ant after the other would be struck off with great celerity and ease, and I fancied that some wasps were much cleverer than others. In those cases where it succeeded in clearing the leaf, it was never left long in peace.   Fresh relays of ants were continually arriving, and generally tired the wasp out. It would never wait for an ant to get near it, doubtless knowing well that if its little rival once fastened on its leg, it would be a difficult matter to get rid of it again.   If a wasp first obtained possession, it was able to keep it; for the first ants that came up were only pioneers, and by knocking these off it prevented them from returning and scenting the trail to communicate the intelligence to others.

Before leaving this subject, I may remark that just as in plants some glands secrete honey that attracts insects, others a resinous liquid that repels them, so the secretions of different genera of the homopterous division of the Hemiptera are curiously modified for strikingly different useful purposes.   We have seen that by many species of plant-lice, scale-insects, and leaf-hoppers, a honey-like fluid is secreted that attracts ants to attend upon them. Other species of aphides (*Eriosoma*) that have no honey-tubes, and many of the Coccidæ, secrete a white, flocculent, waxy cotton, under which they lie concealed.   In many of the Homoptera, this secretion only amounts to a white powder covering the body, as in some of the Fulgoridæ. In others it is more abundant, and it reaches its extreme limit in a species of *Phenax* that I found at Santo Domingo.   The insect is about an inch in length, but the waxy secretion forms a long thick tail of cotton-like fibres, two inches in length, that gives the insect a most curious appearance when flying.   This flocculent mass is so loosely connected with the body that it is difficult to catch the insect without breaking the greater part of it off.   Mr. Bates has suggested that the large brittle wings of the metallic Morphos may often save them from being caught by birds, who are likely to seize some portion of the wide expanse of wing, and this, breaking off, frees the butterfly. Probably the long cumbersome tail of the *Phenax* has a similar use. When flying, it is the only portion of the insect seen ; and birds trying to capture it on the wing are likely to get only a mouthful of the flocculent wax. The large Homoptera are much preyed upon by birds. In April, when the Cicadæ are piping their shrill cry from morning until night, individuals are often seen whose bulky bodies have been bitten off from the thorax by some bird. The large and graceful swallow-tailed kite at that time feeds on nothing else. I have seen these kites sweeping round in circles over the tree-tops, and every now and then catching insects off the leaves, and on shooting them I have found their crops filled with Cicadæ.

The frog-hoppers, besides exuding honey in some genera and wax in others, in a third division emit, when in the larval state, a great quantity of froth, in which they lie concealed, as in the common " cuckoo-spit " of our meadows.

confusum Duval, as affected by atmospheric moisture. Ecol. Monogr. 2: 261–304.

Landahl, H. D. 1955. A mathematical model for the temporal pattern of a population structure, with particular reference to the flour beetle. Bull. Math. Biophysics 17: 63–77.

Lloyd, M. 1957. Productivity, cannibalism, and population size in two laboratory strains of *Tribolium castaneum*. Ph.D. dissertation, Univ. of Chicago.

———. 1961. The artificial production of 'pink' flour. Tribolium Info. Bull. 4: 22–24.

———. 1965. Laboratory studies with confined cannibalistic populations of flour beetles (*Tribolium castaneum*) in a cold-dry environment. I. Data for 24 unmanipulated populations. Tribolium Info. Bull. 8: 89–123.

——— & H. S. Dybas. 1966. The periodical cicada problem. I. Population ecology. Evolution 20: 133–149.

——— & T. Park. 1962. Mortality resulting from interactions between adult flour beetles in laboratory cultures. Physiol. Zool. 35: 330–347.

Mann, H. B. & D. R. Whitney. 1947. On a test of whether one or two random variables is stochastically larger than the other. Ann. Math. Stat. 18: 50–60.

Mertz, D. B. 1965. Age-distribution and abundance in populations of genetic strain cIV-a of the flour beetle, *Tribolium castaneum*. Ph.D. dissertation, Univ. of Chicago.

———, T. Park & W. J. Youden. 1965. Mortality patterns in eight strains of flour beetles. Biometrics 21: 99–114.

Park, T. 1934. Observations on the general biology of the flour beetle, *Tribolium confusum*. Quart. Rev. Biol. 9: 36–54.

———. 1945. Life tables for the black flour beetle, *Tribolium madens* Charp. Amer. Nat. 79: 436–444.

———. 1948. Experimental studies of interspecies competition. I. Competition between populations of the flour beetles, *Tribolium confusum* Duval and *Tribolium castaneum* Herbst. Ecol. Monogr. 18: 265–308.

———. 1954. Experimental studies of interspecies competition. II. Temperature, humidity, and competition in two species of *Tribolium*. Physiol. Zool. 27: 177–238.

——— & M. B. Frank. 1948. The fecundity and development of the flour beetles, *Tribolium confusum* and *Tribolium castaneum*, at three constant temperatures. Ecology 29: 368–374.

——— & ———. 1950. The population history of *Tribolium* free of sporozoan infection. J. Anim. Ecol. 19: 95–105.

———, E. V. Gregg & C. Z. Lutherman. 1941. Studies in population physiology. X. Interspecies competition in populations of granary beetles. Physiol. Zool. 14: 395–430.

———, P. H. Leslie & D. B. Mertz. 1964. Genetic strains and competition in populations of *Tribolium*. Physiol. Zool. 37: 97–162.

———, D. B. Mertz, W. Godzinski & T. Prus. 1965. Cannibalistic predation in populations of flour beetles. Physiol. Zool. 38: 289–321.

Pearl, R., T. Park & J. R. Miner. 1941. Experimental studies on the duration of life. XVI. Life tables for the flour beetle *Tribolium confusum* Duval. Amer. Nat. 75: 5–19.

Rich, E. R. 1956. Egg cannibalism and fecundity in *Tribolium*. Ecology 37: 109–120.

Ricker, W. E. 1954. Stock and recruitment. J. Fish. Res. Bd. Canada 11: 559–623.

Sonleitner, F. J. 1961. Factors affecting egg cannibalism and fecundity in populations of adult *Tribolium castaneum* Herbst. Physiol. Zool. 34: 233–255.

Stanley, J. 1932. A mathematical theory of the growth populations of the flour beetle, *Tribolium confusum* Duv. Canad. J. Res. 6: 632–671.

Stonehouse, B. 1962. Ascension Island and the British Ornithologists' Union Centenary Expedition 1957–59. Ibis 103b: 107–123.

Strawbridge, D. W. 1953. Population dynamics of the flour beetle, *Tribolium castaneum* Herbst. Ph.D. dissertation, Univ. of Chicago.

Watt, K. E. F. 1955. Studies on population productivity. I. Three approaches to the optimum yield problem in populations of *Tribolium confusum*. Ecol. Monogr. 25: 269–290.

Welch, B. L. 1949. Further note on Mrs. Aspin's tables and on certain approximations to the tabled function. Biometrika 36: 293–296.

ON THE POLLINATION ECOLOGY OF *FICUS SYCOMORUS* IN EAST AFRICA

J. GALIL AND D. EISIKOWITCH

Department of Botany, Tel-Aviv University, Israel

(Accepted for publication April 26, 1967)

Abstract. Pollination and seed setting in *Ficus sycomorus* have been investigated in East Africa. *Ficus sycomorus* is monoecious, each fig bearing both male and female flowers. Inside the figs 6 sycophilous wasps develop: *Ceratosolen arabicus, Ceratosolen galili* and *Sycophaga sycomori* (primary sycophiles), and *Apocrypta* sp., *Eukoebelea* sp. and *Sycoryctes* sp. (secondary sycophiles). The structure and behavior of these wasps and their bearing on pollination and seed production are studied.

Ceratosolen arabicus is the legitimate pollinator of *Ficus sycomorus*. It oviposits chiefly into short-styled female flowers, thus ensuring seed setting in the long-styled ones. It is a mutualistic symbiont of the fig. *Sycophaga sycomori* oviposits into both short- and long-styled flowers, and does not cause seed setting. It is a competitor of *Ceratosolen*, but a parasite of the fig. *Eukoebelea, Apocrypta* and *Sycoryctes* are inquilines, making use of galls induced by the activity of the primary sycophiles. They do not interfere with seed production in pollinated flowers not occupied by *Ceratosolen* or *Sycophaga*.

380

J. GALIL AND D. EISIKOWITCH Ecology, Vol. 49, No. 2

INTRODUCTION

Ficus sycomorus L.—the sycomore tree belongs to the section *Sycomorus* of the genus *Ficus*. The section is chiefly African, and the natural distribution area of *Ficus sycomorus* extends from South Africa in the south up to Sudan and Ethiopia in the north. Yemen, in the southwestern corner of the Arabic peninsula, is included as well.

In ancient times, perhaps with the help of man, *Ficus sycomorus* migrated to the north, and is still cultivated in various countries along the eastern and southern shores of the Mediterranean. It played a very important role in the economic and cultural life of the ancient Egyptians, and afterwards in that of the Jews, in Biblical times, as a first-class timber, fruit and shade tree.

From ancient times (Theophrastus 372–287 bc) it has been known that *Ficus sycomorus* does not produce viable seeds in Egypt, and that the peasants propagate it by cuttings or stakes (Brown and Walsingham 1917). Since the legitimate pollinators are absent from the Mediterranean countries the pollination ecology of this tree cannot be studied there. Such research can be carried out only in tropical Africa or Yemen, where *Ficus sycomorus* is pollinated normally and produces viable seeds.

MATERIALS AND METHODS

In order to study the pollination ecology of *Ficus sycomorus* two trips to East Africa were made in September to October 1964, and in January to February 1966. During the first trip many specimens were investigated from wide areas in Kenya and Tanzania, while during the second trip the study was concentrated in one place only. The research station was set up at Magadi, a settlement of the I.C.I. Company, about 100 km to the south-west of Nairobi, the capital of Kenya.

In East Africa *Ficus sycomorus* is found chiefly in riverside forests. It grows abundantly along the banks of the Uvaso-Ngiro River, about 30 km to the west of Magadi. In their natural habitat the trees grow luxuriantly reaching more than 25 m in height and about 4 m in trunk diameter. Small trees and cuttings have been transferred from the river banks to the grounds of the settlement. Despite adverse soil conditions they developed well, owing to watering and cultivation. These trees are still young and small, suitable for observation and experimentation. Their syconia are inhabited by a complete series of fig-wasps, including the legitimate pollinators, and seeds are produced regularly.

A single developmental cycle of the fig of *Ficus sycomorus* in East Africa lasts from 6 to 7 weeks.

Because of our short stay at the site, controlled pollination experiments could not be carried out, and our research concentrated on the investigation of a large number of syconia from various trees, taken at all the developmental phases. For special tests samples of these figs were fixed in F.A.A. and afterwards studied in the Botany Department of Tel-Aviv University. The sections were prepared according to the paraffin method and stained with safranin-fast green. The fig insects were determined by Dr. J. T. Wiebes of the Museum of Natural History in Leiden, Holland.

THE INFLORESCENCE AND THE FLOWERS

At Magadi, *Ficus sycomorus* flowers throughout the year. The inflorescences (= syconia) develop in great numbers in short panicles on the trunk and main branches. The oblong syconia are borne on short peduncles.

Ficus sycomorus is monoecious and both male and female flowers develop in the same syconium. The numerous female flowers cover most of the inner surface of the syconium. Each flower consists of 3 to 4-perianth lobes and a central pistil with one style and a rounded stigma. There is no differentiation into separate seed and gall flowers. All the female flowers can produce seed or galls, as the case may be (see below). The style length ranges from 0.8 to 1.5 mm. Since the long-styled flowers are sessile and the short-styled ones are carried on peduncles of various lengths, all the

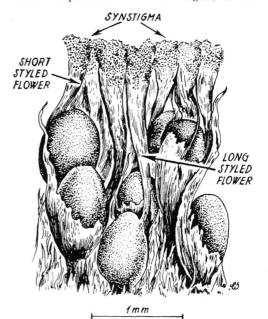

SYNSTIGMA

SHORT STYLED FLOWER

LONG STYLED FLOWER

1 mm

FIG. 1. Female flowers.

stigmata are approximately at the same distance from the inner wall of the syconium (Fig. 1). Due to a partial interlacing of neighboring stigmata by means of their papillae a continuous concave surface is formed which lines the cavity of the syconium. Although the connections between the individual stigmata are quite weak and they are easily separated, even here a collective stigma is produced which precludes the entry of the wasps between the styles or ovaries. Such a stigma may be called "collective stigma" or "synstigma."

The entrance to the syconium, the ostiole, is closed by numerous scales. The outermost are overlapping, while the inner ones are directed

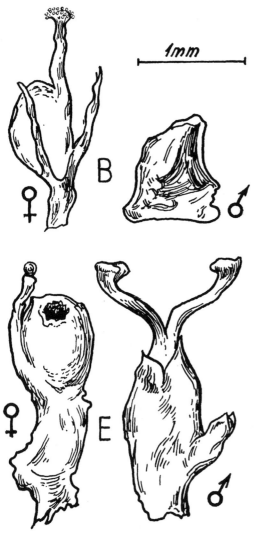

FIG. 2.   Male and female flowers at phases B. and E.

towards the cavity of the syconium. The male flowers are arranged in 2 to 3 rows at the upper part, close to the entrance scales. Each of them consists of 2 to 3 perianth lobes and 2 stamens. As usual in the genus *Ficus* the syconium is strictly protogynous and there is an interval of several weeks between the maturation of the female and that of the male flowers.

The Sycophilous Wasps of Ficus sycomorus

According to the definition of Grandi (1961), the syconium is a "microhabitat" in which several insects live, the faunula of the syconium. Some of these insects are mere pests, while others belong to various types of symbionts the lives of which are intimately bound with the developmental cycle of the syconium. Only the real sycophiles developing in the ovaries of the female flowers will be considered here. Occasional pests, such as ants and certain beetles sometimes found inside the syconia, will not be dealt with.

In the present paper the usual classification of the fig wasps (Grandi 1963) will be adopted. According to it, the real sycophiles belong to two families: Agaonidae (including Agaoninae and Sycophaginae) and Torymidae (Idarninae) of the superfamily Chalcidoidea. In his instructive paper which summarizes the present knowledge of fig biology Grandi (1961) states: "Usually we find within the syconia of a certain fig species a single Agaonine, frequently associated with a Sycophagine, but the Idarninae are often numerous." In the syconia of *Ficus sycomorus* in East Africa a complete series of fig wasps was found.

Since the main purpose of the present research is ecological and not taxonomic, only the outstanding features of the various fig wasps bearing on the pollination process will be mentioned. For further details the reader is referred to the papers of Grandi (1917) and Wiebes (1964).

1. *Ceratosolen arabicus* Mayr. In East Africa the chief pollinator of *Ficus sycomorus* is the small chalcidoid wasp *Ceratosolen arabicus* (Agaonidae, Agaoninae) which ensures seed production in most cases. It is very common in the syconia of *Ficus sycomorus* in Kenya and Tanzania. Several writers mention it in connection with *Ficus sycomorus* from Eritrea, Ethiopia, Somalia and Yemen (Wiebes 1964).

As the other fig wasps, *Ceratosolen arabicus* has a distinctly pronounced sexual dimorphism. The females are agile winged insects of very delicate structure, about 2.5 mm long. They are distinguished from the females of the other wasps inhabiting *Ficus sycomorus* by their light brown color, depressed head and the typical structure of

262   J. GALIL AND D. EISIKOWITCH   Ecology, Vol. 49, No. 2

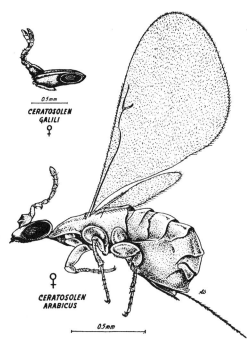

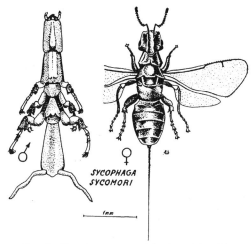

FIG. 4. *Sycophaga sycomori* (male and female).

FIG. 3. *Ceratosolen arabicus* (female).

the proximal antennal segments. The first segment is greatly thickened, and the third bears a characteristic hook on the side (Wiebes 1964). The ovipositor is relatively short, about 0.9 mm (Fig. 3).

The male is a light-brown, wingless, crawling insect. The head and the jaws are especially strong. As in other Agaoninae, the distal segments of the abdomen are tube-like (solenogaster), generally folded downwards and forwards, under the broad anterior ones.

2. *Ceratosolen galili* Wiebes. In East Africa, *Ceratosolen arabicus* is generally accompanied by *Ceratosolen galili* which is perhaps more abundant in Mombasa than in the interior of the continent.

The two species are quite similar in body size and in length of ovipositor, but *Ceratosolen galili* is readily distinguishable by its dark color and comparatively small eyes (Fig. 3). The males also are quite similar (Wiebes 1964).

3. *Sycophaga sycomori* L. (Agaonidae, Sycophaginae) is widespread throughout East Africa. Sexual dimorphism is highly developed (Grandi 1917). Similar to *Ceratosolen,* the females have "the same depressed head, a depressed thorax, spines and combs on fore and hind tibiae which are characteristic of the Agaoninae and apparently having a function while entering the receptacles of the figs through the ostioles" (Wiebes 1961).

The female of *Sycophaga sycomori* is easily distinguishable from that of *Ceratosolen* by its black color, longer ovipositor (up to 1.75 mm) and antennae which lack the modifications of the first and third segments. In the male the abdomen is straight and its last segments are not tubular. Close to its wider tip it bears two characteristic very long filaments (Fig. 4).

4. The Idarninae. In the syconia of *Ficus sycomorus* in East Africa three additional wasp species are often found, namely *Apocrypta* sp. (Fig. 5), *Eukoebelea* sp. and *Sycoryctes* sp. (Torymidae, Idarninae).

As in previously-mentioned sycophyles, here too sexual dimorphism is highly developed. The females are easily identified by their vivid coloring and very long ovipositors. As they do not enter the figs but insert their eggs from the outside through the peel of the syconium, their heads are not depressed and the ovipositors are very long, reaching 4 mm in *Apocrypta*, 5 mm in *Sycoryctes,* and 8 mm in *Eukoebelea.* From the morphological point of view the ovipositors of the three genera differ considerably from one another (Wiebes 1966). The males are wingless, with a straight abdomen. The male *Eukoebelea* is very similar to the male *Sycophaga.*

The developmental cycle of the syconium of Ficus sycomorus

Since the life history of the syconium of any fig species cannot be understood without its wasps, the developmental cycle of the syconium of *Ficus sycomorus* will be considered here in connection with *Ceratosolen arabicus,* its chief pollinator in

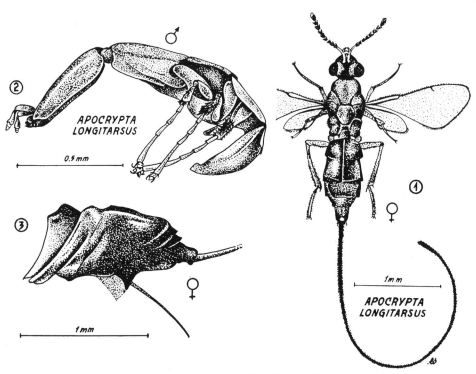

FIG. 5.   Apocrypta sp. 1—female; 2—male; 3—abdomen of female.

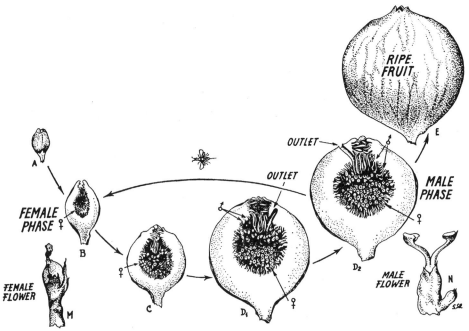

FIG. 6.   Developmental cycle of the syconium.

264   J. GALIL AND D. EISIKOWITCH   Ecology, Vol. 49, No. 2

East Africa. As is usual in figs, the cycle may be divided into five phases (Fig. 6), as follows:

Phase A (Pre-female). The young syconium appears as a small protrusion in the axil of the subtending scale on the inflorescence branch. In the beginning it is enveloped in the three bracts situated at its base. The ostiole is still closed by the overlapping entrance scales.

Phase B (Female). The female flowers reach maturity and the stigmata become receptive. The male flowers are still very small, enclosed within the perianth lobes (Fig. 2). The ostiolar scales withdraw slightly one from the other so that very narrow slits may be detected between them. At this phase the impregnated females of *Ceratosolen arabicus,* which have recently emerged from older syconia, penetrate between the entrance scales. The wasp pushes herself between the scales, leaving her wings and even the distal segments of her antennae at the entrance. Some of the wasps manage to enter the cavity while others die and are crushed between the scales. Within the syconium cavity 1 to 10 live female wasps may be found. By staining with cotton blue it is very easy to ascertain that these females carry pollen grains.

The wasps oviposit into the ovaries through the stigmata and the styles. Microtome sections through numerous pistils show that chiefly the short-styled ovaries are occupied. As in the common fig, the eggs are deposited between the inner integument and the nucellus, generally one egg into each ovule (Fig. 7).

Phase C (Interfloral). This phase is comparatively long, lasting for 3 to 4 weeks. In the ovaries of the long-styled flowers the embryos of *Ficus sycomorous* develop, while in the ovaries of the short-styled ones the larvae of the wasp grow from the eggs which were deposited there during the previous phase.

The ovaries harboring the wasps develop into galls. They swell considerably and protrude into the cavity of the syconium. Their outer cell layers sclerify. The larvae feed on the tissues of the ovules.

Phase D (Male). The wasps complete their life cycle and reach maturity before the seeds manage to ripen. At first the behavior of the insects is quite similar to that of *Blastophaga psenes* described by Grandi (1929). The males emerge into the syconium cavity before the females. By means of their strong jaws they puncture the walls of the female galls and impregnate the females within. The fertilized females widen the holes and emerge into the cavity of the syconium.

From this point the behavior of the insects differs from that described for *Blastophaga psenes.* The entrance scales of the syconium do not withdraw from each other and the syconium does not open at all. At this phase the male flowers remain closed, the filaments do not elongate and the ripe anthers are still enclosed within the perianth lobes. For all practical purposes the male flowers constitute a part of the wall of the syconium.

With fertilization, the *Ceratosolen* males have not yet completed their biological function, as is the case in most *Ficus* species. At this stage many males assemble at the upper part of the syconium and start tunnelling the wall exactly through the zone of the still closed male flowers at the side of the ostiole (Fig. 8). As a result several anthers are destroyed and fall to the bottom

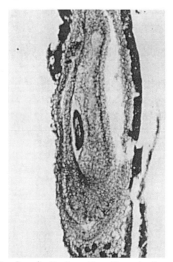

FIG. 7. Longitudinal section through the ovule of *Ficus sycomorus,* showing egg of *Ceratosolen arabicus.*

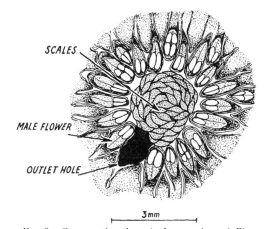

SCALES

MALE FLOWER

OUTLET HOLE

3mm

FIG. 8. Cross section through the syconium of *Ficus sycomorus,* at phase D.

of the syconium. The pollen sacs are ruptured and pollen is scattered along the tunnel. While they are engaged in boring of the holes the males almost fill the tunnel. They bite their way through the syconium wall and proceed slowly towards the exterior. Those of the males which reach the outside crawl out onto the surface of the syconium and eventually drop to the soil. However, the majority of the males remain within the syconium and die there.

Generally only one exit hole is bored, but two or even three holes are found occasionally. The number of males participating in the boring of a single hole may reach 30 to 35.

When the tunnel is finished, the females follow the males through it and fly away. As the females crawl along the narrow passage, their bodies become coated with pollen grains which are carried onto the younger syconia, now at phase B (female).

By boring these exit tunnels the males of *Ceratosolen* fulfill an essential role in the development of both the wasp and the sycomore tree. At phase D (male) the syconium is quite large and its wall, together with the male flowers, reaches about 4 to 5 mm in thickness. The females are unable to tunnel the wall and die within the syconium cavity unless the exit is bored by the males. When for some reason a too small number of males develops in a syconium, it becomes a death trap for the females.

Phase E (Postfloral). After the exit of the female wasps, the post-floral changes typical for endozoochoric fruit occur in the syconium. It increases in size, softens and becomes rose-colored. The separate fruits ripen within it. These are small druplets each containing an elongated yellow stone. When the hard endocarp of the stone is broken, the curved embryo embedded within the endosperm is easily detected. Generally, ripe druplets are found only in sessile or almost sessile long-styled flowers, not occupied by *Ceratosolen*. The pedunculate short-styled ovaries, from which the wasps emerged at phase D, are now perforated and empty (Fig. 2).

At phase E the male flowers have already opened and their stamens protrude into the cavity of the syconium (Fig. 2). Most anthers are still closed while in some of them narrow slits may be seen. Their pollen has not been scattered. Evidently, these stamens have no role in pollination, since the female wasps have already left the syconia.

Fruit dispersal is carried out by birds, bats and monkeys. Various tribesmen, especially boys, also eat the fruit (Dale and Greenway 1961), although it is of inferior quality.

TABLE 1. Population of Syconia at phase B in various trees

Tree	Date	Syconium	Number of *Ceratosolen*	Number of *Sychophaga*
I	11 Jan. 66	1	0	10
		2	2	3
		3	2	2
		4	0	2
		5	4	0
		6	10	0
Total			18	17
II	11 Jan. 66	1	3	0
		2	1	0
		3	13	0
		4	2	1
		5	0	0
		6	4	0
Total			23	1
III	13 Feb. 66	1	1	4
		2	1	2
		3	0	6
		4	1	17
Total			3	29

Colonization of syconia and occupation of ovaries

Occasionally at the receptive phase (B) only females of *Ceratosolen arabicus* are to be found in the vicinity of the syconia. In such cases the syconia become inhabited only by *Ceratosolen arabicus* and the picture is the same as described above. Generally, however, additional insect species are found there and the situation becomes more complicated. As the composition of the faunula inside the syconia is very important for seed setting, many syconia at late B phase were investigated immediately after the wasps entered them. The number of *Ceratosolen* and *Sycophaga* wasps in the syconia was determined (Table 1).

These observations show that practically every possible numerical relationship between the two wasp species may be found. In some syconia there are only *Ceratosolen* or only *Sycophaga* while in others a mixed population is found. Even on the same tree, after a short interval of time the composition of the faunula in the new syconia at phase B may change completely. Neighboring syconia can be inhabited by different wasps.

Evidently, the extent of population of a syconium at phase B and the numerical relationship between *Ceratosolen* and *Sycophaga* wasps within it are conditioned by the size and composition of the wasp population leaving the syconia at phase D in its vicinity, and also by the number of young syconia prepared to receive them.

In addition, many syconia at phase D were examined before the emergence of the newly

J. GALIL AND D. EISIKOWITCH   Ecology, Vol. 49, No. 2

TABLE 2. Percentage of seeds, galls and empty pistils found in phase D syconia, containing *Ceratosolen* only, *Sycophaga* only or both species, in short-styled and long-styled flowers

Faunula of syconium	Short-styled flowers			Long-styled flowers		
	Seeds %	Galls %	Empty %	Seeds %	Galls %	Empty %
Ceratosolen........	12.3	87	0.7	85	6.6	8.4
Sycophaga........	0	53	47	0	53.1	46.9
Ceratosolen+Sycophaga....	3.8	71	25.2	56	42	2

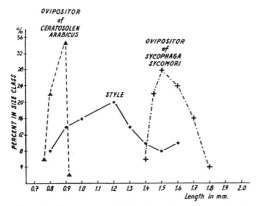

FIG. 9. Percentage distribution of wasp species by ovipositor length classes compared with percentage distribution of female flowers by style length classes.

hatched wasps, so that it was possible to study the relationship between seed setting and the composition of the faunula. As in the syconia at phase B, here too some of them contained only *Ceratosolen, Sycophaga,* or both species together (Table 2).

As a general rule, when only *Ceratosolen* were present, numerous seeds were produced, most of them within the sessile ovaries. On the other hand, in syconia harboring only *Sycophaga* no seeds were formed. Even when only a part of the pistils was occupied by *Sycophaga* and many shrunken female flowers have been left among the galls, no seeds were detected. It is quite evident that owing to their slightly longer ovipositor (Fig. 9) *Sycophaga* females may oviposit even into the long-styled pistils. As a result may sessile ovaries produce galls. The empty flowers among the galls prove that in this case the presence of *Sycophaga* wasps in the long-styled flowers is not the only cause of the non-production of seeds. The effectiveness of pollination by *Sycophaga* may be questioned. Perhaps the behavior of *Sycophaga* does not encourage seed setting, so that, although some pollination had taken place, no seeds develop. It is interesting to note the presence of seeds in syconia populated both by *Ceratosolen* and *Syco-*

phaga. This point will be dealt with in the discussion.

The role played by Idarninae in the colonizing of the syconia and subsequent seed setting is quite different. It has already been stated that these wasps oviposit into the syconia at the beginning of phase C, after these have already been inhabited by *Ceratosolen* or *Sycophaga*. Oviposition is effected from the outside, through the peel of the syconium. As it is not possible to determine from the outside the precise site of oviposition, the relationship of the Idarninae with the other wasps and its effect on seed setting may be studied only indirectly. One of the trees at Magadi provided valuable information.

This tree was loaded with ripe fruit at phase E, rose-colored and soft. Contrary to expectations, most of its syconia were still closed, without any exit holes, and contained many wasps mostly Idarninae. Many syconia had already dropped to the soil. Some of them contained live wasps, others dead ones. A few *Ceratosolen,* both male and female, could be detected among the multitude of Idarninae. All these figs contained many seeds, mainly in the long-styled, sessile ovaries.

It is not difficult to reconstruct the history of these syconia. Since they produced ripe seeds it is evident that they were inhabited first by *Ceratosolen* wasps, as only they cause effective pollination. The females of Idarninae do not enter the syconia and play no part in pollination. Female *Ceratosolen* pollinated the flowers and oviposited into the short-style pistils. Later, a large number of Idarninae was liberated in the vicinity and attacked the young syconia, then at the beginning of phase C. As in this case the attack was particularly strong, the Idarninae managed to occupy most of the ovaries already occupied by *Ceratosolen*. Although almost all the *Ceratosolen* galls thus became occupied by Idarninae, the long-styled ovaries into which *Ceratosolen* had not oviposited remained intact and produced normal seeds.

The fact that the Idarninae oviposit into ovaries already occupied by *Ceratosolen* or *Sycophaga* and do not destroy pollinated flowers, not occupied by primary sycophiles, was apparent in a few syconia from the same tree. The great majority of the female flowers found in them, both long and short-styled, produced normal seeds. Idarninae-occupied galls were rare. These were true seed syconia. It is clear that even here the syconia must have been first occupied by *Ceratosolen*. Presumably the female *Ceratosolen* which entered these syconia were very weak and although they did bring pollen and pollinated the flowers, very little oviposition took place, and only a few ovaries

Early Spring 1968   POLLINATION ECOLOGY OF *FICUS SYCOMORUS* IN EAST AFRICA   *267*

became inhabited by the female *Ceratosolen* before their death, but later on only these were occupied by the Idarninae when they replaced the *Ceratosolen*. In this way, despite the prevalence of Idarninae in the vicinity of the syconia in question, the seed ovaries were not occupied by them.

The above observations lead to several conclusions of significance for the understanding of the relationships between the Idarninae and the other sycophiles of *Ficus sycomorus*.

1. The Idarninae develop only in ovaries previously occupied by *Ceratosolen* or *Sycophaga*. They are secondary sycophiles.

2. The Idarninae do not interfere with seed setting in pollinated flowers which do not harbor either *Ceratosolen* of *Sycophaga*.

3. The production of normal seeds by both short and long-styled flowers in this case, and the development of *Sycophaga* in the ovaries of long-styled flowers observed previously clearly show that all the female flowers in the syconium are the same. There is no real differentiation into gall and seed flowers.

r. The male Idarninae do not bore exit holes, so that whenever there are only a few *Ceratosolen* males inside the syconium the female Idarninae remain entrapped. The syconium reaches phase E with the latter still inside. Eventually they die in the trap, unless a fruit-eating bird or bat damages the wall of the syconium and thus releases them.

DISCUSSION

For the understanding of seed setting in *Ficus sycomorus* the life history of each syconium should be observed separately. The population of sycophilous wasps in the vicinity of the young syconia changes from day to day and even from hour to hour, so that two neighboring syconia may differ from each other considerably.

The interrelationships between the syconia and the sycophilous wasps bear not only on structural details but also on various aspects of floral phenology and on behavioral patterns of the insects. The loading of pollen is connected with one of the main peculiarities of *Ficus sycomorus,* namely the non-opening of the syconia at phase D. This phenomenon is clearly related with several characteristics of the flowers and wasps, such as the delay in the opening of the male flowers, in the elongation of the filaments and in the opening of the anthers. Clearly this situation could not have developed unless the males of the sycophile wasps tunnelled their way out through the syconium wall exactly at the zone of the still closed male flowers.

At least two other instances are known of figs which do not open by themselves at phase D and

require the help of insects, i.e. in *Ficus roxburghii* (Cunningham 1889) and in *Ficus macrophylla* (Pemberton 1921). In each case the problems of pollen scattering and liberation of the females are solved differently. The tunnelling of the exit holes by males and not by the females in *Ficus roxburghii* and in *Ficus sycomorus* seems especially significant. The boring of a long tunnel through a thick and sticky syconium wall at phase D by female wasps would damage these tiny insects, especially their delicate wings, thus rendering them unable to perform their future tasks.

The tunnelling of the syconium wall is done by the males of *Ceratosolen* and *Sycophaga* only. When both are present generally only those of *Ceratosolen* perform this function. If the number of males is too small, no exit holes are bored and the insects remain entrapped inside the syconium. The normal development of the syconium is thus based on a very delicate equilibrium between the number of males and females of the primary sycophiles on one hand and the rate of occupation of the ovaries by the Idarninae on the other. A disturbance of this equilibrium leads to the entrapping and eventual destruction of the faunula within.

Although only a part of the anthers are destroyed by the males and little pollen is scattered within the syconia, pollen grains were found on the bodies and wings of both *Ceratosolen* and *Sycophaga*, generally more on the former. Apparently the males of *Ceratosolen* are more active in destroying the anthers and in scattering pollen while boring the tunnels. When both species are present, *Ceratosolen* leaves the syconium first, carrying most of the scattered pollen. Germinating pollen grains were found on the stigmata of female flowers at phase B, after the wasps had entered the syconia. Even the females of Idarninae may carry pollen, but as they do not enter the young syconia at phase B at all, this pollen is useless for pollination.

The special role of *Ceratosolen arabicus* in ensuring seed setting in *Ficus sycomorus* even in the presence of *Sycophaga* was apparent during the examination of figs at phase D, carried out in Mombasa, on February 17, 1966. Of the 100 figs investigated, only 2 contained *Ceratosolen arabicus* together with *Sycophaga* and Idarninae. Only these 2 produced seeds, while the others, harboring *Ceratosden galili, Sycophaga* and Idarninae, were seedless. Although *Ceratosolen galili* has a short ovipositor its role in seed production in *Ficus sycomorus* is not evident.

Ceratosolen arabicus is a mutualistic symbiont (Table 3, Fig. 10) of *Ficus sycomorus,* his characteristics and behavior being in harmony with the

268 J. GALIL AND D. EISIKOWITCH Ecology, Vol. 49, No. 2

TABLE 3. Summary of the characteristics of the sycophile wasps of *Ficus sycomorus* and their relationships with the tree and the chief pollinator

	CHALCIDOIDEA			
	AGAONIDAE		SYCOPHAGINAE	TORYMIDAE
	AGAONINAE		SYCOPHAGINAE	IDARNINAE
	Ceratosolen arabicus	Ceratosolen galili	Sycophaga sycomori	Apocrypta Eukoebelea Sycoryctes
Head Depressed	+	+	+	−
Entry into Syconium	+	+	+	−
Ovipositor	short	short	medium	long
Oviposition	through style	through style	through style	through peel (from outside)
Ovary Occupation	short styled	short styled	short & long styled	short & long styled
Gall Induction	+	+	+	
Sycophily	primary	primary	primary	secondary
Pollination	+	+	(+)	−
Ovary Protection	+	−		
Interference with Seed Setting			+	−
Tunnelling by Males	+	+	+	−
Seed Setting	+	+	−	−
RELATIONSHIP				
to F. Sycomorus	Mutualistic Symbiont	Mutualistic Symbiont	Parasite	Parasite
to Ceratosolen			Competitor	Inquiline

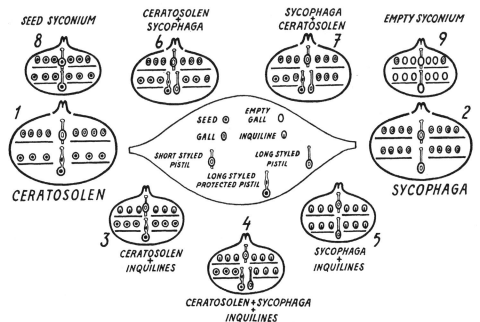

FIG. 10. Diagram summarizing seed-setting in syconia populated by *Ceratosolen* only, *Sycophaga* only and by both of them (above) and the effect of Idarninae on seed production in the previous syconia (below).

requirements of the tree. On the other hand, for *Sycophaga sycomori* the situation is quite different. Here the ovipositor is long enough to allow occupation of both short, and long-styled flowers. Whenever the syconium is inhabited by *Sycophaga* only, many ovaries are destroyed by the insects, but even in this case not all the pistils are occupied. Although there is some prospect of pollination, generally no seeds are formed. Thus, as regards *Ficus sycomorus*, *Sycophaga* is a mere parasite destroying the ovaries without bringing any benefit. Its relation with *Ceratosolen* is that

Early Spring 1968   THE GREEN SEA TURTLE *CHELONIA MYDAS* (L.)   269

of a competitor (Table 3, Fig. 10), as it occupies ovaries which otherwise could be inhabited by the latter.

However, the interrelations between *Ceratosolen* and *Sycophaga* are not as simple as they may appear. It has already been shown that syconia inhabited by both *Ceratosolen* and *Sycophaga* generally produce seeds. If the occupation of ovaries were conditioned by the length of the ovipositor only, the *Sycophaga* would oviposit into the long-styled flowers, and thus most of the ovaries within the syconium would be destroyed. The presence of seeds in syconia inhabited jointly by *Sycophaga* and *Ceratosolen* suggests the possibility of the existence of some additional factor, brought apparently by *Ceratosolen,* which protects at least a part of the long-styled ovaries against oviposition by *Sycophaga.* The problem is of great biological interest and deserves further study.

The effect of the Idarninae on seed setting is only indirect, by decreasing the population of *Ceratosolen arabicus,* thus impairing the prospects of pollination in the following generation. Their relationship with *Ficus sycomorus* is that of parasites nourished on plant tissues. On the other hand they are inquilines (subtenants) of *Ceratosolen,* making use of the galls developed as a consequence of the activity of the primary sycophiles. Here is a clear example of gall insects, which need certain galls for their normal development, but are unable to induce the formation of these galls (Mani 1964). The same situation was described for *Philotrypesis caricae* in the common fig (Joseph 1955, Grandi 1930, 1961).

ACKNOWLEDGMENTS

Our thanks are due to Dr. J. T. Wiebes of the Rijksmuseum of Natural History, Leiden, for the identification of the wasps. We are indebted to the Directors of the Soda Ash Company at Magadi, Kenya, especially to Mr. Walter Rouse for their hospitality, help and interest in our work during our stay. We also wish to express our gratitude to Mrs. B. Sapir and to Mrs. A. Gour for the many helpful suggestions, and also to Mr. S. Scheffer for the fine drawings.

LITERATURE CITED

Brown, T. W., and F. G. Walsingham. 1917. The sycamore fig in Egypt. The J. of Hered. **8**: 3-12.

Cunningham, D. D. 1889. On the phenomena of fertilization in *Ficus roxburghii* Wahl. Ann. Roy. Bot. Gdns. Calcutta **1**: 13-51.

Dale, I. R., and G. J. Greenway. 1961. Kenya trees and shrubs. Nairobi Buchanan's Kenya Estates Limited. London.

Grandi, G. 1917. Contributa alla conoscenza degli Agaonini (Hymenoptera chalcididae) dell' Eritrea e dell' Uganda. Bull. Soc. Ent. Ital. **48**: 3-42.

———. 1929. Studio morfologico e biologico della *Blastophaga psenes* L. Boll. Lab. Ent. Bologna **2**: 1-147.

———. 1930. Monografia del Gen. *Philotrypesis* Forst. Boll. Lab. Ent. Bologna **3**: 1-181.

———. 1961. The hymenopterous insects of the superfamily *Chalcidoidea* developing within the receptacles of figs. Boll. Instit. Ent. Univ. Bologna **26**: 1-13.

———. 1963. Catalogo ragionato degli Agaonini del mondo. Boll. Instit. Ent. Univ. Bologna **26**: 319-373.

Joseph, K. J. 1955. Observations sur la biologie de *Philotrypesis caricae* L. C. R. Acad. Scienc. Paris **241**: 1624-1625.

Mani, M. S. 1964. Ecology of plant galls. W. Junk, The Hague.

Pemberton, C. E. 1921. The fig wasp of the Moreton Bay fig. The Hawaiian Planters Rec. **24**: 297-319.

Theophrastus. Inquiring into plants. Translated by A. Hort, 1961. Vol. 1, Book IV: 203. W. Heinemann, London.

Wiebes, J. T. 1961. Indomalayan and Papuan fig wasps (Hymenoptera, Chalcidoidea) 1. *Grandiana wassae* nov. gen., nov. spec. (Idarninae), with remarks on the classification of the Sycophaginae. Nova Guinea Zool. **14**: 245-252.

Wiebes, J. T. 1964. Fig wasps from Israeli *Ficus sycomorus* and related East African species (Hymenoptera, Chalcidoidea). Agaonidae. Entom. Ber. **24**: 187-191.

Wiebes, J. T. 1966. The structure of the ovipositing organs as a tribal character in the Indo-Australian Sycophaginae Torymidae (Hymenoptera, Chalcidoidea). Zool. Meded. **41**: 151-159.

Biologically Active Compounds
in Orchid Fragrances

Function of natural plant products in orchid flower odors
and the attraction of specific pollinators are described.

Calaway H. Dodson, Robert L. Dressler, Harold G. Hills,
Ralph M. Adams, Norris H. Williams

Species-specific attraction of pollinators is characteristic of many of the more highly evolved species of orchids (1). In those orchids the pollinating agents isolate and prevent hybridization between compatible populations. The development of numerous species in the orchid family (more than 10 percent of all species of flowering plants are orchids) can probably be attributed in large part to the attraction of particular kinds of pollinators. Some of the most bizarre pollination systems known function in attraction of specific pollinators; among them are food and prey imitation, sexual deception, and pseudoantagonism (1). Generally, the pollinators are attracted by means of brightly colored flowers or strong fragrances associated with the production of nectar. Bees, butterflies, moths, flies, and birds are the most common kinds of orchid pollinators; bees predominate (1). Much of the floral variation of orchids is a result of morphological rearrangements necessary to accommodate the physical characteristics of such diverse pollinating organisms.

Fragrance is often the dominant means of attraction, particularly in moth-pollinated flowers, which are searched out and visited at night. Many bee- and fly-pollinated species of orchids depend upon fragrance as an attractant and then reinforce that stimulus with flower colors and elaborate structural arrangements. Fragrances may attract a broad spectrum of pol-

linators; in these cases, structural modifications, which exclude all but one or a few kinds of pollinators, become critical. This is particularly true where such modifications are necessary to maintain the integrity of closely related and interfertile species which occur together.

Euglossine Bees as Orchid Pollinators

The evolution of certain orchids in tropical America is related to the presence of euglossine bees (tribe Euglossini, subfamily Bombinae—closely allied to the honey bees and especially the bumblebees). Male bees are specifically attracted to certain fragrances. This phenomenon has been partially elucidated during the past 10 years. The visits of euglossine bees to orchids were first reported by Cruger (2) and discussed by Darwin (3) in his classic treatise on the modifications of the orchid flower. In succeeding years there were additional reports of euglossine bees visiting orchids, but in all cases the observers assumed that the bees were visiting the flowers to obtain some kind of food. The flowers involved do not contain nectaries, and it was thus assumed that the bees gnaw on the flowers. Observers may have been misled by flowers that had been partly eaten by crickets, cockroaches, or other chewing insects. Ducke (4) made many observations of euglossine bees and noted that only male bees were visiting most orchid flowers, but he also believed, as did Porsch (5) and Allen (6), that the bees were eating the flower tissues. Dodson and Frymire (7) were the first to note that the bees do not chew on the flowers, but scratch or brush on the surface, frequently stop-

ping to hover nearby. They observed that the bees became less wary after visiting a flower for a few minutes, and seemed to become "drunk" or intoxicated in some manner.

Dodson and Frymire suggested that bees were detecting and absorbing some substance by the "brushes" which are found on the front legs of euglossine males. Vogel (8) made similar observations and presented evidence that the bees might be depositing some substance in their inflated hind tibiae. He did not attach much significance to this and suggested that the flowers were mimicking the sexual odors of the female bees and that the flowers were morphologically simulating the bee's nest cells. He suggested that the males arrived in search of females and scratched on the surface of the flower in frustration when no female could be found; however, the systematic and continued brushing of the bees at specific places on the flower does not lend itself to the idea of "scratching in frustration." Similar observations on flowers of other plant families which produce the same fragrance components as orchid flowers also weaken this idea. For example, *Spathiphyllum cannaefolium* (Dryand.) Schott, *Anthurium* spp. (both in the Araceae), *Gloxinia perennis* (L.) Fritsch and *Drymonia turrialvae* Hanstein. (both in the Gesneriaceae) elicit the brushing behavior by the bees (9). After further observations Vogel was convinced (as were we) that the bees were gathering some substance which they placed in their hind tibiae, he called this *Duftstoff* or "odor substance" (8) and suggested that the males were utilizing it as a borrowed pheromone to assist in marking their territories or to attract females by adding it to their own tibial secretions. Our observations suggest odor marking, but the flowers never attract female bees. If the odor substances are used unmodified, as a borrowed pheromone, it must be for a different purpose than sexual attraction of female bees.

Natural History of Euglossine Bees

Euglossine bees (more than 200 species) are restricted to the tropical regions of the Western Hemisphere. They are divided into six genera: *Eulaema*, *Euglossa*, *Euplusia*, *Eufriesea*, *Exaerete*, and *Aglae*. *Eulaema*, *Euglossa*, and *Euplusia* are most frequently associated with orchid flowers; the other three genera rarely visit

Dr. Dodson is associate professor of botany at the University of Miami, Coral Gables, Florida; Dr. Dressler is biologist at the Smithsonian Tropical Research Institute, Balboa, Canal Zone; Dr. Hills is a postdoctoral fellow in the biology department of the University of Miami; Dr. Adams is assistant professor of biology at Florida Atlantic University, Boca Raton, Florida; and Mr. Williams is a doctoral candidate at the University of Miami.

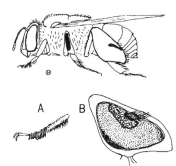

Fig. 1. Male euglosine bee. (A) Tarsal brushes; (B) section showing the glandular interior of the posterior tibia.

orchids. *Eulaema* consists of about 17 species of large hairy bees, and *Euplusia* has about 40 species which are superficially similar to species of *Eulaema*. *Euglossa* consists of over 100 species (more than twice the number of species that were recognized when we began our study in 1959) of small to medium-sized, brilliantly metallic blue, green, or golden bees that are sparsely hairy. All of these bees are rapid fliers and tend to be very wary. The males are characterized by brushes on the front tarsi and by greatly inflated hind tibiae which bear "scars" [openings densely covered by hairs, through which liquids may pass (Fig. 1)]. The mid-leg also shows a "velvet" area on the tibia, but its function is unknown. The brushes and scars are not as well developed in *Exaerete* and *Aglae* as in the other genera.

The feeding behavior of *Euglossa*, *Eulaema*, *Euplusia*, and *Eufriesea* is essentially similar although nesting behavior is characteristic for each genus (*10*). *Exaerete* and *Aglae* are parasitic

bees that lay their eggs in the nests of other euglossine bees. The females of the nonparasitic genera forage for materials for nest construction and food for storage in the nest cells. In most species there appears to be little division of labor, and each female constructs her own nests and cells. In some species of *Eulaema* and *Euglossa* several females may occupy a single large nest and apparently cooperate in its construction and provisioning (*10*); however, there is no evidence of caste formation.

Males leave the nest immediately upon emerging and do not return. They live a vagabond life, feeding on nectar-producing flowers and visiting orchid flowers (and other flowers that produce the same odors as orchids). The males are known to live as long as 6 months (*10*), which is considered to be very long for male bees.

The male establishes a display site which he defends and patrols in a manner typical of his species. Some choose a limb or a small tree trunk, land on it for a moment, and then fly a prescribed pattern before returning and landing again. Others fly a zigzag pattern, buzzing as they fly over or near the site without landing. This behavior may continue for hours and frequently occurs on several succeeding days at the same spot. Other males of the same species frequently may be attracted by the activity of the first bee and hover nearby. Apparently a fragrance is left at the spot where landing takes place, for if one male is captured a new male frequently takes its place at the same spot the following day. While the bee is on the tree, he buzzes loudly every few seconds, and a fine mist can be seen to emanate from the posterior portion of the bee (it has not been

possible to determine if the emanation is from the abdomen or the legs). The female is attracted either by the loud buzzing, by the flight pattern, or by the odor produced by the male. Copulation takes place near the site (*10*).

Visits to Flowers

It has been established that euglossine bees are attracted to odors (*5*, *10*). Most of the flowers visited by euglossine bees produce a strong fragrance and, even if the flowers are hidden from view, the bees will seek them out. Adams (*11*) placed flowers of *Catasetum maculatum* L. C. Rich ex Kunth inside a clear plastic insect trap, left the flowers for a few minutes, and then removed them. Bees were attracted to the residual odor in the trap.

The bees characteristically approach the flowers from downwind, stopping to examine any object in their path as they search for the source of the odor. When the bees arrive at the flower they are generally very wary, hovering and darting away only to return and hover again as they test the fragrance. Immediately after landing on the flower, the bees begin to rub the lip of the flower with their tarsal brushes. While the bees are brushing, their antennae are extended and depressed so that the bees seem to be continually sampling the odors near the surface where they are brushing. After 30 to 60 seconds of brushing, the bees resume flight and hover downwind in front of the flower, rubbing the tarsal brushes against the scars on the swollen tibiae. They then return to the flower, resume brushing, and repeat the process.

Chromatographic analysis of the contents of the tibiae indicate that the odor substance is transferred from the tarsal brushes to the hind tibiae, where it is evidently absorbed through the scars. The tibiae contain the same odor substances as those of the fragrance produced by the flowers visited (*8*, *11*).

Once a bee has landed and brushed, it becomes less wary and can often be caught by hand. Formerly we believed that the bees became "intoxicated" by the materials obtained by rubbing on the flowers (*7*, *10*), but recent observations indicate that female euglossine bees react in much the same manner when collecting resin for nest construction. Once they begin collecting the resin and transferring it to the pollen baskets, they are much less wary. It is unlikely that the resin "intoxicates" the female bee; therefore, it

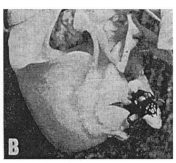

Fig. 2. (A) Male bees of *Euplusia superba* visiting the flowers of *Coryanthes rodriguezii* at Iquitos, Peru. The bees rub on the upper portion of the lip and fall into the bucket-shaped lower portion which is filled with water from glands on either side of the column. (B) One of the bees crawling out of the bucket under the stigma and anther of the flower. As the bee crawls out the pollen masses adhere to the dorsal abdomen.

seems more likely that the "drugged" aspect of the behavior of both male and female bees results from "concentration" rather than from a physiological reaction to substances produced by the plants.

While visiting orchids, the bees, whether drugged or not, often slip and fall. The flower surfaces may be very smooth, which increases the frequency of slipping, and the structure of the flower may be such that the bee falls in an awkward position, or finds its wing movements hampered by projections of the flower, so that it must fall a few centimeters before it can right itself and continue flight. Falling is especially frequent when the bee releases the flower to hover and transfer the fragrance material to the tibial organs. In a number of species this falling is an essential part of the pollination mechanism (Figs. 2 and 3).

Some orchids pollinated by euglossine bees are relatively simple morphologically (Fig. 4) and are visited and pollinated in the same manner as many other orchids. Others have quite bizarre structures and pollination mechanisms. The pollinaria (pollen masses and associated structures which attach the pollinia to the pollinator) are attached to the bee in specific places and are transported to the stigma of another flower of the same species. Because of variation of the point of attachment of the pollinarium, (behind the head, behind the thorax, on top of the thorax, on the front of the head, under the abdomen, on the legs, and so forth (9), and because of the varying positions of the stigma in relation to the posture of the entering bee, it is possible for several sympatric species of orchid to be pollinated by the same bee species without hybridization occurring (9, 10). The more complex flowers, such as Gongora spp. and Stanhopea spp., have correspondingly more complicated pollination systems. In these genera pollination is accomplished by a bee falling through the flower and picking up or depositing the pollinarium as the bee passes the end of the column (Fig. 3). In the genus Coryanthes the apical portion of the lip forms a "bucket" into which water drips from glands on the side of the column (Fig. 2). The bee falls into the water in the bucket and must crawl under the stigma and the anther to escape from the flower.

Flowers which are pollinated by euglossine bees [euglossine orchids (9)] usually have highly specific odors which attract only one or only a few species even in areas where many spe-

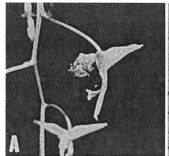

Fig. 3. (A) Male *Euglossa gorgonensis* rubbing on the lip of *Gongora* aff. *quinquenervis* (Guapiles 3). (B) Male *Euglossa cyanura* falling and sliding off the column of *Gongora tricolor*. When attempting to fly from the flower to transfer the compounds from the tarsal brushes to the tibial organs, the bee falls. When it passes the end of the column, the pollen masses adhere to the thorax. The pollen masses are inserted into the stigma of a succeeding flower in the same manner.

cies of bees occur. In Panama, *Gongora tricolor* (Lindl.) Reichb. f. is visited only by *Euglossa cyanura* Cockrell, while in the same area *Gongora quinquenervis* Ruiz & Pavon is visited by five other species of *Euglossa*. There are other species of euglossine orchids which also attract several species of bees, but generally any species of orchid will be pollinated by only one or very few species of bee. In some instances where an orchid species attracts several species of bee, some of the bees are accessory visitors (species which are of the wrong size or behavior to effect pollination). At Cerro Campana in Panama, *Stanhopea* aff. *inodora* Lodd. ex Lindl. is pollinated by a large bee, *Eulaema ornata* (Mocsary). The flower is also visited by several species of *Euglossa* which are too small to effect pollination. These bees rarely enter the lip of the flower, where the normal pollinator would brush, but tend to brush on the sepals and petals. This behavior is a frequent phenomenon in euglossine orchids and permits pollination by a single species of bee, even when the chemical attraction is not specific.

In other euglossine orchids dimensions of the flower may serve as isolating mechanisms through adaptation to large or small bees; however, morphological isolating mechanisms alone are rarely sufficient to assure specific pollination. In central Panama there are 60 known species of euglossine bees and probably 40 of these species could be found in any favorable orchid habitat in the area. Adaptation to size of pollinator and placement of pollinaria are not sufficient to provide the specificity necessary to prevent hybridization between many interfertile species.

Strong attraction of euglossine bees to specific fragrances produced by the flowers provides the necessary reproductive isolation to maintain the integrity of interfertile species.

Components of Floral Fragrances

Orchid floral fragrances are diverse in their composition. Gas chromatographic analysis of the fragrances of 150 species from 25 genera (largely euglossine-pollinated species) indicate approximately 50 different compounds in orchid flower fragrances (10). Most species produce from seven to ten compounds, but some produce as many as 18 or as few as three. Of the 50 compounds present, 16 have been identified by relative retention times on two columns, enrichment, smell (most of

Fig. 4. Male *Eulaema polychroma* visiting the morphologically simple flower of *Pescatoria wallisii*. While the bee rubs the lip, the pollen masses adhere behind the head.

Fig. 5. Male bees attracted to blotter paper saturated with 1,8-cineole. (Left) *Eulaema nigrita*; (middle) *Euglossa dodsoni*; (right) *Euglossa asarophora*.

the compounds are common perfume or flavor ingredients), and biological activity (*10–13*). Ten additional compounds have been tentatively identified and have proven to attract euglossine bees.

Not all compounds are produced with equal frequency. Almost 60 percent of the species sampled produce 1,8-cineole, but less than 5 percent produce methyl cinnamate. The amount of a compound in a fragrance also varies; for example, 1,8-cineole forms about 90 percent of the odor of *Stanhopea cirrhata* Lindl., but only about 7 percent of the fragrance of *Catasetum maculatum* L. C. Rich. ex Kunth. The percentage of a compound in a fragrance may not determine its overall smell to humans; for example, methyl cinnamate forms only 1 percent of the total fragrance of *Catasetum roseum* (Lindl.) Reichb. f., yet the floral fragrance of that species is reminiscent of cinnamon.

Field Tests of Compounds

To determine the effects of the identified compounds on the bees, field tests were carried out in tropical America. The first series of tests, in central Panama in early February 1968, were to determine the kinds of bees attracted to pure compounds and to mixtures of compounds. A second series of tests designed to survey the attraction potential of the compounds and to determine geographical distributions of the bees, was made from February to August 1968 in Mexico, Guatemala, El Salvador, Honduras, Nicaragua, Costa Rica, Panama, Colombia, Ecuador, Venezuela, and Trinidad.

The first series of tests took place in the central portion of Panama on both sides of the Canal Zone. Rainfall and vegetation of the three sites—Cerro Jefe east of Panama City, Santa Rita Ridge east of Colon, and Cerro Campana west of Panama City—are similar, and all three sites were known to have numerous euglossine bees.

Blotter papers (5 by 5 centimeters) were saturated with the compounds to be tested and tacked 2 to 5 meters apart on logs or tree trunks in forest areas (Fig. 5). The tests were made between 7 a.m. and 1 p.m.—when euglossine bees are most active. All bees attracted were captured and killed for species determinations and body counts. Blotter papers were replenished when a compound appeared to have evaporated—some of the compounds are very volatile while others last for several days.

During a 5-day test period in central Panama, 42 of the 60 species known from that area were attracted. Of the other 18 species, some were present at the time of the tests but were not attracted. Some of the unattracted species are seasonal or extremely rare, and they may not have been present. Subsequently, 12 of the 18 species have been attracted to the original or to additional compounds. Six species remain unattracted.

During the Panama tests, pure compounds and mixtures of pure compounds were assayed. In pure form 1,8-cineole, methyl salicylate, and benzyl acetate acted as general attractants. Two compounds, α-pinene and β-pinene, failed to attract.

During the 5-day test period, 1,8-cineole attracted 433 male euglossine bees (no other kinds of bees were at-

tracted) representing 35 species; methyl salicylate attracted 113 individuals of 11 species; and benzyl acetate, 36 individuals of 6 species. When one part 1,8-cineole and 39 parts benzyl acetate were mixed (the approximate proportions of these compounds in the fragrance of *Stanhopea tricornis* Lindl.) only 49 individuals from 8 species were attracted. When α-pinene was added to the mixture of 1,8-cineole and benzyl acetate in the same proportion found in the same orchid, only six individuals of two species were attracted. The species were *Eulaema meriana* (Olivier), the known pollinator for *Stanhopea tricornis* in its native habitat in Colombia and Ecuador, and *Euglossa dodsoni* Moure, a bee much too small to effectively pollinate *S. tricornis*.

In the second series of tests pure compounds were tried at numerous sites in tropical America. Additional compounds not tried in the first series were eugenol, methyl cinnamate, bornyl acetate, α-phellandrene, and myrcene. Piperonal and indole were tried only in Panama, whereas vanillin was tested in Panama and Ecuador. All of these compounds attracted bees. Vanillin and piperonal have not been positively identified as components of orchid fragrances, but the odor of vanillin is reminiscent of the fragrance of *Stanhopea oculata* (Lodd.) Lodd. ex Lindl., *Catasetum russellianum* Hook, and *Mormodes uncium* Reichb. f. Bees attracted to these orchids were also attracted to vanillin.

The most effective general attractant has been 1,8-cineole except in western Mexico where eugenol was as effective in general, and more effective with particular kinds of bees (Table 1). Methyl cinnamate was more effective in Mexico than in Ecuador, Colombia, or Venezuela. The other compounds tested attracted fewer species and were effective only in certain areas. In Mexico and Panama, d-carvone attracted several species of *Euplusia*. Bornyl acetate, anethole, geraniol, pulegone, linalyl acetate, and α-phellandrene each attracted a few species but only in Panama and Costa Rica. Myrcene attracted six species in Panama, Colombia, and Ecuador and was the only compound to attract females (two were seen to hover near the blotter).

The absolute concentration of the compounds seemed of little consequence in most cases. Totally saturated pads were most effective in attraction except those saturated with β-ionone and anethole. β-Ionone was most effective in cases where only a *single* drop was placed on the blotter whereas blotters saturated with anethole attracted bees only after 2 to 3 days of exposure. In all cases the bees behaved in the same manner at the liquid-soaked blotters as at flowers. They hovered in front of the pad testing the fragrance, landed and rubbed the blotters, launched into flight and rubbed the tarsal brushes on the tibial scars, and became less wary.

The general attractants are the most frequently produced odor compounds in orchid flowers. Over 70 percent of the attracted species of euglossine bees are drawn to 1,8-cineole, which is produced by 60 percent of the orchid species sampled (14). Benzyl acetate occurs in about 25 percent of the orchid species sampled and attracts 10 percent of the bee species, while methyl salicylate occurs in 4 percent of the orchids and attracts 20 percent of the bee species. Many species of bees were attracted to several compounds, but some were attracted to only one compound (14). Eulaema cingulata (Fabricius) was attracted to nine of the compounds tested, but was not attracted to 1,8-cineole. This is one of the most frequent pollinators of orchids and can be very selectively attracted to certain orchid fragrances (10).

The combination of two attractants modifies the attraction potential of the total fragrance and often fails to draw in species that would visit one of the attractants in pure form. The addition of a third compound (such as α-pinene) may further reduce the numbers of species attracted. This selectivity of mixtures is very significant, and some combinations of compounds will attract only one or very few bee species, even though some of the ingredients would,

by themselves, attract many species. The differential production of fragrance components by different orchid species may thus limit the number of bee species attracted when numerous species are present. Once the number of species attracted has been reduced, mechanical isolation can play a more effective role in pollinator specificity.

Conclusions

Many orchids pollinated by male euglossine bees produce compounds in their fragrances which attract particular species of bees. No food is provided by the flowers. The bees collect the fragrance components which they store in their hind tibiae. Why do the bees collect these materials? We have little documented evidence at present to answer that question, but we offer three possibilities.

1) Male euglossine bees live longer than is normal for other male bees and some evidence exists (10) that the bees die if deprived of the compounds. The bees may metabolize the compounds to cover some natural deficiency.

2) Male euglossine bees may convert the compounds into sex attractants. Female bees are not attracted to the pure compounds, but they are somehow attracted to the territorial displays of the males, and they copulate at the site (10).

3) Males may use the compounds to attract other males of the same species, so that several males are present at the mating site. This occurs in other arthropods (15) and probably tends to insure fertilization of the occasional female which passes by. The female euglossine bees may be attracted by the

loud buzzing of the males rather than by chemical sex attractants.

In an atmosphere saturated with certain of the compounds, the bees tend to die quickly. The presence of the collecting and storage organs at distal portions of the legs rather than in the body cavity may protect the organisms from the compounds. If the compounds are deleterious to the bees when taken internally, then the bees could not collect them with the tongue and store them in the body. A male Euglossa sp. (an unnamed species designated as "RD 725") which emerged from a nest in our laboratory at Miami was allowed to collect pure cineole for 3 days and was then dissected and examined for the presence of cineole in various parts of its body. Cineole was found only in the tibial organ.

Whatever the reason for the collection of the fragrance compounds, the bees have had a great effect on the evolution of the orchids which produce the compounds. Speciation in these orchids could occur by minor genetic changes affecting the production of fragrance components (16). The production of additional components or the failure to produce a component could change the attraction potential of the fragrance of a genotype. If a different species of bee is attracted and the pollinator of the parental form is not attracted, a new reproductively isolated population could develop. For example, the members of the population of Stanhopea tricornis at Santo Domingo, Ecuador, have a slightly different combination of odor components from the population at Turbo in Colombia (Fig. 6). Both are probably pollinated by the same species of bee

Table 1. Numbers of male euglossine bees collected while visiting some of the primary attractants at various localities in tropical America. (A) 1,8-Cineole; (B) benzyl acetate; (C) eugenol; (D) methyl salicylate; and (E) methyl cinnamate.

Locality	Total (No.)	Average/day (No.)	Species (No.)	Visitors at attractant				
				A	B	C	D	E
Eastern Mexico	203	29	9	167	3	12	1	20
Western Mexico	119	39	5	40	4	74		1
Southern Mexico	605	201	9	530	1		1	6
Guatemala	68	11	6	47	1	15	1	3
El Salvador	31	10	6	10	2	16		3
Honduras	28	28	8	20	1	2	5	
Nicaragua	73	18	4	61	1	1	10	
Northern Costa Rica	88	22	17	56	6	11	5	
Southern Costa Rica	93	31	20	87	1		5	
Panama	927	46	48	685	38	28	153	23
Eastern Colombia	160	16	42	133		3	24	
Western Colombia	29	14	6	16			8	5
Eastern Equador	427	42	18	157	24	11	229	6
Western Ecuador	121	30	13	117	1		2	1
Eastern Venezuela	89	44	18	70	1		12	4
Western Venezuela	173	43	15	152	14		6	1
Guianas	107	21	4	107				
Trinidad	244	81	13	114	69	15	41	5
Totals	3585	38	85	2569	167	188	502	78

[*Eulaema meriana* (Olivier) pollinates this species in Ecuador]. Further fragrance changes could attract different species of bees and reproductively isolate the two populations.

This system would permit sympatric speciation, which we believe is occurring in the genus *Gongora* in Central America. Extensive populations of *Gongora* aff. *quinquenervis* Ruiz & Pavon occur in Costa Rica and Panama. The plants are essentially the same in all external characters, but the flowers tend to be variable in color within a given population, and in some cases morphological characters of the lip of the flower may vary. Early taxonomic treatment had separated several forms on the basis of color, but recent taxonomists have reduced all gongoras which resemble *G. quinquenervis* to that species. At Guapiles, in Costa Rica, a large population of *Gongora* produces flowers which are structurally quite similar but which diverge in color, fragrance spectra, and pollinators. One form, *G. unicolor* Schltr., produces flesh-pink flowers and a sweet fragrance which we are unable to analyze with the gas chromatograph. It is recognizable only by the color of the flowers and the fragrance it produces, yet it is pollinated by a bee, *Euglossa purpurea* Friese, which does not visit any of the other members of the group. The other members of the group produce flowers which are nearly indistinguishable from one another in form, but vary widely

Table 2. Pollination spectrum of the Orchidaceae indicating the percentage of orchid species pollinated by various agents. [Taken from van der Pijl and Dodson (*1*)]

Orchid species (%) pollinated by:			
Hymenoptera		Other agents	
Wasps	5	Moths	8
Lower bees	16	Butterflies	3
Carpenter bees	11	Birds	3
Euglossine bees	10	Flies	15
Social bees	8	Mixed agents	8
Mixed bees	10	Apomictic	3

in color from white flecked with red to completely wine red. Two fragrance types (Fig. 7) associated with pollinators, were designated "Guapiles 3 and 4." The plants designated "Guapiles 3" attracted *Euglossa gorgonensis* Cheesman while "Guapiles 4" attracted *E. bursigera* Moure. Only one of the three types can be distinguished (*G. unicolor* —by color of the flower) when pollinator data and fragrance spectra are ignored. The indication is that adaptation radiation to different pollinators is taking place. One form, *G. unicolor*, has reached a point of color differentiation. In time the other two forms might develop morphological differences easily recognizable by taxonomists.

We have discussed orchid speciation based on attraction of specific kinds of euglossine bees. These orchids constitute about 10 percent of the species in the family. How did the other 90 percent accomplish comparable speciation? We know that most of the members of the

genera *Brassavola, Epidendrum, Habenaria,* and *Campylocentrum* in the neotropics and *Angraecum, Aerangis* and *Platanthera* in the Old World tropics are adapted to pollination by night-flying moths. Orchids adapted to moth pollination are characterized by white or light green flowers, strong fragrances at night, and long nectar tubes. Because of the difficulties in observing night pollination, few data have been accumulated concerning pollinator specificity in these genera. These genera contain intrageneric interfertile species, many of which are sympatric, but few reports of natural hybrids exist. Preliminary studies with gas chromatography of species of *Brassavola* and *Angraecum* indicate that species-specific fragrances are produced.

Similar situations appear to exist with such fly-pollinated genera as *Pleurothallis* in the neotropics and *Bulbophyllum* in the Old World tropics. Both genera are very large (near 1000 species) and have allied genera with numerous species. Scattered observations indicate that the species are isolated by pollinator specificity (*10, 17*). Further study may demonstrate that differential fragrance spectra are involved in pollinator specificity.

About 33 percent of the species of orchids are covered by the euglossine bee-, moth-, and fly-pollinated classes (Table 2). Obviously specific attraction by fragrance is not the only factor in the evolution of the family; however,

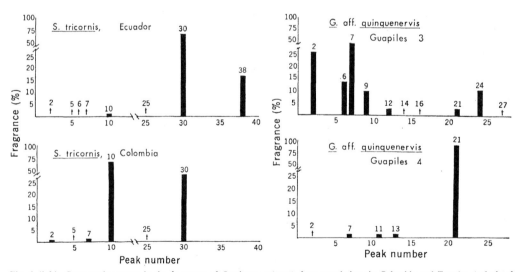

Fig. 6 (left). Compounds present in the fragrance of *Stanhopea tricornis* from populations in Colombia and Ecuador (calculated from gas chromatographs of the floral fragrances).   Fig. 7 (right). Compounds present in the fragrance of two kinds of *Gongora* closely related to *Gongora quinquenervis* Ruiz & Pavon which occur together in a large population at Guapiles, Costa Rica.

the majority of the large genera are covered by this system. An exception is *Dendrobium* (estimated to consist of 1600 species) which occurs throughout tropical Asia and Australia. Here spatial isolation on islands, flower color, and periodicity in flowering (*1*) may have played a more important role. In *Dendrobium* social bees, which are not instinctively associated with attraction by specific fragrances, join with flies, birds, and butterflies as pollinators.

Summary

Certain orchids in tropical America have become adapted to pollination by male euglossine bees. The bees are attracted by floral fragrances, and the chemical composition of the fragrances determines which species are attracted. The male bees collect the fragrance materials directly from the flower by rubbing the surface of the flower with special tarsal brushes. The bees launch into flight, transfer the fragrance materials, and store them in swollen glandular tibiae of the rear legs. The contents of the tibiae after floral visits were analyzed by gas chromatography; they were the same as the floral fragrance.

Approximately 50 compounds are present in euglossine orchid fragrances, and some species may produce as many as 18 of the compounds. Other species produce fewer compounds. Certain of the compounds, when presented to the bees in tropical America, proved to attract many species of euglossine bees. Other compounds attracted only a few species although in some cases no bees were attracted. Combinations of the compounds attracted markedly fewer species than pure compounds. Appropriate combinations of compounds, in the proportions found in orchid fragrances, attract the same bees which are attracted by the flowers. Speciation and reproductive isolation in euglossine bee-pollinated orchids appears to be based on specific attraction of pollinators to odors produced by the orchid flowers; the substances are believed to play a role in the life cycle of the bees.

References and Notes

1. L. van der Pijl and C. H. Dodson, *Orchid Flowers, Their Pollination and Evolution* (Univ. of Miami Press, Miami, Fla., 1966).
2. H. Cruger, *J. Linn. Soc.* **8**, 129 (1865).
3. C. Darwin, *The Fertilization of Orchids by Insects* (London, 1862 and 1877).
4. A. Ducke, *Bol. Mus. Paraense* **3**, 1 (1902).
5. O. Porsch, *Oester. Bot. Z.* **102**, 117 (1955).
6. P. A. Allen, *Amer. Orchid Soc. Bull.* **19**, 528 (1951); *Orchid J.* **1**, 226 (1952); *Ceiba* **4**, 121 (1954).
7. C. H. Dodson and G. P. Frymire, *Mo. Bot. Gard. Bull.* **49**, 113 (1961).
8. S. Vogel, *Oesterr. Bot. Z.* **110**, 308 (1963); *ibid.* **113**, 302 (1966).
9. R. L. Dressler, *Atlas Simp. Biota Amazonica* **5**, 171 (1967); *Evolution* **22**, 202 (1968); *Rev. Biol. Trop.* **15**, 143 (1968).
10. C. H. Dodson, *Amer. Orchid Soc. Bull.* **31**, 525 (1962); *Agentes de Polinizacion y su Influencia sobre la Evolucion en la Familia Orquidacea* (Univ. Nac. Amazonia Peruana, Iquitos, Peru, 1965); *J. Kans. Entomol. Soc.* **39**, 607 (1966); *Atlas Simp. Biota Amazonica* **5**, 1 (1967); in *Biochemical Coevolution* (Oregon State Univ., Corvallis, 1968).
11. R. M. Adams, thesis, University of Miami (1968).
12. C. H. Dodson and H. G. Hills, *Amer. Orchid Soc. Bull.* **35**, 720 (1966); H. G. Hills, N. H. Williams, C. H. Dodson, *ibid.* **37**, 967 (1968).
13. H. G. Hills, thesis, University of Miami (1968).
14. For the tabulation (numbers of male euglossine bees of each species collected at 11 orchid fragrance compounds and at 12 floral fragrance compounds, some of which may be present in orchid fragrances), order NAPS Document 00475 from ASIS National Auxiliary Publications Service, % CCM Information Sciences, Inc., 22 West 34 St., New York 10001, remitting $1 for microfiche.
15. C. G. Butler, *Biol. Rev. (Cambridge)* **42**, 42 (1967).
16. M. J. Murray, *Genetics* **45**, 925, 931 (1960).
17. H. N. Ridley, *Ann. Bot.* **4**, 327 (1890).
18. Supported by NSF grants 6B-6409 and 6B-7142. We thank J. Clegg and W. Evoy (University of Miami) for their comments and discussion of aspects of insect behavior.

EVOLUTIONARY ASPECTS OF FRUIT-EATING BY BIRDS

D. W. SNOW

Received on 3 March 1970

Forty years ago Schuster (1930) pointed out that although ornithologists had long realised the importance of fruits as a source of food for birds, the references to fruit-eating were widely scattered in the literature and no synthesis was available. Schuster under-took such a synthesis for European birds, but he made it quite clear that it was no more than a first step; what he did was simply list, with references, the fruits which had been reported to be eaten and the bird species concerned. Economic botanists too have naturally been interested in birds as disseminators or destroyers of fruits, but here again the published work seems not to have progressed much beyond the listing of records. For Europe, the work of Turček (1961) represents a synthesis from both the ornitho-logical and economic botanical points of view. McAtee (1947) lists references to fruit-eating by North American birds.

For the theoretical botanist the subject is of considerable importance, since dispersal of the seeds by animals (zoochory) is now held to be an extremely ancient adaptation of flowering plants; contrary to previous opinion, there is reason to suppose that it was an earlier evolutionary development than dispersal by wind (anemochory) (Corner 1964, van der Pijl 1966, 1969). Thus one must envisage a very long mutual interaction between plants and birds, which has resulted in very beautiful adaptations on the part of the plants. Ridley (1930) gives the classic account, and many examples are cited in botanical textbooks; but the botanical discussion has centred largely on the evolution of fruit structure, a technical and controversial matter (van der Pijl 1966) which is not directly relevant to the broader aspects of the subject which it is proposed to discuss here.

In spite of the considerable literature which now exists on the subject of fruits and fruit-eating, of which a few key references have been given above, it seems that the general evolutionary aspects of fruit-eating have been largely or completely neglected. My aim here is to try to fill this gap at least in a preliminary way. This paper does not aim to be a complete treatise on seed-dispersal by birds. Much of it is speculative, but this is unavoidable at the present stage, because proof of the ideas advanced would be extremely hard to obtain, though theoretically possible. Indeed, a major difficulty has been to obtain the most elementary data on certain points. For example, although the seasons of ripening of different fruits in different geographical areas are of fundamental importance for the purpose in hand, even modern floras fail almost without exception to provide this information with any degree of exactness. The admirable series of papers appearing in the 'Journal of Ecology' under the general title " A biological flora of the British Isles " unfortunately has so far dealt with few bird-dispersed plants.

THE EVOLUTION OF FRUITS

I include in the discussion all fruits which have a fleshy part that is eaten by birds, whatever their technical botanical description and derivation—drupes, berries and arillate fruits. This is justifiable for the present purpose, as the assumption is made that the fleshy parts, whatever their anatomical origin, are functionally analogous in so far as they are the parts digested by the fruit-eating birds which exploit them. As already mentioned, the early stages in the evolution of fruits are still controversial. Corner (1954) in his " durian theory " has argued that the primitive fruits of flowering plants were dehiscent arillate carpels or capsules, the edible aril being an adaptation for dispersal by animals. This theory has been challenged by van der Pijl (1966), but both agree that dispersal by animals is primitive; and whatever their early evolutionary history, nearly all botanists agree that fleshy fruits are adapted to dispersal by birds and other animals.

Probably " saurochory " (dispersal by reptiles) was the most primitive condition. Saurochory still occurs, and van der Pijl has suggested that saurochorous fruits are characterised by an attractive odour and by being borne basally on the trunk.   As birds and mammals evolved and proliferated they undoubtedly became the main dispersal agents.   We are not concerned here with mammals, but it may be noted that fruits adapted for dispersal primarily by mammals tend to be scented, often with a fetid smell, dull in colour, and in many cases very large.   Bat-dispersed fruits are a special case, characterised additionally by permanent attachment and exposure away from the foliage, especially hanging below it or attached to the trunk (van der Pijl 1957, 1969).

Corner and van der Pijl both agree that the early evolution of fruits of the kind with which we are here concerned was essentially tropical.   The earlier idea, that wind-dispersal is more primitive, was the result of the northern bias of most botanists.   Wind-dispersal should rather be seen as a specialisation, an adaptation to less favourable conditions encountered as the early fruiting plants spread to higher latitudes or more severely seasonal environments.   Thus there is a tendency for large, mainly tropical families with mainly zoochorous fruits to have a few species in temperate regions adapted for wind-dispersal—for example the Oleaceae, represented by many drupe-bearing tropical or subtropical genera and by the wind-dispersed ash (*Fraxinus*) in the north.

SEED DISPERSAL VS. SEED DIGESTION

Typically, dispersal of fleshy fruits is effected by birds which digest the fleshy part and void the seed or seeds intact.   These, in fact, are the true fruit-eating birds in the sense in which the term is used here.   The fruits may however be eaten for the sake of their seeds by other birds which have, so to speak, broken through the essentially sym-biotic relationship maintained between plant and legitimate fruit-eater.   Thus many parrots feed on the seeds of fleshy fruits, discarding the fleshy parts, as does the Hawfinch *Coccothraustes* when feeding on *Prunus* and *Crataegus* fruits.   Some pigeons (e.g. *Columba* species) grind up the seeds in fruits which they eat; but the true fruit-pigeons digest only the fleshy parts and pass the seeds through the gut (e.g. *Globicera*, Wood 1924; *Ducula* and *Ptilinopus*, Cadow 1933).   In some cases unripe fruits may be eaten and the soft seeds digested, while later, when the fruits ripen, the seeds are left undigested (e.g. ivy berries eaten by *Columba palumbus;* Heim de Balsac 1928).   Such cases of seed destruc-tion will not be further considered; they may be regarded as ecological by-ways, important enough for the birds concerned but out of the main stream of the evolutionary develop-ment of fruit-eating.

The presence of toxic or irritant substances either in the seeds or in the fleshy parts of fruits has been assumed to be a defence mechanism on the part of the plant against digestion of the seed by fruit-eating birds (and other animals).   This is probably correct, but there seem to be a puzzlingly large number of anomalies, cases where seeds apparently protected by toxic substances are eaten, some of which are discussed by Heim de Balsac (1928), who considered that these anomalies invalidated the general hypothesis.   The fact that fruits of *Atropa belladonna* are eaten by birds, and indeed seem to be adapted to dispersal by this means, although their flesh is highly poisonous to man, suggests that each case needs to be examined in detail, with regard to the various kinds of animals that might either disperse or destroy the seeds.

What is perhaps as striking as the apparent defence of some seeds against digestion is the way in which some apparently very vulnerable seeds are not digested by fruit-eating birds.   For example the fruits of some of the Lauraceae, a mainly tropical family pre-eminently adapted for dispersal by birds, have a rather dense pericarp surrounding a relatively very large, comparatively soft seed.   And yet in the stomach of the Oilbird *Steatornis caripensis* and some cotingids the pericarps are cleanly stripped off without a mark being made on the seed.

A number of cases have been reported where the germination of seeds is facilitated by their previous passage through the digestive tract of a vertebrate, as in the case of the Galapagos tomato and giant tortoise reported by Rick & Bowman (1961), who summarise previous literature.   The evidence for birds appears to be slight.   This has been regarded as a refinement of the symbiotic relationship between plant and dispersal agent, an adaptation to ensure distant dispersal; but it is theoretically puzzling, because there is no obvious advantage in germination being prevented, or made less likely, in those fruits which fall beneath the parent plant or are otherwise scattered without being eaten by an animal.   It may be that in such cases the plant has become adapted to dispersal by an agent which retains the seed for a long time in its digestive tract (as the tortoise does), or in some other way subjects it to harsh treatment, and that the need to be able to resist this treatment has resulted in the development of a protective coat which, in the absence of the treatment, impairs germination.

Although they are outside the scope of this discussion, the general principles involved in the dispersal of two types of " dry " fruits may be briefly considered.   Several kinds of nuts are stored by birds (and mammals) and very effectively dispersed in this way, because some are always forgotten or lost or the individual that stored them dies.   It is not possible to be certain whether or not the nutritive content of such fruits has been enhanced by the need to be attractive as a food; but it seems very likely that this is so, at least in some cases, because the plant may be completely dependent on the dispersal agent for its spread over any considerable distance, especially up hill.   Too small a nut would presumably not be worth storing.   Futhermore, the planting of, for example, oak trees by Corvidae, which bury acorns over wide areas often where there are no other large plants, may well be so effective a means of dispersal for the plant that the consumption of a very large proportion of the fruit crop may be a minor disadvantage.   By comparison, the true fruit-eating birds which regurgitate the seeds intact must usually tend to produce a more localised scattering of the seeds, which instead of being planted in earth must often fall on stony ground.   The oak tree's strategy for dispersal should therefore be regarded as an efficient one but one that is off the main evolutionary line which is being considered here.   It will naturally be an appropriate strategy only in latitudes or climates where there is a seasonal food shortage for birds.

Other dry fruits produce seeds which are eaten by birds, with no concomitant advantage to the parent plant.   Such are grasses, many Compositae and many trees with wind-dispersed fruits.   Here the evolutionary trend has been towards abundant seed, usually of small or very small size.   Such seeds presumably cannot, for reasons of size, evolve any effective defence against birds which are structurally adapted to feed on them, but this disadvantage presumably does not outweigh the advantage gained by their very large numbers, which will normally ensure that many are dispersed for every one eaten (even though in certain circumstances a seed crop may locally be entirely eaten by birds).   Corner (1964) has shown that small, dry fruits are a comparatively late development in the evolution of plants; so it is significant that small seed-eating birds belong to only a few phylogenetic lines and that the two main groups (Ploceidae and Fringillidae*) are among the most " advanced " and show little major structural diversity, although they have speciated abundantly.   Apparently only a few avian stocks were able to take advantage of the new food supply, but those that did so found a range of new niches available and underwent rapid speciation.

---

* The classification follows Van Tyne & Berger (1959), as also the numbers of species in different families, given on p. 199.   Differences of opinion on the classification of these groups do not affect the main points which are being made here.

THE STRATEGY OF FRUITS FOR DISPERSAL BY BIRDS

Apart from the possible defences evolved by the seed against digestion, which have been considered briefly above, a number of " strategies " have been adopted by fruits in connection with their dispersal by birds.

COLOUR

The attractive colours of ripe fruits are universally known and will only be summarily mentioned here. Ridley (1930) gives many examples and Turček (1963) has shown statistically that red and black are the most highly preferred colours. Blue is another favoured colour, and combinations of these three colours, involving neighbouring structures as well as the fruits themselves, are well known and have been figured in botanical textbooks. It should be pointed out that there is still matter for further study here: it is such a general rule that fruits change colour on ripening from an inconspicuous, possibly even cryptic, colour to a conspicuous colour that there can be little doubt that the colour change is a signal to the frugivore that the fruit is ripe, and the frugivore's response (perhaps innate) ensures that normally only ripe fruits are taken. But it is not immediately clear why unripe fruits, which must have some nutritive value and certainly are often easy enough to find, are not more commonly taken. Corner (1964) attributes the immunity of unripe fruits to a chemical defence, the concentration in their flesh of tannins, alkaloids and sour acids. Biochemical analysis (of cultivated varieties) shows that the concentration of sugars increases at ripening at the expense of poly-saccharides (Niethammer & Tietz 1961), as common experience would lead one to suspect, resulting in a more nutritious food. Probably both these processes combine to ensure that any tendencies to exploit unripe fruits carry little or no selective advantage for a fruit-eating bird.

ACCESSIBILITY

The accessibility of fruits adapted for dispersal by birds has been discussed by Ridley (1930) and others. In general, such fruits are borne terminally. Accessibility may also be taken to include the ease with which fruits may be picked, and here two opposing selec-tive forces probably operate: fruits should not fall too easily, but they should not be so firmly attached that birds cannot pick them. This may seem a trivial point but it is worthy of attention. In Trinidad some palm fruits (*Bactris* spp.) are apparently too firmly attached to be picked by the Bearded Bellbird *Procnias averano* (B. K. Snow 1970), which takes other fruits of the same size in the same habitat; but they are taken by the heavier Oilbird and probably by other large frugivorous birds. Among closely related fruits, one species may persist on the parent plant, while another may drop after a short time (e.g. *Frangula* and *Rhamnus*; Godwin 1943). Perhaps the dropping of fruits has been favoured by selection in species to the extent that alternative, ground-feeding dispersers are available.

FOOD VALUE OF FRUITS

In simple terms, a fruit must be able to offer sufficient nourishment to a bird for it to be worth eating; but there is a limit to the resources which a plant can devote to this. Furthermore, there must be a balance between the nutritive value of the fleshy part of the fruit and the mass of the seed (useless for the bird) which is dispersed with it. This will be referred to again later, with respect both to the nutritive value of the part that is eaten and to the size and numbers of the enclosed seeds. At this stage it is sufficient to point out that on theoretical grounds the condition found in any particular fruit will be expected to be the result of a compromise, or balance, between these conflicting demands and possibilities.

198   D. W. SNOW   Ibis 113

ABUNDANCE OF FRUIT

Here again there are conflicting selective forces. The main trends are well known: in simple terms, a plant can produce a few large seeds containing ample reserves for the developing seedling, or a large number of small seeds each of which has a small chance of survival. Among trees, large-seeded fruits are characteristic of climax plant associations, especially tropical forest, where seedlings need to have ample reserves while waiting to take advantage of the occasional space created by a tree fall or other rare catastrophe; while in secondary or open vegetation fruits with many small seeds are the rule, since a premium is set on efficient dispersal to take advantage of the many spaces available.

Whatever the size and other characteristics of the fruit evolved under the various selective forces operating, the individual plant which fruits most abundantly will, other things being equal, have a selective advantage over those that are less prolific. Similarly, the plant with the most accessible and attractive fruit will have the advantage. The result must be that fruit will be produced as abundantly, and as conspicuously, as possible, within the limitations imposed by the other factors. The ecological implications of this general condition will be discussed in the next section.

CONSEQUENCES FOR FRUGIVOROUS BIRDS

The characteristics of fruit as a food for birds, discussed in the last section, must ntail two important consequences for the birds exploiting them, one ecological and the ther evolutionary.

(1) Natural selection will have tended to promote abundance and conspicuousness in fruit, as already mentioned. In these respects the long-term effects of their being eaten on their subsequent availability will be exactly the opposite of the long-term effects of predation on insects on their availability. Predation by birds on insects must have the immediate effect of making them less abundant; but more importantly, it must have the long-term effect of making them less conspicuous and therefore less available, as it is the selective agent directly responsible for promoting cryptic characteristics, of both structure and behaviour. Hence it may be expected on theoretical grounds that fruit will constitute, at the seasons when it is available, an abundant food supply which is easily obtained, whereas insects will constitute a less abundant food supply and one which is less easily located. It is surely for this reason that lek behaviour, which entails the presence of the displaying birds on their display perches for the greater part of the day, has evolved in some groups of frugivorous tropical forest birds, but not in insectivorous birds (Snow 1963).

(2) It must be part of the strategy of fruits not only to be conspicuous but also to be accessible to as many dispersal agents as possible, i.e. to as many different bird species as possible. That many fruits are in fact fed on by many different bird species has been noted by several observers, and in the tropics the number of species exploiting a single fruit tree may be strikingly high; thus Beebe (1916) recorded 51 species feeding on the fruit of a single tree (" wild cinnamon ") at Pará, Eisenmann (1961) recorded 24 species feeding on *Cecropia* fruit in Panama, and Land (1963) recorded 20 species feeding on *Miconia trinervia* fruits in Guatemala. By contrast, predation on insects promotes their inconspicuousness. There are many different ways in which inconspicuousness may be achieved, and correspondingly many different searching techniques will be necessary for potential predators. Hence there must be far more different feeding niches for insectivorous than for frugivorous birds, and this is almost certainly the basic reason for the much greater number of species in insectivorous families than in the specialised frugivorous families of birds. Of course many other factors must have been concerned in the history of speciation and the number of species now extant in any modern bird family, but it may be suggested that the differences between the number of species in the

following four mainly neotropical suboscine passerine families are due primarily to the consequences of their differences in diet:

mainly frugivorous	Cotingidae	90 species
	Pipridae	59 species
mainly insectivorous	Formicariidae	222 species
	Tyrannidae	365 species

SEASONAL FACTORS

The foregoing discussion has taken no account of the fact that fruit is typically produced seasonally. Seasonality of fruits poses a problem both to the fruit-eating birds and to the parent plants which is, at its simplest, that a seasonal fruit does not produce an adequate food supply for a fruit-eating bird, and if it loses its population of fruit-eating birds it loses its agents of dispersal. Of course the problem can be circumvented if birds are catholic enough in their diet to feed on other foods when fruits are unavailable, and this is in fact what happens in the more seasonal environments, where specialised fruit-eaters cannot exist. In the less seasonal, tropical environments specialised fruit-eaters can and do exist; but it may be expected that both in the tropics and in temperate latitudes there will have been interactions between fruits and birds which must have played a part in determining the seasonal succession of fruits, whether spread over the whole year or only part of the year. Some of these interactions are considered below.

TEMPERATE LATITUDES

The following discussion refers only to the situation in Europe, and even here the data available are far from adequate, so that the interpretation must be considered provisional and partly speculative. Early-maturing fruits (late summer–early autumn) tend to be very succulent, with a high water content, and probably with a low protein and fat content. Such fruits tend to go bad, dry up or fall off if not eaten; they therefore form a rather short-lived food supply. Fruits which mature later tend to be drier and more nutritious, and to persist for longer on the plant if not eaten; they thus provide a food supply well adapted for wintering birds. Analyses of some British wild fruits, illustrating these points, are given in Table 1. Although a succulent fruit presumably needs a shorter time to mature than a drier and more nutritious fruit, the time needed for maturation is

TABLE 1
Percentage composition of some British and tropical wild fruits

	Seed (as % of total weight)	Constituents of pericarp by weight (%)		
		Water	Protein	Fat
British				
Early-maturing				
Sambucus niger	5	90	?	?
Solanum dulcamara	?	*c.* 90	?	?
Rubus idaeus	?	85	2·5	1·4
Autumn–early winter				
Crataegus monogyna	23	73	1·2	1·0
Prunus spinosa	13	80	0·7	0 3
Ilex aquifolium	35	73	1·5	1·2
Rosa sp.	29	63	2·0	0·4
Late-maturing				
Hedera helix	49	73	5·3	3·4
Tropical fruits eaten by specialised frugivorous birds				
Ocotea wachenheimii (Lauraceae)	42	75	3·5	8·5
Lauraceae sp.	34	54	5·0	16·3
Lauraceae sp.	54	63	3·7	8·1
Dacryodes sp. (Burseraceae)	54	60	4·4	9·6
Didymopanax morototoni (Araliaceae)	11	68	3·8	10·7

200   D. W. SNOW   IBIS 113

apparently not the only factor involved in determining the time of ripening, since the intervals between flowering and fruiting are diverse in both classes. It is therefore reasonable to suppose that in each plant species both the nature of the fruit and the fruiting season are adapted to secure the most efficient dispersal by frugivorous birds, not in isolation but in a context of competitive interaction with other plant species. It can hardly be expected, however, that these interactions can now be understood except in broad outline, since the natural vegetation has been so extensively altered by man.

Succulent fruits seem to be especially suitable for migrants laying down premigratory fat, as has been reported in southern France by Blondel (1969) and in Spain by Mead (1966). A parallel case has also been reported from the southern edge of the Sahara, where small migrants laying down fat before making the northerly crossing of the desert in spring feed largely on the succulent berries of *Salvadora* bushes (Fry *et al.* 1970). The fact that such fruits are typically poor in proteins is presumably no disadvantage for a bird whose immediate need is to lay down a reserve of fat in a short time.

Many land-birds migrate south from northern Europe in autumn, including nearly all the fruit-eaters. In middle latitudes of Europe a large passage of northern birds takes place with its peak in October, and many of these birds continue south, arriving in the Mediterranean area, their winter quarters, in late autumn. In conformity with this southward movement of the main bulk of frugivorous birds, fruits tend to ripen in late summer or early autumn in Scandinavian latitudes; further south, in central Europe, ripe fruits are available from late summer to early winter; while in the Mediterranean area winter is the main time when ripe fruits are available (Tutman 1969). There seems also to be a trend, from north to south, towards less succulent, drier and more nutritious fruits with a higher fat content. Far more analyses are needed before this can be more than a tentative suggestion; but the prevalence of succulent fruits of *Vaccinium* and *Empetrum* spp. in the north may be contrasted with the drier fruits of *Juniperus* spp. and the oily fruits of *Olea*, *Laurus* and *Ligustrum* in the south. It is notable that the fruit of ivy (*Hedera helix*), with an essentially southern distribution, has a relatively very high fat and protein content (Table 1). It is a reasonable hypothesis that, just as the succession and types of fruits ripening at different seasons in any one area are adapted to the seasonally changing bird population, so the latitudinal differences in type of fruit and season of ripening are adapted to the seasonally shifting bird populations.*

Even at the latitude of Britain there are barely two months in the year when no fruits are available. The latest fruits (ivy) remain, and are eaten, as late as May or even June, while the earliest fruits of the next season are available in July, and a few even in June. Without ivy, the fruitless period would be considerably longer. It is noteworthy that ivy is the single European species of an essentially tropical plant family and retains some of the characteristics of a tropical fruit—high nutritive content (Table 1), long period of maturation, and a fruiting season that helps to promote a year-round fruit supply. It is also, apparently, the main northern European wild fruit that is regularly fed to the young by thrushes (*Turdus* spp.).

TROPICAL LATITUDES

The examples here are taken from Trinidad, and for the same reasons as were given in the preceding section the discussion must be considered speculative.

---

* It might be that the climate of the Mediterranean region, with its very dry summer, is less favourable for the ripening of fruits in late summer and early autumn than in winter; but this seems unlikely, because a number of succulent fruits do ripen at this time (Blondel 1969). There is scope for a comparison between fruiting seasons, and the shifting bird populations, in the Mediterranean area with the situation in Mexico and the southern United States, where at similar latitudes the rainfall comes mainly in the summer, not in the winter. Such a comparison might afford a critical test of the extent to which fruiting seasons are adapted to the bird population rather than to the climate.

In the tropics there is an apparent tendency for succulent fruits to ripen quickly, to be small and many seeded, and to be characteristic of secondary forest. By contrast, trees of primary forest tend to have larger, drier and more nutritious fruits. Thus some of the distinctions between early and late fruits in Europe are distinctions of habitat in the tropics. The size and number of seeds are however primarily an adaptation to habitat in both regions (p. 198).

The rather large, dry and nutritious fruits of primary forest trees constitute the main food supply of the specialised fruit-eating birds which are absent from temperate latitudes. The palms, Lauraceae and Burseraceae are outstanding in Trinidad, and apparently elsewhere in neotropical forests. It is especially noteworthy that the most specialised fruit-eating birds feed their young wholly on the fruits of such trees (Snow 1962, B. K. Snow 1970), while less specialised frugivorous birds feed their young largely on them, as Skutch has reported for several central American birds. Clearly the existence of the very specialised fruit-eating birds depends on the existence of such fruits, and without doubt there has been a mutual evolution.*

The relatively nutritious pericarp of such fruits should probably be seen as a consequence of the large size of the seed, for the following reasons. There was probably selection for large seeds in the trees concerned, as members of primary forest communities, independently of their relationship with their dispersal agents. Given a large seed, i.e. a large amount of " ballast " of no direct use to the fruit-eating bird, it is presumably necessary to concentrate a rather thin layer of nutritious pericarp round it, to make it an adequate food. (The alternative, a large seed surrounded by a very large amount of less nutritious pericarp, would probably make unacceptable demands on the tree and, especially, would require the potential fruit-eater to be of a size that would be inadaptive in relation to other environmental and physical demands.) Doubtless the sizes of both fruits and fruit-eating birds have been determined by the interaction between these various factors. A tropical or subtropical climate, permitting the slow maturation of fruits over a period of months with the accumulation of fats and proteins, must have been an essential pre-existing condition. If this argument is correct in its essentials, it follows that the very specialised fruit-eating birds have been able to evolve because a large seed size has been of selective advantage in tropical forest trees; and it is not surprising that there are, apparently, few very specialised fruit-eating birds that are very small, because fruits of the sizes available to them will tend not to be very nutritious. Thus manakins (Pipridae) in neotropical forests, although fruit-eaters to a large extent, take a significant quantity of insects and feed their young partly on them. (The specialised eaters of mistletoe fruits, *Dicaeum* spp. in the Old World and *Euphonia* spp. in the New World tropics, are striking exceptions to this rule, and would repay further investigation.)

In Trinidad there is a constant succession of ripe fruits throughout the year, of both succulent and more nutritious, drier kinds. I have suggested in an earlier paper (1966) that in the genus *Miconia* (Melastomaceae) the staggering of fruiting seasons of very similar species may be the outcome of interspecific competition for dispersal between the plants: any species fruiting at a time when as few other species as possible were in fruit would have a selective advantage. In any forest environment where there is a rich variety of trees, and seasonal climatic factors are not marked enough to have an overriding effect on the determination of flowering and fruiting seasons, this kind of process may be expected. The fruit-eating birds, by acting as agents of this selection, will thus promote the development of their own food supply. The symbiosis may have played a significant part in the evolution of the whole ecosystem.

---

* It is probable that the paucity of specialised frugivorous birds in the Ethiopian region compared with the Neotropical and Oriental regions is ultimately attributable to the fact that the Lauraceae, and secondarily perhaps the palms, are so poorly represented in Africa.

SUMMARY

In spite of a considerable literature on fruit-eating, the general evolutionary implications of fruit as a source of food for birds have been neglected. A preliminary attempt is made to explore the evolutionary and ecological consequences of fruit-eating, considered as a mutual interaction between parent plant and dispersal agent.

The relationship considered is that obtaining between fleshy fruits and the " legitimate " fruit-eating birds which digest the fleshy part of the fruit and void the seed intact. Evolutionary aspects of seed-eating are also briefly discussed.

The " strategies " adopted by fruits for dispersal by birds result in the production of abundant food supplies which are easy of access and exploitable by many species of birds. By contrast, the predation of birds on insects leads to a heterogeneous, sparse and cryptic food supply, to exploit which many different hunting techniques are necessary. Two important evolutionary developments in birds are attributed to these differences in food supply: there tend to be more species in families of insectivorous than of frugivorous birds, and lek behaviour in tropical forest has evolved in predominantly frugivorous birds.

The seasonal succession of fruits in temperate latitudes is discussed, and contrasted with the situation in the tropics, using examples from Europe and Trinidad. In general, the succession of ripe fruits in Europe seems to be adapted to the seasonal shifts of the bird populations, and the more nutritious fruits tend to have a more southerly distribution and to ripen later than the more succulent fruits. In the tropics the distinction between nutritious and succulent fruits seems to be largely one of habitat.

The constant succession of ripe fruits throughout the year in the tropics probably depends on competition for dispersal by frugivorous birds, which thus ensure the maintenance of their own food supply. This may be regarded as a symbiosis at the level of the ecosystem.

REFERENCES

BEEBE, C. W. 1916. Notes on the birds of Pará, Brazil. Zoologica 2 : 55–106.
BLONDEL, J. 1969. Synécologie des passereaux résidents et migrateurs dans le midi méditerranéen français. Centre Régional de Documentation Pédagogique, Marseille.
CADOW, G. 1933. Magen und Damen der Fruchttauben. J. Orn., Lpz. 81 : 236–252.
CORNER, E. J. H. 1954. The evolution of tropical forest. From J. S. Huxley, A. C. Hardy & E. B. Ford (Eds.), Evolution as a process. London: Methuen.
CORNER, E. J. H. 1964. The life of plants. London: Weidenfeld & Nicolson.
EISENMANN, E. 1961. Favorite foods of neotropical birds: flying termites and Cecropia catkins. Auk 78 : 636–638.
FRY, C. H., ASH, J. S. & FERGUSON-LEES, I. J. 1970. Spring weights of some Palaearctic migrants at Lake Chad. Ibis 112 : 58–82.
GODWIN, H. 1943. Biological flora of the British Isles. Rhamnaceae. J. Ecol. 31 : 66–92.
HEIM DE BALSAC, H. 1928. Fragments de bromatologie ornithologique. Revue fr. Orn. scient. prat. 12 : 54–66.
LAND, H. C. 1963. A tropical feeding tree. Wilson Bull. 75 : 199–200.
MCATEE, W. L. 1947. Distribution of seeds by birds. Am. Midl. Nat. 38 : 214–223.
MEAD, C. 1966. Premigratory weights of transsaharan migrants. Ringers' Bull. 2 : 15–16.
NIETHAMMER, A. & TIETZ, N. 1961. Samen und Früchter des Handels und der Industrie. Den Haag: W. Junk.
PIJL, L. VAN DER. 1957. The dispersal of plants by bats (chiropterochory). Acta bot. neerl. 6 : 291–315.
PIJL, L. VAN DER. 1966. Ecological aspects of fruit evolution. Proc. K. ned. Akad. Wet. (Ser. C), 69 : 597–640.
PIJL, L. VAN DER. 1969. Principles of dispersal in higher plants. Berlin: Springer-Verlag.
RICK, C. M. & BOWMAN, R. I. 1961. Galápagos tomatoes and tortoises. Evolution, Lancaster, Pa. 15 : 407–417.
RIDLEY, H. N. 1930. The dispersal of plants throughout the world. Ashford, Kent: L. Reeve & Co. Ltd.
SCHUSTER, L. 1930. Ueber die Beerennahrung der Vögel. J. Orn., Lpz. 78 : 273–301.
SNOW, B. K. 1970. A field study of the Bearded Bellbird in Trinidad. Ibis 112 : 299–329.
SNOW, D. W. 1962. The natural history of the Oilbird, Steatornis caripensis, in Trinidad, W.I. Part 2. Population, breeding ecology and food. Zoologica 47 : 199–221.
SNOW, D. W. 1963. The evolution of manakin displays. Proc. XIII Int. orn. Congr. : 553–561.
SNOW, D. W. 1966. A possible selective factor in the evolution of fruiting seasons in tropical forest. Oikos 15 : 274–281.
TURCEK, F. J. 1961. Oekologische Beziehungen der Vögel und Gehölze. Bratislava.
TURCEK, F. J. 1963. Color preferences in fruit- and seed-eating birds. Proc. XIII Int. orn. Congr. : 285–292.
TUTMAN, I. 1969. Beobachtungen an olivenfressenden Vögeln. Vogelwelt 90 : 1–8.
VAN TYNE, J. A. & BERGER, A. J. 1959. Fundamentals of ornithology. New York : John Wiley.
WOOD, C. A. 1924. The Polynesian fruit pigeon, Globicera pacifica, its food and digestive apparatus. Auk 41 : 433–438.

Dr D. W. Snow, Sub-Department of Ornithology, British Museum (Natural History), Tring, Hertfordshire

6

Case Studies of Arthropod Diversity and Distribution

Scott E. Miller, Vojtech Novotny, and Yves Basset

Because insects and other arthropods exhibit such striking diversity in the tropics, these taxa have provided models for the development of many key topics in tropical biology. Some of these topics are emphasized elsewhere in this book, including parts 3, 5 (mimicry and pollination), 4 (plant-herbivore relations), and 10 (ecosystem ecology). This part highlights three papers that helped fuel major discussions of both pattern and process in the diversity of tropical arthropods and other organisms. Erwin (1982; paper 28) laid out a set of testable hypotheses that led to major reinterpretation of the magnitude of tropical diversity. The series of studies in Haddow, Corbet, and Gillett (1961; paper 27) were an early and elegant view of vertical stratification of insects in tropical forests. Wilson (1958; paper 26) wrote the first in a series of papers based on observations of ants in Papua New Guinea that led to major discussions of heterogeneity, ant mosaics, and taxon cycles. The discussion below will show that these are still important topics in tropical biology.

How Many Species Are There?

For most of the twentieth century, the total number of insects in the world was assumed to be around 2 million. For example, Sharp (1895) and Frost (1942) gave estimates of 2.5 million and 2 million, respectively. Sabrosky (1952) reviewed knowledge of insect diversity at that time and said "workers in the division of insect identification of the [United States] Department of Agriculture estimate that [by] 1948 approximately 686,000 different species of insects" had been described in the world (1952, 1). For the total including undescribed species, Sabrosky (1952) stated "recent guesses vary from 2,500,000 to 10,000,000 different kinds" and "[t]he final roll call may be far short of 10 million but it seems sure to be somewhere in the millions" (1952, 2).

Some twenty years ago, in an ingenious and visionary paper, Erwin (1982) suggested that there may be as many as thirty million species of insects, instead of the previously estimated two or so million species. His conclusions were

The authors thankfully acknowledge support from the U.S. National Science Foundation, which has enabled their collaborative research on arthropod diversity and distribution.

Remarkable beetles found at Simunjon, Borneo. From Wallace (1869)

based on beetles sampled in insecticidal fogging of nineteen individuals of the tree *Luehea seemannii* in Panama (Erwin and Scott 1980; see Basset et al. 1996 for a table summarizing the assumptions and steps in the estimate). Subsequently, Erwin (1988) admitted that he was surprised by the attention that his calculations received and the controversy they generated, stating that he had simply advanced a hypothesis that could be tested rigorously, and suggested that this "must begin by refining of our knowledge about host specificity of insects in tropical forests" (1988, 123).

Although many papers have debated Erwin's conclusion, very few have actually attempted to test his assumptions, in particular the proportion of host-specific insect herbivores associated with different species of tropical trees (e.g., Stork 1988; Erwin 1988; May 1988, 1990, 2000; Thomas 1990a; Hammond 1992; Gaston 1991; Hodkinson and Casson 1991; Basset et al. 1996). Erwin's paper raised many questions regarding how to properly assess the number of host-specific arthropod species in general, and in the tropics in particular. One issue is the problem of transient species that are dispersing from tree species not under direct study (Janzen 1976; Stork 1993). Specialist species may be collected on other tree species besides their normal hosts. With greater diversity of plant species within the study site, more transient species are likely to be collected on the foliage of study trees (Basset 1999; Novotny and Basset 2000).

Another issue is the varying degree of host specificity observed among taxonomic groups. For example, wood-eating guilds of beetles rarely feed on living tissues and are therefore often much less host specific in the tropics than leaf-feeding beetles (Basset 1992). Studies of herbivorous insects associated with single plant genera in the Neotropics have recognized 30 percent monophagous (single-host-feeding) species on *Passiflora* (Thomas 1990b) and 10 percent monophagous geometrid moths and 26 percent monophagous species of weevils on *Piper* (Marquis 1991). But several recent studies have found much lower host specificity

across broader assemblages of hosts. In a study of leaf-chewing insects on ten tree species in Papua New Guinea, Basset et al. (1996) found 4.3 percent of the beetles were restricted to one of the ten tree species. In a much larger study of host specialization of leaf-chewing insects on sixty-two species of woody rain forest plants, Novotny, Basset, and Miller (in preparation) found that most herbivore species had wide host plant ranges within plant genera, but were restricted to only a few genera. A similar pattern has been found for tropical mites that feed on nectar in hummingbird-pollinated flowers (Naskrecki and Colwell 1998). Because speciose plant genera (such as *Ficus* and *Psychotria*) are a characteristic feature of tropical floras, the large overlap among herbivore communities on congeneric plants means that the total number of herbivores is lower than might otherwise be expected. Similar low host specificity at the plant species level was found by Wagner (1998) from canopy fogging in Uganda, and Tavakilian et al. (1997) in rearing cerambycid beetles from trees in French Guiana.

Moreover, tropical tree species may support very different ratios of specialist species, varying with host plant, forest characteristics, and geographic locations (Basset 1992, 1999). For example, chrysomelid beetle samples obtained in Panama (Erwin and Scott 1980) and the Peruvian Amazon (Farrell and Erwin 1988) were dominated by Alticinae, whereas in chrysomelid samples from Papua New Guinea (Basset and Samuelson 1996) and Borneo (Stork 1991) Eumolpinae dominated. Since Alticinae are often more host specific than Eumolpinae (e.g., Jolivet 1988), the overall proportions of specialists on particular tree species in the Neotropics may be higher than these in the Old World tropics.

Aside from differences in taxonomic composition of the overall fauna, tropical regions also differ in overall diversity. Although data on regional diversity are too poor for comparisons among most beetle taxa, it is well known that butterfly faunas differ markedly across regions. Within equal-sized areas, species richness of butterflies in the Oriental region is about half that in the Neotropics (Robbins 1993). Finally, the relative diversity of canopy versus soil faunas remains a subject of conjecture (Stork 1988; Hammond 1992; André, Lebrun, and Noti 1992). Much more work is needed on soil biota (see also the discussion of Fittkau and Klinge 1973 [paper 45]).

As illustrated by the papers cited above, vigorous discussion of how to predict the global number of arthropods continues. Current evidence from the major museum collections of sorted and labeled insect species, whether described or undescribed, does not support the larger estimates, and insect taxonomists broadly concur from this that although there may be up to five million species of insects in the world, there are probably less than ten million (Nielsen and Mound 2000). In a recent review, May (2000) settled on a "best guess" of four million species.

Although the magnitude of undescribed insects in the Andean region may be extremely high, this does not appear to be the case in other regions. Scholtz and Chown (1995) analyzed taxonomic knowledge of insects in southern Africa and considered "a doubling in [species] numbers to be the upper limit of the increase in species richness" in the region (125). In a detailed review of present knowledge of ants (Hymenoptera: Formicidae) of tropical Africa, Robertson (2000) suggests that about half the species of ants have been described—a figure that concurs approximately with these recent world insect diversity estimates.

Several factors contributed to the influence of Erwin's paper. First, his study suggested that there are many more insect species than previously thought, even if the magnitude of the number is still not agreed. Second, this was part of the first comprehensive quantitative analysis of fogging samples to the morphospecies level. Third, Erwin was the first to articulate a set of quantitative assumptions about global insect species richness in a sequence that could be discussed and tested. This step, in addition to the unexpected magnitude of the result, gained the attention not only of insect taxonomists, but also the broader scientific community and

ultimately conservationists. But sadly, this discussion also points out two other features of tropical insect research—the low availability of data and how slowly the gaps are being filled.

Vertical Patterns of Species Distribution

A large body of literature focuses on arthropod samples obtained from the forest "canopy," usually referring to samples obtained fifteen meters or more above the ground, with various methods (reviewed in Basset 2001). Most entomological studies, either with insecticidal fogging (e.g., Erwin 1995), with light traps (e.g., Sutton, Ash, and Grundy 1983; Wolda, O'Brien, and Stockwell 1998), or by felling trees (Amedegnato 1997; Basset, Charles, and Novotny 1999), cannot sample the upper canopy selectively. Recently, entomologists have been able to sample selectively the upper canopy either with fixed canopy cranes (Wright and Colley 1994) or a mobile canopy raft and sledge (Hallé and Blanc 1990), offering the promise of deeper biological understanding. These studies have generally found significant differences in composition and abundance of arthropods at different vertical levels in the canopy, but questions of what is actually being sampled and lack of understanding of the biology of the organisms has limited the conclusions that can be made. Some studies find greater abundance at higher levels (e.g., Basset, Aberlenc, and Delvare 1992), while others find greater abundance at lower levels (e.g., Wolda, O'Brien, and Stockwell 1998) or no significant differences are observed (e.g., Intachat and Holloway 2000).

Much of this recent ecological literature would leave the reader with the impression that the study of vertical stratification was invented only in the 1970s. On the contrary, there is a diverse literature, much of it in medical entomology journals, on much earlier efforts to study vertical stratification of biting flies and other economically important insects (e.g., Bates 1944; Mattingly 1949). Early efforts to study stratification outside of medical entomology included those of Allee (1926) on

Barro Colorado Island, Panama, Hingston (1930) and associates in Guyana, and Paulian (1947) in Ivory Coast. The methods may have been primitive by today's standards, but the logistic scale of samples taken on various kinds of platforms suspended in trees remains impressive.

Here we highlight one of the more impressive efforts of Haddow, Corbet, and Gillett (1961) in Africa—a 120-foot (36-m) tower, originally built at Mpanga, Uganda, in 1958 for mosquito studies. The tower was moved to a nearby site at Zika in 1960, and has been in more or less continuous use up to the present. The Zika site is near Entebbe, in a small forest fringing Lake Victoria. Zika has been the site of fairly intensive biodiversity research since 1946, including studies of vegetation, biting flies, dragonflies, other insects, birds, and mammals (Buxton 1952; Davenport, Howard, and Dickinson 1996). This was the first time that a fixed tower was used as a long-term research platform in a tropical forest. When it was built, the tower represented the same kind of leap forward in the application of technology as the new generation of canopy cranes when they were developed in the 1990s. Studies on the tower stratified samples in multiple ways—around the clock, through the seasons, and vertically through the forest and above the canopy.

Haddow's team found that values of some climatic parameters showed little variation vertically (temperature and saturation deficiency, a measure of humidity), whereas others did (wind and light). Vertical stratification was observed in breeding sites of mosquitoes. Patterns of stratification varied among different insect groups, and in some groups, males and females exhibited different patterns. Because of the cycles involved in flight patterns, some kinds of traps gave biased views of overall population activities. Haddow's group also published some of the first detailed observations of insect behavior above the canopy, noting especially the swarming activities of mosquitoes. The data were used in broader discussions of interactions between endogenous (genetic) and exogenous (environmental) components in determining insect behavior patterns (Corbet 1966).

Many abiotic and biotic characteristics of the upper canopy are different from other forest layers below. Irradiance, air temperature, wind, fluctuation of relative humidity, and dew formation at night are notably higher in the upper canopy than in the understory (Parker 1995). Leaf area density and the abundance of young leaves, flowers, and seeds are also usually higher in the upper canopy than lower levels (Parker 1995). For example, in a rain forest in Cameroon, the environmental and biophysical conditions characteristic of the top canopy layer are more like those of chaparral shrub vegetation than of the rain forest ground-layer vegetation. The implications for the distribution of insect herbivores along vertical gradients in tropical rain forests may be significant. Insect herbivores foraging and feeding in the upper canopy encounter serious hygrothermal stress during day and water condensation at night. Conversely, the supply of young leaves available to them is greater than in the lower forest strata. As discussed by Basset et al. (2001) this suggests several possible strategies for coping with this apparently conflicting situation: (1) a specialized and distinct fauna, well adapted to the extreme microclimatic conditions of the upper canopy; (2) interchanges of fauna between the upper canopy and lower layers, e.g., individuals resting in lower layers by day and moving up to feed at night, perhaps taking advantage of air movements (Sutton 1989); or (3) both strategies above.

In a study of abundance, activity, and species richness of arthropods in the upper canopy and understory of a lowland rain forest using the "canopy raft" in Gabon, Basset et al. (2001) found that the density and abundance of many arthropod higher taxa and species were significantly higher in the upper canopy than in the understory. Arthropod activity was also higher during day than night. In particular, insect herbivores were more than twice as abundant and twice as speciose in the upper canopy as in the understory, probably responding to higher and more diverse food resources. Faunal overlap between the upper canopy and understory was low. Herbivore turnover between day and night was rather high in the upper canopy and no strong influx of insect herbivores from lower foliage to the upper canopy was detected during night. This suggests that insect herbivores of the upper canopy may be resident and well adapted to environmental conditions there.

It is premature to draw general conclusions about the vertical distribution of insects in tropical forests. We simply do not have enough data yet. Long-term studies, such as that of Roubik (1993), suggest that temporal movements up and down in response to changes in the environment (food and nectar sources, as well as microclimate) and the insect populations (mating behaviors, for example) are of critical importance and can be seen and understood only with long-term observations. Regular vertical movements of insects reach an extreme in seasonally inundated forests (Adis 1984). May (1999) points out that most ecological research is still relatively short term, often limited by the length of Ph.D. programs and research grants.

Patchy Distributions of Ant Species

Based on extensive fieldwork in Papua New Guinea in 1955, Wilson published a series of papers documenting the taxonomy, ecology, speciation patterns, and biogeography of the Melanesian ant fauna. The paper we reprint here (Wilson 1958) dealt with the patchiness, or heterogeneity, of the local distribution of ant species. Leston (1973), building on the concept of ants being discontinuously distributed through the three-dimensional space as described by Wilson (1958), Greenslade (1971), Schneirla (1971), and others, characterized ant "mosaics" in cocoa plantations and forests in West Africa. Leston's concept of ant mosaic includes dominant species being distributed in a three-dimensional pattern, with lacunae in which less dominant species are able to persist, although other dominant species are excluded from the territory. Dominant species are usually nonnomadic, arboreal, multinested, sugar-loving, and predatory, practicing mutualism with Homoptera (such as scale insects), and with the potential for rapid population growth.

Aside from the ecological interest, manipulation of such mosaics in plantation crops could have practical applications in pest control. The distribution of arboreal ants in both plantations and natural forests has now been studied in West Africa, Brazil, Borneo, New Guinea, Solomon Islands, and Australia (Dejean et al. 2000; Floren and Linsenmair 2000; Greenslade 1971; Majer 1993; Room 1975). Although many aspects of Leston's description hold true, all the elements are not always present and the complex factors effecting community organization are not fully understood. Thus, although the concept is useful (Dejean et al. 2000), it needs further study before it is widely accepted. One element that remains clear is the overwhelming ability of ants to dominate their environment (Wilson 1990).

The taxon cycle. Wilson (1959b) provided a more formal description of the ecological diversification and stratification of the ant fauna. Insular species evolve through a series of stages from newly arrived colonists, indistinguishable from their mainland relatives, to highly differentiated endemics, which ultimately become extinct. Wilson (1959a) described patterns of speciation, adaptive radiation, and dispersal of Melanesian ants, and characterized a "cyclical pattern of expansion, diversification, and contraction . . . account[ing] for later evolutionary events following initial dispersal" (143). This cyclical pattern was further characterized and named the taxon cycle in a subsequent paper (Wilson 1961). Wilson later extended some of the concepts further, including composition and dominance in local ant faunas (Wilson 1976). A related taxon pulse was characterized by Erwin (1979).

Both concepts are based on common assumptions: (1) habitat specialization is largely irreversible in a lineage, (2) ecological specializations arise in a center of origin, and (3) dispersal events leading to current distributions can be ascertained (see Liebherr and Hajek 1990 for further discussion and comparison). The taxon cycle concept has been applied with success to staphylinid beetles in the Solomon

Islands (Greenslade 1972a, 1972b, later expanded into discussion of adversity selection in Greenslade 1983), West Indian birds (Ricklefs and Bermingham 1999), *Anolis* lizards (Miles and Dunham 1996), and fishes in the Lake Victoria region (Kaufman 1997), but unsuccessfully to West Indian ground beetles (Liebherr and Hajek 1990). As noted by Brown and Lomolino (1998), "given its ability to integrate distributional, ecological, and evolutionary phenomena, Wilson's theory of taxon cycles merits far more attention and more rigorous assessment" (447). In turn, the taxon cycle inspired the more expansive taxon pulse hypothesis (Erwin 1979, 1998), which has been little tested beyond ground beetles (see Liebherr and Hajek 1990 for comparison of taxon cycle and taxon pulse). Rigorous tests of the taxon cycle and the pulse hypothesis require accurate cladistic taxonomies, which are still only rarely available for tropical arthropods (see Liebherr and Hajek 1990 for further discussion).

Both Wilson (see his autobiographical note —Wilson 1985) and Erwin were influenced by the earlier notions of faunal dominance of P. J. Darlington (Darlington 1957, 1971). It is also interesting to note the importance of carabid beetles and ants in the development of ideas by Darlington, Wilson, Erwin, and many others (Ball 1985). Wilson's studies, along with subsequent papers (Wilson and Taylor 1967a, 1967b), remain among of the most comprehensive biogeographical studies of any insects in the Pacific Basin (Miller 1996) and also provided the background for the equilibrium theory of island biogeography (MacArthur and Wilson 1967).

Conclusion

Elegant and testable hypotheses laid out many years ago remain poorly tested and provide clear evidence that much interesting work remains to be done in the evolutionary biology of tropical insects. Forty years ago, Wilson laid out the taxon cycle model, and also contributed the foundation for Leston's proposal, thirty years ago, of the ant mosaic model. Twenty years ago, Erwin made a chain of hypotheses about insect diversity. While Erwin's conclusions fueled discussions about the scale and conservation of biological diversity, the underlying assumptions remain poorly tested. Although Haddow, Corbet, and colleagues did not contribute explicit hypotheses about insect stratification, their bold experiments in the forests of Uganda challenged existing assumptions that remain inadequately tested forty years later. This commentary also shows that it is indeed difficult to identify single seminal papers because of the cumulative growth of theories, and data to test them, over time. Much of tropical insect ecology remains in the case study phase, and generalizations across continents are still difficult to make for most topics. New techniques of sampling, analysis, and information management (e.g., Longino and Colwell 1997; Basset et al. 2000) are facilitating a new generation of long-term research accumulating large data sets that should help fill these gaps.

Reprinted Selections

E. O. Wilson. 1958. Patchy distributions of ant species in New Guinea rain forests. *Psyche* 65:26–38

A. J. Haddow, P. S. Corbet, and J. D. Gillett. 1961. Entomological studies from a high tower in Mpanga Forest, Uganda. Introduction and abstracts to parts 2, 4, 5, and 6. *Transactions of the Royal Entomological Society of London* 113:249–253, 269, 283, 300, and 314, plates I–II

T. L. Erwin. 1982. Tropical forests: Their richness in Coleoptera and other arthropod species. *The Coleopterists Bulletin* 36:74–75

PATCHY DISTRIBUTIONS OF ANT SPECIES IN NEW GUINEA RAIN FORESTS

By EDWARD O. WILSON
Biological Laboratories, Harvard University

While recently engaged in field work in New Guinea the author had several excellent opportunities to study local areal distribution of rain forest ants. During one three-week period in April, 1955, a walk was made from Finschhafen, on the eastern tip of the Huon Peninsula, west for a distance of 45 kilometers through the midmountain rain forests of the Dedua-Hube regions to Tumnang and Laulaunung, thence south for thirty kilometers to Butala on the southern coast. In the vicinity of Lae intensive collecting was conducted over a distance of twelve kilometers in recently continuous lowland rain forest within the triangle formed by Didiman Creek, Bubia, and the section between the Busu and Bupu Rivers.

Areal distributions of individual species were found to be almost universally patchy, despite the external appearance of uniformity of the rain forest environment. Furthermore, in the cases of species abundant enough to be studied in some detail, the patchiness seemed to obtain at two levels of distribution, which for purposes of description here will be referred to as "microgeographic" and "geographic".

Microgeographic patchiness. The species common enough to be studied in detail are also relatively adaptable, occurring usually in spots of variable canopy density (see below) and sometimes in more than one major forest type (e.g., *Leptogenys dimunuta* (Fr. Smith), which ranges from medium lowland rain forest to dry, monsoon forest). In this respect, at least, they seem to be no more specialized than the majority of temperate ant species. At the same time, they show definite preferences for certain local environmental con-

---

EXPLANATION OF PLATE 3

Plate 3. Primary medium-aspect rain forest near the lower Busu River, Northeast New Guinea. A bulldozer trail cuts through the lower left hand corner of the picture.

PSYCHE, 1958   VOL. 65, PLATE 3

WILSON — NEW GUINEA RAIN FOREST

ditions. At the Busu River and in other lowland rain forest sites investigated, ant species tended to be segregated into local areas, sometimes a hectare in extent or less, which could be distinguished from adjacent areas by their specific canopy densities. When the total range of possible canopy densities at the Busu River, from the open aspect that fringes savanna areas, to the most closed aspect, ordinarily found covering sloughs, was arbitrarily divided into three divisions (open, medium, dense) and their faunas studied, the following microgeographic segregation of ant species was noted.

"Open rain forest". (Plate 5) Broken canopy; considerable ground insolation; leaf litter 2 to 15 cm. thick; leaf mold present but thin and relatively dry; soil loose, well aerated, and relatively dry; moss scarce on both ground and tree trunks; A-stratum trees generally less than thirty meters high; lianes and plank buttresses much less common than in other two divisions; recumbent vines common on ground; soil and rotting logs generally thoroughly penetrated with dense root and rhizome growth; undergrowth relatively dense; sufficient to make human progress across the forest floor difficult. This is the aspect of old second-growth forest and may be created naturally by the fall of large forest trees or, in mountainous areas, by rockslides. It is also a more or less permanent feature of the fringe of forest, generally one to two hundred meters wide, that borders savanna areas. Occasional spots deep within rain forest approach the open aspect even though an immediate cause, such as a large fallen tree, is not in evidence. Ant species that appear to reach their maximum density in open rain forest at the Busu River included *Platythyrea parallela* (Fr. Smith), *Diacamma rugosum* (Le Guillou), *Odontomachus simillimus* (Fr. Smith), and *Cardiocondyla paradoxa* (Emery). In the canopy of the open forest, species of *Crematogaster*, especially subgenus *Xiphocrema*, and of *Technomyrmex* increased generally, while those of *Iridomyrmex* decreased.

"Medium rain forest". (Plates 3, 4). By far the largest lowland area in the Lae area is covered by forest of the following aspect: closed canopy; ground insolation slight;

leaf litter as in open aspect; underlying leaf mold rich and moist; soil loose, well aerated and drained and relatively, moist; moss common on the surface of the ground, on rotting wood lying on the ground and on tree trunks; A-stratum trees average 40 meters or more in height; plank buttresses common; lianes and epiphytes abundant; under growth sparse, making human progress across the forest floor easy. The majority of endemic ant species are concentrated in this division. Examples of genera that reached maximum density (in 1955) on the floor of the Busu forest included *Ponera, Myopias, Ectomomyrmex, Pheidole, Strumigenys, Rhopalothrix, Myrmecina,* and *Pristomyrmex.* In the canopy *Iridomyrmex* heavily predominated.

"Dense rain forest". Closed canopy; little or no ground insolation; leaf litter thin, with one-quarter or more of the ground surface completely bare; leaf mold very poorly developed; soil dense, less well drained and moister than in medium forest; parts of the ground surface occasionally holding shallow pools of water after heavy rains; moss abundant, especially on larger rotting logs; A-stratum trees as tall as in medium forest; plank buttresses common; lianes and epiphytes abundant; undergrowth very sparse, even more so than in medium forest. Ants reaching maximum density in various strata of this division at the Busu River included some species of *Pheidologeton, Tetramorium, Leptomyrmex* and *Iridomyrmex.*

Careful analysis would probably reveal many finer details of microgeographic segregation than those indicated here, for the rain forest is an extraordinarily complex mosaic of local habitats, exhibiting seemingly endless nuances and combinations of erosion states, growth and death of vegetation, composition of leaf mold, and other environmental features. Ant species did not appear to be limited to any of these particular divisions within the rain forest proper. At most, the divisions probably serve as density foci, from which the species are constantly pressing out into adjacent, less favorable habitats,

Geographic patchiness. Ant species apparently show extensive and unpredictable variation in population density over short geographic distances above and beyond that already noted with respect to microgeographic habitat segregation. This phenomenon was first observed in the Hube area of the Huon Peninsula, where, through a few kilometers distance in seemingly uniform mid-mountain forest, dominant species of the genera *Aphaenogaster* (*Planimyrma*), *Meranoplus,* and *Leptomyrmex* showed conspicuously irregular density patterns. The impression was gained that even within the most favored habitats these species showed irregular density patterns. This type of discontinuous distribution is superimposed on the mosaic, habitat-correlated microgeographic patchiness, and the two conditions probably grade into each other. It can be predicted that superimposition of the two levels of patchiness will result in very irregular and complex individual species distributions, which in turn will have a profound effect on the differentiation of local faunas at localities separated by as little as a few kilometers distance. Such an effect was in fact observed in the lowland rain forests of the Lae area, as described below

Differentiation of local faunas in the Lae area. In 1955 most of the area to the north of Lae and east of the nearby Busu River was covered with a mixture of primary and secondary rain forest, with occasional savanna enclaves. Native villages were not numerous, and native agriculture had not made serious inroads into the forest. In the vicinity of Bubia, to the northwest of Lae, extensive land was under cultivation, partly by the Government Agricultural Experiment Station, but even here the forest was still partly intact, and primary tracts were still accessible[1].

[1] According to both Mr. Henry G. Eckhoff and Mr. Carl M. Jacobson (pers. commun.), who were among the first European settlers of the Lae district, extensive clearing of the forests of this area is a comparatively recent event. Prior to 1925 the only European settlement was the mission station at Malahang, on the coast near Lae. In 1925 a small amount of ground was cleared at Didiman Creek to establish the Goverment Agricultural Experimental Station. Between 1925 and 1930, further clearing proceeded in the vicinity but was still restricted to the present town limits of Lae. Mr. Eckhoff, who arrived in 1928, states that in 1929-30, "My wife and I were the only residents of Lae other than the air freighting companies. There were no other agricultural activities". The next principal development was the establishment of a poultry farm just outside the Lae township by Mr. Jacobson. During the Second World War a road was built from Lae through Bubia to the airfield at Nadzab. Since 1945 clearing for agricultural purposes has proceeded to a limited extent of either side of this road.

Three localities within this forested area were chosen as sites of intensive collecting (see figure 1). The Busu-Bupu forest was the least disturbed of the three; lumbering operations had commenced in the collecting area only the year before, and most of the forest seemed in primary condition. The Didiman Creek site contained a tract of forest, at least partly second-growth in nature, that had been preserved within the Government Agricultural Experimental Station on the northern edge of Lae. At Bubia, extensive forest tracts, primary at least in part, extended to the east of the Jacobson Plantation. The forest tracts at these three localities represent relict segments of what can reasonably be assumed to have been continuous, predominantly primary lowland forest as recently as thirty years ago. Bubia and

TABLE I.

	BUBIA	DIDIMAN CR.	BUSU R.
Cardiocondyla paradoxa Emery	X	XX	XX
Crematogaster (Acrocoelia) irritabilis (Fr. Smith)	X	XXX	—
Crematogaster (Rhachiocrema) sp. nov.	—	XX	—
Tetramorium validiusculum Emery	XXX	X	XX
Tetramorium ornatum Emery	—	XX	XX
Triglyphothrix fulviceps Emery	—	XX	XX
Aphaenogaster dromedarius Emery	—	—	XX
Meranoplus hirsutus (Fr. Smith)	X	—	XX
Leptomyrmex fragilis (Fr. Smith)	XX	—	XX
Pseudolasius breviceps Emery	XXX	XX	X

Subjective estimates of relative abundance of some dominant ant species at three neighboring localities in New Guinea. A dashed line means absent, or at least never observed; a single X, present but collected only once or twice; double-X moderately abundant; triple-X among the two or three most abundant species at the locality. Since collecting trips were wide-ranging, these estimates reflect most closely the relative abundance of colonies, rather than number of workers or biomass. Further explanation in text.

Busu-Bupu regions were almost connected by continuous forest even as late as 1955. There is no reason to believe

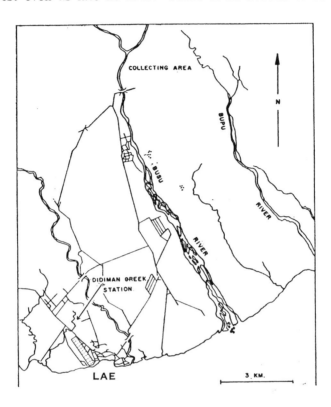

Figure 1. Map of the Lae area in 1955, showing Didiman Creek and the Busu-Bupu area, two of the collecting stations studied with respect to local distribution of species. The third station, Bubia, is located 12.5 kilometers to the northwest of the town of Lae.

EXPLANATION OF PLATE 4

Plate 4. Floor of primary medium-aspect rain forest near lower Busu River. An overhead tree has just been felled to allow in an unusual amount of sunlight. The exposed portion of the machete is approximately 20 inches, or 50 centimeters, in length. The greatest concentration of species and individual colonies to be found anywhere in New Guinea nest in small pieces of rotting wood in this situation.

that the forests at the three localities, or the ant faunas in
them, had been seriously disturbed by man. All three localities contained rich endemic Papuan faunas, with virtually
no infi tration of introduced species.

Subjective impressions of the relative abundance of several of the dominant ant species are presented in Table 1. In
each of the three localities, all of the major microgeographic
areal divisions were studied. Each locality was visited at
least twice during the author's two month stay in the Lae
area, and a minimum of four days devoted to intensive collecting. Under these conditions, only the commonest species
could be compared, but differences in local abundance of
these were so striking that it seems safe to predict that
similar patchy distributions are exhibited by other, less dominant members of the fauna.

DISCUSSION: THE EVOLUTIONARY IMPLICATIONS OF PATCHINESS

In any appraisal of comparative ecology, the New Guinea
ant fauna is to be characterized first of all by the exceptional
richness of its species and the great size of its biomass. The
present study has shown that in addition to sheer size, an
additional factor adds greatly to the total faunal complexity.
This is the discordant patchy distribution of individual
species. The fractioning of species into small subpopulations
that are partially isolated from one another probably results
in relatively high rates of evolution, whether through random drift or differential selective pressures or both (see for
instance Kimura, 1955, and Ford, 1955). Moreover, as a
result of discordant patchiness, no two localities harbor
exactly the same fauna. Considering that several hundreds
of species are thus involved, it is clear that the spatiotemporal structure of the entire New Guinea fauna must
present the appearance of a great kaleidoscope. The effects
of such a structure on the evolution of individual species of

---

EXPLANATION OF PLATE 5

Plate 5. Floor of primary open-aspect rain forest near the lower
Busu River. The undergrowth at this spot is made up preponderantly of
an unidentified speces of *Selaginella*.

ants, as well as of other kinds of animals, must be considerable. It very possibly hastens the genetic divergence of local populations and plays an important role in the "exuberance" and amplitude that characterizes evolution in the tropics. Probably as the fauna increases in size, in passing from temperate to tropical areas or from small islands to large ones. the diversifying effects of a kaleidoscopic population structure increase exponentially.

There is abundant evidence that similar features of population structure occur in other groups of organisms in tropical forests. Aubrevi'le (1938), in his "mosaic" or "cyclical" theory of regeneration, has described a kaleidoscope pattern in forest trees of the Ivory Coast. Richards (1952) doubts whether the mosaic theory holds for all rain forest associations, but accepts its validity in special cases where certain conditions have been met.

"The poor regeneration of the dominant species in African Forests seems in all probability to indicate that the composition of the community is changing. If the forest is in fact 'untouched and primitive', as Aubreville claims . . . . the changes must be cyclical as the Mosaic theory imp'ies. On the other hand, if the community has undergone disturbance in the past, the present combination of species [in a given sample plot] may be a seral stage and the changes part of a normal (not cyclical) process of development toward a stable climax".

Moreau (1948) finds patchiness a common feature in the distribution of rain forest birds in Tanganyika. Where a species is absent from a locality, it is usually replaced by a related species (from the same family), but not always, leaving some inexplicab'e gaps. The following example is typical:

"Nearly all the montane forests of eastern Africa from Kenya southward are occupied by one or both of the little barbets, *Pogoniulus bilineatus* and *Viridobucco leucomystax*. On Hanang Mountain, where both these species are missing, *Pogoniulus pusillus,* normally a bird of deciduous trees at lower altitudes, appears in the mountain forests

(Fuggles-Couchman, unpublished). But this does not happen in the neighboring forests of the Mbulu District, where the fruit-eating barbets are not represented at all."

Additional examples from other animal groups and other parts of the tropics (as well as the temperate zones) could be cited to show that patchiness is a widespread phenomenon, on both a very local (microgeographic) and broader (geographic) scale. To all such cases Richards' conditions must be applied, i.e., it must be asked whether patchiness has not arisen exclusively as a result of man-made disturbances. But patchiness as a result of natural disturbances, such as tree falls and stream erosion, is a good possibility also, and should be considered in the future. In the author's present opinion, much of the patchiness observed in New Guinea ant populations has actually arisen through natural disturbances, since enclaves of second-growth vegetation are a normal feature of remote, undisturbed forest. This argument has been taken up in somewhat more detail elsewhere (Wilson, 1959).

SUMMARY

The population structure of individual Papuan ant species is shown to be generally irregular. Patchiness exists at both a local, clearly ecological level, and a broader, "geographic" level not easily correlated with environmental influences. The combined irregularities in the distributions of multiple species result in distinct shifts of faunal composition and relative abundance over distances of only a few kilometers even in relatively continuous, homogeneous rain forest. The theoretical implications of discordant patchiness with respect to rapid evolution are discussed.

LITERATURE CITED

AUBREVILLE, A.
  1938. La forêt coloniale: les forêts de l'Afrique occidentale française. Ann. Acad. Sci. Colon., Paris, 9: 1-245.
FORD, E. B.
  1955. Rapid evolution and the conditions which make it possible. Symp. Quant. Biol. (Cold Spring Harbor), 20: 230-238.

KIMURA, M.
  1955. Stochastic processes and distribution of gene frequencies under
        natural selection. Symp. Quant. Biol. (Cold Spring Harbor),
        20: 33-53.

MOREAU, R. E.
  1948. Ecological isolation in a rich tropical avifauna. J. Animal Ecol.,
        17: 113-126.

RICHARDS, P. W.
  1952. *The tropical rain forest.* Cambridge University Press.

WILSON, E. O.
  1959. Adaptive shift and dispersal in a tropical ant fauna. Evolution
        (in press).

ENTOMOLOGICAL STUDIES FROM A HIGH TOWER
IN MPANGA FOREST, UGANDA

Manuscript received 29th September, 1960

(Read 7th December, 1960)

With 2 Plates and 35 Text-figures

CONTENTS

I. INTRODUCTION

By A. J. HADDOW, PHILIP S. CORBET AND J. D. GILLETT

(East African Virus Research Institute, Entebbe, Uganda)

THE East African Virus Research Institute is concerned with the arthropod-borne viruses of man and animals in East Africa, and particularly with those which are transmitted by mosquitoes. The high steel tower, from which the studies here reported were carried out, was designed mainly for the study of biting Diptera which might be concerned in virus transmission, but workers in other fields have also found it suitable for their studies, some of which are included in the present series.

The first studies on the vertical distribution of biting Diptera in Africa were carried out almost concurrently in Kenya and Uganda. The results obtained in

250   *Entomological studies from a high tower in Mpanga Forest, Uganda*

banana plantations in the Semliki Valley, Uganda, were published by Haddow (1945b), those from the Kaimosi Forest, Kenya, by Garnham, Harper and Highton (1946) and those from the Semliki Forest, Uganda, by Haddow, Gillett and Highton (1947). Another interesting group of catches was carried out at this time in the Entebbe area by Dr. K. Goodner, a member of the International Health Division of the Rockefeller Foundation, but the results were not published and are available only in the annual reports of the Yellow Fever Research Institute, Entebbe.

The work in the Semliki Forest mentioned above consisted mainly of 24-hour catches with human bait carried out simultaneously at a number of levels above ground, with controls at ground level. These studies, made in 1944–45, were accompanied by observations on microclimate. It was found that, as in South America, certain species bite mainly in the canopy, others in the understorey and others at ground level. The highest station established was at 82 feet, in a semi-emergent tree, the platform being well above the main canopy level. Here, though the canopy species were reduced in abundance, they were still prevalent and at once the question arose as to whether there might not be a good deal of activity in the free air above the forest.

During the succeeding years numerous tree platforms were erected—40 in the Semliki Valley and 7 near Entebbe. Extensive studies were carried out, about five hundred 24-hour catches being made. Meanwhile the problem of activity above the forest remained unsolved, though it was becoming more and more obvious that it was one of major significance. Thus the males of certain important species are seldom or never found in nature, a finding paralleled by work in South America on the genus *Haemagogus*, where the males of certain species were never obtained except by rearing from larvae (Kumm, Osorno and Boshell, 1946). It was suspected that such males might be found in and above the canopy and that their incidence there might be investigated by light-trapping. A more important point was that, apart from some early references, almost nothing was known of the swarming of African mosquitoes with the exception of *Anopheles funestus* Giles (Harper, 1944) and *A. gambiae* Giles (Muirhead Thomson, 1948). It seemed likely that swarming might occur over emergent trees in the forest and that the crepuscular periods would be, as in the case of European species, the important times (*see, for example*, Marshall, 1938). Evening twilight was already known to be a time of great activity in many species (Kerr, 1933; Haddow, Gillett and Highton, 1947; Lumsden, 1952) and it was felt that, should swarming over the forest occur in this period, it might well be at a time at which dispersal of mosquitoes to surrounding areas might occur. Thompson (1953) has shown that in calm weather in woodland there is a slow, almost continuous interchange of air between the upper and lower levels. Wellington (1945), however, has pointed out that as tropical forest is darker than the surrounding landscape, very rapid radiation of heat occurs at canopy level after sunset. Thus, though air within the forest is almost a closed system by day, thermals may tend to develop over it at sunset, and these may help to carry small insects to considerable heights and distances. It is known that aphids are carried to great heights daily (*see, for example*, Johnson, 1953) and it has been shown that mosquitoes may also occur in the upper atmosphere to heights of at least 5,000 feet (Glick, 1939).

Apart from swarming activity it was felt that mosquitoes might leave the forest in response to the influence of environmental factors. It was known that at ground level the microclimatic boundaries of the forest may break down at certain times and under certain conditions, permitting sylvan species to move out into surrounding environments (Boshell and Osorno, 1944; Haddow, 1945a). Further, it had been shown that the microclimate of the forest canopy may not differ very greatly from that in the open air (Allee, 1926; Haddow, Gillett and Highton, 1947). Shannon (1931a and b) had pointed out that most metallic mosquitoes are diurnal, and Bates (1944) had shown that many of them are arboreal. He suggested that the coloration was connected with life in an " unfavourable " (*i.e.* rather dry) environment and showed (1947) that *Haemagogus*—typical members of this arboreal group—survive best in rather dry air which is actually circulating. It seemed, therefore, that some of the arboreal and diurnal African mosquitoes which have metallic colours—such as *Aedes longipalpis* (Grünberg)—might well be able to " break the barrier " and rise above the forest. The question appeared to call for thorough investigation.

It was decided that a high tower with catching-platforms and climate stations at regular levels was required, but many years passed before funds could be obtained. Finally, with the aid of a grant from the World Health Organisation, work was begun and the tower (Plates I and II) was completed in 1958. It is constructed of steel, and has wooden platforms at ground level, 30 feet (in the understorey), 60 feet (in a dense part of the canopy), 90 feet (above the main canopy but in the zone of numerous emergent trees) and 120 feet (high above the main canopy and on a level with the tops of the highest emergent trees in its vicinity). Standard meteorological screens were set up at 6 feet and on platforms at 50 and 110 feet. From time to time series of thermohygrograph readings were carried out in these screens. It was not possible to keep the instruments running throughout the period of almost a year during which mosquito studies were in progress, but the series of recordings covered both dry and wet seasons. Run-of-the-wind anemometers were used to study wind flow at various heights (Part II, p. 258) and a visiting worker made studies on light (Part III). Unfortunately another visitor, who studied rainfall at various levels, did not realise that our intention was to publish the work all at one time and his contribution has appeared elsewhere (Hopkins, 1960). Bamboo pots for mosquito oviposition were attached to the tower at vertical intervals of ten feet from ground level to the top.

Much thought was given to the placing of the tower. For 14 years the Institute staff had been working in a small forest at Zika near Entebbe, and this seemed in many ways suitable. There were, however, certain difficulties and finally it was decided to build in the Mpanga Research Forest, west of Kampala. Some of the advantages were administrative, but the most important was that, as this forest is maintained for research by the Forest Department of the Uganda Protectorate, it was thoroughly known and mapped, and the plant ecology had been studied in considerable detail. Some blocks of the forest are used for particular research projects, others for exploitation in the normal way, and others again are maintained in a state of nature.

An admirably terse description of the forest has been given in a pamphlet circulated by the Forest Department (Ref. GPUP–2015–IM–8–55, Entebbe, May 1955) and it is felt that the writers cannot do better than quote this *verbatim* :

" POSITION : 0°12′–13′N., 32°17′–18′E. 25 miles (40 km.) west of Kampala on Masaka road, about 10 miles (16 km.) north of Lake Victoria. Forest Reserve of 1,121 acres (450 ha.). ALTITUDE : 3,800′ (1,160 m.). CLIMATE : Rainfall mean about 45″ (1130 mm.), lowest recorded fall about 35″ (890 mm.) and highest about 66″ (1670 mm.) with 2 to 4 months of less than 2″ (50 mm.). Temperatures from 50°F. (10°C.) to 92°F. (33°C.), mean about 75° F. (24°C.). Relative humidities from 60 per cent. to 95 per cent. TOPOGRAPHY : Level valley flanked by gentle slopes of low hills, draining N.W. to join the south-flowing Nakyetema swamp. SOIL : Swamp : blue-grey heavy clays with some peat, pH. about 5. Slopes : deep lateritic red-earth with murram gravel over highly decomposed gneiss and quartzite, occasional ironstone outcrops, pH. 5 to 6. FOREST TYPES : Swamp : permanently flooded or water-logged *Mitragyna-Macaranga-Phoenix* association with some *Erythrina* and *Spondianthus*, over *Euphorbia teke* and acanth-marantaceous herb layer with much *Dracaena laxissima*. Developed from *Cyperus papyrus* with all seral stages. Slopes : well developed *Celtis-Aningeria* association up to

160′ (50 m.) top height, rich in species of seral stages from *Pennisetum Hyparrhenia* grassland, of the genera *Albizzia, Piptadenia, Lovoa,* over dense *Acalypha-Dracaena fragrans* shrub layer, over almost continuous *Leptaspi*: ground layer. REFERENCES : Locality described by A. S. Thomas, *Journ Ecol.* **33** : 24–30 (1945). Papyrus-forest sere by W. J. Eggeling, *Journ. Ecol.* **23** : 422 (1935) ''.

The site selected was in a swampy valley and the tower stands at the junction of swamp and slope forest. A small perennial stream flowing from a hill-foot seepage passes within a few yards of the base. During building the greatest care was taken not to cut trees or branches and to disturb the undergrowth as little as possible. The tower rises, itself like a forest tree, through a dense stand of timber in which *Pseudospondias microcarpa* (A. Rich.) Engle., *Erythrina excelsa* Bak., *Canarium schweinfurthii* Engl. and *Entandrophragma angolense* (Welw.) C.DC. are prominent. Slightly further down the valley wetter conditions lead to a dominance of *Pseudospondias*. Prominent among understorey trees is *Euphorbia teke* Schweinf. *ex* Pax, and the shrub layer is largely composed of *Dracaena fragrans* Ker-Gaul whose topmost axils provide a breeding-ground for mosquitoes of the genus *Eretmapodites*.

The tower was built beside a hugh tree (*E. excelsa*) as it was felt that this might provide a swarming focus. Actually, as will be described in Part V, the tower itself has proved to be a focus for swarming Diptera belonging to many different groups.

When first erected, the tower rose through a particularly dense patch of forest in which an important feature was an exceptionally heavy growth of lianas and of epiphytic ferns and orchids. It was considered that this dense concentration of plants in the canopy would give good harbourage for resting mosquitoes. Among the lianas, and forming a crucial support for the tangled mass, is one of exceptional size. At about 50 feet from its origin it is still over 30 inches in girth and its length the writers estimate as not less than 400 feet. It originally passed, close beside the tower, through the crown of three *Pseudospondias* of medium size. During a severe storm one of those was uprooted, and the other two now had to bear the immense weight of this liana, plus that of numerous other smaller specimens together with the masses of epiphytes with which they were covered. This proved too great a load and, after a few weeks, one of the *Pseudospondias* snapped off at about 12 feet above ground. The other fell subsequently, uprooted by the additional weight it now bore. The result was that the tower is now rather exposed on one side at understorey level though still closely surrounded on the others. In the outcome, no apparent difference in the catches was obvious. This agreed with past experience at Zika where on one occasion a large semi-emergent tree standing beside one of the platforms fell, bringing down many branches from other trees with it and leaving a considerable gap in the canopy. No change in the catch results was, however, apparent.

Before the tower was built, catches of various kinds were carried out in order to investigate the local fauna. Taken together with the subsequent work on the tower, the records of those collections have revealed the presence of a considerable number of species. Not all of these were common in the catches which will be described in greater detail in the subsequent papers that form parts of this series, and it is therefore convenient to give at this stage the complete list of biting Diptera taken in the Mpanga Forest at any time by Institute staff. The names are given in full in Appendix A to permit the use of abbreviated names in the following papers. The nomenclature of Stone, Knight and Starcke (1959) has been followed for mosquitoes as, though some of the names are not those generally used in the British Commonwealth, this is the only up-to-date and complete list available. Where contracted names have been employed, *Ae.* is given for *Aedes* to avoid confusion with *Anopheles*, which is given as *A.* Biting Diptera referred to below which are not known from Mpanga are listed in Appendix B. Certain other (non-biting) insect groups have also been studied on the tower. These form the subject of separate papers in this series, in which the species are listed in full.

All the papers referred to in this and subsequent parts in the series have been combined in a single list at the end. When another paper in this series is cited in the text, it is referred to simply by its part number.

In mosquito catching our standard procedure is to adjust the clock so that 1800 hours " catch time " corresponds to the actual time of sunset. As Mpanga is very close to the equator, sunrise is very close to 0600 hours "catch time ".

The measure of central tendency used in these papers is the logarithmic transformation introduced by Williams (1937, 1939). Formerly it was usually referred to as " Williams' modification of the geometric mean ". This definition was considered to lack precision, and the term " Williams' Mean " (designated by the symbol M_w) is considered preferable (Haddow, 1960).

The term " circadian " is a recent one (Halberg, Halberg, Barnum and Bittner, 1959). Originally it implied a period differing from 24 hours by not more than a few hours. By most workers it is now taken to imply a period approximating to 24 hours.

In conclusion we wish to thank the many workers in different fields who contributed to the actual building of the tower, particularly Mr. J. D. Smithers of H. Young & Co. (East Africa) who designed it, Mr. B. C. Eccleston, Supervisor, Provincial Engineer's Office, Public Works Department, Uganda, who designed the foundations, Mr. F. W. Volrath, Transport Officer, Public Works Department, who solved a difficult transport problem for us and Mr. K. P. Dewar, also of the Public Works Department, who actually built the foundations. We are indebted to Mr. H. C. Dawkins, Ecologist, Forest Department, Uganda, for much information concerning the Mpanga Forest and for permission to quote the description printed above, and to Mr. D. J. Bargman of the East African Meteorological Department for help in installing and calibrating the recording instruments.

(*APPENDIX A* overleaf)

Trans. R. Ent. Soc. Lond.   Vol. 113

PLATE I

The 120-foot steel tower in the Mpanga Forest, Mengo District, Uganda.

A. J. Haddow and others

Trans. R. Ent. Soc. Lond.   Vol. 113   PLATE II

The 120-foot steel tower in the Mpanga Forest, Mengo District, Uganda.
(Photo. Prof. A. W. Woodruff)

A. J. Haddow and others

ENTOMOLOGICAL STUDIES FROM A HIGH TOWER
IN MPANGA FOREST, UGANDA

II. OBSERVATIONS ON CERTAIN ENVIRONMENTAL FACTORS
AT DIFFERENT LEVELS

By A. J. Haddow and Philip S. Corbet

(*East African Virus Research Institute, Entebbe, Uganda*)

Summary

1. Series of readings were made with the help of recording instruments in the Mpanga Forest, Uganda. The main environmental factors studied were temperature, saturation deficiency, wind direction and wind speed. These readings were made at 116–120 feet (above the canopy), 56–60 feet (in the canopy) and 6 feet (" ground level ").

2. Where temperature and saturation deficiency were concerned, the differences between the canopy and the air above it were small at all times. During the day the readings at ground level were lower than those above, but the differences were much smaller than those recorded elsewhere by other workers. On the other hand, there were very striking differences at all levels between days on which rain fell in the afternoon and days when it did not. Differences between days were, in fact, more important than differences between levels. By night there was no significant difference between the levels, and there was therefore no microclimatic barrier to prevent the diffusion of mosquitoes from the forest into the atmosphere above it at this time.

3. The ratio of wind flow above the canopy to flow in the canopy to flow at ground level was approximately 150 : 16 : 1. At ground level recordable wind was virtually confined to the afternoon and even in the canopy there was very little wind by night. Above the canopy there was much wind by day, with a maximum in mid-afternoon. After sunset, however, there was very little flow even at this level, and once again it seemed to present little or no barrier to the upward diffusion of mosquitoes by night. The prevailing winds were south to south-westerly at all times of the day and night.

4. It is pointed out that at ground level in forest light intensity may be biphasic, with peaks in the morning and afternoon and a period of lesser intensity around midday. The biting cycle of many ground-haunting mosquitoes shows a similar pattern.

ENTOMOLOGICAL STUDIES FROM A HIGH TOWER
IN MPANGA FOREST, UGANDA

IV. MOSQUITO BREEDING AT DIFFERENT LEVELS
IN AND ABOVE THE FOREST

By PHILIP S. CORBET

(*East African Virus Research Institute, Entebbe, Uganda*)

SUMMARY

1. Mosquito breeding in natural sites and bamboo sections was studied in Mpanga Forest. Observations extended from the ground to a height of 120 feet, about 50 feet above the canopy.

2. Several species exhibited a non-random vertical distribution of larval occurrence. *Toxorhynchites brevipalpis, Aedes africanus* and *Eretmapodites semisimplicipes* were commonest at ground level, and *Aedes apicoargenteus* above the canopy.

3. Predatory mosquitoes predominated below the canopy, particularly at ground level, where they are presumed to have affected the numbers of *Ae. africanus*. The observed vertical distribution of *Ae. apicoargenteus*, however, is shown to have resulted from a site preference and not from predation. It is stressed that these two factors should be clearly distinguished in future studies of mosquito breeding where predators are involved.

4. Results are discussed and compared with those of other workers. Two other insectivorous inhabitants of forest tree-holes are briefly mentioned.

ENTOMOLOGICAL STUDIES FROM A HIGH TOWER
IN MPANGA FOREST, UGANDA

V. SWARMING ACTIVITY ABOVE THE FOREST

By A. J. Haddow and Philip S. Corbet

(*East African Virus Research Institute, Entebbe, Uganda*)

Summary

1. Mosquito swarms form almost nightly over a 120-foot tower in the Mpanga Forest, Uganda. Several species usually swarm together, and members of other insect groups may also be present. Different species may begin swarming at different times, but all tend to end swarming at about the same time. Evening swarming is confined to the single hour after sunset with a peak in the period 20–35 minutes after sunset. The light changes in the post-sunset period are discussed in relation to swarming behaviour.

2. Dawn mosquito swarms occur with less regularity. They are small and of short duration, and only a few species are involved. At dawn, however, male tabanids of various species swarm regularly over the forest.

3. Mating was not observed, though females were regularly present in the mosquito swarms. Taking all species together, the percentage of females was small, but the sex ratio varied from one species to another and in some cases the females outnumbered the males.

4. Some of the more important literature is reviewed and the function of swarming is discussed, but the conclusion is reached that there is not yet sufficient evidence for an explanation of the phenomenon.

ENTOMOLOGICAL STUDIES FROM A HIGH TOWER
IN MPANGA FOREST, UGANDA

VI. NOCTURNAL FLIGHT ACTIVITY OF CULICIDAE AND
TABANIDAE AS INDICATED BY LIGHT-TRAPS

By Philip S. Corbet

(*East African Virus Research Institute, Entebbe, Uganda*)

Summary

1. Fifteen all-night catches with mercury-vapour light-traps were made at five levels on a tower in Mpanga Forest, Uganda. Each trap was emptied hourly, and the Culicidae and Tabanidae which had been caught were identified and counted.

2. The light-traps sampled a more diverse mosquito population than did catches using human-bait at the same site.

3. Males comprised 84·5 per cent. of the 1951 mosquitoes caught, and about 76 per cent. of the 59 tabanids.

4. Mosquitoes most commonly encountered were species of *Uranotaenia*, *Mansonia* and *Culex*. Within a species, activity varied according to level, but males and females usually showed a similar vertical distribution. Nocturnal flight activity, as indicated by the light-trap catches, was cyclical, and usually occurred in two broad waves, males predominating in the first and females in the second. At higher levels, the peak of male activity usually occurred earlier, and the pattern of female activity tended to be better defined. Thus the catches provided evidence for vertical movements.

5. In tabanids there were well-defined differences between males and females : males were only caught above the canopy, and females mainly below it ; males flew mainly in the hour before sunrise, and females in the second hour after sunset.

6. It is suggested that light-traps only sample mosquitoes engaged in non-specific flight activity, and that for this reason the flight patterns they reveal are unlikely to correspond to those of more specific activities such as biting.

7. It is suggested that the rhythmic flight activity recorded in this work has a strong endogenous component. The interplay of endogenous and exogenous rhythms in daily cyclical activity of mosquitoes is briefly discussed.

The Coleopterists Bulletin, 36(1):74–75. 1982.

TROPICAL FORESTS: THEIR RICHNESS IN COLEOPTERA AND OTHER ARTHROPOD SPECIES

TERRY L. ERWIN

National Museum of Natural History, Smithsonian Institution,
Washington, DC 20560

ABSTRACT

Extrapolation from data about canopy insects collected by fogging methods together with estimates of tropical plant host specificity indicate that one hectare of unrich seasonal forest in Panama may have in excess of 41,000 species of arthropods. Further extrapolation of available data based on known relative richness of insect Orders and canopy richness leads to the conclusion that current estimates of Arthropod species numbers are grossly underestimated; that there could be as many as 30 million species extant globally, not 1.5 million as usually estimated.

Since the early days of naturalists, there has been the question of how many species there were in the forests of the tropics. Bates (1892) wrote of collecting more than 700 species of butterflies within an hour's walk of his home in Para, Brazil. Many have guessed that the arthropod fauna of the world today contains between 1.5 to 10 million species. No hard data are available however, and these estimates are less than reliable and as a result misleading. In a recent paper, Erwin and Scott (1980) provided the first hard data with regard to the Coleoptera fauna of a single species of tree in the tropical seasonal forest of Panama. Also recently, Peter Raven of the Missouri Botanical Gardens wrote me with the same inquiry that Bates had pondered—"How many species are there in one acre of rich tropical forest?" With the hard data available from the Panama study, I set out to give as close an estimate as possible and was shocked by my conclusions.

The tropical tree *Luehea seemannii* is a medium-sized seasonal forest evergreen tree with open canopy, large and wide-spaced leaves. The trees sampled (n = 19) had few epiphytes or lianas generally, certainly not the epiphytic load normally thought of as being rich. These 19 trees over a three season sampling regime produced 955+ species of beetles, excluding weevils. In other samples now being processed from Brazil, there are as many weevils as leaf-beetles, usually more, so I added 206 (weevils) to the *Luehea* count and rounded to 1,200 for convenience. There can be as many as 245 species of trees in one hectare of rich forest in the tropics, often some of these in the same genus. Usually there are between 40 to 100 species and/or genera, so I used 70 as an average number of genus-group trees where host-specificity might play a role with regard to arthropods. No data are available with which to judge the proportion of host-specific arthropods per trophic group anywhere, let alone the tropics. So conservatively, I allowed 20% of the *Luehea* herbivorous beetles to be host-specific (i.e., must use this tree species in some way for successful reproduction), 5% of the predators (i.e., are tied to one or more of the host-specific herbivores), 10% of the fungivores (i.e., are tied to fungus associated only with this tree), and 5% of the scavengers (i.e., are associated in some way with only the tree or with the other three trophic groups) (Table 1).

THE COLEOPTERISTS BULLETIN 36(1), 1982 75

Table 1. Numbers of host-specific species per trophic group on *Luehea seemannii* (Figures from Erwin and Scott, 1980).

Trophic group	# Species	% Host-specific (estimated)	# Host-specific (estimated)
Herbivores	682	20%	136.4
Predatores	296	5%	14.8
Fungivores	69	10%	6.9
Scavengers	96	5%	4.8
	1,200+		162.9

Therefore, *Luehea* carries an estimated load of 163 species of host-specific beetles, a rather conservative estimate of 13.5%. I regard the other 86.5% as transient species, merely resting or flying through *Luehea* trees. If one hectare has 70 such genereic-group tree species, there are 11,410 host-specific species of beetles per hectare, plus the remaining 1,038 species of transient beetles, for a total of 12,448 species of beetles per hectare of tropical forest *canopy*.

Beetles make up an estimated 40% of all Arthropod species, therefore there are 31,120 species of Arthropods in the canopy of one hectare of tropical forest. Based on my own observation, I believe the canopy fauna to be at least twice as rich as the forest floor and composed of a different set of species for the most part, so I added ⅓ more to the canopy figure to arrive at a grand total of *41,389 species per hectare* of scrubby seasonal forest in Panama! What will there be in a rich forest? I would hope someone will challenge these figures with more data.

It should be noted that there are an estimated 50,000 species of tropical trees (R. Howard, via R. Eyde, pers. comm.). I suggested elsewhere (Erwin and Adis 1981) that tropical forest insect species, for the most part, are not highly vagile and have small distributions. If this is so, and using the same formula as above starting with 162 host-specific beetles/tree species then there are perhaps as many as *30,000,000* species of tropical arthropods, *not* 1.5 million!

LITERATURE CITED

BATES, H. W. 1892. The Naturalist on the River Amazons. A record of adventures, habits of animals, sketches of Brazilian and Indian life, and aspects of nature under the equator, during eleven years of travel. John Murray, London. 285 p.

ERWIN, T. L., AND J. ADIS. 1981. Amazonian inundation forests: Their role as short-term refugia and generators of species diversity and taxon pulses. *In:* G. Prance, ed. Biological diversification in the tropics. Columbia University Press, New York. 714 p.

ERWIN, T. L., AND J. C. SCOTT. 1980. Seasonal and size patterns, trophic structure, and richness of Coleoptera in the tropical arboreal ecosystem: The fauna of the tree *Luehea seemannii* Triana and Planch in the Canal Zone of Panama. Coleopterists Bulletin 34(3):305–322.

7

Terrestrial Vertebrate Diversity

B. A. Loiselle, R. W. Sussman, and the Earl of Cranbrook

In 1977, John Terborgh wrote that "the species diversity problem has been under intensive investigation by ecologists and biogeographers for the past 20 yr. Yet we are still far from a global understanding of the many diversity patterns in nature" (1007). Nearly twenty-five years later, one might argue that we are not much closer to that understanding, although the past twenty-five years have been productive ones. Moreover, much of the focus on tropical vertebrate diversity in very recent years has shifted to asking how we might conserve species and habitats, given the current patterns of deforestation and habitat modifications (see part 11). Indeed, a search of the recent literature revealed that most papers published in the past five years on tropical vertebrate ecology focus on responses of such communities to forest fragmentation or abundance patterns in human-modified ecosystems (e.g., plantations, selectively logged forests, agroforestry plots).

The set of foundational papers selected for this part were published from 1962 to 1978. These studies have stimulated and shaped much of the current ecological research on vertebrates in tropical forests.

Resource Partitioning and Vertebrate Diversity

The authors of these papers and their contemporaries recognized that tropical humid forests contained many more vertebrate species than did temperate forests. Before the 1960s many well-known studies documented high vertebrate diversity at a number of tropical sites, including studies on birds (e.g., J. P. Chapin's work in the Belgian Congo [1932–54]; Moreau's work in East Africa [1936a, 1950]; A. Wetmore's studies in southern South America [1926]; A. F. Skutch's bird studies in Costa Rica [e.g., 1950, 1954]; F. M. Chapman's studies in northern South America [1917, 1926]; C. E. Hellmayr's studies in South America [1918–38]), herpetofauna (L. C. Stuart's work in Guatemala [1950, 1951]), and mammals (e.g., W. C. Allee's studies in Panama [1926], I. T. Sanderson's work in Cameroon [1940], G. M. Allen and H. J. Coolidge's studies in Liberia [1930], B. L. Lim's study on Asian bats [1960]). Yet prior to the 1960s, biologists believed that the mechanisms underlying high diversity were largely based on historical processes, arguing that geologically older areas contain more species than do younger areas

Flying frog. From Wallace (1869)

(Wallace 1876, Willis 1922; but see Dobzhansky 1950, Corner 1954; also see part 3).

The 1960s, critically, saw the extension of two revolutionary tools for field-workers in tropical forests: the mist-net and the catch-alive trap. For birds and small mammals, unprecedented quantitative data became available on species occurrence, numbers, mobility, and periodic activities. In the 1960s and 1970s this new information led to advancements in ecological theory, particularly relating to community ecology (Kingsland 1985, Schluter and Ricklefs 1993). The result was that ecological interactions, especially competition, were pushed to the forefront as explanations for diversity patterns (Schluter and Ricklefs 1993; see part 3). Consequently, the motivation for many studies conducted in the 1960s and the following two decades was to understand not only why tropical forests harbored such high vertebrate diversity, but also to understand how so many species could coexist in the same patch of forest. The prevalent ideas at the time were influenced strongly by David Lack (1944), who had proposed that coexistence of closely related species occurs because such species partition resources. These ideas were expanded upon by G. E. Hutchinson (1959) as he developed concepts of the multidimensional niche and explained how resources can be partitioned among species. MacArthur and colleagues then connected niche theory to the problem of species diversity (see part 3). Perhaps most importantly, MacArthur (1965) proposed that competitive interactions limit species packing in niche space (see also MacArthur and Levins 1967). Thus, in saturated environments, "the number of species expected is the usable range of resources divided by the limiting similarity of resources which can be used by coexisting species" (MacArthur 1965, 522). Given such patterns of limited similarity, more species are expected to occur in sites with greater complexity of vegetation (i.e., more vegetation layers) as such sites provide more ecological opportunities to accommodate species (MacArthur and MacArthur 1961; see also Dobzhansky 1950, Pianka 1967, part 3 of this volume). The importance of competition had long been recognized by biologists. For example, in 1859 Charles Darwin wrote that

[i]t is the most closely allied forms—varieties of the same species and species of the same genera—which, from having nearly the same structure, constitution and habits, generally come into the severest competition with each other; consequently each new variety or species during the progress of its formation, will press hardest on its nearest kindred, and tend to exterminate them. (Darwin 1959, 101)

Yet, it was not until the 1960s that the concepts of interspecific competition and resource partitioning were connected to species diversity questions (see part 3 for further discussion).

The approach taken to understanding vertebrate diversity patterns in tropical forests has varied, including detailed studies at a single locality (e.g., Crump 1978, Fogden 1972, Charles-Dominique et al. 1981), broad-scale comparisons along environmental (e.g., Terborgh 1971, 1977; Medway 1972a) or latitudinal (Pianka 1966, Karr 1971, Cody 1975) gradients, and comparisons among sites within or between continents (e.g., Karr 1976). As Terborgh (1977) noted, "[Local] diversity is a complex community phenomenon, not just a number which can be 'explained' with one or more competing hypotheses" (1017). Processes operating at one scale (e.g., environmental gradient) are likely to play only minor roles at other scales (e.g., interregional comparisons). In addition, locally important processes most likely differ among the sets of species considered. Hence it is not surprising that attempts to generate global hypotheses to explain diversity patterns have fallen short of their goal.

While at the Institute of Medical Research (IMR) at Kuala Lumpur and later for a short stint in northern Queensland, John L. Harrison integrated work on arboviruses and their hosts and vectors with trapping surveys of small mammals. From accumulated observations, he reviewed patterns of niche segregation among a broad variety of tropical mammals in Malaysian and Australian rain forests (Harrison 1954, 1962, 1969). The interpretive descriptions of rain forest plots by Paul W. Richards (1952) and the school of foresters in Brunei (Ashton 1964; see also parts 8 and 12) were instrumental in assisting both Harrison and later Terborgh in recognizing structure within a complex vegetation community. Both Harrison and Terborgh used vertical layers defined by Richards (1952) to describe patterns of niche segregation among tropical vertebrates. Harrison (1957, 1962) redefined Richards's layers into vertical units used by mammals and birds, which included flying animals above the canopy, canopy animals, middle-zone flying and scansorial animals, large ground animals that are restricted to the ground, and small ground animals that can climb or otherwise use lower vegetation. In a paper reprinted here, he synthesized his categorization of mammals and birds into a diagram (Harrison 1962, 61, fig. 2) which integrated diversity of each group within each layer, food resources used, and connections among various groups. This food chain was revolutionary at the time and was later adopted or imitated by others, including R. E. Moreau (1966). Harrison emphasized the upper canopy as the "primary producing layer" that plays a major role in supporting the diverse assemblage of mammals. Harrison's diagram reflects how food resources directly or indirectly produced in the canopy (fruits, flowers, insects) serve to provide other food to animals living in other vertical layers. Impressed by the complexity of tropical rain forests, Harrison's goal was not to explain all components of diversity in his food chain diagram, but rather to provide a hypothetical framework into which other observations could be placed. Harrison's studies, therefore, provided a framework for segregating species into different zones within tropical forests and defining functional groups, but did not address the perplexing question of how so many species could coexist within the same forest. The importance of primary productivity and habitat complexity to tropical diversity, although not directly stated, were hinted at in the article; such theories were developed just a few years later as mechanisms to explain diversity

patterns (see parts 3 and 9 for further discussion).

Habitat Complexity and Resource Productivity

John Terborgh and his colleagues, most notably John Weske, set out to examine diversity patterns along an environmental gradient in Peru (Terborgh 1971, 1977; Terborgh and Weske 1969, 1975). In the mid-1970s the positive relationship between bird diversity and habitat complexity (i.e., foliage height diversity) had been demonstrated in a number of biogeographic regions (Karr 1971; MacArthur 1964; MacArthur, Recher, and Cody 1966; Recher 1969). Yet Terborgh challenged the dogma at the time and questioned whether or not habitat complexity and the opportunities it offers for greater niche segregation really provided a causal explanation for diversity patterns.

Building on his ornithological surveys while at the IMR, H. Elliott McClure led an unprecedented international bird-banding program that ran from 1963 to 1971, with collaborators across tropical Asia from India to Taiwan (McClure 1974). Although the emphasis was on migratory species, some participants used the opportunity to investigate local rain forest bird faunas, showing for the first time that migrants play a significant role in community ecology in Asian tropical rain forests (Wells 1969, Fogden 1972, Medway and Wells 1976). Elsewhere, ecological studies on bird communities by Terborgh and his contemporaries (e.g., James Karr, F. Gary Stiles, Jared Diamond, Harry Recher, and Martin Cody, among others) stimulated not only a whole new generation of tropical ornithologists, but also contributed greatly to advances in community ecology theory and provided rich empirical data sets on bird communities throughout the tropics. Terborgh's intimate knowledge of the bird fauna of the Apurimac Valley (Cordillera Vilcabamba) of Peru revealed a number of subtle patterns in bird community structure. Moreover, the years of studies played no small part in leading Terborgh to develop into one of the recognized conservation leaders of our time. In the introduction to the last paper to be published on the Vilcabamba dataset, Terborgh (1985) wrote that "[this paper], in a sense, [is] an epitaph for an environment that no longer exists." After witnessing the nearly complete destruction of the forest over "so brief a period," he advised us that "there is no time to lose" (1237).

Several ideas emerged from Terborgh's (1977) investigation of diversity patterns along an elevational gradient, which is reprinted here. First, the positive correlation between foliage height diversity and bird diversity was confirmed, but found to mask different responses by functional groups (e.g., insectivores, frugivores, nectarivores). Thus, habitat complexity failed as a general explanation for bird diversity patterns. Instead, the importance of food resources and productivity emerged as important contributors to diversity patterns in this system. Second, complementing Janzen's (1973a, 1973b) findings regarding arthropod diversity and density in Costa Rica, Terborgh reported a midelevation bulge in density and diversity of insectivorous birds (1977, 1013, fig. 7). He attributed this "hot spot" to a greater abundance of insect food resources, proposed to result from greater primary plant productivity. Scott (1976) reported a similar altitudinal trend in diversity of leaf litter herpetofaunas in Costa Rica and also attributed this to greater forest productivity at intermediate elevations. (It must be noted here, however, that no study has yet been made of variation in plant productivity with elevation in the tropics.) The increased density *and* diversity as a result of a putatively more productive environment are due to greater availability and variety of essential food resources (cf. Janzen 1973b). Third, Terborgh placed in perspective the complexities of addressing the species diversity problem. Terborgh stresses that factors influencing diversity patterns "overlie in an intricate mosaic." In other words, searches for simple (or single) explanations are bound to fail. For example, Terborgh noted the importance of geographic scale when he stated that

evolutionary and historical processes, rather than ecological factors, are likely to dominate explanations in interregional comparisons (see also MacArthur 1969, Karr 1976, and parts 2 and 3). The importance of scale and evolutionary and geologic history, in addition to ecological factors, in influencing species diversity and community structure was to emerge as an important research area in the 1980s and 1990s (see Ricklefs and Schluter 1993).

Social Behavior and Ecology

The underlying importance of evolutionary history in influencing niche partitioning is apparent in the detailed studies of Annie Gautier-Hion and colleagues (Gautier and Gautier-Hion 1969; Gautier-Hion 1971, 1978). Building on a number of autoecological studies of primates in northeast Gabon, Gautier-Hion 1978, reprinted here, examined food niches of coexisting species in undisturbed and disturbed rain forests of the region. Average weights of the coexisting primates varied nearly continuously, and in some instances, primates occupied different vertical zones. Within three sympatric *Cercopithecus* species, however, niche segregation was less obvious. These primates had similar social organization and two of the three species foraged at essentially the same heights, and often traveled and foraged together. Although the species differed subtly in diet (i.e., how they fed on arthropod resources), fruit was the principal food for all. Rather than competing for food resources, Cercopithecines are viewed as cooperating and are hypothesized to benefit from occurring in mixed feeding groups. The degree to which phylogeny or ecology influences the observed overlap in feeding strategies was not discussed, but the importance of phylogeny in explaining species' ecology and behavior was mentioned briefly. Gautier-Hion's study was noteworthy in its efforts to link social behavior and ecology of a group of primates. The history of such detailed field studies in anthropology goes back several decades and includes the pioneering studies of C. R. Carpenter on gibbons in southeast Asia (Carpenter 1940). Carpenter's work stimulated much other research, including Booth's work in Africa (1956), Chivers's extensive studies on socioecology of primates in Malaysia (e.g., Raemaekers and Chivers 1980), Sussman's and Tattersall's studies in Madagascar (e.g., Sussman 1974, 1977; Tattersall 1982), and Charles-Dominique's (1971, 1977) research on African nocturnal prosimians. Several complementary studies were also occurring in the Neotropics at the time of Chivers's and Gautier-Hion's work, including studies on primate ecology and behavior in dry forests of Costa Rica (Freese 1977) and humid forests of Central and South America (e.g., Hladik and Hladik 1969, Klein and Klein 1975, Kinzey 1977, Terborgh 1983).

Not surprisingly, studies on the evolution of social organization in primates have long interested primatologists, and such studies have provided an important framework for research in natural history and ecology. The paper by Crook and Gartlan (1966), reprinted here, integrated what was then known about the social organization of primates and proposed hypotheses concerning the adaptive significance of such behaviors. In particular, environmental characteristics such as habitat complexity, food limitation, and predation risk were identified as key factors influencing population characteristics and social organization of primates. For example, a change from a diet of insects to one of fruits and leaves was proposed to result in the formation of larger social groups. Further, Crook and Gartlan (1966) attribute the greater species diversity of primates in forests to "availability of numerous niches in forest where primate populations have specialized in terms of diet, vertical zonation, daily rhythms, etc." (1201). The existence of geographic barriers in forests was also believed to be greater than in open country, thus promoting greater speciation rates in forest habitats. Crook and Gartlan's (1966) synthesis provided an important framework for many of the studies discussed in the previous paragraph, and for behavioral ecology in general.

Reproductive Diversity in Frogs

Like those who studied primates and birds, Marty Crump (1974) became intrigued by the great diversity of frog species found at a single site in Ecuador and questioned how so many species could coexist in the same forest. Explanations for such high diversity, however, largely followed a different theme than for patterns observed in birds and primates. In a landmark paper reprinted here, Crump (1974) attributed coexistence of frog species to the reproductive diversity exhibited by these anurans. She described ten reproductive modes from purely aquatic egg and tadpole stages to direct development, where froglets hatch directly from eggs deposited on land, and both young and egg are not dependent on water. On a larger geographic scale, the importance of such diversity in reproductive modes for species richness of leaf litter frogs was also noted by Scott (1976), who attributed lower frog diversity in Borneo when compared to Costa Rica to the fact that all litter frogs in Borneo are dependent on water for larval development.

A number of factors, including historical events, seasonality of breeding habitats, and predation, were proposed by Crump (1974) as important factors influencing the radiation of anurans. In particular, the importance of changing environments during the Pleistocene and subsequent strong selection on reproductive characters to adapt to these changing conditions was considered a key factor in anuran radiation in the Neotropics. Predation of eggs and young and competition for limited aquatic breeding sites, however, were also highlighted as important factors influencing life history evolution and reproductive diversity of frogs. A major contribution of Crump (1974) was the in-depth analysis of life history characteristics of this community of anurans. Like other papers highlighted in this part, Crump 1974 provided a framework from which to evaluate patterns of frog diversity, as well as to examine behavioral adaptations to various reproductive modes exhibited by this group.

Seasonal Dynamics in Vertebrate Communities

Many studies on vertebrate communities focused on spatial or geographic variation in diversity, rather than temporal variation. In fact, the dogma was that tropical vertebrate populations were rather sedentary and did not change markedly across the year, especially in the relatively aseasonal environments of tropical wet forests. Ornithological studies by Davis (1945a, 1945b) in southeast Brazil and Fogden (1972) in Sarawak demonstrated the seasonal dynamics of bird communities (Fogden's paper is reprinted here). Later studies in Central and South America (e.g., Stiles 1975, Karr and Freemark 1983, Terborgh 1983) would confirm the dynamic nature of vertebrate communities. Year-round availability of resources, such as fruits and flowers, is one explanation for greater vertebrate diversity in tropical regions when compared to temperate or highly seasonal tropical habitats (Fleming 1973, Karr 1976, Orians 1969). Yet variability in the abundance of food resources occurs even in such aseasonal environments (e.g., McClure 1966, Fogden 1972, Wolda 1978), and such fluctuation may impact abundance, distribution, and reproductive behavior of birds and other vertebrates (e.g., Moreau 1936b, Ward 1969, Fogden 1972, Medway 1976; see review by Van Schaik, Terborgh, and Wright 1993). Fogden (1972) supported the idea that food resources (bottom-up forces) were ultimate factors influencing population and reproductive dynamics of birds. Based on reproductive patterns he observed in Sarawak, Fogden (1972) believed, as did Lack (1968), that food limitations were responsible for low reproductive rates of birds. Fogden (1972), however, did not discuss the role of predation in influencing clutch sizes and reproductive rates of birds. The debate over food limitation or predation as selective forces in clutch size evolution in birds was shortly to generate a considerable number of empirical and theoretical studies (e.g., see Ricklefs 1977, 1989; Martin 1992).

Studies on tropical vertebrate communities have provided excellent examples of niche segregation, adaptive radiation, and convergent evolution. Studies prior to 1960 largely described patterns of species occurrence, while those of the 1960s and 1970s began to examine the question of how so many species can coexist in tropical forests. With the development of community ecology theory, studies shifted in focus to provide explanations for high diversity and species coexistence. Each decade added more detailed information about these communities, while at the same time revealing the underlying complexities due to changing species composition in space and time, and temporal variation in resources, species interactions, and population dynamics. The past twenty years have been characterized by further theoretical development, which has broadened the focus of community studies (e.g., Ricklefs and Schluter 1993). At the same time, we have witnessed unprecedented ecological change as a consequence of rampant commercial logging and accelerating forest conversion to other land uses. The research community has responded with a new emphasis on studying vertebrate communities in disturbed ecosystems. In large part, the research questions have changed from how so many species can coexist in a forest to how many species we can expect to lose even before they become formally described and documented.

Reprinted Selections

J. L. Harrison. 1962. The distribution of feeding habits among mammals in a tropical rain forest. *Journal of Animal Ecology* 31:53–56, 60–63

J. H. Crook and J. S. Gartlan. 1966. Evolution of primate societies. *Nature* 210:1200-1203

M. P. L. Fogden. 1972. The seasonality and population dynamics of equatorial forest birds in Sarawak (excerpt). *Ibis* 114, no. 3: 334–42. Reproduced with the kind permission of the British Ornithologists' Union

M. L. Crump. 1974. Reproductive strategies in a tropical anuran community. *Miscellaneous Publications, Museum of Natural History, University of Kansas* 61:4, 44–57

J. Terborgh. 1977. Bird species diversity on an Andean elevational gradient. *Ecology* 58:1007-1019

A. Gautier-Hion. 1978. Food niches and coexistence in sympatric primates in Gabon. In *Feeding Behavior in Relation to Food Availability and Composition,* edited by C. M. Hladik and D. J. Chivers, 269–72, 277–86. Academic Press, New York

53

THE DISTRIBUTION OF FEEDING HABITS AMONG ANIMALS IN A TROPICAL RAIN FOREST

By J. L. HARRISON

Queensland Institute of Medical Research*

Tropical Rain forest is an enormously complicated habitat, of which the animals have been so far but little studied. Our knowledge of these animals, however, is now emerging from the taxonomic stage, and the botanical studies, upon which the zoological are inevitably based, are now sufficiently advanced to support this. In particular the invaluable work of Richards (1952) has done much to draw together scattered knowledge and make it available to the non-botanist.

The great difficulty in the study of Rain forest is one of integration. It is literally true to say that one cannot see the wood for the trees. There is no one position in which one can stand and get a good view of a complete sample of forest, and it is correspondingly difficult to visualize the relationships between, say, animals living on the forest floor and those out of sight in the canopy, perhaps a hundred feet above. In such circumstances, ideas and patterns into which one can fit (or fail to fit) one's observations assume a special value. The present paper uses the results of some observations, made over the last decade, on the food of mammals in Malaysian and Australian Rain forests to draw up a simple scheme of the classification of feeding habits within forest of this kind.

THE STRUCTURE OF TROPICAL RAIN FOREST

This subject is discussed at some length in most ecological text-books, but, since the terminology varies slightly, it needs to be summarized for the present purpose.

Physically, Rain forest is composed of woody plants. The trees of the main storey rise on 30 m or more of slim, bare trunk to small, compact crowns, which are usually more or less in contact. Below and between these are the smaller trees, of the under-storey, either young specimens of the giants, or smaller species, which fill up small gaps and generally reinforce the overhead cover, so that there is no clear view of the sky. Beneath the trees are layers of shrubs, and of sparse herbage which are developed in inverse proportion to the completeness of the overhead cover, so that Rain forest with a completely unbroken canopy is relatively bare underfoot. The whole of this structure is bound together with lianes (woody climbing plants) and plentifully sprinkled with epiphytes.

Taxonomically there is a bewildering array of species. Exceptionally stretches may be dominated by one species of tree, but normally the variety is such that two trees of the same species are rarely in view at the same time. Thus Wyatt-Smith (1949) records 227 species among the 559 trees per hectare in Lowland Rain forest near Kuala Lumpur, of which the most abundant species comprised less than 7%. When a major tree falls the resulting space is filled by the sudden rapid growth of the smaller trees, one of which will usually win the race to fill the gap. A tree is thus rarely replaced by another specimen of its own species, and the diversity is maintained.

To this diversity is added a comparative lack of seasonal variation, so that flowering and fruiting of the various species are spread throughout most of the year. Thus, even

* Now at Nanyang University, Singapore, 22.

though the trees of one species may fruit together, the individuals are so scattered that there is little variation in the availability of flower or fruit. They are never specially abundant, but on the other hand they are usually present.

Much thought has gone into elaboration of the classification of the horizontal layers into which the forest may be divided. Richards (1952) uses a system of five layers, A to E, which we may describe, for Malaysian conditions (using data from Wyatt-Smith 1952), as: A—the emergent layer, the tops of the tallest trees projecting above the general level of the forest, 30-45 m high or more in Malaya; B—the main storey, 20-30 m high, which usually forms a continuous canopy; C—the under-storey; D—the shrub layer; and E—the herb layer.

Different forests differ in the degree to which any one of these layers may provide an effective ground cover. Thus the main storey, B, may be so dense as virtually to exclude light from the under storey, C; or it may be discontinuous, so that the effectively complete cover is provided by the under-storey.

These three storeys, however, are a refinement of classification into which, at present, the zoologist has insufficient data to fit his animals. It may be summarized by saying that in Tropical Rain forest the 'canopy', consisting of layers A to C, forms a complete unbroken vegetable layer, which effectively excludes bright light (other than sun-flecks) from the forest floor, and which provides a continuous zone within which animals may move.

ZONATION OF ANIMAL LIFE

There is no doubt that, as our knowledge increases, it will be possible to correlate different animal communities with the different layers enumerated above. Colquhoun & Morley (1943) found it necessary to distinguish five layers in an English oak-wood to accommodate a bird fauna of less than thirty species, so the subdivisions necessary to define niches for the three hundred or more birds of Malayan forest can well be imagined. With such a bewildering array of possibilities, it is clearly desirable to provide some simple, basic scheme of classification.

Mammals provide a good subject for a classification of this sort, and, as a result of many years collecting in Malaysia, a clear impression had been gained as to where any one species was to be found. Some years ago, an attempt was made to follow such examples as those of Allee (1926), and divided up the species of mammals, other than bats, recorded from forests of the Malay Peninsula into three zones, using this impression as criterion. The result, in numbers of species was (Harrison 1957):

Canopy mammals	23 species
Under-canopy mammals	23 species
Ground mammals	51 species*

Having obtained this classification an attempt was made to work backwards and define the layers represented by them. The classification was then found to be unsatisfactory in two particulars. The group of 'under-canopy animals', although representing a recognizable community, did not correspond to any layer that could be called an 'under-canopy'; rather they were animals with a vertical distribution, to be found both in the canopy and on the ground. Secondly the group 'ground mammals' appeared to contain two different elements: small mammals, such as rats, with considerable climbing abilities, which were

---

* A misprint in Harrison (1957) shows nineteen 'ground rats' instead of the correct figure of nine.

not always easy to differentiate clearly from the 'under-canopy' group; and large animals, such as elephants and deer, with no climbing ability, but which were able to crop leaves from the bushes and smaller trees.

Table 1. *Malayan mammals: numbers of different species known to occur in the Lowland forest of the Malay Peninsula classified by level and by feeding habits*

F = Fruit; L = leaves; V = vegetable matter; I = insects, etc.; C = carnivorous

Group	Genus or sub-family	No. of species	Feeding habits
1. Canopy mammals (23)			
Primates	*Hylobates* (gibbons)	2	2 F
	Presbytis (leaf monkeys)	3	3 L
	Nycticebus (slow loris)	1	1 FI
Rodents	*Ratufa* (giant squirrels)	2	2 F
	Flying squirrels	10	4 F, 6 IF
	Arboreal rats (*Hapalomys*, etc.)	3	3 F
Other mammals	*Cynocephalus* (flying lemur)	1	1 L
	Ptilocercus (pen-tail tree-shrew)	1	1 I
2. Middle-zone mammals (21)			
Primates	*Macaca* (monkeys)	2	2 IF
Carnivores	*Martes* (marten)	1	1 C
	Prionodon (linsang)	1	1 C
	Paradoxurinae (civets)	5	5 IF
	Neofelis (clouded leopard)	1	1 C
Rodents	*Callosciurus* (tree squirrels)	7	7 IF
	Rattus (tree rats)	2	1 F, 1 IF
Insectivores	*Tupaia* (tree-shrews)	2	2 IF
3. Large ground mammals (17)			
Elephant	*Elephas*	1	1 L
Perissodactyls	*Didermocerus* (rhinocerus)	1	1 L
	Tapirus (tapir)	1	1 L
	Sus (pigs)	2	2 V
Artiodactyls	Cervidae (deer)	2	2 L
	Tragulus (mouse deer)	2	2 F
	Bos (Gaur)	1	1 L
Carnivores	*Panthera* (tiger and leopard)	2	2 C
	Helarctos (bear)	1	1 IVC
	Cuon (wild dog)	1	1 C
Rodents	Hystricidae (porcupines)	3	3 V
4. Small ground mammals (28)			
Carnivores	Viverrinae (civets)	4	4 IF
	Felis (small cats)	4	4 C
	Mustela (stoat)	1	1 C
Rodents	*Lariscus* and *Rhinosciurus* (ground squirrels)	2	1 F, 1 I
	Rattus (ground rats)	6	1 V, 5 IV
	Rhizomys (bamboo rats)	2	2 V
Insectivores	Erinaceidae (moonrat and short-tailed shrew)	2	2 I
	Soricidae (shrews)	6	6 I
Others	*Manis* (scaly anteater)	1	1 I

The mammal communities may, therefore, be re-defined as follows: (1) THE CANOPY MAMMALS confined to the continuous leafy layer which provides a complete and continuous cover (corresponding to Richards's layers A, B, and C); these animals normally have no contact with the ground. (2) MIDDLE-ZONE MAMMALS of scansorial habit which range

56   *Feeding habits in Rain forest*

vertically up and down the tree-trunks between the canopy and the ground. (3) LARGE GROUND MAMMALS, living on the ground surface, too heavy for scrambling among bushes, and with no climbing ability. (4) SMALL GROUND MAMMALS which live on and in the ground surface, ranging on to bushes, fallen trees, and the lower parts of tree-trunks (Richards's layers D and E). It is comparatively easy to allot mammals to one or another of the groups defined in this way, and this has been done in Table 1 for all the species recorded from Lowland Forest in Malaya (Harrison 1957). Occasional allocations are arbitrary. Thus, the Malay bear (*Helictus*) has been allotted to group (3) on size, although its climbing ability could put it into group (2). *Neofelis* has been allotted to group (2), and *Panthera pardus* to group (3), although there is not a great deal of difference in their climbing abilities. This, however, is saying no more than that not all animals will fit into an arbitrary scheme of classification.

Feeding habits within zones

Normal food is much more difficult to determine than normal dwelling place, especially for the smaller species. Luckily the results of a number of stomach examinations are now available (Harrison 1954, and in press, a), and it is possible to decide with reasonable confidence what the various species normally eat. The results of these decisions have been summarized in Table 1, classified as: L for leaf, F for fruit and nectar, V for vegetable, I for insect-eating, and C for carnivorous. 'Vegetable' is an all-embracing term for vegetable matter of all kinds, mostly tubers, stem and bud material, but including fruit, leaves and, presumably, fungi; the class is included for such animals as ground rats which appear to eat a very wide range of foods. All invertebrates eaten, and some small vertebrates, such as small geckos, have been included in I for insects, but the flesh of the larger vertebrates comes under C for carnivorous. Species taking a mixed diet are shown with two or more food groups — thus, most rats are IV eating both insects and vegetable matter.

Table 2. *Malayan mammals: summary of the numbers of species by zone and feeding habits and (in parentheses) their percentages of the whole fauna*

		No. of species with diet of:			
Zone	No. of species	Plant (F, L and V)	Mixed (IV, IF, etc)	Insect (I)	Flesh (C)
Canopy	23 (26)	15 (17)	7 (8)	1 (1)	0
Middle zone	21 (24)	1 (1)	17 (19)	0	3 (3)
Large Ground Mammals	17 (19)	13 (15)	1 (1)	0	3 (3)
Small Ground Mammals	28 (31)	4 (4)	9 (10)	10 (11)	5 (6)
Total	89 (100)	33 (37)	34 (38)	11 (12)	11 (12)

When the numbers taking plant foods of all kind, mixed, insect, or flesh food, are added together by zones we get the distribution shown in Table 2. It is at once clear that the mammals of each community exhibit a characteristic pattern of feeding. The canopy mammals are predominantly plant feeders, the middle-zone mammals are overwhelmingly mixed feeders, the small ground mammals are about equally mixed feeders or insectivorous, while the large ground mammals are overwhelming plant feeders — indeed the sole exception (the Malay Bear) has already been noted as possibly more correctly to be placed in the middle zone. Carnivores are generally distributed, although, having a wide range of movement, none can be considered as confined to the canopy.

BATS

Bats have, so far, been left out of this discussion, because our knowledge of them is so much less complete than for other mammals or birds. Some seventy-two species are recorded from the Malay Peninsula, all of which can be considered forest species. Of these eleven are fruit-bats (Megachiroptera), feeding mostly on fruit or nectar and spending much of their time hanging or scrambling in the canopy. The remaining sixty-one are Microchiroptera ('insectivorous bats') either truly insectivorous, or carnivorous (on small birds, etc.), living in tree-holes, caves, or other small cavities, and hunting mostly in the air beneath the canopy, or sometimes above it. With our present knowledge, no more than an informed guess is possible for the allocation of these species to zones, but it would probably be fair to allot them as follows:

Upper air	5 all insectivorous	(7%)
Canopy	11 all plant feeders	(15%)
Middle zone, flying	51 insectivorous	(71%)
	5 carnivorous	(7%)

The Australian Rain-forest species are even less well known than the Malayan. Tate (1952) records twenty-six species from the Cape York Peninsula, noting three of them as from open forest, and five as probably from Rain forest. Counting the remaining eighteen as Rain-forest species also, and guessing at the habits of most (a reasonable procedure, as they are closely related to the Malayan species) we get:

Canopy .	3 plant and 1 mixed feeder (13% and 4%)
Middle zone, flying	18 insectivorous and 1 carnivorous (79% and 4%)

DISCUSSION

A synthesis of these classifications is presented in Fig. 1. Owing to the great excess of numbers of species of birds over mammals, the percentage distributions of birds, bats and other mammals have been taken as equivalent and it is the mean percentage of the three which is represented by each block of the diagram, but in fact the total numbers of species of all groups is found to give a similar pattern of distribution. It is to be noted that the Malayan and the Australian agree very closely, although the species and even families of animals concerned are not the same.

The birds and mammals of both Malaysian and Australian Tropical Rain forests may, therefore, be assembled into the following six communities:

(1) UPPER AIR COMMUNITY: Birds and bats which hunt above the canopy; mostly insectivorous, but with a large proportion of carnivores.

(2) CANOPY COMMUNITY: Birds, fruit-bats, and other mammals confined to this zone; predominantly feeding on leaves, fruit, or nectar, but with a few insectivorous and mixed feeders.

(3) MIDDLE-ZONE FLYING ANIMALS: Birds and insectivorous bats; predominantly insectivorous, with a few carnivores.

(4) MIDDLE-ZONE SCANSORIAL ANIMALS: Mammals which range up and down the trunks, entering both the canopy and ground zones; predominantly mixed feeders, with a few carnivores.

(5) LARGE GROUND ANIMALS: Large mammals and rarely birds living on the ground, without climbing ability, but of great range, either by reaching up into the canopy, or by

J. L. Harrison   61

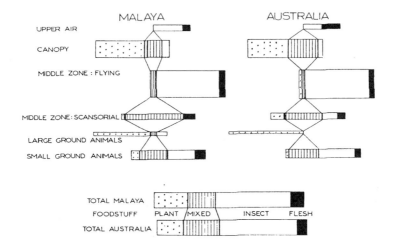

Fig. 1. Patterns of the distribution of feeding habits in Malaya and Australia compared. Areas are proportional to mean percentages of the total numbers of species; Malaya: 306 birds, 72 bats, and 89 other mammals (total 467); Australia: 117 birds, 23 bats, and 28 other mammals (total 168). The vertical scale represents proportion of the total in that zone, the horizontal scale proportions of those in the zone with each diet.

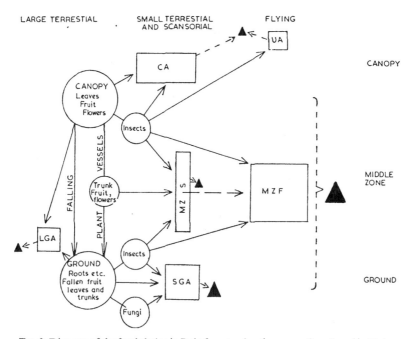

Fig. 2. Diagram of the food chains in Rain forest, using the proportions found in Malaya. Sources of foods are represented by circles, the principal groups of mammals and birds by rectangles, and the attendant predators by black triangles. Areas of the rectangles and triangles are proportional to numbers of species. CA = Canopy Animals, LGA = Large Ground Animals, MZF = Middle-Zone Flying animals, MZS = Middle-Zone Scansorial animals, SGA = Small Ground Animals, UA = animals of the Upper Air.

covering a large area of forest; plant feeders, feeding largely by browsing on leaves, but exceptionally feeding on fallen fruit (*e.g.* mouse-deer and cassowary), or rooting for tubers, etc. (pigs), with attendant large carnivores.

(6) SMALL GROUND ANIMALS: Birds and small mammals, capable of some climbing, which search the ground litter and the lower parts of tree-trunks; predominantly either insectivorous or mixed feeders, but with a fair proportion of vegetable feeders, and some carnivorous.

The relation between these groups is expressed as a diagram of food-chains in Fig. 2. The canopy is clearly the primary producing layer, and the herbivorous animals are either confined to it, or, as ground animals, are big enough to reach the lower parts of it from the ground. Animals confined to the canopy are therefore usually leaf, nectar, or fruit eating. Large ground mammals may be big enough to browse on the leaves of the lower parts of the canopy, or they may use their speed and range of movement to seek places where, as noted above, the canopy in effect comes down to ground level.

Food material manufactured in the canopy can be distributed by the falling of fruit, leaves and branches, or through the vessels of the plant to form trunks, buttresses, roots and storage organs. A few ground-dwelling animals may be expected to rely upon fallen fruit, but dead leaves and fallen trunks cannot be utilized directly by vertebrates. Fungi and insects, however, can make use of this material, and can make it available to vertebrates in the form of their own bodies, so that the majority of the ground-dwelling vertebrates may be expected to search for insects and fungi among the ground litter.

In the middle zone fruit is available borne directly on the trunks of trees (*e.g.* many figs) or by epiphytes, from which also leaves are available. The most abundant food, however, will be insects derived either from the ground, or from the canopy, and distributed by flight. The most successful middle-zone feeders can therefore be expected to be insectivorous birds and bats, capable of catching insects on the wing. Middle-zone mammals will find food less easily, and may be expected to exploit a wide range of possible foodstuffs.

It may be helpful to draw a comparison between the Rain forest and a body of water such as a lake or sea. The canopy represents the phytoplankton, exploited directly by insects, comparable to zoo-plankton, and larger animals comparable to nekton. Food is carried down to the deeper layers and to the bottom (*i.e* the middle zone and the ground) in the form of fallen leaves, fruit and insect bodies, comparable to the bodies of planktonic organisms, there to be exploited by middle-zone birds and bats corresponding to nektonic organisms of the deeper layers; middle-zone mammals, corresponding to periphytic organisms; and small ground mammals, corresponding to benthic organisms. The large ground mammals are perhaps to be compared to whales; but we must not push an analogy too far.

The declared object is, not to produce a complete scheme of classification, but to select a pattern from a confusing mass of observations into which further observations may be fitted, or, what is more stimulating to thought, into which further observations may fail to fit.

SUMMARY

Based on experience in Malaysia and Australia, a classification is proposed of the birds and mammals of Tropical Rain forest into six communities defined by the level at which

J. L. Harrison   63

they occur and their range of foodstuffs. The communities are: (1) Upper Air, insectivorous and carnivorous birds and bats; (2) Canopy, birds and mammals feeding largely on leaves and fruit; (3) Middle-zone flying, mainly insectivorous birds and bats; (4) Middle-zone scansorial, mammals of mixed feeding habits ranging up and down the trunks; (5) Large Ground, large herbivorous species; and (6) Small Ground, small mammals and birds of varied diet searching the forest floor.

REFERENCES

Allee, W. C. (1926). Distributions of animals in a Tropical Rain forest with relation to environmental factors. *Ecology* 7, 445-68.

Colquhoun, M. K. & Morley, A. (1943). Vertical zonation in woodland bird communities. *J. Anim. Ecol.* 12, 75-81.

Gibson-Hill, C. A. (1949). An annotated check-list of the birds of Malaya. *Bull. Raffles Mus.* 20, 1-299.

Harrison, J. L. (1954). The natural food of some rats and other mammals. *Bull. Raffles Mus.* 25, 157-65.

Harrison, J. L. (1957). Malaysian parasites — XXXIII. The hosts. *Stud. Inst. Med. Res. Malaya,* 28, 409-26.

Harrison, J. L. (in press, a). The natural food of some Malayan mammals. *Bull. Raffles Mus.*

Harrison, J. L. (in press, b). Mammals of Innisfail — I. Species and distribution. *Aust. J. Zool.*

Keast, A. (1959). Australian birds: their zoogeography and adaptions to an arid continent. Chapter VI in *Biogeography and ecology in Australia.* (pp. 89-114). Den Haag.

Leach, J. A. (1958). *An Australian Bird Book.* 9th ed. Revised by P. C. Morrison. Melbourne.

Madoc, G. C. (1956). *An Introduction to Malayan Birds.* Kuala Lumpur.

North Queensland Naturalists' Club, & Whittell, H. M., (1949). *List of Birds occurring in North Queensland.* N.Q.N.C. Publication 5.

Richards, P. W. (1952). *The Tropical Rain-forest, an Ecological Study.* Cambridge.

Smythies, B.E. (1953). *The Birds of Burma.* Edinburgh.

Tate, G. H. H. (1952). Results of the Archbold expeditions. No. 66: Mammals of Cape York Peninsula, with a note on the occurrence of rain-forest in Queensland. *Bull. Amer. Mus. Nat. Hist.* 98 (7), 567-616.

Troughton, E. (1946). *Furred Animals of Australia,* 3rd ed. Sydney.

Wyatt-Smith, J. (1949). A note on tropical lowland evergreen Rain forest in Malaya. *Malayan Forester,* 12 (2), 1-6.

Wyatt-Smith, J. (1952). Malayan forest types (part 1). *Malay. Nat. J.* 7, 45-55.

1200　　　　　　　　　　NATURE　　　　　　JUNE 18, 1966 VOL. 210

EVOLUTION OF PRIMATE SOCIETIES

By Dr. J. H. CROOK and J. S. GARTLAN

Department of Psychology, University of Bristol

RESEARCH on primate behaviour has tended to concentrate on similarities rather than differences between taxa, thereby allowing authors to make generalizations concerning the evolution of primate and human societies based on the characteristics of single species[1]. Recent developments in field investigation[2], however, now provide a range of information clearly demonstrating the contrasts that exist even between species the behaviour and ecology of which appeared superficially alike previously. The number of species sampled remains small but enough is known to permit a preliminary examination of the range of social systems uncovered and their functional significance in the habitats concerned. Analysis of function provides some understanding of the selection pressures responsible for adaptive change in social structure, and, given information regarding relevant ecological change in past time, allows the construction of evolutionary hypotheses.

The present approach is based first on the ethological and ecological results of recent field investigations[3]; secondly, on a methodology of evolutionary analysis of social systems used in recent ornithological work[4,5]; and, thirdly, on recent research in the palaeoecology and palaeontology of African primates[6]. Our purpose is to direct attention to patterns of relationships inherent in the data now available and to begin the task of ordering it. The hypothesis put forward gains strength from two aspects not treated here, namely cases of parallel adaptive radiation among African, Malagasy and Asian primates and intra-specific adaptations to local differences within habitats of single species. Detailed field investigations will, in due course, test the ideas suggested.

Grades of Social Organization

Ornithological investigations have shown that patterns of social organization determining population dispersion are intimately linked to species ecology—the whole interrelationship of behavioural features being co-adapted to certain aspects of the environment forming major selection pressures. In Table 1 we attempt to allocate species recently investigated to a series of 'Grades'[7] representing 'levels' of adaptation in forest, tree savannah, grassland and arid environments respectively. Anatomical investigations of fossil and living material reveal a progressive adaptive radiation from forest-dwelling insectivorous primates to larger open country animals predominantly vegetarian. It is not surprising, therefore, to find correlated trends in the behavioural data[8]. Table 1 reveals a shift from insectivorous, nocturnal forest animals with markedly solitary habits and a population dispersion based on aggressive contacts through a range of fruit- or leaf-eating forms (diurnal; very small family groups or larger parties showing defensive behaviour of a variety of types in 'territorial' encounters with neighbours but, otherwise, little intra-group aggression, sexuality or inter-male competition) to vegetarian browsers of open country normally living in well-structured troops or herds, usually in home ranges and showing much sexuality (often seasonal) and inter-male competition.

The aboreal grades contain several species while fewer are allocated to those of open country. In Table 1 this reflects a large species contingent from Petter's investigations on the lemurs[9]; however, in general, the numbers of forest species do exceed those of open country forms. This is because of the availability of numerous niches in forest where primate populations have specialized in terms of diet, vertical zonation, daily rhythms, etc. The limited ranges of the population units and their confinement to forests means that geographical barriers impose a more extensive speciation than in open country where species show great adaptability in exploiting a considerable range of habitats.

In common with their insectivorous ancestors, the co-adaptations of Grade I primates are clearly related to their nocturnal insect-hunting habits. Two leaf-eating

Table 1. ADAPTIVE GRADES OF PRIMATES (SEE TEXT)

Species, ecological and behavioural characteristics	Grade I	Grade II	Grade III	Grade IV	Grade V
Species	*Microcebus* sp. *Chierogaleus* sp. *Phaner* sp. *Daubentonia* sp. *Lepilemur* *Galago* *Aotus trivirgatus*	*Hapelemur griseus* *Indri* *Propithecus* sp. *Avahi* *Lemur* sp. *Callicebus moloch* *Hylobates* sp.	*Lemur macaca* *Alouatta palliata* *Saimiri sciureus* *Colobus* sp. *Cercopithecus ascanius* *Gorilla*	*Macaca mulatta*, etc. *Presbytis entellus* *Cercopithecus aethiops* *Papio cynocephalus* *Pan satyrus*	*Erythrocebus patas* *Papio hamadryas* *Theropithecus gelada*
Habitat	Forest	Forest	Forest–Forest fringe	Forest fringe, tree savannah	Grassland or arid savannah
Diet	Mostly insects	Fruit or leaves	Fruit or fruit and leaves. Stems, etc.	Vegetarian-omnivore Occasionally carnivorous in *Papio* and *Pan*	Vegetarian-omnivore *P. hamadryas* occasionally also carnivorous
Diurnal activity	Nocturnal	Crepuscular or diurnal	Diurnal	Diurnal	Diurnal
Size of groups	Usually solitary	Very small groups	Small to occasionally large parties	Medium to large groups. *Pan* groups inconstant in size	Medium to large groups, variable size in *T. gelada* and probably *P. hamadryas*
Reproductive units	Pairs where known	Small family parties based on single male	Multi-male groups	Multi-male groups	One-male groups
Male motility between groups	—	Probably slight	Yes—where known	Yes in *M. fuscata* and *C. aethiops*, otherwise not observed	Not observed
Sex dimorphism and social role differentiation	Slight	Slight	Slight—Size and behavioural dimorphism marked in *Gorilla*. Colour contrasts in *Lemur*	Marked dimorphism and role differentiation in *Papio* and *Macaca*	Marked dimorphism. Social role differentiation
Population dispersion	Limited information suggests territories	Territories with display, marking, etc.	Territories known in *Aloutta*, *Lemur*. Home ranges in *Gorilla* with some group avoidance probable	Territories with display in *C. aethiops*. Home ranges with avoidance or group combat in others. Extensive group mixing in *Pan*	Home ranges in *E. patas*. *P. hamadryas* and *T. gelada* show much congregation in feeding and sleeping. *T. gelada* in poor feeding conditions shows group dispersal

No. 5042 JUNE 18. 1966   NATURE   1201

forms are exceptions requiring further explanation. The switch to frugivorous or leaf-eating habits in Grades II and III is linked with diurnal activity and the formation of larger social groups. As with many birds, this development is linked to the change from a diet requiring individual hunting to food sources often locally distributed and at which social responses allow congregation for exploitation in common. 'Family bands' of very small size and larger multi-male social units in forest are often markedly 'territorial', in that defensive behaviour involving displays and/or marking in relation to neighbouring groups is shown. While the behaviour may defend a discrete area, this has not often been demonstrated; nevertheless, it does ensure an over-dispersion of population units.

The small size of social units in many forest frugivores is probably related to limiting conditions of food supply occasioned by the relatively stable conditions of tropical rain forest. A non-seasonal climate with a moderately constant availability of various fruits presumably allows increase in numbers to a ceiling imposed by periodic food shortages due to local food crop failures. In this situation the addition of young to the population may be difficult—recruitment necessarily balancing mortality. Breeding appears to be non-seasonal and this may explain the low frequency of copulations observed in some of these species[10,11]. The 'territorial' behaviour of forest groups may be interpreted as ensuring an adequate provisioning area for the individuals comprising them. It remains difficult, however, to apply this argument to all leaf-eaters.

In the dry forest, savannah and steppe conditions of Grades IV and V marked climatic seasonality with a harsh period of aridity, and food shortage probably imposes high seasonal mortality rates especially on old or infirm animals. In the rainy season, food for the remainder is superabundant and vigorous seasonal breeding[12] can replenish the population without risks of failures from food shortage in rearing young. It is as yet unclear whether the timing of the breeding seasons confers advantages during pregnancy, lactation or in terms of food supply for young animals; however, in principle, the effects with regard to survival may be the same.

Outside the forest the social units are generally larger and this appears to result from open country conditions of predation and food supply affecting ground dwelling populations. Savannah primates face a number of predators and scattering undoubtedly decreases the chances of individual survival. Groups of *Papio* baboons and *Rhesus* monkeys show a marked cohesion permitted ecologically by local food abundance allowing congregation without risk of over-exploitation.

One of the effects of increased group size in open country terrestrial primates is marked competition between males for females and the consequent intra-sexual selection of male characteristics. The open nature of the terrain allows every troop member to be aware of its companion's activities, and the cohesion of most troops makes this doubly sure. The seasonality of mating activities further means that many males are particularly active sexually at the same time, when, in the absence of structural equilibration in the troop, fierce competition and fighting would result. Again some Japanese observations[13] suggest that with increased numbers the socionomic sex ratio of *Macaca fuscata* troops increases so that there are fewer females to be shared among the males. This, they observe, may be a factor occasioning the splitting off of small groups from a troop and the exclusion of 'all male' parties. Finally there is a possibility that female 'open-country' primates may be sexually attractive for longer periods per oestrus cycle than is the case for forest animals[14]. All these factors enhance intra-sexual selection producing sexual dimorphism in size, appearance, and also in behaviour. The marked aggressiveness of male baboons and rhesus monkeys results in

differential access to females, and is correlated with the promiscuous behaviour of oestrus females prior to their mating exclusively with the troop despot at about the time of greatest receptivity.

The increased size and aggressive nature of these males are considered to have been pre-adaptive to their role in troop defence. Males disperse around the periphery of moving troops and co-operate against common danger (see, for example, refs. 15 and 16). We do not think size and aggressiveness originated directly as a response to predation (compare with refs. 17 and 18), but the organization of the troop and male co-operative tendencies in defence undoubtedly did so.

Within Grade IV we have included not only typical forest fringe and savannah woodland species such as *Papio cynocephalus* and *Macaca* sp. but also a number of forest forms, which, in secondary habitats provided by human destruction of woodlands, show social organization in some degree similar to these. Characteristic of all the members of this Grade is a marked adaptability revealed in investigations of the species in contrasting habitats. The *Cercopithecus aethiops* population on the rich but small Lolui Island has 'territorial' behaviour not apparent in unlimited but impoverished conditions where the animals have much larger home ranges[19]. Similar, though often less investigated, accounts are available for the langur (*Presbytis entellus*), chimpanzee and baboon. These variations in social systems appear owing to the plasticity of intra-group relations possible in these forms—a plasticity of undoubted survival value in forest-fringe environments.

Grade IV systems seem therefore to be the result of (i) open country conditions of food supply and predation favouring increase in group size, and (ii) intra-sex selection increasing size and aggressiveness of males, thereby producing (iii) marked group structuring and, in some forms, the protective functions of males acting in unison against predators. Changes from Grade IV to Grade V are related to the occupation of habitats in which food supplies are less abundant, and, at least seasonally, more sparsely and infrequently distributed in the environment. In such areas it would be advantageous for groups of Grade IV animals to fragment into smaller, more widely ranging parties to avoid local over-exploitation of food. Indeed there is evidence from *Papio cynocephalus* populations in arid African areas and from *Macaca fuscata* in northern Japan that group size decreases at the limit of the species geographical range. This is probably in part the result of a low population density, their group organization remaining typical of Grade IV. Small groups of this kind are, however, not very efficient population units. The presence of several large males, only functional in mating and playing no part in rearing young, results in the consumption of much food not used in maintaining the species. Furthermore, the role of the male in protection is less efficient in small groups. In these habitats the 'one-male groups'[20] of *Papio hamadryas*, *Erythrocebus patas* and *Theropithecus gelada* are more adaptive in that less food per reproductive unit goes to individuals not involved in rearing young. The exclusive possession of a 'harem' probably increases inter-male competition for females still further and the occurrence of 'all male' population units indicates a considerable degree of exclusion of potential reproductives from breeding. The intense intra-sexual selection is again doubtless the main factor increasing the dramatic appearance of *P. hamadryas* and *T. gelada* males through the growth of large capes on the backs of these animals[21]—an apparent increase in size not requiring much utilization of energy for its maintenance and providing the animals with a distinctly ferocious appearance enhanced by demeanour and facial expressions.

The differently co-adapted characteristics of the three Group V species suggest clearly the interaction of selection pressures from food shortage, predation and habitat

1202   NATURE   JUNE 18, 1966   VOL. 210

topography in slightly different environments. Thus *T. gelada* in the Ethiopian mountains forms herds in good feeding conditions that split into separately foraging harem groups as conditions deteriorate[16]. Sleeping sites on ever-present cliffs are super-abundant. *P. hamadryas*, although forming 'one-male groups', apparently shows less dispersal because of the limited number of sleeping sites available (rock cliffs, outcrops, etc.) in the single area so far investigated in detail[20]. The patas monkey of open savannah grasslands never forms herds, individual 'one-male groups' keeping apart[22]. There are no rocky sleeping sites and plenty of predators. At night the animals disperse into separate trees and re-assemble for the morning. The male does not adopt the aggressive defence tactics of *Papio* and *Theropithecus;* rather he plays the part of watchdog, showing alert and diversionary behaviour in relation to predators. He does not exert dominance over the group in the same way as the other two species.

The behavioural features of the Grade V species are thus maintained by three main environmental selection pressures the characteristics and range of lability of which are relatively constant within the three habitats. They contrast markedly with the differing values of these same pressures, maintaining the Grade IV organizations in a richer habitat. Signal flow diagrams relating the environmental input of information and the adaptive response of the population in terms of numerical size, population dispersion and social structure are prepared for each of these types. A generalized diagram to which the characteristics of any one of these systems may be fitted is shown in Fig. 1.

The Great Apes and Man

Clearly in Table 1 the Pongidae do not fit easily into categories imposed primarily by investigations of cercopithecid primates. Nevertheless, *Hylobates*, in spite of its adoption of brachiation, has much in common with other tree-top frugivores. Similarities between *Gorilla* and *Pan* to other animals in their Grades are much less clear—a function in part doubtless of their pongid status. Reynolds[23] has clarified the adaptive significance of contrasts in social systems between these two genera.

The development by *Pan* of a simple tool-using culture[24,25] suggests a social condition close to that of early hominids, but we do not accept the suggestion[26] that this necessarily implies a regression from a more human condition. Palaeontological investigations suggest a radiation of early hominids from dryopithecine stocks in circumstances similar to those controlling the transitions from Grade IV to V in the cercopithecids. While *Ramapithecus* and *Paranthropus* were herbivores[27], *Australopithecus* shows evidence from dentition of a more omnivorous food habit including meat eating. Early hominids faced with seasonal food shortage in savannahs probably had initially a social organization not unlike that of the chimpanzee and perhaps formed later either groups guarded by weapon-bearing males or moved in one-male family units—the males playing a part of guardian and watchdog. Possession of weapons would have substituted for gross sexual dimorphism in size. The creatures doubtless retained the ability to congregate in conditions of plenty and in sparsely distributed rocks or tree shelters. These would soon have become bases for hunting raids. Shortage of vegetable food would have accelerated the adoption of weapons for killing animal prey while the trend towards bipedalism, already providing speed in escape from danger, allowed the use of arms in wielding weapons and speed in the chase. The fact that with *Pan* 'all-male groups' occur suggests a source for the loyalty and co-operation necessary in the development of group hunting expeditions. Certainly the biomass of animals suitable for hunting was abundantly present in the grassland savannah of Pleistocene Africa[28], but probably only in *Australopithecus* did an increased reliance on meat lead to major changes in social structure[29].

Sexual Selection

The form of a primate social system is a function not only of selection pressures of the environment. As we have seen, sexual selection, especially in terrestrial societies, plays an important part. Wickler[30] has recently stressed this factor as an ultimate determinant of morphological signals functional in the sexual and agonistic behaviour of certain primates. It would seem that the structures concerned have been derived from skin colour changes occurring in certain phases of the oestrus cycle and for which no signal function is known[31]. Wickler suggests that the coloured buttocks normally present in certain species function in protecting the less dominant males from the despots during quarrels in the troops. Weaker or junior males 'present' to larger animals thereby stimulating a mounting gesture rather than aggression. He considers this to be a case of 'intra-specific mimicry', the male

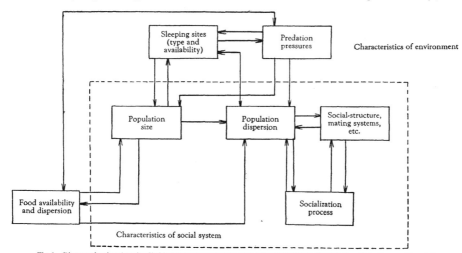

Fig. 1. Diagram showing the role of habitat factors maintaining a specific social system through time in a given environment

No. 5042   JUNE 18, 1966   NATURE   1203

buttocks being copies of the feminine original. Again the curiously shaped patch of bare skin on the chest of *Theropithecus gelada* in both sexes, which undergoes cyclical changes including peripheral vesicle formation in the female[22], has a resemblance in pattern and colour to the perineal skin of the female at oestrus. Wickler considers the chest patches to be substitutes for signals given posteriorly in presentation for mating and he implies, though he does not state, that the chest patches of the males function in a similar way as the coloured buttocks of other male baboons.

Recent investigations (by J. H. C.) in Ethiopia have shown that males do indeed examine the chests of females in oestrus prior to certain copulations, probably those occurring early in an oestrus cycle. Quantitative data show, however, that the colour changes on chest and ischial areas are not in phase. Lactating mothers and non-oestrus females have the reddest behinds. It seems odd that if the red chest colour is attractive to males the perineal areas should be most red at precisely the time when mating would be inappropriate. Long nipples in the mid-line of the chest, assumed by Wickler to be signal imitations of the vulva, appear to arise in the course of suckling. Preparous females have small nipples spaced apart, but, when in oestrus, are nevertheless frequently mated. The role of nipple shape and position in sexual signalling prior to copulation is thus in doubt.

The gelada spends a considerably greater time sitting down than does *Papio doguera* in the same area. A chest signal as an indicator of female sexual condition would therefore be more appropriate than an ischial one. It does not appear essential, however, for the signal to be an exact copy of the ischial design—and indeed we find that it is not. In view of the baby and juvenile geladas' prolonged interest in the nipples—with which they play as well as from which they obtain nourishment—adult concern with this area is readily understandable and any colour changes are likely to develop a significance. The extent to which chest patches really copy the behind remains largely subjective. There is no evidence that the chest patch of the male gelada functions in a manner analogous to Wickler's suggestions for the buttocks in males of other species.

Wickler's hypothesis deserves critical scrutiny as it could have considerable significance in the investigation of human sexual aesthetics. The shape of the human mammary glands is not apparently 'essential' for it is not found in the great apes. Possibly they have acquired their function as a sexual releaser in a manner analogous to the evolutionary process suggested for the female gelada's chest. The development could have arisen in co-adaptation with the adoption of the upright bipedal stance in the early Hominidae and the use of the frontal position in mating. However, it is not so much the shape of the human breasts that is the critical sexual releaser as the visual stimulus provided by the nipple and the areolar zone around it[23]. While "intraspecific mimicry" might account for the shape of these organs it seems that normal Darwinian sexual selection (that is, inter-sexual selection) could account for the enhancement of structural features around the nipples. Further research into the significance and evolution of such signals in both non-human primates and man will be of considerable interest.

[1] Washburn, S., and DeVore, I., in *Social Life of Early Man*, edit. by Washburn, S. L., 91 (New York, 1961).
[2] Hall, K. R. L., *Symp. Zool. Soc. Lond.*, **14**, 265 (1965).
[3] DeVore, I., (ed.), *Primate Behavior* (New York, 1965).
[4] Crook, J. H., *Behaviour Monograph*, 10 (1964).
[5] Crook, J. H., *Symposium Zool. Soc. Lond.*, **14**, 181 (1965).
[6] Howell, F. C., and Bourlière, F. (eds.), *African Ecology and Human Evolution* (Chicago, 1963).
[7] Huxley, J. S., *Systematics Assoc. Publ.*, **3**, 21 (1959).
[8] Hill, W. C. Osman, *Proc. Roy. Soc. Edin.*, **66**, pt. 1 (No. 5), 94 (1955).
[9] Petter, J. J., *Mem. Mus. Hist. Nat. Paris.*, A, **27**, (1), 1 (1962).
[10] Jay, P., in *Primate Behavior* (New York, 1965).
[11] Schaller, G. B., in *Primate Behavior* (New York, 1965).
[12] Lancaster, J. B., and Lee, R. B., in *Primate Behavior* (New York, 1965).
[13] Itani *et al.*, *Primates*, **4**, No. 3 (1963).
[14] Chance and Mead, S. E. B. Symp. VII, 395 (1953).
[15] Hall, K. R. L., and Devore, I., in *Primate Behavior* (New York, 1965).
[16] Crook, J. H., *Symp. Zool. Soc. Lond.* (in the press).
[17] DeVore, I., and Washburn, S. L., *African Ecology and Human Evolution* (Chicago, 1963).
[18] Chance, M. R. A., *Primates*, **4**, 1 (1963).
[19] Gartlan, J. S., and Brain, C. K. (in the press).
[20] Kummer, H., and Kurt, F., *Folia. Primat.*, 1, 4 (1963).
[21] Jolly, C. H., *Man*, **63**, No. 222 (1963).
[22] Hall, K. R. L., *J. Zool.*, **148**, 15 (1966).
[23] Reynolds, V., *American Anthropologist*, **67**, 3, 691 (1965).
[24] Goodall, J., *Primate Behavior* (New York, 1965).
[25] Koortlandt, A. (personal communication).
[26] Koortlandt, A., and Kolj, M, *Symp. Zool. Soc. Lond.*, **10**, 61–88 (1963).
[27] Robinson, J. T. *African Ecology and Human Evolution* (Chicago, 1963).
[28] Bourlière, F., *African Ecology and Human Evolution* (Chicago, 1963).
[29] Crook, J. H., in *Symp. "Biology of Co-operation", Eugenics Review* (in the press).
[30] Wickler, W., *Naturwiss.*, **50**, 481 (1963).
[31] Rowell, T. E., *J. Reprod. Fertil.*, **6**, 193 (1963).
[32] Harrison Matthews, L., *Trans. Zool. Soc. Lond.*, **28**, 7, 543 (1956).
[33] Goodhart, C. B., *New Scientist*, **23**, 558 (1964).

The Seasonality and Population Dynamics of Equatorial Forest Birds in Sarawak
M. P. L. Fogden

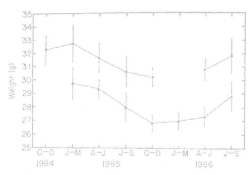

FIGURE 19. Seasonal changes in the mean weight of *Pycnonotus eutilotus* and *P. plumosus* at Semengo, 1964–66. The samples for each period of three months contain at least 20 individuals. The vertical bars represent one standard deviation. ●, *Pycnonotus eutilotus*; ▲, *P. plumosus*.

And again, in Ward's study, muscle weights of *P. goiavier* were apparently increasing during October, which is the lean season in Singapore. On the other hand, if fruit is very scarce, as it was at Semengo in the second half of 1965, weights of frugivorous species may not recover until fruit increases. Figure 19 shows this clearly in the case of *P. eutilotus* and *P. plumosus*.

This explanation of the annual cycle of body and muscle weights accounts for the conclusions drawn from the data in Figure 18 and listed above, and also accounts for the general correlation between low muscle weights and moult that was noted by Ward.

THE LEAN SEASON AND FOOD AS A LIMITING FACTOR

There is a considerable body of circumstantial evidence that food limits bird populations in the Sarawak forest, and that the lean season, when insects are least abundant, is a critical period for insectivorous birds. That this is so is suggested by the fact that the annual cycle of insectivorous birds is organised so that during the lean season there is a complete cessation of any activities that increase their energy demands beyond a simple maintenance level. Breeding, parental care of young and moulting come to a halt at the beginning of the lean season. Moult that is incomplete is arrested. Furthermore, foraging is made as efficient as possible by birds joining mixed foraging flocks. These assemblages of insectivorous birds reach a maximum size during the lean season, and their primary function is to increase foraging efficiency (Fogden 1970, and in prep.). Populations appear to be regulated at the time of the juvenile dispersal, shortly before the lean season, when there is much territorial activity. By contrast, there is a conspicuous lack of singing and other territorial activity during the lean season itself. All these facts strongly suggest that the lean season is a period of great food shortage.

The lean season is also a period of food shortage for species with a mixed diet of insects and fruit, at least in some years. This is shown by Ward's (1969b) study of the diurnal fat cycles of *Pycnonotus goiavier* in Singapore, where the lean season is in October. Ward showed that *P. goiavier* requires 0·6 g of fat for overnight metabolism, and that during October 1964, 1965 and 1966, but during no other months in any year, there were some birds going to roost with less than this required amount of fat. Such birds would have been forced to break down other tissues to obtain energy, a process that is kinetically inefficient and which, if continued, quickly results in death. This is direct evidence that food might be sufficiently scarce during the lean season to cause mortality through starvation.

However, the view has already been put forward that the lean season is not necessarily always a period of food shortage for species, such as *P. goiavier*, which eat fruit as well as insects, because fruit is often abundant during the lean season.   Infact, Ward (1969a) showed that muscle weights of *P. goiavier* were increasing during October 1966, which argues that the month was not particularly severe for at least a part of the population he was studying.   Fruit is a poor source of protein, and its importance lies in its being a relatively good source of energy.   If all the energy requirements of a bird are easily met during the lean season by an abundant fruit supply, then it is possible that a relatively small and irregular protein intake would suffice to increase body and muscle weights.   This might explain the relatively high body weights of *Pycnonotus* species at Semengo during the lean season in 1964 (Fig. 19), and the increase in muscle weights of *P. goiavier* in Singapore.

It is probable that fruit is also of great importance during the breeding season; certainly this was true at Semengo, where species of *Pycnonotus*, and other species with a mixed diet, were observed to eat fruit whenever it was available, even when insects were abundant.   This is probably because fruit represents a readily available source of energy which can be collected quickly, thereby leaving time to forage for protein-rich insect food to feed to growing young or, alternatively, at other times of the year, to satisfy protein demands for amino acids for feather synthesis or the recovery of muscle weights.   When fruit is not readily available, which is a possibility at any time of the year, such species have to rely on insects for all their requirements, and there is evidence that they are not sufficiently specialised to acquire insects in the necessary quantities to satisfy both their energy requirements and their protein requirements for breeding, moulting or recovery from low muscle weights.

The evidence for these suggestions comes from the two annual cycles of *Pycnonotus* species at Semengo between October 1964 and September 1966.   The data mainly concern *P. eutilotus* and *P. plumosus*, but other species conformed to the same pattern. Fruit was plentiful in the study area from October 1964 to September 1965.   Weights of *Pycnonotus* species were already quite high in October (Fig. 19) and the lean season apparently presented no difficulties.   A successful breeding season followed (Table 1), while the timing of their moult was similar to that of insectivorous species and lasted 4–5 months (Fig. 9).   However, from October 1965 to August 1966 fruit was remarkably scarce in the Semengo area, and for a considerable distance around.   Many trees fruited, but crops were small and continued for shorter periods than normal.   As a result, species of *Pycnonotus* fed mainly on insects from October onwards, and the weights of most individuals remained low throughout (Fig. 19).   Some individuals attempted to breed, but most were unsuccessful, and the average proportion of juveniles in the trapped population was less than 2% in 1966, as compared with 14% in the previous year. Attempts to breed stopped early, and most birds began to moult in March, two to three months earlier than in 1965, while the moult itself was slower, lasting about 23 weeks (Fig. 10).   Fruit eventually became plentiful again in August 1966, and there was a rapid recovery in the weights of most birds (Fig. 19).   This whole sequence of events appears to revolve around the availability of fruit.   The consequence of a shortage of fruit is dependence on insects, and this evidence suggests that species of *Pycnonotus* are unable to breed successfully while feeding on insects alone.   As Ward (1969 a) pointed out, it may be more than a coincidence that *P. goiavier* also had a poor breeding season in Singapore in 1966.

Specialised frugivorous species resemble those with a mixed diet in not necessarily being affected by the lean season, but they differ in that a shortage of fruit results in a substantial part of their populations moving elsewhere.   For example, not a single individual of the frugivorous dove *Chalcophaps indica* was seen, heard or netted at Semengo between October 1965 and August 1966, though they were common when fruit was plentiful. Other frugivorous species, such as *Calyptomena viridis* and *Irena puella*, were also rare at Semengo when fruit was scarce.

In summary, the lean season is an annually recurring period of food shortage for insectivorous species. Its timing and regularity results from the consistency of the annual rainfall pattern, which affects primary productivity and, hence, insect abundance. By contrast, the lean season is not necessarily a period of food shortage for species that eat fruit as well as insects, because fruit may be abundant at any time of the year. However, such species are likely to be at a disadvantage whenever a period of fruit shortage coincides with the lean season; they then have to forage for insects, for which they are less well adapted than specialised insectivorous species. There is also evidence that such species are unable to breed successfully when a fruit shortage coincides with the breeding season. As fruit is an erratic and unreliable food supply, their reproductive success varies considerably from year to year.

EVIDENCE OF A LESS THAN ANNUAL CYCLE IN TWO SARAWAK BIRDS

There is evidence that two species, the babbler *Stachyris erythroptera* and the spider-hunter *Arachnothera longirostris*, have a less than annual cycle with a periodicity of rather more than nine months. During the course of this study both species were more or less in phase with each other, with a tendency for *A. longirostris* to be slightly ahead with its moult.

Both species had distinct peaks of breeding activity from March to May 1964, December 1964 to February 1965, late October to December 1965, and August to October 1966, with complete moult cycles between each breeding season. The timing and

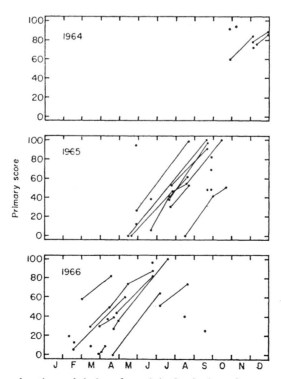

FIGURE 20. The rate, duration and timing of moult in *Stachyris erythroptera* at Semengo in 1964, 1965 and 1966.

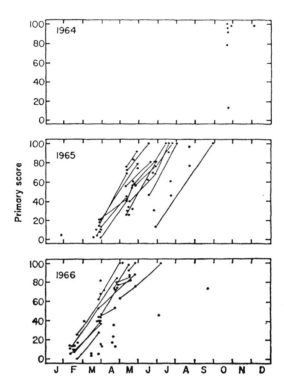

FIGURE 21.   The rate, duration and timing of moult in *Arachnothera longirostris* at Semengo in 1964, 1965 and 1966.

duration of the moult are shown in Figures 20 and 21.   The bulk of the population of both species were fairly synchronised, the moult of individuals taking about 17 weeks in *S. erythroptera* and 14 weeks in *A. longirostris*, the latter being one of the quickest moults among Sarawak birds.   A further piece of evidence in support of a less than annual cycle in *S. erythroptera* comes from the moult condition of specimens in the Sarawak Museum that were collected in the Kuching area between 1891 and 1956.   The primary score of these specimens is plotted in Figure 22, together with the scores of specimens of *S. nigricollis*, *S. poliocephala* and *S. maculata* for comparison.   The timing of the moult of almost all the specimens of the latter three species is clearly similar to that of *S. nigricollis* and *S. poliocephala* at Semengo in 1965 and 1966 (Fig. 16), even though the specimens were collected over a period of more than 60 years.   By contrast, the records of moult of the specimens of *S. erythroptera* are scattered throughout all 12 months of the year.   This is precisely what would be expected of specimens of a species with a less than annual cycle that were collected in many different years.

    In both *S. erythroptera* and *A. longirostris*, just as in other Sarawak birds, successful breeding is quickly followed by a moult which coincides, at least in *S. erythroptera*, with a period of prolonged parental care of juveniles.   Both species differ from others in that the moult is followed immediately by another breeding season.   Why these species are able to breed sucessfully at any time of the year, when others cannot, is not known. Nor is it known why individuals remain synchronised in these circumstances.

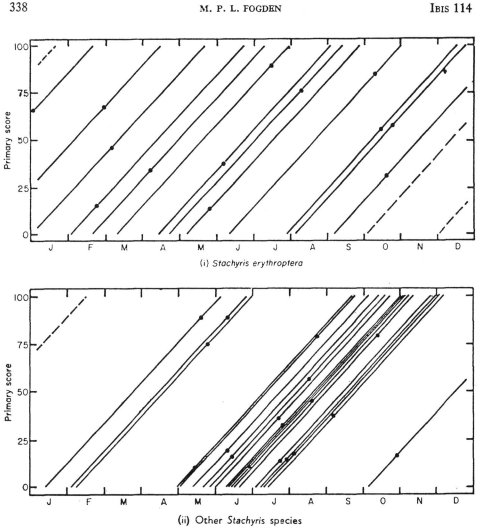

(i) *Stachyris erythroptera*

(ii) Other *Stachyris* species

FIGURE 22. The rate, duration and timing of moult in *Stachyris erythroptera*, based on skins in the Sarawak Museum collected in the vicinity of Kuching. Data on the moult of *S. nigricollis*, *S. poliocephala* and *S. maculata* from the same source are given for comparison.

THE PROXIMATE FACTORS INITIATING BREEDING

Moreau (1936), writing of East Africa, and Ward (1969a), writing of southeast Asia, both rejected the idea that changes in photoperiod can be responsible for bringing birds into breeding condition at the appropriate time in equatorial regions, because the changes in day-length are exceedingly small. Photoperiod seems similarly unlikely as a proximate factor in Sarawak. In southeast Asia breeding seasons generally follow soon after the beginning of the period of heaviest rainfall but, as heavy rain can and does fall at other times of the year as well, rainfall by itself can hardly act as a proximate factor for breeding. It is possible that a subtle combination of such factors, such as vegetation changes, changes in rainfall pattern, continuous high humidity, etc., could act in the necessary way, though, as Ward pointed out, a response to such a combination of factors would be difficult to prove. It would also be difficult to evolve and does not appear to be a very likely possibility. Ward suggested, however, that " the level of tissue protein may have important repercussions on the timing of both reproduction and moult, and might even be the main regulating mechanism. Although seasonal changes in the level of tissue protein must be geared to changes in protein availability (i.e. in insect food abundance), internal regulation by this means would not require any perception of an environmental change through the external sense organs." I have come to a similar conclusion in this study as a result of the annual cycles of weight changes that were observed at Semengo. According to this hypothesis, a bird will come into breeding condition whenever its protein level is sufficiently high. For reasons that have been discussed, this is normally at the time when insects increase in abundance soon after the beginning of the annual monsoon. However, it is highly likely that circumstances could result in some birds getting into good protein condition at other times of the year, and these could account for the not inconsiderable number of birds that breed or attempt to breed outside the normal season. However, such attempts are even less likely to be successful than those in the normal season, so most birds would quickly be brought back into line with the rest of the population. The hypothesis also accounts for, and is supported by, the lack of breeding by species of *Pycnonotus* at Semengo in 1966. Among the species for which data are available, they alone failed to increase in weight at the beginning of the breeding season, and they alone failed to breed that year. Given that less than annual cycles occur, as they appear to do in the case of *Stachyris erythroptera* and *Arachnothera longirostris*, the hypothesis also accounts for the way in which a bird can come into breeding condition at a different time each year, a phenomonen that is difficult to explain in terms of environmental triggers. It does not, of course, explain why these species are able to breed successfully at different times of year.

A COMPARISON OF SEASONALITY AND REPRODUCTION IN EQUATORIAL FOREST AND TEMPERATE WOODLAND

The organisation and timing of the annual cycle of forest birds in Sarawak is summarised in Figure 23. It is as strongly seasonal as that of birds in a less climatically stable environment, such as temperate woodland, all those activities which result in increased energy and/or protein demands, namely breeding, prolonged parental care, moulting and dispersal, being timed to occur when food is relatively more abundant. However, in spite of their similar seasonality, some features of reproduction in the two environments are very different. Whereas large and repeated broods are the rule in temperate woodland, prolonged parental care of a small brood is the rule in equatorial forest. The result is very low reproductive success in equatorial forest as compared with temperate woodland, and low as compared with high mortality rates. The basis for these differences is the amount of seasonal variation in the abundance of food in the two environments, which is probably several thousand-fold in temperate woodland, but only a few-fold in equatorial forest. In temperate woodland food is so abundant during

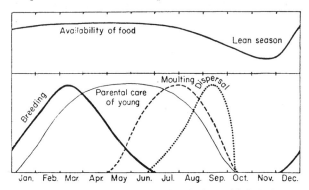

FIGURE 23. A summary of seasonality in forest birds in Sarawak.

the breeding season that young inexperienced birds can be left after a short while to fend for themselves. In equatorial forest food is relatively difficult to find throughout the year. There is a popular conception that life in a lush equatorial forest must be very easy for birds and other animals. This is true in so far as adult birds have a very long life expectancy compared with small birds elsewhere. But, paradoxically, the low adult mortality rate is a consequence of the relative scarcity of food in equatorial forest, which results in very low reproductive rate.

ACKNOWLEDGMENTS

I am most grateful to Dr D. Lack F.R.S. for making available the facilities of the Edward Grey Institute, Oxford, and for criticising an early draft of this paper, and to Dr P. Ward and Dr P. S. Ashton who read all or part of a later draft and suggested many improvements. Particular thanks are due to my wife who read and improved the paper at all stages, in addition to drawing the figures and helping in many other ways.

The study would not have been possible without the great help and support of Tom Harrisson who, as Curator of the Sarawak Museum, encouraged me to make the most of its facilities. The mist-netting study would not have been possible without the help of many members of the Museum staff, but particularly Lian Labang, Gaun anak Sureng and Ambrose Achang. Thanks are due to many other people for their help and advice, particularly to Dr G. H. L. Rothschild, who kindly allowed me to use his data on the abundance of insects at Semengo, and Dr H. Elliot McClure, who kindly made available an equipment grant in his capacity as Director of the United States Armed Forces Migratory Animal Pathological Survey.

SUMMARY

This two-year study of the seasonality and population dynamics of equatorial forest birds was carried out in the Semengo Forest Reserve in Sarawak. Sarawak has one of the most non-seasonal climates in the world, characterised by heavy all-year-round rainfall, uniform moderately high temperatures and high humidity. Nevertheless, rainfall increases during the northeast monsoon, from December to February, and results in increased leaf production.

The two main types of bird food differ in their seasonality and distribution. Insects are relatively evenly distributed in both space and time, and fluctuation in their numbers is only a few-fold during the course of the year. Insect numbers are related to leaf production, and hence they are most abundant during and after the northeast monsoon, and least abundant in November, just before the monsoon. The latter period is termed the lean season. By contrast with insects, fruit is patchily distributed and erratic in its seasonality. There may be long periods when fruit is abundant, and others when there is little fruit over wide areas. There is no annually recurring period when fruit is always scarce, as there is in insects. This results in some differences in breeding biology between insectivorous and frugivorous birds.

The breeding season of forest birds is sharply defined, lasting from about December to June, this being the period when insects are most abundant. This applies to frugivorous as well as insectivorous species, perhaps because of the need to provide a protein rich diet in the form of insects to their nestlings. Food is almost certainly the ultimate factor controlling the timing of the breeding season.

Most species have small clutches and suffer a very high rate of nest predation, though young survive well once they have fledged, for they have no important predators. Those juveniles that fledge successfully attain independence from their parents in September and October, at which time there is a general dispersal of juveniles which coincides with adults singing and re-establishing their territories. It appears that the population is effectively regulated at this time, and that the only juveniles to survive are those that manage to establish territories. This period of population regulation occurs just before the lean season. The annual recruitment and adult mortality are very low, being in the region of 10%.

After the young fledge there is a long period of parental care, including feeding, which may last for as long as 6–7 months in insectivorous species. Since this effectively prevents second broods, prolonged parental care must have some compensating advantage. This is probably related to the need to provide the young with sufficient time to learn by experience how to find and recognise the great diversity of highly cryptic insects upon which they feed.

Moult is fairly synchronised between both species and individuals. In the majority of species it occurs between May and October, being timed to end before the onset of the lean season, and is rather slow, taking from 17–20 weeks. In woodpeckers and terrestrial babblers the moult is exceptionally slow, taking up to 40 weeks in the former. There is evidence that some birds of many species do not moult every year.

Seasonal changes in body weight were noted in several species, which appear to be due to changes in muscle protein levels. Weights peak early in the breeding season and thereafter decline, remaining low until the following breeding season. It is suggested that the initial fall in body weights is caused by the stresses of breeding, and that for some months a recovery is prevented by the stresses of parental care of young, moulting and the lean season. High protein levels are regarded as a protein store which enables birds to neglect their own feeding and nutrition, and concentrate on breeding activities.

There is evidence that the lean season is a period of food shortage for insectivorous birds, and that it effectively limits their numbers. This is particularly suggested by the complete cessation during the lean season of any demands beyond a simple maintenance level. By contrast, the lean season is not necessarily a period of food shortage for species that eat fruit as well as insects, because fruit is often abundant during the lean season. However, there is evidence that such species are at a disadvantage when a period of fruit shortage coincides with the lean season, and that they are unable to breed successfully if fruit is scarce during the breeding season.

Two of the species studied, *Stachyris erythroptera* and *Arachnothera longirostris*, have a less than annual cycle with a periodicity of about nine months. Why these species are apparently able to breed at any time of the year is not known. Nor is it known why individuals remain synchronised in these circumstances, as they do.

Photoperiod and rainfall are rejected as possible proximate factors controlling the timing of the breeding season. It is suggested that the main regulating factor is the protein condition of individual birds, and that they come into breeding condition whenever their protein level is sufficiently high. This is generally at the beginning of the monsoon when insects increase in numbers, but birds with high protein levels at other times of the year account for the not infrequent attempts to breed out of the normal season.

The characteristic features of reproduction in equatorial forest birds, namely small clutches, the lack of second broods and prolonged parental care, result in low reproductive success and low adult mortality and are directly related to the relatively small seasonal variation in food abundance.

REFERENCES

ASHMOLE, N. P. 1962. The Black Noddy *Anous tenuirostris* on Ascension Island. Ibis 103 b : 235–273.

ASHMOLE, N. P. & TOVAR S., H. 1968. Prolonged parental care in Royal Terns and other birds. Auk 85 : 90–100.

BAKER, J. R., MARSHALL, A. J. & HARRISSON, T. H. 1940. The seasons in a tropical rain forest (New Hebrides). Part 5 Birds (*Pachycephala*). J. Linn. Soc. (Zool.) 41 : 50–70.

BATES, G. L. 1908. Observations regarding the breeding season of the birds of southern Kamerun. Ibis (9)2 : 558–570.

CHAPIN, J. P. 1932–54. The birds of the Belgian Congo. Bull. Am. Mus. nat. Hist. 65, 75, 75A, 75B.

CORBET, A. S. & PENDLEBURY, H. M. 1956. The butterflies of the Malay peninsula. London.

CORNER, E. J. H. 1940. Wayside trees of Malaya. Singapore.

EVANS, P. R. 1966. Autumn movements, moult and measurements of the Lesser Redpoll *Carduelis flammea cabaret*. Ibis 108 : 183–216.

FOGDEN, M. P. L. 1970. Some aspects of the ecology of bird populations in Sarawak. D. Phil. Thesis, Oxford University.

GIBSON-HILL, C. A. 1952. The apparent breeding seasons of land birds in North Borneo and Malaya. Bull. Raffles Mus. 24 : 270–294.

MARLER, P. 1956. Behaviour of the Chaffinch *Fringilla coelebs*. Behaviour, Suppl. 5.

McCLURE, H. E. 1966. Observations on fruiting and flowering seasons in a Malayan forest. Malay. Forester 29 : 193–201.

MICHENER, H. & MICHENER, J. R. 1940. The molt of house finches of the Pasadena region, California. Condor 42 : 140–153.

MILLER, A. H. 1959. Reproductive cycles in an equatorial sparrow. Proc. natn. Acad. Sci. U.S.A. 45 : 1095–1100.

MILLER, A. H. 1961. Molt cycles in equatorial Andean Sparrows. Condor 63 : 143–161.

MILLER, A. H. 1962. Bimodal occurrence of breeding in an equatorial sparrow. Proc. natn. Acad. Sci. U.S.A. 48 : 396–400.

MILLER. A, H. 1963. Seasonal activity and ecology of the avifauna of an American equatorial cloud forest. Univ. Calif. Publs. Zool. 66 : 1–78.

MOREAU, R. E. 1936. Breeding seasons of birds in East African evergreen forest. Proc. zool. Soc. Lond. 1936 : 631–653.

MOREAU, R. E. 1950. The breeding seasons of African birds. I. Land birds. Ibis 92 : 223–267.

NEWTON, I. 1966. The moult of the Bullfinch *Pyrrhula pyrrhula*. Ibis 108 : 41–67.

PIECHOCKI, R. 1955. Ueber Verhalten, Mauser und Umfärbung einer gekäfigten Steppenweihe (*Circus macrourus*). J. Orn. 96 : 327–336.

PITELKA, F. A. 1958. Timing of molt in the Steller Jays of the Queen Charlotte Islands, British Columbia. Condor 60 : 38–49.

RICHARDS, P. W. 1952. The tropical rain forest. Cambridge University Press.

RUWET, J. C. 1964. La périodicité de la reproduction chez oiseaux du Katanga. Gerfaut 54 : 84–110.

SEAL, J. 1958. Rainfall and sunshine in Sarawak. Sarawak Mus. J. 8 : 500–544.

SELANDER, R. K. 1958. Age determination and molt in the Boat-tailed Grackle. Condor 60 : 355–376.

SKUTCH, A. F. 1950. The nesting season of Central American birds in relation to climate and food supply. Ibis 92 : 185–222.

SMYTHIES, B. E. 1960. The birds of Borneo. London.

SNOW, D. W. 1962. A field study of the Black-and-white Manakin *Manacus manacus* in Trinidad. Zoologica 47 : 65–104.

SNOW, D. W. 1963. The natural history of the Oilbird *Steatornis caripensis* in Trinidad. Zoologica 47 : 199–221.

SNOW, D. W. 1967. A guide to moult in British birds. British Trust for Ornithology, Field Guide No. 11.

SNOW, D. W. & SNOW, B. K. 1964. Breeding seasons and annual cycles of Trinidad land-birds. Zoologica 49 : 1–39.

VOOUS, K. H. 1950. The breeding seasons of birds in Indonesia. Ibis 92 : 279–287.

WARD, P. 1969 a. The annual cycle of the Yellow-vented Bulbul *Pycnonotus goiavier* in a humid equatorial environment. J. Zool., Lond. 157 : 25–45.

WARD, P. 1969 b. Seasonal and diurnal changes in the fat content of an equatorial bird. Physiol. Zoöl. 42 : 85–95.

WARD, P. & D'CRUZ, D. 1968. Seasonal changes in the thymus gland of a tropical bird. Ibis 110 : 203–205.

WILLIAMSON, K. 1957. The annual post-nuptial moult in the Wheatear *Oenanthe oenanthe*. Bird-Banding 28 : 129–135.

Dr. M. P. L. Fogden, Edward Grey Institute, of Field Ornithology, Department of Zoology, South Parks Road, Oxford OX1 3PS

Reproductive Strategies in a Tropical Anuran Community
M. L. Crump

INTRODUCTION

If it is not small enough to eat nor large enough to eat you, and does not put up a squawk about it, mate with it. D. L. Jameson (1955).

But, reproduction in frogs is more complicated than Jameson's whimsical statement indicates. Six years ago, when I collected my first tropical frogs, I was immediately impressed with the diversity of the fauna. My first surprise was finding more than 35 sympatric species of frogs within the first week. I encountered the flashy and gaudy color patterns, such as those of the *Hyla leucophyllata* group, and the morphological oddities, such as *Hemiphractus* and *Pipa*. However, the most impressive aspects of the diversity were the bizarre modes of reproduction. Being a temperate–zone biologist, I was accustomed to the "generalized" life history of frogs—egg deposition in water, aquatic larval development, metamorphosis, following which the frogs spend most of their lives on land. But many tropical species lay their eggs out of water and have aquatic larvae, and others have completely eliminated the tadpole stage. It seems as though evolutionary forces operant on tropical frogs favored more "imaginative" life histories than those of temperate frogs.

The greatest anuran species richness of any area in the world studied to date is found at Santa Cecilia, Ecuador (81 species). Upon examination of the modes of reproduction (egg deposition site and type of development), it is apparent that a great diversity of modes exists—probably the greatest in any known region. It seems reasonable to assume that as anuran speciation occurred in the tropics, the evolutionary thrust included this diversity of reproductive modes. Environments, as measured by niche diversification, life span of the habitat, and climatic variables, as well as competition and predation no doubt operated on the genetic potential of organisms in bringing about physiological, morphological, and behavioral changes. These influenced and were influenced by the evolution of reproductive diversity.

The premise of this study is that the reproductive diversity at Santa Cecilia allows coexistence of a great number of anuran species by means of partitioning of breeding sites. In order to investigate this premise, I have analyzed the reproductive strategies operant within a diverse community of Neotropical frogs. Several aspects of the reproductive characteristics of each species of frog are considered: (1) behavioral and morphological adaptations, (2) habitat partitioning as judged by egg deposition site, (3) temporal partitioning of the environment judged by breeding seasonality, (4) size-fecundity relationships, (5) volumetric relationships of female to egg-complement volume, and (6) developmental relationships (number of eggs deposited, size of eggs, number of days until hatching, size at hatching), as related to the egg deposition and developmental sites. The data are synthesized into a discussion incorporating interpretation of reproductive strategies in terms of spatial and temporal environmental partitioning, reproductive effort of the adult frogs, and the ecological and evolutionary significance of the reproductive diversity.

ACKNOWLEDGEMENTS

I am extremely grateful to the many persons who assisted in the conception, gestation, and finally in the deliverance of this study. Dr. William E. Duellman first aroused my curiosity concerning anuran reproductive strategies years ago and later served as chairman of my doctoral committee. For all of this, and especially for instilling within me a love for the tropics, I am indebted.

SYNTHESIS OF RESULTS BY
REPRODUCTIVE MODE

The 30 species that deposit eggs in water (mode 1) demonstrate a wide range in each of the reproductive variables. Included in this mode are the smallest (19.1 mm snout-vent length) to the next-to-the-largest species (132.6 mm) at Santa Cecilia. Fecundity ranges from 143 eggs for *Sphaenorhychus carneus* to more than 8500 eggs for *Bufo marinus*. On an overall basis, larger species produce more eggs ($P < 0.01$). However, only three of the 16 species tested show a significant correlation between snout-vent length and fecundity. The range in maximal ovarian egg diameter is 1.0 to 2.0 mm, which together with snout-vent length and fecundity yields a wide range in the ovarian size factor index (6.22 to 97.26). The larger the body volume, the greater the egg complement volume. Sexual dimorphism in snout-vent length ranges from essentially none (female-to-male ratio of *Hyla punctata* = 1.01) to the female being half again the size of the male (ratio = 1.51 for *Hyla geographica*). Species with the largest clutch sizes also have the largest ovum diameters. There is no apparent relationship between ovum diameter and intraoval developmental time, although this may be due to only slight range in variation of both variables. There is no significant relationship between either developmental time or hatchling size and the "permanence" of the environment. All of the species have at least slightly pigmented eggs. Some species breed in ephemeral and/or temporary water, others in permanent water. Fecundity is not significantly greater ($P < 0.4$) in those species breeding in ephemeral–temporary water than for those breeding in more permanent water. Some species breed in the forest, others in forest-edge environments, and others in disturbed, open areas; the breeding habitat is unknown for many of the species. Species breed continually, opportunistically, or sporadically.

Nyctimantis rugiceps is the only representative of mode 2 reproduction. No gravid females were found. Males call continually throughout the year from water-filled tree cavities (often bamboo trees) in both forest and forest-edge environments. It is assumed that eggs are deposited in the cavities and that larval development occurs therein.

Mode 3 reproduction is represented only by the large tree frog, *Hyla boans* (mean female snout-vent length = 99.0 mm). The mean number of ovarian eggs is 3154.8, and the maximum ovarian egg diameter is 2.0 mm, yielding an extremely high ovarian size factor of 63.73. Larger females (snout-vent length) produce significantly more eggs ($P < 0.05$). Males are slightly larger than females. Eggs are heavily pigmented. The only breeding site of *H. boans* is along the edge of the river. Breeding is sporadic, usually during drier periods when the river level is low.

Thirteen species deposit eggs on vegetation above water (mode 4). These range in size from small tree frogs (20.9 mm snout-vent length, *Hyla brevifrons*) to the large *Phyllomedusa tarsius* (105.3 mm). Likewise, fecundity exhibits a wide range, from 18 eggs of *Centrolenella munozorum* to over 1000 eggs for *Phyllomedusa vaillanti*. On an overall basis, larger species produce more eggs ($P < 0.05$). Only three of the eight species tested for size-fecundity correlations show a significant relationship ($P < 0.05$). Maximal ovarian egg diameter ranges from 1.0 to 3.5 mm, yielding a wide spectrum of ovarian size factors (1.17 to 28.28). There is a trend for species with larger body volumes to have larger ovarian egg complement volumes. The female-to-male snout-vent length ratios range from 1.09 for *Hyla bokermanni* to 1.51 for *Phyllomedusa vaillanti*. Tadpoles of species of mode 4 take longer to hatch than those of species that deposit eggs directly in water. With the exception of two species, there is a positive relationship between ovum diameter and number of days until hatching. The sprinkling of water onto the egg clutch speeds up the developmental process and initiates hatching in some species. Species of this_ reproductive mode have a significantly lower egg mass relative to body length than those species that deposit eggs in water. Egg pigmentation ranges from none to heavy. Species breed over still and running water, in ephemeral, temporary, and permanent situations. Breeding occurs in forest, forest-edge, and disturbed, open areas. None of the species breeds continually; of those known, all are opportunistic or sporadic breeders.

Five leptodactylids produce foam nests and have aquatic larval development (mode 5); quantitative reproductive data are available for three of these. Snout-vent length ranges from 33.6 mm (*Leptodactylus discodactylus*) to 68.2 mm (*Leptodactylus wagneri*), and fecundity from 234.8 eggs to 1740.0 eggs for the same two species, respectively. Maximal ovarian egg diameter ranges from 1.0 mm for *L. discodactylus* to 2.5 mm for *L. mystaceus*. The ovarian size factors range from 6.99 to 38.27. Sexual dimorphism in size ranges from practically none (female-to-male snout-vent length ratio = 1.07, *L. mystaceus*) to 1.41, *L. wagneri*. *Leptodactylus wagneri* is the only one of these three species with egg pigmentation. Breeding habitats are known for three species: *L. mystaceus* and *L. wagneri* breed in open, disturbed areas and in forest-edge environments, and *L. pentadactylus* breeds in forest and forest-edge situations. *Leptodactylus mystaceus* is considered to be a continuous breeder, and *L. pentadactylus* a drier-period, sporadic breeder.

Five dendrobatids deposit terrestrial eggs and the larvae subsequently are carried to water on the dorsum of the adult (mode 6). All are small frogs (snout-vent lengths from 17.8 to 25.6 mm) and have low fecundity (8.9 to 22.7 eggs). *Dendrobates pictus* is the only species having a significant ($P < 0.05$) correlation between snout-vent length and fecundity. Maximal ovarian egg

diameter ranges from 1.5 to 3.0 mm; the ovarian size factors all are extremely low (0.66 to 1.77). Volumetric data were taken for three species; as expected, the species with the greatest snout-vent length (*Dendrobates pictus*) has the greatest body volume and egg complement volume. There is little variation in sexual dimorphism in snout-vent length (female-to-male ratios range from 1.04 to 1.16). Eggs are moderately pigmented in all species. All species breed in forest and/or forest-edge environments based on calling activity of the males and occurrence of gravid females. Based on the occurrence of gravid individuals and juveniles, it is suggested that all species except *Colostethus sauli* (for which there are few data) are continuous breeders.

Leptodactylus andreae is the only species that produces a foam nest in which the larvae undergo complete development (mode 7). The mean snout-vent length of gravid females is 26.7 mm, and the mean number of mature ovarian eggs is 8.7. There is no significant correlation between snout-vent length and fecundity. The maximal ovum diameter is 3.0 mm; the ovarian size factor is low (0.98). Females are significantly ($P < 0.001$) larger than males, although the female-to-male snout-vent length ratio is low (1.09). The eggs are unpigmented. Gravid females were found sporadically throughout the year in forest and forest-edge environments.

Fourteen species of *Eleutherodactylus* deposit terrestrial or arboreal eggs which undergo direct development (mode 8). Most species are small, ranging in snout-vent length from 19.0 to 44.5 mm. Fecundity is low (4.8 to 43.0 eggs) and ovarian egg diameter is large (2.0 to 3.5 mm). The ovarian size factors are correspondingly low, ranging from 0.66 for *E. paululus* to 3.54 for *E. conspicillatus*. Generally, larger species produce more eggs ($P < 0.01$). Three of the nine species tested show significant correlation ($P < 0.05$ to 0.01) between snout-vent length and fecundity. Volumetric data are available for four species. The larger the mean snout-vent length of the species, the larger is the mean body volume and egg complement volume. Females are significantly larger than males ($P < 0.001$) in each of the ten species examined; the female-to-male ratios are large, ranging from 1.24 to 1.54. Developmental data are available for only two species. An *E. martiae* deposited eight eggs (mean diameter = 3.5 mm); one egg hatched 26 days later; hatchling size was 5.0 mm. An *E. pseudoacuminatus* deposited seven eggs (mean diameter = 3.5 mm); two eggs hatched 30 days later; each hatchling was 5.0 mm snout-vent length. Eggs of all species are unpigmented. Some species breed in the forest, others at the forest-edge, and others in disturbed, open areas; breeding sites of several species are unknown. Gravid females of three species are found throughout the year, and are presumably continual breeders. Gravid females of seven species are found sporadically.

Hemiphractus proboscideus is the only terrestrial species which presumably provides complete parental care for young which undergo direct development (mode 10). No gravid females were found. Because all individuals (adults and young) were found in mature or second-growth forest, it is assumed that breeding occurs there. No information is available on breeding frequency.

The mode of reproduction is unknown for three leptodactylids (*Edalorhina perezi*, *Ischnocnema quixensis*, and *Lithodytes lineatus*). These species range in snout-vent length from 38.0 mm (*E. perezi*) to 52.9 mm (*I. quixensis*), and number of mature ovarian eggs ranges from 35.1 (*I. quixensis*) to 195.0 (*L. lineatus*). The low fecundity of *I. quixensis* suggests that development might be direct. On the other hand, the size of the ovarian complement of *L. lineatus* suggests the possibility of egg suspension in a foam nest. Size-fecun-

dity relationship was examined for *I. quixensis*; there is no significant correlation. The maximal ovarian egg diameter is 4.0 mm for *I. quixensis* and 2.0 mm for the other two species; the ovarian size factors range from 2.65 to 7.65. Female *I. quixensis* are 1.23 times as large as males. Eggs are unpigmented in all three species. The breeding habitats of the species are unknown; gravid *I. quixensis* were found throughout the year, suggesting that the species is a continuous breeder.

The greatest amount of variation in the reproductive characters examined occurs among the species that deposit eggs in bodies of water other than tree holes or constructed nests. This may be due to the fact that this is the largest group (30 of the 74 species). Or, it may be the result of a wider spectrum of morphological and physiological possibilities (related to the energetics of reproduction) available to the species. The least amount of variation is found among the five species that carry their larvae to water. The character states of eight reproductive variables for each of the 74 species are summarized in coded form in table 20 (see Table 19 for translation of code). The following outline indicates the relationship of the species within each reproductive mode:

I. Eggs Deposited in Water; Tadpoles Develop in Water
   A. Eggs Deposited in Ditches, Puddles, Swamps, Ponds, Lake, and Streams (32 species)
     1. Large body size (SVL > 60 mm)
       a. Less than 600 eggs
         (1) *Osteocephalus taurinus*
       b. 1000 to 3000 eggs
         (1) *Bufo typhonius*
         (2) *Hyla geographica*
         (3) *Hyla lanciformis*
         (4) *Phrynohyas coriacea*
         (5) *Rana palmipes*
       c. More than 8000 eggs
         (1) *Bufo marinus*
       d. Fecundity unknown
         (1) *Bufo glaberrimus*
     2. Medium body size (SVL = 30 to 60 mm)
       a. Less than 500 eggs
         (1) *Hyla alboguttata*

(2) *Hyla granosa*
(3) *Hyla punctata*
b. 500 to 800 eggs
  (1) *Hyla fasciata*
  (2) *Hyla funerea*
  (3) *Hyla garbei*
  (4) *Hyla rubra*
  (5) *Osteocephalus buckleyi*
c. More than 800 eggs
  (1) *Hyla calcarata*
  (2) *Hyla marmorata*
  (3) *Osteocephalus lepreurii*
  (4) *Hamtophryne boliviana*
3. Small body size (SVL < 30 mm)
a. Less than 175 eggs
  (1) *Dendrophryniscus minutus*
  (2) *Sphaenorhynchus carneus*
b. 200 to 300 eggs
  (1) *Hyla minuta*
  (2) *Hyla parviceps*
  (3) *Hyla rhodopepla*
  (4) *Chiasmocleis bassleri*
  (5) *Chiasmocleis anatipes*
  (6) *Chiasmocleis ventrimacu-lata*
c. More than 500 eggs
  (1) *Hyla cruentomma*
d. Fecundity unknown
  (1) *Hyla riveroi*
B. Tree Cavity
1. *Nyctimantis rugiceps*
C. Constructed Basin
1. *Hyla boans*
II. Eggs Deposited out of Water; Tadpoles Develop in Water (23 species)

A. Eggs Deposited on Vegetation Above Water
1. Less than 30 eggs
a. *Centrolenella midas*
b. *Centrolenella munozorum*
2. More than 60 eggs
a. Eggs unpigmented; usually > 2.0 mm diameter
  (1) Small egg mass relative to body length (ovarian size factor < 5.0)
    (a) *Phyllomedusa palliata*
    (b) *Phyllomedusa tomopterna*
  (2) Large egg mass relative to body length (ovarian size factor > 15.0)
    (a) *Phyllomedusa tarsius*
    (b) *Phyllomedusa vaillanti*
b. Eggs slightly to heavily pigmented; usually < 2.0 mm diameter
  (1) Small body size (SVL < 25 mm); less than 100 eggs
    (a) *Hyla bokermanni*
    (b) *Hyla brevifrons*

TABLE 19.—CODE OF REPRODUCTIVE STRATEGY CHARACTERS.

I. Mean Female Snout-Vent Length
  1) ≤ 30.9 mm   4) 61.0-75.9 mm
  2) 31.0-45.9 mm 5) 76.0-90.9 mm
  3) 46.0-60.9 mm 6) ≥ 91 mm

II. Mean Number Mature Ovarian Eggs
  1) 1.0-10.9   11) 301.0-400.9
  2) 11.0-20.9   12) 401.0-500.9
  3) 21.0-30.9   13) 501.0-600.9
  4) 31.0-50.9   14) 601.0-700.9
  5) 51.0-75.9   15) 701.0-800.9
  6) 76.0-100.9 16) 801.0-1000.9
  7) 101.0-150.9 17) 1001.0-2000.9
  8) 151.0-200.9 18) 2001.0-3000.9
  9) 201.0-250.9 19) 3001.0-5000.9
  10) 251.0-300.9 20) ≥ 5001

III. Maximum Ovarian Egg Diameter
  1) ≤ 1.0 mm   5) 2.6-3.0 mm
  2) 1.1-1.5 mm 6) 3.1-3.5 mm
  3) 1.6-2.0 mm 7) ≥ 3.6 mm
  4) 2.1-2.5 mm

IV. Ovarian Size Factor
  1) 0.01-5.00   7) 30.01-35.00
  2) 5.01-10.00   8) 35.01-40.00
  3) 10.01-15.00 9) 40.01-45.00
  4) 15.01-20.00 10) 45.01-50.00
  5) 20.01-25.00 11) ≥ 50.01
  6) 25.01-30.00

V. Sexual Size Dimorphism (♀/♂ SVL)
  1) 0.91-1.00   5) 1.31-1.40
  2) 1.01-1.10   6) 1.41-1.50
  3) 1.11-1.20   7) 1.51-1.60
  4) 1.21-1.30

VI. Breeding Habitat ("Non-aquatic" includes constructed basin + tree hole)
  1) Aquatic—forest
  2) Aquatic—forest edge
  3) Aquatic—disturbed area
  4) 1 & 2
  5) 1 & 3
  6) 2 & 3
  7) 1, 2, & 3
  8) Aquatic—unknown
  9) Non-aquatic—forest
  10) Non-aquatic—forest edge
  11) Non-aquatic—disturbed area
  12) 9 & 10
  13) 9 & 11
  14) 10 & 11
  15) 9, 10, & 11
  16) Non-aquatic—unknown
  17) Unknown

VII. Frequency of Breeding
  1) Continuous   3) Sporadic
  2) Opportunistic 4) Unknown

VIII. Egg Pigmentation
  1) Unpigmented
  2) Slightly pigmented
  3) Moderately to heavily pigmented
  4) Unknown

TABLE 20.—CHARACTER STATES OF EIGHT REPRODUCTIVE CHARACTERS FOR 74 SPECIES OF FROGS, BY REPRODUCTIVE MODE.

See Table 19 for translation of character states. An asterisk indicates data from Lago Agrio (16 km. from Santa Cecilia).

Species	X̄ ♀ SVL	X̄ N Eggs	Maximum Egg Diameter	Ovarian Size Factor	Sexual Size Dimorphism	Breeding Habitat	Breeding Frequency	Egg Pigmentation
MODE 1								
B. glaberrimus	..	..	..	..	..	8	4	4
B. marinus	6	20	2	11	4	3	3	3
B. typhonius	4	17	3	9	6	4	1	3
D. minutus	1	7	1	2	5	8	1	3
H. alboguttata	2	12	2	4	6	8	3	3
H. calcarata	3	17	2	7	6	4	3	3
H. cruentomma	1	13	1	5	2	4	3	3
H. fasciata	3	13	2	4	5	8	1	3
H. funerea	2	13	1	3	3	4	3	3
H. garbei	2	13	2	4	3	7	1	3
H. geographica	4	18	1	9	7	1	3	3
H. granosa	2	12	2	4	2	1	3	3
H. lanciformis	5	17	3	8	3	6	1	3
H. marmorata	3	16	2	6	4	7	2	3
H. minuta	1	9	1	2	3	8	4	3
H. parviceps	1	9	1	3	5	4	1	3
H. punctata	2	11	2	3	2	7	3	3
H. rhodopepla	1	10	1	3	4	7	2	3
H. riveroi	..	..	..	..	..	8	4	4
H. rubra	2	13	2	4	3	6	2	3
O. buckleyi*	3	13	1	3	..	8	4	3
O. leprieurii*	3	16	1	3	..	8	3	3
O. taurinus	5	13	1	2	..	8	4	3
P. coriacea	4	17	3	9	..	8	4	3
S. carneus	1	7	1	2	..	1	4	2
C. anatipes	..	..	..	..	..	1	4	..
C. bassleri	1	9	1	2	..	8	4	3
C. ventrimaculata	1	9	1	2	..	8	4	3
H. boliviana	2	17	1	9	4	4	3	3
R. palmipes	6	18	3	10	4	7	1	3
MODE 2								
N. rugiceps	..	..	..	..	..	12	4	4
MODE 3								
H. boans	6	19	3	11	1	10	3	3
MODE 4								
C. midas	1	3	2	1	..	8	4	2
C. munozorum	1	2	2	1	..	1	4	1
H. bifurca	2	8	2	2	4	6	2	3
H. bokermanni	1	6	2	2	2	7	2	2
H. brevifrons	1	6	1	1	3	2	2	2
H. favosa	2	12	1	3	..	4	4	3
H. leucophyllata	2	13	2	5	4	4	3	2
H. sarayacuensis	2	7	3	2	5	7	2	2
H. triangulum	2	13	2	4	6	7	2	3
P. palliata	3	5	4	1	2	4	3	1
P. tarsius	6	13	5	4	4	4	3	1
P. tomopterna	3	5	6	1	4	4 —	3	1
P. vaillanti	5	17	3	6	7	1	3	1
MODE 5								
L. discodactylus	2	9	1	2	4	8	4	1

CRUMP: REPRODUCTIVE STRATEGIES IN A TROPICAL ANURAN COMMUNITY   49

TABLE 20.—CHARACTER STATES OF EIGHT REPRODUCTIVE CHARACTERS FOR 74 SPECIES OF FROGS, BY REPRODUCTIVE MODE.—*Continued.*

See Table 19 for translation of character states. An asterisk indicates data from Lago Agrio (16 km. from Santa Cecilia).

Species	$\bar{X}$ ♀ SVL	$\bar{X}$ N Eggs	Maximum Egg Diameter	Ovarian Size Factor	Sexual Size Dimorphism	Breeding Habitat	Frequency Breeding	Egg Pigmentation
L. mystaceus	3	10	4	3	2	6	1	1
L. pentadactylus	--	--	--	--	--	4	3	3
L. wagneri	4	17	2	8	6	6	4	3
P. petersi	--	--	--	--	--	8	4	1
MODE 6								
C. marchesianus	1	2	2	1	2	12	1	3
C. sauli	1	2	2	1	3	9	4	3
D. parvulus	1	1	5	1	3	12	1	3
D. pictus	1	2	3	1	3	12	1	3
P. femoralis	1	3	3	1	3	12	1	3
MODE 7								
L. andreae	1	1	5	1	2	12	3	1
MODE 8								
E. acuminatus	1	2	4	1	7	9	3	1
E. altamazonicus	1	2	4	1	7	9	3	1
E. conspicillatus	2	4	6	1	6	9	3	1
E. croceoinguinis	1	1	5	1	5	9	1	1
E. diadematus	2	4	4	1	--	16	4	1
E. lacrimosus	1	1	4	1	4	9	3	1
E. lanthanites	2	3	5	1	6	12	1	1
E. martiae	1	1	3	1	6	12	3	1
E. ockendeni	1	2	5	1	5	9	3	1
E. paululus	1	1	4	1	--	16	4	1
E. pseudoacuminatus	1	1	5	1	4	10	3	1
E. quaquaversus	1	3	4	1	--	16	4	1
E. sulcatus	--	--	--	--	--	16	4	1
E. variabilis	1	1	5	1	6	14	1	1
MODE 10								
H. proboscideus	--	--	--	--	--	9	4	1
MODE UNKNOWN								
E. perezi	2	6	3	1	--	17	4	1
I. quixensis	3	4	7	1	4	17	1	1
L. lineatus*	3	8	3	2	--	17	4	1

(2) Medium body size (SVL > 30 mm); more than 100 eggs
  (a) Less than 200 eggs
    (1) *Hyla bifurca*
    (2) *Hyla sarayacuensis*
  (b) More than 450 eggs
    (1) *Hyla favosa*
    (2) *Hyla leucophyllata*
    (3) *Hyla triangulum*
B. Eggs Suspended in Foam Nest
  1. Large body size (SVL > 60 mm); eggs moderately pigmented; males with prepollical spine
    a. *Leptodactylus pentadactylus*
    b. *Leptodactylus wagneri*
  2. Small to medium body size (SVL < 60 mm); eggs unpigmented; males lacking prepollical spine
    a. Foam nest produced on surface of water
      (1) *Leptodactylus discodactylus*
      (2) *Physalaemus petersi*
    b. Foam nest produced in burrow
      (1) *Leptodactylus mystaceus*
C. Terrestrial Eggs; Larvae Carried to Water on Dorsum of Adult
  1. Fewer than 10 eggs
    a. *Dendrobates parvulus*

2. 11 to 20 eggs
   a. Smaller egg mass relative to body length (ovarian size factor < 1.20)
      (1) *Colostethus marchesianus*
      (2) *Colostethus sauli*
   b. Larger egg mass relative to body length (ovarian size factor 1.60)
      (1) *Dendrobates pictus*
3. More than 20 eggs
   a. *Phyllobates femoralis*
III. Eggs and Young Completely Independent of Standing Water (16 species)
   A. Tadpoles Develop Within Foam Nest
      1. *Leptodactylus andreae*
   B. Direct Development
      1. No, or limited parental care
         a. Larger body size (SVL > 35 mm); more than 25 eggs
            (1) *Eleutherodactylus conspicillatus*
            (2) *Eleutherodactylus diadematus*
            (3) *Eleutherodactylus lanthanites*
         b. Smaller body size (SVL < 35 mm); less than 25 eggs
            (1) Less than 10 eggs
               (a) *Eleutherodactylus croceoinguinis*
               (b) *Eleutherodactylus lacrimosus*
               (c) *Eleutherodactylus martiae*
               (d) *Eleutherodactylus paululus*
               (e) *Eleutherodactylus pseudoacuminatus*
               (f) *Eleutherodactylus variabilis*
            (2) More than 10 eggs
               (a) *Eleutherodactylus acuminatus*
               (b) *Eleutherodactylus altamazonicus*
               (c) *Eleutherodactylus ockendeni*
               (d) *Eleutherodactylus quaquaversus*
         c. Size and fecundity unknown
            (1) *Eleutherodactylus sulcatus*
      2. Complete parental care
         a. *Hemiphractus proboscideus*

DISCUSSION

Among the 81 species of frogs known to occur at Santa Cecilia, ten modes of reproduction are represented, and many reproductive strategies are operant. The key aspects involved in reproductive strategies are (1) size of female, (2) ovarian complement and clutch size, (3) diameter of eggs, (4) egg deposition site, (5) type of development, and (6) frequency of breeding. Presumably, each species possesses an optimal set of reproductive characters for maintenance of its population. Some species produce many eggs relative to their body size, others few. Some produce large eggs, others small. Some species breed continually, others sporadically. Cole (1954), in discussing variations in life history patterns, considered the following as axiomatic, ". . . that the reproductive potentials of existing species are related to their requirements for survival; that any life history features affecting reproductive potential are subject to natural selection; and that such features observed in existing species should be considered as adaptations, just as purely morphological or behavioral patterns are commonly so considered." Keeping these assumptions in mind, we can ask, why does the great diversity in anuran species and their reproductive modes exist at Santa Cecilia?

Historical Zoogeography.—Vuilleumier (1971) suggested that the present biotic patterns in South America have been determined by paleoecological changes during the Pleistocene. The evidence is based on analyses of speciation patterns of the flora and fauna throughout the continent and on paleobotanical and geological studies that document climatic events. Many areas of disjunction, hybridization, secondary sympatry, and introgression seem to exist in the Amazon Basin. Haffer (1969) proposed that climatic oscillations during the Pleistocene resulted in alternating series of contractions and expansions of the rainforest in lowland tropical South America. He postulated that during dry phases the forest covered only small, disjunct areas; these isolated regions would have acted as refugia for forest animals. Local selection pressures would have resulted in differentiation among the populations of species inhabiting different forest refugia. During the wetter phases, the forests expanded; where previously isolated populations came together, they formed the present complex patterns typical of zones of secondary contact. One of the nine forest refugia postulated by Haffer is the Napo region, in which Santa Cecilia is located. Vanzolini and Williams (1970) also concluded that the Napo region was a forest refugium from a study of morphological variation of *Anolis chrysolepis* from the Amazon Basin. In certain areas, large blocks of characters are correlated with one another and vary geographically in the same direction; these areas were termed "core areas," and were thought to be those regions in which populations had evolved as a unit. One of the four core areas is the lower eastern slopes of the Andes, including the area of Santa Cecilia. Similar patterns of speciation in the upper Amazon Basin were hypothesized for the *Leptodactylus marmoratus* group (Heyer, 1973) and for the *Hyla parviceps* group (Duellman and Crump, 1974).

If Santa Cecilia were indeed part of a forest refugium during the Pleistocene, the high species richness in great part may be explained on that basis. There was probably strong selection favoring the evolution of reproductive diversity to cope with the changing environment. Selective factors operant at the species level would encourage those modes of reproduction best adapted to the environment.

The specific geographical location of Santa Cecilia probably serves as another contributing factor to the high species richness. The site is peripheral to both the Amazon Basin and the eastern slopes of the Andes. Certain species are widespread Amazonian species; others occur only in the upper Amazon Basin, and others principally inhabit lower Andean slopes. Possibly many of the species at Santa Cecilia are living at or near their ecological limits; this may explain why many of the species are seemingly rare.

Aquatic Larvae Versus Direct Devel-

opment.—About 20 per cent of the total species of frogs at Santa Cecilia are independent of open bodies of water in that the young undergo direct development. Orton (1949) pointed out that direct development occurs in 10 of the 13 families of frogs then considered valid. She noted the occurrence of direct development in the Pipidae, Microhylidae, Ascaphidae, Pelobatidae, Leptodactylidae, Bufonidae, Atelopodidae, Dendrobatidae, Hylidae, and Ranidae. Orton stated that on one hand there is the tendency toward elimination of the tadpole stage (direct development), while in the opposite direction, there is the tendency toward greater complexity of the tadpole stage, represented by many species. She considered this paradox to be "an excellent example of the random nature of evolutionary trends."

Istock (1967) proposed that complex life cycles (defined as the condition "when the individuals of a species consistently pass through 2 or more ecologically distinct phases") are inherently unstable over evolutionary time. His proposal is based on the assumption that the evolutionary adaptations of the different phases are essentially independent, and that this independence is responsible for the fact that the ecological advantages of neither phase are fully realized. He suggested that through evolutionary time selective forces are generated that favor the reduction or loss of one of the phases. One example he cited is that of the loss of the larval stage in some frogs. However, Istock did not discuss the fact that there are no neotenic tadpoles. Wassersug (1974) attributed this phenomenon to the functional morphology of tadpoles.

Elimination of the aquatic larval stage offers several advantages: competition with other aquatic animals is avoided, vulnerability to aquatic predators is absent, and "unpredictability," in terms of the environment evaporating or becoming unfavorable, is eliminated.

On the other hand, there has been vast radiation in tadpole morphology, and the majority of species of frogs have tadpoles. The maintenance of the larval stage may be considered the result either of presence or of absence of selective forces. Perhaps selection favored the continuing existence of tadpoles in some species. (See Wassersug, 1974, for a discussion concerning the adaptive advantages of the larval stage in anurans.) Or, perhaps selection favored direct development. In those environments with highly unstable paleoclimatic histories, the most successful strategy may have been the elimination of the larval stage. However, it may be that the hylids, bufonids, and ranids, among others that presently occur at Santa Cecilia, evolved during a more stable climatic regime—in environments with plentiful and open bodies of water, such that there was no advantage of becoming more terrestrial. The absence of these selective forces, then, may have resulted in the maintenance of the larval stage.

Size and Fecundity.—The widespread tendency of animal groups to evolve toward larger physical size is implied in Cope's writings (1887 and 1896). The most recent analysis of this phenomenon (now referred to as Cope's Rule) was presented by Stanley (1973), whose premise was that for every evolving population there would be some optimal body size for the niche it occupies. Whether evolution is towards size increase or decrease depends on whether the mean body size in the original population is smaller or larger than this optimum. The niche and/or optimal body size may change through time, leading to the evolution of a new body size. Numerous examples indicate that most populations approach optimal body size from smaller rather than from larger sizes. One exception is amphibians, which have evolved from "medium-sized" ancestors rather than "small." Stanley suggested that perhaps an important consideration is the fact that the origin of amphibians was associated with a new environmental medium. He suggested that large size initially may

have been a necessity to provide a high surface-to-volume ratio, because of dehydration problems associated with cutaneous water loss. Stanley noted that many small species of animals are morphologically unspecialized, whereas nearly all relatively large species are structurally specialized; "major adaptive breakthroughs" occur at relatively small body sizes.

Lending support to Stanley's contention, Salthe and Duellman (1973) suggested that "small body size in frogs is a preadaptation for reproductive experimentation." Within the anuran fauna at Santa Cecilia, some of the most "specialized" modes of reproduction (modes 6-8) are represented by relatively small species. Most large species have a relatively generalized mode of reproduction.

A constraint to the evolution of new body size may be the sizes of sympatric species. Several studies have been carried out concerning the sizes of species in a community (Hutchinson, 1959; Schoener, 1965; 1970). These studies reveal that body size ratios (ratio of largest species to the next-largest species) show a regular progression of size among species within a community. The proposed explanation is that individual species may be dividing the size of the food items according to their own body sizes. There may be selection for the evolution of different sizes to avoid overlap in prey size. Thus, even though it may be advantageous for a species to increase its body size for reproductive purposes, it then may not compete as well for food. Caldwell (1973) found a similar regular progression of body size ratios in communities of tree frogs in Oaxaca, México. She suggested that competition for food was possibly an important factor influencing body size. C. Toft (personal communication) came to a similar conclusion from preliminary observations on forest-floor frogs (*Eleutherodactylus* and dendrobatids) in Perú.

Numerous studies on the relationship between female size and fecundity in animals have been carried out. Rensch (1960) showed that large-sized species of different groups of cold-blooded vertebrates produce more eggs than small species of the same groups. Tinkle, Wilbur, and Tilley (1970) examined interspecific relationships between size and fecundity within single-brooded, multiple-brooded, oviparous, viviparous, early-maturing, late-maturing, temperate, and tropical groups of lizards. In all groups except late-maturing and tropical, larger species have significantly more eggs than smaller species. Salthe (1969) noted the interspecific relationship between snout-vent length and fecundity in salamanders is dependent upon the body length. Clutch size increases slowly with increasing size of small species, but increases at a greater rate with increasing size of larger species. Tilley (1968) showed that four of five sympatric species of *Desmognathus* have a positive correlation between snout-vent length and fecundity, both intraspecifically and interspecifically. Salthe and Duellman (1973) concluded that within a given reproductive mode there is a positive correlation between female snout-vent length and clutch size in frogs. My data on the frogs at Santa Cecilia support this contention; within a given reproductive mode, as female body length increases, fecundity increases interspecifically (Table 10 and Fig. 5).

Natural Selection.—The theory of "*r* and *K* selection" has received much attention recently. The terms (Cody, 1966; MacArthur and Wilson, 1967) refer to the two components of natural selection; *r* (intrinsic rate of natural increase) is the density-independent component and *K* (carrying capacity) is the density-dependent component. Pianka (1970) emphasized that no species is completely "*r*-selected" or completely "*K*-selected"; he suggested that selection should be thought of as a continuum, from *r* to *K*. The strategy at the *r*-end is productivity; mortality is often catastrophic and density-independent. Spe-

cies at the *K*-end of the continuum capitalize on efficiency; the strategy is to increase efficiency of environmental resource utilization and to produce a few extremely fit offspring. In *K*-selection, mortality is usually density-dependent.

A combination of the following four components of *r* are useful in determining the relative position of a species on the *r-K* continuum: (1) fecundity, (2) longevity, (3) age at first reproduction, and (4) number of breeding times per lifetime. In addition, one needs to know death rates and whether mortality is mainly density-dependent or independent. The only parameter affecting *r* measured in my study at Santa Cecilia is fecundity. Because the spread of fecundity is so large (means from 4.8 to 8598 eggs) for the species of frogs, the measure is probably of considerable importance and is used here as a crude estimate of *r*.

Using fecundity as the measure of *r*, the fauna can be positioned along the continuum. Those species which deposit many small eggs in unprotected bodies of water are referred to the *r*-end. These include many of the species from mode 1. Next are the members of mode 1 with lower fecundity, followed by *Hyla boans* which constructs a nest. Intermediate groups, following the continuum to the right are: (1) mode 4 (*Centrolenella*, *Hyla*, and *Phyllomedusa*), (2) mode 5 (*Leptodactylus* and *Physalaemus*), (3) mode 6 (the dendrobatids), and (4) mode 7 (*Leptodactylus andreae*). The preceding species exhibit neither an extreme *r* nor *K* strategy. They allocate more energy into the search for appropriate oviposition sites than do the species which deposit eggs in open water. Much energy probably is spent in the production of foam nests and in the transportation of tadpoles to open water. The two *K*-strategist groups are the 14 species of *Eleutherodactylus*, which deposit few, large eggs out of water, and *Hemiphractus* which presumably provides complete parental care to the eggs and young. All 15 species have direct development. (Fecundity in the latter species has not been measured at Santa Cecilia, but an individual from the nearby locality of Puerto Libre had 26 mature ovarian eggs.)

The next aspect considered is the relationship between fecundity, position on the r-K continuum, and the environment. Those species which deposit many eggs in open bodies of water (r-strategists) generally breed in unpredictable environments such as ephemeral or temporary puddles, ditches, and ponds in open, disturbed or forest-edge areas. Examples of these species are *Bufo marinus* and many *Hyla*. Probably one of the biggest mortality factors is evaporation of the aquatic habitat, obviously a density-independent factor. The frogs have no way of predicting whether the water will persist long enough for the eggs to hatch and the tadpoles to metamorphose. The strategy is to breed repeatedly throughout the year (these species are generally continuous or opportunistic breeders), and to deposit many eggs at a time. The K-strategists are generally found in second-growth or mature forest. They are completely independent of open bodies of water. The species do not form breeding congregations, but are more widely dispersed in the forest. The life-span of the oviposition and developmental sites are more predictable than those of r-strategists. For these reasons, catastrophic mortality is probably relatively uncommon, and overall mortality is more density-dependent.

There is no apparent relationship between population density and relative position on the r-K continuum. (Densities are merely estimates based on field observations and are not the result of quantitative sampling methods.) The most abundant species are located all along the continuum. These are tree frogs which congregate at temporary ditches and ponds (e.g., *Hyla bifurca, parviceps, rhodopepla, triangulum*), *Bufo typhonius* and *Dendrophryniscus minutus, Leptodactylus mystaceus*, two dendrobatids (*Colostethus marchesianus*

and *Dendrobates parvulus*), and several species of *Eleutherodactylus* (e.g., croceoinguinis, lanthanites, and variabilis). Rare species are represented by most of the modes of reproduction, some more towards the r-end and some more towards the K-end of the continuum. The low population densities (if not the result of sampling bias), may be due to one or all of the following reasons: the species may be living at the border of their ecological tolerance; collecting pressure in past years perhaps depleted populations; some species may require a long time to reach sexual maturity; and, individuals may breed only once per year, or even less frequently.

Reproductive Effort.—As in other vertebrates, the energy commitment in terms of gametes is much greater for the female frog than for the male. Spermatozoa are produced cheaply. Males often call indiscriminately, whether or not conditions for breeding are adequate, much less optimal. For example, males were often found calling from dry swamps. It seems to be advantageous for males to be reproductively ready continuously. However, females produce gametes with larger amounts of stored energy. Because the energy commitment of females is so much greater, it is advantageous to be reproductively ready only at the most favorable times. There is no doubt stronger selection against error in the female; she must "predict" when conditions are favorable and respond to the male accordingly.

There is much variation in the timing of ovulation and actual egg deposition among species. Pairs of *Eleutherodactylus* often were observed in amplexus for several hours in the forest. Frequently, the female of the amplectant pair still had not ovulated the following day (observed by dissection). On the other hand, females of most hylids which breed in congregations do not come to the breeding site until they have ovulated. Much less time is spent in amplexus for these species than for *Eleu-*

therodactylus. It is suggested that ovulation before entering the breeding site is a behavioral adaptation reducing vulnerability of the pair to potential predators. The chance of a predator encountering an amplectant pair of tree frogs at an aquatic site amidst a large congreation of calling individuals is perhaps greater than that of a predator encountering a pair of *Eleutherodactylus* isolated in the forest. *Bufo marinus* is an exception; although the species congregates and breeds in ditches in open areas, pairs often remain in amplexus for several hours (and up to six days in captivity). Possible reasons they are able to afford this behavior are their toxic skin secretions and large size; *B. marinus* probably has very few natural predators. *Phyllomedusa,* which also have poisonous skin secretions, remain in amplexus at breeding sites for several hours.

Energy allotted to reproduction ("reproductive effort") is partitioned differentially for each species among egg production, sperm production, courtship, vocalization, territoriality, parental care, frequency of breeding, and nest-building. Members of mode 1 represent the simplest situation. Males congregate at aquatic breeding sites and call. Some species call continuously even though there may be no water present and females are not present at the site; males of other species call only following heavy rains. The reproductive energy allotment of males is divided into sperm production and calling, for there is no apparent courtship, territoriality, or parental care involved. The reproductive energy of females is channeled into egg production. It is not known how frequently individuals breed, but based on the immature complement found in nearly every gravid female, it is suggested that females breed repeatedly throughout the year.

Hyla boans represents a slightly more complicated situation. Males expend energy calling, constructing nests, and possibly defending the nests. Females take no part in these activities, but put energy into a relatively large egg clutch.

Frogs that deposit eggs on vegetation above water probably expend more energy in choosing oviposition sites than do frogs of mode 1 type of reproduction. Some species (such as *Hyla bokermanni* and *H. sarayacuensis*) deposit eggs in many small clutches, spread out on several leaves, probably requiring more energy than single oviposition. It is assumed that reproductive energy for most species is spent in calling, sperm and egg production, and searching for oviposition sites. Male *Phyllomedusa tarsius* expend energy in folding leaves around the egg clutch. Some of the energy allotment of the female is used in the production of empty gelatinous capsules, probably formed in the oviduct.

Males of the species that produce foam nests (modes 5 and 7) spend energy in constructing the nest during amplexus, in addition to the energy used in calling. Aggressive behavior has been reported for leptodactylids (Brattstrom and Yarnell, 1968), but was not observed in any of the species at Santa Cecilia. Reproductive energy in the female is channeled into egg production. *Leptodactylus andreae* produces few, large eggs, each one representing a large energy investment. The eggs of *Leptodactylus mystaceus,* likewise, are relatively large, but fecundity is much greater for this species than for the former, relative to body size.

The dendrobatids represent a more complex situation. It is probable that (at least for *Dendrobates*) elaborate courtship and territoriality are important aspects of the breeding process. These have been described for several dendrobatids (Crump, 1972; Duellman, 1966; Goodman, 1971; Sexton, 1960; Silverstone, 1973; Test, 1954; Wardenier, 1973). From my studies on *Dendrobates granuliferus* in Costa Rica (Crump, 1972), I concluded that territoriality is an energetically expensive activity in high density populations based on the frequency of observed encounters. Territories are defended by physical combat lasting up to several minutes. Courtship is elaborate and probably costly in energy. Much time (and energy) is spent by the female searching for an appropriate oviposition site. However, in *Dendrobates auratus* the male chooses the site (Wardenier, 1973). No courtship activity or territoriality was observed for the five species at Santa Cecilia, but combat activity has been observed between male *Dendrobates pictus* in Perú (C. Toft, personal communication). Males call but do not congregate. It is assumed that the tadpoles of all five species are transported to water on the dorsum of the males or females. This form of parental care potentially requires much energy on the part of either sex. Fecundity is low, and the eggs are heavily yolked and large.

The strategy of the 14 species of *Eleutherodactylus* is the production of a few, large eggs. Presumably each egg is energetically costly. The eggs are deposited in relatively protected areas (e.g., amidst leaf litter and under tree bark). Males call but do not congregate. No parental care or elaborate courtship was observed; in captivity, males mount the females in simple amplexus, without preliminary courtship.

Eggs and Larvae in the Aquatic Environment.—The egg stage probably is more vulnerable to predators than the tadpole or adult stages because eggs are immobile, and therefore unable to escape predators. At Santa Cecilia members of five of the eight families show some means of protecting eggs rather than depositing them in open bodies of water. These adaptations (e.g., eggs deposited on vegetation above water, in foam nests, on land) undoubtedly have arisen independently. However, upon hatching, the tadpoles are left to fend for themselves in the aquatic environment, and are dependent on it until metamorphosis.

Chief predators on anuran eggs are aquatic insects, fish, and snakes. Several studies have been carried out in order to examine the effects of anuran eggs on predators. Licht (1968, 1969) demonstrated that eggs of several species of *Bufo* were unpalatable and toxic when ingested by potential vertebrate and invertebrate predators. Licht (1969) found that eggs of *Rana* and *Hyla*, however, were palatable and nontoxic to the same potential predators. Grubb (1972) examined differential predation of fish (*Gambusia*) on the eggs of *Acris, Bufo, Gastrophryne, Hyla, Pseudacris, Scaphiopus,* and *Rana*. None of the eggs seemed to have toxic effects on the fish. Grubb found that the fish ate a significantly larger number and greater volume of eggs of those species that generally breed in temporary as opposed to permanent water. His explanation for this is that species that deposit eggs in temporary water generally have less firm gelatinous capsules. Aquatic predators (especially fish) are more abundant in permanent water than in temporary water. Perhaps the firmer egg capsule typical of permanent water breeders serves as a mechanical defense against predators.

The relationship between egg pigmentation and the aquatic environment is not intuitively obvious. The melanin of eggs may promote absorption of radiant heat energy and/or shield the eggs from ultraviolet radiation. In either case, those eggs exposed to light are pigmented, whereas those sheltered from direct sunlight generally lack pigment. Species that deposit eggs in shallow bodies of water (e.g., *Bufo marinus, Hyla lanciformis, H. marmorata, H. rubra*) have heavily pigmented eggs. The melanin likely promotes more rapid development in the warm water, and thus is a selective advantage in temporary habitats.

There are far fewer species of frogs that breed in the large, permanent bodies of water at Santa Cecilia than in the smaller, ephemeral and temporary environments. One explanation is related to potential predator pressure. The permanent aquatic habitats at Santa Cecilia are deep, and fish are abundant. The temperature of the water is much cooler than that of small aquatic sites. Because rate of development is directly related to water temperature, perhaps there is a penalty for breeding where development is less rapid and eggs and tadpoles are exposed to predators for a greater length of time. Most of the species that breed in permanent water have large egg clutches, possibly a preadaptation to high egg and larval mortality.

There is no significant difference in fecundity, intraoval developmental time, or hatchling size between species that deposit eggs in ephemeral or temporary water and those that deposit eggs in more permanent water. This is probably the result of balancing hazards. In other words, neither environment may be inherently more advantageous than the other. In the temporary environment, the greatest hazard probably is unpredictability of the life span of the habitat, whereas in the more permanent habitat, it is probably the greater number of aquatic predators.

SUMMARY AND CONCLUSIONS

Eighty-one species of frogs representing ten modes of reproduction (defined as a combination of type of development and oviposition site) are known from Santa Cecilia, Ecuador. The study site is in an aseasonal environment in the upper Amazon Basin. Several explanations are offered for the extremely rich anuran fauna. Paleoclimatic instability may account for the extensive speciation which occurred in the lowland tropics of South America. The diversity of reproductive modes probably represents adaptive responses to changing environments.

There are many reproductive strategies operant in the anuran community. Some species put all their reproductive energy allotted into egg and sperm production and vocalization. Other species expend energy for constructing nests, courtship, territoriality, and parental care. Some species produce a few large eggs presumably high in energy content, others distribute energy through thousands of small eggs. Species that deposit many eggs directly in water (r-strategists) generally breed in unpredictable, ephemeral or temporary environments. The K-strategists are those species that are completely independent of open bodies of water; they deposit terrestrial or arboreal eggs which have direct development. The breeding sites of the latter species are considered to be more predictable and less hazardous than those of the former.

Approximately 46 per cent of the species of frogs deposit eggs directly in water; the remainder have specialized oviposition sites and/or direct development. Many of these species have specialized behavioral and/or morphological adaptations toward terrestriality. Behavioral modifications include construction of a basin in the mud for egg deposition, oviposition on vegetation above water, production of a foam nest in which the eggs are suspended, and oviposition on land with subsequent carrying of the tadpoles to water on the dorsum of the adults. Morphological modifications include prepollical spines and horny nuptial excrescences that presumably aid in grasping the female during amplexus. Generally those species that deposit eggs in exposed situations have pigmented eggs, whereas species that deposit eggs in sheltered sites have eggs lacking pigment. Hatchling *Eleutherodactylus* have "egg teeth" (horny projections on the tip of the snout) used in ripping the jelly capsule of the nonaquatic egg during hatching. Juvenile *Hemiphractus proboscideus* presumably are attached to the dorsum of the female by flat gills.

The premise on which this study is based is that because the number of aquatic breeding sites is less than the number of species, the sites represent a potentially limiting resource. Spatial and temporal utilization of the sites was

References

Brattstrom, B. H., and R. M. Yarnell. 1968. Aggressive behavior in two species of leptodactylid frogs. *Herpetologica* 24: 222–28.

Caldwell, J. P. 1973. Tropical tree frog communities: patterns of reproduction, size, and utilization of structural habitat. Ph.D. diss., University of Kansas.

Cody, M. L. 1966. A general theory of clutch size. *Evolution* 20:174–84.

Cole, L. C. 1954. The population consequences of life history phenomena. *Quart Rev Biol* 29:103–37.

Cope, E. D. 1887. The *origin of the fittest*. New York: D. Appleton and Co.

———. 1896. *The primary factors of organic evolution*. Chicago: Open Court.

Crump, M. L. 1972. Territoriality and mating behavior in *Dendrobates granuliferus* (Anura: Dendrobatidae). *Herpetologica* 28:195–98.

Duellman, W. E. 1966. Aggressive behavior in dendrobatid frogs. *Herpetologica* 22:217–21.

Duellman, W. E., and M. L. Crump. 1974. Speciation in frogs of the *Hyla parviceps* group in the upper Amazon Basin. *Occas Pap Mus Nat Hist Univ Kansas* 23:1–40.

Goodman, D. E. 1971. Territorial behavior in a neotropical frog, *Dendrobates granuliferus. Copeia* 1971:365–70.

Grubb, J. C. 1972. Differential predation by *Gambusia affinia* on the eggs of seven species of anuran amphibians. *Amer Midl Natur* 88:102–8.

Haffer, J. 1969. Speciation in Amazonian forest birds. *Science* 165:131–37.

Heyer, W. R. 1973. Systematics of the *marmoratus* group of frog genus *Leptodactylus* (Amphibia, Leptodactylidae). *Contrib in Science Nat Hist Mus Los Angeles Co* 251:1–50.

Jameson, D. L. 1955. Evolutionary trends in the courtship and mating behavior of *Salientia Syst Zool* 4:105–19.

Lutz, B. 1947. Trends toward non-aquatic and direct development in frogs. *Copeia* 1947 (4):242–52.

———. 1948. Ontogenetic evolution in frogs. *Evolution* 2:29–35.

———. 1960. Fighting and an incipient notion of territory in male tree frogs. *Copeia* 1960 (1):61–63.

MacArthur, R. H., and E. O. Wilson. 1967. The theory of island biogeography. Princeton: Princeton University Press.

Orton, G. L. 1949. Larval development of *Nectophrynoides tornieri* (Roux) with comments on direct development in frogs. *Ann Carnegie Mus* 31:257–76.

Pianka, E. R. 1970. On *r-* and *K*-selection. *Am Nat* 104:592–97.

Rensch, B. 1960. Evolution above the species level. 2d ed. New York: Columbia University Press.

Salthe, S. N. 1969. Evolutionary relationships in the reproductive modes and the numbers and sizes of ova in the urodeles. *Amer Midl Natur* 81:467–90.

Salthe, S. N., and W. E. Duellman. 1973. Quantitative constraints associated with reproductive mode in anurans. In *Evolutionary Biology of the Anurans,* ed. J. L. Vial. Columbia: University of Missouri Press.

Schoener, T. S. 1965. The evolution of bill size differences among sympatric congeneric species of birds. *Evolution* 19:189–213.

———. 1970. Size patterns in West Indian *Anolis* lizards, II: Correlations with the sizes of particular sympatric species—displacement and convergence. *Am Nat* 104:155–74.

Sexton, O. J. 1960. Some aspects of the behavior and of the territory of a dendrobatid frog, *Prostherapis trinitatus. Ecology* 41:107–15.

Silverstone, P. A. 1973. Observations on the behavior and ecology of a Colombian poison-arrow frog, the Kokoépá (*Dendrobates histrionicus* Berthold). *Herpetologica* 29:295–301.

Stanley, S. M. 1973. An explanation for Cope's rule. *Evolution* 27:1–26.

Test, F. H. 1954. Social aggressiveness in an amphibian. *Science* 120:140–41.

Tilley, S. G. 1968. Size–fecundity relationships and their evolutionary implications in five desmognathine salamanders. *Evolution* 22:808–16.

Tinkle, D. W., H. M. Wilbur, and S. G. Tilley. 1970. Evolutionary strategies in lizard reproduction. *Evolution* 24:55–74.

Vanzolini, P. E., and E. E. Williams. 1970. South American anoles: The geographic differentiation and evolution of the *Anolis chrysolepis* species group (Sauria, Iguanidae). *Arquivos de Zool* 19 (3–4):125–298.

Vuilleumier, B. S. 1971. Pleistocene changes in the fauna and flora of South America. *Science* 173:771–80.

Wardenier, R. J. A. 1973. Verslag van het Keweken met *Dendrobates auratus. Lacerta* 11:167–71.

Wassersug, R. J. 1974. The adaptive significance of the tadpole stage with comments on the maintenance of complex life cycles in anurans. *Am Zoologist* 15:405–17.

Ecology (1977) **58**: pp. 1007–1019

BIRD SPECIES DIVERSITY ON AN ANDEAN
ELEVATIONAL GRADIENT[1]

JOHN TERBORGH

Department of Biology, Princeton University, Princeton, New Jersey 08540 USA

Abstract. This paper analyzes patterns of bird species diversity on an elevational transect of the Cordillera Vilcabamba, Peru. Major changes in climate and vegetation are encompassed by the transect which extended from the Apurimac Valley floor at 500 m to the summit ridge of the range at > 3,500 m. Four vegetation zones are easily discerned—lowland rain forest, montane rain forest, cloud forest, and elfin forest. In progressing upwards there is a monotonic trend toward decreasing canopy stature and reduced number of plant strata.

The vegetation gradient provided the opportunity to examine the relation between bird species diversity and habitat complexity in an entirely natural setting. The decrease in forest stature with elevation was closely paralleled by decreasing avian syntopy (the total number of bird species cohabiting the forest at a given elevation). Bird species diversity was shown to be highly correlated with foliage height diversity, using either four or five layers in the foliage height diversity calculation ($r = .97$), and less well correlated using three layers, as defined previously by MacArthur ($r = .84$). At this superficial level the trend in bird species diversity seemed to be adequately explained as a response to the vegetation gradient.

This preliminary conclusion was found to be illusory when the elevational trend in syntopy was reexamined separately for three major trophic subdivisions of the fauna. The number of insectivores decreased 5.2-fold from the bottom to the top of the gradient, frugivores decreased by a factor of 2.3, and nectarivores showed no change. It was now clear that the diversity in each of these trophic categories was responsive to environmental influences other than, or in addition to, the gradient in habitat structure. Additional factors implicated by the available evidence are competitive interactions with other taxa at the same trophic level, changing composition of the resource base as a function of elevation, and declining productivity at high elevations.

Analysis of netted bird samples revealed an unexpected diversity maximum in the lower cloud forest zone. The immediate cause of this was a relaxation of the vertical stratification of foraging zones, such that an anomalously large fraction of the species present entered the nets. The excess diversity was found to consist almost entirely of insectivores. Several factors appear to contribute to the ultimate causes of the diversity maximum: greater patchiness of the montane forest due to the rugged topography, a higher density of foliage near the ground, and possibly increased resource productivity. A correlation between diversity and density in the netting results suggested a causal connection mediated via resource levels.

The conclusion is that diversity is a complex community property that is responsive to many types of influences beyond simply the structure of the habitat.

Key words: Andes; birds; ecotone; environmental gradient; foliage height diversity; Peru; species diversity.

INTRODUCTION

The species diversity problem has been under intensive investigation by ecologists and biogeographers for the past 20 yr. Yet we are still far from a global understanding of the many diversity patterns in nature. In studies involving birds, success has been limited to exposing empirical relationships that serve to predict diversity patterns within but not between biogeographic provinces. A knowledge of the foliage height profile of a habitat in eastern North America, for example, allows a fairly accurate prediction of its bird species diversity (MacArthur 1964), but the same empirical relationship fails if we use it to try to predict the bird species diversity of a tropical habitat (Terborgh and Weske 1969). Similarly, one may be able to predict the number of bird species inhabiting an oceanic island from the species-area and species-distance re-

gressions of other nearby islands (Diamond 1973), but the prediction fails if we apply it to islands in another ocean. Clearly we have a better feeling for the environmental regulation of diversity within biogeographic provinces than we do for what causes the differences between them.

The most thoroughly documented noninsular pattern is the positive relation between bird species diversity and measures of habitat complexity, a relation that has been shown to hold, with scaling adjustments, within several biogeographic regions (MacArthur et al. 1966; Recher 1969; Karr 1971). The notion that complex habitats provide greater opportunities for resource subdivision has intuitive appeal. Nevertheless, the causal chain that links habitat structure with consumer diversity is by no means simple, and may involve a number of branching or independent connections. Furthermore, the causal links may differ from one set of species to another. Much of the work on diversity to date has concentrated on establishing the

[1] Manuscript received 5 August 1976; accepted 21 January 1977.

1008   JOHN TERBORGH   Ecology, Vol. 58, No. 5

empirical relations between habitat structure and diversity; the causal connections have been relatively little explored. It is this last aspect of the diversity problem that motivates the present article.

The measurements of habitat structure and species diversity come from an elevational transect of the eastern Peruvian Andes. The stature and vertical layering of the vegetation on the transect change in a systematic fashion with elevation, providing a monotonic natural gradient of habitat complexity. I will first examine the relation between avian diversity and two measures of habitat complexity: forest stature and foliage height diversity. I will then show that a strong correlation between species diversity and these measures of habitat complexity is partly fortuitous and masks probable responses to a changing trophic organization of the community, the presence and absence of other taxa in the same trophic levels, and variations in resource productivity along the gradient.

THE VILCABAMBA ELEVATIONAL GRADIENT

With the help of several colleagues and Peruvian assistants, I conducted an intensive survey of the elevational distribution of birdlife along a transect of the West-facing slope of the Cordillera Vilcabamba in Central Peru (approximate location, 12°35′S, 73°40′W). This was accomplished in a series of six expeditions during the period of 1965 to 1972. Descriptions of the climate and vegetation along the transect have been published in a number of previous articles, and so I will reiterate only essential points here (Terborgh 1971, 1973a; Terborgh and Dudley 1973).

Temperature is the climatic variable most closely associated with elevation ($T = -0.56°C/100$ m gain in elevation), though the amount of cloudiness and the frequency of rainfall increase noticeably toward the upper end of the transect. Superimposed on the smooth temperature gradient are four structurally and (to a lesser degree) floristically distinct vegetation formations: lowland rain forest, montane rain forest, cloud forest, and elfin forest. They are characterized, in this order, by declining stature and reduced vertical stratification.

I concur with Richards (1952) that lowland rain forest on good sites contains five vertically distinct strata, ranging from a 50- to 60-m A-story of giant emergents down to a 0.5-m herbaceous D-story. (One can satisfy himself of this by counting the vertically superimposed crowns beneath emergents. The most frequent number is five.) On our transect, lowland rain forest occupied only the flat Apurimac Valley floor. (Virtually none remains at present.) Montane rain forest (650–1,385 m) is floristically similar but lacks the emergent stratum. Gradual trends toward reduced canopy height and increased foliage density in the understory are discernible as one climbs upward. This continues through the cloud forest belt (1,385 to roughly 2,500 m), which in the Vilcabamba is structur-

ally chaotic due to the extremely steep and irregular terrain. Frequent treefalls and landslides result in an irregular canopy that admits a great deal of light into the understory, with a consequent proliferation of climbing bamboo (Chusquea spp.). Elfin forest, the uppermost vegetation zone, first appears on ridge tops at ≈2,500 m in the form of stunted, nearly impenetrable thickets. On good sites, elfin forest may include three strata, corresponding roughly to trees, shrubs, and herbs, but on steep slopes or in poorly drained areas where sphagnum peat accumulates, there are only scattered low trees and a grassy understory. Elfin forest and cloud forest interdigitate on ridges and slopes between 2,400 and 2,700 m. In many places the transition between them is marked by an abrupt drop in canopy height from 20 m or so down to 8 m or less. Although the elfin forest zone is visibly patchy due to the effects of irregularities in exposure and soil conditions, the overall trend toward structural simplification and reduced stature of the vegetation continues to timberline (3,500 m).

AVIAN SYNTOPY AND HABITAT COMPLEXITY

We recorded syntopy as the total number of bird species regularly using the forest within ±30 m elevation of our 9 bush camps. The lists were compiled from sight, sound, and netting records, as described previously (Terborgh 1971). Only forest-dwelling species were counted. Thus the totals for each site omit a few species that were obvious vagrants from other habitats or that use the forest discontinuously along stream margins or in treefall openings. Although the syntopic species at any elevation differ greatly in abundance, from large eagles with territories of several square kilometres to common small passerines, all coexist in the matrix of the forest. In compiling the results my colleagues and I invested a total of 13 party-months on the transect, including 3 wk or more at each of the 9 bush camps. The thoroughness of the effort can be judged by the fact that the final expedition in 1972 added only two new species to a cumulative total of 600.

Figure 1 reveals that forest stature and avian syntopy vary with elevation in a strikingly parallel fashion. The parallelism falters only at the lowland forest-montane forest ecotone where the giant 60-m emergent stratum drops out of the vegetation. However, 60-m trees are rare, even in the best lowland stands, and nowhere does a closed canopy form at heights >30–40 m. A biologically more realistic index of the stature of the lowland forest would be a weighted mean of the heights of unshaded canopy trees. This would fall in the range of 30–45 m and would preserve the parallelism with the syntopy curve over the entire gradient.

As discussed above, the number of vertically superimposed plant strata in the Vilcabamba vegetation formations is closely correlated with the overall

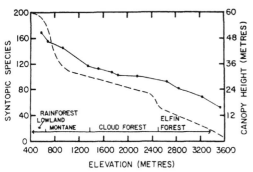

FIG. 1. Avian syntopy (solid line) and forest stature (dashed line) vs. elevation in the Cordillera Vilcabamba. Vegetation zones indicated above the abscissa. Syntopy is the number of species regularly using the forest within ± 30 m of each station. Canopy height represents the mean height of the tallest tree stratum.

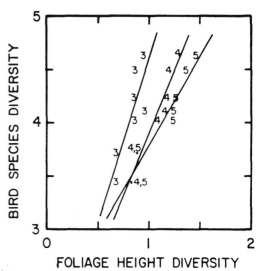

FOLIAGE HEIGHT DIVERSITY

FIG. 2. Bird species diversity vs. foliage height diversity in the Cordillera Vilcabamba. Numbered points refer to the number of foliage layers used in computing the foliage height diversity. Lines represent least squares regressions with correlation coefficients, $r_3 = .84$; $r_4 = .97$; $r_5 = .97$. Further methodological details in text.

stature of the forest. Thus, the data associate the richer low-elevation communities with a taller, more complex and highly stratified habitat. Expressed in this form, the results suggest nothing new.

Bird species diversity vs. foliage
height diversity

To see whether the conclusions reached using a crude and easily obtained measure of habitat complexity—stature—would hold up under more conventional methods of analysis, we determined the foliage height profile of the forest at seven elevations. Foliage densities were measured with MacArthur's checkerboard technique (MacArthur and MacArthur 1961) up to 6 or sometimes 9.14 m [20 or 30 feet], which is as high as we could elevate the checkerboard. Educated guesswork served to fill in the rest of the profile. (For some examples, see Terborgh and Weske 1969.) Foliage height diversities were then computed on the basis of 3 layers (0–2′, 2–25′, >25′), 4 layers (0–2′, 2–10′, 10–50′, >50′), and 5 layers (0–2′, 2–10′, 10–30′, 30–90′, >90′). The intervals for the 3- and 4-layer calculations were those used by MacArthur et al. (1966), while those for the 5-layer calculations were based on Richard's (1952) description of the 5 strata of lowland rain forest.

Bird species diversity is not directly measurable in tropical forest because of the presence of many cryptic species that are rarely observed, and because there is little diurnal or seasonal overlap in the vocal activity periods of many species. Thus it was necessary to estimate bird species diversity from syntopy values by assuming that community equitability is constant at all elevations. Some confidence in this procedure can be obtained from the fact that the species equitabilities of netted samples cluster tightly in the range of 0.7 to 0.8 with no apparent elevational trend (Fig. 6, and see Table 1 in Terborgh and Weske 1975). Because large birds, which are poorly sampled by nets, tend to be

less common than small ones, a lower value, arbitrarily set at 0.6, was used to convert syntopy values to estimates of the number of equally common species. The natural logarithms of these estimates represent bird species diversity. (Letting $H = \Sigma\, p_i \ln p_i$, $\exp^H$ gives the number of equally common species and $\exp^H/S$ = equitability, where S = the total number of species in the sample.) We have just obtained estimates of H by proceeding through this backwards, i.e., $H = \ln (0.6S)$. Even if equitability does vary somewhat from station to station, most of the variation will be wiped out by taking the logarithm.

Bird species diversity correlates well with foliage height diversity on the Vilcabamba gradient, regardless of how many layers are used in computing the latter (Fig. 2). A better fit is obtained with 4 or 5 layers because foliage height diversity measurements based on 3 layers do not discriminate between forests in which most of the foliage is above 7.6 m.

Variation in habitat complexity explains a large fraction of the variance in avian syntopy/diversity on the Vilcabamba elevational gradient, whether one takes into account the details of the vertical organization of the vegetation, as with the foliage height diversity index, or uses only the simple metric of overall forest stature. Investigations in other parts of the world have frequently, though not invariably, produced similar results, except that values of bird species diversity corresponding to a given foliage height diversity have in general been much lower (MacArthur 1964; MacArthur et al. 1966; Recher 1969; Terborgh and Weske

1969; Karr and Roth 1971). It is likely that regional differences are better explained by evolutionary histories of their samples than by postulating as yet undiscovered distinctions in the quality of habitats (Vuilleumier 1972; Cody 1975; Karr 1975; Pearson 1976, and later discussion).

At this point one could easily close the paper with the statement that the Vilcabamba results have merely confirmed a common empirical relationship. When one examines the underlying details, however, a much more complicated picture emerges.

Trophically independent subdivisions of the avifauna

Instead of looking at the very broad pattern described by the entire forest-dwelling avifauna, it is of interest to examine its component subdivisions to see whether they all respond similarly to the gradient. Discounting raptors and vultures, tropical avifaunas can be fairly discretely partitioned into three trophically distinct subdivisions: insectivores, frugivores (including granivores), and nectarivores. A minority of species that feed on nearly equal mixtures of insects and fruit (mainly tanagers and some honeycreepers), or of fruit and nectar (certain honeycreepers) were split evenly between the respective categories. Species that feed on markedly uneven mixtures were assigned to the category representing the major component of their diets. For example, flycatchers that seasonally take some fruit were nevertheless included as insectivores, and some manakins and certain cotingids that occasionally catch insects were classified as frugivores. To a first approximation at least, the subdivisions are trophically, and therefore competitively, independent of one another. Now, if structural complexity of the habitat were the controlling factor in the diversity of birds in general, the three major subdivisions of the avifauna should all respond in a like manner to the vegetational gradient. But they do not (Fig. 3). The trends are strikingly different. Syntopy among insectivores undergoes the greatest change with elevation (>5-fold). Frugivores decline less sharply (2.3-fold) while syntopy in nectarivores is entirely independent of the gradient.

The simple parallelism between vegetational complexity and avian syntopy has vanished, leaving in its place a trio of contrasting cases to be examined individually in the light of the special circumstances pertaining to each. My interpretations, while largely anecdotal, are nevertheless based on what I regard as sound biological evidence.

Insectivores.—Why should insectivores decline most precipitously with elevation? The answer to this seems to be compounded of several trends. First, it could be expected that insectivores would be most severely affected by structural simplification of the habitat. While fruit and flowers can be carried on a plant in only a limited number of ways, insects can

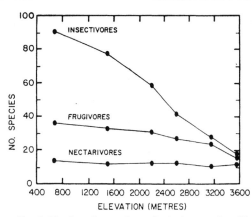

FIG. 3. Number of syntopic species in three tropic guilds vs. elevation in the Cordillera Vilcabamba. From the bottom of the gradient to the top, syntopy in the guilds decreases by the following factors: insectivores 5.1-fold; frugivores (including granivores) 2.3-fold; nectarivores 1.2-fold. Further details in text.

conceal themselves or escape by a great variety of means. Diamond (1973) has shown, for example, that fruit-eating birds in the southwest Pacific sort mainly by size, while, in contrast, it is routine to find several like-sized insectivores sharing the same habitat and segregating by subtle behavioral differences (MacArthur 1958). The simple fact that most avifaunas contain much larger numbers of insectivorous species and families than of taxa specialized on other types of resources testifies to the vast array of behavioral and morphological specializations that can be effectively employed in pursuit of insect prey (Lein 1972; Keast 1972).

Beyond the obvious generalization that structurally complex vegetation offers more opportunities for specialized techniques of harvesting insects, one can make a few more particular statements about how such opportunities decrease on the Vilcabamba gradient. One clear case is that of bark-feeding birds (woodpeckers, Picidae, and woodcreepers, Dendrocolaptidae). As many as 30 species in these two families can be found in a single locality in the lowlands where the variety of bark substrates is impressive: giant trunks, tiny twigs, swinging vines, bamboo canes, termite nests, bromeliads, rotting knot holes, etc. Near timberline the situation is drastically different. The trees are low, spindly, and nearly uniform in size, and moreover, because of the festoons of mosses and lichens that cling to most trunks and branches, there is very little exposed bark. Here the bark-feeding "guild" is comprised of a single small woodpecker. Terrestrial insectivores that forage in the leaf litter are another case. A dozen or more species may coexist in the lowlands, while above 2,400 m there is only one, a species of antpitta (*Grallaria*). The floor of the upper montane forest is a cold damp carpet of sphagnum;

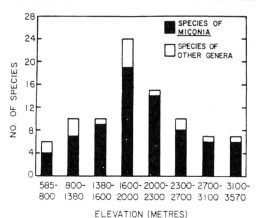

FIG. 4. Number of species in the ornithochoric plant family Melastomataceae occurring in eight arbitrary elevation zones in the Cordillera Vilcabamba. *Miconia* is the predominate genus at all elevations. Redrawn from Mardres (1970).

there scarcely is any leaf litter. One can search through the sphagnum at length without finding any arthropods at all (Terborgh and Weske 1972).

This brings up another probable cause for the decline in insectivores: a scarcity of insects at high elevations. Several major groups including ants and termites appear to drop out altogether above 2,500 m, while others (Lepidoptera, Orthoptera, Diptera, Coleoptera, Hymenoptera) are conspicuously less abundant. Netting yields indicate that the biomass of insectivorous birds drops some 20- to 30-fold between midelevations (≈1,500 m) and timberline, as will be shown later. Reduced syntopy among insectivores at high elevations can thus be explained as a response both to simplified vegetation and to a reduced food resource base.

Frugivores.—Syntopy among fruit- and seed-eating birds shows a more moderate 2.3-fold decrease with elevation. It could be that this merely reflects reduced opportunities for vertical partitioning of resources, though I believe that other factors are involved as well. For one, the availability of fruit crops is considerably more seasonal in the lowlands (Smythe 1970) than it appears to be at high elevations where many plants bear fruits and flowers continuously for long periods. For another, the bulk of the lowland fruit crop is harvested by mammals. At one site in the Peruvian lowlands we found that the biomass of frugivorous primates was approximately 400 kg/km², a value that is well above any reasonable estimate of the biomass of frugivorous birds in the same forest (Janson 1975). But this is by no means the whole picture, as other less easily censused mammalian groups may consume more fruit than do the primates, e.g., bats, rodents, peccaries, marsupials, procyonids. Most of these animals drop out of the Andean fauna below 2,000 m, and many of them below 1,000 m. In spite of their powers

of flight, frugivorous bats respond more like other mammals than like birds. Below roughly 1,300 m our mist nets (on the few occasions we left them open) captured more frugivorous bats at night than birds of all species by day. Above this level the reverse was true and we routinely left nets open at night. These observations suggest that birds, by default, harvest a much greater proportion of the fruit crop at middle and upper elevations than they do in the lowlands. Moreover, it is possible that more suitable fruit is available, as the incidence of several ornithochoric plant families increases sharply in the upper montane forest (e.g., Ericaceae, Rubiaceae, Melastomataceae—Fig. 4).

Why then, if all these things are true, does the number of frugivorous bird species not increase with elevation? Although the proportion of fruit-eating birds in the community does increase markedly, the number of species does not. Part of the answer may lie with the reduced potential for spatial partitioning of the resource in structurally simplified vegetation. (Terrestrial frugivores, for example, drop out entirely above 2,800 m—because of the sphagnum?—though lowland forests may accommodate as many as 6 or 8.) There may be other influences as well, such as declining plant productivity at high elevations. Though the elevational variation in syntopy among frugivorous birds plots as a deceptively simple monotonic trend, it is clear that the underlying causality is complex and still largely unresolved.

Nectarivores.—The situation with regard to nectar-feeding birds is also complex. In the lowlands there is a pronounced vertical stratification of species. Nets capture little else than hermits (subfamily Phaethorninae) while several genera of trochiline hummingbirds and a number of honeycreepers occupy the canopy. Conditions in the lowland forest militate against high densities of nectarivores. Flowering tends to be markedly seasonal, and only a few species are in bloom at any time (Janzen 1967; Frankie et al. 1974). A large majority of the plants are entomophilous (Faegri and Pijl 1971). All these circumstances are reversed at high elevation. The climate is much less seasonal, a large proportion of the plants have flowering periods that last for months (Nevling 1971), and the flora is rich in ornithophilous genera and families (e.g., Ericaceae, Loranthaceae, Loganiaceae, Onagraceae, Bromeliaceae, Verbenaceae, etc.). Whereas hummingbirds and honeycreepers usually comprise <10% of the individuals in lowland net samples, these 2 families frequently constitute half of the catch near timberline. The roughly constant number of nectarivores over the whole gradient may result from a fortuitous balance of two countervailing influences: greater opportunities for vertical partitioning of nectar resources in the lowland forest vs. more abundant and more constant supplies of these resources at high elevations.

1012   JOHN TERBORGH   Ecology, Vol. 58, No. 5

In summary, we first found that the overall trend in avian syntopy along the elevational gradient closely paralleled a gradual telescoping of the forest. However, a very rudimentary trophic breakdown of the fauna clearly demonstrated the folly of taking a good correlation too seriously in the absence of compelling *a priori* logic. Each trophic subdivision of the fauna responds to the gradient in a strikingly individualistic fashion. In every case the causal mechanisms seem to be compounded of several more or less independent influences. The structure of the habitat seems to play a role in every instance, but superimposed on it are effects that derive from major decreases (insects) or increases (nectar) in the availability of food resources, or from the dropout of a major class of competitors (frugivorous mammals). The structure of the habitat *per se* is by no means the only determinant of avian diversity.

Diversity In Netted Population Samples

Now that we have examined the pattern of avian syntopy on the elevational gradient, we can ask whether a similar pattern holds for the component of the fauna that frequents the forest understory. First, a few methodological comments.

Netting method

Mist nets capture birds using the airspace between 0.1 and 2 m above the ground. The size we use (12 m long, 36 mm mesh) is maximally efficient for birds in the 8- to 60-g range; smaller species occasionally slip through the mesh and larger ones frequently bounce out without becoming entangled. Our standard procedure is to construct long end-to-end lines of 20 or more nets (up to 50) and to operate them for periods of 4 to 8 consecutive days. At the end of such a run, >80% of the resident population will have been captured, as can easily be verified by checking for bands on birds observed in the vicinity. Population density estimates can be obtained by making use of the fact that daily catch rates (of previously unmarked individuals) decline in a log-linear fashion with time. Regression analysis then yields a statistic that we call the projected population per net (see caption of Fig. 8 and Terborgh and Faaborg 1973 for further details).

As a sample accumulates the number of species captured increases, rapidly at first, and then gradually to a plateau because of the many inefficiently trapped terrestrial and canopy-dwelling species present at most sites. Diversity estimates that are statistically independent of the density measurements are obtained by basing them on the first 100 individuals captured. (More than 100 individuals are always contained in the density estimates.)

Species diversity in net samples

Now let us attempt to anticipate how diversity, as sampled with mist nets, might vary with elevation. Re-

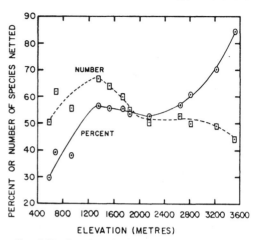

FIG. 5. Number of species contained in samples of 300 mist netted birds (dashed line), and the percent this represents of total syntopy (solid line) vs. elevation in the Cordillera Vilcabamba.

call first that the total number of species present (syntopy) declines from 170 in the lowland forest to 52 at timberline, a 3.3-fold decrease. However, the stature of the habitat also decreases by an equal or greater factor, suggesting that the concentration of species in a standard vertical slice of the forest may not change very much. Moreover, we can expect the nets to capture a much higher proportion of the whole community toward the upper end of the gradient where the vegetation is low.

This does indeed happen, but with some unanticipated kinks. The fraction of the entire syntopic community that is captured in a standard net sample of 300 individuals increases from ≈30% in the lowlands to >85% at timberline. But instead of rising as the mirror image of the forest stature curve, as might be expected, the curve displays a prominent shoulder between 1,200 and 2,000 m (Fig. 5). In the absence of any major changes in forest stature in this region, the result is puzzling. An anomalously large fraction of the community is captured in the lower cloud forest zone with the consequence that netted species diversities rise to a pronounced peak (Fig. 6). The high diversities are not due to the presence of additional species, as the syntopy curve (Fig. 1) clearly shows, but rather to an unexpected local relaxation in the vertical stratification of the community. Neither is the high diversity explained simply by an increased incidence of canopy species in the samples, because the inclusion of inefficiently captured species results in reduced equitabilities and little or no change in diversity. To the contrary, equitabilities are high in the region of the diversity peak. Elsewhere on the transect the results are much as anticipated; comparing the bottom and the top of the gradient, the net samples contain roughly equal diversities, in spite of the large difference in syn-

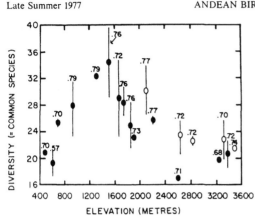

FIG. 6. Number of equally common bird species ($=\exp - \Sigma p_i \ln p_i$) contained in netted samples of 100 individuals vs. elevation in the Cordillera Vilcabamba. Vertical bars represent the range of values obtained at stations sampled on 2 or more yr. Open points indicate lines where nets ran along exposed ridgetops (cejas) as distinguished from broad slopes or level ground (closed points). Numbers give the mean equitability ($=\exp - \Sigma p_i \ln p_i/S$) of the sample(s) at each station.

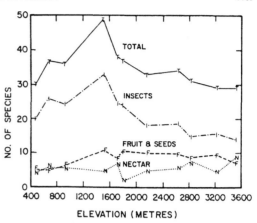

FIG. 7. Trophic composition of net samples vs. elevation in the Cordillera Vilcabamba. Criteria are the same as in Fig. 3.

topy. The problem that remains is how to account for the anomalous midelevation peak.

The midelevation diversity peak

An increased concentration of foliage at the level of the nets might contribute to greater coexistence, as has been demonstrated in some other studies (Karr and Roth 1971; Willson 1974). There may be some evidence for this, as shall be discussed later. However, the elevational patterns do not accord. Netted bird diversity is at a maximum between 1,400 and 1,600 m while the thickest understory occurs between 2,000 and 3,000 m.

Though the structure of the habitat may be of some ultimate significance in regulating the diversity pattern, it is possible that better insights may be derived by examining the more proximal clues offered by the organization of the avian community itself. The community undergoes pronounced compositional shifts as its trophic structure changes, and as a result of a nearly constant rate of species turnover with elevation (Terborgh 1971). Whole guilds wax and wane, or drop out altogether. Obligate army ant followers are a good example. Members of this guild are among the commonest species in lowland net samples. Their relative abundance and the number of species decline steadily with elevation until the last of them drops out near 2,000 m. Earlier I mentioned the cases of the bark-gleaning guild and terrestrial insectivores. There are many more examples, including ones that entail increases with elevation, as well as decreases.

Given that such marked compositional shifts involve guilds that depend on a wide range of distinct food and habitat resources, it is at least conceivable that there might be some point on the gradient at which the spectrum of available resources allowed a maximum number of guilds to coexist.

Equitability of faunal components

Using the same rough breakdown of the fauna into insectivores, frugivores, and nectarivores, we note the surprising result that the midelevation diversity peak is almost entirely attributable to an increased concentration of insectivores (Fig. 7). At this crude level at least, enhanced equitability of trophic guilds is not the answer.

To pursue the matter further we focus on insectivores, in particular, the six most important families: Tyrannidae (flycatchers)—59 spp.; Formicariidae (antbirds)—43 spp.; Furnariidae (ovenbirds)—26 spp.; Dendrocolaptidae (woodcreepers)—16 spp.; Troglodytidae (wrens)—8 spp.; and Parulidae (warblers)—8 spp. (Numbers are all species inhabitating the gradient; many are not readily captured in nets.) Significantly, each of the four largest of these families possess a distinctive and characteristic type of foraging behavior. There are a few exceptions in each family, but to a first approximation woodcreepers glean the bark of trunks and major limbs, antbirds are foliage gleaners, ovenbirds have a creeping habit and are partial to searching through epiphytes and dead leaves, and flycatchers hawk or hover-snatch. The deployment of such conspicuously different foraging techniques probably implies differential resource utilization, as Hespenheide (1975) has shown for a number of tropical and temperate insectivores. It is not immediately obvious, however, why the proportions of these families should vary so strongly with elevation (Table 1). Antbirds predominate in the lowlands, contributing more species to the net samples than the other five families combined. But by 2,500 m they have virtually dropped out of the fauna. Flycatchers and ovenbirds, on the other hand, prevail near the top

1014   JOHN TERBORGH   Ecology, Vol. 58, No. 5

TABLE 1. Representation of major insectivorous families in Vilcabamba net samples (first 300 individuals). Number of species

Family	Elevation (m)									
	585	685	930	1,350	1,520	1,730	1,835	2,215	2,640	3,510
Dendrocolaptidae	4	4	4	3	2	1	3	3	0	0
Furnariidae	4	4	5	10	9	8	7	4	5	3
Formicariidae	15	12	9	8	9	8	6	4	1	0
Tyrannidae	4	9	11	10	11	8	9	6	10	6
Troglodytidae	1	1	1	3	2	3	2	3	1	0
Parulidae	0	2	2	1	3	3	2	3	3	1
Total	28	32	32	35	36	31	29	23	20	10

of the gradient. The unexpectedly high net diversity at midelevations is clearly a consequence of the good and strikingly equitable representation of all the families of insectivores. Since each of the distinctive family foraging modes requires appropriate substrates, the key to the problem lies in understanding how the midelevation forest provides such a wealth of foraging opportunities.

Structural heterogeneity of the midmontane forest

Mid- and high-elevation forests are far more heterogeneous in the horizontal plane than are lowland forests. In part this is an inevitable consequence of mountain topography, with its ridges, slopes, and ravines. The continuity of the forest is frequently interrupted by landslide tracks and deep stream gorges; tree heights vary greatly between sheltered ravines and exposed ridgetops. All these irregularities create a variety of "edge" situations that are exploited by flycatchers. Climbing bamboos (*Chusquea* spp.) invade old landslides and treefalls, forming impenetrable thickets that are the home of certain ovenbirds, antbirds, and wrens. Where rising air currents are deflected by slopes and ridges, the forest becomes choked with a profusion of mosses and other epiphytes that carpet all exposed surfaces, both vertical and horizontal. The thick mats of mosses, lichens, and ferns offer a novel substrate that is exploited by a great array of creeping birds, notably ovenbirds and certain wrens. In addition, the forest harbors a full spectrum of the more conventional types of bark and foliage gleaners that are so prevalent in the lowlands. In sum, the steep terrain, irregular canopy, and an extraordinary variety of arboreal substrates all contribute to the microspatial heterogeneity of the midmontane forest of the Cordillera Vilcabamba. Lowland forests, in contrast, are more regularly stratified in the vertical plane, and less heterogeneous in the horizontal plane. (Such structural differences between forests, while potentially important to bird diversity, are not registered in foliage height diversity measurements because horizontal variation in foliage density is averaged in the computation.)

Is the elevational pattern of bird species diversity

adequately explained by the structural heterogeneity of the midmontane forest? No. What does seem to be accounted for is the more equitable representation of the principal families of insectivores. But there are other features of the pattern that are not explained, such as why there are decidedly fewer insectivores at 2,200 m than at 1,500 m (Table 1), even though at the higher elevation the forest still contains large trees and remains extremely heterogeneous, as is affirmed by the high family equitability. For the answer to this question we must inquire into the causes of the declining role of insectivory toward the upper end of the gradient. This will be taken up in the next section.

AVIAN DENSITY, SPECIES DIVERSITY, AND RESOURCES

Population density estimates derived from 4-day net runs yield an elevational pattern that closely parallels the trend in species diversity (Fig. 8). A high degree of correlation between the two sets of results is confirmed by plotting them together in a scatter diagram (Fig. 9). Maximum levels of both density and diversity coincide in a narrow elevational belt corresponding to lower cloud forest. Two quite independent questions are posed by the findings: (1) is a causal interrelationship implied by the correlation of density and diversity, and (2) what features of the changing conditions on the gradient could account for the pattern of avian abundance in the understory? These questions will be taken up in order.

Density and diversity

Our earlier experience with the parallelism between syntopy and forest stature provided a trenchant reminder to proceed with caution in the interpretation of correlations. In the present case it is not even clear which is the independent variable. There are plausible arguments on both sides. At one extreme, it could be held that the number of individuals in a community is a function of the number of species it contains. This is what one could expect if avian niches were rigidly unresponsive to variations in the intensity of interspecific competition. Though something like this may occur in the impoverished Pacific islands studied by Diamond (1971*b*), a large body of evidence indicates that in gen-

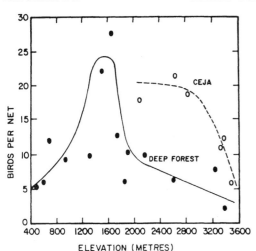

FIG. 8. Avian population density vs. elevation in the Cordillera Vilcabamba. The ordinate gives the projected population per net, computed from the first sample taken at each station as $[N/n]/[1 - (Cf/Co)]$, where N = the number of different individuals in the sample, n = the number of nets used, Cf = the final and Co = the initial capture rates (in birds per net-day). Cf and Co are taken from the log-linear regression of capture rate vs. accumulated net-days of sampling. Further details on this method are given in Terborgh and Faaborg (1973). Open points represent ceja lines, as described in the caption of Fig. 6. Single values only are given for each station because banded birds are adept at avoiding nets, hence lower values are obtained when repeat measurements are made on subsequent years.

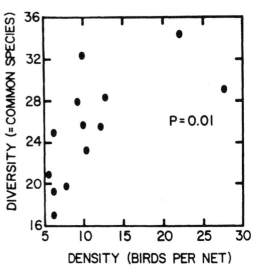

FIG. 9. Scatter plot of bird species diversity vs. population density in Vilcabamba net samples. Values were taken from the closed (deep forest) points in Figs. 6 and 8. The correlation is highly significant, $P = .01$.

eral birds are capable of almost unlimited competitive release (Crowell 1962; Diamond 1971*a*; MacArthur et al. 1972, 1973). Indeed, our own efforts to determine the limits of competitive release among Caribbean birds have been notably unsuccessful. Tiny islands with only 10 or 12 species support avian biomasses that equal or exceed those of much larger species rich islands (Terborgh and Faaborg 1973; Terborgh et al. 1977). Among Caribbean bird communities at least, densities are more or less constant over a wide range of diversities. Thus it seems doubtful that diversity could be the independent variable in Fig. 9.

An intermediate proposition would be the following. Since we have already noted that the equitability of insectivorous families increases sharply from the lowlands to middle elevations, apparently in response to a greater structural heterogeneity of the habitat, it is possible that a broader spectrum of foraging opportunities would contribute to an increase in both density and diversity. Though this cannot be rejected as a partial explanation, there are additional facts that remain unresolved. One is the decline in number of insectivores between 1,500 and 2,200 m, a zone in which family equitability is high and within which there is little perceptible change in the character of the forest.

Another is that the relative increase in density in Fig. 9 exceeds the relative increase in diversity. If the high diversity of the lower cloud forest region were simply a response to the presence of additional foraging opportunities, one would indeed find more species, but the average abundance per species would remain the same or decrease; certainly it would not increase. But in our results it does. To account for this it seems necessary to postulate that at least some of the extra diversity is a consequence of increased density.

An increased density of birds in the understory could result from a greater concentration of foraging substrate (foliage), reduced mortality (predation, disease, etc.), or a higher productivity of food resources. Greater amounts of foliage in the understory might result in increased foraging activity at net level, though, as mentioned above, maximum foliage densities near the ground are attained above 2,000 m where both density and diversity are declining. We have no information on mortality factors, nor is it clear what effect local variations in predators, parasites, etc. would have on diversity. Specialized bird hawks (*Micrastur, Accipiter*) occur in low numbers over the entire gradient. To me the most plausible cause of the midelevation "hot spot" is a greater abundance of food resources.

A more productive environment could support both a more numerous and more diverse community because it could provide essential food resources in greater amounts and in greater variety. But why should avian resources, especially insects, reach a peak in the lower cloud forest zone? Most of what follows is admittedly *a posteriori* rationalization,

Ecology, Vol. 58, No. 5

though some of the corroborative evidence is independently derived.

Productivity and the environmental gradient

The problem has two parts: why do bird densities increase from the lowlands upward into the cloud forest, and why do they then decrease at still higher elevations. In discussing this I shall assume only that there is some proportionality between the density of bird populations and the productivity of the resources that sustain them.

Taking the second part of the problem first, what is the evidence that the availability of insects may decline toward the upper part of the gradient? (1) Subjective impressions. Ants, termites and flying insects—hymenoptera, flies, cicadas, lepidoptera—are omnipresent in low-elevation forests. At night there is a constant din of insect noise, and heaps of scorched bodies accumulate under the pressure lantern. In contrast, the nighttime silence at high elevation is broken only by an occasional owl or frog. The lantern attracts nothing more than a few moths. During the day one sees no ants or termites and only an occasional butterfly during the brief periods of sunshine. (2) The number of syntopic insectivores decreases by a factor of 5 between the bottom and top of the gradient. (3) The rate at which nets capture insectivorous birds decreases by more than 10-fold between 1,500 and 3,500 m (Fig. 8). If we take into account the fact that nets sample a much larger fraction of the high-elevation community (Fig. 5), the disparity becomes something like 20- to 30-fold. (4) Janzen (1973b) has shown that arthropod density and diversity decrease sharply at high elevations in Costa Rica. While these are all statements of circumstantial evidence, taken together they argue plausibly that the decrease in diversity of insectivorous birds above 1,500 m is due at least in part to a declining resource base.

The evidence that insect densities increase upwards from the lowlands to a midelevation maximum is far less compelling. (1) There is no corresponding increase in the number of avian insectivores, only in the overlap of their foraging zones. (2) The increased capture rates could be at least partly an artifact of this and other circumstances, such as the irregular terrain. (3) Greater concentrations of foliage near the ground could result in increased foraging activity at net level in the absence of any real increase in bird numbers. (4) Still another possibility is the preemption of resources that are harvested by other taxa at lower elevations. Highly insectivorous squirrel monkeys (*Saimiri sciureus*) abound in the undisturbed lowland forest, but these animals drop out at the base of the mountains around 600 m. In the one locality for which we have reliable census data, the squirrel monkey population ($\approx$80/km²) has a biomass roughly equal to that of all avian insectivores in the same forest (Janson 1975). Thus, though the densities of insectivorous birds do

appear to increase at midelevations, there is little in our experience to suggest that insects do also. (5) The only direct evidence comes from Janzen's (1973a,b) sweep net survey of an elevational transect in Costa Rica in which he found maximum numbers of arthropod species and individuals in lower montane forest between 1,000 and 1,500 m. Indeed, the elevational pattern of arthropod density and diversity in his sweep net samples parallels that of our mist net results so closely as to merit further discussion.

I agree with Janzen in the feeling that the elevational pattern in arthropod abundance reflects an underlying variation in plant primary productivity. Neither of us has any direct evidence; yet there is sufficiently compelling circumstantial arguments to excuse a few lines of speculation. Janzen (1973b) maintains that net productivity can be expected to increase at midelevation because of reduced nighttime temperatures and the attendant savings in energy lost to respiration. At higher elevations, diurnal as well as nocturnal temperatures are severly depressed, resulting in lower productivity. Whether one accepts this argument or not, there are a number of additional grounds for rationalizing a midelevation productivity maximum.

First, several aspects of the lowland environment are ameliorated at midelevations in ways that would be expected to enhance photosynthetic activity.

1) Prolonged dry spells (>1 wk) are rare to nonexistent at midelevations, and accordingly there is no deciduousness, even in the tallest trees. On the other hand, droughts of a month or more are a routine annual event in the lowlands where most of the taller trees drop their leaves for some portion of the dry season, and many subcanopy species reduce their leaf volumes.

2) Middle elevations characteristically experience a propitious daily weather regimen in which the mornings and late afternoons tend to be sunny, and middays and early afternoons cloudy or rainy. Light intensity and temperature in the canopy are thus moderated through the day, mitigating the conditions that produce a midday photosynthetic depression. The Apurimac Valley lowlands, at least during the dry season, tend to be shrouded in mists for the early morning hours, and hot, dry, and sunny through the middle of the day.

3) Retarded rates of organic decomposition at middle and higher elevations may mean a more gradual release of mineral nutrients. This should imply a more continuous rate of growth than is possible in the lowlands where nutrients are released from the leaf litter in a burst at the beginning of the rainy season (Richards 1952).

4) The duff mat (25 cm thick at 1,800 m) that develops on the forest floor above 1,000 m soaks up water like a sponge, retarding runoff and buffering the superficial layers of the soil against desiccation.

Even if one were satisfied that these circumstances

pointed to rising productivity above the lowlands, it would remain to be explained why there seems to be a decline at still higher elevations. Again, there appear to be a number of contributory circumstances.

1) Reduced light intensity. The amount of cloudiness becomes extreme toward the top of the range. Even in mid dry season the summit ridge receives <20 h of sun a week, and most of this comes before 0800 when there may still be frost on the ground.

2) Low temperatures, especially low root temperatures, may adversely affect growth via retarded nutrient uptake.

3) Permanently high humidities imply low transpiration rates, another factor that could hamper nutrient uptake (Baynton 1969; Gates 1969; Weaver et al. 1973).

4) A ubiquitous carpet of sphagnum above 2,000 m lowers the pH to 4–5 in the root zone (our measurements), perhaps further exacerbating a scarcity of nutrients.

5) Drastically retarded organic decomposition at high elevations leads to the accumulation of thick peat deposits that could sequester nutrients in forms that are not readily taken up by roots.

Finally, I wish to present a piece of anecdotal evidence that to me very convincingly illustrates the existence of an optimal productivity zone in the lower montane region. It is the pattern of recent agricultural settlement in the eastern Andean sectors of Colombia, Ecuador, Peru, and Bolivia. The first colonists to arrive in an unexploited area invariably choose sites within the elevational span of 500 to 1,200 m. In most places the terrain above this level becomes too steep to cultivate easily. But even so, as the pressure of immigration continues, late-arriving settlers prefer to hack out pitiful little plots on 30 to 40 degree slopes, rather than to invade the expansive Amazonian flat lands. These people know what they are doing. It is common knowledge, gained by trial-and-error experience, that it is futile to attempt to cultivate food and cash crops much below 500 m. In Colombia, where the pressure of overpopulation is most severe, agricultural settlement has spread practically to timberline, while vast expanses of lowland forest remain virtually uninhabited. The behavior of peasant farmers is probably as good a bioassay for inherent productivity (with a correction for steepness of the terrain) as any we have.

I would not have dwelt so long on these speculative matters had I not been impressed by the striking parallels between Janzen's results and ours. In both cases maximum species diversities occurred in areas supporting maximum densities of individuals. It is tempting to imagine that an increased abundance of resources in a complex environment like a tropical forest could allow a greater array of foraging specializations to achieve profitability, thus accounting for enhanced diversity. While this interpretation has a commonsensical appeal it is only suggested, not proven, by the data on hand.

BIRD SPECIES DIVERSITY IN PERSPECTIVE

The primary lesson of our examination of bird species diversity patterns in the Cordillera Vilcabamba is that diversity is a complex community phenomenon, not just a number which can be "explained" with one or another competing hypothesis. Contributory factors overlie in an intricate mosaic, so that one cannot even be assured of unidirectional trends in moving along major environmental gradients. Carefully conducted comparisons are at present our most effective means for dissecting out the important variables.

Influences of history and geography may dominate when the geographical scale of a comparison is large. Thus the factors which appear to control the trends within the 30-km Vilcabamba transect—habitat structure, abundance and qualitative balance of food resources, presence or absence of other taxa at the same trophic levels—may play minor or negligible roles in interregional comparisons. The richest mature forests in North America, for example, harbor barely half as many bird species as the stunted 4-m elfin shrubland astride the cold, mist-shrouded Vilcabamba summit ridge. Clearly the differences in habitat complexity and productivity run the wrong way to explain this seemingly paradoxical contrast. I side with MacArthur (1969) in thinking that evolutionary processes (speciation, immigration, and extinction) are largely at the root of such interregional differences, as I have already expounded elsewhere (Terborgh 1973b).

The possible causal connections between productivity and diversity remain problematical. An increased abundance of resources could provide sustenance for additional species through either or both of two mechanisms: the availability of broadened resource spectra or the availability of the same basic spectrum of resources in a greater variety of sites in a complex environment. It goes without saying that a necessary condition for a positive response to a high productivity site is the presence of appropriately adapted species in adjacent habitats. Merely fertilizing a pond or a piece of grassland may not provide an adequate test, because it creates a novel situation to which many of the species present are not adapted. Resource spectra may consequently narrow instead of broaden.

Diversity has proven difficult to study because it lies at the end of a number of interacting causal chains, often several steps removed from the things we are able to measure. Even if we could measure the whole gamut of proximate variables—the precise habitat needs of individual species, resource spectra, the pressure of interspecific competition, etc.—we would still have to contend with historical/evolutionary influences in accounting for interregional contrasts. The contribution of this work has not been in resolving issues so much as in demonstrating the composite nature of the diversity problem and the essentiality of reducing it to its component parts as a precondition for further understanding.

ACKNOWLEDGMENTS

This article is based on results that were gathered over an 8-yr period on 6 expeditions to the Apurimac Valley and Cordillera Vilcabamba. So many people contributed to the undertaking that it is impossible to name them all individually, but a few deserve special mention. I am especially grateful to John Weske, my closest collaborator on 5 of the expeditions, for major contributions to the fieldwork and for assisting in the preparation of the manuscript. Many of the data presented here were included, in preliminary form, in his doctoral thesis (Weske 1972). Perhaps our greatest assets in the exploratory work were the strength, resourcefulness, and reliability of our two perennial assistants, Klaus Wehr and Manuel Sanchez. Our base camp for all the expeditions was at Hacienda Luisiana, where we received extraordinary assistance and hospitality from its owner, Jose Parodi V. Invaluable storage facilities at the Museo de Historia National were provided by the director, Ramon Ferreyra.

Financial support of one or more of the expeditions was received from the American Philosophical Society, the Chapman Fund of the American Museum of Natural History, the National Geographic Society, and the National Science Foundation (GB-20170). We are grateful for their sustained interest in the research.

LITERATURE CITED

Baynton, H. W. 1969. The ecology of an elfin forest in Puerto Rico, 3. Hilltop and forest influence on the microclimate of Pico del Oeste. J. Arnold Arbor. Harv. Univ. 50:80–92.

Cody, M. L. 1975. Trends toward a theory of continental species diversities: bird distributions over Mediterranean habitat gradients, p. 214–257. In M. L. Cody and J. M. Diamond [eds.] Ecology and evolution of communities. Belknap, Cambridge, Mass.

Crowell, K. 1962. Reduced interspecific competition among the birds of Bermuda. Ecology 43:75–88.

Diamond, J. M. 1971a. Ecological consequences of island colonization by southwest Pacific birds, I. Types of niche shifts. Natl. Acad. Sci. Proc. 67:529–536.

———. 1971b. Ecological consequences of island colonization by southwest Pacific birds. II. The effect of species diversity on total population density. Natl. Acad. Sci. Proc. 67:1715–1721.

———. 1973. Distributional ecology of New Guinea birds. Science 179:759–769.

Faegri, K., and L. van der Pijl. 1971. The principles of pollination ecology (2nd ed.). Oxford.

Frankie, G. W., H. G. Baker, and P. A. Opler. 1974. Comparative phenological studies of trees in tropical wet and dry forests in the lowlands of Costa Rica. J. Ecol. 62:881–919.

Gates, D. M. 1969. The ecology of an elfin forest in Puerto Rico, 4. Transpiration rates and temperatures of leaves in cool humid environment. J. Arnold Arbor. Harv. Univ. 50:197–209.

Hespenheide, H. A. 1975. Prey characteristics and predator niche width, p. 158–180. In M. L. Cody and J. M. Diamond [eds.] Ecology and evolution of communities. Belknap, Cambridge, Mass.

Janson, C. H. 1975. Ecology and population densities of primates in a Peruvian rainforest. Undergraduate thesis, Princeton University. 96 p.

Janzen, D. H. 1967. Synchronization of sexual reproduction of trees within the dry season in Central America. Evolution 21:620–637.

———. 1973a. Sweep samples of tropical foliage insects: description of study sites, with data on species abundances and size distributions. Ecology 54:659–686.

———. 1973b. Sweep samples of tropical foliage insects: effects of seasons, vegetation types, elevation, time of day, and insularity. Ecology 54:687–708.

Karr, J. R. 1971. Structure of avian communities in selected Panama and Illinois habitats. Ecol. Monogr. 41:207–233.

———. 1975. Production, energy pathways and community diversity in forest birds, p. 161–176. In F. B. Golley and E. Medina, [eds.] Tropical ecological systems. Springer-Verlag, N.Y.

Karr, J. R., and R. R. Roth. 1971. Vegetation structure and avian diversity in several new world areas. Am. Nat. 105:423–435.

Keast, A. 1972. Ecological opportunities and dominant families, as illustrated by the Neotropical Tyrannidae (Aves). Evol. Biol. 5:229–277.

Lein, M. R. 1972. A trophic comparison of avifaunas. Syst. Zool. 21:135–150.

MacArthur, R. H. 1958. Population ecology of some warblers of northeastern coniferous forests. Ecology 39:599–619.

———. 1964. Environmental factors affecting bird species diversity. Am. Nat. 98:387–397.

———. 1969. Patterns of communities in the tropics. Biol. J. Linn. Soc. 1:19–30.

MacArthur, R. H., and J. W. MacArthur. 1961. On bird species diversity. Ecology 42:594–598.

MacArthur, R. H., J. M. Diamond, and J. R. Karr. 1972. Density compensation in island faunas. Ecology 53:330–342.

MacArthur, R. H., H. Recher, and M. Cody. 1966. On the relation between habitat selection and species diversity. Am. Nat. 100:319–332.

MacArthur, R. H., J. MacArthur, D. MacArthur, and A. MacArthur. 1973. The effect of island area on population densities. Ecology 54:657–658.

Mardres, J. H. W. 1970. Distribution of Melastomataceae along environmental gradients in Peru and the Dominican Republic. Master's thesis, Univ. of Maryland. 73 p.

Nevling, L. I., Jr. 1971. The ecology of an elfin forest in Puerto Rico, 16. The flowering cycle and an interpretation of its seasonality. J. Arnold Arbor. Harv. Univ. 52:586–613.

Pearson, D. L. 1976. The relation of foliage complexity to ecological diversity of three Amazonian bird communities. Condor 77:453–466.

Recher, H. F. 1969. Bird species diversity and habitat diversity in Australia and North America. Am. Nat. 103:75–80.

Richards, P. W. 1952. The tropical rainforest. Cambridge Univ. Press, Cambridge. 450 p.

Smythe, N. 1970. Relationships between fruiting seasons and seed dispersal methods in a Neotropical forest. Am. Nat. 104:25–35.

Terborgh, J. 1971. Distribution on environmental gradients: theory and a preliminary interpretation of distributional patterns in the avifauna of the Cordillera Vilcabamba, Peru. Ecology 52:23–40.

———. 1973a. Vilcabamba Birdlife. Explor. J. 51:48–56.

———. 1973b. On the notion of favorableness in plant ecology. Am. Nat. 107:481–501.

Terborgh, J., and T. R. Dudley. 1973. Biological exploration of the Northern Cordillera Vilcabamba, Peru. Natl. Geogr. Soc. Res. Reports, 1966 Projects, p. 255–264.

Terborgh, J., and J. Faaborg. 1973. Turnover and ecological release in the avifauna of Mona Island, Puerto Rico. Auk 90:759–779.

Terborgh, J., and J. S. Weske. 1969. Colonization of secondary habitats by Peruvian birds. Ecology 50:765–782.

———. 1972. Rediscovery of the Imperial Snipe in Peru. Auk 89:497–505.

———. 1975. The role of competition in the distribution of Andean birds. Ecology 56:562–576.

Terborgh, J., J. Faaborg, and H. J. Brockmann. 1977. Island colonization by Lesser Antillean birds. Auk. *In press*.

Vuilleumier, F. 1972. Bird species diversity in Patagonia (temperate South America). Am. Nat. 106:266–271.

Weske, J. S. 1972. The distribution of the avifauna in the Apurimac Valley of Peru with respect to environmental gradients, habitat, and related species. Ph.D. thesis, Univ. of Oklahoma. 137 p.

Weaver, P. L., M. D. Byer, and D. L. Bruck. 1973. Transpiration rates in the Luquillo Mountains of Puerto Rico. Biotropica 5:123–133.

Willson, M. F. 1974. Avian community organization and habitat structure. Ecology 55:1017–1029.

FOOD NICHES AND COEXISTENCE IN SYMPATRIC PRIMATES IN GABON

ANNIE GAUTIER-HION

Station Biologique de Paimpont,
Université de Rennes, 35380 – Plélan-le-Grand, France.

INTRODUCTION

The Laboratory of Equatorial Primatology and Ecology of the C.N.R.S. (Centre National de la Recherche Scientifique) is located in north-eastern Gabon, in the midst of the equatorial rain forest. Apart from the five nocturnal prosimians, eleven species of simian primate are found there. All except the gorilla have been the subject of more or less long-term studies conducted by the various research-workers at the Laboratory (Table I). Among the simian species, only the mandrill and the crested mangabey are strictly allopatric. The former is approximately limited to the south by the Ivindo river, whereas the western limit of the latter coincides with the left bank tributaries of this river (Fig. 1).

The aim of this paper is to make a comparative analysis of the ecological niches of some of these species. For each species studied, the ecological preferences will be described, followed by a comparison of their dietary compositions.

METHODS

Because current methods of calculating time spent feeding, and Hladik's (1973) techniques of direct observation were both unsuitable under our working conditions, a large number of stomach contents were collected so that the mean composition and seasonal variation of the monkeys' diets could be studied.

The stomachs were taken from specimens freshly shot by local hunters who still eat monkey meat as well as that of duikers and wild pigs. They were fixed in 10% formalin. The contents of each stomach were then washed and filtered through a series of sieves. A large-meshed first sieve (mesh size= 16 mm^2) retained the larger seeds and pieces of fruit and facilitated recognition of the smaller particles of the second (4 mm^2). The homogeneous and partly digested composition of this latter fraction can be used to estimate the composition of the fraction from the third sieve (0.01 mm^2), which is impossible to analyse into separate components.

The fraction from each sieve was sorted separately with a binocular microscope into various categories such as: fruit, leaves, animal matter, and so forth. These categories were weighed separately, after drying to constant weight.

The overall composition of the stomach contents was then evaluated in percentages of the total dry weight of the content. This total does not

TABLE 1

Diurnal-Primate fauna of N-E Gabon

DIURNAL PRIMATE SPECIES N-E GABON	AUTHORS	NATURE OF THE STUDIES
Gorilla gorilla	-	-
Pan troglodytes	C.M. Hladik (1973)	Feeding behaviour
Mandrillus sphinx	P. Jouventin (1975)	Socio-ecology
Colobus guereza	A. Gautier (this paper)	Diet
Cercocebus albigena	A. Gautier (this paper)	Diet
Cercocebus galeritus	R. Quris (1975, 1976)	Socio-ecology
Cercopithecus nictitans }	J-P. et A. Gautier (1969, 1974)	Socio-ecology
Cercopithecus pogonias }		
Cercopithecus cephus }	A. Gautier (this paper)	Feeding behaviour
Cercopithecus neglectus	A. et J-P. Gautier (in prep)	Socio-ecology
Miopithecus talapoin	A. Gautier (1970, 1971, 1973)	Socio-ecology

Food niches in sympatric primates   271

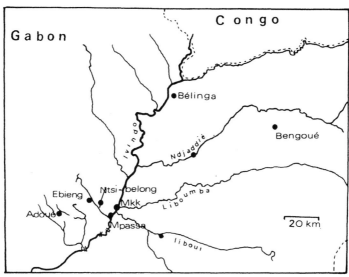

Figure 1. The various study sites in N-E Gabon; the C.N.R.S. laboratory is located at M'passa. Thanks are due to P. Charles-Dominique, G. Dubost, L. Emmons, J.P. Gautier and R. Quris, who helped me collect material there.

include the big seeds if they have not been crushed, since the latter appear to be used as roughage. One *Cercocebus albigena*, for example, swallowed 69 seeds of a Myristicacae (*Pycnanthus* or *Coecolaryon*) (length: $\frac{ca}{\pm}\cdot 2$ cm; weight: $\frac{ca}{\pm}\cdot 5$ g), of which only the arils were eaten. These seeds can occupy 3/4 of stomach volume and they are found undamaged in faeces.

Stomach contents from nearly 200 individuals have been collected within a radius of about thirty kilometres around M'passa (Fig. 1). 109 have been analysed to date and the results are presented here in a preliminary account which does not include seasonal variations.

The analysis is based essentially on the four *Cercopithecus* species and *Miopithecus talapoin* but data have been included for 15 stomachs from *C.albigena* and two from *Colobus guereza*, though there is very little ecological data available for these species in Gabon. This report also includes the results from Quris' studies (1975, 1976) on *Cercocebus galeritus*, which were obtained with methods similar to ours.

Analysis of diet through the study of stomach contents seems to be the most objective procedure from a quantitative view point (see Hladik, 1976); but the use of dry weights is open to criticism. Obviously, one may expect that dessication acts differently according to the nature of the food, though a recent study conducted by Hladik (pers. comm.) demonstrates that for two species of *Presbytis*, the differences between the proportions obtained from fresh weight and those from dry weight are virtually negligible. Hladik's analysis, however, does not include animal matter, which is probably the category most altered, and hence most underestimated, by dry weight measurement.

272   Annie Gautier-Hion

THE FOREST AND ITS CLIMATE

N.E. Gabon has a hot humid equatorial climate and an evergreen tropical forest, in spite of the relatively low annual rainfall.

Mature rain forest forms the most substantial part of the vegetation. It is a high, species-rich forest with an open under-storey (919 identified plant species: see Hladik, 1973). The work of A. Hladik (1977) is now providing initial indication of its phenology.

The riparian forest presents different formations depending on the appearance of the river banks. If the latter are flat, they are periodically flooded and covered with a relatively low forest with characteristic tree species, such as *Uapaca sp., Macrolobium sp.* and various palm-tree species. Its understorey is usually very dense. If the banks are steep, however, they are covered with a relatively high forest very similar in species composition to the mature rain forest. Finally the riparian forest can be composed of secondary growth, especially in places where there used to be villages of tribes living on the river banks.

PRIMATE SPECIES INHABITING RIPARIAN FOREST

The species

There are three monkey species of riparian forest: *Cercocebus galeritus* (the crested mangabey), *Cercopithecus neglectus* (the De Brazza monkey) and *Miopithecus talapoin* (the talapoin). These species are never encountered in areas lacking broad rivers, and their home ranges always include a portion of river bank. They are therefore not found in mountainous regions.

The mean body weights of adult males and females are indicated on Fig. 2. The lightest species, *M. talapoin*, shows weak sexual dimorphism in weight. In contrast, the heaviest species, *C. neglectus* and *C. galeritus*, exhibit strong sexual dimorphism in weight (Gautier-Hion, 1975).

Habitat occupation

Cercocebus galeritus. The crested mangabey has been studied by Quris (1975, 1976) in a zone near the Liboui river (Fig. 1). In this area, the monkeys spent 95% of their time in periodically flooded forest. The home ranges of the different troops are spaced along the river bed. The home range of the troop which was regularly followed, covered a total area of nearly 2 km^2, while the daily ranging distance attained an average of 1300 m.

The basic social unit seems usually to be a harem including an average of ten animals. The different harems, whose home ranges exhibit partial overlap, can be temporarily mixed. The overall density of *C. galeritus* is estimated to be 7.7 to 12.5 individuals/km^2 (Table 2).

Cercopithecus neglectus. The De Brazza monkey is well distributed along the rivers and also occurs on the islands. It occurs essentially in periodically flooded forest, but it is also present in places where the river banks are steep. On the flanks of the M'passa plateau (Fig. 1), troops of De Brazza monkeys colonising the Ivindo banks have home ranges including essentially primary and secondary forests.

The day ranges of the troops do not exceed an average of 400-500 metres. The troops include 3 to 6 members living in small home ranges (0.04 to fairly uniform rate of movement of troop members, added to the cumulative movement of branches and leaves, increases the chance of provoking potential prey to take flight. Consequently, the talapoin is a wide-ranging primate, especially in relation to its small size.

The De Brazza monkey displays a quite opposite strategy. It lives in small troops, in small home ranges, and its daily movements are especially limited. These quiet monkeys always walk slowly and silently, avoiding leaping from branch to branch. They take their food very quietly, staying in a same fruiting tree for more than an hour. The daily diet is not diversified. Between the two or three trees visited each day, the monkeys stay motionless hidden in the foliage. The same tree can be visited daily throughout its fruiting period. For the De Brazza monkey, the strategy of habitat use appears to be very intensive.

More studies are needed to clarify the ecological status of *C. galeritus*. In N.E. Gabon, this species lives in close sympatry with *C. neglectus*; it occurs at the same levels of the flooded forest and its mean diet composition is very similar. The most striking differences are found between the daily movement patterns, the daily range length being three to five times greater for the *galeritus* troops. Thus, the home ranges of one troop of this species may encompass the home ranges of four troops of *C. neglectus*. The pattern of habitat use is hence less intensive for *C. galeritus*.

The very low population density found by Quris (1975) in Gabon for this mangabey subspecies (about 10 ind/km²), compared with the very high density found by Homewood (1975) for a related subspecies, in East Africa (up to 300 ind/km²), may be explained as the result of interspecific competition with *C. neglectus*. Living at the limit of its distribution area in Gabon, *C. galeritus* is also perhaps living at the limits of its adaptation capacities (see Quris, 1976).

The three species described are not the only ones to live in riparian forest, since all the diurnal primates species can be found there. For *C. nictitans*, *C. pogonias*, *C. cephus*, *C. albigena*, *C. guereza*, *M. sphinx* and the great apes, however, the riparian forest constitutes a marginal habitat which is only partially used (certain zones are not accessible to them) and temporarily exploited (especially when certain large trees are covered with fruit).

PRIMATE SPECIES INHABITING THE MATURE RAIN FOREST

The species

One *Colobus*, one *Cercocebus*, and three *Cercopithecus* species are found in mature rain forest and, more rarely, in secondary growth. The first two, the heaviest (Fig. 2), have been largely exterminated by hunters in the most populated regions, and their ecology has not yet been studied. They are nevertheless found in sympatry with the *Cercopithecus sp.*, notably in the mountainous regions of Belinga and Bengooue and near the Ndjaddie and Liboui river (Fig. 1). The mandrill, the gorilla and the chimpanzee are also present, but the ecological preferences of these species remain to be studied in detail.

The present comparison will be based essentially on the three *Cercopithecus* species; namely *C. nictitans*, *C. cephus* and *C. pogonias*.

Fig. 2 indicates the mean body weights of adult males and females. It shows that a continuous range of weights exists when the three species are

considered together. *C. pogonias* and *C. cephus* show a moderate sexual dimorphism for their weights whereas dimorphism is more accentuated in *C. nictitans* (Gautier-Hion, 1975).

Habitat occupation

The main characteristics of the three *Cercopithecus* species is that they
occur significantly more in polyspecific troops than in monospecific ones.
These mixed troops can include either *C. nictitans* + *C. cephus*, or *C. nictitans* + *C. pogonias*, or *C. nictitans* + *C. cephus* + *C. pogonias* (Gautier and
Gautier-Hion, 1969).
The stability of such mixed troops may be lasting. Thus a bispecific
troop including 13 *nictitans* and 13 *pogonias*, which was followed during
three months in the main dry seasnn, was found to be consistently mixed for
more than 97% of the time. The monkeys shared the same daily travel patterns, activity rhythms and sleeping sites. They also occurred simultaneously in the same fruiting trees (Gautier-Hion and Gautier, 1974). The same
bi-specific troop, when followed for a further three months again in the
short dry season, was still found to be constantly mixed (pers. obs.).
Such examples are quite common in Gabon, and the difficulty is to find
one consistently monospecific troop to follow. However, some specific ecological preferences can be stressed.
Both *C. nictitans* and *C. pogonias* preferentially inhabit the mature rain
forest and ocacsionally old secondary growth. *C. cephus* also colonises the
primary forest, where it prefers the densest places, such as natural areas
of tree falls. Nevertheless, this species also frequents secondary forest,
where it may associate with the talapoin monkey with which it approaches
degraded areas close to villages.

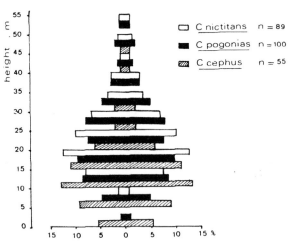

Figure 5. Vertical distribution of C. nictitans, C. pogonias *and* C. cephus
*in the same mature rain forest habitat (n = number of sightings
for the different height classes).*

Fig. 5 shows the vertical distributions of these three species in a
given zone of primary forest. *C. cephus* colonises relatively lower strata

than the other two species: 77% of the observations were made at heights below twenty metres. On the contrary, *C. pogonias* and *C. nictitans* tend to occupy comparable higher levels, 55 and 56% of the observations were made at heights above twenty metres.

The troops of *C. nictitans* contain an average of 20 individuals, those of *C. pogonias* about 15 and those of *C. cephus* about 10. But troop-size is heavily dependent upon hunting. Vestigial troops containing only a few individuals can be observed in unprotected areas, whereas troops containing as many as 28 *nictitans* or 17 *cephus* have been observed in protected areas.

The home range size and the day range length vary according to the number of associated individuals. Large polyspecific units may cover more than eighty hectares. Yet, two facts stand out from the observations of the rare monospecific troops. On the one hand, *C. cephus* monkeys living in monospecific social units tend to have smaller home ranges (mean size about 25 hectares). On the other hand, monospecific troops of *C. pogonias* cover larger home ranges and travel more than polyspecific ones (Gautier, pers. obs.; Table 3.).

The troops of all three species typically include one sexually and socially mature male. But in *C. pogonias* notably, this social leader is frequently assisted in his defensive behaviour by a second sexually mature male.

The population density varies from 20 to 40 ind/km^2, though it is generally higher for *C. nictitans*. If the three species are mixed, the total density can reach about 70 ind/km^2.

A third species seems to share the same ecological preferences for the highest levels of mature rain forest as *C. pogonias* and *C. nictitans*, namely *C. albigena*, a typically arboreal monkey which can be found in mixed troops with either *Cercopithecus* species. This monkey species, however, seems to range over larger areas than the *Cercopithecus*.

The mandrill is partly terrestrial and very often located in the lower strata of the forest. Its large troops (up to 200 or 300 monkeys) live in especially large home ranges (up to 50 km^2: Jouventin, 1975). As for the *guereza*, it seems to live in troops of about ten animals, ranging over relatively small home ranges.

Diet composition

Quantitative study. Contents of 74 stomachs from individuals of the three *Cercopithecus* species have been analysed. Fig. 6 gives their average composition in percentage of the ingested dry weight and also includes the data so far obtained for *C. albigena* (n = 15) and *C. guereza* (n = 2). All the species considered, except for the *guereza* (for which the data are insufficient), are primarily frugivorous. Between the three *Cercopithecus*, a consistent gradient is revealed. For the *Cercopithecus spp.*, a high percentage of the stomach contents analysed, have been collected in the major dry season. The results might be different when collection and analysis of stomachs from all times of year has been completed. Probably, the mean percentage of insects will be increased, and the mean percentage of leaves decreased, but the preliminary results indicate that the gradient between the three species, will not be drastically modified.

If one considers first *C. pogonias*, then *C. cephus* and finally *C. nictitans*, the following points are noted: (1) that the frugivorous tendency decreases (84%, 79%, 61%); (2) that the insectivorous tendency also decreases (14%, 10%, 8%); (3) that the folivorous tendency increases (2%, 8%, 28%).

TABLE 3

Ecological data on the three Cercopithecus spp. of the mature rain forest

SPECIES	VERTICAL DISTRIBUTION	HOME RANGE SIZE, Km2	DAY RANGE LENGTH, m	MEAN GROUP SIZE	POPULATION DENSITY/Km2	GROUP STRUCTURE
Cercopithecus nictitans	middle, higher strata (10-30)	0.550 to 0.800 Km2	± 1500 m	20	20 to 40	one sexually and socially mature ♂
Cercopithecus pogonias	middle, higher strata (10-30)	0.550 to 1.000 Km2	1500 to 2000 m	15	20 to 25	one sexually and socially mature ♂
Cercopithecus cephus	middle strata (5 - 20m)	0.200 to 0.500 Km2	500 to 1000 m	10	20 to 30	one sexually and socially mature ♂

Food niches in sympatric primates   281

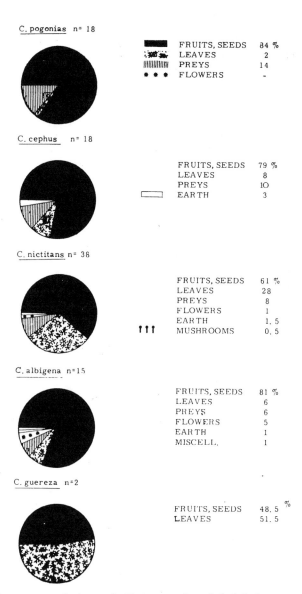

Figure 6. *Mean diet composition of five species inhabiting mature rain forest (in % of total dry weight of stomach contents).*

At one extreme, there is a frugivorous-insectivorous monkey, *C. pogonias* and at the other, a frugivorous-folivorous one, *C. nictitans*. *C. cephus* occupies a middle position and has the least specialised diet.

   C. albigena appears to be a highly frugivorous monkey. Its mean diet composition is relatively close to that of *C. cephus*. It seems particularly fond of flower buds. In September, for instance, flower buds may constitute more than 23% in dry weight of the total bulk of ingested food.

C. guereza, the only colobine present in the study area, is not a strictly folivorous monkey. The analysis of four stomach contents (not all included in Fig. 6) yielded: leaves - 62%; fruit - 37%; insects - 0.1%; earth - 0.6%. The contents of one stomach included nearly 40% of fruit, although collected in June, at a time when fruit-production is limited. This is a high percentage as compared to the average of 55% of fruit eaten during the same month by *C. nictitans* (n = 14).

Jouventin (1975) described the mandrill as a particularly eclectic omnivorous animal, having quite a varied diet. A number of studies on the feeding behaviour of this monkey, however, are necessary before contrasting the "non-specialised" mandrill with other primates species which might be "adapted to a definite stratum or to some particular food items". The various food categories ingested by the mandrill are the same as those found in the stomachs of the other monkey species of Gabon. The single stomach of a mandrill which was analysed contained the following: fruit - 88%; earth - 5.1%; insects - 3.6%; fibres and leaves - 2.7%; lichens - 0,6% (percentage of dry weight). Two intestines examined by Jouventin and myself give similar results, namely a great quantity of fruit and seeds, a few leaves and some animal matter.

For the chimpanzee, the Hladik's results (1973) obtained from direct observations on tame animals reintroduced into the forest, show a frugivorous-folivorous diet, very similar in its global composition to that of *C. nictitans* (fruit - 68%: vs. 61%; leaves - 28%: vs. 28%; animal matter - 4%: vs. 8%).

Qualitative study. The characterisation of diet according to large categories such as "frugivorous" or "folivorous" is obviously an oversimplification. Without dealing here with a detailed qualitative analysis of the nature of the ingested food items, the main features can be given, including some data of riparian forest species.

Fruit. Except for fruit with hard shells, only crushed by the largest monkeys, many ingested fruit species can be found in the diet of most diurnal primates (cf. Gautier-Hion, 1971; Hladik, 1973; Gautier-Hion and Gautier, 1974; Quris, 1975). Further, no main plant species seems to predominate in the diet of one monkey species, as it is often the case in poorer habitats (as for *Colobus badius* or *Cercopithecus sabaeus* in Senegal (Gatinot, 1975; Galat, pers. comm.). According to the season, however, there clearly exist some main plant species which are simultaneously eaten by all the monkey species, and also by many other frugivorous mammals. The most obvious example is found during the main dry season during which many diurnal primate species eat great quantities of arils of Myristicacae. Moreover, some plant species which yield fruit virtually throughout the year (e.g. *Cissus* species), are regularly used by many species.

Leaves. This category includes the leaves and the fibrous plant matter from various sources (petioles, stems, sap-woods or bark). The "real" leaves (essentially the laminae) are eaten by the "real" folivorous monkeys, namely the *guereza*, the chimpanzee and *C. nictitans* (folivorous tendency - that is to say percentage of leaf material by dry weight - > 25%). For the species with a medium folivorous tendency (5 < t > 15%), the plant material eaten comprises both leaves and fibres, which is the case for *C. albigena* and *C. galeritus*, *C. cephus* and *C. neglectus*. Finally, the least folivorous species (t ≤ 2%), namely *C. pogonias* and *M. talapoin*, only eat fibres. Among the species of the riparian forest, some aquatic weeds can also be found in stomach contents.

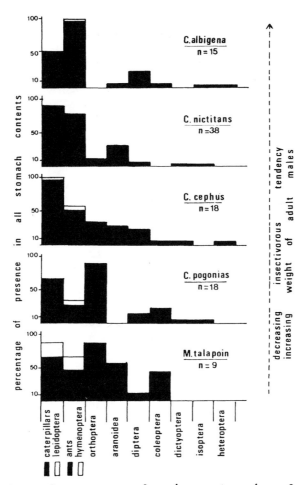

Figure 7. Percentage of occurrence of various categories of prey in the stomach contents of five Cercopithecine species.

Animal matter. Without giving a detailed list of the species, Fig. 7 sums up the tendencies of each monkey species to eat various animal prey, stressing the percentage of occurrence of each category recognised in all stomachs (e.g. 100% of ants for *C. albigena* means that ants were recorded in all of the analysed contents, without taking into account their abundance in the contents of any stomach).

Fig. 7 shows that caterpillars and ants are the main forms of animal prey eaten, followed by orthopterans and spiders. Two tendencies can be recognised: (1) the really insectivorous species (t $\geq$ 10%) such as *M. talapoin*, *C. pogonias* and to a lesser degree *C. cephus* eat both cryptic but mobile prey species which they catch in flight (such as orthopterans) and more sedentary prey which they find on leaves or on bark, such as caterpillars, ants or various larvae; (2) the less insectivorous species eat almost exclusively sedentary prey (notably caterpillars and ants), as is the case for *C. nicti-tans* and *C. albigena*.

Moreover, the data relating to the relative abundance of each category show: (1) that *C. albigena* is almost exclusively an ant-eater (eggs, larvae and adults). Although caterpillars are often found in the stomachs, they are always in small quantities; (2) that *C. nictitans* is primarily a caterpillar eater rather than an ant-eater; (3) that *C. cephus* is less specialised, eating some caterpillars and various larvae, fewer ants, and some orthopterans; (4) that *C. pogonias* is mainly a predator of orthopterans; (5) that *M. tala-poin* eats a large range of prey categories. The talapoin is the only diurnal primate species which regularly catches butterflies and moths and various hymenoptera in addition to ants. It is also a predator of spiders.

It is striking that termites are rarely eaten. They were only once found to be present in large number, in a stomach of *C. albigena*, in the form of larvae mixed with some earth from the termite mound.

Hladik (1973) has described accurately the nature of the prey species eaten by the chimpanzee. Like *C. albigena* and *C. nictitans*, the chimpanzees of Gabon eat a great number of ants but only a few termites. They are also predators of bird nests.

An efficient technique for eating bird eggs has been described for wild talapoin monkeys (Gautier-Hion, 1971b). With its sharp canines, the tala-poin makes a hole in the egg and slowly sucks up the liquid, without ingesting any pieces of shell. A similar method can be observed with *C. pogonias* and *C. cephus*. It leaves hardly any trace which can be easily identified in the stomach, and this obviously explains why no single stomach has revealed the presence of egg. In the cheek-pouch of a freshly-shot male *C. cephus* an egg containing a fledgling was found. One must add that, in captivity, both *C. albigena* and *M. talapoin* show a high carnivorous propensity. Every mouse or bird crossing the monkeys' enclosures is vigorously hunted, killed and eaten. In talapoin monkeys, the prey is usually shared, each group member pulling off a piece of meat.

These specific food choices show a further degree of specificity in terms of the feeding niches. If the three *Cercopithecus* species of mature forest are again compared, one can see: (1) that *C. pogonias* is not only much less 'folivorous' than *C. nictitans* but also scarcely eats 'real' leaves; (2) that *C. nictitans* is not only less insectivorous than *C. pogonias*, but also does not prey on the same insect species (e.g. 10% of orthopterans for *C. nictitans* vs. nearly 90% for *pogonias*); (3) that *C. cephus* again occupies an intermediate position between the other two species, feeding both on leaves and fibres as well as on caterpillars and orthopterans.

Discussion

At first sight, the three *Cercopithecus* species of mature rain forest have a relatively similar way of life. They live in medium-sized troops, within which one male plays the social leader role, in medium-sized home ranges and show a common tendency to form mixed troops. The parallel is especially obvious between *C. pogonias* and *C. nictitans*, which both prefer the higher levels of mature rain forest. These two species can be most easily differentiated on the basis of their food habits. On the contrary, *C. cephus* which occupies a slightly different niche, exploiting lower levels of the forest and colonising more degraded habitats, has a less differentia-ted diet both in terms of its global composition and in terms of its specific food choices.

Nevertheless, these differences are not markedly significant and they are blurred by the very existence of mixed troops which, for months or years, occupy similar areas and gather fruit simultaneously in the same trees. In fact, competition for fruit is not obvious. On the other hand, competition for Arthropods is reduced by different feeding behaviour, one species catching insects on the wing, the other searching on trunks and branches, and the third catching its prey both ways.

These long lasting associations between the three monkey species must be viewed more in terms of co-operation than in terms of competition. The polyspecific social unit, which may possess a supra-specific social organisation (Gautier-Hion and Gautier, 1974), must be considered as an entity, which exploits its environment by means of a complementary strategy. The continuous gradient revealed both in the weights of adult males and females of the three species and in the forest levels occupied, as well as in food habits, provides a good reflection of this complementarity between the three cercopithecines.

In fact, each population seems to benefit from the others. The formation of polyspecific troops, by increasing the number of group members without increasing intraspecific competition, multiplies the numbers of eyes able to catch sight of the predators and can also lead to an enlargement of the feeding area. This is obvious for *C. cephus* which travels significantly less when living in monospecific groups than when associated with other species. Obviously a large area is more heterogeneous than a small one. The same fruiting tree will only be visited every three or four days; the plant species the monkeys are able to eat will be more numerous and the number of individual trees visited per given species higher. In addition, *C. pogonias* troops take advantage of the movements made by all troop members to catch prey which take flight. Accordingly, this species reduces its daily range length (see Gautier-Hion and Gautier, 1974).

One must add that such life in mixed troops is only possible thanks to an interspecific gregarious tendency which is not to be found in *C. neglectus*, for instance.

CONCLUSIONS

(1) A wide-range of different patterns of social organisation can occur among forest-dwelling sympatric species. Thus, among the most terrestrial species, one can find both very large and wide-ranging troops, such as the mandrill, and very small localized ones, such as in the De Brazza monkey. The same is true for the most arboreal species, for instance with *M. talapoin* and *C. cephus*.

(2) A negative correlation is found between the specific body weights and the amount of animal prey ingested (the three most insectivorous species: *M. talapoin, C. pogonias* and *C. cephus* are the three lightest species). An approximate inverse correlation is found for leaf material.

(3) The three species most closely related phylogenetically, *C. nictitans, C. pogonias* and *C. cephus*, which also show the most extensive sympatry do not exhibit striking differences in their diet but only subtle specialisations. Moreover, the work in progress shows that the seasonal variations in their diets may be more important than inter-specific differences.

(4) Although both striking and subtle differences can be found in specific food habits, it seems impossible to relate simply dietary characteristics

to social organisation, or food availability to group size. Such correlations must take into consideration both differences in feeding choice and in the overall strategies displayed. The best example is provided by the quiet *C. neglectus*, whose entire strategy is in keeping with its morphological features (it is a heavy, inactive monkey) and with its behavioral traits (it possesses notably poorly-developed intercommunication signals: Gautier, 1975). Moreover, it retains some primitive characteristics, such as 'freezing' posture in response to the predators and olfactory marking (pers. obs.). Such behavioral patterns are quite well fitted to a way of life in small units, on small home ranges and all contribute to the niche specificity.

(5) No clear correlation can be established between the kind of diets of the sympatric species and their population densities. Precise evaluations of biomasses, based upon limited data, only show: (a) that the most insectivorous species, namely *M. talapoin*, has a slightly smaller biomass than the *Cercopithecus* species (0.6 kg/ha and about 1 kg/ha); (b) that among the three associated *Cercopithecus*, the most folivorous, *C. nictitans*, seems to have the highest biomass (0.8 to 1.1 kg/ha) and the most insectivorous, *C. pogonias*, the smallest one (0.6 to 0.7 kg/ha). In contrast, the two riverine species (*C. neglectus* and *C. galeritus*), which exhibit a similar diet, have quite different biomasses (1 kg/ha and 0.3 kg/ha).

In fact, in Gabon, we do not know whether food availability really is a limiting factor or whether the habitat has attained its carrying capacity, mainly because we cannot evaluate precisely the hunting pressure. Moreover, we cannot speak about competition for fruit, for instance, without taking into consideration the numerous frugivorous sympatric birds and mammal species. Only long-term quantitative studies on the phenology of this highly complex forest and on the seasonal availability of all kinds of food will permit fuller interpretation of such results.

REFERENCES

Gatinot, B.L. (1975). Ph.D. thesis, 3rd cycle. University of Paris 6.
Gautier, J.P. (1975). Ph.D. thesis. Universite de Rennes.
Gautier, J.P. and Gautier-Hion, A. (1969). *Terre et Vie*, 23, 164-201.
Gautier-Hion, A. (1970). *Folia primat.*, 12, 116-141.
Gautier-Hion, A. (1971a). *Terre et Vie*, 25, 427-490.
Gautier-Hion, A. (1971b). *Biol. gabon.*, 7, 295-391.
Gautier-Hion, A. (1973). *In* "Comparative ecology and behaviour of Primates" (R.P. Michael and J.H. Crook, eds), pp. 148-170. Academic Press, London.
Gautier-Hion, A. (1975). *Mammalia*, 39, 365-374.
Gautier-Hion, A. and Gautier, J.P. (1974). *Folia primat.*, 22, 134-177.
Hladik, C.M. (1973). *Terre et Vie*, 27, 343-413.
Hladik, C.M. (1976). *In* "Primate Ecology: studies on feeding and ranging behaviour in lemurs, monkeys and apes" (T.H. Clutton-Brock, ed.). Academic Press, London.
Hladik, A. (1977). *In* "The Ecology of Arboreal Folivores" (G.G. Montgomery, ed.). Smithsonian Institution, Washington.
Homewood, K. (1975). *Oryx.*, 13, 53-59.
Jouventin, P. (1975). *Terre et Vie*, 29, 493-532.
Quris, R. (1975). *Terre et Vie*, 29, 337-398.
Quris, R. (1976). *Terre et Vie*, 2, 193-209.

8

Floristic Composition and Species Richness

Robin L. Chazdon and Julie S. Denslow

> A definitive kind of order exists in the closed forest in spite of the diversity of species.
> —A. Aubréville, *La forêt coloniale* (1938)

The bewildering floristic diversity of tropical rain forests has inspired and challenged botanists for centuries. Could Darwin's "chaos of delight" become transformed into Aubréville's "definitive kind of order"? Following the lead of astute tropical naturalists (see part 1), early twentieth-century botanists began major efforts to describe and understand patterns of plant species richness in tropical forests. Their studies focused on two central areas of inquiry: first, enumerating and comparing species richness within particular areas and, second, examining patterns of floristic composition in relation to environmental variables. Both types of analyses required a field-based knowledge of the identification of plant species, which has greatly advanced since the 1920s.

In this part, we reprint excerpts from four articles that stimulated new lines of research and strongly influenced current ways of thinking about floristic composition and species richness of tropical forests. Aubréville's detailed studies of the closed forests of Côte d'Ivoire ex-

emplify the power of synthesizing ecological and taxonomic perspectives (Aubréville 1933, 1936, 1938). This excerpt from his work (translated into English by Eyre and published in Eyre 1971) summarizes Aubréville's thinking about tropical moist forests. Aubréville (1938) rejected the temperate-based notion of a stable, climax tree community in favor of what Richards (1952) came to call a mosaic or cyclical theory of regeneration (see part 9). In his view, species composition of dominant trees varies spatially as well as temporally, and there is no single permanent equilibrium between local site characteristics and characteristic species. Aubréville's writings gave rise to much debate (Richards 1952; Poore 1968) and stimulated the development of nonequilibrium views of species composition that later strongly influenced ecological thinking (see parts 3 and 9).

In his pioneering synthesis, Richards (1952) posed the question of whether tropical rain forests represent one big floristic association or whether discrete communities can be associ-

Interior of primeval forest on the Amazon. From Bates (1864)

ated with particular soil types or other local site characteristics. The "question of the association" in tropical forests, first raised in the selection reprinted here and elaborated in a later paper (Richards 1963), stimulated a wide range of quantitative analyses of rain forest species composition in relation to environmental variables (Ashton 1964; Jones 1955, 1956; Poore 1963, 1968; Schulz 1960). Ashton (1964) provided the first rigorous evidence that variations in community composition within rain forests of Brunei reflect variations in topography and soil properties. We reprint here two selections from Ashton's pioneering application of ordination techniques in addressing the nature of tropical forest associations in relation to environmental factors.

Following early studies of tropical forest vegetation in British Guiana by Davis and Richards (1934), Black, Dobzhansky, and Pavan (1950) attempted to enumerate the number of tree species above 10 cm dbh in equatorial forests of Brazil. This notable work was continued by Pires, Dobzhansky, and Black (1953) in a study reprinted here. This effort to obtain more robust estimates of the number of tree species in a terra firme forest in Pará, Brazil, was among the first applications of Preston's lognormal distribution (Preston 1948) in tropical forests. Moreover, this study was pioneering in recognizing the significance of rare species for estimating total species richness within a study area. The nature of rarity of tropical tree species is critically important for ecologists, conservationists, and foresters (Ashton 1998; Hubbell and Foster 1986c; Pitman et al. 1999).

These papers provided conceptual and analytical foundations for much of the literature on floristic composition in tropical forests that we review here. Early studies lacked a geographic-scale understanding of species distributions, and were therefore more limited in global perspective. Improvements in transportation, logistics, facilities, and communication, as well as advances in taxonomy and field identification techniques, have added considerably to a global database of species distributions, although we still have limited knowledge. Sadly, further

pursuits of this knowledge are now seriously threatened by the loss of the accessible tropical forest flora and associated biota due to degradation, fragmentation, and conversion to nonforest uses (see part 11). Studies of floristic composition in tropical forests are now as critical to conservation biology as they are to ecology and evolutionary biology.

Floristic Composition and the Concept of the Association in Tropical Forests

Early plant ecologists working in tropical forests faced tremendous challenges due to high species richness and complex vertical structure. At any one time, the majority of trees are not in fruit or flower, rendering species identification difficult. Binoculars are necessary to examine leaf characteristics. Obtaining specimens often requires felling trees, shooting down branches with a gun, or employing human tree climbers. In some cases, specially trained monkeys have also been employed. Added to these logistic problems are methodological difficulties associated with sampling and selection of "representative areas" (Poore 1963). These issues continue to challenge researchers in tropical forests, where low density of many species results in their absence from small sample plots (see below). To demonstrate variation in species composition as a function of environmental variation requires that species abundances vary across an environmental gradient. If many species have low abundance and are poorly sampled because of rarity, documenting spatial variation in abundance and in patterns of species association becomes difficult.

Early studies lacked resources to aid in species identification that characterize many current studies of floristic composition, such as local floras and herbaria. Yet these early investigations clearly revealed that tropical forest regions contained both single-dominant (monodominant) and mixed forest associations. In a detailed account of floristic composition of communities along Moraballi Creek, British Guiana, Davis and Richards (1934) distinguished five main communities; four were dominated by a distinct tree species and one was described as a mixed forest association with many codominant species. Beard (1946) also describes one of these single-dominant associations (dominated by *Mora excelsa*) from Trinidad. A large number of tree species were common to each of the five communities, but with different relative proportions. Davis and Richards (1934) concluded that the species composition within each of these communities is determined by soils and topography, and that the mixed forest occurs on the optimal soil type. Single-species dominance was associated with unfavorable soil characteristics. This theme is developed at great length by Richards (1952).

Following the studies in British Guiana, Richards visited northern Sarawak, where a completely different flora awaited study. Here, he distinguished four types of primary forest communities, two in the lowland areas and two in the montane and submontane regions (Richards 1936). In the lowlands, the mixed forest and heath forest differ markedly in physiognomy and floristic composition. In the mixed forest, the Dipterocarpaceae comprise at least 44 percent of trees that are 16 inches (40.6 cm) in diameter or more. This level of family dominance among canopy trees occurs generally in lowland forest of the west Malesian region (the Sunda Shelf as far east as Borneo), and in Borneo these forests became known as mixed dipterocarp forests (Richards 1952). The heath forest community is associated with bleached sand soils that were thought to cause "physiological xeromorphy" due to mineral deficiencies in the highly acidic soil (see part 10). Similar to the white sand forests observed in Guiana, these heath communities are composed of fewer tree species and show greater dominance of a small number of species than do nearby mixed forests. Richards (1952, 1973) concluded that these parallel patterns of edaphic differentiation are due to effects of similar climates and soils acting on completely different regional floras.

Most studies of mixed tropical forest communities supported Gleason's (1926) view of the individualistic nature of community com-

position, based on studies of temperate plant communities. Aubréville's (1938) descriptions of the dense forest of the Ivory Coast provided the fullest account available of variations in mixed forest floristic composition over a large area. Of an estimated 596 species of large trees in the whole of Ivory Coast, a single hectare contained about forty species (diameter limits were not stated). The dominant species varied from site to site, but together constituted a group of no more than twenty species. Aubréville proposed that the dominant species in any one spot change continually in space and time. Richards (1952) termed this the "mosaic theory" of forest regeneration (see also part 9). In the text reprinted here, Aubréville noted that young individuals of many of the dominant canopy species are locally scarce, a phenomenon also described in detail by Jones (1956), who tested Aubréville's mosaic hypothesis in the Okomu forest reserve in southern Nigeria (see part 9). Aubréville (1938) also conceded that communities may vary as a function of edaphic conditions (see part 10).

Ashton (1964) described his rigorous effort to determine whether mixed dipterocarp forests of Brunei represented a single uniform association or whether species composition varies spatially according to environmental factors, such as soils or topography. In the selections reprinted here, he describes relationships between species composition and environmental gradients in two separate areas, Belalong and Andulau, based on ordinations using the method of Bray and Curtis (1957). In both areas, the primary axis of floristic variation among communities was related to soil moisture, with valley plots clustering together at one end and ridge plots clustering at the other end. Underlying these patterns are narrow, but overlapping ecological ranges of most of the dipterocarp species (Ashton 1964, 49). These findings may reflect, in part, Ashton's selection of topographically homogeneous study plots within ridge crests, hillsides, or valleys and the fact that intermediate areas were not sampled.

Efforts to understand the nature of floristic

associations in tropical wet forests stimulated application of a variety of analytical approaches, following Ashton's lead (Poore 1968; Austin and Greig-Smith 1968). Austin, Ashton, and Greig-Smith (1972) reanalyzed Ashton's Brunei data set using more powerful quantitative methods, and Greig-Smith, Austin, and Whitmore (1967) used quantitative methods to distinguish six floristic types on Kolombangara in the Solomon Islands. Further numerical analyses have been applied to develop classification systems for tropical forest communities (Hall and Swaine 1976) as well as to link patterns of floristic composition with environmental factors and with autecological characteristics of individual tree species (Webb et al. 1967; Williams et al. 1969; also see part 9). Many studies have shown that species distributions are influenced by edaphic factors at the plot or transect scale (e.g., Ashton 1989; Clark, Palmer, and Clark 1999; Hubbell and Foster 1986b; Newbery and Proctor 1984; Svenning 1999; Tuomisto and Ruokolainen 1994), though often quantitatively rather than qualitatively (e.g., Whitmore 1973). In a study of 325 species in a Bornean rain forest, Webb and Peart (2000) examined species associations with habitat variables for seedlings as well as for adult individuals. Their principal component analyses showed that tree species composition among sample plots was strongly associated with topography and soil characteristics. Moreover, 21 of 49 species tested as adults showed significant habitat associations. In contrast, only 5 of 22 species showed significant habitat associations for seedlings (Webb and Peart 2000). Throughout the tropics, landscape-scale and regional patterns of floristic composition are overall determined by biogeographic factors (discussed in part 2), then by catastrophic disturbances (discussed in part 9), followed by topography, including edaphic factors (Baillie et al. 1987; Clark et al. 1995; Clark, Clark, and Read 1998; Duivenvoorden 1996; Kahn and de Castro 1995; Salo et al. 1986; Swaine 1996; Tuomisto et al. 1995; Whitmore 1973, 1974).

The question of what constitutes a "repre-sentative area" or a "representative sample" continues to plague analyses of tropical forest associations. At Pasoh forest in the center of the Malay peninsula, Wong and Whitmore (1970), using plots of 0.4 ha, found no indication that species groups were correlated with soil types. A second study at the western end of Pasoh, using larger plots, revealed correlations between floristic composition and microtopography (Ashton 1976). In Ashton's Brunei study, sample plots of 0.4 ha were sufficiently large to yield meaningful ordination results (Ashton 1964), whereas Poore (1968), working in the Malay Peninsula, found that plots measuring 2–5 ha were needed to contain a representative sample of the common, important species. The size classes of stems included in the sample further influences the appropriate size for representative sample plots. For example, Gentry (1988a) and Clinebell et al. (1995) claim that 0.1 ha plots that include all stems above 2.5 cm dbh represent the floristic composition of the whole forest better than do tree plots including only individuals measuring 10 cm dbh or more. The location and size of study plots and the distance between them can strongly influence the outcome of quantitative analyses. Yet few studies use unbiased sampling techniques to quantify vegetation and edaphic factors and to assess the spatial scale of floristic variation (Clark, Palmer, and Clark 1999).

The controversial issue raised by Richards (1952, 1963) of the nature of tropical forest associations appears to have been resolved for large, geographically heterogeneous regions with pronounced variation in environmental factors, but the application of the concept of the association remains problematic for smaller plots within relatively homogeneous areas, such as 50-ha monitoring plots (Condit 1995). Based on studies in a 50-ha plot on Barro Colorado Island, Panama, Hubbell and Foster (1986a) challenged the view that patterns of species composition in tropical forests are structured by underlying environmental factors. They proposed that, at this scale, chance and history play an important role in structuring vegetation communities (see part 9). In contrast to Ashton's (1964, 1969) view of narrow ecological ranges and specialized tree distributions, Hubbell and Foster (1986a) found that 70 percent of the tropical tree species above 1 cm dbh in their plot are generalists, at least with respect to light environments. The community drift model (Hubbell 1979) predicts that local species composition is determined by random walk processes acting within a regional species pool, rather than niche specialization and competitive exclusion. Based on this model and on the scale of these fairly homogeneous plots, tropical forests are predicted to lack well-defined tree communities. In a comparison of species richness in three 50-ha forest plots, Condit et al. (1996, 1988) suggest that plots in Peninsular Malaysia and on Barro Colorado Island behave as single large communities at drift, as predicted by this null model. Nevertheless, within the 50-ha plot on Barro Colorado Island, species richness is 30–50 percent higher on mesic slopes than on the seasonally drier plateau or the seasonally flooded swamp, suggesting that species composition in this forest may be more influenced by topography and soil properties than by light environments (Hubbell 1998; see also Lieberman et al. 1995).

Global and Regional Patterns of Plant Diversity

Tropical botanists have long sought to understand how the world's tropical forest regions compare in terms of floristic diversity. Richards (1952) compiled the first descriptive set of data on global patterns of tree species richness. The Indo-Malayan rain forest, although smaller than those of tropical America or Africa, was thought to be the richest in plant species. African forest formations were floristically less diverse and more spatially homogeneous. The richest tropical rain forests discovered so far contain more than two hundred species of trees over 10 cm dbh per hectare (which means that every second or third tree is a distinct species). Most of these plots are in Asia (Whitmore 1984b), but a

growing number have been described from South America (Gentry 1988b; Valencia, Balslev, and Paz y Miño 1994; Oliveira and Mori 1999). In the Neotropics, the greatest local (alpha) richness is mostly in western Amazonia close to the Andean foothills (Balslev et al. 1998), but similar richness has recently been found in the central basin near Manaus (Oliveira and Mori 1999). Two 1-ha plots near Iquitos, Peru, contain nearly three hundred species of at least 10 cm dbh (Gentry 1988b, 1992). In Asia the richest forests are in Borneo and adjacent Peninsular Malaysia (Appanah, Gentry, and LaFrankie 1993; Ashton 1977; Whitmore 1984b) and in Africa the most species-rich forests for woody plants are in wetter areas of West Africa and on the eastern slopes of the Congo basin in Central Africa (Gentry 1992). The maximum number of species of trees of 10 cm dbh or more recorded in Africa is 73 species per hectare (Whitmore and Sidiyasa 1986).

Prance (1977) summarized available data on estimated number of plant species throughout the world's tropics. Tropical Africa was estimated to have 30,000 species of flowering plants, tropical Asia 35,000, and tropical America 90,000 (37.5% of the world total). The American tropics were less well known botanically, however, than the other two regions, and this remains true today. The flora of African rain forests is relatively species poor compared with floras of the New World and Asian tropics (Richards 1973), although in a few areas of humid tropical Africa small plots may contain as many tree species of 10 cm dbh or more as do most rain forests in Asia and America (Whitmore 1975; Gentry 1992). Africa is poor in certain plant families that are considered to be characteristic of tropical regions, such as the Arecaceae, Orchidaceae, Lauraceae, Myrtaceae, and Myristicaceae, and has only a handful of bamboo species. Richards (1973) attributed the depauperate African flora partly to extensive human impact. Raven and Axelrod (1974, excerpted in part 2) attributed it to climatic drying, especially during the Pleistocene. When moist-climate floras were forced into refugia during past periods of dry climate (see part 2), there were few wet mountainous refugia in Africa (in contrast to America and Asia) in which mesic elements could persist (Morley 2000). Areas of high species richness and local endemism in humid tropical Africa coincide with putative Pleistocene refugia in regions of upper Guinea, Cameroon, Gabon, central Congo, and eastern Congo (Maley 1987). Major centers of endemism are located within humid tropical Africa (the Guineo-Congolian of White 1979), which has overall 62 percent of species strictly endemic and 29 percent near endemic.

Although trees are the most obvious feature of tropical forests, species in other life forms contribute heavily to their high floristic diversity (Balslev et al. 1998). Whitmore, Peralta, and Brown (1986) found 233 vascular plants on a 100 m^2 (0.01 ha) plot in northeastern Costa Rica. Foster (1990) and Gentry (1990a) found that in Amazonia and Central America up to 50 percent of the plant species at individual sites are herbs and shrubs. Gentry and Dodson (1987a) recorded 365 species in a 1000 m^2 (0.1 ha) plot in western Ecuador. Over a third of the species and almost half of the individual plants were epiphytes. Only 32 species of trees of 10 cm dbh or more were sampled, although the number of tree species in the 0.1-ha plot increases to 117 if seedlings and samplings are included. In another 1-ha study plot in western Ecuador, botanists encountered 175 species of epiphytes (21 percent of the total number of species; Valencia et al. 1994) and 96 species of herbs (12 percent of the total number of species; Poulsen and Balslev 1991).

Condit et al. (1996, 1998) included all woody stems of 1 cm dbh or more in their comparative studies of species richness and species accumulation in three 50-ha plots. Their analysis showed that the diameter limit had little influence on relationships between stem density and species richness in these plots. Total numbers of species were highest in the Pasoh plot (817 species). The dry forest plot at Mudumalai, southern India, had the fewest species (71), whereas the plot on Barro Colorado Island had an intermediate species richness (303 species). Stem density was also highest for Pasoh and lowest for Mudumalai (Condit et al. 1996, 1998).

Species Distributions, Rarity, and Estimation of Species Richness

In one of the first studies of species diversity and population density of trees in Amazonia, Black, Dobzhansky, and Pavan (1950) laid out three 1-ha plots; two in dryland (terra firme) forests and one in flooded (igapó) forest. They found that among trees of at least 10 cm dbh, over one-third of the species were represented by a single individual. They also observed that "the number of species found in a sample depends to a great extent upon the number of individuals classified, and the observed differences in the diversity of species may well be spurious. This emphasizes the necessity of caution in drawing conclusions, on the basis of small samples, regarding the diversity of species in floras, faunas, or ecological associations" (Black, Dobzhansky, and Pavan 1950, 421).

Tropical botanists have long recognized the problems associated with gathering species richness data from small sample plots or transects. But until very recently, most of the floristic data available for tropical forests were taken from single rectangular plots 0.1 to 1 ha in size (Gentry 1982, 1988a; Lang, Knight, and Anderson 1971). Holdridge et al. (1971) used 0.1-ha plots to compare tree species composition among a wide range of Neotropical forest types. In his widely cited review of patterns of Neotropical plant species diversity, Gentry (1982) compared data from 0.1-ha plots in eleven Neotropical plant communities, including lianas, trees, and shrubs above 2.5 cm dbh. These data cannot be closely compared with other studies, however, because Gentry used long, linear plots, 2 m × 50 m in size. Even in large 50-ha forest plots, species area curves for individuals above 1 cm dbh do not reach an asymptote (Condit et al. 1996, Condit et al. 1998). The 50-ha plot at Pasoh captures an estimated 50 percent of the available species found in this forest type (Kochummen, LaFrankie, and Manokaran 1990). Given these difficulties, can we adequately characterize and compare species richness and species composition among different tropical forests?

Pires, Dobzhansky, and Black (1953), in a paper reprinted here, sought to address this question, using data from a 3.5-ha plot near Belém, Brazil. Following Black, Dobzhansky, and Pavan (1950), they fit their species abundance data to Preston's lognormal distribution. Based on these data, they estimated that an additional seventy species that could be expected to occur within the sampled association were absent from the plot. They recognized that it is the rare (and often undetected) species that contribute so greatly to species richness in tropical forest communities. Differences in species richness between the rich forests of northwestern Borneo and the relatively species-poor wet forests of southern Sri Lanka are almost entirely attributable to differences in the number of species occurring at low densities (Ashton 1989). Ashton (1998) echoes this theme when he states, "The variation in the number of species in exceptionally low population densities, especially in members of congeneric species series, is the chief cause of variation in species richness with habitat" (505–6). Rare species form an important component of tropical floras, yet they are poorly sampled in many ecological studies.

Rarity is, indeed, a characteristic feature of tropical forest trees (Wallace 1878; part 1). Yet there are many kinds of rarity, as exemplified by the scheme developed by Rabinowitz (1981), which Pitman et al. (1999) applied to a dataset from twenty-one tree plots in lowland tropical moist forests in the Manu River basin in southeastern Peru. In plots ranging in size from 0.87 to 2.5 ha, all trees of 10 cm dbh or more were identified (when possible) and mapped. The plots spanned four distinct habitat types, classified as terra firme, floodplain, successional, and swamp. They found that that 88 percent of the 829 species and morphospecies occurred at densities below 1/ha and 253 species were repre-

sented by a single individual. Only 15–26 percent of the tree species occurred in a single forest type. Based on these results, Ricklefs (2000) states, "When the abundance of many species averages one individual per hectare, local assemblages of species within hectare plots have little meaning" (84).

Comparative studies examine not only differences in species composition but also differences in total species richness (Condit et al. 1996). Given these serious questions about the comparative value of observed species richness for small plots, how can we better apply the many past and current datasets from tropical forests? One approach is to nest these small plots within larger areas and to conduct analyses at several different spatial scales. Another approach is to estimate total species richness, based on data collected from samples within plots or from transects, as first done by Black, Dobzhansky, and Pavan (1950). According to Colwell and Coddington (1994), however, the lognormal distribution does not fit species abundance data well for many temperate and tropical communities. For three 50-ha forest plots, Condit et al. (1996, 1998) found that Fisher's alpha, a parameter of the log series (Fisher, Corbet, and Williams 1943), provides a stable predictor of tree species richness when the number of stems exceeds two thousand.

Another set of approaches for estimating species richness within designated areas is based on techniques involving extrapolation of species accumulation curves (Colwell and Coddington 1994) or through analyses of species-area relationships. Recently, Plotkin et al. (2000) have developed a new approach to predicting species diversity of stems 1 cm or more in dbh in tropical forests, based on an extended model of the species-area relationship. Their approach predicts diversity within a 50-ha plot with an average error of 3 percent, based on smaller-scale samples (Plotkin et al. 2000). Several nonparametric estimators have also proved useful in species richness estimation for a variety of taxa, including woody plants (Chazdon et al. 1998; Colwell and Coddington 1994; Palmer 1991). Further studies are needed to compare the performance of different species richness estimators throughout the tropics.

Researchers have recently come to realize what Black, Dobzhansky, and Pavan discussed in their pioneering study (1950), that species richness is intimately related to density. Thus, comparisons of species richness among topographic classes, habitats, plots, or regions that differ in overall density may be confounded (Lieberman et al. 1995; Denslow 1995; Chazdon et al. 1998; Condit et al. 1998). Accounting for effects of density on species richness can be done by comparing the number of species within a sample of a constant number of individuals, as demonstrated by studies by Terborgh, Foster, and Nuñez (1996) and Condit et al. (1996, 1998). Alternatively, for plot sizes well below the asymptote of the species area curve, density can be included as a covariate in regression analyses (Clinebell et al. 1995).

Species Richness in Relation to Environmental Gradients

It has long been established that floristic richness is highest near the equator and decreases toward the poles, a pattern consistent with many other biological groups (part 3). Within tropical regions, altitudinal zonation became a major theme of early studies of floristic composition and vegetation classification. Many of these early studies focused on identifying the altitudinal limits of vegetation types, forest physiognomy, and floristic distributions in tropical regions throughout the world (Beard 1944; Grubb et al. 1963; Grubb and Stevens 1985; Grubb and Whitmore 1966; Holdridge et al. 1971; Richards 1936; Steenis 1936; Symington 1943).

Few studies, however, had examined latitudinal and environmental gradients of floristic richness in detail until Alwyn Gentry began compiling data using a standardized sampling technique (Gentry 1982, 1988a). Gentry (1988a) and Clinebell et al. (1995) used a rapid inventory approach at sixty-nine Neotropical localities in ten linear subplots of 2 × 50 m (total area of 0.1 ha), including all stems above 2.5 cm

dbh. Their samples include many saplings, vines, shrubs, and hemiepiphytes, which are typically ignored in forest inventory studies. Annual rainfall and rainfall seasonality were the two most important variables for explaining variation in species richness among the localities; species richness increases with annual rainfall and decreases with the number of months with less than 60 mm precipitation (Clinebell et al. 1995). Givnish (1999) comprehensively reviewed a large literature on the causes of gradients in tropical tree diversity worldwide. The number of woody species in tropical forests generally increases with rainfall, forest stature, soil fertility (after controlling for effects of rainfall), rate of canopy turnover, and time since catastrophic disturbance (Givnish 1999).

Conclusion

The papers reprinted in this part serve as an inspiration for those who hope to advance the state of knowledge of tropical botany and floristics. These studies are key to understanding underlying ecological patterns of species composition and diversity. Comparisons among studies of floristic composition, species richness, and environmental gradients in tropical plant diversity are still hampered by site differences in overall density, size and shape of sampling units, and in size class and life form distributions of vegetation. Only recently have standardized methodologies been applied across a large number of geographic areas, permitting rigorous statistical and taxonomic comparisons. We are far from being able to make strong generalizations, but we have made much progress in describing floristic patterns within particular study areas. High rates of deforestation and fragmentation will limit our ability to decipher these vegetation patterns in the future (see part 11). Even protected areas are vulnerable to effects of climate change on species abundance patterns (Condit, Hubbell, and Foster 1996).

The scope of floristic studies has broadened greatly since the early studies described here, as is evidenced by a recent two-volume compilation on forest biodiversity and monitoring (Dallmeier and Comiskey 1998, 1999). Some tropical forest inventories now include nonwoody life forms, such as vascular epiphytes (Kress 1986, Gentry and Dodson 1987b) and understory herbs (Gentry and Emmons 1987), and standard protocols are being developed for both small and large monitoring plots (Condit 1997, Dallmeier, Kabel, and Rice 1992). The number of field stations, reserves, and monitoring sites has increased substantially throughout the tropics. These factors, combined with the development of extensive taxonomic data bases and local floras, yield optimistic projections for progress in understanding patterns of floristic composition and species richness in tropical forests.

Reprinted Selections

A. Aubréville. 1938. Regeneration patterns in the closed forest of Ivory Coast. In *World Vegetation Types,* edited by S. R. Eyre, 41–55. London: Macmillan, 1971. [A translation by S. R. Eyre from La forêt Coloniale. *Académie des Sciences Coloniales: Annales* 9:126–37.]

P. W. Richards. 1952. Composition of primary rain forest (II). In *The Tropical Rain Forest,* 248–54. Cambridge: Cambridge University Press. Reprinted with the permission of Cambridge University Press

J. M. Pires, T. Dobzhansky, and G. A. Black. 1953. An estimate of the number of species of trees in an Amazonian forest community. *Botanical Gazette* 114:467–477

P. S. Ashton. 1964. Ecological studies in the mixed dipterocarp forests of Brunei State (excerpts). *Oxford Forestry Memoir* 25:37–41, 47–61

2 Regeneration Patterns in the Closed Forest of Ivory Coast

A. AUBRÉVILLE

Translated by S. R. Eyre from 'La Forêt Coloniale', *Académie des Sciences Coloniales: Annales*, IX (Société d'Editions Géographiques, Maritimes et Coloniales, Paris, 1938) 126–37.

DESCRIPTIVE STUDY OF THE COMMUNITIES

A DEFINITE kind of order exists in the closed forest in spite of the diversity of species. Each locality has certain dominant or abundant species, but a statement regarding their relative numbers is only valid for a restricted area. They change very quickly from place to place. In a neighbouring locality a rise in the numbers of new dominants will be apparent while those of the first area are scarcely represented. This is because the gregarious species, with fairly rare exceptions, are not distributed continuously throughout their range. They are distributed throughout the forest as are the spots on the skin of a panther – in groups, outside which they are thinly scattered. So marked is this that, when surveying along a track, one may fail to see certain dominant species of the region because they are grouped outside the particular line being followed. Nevertheless, the longer the line of transect, the greater the chance of observing all the characteristic species of the region. Conversely, if a patch in the form of a long narrow band (a fairly common phenomenon) is traversed longitudinally by the surveyor, he will be tempted to conclude that the species which *appears* to him to be widespread and abundant in the area as a whole is, in fact, growing only within a few feet of the path he has followed.

Quite frequently the species which are abundant or dominant in the forest are fairly few in number. It is because of this that certain phytogeographers, such as Chipp [1], have applied the association concept to the equatorial forest; this is a little surprising in view of the long list of species which compete here for light and space. Moreover, as pointed out by Gaussen [2], the term 'association' is not very appropriate: 'It is not implied that the plants provide each other with any protection whatsoever. Generally speaking they are competitors.' The usual groupings cannot be regarded as having only one or two dominant and abundant species, as a number of cases cited below will show. Within the same floristic region it is impossible, in every locality, to identify, as Chipp has done, two species which characterise the community. In fact the equatorial forest 'association' (to use the convenient term but the one which leads to confusion) is much more complex than this. It is made up of any combination of the gregarious species which are characteristic of a formation. It is possible that one or two of these species appear more frequently as dominants than do the others. It does not follow, however, that they alone characterise the community since they may not be found over wide areas covered by the same formation. But let us return to the rather over-simplified associations of Chipp. One might think that in the formation normally regarded as being coterminous with the *Lophira–Cynometra* association, for example, one is bound to find these two abundant or dominant species everywhere in association with each other. There is, in fact, little likelihood of this. The same association appears in Ivory Coast but does not have any more importance than other associations. It is inevitably associated with 'rain forests' certainly, just as are the *Lophira–Entandrophragma* association, the *Tarrietia–Anopyxis* association and many others; in the same way *Triplochiton–Piptadenia* must be associated with 'deciduous forests'.

In the various parts of the rain forest in the Man region in Ivory Coast, taking only the dominant species, one is able to distinguish the following associations:

1. *Alstonia congensis*
   Bussea occidentalis
   Carapa procera
   Chidlovia sanguinea

2. *Lophira procera*
   Uapaca guineensis
   Chidlovia sanguinea
   Coula edulis
   Carapa procera

3. *Petersia africana*
   Parinarium kerstingii
   Piptadenia africana
   Calpocalyx brevibracteatus

4. *Turreanthus africana*
   Petersia africana
   Chidlovia sanguinea
   Coula edulis

5. *Tarrietia utilis*
   Lophira procera
   Turreanthus africana
   Coula edulis
   Chidlovia sanguinea

6. *Piptadenia africana*
   Tarrietia utilis
   Funtumia africana

Regeneration Patterns in Closed Forest of Ivory Coast   43

7. *Piptadenia africana*
    Ceiba pentandra
    Copaifera ehie
    Petersia africana
    Chidlovia sanguinea
    Bussea occidentalis

8. *Petersia africana*
    Piptadenia africana
    Tarrietia utilis
    Triplochiton scleroxylon
    Bussea occidentalis
    Chidlovia sanguinea

9. *Petersia africana*
    Chidlovia sanguinea

10. *Lophira procera*
    Petersia africana
    Tarrietia utilis
    Piptadenia africana
    Placodiscus boya
    Ochtocosmus africanus, etc.

11. *Petersia africana*
    Piptadenia africana
    Funtumia africana

12. *Petersia africana*
    Chlorophora excelsa
    Chidlovia sanguinea

The following species often recur as dominants: *Lophira procera, Chidlovia sanguinea, Petersia africana, Bussea occidentalis, Tarrietia utilis, Piptadenia africana, Turreanthus africana, Coula edulis, Calpocalyx brevibracteatus* – nine in all. At each observation point there is a different combination of several of them along with one or two other species.

Moreover, to give a more exact impression of the average composition of the plant population, it is necessary to add the following species which are often quite abundant: *Uapaca guineensis, Parkia bicolor, Anopyxis occidentalis, Erythrophleum ivorense, Funtumia africana, Parinarium kerstingii, Octoknema borealis.*

All these species are characteristic of the 'rain forests'. Consequently, the citing of just one association, dominated by two species chosen from amongst the most extensive ones, to represent the Man area, would provide only a very arbitrary picture.

What is said below regarding the Man example could equally well be said about the survey we have made in the different regions of the colony. In the 'rain forests' in the hinterland of Tabou there appear, apart from some of the species already listed, some other dominant ones, such as *Cynometra ananta, Strombosia pustulata, Scytopetalum tieghemii, Pachylobus deliciosus, Dalium aubrevillei, Protomegabaria stapfiana, Calpocalyx aubrevillei, Parkia bicolor, Monopetathus* sp., *Diospyros sanza minika.*

In fact one can form the following impression of the closed forest. Some of the environmental conditions which hold sway over a vast area bring into existence a certain type of forest made up of a large number of species having the same biological requirements. At each point in the forest a particular set of these species dominates, but the composition varies spatially. Out of the total number of species, twenty or so become dominant more frequently than the rest. These twenty, most particularly, characterise the formation.

A census carried out over an area of 210 ha. in the Banco forest reserve in coastal 'rain forest' confirms this point. 5703 trees with a diameter of at least 0·50 m. were counted in this forest management operation. The main species were as follows:

Dominant species		per cent
'Avodiré'[1]	*Turreanthus africana*	18
Red ironwood	*Lophira procera*	10
'Adjouaba'	*Pachylobus deliciosa*	10
Stinkwood tree	*Petersia africana*	7

Fairly abundant species		
'Lo'	*Parkia bicolor*	4·8
'Dabéma'	*Piptadenia africana*	4·5
Oil-bean tree	*Pentaclethra macrophylla*	3·7
Akee apple	*Phialodiscus bancoensis*	3·3
'Melegba'	*Berlinia acuminata*	3·1
African walnut	*Coula edulis*	3·0
'Aramon'	*Parinarium kerstingii*	2·4
'Poé'	*Strombosia pustulata*	2·3
'Bodioa'	*Anopyxis occidentalis*	2·2
Guinea plum	*Parinarium tenuifolium*	2·1

Thus *four dominant species* comprised about 45 per cent of the large tree population, *ten abundant species* formed 33 per cent, and *fifty scattered species* accounted for no more than 22 per cent.

DYNAMIC STUDY OF THE CLOSED FOREST

After man has destroyed the primeval forest in order to cultivate the humus-rich soil, a new forest community soon takes possession of it. The appearance and floristic content of the vegetation are modified. The new community is 'secondary forest', so called by M. Chevalier in contradistinction to the pre-existing virgin forest, which is termed 'primary'. Certain phytogeographers do not approve of these terms,

---

[1] Common names in quotation marks are the original French renderings of native names presented by the author. Where possible English equivalents from F. R. Irvine's *Woody Plants of Ghana* (1961) are given here [Ed.].

doubtless because, for them, the flora and the physiognomy of a plant community are constantly modified by diverse influences until a final stage in stable equilibrium is reached, with maximum biological production preordained for each locality, which they call 'the climax'. Thus, before a plant community reaches its final state, it will pass through numerous intermediate stages. Under the climatic conditions of lower Ivory Coast, the so-called 'secondary' forest is one of these unstable stages, but it is not necessarily the 'second' one. As for the forest communities which appear to be 'primary', they are not necessarily final stages or climaxes. Nevertheless, for practical purposes, and seeing that we do not have any more meaningful expressions, these terms may be accepted as having some meaning. The closed primary forest is a formation of large trees, normally having a hard wood. The total canopy is very dense, direct sunlight does not reach the ground, and a man can walk about freely. Secondary forest originates under conditions which are well understood. It is composed of a particular set of species and generally it changes back only slowly to the primary forest type. When the secondary species are fairly large, they provide only a thin cover (as in the case of the umbrella tree, *Musanga smithii*) beneath which the seeds of primary forest species germinate successfully. Thus, at length, the primary forest is re-established. Doubtless its floristic composition will no longer be that of the pre-existing one destroyed by man, but the physiognomy will become the same as that of a 'primary' forest.

One could reserve the name 'primary forest' for the forest which has never been modified by man. The true virgin forest doubtless exists in Ivory Coast within generally inhabited regions, although it is never possible to be certain that any particular area has not actually been worked over centuries ago. Thus there is no recognisable difference between forests which are incontestably virgin since remote times, and *ancient* forests which are found in regions which were worked over by man a long time ago. They have the same species and the same associations of species.

It is only the forests which have re-formed recently which have a special floristic composition. A number of large trees still survive which are of secondary origin such as the black bark (*Terminalia ivorensis*), 'iroko' (*Chlorophora excelsa*), 'fraké' (*Terminalia altissima*), oil palm (*Elaeis guineensis*), 'Bahé' (*Fagara macrophylla*), silk cotton tree (*Ceiba pentandra*), 'ouochi' (*Albizia zygia*), 'eho' (*Ricinodendron*

46   *A. Aubréville*

africanum), 'loloti' (*Lannea acidissima*) and African tragacanth
(*Sterculia tragacantha*). One must not infer from this that each time
one finds these species in closed forest, this is evidence for former
felling and burning: in the 'rain forests', they are able to invade
into gaps which occur sporadically due, for example, to the falling of
large trees. In the 'deciduous forests', moreover, they are often true
climax species. The oil palm is an exception: it never occurs in virgin
forest. If it is found, this is evidence of former occupation by man.
In fact one never finds young oil palms beneath the cover of old
forest.

It is very easy to study the successive stages in woodland reestablishment on ground which has been cleared by indigenous
cultivators and then abandoned to the wild. It is always the same
species which invade first, the chief ones being as follows. The
umbrella tree (*Musanga smithii*) forms pure, uniform stands. Representatives of the Euphorbiaceae are numerous, there being several
spiny species of *Macaranga*, the 'lié' (*Phyllanthus africanum*), the
beard tree (*Tetrorchidium didymostemon*) and the 'tougbi' (*Bridelia
micrantha*). The Leguminosae are represented by two species of
Albizia, the 'bangbaye' and the 'ouochi' (*Albizia sassa* and *A. zygia*).
Some other abundant species are as follows:

Ulmaceae:	'adaschia' (*Trema guineensis*)
Hypericaceae:	'ouombé' (*Haronga paniculata*)
Compositae:	'iaonvi-poupouia' (two species of *Vernonia*)
Loganiaceae:	cabbage palm (*Anthocleista nobilis*) and *Gaertnera paniculata*
Verbenaceae:	several species of *Vitex* and *Premna hispida*
Rutaceae:	several species of *Fagara*
Apocynaceae:	'déchavi' (*Rauwolfia vomitoria*), some species of *Conopharyngia* and the two species of *Funtumia* (*F. elastica* and *F. africana*)
Rubiaceae:	some *Canthium*, *Grumilia*, etc.
Moraceae:	some *Ficus*, African bread fruit (*Treculia africana* and some *Myrianthus*
Myristicaceae:	African nutmeg (*Pycanthus kombo*)
Anacardiaceae:	'loloti' (*Lannea acidissima*)
Combretaceae:	black bark (*Terminalia ivorensis*)

Subsequently, other species make their appearance in the shade of
the first ones. They vary very much from place to place, coming as
they do from neighbouring communities.

It is more difficult to study changes over a period of time in the different forest successions which make up an old forest of the 'primary' type. The species of secondary scrub have a rapid rate of growth; in some months, in some years, one can observe the development of this scrub very well, but the situation is different in the high forest. Chipp has initiated investigations into this kind of situation in the forest of the Gold Coast [1]. He has recognised the *Lophira–Cynometra* as a final optimum stage or 'climax' in the thick forest. Neighbouring stages he has correlated with slightly different environmental conditions and regarded as pre-climaxes: *Lophira–Entandrophragma*, *Entandrophragma–Khaya* and *Triplochiton–Piptadenia*. According to him the *Anopyxis–Tarrietia* and *Chlorophora–Landolphia* associations only represent temporary stages, though they are sufficiently stable to persist for a very long period.

The point already made in the foregoing descriptive study of communities regarding these 'climax' associations can be repeated here. They certainly correspond very closely to apparently stable forms in the forest, but in our opinion this view of the facts is oversimplified since a large number of other combinations of species could equally well be regarded as the climax. The climax or pre-climax communities *Lophira–Entandrophragma* and *Anopyxis–Tarrietia* are to us merely selected examples, more theoretical than real, from the climax of the 'rain forest' formation. Similarly the climax associations *Triplochiton–Piptadenia* and *Chlorophora–Landolphia* are selected examples from the corresponding climax 'deciduous forest'. The pre-climax *Entandrophragma–Khaya* may represent transition types between 'rain forests' and 'deciduous forests'.

In real terms, all those groupings of dominant species from which examples have been cited with regard to our surveys in the Man region are climaxes. The 'rain forest' or the 'deciduous forest' are final forms in stable equilibrium with environmental conditions and they possess very numerous climaxes (any combination whatsoever out of a large number of abundant species in the formation).

Moreover, is it not agreed that the term 'climax' should be applied strictly to those groupings of dominant species which characterise 'synecies' in the closed forest (to use the vocabulary of the phytosociologist)? The communities under discussion must be final, stable 'synecies', unless it can be demonstrated that they tend to become more and more homogeneous and ultimately to be reduced to only a few climax types (as Chipp's thesis would suggest). In fact they do not persist in the same condition, and it is possible that *none of them* can be considered to be the last rung of the ladder.

Not only do the synecies vary spatially (in the ways that we have shown), they also do so in time without ever culminating in a definite climax. Before presenting some facts which support our hypothesis, it is relevant to note that if, within a virgin forest of considerable extent but with identical environmental conditions (one can still find this despite the fact that today the remains of it are more and more exploited by the natives), the 'synecies' develop towards a single climax, it seems likely that one ought to be able to demonstrate a certain homogeneity of population. In fact none is to be found: the population make-up varies just as capriciously as in forests where one has reason to suspect the former influence of man – just as much as one might expect in forests which were still seeking their final point of equilibrium.

Let us consider a few facts. One can frequently find in the primary forests (possibly virgin) that there is a great difference between the species-composition of the adult tree population and that of the developing one which is destined to replace it. Often an abundant species in the community is not regenerating in the undergrowth. The natives express this situation by saying that these trees 'never make little ones'. Sometimes in fact our surveyors had difficulty in finding young individuals of a species in order to fell them; we only encountered large individuals from which it was impossible to collect herbarium specimens. I remember in particular in the vicinity of Abengourou, having encountered for the first time a community of a very large tree with a very hard wood – the asamela (*Afrormosia elata*) – we searched for a long time, without any success, for a young tree of this species so that we could cut it down easily. We were forced to resign ourselves to felling a large tree. The natives of that place maintained that the tree 'did not make little ones'. On the other hand one finds areas invaded by seedlings and young plants of species of large trees which are quite absent from the upper layers of the forest.

We have also the example from the forest reserve of Massa Mé where we formerly carried out a census over an area of about 1·4 ha. in the interior of untouched primeval forest, on a stony, laterite soil. The forest is very old, the canopy dense, the soil unmodified and there are few lianes. Above all, the highest stratum is composed of very thick, widely-spaced trees – the criterion for a very ancient forest.

All the trees having a diameter of 5 cm. or more were counted, as well as all the young individuals belonging to some selected species. The inventory is shown in Table 2.1.

The species-composition on this area, which was taken at random in the forest, is very varied, since seventy-four different species were found in it. It is immediately noticeable how the species at the head of the list, which form the upper stratum, are poorly represented in the lowest stratum and in the undergrowth. Among the very large trees, the 'dabéma' (*Piptadenia africana*) predominates. The impression which this species gives in reality is more striking than might be thought from a mere reading of the figures, for the vast, flattened crowns of the 'dabémas', with their large aerial spread and conspicuous buttresses, lead surveyors to believe that they have found a considerable population of them. Nevertheless, in the future, the 'dabéma' will almost disappear from this patch of land since there are only two saplings for replacement. The stinkwood tree (*Petersia africana*) will doubtless hold its own but the following very large species will disappear completely: African elemi (*Canarium sweinfurthii*), 'lo' (*Parkia bicolor*) and Guinea plum (*Parinarium tenuifolium*).

What will the future population of large trees be, if we imagine that all the present saplings of 10 to 20 cm. diameter will one day be competing for the light? In Table 2.1, all the names of species which are capable of attaining very large size are given in capitals. It is obvious that the struggle will be severe. If certain species now occupying the forest canopy are about to decline, a large number of others are ready to replace them. At the end of the list it can be seen that very large species are represented, each by a single pole. Consequently they must have established themselves here quite recently. These species are: the African mammy apple (*Mammea africana*), the red ironwood (*Lophira procera*), the bark-cloth tree (*Antiaris welwitschii*), the sasswood tree (*Erythrophleum ivorense*) and the 'bodioa' (*Anopyxis occidentalis*). It is impossible to have any idea as to which will be the future dominants, but it is clear that plenty of combinations are possible and that the advance towards a climax (if such a thing can be visualised for equatorial formations) is a very indirect one.

The inventory of young plants of the abundant species is equally interesting, since it is established that species such as the 'niangon' (*Tarrietia utilis*), the scented guarea (*Guarea cedrata*) and the 'avodiré'

TABLE 2.1

Systematic name	Family	Seedlings	Metres											
			0·1	0·2	0·3	0·4	0·5	0·6	0·7	0·8	0·9	1·0	1·2	1·5
PIPTADENIA AFRICANA	Leg.	–	1	1	1	–	1	1	–	1	–	1	1	2
PETERSIA AFRICANA	Leg.	–	4	3	2	1	1	2	–	1	–	1	–	–
KHAYA IVORENSIS	Mel.	12	1	–	–	1	–	1	–	1	–	–	1	–
CANARIUM SWEINFURTHII	Bur.	–	–	–	–	–	–	1	–	–	–	–	–	–
KLAINEDOXA GABONENSIS	Irv.	–	–	–	–	1	–	1	–	1	–	–	1	–
PARKIA BICOLOR	Leg.	–	–	–	–	–	–	1	–	–	–	–	–	–
PARINARIUM TENUIFOLIUM	Ros.	–	–	–	–	–	1	1	–	–	–	–	1	–
Pachylobus deliciosa	Bur.	–	46	37	11	2	1	–	–	–	–	–	1	–
Funtumia africana	Apoc.	–	3	2	2	–	–	1	–	–	–	–	1	–
Diospyros sanza minika	Eb.	–	45	27	2	2	1	1	–	–	–	–	–	–
STROMBOSIA PUSTULATA	Olac.	–	43	13	4	2	–	–	–	–	–	–	–	–
SCOTTELIA CORIACEA	Flac.	–	15	7	3	2	2	–	–	–	–	–	–	–
Monodora myristica	Anon.	–	3	6	3	2	–	–	–	–	–	–	–	–
PARINARIUM KERSTINGII	Ros.	–	2	4	2	1	2	–	–	–	–	–	–	–
HANNOA KLAINEANA	Sim.	–	16	6	2	–	–	–	–	–	–	–	–	–
Allanblackia parviflora	Gutt.	–	15	3	3	1	–	–	–	–	–	–	–	–
Scythopetalum tieghemii	Scyt.	–	3	3	1	4	–	–	–	–	–	–	–	–
Calpocalyx brevibracteatus	Leg.	–	16	5	2	2	–	–	–	–	–	–	–	–
Cola maclaudii	Sterc.	–	3	6	1	–	–	–	–	–	–	–	–	–
DANIELLIA Aff. THURIFERA	Leg.	–	3	2	1	1	2	–	–	–	–	–	–	–
Protomegabaria stapfiana	Euph.	–	5	3	1	2	–	–	–	–	–	–	–	–
Trichoscypha arborea	Anac.	–	2	5	–	–	–	–	–	–	–	–	–	–
Panda oleosa	Pand.	–	–	3	–	2	–	–	–	–	–	–	–	–
Cola nitida	Sterc.	–	6	5	–	–	–	–	–	–	–	–	–	–
IRVINGIA GABONENSIS	Irv.	–	2	3	1	1	–	–	–	–	–	–	–	–

Species	Family						
ENTANDROPHRAGMA ANGOLENSE	Mel.	3	3	2	2	–	–
Diospyros kamerunensis	Eb.	–	22	4	1	–	–
GUAREA CEDRATA	Mel.	7	7	2	1	–	–
TARRIETIA UTILIS	Sterc.	53	6	2	1	–	–
AMPHIMAS PTEROCARPOIDES	Leg.	–	6	2	–	1	–
PHIALODISCUS PLURIJUGATUS	Sapi.	–	2	2	1	–	–
Baphia pubescens	Leg.	–	10	3	–	–	–
Enantia polycarpa	Anon.	–	3	3	–	–	–
Isolona campanulata	Anon.	–	5	3	–	–	–
Aporrhiza rugosa	Sapi.	–	3	3	–	–	–
ENTANDROPHRAGMA CYLINDRICUM	Mel.	1	–	2	–	–	–
TURREANTHUS AFRICANA	Mel.	48	4	–	1	1	–
AFZELIA BELLA	Leg.		3	–	2	1	
Albizzia zygia	Leg.		1	2	–		
Trichilia thompsonii	Mel.		1	1	1		
Coula edulis	Olac.		1	2			
Pleiocarpa mutica	Apoc.		7	2			
Vitex micrantha	Verb.		3	2			
Garcinia polyantha	Gutt.		4	2			
MACROLOBIUM CHRYSOPHYLLOIDES	Leg.		3	3	1		
Discoglypremna caloneura	Euph.		5	1			
Ricinodendron africanum	Euph.		–	1			
Tylostemon mannii	Laur.		2	1			
Trichilia heudelotii	Mel.		2	1			

TABLE 2·1—cont.

Systematic name	Family	Seedlings	Metres				
			0·1	0·2	0·3	0·4	0·5
Lannea acidissima	Anac.		–	–	–	–	1
Octoknema borealis	Oct.			1			
Xylopia elliotii	Anon.		3	1			
Pycnanthus kombo	Myr.		4	–		1	
Cola mirabilis	Sterc.		37	1	–		
Myrianthus arboreus	Mor.		12	–	1		
Conopharyngia durissima	Apoc.		8	1			
Phyllanthus discoideus	Euph.		2	1			
Bridelia micrantha	Euph.		–	1			
Napoleona sp.	Lecy.		9				
Omphalocarpum sp.	Sapi.		5				
Fagara macrophylla	Rut.		4				
Uapaca guineensis	Euph.		3				
MAMMEA AFRICANA	Gutt.		1				
LOPHIRA PROCERA (ALATA)	Och.		1				
ANTIARIS WELWITSCHII	Mor.		1				
ERYTHROPHLEUM IVORENSE	Leg.		1				
ANOPYXIS OCCIDENTALIS	Rhiz.		1				
Anthocleistha nobilis	Log.		1				
Scaphopetalum amoenum	Sterc.		5				
Microdesmis puberula	Euph.		3				
Baphia nitida	Leg.		3				
Carapa procera	Mel.		1				
Randia genipaeflora	Rub.		1				
CHLOROPHORA EXCELSA	Mor.	1	–				

(*Turreanthus africana*), although they have no seed parents either in the area concerned or in the immediate vicinity, seem to invade the undergrowth. Their arrival is recent.

Such examples of detailed surveys are interesting but, unfortunately, rare. In order to draw up such an inventory of the forest, it is necessary to have at one's disposal several excellent native surveyors. Such surveys would demonstrate, without doubt, that there is not always a close correspondence between the actual population of dominant species and that which is waiting in the undergrowth to replace it. They would direct attention to the confusion that exists between the static view of the plant association in the equatorial forest and the dynamic one of the climax. In the area that we have surveyed, the traveller sees, as we have said, a community characterised by *Piptadenia africana*. This is a false impression: the only species which are really in possession of the soil and which appear to have a firm hold are found in the lower levels of the forest. Here these are the 'adjouaba' (*Pachylobus deliciosa*), the flint bark (*Diospyros sanza minika*), the 'poé' (*Strombosia pustulata*), the odoko (*Scottelia coriacea*) and perhaps the stinkwood tree (*Petersia africana*).

Chipp has cited the red ironwood (*Lophira procera*) as a typical species of the climax in these forests of warm and very humid lands – formations which have a dense canopy and which epitomise the maximum development of a vegetation community. Now we have often observed – without, unfortunately, being able to make a detailed count – that beneath very old high forest in which the red ironwood dominated, one found few young plants of this species. There is nothing surprising in this if one knows about the light-demanding propensities of *Lophira procera*. It makes only a sorry rate of growth beneath dense shade, whereas it grows luxuriantly and rapidly in full sunlight. The red ironwood invades secondary scrub, roadsides and river banks without difficulty, indeed everywhere where it finds a little sunlight. Its fruits are winged and its colonising ability is great. But how could such a species be a typical element in a climax of dense, dark 'rain forest'?

Again, let us compare two species of large tree as seen from a census taken from management fellings in 80 ha. of primary forest in the Banco reserve (Table 2.2). In the series, it is quite normal to find a progressive decrease in the numbers of African walnut (*Lovea klaineana*) as diameter increases. The small number of large trees,

TABLE 2.2

	Metres													
	0·05	0·10	0·20	0·30	0·40	0·50	0·60	0·70	0·80	0·90	1·00	1·10	1·20	1·30
African walnut (*Lovea klaineana*)	199	47	28	12	8	5	4	3	1	1				
'Dabéma' (*Piptadenia africana*)	3	16	27	32	38	45	44	25	27	24	21	6	6	1

those which have passed the sapling stage, indicates that this species only established itself in the community a short time ago and that it is tending to occupy a more and more important position. On the other hand, one cannot but be astonished at the large number of old 'dabémas' (*Piptadenia africana*) in comparison to the scarcity of young trees. Is one not compelled to recognise on the one hand a rapidly expanding species and, on the other, one which is now dominant but which is going to decline?

M. Brillet, Inspecteur des Forêts in Indo-China, has cited [3] the very interesting case of the 'lim' (*Erythrophleum fordii*), a beautiful species in Tonkin. In the forests where old 'lims' are abundant one would find only very few seedlings of this species around seed parents – in most cases none at all. On the other hand, elsewhere one would find pure stands of 'lim' composed of *poles* of the same age.

REFERENCES

[1] CHIPP, T. F. (1927) *The Gold Coast Forest: A Study in Synecology.*
[2] GAUSSEN, HENRI (1933) *Géographie des Plantes.*
[3] BRILLET, M. (1927) *Les Annales Forestières de l'Indochine.*

The Tropical Rain Forest
P. W. Richards

CHAPTER 11

COMPOSITION OF PRIMARY RAIN FOREST (II)

Most Tropical Rain forests, as has already been stated, are of mixed composition, though the Rain forest does not always consist, as earlier observers supposed, of associations without single dominants. Though primary communities with single dominants occur, as we shall see, in all the main geographical divisions of the rain forest, British Guiana appears to be exceptional both in the number of single-dominant communities which occur and in the large area which they cover. Even at Moraballi Creek the Mixed forest is the most widely distributed forest type and probably occupies a larger proportion of the ground than any other community. In some parts of the tropics, for instance throughout West Africa, single-dominant climax primary communities seem to be absent, or nearly so, and all the primary forest on well-drained sites appears to form a single, very extensive mixed community, which fluctuates in composition from place to place, but is almost impossible to separate into more than one distinct association. The Mixed forests of British Guiana and Borneo are thus typical Rain forests in that they show scarcely any tendency towards single-species dominance.

COMPOSITION OF MIXED RAIN FOREST

Composition in small samples

The floristic composition of two sample plots of typical Mixed forest was described in some detail in the last chapter. In Table 28 the data for these plots are compared with those for some other small samples of mixed communities and in Table 25 (Chapter 10) figures were given for the number of species in sample areas of Mixed forest in various localities. From both tables several interesting facts emerge, but the significance of all of them is not at present easy to estimate. It is evident from Table 28 that even in widely separated regions Mixed Rain forest shows considerable uniformity in the general features of its composition. The facts also suggest that the Mixed forest of different geographical regions shows small local peculiarities in its composition, though from a small number of samples it would be unwise to draw very definite conclusions.

The number of species per unit area shows a considerable range, especially among trees of the smaller diameter classes. In any one district the number is fairly constant, the differences between different districts probably depending mainly on the floristic richness of the region as a whole. This, as was suggested earlier, seems to depend on historical factors rather than on the environment at the present day. Only for the West African forest is a considerable number of figures for species per unit area available; in addition to the data given in the table, other figures have been published by Jentsch (1911), Mildbraed (1930*a*, 1930*b*, 1933*b*) and Richards (1939). It is uncertain whether the table covers the whole range of variation in floristic richness. Jentsch's plots in the Cameroons, which are not directly comparable with the author's figures, are possibly even richer than the Mt Dulit Mixed forest plot; on the other hand, some small areas of Rain forest may have fewer species per unit area than the relatively poor Mauritius plot (the poverty of which may be due to its situation on an oceanic island).

TABLE 28. *Composition of Mixed Tropical Rain forest*

			Africa		
Locality	Asia Mt Dulit, Sarawak	S. America Moraballi Creek, Brit. Guiana	Okomu Forest Reserve, Nigeria	Massa Mé Forest Reserve, Ivory Coast	Crown land Macabé, Mauritius (alt. 550 m.)
Source of data	Richards (1936)	Davis & Richards (1933–4)	Richards (1939)	Aubréville (1938)	Vaughan & Wiehe (1941)
Size of plot in hectares (approx.)	1·5	1·5	1·5	*c.* 1·4	1·0
No. of trees per hectare:					
4 in. (10 cm.) and over	—	432	390	530	1710
8 in. (20 cm.) and over	184	232	223	214	331
16 in. (41 cm.) and over	44	60	47	39*	60
No. of species:					
4 in. (10 cm.) and over	—	91	70	74	52
8 in. (20 cm.) and over	98	55	51	58	33
16 in. (41 cm.) and over	32	32	31	*c.* 23	11
Ratio individual/species:					
Species 4 in. (10 cm.) and over	—	7·1	8·3	10·0	32·9
Species 8 in. (20 cm.) and over	2·7	6·0	6·2	5·2	10·0
Species 16 in. (41 cm.) and over	1·9	2·8	2·3	2·4	5·5
Percentage of most abundant species: 4 in. (10 cm.) and over	—	*Pentaclethra macroloba* 11	*Strombosia retivenia* 30	*Pachylobus deliciosus* 15	*Eugenia glomerata* 18
8 in. (20 cm.) and over	'Medang lit' 5	*Pentaclethra macroloba* 13	*Strombosia retivenia* 35	*Pachylobus deliciosus* 17	*Eugenia glomerata* 19
16 in. (41 cm.) and over	'Marakah batu' 'Meranti daging' each {10 {10	*Eschweilera sagotiana* 16	*Pausinystalia* sp. (or spp.) 14 (or less)	*Piptadenia africana* 13	*Mimusops maxima* 25

* Figure for trees 40 cm. diam. and over.

The number of species will of course depend partly on the number of individuals per unit area. This may vary within wide limits and, as the Moraballi Creek communities show, is related to soil and other conditions of the environment. In the mixed Evergreen Seasonal forest of Trinidad the number of trees per acre in the wetter districts is nearly double that in the drier (Beard, 1946*b*, p. 63).

The ratio of individuals/species has been termed the *Mischungsquotient* by Mildbraed (1930a), who considers it a useful means of characterizing different types of rain-forest community. Mildbraed, however, overlooks the obvious fact that while the number of individuals varies linearly with the size of sample plot, the number of species does not (see species/area curves, Fig. 34). The *Mischungsquotient* can therefore only be used for comparing plots of the same size. In the examples in Table 28, if we omit the Mauritius plot which has an abnormally large number of individuals per unit area and a small number of species, its range of variation is not great. On all the plots the average number of individuals per species is greater for trees of the smaller diameter-classes than for the larger.

TABLE 29. *Number of species represented by* 1, 2, 3, ... *individuals in Mixed and Single-dominant Rain forests*

Number of individuals

	1	1–5	1–10	11–20	21–30	31–40	41–50	51–60	61–70	71–80	81–90	91–100	Over 100
Mixed forests:													
1. Moraballi Creek, British Guiana	21	68	79	4	4	1	2	—	1	1	—	—	—
2. Okomu Forest Reserve, Nigeria	23	48	58	7	2	1	—	—	1	—	—	—	1
3. Mt Dulit, Borneo*	41	85	97	1	—	—	—	—	—	—	—	—	—
Single-dominant forests (or associations with tendency to single-species dominance):													
4. Mora (*Mora excelsa*) forest, Moraballi Creek, British Guiana	22	41	47	9	1	2	—	—	—	—	—	—	1
5. Morabukea (*Mora gonggrijpii*) forest, same loc.	25	49	61	3	3	1	—	—	—	—	—	—	1
6. Greenheart (*Ocotea rodiaei*) forest, same loc.	31	63	78	6	—	3	2	2	—	2	—	—	—
7. Wallaba (*Eperua falcata*) forest, same loc.	14	45	55	11	4	—	1	—	—	—	—	—	3
8. Freshwater Swamp forest, Shasha Forest Reserve, Nigeria	11	19	24	6	2	3	—	—	—	1	—	—	1
9. Heath forest, Koyan Valley, Borneo*	18	39	47	7	—	—	2	—	—	—	—	—	—
10. Heath forest, Marudi, Borneo*	13	42	49	3	1	2	1	—	—	—	—	—	—
11. Ironwood (*Cynometra alexandri*) forest, Budongo, Uganda	3	3	5	2	—	—	—	1	1	—	—	—	2

* For trees 8 in. (20 cm.) diameter and over (other data for trees 4 in. (10 cm.) and over). 1–10 from Davis & Richards (1933–4), Richards (1936, 1939); 11 from Eggeling (1947).

The percentage of the most abundant species shows a number of features which are possibly significant. On all the plots the most abundant species in the diameter class '4 in. and over' is different from that in the class '16 in. and over'. Thus the species which approaches nearest to dominance among the larger trees does not form the largest proportion among the smaller. Each stratum probably has a different 'most abundant' species. Among the larger trees (16 in. and over) no one species forms more than about one-sixth of the stand, except in the Mauritius forest where one species forms about one-quarter. On three of the plots in the table the most abundant species in the '4 in. and over' and '8 in. and over' classes forms a *smaller* proportion of its class than the most abundant species in the '16 in. and over' class; in other words, there is even less tendency towards single-species dominance among the lower strata of the forest than among the upper. In the two West African plots, of which the opposite is true, the upper strata may have been artificially depleted by felling.

The 'mixed' nature of these forests may also be expressed in another way, by stating the number of species in each plot represented by 1, 2, 3, ... individuals. The results for several Mixed forest plots (and for comparison some plots of single-dominant communities) are given in Table 29. It will be observed that in Rain forests of all types the great majority of the species are represented by very few individuals. In both Mixed and Single-dominant forests at least half the species present are represented by five individuals or fewer on a 400 × 400 ft. plot (equivalent to from less than 1 % to about 2 % of the stand, depending on the number of individuals per unit area) and considerably more than half by ten individuals or less. In the Mt Dulit Mixed forest as many as eighty-five species, out of a total of ninety-eight (8 in. diam. and over) are represented by five individuals or fewer. In Mixed forest it is rare for any species to be represented by more than 100 individuals (the Mixed plot at Okomu Forest Reserve, Nigeria, is exceptional in this respect), but in Single-dominant forests several species (three in the case of the Guiana Wallaba forest) reach this level of frequency.

Variations in Mixed forest over large areas

So far only small uniform samples of Mixed forest have been discussed; it is also necessary to consider how the composition varies over much larger areas. Does the Mixed forest over an extensive area or a whole geographical region vary in composition in a regular manner or does the composition merely fluctuate fortuitously from place to place? If regular changes in composition exist, can different mixed associations dependent on variations of soil or climate be recognized within any one region? Are the variations in the composition of the tree-layers correlated with variations in the composition of the undergrowth (shrub- and herb-layers)? These questions have been answered in various ways, depending on different authors' conceptions of the nature of an association.

The evidence is at present insufficient for a definite answer, but some of the data deserve consideration.

Meijer Drees (1938) compared statistically the composition of small sample plots of 'high forest' (Mixed Rain forest) in the Netherlands Indies and concluded that only one association was present. In the lowland rain forest of Trinidad (Evergreen Seasonal forest of Beard) Marshall (1934) recognizes three 'associations': the *Carapa guianensis-Eschweilera subglandulosa* association, the *Mora excelsa* association and the *Carapa guianensis-Licania biglandulosa* association. In the first of these he distinguishes four 'subdivisions' of different composition, each occurring under slightly different conditions of soil and topography. Marshall's *Mora* 'association' is a single-dominant type and is here regarded as a consociation. The forest communities of Trinidad have been reclassified by Beard (1946*b*), who treats all the Evergreen Seasonal forest as a single *Carapa-Eschweilera* association with four 'faciations'. All Marshall's 'associations' and 'subdivisions', including the single-dominant *Mora* community, are regarded by Beard as faciations.

The 'closed forest' of the Gold Coast is considered by Chipp (1927) to form several communities: a *Cynometra-Lophira* association, and *Lophira-Entandrophragma*, *Entandrophragma-Khaya* and *Triplochiton-Piptadenia* 'pre-climaxes'. The last is equivalent to what is usually termed Mixed Deciduous forest (see Chapter 15) and the application to it of the term 'pre-climax' is open to criticism. The other communities correspond to the Mixed Rain forest of Nigeria and the Ivory Coast, but it should be noted that the species after which they are named are not the only or even the chief, dominants; they are merely abundant A story species selected more or less arbitrarily.

Chipp's concept of the association has been criticized by Aubréville (1938), who holds that no true associations are distinguishable in the Mixed Rain forest of West Africa. Before considering Aubréville's criticisms, it will be useful to summarize his own description of the composition of the *forêt dense* of the Ivory Coast, which is contiguous to that of the Gold Coast. This is the fullest account available of the variations in composition of Mixed forest over a large area.

Aubréville shows, first of all, that the individual tree species composing the rain forest have several different types of distribution. Many, e.g. *Lophira procera*, are found more or less throughout the rain-forest area; others are much more local. Some are limited to a single compact area, which may be comparatively large, as in *Chidlovia sanguinea*, or only a few square kilometres in extent, as in *Stemonocoleus micranthus*. Others again have discontinuous areas, e.g. *Entandrophragma utile*. The causes of these puzzling differences of distribution in what was probably until recently a continuous and apparently uniform tract of forest are obscure and probably historical. (A theory to account for the rather similar problems of distribution in the Guiana rain forest has been put forward by Davis (1941).)

Because of these differences in the distribution of its species, the forest must necessarily differ in composition from place to place. Though there are estimated to be some 596 species of large trees in the forest of the whole of the Ivory Coast, the number in any one locality is much smaller. On a single hectare there are about forty (diameter limits not stated) and on a slightly larger homogeneous area about seventy.[1] Each locality has a characteristic assemblage of abundant species, which do not exceed twenty in number. Often the population consists of one to four 'dominant' species ('dominant' is used by Aubréville in a sense different from that adopted here) and one to six 'abundant' species; the numerous other species are represented by single, or very few, individuals. The 'dominant' and 'abundant' species vary from place to place; a species which is 'abundant' in one locality may be almost absent in a neighbouring one. Over a wide extent of country almost every possible combination of species is met with, but the 'dominants' are always a selection from a group of not more than perhaps twenty species. Thus the forest is a collection of species of similar ecological requirements which occur in combinations fluctuating in composition from place to place.

These combinations vary not only in space, but, according to Aubréville, they also vary in time, the forest at any one spot continually changing in composition. Aubréville's theory of forest regeneration, which we have called the Mosaic theory, has already been discussed in Chapter 3.

If this is an accurate picture of a large tract of Mixed forest, it follows that no true associations can be recognized in it. Chipp's 'association' and 'pre-climaxes' would thus represent merely a few arbitrarily chosen combinations of species, constant neither in time nor in space. The whole Mixed forest in this case must be regarded as a single association of fluctuating composition.

Aubréville admits that where there are peculiar local soil conditions, true associations may exist. In these the population is more homogeneous than in the Mixed forest and at times one may meet with almost pure stands of one species. An example of these 'edaphic associations' is the combination of species characteristic of river banks in the Ivory Coast, including *Cynometra megalophylla*, *Hymenostegia emarginata*, etc. This combination of species is probably to be regarded as a fragment of a riparian community similar to the creekside Mora forest of Guiana and the West African Fresh-water Swamp forest described in Chapter 13), rather than as an association of the Mixed forest.[2]

This account of the composition of the Ivory Coast forest agrees well with Mildbraed's (1930a, 1930b) description of the Likomba forest in the Cameroons,

[1] The number of species on the author's sample plot (area 1·5 ha.) of Mixed forest in the Okomu Forest Reserve, Nigeria, was seventy (4 in. and over).

[2] Groups of species characteristic along the banks of rivers and streams are of course found in all types of Rain forest, just as *Alnus*, *Salix*, etc., by temperate rivers. Examples are the 'Saraca streams' fringed by *Saraca* spp. and the 'Neram rivers' fringed by *Dipterocarpus oblongifolius* in the Mixed forest of Malaya (Corner, 1940, p. 42). Some of these species are probably confined to the actual river margin and are not found in wider belts of riparian forest.

a much smaller area. There he found a marked preponderance of certain species in certain areas, but concluded that the forest was a mixture of species in varying proportions rather than a series of true associations.

For a Mixed forest community to qualify for recognition as a distinct association it should have a characteristic composition remaining constant over a wide area, the most abundant species must retain their places permanently and not give way to others, and we should also expect that a characteristic floristic composition would be shown in all the strata, including the shrubs and herbs. The evidence is inadequate, but, it must be admitted, the presence of several associations in the Mixed Rain forest within a single geographical region has not yet been clearly established.

Family dominance in Mixed forest

Reference has already been made to 'family dominance' in Mixed forests, that is to say, the numerical preponderance of species of the same family or of a group of related genera in some types of Mixed forest. The most striking example is the family dominance of the Dipterocarpaceae in the lowland tropical forests of the Indo-Malayan region west of Wallace's line. In the greater part of the Rain forest (mainly mixed in composition) from Ceylon to Indo-China and Borneo the dominance of this family is well marked and a number of species of one or several genera are usually among the most abundant species in any one area. It would also be possible to speak of the family dominance of Leguminosae in some South American forests, or of Meliaceae in some West African forests. The significance of the phenomenon, which is certainly widespread, is not understood. It is usually believed that competition between plants or animals is most severe between the most nearly related species. On this view it is surprising to find several species of the same genus or family co-dominant in the same habitat. Family dominance probably deserves further study because of the light it may throw on competition in mixed forest communities, still a very obscure subject.

COMPOSITION OF RAIN FOREST WITH SINGLE DOMINANT SPECIES

Among the primary forest communities in British Guiana and Borneo described in the last chapter there were four, the Mora, Morabukea, Greenheart and Wallaba types of Moraballi Creek, in which a single species of tree forms a substantial proportion of the whole stand and may therefore be regarded as the only dominant species; in another of these communities, the Heath forest of Borneo, no one species could be said to be actually dominant, but there was a 'tendency' towards single-species dominance.

All five of these forest types appear to be climax communities in stable equilibrium with their environment. There is nothing to suggest that any of

LITERATURE CITED

1. BROWN, C. A.; HOLDEMAN, Q. L.; and HAGOOD, E. D. Injuries to cotton by 2,4-D. Louisiana Agr. Exp. Sta. Bull. 426. 1948.
2. DUNLAP, A. A. 2,4-D injury to cotton from airplane dusting of rice. Phytopathology 37:636–644. 1948.
3. ERGLE, D. R., and DUNLAP, A. A. Responses of cotton to 2,4-D. Texas Agr. Exp. Sta. Bull. 713. 1949.
4. ERGLE, D. R., and McILRATH, W. J. Germination of seed harvested from cotton plants damaged by 2,4-D. Texas Agr. Exp. Sta. Progress Rept. 1394. 1951.
5. McILRATH, W. J.; ERGLE, D. R.; and DUNLAP, A. A. Persistence of 2,4-D stimulus in cotton plants with reference to its transmission to the seed. BOT. GAZ. 112:511–518. 1951.

6. STATEN, G. Contamination of cotton fields by 2,4-D or hormone-type weed sprays. Jour. Amer. Soc. Agron. 38:536–544. 1946.
7. WATSON, D. P. An anatomical study of the modification of bean leaves as a result of treatment with 2,4-D. Amer. Jour. Bot. 35:543–555. 1948.

DEPARTMENT OF BOTANY
UNIVERSITY OF CHICAGO
CHICAGO 37, ILLINOIS
AND
TEXAS AGRICULTURAL EXPERIMENT STATION AND
BUREAU OF PLANT INDUSTRY, SOILS, AND
AGRICULTURAL ENGINEERING
COLLEGE STATION, TEXAS

AN ESTIMATE OF THE NUMBER OF SPECIES OF TREES IN AN AMAZONIAN FOREST COMMUNITY

J. MURÇA PIRES, TH. DOBZHANSKY, AND G. A. BLACK

Introduction

A remarkable diversity of species of trees exists in tropical forest communities, and particularly in those of the Amazonian Hylea. Following the work of DAVIS and RICHARDS (2) in British Guiana, BLACK, DOBZHANSKY, and PAVAN (1) made counts of the numbers of species of trees 10 cm. or more in diameter on several 1-hectare plots in equatorial Brazil. From 59 to 94 species per plot were found. These numbers were admittedly far short of the total numbers of tree species in the forest communities sampled. On every plot about a third of the species were represented by single individuals, making it virtually certain that counts on larger plots would reveal the existence of many additional species of trees in the same communities. If the species are divided into "octaves" of frequencies, as suggested by PRESTON (5), the leftmost octave is always as large as, or larger than, the next to the right of it.

This also shows that many species present in the communities were not found on the plots studied. In August, 1952, we made an attempt to obtain a fuller estimate of the number of tree species in a terra firme community in the state of Pará, in Brazil, by making a count on a plot of a larger size than used previously, namely, on 3.5 hectares. The results of this attempt are reported in the present article.

Material and methods

The technique used by BLACK et al. (1) was followed also in the present investigation. We chose, because of its relative accessibility, a luxuriant and virgin terra firme forest near the village of Tres de Outubro, between Castanhal and the River Guamá, some 120 km. from Belém, state of Pará, Brazil. In this forest a territory was selected which was reasonably flat and which did not show any obvious nonuniformities. An experimental plot of

3.5 hectares was laid out, subdivided by strings into thirty-five strips of equal area, namely, 1000 sq. m. Of the strips, thirty were 100 × 10 m., and five were 50 × 20 m. each. On each strip the trees 10 cm. or more in diameter were examined and recorded (table 1). For each tree we attempted to obtain an identification by the four tree specialists, Nilo Tomaz da Silva, Antonio da Silva, Feliciano Alves Ferreira, and Themistocles Gedes, who worked with us. The vernacular names given by these men were recorded. In all cases of doubt, as well as when no vernacular names were given, herbarium specimens were obtained for later identification and comparison with determined specimens in the herbaria of the Instituto Agronomico do Norte and of the Museu Goeldi at Belém. These herbarium specimens are preserved at the former institution under numbers indicated in table 1 in parentheses. As in previous work, we were unable to ascertain the scientific names of some of the species encountered on the plot and, in some instances, even the generic names. This fact is unfortunate, but it does not seriously interfere with our task, which is an attempt to estimate the number of species. What we need is, first of all, to distinguish the species collected, and we are confident that this has been accomplished in all or almost all cases; whether or not these species could also be named is secondary in this particular investigation.

Number and frequency of species. —A total of 179 species was found among the 1482 individual trees counted on the plot. Among these trees, 55.9% had trunks 10–20 cm., 30.5% trunks 20–40 cm., and 13.6% trunks more than 40 cm. in diameter at chest height.

Numbers of species represented by different numbers of individuals are shown in table 2. It can be seen that 45 species, or about one-quarter of the total, were represented by single individuals each, 27 species by two individuals each, etc. The five most common species were *Eschweilera krukovii* (171 individuals), *E. odora* (86), *Micropholis guianensis* (51), *Rinorea passoura* (41), *Trichilia smithi* (40), and *Sterculia* sp. (39).

The family Leguminosae was represented on the plot by the largest number of species, namely, 30, and by 174 individuals. The next most diversified family was Sapotaceae, with 25 species and 266 individuals. Lecythidaceae was represented by only 5 species but by 273 individuals, since the two species of *Eschweilera* belong here. The number of families represented was 48. No species and no family can, accordingly, be considered dominant or even approaching the status of dominance.

Uniformity of the plot.—It is evident that the number of species of trees found in a plot as small as 3.5 hectares can give reliable information about the diversity of species growing together in the same facies, or community, only if the territory of the plot is uniform. It will be misleading if many species are more likely to occur in some parts of the plot than in others. Although an effort was made to avoid such nonuniformities in choosing the territory (see above), only statistical tests can evaluate the degree of success of this effort.

Table 3 shows the numbers of individual trees and the numbers of species found in each of the thirty-five strips into which the territory of the plot was subdivided. The smallest number of individuals on a strip was 23 and the largest 57; the smallest number of species was 20 and the largest 37. There exists, as expected, some positive correlation be-

TABLE 1

NUMBERS OF INDIVIDUALS OF TREE SPECIES FOUND ON 3.5 HECTARES OF "TERRA
FIRME" FOREST NEAR CASTANHAL, PARÁ, BRAZIL

SCIENTIFIC NAME AND HERBARIUM REFERENCE*	COMMON NAME	No. OF INDIVIDUALS CLASSED BY TRUNK DIAM. AT CHEST HEIGHT		
		10–20 cm.	20–40 cm.	Over 40 cm.
Palmae				
Oenocarpus distichus Mart.............	Bacaba	3	0	1
Musaceae				
Ravenala guianensis (Endl.) Benth.........	Sororoca	1	0	0
Moraceae				
Bagassa guianensis Aubl...............	Tatajuba	1	0	0
Perebea laurifolia Tul....	Mão de gato	1	0	0˙
Ogcodeia sp.? (4095)...........	....	6	2	1
Helicostylis sp.?...........	Mão de gato	5	4	0
Brosimum paraense Hub....	Amapá	5	1	1
Coussapoa sp.?...........		0	2	0
Cecropia bureaniana A. Richt....	Imbauba vermelha	5	0	0
C. obtusa Trec....	Imbauba branca	1	2	0
Moraceae gen.? (4184)...........	....	2	0	0
Proteaceae				
Proteaceae gen.? (4180)...........	....	1	0	0
Olacaceae				
Liriosma sp.?...........		8	2	0
Minquartia guianensis Aubl....	Acariquara	4	1	0
Heisteria sp.? (4181)...........		0	1	0
Olacaceae gen.? (4179)...........		2	0	0
Nyctaginaceae				
Neea sp.? (4177)...........		2	5	0
Neea sp.? (4169)...........		0	2	0
Menispermaceae				
Abuta sp.?...........		3	0	0
Anonaceae				
Guatteria elongata Benth....	Envira	1	0	0
Duguettia sp.? (4171)...........		1	0	0
Anona sp.? (4170)...........		0	1	0
Anona sp.? (A. Silva 54)...........	Envira preta	3	4	0
Anonaceae gen.? (4172)...........	Envira preta	0	4	0
Myristicaceae				
Iryanthera paraensis Hub....	Ucuuba	3	2	2
Compsoneura sp.?...........		1	0	0
Lauraceae				
Lauraceae gen.? (4155)...........	Louro rosa	1	1	0
Lauraceae gen.? (4156)...........	Louro	2	1	1
Lauraceae gen.? (4157)...........	Louro	3	0	0
Lauraceae gen.? (4158)...........	Louro	1	1	0
Lauraceae gen.? (4159)...........	Louro	4	1	0
Lauraceae gen.? (4160)...........	Louro	0	0	1
Rosaceae				
Licania sp.? (4132)...........	Caripé	2	2	0
Licania sp.? (4133)...........		0	1	0
Licania sp.? (4134)...........	Pintadinho	8	9	0
Couepia hoffmanniana Kl. (4146)...........	Cariperana	17	7	2
Couepia sp.? (4135)...........	Pajurá	1	0	1

* Number in parentheses indicates herbarium specimen at the Instituto Agronomico do Norte, Belém, Pará, Brazil.

TABLE 1—*Continued*

SCIENTIFIC NAME AND HERBARIUM REFERENCE*	COMMON NAME	No. OF INDIVIDUALS CLASSED BY TRUNK DIAM. AT CHEST HEIGHT		
		10–20 cm.	20–40 cm.	Over 40 cm.
Connaraceae				
Connarus angustifolius (Radlk.) Schellenb.	Barbatimão	1	0	0
Leguminosae				
Inga alba (Ew.) Willd.	Inga	1	0	0
I. brachystachys Ducke	Inga de sapo	5	1	0
I. capitata Desv.	Inga	7	1	0
I. fagifolia Willd.		1	0	0
I. heterophylla Willd.	Inga	2	8	1
I. ingoides (Richr.) Willd.	Inga	2	0	0
I. thibaudiana DC.	Inga	7	2	0
Enterolobium schomburgkii Benth.	Orelha de negro	1	2	1
Pithecolobium pedicellare (DC.) Benth.		1	2	5
P. cf. *racemosum* Ducke	Angelim pedra	4	5	2
P. trapezifolium (Vahl.) Benth	Ingarana	3	1	0
Mimosa sp.?	Rabo de camaleão	3	0	0
Stryphnodendron pulcherrimum (Wild) Hochz.	Visgueeiro	2	0	0
Piptadenia psylostachya Benth.	Timborana	6	9	4
Parkia sp.? (4128)		1	0	2
Dimorphandra multipora Ducke (4123) (= *D. pullei* Amsh.?)		0	0	1
Copaifera reticulata Ducke	Copaiba	0	0	1
Hymenaea sp.?		0	0	2
Bauhinia alliscandens Ducke	Escada de jabotí	7	0	0
Cassia apoucouita Aubl.	Coração de negro	0	0	1
Vouacapoua americana Aubl.	Acapú	12	7	10
Sclerologium paraense Hub.	Tachí	4	5	5
Diplotropis purpurea var. *belemensis* Ducke		1	0	0
Bowdichia nitida Spruce	Sucupira	2	1	2
Ormosia coutinhoi Ducke	Boiussú	0	0	1
O. nobilis Tul.	Pau de bixo	1	1	0
Poecilanthe effusa (Hub.) Ducke	Tento	10	4	0
Platymiscium filipes Benth.		0	1	0
Hymenolobium excelsum Ducke	Angelim rajado	1	0	0
Andira retusa HBK	Mangabarana	0	0	2
Humiriaceae				
Vantanea cupularis Hub.? (4143)	Uchirana	4	11	7
Vantanea sp.? (4144)		0	2	0
Erythroxylaceae				
Erythroxylum sp.?		2	0	0
Rutaceae				
Xanthoxylum sp.? (4176)	Tamanqueira	4	0	0
Euxylophora paraensis Hub.	Pau amarelo	2	5	7
Simarubaceae				
Simaruba amara Aubl.	Marupá	1	0	0
Simaba cedron Planch.	Pau para tudo	13	0	0
Burseraceae				
Protium heptaphyllum (Aubl.) Marsh.	Breu branco	14	9	2
P. hostmannii Engl.	Breu	27	2	0
P. (= *P. heptaphyllum?*) (4121)	Breu branco	14	9	2
P. polybotryum Engl.		20	15	0
P. sagotianum Marsh.	Breu inhambú	5	1	1
Protium sp.? (4118)	Breu sucuruba	23	8	2
Protium sp.? (4119)		6	3	3
Protium sp.? (4122)	Breu	1	1	0

TABLE 1—*Continued*

SCIENTIFIC NAME AND HERBARIUM REFERENCE*	COMMON NAME	No. OF INDIVIDUALS CLASSED BY TRUNK DIAM. AT CHEST HEIGHT		
		10–20 cm.	20–40 cm.	Over 40 cm.
Meliaceae				
Cedrela sp.?	Cedro	0	1	0
Carapa guianensis Aubl.	Andiroba	1	2	0
Trichilia smithi C. DC. (4149)		29	10	1
Malpighiaceae				
Byrsonima amazonica Griseb.	Murucí	8	3	0
Vochysiaceae				
Qualea albiflora Warm.	Quaruba	2	3	4
Erisma uncinatum Warm.	Quaruba	5	1	0
Euphorbiaceae				
Discocarpus sp.? (4163)		3	4	0
Croton matourensis Aubl.	Caferana	0	0	1
Aparisthmium cordatum (Juss.) Baill.		2	1	0
Sagotia racemosa Baill.	Arataciuba	12	0	0
Sapium sp.?	Murupita	0	2	0
Anacardiaceae				
Anacardium giganteum Engl.	Cajú-assú	1	0	0
Thyrsodium paraense Huber	Amaparana	2	0	0
Astronium sp.? (4148)		1	0	0
Celastraceae				
Goupia glabra Aubl.	Cupiuba	1	2	4
Icacinaceae				
Dendrobangia boliviana Rusby		2	0	1
Discophora sp.? (4150)		1	0	0
Sapindaceae				
Talisia megaphylla Sagot.		3	0	0
Tiliaceae				
Sloanea porphyrocarpa Ducke		0	1	1
Sloanea sp.? (4165)	Urucurana	2	0	0
Apeiba petoumo Aubl.	Pente de macaco	6	4	5
Bombacaceae				
Bombax longipedicellatum Ducke		0	0	1
Sterculiaceae				
Theobroma subincanum Mart.	Cupuí	5	1	0
Sterculia sp.?	Tacacá	16	14	9
Caryocaraceae				
Caryocar glabrum Aubl.	Piquiarana	1	2	2
Quiinaceae				
Quiina obovata Tul.		0	1	0
Touroulia guianensis Aubl.		0	1	0
Lacunaria crenata (Tul.) A. C. Smith		5	0	0
L. jenmani (Oliv.) Ducke		1	0	0
Guttiferae				
Clusia grandiflora Splitg.	Apuí	2	1	0
Tovomita sp.?		1	0	0
Symphonia globulifera L.f.	Ananí	4	1	1
Violaceae				
Rinorea passoura O. Ktze.		43	0	0
Leonia glycycarpa R. et P.	Envira de sapo	9	0	0

TABLE 1—*Continued*

SCIENTIFIC NAME AND HERBARIUM REFFRENCE*	COMMON NAME	NO. OF INDIVIDUALS CLASSED BY TRUNK DIAM. AT CHEST HEIGHT		
		10–20 cm.	20–40 cm.	Over 40 cm.
Flacourtiaceae				
Casearia javitensis H.B.R.		2	0	0
C. silvestris Ew.?		0	1	0
Casearia sp.? (4182)	Envira	2	1	0
Thymelaeaceae				
Lophostoma calophylloides Meissn.		8	0	0
Lecythidaceae				
Lecythis sp.?	Sapucaia	0	0	4
Eschweilera krukovii Smith	Atereua	62	85	24
E. odora (Poepp.) Miers	Matamatá	37	41	8
Couratari pulchra Sandw.	Tauarí	0	5	2
Holopyxidium jarana Ducke	Jarana	0	1	4
Combretaceae				
Terminalia amazonica (Gmel.) Excell.	Tanimbuca	3	4	0
Myrtaceae				
Myrcia deflexa D.C.		2	0	0
Myrtaceae gen.? (4151)	Murta	1	0	0
Myrtaceae gen.? (4152)	Murta	4	0	0
Myrtaceae gen.? (4153)		3	0	0
Myrtaceae gen.? (4154)	Murta	5	0	0
Melastomaceae				
Mouriria huberi Cogn.		1	1	0
M. nervosa Pilger		2	0	0
M. plaschaerti Pulle		4	0	0
Miconia guianensis Aubl.	Buchuchú	14	1	0
Araliaceae				
Didymophanx morototoni (Aubl.) D. & P.	Morototó	2	0	2
Sapotaceae				
Pouteria egregia Sandw.	Abiurana	1	4	4
P. engleri Eyma (4096)	Abiurana	4	1	2
P. glomerata Radlk. (4107)	Abiurana	7	4	2
P. reticulata (Engl.) Eyma (F. 24889)	Abiurana	4	1	3
Pouteria sp.? (4101)	Abiurana	6	4	4
Pouteria sp.? (4102)	Abiurana	1	0	0
Pouteria sp.? (4103)	Abiurana	9	4	0
Pouteria sp.? (4104)	Abiurana	12	5	0
Pouteria sp.? (4105)	Abiurana	25	7	3
Pouteria sp.? (4106)	Abiurana	0	0	2
Pouteria sp.? (4108)	Abiurana	1	0	0
Micropholis sp.? (4113)		0	1	0
M. acutangula (Ducke) Eyma		11	11	2
M. guianensis (ADC) Pierre	Mangabarana	28	14	6
Pradosia huberi Ducke	Guajará bolacha	0	0	1
P. praealta Ducke	Casca doce	1	0	2
Manilkara amazonica Standley	Maparajuba	4	0	1
Sapotaceae gen.? (4098)	Abiurana	0	0	1
Sapotaceae gen.? (4099)	Abiurana	0	1	0
Sapotaceae gen.? (4109)	Abiurana	7	4	3
Sapotaceae gen.? (4111)	Abiurana	4	3	1
Sapotaceae gen.? (4114)	Abiurana	3	1	0
Ebenaceae				
Diospyros melinoni (Hiern.) A. C. Smith		7	0	0

TABLE 1—*Continued*

Scientific name and herbarium reference*	Common name	No. of individuals classed by trunk diam. at chest height		
		10–20 cm.	20–40 cm.	Over 40 cm.
Apocynaceae				
Rauwolfia paraensis Ducke		1	0	0
Ambelania tenuifolia Muell.	Pepino	3	0	0
Lacmellia aculeata (Ducke) Monach.	Pau de colher	9	2	0
Parahancornia amapa Ducke	Amapá	1	1	0
Couma guianensis Aubl.	Sorva	0	1	0
Plumeria sp.?	Sucuuba	1	0	0
Aspidosperma desmanthum Benth.	Araracanga	4	0	1
A. nitidum Benth.	Carapanauba	1	4	1
Geissospermum sp.? (F. 23576)	Acariquararana	2	0	0
Geissospermum sp.?	Acariquararana	0	0	1
Boraginaceae				
Cordia goeldiana Huber	Frejó	0	0	1
C. scabrida Mart. (?)		0	1	0
Verbenaceae				
Vitex triflora Vahl.	Tarumán	1	0	0
Bignoniaceae				
Tabebuia sp.?	Pau d'arco	0	1	2
Rubiaceae				
Amaioua guianensis Aubl.	Puruirana	4	0	0
Chimarrhis turbinata DC.	Pau de remo	1	2	2

TABLE 2

NUMBERS OF SPECIES REPRESENTED BY DIFFERENT NUMBERS OF INDIVIDUALS ON 3.5-HECTARE PLOT

Individuals	Species	Individuals	Species	Individuals	Species	Individuals	Species
1	45	9	6	19	1	33	1
2	27	10	1	20	1	35	2
3	15	11	5	21	1	39	1
4	13	12	2	22	1	40	1
5	12	13	3	24	1	41	1
6	5	14	5	25	1	51	1
7	12	15	2	26	1	86	1
8	6	17	2	29	2	171	1

TABLE 3

TOTAL NUMBER OF SPECIES, NUMBER OF "NEW" SPECIES, AND NUMBERS OF INDIVIDUALS FOUND IN EACH OF THIRTY-FIVE STRIPS ON 3.5-HECTARE PLOT

Strip no.	Total species	New species	Individuals	Strip no.	Total species	New species	Individuals
1	28	28	42	20	22	3	35
2	37	25	52	21	29	3	43
3	32	11	53	22	21	2	39
4	29	10	44	23	23	2	41
5	30	12	47	24	29	1	44
6	25	6	38	25	29	3	41
7	24	5	38	26	30	2	44
8	26	4	48	27	29	3	46
9	32	6	42	28	27	3	37
10	24	1	43	29	22	1	32
11	29	8	41	30	21	2	32
12	28	5	41	31	33	5	57
13	33	3	45	32	26	2	46
14	29	5	41	33	23	.....	46
15	33	4	45	34	20	1	52
16	25	4	35	35	30	.....	55
17	34	4	40				
18	27	4	34	Total	179	179	1482
19	20	1	23				

tween the number of individuals and the number of species found on a plot.

A more conclusive test can be made as follows: Suppose that the average number of trees of a certain species per strip is m (m is, then, the number of trees of that species on the plot divided by the number of the strips of which the plot is composed). If the distribution of the trees of

viduals would be less frequent than expected on the basis of randomness. These possible deviations from randomness are sometimes called in the ecological literature "overdispersion" and "underdispersion," respectively (cf. GOODALL, **3**). This is a misleading terminology, since "overdispersion" is obviously due to grouping and "underdispersion" to re-

TABLE 4

EXPECTED AND OBSERVED NUMBER OF STRIPS WITH DIFFERENT NUM-
BERS OF INDIVIDUALS OF CERTAIN SPECIES OF TREES

No. OF IN-DIVIDUALS	ESCHWEILERA KRUKOVII		E. ODORA		MICROPHOLIS GUIANENSIS		RINOREA PASSOURA		TRICHILIA SMITHI		STERCULIA SP.	
	Exp.	Obs.	Exp.	Obs.	Exp.	Obs.	Exp.	Obs.	Exp.	Obs.	Exp.	Obs.
0......	0.3	1	3.0	4	8.1	9	10.2	15	11.2	13	11.5	12
1......	1.3	4	7.4	8	11.9	11	12.6	10	12.8	10	12.8	12
2......	3.1	4	9.1	10	8.7	7	7.7	3	7.3	8	7.1	8
3......	5.1	4	7.4	4	4.2	6	3.2	5	2.8	2	2.7	1
4......	6.3	3	4.5	4	1.5	2	1.0	0	0.8	2	0.7	2
5......	6.1	2	2.2	2	} 0.6	0	0.3	2	0.2	0	0.2	0
6......	5.0	7	0.9	2								
7......	3.5	4	} 0.5	1								
8......	2.1	4										
>8......	2.1	2										

that species on the plot is at random, the proportion of strips with r trees is given by the Poisson formula,

$$\frac{e^{-m}m^r}{r!},$$

where e is the base of natural logarithms. If, on the other hand, trees of the same species tended to occur in groups, either because of nonuniformities of the terrain or because of inefficient seed dispersal, the numbers of strips with few and with many trees of the same species would tend to be greater than expected on the basis of the Poisson formula. Finally, if the presence of a tree of a given species were to diminish the probability of other individuals of the same species growing within a certain distance from it, then the strips with few and with many indi-

pulsion between individuals of the same species.

The numbers of strips on the experimental plot observed and expected, from Poisson's formula, to contain various numbers of individuals of the six commonest species are given in table 4. A glance at the table shows that the agreement between the observed and the expected figures is in most cases quite close. A more sensitive test is afforded by calculating chi-squares for the various species. For this purpose, the adjacent classes containing small numbers of individuals have been combined so that the aggregate expected numbers of strips would be no less than three. The results are given in table 5.

The deviations between the expected and the observed numbers in no case reach the conventional level of significance. The joint chi-square has a probability of chance occurrence just under 0.5. The distribution of at least these six species on our plot does not appreciably deviate from uniformity.

Finally, we attempted to correlate the occurrence of certain species of trees with minor variations in the characteristics of the terrain in the different strips. Three species recorded on our plot—namely, *Ravenala guianensis*, *Platymiscium filipes*, and *Symphonia globulifera*—are known to be forms which occur commonly on wet ground (igapo) or in periodically inundated places (varzea), in the Amazonian rain forests. Their presence in the terra firme forest community was, to this extent, atypical and suggested that the strips where they were found may be characterized by a greater water content in the soil. We have also noted the fact that three of the thirty-five strips into which our plot was divided contained parts of a small depression with wet soil. A check disclosed, however, that only two out of the six *Symphonia* trees, and neither *Ravenala* nor *Platymiscium*, grew on these or on the adjacent strips. These members of the igapo and varzea associations thus occur, though with low frequencies, also in terra firme forests.

RARE AND UNDETECTED SPECIES.— The forest community in which our plot was laid out is evidently so rich in species that, even with a plot 3.5 hectares in area, 45 out of 179 species were represented by single individuals each. Table 3 shows not only the numbers of species recorded on each of the thirty-five strips on this plot but also the numbers of species found on each strip which have not been found on any of the strips studied before ("New species"). Thus, strip no. 1 contained 28 species, all of which ob-

viously were found for the first time; strip no. 2 had 37 species, 12 of which were recorded also on no. 1 and 25 of which were "new"; strip no. 3 had 32 species, 21 of which were found also on no. 1 or on no. 2, or on both, and 11 which were new, etc. By the time strips nos. 10–19 were reached, the average number of new species per strip fell to about 4. On strips nos. 20–29 the number of new species was 3 or less. Strip no. 31 had 5 new species, but nos. 33 and 35 had

TABLE 5

Species	Chi-square	Degrees of freedom	Probability
Eschweilera krukovii..	10.09	5	0.07
E. odora............	2.13	4	.75
Micropholis guianensis	0.93	3	.8
Rinorea passoura.....	7.10	3	.07
Trichilia smithi......	0.99	3	.8
Sterculia sp..........	0.27	3	0.99
Total.............	21.51	21	0.45

none. There can be scarcely any doubt that if we could have extended our plot farther, new species would have been added to the list, although the rate of addition would become progressively slower.

To obtain even a very rough estimate of the total number of species in the forest community which we have studied, a hypothesis must be made concerning the relationships between the common and the rare species. Among the various hypotheses suggested, that of PRESTON (5), who assumed that common and rare species are distributed according to a probability curve, seems to us most reasonable, although we are aware of the objections raised against it (3). The distribution of the 179 species found in our plot into PRESTON's "octaves" of frequencies is as shown in table 6.

476   BOTANICAL GAZETTE   [JUNE

The three leftmost octaves (1, 2–3, 4–7) contain about the same numbers of species. Here it may be recalled that on the 1-hectare plot used by BLACK *et al.* (1) and on the 1.49-hectare plot used by DAVIS and RICHARDS (2) the leftmost octave was always the largest. This indicates that more than half the species present in the community have actually been found on the 3.5-hectare plot here described. Assuming with PRESTON that the curve of species frequencies is symmetrical and assuming further that the

liance should be placed, however, on this estimate until it is checked by further observations.

COMPARISON OF DIFFERENT FACIES OF THE SAME ASSOCIATION.—The 3.5-hectare plot described here is located some 120 km. to the east of the 1-hectare plot in the terra firme forest near Belém studied by BLACK *et al.* (1). Superficially the aspects of both forests are similar, but their species composition proved to be far from identical. The number of species and their frequencies

TABLE 6

	Octaves								Total
	1	2–3	4–7	8–15	16–31	32–63	64–127	128–255	
No. of species.....	45	42	42	30	11	7	1	1	179

2–3 octave in table 6 is the modal one, an attempt may be made to estimate the total number of species in the community studied. We are indebted to Messrs. HOWARD LEVENE, T. PROUT, and R. LEWONTIN for making the necessary calculations. Professor H. LEVENE, using a method somewhat different from that used by PRESTON, estimated the total number of species in the Castanhal community as approximately 250. The median frequency is 1.85 individuals, and the value of PRESTON's a is 0.308. The method of GRUNDY (4), using the values 1.85 and 0.308, gives the expected number of species as 246, in good agreement with the result above, and the expected number of species represented by one individual as 45.5, which happens to agree almost exactly with the observed figure, 45. Taking these estimates at face value, the terra firme forest community which we studied should contain 67–71 tree species which we failed to encounter. No re-

TABLE 7

NUMBERS OF SPECIES REPRESENTED BY DIFFERENT NUMBERS OF INDIVIDUALS ON 1-HECTARE BELÉM PLOT AND ON FIRST TEN STRIPS AT CASTANHAL

INDIVIDUALS	SPECIES		INDIVIDUALS	SPECIES		INDIVIDUALS	SPECIES	
	Belém	Castanhal		Belém	Castanhal		Belém	Castanhal
1....	33	43	9..	4	3	20...	1	0
2....	15	19	10..	0	0	23...	0	1
3....	15	10	11..	0	4	25...	1	0
4....	3	10	12..	1	0	30...	0	1
5....	4	6	13..	0	1	37...	2	0
6....	2	3	16..	0	2	39...	0	1
7....	3	1	17..	2	0	49...	1	0
8....	0	2	18..	0	1	Total	87	108

on the Belém plot and on the first ten strips of the Castanhal plot compare as shown in table 7.

The Castanhal facies of the terra firme forest association seems to be significantly richer in species than the community examined near Belém. Furthermore, they proved to be qualitatively distinct, as shown by comparison of the list in table 1 of the present paper with table 2 of that of BLACK *et al.*, as well as by a preliminary check of herbarium specimens of both collections.[1] As many as 33 of the 87 species found at Belém were not seen at Castanhal, and 125 of the 179 species found at Castanhal were not seen at Belém. Some of the species recorded in one but not in the other place are known to be widely distributed in the terra firme forests of Pará, and their absence in one of our samples is in all probability accidental. On the other hand, *Micropholis guianensis* and *Rinorea passoura*, which are among the commonest species at Castanhal, have not been recorded at all at Belém, while *Vochysia guianensis* is common on the Belém plot but not re-corded at all at Castanhal. It is evident that different facies of the so-called terra firme forests of Pará are actually very distinct in species composition and that any estimates of the total species diversity that may be arrived at will describe the situation only in the particular facies in which they are made. The importance of studies in this field for rational exploitation of the forest resources of Amazonia is clear without further comment.

Summary

1. As many as 1482 trees 10 cm. or more in diameter, belonging to 179 species, have been counted on a 3.5-hectare plot in a virgin terra firme forest near Castanhal, Pará, Brazil. Evidence is given that the distribution of at least the common species over the territory of the plot is uniform, and the inference is drawn that about 70 species which may occur in the association sampled have not been encountered on the plot.

2. Comparison of the species composition of the sample described in the present paper with that on a plot some 120 km. away studied by BLACK *et al.* (1) shows very considerable differences. The number of species in the different facies of the terra firme association in Amazonia may be much larger than found in the samples studied so far.

---

[1] Some of the species found on the Belém plot in 1949 and listed in table 2 of the publication by BLACK *et al.* (1) under herbarium reference numbers of the 8000 series have now been identified as follows: no. 8124 = 8085 = *Protium polybotryum;* 8101, 8105 = *P. aracouchini;* 8117, 8062 = *P. hostmannii;* 8135, 8163 = *P. heptaphyllum;* 8116 = *Protium* sp., no. 4118 of Castanhal; 8070 = *Ogcodeia* sp., no. 4095 of Castanhal; 8127 = louro no. 4156 of Castanhal; 8161 = louro 4158 of Castanhal; 8064 = *Cuepia hoffmanniana;* 8112 = 8097 = *Inga heterophylla;* 8079 = *Pouteria* sp. not found at Castanhal; 8146 = 8133 = *Micropholis* no. 4113 of Castanhal; 8080 = *Mouriria huberi;* 8104 = 8125 = *Qualea albiflora;* 8151 = *Myrcia* sp. not found at Castanhal.

LITERATURE CITED

1. BLACK, G. A.; DOBZHANSKY, TH.; and PAVAN, C. Some attempts to estimate species diversity and population density of trees in Amazonian forests. BOT. GAZ. 111:413–425. 1950.
2. DAVIS, T. A. W., and RICHARDS, P. W. The vegetation of Moraballi Creek, British Guinea. Part II. Jour. Ecol. 22:106–155. 1934.
3. GOODALL, D. W. Quantitative aspects of plant distribution. Biol. Rev. 27:194–245. 1952.
4. GRUNDY, P. M. The expected frequencies in a sample of an animal population in which the abundances of species are log-normally distributed. Biometrika 38:427–434. 1951.
5. PRESTON, F. W. The commonness and rarity of species. Ecology 29: 254–283. 1948.

Ecological Studies in the Mixed Dipterocarp Forests of Brunei State
P. S. Ashton

2.   SOME RELATIONSHIPS BETWEEN ENVIRONMENTAL AND VEGETATION GRADIENTS EXPRESSED IN THE ORDINATIONS

The real test of the value of the ordination in this study is whether the position of the plots on the axes, based on properties of the plant communities they represent, bear any relationships to environmental gradients I have studied.   In figs. 10-13 and figs. 15 and 16, which should be superimposed on fig. 10, the plots sampled in each physiographic unit are enclosed by the lines.

'*x*' *axes*.   In both the ordinations the valley plots are orientated together at one end, and the ridge plots at the other; in both the ridge plots are more tightly clustered than the valley plots and occupy a shorter length of the axis (excluding the high ridge plots at Belalong).   This reflects the great variability in habitat conditions in the hillsides and valleys.   At Belalong, the way in which the hillside plots are ordered bears a close relationship with their topographic position (see fig. 2, where approximate contours are included).   There is an almost complete segregation of the river side plots sampled in the deep narrow valley of the Belalong, which are grouped to the far left of the axis, and those from the broad valley of the Temburong, which have a position in the centre of the area of the lower hillside plots.   From this one might deduce that there is lower humidity of the soil conditions in Temburong valley plots, caused in part by the breezes which pass up the broader river valleys in hilly districts; these would not be influential in the narrow Belalong valley where the crowns of the trees often meet over the river (plates 14, 15).   The evidence available suggests that the '*x*' axis at Belalong corresponds to a humidity gradient, with the very sticky valley soils at one end and the friable shale lithosols at the other; I have already suggested that this sequence is related also to an increasing 'physiological depth' of the soil, from humid to drier conditions, and to a decrease in pH from c. 4.6 to c. 4.0, with rapid decomposition in the more basic to raw humus accumulation in the more acid conditions.   There will also be an increase in light intensity at the forest floor from the valley to the high ridge plots.   Plots 46-50, on shale lithosols at the highest altitudes, are far separated on this axis from the other plots.   This graphically expresses the very different conditions at these stations.   As the ridge plots are more or less separated from the hillside plots there is some relationship with change in altitude; the long sections occupied by the riparian plots and the groups of hillside plots at different altitudes, and the disproportionate gap between plots sited below and above 600 m., suggests that the effect of altitudinal climatic changes is only indirect, through its effect on soil conditions.   Observations throughout Brunei confirmed that the primary gradient in floristic variation is that expressed in the Belalong '*x*' axis, and that direct altitudinal changes are secondary and obscured by soil gradients; this is further discussed in later chapters.   There appears therefore to be a close similarity in the relationship between environment and floristic variation between the forests of Brunei and those studied by Whittaker (1956) in the Great Smoky Mountains, United States.

The Andulau '*x*' axis shows a similar arrangement.   Comparison with Table 3 shows that hillside plots with stickier soils occur mainly to the left of the sandier plots; this seems true also of the valley plots, though it is less convincing owing to their internal heterogeneity.   In both valley and hillside there are some plots that seem not to be correctly ordinated, however; plot no. 8 is apparently too far to the left to agree with my field observations, plots 1 and 2 are too far to the right. It is hardly surprising to find some anomalies in view of the limitations of the data. I here again suggest that this axis is related to rooting depth, friability near the surface, pH, and light intensity at the forest floor. Only one of the twenty valley plots overlapped with the hillside plots on this axis, and this, no. 19, was on sandy soils at the head of a valley, similar to pits 24 and 25.

At both areas, therefore, there is a gradient along the 'x' axis corresponding to a change from mesic to relatively xeric soil conditions, thus paralleling the 'x' axis of Bray and Curtis, and equating with the unidimensional continuum originally introduced by Curtis and McIntosh (1951). This demonstrates the universal importance of Milne's (1947) concept of the soil catena in relation to plant community changes, and disproves the idea that Dipterocarp forest is a uniform climatic climax formation.

'y' axes. At Belalong the upper hillside plots show the greatest variation in their positions, then those of the lower hillsides, riversides and finally ridges. The majority of plots are placed towards the lower ends of the axis and the other half of it is occupied entirely by plots on steep hillsides (see fig. 2). There appears to be a relationship between the 'y' axis plot positions and slope, though the plots at the lower end are on spurs and undulating land and not ridges. There appears to be a similar relationship also with depth of humus, total carbon content, and factors related to them. I have already suggested that available nutrients will probably be highest on low spurs; this could be an explanation of the position of the plots on this axis.

At Andulau the 'y' axis again appears to be related to similar phenomena. Comparison of axis positions of the hillside plots with their approximate steepness in Table 3 shows that the steepest are placed higher on the axis than the less steep, though plot 32, occupying low undulating land, is anomalous in its position. The ridge plots occupy mostly lower positions than the hillsides; plots 46, 47, and 48, which are placed above the others on the axis, are all situated on spurs sloping down to the Lumut valley. Of the valley plots, the lowest are those with a constantly high water table, while the upper are those with a variable water table. Plot 6 was an anomalous plot in a broad sandy valley, with swampy conditions at one end; the soils throughout were strongly bleached, with deep raw humus accumulations. The axis expresses the close relationship between the vegetation on the peaty valley soils and that on the leached hill soils. There is a tendency for the plots in the broader lower parts of valleys to be lower on this axis than those higher up, as might be expected. The continuum along the Andulau 'y' axis appears therefore accompanied by a change downwards from hillside soils with little surface organic matter or leaching down to bleached alluvial soils and yellow leached podsolic soils with deep layers of organic material. The ordination implies that these tendencies are independent of the clay/sand ratio in the valley plots and depend more on drainage, which confirms field observations.

'z' axes. No relationship could be found between the 'z' axes and environmental gradients. x/z and y/z axis diagrams (figs. 11-13) show that in both Andulau and Belalong there is complete overlapping of physiographic units on the 'z' axis. It is probable that the 'z' axes represent residual variation due to the limitations

of the sampling procedure and to the effects of non-random species distribution in any one habitat. Comparison of distribution of dipterocarp species along this axis (figs. 17, 18), and the apparently random distribution of species mid-points, tends to support this.

3. FLORISTIC VARIATION WITHIN THE DIPTEROCARP FORESTS; GENERAL CONSIDERATIONS

It has already been pointed out that the 'x' axis approximates to Curtis and McIntosh's (1951) continuum; owing to the nature of the ordination it is to be expected that the principal trend of variation of the community will be expressed along the primary axis. This is particularly so in the present case, where the comparatively high expected sampling error will partially obscure secondary variation gradients.

In order to plot the behaviour of different species along the 'x' axis I have taken as an approximation the mean value of successive groups of 5 plots. The choice of plots in the sectors along the K. Belalong axis is derived from the two shorter axes given in fig. 14; the hillside sectors being obtained from the plots 1-34 axis, and the ridge sectors from the plots 21-50 axis. Mean values for the 5 acres of Heath forest at Badas and Bt. Puan enumerated are included for comparison.

In fig. 19 the number of species along the two 'x' axes is plotted as totals per 5 acre sector. There is a very marked difference between the Andulau and Belalong plots — most surprising is the greater number in the Heath forest plots than in those of most Dipterocarp forest plots at Belalong; these differences are in part related to the lower density of trees at Belalong, though the lower ridge plots at Belalong have a comparable density to plots at Andulau. The curve showing total number of species per 5 acres at Belalong is seen to be related to that connecting median 'y' axis locations of each five plot sector along the 'x' axis (fig. 23).

Species/area curves for groups of five plots in different habitats are shown in fig. 20. In each habitat, groups of five plots were chosen which shared high community coefficients with one another; though I do not pretend that these areas of five acres are homogeneous, they are as uniform as can be obtained in the areas under study and I venture to question whether the figures included from elsewhere for comparison are equally uniform. The plots chosen were as follows :

> Andulau valley : 8,12,3,18,4.
>
> Andulau ridge : 40,41,44,36,37.
>
> Belalong lower hillside : 3,6,7,13,14.
>
> Belalong upper hillside : 21,22,23,26,29.
>
> Belalong 700 m. ridge :   46,47,48,49,50.

In the initial $\frac{1}{2}$ acre the steepness of the curve is related to the density within the plots; in floristically poorer types the curve subsequently begins to level out more rapidly than in the floristically richer ones.

The high shale ridges at Belalong are clearly the poorest in species. Though the Heath forest at 5 acres still has more species than the Belalong hillside Dipterocarp forest, the curve is levelling out more rapidly than the two Belalong curves. The Andulau valley curve is somewhat higher than the ridge curve; both are considerably higher than others from Brunei, and show little sign of levelling out.

The figures superimposed from other areas (obtained from data summarised by Richards (1945), Wyatt Smith (1949), Black et al. (1950), Cousens (1951), and Schultz (1960) are based either on trees exceeding 4 in. or 10 cm. diam. (12.37 in. girth), but this is unlikely to cause appreciable differences in the comparative values. The floristic poverty of African rain forest compared with S. American and Malaysian types is confirmed, and demonstrates that they are comparable in richness with the stunted ridge forest on shale lithosols in Brunei. The S. American figures, though appreciably lower than the Andulau plots, are in some cases higher than those at Belalong, while the data from Malaya shows the greatest richness — in the forests on the old rocks of the Sunda Shelf. Dipterocarp forest is therefore not always richer floristically than rain forest in other regions; under optimum edaphic conditions, such as occur in Malaya, this seems to be true though much more data is needed from S. America.

Species/individual curves (fig. 21) for Belalong Dipterocarp forest below 650 m. however are closely similar to those from the Andulau ridge plots, whereas the Heath forest curve is much lower. The curve for shale lithosols remains lower than that for Heath forest. Thus the disparity between Andulau and lower altitude Belalong species/area curves can be mainly attributed to the greater density of individuals at Andulau F.R.

Number of individuals per species plotted as means per acre along the 'x' axes (fig. 19) in fact show lower ratios at Belalong than Andulau, except on high ridges. The graphs indicate that the floristically richest sites in both areas are on clay rich relatively well drained soils. At Andulau the individual/species ratio increases with decreasing 'physiological' depth of soil in the valleys, and with increasingly xeric conditions on the hills.

Species/area curves for trees exceeding 25 in. (c. 20 cm. diam.) girth (fig. 22) shows that though the Heath forest is floristically relatively rich in the lower girth classes, the number of species reaching higher girth classes falls off more rapidly than in any of the Belalong or Andulau sites, including the forest on shale lithosols. At this girth-class figures for Bt. Lagong, Malaya, are somewhat lower than the Andulau figures, while those for S. Menyala F.R., Malaya, are hardly higher than Brunei Heath forest; it appears that it is in the smaller girth classes that Malayan forest is floristically richer.

Comparison with Richards' data from Mt. Dulit Mixed forest (i.e. Dipterocarp forest) and Marudi Heath forest, in which trees exceeding 8 in. (c. 20 cm.) diam. were recorded, show remarkably almost identical figures for Heath forest at Badas and Marudi; the terraces in the two areas are part of the same formation. His Mixed forest plot was considerably richer, however. It seems likely that his plot is heterogeneous; it would be difficult to select a site of 122 m. square (the size of his plot) that was not. The fact that one side ran along a ridge and that the plot was situated on a low hill suggests that there were considerable variations in soil texture. Of the identifiable species present *Oncosperma horrida*, *Kurrimia paniculata*, Binuah (*Octomeles sumatrana*), Pelajau (*Pentaspadon motleyi*),

Dyera costulata (plate 17), *Antiaris toxicaria* (plate 18), and Kapur Paji (*Dryobalanops lanceolata*) are all more or less confined to clay rich soils on hillsides, the first three in particular being found in damp places. Yet he elsewhere (p. 22) records *Gleichenia linearis, Eurycoma longifolia* and *Anisophyllea disticha* on the ridges in the vicinity. In Brunei these species are exclusively confined to sandy soils (see plate 29). The fact that he states that the vegetation was most dense on the narrowest ridges, contrary to my observations on shale below 600 m. at K. Belalong, suggests that his sharp ridges were supported by hard sandstone strata.

As has been stated earlier, in forest communities, when comparisons are being made between plots comprising groups of individuals of very disparate sizes, density comparisons are weighted in favour of small trees, while measures such as basal area are weighted in favour of the larger trees. Cain et al. (1956) have shown, in studies of limited areas of rain forest on the lower Amazon, that the Importance Value of Curtis (1947), that is, the summed relative density, relative frequency (species presence values for a given number of plots relative to summed presence values for all species considered for the plots) and relative basal area for a species in a stand, is a useful tool in the description of tropical as well as temperate forest communities. Though this measure can be criticised in that it is an arbitrary combination of different community properties, by combining the above weighted measures it provides a better indication, according to its proponents, of species importance in tree communities than the single measures available. Using it Cain effectively demonstrated the absence of single species dominance in a sample of tropical rain forest. The 25 leading species in the six different groups of five plots adopted earlier are shown in Table 9. The numbers refer to the sectors along the 'x' axes (counting from the left) from which the plots were selected. The importance value is here calculated using relative frequency in a sector of 5 plots. Only the Heath forest has a species, *Agathis alba,* with distinct dominance, and in all the other examples there is no clear dominance using this criterion; in fact the leading species always has an Importance Value several units lower than *Vochysia guianensis* in Cain's South American plot.

In fig. 24 I have plotted the Importance Values of all species that become leading species in any one or more sectors along the two 'x' axes. At Belalong there is an inverse relationship between the curve connecting maximum importance values with the median 'y' axis locations curve (fig. 23), the highest figure being recorded in the area of the lower hillsides plots. At Andulau there is a difference between the valley and the hill sectors, and a steep rise at each end of the axis. Comparison with individual/species curves (fig. 19) for the 5 acre sectors along the 'x' axis supports Richards' (1952, 242, 260) comment that there is an inverse relationship between dominance and floristic richness.

A surprising effect contrasting the two areas is that whereas at Belalong all the leading species are dipterocarps, at Andulau in only two sectors is a dipterocarp the leading species, the importance value giving apparent bias to the smaller yet more abundant trees.

4. STRUCTURE AND PHYSIOGNOMY

Richards (1936) has already compared the physiognomy and structure of the 'Mixed,' that is Dipterocarp, forest, and 'Heath' forest at Mt. Dulit, Sarawak.

CHAPTER III

THE ROLE OF THE DIPTEROCARPACEAE IN THE LOWLAND MIXED RAIN FOREST FORMATION.

1. THE FAMILY

FIG. 39 demonstrates that Dipterocarpaceae are floristically richest relative to other families on well, but not excessively, drained soils, particularly on ridges.

It is generally assumed that Dipterocarpaceae are the dominant family, that is, that they form the most abundant constituents among the upper stories, of the lowland evergreen forests on the better soils in western Malaysia. So far no estimate of variation in family dominance in different habitats in one area has been made or the degree of dominance compared with other leading families.

Dipterocarp dominance, expressed as the family importance value (defined on page 41), along the two 'x' axes (fig. 40) is greatest on well drained, but not highly leached, soils on ridges. At Belalong there is a second peak on the less steep lower hillsides and spurs. The Euphorbiaceae become the leading family in the fresh water swamps at Andulau, though not as markedly so as the Dipterocarpaceae elsewhere. In the Heath forest studied, species importance value of *Agathis* (63.6) far exceeds the maximum importance value of any other single species or family, in this respect differing from the structurally similar higher shale ridge forest, where Dipterocarpaceae remain the leading family; in Heath forest on shallow podsols, however, *Agathis* is frequently absent. The plots on residual soils at Belalong show more variation that those at Andulau, the damper hillside plots showing the lowest values, and the lower ridges the highest values; this reflects the more extreme physiographic and drainage conditions in that area.

FIG. 41 confirms that the family is most dense in the highest girth classes in places where it is floristically richest; at Andulau all trees exceeding 108 in. girth in the ridge plots were dipterocarps. This confirms similar observations in Malaya (Wyatt Smith, 1949; Cousens, 1951). Anderson (1957) summarised data obtained in 1933, giving percentage representation of the family at different diameters, from enumerations including all habitat conditions in Andulau F.R.; he quoted dipterocarps as representing 60% of all trees above 16 in. diam. (50 in. girth), 68% above 20 in. (63 in. girth), 72% above 24 in. (75 in. girth), and 88% above 32 in. (101 in. girth). These figures appear very high, but it is not known how much Fresh Water Swamp forest, where the family has a relatively low density, was included. Dipterocarps are also not well represented in the highest girth classes in Heath forest; or in Belalong riparian forest, where in particular *Swintonia acuta* (plate 36), *Saraca longistyla* (plate 37), and *Pometia pinnata* are frequent large trees.

Whitford (1909) estimated relative density of dipterocarps among trees exceeding 40 cm. diam. (49.5 in. girth) in Philippine forest surveys; his results varied from 33% (Mindoro delta plain) to 89% (Negros). This latter figure was exceptional, and 6 of the 9 sites were below 50%. By comparison, Belalong ridges below 650 m. had 53% of all trees exceeding c. 38 cm. diam. (48 in. girth), Andulau ridges

54%, Andulau valleys 27%, and Heath forest 21%. There is therefore little difference between most of Whitford's figures and my own, though no Dipterocarp forest in Brunei would approach his Negros figures. Wyatt Smith (1949) summarised comparable data from six areas in Malaya. Percentage dipterocarp representation for trees exceeding 16 in. diam. (50 in. girth) varied between 24.4% at Bt. Lagong to 43.4% at S. Menyala. Cousens (1951), summarised by Wyatt Smith (loc. cit.) obtained figures of 50.0% and 55.5% at Rengam F.R., but as the area enumerated was small the figures may overestimate the average there. Cousens (1959) found that dipterocarps represented 48% of all trees exceeding 48 in. girth over 154.7 acres over a variety of habitats in S. Pangkor F.R., E. Malaya.

Wyatt Smith (1954), in a paper written after a visit to forests in Negros, observed that the proportion of dipterocarps in the higher girth classes seemed to increase from Malaya eastwards to the Philippines. The present evidence suggests that dipterocarp representation varies so much from one habitat to another within one area that this generalisation is meaningless; I suspect that if figures were available from the seasonal *Dipterocarpus* forests of Thailand and Burma they would produce higher figures than those of Whitford for Negros.

Table 12 shows maximum density per acre reached by single species for trees exceeding 16 in. diam., 40 cm. diam., or 48 in. girth, for Badas, in the sectors along the two Brunei 'x' axes, and in Dipterocarp forest enumerations recorded by Whitford (1909), Wyatt Smith (1954), and Cousens (1958).

Variation in this quantity along the 'x' axes is seen to be closely related to variation in maximum importance values already discussed (fig. 24). On well drained, but not strongly leached, soils in Brunei dipterocarps without exception represent the most abundant trees in the size classes under discussion; besides the species in the table *Shorea geniculata* and *S. curtisii* at Andulau, and *S. faguetiana*, *Dryobalanops lanceolata*, and *Dr. beccarii* at Belalong were also abundant trees in the plots on these soils. At Andulau the most abundant species above the chosen girth in each of the four alluvium sectors, and the first hillside sector, were not dipterocarps; one of the species in the second Belalong sector also was not.

The maximum density figures in Brunei are closely comparable with those quoted from Malayan forests; by contrast, however, two out of the three Malayan examples are represented by species which are not dipterocarps. Philippine figures are uniformly higher, and the only Brunei figure comparable to the very high density of *Parashorea plicata* recorded by Whitford at Masbate is that for *Agathis* in Heath forest. In single acre plots in Brunei, however, *S. multiflora* reached a relative density of 28% in plot 39 at Andulau in the girth class under discussion, and at Belalong *S. laevis* reached 29.4% in plot 49; these high figures can be attributed to the clustering of species due to non-random distribution.

Relative density of, for instance, *Dipterocarpus tuberculatus* in the 'dry dipterocarp forests' of Thailand and Burma, described by Troup (1921), Champion (1936), and others, must far exceed Whitford's highest figures, as also would the figure for *S. albida* in the Brunei and Sarawak peat swamps. Family and single species dominance in Dipterocarpaceae, using the present criterion, seems to increase from non-seasonal to seasonal conditions, and from well drained relatively basic to poorly drained acid soils rather than from east to west, while species richness decreases.

2. *ECOLOGICAL DISTRIBUTION OF GENERA AND SPECIES*

In fig. 42 the Importance Values, relative to total dipterocarp values, of the principal genera, and the larger sections of *Shorea,* are plotted along the 'x' axes. It is seen that the general tendency of the family is not echoed by each section; *Dipterocarpus* shows a preference for ridges (the high values at the left hand end of the Belalong axis are caused by the single riverain species *D. oblongifolius*); Richetioides reaches its optimum on more friable soils, where raw humus accumulation is present. Sections Mutica and Brachyptera reach their highest relative importance under relatively humid conditions.

In figs. 43 and 44 the importance values of selected species are plotted along the 'x' axes, and show that Curtis' method confirms subjective observations (see table 14) and is a useful tool in describing species distribution in rain forest.

In Table 13 the basal area and frequency data of all dipterocarps recorded from all plots are arranged as means per acre along the 'x' axes. It demonstrates the narrow ecological ranges of most species, and the continuous overlapping spectrum of species ranges along the axes. Owing to the unavoidability of including a certain amount of environmental variation in each plot the breadth of the specific ranges is somewhat exaggerated, which can explain why in some cases they are broader than recorded in subjective estimates.

Widespread species grow to different sizes in different habitats; thus *S. multiflora* and *S. laevis* never grow to the same girths on shale lithosols that they do elsewhere (fig. 45). This effect is only discernable in the few species which are common throughout the limited area sampled.

Bray and Curtis (1957) showed that the distribution of species plotted on their ordination threw further light on their ecological behaviour. Dipterocarps occurring on the Andulau and Belalong ordinations are plotted on the x/y axis diagrams in figs. 46-56, which should be examined in conjunction with figs. 15 and 16, which should be superimposed on them. They demonstrate that the overlapping mosaic formed by the ecological distribution of the different species is multi-dimensional, and help to provide preliminary interpretations of species ranges in terms of their environment. The tendency for dipterocarps to be clustered on more level well drained sites is confirmed. Sections Mutica and Brachyptera of *Shorea,* and *Hopea* and *Vatica* which are mainly small trees, show wide distribution in contrast to the clustering of sections Richetioides and Shorea on the more level sites, especially at Belalong. The distribution of the four species of *Dryobalanops* on the ordinations (fig. 48) particularly well shows the value of this method in tropical forest ecology. Thus the mutual occurrence of *Dr. rappa* and *Dr. aromatica* in plot 6 at Andulau, whose soils I have already commented on, goes a long way to explain why the two species also occur together on sandy ridges at Lawas and in the Ulu Ingei.

Fig. 57 shows the patterns of some species occurring in both Andulau and Belalong ordinations. They fall into four groups :

(a) Widespread in Andulau, confined to well drained friable soils on level ground at Belalong.

50   ASHTON — ECOLOGICAL STUDIES IN THE MIXED

(b)   Species with more limited distribution :

(i)   Those confined to areas of high humidity and clay content.

(ii)   Those confined to latosolic soils; on ridges below 650 m. at Belalong, and towards the centre of the Andulau 'x' axis.

(iii)   Species occurring on the most friable soils at Andulau and also at Belalong on the higher ridges.

Species occurring in both areas are possibly less dependent on the 'physiological depth' of the soils, which differs so markedly in the two areas. Species such as *S. andulensis, S. pilosa, S. kunstleri, S. curtisii, D. crinitus, V. bantamensis, D. geniculatus, S. smithiana, S. mecistopteryx,* and *S. slooteni,* at Andulau; and *D. humeratus, H. bracteata, Dr. beccarii,* and *S. laevis,* at Belalong, are by contrast all species found most abundantly on latosols, but have only been recorded either on sandy or clay latosols.

It would not be expected that the full range of habitats occupied by the less common species would be exhibited in limited ordinations such as these. *S. ochracea, S. ovalis, H. subalata, V. oblongifolia* and *S. myrionerva* occur in only one of the ordinations, but are found outside the plots in both areas.

It was my initial exploration of the forests in 1957-8 that led me to realise that dipterocarps had more or less clearly defined ecological distributions. I presented a paper at Bogor (1958) before I had had the opportunity of checking my observations with quantitative studies, and included a table showing the altitudinal and edaphic distribution of 103 species. Data is now available for all species in Brunei and is summarised for all except montane species in Table 14. Thus the spectra observable on the ordinations are small sections of a much larger pattern of overlapping species ranges extending through all forest types except the mangrove.

This table demonstrates that, in the small area of Brunei, species are limited in altitude more by the altitudinal limits of the soils on which they occur than by any more direct climatic influence, a deduction already drawn from considerations of the Belalong ordination. Thus the species of yellow podsolic soils and sandy latosols are mainly confined to below 400 m. (the summits of Bt. Teraja and Bt. Biang), yet I found *H. beccariana* on a small patch of yellow podsolic soil on G. Pagon at 1,650 m. Thus also *S. teysmanniana,* previously known only from the lowlands, occurs in peat swamp on a relict fragmented peneplain at 650 m. on Bt. Bubong Rumah (Lawas), and *S. coriacea, S. longiflora, Dacridium beccarii var. subelatum* and *Ploiarium alternifolium,* plants typical of peaty conditions at low altitudes occur on the old topographic remnant already alluded to in the Ulu Temawai at 1,000 m. E.F.W.O. Brunig has recently also discovered *S. albida,* the gregarious dominant tree of the lowland peat swamps, also growing gregariously in association with many peat swamp species at c. 1,300 m. (4,000 ft.) on the Merurong plateau, N.E. Sarawak. Further, I am unable to distinguish between lowland and hill *Agathis* sp. in Brunei. In the lowlands it is confined to podsols, and grows gregariously on similar soils in the mountains. My map (fig. 58) of these gregarious colonies (from ground surveys extrapolated with aerial photographs) closely follows Wilford's (1961) map delineating areas of old topography. The gentle topography of those areas provides the only situation in the otherwise steeply dissected mountains where the deep podsols can develop.

S. ovata, S. curtisii, and *V. mangachapoi,* which occur on friable lowland sites in Brunei, are typical of high altitudes in Malaya, whereas *D. eurynchus* and *C. malayanum,* typical of high ridges in Brunei, occur on sandy soils at low altitudes elsewhere. This seems to be essentially another manifestation of the same phenomenon as has been observed when considering the distribution of species common to both Andulau and Belalong ordinations. At least below c. 1,300 m. therefore it appears that soil distribution is paramount in influencing altitudinal distribution of dipterocarps and possibly many other families too.

I have already indicated that the physiographic remnants of the Temawai and elsewhere may be contemporary with the submerged land surface of the South China Sea, the former having been upthrust by compensatory movements. There is no evidence to suggest, however, that these *Agathis* forests have a relict flora with an origin contemporary with the old land surface; the distribution of these species can be explained in terms of soil distribution alone. Pollen analysis and dating of the peat deposits in those areas might yield more cognate historical evidence.

Thus, whereas I have found few typical representatives of the Dipterocarp forest flora above 1,450 m. altitude, many representatives of the Heath forest flora are not only found above this altitude, but represent some of the most abundant trees occuring up to 1,900 m., the summit of Gunong Pagon Periok, the highest mountain in Brunei. *Calophyllum depressinervosum* Hend. et Wyatt-Smith, *Kayea elmeri* Merr., *Memecylon lanceolatum* Cogn., *Eugenia bankense* Hassk., *E. alcinae* Merr., *E. leucoxylon* Korth., *Tristania pentandra* Merr., *Ternstroemia aneura* Miq., *Stemonurus umbellatus* Bl., *Horsfieldia polyspherula* Hook. f., *Tetractomia holttumii* Ridl., and *Myrsine umbellulata* (Wall) Mez. in particular are trees so abundant in the forests of the montane ridges as to characterise them; yet they also occur abundantly on podsolic soils down to sea level.

Conversely several species, previously known almost entirely from mountain tops, and found in Brunei in the stunted mossy forest of the more exposed sandstone mountain ridges above 1,400 m., have been found on similar exposed rocky summits at lower altitudes; there a similar vegetation of small gnarled trees is also to be found. Examples are particularly evident among Ericaceae, representatives of which are characteristic of these sites : The rare *Rhododendron orbiculatum* Ridl. is found on the summit ridge of Gunong Pagon at 1,900 m., and has also been collected on the rocky summit of Bt. Tanggoi at only 850 m., where the other shrubs *R. quadrasianum* Vidal, v. *villosum* J.J.S., *R. durionifolium* Becc., and *Vaccinium clementis* Merr., all characteristic of montane forest in Brunei and on Kinabalu, are found abundantly. Thus also *Xanthomyrtus flavida* Stapf., another typical Kinabalu tree, occurs on the ridge of Bt. Sagan, Limbang, Sarawak, at 650 m., where also *Vaccinium clementis* occurs. *Rhododendron longiflorum* Lindl., v. *longiflorum,* * *R. brookeanum* Low ex Lindl., and *Vaccinium bancanum* Miq.* are three other species occuring frequently on montane ridges, and widespread in the lowlands on rocky summits, as at Bt. Tanggoi, Bt. Sagan, Bt. Biang (400 m.) and Bt. Patoi

---

* R. longiflorum and V. bancanum are characteristic species of quartzite ridges in the lowlands of Malaya, according to Reid (1959).

(250 m.). The montane dipterocarp *Shorea monticola* Ashton, locally frequent in tall forest on gentle slopes among boulders above 1,500 m., is also found on the summit of Bt. Belalong at 900 m., and *Tristania anomala* Merr., one of the most abundant larger trees on montane ridges, is locally abundant also on shale lithosols down to 600 m.

Perhaps the most outstanding example of this phenomenon is the flora of the summit of Bt. Batu Ketam in the Ulu Ingei, an exposed narrow knife-edge sandstone ridge bearing stunted forest at only 250 m. (850 ft.). Here I have collected *R. durionifolium,* and also the rare *Microtropis suborbiculatum* Merr., collected flowering there also by Brunig and previously only known from high mountains as on Kinabalu. Another species there, *Eugenia ampullaria* Stapf., has only been found elsewhere in Brunei by me on montane ridges above 1,400 m.

Whereas the tree flora of exposed rocky ridges is physiognomically and in part floristically similar at all altitudes, the striking difference between the vegetation in these places above and below c. 1,400 m. is that below this altitude the formation of deep moss tussocks and blankets, on the ground and up the bases of the trees, is absent; absent too is the rich flora of epiphytic and terrestrial herbs, orchids and ferns and other cryptogams. This may be attributable directly to climatic factors. I have earlier described how the higher summits are cloaked in cloud during the hottest part of the day, whereas the structurally similar forest on similar summits at lower altitudes, with its diffuse open canopy, exposes the ground directly to the sun, so that greater extremes of temperature can be expected there even than in the Dipterocarp and Heath forest. Though I have shown that, probably owing to edaphic similarities, the 'mor' bearing soils at low altitudes in Brunei bear vegetation with floristic, and sometimes structural relationships to montane vegetation, thus obscuring altitudinal zonation, there are still prominent differences in the tree flora which suggest that climate must still be considered highly important in directly influencing the altitudinal distribution of its members above and below 1300 m. Very many species characteristic of humic podsols at low altitudes, of which all the Heath forest Dipterocarpaceae can be cited as examples, seem to be absent on similar montane soils above 1,500 m.; the montane ridge forests in Brunei thus resemble a floristically poor Heath forest, but possess also several additional species which seem never to be found in the lowlands. Examples are *Podocarpus imbricatus* Hook. f., *Phyllocladus hypophylla* Hook. f., *Dacridium falciforme* Parl.; *Weinmannia dulitensis* Airy Shaw, *Ascarina philippinensis* C. B. Rob., *Drymys piperita* Hook. f., *Xanthomyrtus taxifolia* (Ridl.) Merr., *Elaeocarpus fulvotomentosus* Knuth., *Rhododendron stenophyllum* Hook. f., *R. crassifolia* Stapf, *Dyplicosia sucifolia* Airy Shaw, *Vaccinium tenerellum* Sleum., and several species in the *Fagaceae* and *Lauraceae.*

I emphasize therefore that van Steenis' (1935) concept of the 'microtherm' species, confined to high altitudes on tropical mountains by the direct influence of climatic factors is in no way challenged. I do suggest however that many species, particularly trees, that in areas other than Borneo are considered to be true 'microtherm' species, may in fact be confined there owing to the confinement of their edaphic environment to mountains in those regions.

Dames (1955, 146) states in reference to W.C. Java that 'it is interesting that the transitional zone observed by botanists, situated at 700-1000 m., wholly coincides with the pedological zone of transition'; that is, the transition from tropical rain forest to submontane rain forest described by Van Steenis (1935) coincides with the transition to brown humic mountain soils characterised by 'mor' accumulation and leaching. It therefore appears that the presence of widespread 'mor' bearing soils in lowland Sarawak and Brunei, associated with the arenaceous sedimentary lithology, combined possibly with the geologically recent upthrusting of the inland areas, has led to the obscuring of altitudinal floristic zonation below 1300 m.

3. CLASSIFICATION OF DIPTEROCARP FOREST COMMUNITIES

Symington (1943) suggested a classification system for Malayan forests that was later elaborated by Wyatt Smith (1952-3, 1961). He recognised a main dichotomy into 'the main (climatic) climax formations,' including Dipterocarp forests, and 'edaphic climax formations,' including among others Heath and Peat Swamp forests. I have already shown that such a dichotomy is untenable, and within all forests studied here soils and drainage were influencing floristic composition such that it is not possible to distinguish any types as 'climatic climax' communities. Wyatt Smith (1961) included the Heath forest as a type of Dipterocarp forest, but did not discuss this decision in terms of climatic climax theories. Symington divided Malayan Dipterocarp forests floristically more or less arbitrarily into three types on an altitudinal basis : 'Lowland Dipterocarp forests,' from sea level to 1000 ft.; 'Hill Dipterocarp forests,' to c. 2500 ft.; and 'Upper Dipterocarp forests,' to c. 4000 ft. All tend to occur at lower altitudes on isolated mountains and near the coast ('massenerhebung effect'); he presumably assumed that climate itself was the direct cause of this zonation in his 'climatic climax formations'. Wyatt Smith (1961) maintained this broad altitudinal classification, but reiterated Garfitt's (1940) contention that as it stood it was no longer adequate; he subdivided Lowland Dipterocarp forests into 11, and Hill Dipterocarp forests into 5, types on a floristic basis. Only a short description of each type is given, and the commoner species quoted; it is not stated how the existence of these forest types have been proved in the field, and how discrete they are from one another; in only four of the types can the existence of related edaphic factors be detected.

Symington's altitudinal scheme is not applicable to the area under study. Floristic changes related to edaphic and physiographic gradients obscure any altitudinal climatic zonation that might exist. Further, according to Wyatt Smith (1952), the three main Malayan types differed floristically but not structurally. The stunted Dipterocarp forests on high shale ridges in Brunei therefore are in no way a manifestation of Symington's 'Upper Dipterocarp forest'. The structural differences observed on different soils in Brunei have not been observed in Malaya.

The ordinations provide a method of assessing whether the plant communities sampled are divided into a number of discrete units, or whether there is continuous variation. If the plots form isolated clusters on the ordinations, then the former is suggested, though the restriction of plots to one physiographic unit will exaggerate any existing differentiation between the flora on these units; if they are diffusely distributed, then the latter holds good, and any classification must be arbitrary.

In fact, on both our x/y axes ordinations (fig. 10) there is a marked tendency. for the plots to cluster — these clusters can be considered equivalent to the 'noda' of Poore (1955-6). At Andulau one occurs at the right hand end of the 'x' axis in the region where the ridge plots are centred, but the valley plots are diffuse. On the x/y ordination the valley plots are almost completely separated from the hillside and ridge plots, the latter two showing considerable overlap; this implies that there is a rather clearly defined boundary between the communities on alluvial and hill soils, and reflects the relatively abrupt physiographic boundary between hillsides and alluvium; while there is no clear differentiation between hillsides and ridges.

At Belalong, the ridges below 650 m. form one cluster, and those above form another far separated from all other plots. The flora of the shale lithosols is thus very clear'y defined; the structural and physiognomic differences have already been described. Whitford (1906) has described a structurally similar forest on ridges at 750 m. on Mt. Merivales, Luzon, though differing floristically and without dipterocarps. He attributed the nature of the vegetation to wind desiccation, and produced evidence that the soils were not appreciably different from others. Wind conditions are clearly different from Mt. Merivales in Temburong, and soil differences are very evident between plots. There is an ill-defined further cluster at the lower left hand end of the Belalong x/y axis ordination, where the lower hillside plots on gently sloping land are situated; there is also a complete separation of hillside from ridge plots; this is again justified in terms of the abrupt physiographic changes.

Apart from the shale lithosol plot cluster, all others are ill-separated from one another. They produce a more or less stepped continuum along the 'x' axes. In Brunei abrupt transitions from one forest type to another are the exception rather than the rule, imposed by abrupt changes in the environment which can be attributed to one of the following factors :

(a)   Abrupt lithological changes.

(b)   Abrupt physiographic boundaries; sharp ridges or sharply differentiated valley alluvium.

(c)   Clearly defined maximum flood levels.

The transitional zone between pure sandstone rocks, interlaminated shale and sandstone, and pure shale rocks is usually narrow, so that plant communities on them can be defined clearly from one another geographically (I do not though imply by this that there is an abrupt boundary between plant communities in the transition zone). Likewise, Peat Swamp and Heath forests are generally clearly delineated. It is on hills with shale sides and a sandstone 'backbone' that intergrading is most gradual, with clay flora on the slopes, yellow podsolic flora on the saddles, and frequently Heath forests on the crests.

A series of single plots were laid out at Bt. Patoi to demonstrate transitions between these types. They were arranged as in fig. 59; each was 22 yards (1 chain) square, or 1/10 acre, and all trees exceeding 2 in. girth and 10 ft. high were enumerated. The ecological range of the constituent species in terms of the percentage in each plot recorded at Andulau, Belalong, and Badas and Bt. Puan gives an approximation to the floristic affinities. The scarp slopes show a sharp boundary between the clay hillside flora and the sandy podsol flora of the flat plateau; where the sandstone pavement is eroded away by a stream the eroding sand mixes with the clay below to form yellow podsolic soils and the flora has affinities with that at Andulau. The abrupt change on the scarp slope at Bt. Patoi is comparable with those recorded at Moraballi Creek, British Guiana, by Richards (1933-4). He recognised five distinct forest types, occupying more or less well defined steps in a habitat gradient from xeric to mesic conditions, thus being similar to my 'x' axes. There was an abrupt boundary between Mora forest on alluvium and Morabukea on undulating land; the latter was not clearly demarcated from Greenheart or Mixed rain forest owing to gradual transitions in the soil conditions. There was another abrupt boundary between the Greenheart and the Wallaba forest on podsols owing to an abrupt change in the substratum. Schultz (1960) considered that abrupt changes in Surinam were the exception rather than the rule, which is my experience in Brunei.

Richards, Tansley, and Watt (1940) have emphasised the importance of classifying vegetation according to the plant constituents of which it is formed, as opposed to some habitat factor which is assumed to be correlated with community variations.

Though the forest structure varies and is to some extent characteristic of different forest types in Brunei, differences within, for instance, the Dipterocarp forest are impossible to detect without careful measurement and are hence not suitable for use in a practical classification. Such a method seems more applicable in rain forest near its climatic limits, as that studied by L.J. Webb (1959), where climatic differences combine with physiographic and edaphic factors to produce great variation in forest structure.

Schultz (1960, 212) states that in Surinam 'the extensive hylean forests, where man-made discontinuities are still of rather rare occurrence, form the best illustration of species individuality . . . . . which ideas are familiar as Gleason's (e.g. 1926) "individualistic concept of the plant association".' This statement can be applied equally to dry-land forest in Brunei. The distribution of species in Appendix III, and of dipterocarps on the 'x' and 'y' axes, confirms Gleason's view. The forest at any place is made up of the species that can compete successfully in the habitat of the place; the habitat usually varies continuously. Any classification into communities must be partly arbitrary therefore, but I feel that for practical purposes some attempt at classification is justifiable and necessary. These conclusions therefore echo those of Whittaker (1956), whose work on the forests of the Great Smoky Mountains of the United States I have already referred to; his observations on floristic variation are strikingly similar to those observed in Brunei.

The great floristic richness and dominance of Dipterocarpaceae on well drained mesic sites is so marked as to be the most distinct feature of them, distinguishing forests in these habitats from Heath and Peat Swamp forests; dipterocarps are also very well represented in the forests on shale lithosols. I therefore propose that the general term Mixed Dipterocarp forests is appropriate for all primary forests on yellow or red residual soils in Brunei. The Andulau plots on alluvium seem to be in a transitional type between Mixed Dipterocarp forests and Fresh Water Swamp forests, hence the lack of a plot cluster on the ordination; Euphorbiaceae have replaced the Dipterocarpaceae as leading family, measured in terms of the Importance Value.

Within these plots there are tree species which are abundant and whose ranges more or less coincide with the plot clusters in the ordinations; they could be used to categorise them. Clearly, classification systems based on co-dominance in this case cannot be applied, and Tansley's (1939) hierarchy of association, consociation, and society, which Beard (1946) found possible to adopt in Trinidad vegetation, is unacceptable in Brunei. The Braun Blanquet system, which has been critically assessed by Poore (1955, 1956), offers a useful alternative in that priority is given to fidelity and constancy rather than to dominance. Within the Mixed Dipterocarp forest dipterocarp species themselves, owing to their size, ease of identification, and well defined ecological ranges, are eminently suited to this purpose, and it has been found possible, using the criteria of high fidelity and constancy, to select species on the basis of the ordinations and form a classification of forest types occurring in the areas under study (Table 15). The species selected are mapped on the ordinations in fig. 60, from which their high fidelity and constancy can be seen; their density per acre along the 'x' axes can be referred to in Table 13. At the highest hierarchic level no species are available to use for classification. The use of a family, such as I have done, is not entirely satisfactory as the criterion of fidelity is not fulfilled, and in fact the family had to be chosen largely on the criterion of dominance. It is therefore only at the lower hierarchic levels that Braun Blanquet criteria could be applied.

D.A. Webb (1954) has pointed out the disadvantages of using a hierarchic system to classify vegetation; the absence of a phylogenetic relationship between plant communities, and the many, not necessarily related, variation gradients that occur between them, advocate a multifactorial classification system. Classification is only worthwhile if it serves a useful purpose, and if the system adopted is convenient to use. I have shown earlier that in the forests of Brunei the primary variation gradient in vegetation, related to soil porosity and drainage, is far more prominent than other gradients; other gradients in fact are not perceptible enough to be usefully classified. I have also stated that areas of one type of rock, hence one range of soil porosites, are the rule rather than continuous lithological intergradations. These two facts have led me to adopt the present hierarchic system as most convenient, though if larger areas and a wider range of habitats were studied this would probably not be true.

At Andulau the Mixed Dipterocarp forest plots on yellow sandy latosols form a continuum with those on yellow podsolic soils, only the latter being grouped in a well defined cluster. In other areas the two are frequently discrete, but my data is at present not adequate to be able to suggest a nomenclature for the forest on sandy latosols, though *A. grossivenia* appears to be suitable both from the evidence of the ordination and subjective observation elsewhere.

With a knowledge of the lithology of an area, and a field survey of the forest from a few places in it, it would be possible to produce a primary vegetation map using the present classification. Intermediate zones between types, such as are evident on the ordinations, occupy narrow zones geographically. I have, with the use of aerial photographs, prepared data for such a map. It cannot be completed until the contour map of Brunei, originally scheduled for 1961, is completed; this would be used as a base.

Though I have adopted Braun Blanquet criteria in my classification, my sampling method and arrangement of plots is very different. Provided the limitations of a system, as those which are presented by the absence of clearly defined boundaries, are fully realised, a classification such as that proposed in my opinion can serve a useful purpose in descriptive rain forest ecology.

4. *THE RELATIONSHIP BETWEEN EDAPHIC PREFERENCES OF DIPTEROCARPS IN BRUNEI AND THEIR DISTRIBUTION*

In Table 14 I have divided the Brunei dipterocarps into broad groups according to the centres of their edaphic ranges, demarcated by the heavy vertical lines. In Table 16 the number of species from each group recorded from different areas of western Malaysia is summarised (details for each species can be referred to in my manual). Some areas, notably Sumatra and C. Borneo, are poorly represented as they have been little explored. Examples of distribution patterns for species occurring on various soil types are given in figs. 61-65.

Peat swamp species are obviously confined to areas where their habitat occurs.

The species of deep podsols have a disjunct distribution from Brunei throughout the Sarawak lowlands, and westwards to the lower Kapuas terraces of W. Borneo; a few occur in the Heath forests of S. Borneo and Riouw, and one in E. coastal Malaya. The podsols of east coastal Malaya where others might have occurred have mostly been under cultivation; their primary flora is little known.

Those found on shallow podsols are more widespread; *S. venulosa* and *C. malayanum*, for instance, occur on shale lithosols, which resemble podsols in their friability and presence of 'mor', and are found on the similar acid soils occurring surprisingly on highly porous ultrabasic rocks in North Borneo. *V. mangachapoi* is found in both the Philippines, North Borneo and in Malaya similarly on high hills.

Species of yellow podsolic soils have an essentially similar distribution to those of deep podsols, with aggregations in S. Borneo and Riouw, complete absence in the greater part of North Borneo and in E. and C. Borneo, and a small representation in E. Malaya. There are two exceptions : *H. beccariana,* which occurs on 'sandy coastal hills' in Malaya and also at high altitudes, and *Dr. aromatica,* which occurs in Malaya on arenaceous soils in the east, and on similar soils overlying quartzite in the west; and also in Sumatra where its edaphic habitat has not been described. My Andulau ordination shows it to be one of the ecologically most widespread species on yellow podsolic soils (compare figs. 48 and 62).

Species of sandy latosols are well represented in E. North Borneo however, while in Malaya the majority are widespread in the lowlands; *S. curtisii,* however, is characteristic of high granite ridges in Malaya, where the soils will be more friable than hillside soils.

Species widespread on both yellow podsolic and latosol soils show distributions of the previous two types. Those occurring widespread, but mainly on sandy and clay latosols, reflect their wide ecological distribution in a tendency for widespread distribution elsewhere; they are relatively well represented both throughout Borneo and in C. and E. Sumatra, and of the five occurring in Malaya, none is confined to the east coast.

The few species more or less confined to shale lithosols in Brunei are in some cases found on sandy soils at low altitudes elsewhere, such as *D. eurynchus*, which is said to occur in such places in W. Borneo, Bangka, Sumatra, Riouw, and E. Malaya. The relationship between the flora of the friable soils on high ridges and sandy soils at low altitudes has already been discussed.

Dipterocarps confined in Brunei to soils derived from pure shale show a different distribution pattern from those so far considered. Of the 53 species in all, only 5 are yet recorded from lowland central Sarawak! Of the 16 found in Malaya, all but two are widespread or characteristic of the central granite mountains. They are more widespread in C. and S. Borneo than others, and no fewer than 7 are found on the igneous mountains of Sumatra. Whereas species mostly found on clay latosols on ridges are very widespread, the 15 species of clay lithosols with 2 exceptions are endemic to Borneo. Of the exceptions *S. leptoclados* is only known outside Borneo in Panti F.R. Johore. In fig. 69 I have plotted distribution on the Belalong ordinations of some ecologically narrow ranged species endemic to Borneo, and in fig. 68 some others of widespread geographical distribution.

Of the riparian species, *D. oblongifolius*, *S. myrionerva* and *H. ?acuminata* are confined in Brunei to clay overlying shale rocks on river banks, not occurring on alluvium. Their distribution reflects this — one confined to mountains of S.W. North Borneo and inland Sarawak, one endemic, and one found along the mountain torrents throughout Central Borneo and also those of the Malayan hills. *D. apterus*, occurring only on sandy alluvium, occurs in Sarawak, W. Borneo, the Anambas, and E. Malaya. *V. umbonata* and *S. seminis* are widespread on alluvium and occur throughout Borneo, and the latter also in the Philippines. *H. fluvialis* and *S. macrophylla*, both found on clay soils mainly by rivers, are both endemic to Borneo.

Soils will not, of course, be the only environmental factor influencing distribution. The biotic environment will change geographically, owing to the different ranges of the species components of the community, and species occurring on one soil type in Brunei may occur on quite different soils elsewhere. Nevertheless, the species groups discussed do have characteristic geographical ranges, and this may throw further light on the recent history of the family.

These observations may throw light on the tertiary and quaternary evolution of Dipterocarpaceae in W. Malaysia. The great area of sedimentary rock that came above the sea towards the end of the tertiary in northern and S.E. Borneo laid bare an enormous new surface for plant colonisation. From fossil evidence it appears that most genera, and probably many if not most of the species as we now know them, were already extant at that time.

The relationships between soils in Brunei and those in Malaya have already been discussed. It is not surprising that the flora of the old Sunda-land igneous rocks (see fig. 66) is therefore represented almost without exception on clay and sandy latosols in Brunei. The clay hillsides, being subject to more rapid erosion in the steeply dissected physiography of Brunei's tertiary shales than the hillsides of the mature rounded physiography of the old Malayan mountains, produce a different steep hillside habitat, much more localised on old land surfaces; hence the dipterocarp flora is largely endemic. Most species of the old Sunda 'coign', such as *S. platyclados, D. gracilis, A. costata, A. laevis, S. parvifolia, S. exelliptica, S. lamellata, V. odorata, H. sangal,* and *S. maxwelliana* were, owing to their ecological range, only able to spread into the new areas where conditions were similar to the old environment. Others had become adapted to particular sites where weathering had proceeded in a different way. The species adapted to the deep highly weathered soils of the lowlands were able to spread onto the deep sandy latosols of the interlaminated sedimentary rocks—*D. crinitus, S. kunstleri, S. ovalis, V. nitens, H. subalata, D. verrucosus,* and *S. multiflora.* Others, adapted to the relatively friable soils of the ridges, spread into similarly friable soils at low altitudes, such as *S. ovata, S. curtisii,* and *V. mangachapoi.*

Triassic quartzitic rocks in E. Malaya have weathered in situ to sandstone, according to Owen (1950) and others, since the upper cretaceous. Yellow leached sandy soils have probably been in existence there therefore at least since the lower tertiary, so that when the new Bornean land mass appeared a group of species was possibly already evolved there capable of spreading into the new areas, such as *D. apterus, C. melanoxylon, D. lowii, Dr. aromatica, H. nutans, D. sarawakensis,* and *D. rigidus.* These species at present have a disjunct distribution, occurring in northern Borneo, E. Malaya, and in some cases S. Borneo and Sumatra; they must have been able to penetrate down through E. Sumatra and Riouw to S. Borneo, and from Johore to Sarawak and Brunei; they have not as far as we know penetrated into the S. E. Borneo sedimentary area, possibly because the deposits are more argyllaceous. Since that time, though Malaya, Sumatra, and W. Borneo were connected until geologically recently, the Malayan flora on these soils has been separated from that of Sarawak and Brunei by the main drainage valley of the Sunda land mass, which ran between W. Borneo and E. Sumatra northwards. At the same time, the S. Bornean flora was separated ecologically by the igneous area of C. and W. Borneo.

In Borneo, particularly in the north and east, there seems to have been a second period of speciation, giving rise to many of the present endemic species. The species of podsols and yellow podsolic soils not endemic to northern Borneo are: *U. borneensis, D. borneensis, D. rigidus, D. sarawakensis, Dr. aromatica, S. materialis, H. nutans* and *H. philippinensis. H. philippinensis* is represented in Borneo by a separate subspecies and in the Philippines apparently occurs on different soils. It is interesting that the other widespread species belong to *Upuna, Dipterocarpus* and *Dryobalanops,* which I consider old and isolated groups, and the Type sections of *Hopea* and *Shorea,* which on taxonomic evidence appear to be the most ancient groups in those genea.

There was a land connection at least until the end of the tertiary across the South China Sea to Indochina. Dipterocarp species, because they are usually emergent trees and thus easily affected by climatic changes, rarely range from non-seasonal to monsoon areas, and the floristic relation between Borneo and Indochina is very slight in the family. The rare *D. lamellatus* of Labuan and S.W. North Borneo, however, is closely allied to *D. intricatus* of the sandy Mekong delta, while specimens recently received at Paris from coastal S.W. Indochina represent a taxon allied to *S. matarialis* which has been called *S. falcata*.

The area left by the receding S.E. Borneo tertiary sea seems to have been occupied by species growing in Brunei on soils of high clay content. There appears to be a phytogeographic connection from Brunei across southern North Borneo to the east coast, as witnessed by the ranges of *S. mecistopteryx, S. acuminatissima, S. amplexicaulis, S. agami, D. exalatus, H. wyattsmithii, S. smithiana, S. slooteni, D. verrucosus, D. acutangulus* and *C. melanoxylon*. Of these, the first eight are confined to that area.

While an evolutionary explosion was taking place in the sandier soils, another was occurring on the clays and shales, resulting in the highly endemic hillside flora.

Foxworthy (1946), and Merrill (1923) hold to the opinion that the origin of the Dipterocarpaceae lies in the area between Malaya and the Philippines, with the main centre in Borneo. This argument, based on the present richness of species in that area, is not supported by Croizat (1952). Croizat recognises two main migration routes taken by the plants which have colonised the unstable land area between the stable Sunda 'coign' and the New Guinea 'coign' : one from S.E. Indochina through Malaya and the Riouw Archipelago to Java and Bali; the other from New Guinea north-west to Celebes and the Philippines. He thus considers Borneo a backwater, unimportant in the primary spread of species into the new lands, but the home of a secondary ebullition which has led to its present floristic richness. He cites Dipterocarpaceae as an example of a family of Gondwanaland origins which have shown two periods of speciation. As a species of the first period, he cites *S. platyclados*, which he notes occurs in the Gajo Lands of Sumatra (in the central igneous mountain chain), and at Kinabalu, both 'classic stations of primary distribution'. As species of the second period, he cites *S. seminis*, sharing a common origin with *S. sumatrana* of Sumatra and Malaya in a species of the first period that spread over the area and then underwent further speciation. The latter he further uses, with *V. mangachapoi*, to support his contention that there has been an intermittent land connection with the Philippines until comparatively recent times, an idea also supported by Merrill. The present data support Croizat's arguments. 'Old' species with wide distribution occurring in the Philippines include *D. gracilis, D. hasseltii* (not known from Brunei, but occurring in Malaya, Sumatra, Java, Central Borneo and the Philippines), and also *V. mangachapoi* (now found to have a Malayan distribution). *Anisoptera curtisii* of Malaya and Sumatra is represented by the closely allied *A. grossivenia* in Borneo, and by *A. aurea* in the Philippines, a good example of speciation of the second period. *S. fallax* of Borneo is represented in the Philippines by the closely allied *S. squamata*, and *S. leptoclados* by *S. polysperma*. *P. malaanonan*, which is very widespread and abundant in the Philippines, occurs also in N.E. Borneo, suggesting that it has spread into Borneo from the Philippines fairly recently, thus supporting the argument of a recent land connection.

DIPTEROCARP FORESTS OF BRUNEI STATE 61

5. COMPARISON WITH OTHER FAMILIES

The total frequency and basal area data for all species recorded as means per acre in 5 acre sectors along the two 'x' axes and at Badas and Bt. Puan is included in Appendix III; they are arranged in families, and for each species the maximum girth recorded is included to give an indication of the structural role of the species in the forest.

Many families show wider specific ranges than dipterocarps, and vary in a more uneven manner along the ordination axes. This may be caused in part by three sources of error in the sampling procedure : (a) Accurate determinations could not be guaranteed for non-dipterocarps. (b) Many families are composed mainly of understory trees; they may be able to occupy small pockets of a different soil type within a plot. (c) Schultz (1960) noted in Surinam that many understory species tend to form locally gregarious communities. They may be expected to respond to a different set of environmental factors from large trees; as the ordination is weighted in favour of the larger trees these variations may not be shown up.

That species of all families do not have the same narrow ecological ranges as dipterocarps is seen in fig. 70, in which Moraceous trees are distributed on the ordinations. These trees have been accurately identifiable as many have edible fruit and are hence well known. The fact that they depend on animals for dispersal may have some bearing on the evolution of different breadths of ecological range in the two families.

References

Anderson, J. A. R. 1957. The enumeration of 235 acres of Dipterocarp forest in Brunei. *Mal For* 20:144.

Ashton, P. S. 1958. Notes on the primary vegetation and soils of Brunei. *Proc UNESCO Symposium on Humid Tropics Vegetation*, Tjiawi, Indonesia.

Beard, J. S. 1946. The natural vegetation of Trinidad. *Oxf For Mem* 20.

Black, G. A., T. Dobzhansky, and C. Pavan. 1950. Some attempts to estimate species diversity and population density of trees in Amazonian forests. *Bot Gaz* 413.

Bray, J. R., and J. T. Curtis. 1957. The ordination of upland forest communities in southern Wisconsin. *Ecol Monogr* 27:325.

Cain, S. A., G. M. de Oliveira Castro, J. Pires, N. T. da Silva et al. 1956. Applications of some phytosociological techniques to some Brazilian rain forest. *Amer J Bot* 43:911.

Champion, H. G. 1936. A preliminary survey of the forest types of India and Burma. *Indian For Rec*, n.s. (Silviculture), 1:1.

Cousens, J. E. 1951. Some notes on the composition of lowland tropical rain forest in Rengam Forest Reserve, Johore. *Mal For* 14:131.

———. 1958. A study of 155 acres of tropical rain forest by complete enumeration of all large trees. *Mal For* 21:155.

Curtis, J. T. 1947. The palo verde forest type near Gonaives, Haiti, and its relation to the surrounding vegetation. *Caribb For* 8:1.

Curtis, J. T., and R. P. McIntosh. 1951. An upland forest continuum of the prairie-forest border region of Wisconsin. *Ecology* 32:476.

Dames, T. W. G. 1955. *The Soils of East Central Java*. Contributions to the General Agricultural Research Station, Bogor.

Foxworthy, F. W. 1946. Distribution of the Dipterocarpaceae. *J Arn Arb* 37:347.

Garfitt, J. E. 1940. Malayan forest types. *Mal For* 10:136.

Gleason, H. A. 1926. Some applications of the quadrat method. *Bull Torrey Bot Club* 53:20.

Merrill, E. D. 1923. Distribution of the Dipterocarpaceae. *Phil J Sc* 23:1.

Milne, G. 1947. A soil reconnaissance journey through parts of Tanganyika territory: December 1935 to February 1936. *J Ecol* 35:192.

Owen, G. 1950. A provisional classification of Malayan soils. *J Soil Sci* 2:20.

Poore, M. E. D. 1955–56. The use of phytosociological

methods in ecological investigations. *J Ecol* 43:226, 606; *J Ecol* 44:28.

Richards, P. W. 1936. Ecological observations on the rain forest of Mount Dulit, Sarawak. *J Ecol* 24:1, 340.

———. 1945. The floristic composition of primary tropical rain forest. *Biol Rev* 20:1.

———. 1952. *The Tropical Rain Forest.* Cambridge.

Richards, P. W., A. G. Tansley, and A. S. Watt. 1940. The recording of structure, life form, and flora of tropical forest communities as a basis for their classification. *J Ecol* 28:224.

Schultz, J. P. 1960. Ecological studies on rain forest in Northern Suriname. *Verh. K. Ned. Akad. Wet., Afd Natuurkunde,* ser. 2., 53(1).

Steenis, C. G. G. J. van. 1935. On the origin of the Malaysian mountain flora. II. Altitudinal zones, general considerations and renewed statement of the problem. *Bull Jard Bot Btzg,* ser. 3, 13:289.

Symington, C. G. 1943. Foresters manual of dipterocarps. *Mal For Rec* 16.

Webb, D. A. 1954. Is the classification of plant communities either possible or desirable? *Soertryk af Botanisk Tidsskrift* 51:362.

Whitford, H. N. 1906. The vegetation of the Lamão Forest Reserve. *Phil J Sc C* 1:373, 637.

———. 1909. Studies on the vegetation of the Philippines. 1. The composition and volume of the Dipteroearp forests of the Philippines. *Phil J Sc C* 4:699.

Whittaker, R. H. 1956. A study of summer foliage insect communities in the Great Smoky Mountains. *Ecol Monogr* 22:1.

Wilford, G. E. 1961. *The Geology and Mineral Resources of Brunei and Adjacent Areas of Sarawak.* Brit. Borneo Geol. Surv., Kuching, memoir no. 10.

Wyatt Smith, J. 1949. A note on the tropical lowland evergreen forest in Malaya. *Mal For* 12:58.

———. 1952. Malayan forest types. *Mal Nat J* 7:45, 91.

———. 1954. Forest Memories of the Philippines. *Mal For* 17:135.

———. 1961. A note on the fresh-water swamp, lowland, and hill forest types of Malaya. *Mal For* 24, 2:110.

9

Forest Dynamics and Regeneration

David F. R. P. Burslem and M. D. Swaine

Tropical forest ecologists and tropical foresters concerned with regeneration have emphasized the importance of the disturbance to forest canopies created when large living or dead trees fall to the ground, thus initiating a process of succession in the gaps so formed. In this context, "dynamics" refers to the study of changes over time in the composition of the regenerating community, rather than to the study of population dynamics of tropical trees per se. In this part we present a selection of papers that have been important to the historical development of research on tropical forest dynamics and regeneration, and in some cases remain widely cited by contemporary authors. We have deliberately selected studies that illustrate the range and scales of disturbance events that provide the context for research on dynamics and regeneration in tropical forests.

Studies of disturbance, canopy gap formation, and successional development in gaps have been fundamental to many long-running debates in tropical forest community ecology (Whitmore 1974, 1978, 1984a; Grubb 1977, 1996; Denslow 1980, 1984; Hubbell and Foster 1986a, 1986b; Hubbell et al. 1999). Four major questions have guided the study of forest dynamics. How do canopy gaps determine patterns in tropical forest community composition? What is the contribution of disturbance events, on a variety of scales, to maintenance of species richness in tropical forests? To what extent does the autecology of tropical tree species reflect their varying requirements for regeneration in canopy gaps? What are the implications of successional processes and disturbance for the equilibrium status of tropical forests? In this part, we will focus on describing the historical development of research aimed at answering the second, third, and fourth questions and attempt to highlight those studies that have laid a foundation for future work.

Pattern and Process in Tropical Forest Communities

Historically, research investigating patterns in tropical forest species composition has not been conducted independently of research investigating the processes that generate the patterns. Hence the division of material between parts 8 (on patterns) and 9 (on processes) of this book is a somewhat artificial distinction that has led to an inevitable overlap in content, although spatial patterns will be dealt with only briefly here.

The notion that tropical forest species com-

Ficus with buttresses. Tabula XVI from K. F. P. von Martius, ed. (1794–1869), *Flora Brasiliensis*

position is spatially variable, and that this variability may be generated during regeneration, was discussed by Aubréville (1938 [paper 35]). This theory was called the "mosaic" or "cyclical" theory of regeneration by Watt (1947) and Richards (1952), and was promoted by them as an expression, for tropical forests, of the classical view of pattern and process in plant communities. Aubréville's theory proposed that the spatial variability in the dominant species in a forest was caused by the failure of some species to regenerate beneath their own canopy. An inevitable outcome of this behavior must be that the future species composition of the canopy dominants will change in favor of the species currently most abundant in the seedling and sapling communities, but persistence of all species within the landscape is guaranteed by the coexistence of forest patches with varying compositions. The original evidence for this theory came from Aubréville's studies in Côte d'Ivoire (see part 8, paper 35), but similar patterns have been observed in other tropical forests, for example by Eggeling (1947; paper 39) and Whitmore (1974; paper 43). However, an ambiguity in the presentation of Aubréville's data by Richards (1952) has led to misinterpretation of the strength of the evidence for this theory, and data from Ghanaian forests do not support it (Hall and Swaine 1976; Swaine and Hall 1988).

Aubréville's work stimulated two direct lines of research: investigations of the mechanisms underlying the patterns described and of the consequences of these patterns for the equilibrium status of tropical forest communities. One of the first experimental studies of (sub)tropical forest regeneration (Webb, Tracey, and Williams 1972) is reprinted in full in this part (paper 42). This study was designed as a test of Aubréville's ideas as well as questions taken from Richards (1952), Jones (1956), and Schulz (1960). Analysis of the distribution and abundance of trees of all sizes in an experimental clearing twelve years after it was created showed that the patchiness in species composition observed in mature-phase forest had already been established by then, and that these patches were largely determined by the local availabil-

ity of seed trees (Webb, Tracey, and Williams 1972). This paper is important because the authors draw attention to the role of chance events in the determination of the outcome of regeneration in gaps and highlight the significance of patterns in tropical forest composition at different spatial scales. The relative importance of chance events in tropical forest regeneration has been investigated in detail by Hubbell and coworkers in Neotropical forests and was one of the stimuli for the creation of a network of very large plots (16–50 ha) at a range of tropical forest sites from the early 1980s (Hubbell 1979; Hubbell and Foster 1986a, 1986b, 1987; Hubbell et al. 1999). The importance of dispersal limitation for determining the outcome of regeneration in gaps has recently been confirmed for pioneer trees growing on the fifty-hectare plot on Barro Colorado Island, Panama (Dalling, Hubbell, and Silvera 1998).

Forest Growth Cycle, Gap Phase Dynamics, and Species Richness

Drawing on ideas expressed in a different context by Watt (1947), Whitmore (1975, 1978) described and illustrated the "forest growth cycle" for tropical forests, defined as a "state of dynamic equilibrium" that "may be subdivided . . . into three phases: the gap phase, the building phase, and the mature phase" (Whitmore 1978, 639). Whitmore emphasized that these phases should be considered as abstract concepts rather than distinct entities, but this has not prevented a literature on the definition of gaps and their boundaries from developing (Brokaw 1982; Popma et al. 1988; Lieberman, Lieberman, and Peralta 1989). It is now widely recognized that a continuum of irradiance conditions and microclimates exist in forests on many spatial scales, and that conditions at a given site can be highly dynamic (Chazdon 1988; Brown 1993).

Although the forest growth cycle is essentially a descriptive concept, its exposition contributed to a large body of research from the 1980s on "gap phase dynamics." Much of this work has tested hypotheses concerning the mechanisms of tropical forest regeneration (e.g., Brokaw 1985; Uhl et al. 1988; Brown and Whitmore 1992). These studies were mostly formulated at a time when canopy gaps were considered to be all-important for processes ranging from tree growth and reproduction to maintenance of species richness (Hartshorn 1978; Denslow 1980, 1984; Whitmore 1984a). Many of the latter studies are still continuing, but it is already clear that some of the earlier ideas are in need of revision (Grubb 1996; Brown and Jennings 1998).

Three examples will illustrate how these debates have developed. The first comes from the observation that gaps in the litter layer are important for the regeneration of some tree species, such as those studied on Barro Colorado Island, Panama, by Molofsky and Augspurger (1992). Grubb (1996) suggested that the distribution of litter gaps is independent of that of canopy gaps and that litter gaps may be all-important for the regeneration of some species. A second example that illustrates how ideas have shifted since the 1980s may be illustrated by the long-running gap-creation experiment at Danum Valley in Sabah, Malaysia, which has shown that the outcome of regeneration in gaps is determined by processes occurring prior to gap creation, as well as species-specific responses to the gap environment (Brown and Whitmore 1992; Whitmore and Brown 1996). A third example of a more recent development in this field is the finding that competition for below-ground resources may also limit seedling growth and survival in tropical forests (Coomes and Grubb 1998; Ostertag 1998; Lewis and Tanner 2000), a finding that was predicted by tropical foresters decades earlier (Wilkinson 1939; Fox 1973).

The potential for forest structural heterogeneity created by the phases of the forest growth cycle to contribute to maintenance of tree species richness has been a theme of tropical forest community ecology for over two decades (Grubb 1977; Denslow 1980, 1984; Whitmore 1984a) and a large number of experimental and observational studies have addressed this issue (reviewed in Denslow 1987

and Brown and Jennings 1998). The importance of differences in gap size for coexistence of species at the extremes of the shade tolerance gradient in tropical forests was first demonstrated by Kramer (1933, cited by Whitmore 1978), but the relative importance of heterogeneity in forest structure to maintenance of species richness within the large functional group of nonpioneer species remains highly controversial. Orians (1982) suggested that within-gap heterogeneity might contribute to the maintenance of tree species richness by micro-site partitioning among coexisting species, and some support for this hypothesis has been presented for a tropical wet forest in Costa Rica (Brandani, Hartshorn, and Orians 1988). Recent studies show the potential for niche partitioning among rain forest tree species along a gradient of light availability (Kobe 1999). However, observational studies do not suggest that gap-size partitioning actually plays a significant role in maintenance of tropical tree species richness (reviewed in Brown and Jennings 1998 and Brokaw and Busing 2000).

Autecology and Functional Groups

The classification of tropical trees into functional groups or ecological species groups according to their autecological characteristics has been a central theme of tropical forest ecology research for over forty years, and a confusing terminology has evolved (Swaine and Whitmore 1988). Three of the papers reprinted in this part illustrate the development of these ideas (Steenis 1958 [paper 40]; Budowski 1965 [paper 41]; Whitmore 1974 [paper 43]). Steenis (1958) first recognized a distinct group of species with "soft wood, swift growth and limited life-span" (212) and contrasted the behavior and ecology of these "nomad" species with the remaining, "stationary," species. Steenis (1958) summarized the "pioneer qualities" of the nomads and introduced a degree of complexity by noting that "a few nomads are long lived" (212). This complexity was developed by later workers, including Budowski (1965) and Whitmore (1974, 53, table 7.6), both of whom expanded the number of species groups identified to four. More recent reviews and empirical studies have attempted to codify the nomenclature and determine the nature of the traits that distinguish members of different species groups. For example, Denslow (1987) recognized three species groups arrayed along a continuum of light demand, while Swaine and Whitmore (1988) recommended a simple dichotomy of species into pioneer and nonpioneer (or climax) groups and proposed that pioneers are uniquely identifiable by possessing "seeds that only germinate in canopy gaps open to the sky and which receive some full sunlight" and an inability to "survive in shade" (33).

These attempts at functional group identification have not passed without comment and criticism as their predictions have begun to be tested (e.g., Alvarez-Buylla and Martinez-Ramos 1992; Clark and Clark 1992; Grubb 1996). Part of the difficulty arises, for example, because different authors, or even the same author, use different terms to refer to the same entity. A continuing debate focuses on whether distinct functional groups can be distinguished by the possession of a distinguishing trait, or whether the ecological species groups represent two extremes of a successional gradient. Quantitative comparative analyses of tropical trees for the traits thought to define functional groups have only been attempted relatively recently, and tend to support the existence of a continuum of successional status rather than uniquely identifiable functional groups (e.g., Zimmerman et al. 1994). Most of the suggested traits relate to characteristics of the juvenile stages of the plant, such as seed size and requirements for germination and establishment, although adult mortality and recruitment rates and wood density are also sometimes included.

Further complexity has been added by the suggestion that there is not a single continuum of relative light demand or successional status among tropical forest trees, because species change their relative light demand during ontogeny such that "cross-overs" might exist (Thompson, Stocker, and Kriedemann 1988;

Clark and Clark 1992; Grubb 1996). This remains a poorly studied area of tropical forest ecology. Future research will need to adopt a comparative approach to investigating the ecological significance of differences or similarities in traits between species, as used by Grubb and Metcalfe (1996) to examine the relationship between seed size and establishment conditions in tropical Australian rain forest plants. Phylogenetically controlled contrasts suggested that seed size ranked low down on the "hierarchy of characteristics enabling plants to become established in the shade" (Grubb and Metcalfe 1996, 512). We advocate that a similar approach be adopted in future comparative research on the autecology of tropical forest plants.

Succession and the Equilibrium Status of Tropical Forests

So far in this part we have focused on the literature on small-scale disturbance events and internal forest dynamics through gap colonization processes. However, in order to review the historical development of tropical forest dynamics and regeneration thoroughly, it is necessary to acknowledge the emerging recognition that large-scale disturbance events, and the ensuing successional processes, may be crucial to understanding the dynamics and diversity of many tropical forest communities (see also part 3).

The extract of the paper by Eggeling (1947) reprinted here describes the dynamics of colonization of grassland by woodland in Budongo Forest, Uganda. Eggeling showed that a predictable sequence of forest types developed on a timescale of decades as a result of woody plant succession at this site, and presented data that show nonlinear changes in the diversity of trees in forest stands over time. Although a number of primary tropical vegetation successions had been described previously (for example the primary succession on Krakatau was reviewed by Richards [1952]), it was the Budongo data that Connell (1978) used to derive his intermediate disturbance hypothesis (paper 16). Connell's model proposed that the diversity of communities is maximal at the midpoint of succession or in sites where disturbance intensity or frequency are intermediate in scale. According to Connell, early successional communities are dominated by a species-poor assemblage of pioneers. Species diversity increases during succession, but declines in late succession through competitive exclusion in the absence of extrinsic disturbance. Thus only the late-successional, species-poor communities can be regarded as being at "equilibrium" with respect to their composition or richness.

The implications of this model for the equilibrium status of tropical forest communities are profound, but supporting evidence is not conclusive. Species-poor tropical forests are not uncommon, particularly in tropical Africa (Hart, Hart, and Murphy 1989; Connell and Lowman 1989), but research is needed to determine the mechanisms that generate and maintain their low diversity (see part 8). By reanalyzing long-term tropical forest data sets, Sheil (1996, 1997, 1999) and Burslem and Whitmore (1999) have argued that the positive relationship between rates of forest turnover and measures of species diversity in both local and global comparisons (Phillips et al. 1994) supports Connell's hypothesis (cf. Phillips et al. 1997).

By acting as one of the stimuli for the development of the intermediate disturbance hypothesis, Eggeling's (1947) paper represents an important landmark in understanding tropical forest dynamics and regeneration at temporal and spatial scales greater than those encompassed by an individual tree. The more recent recognition of the importance of large-scale disturbance events has further broadened our understanding of the processes and scales that influence tropical forest dynamics and regeneration. The paper by Whitmore (1974), part of which is reprinted in this part (paper 43), was influential because it reported changes in forest structure and composition on the South Pacific island of Kolombangara over a six-year interval during which the forest was impacted by a cyclone, whereas earlier studies (e.g., Webb 1958; Wadsworth and Englerth 1959) had reported static responses to isolated events. The study of the effects of large-scale disturbances on tropical ecosystems has since developed into a substantial discipline in its own right. The list of disturbance factors that are known to influence tropical forest dynamics over long timescales also includes landslides, earthquakes, volcanoes, lightning, drought and fire, epidemic herbivory, and anthropogenic effects (reviewed by Whitmore and Burslem 1998), although most of the studies of these factors have not had the benefit of censuses conducted before and after disturbance. Research on forest responses to severe windstorms is particularly well advanced in the Caribbean (see Walker et al. 1991). The key finding emerging from studies of tropical windstorms is that tree species composition and relative abundance in forests impacted by severe windstorms are not markedly different from the predisturbance state (e.g., Bellingham, Tanner, and Healey 1995). In fact, recent studies show that hurricane disturbance can actually lead to higher species richness during recovery compared to undisturbed forest (Vandermeer et al. 2000). The high resistance to disturbance is determined, in part, by the predominance of sprouting as a mechanism of forest recovery (Bellingham, Tanner, and Healey 1994). The prevalence of resprouts among the stems damaged by hurricane Joan in Nicaragua led Yih et al. (1991) and Boucher et al. (1994) to propose a "direct regeneration" model of forest recovery, in which "species dominant in the first years after the disturbance will be the same as the species which were dominant before the disturbance" (Boucher et al. 1994, 127). If validated, this model would challenge the notion that large-scale disturbance by high winds prevent the establishment of an "equilibrium" species composition in disturbed tropical forests.

Conclusion

The history of research on tropical forest dynamics and regeneration reflects its early origins in temperate forest ecology and tropical forestry. For example, the concepts introduced into tropical ecology by Richards, Whitmore, and Webb, Tracey, and Williams reflect their theoretical origins in the "pattern and process" view of plant communities proposed by Watt (1947), while the work of Eggeling (1947) in Uganda was designed in part to underpin his work in forest management. More recently, theoretical and empirical advances in tropical forest dynamics and regeneration have begun to influence the development of techniques and theory in ecological research beyond the tropics, as predicted by Richards (1963). Concepts that were pioneered in tropical forests range from the roles of density dependence and recruitment limitation as factors contributing to the maintenance of tree species richness (Janzen 1970 [paper 17]; Connell 1971; Hubbell et al. 1999; see also part 4) to the importance of sunflecks in the carbon balance of seedlings in the shade (Chazdon 1988). The ongoing concentration of research effort in the dynamics and regeneration of tropical forests suggests that the increasing contribution of tropical

ecology to the development of ecological theory is set to continue well into the future.

Reprinted Selections

W. J. Eggeling. 1947. Observations on the ecology of the Budongo rain forest, Uganda (excerpt). *Journal of Ecology* 34:37–39

C. G. G. J. van Steenis. 1958. Rejuvenation as a factor for judging the status of vegetation types: The biological nomad theory. In *Study of Tropical Vegetation*. Proceedings of the Kandy Symposium, 212–15, 218. Paris: UNESCO

G. Budowski. 1965. Distribution of tropical American rain forest species in the light of successional processes. *Turrialba* 15:40–42

L. J. Webb, J. G. Tracey, and W. T. Williams. 1972. Regeneration and pattern in the subtropical rain forest. *Journal of Ecology* 60:675–695

T. C. Whitmore. 1974. Change with time and the role of cyclones in tropical rain forest on Kolombangara, Solomon Islands. Paper 46, pp. 8, 26–30, 36–42, 52–59. Oxford: Commonwealth Forestry Institute

PAPER 39

Observations on the Ecology of the Budongo Rain Forest, Uganda
W. J. Eggeling

Richards (1939) has pointed out that in Nigeria the rainfall during the wet season must be more than adequate for the needs of vegetation everywhere in both the forest zones and that, contrary to expectation, the boundary between them is determined neither by the length of the dry season nor by the total rainfall during the dry months. He suggests the possibility that in Nigeria the dividing line between Rain Forest and Mixed Deciduous Forest is determined primarily not by the rainfall itself but by some factor correlated with it such as the distance inland reached by moist air from the sea during the dry season. The dry season at Budongo is less severe than at any of the Rain Forest stations for which Richards gives figures. Rainy days, too, are more numerous and better distributed (Table 5). This latter factor and the proximity to Budongo of two large bodies of inland water (Lake Albert on the west and Lake Kioga on the east) are probably important.

Table 5. *Rainfall and rainy days at Budongo, Uganda, and Akilla, Nigeria*

	Jan.	Feb.	Mar.	Apr.	May	June	July	Aug.	Sept.	Oct.	Nov.	Dec.	Year
Mean monthly rainfall (mm.):													
Budongo	23	77	129	188	173	134	98	155	153	160	132	73	1495
Akilla	28	35	96	180	196	407	419	134	252	242	80	11	2080
Mean no. of rainy days:													
Budongo	5	9	13	19	20	15	12	16	15	18	16	9	167
	(3)	(7)	(11)	(16)	(16)	(11)	(10)	(15)	(15)	(16)	(14)	(7)	(141)
Akilla	1	3	8	9	13	18	17	13	18	16	8	1	125

Numbers in brackets indicate rainy days at Kyatarugo estate, 3·5 km. (2¼ miles) from the edge of Budongo (years 1916–32 and 1939–42). Budongo figures (from the station at the Mile 55 Camp, Busingiro) cover the 10-year period August 1933–July 1943. The Akilla figures (from Richards, 1939) are for the years 1921–34.

Chief types of forest. At Budongo, in addition to Swamp Forest (edaphic climax), which is relatively unimportant, three main types of forest belonging to a single sere are recognized. They are Colonizing Forest (seral), Mixed Forest (seral), and Ironwood Forest (climatic climax). Colonizing Forest, the youngest type, occurs in two forms. In the first, Colonizing (*Maesopsis*) Forest, the dominant large tree is *Maesopsis eminii*; in the second, Colonizing (Woodland) Forest, *Maesopsis* is either absent or scarce. Mixed Forest is the mid-way stage in the development of Colonizing Forest to Ironwood Forest. It is the richest of the forest types and its canopy is composed of many species. In Ironwood Forest, *Cynometra alexandri* is dominant, forming over 75% of the canopy.

Mixed Forest (60%) and Ironwood Forest (32%) cover by far the great part of Budongo. Colonizing Forest accounts for a further 6% and Swamp Forest (2%) for the remainder.

Colonization and succession. Grassland and forest are normally separated, in Bunyoro, by a narrow belt of *Acanthus arboreus* Forsk. (E. 1460), a prickly shrub which attains 3·5 m. (12 ft.) in height. Around much of Budongo the forest is expanding and every year sees a few more yards won from the grassland. Expansion is most rapid in *Acanthus* areas, where reduced grass competition and lessened shade afford conditions suitable for the regeneration of *Maesopsis*, the principal tree colonizer. In such areas, *Maesopsis* Forest results.

Where *Acanthus* is absent, and especially on murram ridges and on patches of shallow soil, expansion is slower. Here *Albizzia* spp., *Caloncoba schweinfurthii*, *Croton* spp., *Dombeya mukole*, *Olea welwitschii*, *Phyllanthus* spp., *Sapium ellipticum*, *Spathodea campanulata* and a few other species do most of the colonizing. By degrees they invade the grassland (usually first occupying the bases of termite mounds and thence spreading outwards),

584

38   *The ecology of the Budongo rain forest, Uganda*

partly kill out the grass, afford protection to undershrubs and herbs, and produce conditions which lead to the gradual formation of Woodland Forest.

The formation of *Maesopsis* Forest and Woodland Forest can be much hastened by fire protection. For this reason, bays of grassland lying between strips of gallery forest usually thicken very quickly. Fires in such areas are less fierce than elsewhere because the surrounding forest reduces fanning by wind.

Maesopsis Forest persists, as such, at Budongo, for only one generation. While the crop is young there is a regular distribution of age classes, but as the trees become older the smaller specimens become suppressed, the canopy thins, the lower stories and undergrowth thicken, *Maesopsis* fails to regenerate, and less violently light demanding Mixed Forest species make their appearance.

The development of Woodland Forest to Mixed Forest is similar. Following the suppression of grass and the formation of a canopy, the stand of colonizers is gradually invaded by more truly forest species such as *Celtis* spp., *Funtumia* spp. and *Maba abyssinica*. There is a tendency for *Maesopsis*, too, to appear, but not in numbers.

The replacement of Mixed Forest by Ironwood Forest takes much longer than the preceding stage of the succession. The climax dominant (*Cynometra*) makes its first appearance before Mixed Forest reaches its optimum development, but its presence in the young stages is apt to be overlooked because it is not at first a fast-growing species and attention is captured by the more conspicuous saplings of light-demanders. By degrees, however, the ironwood becomes noticeable as it pushes its way through undergrowth and understory. It is catholic in its tastes and establishes itself everywhere. As more and more *Cynometra* appear, Mixed Forest species fail to regenerate, existing stems fall and are not replaced, and climax Ironwood Forest forms. The reason for the failure of Mixed Forest species to resist the invasion of the *Cynometra* is as yet imperfectly understood. Possibly they are unable to withstand the competition of its roots. The shade in Ironwood Forest is not unduly dense, and as a rule the purer the crop the thinner the undergrowth. There appears to be quite sufficient light for all but the most light-demanding of the Mixed Forest species, so that shade does not account, as was at first believed, for their failure to regenerate.

In Table 6 an attempt is made to indicate succession by listing the most abundant species in sample plots in the different types of forest. In Fig. 4 the instability of the seral types is expressed in graphical form.

Spread. An examination of the areas of Colonizing Forest shows conclusively that within the last thirty years Budongo has spread considerably. The evidence includes the presence of relict *Terminalia velutina* and of derelict termite mounds of a grassland type well within the forest, and is confirmed by a comparison of old and present-day maps.

To take a convenient example, Map 2 shows part of a recent stock-map of a portion of Budongo immediately north of Busingiro. Towards the top of the map is an area of Colonizing Forest known as Mpembeje. A typescript report (M.P. 67/32) in the files of the Uganda Forest Department states that in 1910, when the first survey of Budongo was made, the whole of this bay-like area was grassy. In the words of the writer (M. T. Dawe) the tree vegetation was 'mainly *Terminalia velutina*', the area being shown as grassland on the map accompanying the report. Air photographs taken in 1931 reveal that in that year no grass remained and that the whole bay had become closed forest.*

* For details of composition see Tables 10 and 11. S.P. 1 is situated almost in the centre of the bay; S.P. 2 in its south-west corner.

Table 6. *Total number of individuals of species which are represented on three or more sample plots by four or more trees exceeding 20 cm. (8 in.) diam. (Swamp Forest excluded)*

Maximum abundance in	Species	Colonizing (Woodland) Forest (S.P. 1)	Colonizing (*Maesopsis*) Forest (mean of S.P. 2 and 3)	Ecotone (S.P. 4)	Mixed Forest (mean of S.P. 5 and 6)	Ecotone (mean of S.P. 7 and 8)	Ironwood Forest (mean of S.P. 9 and 10)
Colonizing Forest	*Maesopsis eminii* Engl.	—	74	27	—	—	—
	Olea welwitschii Gilg & Schellenb.	48	54	31	—	—	—
	Spathodea campanulata Beauv.	23	10	4	—	—	—
	Sapium ellipticum Pax	14	12	8	—	—	—
	Caloncoba schweinfurthii Gilg	131	164	6	—	1	—
	Phyllanthus discoideus Muell. Arg.	19	32	32	1	1	—
	Erythrophleum guineense G. Don	15	15	5	2	1	—
Ecotone	*Funtumia* spp.*	1	32	104	20	23	—
Mixed Forest	*Trichilia prieuriana* A. Juss.	—	—	2	20	2	—
	Alstonia congensis Engl.	—	4	2	10	8	1
	Mahoganies†	—	—	2	15	7	1
	Chrysophyllum spp.‡	1	8	6	71	11	1
	Celtis spp.§	23	61	90	319	141	72
Ecotone	*Rinorea ardisiaeflora* O. Ktze.	—	—	5	13	70	27
Ironwood Forest	*Cynometra alexandri* C. H. Wright	—	—	—	36	55	119
	Lasiodiscus mildbraedii Engl.	—	—	—	—	118	258

* *Funtumia elastica* Stapf; *F. latifolia* Stapf ex Schltr.

† *Entandrophragma cylindricum* Sprague; *E. utile* Sprague; *Khaya anthotheca* C.DC.

‡ *Chrysophyllum albidum* G. Don; *C. perpulchrum* Mildbr. ex Hutch. & J. M. Dalz.; *Chrysophyllum* n.sp.? (E. 2248).

§ *Celtis brownii* Rendle; *C. durandii* Engl. var. *ugandensis* Rendle; *C. soyauxii* Engl.; *C. zenkeri* Engl.

Similar evidence of the rapid expansion of Budongo is available for a number of other areas, and it is probable that the forest has been spreading for some time. The present proportions of the main types of forest bear out this view, since only a third of the forest is old enough to carry the climax type.

IV. Methods: Description of Plots

(1) Methods

Floristic composition was studied in eleven sample plots (S.P.), three situated in Colonizing Forest, two in Mixed Forest, two in Ironwood Forest, one in Swamp Forest, one in an ecotone between Colonizing Forest and Mixed Forest, and two in ecotones between Mixed Forest and Ironwood Forest.

Stratification was studied by means of four profile plots (P.P.), one in each of the two kinds of Colonizing Forest, one in Mixed Forest and one in Ironwood Forest.

The sample plots, 122 m. (400 ft.) square (= 1·418 ha. = 3·673 acres), were marked out by chain and compass. Each was divided into four strips 122 × 30·5 m. (400 × 100 ft.), and all trees over 10 cm. (4 in.) d.b.h. were measured, each strip recorded separately.*

* If sample plots are enumerated in strips, curves can be prepared showing the relationship between number of species and area *within* the plots. 'Each strip is treated as a separate unit, then by taking the average number of species on the four strips, on the six possible combinations of three strips, and the number on the whole plot, four points are obtained through which a species/area curve can be drawn' (Richards, 1939). In the case of S.P. 1, 2, 3, 8, 9 and 10, the curve was found to be flattening out at the area of the whole plot. In the case of S.P. 4, 5, 6 and 7 it was still rising slightly, and in the case of S.P. 11 (Swamp Forest) was rising steeply. For this latter plot alone, therefore, the area sampled was less than the 'minimal area' for trees 10 cm. (4 in.) diam. and over. Results are expressed in an abbreviated form in Fig. 5, where mean curves are shown for the various types of forest.

Rejuvenation as a Factor for judging the Status of Vegetation Types: the Biological Nomad Theory

by

Dr. C. G. G. J. van Steenis

Rejuvenation (regeneration) of a tropical climax rain forest is comparable to the growth of an organism in which the cells are continuously regenerated, because the individual specimens, after having completed their life cycle, are replaced by other specimens of the same species. Seedlings and juvenile individuals are present in the forest in various age classes.

In this comparison of the forest with an organism, the only difference is that the organism has generally a life-span that can be measured in human terms of time and is at most 4,000 years in exceptional cases, whereas the climax-forest is so long lived that its life-span can only be measured in terms of geological time.

This rejuvenation in the climax rain forest takes place for each species, humble or tall, whether a herb, a liana, or a tree, each occupying its own niche and having its own function in this organism. The length of the life cycles is, therefore, very different for different participants, and varies from one year to several hundreds of years; but the regeneration as expressed in these life cycles is performed in an average mutual balance.

The participants of this organism, this climax rain forest, can be called stationary species, or dryads.

There is, however, another class of species which I call temporary species or nomads. They cannot rejuvenate in the rain forest and can maintain themselves only at its borders.

The reason for this lies in the particular needs of their germination and early juvenile growth, which is intolerant of shade. To this is sometimes added an additional need for certain high temperatures for seed germination itself, as for example with teak, or the need of having the seeds in direct contact with the mineral soil in order to germinate, as for example with pine.

There is no question but that this class of nomad plants belongs to the rain forest in the wider sense. A few of them may be of alien origin and have been imported in historic time, but in Malaysia the majority of them are indigenous and autochthonous and even

large genera consist almost wholly of nomads, for example *Macaranga*, *Pipturus*, *Mallotus*, and many others.

The majority are short lived and are often termed weed trees because of their soft wood, swift growth and limited life-span. The demand for more or less open country for their swift growth marks them as suitable for secondary growths (seral succession series). A few nomads are long lived; these will be discussed below.

To return to my comparison with the rain forest as an organism, the nomads fulfil a function for the rain forest similar to the role of the lymph coagulating to form a scab for the skin, which falls off after having completed its function of closing a wound. The function of nomads in the rain forest is limited but occasionally needed in various places.

The forming of such a rain forest scab is needed in all places where forest has been destroyed by natural causes or new soil has been formed, for example on the slopes along river courses and in ever-changing river bottoms, in deltas, on undercut slopes along streams followed by earth slides, on volcanic mud streams, on lava streams; also in all other spots where the forest balance has been upset, as where mature or over mature trees have crashed down or wind or lightning has made openings in the forest. The latter cases often happen in tropical forests in which the root systems of trees are generally very superficial.

All these open places, by the native people often called the "eyes" of the forest, are rapidly filled with succession seres of nomads in the shade of which the ultimately larger and longer-lived emergents of the canopy and the larger upper and understorey trees germinate. The seedlings of the latter grow up, thin and slender in shape as pole trees with a straight unbranched bole and a remarkably small apical crown, their habit indicating the striving for light. Their growth is at first considerably slower than that of the weed trees, but increases with age; in this way they overtake the weed trees and some of them will succeed in developing into mature trees and finding their proper niche, sorting themselves out according to their final size in the upper strata of the canopy. A good description of this overtaking and telescoping process has been given by F. Kramer [2] [1] in his study on the regeneration of the West Java rain forest on the slopes of Mount Gedeh.

For some time it was a problem to me where these nomads came from, where they originated—but this problem was cleared up when I prepared my thesis on the Malaysian *Bignoniaceae.* Among them is the genus *Oroxylum,* consisting of one species only. *O. indicum* is found over an immense area of about 6,000 by 5,000 kilometres from the Himalayas to Central Malaysia and from South China and the Philippines as far as Timor.

It is not a rare species today, but it is not common in the sense that it can be located every 10 square kilometres. Its large fine-winged seeds are very suitable to wind dispersal. It is entirely confined to the secondary forest and other seral growths. Its life-span is, for a tree, short, and it attains only small dimensions. If the localities where its occurs are mapped, the picture obtained is one of isolated dots and spots and short and interrupted stripes, most localities consisting of only a few specimens.

It is certain that it is far more abundant in the present vegetation cover than it will have been in the times when man had not yet started his destruction of the forest, as most of the localities where *Oroxylum* now occurs are in secondary growths made by man. It is possible that its area before the advent of man was somewhat smaller than at present. This does not affect the problem, however, as the ecology of *Oroxylum* has remained the same as it was.

Furthermore it has no near allies among rain forest *Bignoniaceae* from which it might have originated in recent time; it is taxonomically isolated and this makes it a specially interesting clear-cut case to discuss.

It can have thrived only in the open places alluded to above i.e. those caused by natural agencies. In that case it was naturally in prehistoric time a rare species, before man, by destroying forest on a grand scale, enlarged the area suited to the life-cycle of *Oroxylum.* When that happened *Oroxylum* got its chance and multiplied enormously and possibly extended the frontiers of its range.

The same story holds for all these autochthonous pioneers which live as nomads, because the suiting localities are also short-lived: as soon as the open spot has been covered by seral growth the forest components come in and in a few decades will overgrow the seral stands. After half a century none of these will survive, all possibility for their maintaining themselves being suppressed.

Here the function of the "scab" comes clearly to the fore. The large emergents, which are to form the frame of the forest, owe the possibility for their upgrowth in youth in the open places to the presence of the nomads; the "scab" enables the final tissue of the balanced rain forest to restore itself.

Attention should be given to the fact that, originally, the nomads were in all probability the humblest of all plants. Through their special needs for light for their germination and growth they were and are, powerless against the overwhelmingly vigorous rain forest growth. *They were originally of rare occurrence, as the potential surface of the area suiting their needs was very restricted and everchanging.*

It is man, who, by his wholesale destruction of the primary forest, enabled the colossal increase in their numbers and possibly even in the number of species.

This principle of ecological balance and its shift, based on autecological tolerance, does not hold exclusively for one factor. Similar happenings and reasoning could be applied if other factors were the limiting ones, changes of temperature, changes of precipitation, and so on.

The principle holds of course equally well in the animal kingdom. The following is an authentic example serving to prove its usefulness. Dr. E. Mayr, the well-known ornithologist, visited West New Guinea and explored the avifauna of the extensive grasslands between Sentani Lake and Hollandia. He reported [3] the occurrence of special grassland-adapted subspecies of birds in these grassfields. Basing himself on the idea that the origin of subspecies cannot be very recent but requires Lamarckian periods, he assumes that these grass wastes are autochthonous and is furthermore of the opinion that they were much commoner and wider spread in New Guinea than they are today, although he knew that botanists and foresters shared the opinion that they were man made and actually extending themselves.

In applying the principle of shift in numbers through tolerance to this case I have suggested [5, 6] that closer examination of open spots in untouched Papuan forest would show the presence of these bird races in the original niche from where they had extended their area to the man-made open grass wastes which later offered conditions suiting their ecological tolerance.

Soon afterwards this conclusion was checked and proved to hold. I discussed the problem with Mr. A. L. Rand in 1938 at Bogor while he was preparing the Third Archbold Expedition to New Guinea; he apparently had a similar idea and was able to find Mayr's nomad subspecies in naturally open spots in primary vegetation [1].

In this connexion I call attention to the man-bound sparrow in Europe; if this bird existed in nature before man, it was in all probability a rare bird; since then it has immensely increased in numbers.

1. The figures in brackets refer to the bibliography on page 218.

The biological nomad theory

Hunting tribes have always employed the nomad theory: in using fire, grass is encouraged and grasslands and savannas and the fauna adapted to them extend enormously in numbers.

There is every reason to study the ecology of the nomad plants, as they are extremely valuable to mankind today, in various ways (shade trees, green manures, reafforestation, erosion control, etc.).

I estimate that about 20 per cent of the Malaysian flora consists of nomads. Certain families are very rich in nomads, e.g. *Urticaceae, Moraceae, Verbenaceae, Ruphorbiaceae, Gramineae, Leguminosae,* and *Ulmaceae*.

It is possible that a number of new species have originated in rather recent time as a result of new possibilities for hybridization, which arose when the balance in the natural populations was upset and the nomads began to spread to and settle in areas which they could not reach in the balanced climaxes, or in sufficient numbers. New perspectives were opened to gene combinations which had no chance in the primary vegetation but were adapted to the new circumstances and the new type of competition requiring emphasis on other tolerance capacities than before. Geneticists and taxonomists have suggested such a recent origin of nomad species in various areas of the world, e.g. in North America, the Mediterranean, the African savannas, Australia, Tasmania, and New Zealand.[1]

As I said before, the majority of the pioneer nomads are short lived, but a certain number of them have a long life cycle, of a hundred years and more. For example, *Pinus merkusii*, which is very rare in the montane rain forest in North Sumatra and Luzon and Mindoro and grows only locally in the "eyes" of the primary forest on very steep stony ridges, on landslides regularly torn open by earthquakes. It seeds easily on the new soil of mudstreams (lahars) and lava streams. Its seeds need light and contact with mineral soil for germination; its seedlings cannot stand the shade of broad leaved trees. These conditions and a reasonable resistance against fire enables it to invade in great quantities the man-made grass wastes, where it appears in pure stands. These pure grass stands are consequently a secondary forest type though they remain quite stable under anthropogenous conditions (fire, cattle) which keep it pure and create the favourable conditions for germination and regeneration.

If such stands are left to themselves, as can be observed on volcanic mudstreams, leafy shrubs and later also trees invade the pine stands and a shade cover grows up in it, prohibiting germination and seedling growth of pine. If diaspores of the primitive forest are available the succession will gradually turn towards a mixed rain forest composition. The existing pine trees, however, have their crowns above this upgrowing mixed forest, in which they thrive excellently. Even in climax rain forest they tower above it and may reach a height of 70 metres in little more than a century. Their rejuvenation however is shut off, although the old trees remain to act as mother seed trees for spotwise rejuvenation in the "eyes" of the forest.

This example shows that, if we know exactly the factors involved in the rejuvenation cycle, the interpretation of such forest types at once becomes clear. And the essential thing to look for in a forest type is to see whether each of the main components of the forest is presented by various age classes.

Many other cases could be mentioned to show this universal application. On Mount Glorious in Queensland, aggregates of *Eucalyptus grandis* occurred (1950) in mixed rain forest without any juveniles; all the *Eucalyptus*, of huge size, were of about the same age class, 50 metres tall, bole diameter about 1½ metres, age possibly 70 years. The mixed rain forest is apparently recovering and has encroached on a pioneer stand of this *eucalypt*.

Excellent examples are given by Mr. R. N. Parker [4] in a discussion on the ecological status of the Himalayan fir forests. In Africa there will doubtless be a number of nomad species and in North America a number of nomads occur among the pines, in *Quercus* and the douglas fir. In Malaysia there are many examples of long-lived nomad trees, e.g. all the *Eucalypts* (except *Euc. deglupta*), *Casuarina montana, C. papuana, Tectona grandis, Pinus merkusii* and *Pkhasya*, certain bamboos, tree ferns, palms, etc.

Among the trees of the coastal *Barringtonia* formation *Casuarina equisetifolia* represents a nomad, as the stands are formed as pioneer aggregates on freshly accumulated sand, but once established they have no possibilities for maintaining themselves by continuous regeneration.

It appears that acute and detailed observation of regeneration and its conditions, in short the ecology of the life cycle, is essential for the understanding of the status and the ecological balance of a forest.

It is a powerful methodological tool for botanists and foresters who know the ecology of trees to distinguish between primary and secondary forest. Its application has shown that the general assumption that mangrove forest is seral is erroneous. This opinion was based on observations along accrescent coasts where the environment is shifting. In places where the coastline is not moving seaward the mangrove forest is stationary with free regeneration.

The tool, provided by the nomad theory for practical sociology, enabling a better judgement of vegetation by regeneration study, cannot be employed directly in the one-storeyed monsoon forest. Estimation of the status of types in monsoon forest is far more difficult.

The nomads possess, by necessity of their precarious existence in scarce temporary habitats in the primitive forest, a number of characters of distinct survival value,

1. This will be treated more extensively in Ser. I, Vol. 5, Part 3 (in the press) in a general chapter on the delimitation of species. The idea was long ago advanced by Bentham and some decades ago again stressed by Hugo de Vries as I have recorded in *Flora Malesiana Bull.* 1949, Vol. I, No. 5, pp. XL–XLI, LXV–LXVIII.

which characters enable them to cope with their struggle for a place to live.

These characters I have elsewhere described as pioneer qualities [7]. Ecologically they are destined for maintenance, and appear to us in secondary vegetation as an expression of tenacity and of aggressive nature. They are the result of selection on the basis of tolerance in the process of variation and speciation.

They comprise: rapid growth, generally a profusion of flower and seed often independent of seasons and continuous throughout the year, production of flowers and seeds already in juvenile stages, great quantities of seed, per individual plant, structures in seed or fruit leading to seed reserves (dormancy), efficient structures for seed dispersal, great capacity for producing suckers from the stem-base or roots, qualities of bark for resistance against drought, heat, and fire, in general a wide tolerance against conditions of soil and climate and often of temperature, frequent occurrence of underground parts for survival (underground branching system, lignotubers, bulbs, corms, rhizomes, tubers, etc.), in short an array of fighting qualities marking them as tenacious plants.

It is of course by no means by intention to identify the nomads with the weed trees of the rain forest only. Nomads are found as an accessory category to probably every vegetation type.

In European and other temperate countries there are very few plants which can be compared with the seral weed trees of the rain forest succession. But an approach is made towards their ecology by the study of a few typical invaders of felled areas *(Kahlschlagpflanzen)*, for example *Epilobium augustifolium*. Dr V. Westhoff (Wageningen) was so kind to inform me (May 1956), from literature and from his personal experience and from information from Dr. D. Bakker (Zwolle), that there is abundant evidence in favour of the idea that its gregarious occurrence in fellings is due to newly arrived seed. This opinion is shared by British and other European ecologists; Salisbury [8] has given ample

arguments for this and the detailed experience of Dr. Westhoff is entirely in agreement with it.

It seems to me that there is a very sharp demarcation between the two classes: stationary species and nomads, although there are, among the nomads, some which usually come late in the succession series. On the other hand the succession series does not always start with the same species succeeded by a fixed other species and another and always end with the same final one. This varies from place to place and is mostly a matter of chance and opportunity. Stands of seral nomads are often very different in specific composition. Though I will not go as far as to say that there is no relation between the species of nomads with climate and soil —to which they are often rather indifferent—there is no question that the hypothesis of Treub, proposed after a very superficial visit to Krakatao, that revegetation on new soil would to some degree reflect a supposed phylogenetical series of organisms each preparing the way for its follower, is an adequate picture of what actually takes place in nature. Many subsequent data have shown that this idea is refuted by the facts.

Succession series in tropical rain forest are generally not fixed floristic series but merely physiognomic and structural in a gross series: herbs, shrubs, small trees, large trees.

In my practical experience I have observed a sharp difference in the field between nomads and stationary species. Though the demand for light in the germination of either the nomads and the stationary rain forest species may be different for different species, there is no gradual series of transitions which would tend to blot out the whole nomad concept.

The nomads can be defined as those plants whose life cycle and/or other ecological characters do not fit into the closed cover of the undisturbed climax and which can maintain themselves only under disturbed conditions either by nature or by man on the "margin" of the pertaining climax.

The biological nomad theory

such nomads species exotic to the regions concerned. I would refer to the performance of certain *Eucalyptus* species mainly of *E. Robusta* in bridging or short circuiting natural succession from grassland to closed forest. Another exotic of special interest in wet evergreen forest is *Swietenia macrophylla*. This has been introduced into plantations of other species and under shelter of natural forest is spreading underneath the canopy forest which from one cause or another has been slightly oepened.

DR. PURI. I should like to comment on the remark by Dr. van Steenis about *Shorea robusta*, that it is not a nomad or seral, but is a seral community and has been kept in that condition by the biotic factor—fire control in dry regions and fire in moister parts. In these forests, regeneration is greatly helped by silvicultural practices such as shrub cutting, weeding, etc.

Regarding conifers. I mean all the species of conifers and they are all seral to one or the other community of oak.

Bibliography / Bibliographie

1. (a) *Bull. Amer. Mus. nat. Hist.* 1935, no. 68, p. 534-556, 557; 1940, no. 77, p. 377.
   (b) *Amer. Mus. Novit.* 1941. no. 1122, p. 1, 3.
   (c) *Bull. Amer. Mus. nat. Hist.* 1942, no. 79, p. 284-285.
2. KRAMER, F. "Onderzoek naar de natuurlijke verjonging en uitkap". *Preanger gebergtebosch*, p. 1-181 (*Meded. Boschbouwtproefst. Btzg.* no. 14). Thesis, Wageningen, 1926.
3. MAYR, E. *Novit. zool.* 1930, no. 36, p. 25.
4. PARKER, R. N. *Ann. Rev. Bot. Gard. Calc.* 1942, p. 125-128.
5. STEENIS, C. G. G. J. VAN. *Tijdschr. ned. aardrijksk. Genoot.* 1935, no. 52, p. 188-189.
6. ——. *Bull. Jard. Bot. Btzg.* 1953, vol. III, no. 13, p. 369.
7. ——. *Verslag 28ste Verg. Ver. Proefst. Pers. (Ned. Ind.)*, 1941, p. 195-205.
8. SALISBURY. *The reproductive capacity of plants.* 1942. p. 22. 49, 186, 215, 219.

Distribution of tropical American rain forest species in the light of successional processes[*][1]————————GERARDO BUDOWSKI[**]

COMPENDIO

Dentro del bosque húmedo tropical, las especies que integran las diferentes etapas de la sucesión, muestran ciertas características definidas en su distribución.

Las especies pioneras y las secundarias tempranas tienen una distribución amplia. Las especies secundarias tardías son deciduas y pueden alcanzar un tamaño considerable cuando llegan a una edad avanzada. Ellas forman parte del climax en los bosques secos o deciduos. En las comunidades climax se encuentra mucho endemismo; allí, aún cuando la heterogeneidad de especies es la regla, pueden darse casos de dominancia de una o pocas especies debido a la influencia de ciertos factores edáficos. —El autor.

Introduction

DISTRIBUTION patterns of rain forest species are the result of many inter-acting factors among which climate, soils, relief and historic geology have been treated in detail. There are also some studies on the role of wind, animals and water in seed dispersion.

However, there is still another important factor, namely plant succession, which bears important implications on distribution patterns and which, for the tropical rain forest, as unjustly received scanty attention.

The present study attemps to show certain relationships between successional processes and distribution patterns for the tropical American lowland forests. The areas studied cover large extensions in northern tropical America and Central America with a mean annual temperature over 22°C. (71.6ºF) and a mean annual rainfall over 2,000 mm. (approximately 80 inches).

The classifying of communities in their proper successional status

In order to appreciate the relationship between successional patterns and the distribution of rain forest species, it is essencial that successional seral stages be recognized. This can be done by recording carefully a series of critical floristic, physiognomic and structural features which will give enough clues for classifying the different seral stages. These stages can be called —for convenience— pioneer, early secondary, old secondary and climax, and comprise the critical characters shown in Table 1, which were taken from a series of plots of which age and past intervention were well known (2, 3).

The generalizations shown on the table have been simplified to indicate relative values rather than absolute numerical ones, since the latter would be very difficult to render in detail at this stage. However, experience has shown that the recording of these characters does not offer a serious problem to those who have a fair acquaintance with tropical rain forest vegetation.

When such classification is achieved, a distinct relationship between distribution patterns of some species and their proper successional status can be found.

The distribution patterns of pioneers and early secondary species

These two groups, here lumped together for convenience, are found over areas of very different climatic and edaphic conditions. Under conditions of closed undisturbed forest the presence of species of these successional stages is limited to openings or gaps made by falling trees landslides or other accidents including,

* Received for publication January 29, 1965.
1/ Presented to the 10th International Botanical Congress. Edinburgh, August, 1964.
** Head, Forestry Program, Inter-American Institute of Agricultural Sciences Training and Research Center, Turrialba, Costa Rica.

Table 1.—Characteristics of arboreal components of seral stages in tropical American humid forests.

	Pioneer	Early secondary	Late secondary	Climax
Age of communities observed, years	1-3	5-15	20-50	more than 100
Height, meters	5-8	12-20	20-30, some reaching 50	30-45, some up to 60
Number of woody species	few, 1-5	few, 1-10	30-60	up to 100 or a little more
Floristic composition of dominants	Euphorbiaceae, Cecropia, Ochroma, Trema	Ochroma, Cecropia, Trema, Heliocarpus most frequent	mixture, many Meliaceae Bombacaceae, Tiliaceae	mixture, except on edaphic association
Natural distribution of dominants	very wide	very wide	wide, includes drier regions	usually restricted, endemics frequent
Number of strata	1, very dense	2, well differentiated	3, increasingly difficult to discern with age.	4-5, difficult to discern
Upper canopy	homogeneous, dense	verticillate branching, thin horizontal crowns	heterogeneous, includes very wide crowns	many variable shapes of crowns
Lower stratum	dense, tangled	dense, large herbaceous species frequent	relatively scarce, includes tolerant species	scarce, with tolerant species
Growth	very fast	very fast	dominants fast, others slow	slow or very slow
Life span, dominants	very short, less than 10 years	short, 10-25 years	usually 40-100 years, some more	very long, 100-1000, some probably more
Tolerance to shade, dominants	very intolerant	very intolerant	tolerant in juvenile stage, later intolerant	tolerant, except in adult stage
Regeneration of dominants	very scarce	practically absent	absent or abundant with large mortality in early years	fairly abundant
Dissemination of seeds of dominants	birds, bats, wind	winds, birds, bats	wind principally	gravity, mammals, rodents birds
Wood and stem, dominants	very light, small diameters	very light, diameters below 60 cm.	light to medium hard, some very large stems	hard and heavy, includes large stems
Size of seed, or fruits dispersed	small	small	small to medium	large
Viability of seeds	long, latent in soil	long, latent in soil	short to medium	short
Leaves of dominants	evergreen	evergreen	many deciduous	evergreen
Epiphytes	absent	few	many in number, but few species	many species and life forms
Vines	abundant, herbaceous, but few species	abundant, herbaceous but few species	abundant, but few of them large	abundant, includes very large woody species
Shrubs	many, but few species	relatively abundant but few species	few	few in number but many species
Grasses	abundant	abundant or scarce	scarce	scarce

42   TURRIALBA: VOL. 15, NUM. 1, TRIMESTRE ENERO-MARZO 1965

of course, man-made clearings. These are the "biological nomads" as they have been rightly called by van Steenis (5, 6). However, these species are also found in other niches such as the river banks, the edges of swamps and, in some cases, they are also components of the early stages of succession of the drier formation, i.e., the deciduous forest, although they are not deciduous themselves. The obvious implication is that these species are well adapted to drought, be it lack of rainfall or physiological, through flooding. Very poor soils or rocky outcrops also constitute niches where these species take refuge. Their seed dissemination mechanism is very efficient. The small seeds are not only produced profusely but can remain dormant for a considerable period under the shade of high canopy species until full sunlight triggers their germination.

The distribution of pioneers and early secondary species has of course, considerably increased over the last 50 years as a result of man's impact on the vegetation.

The distribution pattern of late secondary species

The most striking characteristic of these species is their deciduousness, even in areas of very heavy rainfall. The most significant factor in connection with distribution is that many of the species are also found in drier habitats, mainly the deciduous forest or the very dry forest. In some of those formations they actually reproduce well, and hence may be considered as members of the climax. This possibility has been discussed by Troll and Richards (as comments on a paper by Aubert de la Rue (1). It is definitely true for many American species, such as *Goethalsia meiantha, Bursera simaruba, Luehea seemanii, Cordia alliodora*, among others. Possibly *Ceiba pentandra*, of pantropical distribution, enters into that category too. Some of these older secondary species may actually remain in place for centuries and attain great size. This has also been pointed out by van Steenis (5,6), among others. Curiously, then, some of the largest trees of the tropical rain forest may often be old secondary species which have remained in the area for a long period, but do not regenerate. This is certainly the case for some of the valuable Meliaceae, such as *Swietenia macrophylla, Cedrela mexicana* and some Bombacaceae, such as *Bombacopsis sepium* and *Ceiba pentandra*. In Panama and Colombia *Cavanillesia platanifolia* is another outstanding example.

The distribution of climax species

For convenience of definition, a climax community is the end product of a successional sere when a relatively stable —although certainly not static— community has been reached and when changes of floristic composition, structure and physiognomy over the age span of the dominants become insignificant.

The rule in climax communities is a thorough mixture of species whenever drainage is not extreme or impeded. This has been stressed, among others by Richards (4). As soon as one single or a few species become dominant, some edaphic factor, usually related to excessive water —at least during part of the year— can be suspected; but, generally speaking, endemism is frecuent from the floristic standpoint.

In conclusion it is felt that in order to understand distribution patterns of rain forest species much consideration should be given to successional patterns. The classification of communities into their proper successional sequence, a matter which can be achieved by carefully recording indicative floristic, physiognomic and structural characteristics of the communities, seems to be an essential previous step. A large proportion of pioneers, early secondary, old secondary and climax species appears to display a distribution pattern which is typical of their successional status.

Summary

Within the tropical rain forest the species that integrate different seral stages display characteristic distribution patterns. Pioneers and early secondary species have a wide distribution. Late secondary species are deciduous and may attain considerable size when they grow to old age. They are part of the climax in the drier or deciduous forest. Much endemism is found in climax communities; while a mixture of species is the rule, there may be edaphic factors which favor the dominance of one or a few species.

Literature cited

1. AUBERT DE LA RUE, E. Man's influence on tropical vegetation. *In* Proceedings, Ninth Pacific Science Congress, 1957. Bangkok, Secretariat, Ninth Pacific Science Congress. 1958. pp. 81-94.

2. BUDOWSKI, G. Studies on forest succession in Costa Rica and Panama Doctor of Philosophy thesis. New Haven, Yale University, School of Forestry. 1961. 189 p.

3. ——————Forest succession in tropical lowlands. Turrialba 13(1):42-44 1963.

4. RICHARDS, P. W. What the tropics can contribute to ecology. Journal of Ecology 51(2):231-241. 1963.

5. VAN STEENIS, C. G. G. J. Rejuvenation as a factor for judging the status of vegetation types: the biological nomad theory. *In* Study of Tropical Vegetation. Proceedings of the Kandy Symposium, Ceylon 19-21 March 1956. pp. 212-215. 1958

6. ——————Tropical lowland vegetation; the characteristics of its types and their relation to climate. *In* Proceedings Ninth Pacific Science Congress, 1957. Bangkok, Secretariat, Ninth Pacific Science Congress. pp. 25-37. 1958.

REGENERATION AND PATTERN IN THE SUBTROPICAL RAIN FOREST

By L. J. WEBB, J. G. TRACEY AND W. T. WILLIAMS

Rain Forest Ecology Section, C.S.I.R.O. Division of Plant Industry, Brisbane; C.S.I.R.O. Division of Tropical Pastures, Brisbane

INTRODUCTION

According to the classical view of pattern and process by Watt (1947), the plant community in temperate regions consists of 'patches', i.e. aggregates of individuals and species. Each patch is of limited area, and is dynamically related to other patches or phases. To understand the nature of the plant community, and how the individuals and species are put together, involves knowing the relative proportions, size, and arrangement of the patches in space and time.

Watt (*loc. cit.*) tentatively suggested that complex tropical forests may also exhibit pattern and process as in temperate vegetation, and referred to the interpretation of Aubréville (1938), which has now come to be known as the mosaic or cyclical theory of regeneration (Richards 1952). More recently, Daubenmire (1968) has proposed the term serule or microsere for the dynamically related patches which comprise a climax: the changes of the serules which maintain the average composition of a climax community are cyclic, and not unidirectional as in a sere.

Those workers who have studied the floristic composition of tropical rain forest have, in fact, been impressed by the 'patchy' distribution of many of the tree species. Aubréville (*loc. cit.*) compared the occurrence of dominant species to the spots on the skin of a panther. Each patch or cluster of species was separated by only a few feet from another patch, but the size of the patches was not stated.

Schulz (1960) referred to groups of 'leading species' which varied in abundance from place to place, because of site differences or of the patchy distribution noted as characteristic of many species of the tropical forest. Jones (1955) considered it unlikely that units of a mosaic are sharply defined in complex and many-layered tropical communities, and quoted patchiness as one factor contributing to mosaic structure. Richards (1952, 1963) suggested that the mixed forest of a defined tropical region was only a single association of fluctuating composition, and that separate associations were restricted to relatively unfavourable habitats.

As in temperate vegetation, it has been usual to invoke a dynamic interpretation of the mosaic structure of tropical communities, and Aubréville (*loc. cit.*) noted that his patches were constantly in a process of change. Poore (1964) characterized replacement of one species by another at the same place as 'shifting pattern'; but he believed that it was also possible to recognize areas of 'static pattern', where the young of each species tended to regenerate around their parents, so that the floristic composition of the patch remained constant. He did not, however, define the size of individual patches.

Our own work (Webb *et al.* 1967a, 1970) has suggested that if the members of a group of sites are widely separated geographically it is possible to regard them as characterized by conventional floristic associations; but it has been found impossible (Williams *et al.* 1969b) to interpret the pattern of a small (0·4 ha) area without invoking dynamic and autogenic considerations.

In any study of this type it is desirable to distinguish between three phases of investigation. There is first the definition of the static pattern, as it exists in any moment of time. Secondly, there is the description of the floristic changes which accompany the evolution of the pattern. Thirdly, there is the explanation of this evolution, in terms either of environment, or of growth, reproductive characteristics and sociological interactions of the species. If the controlling factors appear to be those of the physical environment (allogenic), the second phase is unimportant; the problem simply resolves itself into the autecology of individual species. There is no doubt of the importance of environmental factors on a geographical scale (see, e.g. Tracey 1969; Webb 1969); but their relevance to small-scale patchiness may be difficult to establish. Richards (1952) noted local peculiarities of soil conditions which may support true floristic associations. Ashton (1964) showed that variations in composition of the complex mixed forests of Brunei closely reflected variations in topography or soil. Poore (1968) suggested that the forest might be composed of a number of groups of species which occupy particular habitats determined by their narrow tolerances, but that these might occur within a matrix of commoner, widely-tolerant, species. This latter interpretation is, however, disputed by Austin & Greig-Smith (1968); and Kershaw (1964) has pointed out that it is virtually impossible to separate small-scale effects due to intrinsic properties of the plants themselves from effects due to microvariations in the environment.

However, if the rain forest is indeed a mosaic, and if this mosaic is the result of competition, a knowledge of the second phase—the description of the total succession—will be essential to understanding it. Such knowledge does not yet exist, since the complete study of regeneration in tropical rain forest would exceed the limits of a human working lifetime. Instead, workers have contented themselves with attempting to define specific questions which, if they could be answered, would at least contribute substantially to an understanding of the problem. The following questions have been extracted from the writings of Richards (1952), Jones (1956) and Schulz (1960).

(1) To what extent are the regenerating species reproducing a forest which has substantially the same form and composition as the surrounding forest? (This is implied also in the 'shifting/static' dichotomy of Poore (1964).)

(2) How do the canopy and emergent trees regenerate and attain their position?

(3) Do the canopy and emergent trees regenerate continuously or intermittently?

(4) What is the normal size- or age-class representation of the canopy trees?

(5) How does the growth-rate of the trees vary during succession?

(6) At what stages does the heaviest mortality of seedlings and saplings occur?

(7) What is the role of chance in regeneration?

If the answers to these questions were known, a fairly good picture of the succession would be available; and it would be reasonable to embark on an investigation into mechanism by observing, for key species, the seed production and the later growth and mortality of seedlings. It is, of course, possible to do this without knowing the total process, and many workers have done so. Interpretation of such observations, however, rests on a logical procedure which is the reverse of that in temperate ecology. Instead of describing a process, and then seeking possible mechanisms, the procedure is now to make observations whose interpretation implies particular mechanisms, and then to

L. J. WEBB, J. G. TRACEY AND W. T. WILLIAMS   677

deduce the nature of the process to which they would give rise. There is nothing invalid *per se* in such work, but it rather easily gives rise to circular arguments: a mechanism is used to postulate a process, which is then explained by the mechanism.

It is clear that direct observation of the processes of rain forest succession is highly desirable. Even though the complete cycle of regeneration or establishment is too long for a single worker to follow, it is still conceivable that a quantitative study of a relatively short time-segment—say, of a few years—might answer some of the questions summarized above. Unfortunately, for many ecologists the tropical rain forest is a community that can be visited only infrequently and for short periods; hence such studies have been limited. One of the most important of these was the Cambridge expedition to Nigeria, whose work in the Okumu Forest Reserve, Benin, has been reported by Jones (1950, 1955, 1956). Interpretation of the results was, however, beset by several difficulties. There was some evidence of early, but undocumented, agricultural occupation of the area, followed by recent light felling; and young regenerating shoots were browsed by elephants. The area was also rich in robust liane species which produced a 'climber tangle' which blanketed the regenerating canopy trees.

Fortunately it has been possible to avoid these difficulties. In a previous paper (Williams *et al.* 1969a) the early stages of succession in an experimental clearing of subtropical rain forest were described and analysed. There is every reason to believe that this was virgin forest. Aboriginal man did not practise agriculture or systematic tree-felling, and there was no evidence of recent logging. Nor has there been any record—or likelihood—of fire within the rain forest, and the only disturbances have been natural wind-throws and occasional cyclone damage. Although there is a liane flora, it is not developed sufficiently early in succession to form the blanketing 'climber tangles' of Benin; and there are no elephants or other large browsing mammals.

The study area was cleared in 1957. In the first twelve months after clearing the floristic composition varied in time but not in space; this phase was dominated by pioneer species whose long-lived seeds were already present in the topsoil of the mature forest. After 12 months there was a dramatic change from a temporal to a spatial pattern, which could be related to micro-site differences resulting from clearing. The last observation described in the earlier paper was made in June 1964; 6 more years have now elapsed, and it seemed likely that a detailed study of the present vegetation might help to answer some of the outstanding questions of canopy development.

This paper describes such a study; the task has been simplified by concentrating particularly on the canopy trees which exercise a controlling influence on species of other synusiae, and carry most of the information about the macro-environment (Webb *et al.* 1967b).

AREA STUDIED AND COLLECTION OF DATA

The study area was located on Mount Glorious, South Queensland (latitude 27° 20′ S, longitude 152° 45′ E) and represented 12-year-old regrowth of moist subtropical rain forest on a basaltic krasnozem. The cleared area of approximately 0·16 ha (0·4 ac) was situated within tall unlogged rain forest, with a road and tracks nearby. Owing to a misunderstanding, a track was bulldozed through the regrowth when it was 7 years old (in 1965), but the area has suffered no further interference. For details of the initial stages of the succession, reference should be made to the earlier paper (Williams *et al.* 1969a).

678   *Regeneration and pattern in rain forest*

The small quadrats used for the earlier study (which had been damaged in part by the bulldozer) were abandoned; and within the cleared area a rectangular plot 40 × 20 m (approximately 0·2 ac) was located, and gridded at 5-m intervals by permanent pegs and plastic-covered wire to provide thirty-two plots (see Fig. 1). Each was further subdivided into four by measuring sticks 2·5 m long; these were marked at 15-cm intervals for the

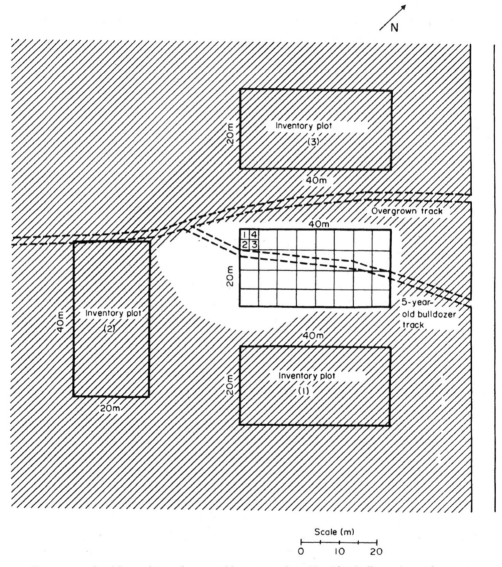

FIG. 1. Location of experimental area and inventory plots. Hatching indicates intact forest.

purpose of recording the co-ordinates of every plant above 5 cm high. The co-ordinates for the 128 sub-plots were converted by computer to an overall set, with the origin at the north-west corner of the area. For each plant its position, height, vitality and botanical identity were noted; in all, seventy-six species were represented among a total of 1775 individuals. Suckers from stumps or from remnants of roots were recorded separately from seedlings.

Table 1. *Inventory of species on the study plot before clearing, and frequency on reference plots (latter as mature canopy trees only)*

Species	Study plot	Reference plots 1	2	3
Acronychia pubescens (F. Muell.) C. T. White	+	−	−	−
Actephila mooreana Baill.	+	−	−	−
Ailanthus triphysa (Dennst.) Alston	−	−	1	−
Alangium villosum (Bl.) Wangerin spp. *polyosmoides* (F. Muell.) Bloemb.	+	1	−	−
Archontophoenix cunninghamiana (Wendl.) Wendl. & Drude	+	2	−	5
Argyrodendron actinophyllum (F. M. Bail.) H. L. Edlin	+	−	−	−
A. trifoliolatum F. Muell.	+	2	3	−
Beilschmiedia obtusifolia (F. Muell. ex Meissn.) F. Muell.	+	−	2	2
Brachychiton discolor F. Muell.	+	−	−	−
Chrysophyllum chartaceum F. M. Bail.	+	1	2	2
Cinnamomum oliveri F. M. Bail.	+	−	−	−
Citronella moorei (F. Muell. ex Benth.) Howard	−	1	1	−
Cryptocarya erythroxylon Maid. & Betche	+	−	−	3
C. glaucescens R. Br.	−	1	−	−
C. obovata R. Br.	+	−	−	−
C. triplinervis R. Br.	+	−	−	−
Daphnandra micrantha (Tul.) Benth.	+	−	−	1
Dendrocnide excelsa (Wedd.) Chew	+	−	2	1
D. photinophylla (Wedd.) Chew	+	−	−	−
Diospyros pentamera (Woolls & F. Muell.) Woolls & F. Muell.	+	−	−	−
Diploglottis australis (G. Don) Radlk.	+	−	−	−
Dysoxylum fraseranum (A. Juss.) Benth.	+	−	−	−
D. rufum (A. Rich.) Benth.	−	−	−	1
Elaeocarpus kirtonii F. Muell. ex F. M. Bail.	−	1	−	−
Elattostachys nervosa (F. Muell.) Radlk.	+	−	−	−
Endiandra muelleri Meissn.	+	2	1	−
Eugenia brachyandra Maid. & Betche	+	−	−	−
E. corynantha F. Muell.	+	−	2	4
E. crebrinervis C. T. White	+	1	−	3
Euroschinus falcata Hook. f. var. *falcata*	+	−	−	−
Ficus macrophylla Desf.	+	−	−	−
F. obliqua Forst. f. var. *obliqua*	−	1	−	−
F. watkinsiana F. M. Bail.	+	1	2	−
Gmelina leichhardtii (F. Muell.) F. Muell. ex Benth.	+	1	−	−
Guioa semiglauca (F. Muell.) Radlk.	+	−	−	−
Helicia glabriflora F. Muell.	−	−	−	4
Litsea reticulata (Meissn.) F. Muell.	+	−	−	−
Mischocarpus pyriformis (F. Muell.) Radlk.	−	1	−	−
Pennantia cunninghamii Miers	+	−	−	1
Podocarpus elatus R. Br. ex Endl.	+	−	−	−
Polyosma cunninghamii J. J. Benn.	+	−	−	−
Pseudocarapa nitidula (Benth.) Merr. & Perry	+	3	1	2
Pseudoweinmannia lachnocarpa (F. Muell.) Engl.	−	1	1	−
Sarcopteryx stipitata (F. Muell.) Radlk.	+	1	1	−
Scolopia brownii F. Muell.	−	−	1	−
Sloanea woollsii F. Muell.	+	3	2	2

To assist interpretation of results, two further sets of information are available. First, the potential sources of seeds are known from a spot-list made of all large trees of potential and actual canopy species before the plot was cleared on 30 November 1970. By an actual canopy species, a tree with at least part of its crown in full sunlight is meant. A presence-and-absence list is given in the first column of Table 1. Secondly, quantitative data for the terminal stage of canopy development in the rain forest under study were obtained in August 1970, when all trees which had actually reached the canopy were counted and identified on three 40×20 m plots in the adjacent mature rain forest. The position of these plots is shown in Fig. 1, and the frequencies of the species concerned are given in the last three columns of Table 1.

Finally, to ensure that no potential seed-parents had been overlooked, a belt 40 m wide round the boundaries of the study area was spot-listed. This list is not reproduced, but will be referred to when necessary. Nor is it profitable to reproduce the entire list of seventy-six species present on the study area. It is, however, necessary to refer in the text to the following pioneer or understorey species that are not included in Table 1.

Acacia melanoxylon R. Br.   *Omalanthus populifolius* Grah.
Citriobatus pauciflorus A. Cunn.   *Sambucus australasica* (Lindl.) Fritsch
Clerodendrum floribundum R. Br.   *Solanum mauritianum* Scop.
Duboisia myoporoides R. Br.   *Tieghemopanax elegans* (C. Moore & F.
Eupomatia laurina R. Br.   Muell.) Viguier
Lantana camara L.   *Trema aspera* (Brongn.) Bl.
Neolitsea dealbata (R. Br.) Merr.   *Wilkiea macrophylla* (A. Cunn.) DC.

One canopy species that proved to be of importance was *Eugenia francisii* F.M. Bail.; it does not appear in Table 1, since there was only a single tree just outside the study plot and outside the boundaries of the three inventory plots. In the previous paper it was incorrectly given as *E. luehmannii* F. Muell. The species here called *Dendrocnide excelsa* is referred to in the previous paper by its earlier name of *Laportea gigas* Wedd.

RESULTS

(1) *Presence/absence analysis of 128 sub-plots*

For this preliminary analysis, the data were reduced to the presence and absence of the seventy-six species in the 128 sub-plots, and the data matrix subjected to normal and inverse information analysis (Williams, Lambert & Lance 1966). The results require examination from two points of view: first, the scale; and secondly, the species-composition of the communities so delimited.

(i) *Scale*

When using an agglomerative hierarchial procedure such as information analysis, two alternative approaches are possible. First, the successive fusions may be constrained so that only contiguous sub-plots fuse. This approach is common in regional geography, where it is desired to consider an area as made up of a small number of discrete sub-areas which shall intermingle as little as possible, small-scale mosaic structure being of no interest. The implications of this approach are considered by Johnston (1970), and some computational details given by Dale, Lance & Albrecht (1971). Alternatively, and more usually in ecology, no such constraint is imposed, and sub-plots are permitted to fuse whatever their spatial relationship. Then three possible outcomes can be usefully distin-

L. J. WEBB, J. G. TRACEY AND W. T. WILLIAMS 681

guished. First, well-defined regions of the area may be separated very early in the construction of the hierarchy. This situation almost always implies a marked environmental discontinuity; it has been particularly well-established in temperate forest studies. At the other extreme, an area may remain as a mosaic of intermingled communities until virtually the completion of the hierarchy. This is the usual outcome of the analysis of sample plots in mature rain forest if the plots are too small; for an example, see Fig. 1(c) of Williams *et al.* (1969b). Lastly, the area may remain a mosaic until high up the hierarchy, when contiguous mosaic areas may abruptly coalesce into well-defined regions, whose size serves to define the scale of the intrinsic vegetation pattern.

The disposition of the classificatory groups of sub-plots is shown at the four-group level in Fig. 2. The area marked A is established early in the hierarchy and remains distinct throughout; it thus behaves as if it represented an environmental discontinuity, and it is in fact the area of disturbance associated with the bulldozer track. The remainder of the area exhibited a fairly intricate mosaic until fusion into the three further groups. The

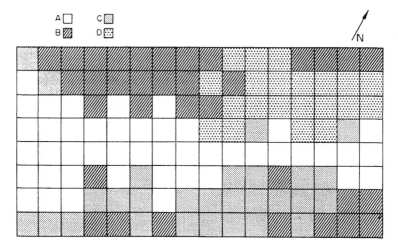

FIG. 2. Presence and absence analysis; spatial configuration at four-group level. For the constitution of the four groups (A, B, C, D) see text.

undisturbed area is thus already showing a 'patchy' structure, and it is interesting to note that the three patches (allowing for occasional sub-plot transgressions) are all of roughly the same size—100–150 m² (1·0–1·5 are).

(ii) *Species composition*

The analysis was first examined as a two-way table at the ten-group level; at this level, only twenty-seven of the species were associated with cell densities of 30% or more, and discussion is confined to these species. The ten-group level proved unrealistically fine for both species and site-groups, and both are discussed at the four-group level. Table 2 lists the species in each of the four species-groups, and shows their disposition between the site-groups.

Species-group 1 is composed of the aggressive introduced shrub *Lantana camara* and the native pioneer shrubs *Solanum mauritianum* and *Trema aspera*. These were at one time scattered over the entire area, but have been eliminated by the intense competition (especially shading) of the later seral species in all except the area (A) defined by the track. The expansion of area (A) at the western boundary of the plot, and the continuing growth of *Lantana camara*, are associated with high light intensity and the persistent dryness and compaction of the soil resulting from frequent passage of the bulldozer during the original (1957) clearing operation.

Species-group 2 is ubiquitous; it consists of two species which sucker freely from residual stumps and roots. It is most dense in the north-eastern corner (area D); this is also the area of highest density of other species.

Species-group 3 consists mainly of species of the mature forest; but it also contains the long-lived pioneer tree *Diploglottis australis* and the relatively short-lived pioneer trees *Omalanthus populifolius* and *Tieghemopanax elegans*. The scattered occurrence of these woody pioneers is to be expected; their seeds are long lived, and were no doubt in the topsoil before clearing. When topsoil is removed from beneath a mature forest canopy in this general region, seedlings of these and other pioneers quickly appear after watering

Table 2. *Site-group/species-group coincidences for presence/absence analysis*

(a) Species–groups

Group 1:	*Lantana camara, Solanum mauritianum, Trema aspera.*
Group 2:	*Daphnandra micrantha, Eupomatia laurina.*
Group 3:	*Archontophoenix cunninghamiana, Argyrodendron actinophyllum, A. trifoliolatum, Cinnamomum oliveri, Citriobatus pauciflorus, Cryptocarya erythroxylon, Dendrocnide photinophylla, Diploglottis australis, Elattostachys nervosa, Eugenia corynantha, Neolitsea dealbata, Omalanthus populifolius, Sarcopteryx stipitata, Sloanea woollsii, Teighemopanax elegans.*
Group 4:	*Actephila mooreana, Alangium villosum, Dysoxylum fraseranum, Eugenia brachyandra, E. francisii, Pseudocarapa nitidula, Wilkiea macrophylla.*

(b) Site–species coincidences

Species-group	A	B	C	D
1	+	−	−	−
2	+	+ +	+ +	+ + +
3	−	+	−	−
4	−	+	+	+ +

Key: + + +, cell-density $\geq$ 75%; + +, cell-density < 75%, $\geq$ 50%; +, cell-density < 50%, $\geq$ 30%; −, cell-density < 30%.

and exposure to sunlight. Individual members of the mature-forest species of group 3 are also to be found scattered haphazardly over the entire plot (apart from area A); but only in area B do they jointly assume an appreciable density.

Species-group 4 consists entirely of species of the mature forest. They are ubiquitous, occurring (though sparsely) even in area A; but they reach a high density only in area D. For both groups 3 and 4 it is important to consider the origin of the plants of the mature-forest species. Not all are necessarily from seed; stump-suckers were observed for *Sloanea woollsii, Actephila mooreana, Pseudocarapa nitidula* and *Wilkiea macrophylla*. The difficulty concerning the remainder is that, so far as is known, seeds of species which belong to late seral stages and to the mature forest are of limited viability, usually not exceeding 2 years, and in some cases only a few weeks, depending on weather conditions. There are, however, exceptions and there is some evidence that seeds of certain of these (e.g. *Eugenia brachyandra*) may retain their viability for at least 3–4 years (M. S. Hopkins, personal communication). Seedlings of the following species were observed within 2 years of clearing the plot, and may therefore be presumed to have established from viable seeds which happened to be in the topsoil: *Archontophoenix cunninghamiana, Cinnamomum oliveri, Citriobatus pauciflorus, Dysoxylum fraseranum, Eugenia brachyandra* and *E. francisii*. The other species established later, presumably from seeds which entered the plot from adjacent trees. Further regeneration from adjacent seed-sources is not, of course, precluded for the species which established early, except perhaps for *Cinnamomum oliveri* and *Dysoxylum fraseranum*, neither of which occurred within the adjacent forest.

(iii) *Conclusions*

The most important finding from this analysis is that a 'patchy' structure apparently unrelated to micro-site differences is already established 12 years after clearing. In the present case, the undisturbed area has become divided into three fairly distinct patches, all of approximately the same small size. An estimate of the average canopy-tree density for a mature plot of this size can be obtained by finding the mean number of trees per plot from the last three columns of Table 1; this is in fact twenty-five. Each canopy tree thus occupies on average about 32 m², so that from each of the patches not more than five trees are likely to survive to reach the canopy.

The second important finding is that floristically these patches do not differ qualitatively but quantitatively; although area D has the highest concentration of species-group 4, and area B the highest concentration of species-group 3, there are no sharply-delimited floristic associations. In other words, the patches represent 'facies' (in the sense used by European phytosociologists) of a single association. These patches do not correspond to any evident environmental discontinuities.

It is desirable to know whether the patches represent different stages of the same sere, or whether the vegetation change is no longer unidirectional, which was interpreted by Daubenmire (1968) as the state in which the seral community becomes the climax. Presence-and-absence studies will not suffice for the investigation of this problem, and it is now necessary to consider the vegetation from the point of view of the quantities and sizes of the species.

(2) *Quantitative spatial relationships*

For the work of this section the complete data-set of 1775 plants exceeded the capacity of the computer programs which it was wished to use; the subset consisting of all plants 0·5 m or more in height, of which there were 661, has therefore been used. The distribution of these on the plot is shown in Fig. 3(a). The central area, characterized by extreme sparsity of records, obviously corresponds closely to the bulldozer track (area A) of Fig. 2. This is related to the habit of *Lantana camara*, which is a dense sprawling shrub or liane, so that relatively few plants monopolize a large area to the exclusion of other plants. The dense area in the north-east corner corresponds roughly with area D of Fig. 2. The next densest area lies in the vicinity of area B of Fig. 2.

The appropriate analytical method for processing these records is the multiple-nearest-neighbour method of Williams *et al.* (1969b). Each plant is compounded with its eight nearest neighbours (the number found optimal in the previous work) to form a 'point-clump', and the resulting 661 point-clumps are used as individuals for classification. With this number of individuals it will be necessary to use a divisive monothetic approach; the divisive analogue of information analysis (Lance & Williams 1968) was used, and, for ease of comparison with Fig. 2, the division was terminated at the four-group level. It is known (Lambert & Williams 1966) that, if clear-cut floristic communities exist within the area under study, the results of the agglomerative and divisive approaches will be almost

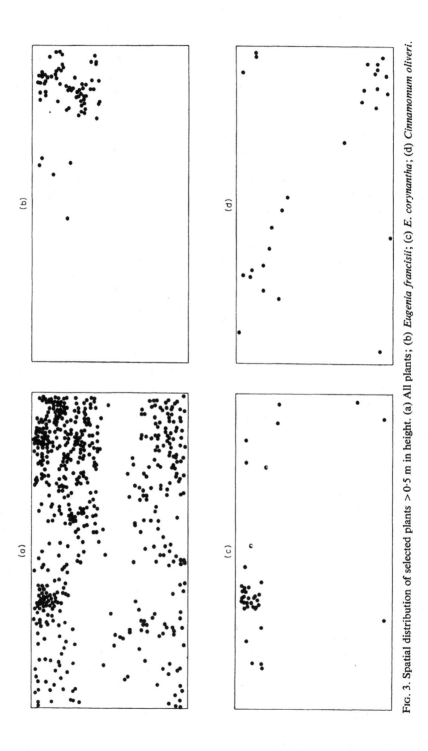

Fɪɢ. 3. Spatial distribution of selected plants > 0·5 m in height. (a) All plants; (b) *Eugenia francisii*; (c) *E. corynantha*; (d) *Cinnamomum oliveri*.

the same. However, if—as even the presence-and-absence analysis has suggested—our 'patches' are essentially assemblages of species extracted by coupled interactions from a uniform set, the monothetic approach is liable to fail in so far as it can do little more than reflect the distribution of the commoner species.

The first division was on *Eugenia francisii*; the negative side then divided on *E. corynantha*, and the double-negative side on *Cinnamomum oliveri*. The disposition of the resulting four groups is shown in Fig. 4. Area I (+*Eugenia francisii*) corresponds quite well with area D of Fig. 2, area II (−*E. francisii*, +*E. corynantha*) with area B, and the all-negative area IV with area A; but area III (−*E.* spp., +*Cinnamomum oliveri*) and the original area C show little correspondence. It may well be that the areas reflect little more than the distribution of the division-species, which therefore requires examination. The distribution of *Eugenia francisii* is shown in Fig. 3(b). The density of this species in the north-east corner is remarkable, and even more so when it is realized that, in addition

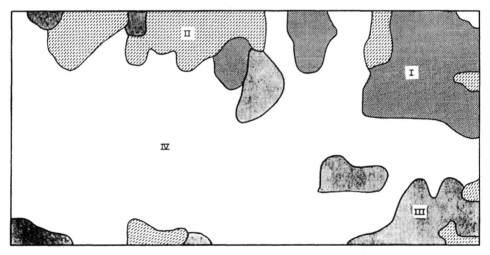

FIG. 4. Multiple-nearest-neighbour analysis at four-group level; for explanation of the four groups (I, II, III, IV) see text.

to the seventy-nine records used in this analysis, there were on the plot a further ninety-six seedlings below 0·5 m in height. This concentration is undoubtedly due to the presence of a single tree of *E. francisii* just outside the north-east corner of the plot, and it provides a striking example of the 'spot-wise regeneration' of van Steenis (1956). However, the danger of using this phenomenon as a basis for the existence of the 'static pattern' of Poore (1964) is shown by the fact that nowhere in the subtropical rain forest of South Queensland has this species been recorded as attaining local dominance; it behaves, in fact, as a typical non-gregarious species, and self-thinning of the seedlings must be very intense. The distribution of *E. corynantha* (forty-two plants) is shown in Fig. 3(c); it is essentially peripheral, and can similarly be related to the proximity of several parent trees just outside the plot. This explanation will not serve for the distribution of *Cinnamomum oliveri* (Fig. 3(d)—twenty-eight plants), since no parent tree could be found within 40 m of the borders of the plot in any direction. Its occurrence on the plot can probably be attributed to germination of seeds which persisted in the topsoil after clearing; the species existed on the plot before clearing, and seedlings were observed within 2 years.

However, its seeds are known to be eaten and dispersed by birds, so that some may have been brought from a considerable distance.

The distribution of even these three species alone demonstrates the importance of the current availability of seed-sources; but the case of *Eugenia francisii* suggests that even abundant seed production and excellent seedling establishment do not confer a certainty of attaining the canopy. Spatial considerations can take us no further; but it is conceivable that the trees of the future canopy are already distinguishable by their superior growth—in other words, that some degree of layering is already beginning to manifest itself. To investigate whether this is indeed the case, the distribution of species within height-classes is examined.

(3) *Size-class distribution*

(i) *General features*

To facilitate retrieval by computer, the heights (recorded in feet or inches) of all

Table 3. *Size-classes*

1	2	3	4	5	6	7
		No.		%	Ditto,	%
Class no.	Upper limit	of records	Diversity	ref. spp.	less suckers	pioneers
1	3 in. (7·6 cm)	34	2·2280	38·2	23·5	0·0
2	6 in. (15·2 cm)	195	2·6519	40·2	24·6	0·5
3	9 in. (22·9 cm)	108	2·3640	43·5	17·6	0·0
4	12 in. (30·5 cm)	244	2·5965	31·6	17·7	1·2
5	15 in. (38·1 cm)	26	1·8054	76·9	19·4	0·0
6	18 in. (45·7 cm)	68	2·1355	29·4	16·2	0·0
7	2 ft (0·6 m)	154	2·6563	28·6	13·0	0·0
8	3 ft (0·9 m)	224	2·6201	25·9	16·5	3·1
9	4 ft (1·2 m)	113	2·6486	31·9	16·9	1·8
10	5 ft (1·5 m)	55	2·2761	36·4	20·1	0·0
11	6 ft (1·8 m)	101	2·6028	33·7	9·9	5·0
12	7 ft (2·1 m)	59	2·5585	32·3	10·1	11·9
13	8 ft (2·4 m)	87	2·4205	39·1	9·2	17·2
14	9 ft (2·7 m)	27	2·0999	22·2	3·7	22·2
15	10 ft (3·0 m)	58	2·1879	22·4	6·9	25·9
16	12 ft (3·7 m)	53	2·3327	39·6	9·4	20·8
17	14 ft (4·3 m)	16	1·4764	68·8	25·1	0·0
18	15 ft (4·6 m)	43	1·9426	18·6	2·3	44·2
19	18 ft (5·5 m)	17	1·6378	35·3	5·9	41·3
20	20 ft (6·1 m)	35	2·0537	20·0	8·6	37·1
21	Over 20 ft	58	2·5757	19·0	10·4	12·1

plants on the plot were divided into twenty-eight classes: 3-in. classes to 18 in.; 19–24 in.; 1-ft classes from 3 ft to 20 ft; 21–25 ft, 25–30 ft; and over 30 ft. Scrutiny of the data showed that five of these classes were empty or nearly so; these were the classes whose upper limit was 11, 13, 16, 17 and 19 ft. As heights above 10 ft were estimated, the observers evidently tended to be biased towards even numbers. Similarly, the three tallest classes were regarded as unreliable, and these were combined into a single class of 'over 20 ft'. This left twenty-one size-classes, whose upper limits (with metric equivalents) are given in column 2 of Table 3. It should be noted that the highest size-classes may be misleading for another reason. 'Height' of a plant such as *Lantana camara* can be interpreted as the length of the longest branch of any one plant, and this was the procedure adopted; but, owing to the sprawling, liane-like, habit of *L. camara*, some of the branches may be very long. In fact, of the fifty-eight records in size-class 21, no less than twenty-nine refer to branches of *L. camara*.

The frequencies are given in column 3 of Table 3. The only marked discontinuity is the conspicuous reduction of the seedling population in size-classes 5 and 6. This may reflect an unfavourable season for the germination and survival of seedlings, or a minor recent burst of germination due to unusually favourable conditions. After this, however, there is an irregular but substantially gradual reduction in numbers of plants with increase in height. Taking all species together, therefore, there is no sign of stratification or layering of plants within the 12-year regrowth of the study area.

It is natural to enquire whether there is any evidence of the gradual development of the high specific diversity characteristic of the mature rain forest. The per-individual Shannon diversities of the three canopy inventory plots of Table 1 and Fig. 1 are 2·4582, 2·3222 and 2·4253 respectively. The Shannon diversities of the twenty-one size-classes are given in column 4 of Table 3; apart from a few aberrant values mostly associated with small numbers of records, they are remarkably constant, and show no trend with time. Moreover, they are already of the same order of magnitude as those of the mature forest. Reference to the previous paper on this area (Williams *et al.* 1969a) shows that this level of diversity was in fact achieved by the third sampling period—6 months after clearing. This illustrates the remarkable ability of a complex system to recover from disturbance such as that imposed in this study.

(ii) *Species composition of size-classes*

It is necessary to know whether canopy species are confined to particular size-classes. As a first test of this, the twenty-two species which occur both on the study plot and on the three inventory plots outside the area were taken. (There were in fact twenty-seven species in the inventory plots; but two of these are 'strangling figs', for which there will not yet be suitable hosts. Of the other three, only *Citronella moorei* occurs closely adjacent to the plot, so that limited availability of seeds may well account for their absence.) For each size-class is calculated the proportion of its records attributable to this reference set of twenty-two species, and these values are given in column 5 of Table 3. Apart from the aberrant values for size-classes 5 and 17, these are remarkably constant. The mean value is 34·9%; the reason that this is higher than 22/76 (i.e. 28·9%) is simply that the twenty-two species include some with very large numbers of records, which gives bias to the mean. Canopy tree species are obviously to be found in all size-classes.

However, it has been previously noted that six of these species were observed to regenerate from suckers. If these species are deleted, and the percentages recalculated for the remaining sixteen, the figures of column 6 of Table 3 are obtained. There is now a marked reduction after size-class 10 (5 ft); the major part of the seedling regeneration of canopy species is represented by smaller trees, and it is evident that the ability to regenerate from suckers confers a considerable advantage in attaining the canopy. It is instructive to compare this size distribution with that of trees known to be relatively short-lived pioneer species. The following are in this category: *Acacia melanoxylon*, *Clerodendrum floribundum*, *Duboisia myoporoides*, *Omalanthus populifolius*, *Sambucus australasica*, *Solanum mauritianum*, *Tieghemopanax elegans*, and *Trema aspera*. The proportions of these ten species represented in the size-class records are given in column 7 of Table 3. It may be noted that the figures increase sharply at exactly the point at which canopy seedling regeneration falls off. The pioneer species are no longer regenerating; they are all light-demanding and apparently intolerant of shade. It may be inferred that the continuing regeneration of the canopy species has reduced the ground light intensity to a level at which pioneer seedlings cannot survive.

Restricted sets of named species with known characteristics have so far been considered, and it will be of interest to ascertain whether similar relationships can be detected in the species-set as a whole. The twenty-one size-classes have therefore been regarded as a set of individuals defined by the presence or absence of the seventy-six species; the resulting 21×76 binary matrix was processed by normal and inverse information analysis. It was found convenient to consider the results in a two-way table at the levels of four size-class groups and seven species-groups. The complete table does not justify reproduction, but the cell-densities have been summarized in Table 4. The distribution was first examined of the twenty-two reference species from the inventory plots among these groups; this has been included in Table 4. It is seen that, as expected, a canopy species can occur in any group, and it is of interest to find out whether any group contains more or fewer of the reference species than would be expected. This can be effected by regarding the columns 'No. of species' and 'No. of reference species' as defining a 7×2 contingency table; owing to the low values for the expectations the exact proba-

Table 4. *Distribution of species within size-classes*

Species group	No. of species	No. of reference species	Cell-densities (%)			
			I	II	III	IV
A	8	4	92	77	85	42
B	6	3	89	90	47	14
C	8	3	75	34	7	4
D	16	7	50	35	40	16
E	7	1	24	16	46	43
F	5	1	0	31	72	67
G	26	3	10	12	7	1

Size-class groups: I = 2, 3, 4; II = 1, 5, 6, 7, 8, 9, 10; III = 11, 12, 13, 15, 16; IV = 14, 17, 18, 19, 20, 21.

bility of this table has been calculated by the method outlined by Goodall (1968); it is 0·429, which would conventionally be regarded as falling far below significance.

Examination of the cell-densities discloses a wider-scale pattern. The four species-groups A, B, C and D are most abundantly represented in the smaller size-classes. The species in these groups mostly belong to the mature forest and do not generally establish early in succession, thus tending to be poorly represented in the large sizes. However, the fact that these mature-forest species are not entirely restricted to the small size-classes suggests that some at least of them are able to grow rapidly even if their establishment is later than that of the pioneers, and their early growth must take place under a canopy of the latter. The species of these groups are in fact shade-tolerant, but there will be rapid growth of saplings when light conditions improve. Species-groups E and F, on the other hand, contain mostly seral woody species, which establish early in succession and consequently preponderate in the largest sizes; the species of group F are completely absent from the smallest size-classes, and their regeneration appears to have ceased. With the exception of one mature canopy species in each group (*Cryptocarya obovata* in E and *Argyrodendron trifoliolatum* in F) all the species concerned are known to be intolerant of shade. Finally, group G is a mixture of seral and mature-forest species. These results thus confirm the inferences from Table 3.

(iii) *Relative abundance of species regenerating*

It has already been noted, for *Eugenia francisii*, that the ability to produce abundant seedlings does not appear to confer any advantages in attaining the canopy; and this phenomenon, too, can now be examined on a broader scale. The seventy-six species were divided into five groups on the basis of their total records on the plot. These groups were as follows: 1-9 records (42 spp.); 10-19 records (11 spp.); 20-29 records (8 spp.); 30-79 records (10 spp.): 80 or more records (5 spp.). The distribution of the twenty-two reference canopy species between these three groups was 11, 3, 2, 4 and 2 respectively; or, if the six species known to sucker are excluded, 11, 2, 1, 1 and 1 respectively. The accurate probabilities for the two resulting contingency tables are 0·952 and 0·949 so that there is no evidence that production of abundant seedlings confers any marked advantage. As extreme examples, *E. francisii* is represented on the plot by 175 records, *Gmelina leichhardtii* by only two; but *Eugenia francisii* is no commoner in the surrounding area than *Gmelina leichhardtii*.

DISCUSSION

(1) *The problem of scale*

The study area, although small, corresponds in size to a very large wind-throw such as might be caused by a cyclone (cf. van Steenis 1956). Because of the removal of the fallen trees by the bulldozer, and the scraping of the soil by the bulldozer blade during clearing, the conditions only partly resemble those which would result from a natural catastrophe. The difficulty of identifying old natural wind-throws of measured area and known age has in the past prevented the comparison of trends following natural and artificial clearing. The early stages of succession would be expected to be very different, but the later stages leading to canopy closure would converge in the two cases. Experience does in fact suggest that the 12-year-old regeneration area in the present study closely resembles the relatively advanced stages of canopy development seen under natural conditions in similar forests. It is therefore considered that the observations made in this study are relevant to the processes of natural regeneration.

The question of scale remains a basic problem. Perusal of references to 'patchiness' or 'monospecific aggregates' in the literature suggests that two completely different scales are involved. The larger of these is well illustrated by work at Davies Creek (Williams *et al.* 1969b) where the tree *Sterculia laurifolia* F. Muell. was commonest on the colluvial shelf C (Fig. 4(b) of that paper), less common on the steeply sloping region B, rare in the gully D, and absent from the ridge-top A. This distribution could be explained by reference to the physical environment. With its shallow root-system and plank buttresses, *S. laurifolia* does not easily establish on steep slopes, and it is usually absent from exposed situations such as ridge-tops. If it could be recognized from the air, it would therefore appear to have a highly contagious distribution; it would in fact exactly conform to one of the 'large aggregates' of van Steenis (1956). The fact that there is no dispute about the reality of such environmentally-determined patches does not mean that their boundaries are easily defined, or that the effective ecological factors can be readily identified. To quote van Steenis, 'Having flown over the central portion of such an aggregate, one notes that individuals of the same species gradually space out and finally fade away'. Furthermore, knowledge of the autecology of rain-forest species is so limited that even a clear-cut pattern may be difficult to interpret in detail.

Aubréville (1938) appears to be thinking in terms of a quite different scale. In this connection, his precise words are significant: 'Si bien qu'en prospectant le long d'une piste, on peut ne pas apercevoir certaines espèces dominantes dans la région, qui se groupent en dehors de l'itinéraire suivi'. This surely implies a scale in terms of a few hundred square metres rather than hectares. Here the work of Poore is critical. In his earlier paper (Poore 1964) on the subject he states that the distributions of *Shorea acuminata* Dyer, and of *Dipterocarpus costulatus* V.Sl., in the Jenka Forest Reserve, Malaya, are contagious; and as evidence he gives maps of the distribution of the larger trees of these species in 24-ha plots. As an exercise in the present study each of these maps was divided into fifty equal sub-plots (each *c.* $10 \times 13 \cdot 5$ m); the distribution between these plots is very close indeed to the Poisson expectations (χ^2 of $1 \cdot 213$ and $4 \cdot 078$, each with 4 d.f.). In a later (1968) paper, Poore re-examined the distribution of these and other species by the pattern analysis of Greig-Smith (1961). The tests used in this technique have aroused some controversy (see, e.g. Goodall 1961, 1963; Greig-Smith, Kershaw & Anderson 1963); but, since the objections related to the possible over-estimation of significance levels, negative results are not in dispute. Poore found no significant patterns until the scale attained the 100- or 200-m level; such patches will be comparable with the 'large aggregates', and are probably environmentally determined. These results suggest that small-scale aggregations are the result of random influences; the meaning to be placed on 'random' in this context is deferred until later in this discussion.

(2) *The specific questions*

The questions extracted from the literature and summarized in the Introduction can now be re-examined. One of these, Q.5 ('How does the growth-rate of trees vary during succession?'), cannot be answered, since no appropriate measurements were made; but at least partial answers are now provided to the other six in the context of this study. However, the answer to Q.1 is implicit in that to Q.7, and Q.1 will therefore not be separately considered. The remaining five questions will therefore provide the framework for this part of the discussion; they are numbered as in the Introduction, but it is convenient to take them in a different order.

Q.2: *How do the canopy and emergent trees regenerate and attain their position?*

There is some terminology difficulty here: the term 'emergent' is used in the present study only for those species, such as Araucarians or strangling figs, that can overtop, as isolated individuals, an otherwise fairly continuous canopy, whereas Jones (1950) appears to use it in the sense of 'canopy tree' as employed here. It is the latter to which attention is at present mostly confined. A wide variety of reproductive strategies appears to be at work. The one missing strategy is that of producing seeds of great longevity; with few doubtful exceptions, our experience suggests that most tree species of the mature rain forest in Australia have short-lived seeds. Such species therefore have no chance of regenerating in a wind-throw if no tree of the species has recently fruited in the vicinity. 'Vicinity' is, however, a broad term. 'Spotwise regeneration'—dispersal by gravity—certainly occurs, as with *Eugenia francisii*, but is only one possible strategy. The seeds of some species are wind-dispersed (e.g. *Argyrodendron* spp. and *Daphnandra micrantha* in the present study area); birds are known to carry seed considerable distances; in the Mount Glorious rain forest, the native rats *Melomys cervinipes* Gould and *Rattus fuscipes* Waterhouse have a range in a straight line of up to 120 m, and 300 m respectively and are responsible for dispersal of seeds (W. J. Freeland, personal communication). The experience of Jones (1950) with *Afzelia* spp. suggests that 100 m is not

L. J. Webb, J. G. Tracey and W. T. Williams   691

an impossible distance for seeds which are not wind-distributed. Limited seed production or germination does not appear to be a disadvantage; the two plants of *Gmelina leichhardtii* of this study are 1·0 and 1·3 m high, and apparently healthy.

A striking feature of the present observation is, however, the importance of suckers as distinct from seeds in the regeneration of tree species. Table 3 shows that suckers have largely, though not quite completely, over-topped seedlings, which must give them an increased chance of attaining the canopy. Although coppicing from the base of the stem, especially after wind damage, has been observed under natural conditions (Nicholson 1965, and present experience), the enhanced suckering in the present area is evidently associated with stumps and roots which had been cut during clearing.

Q.4: *What is the normal size- or age-class representation of the canopy trees?*

It is again clear from Table 3 that in this forest there is no 'normal' size-class: canopy trees are well represented in all size-classes. There is nevertheless a discontinuity based on the method of regeneration, as indicated in the previous paragraph; below about 2 m seedlings predominate, above this suckers predominate. The distribution of the sum of the two is, however, very even among the size-classes. This haphazard size-distribution suggests that it would be unprofitable to regard the different patches as different parts of the same sere, or even as 'serules' as defined by Daubenmire (1968). Instead, there appears to be a situation in which most of the locally-available canopy species are advancing vertically on a remarkably even front, and are continuously reinforced from below. The situation is very different among the pioneer species. There are very few of these below the 'seedling' plateau at 2 m, and their regeneration has almost ceased.

Q.3: *Do the canopy and emergent trees regenerate continuously or intermittently?*

It is obvious from the previous paragraph that the answer must be 'continuously'; but present results provide a possible explanation of how this question has arisen. Consider a forest such as the one studied here but without any suckering; reference to Table 3 shows at once that there would be abundant saplings up to the 2-m level; but between this plateau and the canopy there would be only a small number of medium-sized trees. This would be exactly as the situation reported by Jones (1950) and others for the African forests; and it would be due, not to intermittent regeneration, but to continuous regeneration with a small number of plants 'getting away' in the later stages of succession. Jones advances this as an alternative theory to intermittent regeneration, though he regards it as the less-likely theory; the present results suggest that it is the correct one.

Q.6: *At what stages does the heaviest mortality of seedlings and saplings occur?*

There is as yet no evidence of heavy mortality of canopy species during the 12 years of the present study; there are still, in this limited area, 238 plants of *Eugenia brachyandra*, 175 of *E. francisii*, and 133 (mostly suckers) of *Eupomatia laurina*, to name the most striking cases. It is clear that very high mortality must ensue sooner or later, but the time-scale cannot yet be estimated, nor can there be useful speculation whether this will be due to attacks by insects or fungi, to competition for, e.g. light, nutrients and water, or whether there will be some more active mechanism of self-thinning as is already reported for *Grevillea robusta* A. Cunn. ex R. Br. (Webb, Tracey & Haydock 1967). The view of Fedorov (1966) is disputed when he states that 'no competitive relations ever develop within the populations of most species ... and there is no elimination of individuals within populations such as would ensue from the overpopulation of any area by individuals of the same species'.

Q.7: *What is the role of chance in regeneration?*

This is believed to be the most pertinent question of all, and the last section of this discussion is devoted to it.

(3) *Probability and succession*

Earlier workers have tended to distinguish between two types of processes in the development of vegetation: one orderly and the other fortuitous. On the one hand, an orderly and *determinate* process produces a stand whose floristic composition can be predicted accurately in terms of the available flora, provided the area of the stand is sufficiently large. This process, as Watt (1947) pointed out, accounts for the persistence of pattern in the plant community. In the simplest case, it occurs during succession in a monospecific temperate forest, where, once the dominant has begun to establish, there is only one path open, and such patchiness as exists is composed of different age-classes of one species. Also in the cyclic situations in the relatively simple communities discussed by Watt (1947, 1964), the order of subsequent events is similarly determinate, and the pattern of the community is determined by the dominant where soil and climatic factors are uniform.

On the other hand, in more complex communities, even under uniform environmental conditions, the succession is characterized by departures from orderliness and there is no discernible influence of a dominant species. Such phases of the overall process have been described by Gleason (1926) and noted by Watt (1964) as *fortuitous*, and regarded by Daubenmire (1968) as *unpredictable*; and Gleason has tended to view all vegetation in this light. It is suggested that this antithesis is too extreme; only a truly random or accidental event is completely unpredictable. For this reason, the present authors entirely agree with Goodall (1970) when he says: 'the relation of a species to ecotope space should be considered, not in terms of a discrete cell which the species occupies, but of a diffuse region which could be expressed as a nested set of contour shells representing successively greater probabilities of occurrence'.

How does this concern patchiness? Taken together, the patches in the tropical rain forest—which may differ qualitatively as well as quantitatively in species composition—collectively represent a single floristic association within a uniform environment. The variation of the patches in space and time, however, is related not to niches as traditionally fixed by physical environmental factors, but to a series of biotic reactions which produce niches. These are labile in relation to the life-span of plants within each patch, i.e. such niches are 'floating differentiae' (Watt 1947). Each patch is, as it were, a sociological group culled from a matrix of species dependent on certain environmental features and which form an ecological group.

This situation is not completely unpredictable, in that it is possible to define environmental parameters—including contemporaneous species—which control the floristic composition of any one of the patches within the suite of available species. However, as Richards (1952) points out, no single combination of species is in permanent equilibrium with the environment. Aubréville (1938) regarded the situation as analogous to that in linear algebra where the number of equations (environmental parameters) is less than the number of independent variables (plant species), so that an indefinite number of alternative solutions (species occurrences) will fulfil the required conditions. Even here,

L. J. WEBB, J. G. TRACEY AND W. T. WILLIAMS   693

however, the possible solutions are never *completely* unpredictable; it is usually possible to define boundary-conditions outside which the solutions cannot lie. Similarly, in the tropical rain forest, a patch of regenerated mature canopy cannot include species for which seed sources were unavailable locally when the canopy was opened. Such situations are preferably termed *probabilistic* rather than fortuitous. Rare and truly fortuitous events may, of course, supervene, e.g. cyclones, and determine the size of the gaps in the forest canopy, thus influencing the size and constitution of resultant patches.

It is suggested that, in the past, insufficient distinction has been made between the determinate and probabilistic aspects of pattern in the tropical–subtropical rain forest. In the present particular case, the probability that the early stages of succession will culminate in *Solanum mauritianum* and *Omalanthus populifolius* is so nearly unity that the system can appropriately be treated by deterministic models; but the ensuing stages cannot be so treated. If, as a result of spot-wise regeneration, there is a very large number of plants of a particular species in a limited area, then so long as we are considering only the factor of availability of seedling-source, the probability that all future canopy trees in that place will be of this species is increased. It is not unity, and its value cannot be known unless we are able to assess also the probabilities associated with self-elimination, vulnerability to attack by small mammals or insects, special physiological requirements, or even the influence of previous natural catastrophes such as cyclones or fire. It follows that, as in Aubréville's equation analogy, succession may result in any one of a large number of possible species-combinations which are ecologically compatible, so that, as Watt (1964) remarked, 'no two patches of vegetation are exactly alike'.

It is therefore unlikely that succession initiated in the same place will reproduce the original species-community, i.e. the pattern will normally be 'shifting'. A 'static' pattern would simply be an extreme case, in which the probability associated with a seed-source at one place is sufficiently high to over-ride other probable outcomes; and the greater the size of the disturbed area, the more likelihood of colonization or subsequent invasion by different species to produce a shifting pattern.

From the results of this and previous work it is suggested that tropical rain forest vegetation is best regarded on two levels of organization. On the first level it consists of a determinate framework, on a large or small scale, which is controlled by evident discontinuities of the physical environment. On the large-scale, geographical level, the pattern of vegetation is 'regularly repeating' (Goodall 1970) in relation to the conventional ecological factors of climate, topography and soil. On a smaller scale, variations in the last may be related to less regular patterns, cf. the micro-site differences recognized in the early stages of succession of subtropical rain forest (Williams *et al.* 1969a).

Within this determinate framework of different habitats, the second level consists of a series of patches composed of species which occur probabilistically. The species-constitution of the patches will consequently vary in space and time, and if they are destroyed or become over-mature, they will probably be replaced by another of many possible configurations. The rotation of species at a given site in mature forest may further depend on a deterministic element within the probabilistic framework if certain species are able to influence the site to favour or exclude the establishment of other species or individuals (cf. Webb *et al.* 1967). Such behaviour of a dominant—as defined by Watt (1964)—is necessarily localized in complex communities, and would mean that not all the species of the mature rain forest are ecologically vicarious.

Classical phytosociological techniques are well able to deal with the determinate framework, but they are inappropriate for the study of the labile patches which constitute the finer level of the species organization. It is suggested that this distinction underlies many of the difficulties which have beset workers who have attempted to define the phytosociological structure of the tropical rain forest.

ACKNOWLEDGMENTS

The Queensland Conservator of Forests is thanked for his co-operation for making the study area available for this continuing study. We are also particularly indebted to M. S. Hopkins, Botany Department, University of Queensland, Brisbane, for his assistance in collecting and recording the data.

SUMMARY

References in the literature to the 'patchy' distribution of rain-forest tree species, and to the relationship between this phenomenon and the processes of rain-forest regeneration, are examined critically; it is concluded that direct observations on succession, even over a short time-scale, are needed.

The vegetation (1775 plants of seventy-six species) in a 40 × 20 m plot of 12-year-old regrowth in an experimental clearing in a virgin subtropical rain forest is recorded in detail and analysed by various numerical techniques. A number of specific and hitherto unanswered questions were extracted from the literature and at least partial answers have been obtained to the following problems: (i) the regeneration of the canopy; (ii) the size and age-class representation of canopy spp.; (iii) continuous *v.* intermittent regeneration; (iv) the time scale of seedling and sapling mortality during succession; and, in particular, (v) the role of chance in regeneration.

It is shown that a patchy structure, with patches of area *c.* 100–150 m², has developed, but that the patches differ quantitatively in composition rather than qualitatively. 'Spotwise regeneration' by gravity dispersal of seeds occurs, but experience of this forest type suggests that it is not necessarily followed by a monospecific stand in the same place.

It is concluded that, after the pioneer stage culminating in a temporary canopy, further succession is not unidirectional and is probabilistic rather than determinate. The implications of these findings for the interpretation of rain-forest pattern are discussed, and it is concluded that the pattern will be determinate in its response to recognizable environmental discontinuities, but probabilistic within these on a finer scale, thus producing patchiness.

REFERENCES

Ashton, P. S. (1964). Ecological studies in the mixed Dipterocarp forests of Brunei State. *Oxf. For. Mem.* **25**, 1–75.

Aubréville, A. (1938). La forêt coloniale: les forêts de l'Afrique occidentale française. *Annls Acad. Sci. colon.* **9**, 1–245.

Austin, M. P. & Greig-Smith, P. (1968). The application of quantitative methods to vegetation survey. II. Some methodological problems of data from rain forest. *J. Ecol.* **56**, 827–44.

Dale, M. B., Lance, G. N. & Albrecht, L. (1971). Extensions of information analysis. *Aust. Comput. J.* **3**, 29–34.

Daubenmire, R. (1968). *Plant Communities.* Harper and Row, New York.

Fedorov, An. A. (1966). The structure of the tropical rain forest and speciation in the humid tropics. *J. Ecol.* **54**, 1–11.

Gleason, H. A. (1926). The individualistic concept of the plant association. *Bull. Torrey bot. Club,* **53**, 7–26.

L. J. Webb, J. G. Tracey and W. T. Williams 695

Goodall, D. W. (1961). Objective methods for the classification of vegetation. IV. Pattern and minimal area. *Aust. J. Bot.* **9**, 162–96.

Goodall, D. W. (1963). Pattern analysis and minimal area—some further comments. *J. Ecol.* **51**, 705–10.

Goodall, D. W. (1968). Contingency tables and computers. *Biométr.-Praxim.* **9**, 113–9.

Goodall, D. W. (1970). Statistical plant ecology. *A. Rev. Ecol. Systematics*, **1**, 99–124.

Greig-Smith, P. (1961). Data on pattern within plant communities. I. The analysis of pattern. *J. Ecol.* **49**, 695–702.

Greig-Smith, P., Kershaw, K. A. & Anderson, D. J. (1963). The analysis of pattern in vegetation: a comment on a paper by D. W. Goodall. *J. Ecol.* **51**, 223–9.

Johnston, R. J. (1970). Grouping and regionalizing: some methodological and technical observations. *Econ. Geogr.* **46**, 293–305.

Jones, E. W. (1950). Some aspects of natural regeneration in the Benin rain forest. *Emp. For. Rev.* **29**, 108–25.

Jones, E. W. (1955). Ecological studies on the rain forest of southern Nigeria. IV. The plateau forest of the Okomu forest reserve. Pt I. The environment, the vegetation types of the forest, and the horizontal distribution of species. *J. Ecol.* **43**, 564–94.

Jones, E. W. (1956). Ecological studies on the rain forest of southern Nigeria. IV (cont'd). Pt II. The reproduction and history of the forest. *J. Ecol.* **44**, 83–117.

Kershaw, K. A. (1964). *Quantitative and Dynamic Ecology.* Edward Arnold, London.

Lambert, J. M. & Williams, W. T. (1966). Multivariate methods in plant ecology. VI. Comparison of information-analysis and association-analysis. *J. Ecol.* **54**, 635–64.

Lance, G. N. & Williams, W. T. (1968). Note on a new information statistic classificatory program. *Comput. J.* **11**, 195.

Nicholson, D. I. (1965). A study of virgin forest near Sandakan, North Borneo. *Kuching Symposium on Ecological Research in Humid Tropics Vegetation*, pp. 67–87. UNESCO Sci. Co-op. Office for Southeast Asia.

Poore, M. E. D. (1964). Integration in the plant community. *J. Ecol.* **52** (Suppl.), 213–26.

Poore, M. E. D. (1968). Studies in Malaysian rain forest. I. The forest on Triassic sediments in Jengka forest reserve. *J. Ecol.* **56**, 143–96.

Richards, P. W. (1952). *The Tropical Rain Forest.* Cambridge University Press, London.

Richards, P. W. (1963). What the tropics can contribute to ecology. *J. Ecol.* **51**, 231–41.

Schulz, J. P. (1960). Ecological studies on rain forest in Northern Suriname. *Verh. K. ned. Akad. Wet.*, Afd. natuurk. 2 sect., **53**, 1–367.

Steenis, C. G. G. J. van (1956). Basic principles of rain forest sociology. *Proc. Kandy Symposium on Study of Tropical Vegetation*, pp. 159–63. UNESCO, Paris.

Tracey, J. G. (1969). Edaphic differentiation of some forest types in eastern Australia. I. Soil physical factors. *J. Ecol.* **57**, 805–16.

Watt, A. S. (1947). Pattern and process in the plant community. *J. Ecol.* **35**, 1–22.

Watt, A. S. (1964). The community and the individual. *J. Ecol.* **52** (Suppl.), 203–11.

Webb, L. J. (1969). Edaphic differentiation of some forest types in eastern Australia. II. Soil chemical factors. *J. Ecol.* **57**, 817–30.

Webb, L. J., Tracey, J. G. & Haydock, K. P. (1967). A factor toxic to seedlings of the same species associated with living roots of the non-gregarious subtropical rain forest tree *Grevillea robusta.* *J. appl. Ecol.* **4**, 13–25.

Webb, L. J., Tracey, J. G., Williams, W. T. & Lance, G. N. (1967a). Studies in the numerical analysis of complex rain-forest communities. I. A comparison of methods applicable to site/species data. *J. Ecol.* **55**, 171–91.

Webb, L. J., Tracey, J. G., Williams, W. T. & Lance, G. N. (1967b). Studies in the numerical analysis of complex rain-forest communities. II. The problem of species-sampling. *J. Ecol.* **55**, 525–38.

Webb, L. J., Tracey, J. G., Williams, W. T. & Lance, G. N. (1970). Studies in the numerical analysis of complex rain-forest communities. V. A comparison of the properties of floristic and physiognomic-structural data. *J. Ecol.* **58**, 203–32.

Williams, W. T., Lambert, J. M. & Lance, G. N. (1966). Multivariate methods in plant ecology. V. Similarity analyses and information-analysis. *J. Ecol.* **54**, 427–45.

Williams, W. T., Lance, G. N., Webb, L. J., Tracey, J. G. & Dale, M. B. (1969a). Studies in the numerical analysis of complex rain-forest communities. III. The analysis of successional data. *J. Ecol.* **57**, 515–35.

Williams, W. T., Lance, G. N., Webb, L. J., Tracey, J. G. & Connell, J. H. (1969b). Studies in the numerical analysis of complex rain-forest communities. IV. A method for the elucidation of small-scale forest pattern. *J. Ecol.* **57**, 635–54.

(*Received* 10 *September* 1971)

Change with Time and the Role of Cyclones in Tropical Rain Forest on Kolombangara, Solomon Islands

T. C. Whitmore

2. FOREST TYPES ON KOLOMBANGARA

2.1 INTRODUCTION

Kolombangara Island lies at 157°E, 8°S towards the western end of the New Georgia Islands of the Solomon archipelago.

The island is an extinct Pleistocene volcano and retains the crater rim more or less intact. It is almost circular in outline and almost perfectly symmetrical in relief, only interrupted by a subsidiary volcanic focus, Beacon Hill, in the south-west. The main volcano is composed of olivine pyroxene basalt, and Beacon Hill is composed of hornblende andesite (Thompson & Hackman 1969). There is a very narrow belt of Recent coral reef limestone, about ¼mile (0.4km) wide, round the coast. Shoulder Hill on the north-east is a minor interruption to the regular relief; there is an outwards bulge in the coastline towards the south-east due to extensive mud flows, and in this region there is a more extensive gently sloping region than elsewhere.

Kolombangara is about 18miles (32km) across, the crater rim is about 4miles (6.5km) across (Fig. 2.1†). The land rises from the coast in a gentle slope which steepens inland towards the crater rim, reached at 4900-5400ft (1420-1580m). Drainage is radial and the topography shows a series of fairly broad ridges, narrowing inland, and of steep-sided narrow valleys, generally about 100ft (30m) deep. On the north and north-east coasts the ridges are broader than elsewhere. The crater drains to the south-east.

Just under three-quarters of the island is on 999yr occupation licence to the Lever organisation. The south-west quadrant is under local ownership, except for one small lease to the Seventh Day Adventist mission at Kukundu on the west coast. The main present day villages are in the south-west section; there are a few small coastal settlements on the north, e.g. at Lodomae and Rei Cove and a small settlement on the north-west at Mounga where a sawmill worked for 20 or so years to 1970, and where there is now a Catholic rural training centre. Present day villages and cultivation are more or less restricted to the coast but inland on the Beacon Hill ridge, there are traces of old fortified villages with complex irrigation systems, which have recently been investigated by an archaeologist (D. Yeo, unpublished). Stone foundations of former habitations were found several miles inland on Shoulder Hill during the 1964 forest survey. Since 1968 Levers have been extracting timber on a large scale for export as logs, mainly to Japan, based on a camp at Ringi Cove on the south coast. By late 1972 the forests between Dolo Cove and Bosua Point had been more or less clear-felled by this operation. In these forests, species-poor by comparison with most tropical rain forests, nearly the entire upper canopy is removed, leaving very little residual timber standing.

2.2 DATA

Two forest surveys have been made of Kolombangara. During late 1962 and early 1963 W. R. Evans made enumerations for Levers which covered about 9percent of the area of forest within 5miles (8km) of the coast. This was followed in 1964 by a more detailed survey, the Kolombangara Ecological Survey, of 22 plots of 1.5acres (0.625ha) each, on the

†The figures are to be found at the end of the paper.

4. CYCLONES

4.1 GENERAL

Tropical cyclones (Lamb 1972, pp.131-133) develop between latitudes 10° and 20°. It is believed that there are two prime requirements for their formation. Firstly, a considerable area of very warm ocean is required, with surface temperatures of 27°C or over, and a correspondingly high moisture content of the air. Secondly, most tropical cyclones develop in summer when the intertropical convergence zone makes its furthest advance into the hemisphere concerned.

The 'breeding grounds' where tropical cyclones are born or grown are all over ocean. There is a considerable difference in the typical annual frequency, ranging (for the first half of the twentieth century) from 22 for the N.W. Pacific, to 6-10 in the N.W. Atlantic and 6 in the S.W. Indian Ocean.

There is evidence that, on average and over both hemispheres, the main zones of activity of the atmospheric circulation have been moving somewhat towards the equator as the polar anticyclones have become more pronounced. This trend has been marked since 1960 and is traceable through from a decade or two earlier. It is connected with a global cooling, for which there are a number of independent forecasts, and which is predicted to continue until a minimum is reached in the 1980s which will probably persist to the end of the century (Anon. 1972). Tropical cyclones may never have been appreciably more frequent than in epochs like the present, and at present they are forming nearer the equator than in the recent past.

Observations in the Solomon archipelago fit into this general pattern. Firstly, unpublished Marine Department records since about 1950 show one cyclone in January 1952, followed by a lull and then no fewer than 15 between late 1966 and June 1972, i.e. a marked increase in recent years. These cyclones were indeed most frequent in the southern hemisphere summer, 10 occurred in November-January and none in July-October.

Brookfield (1969) thought cyclones to be more frequent in the south east than the north west of the group, and this is supported by McAlpine (1967) where no mention is made of cyclones in an account of the climate of Bougainville; and by Heyligers (1967) who, in his account of the vegetation of Bougainville, makes no mention of the kind of forest structure which can result from cyclone damage, and such as is reported for the rest of the archipelago by Whitmore (1969). None of the cyclones which occurred between 1952 and 1972 affected the north west of the British Solomons.

Fiji and Queensland, to the south of the Solomons, have long been known to be liable to cyclone damage. The observations in the Solomons therefore support the suggestion that the zone where cyclones are frequent has moved northwards, nearer to the equator. Its northern limit would now appear to be at about 7°S, the latitude of the Shortland Islands (Fig. 4.1).

The world climatological forecasts indicate that the recent cyclone frequency is likely to be maintained until the end of the century, even perhaps increased, though there will probably be considerable year to year variations and minor fluctuations over periods of a few years.

26

Whether these cyclones hit the Solomons depends on the steering of them within the south west Pacific breeding ground, of which the Solomons only occupy a small part. Climatological observations for this region of the world are sparser than for any of the other cyclone zones and prediction from present data would be rash.

Mountain masses of the size of those in the Solomons are too small to interfere with atmospheric circulation to the extent that they will channel cyclones into definite tracks. There is evidence from forest structure and composition on Kolombangara, discussed in the next section, that on a local scale cyclones might be more frequent in some places than others.

Gane (1970) showed that in Fiji cyclones tend to follow tracks so that some places are more prone to damage than others, but the data available were not sufficiently precise for him to be able to make predictions sufficiently accurate to be used to appraise the relative merits of different proposals for land use. Webb (1958) reported that in Queensland local topography steers cyclones and other strong winds to some places more than others. Johnson (1971) observed an area on Erromango, New Hebrides, sheltered by a range of hills from a cyclone of 1959.

4.2 CYCLONE ANNIE

In November 1967 a cyclone formed between Sikaiana and Ontong Java, wrecked the southern half of Ontong Java, passed over the eastern tip of Choiseul, Rob Roy and Wagina and then over Kolombangara, before veering west over north Gizo, then Vella Lavella causing extensive damage in the central east-west lying Oura valley, and then across Baga: see Fig. 4.1. It then moved on to New Guinea where it caused considerable loss of life. Winds reached 100knots (Marine Dept. unpublished memo, K. D. Marten *pers comm.*).

The inhabitants of Taora village on the strait between Choiseul and Rob Roy reported that it lasted there from about 6-11pm. Extensive areas in the vicinity of Koburo peak were affected; the forests on Rob Roy were almost entirely flattened, as ascertained by both ground and aerial reconnaissance in October 1970, but a single valley of undisturbed forest survived and also some stands of *Terminalia brassii* (Groome 1970).

The north of Kolombangara was more heavily damaged than other parts of that island. The percentage of each survey plot which was damaged, computed from observations made in 1971 by Marten is shown on the map Fig. 2.1. It can be seen that forests near Rei Cove and Lodomae were hit hardest, in fact the forests in the area of plot XVIII were so decimated that that plot was completely lost. The three plots furthest inland at Shoulder Hill were less affected than the three nearer the coast. On the west coast the Merusu Cove plots were the least affected of the whole twenty-two, and at Sandfly Harbour some plots were more seriously damaged than others, the overall damage being roughly comparable in degree to that at Shoulder Hill. It seems likely that local relief afforded different degrees of shelter and protection from the high winds of the storm, it is possibly significant that the three furthest inland Shoulder Hill plots lie about 1.3miles (2.1km) west of the peak of Shoulder Hill itself, and the two highest plots at Sandfly

27

Harbour, which were only slightly damaged, lie less than half a mile from two un-named peaks on the western flank. Wadsworth & Englerth (1959) reported marked local differences in the degree of damage caused by a 1956 cyclone on Puerto Rico.

5. SECONDARY SUCCESSION

Most observations on secondary succession in B.S.I.P. have been made on areas from which the timber has been extracted, such areas bear considerable resemblance to forests devastated by cyclone.

Copious growth of the big leaved Convolvulaceae climbers *Merremia* spp. sometimes develops, and these climbers are able to grow over the bare, compacted soil of logging roads and yards, thus protecting the soil from erosion, as well as over the relict forest. Trees are able to grow up under a Merremia mat, carrying it up with them, but some species are often distorted. 'Climber towers' standing amongst low, dense vegetation have been seen from the air in central San Cristobal (K. D. Marten *pers. comm.*), probably these are an example of this kind of regrowth.

On Kolombangara woody climbers are common in the forest and were not completely killed by the destruction of the supporting forest by cyclone Annie, but they fell to the ground and formed a thick tangle. Seedling and sapling trees tend to get bent and broken by such a tangle and forest regrowth is probably slower than in areas with few or no woody climbers. Access by humans is exceedingly difficult. In the Solomons extensive tangles of woody climbers are less likely to remain after logging than after damage by cyclone, because of the mechanical damage caused as logs are dragged out, and the extraction of nearly all the top of canopy trees.

A dense stand of small secondary forest trees commonly develops in felled forest, and grows very rapidly in height, reaching 20-30ft (6-9m) by about 3yr, and ultimately 40-50ft (12-15cm) tall. Such stands are usually of only one or two species in any one place, and the factors which determine composition in different localities remain unknown; availability of seed at the right time is probably one very important factor, and type of soil damage another.

The common components of this group are:

Euphorbiaceae: *Macaranga aleuritoides, M. polyadenia, M. tanarius, M. urophylla* (?) (Suomango); Sterculiaceae: *Melochia umbellata;* Tiliaceae: *Colona scabra, C. velutina, Commersonia bartramia, Trichospermum peekelii, T. psilocladum;* Ulmaceae: *Trema cannabina.*

These species are fast growing, soft-stemmed, short-lived, and do not replace themselves in the same place. Underneath, species of the high forest become established, some at about the same time and some more frequently than others (see chapter 7), and grow up to replace them. It is believed (K. D. Marten, *pers. comm.*) that high forest reforms after devastation more quickly after colonisation by secondary species than if a tangle of woody climbers persists or if *Merremia* develops.

Less often, high forest trees directly colonise open places. Few species are able to do this, but those which do have great ecological importance as indicators of past disturbance, and great silvicultural interest because of their rapid growth, soft, pale timber and gregarious nature. The four main species of this behaviour are

(1) *Endospermum medullosum.* This is the most frequent such species in the Solomons; *E. diadenum (malaccense)* of W. Malesia, closely related (Whitmore 1973), has similar ecology.

(2) *Gmelina moluccana,* which is less common.

29

(3) *Terminalia calamansanai*, whose young soon die except in full light.

(4) *Campnosperma brevipetiolatum* which can grow up in extensive clearings, but is also able to grow up in small gaps in high forest and is a common second-stage species growing under a stand of small secondary forest species.

In addition *Terminalia brassii* whose natural habitat is freshwater swamps germinates copiously and grows vigorously. Trees of 6ft girth at 25yr age stand beside the wartime airstrip at Segi, but the species usually succumbs to competition from others outside swamps (K. D. Marten, *pers. comm.*).

All these five species can grow to 20ft (6m) tall in 3 years.

Further notes on these and other species are given in chapter 7 with the full descriptions of the behaviour of the common big tree species.

30

7. STUDIES ON THE COMMON BIG TREE SPECIES

7.1 INTRODUCTION

Observations were made on all individuals from seedlings to mature trees of the twelve common big tree species on the 33acres (13.7ha) of the detailed ecological survey, over a period of 6.6yr from 1964 to 1971. Additional casual observations were made on the growth of these species in extensive clearings in the forest, in various parts of the Protectorate.

From these studies an attempt will be made in this chapter to outline the ecological behaviour of each species. It will then be possible in chapter 8 to investigate the status the species have in the six forest types and hence the relationship of the forest types to each other.

The different classes of observation will first be described before a description of each species in turn.

7.2 OBSERVATIONS ON FRUITS, SEEDS AND DISPERSAL

Eleven species have fleshy fruits and are presumably dispersed by birds and/or bats, though there is little direct evidence. It must be remembered that the only arboreal mammal in the Solomons is *Phalanger orientalis*, the Australian opossum. *Terminalia calamansanai* has small, winged fruits, presumably adapted for wind dispersal. Seedling populations of *Pometia pinnata*, *Schizomeria serrata* and *T. calamansanai* form mostly near mother trees, indicating poor dispersal. Jones (1956) noted that in a Nigerian rain forest, seedlings were mostly near mother trees in species apparently adapted for wind dispersal, which is the pattern of *T. calamansanai*. Many Dipterocarpaceae, despite having winged fruits, are notorious for their short dispersal distance.

7.3 OBSERVATIONS ON SEEDLINGS

All seedlings of the twelve species were counted five times between 1964 and 1971, as follows:

Aug. 1964		all plots
	26 months	
Oct. 1966		all plots
	23 months	
Aug. 1968		13 plots
	20 months	
April 1970		all 21 surviving plots
	10 months	
Feb. 1971		all 21 surviving plots

The numbers of seedlings per 1ft (0.3m) height class were recorded, seedlings $\geqslant$ 9ft (2.7m) tall being considered as one class.

There are two complete sets of observations from before the November 1967 cyclone, and two more from afterwards (one plot, XVIII, was totally lost in the cyclone). For each species a set of histograms was prepared for each forest plot, to study population size, structure, recruitment and mortality, and from which to infer growth rate. As an example, the set of these histograms for *Campnosperma brevipetiolatum* is reproduced as Fig. 7.1.

In 1964 plot XVI was counted twice. This showed that there are inaccuracies in the counts; more or less the same population structure was

36

recorded each time but there were differences in the numbers in each size class and in the total number. Thus the seedling counts can only be used to follow general trends.

Seedling populations were followed for each plot separately in order to investigate local variation; at the same time consistent similarities within types and differences between types were sought. The extent of canopy destruction by the cyclone was considered when investigating the seedling populations after 1967.

7.4 GROWTH UP INTO THE CANOPY

Table 7.1 gives a summary of the number of stems which attained 6in (150mm) girth in each forest type between 1964 and 1971. A tree which has reached 6in girth has also reached 15ft (4.5m) tall or more and has grown well into the canopy.

TABLE 7.1

Numbers of stems per plot of the twelve big tree species which reached 6in (150mm) girth between 1964 and 1971

forest type	plot number	% damage by 1967 cyclone	CALK	CALV	CAMB	DILS	ELASP	ENDM	GMEM	MARC	PARS	POMP	SCHS	TERC
V	XVII	100	—	—	—	—	3	1	1	2	—	1	—	—
IV	XX	87	4	—	—	—	8	1	—	—	—	—	1	—
IV	XIX	63	—	—	—	—	1	—	—	—	—	—	—	—
II	I	63	—	—	1	—	7	1	—	—	1	1	—	1
V	XI	53	—	—	—	—	—	—	—	—	1	1	—	—
IV	X	50	—	6	—	—	—	—	—	—	—	1	—	—
III	II	43	—	—	1	1	1	—	—	1	1	—	—	—
VI	XII	40	—	1	—	—	—	—	—	1	1	—	—	—
II	XXI	33	—	—	1	—	—	—	—	—	—	4	—	3†
V	XVI	33	1	1	—	—	—	—	—	—	—	—	—	—
VI	XV	33	—	—	—	—	1	—	—	—	—	—	—	—
VI	XIII	27	—	—	—	—	—	—	—	—	—	—	2	—
III	IX	25	—	—	—	3	—	—	—	—	1	—	—	—
I	V	13	—	—	—	—	—	—	—	—	1	—	—	—
III	IV	13	—	—	1	—	—	—	—	—	1	—	—	—
I	VIII	10	1	—	—	1	—	—	—	—	1	—	—	—
III	III	7	1	—	—	—	—	—	—	—	—	—	1	—
I	VI	7	—	—	1	2	—	—	—	—	—	—	—	—
II	XXII	7	—	—	4	1	1	—	—	1	1	—	—	—
I	VII	0	—	—	2	2	1	—	—	—	—	—	—	—
V	XIV	0	—	—	—	—	2	—	—	—	—	—	—	—
totals			7	8	11	10	25	3	1	5	9	9	4	4

* For species abbreviations see appendix 1.
† 2 suckers.

On the 31.5acres (13.1ha) which survived in recognisable form 96 stems of the twelve species reached this size during this 6.6yr period.

Table 7.1 shows that *Endospermum medullosum* and *Gmelina moluccana* have only grown up in plots which received substantial damage to the canopy by the cyclone (but with only 3 and 1 stems respectively), and that most of the *Elaeocarpus sphaericus* recruitment (25 stems) is

37

in such plots. *Calophyllum vitiense* and *Pometia pinnata* show a similar but less marked trend. No other species shows this trend, or any other; instead, 6in (150mm) girth stems have developed throughout the range of amount of canopy damage.

7.5 OBSERVATIONS ON THE TREES

The observations have been described in section 6.1.

7.51 *Growth rates*

For each species the mean girth growth rate of all stems in each 1ft (0.3m) girth class over the whole 6.6yr period 1964.6-1971.2 is shown on Fig. 7.2.

All twelve species show an increase in girth growth rate with girth in the three lowest size classes, from 0.5-3ft (0.15-1.9m), though for most species the correlation is not significant (see below). Such a trend probably follows because on Kolombangara, which bears high forest with only small gaps, some small trees stagnate and others grow up, so that as time progresses it is the bigger ones which are growing faster.

The same trend continues for most species, most notably *Calophyllum kajewskii*. For *Campnosperma brevipetiolatum*, however, there is a tendency to decreasing growth rate from 3ft (0.9m) upwards and for *Dillenia salomonensis* there is no upward trend above 3ft.

The most erratic growth rate curves are shown by the species with fewest individuals; the only meaning which can be given to those for *Elaeocarpus sphaericus*, *Endospermum medullosum* and *Gmelina moluccana* is that they give an indication of the growth individuals are capable of in high forest. (The author has data suitable for calculation of the range of girth growth rates for each size class of each species plus figures for their probability. This analysis is beyond the scope of the present report. The data can be made available to anyone interested to pursue this aspect.)

TABLE 7.2

Mean annual girth increment, 1964-1971, of the twelve big tree species in declining order

species*	no. stems	annual increment (inches)	group (see Table 7.6)
CAMB	102	0.96	. . c .
CALK	120	0.71	. b . .
CALV	63	0.65	. b . .
GMEM	27	0.64	. . . d
ENDM	21	0.59	. . . d
ELASP	27	0.54	. . c .
PARS	137	0.54	a . . .
TERC	65	0.48	. . . d
MARC	24	0.44	a . . .
SCHS	39	0.43	a . . .
DILS	155	0.42	a . . .
POMP	74	0.40	. b . .

Mean increments over the 6.6yr period 1964.7—1971.2 of all stems present in 1971.
* For species abbreviations see appendix 1.

Mean growth rate over 6.6yr of measurement is shown for each species in Table 7.2. It varies from 0.96in (24.4mm)/yr for *Campnosperma brevipetiolatum* down to 0.4in (10.1mm) for *Pometia pinnata*. In making the computations extreme values of girth increment (-0.1in/annum and $+3.5$in/annum, or -2.5, $+89$mm) were rejected because these are probably mostly due to mismeasurement. Most rejected stems were growing faster than this upper limit; in so far as these represent exceptional individuals and not mistakes the figures in Table 7.2 are underestimates.

Only four species have stems in most size classes in both north and west coast forests (only 12 missing values out of 80); these are *Calophyllum kajewskii*, *Campnosperma brevipetiolatum*, *Parinari salomonensis* and *Pometia pinnata* and for them an analysis of variance showed a highly significant difference in mean girth increment between west and north coast forests. There are too many missing values to extend this analysis to other species.

7.52 *Correlations between girth growth, girth and crown*

Regression analyses were made on girth measurements taken in 1964.7 and 1967.7 and only a few significant correlations were found between girth growth and original girth, crown exposure and crown form. These are shown in Table 7.3 and discussed in the notes on individual species

TABLE 7.3

Correlations between girth growth between 1964.7 and 1967.7 and original girth (G), crown exposure k_e and crown form (k_f)

species	no. trees	mean growth in/annum	mean girth (in)	mean k_e	mean k_f	F	t values girth	k_e	k_f	r^2 %
west coast (forest types I-III)										
CALK†	41	0.73	53.97	3.0	3.8	*	2.438(*)	0.552(—)	3.347(**)	63
ELASP	10	0.56	12.04	2.9	3.9	*	4.897(**)	1.083(—)	2.030(—)	96
SCHS	16	0.47	28.74	2.8	3.8	*	0.474(—)	3.202(**)	2.787(**)	78
north coast (forest types IV-VI)										
CALK	79	0.61	23.5	2.34	4.05	*	2.293(*)	4.534(**)	3.112(**)	51
MARC	26	0.36	25.1	2.58	3.73	*	0.882(—)	0.906(—)	3.293(**)	56
POMP	78	0.49	39.9	2.76	3.51	*	1.393(—)	1.332(—)	7.253(**)	57

Only the significant correlations are reproduced here.
† For species abbreviations see appendix 1.

below. North and west coast populations were considered separately. The main conclusion is that, over all girths, there is no significant correlation between growth rate and original girth except for *Calophyllum kajewskii* and *Elaeocarpus sphaericus*. The latter correlation is highly significant but there were few individuals under measurement (Fig. 7.2). Highly significant correlations with crown exposure were shown by *Schizomeria serrata* and *Calophyllum kajewskii* and with crown form by *Calophyllum kajewskii*, *Schizomeria serrata*, *Maranthes corymbosa* and *Pometia pinnata*, mostly in only one of the two populations.

The limited success of these attempts to attribute the considerable variability in girth growth to these parameters is due to the high internal variability within natural populations of trees, which is discussed more fully in section 9.32 below, and has also been found elsewhere, for example in Uganda and Suriname (Dawkins 1956, Schulz 1960 p.230). Analyses were not attempted for any other periods because of the limited significance of the results and the difficulty of interpreting those which were significant. Mervart (1970) has recently shown that in western Nigeria growth of individual trees can vary considerably at different times, and if this is generally the case it also complicates such analyses.

7.53 Stand tables analysed

In Fig. 7.2 summary stand tables are shown for all of the twelve common species, these are a compilation of all stems in the six forest types; in Fig. 7.3 separate stand tables are given for each forest type. These latter reveal similar population structure as the summary tables do, but are less clear because they are based on fewer stems.

Two broadly different kinds of population structure are shown by the stand tables, especially by Fig. 7.2.

Firstly, there is a group of species with many more small individuals than large, the numbers decreasing with increasing size. This size-class distribution indicates that these species are reproducing themselves *in situ;* slow growth rate of the smallest sizes plus mortality at all sizes account for the population structure. This kind of species is commonly stated to have a 'positive stand table' (Dawkins 1958). The most marked examples are *Calophyllum vitiense, Dillenia salomonensis* and *Parinari salomonensis.*

The second, contrasting, population structure is shown best by *Campnosperma brevipetiolatum.* This species does not have a preponderance of small individuals, and, taking into account mortality and the slower growth rate of the smallest sizes, has too few small stems to maintain itself. *Endospermum medullosum* and *Gmelina moluccana* also show a similar population structure. Examination of the populations of *Endospermum medullosum* and *Gmelina moluccana* in the separate forest types, Fig. 7.3, shows that some have a few individuals at each of many girths (i.e. they are like the overall picture for these species) and others have a group of individuals of large girth and no small ones. The summary stand table on Fig. 7.2 for *Terminalia calamansanai* shows two separate groups of trees, and *Elaeocarpus sphaericus*, less common, shows a similar population structure. The populations in the separate forest types, Fig. 7.3, exhibit this structure much more clearly and show it also for *Campnosperma brevipetiolatum* (e.g. in forest type I).

These stand tables indicate that this second group comprises species which are not regenerating continuously *in situ.* The number of small stems is inadequate at the prevailing growth rates and allowing for mortality, to replace the existing large ones as these grow larger and die. Instead, reproduction is in pulses. Periodically conditions occur which permit a group of individuals to grow up together. The continued presence of these species in the forest depends on the periodic recurrence of such conditions.

In considering population structure in detail the crown exposure of each tree was also borne in mind. Commonly, it was found that, as would be expected, the larger trees have on average more exposed (i.e. better-illuminated) crowns, but superimposed on this general trend there are detectable differences between species, reflecting their different ecological characteristics, and showing, in a rough way, the amount of light which each needs in order to survive.

Further discussion of the behaviour of individual species is deferred until section 7.9 where all the different lines of evidence will be brought together.

7.54 *Cyclone losses*

Fig. 7.4 shows stems lost at the cyclone, and losses in each type are incorporated in Fig. 7.3. One species, *Campnosperma brevipetiolatum,* stands out as having lost a lot of big trees (13 over 5ft, 1.5m, girth) and they were lost over a wide area.

7.6 OBSERVATIONS IN LARGE CLEARINGS

Secondary succession in the Solomons was briefly described in chapter 5. The occurrence and performance of a species in seral forests is an obvious clue to its status and role in high forest and is therefore briefly given.

7.7 HEIGHT GROWTH

Height growth was measured six times between 1964 and 1971, on an 0.7acre (1.7ha) subsample of plot VI in forest type I, of all individuals of the twelve common species which were $\geqslant$ 6in (150mm) g.b.h., plus a few which were just below this girth. Five species (*Campnosperma brevipetiolatum, Dillenia salomonensis, Elaeocarpus sphaericus, Parinari salomonensis, Schizomeria serrata*) were included in the sample. The area included all phases of the forest growth cycle from a small gap formed by death of a single tree to mature high forest. Analysis was confined to the smaller trees, up to 50ft (15m) tall, which were measured accurately by climbing on each occasion. The results are summarised in Table 7.4 in which a measure of the exposure of each crown to the sky (i.e. its illumination) is included. It can be seen that height growth did not differ in any regular manner between trees with different crown exposure, though only the three lowest of the five exposure classes were represented. *Campnosperma* was growing fastest with four out of six trees adding 1.5-1.8ft (450-540mm) /yr. Two of the three trees of *Elaeocarpus* were growing over 1ft in height a year, *Dillenia* and *Parinari salomonensis* were growing more slowly.

All of the trees under observation are growing much more slowly than do young trees of the same and other species growing in the open in plantations which commonly add 4-7ft (1.2-2.1m) of height per annum at comparable girths, see Table 7.5, and pioneer trees of *Campnosperma brevipetiolatum, Endospermum medullosum, Gmelina moluccana Terminalia brassii* and *Terminalia calamansanai* colonising areas of felled forest have been observed to reach 20ft (6m) tall in 3yr, a similar rate. *C. brevipetiolatum* and *T. calamansanai* grow at about this rate when planted in lines established in logged areas.

In summary, in high forest and in small gaps, height growth of small trees is much slower than in extensive clearings, or in plantations. This is probably due to a combination of intense root competition and incomplete exposure of the crowns to light.

41

TABLE 7.4

Height growth on 0.7acres (0.29ha) in forest type I

tree no.	crown exposure*	height in 1964 (ft)	height added in 6.6yrs to 1971(ft)	annual growth ft/year
Campnosperma brevipetiolatum				
211	2	43.4	11.6	1.8
182	3	33.7	11.3	1.7
196	3	19.6	10.4	1.6
212	3	22.3	9.7	1.5
1101	n.a.	11.8	0.5	0.08
1103	n.a.	20.6	5.4	0.8
Elaeocarpus sphaericus				
206	1	35.3	2.7	0.4
194	2	25.4	7.6	1.2
195	2	20	8	1.2
Dillenia salomonensis				
202	1	20	8+	1.2+
240	1	36	1	0.2
242	1	37.3	—0.3	0
207	2	18	6 ·	0.9
209	2	44.9	0.1	0.02
237	2	17.2	4.2	0.6
238	2	30.6	2.4	0.4
241	2	53.3	4.4	0 6
Parinari salomonensis				
187	1	44.5	5.5	0.6
189	1	43.3	—1.3	0
190	2	40	0	0
193	2	18.3	0.7	0.1
198	2	39	4	0.6
185	3	52	4	0.6
Schizomeria serrata				
197	1	33.6	—0.6	0

* Crown exposure following Dawkins (1958) on a scale from darkest (1) to full light (5)

7.8 THE SPECIES IN DETAIL

7.81 *Calophyllum kajewskii (CALK)*

Fruit a heavy, globose, blue-black drupe, with leathery flesh, 1-1.5in (25-37mm) diameter, presumably dispersed by large birds and possibly by large bats too, though many fruits fall to the ground below the tree where pigs and rats may disperse some; *C. vitiense* is similar.

Seedling populations tiny or large to very large, commonly 300-500 per acre, reaching 1000 (720-1200-2400/ha). Absent or very rare at high elevations (forest types III and VI) except the valley plot IX at Merusu Cove. *Recruitment* is frequent, by local to widespread flushes of several hundred seedlings/acre, occasionally less, growing quickly to 1ft (0.3m) or taller by extensive growth of the hypocotyl and about half dying within a year, though this is often masked by further recruitment. In some places recruitment followed cyclone damage to the canopy, but in

T. calamansanai locally forms dense seedling carpets in large clearings, for instance at Lodomae after the cyclone. Competing growth commonly overtops it and shades it out so that few seedlings survive after six months. *T. calamansanai* can grow very fast in height and reach 20-30ft (6-10.5m) tall and 10-25in (254-635mm) girth in three years. (K. D. Marten, unpublished report.) It is the most impressive species for height growth in the first few years in Forest Department line planting afforestation schemes and is extensively planted. However, trees shorter than *c.* 40ft (12m) tall, planted on Santa Ysabel, were not wind firm to cyclone Ida (K. D. Marten, *pers. comm.*).

Conclusions. Despite its winged fruits, dispersal appears to be poor, and periodically populations of seedlings develop which may be very dense and very large; rapid growth follows for those with good illumination. The seedlings apparently cannot suspend growth and die if there is no space or inadequate light for continued rapid growth. Thus *T. calamansanai* maintains its presence by producing, mainly in the vicinity of mature trees, big flushes of seedlings, of which a few sometimes grow into trees if a canopy opening develops within a few months. It is entirely dependent on gaps for the growth of seedlings up into trees. It is much commoner on north Kolombangara than in any other Solomons' forest studied (chapter 2). In establishment behaviour and population structure it is a nomad species (section 7.9) but is an unusual one in its apparently inefficient dispersal.

7.9 THE ECOLOGICAL STRATEGIES OF THE COMMON BIG TREE SPECIES SUMMARISED

The observations of the previous section on various aspects of the behaviour of each of the twelve species is very tersely summarised in Table 7.6, inevitably with the omission of much detail. The species fall into four groups (a)-(d).

(a) At the top of the table are four species *Dillenia salomonensis, Maranthes corymbosa, Parinari salomonensis* and *Schizomeria serrata* whose seedlings and trees establish in high forest. There is no evidence that gaps are necessary for recruitment or continuing growth in size. Their tree stand tables show a steady decrease in numbers with increasing size. These are typical 'shade bearing' species. It is noteworthy that three of them have the slowest mean girth growth rates (Table 7.2).

(b) The next species, *Calophyllum kajewskii, C. vitiense* and *Pometia pinnata* also establish their seedlings in high forest, though there is some evidence that *C. kajewskii* seedlings can also establish and do well in gaps. This group differs from the first in that there is a lesser preponderance of the smallest sizes of tree and some evidence of trees growing up in gaps. It is concluded that this second group consists of species which, while they can establish their seedlings in high forest, depend for the completion of the life cycle on the occurrence of gaps. The small gaps which are continually forming from the death of single trees and which were not recorded in this survey are probably adequate.

(c) The third group of species consists of *Campnosperma brevipetiolatum* and *Elaeocarpus sphaericus*. As with the previous group, seedlings establish in high forest (and *C. brevipetiolatum* also in gaps). Stand tables show that tree recruitment is intermittent and of groups, which are sometimes large. These species are more dependent than the previous

52

TABLE 7.6

Summary of behaviour, the twelve big tree species

		seedlings			trees	
	species & group	dis-persal[1]	establishment conditions	usual population size	conditions for development from seedlings	distribution
(a)	DILS[2]	poor	*high forest*	medium	*high forest*	W only, common.
	MARC	?	*high forest*	small/med.	*high forest*	uncommon, N>W.
	PARS	?	*high forest*	medium	*high forest*	common everywhere.
	SCHS	poor	*high forest*	small	*high forest*	N & W, esp. high altitude.
(b)	CALK	poor	*high forest* or *small gaps*	big/huge	*high forest* or *gaps*	common, all types except VI.
	CALV	good	*high forest*	small/med.	*high forest* or *gaps*	nearly all N.
	POMP	poor	*high forest* or *disturbed*	mostly small	*high forest, possibly in small gaps*	mainly N.
(c)	CAMB	poor	*high forest* or *gaps*	mostly small	*gaps*	common W>N.
	ELASP	good	*high forest*	medium	*gaps*	uncommon, more on N.
(d)	TERC	very poor	*high forest but soon dying except in gaps*	huge (ephemeral)	*gaps*	patchy, mainly N.
	ENDM	poor	*mostly gaps*	medium	*gaps*	nearly all N.
	GMEM	poor	*mostly gaps*	tiny	*gaps*	uncommon, W & N.

[1]As judged from seedling distribution relative to big trees
[2]For species abbreviations see appendix 1.

group on gaps for the seedlings to grow up. *C. brevipetiolatum* has the fastest mean girth growth rate of all twelve species (Table 7.2). Young trees of both species grow very fast in height in the open.

(d)   The fourth and final group, *Terminalia calamansanai, Endospermum medullosum* and *Gmelina moluccana*, are species whose seedlings mostly establish in gaps (and those of *T. calamansanai* die in shade) and trees only grow up in gaps. They are uncommon in the forests surveyed, especially the western ones. Their girth growth is fairly fast (Table 7.2). All show very rapid early height growth in the open.

Species with the characteristics of this final group are known from many countries. Their continued existence depends on the continuing development of suitable gaps. Such species have been called 'biological nomads' by van Steenis (1958) because they are continually moving their sites. Van Steenis considered that nomad species could be sharply distinguished as a class from stationary species. In the Solomons, however, they are seen to lie at the end of a series of species which require progressively more light, and also differ from each other in the efficiency of dispersal, the frequency with which they produce seedling flushes, the size of such flushes and the persistence of the seedlings once established. It is thus an oversimplification to divide tree species into two sharp classes. This was also found by Schulz (1960 p.228) for Suriname trees, and was suggested first by Fosberg in a comment following van Steenis' 1958 paper. Van Steenis and Schulz both consider seeds of nomad species require light for germination, no tests have yet been made on this requirement in the Solomons. Nomads have 'pioneer' characteristics, and the concept is a valuable one. However, van Steenis (1958 p.215) included amongst their features adaptations to survive fire and dry conditions, such as thick bark, underground lignotubers, etc., which seem, rather, to belong to a quite different category of species, namely those which persist in fire-maintained savanna woodland. His original concept thus needs some modification.

8. THE STATUS OF THE FOREST TYPES ON KOLOMBANGARA

8.1 EVIDENCE FROM THE COMMON BIG TREE SPECIES

Now that the different strategies adopted by the twelve common species for their continuing presence in the rain forest ecosystem have been analysed, chapter 7, we can go on to investigate the status of the six forest types by studying the extent to which the different species are present in each.

The most common of the twelve species in the six forest types are as follows (chapter 2: see note on abbreviations, appendix 1).

West coast:
>   I   DILS/CAMB/PARS+CALK
>   II   CAMB/PARS/CALK/DILS
> III   CAMB/DILS/EUG/PARS/SCHS

North coast:
>   IV   CALK+CALV/CAMB/PARS/MARC+TERC
>   V   TERC/PARS/CALK/ENDM
>   VI   TERC/CALV/SCHS/PARS/ENDM

Fig. 8.1 shows the location of the types. Types III and VI are furthest inland and at the highest elevation.

The three west coast forests are very similar to each other. They contain big stands of *Dillenia salomonensis* and *Parinari salomonensis* (Fig. 7.3), shade bearing species which maintain themselves in high forest (Table 7.6). *Schizomeria serrata*, of similar biology, is one of the common species in type III, at higher elevation. *Calophyllum kajewskii* replaces *S. serrata* in types I and II as one of the four commonest of the twelve species, and is a species which can utilise gaps for both seedling establishment and growth up into trees, though not being tied to them. The one remaining of the twelve species which is very common in these west coast forests, *Campnosperma brevipetiolatum*, does need gaps for ongrowth of seedlings into trees. Its stands in forest types II and III have a big preponderance of the largest sizes (Fig. 7.3), whilst in type I there is also a stand of small trees. The other of the twelve species are represented by only a scattering of trees. This mixture of the twelve species and the structure of their populations indicates that the west coast forests are high forest of long standing in which shade bearing species which reproduce *in situ* have come to predominate. along with some of those which sometimes grow up into trees in gaps. Furthermore, at some time or times in the past there has been a period or periods of the formation of gaps in all three forests types into which *Campnosperma brevipetiolatum* trees grew up which have now attained large girths. In addition. there has been a more recent period of gap formation in type I in which a further group of *C. brevipetiolatum* trees, currently 6in-3ft (150-900mm) girth, has developed. The true nomad species. *Endospermum medullosum, Gmelina moluccana* and *Terminalia calamansanai,* which need gaps for seedling establishment as well as for tree formation, are rare in all three western forests, as is *Elaeocarpus sphaericus* which has similar requirements to *C. brevipetiolatum*.

The north coast forests are more different from each other than the western ones. They all lack *Dillenia salomonensis* which is common throughout the western types. The stand tables of type IV (Fig. 7.3) show that this type has very few stems over 5ft (1.5m) girth of the shade bearing species *Calophylllum kajewskii, C. vitiense, Maranthes corymbosa, Parinari salomonensis, Pometia pinnata* and *Schizomeria serrata*. Most of the big stems belong to species which are believed to require or to benefit from large gaps for the establishment of trees namely *Campnosperma brevipetiolatum, Elaeocarpus sphaericus, Endospermum medullosum, Gmelina moluccana* and *Terminalia calamansanai*. Except for *E. medullosum* these also have small stems. Type V is similar to type IV (Fig. 7.3), though the relative abundance of the species differs. Type VI has, overall, fewer trees. Most trees over 5ft (1.5m) girth are of the three most light dependent 'nomad' species *E. medullosum, G. moluccana* and *T. calamansanai*, with smaller numbers of *C. vitiense, Campnosperma brevipetiolatum, Elaeocarpus sphaericus, Maranthes corymbosa, Parinari salomonensis* and *Schizomeria serrata*.

The species composition and population structure of the north coast forests indicates widescale canopy destruction at some past time followed by the growth of light demanding trees which are now predominant amongst the stems over 5ft (1.5m) girth. Under these, stands of more shade bearing species have established themselves, presumably from seeds provided by a few big trees which survived the disturbance. Thus, currently, the shade bearers are present mainly as small trees. Most of the light demanding species also have a few small trees, including the nomads *Gmelina moluccana* and *Terminalia calamansanai*, but (except on VI) not the other nomad *Endospermum medullosum* (whose seedlings have been noted to be less shade tolerant); and this indicates more recent but lesser canopy disturbance.

8.2 EVIDENCE FROM THE CLIMBERS AND EPIPHYTES

Observations on the big woody climbers on a 13.3percent sample of the survey area, described in section 2.712, point to a history of more recent disturbance on the north than on the west.

The species comprising this synusia are photophytes which colonise forest gaps, grow into the crowns of small trees, and grow up as these trees develop into high forest.

The north coast forests have more climbers per acre, of more species and of smaller average girth than do the west coast forests. These latter forests can be regarded as, on average, to represent a later phase in the life of this climber synusia: many individual climbers have died out, including some species, and those which remain are of greater average girth.

The two synusiae of bole climbers and skiophytic epiphytes are better developed in the west forests than in the northern forests (section 2.73). The niche these synusiae occupy is at its largest in high forest and has been present longest. Again, as with the twelve big tree species, the implication is that the northern forests have a history of more recent extensive disturbance than do the western ones.

8.3 THE NATURE OF THE DISTURBANCE FACTOR

The most likely cause of canopy damage is cyclones. There is evidence that these have increased in frequency in recent years to be comparable at present with such well known cyclone areas as Fiji and the Caribbean (section 9.21); records were not kept until 1950, but the Solomons lie in a cyclone 'breeding ground' (section 4.1) and are likely always to have been occasionally hit. The pattern of destruction on Kolombangara by the November 1967 cyclone (Fig. 4.2, Table 6.2) shows that the north coast plots were much more severely damaged than those on the west coast, and the former, as has been shown, have signs of more extensive previous damage. The cyclone created gaps of different size and there was a considerable difference in the extent of damage between different forest types and different plots. Species of different ecological strategy can be expected to grow to fill the gaps of different size. In conclusion, previous cyclones could have caused a pattern of canopy damage from which the present day forests arose.

There are other factors which have led to extensive damage to forest in the Solomons (Whitmore 1969). North Kolombangara is now uninhabited except for a few tiny coastal settlements, but there was a much bigger population until the turn of the twentieth century when it was decimated in a civil war, and most or all of the few survivors fled (*pers. comm.* elders of Ire Ire village, 1964). The present-day populations of the west coast are related by marriage to those of the Roviana lagoon on New Georgia and may have come from there (K. D. Marten, *pers. comm.*). Regrowth since about 1900 on cultivated land could have given the present day northern forests both structurally and in terms of species and the big *Gmelina moduccana* trees could have been left standing at the time of occupation because of their value for dugout canoes. Earthquake shocks have led to trees snapping off over many acres in Vella Lavella (see Whitmore 1969, p.263), and cannot be ruled out for Kolombangara. The remaining widescale destructive factor, landslide, is unlikely to have operated in these forests except in those stands of each type on steep valley slopes, because lowland Kolombangara slopes only gently upwards.

8.4 THE COMMON BIG TREE SPECIES REPRESENTATIVE

Forest types were defined on the densities of 91 species, of which we have been considering only twelve. We have shown that the presence and density of these twelve in a particular forest type depends to an important extent on the magnitude of a disturbance factor, operating at various stages in the early life of the tree. This same factor can be expected to be important for all or most tree species. Our findings from examination of only part of the species' complement are therefore likely to apply to the whole.

8.5 THE DISTURBANCE FACTOR PRE-EMINENT

The principal floristic difference, as elucidated by the numerical analyses, was between western and northern forest types. This difference, it now appears, results from regrowth of the forest after different degrees of canopy damage in the past. It can therefore be concluded that, on Kolombangara, the principal ecological factor operating on the lowland forests is that which causes canopy damage. Groups of species can be recognised with different ecological strategies adapted to take advantage of different degrees of canopy gap formation, and the magnitude of the disturbance factor determines which group will come to predominate.

8.6 LESSER DIFFERENCES BETWEEN TYPES ANALYSED

The phytosociological analyses also showed differences between the forest types in altitude and topography, in that order, and on the west coast the stands at Sandfly Harbour segregated out. These differences are less important than between the northern and western forests and reflect ecological factors of lesser importance than the disturbance factor.

Individual species differ from each other in many facets of their ecological behaviour, and it is these differences which maintain the species diversity of the Kolombangara forests. The twelve common species fall roughly into groups on the nature of their response to light, i.e. to the disturbance factor (Table 7.6). Besides this, differences between species can be seen in the three stages of life represented by dispersal, seedling establishment and growth of seedlings up into trees. These can be indicated, although their full investigation is beyond the scope of the present enquiry. Superimposed are differences in seed availability, about which there is no information.

8.61 *Dispersal*

Several of the twelve species have patchy distribution and this is presumably due to poor powers of dispersal.

Most striking is the distribution of *Dillenia salomonensis*, which, it will be recalled, is entirely absent from the north coast yet common on the west.

Terminalia calamansanai is much commoner on the north coast than the west and has most seedlings growing near parent trees.

8.62 *Seedling establishment*

Schizomeria serrata is commoner in the forest types at high elevations and *Calophyllum kajewskii* at low ones. There is no consistent difference between types in the extent of (unstable) hillside habitat, and it may be concluded that ecological factors connected with elevation are operating at the stage of seedling establishment.

8.63 *Onward growth of seedlings*

Several species have more widely distributed seedlings than trees.

Calophyllum vitiense has ubiquitous seedlings, but trees are nearly all on the north coast whereas *C. kajewskii*, with equally widespread seedlings, has trees on most plots.

Maranthes corymbosa and *Parinari salomonensis* have similar, widespread, small to medium-sized, seedling populations. *P. salomonensis* is much commoner as a tree.

Elaeocarpus sphaericus, likewise, has seedlings much more widespread than trees. Seedlings of this species can stagnate for long periods under dense shade and grow up fast when a gap occurs above them.

In none of these cases do we know, from only 6.6yr study, if, in the long term, *Calophyllum vitiense*, *Maranthes corymbosa* and *Elaeocarpus sphaericus* will become more common on Kolombangara. However, other forests in the western Solomons also have these species amongst the less common ones, and this indicates that Kolombangara is probably representative. Either these species are everywhere in the process of

58

becoming more common, or, alternatively, it is more likely that they are in equilibrium and failing in competition with other species to gain space to reach maturity, although successful in seedling establishment. The precise cause of failure remains unknown, and it is noteworthy that in two of the cases a closely related species is much more successful. It is possibly significant that in plantations *Elaeocarpus sphaericus* is very prone to insect damage (section 7.85), which indicates a factor which may be operating in the forest to keep its populations diffuse.

8.7 STATUS OF THE FOREST TYPES

In the three west coast forest types I-III, shade bearing species reproducing *in situ* are amongst the commonest of the big tree species, *Campnosperma brevipetiolatum*, which is dependent on gaps for tree establishment, is dying out of types II and III and will only maintain its numbers if a big enough gap develops to allow more trees to establish while there are still potential mother trees within dispersal range. This replenishment has happened in type I. *C. brevipetiolatum* can flower and set seed from about 30 years age onwards (K. D. Marten, *pers. comm.*).

The north coast forests are less stable in composition, with big stands of trees of shade bearers still small in girth and coming up under light demanders which are mostly of large girth and are not, or are only just, maintaining their numbers. In the course of time, and if there is not further extensive canopy destruction, the shade bearers will come to predominate, the composition will become closer to that of the west coast forests, except that *Dillenia salomonensis* is absent.

The balance between species with different ecological strategies with respect to canopy openings will alter if the disturbance factor is not the same in the future as it has been in the past, and, if disturbance becomes less, the north coast forests will come to resemble the west coast ones.

In the three west coast forest types the same big tree species are common, but they occur in different proportions. Subtle differences between forest types, such as these, depend partly at least in differences in reproductive pressure of the various species due to differences in the frequency of fruiting, efficiency of dispersal, success of germination and seedling establishment and ability of seedlings to grow up into trees. Some such differences have been indicated for the twelve common tree species. These factors can be expected to operate differently for the various species in different habitats at each of the stages in life just indicated. Altitude and topography are the two main habitat factors on Kolombangara.

The potential complexity of response is enormous and increases with species richness. Thus we see why the elucidation of forest types in species rich tropical rain forest has proved such a daunting task, the more so in situations where there is not one overriding factor, represented by canopy damage by cyclones on Kolombangara, to act as a major ecological determinant.

The suggestion by Aubréville (1938), which has become known as the mosaic theory, that the pattern of species in space is maintained by fluctuation at one place in time, is seen to represent an over simplification of the mechanism whereby these forests in fact do maintain themselves.

References

Anonymous. 1972. Forecast indications to the year 2000. *Occ Bull Climate Res Unit Univ East Anglia* 4.

Aubréville, A. 1938. La forêt coloniale: Les forêts de l'Afrique occidentale française. *Ann Acad Sci Colon* 9:1–245.

Brookfield, H. C. 1969. Some notes on the climate of the British Solomon Islands. *Phil Trans Royal Soc,* ser. B 255:207–10.

Dawkins, H. C. 1956. The management of natural tropical high forest, with special reference to Uganda. *Inst Pap Commw For Inst,* no. 34.

Gane, M. 1970. Hurricane risk assessment in Fiji. *Commonw For Rev* 49:253–56.

Groome, J. G. 1970. Report on Rob Roy Island. Letter to the Directors, Allardyce Lumber Co., dated October 29.

Heyligers, P. C. 1967. Vegetation of Bougainville and Buka Islands. *Land Res Ser CSIRO Aust* 20:121–45.

Johnson, M. S. 1971. New Hebrides condominium: Erromango forest inventory. *Land Resour Stud Land Resour Div Dir Overseas Surv,* 10.

Jones, E. W. 1955–56. Ecological studies on the rain forest of southern Nieria. IV. The plateau forest of the Okumu forest reserve. *J Ecol* 43:564–94; *J Ecol* 44:83–117.

Lamb, H. H. 1972. *Climates: Present, Past and Future.* Vol. 1. London: Methuen.

McAlpine, J. R. 1967. Climate of Bougainville and Buka Islands. *Land Res Ser CSIRO Aust* 20:62–70.

Mervart, J. 1970. Growth and mortality rates in the natural high forest of western Nigeria. *Niger For Inf Bull* 22.

Schulz, J. P. 1960. The vegetation of Suriname: A series of papers on the plant communities of Suriname and their origin, distribution and relation to climate and habitat. II. Ecological studies on rain forest in northern Suriname. *Verh. K. Ned. Akad. Wet., Afd Natuurkunde,* ser. 2, 53(1).

Steenis, C. G. G. J. van. 1958. Rejuvenation as a factor for judging the status of vegetation types: The biological nomad theory. *Proc Kandy Symposium UNESCO,* 212–18.

Thompson, R. B., and B. D. Hackman 1969. Some geological notes on areas visited by the Royal Society Expedition to the British Solomon Islands. *Phil Trans Royal Soc,* ser. B. 265:189–202.

Wadsworth, F. H., and G. H. Englerth. 1959. Effects of the 1956 hurricane on forests in Puerto Rico. *Caribb For* 20:3–51.

Webb, L. J. 1958. Cyclones as an ecological factor in tropical lowland rain forest, north Queensland. *Aust J Bot* 6:220–28.

Whitmore, T. C. 1969. The vegetation of the Solomon Islands. *Phil Trans Royal Soc,* ser. B. 255:259–70.

10 Ecosystem Ecology in the Tropics

Julie S. Denslow and Robin L. Chazdon

Since the early days of scientific exploration of the wet tropics, individuals have marveled at the high biomass, diversity, abundance, vigor, and productivity of ecosystems. The diversity of life forms, the variety of species preying on other species, the complex physical structure, and the high rates of growth and decay were viewed as evidence of nature unfettered, where resources are abundant and year-round growing conditions optimal. The tropics seemed to promise a new frontier for entrepreneurs bold enough to attempt to harness such natural productivity for human ends.

Upon closer inspection, however, a puzzling inconsistency in this model of tropical rain forest ecosystems became apparent. Many tropical soils are highly weathered and nutrient poor, often with especially low levels of phosphorus and the major cations—potassium, calcium, and magnesium. Early scientific characterizations described forests of high biomass, productivity, and nutrient content growing on impoverished soils (Walter 1936; Milne 1937; Hardy 1936). Based primarily on these early studies, Richards (1952) proposed that tropical forests have closed, tight nutrient cycles with little or no leakage. "The existence of this closed cycle makes it easy to understand why a soil bearing magnificent rain forest may prove to be far

from fertile when the land is cleared and cultivated" (Richards 1952, 220). These ideas were based largely on studies in East Africa, where tobacco crops failed on sites cleared of lush tropical forest in the Usambara hills (Milne 1937). This simplistic but widely accepted notion of closed nutrient cycles was soon replaced by a better understanding of complex rain forest nutrient cycles (e.g., Nye and Greenland 1960).

In this part, we highlight three selections from classic early papers on tropical ecosystem processes that address this paradox. Nye and Greenland (1960) observe that in spite of the high productivity of many tropical ecosystems, indigenous farming practices in the tropics are characteristic of agriculture on nutrient-depleted soils worldwide. The excerpt from Nye and Greenland's 1960 book, *The Soil under Shifting Cultivation* (paper 44), provides an elegant discussion of the importance of soil organic matter and nitrogen dynamics in the maintenance of soil fertility in hot wet tropical climates. Tatuo Kira's (1978) synopsis of his team's effort to understand the components of productivity in a Malaysian forest (paper 46) provided one of the first reliable estimates of primary productivity in tropical rain forest as well as insight into the challenges of scaling up from small discrete measurements in a large, complex, and hetero-

Leaf insect. From Bates (1864)

geneous system. Fittkau and Klinge's (1973; paper 45) depiction of the trophic structure of an Amazonian forest suggests that the link between the structure and diversity of plant and animal communities on the one hand and productivity and nutrient cycling on the other may be a strong one and is based in the detrital community. These early themes remain at the forefront of ecosystem research in the tropics, as researchers continue to examine the causes and consequences of variation in primary productivity; the nature of the interactions among soil microbiota, nutrient availability, and species distributions; and the significance of small- and large-scale heterogeneity in tropical forest environments (see part 9).

Challenges of Ecosystem Studies in Tropical Life Zones

Ecosystem studies of tropical forests present a formidable challenge. The size and complexity of tropical rain forest vegetation creates physical barriers to sampling and measurement protocols that exacerbate the usual methodological challenges to describing processes occurring over large areas and long time frames (Proctor 1987). Landscape-scale variation in tropical forest structure and species composition occurs commonly as a function of topographic position and disturbance history (see part 8). In their pioneering study of mineral cycling in a New Guinea montane forest, Edwards and Grubb (1977) took special care to include ridges and slopes in their sampling regime because of topographic differences in forest and soil structure. Spatial heterogeneity is also a function of disturbance history. Growth-suppressed seedlings and saplings in the light-impoverished tropical forest understory grow more rapidly in the light patches created when canopy trees die (see part 9). For example in the Neotropics, the forest is a patchwork of dense, small trees interspersed among more widely spaced forest giants (Denslow 1995). At the subhectare scale, natural regeneration processes can produce considerable variation in biomass, dead wood mass, leaf:stem ratios, and microclimates. Nutrient cycling processes (Denslow, Ellison, and Sanford 1998) and trophic interactions (Coley 1983) affected by

substrate quality and rates of chemical reactions may vary as well. Species differences in root and foliage nutrient contents, strategies of nutrient conservation, and presence of nitrogen-fixing bacteria may also affect local nutrient processes. Adequate sampling of such spatially heterogeneous ecosystems, if such were possible, would require large numbers of plots.

Resources available for most ecosystem studies have constrained sample sizes to a typical quarter hectare. Brown, Gillespie, and Lugo (1989) observed that the combined area sampled for all studies of tropical forest biomass totaled less than thirty hectares. Early authors lamented the inadequacy of sampling efforts, but tried instead to select representative patches of rain forest, usually focusing on the mature phase (e.g., Kira et al. 1977). Although our awareness of the consequences of this variation in ecosystem structure and process has improved with increasingly detailed studies of different components of the forest ecosystem, the same tradeoffs between sampling intensity and sampling extent confront modern studies of forest canopy and meteorological processes (e.g., Keller et al. 1996).

The geographic heterogeneity of tropical wet forests also confounds generalizations about ecosystem processes (see part 8). Tropical wet forests may occur on nutrient-poor, but well-drained, soils developed on white river sands, on deeply weathered clay Oxisols and Ultisols, on moderately fertile volcanic and alluvial soils, or on deep organic soils that yield nutrients slowly (Vitousek and Sanford 1986). Failure to appreciate these differences has contributed to unwarranted generalizations about tropical ecosystem processes, including nutrient cycling and limitations to primary productivity, and to misconceptions regarding the fragility of tropical soils and the distribution of nutrients in the ecosystem (Jordan 1985; Proctor 1983; Whitmore 1989b).

Nutrient Cycling in the Hot Humid Tropics

We owe much of our understanding of nutrient cycling in tropical forests to early studies not of undisturbed forest, but of the centuries-old practice of shifting cultivation on nutrient-poor tropical soils. While the details vary from place to place, shifting cultivation has been practiced by people of many different origins and cultures working in different climates and on a variety of soils. They clear and burn fallow vegetation, plant their crops without plowing, and, after one or more rotations, abandon the land to the succession of sprouts and seedlings that reestablishes forest (also see part 12). The intervening fallow of few to many years replenishes the fertility of the topsoil and suppresses growth of weeds. P. H. Nye, D. J. Greenland, and their colleagues, working at the University College Faculty of Agriculture at Kade, Ghana, studied the intricacies of nutrient cycling and replenishment underpinning shifting cultivation. By investigating what happens when the cycles are disrupted, they increased our understanding of nutrient processes under intact rain forest as well. These authors approached their subject with a perspective that was at once historical, geographic, synthetic, and mechanistic. *The Soil under Shifting Cultivation* is still a valuable treatise for the detail and the scope of the nutrient-cycling processes they investigated. Many of the issues discussed remain central to ecosystem research in our age of global change (e.g., the role of atmospheric inputs from pollution and dust, the use of radioisotopes to trace pathways, and the importance of anions (especially NO_3^- and HCO_3^-) in the leaching of cations).

This book is also notable for its whole-ecosystem perspective, treating the interconnectedness of vegetation, soil, nutrients, organic matter, disturbance, and production and especially for including the humans in the ecosystem. Nye and Greenland argue that the universality of shifting cultivation is evidence of its utility in restoring nutrients to soils whose fertility declines while the land is cropped and that tropical farmers make rational decisions about farming practices that reflect not only the reality of their ecosystems but their social, political, and economic environments as well. Chapter 3, "The Nutrient Cycle" paper 44, provides the outlines of the processes by which nutrients are lost and restored. Their description of the complex interplay among soil organic matter, nitrogen mineralization, the leaching of cations, and the role of

deep-rooted shrubs and trees in capturing nutrients from the subsoil is elegant in its clarity. Rain forests do not have "leak proof" nutrient cycles, as Richards (1952) had thought, but receive nutrient inputs from dust and rainfall and by transport via roots from deep soil reservoirs. High rates of decomposition and nitrification under wet, warm conditions efficiently leach mobile nutrients such as K^+ from foliage and soil, which are carried electrostatically by the downward movement of anions such as NO_3^- and HCO_3^-. Soil organic matter clearly emerges as central to the cycling of nutrients in tropical soils, and its rapid buildup in depleted soils is key to the restoration of soil fertility under fallow vegetation (Robertson 1984). Nye and Greenland also puzzled over the source of new nitrogen to ecosystems subject to high losses due to leaching. While nitrogen may be supplied through atmospheric fixation, dust, and symbiotic fixation by microbes associated with legumes and other plants, they suggest that the largest component of nitrogen input to tropical forests is fixation from free-living bacteria associated with soil organic matter, a point on which we still lack adequate data for confirmation (Proctor 1987). In any case, nitrogen turnover rates in many tropical soils are very high, the result of high rates of both supply and demand.

Patterns of nutrient cycling differ widely in sites that vary in soil fertility. Jordan and Herrera (1981) suggested that tropical forests can be viewed along a gradient from oligotrophic, on the nutrient-poor extreme, to eutrophic, on the nutrient-rich extreme. Oligotrophic forests exhibit a variety of mechanisms for nutrient conservation, including nutrient scavenging from rainfall, scleromorphic leaves, and a thick root mat with heavy mycorrhizal infection (Jordan and Stark 1978; Jordan, Todd, and Escalante 1979; Sobrado and Medina 1980). Vitousek and Sanford (1986) note that a simple fertility gradient may not fully explain ecosystem-level variation in nutrient cycling, as soil nutrients can limit forest growth in many ways. Accumulating information on nutrient cycling in the world's forests shows that most lowland tropical rain forests on highly weathered soils are more likely to be limited by phosphorus than by nitrogen (Vitousek 1982, 1984).

Primary Productivity

The question of what sustains high productivity on nutrient-poor soil in tropical forests is often linked to the question of how high species diversity is supported (see parts 3 and 8). Primary productivity directly affects population and community processes in several ways. In productive sites, high plant growth rates are translated into high rates of competitive exclusion; canopy openings caused by tree falls are filled rapidly by the release of seedlings and saplings from the forest floor and by ingrowth of bordering trees (Denslow, Ellison, and Sanford 1998; see also part 9). One of the early hypotheses to account for plant richness in tropical forests suggested that, all else being equal, more resources are likely to support more species (see part 3). This hypothesis has attracted more recent attention in the work of Currie and his colleagues (Currie 1991), who suggest a positive relationship between productivity and diversity of both plants and some animal groups at biogeographic scales (but see Gaston 2000). Other authors suggest that a graph of diversity against productivity is humpbacked rather than increasing (summarized in Ricklefs and Schluter 1993). The relationship between productivity and biodiversity remains a controversial topic (Chapin et al. 2000). The long-sustained vigor of this debate clearly shows that linkages between population, community, and ecosystem processes are poorly understood.

Whereas ecosystem functioning had been a focus of inquiry from the beginnings of tropical exploration, the years following the Second World War saw a surge of research on the biosphere on which humans and all other heterotrophic organisms depend and which the growth and activities of the human population can so dramatically alter. Notable among early efforts to describe the productivity and functioning of tropical rain forests was the study of forest recovery following the catastrophic disturbance produced by exposure to a ^{137}Cs radiation source at Luquillo Experimental Forest in Puerto Rico (Odum and Pigeon 1970; Jordan 1971). Innovative approaches to the measurement of large-scale ecosystem processes originated with this project and its leader, Howard T. Odum, who initiated integrative studies of productivity, energy budgets, and dynamics in tropical ecosystems at a time when most ecologists were focused on floristics and community structure (Lugo 1995). The synthesis volume from the Luquillo project provided the first truly comprehensive assessment of a whole tropical ecosystem (Odum and Pigeon 1970). This impressive 1,643-page book includes chapters on community composition, trophic structure, plant physiology and demography, phenology, microorganisms, mineral cycling, and forest metabolism. Odum introduced a number of innovative approaches to the study of whole-ecosystem processes by adapting techniques previously developed for single plants or parts of plants. One of the more spectacular early efforts was the giant plastic cylinder (67 ft high × 60 ft wide [20 m × 18 m]) that Odum and his colleagues erected at Luquillo to estimate carbon budgets in a patch of rain forest (Odum and Jordan 1970), an approach in use today for research on the consequences of atmospheric CO_2 enrichment for plant growth and ecosystem processes (DeLucia and Thomas 2000). Another technological advance was the use of light extinction measurements to estimate leaf area and mass (Odum, Copeland, and Brown 1968) and the use of the infrared CO_2 gas analyzer in the field to study photosynthesis. His pioneering use of mathematical simulation to synthesize results from many measurements into whole-ecosystem models was the forerunner to their use in the International Biological Program (Odum and Pigeon 1970).

The International Biological Program (IBP), a global cooperative effort to understand and compare the functioning of ecosystems with a wide range of environmental conditions, subsequently launched other large-scale projects. The IBP tropical moist forest project grew out of the Joint Thai-Japanese Biological Expedition to Southeast Asia (Ogawa et al. 1965; Kira and Shidei 1967). The site selected was Pasoh Forest, Peninsular Malaysia, where productivity was studied by a predominantly Japanese team led by Tatuo Kira. His summary of these results is reprinted here (Kira 1978; paper 46). This contribution, a synthesis of the work of many researchers, illustrates the analytical approach to the study of ecosystem processes in complex rain forest ecosystems. The carbon cycle is partitioned among a series of separate fluxes among component pools as illustrated, in part, by the comparison of temperate and tropical models of soil organic matter dynamics (Kira 1978, 586, fig 24.13). Estimates of the parts are combined in a simulation model, clarifying the processes that lead to differences in accumulation of soil organic matter under tropical and temperate climatic regimes. Approaches to the same information from different routes provide a check on estimates and assumptions.

Kira points out where the science was inadequate, producing inconsistent results, and where conclusions appear to be robust. In developing methods for measuring productivity in an aseasonal tropical forest, Kira's team was challenged by the lack of the annual growth rings and bud scale scars through which temperate ecologists have estimated annual growth increments over many years. In addition, temperate and tropical ecologists alike wrestle with the difficulty of scaling up from measurements taken at small scales of a few square meters and on single individuals to processes occurring over several hectares and attributable to many individuals. Kira and colleagues addressed both issues by developing allometric relationships between tree size (measured as dbh and height) and biomass of leaves, stems, branches, and roots. Annual net primary productivity was estimated by measuring litter production and changes in tree diameter at intervals over 1.9 years in total.

Although these extrapolations are now known to be fraught with error (see critical examinations by Evans [1972] and Whitmore [1984b]), the studies at Pasoh and, earlier, in Thailand provided insights into the structure and functioning of tropical forests and tests of common assumptions. For example, comparisons with other ecosystems in the western Pacific confirmed the relationship between tree height in tropical forests and the amount and seasonal distribution of rainfall (Kira 1978, 562). In contrast to Richards's (1952) description of a three-layered foliage structure in tropical rain forests trees, foliage at Pasoh was distributed more or less evenly between 35 and 10 m (Kira 1978, 565). Nevertheless, the leaf area index (leaf area per unit land area) at Pasoh (7) was not much larger than that of several temperate forests in Japan (6.4–6.7) (Kira 1978, 568–69), although light levels at the ground were very low. Results from Pasoh and Thailand (Ogawa et al. 1965) confirmed the expected high gross productivity of tropical rain forests and provided further documentation of the variation in productivity among tropical forests in different circumstances. In comparison to temperate forests, net production (26.67 t/ha/yr) at Pasoh was markedly higher than that measured in warm temperate broad-leaved forests of Japan (20.65 t/ha/yr; Kira 1978, 574) and much higher than in Japanese temperate deciduous and coniferous forests (8.74–14.25 t/ha/yr). At the same time these estimates were considerably lower than some earlier estimates of tropical productivity and placed tropical rain forests within the upper ranges of some temperate forest measurements (Lieth and Whittaker 1975). Although gross primary productivity may reach very high values in tropical rain forests, high respiration rates apparently reduce net primary production to values closer to those of some temperate forests in favorable circumstances (Whittaker 1975).

Carbon uptake and storage by tropical forests are of considerable current interest in relation to efforts to curb atmospheric CO_2 enrichment associated with global climate change (Houghton et al. 1983; Detwiler and Hall 1988; Schlesinger 1991; Grace et al. 1995). A large portion of the world's carbon resides in the tropical forest biomass (Jordan 1971; Brown and Lugo 1982). Forest clearing and burning in the tropics thus are a major source of CO_2 and forest regrowth may be a significant sink for CO_2 (Fearnside and Guimarães 1996). Accurate estimates of forest clearing, land-use change, and secondary forest regrowth in the tropics are therefore critical to our understanding of global climate change (Skole and Tucker 1993; Hughes, Kauffman and Jaramillo 1999).

Trophic Structure

Productivity and characteristics of the litter and humus component of the tropical rain forest floor may also be key to the understanding of factors structuring higher trophic levels. We reprint here one of the first attempts to characterize the trophic structure of a tropical forest, by Fittkau and Klinge (1973; paper 45). These authors suggest that the energetic basis of higher trophic levels of the Central Amazonian rain forest is not the living plant biomass, but the litter and the associated detrital community. Moreover, the depauperate insect and vertebrate fauna of their study site might be attributed to the low nutrient content of the litter. They base their hypothesis on a combination of biomass measurements and samples of soil arthropod communities, and they collected anecdotal information suggesting secondary productivity in this forest is limited by nutrients. Their estimates of herbivory rates were in agreement with studies elsewhere in the tropics, e.g., in the Luquillo forest of Puerto Rico (Odum and Ruíz-Reyes 1970) and with observations from temperate forests (Whittaker 1975), where herbivores likely consume somewhat less than 10 percent of annual leaf production. Most energy and nutrients are linked to higher trophic levels through fungi and microfauna such as collembola and mites. Fittkau and Klinge suggest that the microfauna are feeding directly on fungi and bacteria rather than on the decomposing litter.

The nature of the tropical soil community, how it varies between oligotrophic and eutrophic sites, and how it affects the structure of higher trophic levels are still poorly understood. For example, Janzen (1974a) suggested that the extreme nutrient deficiency of the white-sand soils comprising the watersheds of tropical blackwater rivers strongly affected the structure of terrestrial and aquatic food webs. Other authors have found nutrients not to be especially low and have suggested that low pH may directly influence the distinctive plant and animal life on white-sand soils (Proctor 1983; Whit-

more 1989b). Only recently have we begun to address the intricacies of relationships among the soil community and ecosystem processes (Wall and Moore 1999), taking up a theme introduced in the tropics a quarter century ago.

Conclusion

The three papers reprinted here were selected, in part, to represent some of the breadth of early work on tropical ecosystems, but the diversity of ideas and ecosystems cannot be captured so easily. The reader is encouraged to sample the work of numerous other authors whose approach was characterized by the desire to understand how these immense, complex, heterogeneous ecosystems work. Holdridge (1947), for example, provided a model for the classification of vegetation based on the major controls on productivity—temperature and moisture—in widespread use in the Neotropics today. Edwards and Grubb (1977) looked for the causes of change in vegetation stature and physiognomy on tropical mountains (described earlier by Grubb et al. 1963) in changing nutrient budgets. Many of the themes developed more than twenty-five years ago as scientists sought to understand how tropical ecosystems function are now central to current efforts to understand the consequences of forest management on species diversity and survival and on long-term exploitation of forest products for human needs (see part 12).

Reprinted Selections

P. H. Nye and D. J. Greenland. 1960. The nutrient cycle. Chapter 3 in *The Soil under Shifting Cultivation.* Technical Communication 51. Harpendon: Commonwealth Bureau of Soils

E. J. Fittkau and H. Klinge. 1973. On biomass and trophic structure of the Central Amazon rain forest ecosystem. *Biotropica* 5, no. 1: 2–14

T. Kira. 1978. Community architecture and organic matter dynamics in tropical rain forests of Southeast Asia with special reference to Pasoh Forest, West Malaysia. In *Tropical Trees as Living Systems*, edited by P. B. Tomlinson and M. H. Zimmermann, 561–90. Cambridge: Cambridge University Press. Reprinted with the permission of Cambridge University Press

The Soil under Shifting Cultivation

P. H. Nye and D. J. Greenland

(examples 9, 10, 11). The sub-surface horizons do not differ so greatly, and the nutrients stored in the top foot are not markedly less. In still drier regions, such as those under tall bunch-grass savanna, organic-matter levels and nutrients stored are still lower (example 13).

In all these examples the soils have been kaolinitic. In the much less widely distributed rubrisols, brunosols and black earths that may be developed over basic rocks the amounts of Ca and Mg stored in the soil are very much greater owing to the presence of 2 : 1 lattice-type clay minerals. The amounts of N, K and P are not necessarily higher. The analysis of a black montmorillonitic clay developed on a gentle hill slope, supporting high-grass savanna under a rainfall of 43 in. p.a. at Kpong, Ghana (Brammer, 1955), (example 14) illustrates this point.

Comparing now the amounts of nutrients in the vegetation and soil, we find that well developed thicket and Miombo Woodland store considerably less Ca and Mg than the top foot of soil, but amounts of P and K comparable to the readily available amounts in the exchangeable pool. The high-grass savanna, if well wooded, may also store as much P and K as the top foot of soil, but where trees and shrubs are sparse the savannas store far fewer of all nutrients than the soils supporting them.

Chapter 3

THE NUTRIENT CYCLE

Having established the amounts of nutrients in the soil and fallow we now have to consider how rapidly the interchange between them takes place. Knowledge of this nutrient cycle is an essential background to an understanding of the way in which the fertility of the top soil is restored during the fallow period. In addition to evaluating movement of nutrients within the soil-vegetation system, we have also to determine how important are losses from the system by drainage and, for nitrogen and sulphur, by volatilization, as well as gains to the system from the atmosphere.

The complete cycle, together with the loss and gain processes, are illustrated in fig. 1. In discussing the cycle we shall consider firstly the transfer of nutrients between the soil and vegetation, secondly movement of nutrients between different soil horizons, and thirdly the losses from and gains to the soil-vegetation system.

1. Transfer of Nutrients between Soil and Vegetation

The processes concerned in this type of transfer are (a) uptake by the vegetation, (b) removal from the vegetation and return to the soil, as litter, in rain-wash, by burning and in root excretions.

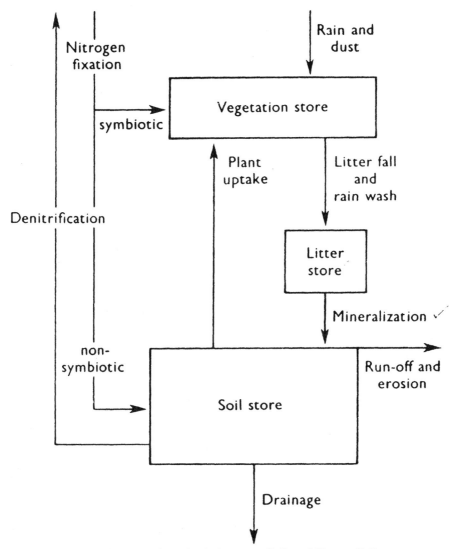

Fig. 1.   The Nutrient Cycle between Soil and Forest Fallow

Further, as litter fall does not add nutrients as such to the soil a further process, (c) mineralization of litter, is involved. We shall consider each of these in turn, and endeavour to give quantitative figures for the amounts of nutrients involved in each process.

(a) *Uptake by the Vegetation*

The total rate of uptake of nutrients (in excess of any that may be excreted back to the soil through the roots) is equal to the increase in storage in the vegetation plus the amount removed from the vegetation. The removals are considered under (b). Typical figures for the annual increase in storage in forest vegetation including roots can be obtained from the data of Bartholomew *et al.* (1953) for forest

35

fallows of up to 18 years of age at Yangambi, and from the data for 40-year-old forest at Kade (Greenland and Kowal, 1960). These are collected below.

Mean Annual Increase in Vegetation Storage (lb./acre)

	N	P	K	Ca	Mg	Forest
Over first 5 years	102	5·6	81	75		Yangambi
Over first 18 years	35	5·3	30	41		Yangambi
*Over first 40 years	36	2·5	15	48	6	Kade
Over first 4 years (excluding roots)	42	3·0	31	39	9	Coastal thicket, Pokoase (Nye, 1958).

* Storage in two very large trees, already standing when the forest regenerated, has been excluded.

It is seen that accumulation during the first five years of growth is more rapid than during the later periods. The reason for the change after the first 5 years, and the subsequent relatively slow increase in storage, is that the leaves and twigs, which are richer in nutrients than other components of the vegetation, rapidly increase to their maximum amount in the fallow, and further storage takes place in the wood and roots. Thus with the exception of P, over half the nutrients stored in the 18-year-old fallow in the Congo had been accumulated by the 5-year-old fallow. It is possible that the difference in the case of P is due to sampling errors since the phosphorus composition of the wood of the 18-year-old fallow, 0·05%, seems high. It will be seen from the data discussed under (b) that the annual increase in storage in the vegetation after the first five years is a relatively small proportion of the total annual nutrient uptake by the vegetation.

The actual uptake and storage may differ somewhat from the figures quoted, particularly if the land is cultivated for more than the usual two to three years, for prolonged cultivation reduces the number of stumps, roots and viable seeds in the ground from which the vigorous regrowth of natural vegetation normally develops. Long-continued cultivation or the incidence of severe erosion might also reduce soil fertility sufficiently to limit the vigour of the regrowth of vegetation. Such an occurrence must however be regarded as exceptional; in all normal circumstances regrowth is, as a matter of experience, extremely rapid and vigorous, and the figures given may be taken as typical of the nutrient absorptions normally occurring.

For the savanna zones it is not easy to obtain a figure for the rate of increase of storage in the vegetation. The annual grass burn causes the return of all nutrients taken up by the grasses to the soil, except the nitrogen and sulphur. Tree density is extremely variable and the age of trees extremely difficult to judge. Tree growth is certainly slow, being severely restricted by fire, and probably by shortage of available nitrogen induced by the grasses. It is therefore impossible to give any meaningful figure for the annual increase of nutrients stored in the trees. It will obviously be much less than the uptake by forest vegetation, and in general it seems unlikely that it will be significant compared with the total uptake. The last example in the table shows that in unburnt thicket vegetation the rate of increase of storage is somewhat less than in young forest vegetation.

(b) *Removal from the Vegetation*

This includes litter fall, rain wash, burning and root excretions. Information on the production of litter and its nutrient content is given in Table 5. They are readily measured by collecting the litter over a period and weighing and analysing it. In moist tropical forest the production amounts to about 5 tons of dry matter per acre, which compares with an average figure of a little over 1 ton per acre in temperate hardwood forests. In the savanna nearly the whole of the herb growth during the rainy season is burnt before the beginning of the following rains. From Table 2, example 11, it will be seen that the material burnt amounts to 3–4 tons per acre in the high-grass savanna. All nutrients except N and S are returned to the soil in the ash. Example 11 also shows that the additional contribution from the leaf fall of the trees will usually be small. In closed Miombo woodland, however, it is possible that figures approaching those quoted for temperate woodland are achieved.

The nutrient content of the litter has generally been taken as a measure of the annual nutrient turnover. However, litter as usually collected in trays consists only of leaves, twigs and small wood. In young forest fallows this is a fairly accurate measure of the return to the soil, but in older fallows some allowance must be made for the fall of branches and stems. This may be estimated in a mature forest fallow by assuming that the annual timber fall is equal to the annual production of wood. Weck (1956) gives an average value for the latter of 10,000 lb. dry wood per acre. This estimate accords well with the annual increase in weight of the fallows for which data were given in Table 2, if some allowance is made for fall of timber during their growth.

Data for the complete nutrient cycle in the 40-year-old forest at Kade are presented in Table 6. The nutrient composition of the timber fall is assumed to be the same as of the dead wood. It will be seen that the effect of timber fall is to increase the turnover of nutrients estimated from litter alone by substantial amounts, especially of calcium (Nye, unpublished).

Another source of nutrient cycling is washing of nutrients from the leaves by the rainfall. It has for many years been recognized that the washing of nutrients from the leaves of crops by rainfall may be an important source of loss from growing vegetation. The extent of the losses reported varies widely according to the treatment of the plants. Mes (1954) and Stenlid (1958) have reviewed the subject. Unfortunately little work has been done with intact growing

TABLE 5

Rate of Litter Production (per annum)

Vegetation	Place	Litter Fall (lb./acre)	Nutrients in Litter (lb./acre)					Authority
			N	P	K	Ca	Mg	
Forest (Musanga dominant)	Congo	13,000 (dry matter)	125	4	93	111	38	Laudelout (1954)
Mixed Forest	"	11,000 (dry matter)	200	6	43	94	46	Nye (unpublished)
Mixed High Forest	Ghana	9,400 (oven dry)	178	6·5	61	184	40	Jenny (1950)
Rain Forest	Colombia	7,000 (oven dry)						" "
" " (Sub-tropical mixed spp.)	Queensland	9,100 (oven dry)						
		6,000 (oven dry—leaf only)	96	5	33	67		Webb (1956)
Temperate Hardwoods	New York	2,700 (dry matter)	17	3	14	66	9	Chandler (1941)

TABLE 6

Nutrient Cycle in High Forest at Kade, Ghana

	Wt. of material (oven dry)	Nutrient elements (lb./acre/annum)				
		N	P	K	Ca	Mg
Rainfall in open— (73 in. in 12 months)		13	0.4	16	11	10
Rainfall under forest— (62 in. in same period)		24	3.7	212	37	26
Rain wash from leaves		11	3.3	196	26	16
Timber fall	10,000	32	2.6	5	73	7
Litter fall (on 12 months' records)	9,400	178	6.5	61	184	40
Total addition to soil surface		221	12.4	262	283	63

plants. Tamm (1953) found nutrient losses from 6 broad-leaf deciduous trees in Sweden averaged 12 lb. K, 0.6 lb. Ca, 1.0 lb. Na per acre following a period in which 9 in. of rain fell. Ingham (1950) has measured the composition of rain water collected beneath a tree on the coast of Natal and in the open during a year in which 49 in. of rain fell. He found that the equivalent of 240 lb. Ca and 9.4 lb. P per acre were added to the surface soil under the tree. He attributed these amounts to the washing away of water-soluble "aerosols" adsorbed from the air by the leaves. His results are unlikely to be applicable to inland areas. Results which have been obtained under the forest at Kade, which is 60 miles from the sea, are shown in Table 6. In comparison with amounts in the litter, remarkably large quantities of potassium and phosphorus, but only small quantities of nitrogen, calcium and magnesium are washed out of the leaves. These findings, which agree in general with earlier work on this subject, establish for the first time the relative importance of rain wash and litter fall for the major nutrients under forest.

The total annual nutrient uptake in the 40-year-old mixed secondary forest at Kade is shown in Table 6. It may be calculated from data in Table 2 and 6 that the annual turnover of nutrients expressed as a percentage of the total capital stored in the vegetation is as follows: N 11%, P 11%, K 32%, Ca 12%, Mg 18%. Of course, in younger forest the turnover is a greater proportion of the storage.

In savannas the annual uptake by grasses is nearly equal to the nutrients stored at the end of the growing season, before serious leaf fall occurs. No data are available for the vigorous natural elephant-grass savannas, but a planted plot at Bambesa, Belgian Congo in the first year of growth produced per acre 26,000 lb. of dry matter and took up 248 lb. N, 20 lb. P, 43 lb. S, 41 lb. Ca, 78 lb. Mg and 275 lb. K (Laudelout, Germain and Kesler, 1954), a performance which compares well with the mature high forest for all nutrients except Ca. We do not know whether this rate of uptake is sustained in older fallows. In the fire-climax high-grass savanna of Andropogoneae, the rate of uptake is much lower, as shown by the figures in Table 2 (example 11). Nye (1958) has given some data indicating that the uptake in the earlier years of such a fallow may be about 50% greater, increasing shortage of nitrogen limiting growth in later years.

A matter requiring further attention is the effect on the soil of the very much greater proportion of Ca and Mg to K circulating under a forest fallow than under a grass fallow. Preliminary indications are that the exchangeable K/Ca ratio in the topsoil is increased by the growth of a grass rather than a broad-leaved fallow (e.g. Nye and Hutton, 1957), and this improvement in the potassium status of savanna soils agrees with their general lack of response to potassium fertilizers, in contrast to the forest soils. The high proportion of non-exchangeable potassium in savanna soils may also be due partly to the grass vegetation as well as to unweathered minerals.

(c) *The Rate of Mineralization of the Litter*

When the litter under a woody fallow has been built up to its maximum level, the rate of mineralization clearly equals the rate of addition. Under tropical conditions this level is rapidly attained, and possible increase in storage of nutrients in the form of litter need hardly be taken into account after a few years of fallow. Greenland and Nye (1959) calculated from the data of Jenny et al. (1949) that when the litter layer had attained its maximum or equilibrium level, 3.25% decomposed in one week, or over one year the amount of litter decomposing was 170% of that found on the forest floor at any one instance. This very high rate of decomposition is to be expected when the annual litter fall is about 5 tons per acre, and the level of litter on the forest floor rather less. The rate at which the maximum level of litter on the forest floor will be attained will also be very high—between one and three years for most tropical forests.

The maximum level of individual nutrients stored in the litter will be even more rapidly attained. The ones that are leached most readily will reach this level most quickly. Bartholomew et al. (1953) have shown that potassium is lost very rapidly from fresh forest litter. After 10 weeks 51% of the N, 61% of the P, 93% of the K, 50% of the Ca, and 82% of the Mg in the original litter had been mineralized. Conversely, reference to Table 2 will show that the ratio Ca/K in the litter of all the forest examples is considerably greater than in the fresh leaves or wood.

II. MOVEMENT OF NUTRIENTS WITHIN THE SOIL

Thanks to the writings of Hardy (1936), Milne (1937) and others it is now well known that in a soil under mature forest the nutrients are maintained in a nearly closed cycle from which few nutrients are lost in the drainage. The downward movement by leaching is nicely balanced by the upward movement into the plant and eventual return to the soil's surface, as well as by the husbanding of a large part of the nutrient reserve in the living vegetation.

The details of this nicely adjusted balance are, however, little understood, and it has even been stated that no downward movement of nutrients occurs under virgin forest. It may be well therefore to examine a little more fully the counterbalancing processes of leaching and uptake, even though quantitative detail is lacking.

(a) *Leaching*

So long as there is percolation down the profile and there are nutrient ions in the soil solution these will be leached. The main anions in the soil solution are NO_8^-, SO_4^-, Cl^-, HCO_8^-. In the slightly acid and acid topsoils such as we are dealing with, the nitrate ion and to a lesser extent the bicarbonate ion are quantitatively the most important. These are little adsorbed by the soil, so that nearly all are in the soil solution. There they are balanced by cations, the most important being Ca^{++}, Mg^{++} and K^+. H^+ plays a very minor role, as also does Al^{+++}, except in very acid soils. It must be appreciated that the total concentration of cations in the soil solution depends on the total concentration of the anions. In particular, a high level of 'biological activity' in a soil, leading to a high level of nitrate ion, implies a corresponding concentration of nutrient cations in the soil solution and therefore ready leaching.

The rate of leaching of a nutrient at any point in the profile will be the product of its concentration in the soil solution and the rate of percolation. Actively growing vegetation reduces leaching losses by

(a) transpiring water and so reducing percolation;

(b) absorbing anions, especially nitrate, from the soil solution;

(c) repressing nitrification (a process extremely important in grass-lands) and so reducing the concentration of anions that would otherwise occur.

Here we may note that the leaching of cations is not directly countered by their uptake, but only indirectly, by removal of anions from the soil solution. If a cation alone were taken up from the soil solution, it would simply be replaced by another from the well buffered exchange complex.

There is no direct evidence of the amount of nutrients being leached from one horizon to another under natural forest, and until lysimetry techniques improve it will be very difficult to obtain this information. Joffe (1932), for example, has attempted such measurements under temperate woodland, using small Ebermayer-type lysimeters, but Kohnke et al. (1940) in a critical review consider the very low percolation figures obtained by this method are due to the drainage water flowing round the collecting funnels. The suction-plate method described by Cole (1958) promises to be much more satisfactory. A particular difficulty associated with tropical soils is the possible occurrence following heavy storms of lateral drainage through the permeable surface layers above the more compact subsoil. Losses by surface run-off under forest are probably small.

This discussion has been centred on the nutrient cations. The phosphate ion is most unlikely to be leached in significant amount beyond the top few inches. The phosphorus concentration of the soil solution in equilibrium with forest subsoils in tropical Africa is usually immeasurably low; so that any phosphorus leached would be adsorbed. Phosphorus is only found in the percolate of lysimeters when high applications of phosphate are made to very light soils.

(b) *Uptake*

Though the total rate of uptake of nutrients can be measured, as we have shown, it is impossible to measure by normal methods the proportion drawn from the different soil horizons. Even were it possible to follow the changes in composition of each horizon during a fallow period, uncertain nutrient changes by addition from litter and leaching take place at the same time. In forest, the distribution of the roots suggests that the great preponderance of feeding occurs in the top soil. It is well known that the enormous buttressed trees of the high forest have shallow root systems and no tap root (Richards, 1952), and it is only the unbuttressed trees, largely understorey species, that have tap roots (Donis, 1948; Foggie, 1957). Jones (1955) has observed in the Nigerian rain forest that the root distribution is similar to that which would be seen in similarly well drained English soils. In the 40-year-old forest at Kade, Greenland and Kowal (1960) found 86% of the roots were in the top foot. The corresponding figure for 15-year-old fallow was 80%. In an 8-year-old forest fallow at Yangambi, dominated by *Musanga cecropioides*, 68% of the roots were in the top 10 inches (results of W. V. Bartholomew quoted by Greenland and Kowal, 1960). It is possible that these figures based on total root weight overemphasize the percentage of the total root-absorbing surface found in the top soil, since this contains a greater proportion of large roots.

In savanna, our general observations are that the range of root systems in the trees is similar to that of the smaller forest trees. Rawitscher (1948) has noted some savanna plants with very deep-rooting systems in the savanna of southern Brazil, and Ferri (1959) found these plants transpired freely through the dry season.

For grasses Laudelout, Germain and Kesler (1954) found among a wide range of species planted in a free-draining soil at Yangambi (73 in. p.a.) that well over 50% of the roots of nearly all species are in the top 8 in. In the natural high-grass savanna dominated by *Schizachyrium semiberbe*, for which data are given in Table 2, Nye (1957) found 30 times as much root in the 0–6 in. as in the 6–12 in. layer of the free-draining sandy soil. In the Transvaal high veldt

Coetzee et al. (1946) record over 50% of the roots in the top 4 in. and over 70% in the top 8 in.

Not only are there few roots in the subsoil, but their activity there may well be lower than in the topsoil because of poorer conditions for feeding. In general the subsoil is much more compact than the topsoil, and the availability of phosphorus and calcium falls away sharply. Use of P^{32} showed that high-grass fallow derived about 30% of its P from layers below 10 in. containing 19% of the roots (Nye and Foster, 1960).

Though the proportion of subsoil feeding may be small it is very important, for it is from this source together with rain and dust fall that losses in 'total' nutrients from the top soil by leaching and cropping are made good. That it occurs to a significant extent is indicated by the fact that the totals of relatively immobile nutrients such as phosphorus and calcium in tropical forest soils are nearly always greater in the topsoil than the subsoil (Nye (1957) for phosphorus, Baley and Chezeau (1954) and Leneuf (1956) for calcium). If 20% of the total uptake calculated in Table 6 for a mature high forest is drawn from below the first foot it represents amounts of 36 lb. N, 2·5 lb. P, 52 lb. K, 55 lb. Ca and 11 lb. Mg per acre "pumped up" per annum. The performance of younger forest fallows should not be much less, since their root system is already established for the suckering species, and their foliage rapidly forms a dense canopy.

It will be noted that on this basis the uptake from the subsoil is about equal to, and for potassium greatly exceeds, the annual increase in storage in the fallow, shown on p. 36. Further evidence that subsoil feeding is sufficient to supply the vegetation store and may also increase the nutrient content of the top soil during the fallow period is given in the next chapter.

III. LOSSES FROM AND GAINS TO THE SOIL-VEGETATION SYSTEM

The loss processes operating are leaching of nutrients out of the rooting zone of the vegetation, removals in run-off water, volatilization of nitrogen through the activity of denitrifying organisms and volatilization of nitrogen and sulphur through oxidation when the vegetation is burnt. Gains consist of additions in rainfall, dust and fixation of atmospheric nitrogen by micro-organisms. The gains and losses of nitrogen due to microbial processes will not be considered here, as they are intimately involved in the carbon and nitrogen cycles considered in detail in the next chapter.

(a) Leaching and Erosion Losses

An approximate upper limit to the amount of leaching and erosion that occurs from the plant-root zone under closed forest may be deduced from the nutrients carried by the River Amazon whose catchment is very largely under closed forest, most of it under rainfall exceeding 70 in. p.a. Russell (1950) calculates from Clarke's (1924) data that the drain of nutrients is 4 lb. K, 33 lb. Ca,

4·5 lb. Mg, 9 lb. Na, 0·4 lb. N (as NO_8), 10 lb. Cl, and 5 lb. S (as SO_4^-) per acre per annum. Most of the cations are balanced by the bicarbonate ion. The very low amounts of nitrate ion are particularly to be noted since, as will be seen, the nitrate ion is usually more important than the bicarbonate ion where leaching from the top soil under cultivation is concerned. The loss of cations by leaching from the actual solum will undoubtedly be less since some of the nutrients in the rivers will come from the deeper zones of primary weathering. Leaching from the solum could only exceed amounts carried away in the drainage system if there were substantial and increasing zones of accumulation of nutrients in the deep subsoil, and these have not been reported from closed-forest areas.

An estimate of the average composition of drainage waters from drier forest soils has been obtained by averaging the composition of 23 rivers draining the moist semi-deciduous forest of Ghana (50–70 in. p.a.) given by Dunn (1947). The composition in Ca and Mg is slightly lower than that reported by Clarke for the Amazon. No figures for K are given. Since under the lower rainfall the drainage will be less than in the Amazon basin, the figures given above may be considered as an upper limit for leaching and run-off losses in the moist semi-deciduous forest region as well.

It will be seen that the amounts of nutrients taken up from the solum and added to the surface each year (Table 6) greatly exceed the maximum losses from the solum by leaching and run-off. The nearly closed cycle of nutrients under tropical forest, with uptake by the vegetation preventing losses in leaching, appears to be borne out. Nevertheless it must be recognized that it is not only absorption into the vegetation and reduction of leaching through increased transpiration (compared with the soil under cultivation) which are responsible. These two factors may be important, particularly in the moist semi-deciduous-forest zone of relatively low rainfall (c. 60 in. p.a.) and neutral topsoils. Here the rainfall during the months when through leaching is liable to occur may be only slightly greater than the amounts of water lost by evaporation and transpiration under a full vegetative cover. In the moist evergreen forest, through leaching may be anything from 20 to 100 in. p.a. or more. Consequently increased transpiration is of relatively little importance. A factor which may be important in preventing further leaching losses is the inhibition of nitrification by the high acidity of these soils. We know little of actual nitrate levels under the forest but it seems likely that they will be low* (p. 108). The concentration of bicarbonate ion will also be very low, and consequently little loss of nutrients can take place because there are no anions to maintain significant concentrations in the soil solution.

Similarly in the savanna zone nitrification is repressed by the grasses, so that once a grass cover is established leaching losses

*Now confirmed experimentally (P.H.N.)

must again be low. Nitrification under forest and savanna fallows is considered in more detail in the next chapter.

The question of losses by erosion is considered in some detail in Part II. Under undisturbed forest and savanna these losses are small.

(b) *Gains from Atmospheric Sources*

The regions of shifting cultivation are remote from industrial districts, and any nutrients they receive directly from the atmosphere are derived primarily from the sea or fine ash from bush fires or dust from deserts. Nitrogen as already mentioned is a special case and we consider here only accession of the chemically combined forms.

Eriksson (1952) and Tamm (1958) have reviewed analytical data on rainfall collected from temperate regions. Much of the data deals with regions near the sea or industrial areas. A fair indication of amounts that might fall in tropical regions remote from the sea is possibly given by the annual supply of elements in rainfall in six agricultural districts of Sweden which is calculated from data given by Tamm as: NH_4-N 1·5, NO_3-N 0·7, K 2·1, Ca 5·3, Mg 1·2, Na 5·7, Cl 8·7, S 5·1 lb. per acre for an average rainfall of 21 in. The amount of P was not recorded in this series, but in another Swedish station it was 0·1 lb. per acre per annum. The amounts collected at Kade shown in Table 6 agree approximately with these results if allowance for a rainfall of 70 in. is made. Numerous estimates assembled by Eriksson, of nitrate N and ammonium N falling in tropical regions, have a median of 7 lb. N per acre per annum.

All the nutrient cations added to the soil in the rain cannot be regarded as an effective gain. A high proportion are balanced in the atmosphere by Cl^- and SO_4^- anions. These anions are but weakly adsorbed by the soil colloid and therefore increase the concentration of the soil solution. When they are leached an equivalent quantity of nutrient cations is lost with them.

It seems likely that in a great area such as the Amazon basin containing for long ages mature soils under high forest, the annual exports of Cl^- and SO_4^- in the drainage waters represent the amounts of Cl^- and SO_4^- added from atmospheric sources plus any small additions from rock decomposition. From figures already quoted this would put the maximum addition of these anions as 10 lb. Cl^- and 5 lb. S as SO_4^- per acre per annum.

The amounts of aeolian dust deposited on vegetation have not been estimated in the tropics. From the figures for Europe quoted by Tamm (1958), 100 lb. per acre is a high figure except on the fringe of desert areas. Doyne et al. (1938) report that a sample of 'harmattan' dust derived from the Sahara and collected in Northern Nigeria contains no P_2O_5, 1·62% K_2O, 5·28% CaO, 2·07% MgO, 0·80% Na_2O.

The main conclusions of this chapter are as follows:—
The rate of turnover of the elements in the nutrient cycle under

forest fallow is very rapid and after the first few years greatly exceeds the rate of storage in the fallow. In addition to the quantities of nutrients in the litter fall, important amounts of potassium and phosphorus are washed out of the leaves of the vegetation. In older fallows significant amounts of calcium are contained in falling dead wood. The annual addition of dry litter under forest is around 10,000 lb. per acre. It decomposes very rapidly; consequently, the litter layer is thin.

The addition of nutrients in the form of rain and dust fall is very small in comparison with their rate of cycling. Estimates of nutrient losses from the solum are scarce but in mature forest soils may be little more than the amounts added in the rain and dust fall.

Much further work is needed on the uptake of nutrients from successive horizons, and transfer from one horizon to another by leaching. Studies of root distributions indicate that in both forest and savanna at least three-quarters of the roots are in the top foot of soil. Root distribution is not a sure guide to feeding activity, but if the uptake from below the top foot is 20% of the total uptake, it is sufficient to account for the annual increase in nutrients stored in the vegetation.

References

Bartholomew, W. V., J. Meyer, and H. Laudelout. 1953. Mineral nutrient immobilization under forest and grass fallow in the Yangambi (Belgian Congo) region. *INEAC Ser Sci* 57. Brussels.

Beley, J., and R. Chezeau. 1954. Characteristiques physiques et chimiques des sols à cacacoyers de la Côte d'Ivoire. *Agron Trop* 9:439–51.

Clarke, F. W. 1924. The data of geochemistry. *US Geol Survey Bull* 770. Washington.

Coetzee, J. A., et al. 1946. Root studies in highveld grassland communities. *South Afr J Sci* 42:105–18.

Cole, D. W. 1958. Alundum tension lysimeter. *Soil Sci* 85:293–96.

Donis, C. 1948. Essai d'économie forestière au Mayumbe. *INEAC Ser Sci* 37. Brussels.

Doyne, H. C., K. T. Hartley, and W. A. Watson. 1938. Soil types and manurial experiments in Nigeria. *Proc 3rd West African Agric Conf* 227–98. Lagos.

Dunn, J. S. 1947. Chemical analyses of Gold Coast rocks, ores and minerals. Appendix: Mineral analyses of Gold Coast waters. *Gold Coast Geol Surv Bull* 15.

Eriksson, E. 1952. Composition of atmospheric precipitation, I: Nitrogen compounds; II: Sulphur, chloride, iodine compounds. *Tellus* 4:215–32, 280–303.

Ferri, M. G. 1959. Aspects of the soil-water-plant relationship in connection with some Brazilian types of vegetation. Presented at CCTA/UNESCO Symposium on vegetation in relation to the soil, Adiopodoumé.

Foggie, A. S. 1957. Forestry problems in the closed forest zone of Ghana. *J W Afr Sci Assoc* 3:131–47.

Greenland, D. J., and J. M. L. Kowal. 1960. Nutrient content of moist tropical forest of Ghana. *Plant and Soil* 12:154–74.

Greenland, D. J., and P. H. Nye. 1959. Increases in the carbon and nitrogen contents of tropical soils under natural fallows. *J Soil Sci* 9:284–99.

Hardy, F. 1936. Some aspects of tropical soils. *Trans 3rd Int Congr Sci* 2:150–63.

Ingham, G. 1950. Effect of materials absorbed from the atmosphere in maintaining soil fertility. *Soil Sci* 70:205–12.

Jenny, H., F. Bingham, and B. Padilla-Saravia. 1948. Nitrogen and organic matter contents of equatorial soils of Colombia, South America. *Soil Sci* 66:173–86.

Joffe, J. S. 1932. Lysimeter studies, I: Moisture percolation through the soil profile. *Soil Sci* 34:123–42.

Jones, E. W. 1955. Ecological studies on the rain forest of Southern Nigeria. *J Ecol* 43:564–94.

Kohnke, H., et al. 1940. A survey and discussion of lysimeters. *US Dept Agric Misc Pub* 372. Washington.

Laudelout, H., R. Germain, and W. Kesler. 1954. Preliminary results on the chemical dynamics of grass fallows and of pastures at Yangambi. *Trans 5th Int Congr Soil Sci* 2:312–21.

Leneuf, N. 1956. Les sols sur 'Roches Vertes' en zone forestière de Côte d'Ivoire. *Trans 6th Int Congr Soil Sci, E*, pp. 573–77.

Mes, M. G. 1954. Excretion (recretion) of phosphorus and

other mineral elements by leaves under the influence of rain. *South Afr J Sci* 50:167–72.

Milne, G. 1937. Essays in applied pedology; I: Soil type and soil management in relation to plantation agriculture in East Usambara. *East Afr Ag J* 3:7–20.

Nye, P. H. 1957. Some prospects for subsistence agriculture in West Africa. *J West Afr Sci Assoc* 3:91–95.

———. 1958a. The relative importance of fallows and soils in storing plant nutrients in Ghana. *J West Afr Sci Assoc* 4:31–49.

———. 1958b. The mineral composition of some shrubs and trees in Ghana. *J West Afr Sci Assoc* 4:91–98.

Nye, P. H., and W. N. M. Foster. 1960. The relative uptake of phosphorus by crops and natural fallow from different parts of their root zone. *J Agric Sci* 56:299–306.

Nye, P. H., and R. G. Hutton. 1957. Some preliminary analyses of fallows and cover crops at the West African Institute for Oil Palm Research, Benin. *J West Afr Inst Oil Palm Res* 2:237–43.

Rawitscher, F. 1948. The water economy of the vegetation of the campos cerrados in southern Brazil. *J Ecol* 36:237–68.

Richards, P. W. 1952. *The tropical rain forest.* Cambridge.

Russell, E. J. 1950. *Soil conditions and plant growth.* London: Longmans.

Stenlid, G. 1958. Salt losses and redistribution of salts in higher plants. *Encyclopedia of Plant Physiology*, vol. 4, pp. 615–37.

Tamm, C. O. 1953. Growth, yield and nutrition in carpets of forest moss. (*Hylocomium splendens*) *Medd Stat Skogsforskn Inst* 43:1–140.

———. 1958. The atmosphere. *Encyclopedia of Plant Physiology*, vol. 4, pp. 233–42.

Weck, J. 1956. Über die Grossenordung der Substanzerzeugung in Baumbeständen verschiedener Vegetationsgebiete. *Allgemeine Forst-und Jagdzeitung*, Bd 127:76–80.

On Biomass and Trophic Structure of the Central Amazonian[1] Rain Forest Ecosystem

E. J. Fittkau and H. Klinge

Max-Planck-Institute of Limnology, Department of Tropical Ecology, D232 Plön/Holstein, Federal Republic of Germany

ABSTRACT

The importance of litter in the total energy flow dynamics of a central Amazonian rain forest near Manaus, Brazil, is discussed. The study area is located in the hinterland of Manaus between the Rio Negro and the Amazon. Its substrate is Tertiary sediment. The area receives 1771 mm rainfall per year, and the soil is classified as yellow latosol. The forest comprises 93,780 dicotyledonous trees and palms per hectare reaching 38.10 meters in height. Over 500 species of palms and dicotyledonous trees above 1.5 m. in height are identified for a 2000 sq. m. plot. The estimate for fresh living dicotyledonous tree and palm biomass is 939.5 metric tons per hectare consisting of 1.9% leaves, 49.7% stems, 21.3% branches and twigs, and 27.1% roots. Lianas, vascular epiphytes, and parasites are estimated to comprise 46.2 mt/hectare in the fresh state. At the soil surface there are 59 mt/hectare of fresh litter. Living animal biomass is about 200 kg/hectare of which half is soil fauna. The high proportion of soil fauna, the type of humus, the decomposition of litter, the apparent dependence of soil fauna on fungi, and the low nutrient content of litter are all factors which strongly support a consumer food chain based almost entirely on dead organic matter. The fungi play a decisive role in concentrating the otherwise limited nutrient resources.

ECOLOGICAL STUDIES carried out in the Amazon region (Fittkau *et al*. 1969) raised further questions concerning the richness of the Amazonian ecosystems, the distribution of their biomass, and importance of overall as well as trophic-level structure. Additional experience obtained through later fieldwork in Amazonia and the results of our studies in hydrobiology, ecology, landscape ecology, pedology, and terrestrial production indicated the importance of finding out what the relationship of all these factors is in the entire central Amazonian[1] rain forest where the predominant soil type is latosol. Also considered must be the geochemical structure of that region, the division of the area as demonstrated by Fittkau (1969, 1970a, 1970b, 1971a, 1971b; fig. 1), and its influence on the nutrient supply available to the biomass in terrestrial and aquatic environments.

A discussion of the bioenergetics of a tropical rain forest is difficult because few studies have been conducted either on the basis of the specific trophic levels involved or on the basis of the whole biomass. As a consequence, a discussion of available nutrients for specific species at various trophic levels is even more difficult. However, comparisons of litter-fall with the soil complex have been published, and the results are interesting enough to investigate the problem further. In a study by Klinge and Rodrigues (1968), the litter-fall of a central Amazonian tropical lowland rain forest was determined

for 1963 and 1964. The average litter-fall for this period shows that 7.3 metric tons (mt) of dry matter per hectare (h) per year are returned to the soil. Dry matter per hectare is made up of 5.6 mt of leaves, or 76.6 percent of the total dry matter; the remainder is composed of flowers, small fruits, and twigs. It is interesting to note that this amount of litter is smaller than the litter-fall reported for tropical rain forests in Africa and Asia (Bray and Gorham 1964). Klinge and Rodrigues (1968) showed that Amazonian litter is poorer in nutrients when compared with litter from other tropical forests. Results from our chemical analyses indicated that the following raw elements occur in the litter returned to the soil in central Amazonia (kg per hectare per year): 2.2 P, 12.7 K, 5.0 Na, 18.4 Ca, 12.6 Mg, and 105.6 N.

In 1970, estimates were made of the amount of woody material involved in litter-fall of the central Amazonian rain forest (Klinge, unpublished). The results of the analyses show that one mt of stems (stem-part of plant between soil surface and first ramification), two mt of branches (ramifications without leaves), and 1.35 mt of twigs (ramifications bearing leaves), bark, etc. are involved.

Because the 1963-1964 litter-fall experiment was not suitable for the measurement of the total fruit-fall, we calculated roughly the amount of fruits involved in annual litter-fall by kind, weight, and number of fruits in a 2000 m² forest plot. Thus, we determined amounts of 0.35 mt of small fruits (up to 5 g in weight) and 0.5-1.0 mt of larger fruits (over approximately 5 g in weight). We

---

[1] In this paper, 'central Amazonia' and 'central Amazonian' refer only to the ecological unit of Amazonia defined by Fittkau (1963) and illustrated in figure 1.

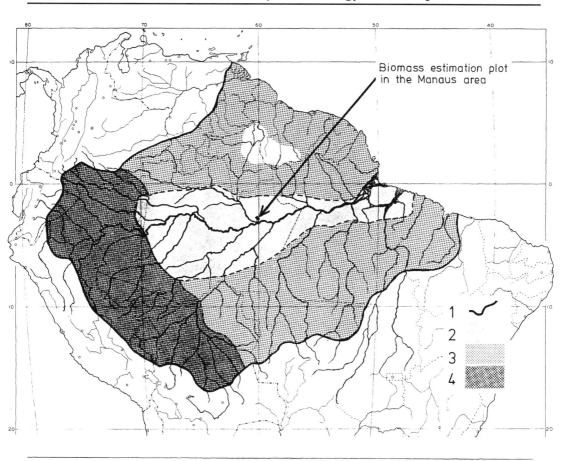

FIGURE 1. Subdivision of Amazonia according to Fittkau (1969). 1—Limit of Amazonian rain forest area. 2—Central Amazonia. 3—Northern and southern peripheral Amazonia. 4—Western peripheral Amazonia.

guess that these amounts are underestimated if we compare our determinations with data for the humid tropical forest on Barro Colorado Island, Panama, as given by Smythe (1970). In a systematic fruit collection experiment, Smythe found about two mt of fruits per hectare per year.

Adding all Amazonian litter fractions, a total of about 11 mt per hectare per year is obtained. This value resembles the litter amount given for a montane rain forest in Puerto Rico which comprises 5.52 mt of small litter-fall, 1.9 mt of log-fall, and 4 mt of brush-fall (Odum 1970). As wood is generally poor in nutrients, the incorporation of so much woody matter in the litter-fall of the central Amazonian rain forest suggests the validity of the above-stated low nutrient content of Amazonian litter.

We also found litter-fall to be seasonal. In the rainy season of 1964 litter-fall was 400 kg per hectare per month; it was 700 kg per hectare per month in the dry season; the maximum for the dry season, measured in September 1964, was 1000 kg per hectare per month. The seasonality of litter-fall is explained by seasonality of rainfall. About 90 percent of the total annual rainfall of 1771 mm per year at Manaus (Walter and Lieth 1960-1967) occurs during the rainy season which lasts generally from May-June to October-November. However, in 1964 the dry season had begun already much earlier than usual.

In the period from June to November 1970, which was unusually rainy, litter-fall was again measured as was the total litter at the soil surface. The results indicate that litter-fall and litter decomposition were rather well balanced because of the high activity of litter decomposers. According to Stark

TABLE 1. *Height classes (meters) and fresh biomass (kilograms) of dicotyledonous trees and palms in central Amazonian rain forest per hectare.*

Height class	<0.2	>0.2 – 0.5	>0.5 – 1.0	>1.0 – 1.5	Subtotal <0.2 – 1.5	>1.5 – 5.0
NUMBERS OF INDIVIDUALS						
Trees	40,725	21,400	12,575	8,950	83,650	6,535
Palms						915
BIOMASS						
Leaves	55	91	128	294	513	3,208
Stem		72	200	609	936	2,993
Twigs and branches						1,132
Total aboveground	55	163	328	903	1,449	7,333
Large roots	25	62	105	247	439	1,542
Fine roots	–	–	–	–	–	–
Total underground	25	62	105	247	439	1,542
Total above and underground	80	225	433	1,150	1,888	8,875
RATIOS						
Aboveground:underground	1:0.5	1:0.4	1:0.3	1:0.3	1:0.3	1:0.2
Leaves:twigs and branches:stem	–	–	–	–	–	1:0.4:0.9
Leaves:wood	–	1:0.8	1:1.6	1:2.1	1:1.8	1:1.3

(1971), decomposition is 5.4 g per m² per day. Klinge (1972a) found a decomposition rate of 0.56 percent per day for leaves, and of 1.5 and 2.3 percent per day for woody litter and fruits, respectively, in the biomass estimation plot.

There is only scattered information regarding the structure of forest which produces the above amounts of litter (Hueck 1966, Lechthaler 1956, Takeuchi 1961). Rodrigues (1967) surveyed a forest and included all trees over 25 cm diameter at breast height (dbh), covering 137,000 hectares in the area of the Manaus-Itacoatiara road. This survey includes the Walter Egler Forest Reserve where the 1963-1964 litter-fall measurements were made. The area studied by Rodrigues also includes a plot which was studied by Klinge and Rodrigues (1971, Klinge 1972a,b,c), for forest biomass estimation. Some results of this recent study are described below.

On a level site at km 64 of the Manaus-Itacoatiara road, a rectangular plot of 2000 m², immediately adjacent the Walter Egler Forest Reserve, was marked off using a nylon line. The plot was subdivided into 40 equal subplots. The area is *terra firma*, i.e., terrain which is never reached by annual river floods. The soil is a yellow latosol of heavy texture (Anonymous 1969). The subsoil is Tertiary sediment (Barreiras Series). The plot was mapped to show the position of all palms and dicotyledonous trees above 1.5 m height and of lianas of more than approximately 5 cm in diameter.

Prior to mapping, all smaller plants were harvested. Total height, stem length, diameter at breast height, and crown diameter of plants above 1.5 m height were measured using a steel tape. Taller plants were measured after felling; smaller plants were measured with a wooden ruler before cutting. In some cases, crown diameters were derived from projections made from the ground.

All leaves, twigs, branches, and stems were separated; leaves by hand, twigs by machete, and branches and stems using a portable chain saw. The fractions were weighed in the field, branches and stems after they were sawed into manageable pieces. Portable balances, weighing up to 100 kg, were used. The root mass of 381 dicotyledonous trees and 51 palms above 1.5 m height was estimated after extraction of the plants by hand or by use of a simple jack. Plants below 1.5 m height were extracted by hand, separated into four height classes and counted, but they were not sampled for taxonomic determinations as in the case of the taller plants. Leaves, shoots, and roots of small plants were also separated and weighed. All fractions of individual dicotyledonous trees and palms of the four height classes under 1.5 m were sampled and weighed, air-dried in the field, and oven-dried in the laboratory at Manaus. All plant parts were finally shipped to Europe for subsequent determinations of nutrients and dry matter. These analyses are still progressing.

The field work extended from mid-June to the

>5.0 – 10.0	>10.0 – 20.0	>20.0 – 25.0	>25.0 – 30.0	>30.0 – 35.0	>35.0 – 38.1	Subtotal 1.5 – 38.1	Total
1,480	725	175	160	55	25	9,155	93,780
45	15	0	0	0	0	975	
1,161	3,253	2,696	3,887	2,277	1,150	17,632	18,145
8,864	37,832	103,241	114,444	126,317	73,410	467,101	467,101
3,193	14,994	53,417	58,419	46,953	21,089	199,197	199,197
13,218	56,079	159,354	176,750	171,547	95,649	683,930	685,379
1,951	6,002	11,952	11,489	10,270	5,356	48,561	49,000
–	–	–	–	–	–	–	206,040
1,951	6,002	11,952	11,489	10,270	5,356	48,561	255,040
15,169	62,081	171,306	188,239	181,817	101,005	732,491	940,419
1:0.2	1:0.1	1:0.08	1:0.07	1:0.06	1:0.06	1:0.07	1:0.4
1:2.8:7.6	1:4.6:11.6	1:19.8:38.3	1:15:29.4	1:20.6:55.5	1:18.3:63.8	1:11.3:26.5	1:11.0:25.7
1:10.4	1:16.2	1:58.1	1:44.5	1:76.1	1:82.7	1:37.9	1:36.8

end of November 1970. During this time many collections were made of large and conspicuous arthropods, amphibians, and reptiles. The vertebrates collected during this time were submitted to Dr. P. Müller, Saarbrücken, Germany, and the invertebrates went to H. Schubart and E. J. Fittkau, Plön, Germany for identification. When evaluating this animal sampling and our observations on animals in central Amazonia made over the last 10 years, we also made use of any information gathered from Indians, settlers, hunters, and professional biologists.

In order to obtain weight data of fauna we listed first those animal taxa (orders, families, etc.) which were observed to have some bearing upon biomass because of their individual weight and/or frequency. Then we estimated density taking into account all observations gathered by ourselves and the above-named sources. Finally, density was converted into weight of the respective group by multiplying weight by density, using average weight of individuals contained in our collections or otherwise determined weight. None of the values thus obtained was adjusted with respect to data found in literature for similar groups in tropical regions elsewhere.

RESULTS AND DISCUSSION

Trees and palms below 1.5 m height were in much greater abundance than taller plants and made up 86 percent of the total plant cover considered (table

1). The number of trees clearly diminishes with height. This relationship is valid particularly for palms which are abundant below 20 m height. The ratios of aboveground biomass, underground biomass, or leaves/branches + twigs/stems, or leaves/wood vary rather consistently from short to tall height classes.

No data are given in table 1 for lianas, epiphytes, and parasites which are represented by the following amounts of fresh biomass: Vascular epiphytes (mainly Araceae, Bromeliaceae, and Orchidaceae), 0.1 mt per hectare; parasites (Loranthaceae), 0.13 mt per hectare; lianas (various families), 46.0 mt per hectare; total 46.23 mt per hectare. Thus we find that lianas are a striking feature of the central Amazonian rain forest, whereas angiosperm epiphytes and parasites are of nearly negligible biomass.

Total weight of the living aboveground biomass of plant origin in the forest is 730.7 mt per hectare. Weight of underground biomass (roots and underground trunks of certain palms) is 255 mt per hectare or 25.9 percent of the total living plant biomass (Klinge, unpublished). Both weights are in agreement with data presented by Rodin and Bazilevic (1964, 1968) and Bazilevic and Rodin (1966). Dead plant biomass at the soil surface (excluding roots) amounts to about 44 mt per hectare of wood and 15 mt per hectare of fine forest detritus, both weights in fresh state. There is, in terms of weight, twice as much stem wood as branch wood.

Total plant biomass of the forest under study is thus about 1100 mt of fresh matter per hectare.

Our herbarium material is actually determined only to the family level. The plant families of which the forest is composed are listed in table 2.

TABLE 2. *Plant families with representatives above 1.5 m height in the central Amazonian rain forest growing on a 2000 m² plot of terra firma latosol.*

Plant family	Numbers of species	Numbers of individuals	Percentage of total individuals
Leguminosae	62	171	8.6
Sapotaceae	43	139	7.0
Lauraceae	40	88	4.4
Chrysobalanaceae[a]	38	96	4.8
Rubiaceae	32	137	6.9
Burseraceae	27	230	11.9
Annonaceae	21	87	4.4
Lecythidaceae	17	132	6.6
Moraceae	17	69	3.5
Palmae	11	196	9.9
Violaceae	10	223	11.2
44 other families	177	409	20.6
Indeterminata	7	9	0.5
Total	502	1986	100.3

[a] Refers to the tribe Chrysobalanoideae of Rosaceae but in the familial sense.

If there are in the literature very little data on total plant biomass of humid tropical forests (Greenland and Kowal 1960, Ogawa *et al.* 1961, 1965, Art and Marks 1971, Rodin and Bazilevic 1964, 1968, Bazilevic and Rodin 1966), there is even less information regarding total animal biomass of these forests (Goodnight and Goodnight 1956, Harrison 1962, Hopkins 1967). A rare exception to this lack of information is the study on structure and metabolism of a red mangrove forest in Puerto Rico (Golley *et al.* 1962). There are, however, good descriptions of the fauna living in humid tropical forests, including Amazonian forests (Bates 1965, Dorst 1967, Mann 1968, Mertens 1948), but information on total animal biomass of Amazonian forests is completely lacking. Meggers (1971) states that the majority of wild animals there are small and solitary. Three studies on the central Amazonian soil fauna (Beck 1967, 1970, 1971) do exist, however. Beck, working chiefly in the hinterland of Manaus, studied mainly meso- and macro-soil fauna on sites comparable to our plant biomass study plot. He presented density data for a series of soil animal groups of which only Isoptera and Formicidae are under-represented owing to the technique of collection which he used (table 3).

The overwhelming predominance of Acarina and Collembola, over all other groups, is easily recognized from table 3. Other important groups of fauna are: Isopoda, Pseudoscorpiones, Araneae, Opiliones, Diplopoda (Chilognatha), Chilopoda, Iso-

TABLE 3. *Soil fauna of central Amazonian terra firma rain forest on latosol. Expressed as 10^6 individuals per hectare; from Beck 1970, 1971.*

10^6 individuals per hectare	Litter	Upper mineral soil	Macro - fauna	Total
Acarina	612	115		727
Collembola	103	16.8	0.34	120
Isopoda	0.7		0.05	0.8
Pseudoscorpiones	2.1		0.09	2.2
Other Arachnida	0.7		0.2	0.9
Diplopoda	2.8		0.1	2.9
Other Myriapoda	3.5		0.03	3.53
Protura	2.8			2.8
Diplura	1.4		0.01	1.41
Larvae of Coleoptera and Diptera	4.0		0.04	4.04
Coleoptera	1.4		0.07	1.5
Isoptera	0.9		0.4	1.3
Formicidae	7.2		1.4	8.6
Aphidina/Coccina	39.4			39.4
Opiliones			0.02	0.02
Blattaria			0.02	0.02
Gryllodea			0.05	0.05
Total individuals	782	144	2.8	929
Biomass (kg)	67.7	12	4.4	84

ptera, Formicidae, Coleoptera and their larvae, and larval Diptera. Moreover, there are regularly present: Scorpiones, Palpigradi, Ricinulei, Uropygi (Schizopeltidia), Symphyla, Pauropoda, Diplopoda (Pselaphognata), Protura, Diplura (Campodeidae and Japygydae), Embiidae, Orthoptera, Phasmida, Forficulidae, Mantodea, Blattaria, Psocoptera, Thysanoptera, Heteroptera, Cicadina, Turbellaria, Hirudineae, Onychophora, Serpentes, Iguanidae, and Dasypodida.

The lack of any precise information on the population density and biomass of termites and ants, which are so numerous in the environment of central Amazonia, is to be regretted. We may refer only to Beck (1971), who assumed that three quarters of the soil fauna, in terms of biomass, are ants and termites in the central Amazonian rain forest. It is, therefore, not possible to evaluate the role of these soil animal groups in the bioenergy flow within the central Amazonian rain forest. It is impossible to evaluate their role from the literature concerning other tropical regions because of contradicting statements regarding the alimentation of specific species and population density of different species in different environments. Regarding termites, see Lee and Wood (1971), and Krishna and Weesner (1970). The data given by Wiegert (1970) for *Nasutitermes costalis* (Holmgren) in a Puerto Rican montane rain forest are inappropriate because of the different type of forest.

The biomass of faunal elements of the central Amazonian rain forest which are important biologically, with respect to production, or because of abundance or size, is given in figure 2. The values have been derived from our general observations over the last 10 years and from observations of others, but not from actual counting and weighing, as stated above. Excepted are: soil fauna, total fresh biomass (84 kg per hectare; Beck 1970, 1971), and certain arthropods and vertebrates which we collected in the biomass estimation plot.

Regarding the zoocoenosis of our forest we found that the following animal groups have a high density: soil fauna (mainly mites and Collembola), Orthoptera (Locustidae, Phasmida), Mantodea, Blattaria, Isoptera, Hemiptera (Heteroptera, Cicadina), and Hymenoptera (Formicidae, Vespoidea). Soil-inhabiting invertebrates are the most conspicuous group comprising the faunal biomass. Below is a detailed discussion of the environment and importance of these soil animals.

The soil contains roots which penetrate more or less one meter into the ground. The main root-bearing zone, however, is only about 30 cm deep. This upper layer contains about half of all fine roots (Klinge 1972c). Because the forest invertebrates listed in figure 2 belong to the soil fauna, and because the soil fauna prefers the uppermost soil layer supplied with organic debris and humified matter, about half the total animal biomass inhabits a zone only 10 cm deep. Thus, in the 40 m vertical range of the ecosystem under discussion, the most important fraction of the zoocoenosis occurs in less than 0.5 percent of the total volume. This fraction of the fauna, however, does not just dwell in this superficial soil layer, but it also feeds on the mostly organic nutrient matter in it.

Regarding alimentation of soil fauna in the tropics, Beck (1970, 1971), in his studies in central Amazonia, and Schaller (1960, 1961), referring to South America and to the tropics in general, stated that tropical soil animals (excluding termites) do not feed so much on organic detritus, as do their counterparts in temperate regions, but also on the fungi which decompose this forest detritus. In explaining this strikingly different feeding behavior between temperate and tropical soil fauna, Beck argues that fungi have optimal growth conditions in the humid tropics where there are constantly high humidity, high temperature, and acidic soil conditions. This argument has also been stated by Eidmann (1942, 1943), Maldague (1958), Maldague and Hilger (1963), and others. Because of these optimal growing conditions for fungi, Beck asserts

further that competition for food between fungi and faunal primary decomposers is much stronger in the tropics than elsewhere. As a consequence of this competition, soil animals are more or less excluded by fungi from the decomposition of organic detritus, and must feed on other material: thus they feed on the fungi themselves. Animal primary decomposers decrease in number, therefore, and secondary decomposers increase accordingly. For secondary decomposers, however, there is not enough organic matter pretreated by primary decomposers. Secondary decomposers also change their food base and change over to feed on fungi. The final result is that fungi become the predominant primary decomposers.

One of the proofs which Beck gives to support his opinion concerns diplopods, which in temperate regions are primary decomposers, while in the central Amazonian rain forest they feed exclusively on fungal mycelia and spores. Regarding other tropical regions, some other authors have reported on fungivorous soil animals. Strickland (1945) referred to fungivorous springtails, beetles, and larval Diptera in Trinidad. Meyer and Maldague (1957) mentioned fungivorous soil animals for the Congo region, Bullock and Khoo (1969) for Malaysia, and Healey (1970) and Coleman (1970) for soil fauna in general.

The surface organic matter or humus of the soil is present as "moder" in the sense of Kubiena (1953), or a "transition between raw humus and mull" (Jacks *et al.* 1966). It is characterized by an absence of mixing of organic and mineral matter, that is, the organic debris layer of moder is separated from the mineral soil below it. The debris layer is well provided with roots and can, therefore, be removed from the mineral soil like a carpet. Moder lacks digging animals or other soil animals which could mix the organic and inorganic components of the soil. There are few Oligochaeta in the central Amazonian rain forest soil and other soil-digging animals are absent (Beck 1971). There are large earthworms (for example, the Glossoscolecidae *Rhinodrilus priollii* Righi), but they do not feed on organic detritus (Beck 1971). These earthworms do not cause active leaf burial, but only incorporate casts among the components of the litter layer. The casts are easily destroyed by rain and are not humic-stained. Madge (1965) observed an earthworm showing similar behavior in a Nigerian rain forest; during the wet season the earthworm, *Hyperiodrilus africanus* (Beddard), produced 36.4 mt of casts per hectare per year. There were 16.4 kg per hectare of earthworms in the soil. In the generally scarce literature on earthworms in tropical rain forest soils

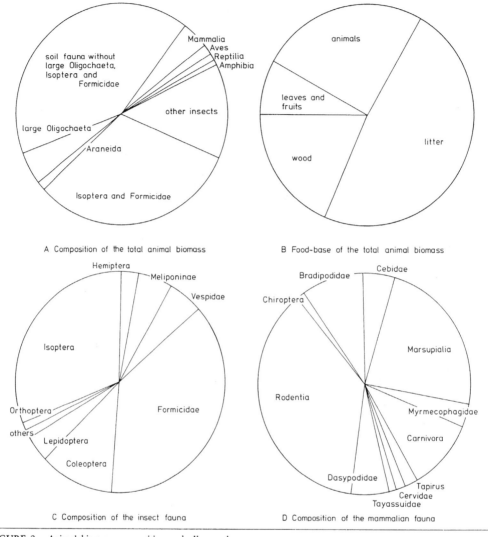

A Composition of the total animal biomass

B Food-base of the total animal biomass

C Composition of the insect fauna

D Composition of the mammalian fauna

FIGURE 2.   Animal biomass, composition and alimentation.

(Bullock and Khoo 1969, Madge 1966, Moore and Burns 1970, Schulze 1967), there is also information on earthworms which feed on leaves of the forest floor (Lyford 1969). Together with *Rhinodrilus priollii*, a large terrestrial leech, *Liostomus* sp., Herpobdellidae, which probably lives on Glossoscolecidae, is found frequently in the Amazonian forest which we examined.

The amount of animal biomass in the central Amazonian rain forest is extremely small when compared with the plant biomass. The poverty in animals is also indicated by the following observations of this forest: Temporary water accumulations in leaves, palm frond bases, etc. are rarely inhabited by animals. Collecting Amblypygi, even by experienced people, is mostly ineffective (even when a high price is offered for one collected specimen). Collecting insects using light traps is also ineffective. The rarity of rodents can be established from the fact that collections for blood parasite studies by the zoology staff of Instituto Nacional de Pesquisas da Amazônia had to be suspended because of the difficulty of securing the animals. Hunting for human food is never effective (even by experienced people). Food wastes at campsites regularly attract only some Scarabaeidae and Diptera. On faeces, only some Diptera may be found. In the biomass estimation plot, one uninhabited wasp nest and one small bee nest were found. Only one Aviculariidae was collected there, and butterflies were seldom observed. Only termites and ants are frequent, judging by the number of their nests in the earth, on the soil surface, and attached to tree trunks and branches, and by the trouble they cause to humans working in the forest. Curculionidae and Cerambycidae are also relatively frequent.

The small percentage of animal biomass compared with the total biomass of the central Amazonian rain forest becomes much more evident if we compare similar figures for African steppes and savannas, or for other tropical forests. In a montane tropical rain forest in Puerto Rico, the animal biomass comprises 0.1 percent of the total biomass (Odum 1970, Odum and Pigeon 1970, Odum *et al.* 1970), while in central Amazonia it comprises only 0.02 percent of the total biomass. In Tanganyika and Uganda grasslands there are 100-300 kg per hectare of large herbivorous animals (Wiegert and Evans 1967). In the East African savanna are 235.6 kg per hectare of these animals, and in Ghana forests there are 0.72 kg per hectare of ungulates and primates (Bourlière 1963). In an East African thornbush savanna, having a dry matter production of 1-7 mt per hectare per year, on each hectare there are 50 kg of ungulates, 4 kg of plant-eating small mammals, and 250 kg of plant-consuming soil animals which feed on the dry matter produced each year. Also present on each hectare are 0.3 kg carnivores (Hendrichs 1970).

It is remarkable that the main part of the animal biomass of the central Amazonian rain forest is present in that part of the ecosystem which is well supplied with forest debris and in which the debris is processed. Correspondingly, the proportion of the animal biomass feeding on living plant matter is rather small. The enormous proportion of wood in the living plant biomass contributes little to the food resources of the fauna. Beetles and their larvae, and termites, are the most important faunal elements feeding on wood. Termites are supposed to be the most effective wood-eaters, but, as stated above, no precise information is available regarding energy and matter flow through this animal group in central Amazonia.

The leaves, which comprise about 2 percent of the living plant biomass of our forest, are utilized by a relatively small number of taxa and individuals (Orthoptera, *Atta,* Coleoptera, Hemiptera, Lepidoptera, sloths, and parrots; primates also consume young leaves, leaf buds, and flowers). Leaf-cutting ants are mostly responsible for the defoliation of small trees

which occur here and there in the forest.

Damage attributable to insect plagues was never observed nor reported (Voute 1945-1946, Schneider 1939). The opinion that a great proportion of the leaves of tropical rain forest plants is consumed by animals before they fall on the soil appears to us to be rather exaggerated and seems not to be generally valid for all tropical forests. Inspection of living leaves in the course of leaf harvest as part of the biomass estimation, as well as of leaves lying on the soil, never showed any signs of heavy attack by animals. Our observations agree with the statement of Madge (1969) who, in a study of litter decomposition in Nigeria, expressed the view that primary food consumption of leaf litter appears to be less in the tropics than in temperate regions. His opinion is also supported by Wanner (1970) who wrote: ". . . direct grazing seems to be a minor pathway of energy flow in rain forest as elsewhere."

There is some controversy in the literature regarding leaves consumed by tropical rain forest animals. The most extreme position is held by Eidmann (1942, 1943) and Büchler (according to Mann 1968) who reported that 25 percent of the leaf matter is consumed by insects in West African and South American forests. Hopkins (1967) estimated that 67 percent of the primary production in a Nigerian rain forest travels along the grazing pathway. Bray (1964), however, estimated the loss of leaf matter due to herbivorous grazing to be 1.5-2.5 percent of the annual leaf production. Odum and Ruiz-Reyes (1970) estimated that 7 percent of the leaf area is consumed by animals of the Puerto Rican Tabonuco rain forest. Cruz Acosta (1964) stated that less than 6 percent of leaf matter was consumed by insects in a Costa Rican rain forest. Chrysomelids and butterfly larvae are mainly responsible for the consumption of living leaves in a West African rain forest (Eidmann 1942). Butterfly larvae were only occasionally observed, and in small numbers, in the central Amazonian rain forest near Manaus.

Cruz Acosta (1964) agrees with Bray (1964) that leaf utilization by animals is correlated with the nutrient content of the leaves. We assume that our finding of a relatively low nutrient content in central Amazonian leaf litter supports this view (Klinge and Rodrigues 1968). Also it has been frequently observed in Amazonia that where fresh mineral soil has been recently dug and exposed to the air, and especially if it is polluted by urine, butterflies, bees, and other insects can be found in large numbers visiting this matter, presumably in search of nutrients. A heavily perspiring man is strongly attacked by *Meliponinae* which suck up the sweat; this circumstance is especially true in the highly oligotrophic Rio Negro area. Both observations seem to us to be an indication of the shortage of nutrients in Amazonia. The physico-mechanical properties and organic composition of leaves will also play a role in making the leaves either attractive or unattractive to animals.

At any given time, fruits and flowers are only present to a small degree (Bourlière 1972) because of the low species density of plants (table 2). These plant organs, therefore, represent only a small food base and do not serve as a continuous source of nutrients for a very important part of the fauna. Meggers (1971) also adheres to our opinion regarding Amazonian *terra firma* forests and points out that in this region the distribution of individuals of the same plant species is scattered so that ripe fruits or seeds are not available in concentrated numbers. She included aboriginal man in her thesis and stated that he, subsisting on wild animals and plants, affected the ecosystem in a way similar to other kinds of large animals.

In the past, reference has been made to a "fauna of tree crowns" in tropical rain forests, thus indicating a specific environment in that part of the ecosystem. Our observations agree with the findings of Harrison (1965) regarding vertebrates in Borneo and contradict the assertion that life in the crowns of trees is highly significant. We have observed certain kinds of adaptations of fauna to a life in the crown area and on bark; for example, protective or cryptic coloration of locusts, mantids, cicadas, beetles, and reptiles. On the other hand, our opinion is that the fungi which inhabit the soil are the main primary decomposers and are highly significant in processing the forest litter and in concentrating the low levels of nutrients stored in the dead organic matter. It is nevertheless true that large amounts of plant matter are produced in the tree crown zone of the forest. But the conversion of the bulk of plant matter to living animal matter must pass through the bottleneck of the dead plant matter which accumulates in the litter layer of the forest soil. This zone is inhabited by soil fungi which can incorporate nutrients of the forest detritus into their mycelia, thus concentrating the limited nutrients and making them available for organisms at the next higher level of the energy pathway.

The critical point in the energy and nutrient transformation is the inability of soil invertebrates to process large quantities of dead plant matter into living matter in strong competition with fungi as described above. Exceptions to this pattern are found in taxa having representatives of microorganisms in their digestive tract, as in ruminants, the tropical termites, and other insects living in symbiosis with microorganisms. These animals can digest large quantities of food, such as wood, to obtain a minimal nutrient level for their existence.

Our contention that the main energy flow is undoubtedly through the detritus food chain (fig. 3) is strongly supported by Cruz Acosta (1964) and by Went and Stark (1968). When studying the biological role of soil fungi in the Amazon rain forest, Went and Stark proposed first a very intensive fungal development, some fraction of which is in the form of mycorrhiza. Then they argue that fungi are the primary decomposers of the forest litter and thus agree with the conclusions of Beck (1970, 1971). Went and Stark further assert that the nutrients liberated during the decomposition of forest litter by fungi are not released into the soil but are transferred to the tree roots through mycorrhizal fungi which are restricted to the surface organic layers of the soil. They believe that the same fungal mycelium acts as primary decomposer and as mycorrhizal mycelium.

The dependence of the lower members of the consumer chain on organic detritus and on microorganisms feeding on it in the terrestrial environment has its parallel in the aquatic environment of central Amazonia in which no primary production has been observed as yet. There is a striking number of such groups of aquatic animals which feed on organic micro-drift and on "detritus" (Fittkau 1967, 1970b, Sattler 1963, 1967).

In conclusion, we believe that in the tropical rain forest of central Amazonia dead organic matter is processed by microorganisms which channel organic matter and nutrients through their own matter into the consumer chain. This type of forest occupies the vast level plain built up by Tertiary sediments (Barreiras Series) of the *terra firma* which is never reached by the annual floods of the drainageways. The hinterland of Manaus where we conducted our studies forms part of central Amazonia and lies between the Rio Negro and the Rio Solimões. It is clearly to be distinguished from the sandy Rio Negro basin, despite the fact that small sand patches are spread throughout central Amazonia. The rain forest of the central Amazonian *terra firma* is characterized by a very high number of dicotyledonous trees and by a great proportion of palms and lianas. Small, slender trees predominate. Total plant biomass of the forest is about 1100 mt of fresh matter per hectare while its animal biomass is only 0.2 mt per hectare. Invertebrates predominate. Insects are well represented. Soil fauna, comprising approximately 50-75 percent of the animal biomass, is the most important group from the points of view of ecology and energy flow. Living plant matter apparently does not serve as the main food base of animals. Seven percent of the animal biomass feeds on living plant matter, except wood, and 19 percent feeds on living and dead wood.

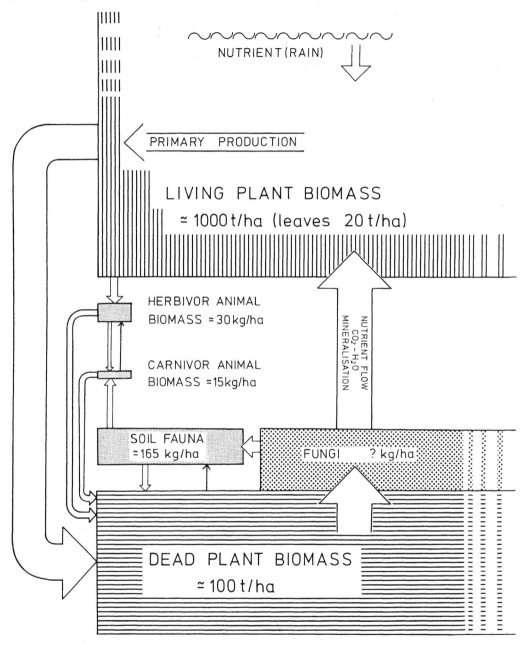

FIGURE 3.   Schematic distribution of biomass and organic matter flow in the central Amazonian rain forest ecosystem.

About half the animal biomass feeds on litter, mainly after it is converted into fungal mycelia.
The food chain is thus built up on transformed litter. Twenty-four percent of the animal biomass is carnivorous and about 2 percent is omnivorous. The preferred utilization of transformed dead matter is believed to be connected with the small nutrient supply of living plant matter and with the ecosystem as a whole. The food chain in the waters of the region supports this thesis (Fittkau 1973).

ACKNOWLEDGEMENTS

Acknowledgement is expressed to Instituto Nacional de Pesquisas da Amazonia for the support given in a cooperative contract between INPA and the Department of Tropical Ecology, Max-Planck-Institute of Limnology. Special thanks are due to W. A. Rodrigues, botany department of INPA, and to his assistants who conducted the forest biomass estimation under the direction of H. Klinge. Gratitude is expressed to Dr. H. Schubart and Dr. P. Müller, for identification of animals, and to Prof. Dr. L. L. Curry, Mount Pleasant, Michigan, U.S.A., and Dr. E. Naguib for translation of the original German manuscript.

LITERATURE CITED

ANONYMOUS. 1969. Os solos da área Manaus-Itacoatiara. Estudos e Ensaios 1. Edição do Setor de Relações Públicas. Estado do Amazônas, Secretaria de Estado da Produção em colaboração com o Instituto de Pesquisas e Experimentação Agropecuárias do Norte (IPEAN). Manaus. Pp. 117.

ART, H. W., AND P. L. MARKS. 1971. A summary table of biomass and net annual primary production in forest ecosystems of the world. Pp. 1–32. *In* H. E. Young (Editor). Forest biomass studies. Life Sciences and Agriculture Experiment Station. University of Maine at Orono.

BATES, M. 1965. South America, flora and fauna. Time, Inc. New York.

BAZILEVIC, N. I., AND L. E. RODIN. 1966. The biological cycle of nitrogen and ash elements in plant communities of the tropical and subtropical zones. Forest. Abstr. 27: 357–368.

BECK, L. 1967. Die Bodenfauna des neotropischen Regenwaldes. *In* Herman Lent (Editor). Atas do simpósio sôbre a biota amazônica 5 Zoologia: 97–101. Conselho Nacional de Pesquisas. Rio de Janeiro.

———. 1970. Zur Ökologie der Bodenarthropoden im Regenwaldgebiet des Amazonasbeckens. Habilitationsschrift. Ruhr-Universität Bochum.

———. 1971. Bodenzoologische Gliederung und Charakterisierung des amazonischen Regenwaldes. Amazoniana 3: 69–132.

BOURLIÈRE, F. 1963. Observations on the ecology of some large African mammals. African Ecol. Human Evol. 36: 43–54.

———. 1972. The comparative ecology of rain forest mammals in Africa and Latin America: some introductory remarks. Pp. 279–292. *In* B. J. Meggers, E. S. Ayensu, and W. D. Duckworth (Editors). Tropical forest ecosystems in Africa and South America: A comparative review. Smithsonian Institution Press. Washington, D.C.

BRAY, J. R. 1964. Primary consumption in three forest canopies. Ecology 45: 165–167.

———, AND E. GORHAM. 1964. Litter production in forests of the world. *In* J. B. Cragg (Editor). Advances Ecol. Res. 2: 101–157.

BULLOCK, J. A., AND B. K. KHOO. 1969. The litter layer. Malayan Nat. J. 22: 136–143.

COLEMAN, D. C. 1970. Food webs of small arthropods of a broomsedge field studied with radio isotope-labelled fungi. *In* J. Phillipson (Editor). Methods of study in soil ecology. Pp. 203–207. Proc. Paris Symposium Methods of study in soil ecology. UNESCO.

CRUZ ACOSTA, A. DE LA. 1964. A preliminary study of organic detritus in a tropical forest ecosystem. Revista Biol. Trop. 12: 175–185.

DORST, I. 1967. South America and Central America, a natural history. Random House, Inc. New York.

EIDMANN, H. 1942. Der tropische Regenwald als Lebensraum. Kolonialforstl. Mitt. 5: 91–147.

———. 1943. Zur Ökologie der Tierwelt. Beitr. Kolonialf. 2: 25–45.

FITTKAU, E. J. 1967. On the ecology of Amazonian rain forest streams. *In* Herman Lent (Editor). Atas do simpósio sôbre a biota amazônica 3 Limnologia: 97–108. Conselho Nacional de Pesquisas. Rio de Janeiro.

———. 1969. The fauna of South America. Pp. 624–658. *In* E. J. Fittkau, J. Illies, H. Klinge, G. H. Schwabe, and H. Sioli (Editors). Biogeography and ecology in South America. Vol. 2. *In* Monographiae biologicae. Vol. 19. W. Junk. N.V. The Hague.

———. 1970a. Limnological conditions in the headwater region of the Xingu river, Brasil. Trop. Ecol. 11: 20–25.

———. 1970b. Esboço de uma divisão ecológica da região amazônica. Pp. 365–372. *In* J. M. Idrobo (Editor). II Simpósio y foro de biología tropical amazónica. Asociación pro Biología Tropical. Editorial Pax. Bogotá.

———. 1971a. Ökologische Gliederung des Amazonasgebietes auf geochemischer Grundlage. Münster. Forsch. Geol. Paläontol. 20/21: 35–50.

———. 1971b. Distribution and ecology of Amazonian chironomids (Diptera). Canad. Entomol. 103: 407–413.

——. 1973. Crocodiles and the nutrient metabolism of Amazonian waters. Amazoniana 4: 103–133.

——, W. JUNK, H. KLINGE, AND H. SIOLI. 1969. Substrat und Vegetation im Amazonasgebiet. 13. Internationales Symposium über Vegetation and Substrat. Rinteln 1969 (in press).

GOLLEY, F., H. T. ODUM, AND R. F. WILSON. 1962. The structure and metabolism of a Puerto Rican red mangrove forest in May. Ecology 43: 9–19.

GOODNIGHT, C. H., AND M. L. GOODNIGHT. 1956. Some observations in a tropical rain forest in Chiapas, Mexico. Ecology 37: 139–150.

GREENLAND, D. J., AND J. M. L. KOWAL. 1960. Nutrient content of the moist tropical forest of Ghana. Pl. & Soil 12: 154–174.

HARRISON, J. L. 1962. The distribution of feeding habits among animals in a tropical rain forest. J. Anim. Ecol. 31: 53–63.

HARRISON, T. 1965. Some quantitative effects of vertebrates on the Borneo flora. Pp. 164–169. In Proceedings Symposium Ecological Research in Humid Tropics Vegetation. Kuching 1963.

HEALEY. I. N. 1970. The study of production and energy flow in populations of soft-bodied microarthropods. In J. Phillipson (Editor). Methods of study in soil ecology. Pp. 175–182. Proc. Paris Symposium Methods of study in soil ecology. UNESCO.

HENDRICHS, H. 1970. Schätzungen der Huftierbiomasse in der Dornbuschsavanne nördlich und westlich der Serengetisteppe in Ostafrika nach einem neuen Verfahren und Bemerkungen zur Biomasse der anderen pflanzenfressenden Tierarten. Säugetierkund. Mitt. 18: 237–255.

HOPKINS, B. 1967. A comparison between productivity in forest and savanna in Africa. J. Ecol. 55: 19–20.

HUECK, K. 1966. Die Wälder Südamerikas. Fischer. Stuttgart.

JACKS. G. V., R. TAVERNIER, AND D. H. BOALCH. 1966. Multilingual vocabulary of soil science. Food and Agriculture Organisation of the United Nations. Rome.

KLINGE, H. 1972a. Biomasa y materia orgánica del suelo en el ecosistema de la pluviselva centro-amazónica. Unpublished paper presented to IV Congreso Latino-Americano de la Ciencia del Suelo, Maracay, Venezuela, 12–18 November, 1972.

——. 1972b. Struktur und Artenreichtum des zentralamazonischen Regenwaldes. Amazoniana (in press).

——. 1972c. Root mass estimation in lowland tropical rain forests of central Amazonia, Brazil. I. Fine root masses of a pale yellow latosol and a giant humus podzol. Trop. Ecol. (in press).

——, AND W. A. RODRIGUES. 1968. Litter production in an area of Amazonian terra firme forest. I, II. Amazoniana I: 287–302, 303–310.

——, AND ——. 1971. Matéria orgânica e nutrientes na mata de terra firme perto de Manaus. Acta Amazonica 1: 69–72.

KRISHNA, K., AND F. M. WEESNER (Editors). 1970. Biology of termites. Vol. 2. Academic Press. New York & London.

KUBIENA, W. L. 1953. The soils of Europe. Consejo Superior de Investigaciones Científicas. Madrid.

LECHTHALER, R. 1956. Inventário das árvores de um hectare de terra firme da zona Reserva Florestal Ducke, Município de Manaus. Publ. No. 3. Instituto Nacional des Pesquisas da Amazônia, Botanica. Rio de Janeiro.

LEE, K. E., AND T. G. WOOD. 1971. Termites and soils. Academic Press. London.

LYFORD, W. H. 1969. The ecology of an elfin forest in Puerto Rico, 7. J. Arnold Arbor. 50: 210–224.

MADGE, D. S. 1965. Leaf litter and litter disappearance in a tropical forest. Pedobiologia 5: 273–288.

——. 1966. How leaf litter disappears. New Sci. 32: 113–115.

——. 1969. Litter disappearance in forest and savanna. Pedobiologia 9: 288–299.

MALDAGUE, M. 1958. Relations entre microfaune et microflore du sol dans la région de Yangambi (Congo-Belge). Agricultura (Louvain) 2: 340–351.

——, AND F. HILGER. 1963. Observations faunistiques et microbiologiques dans quelques biotopes forestières équatoriaux. Pp. 368–374. In J. Doeksen and J. Van der Drift (Editors). Soil organisms. North Holland Publishing Company. Amsterdam.

MANN, G. 1968. Die Ökosysteme Südamerikas. Pp. 171–229. In E. J. Fittkau, J. Illies, H. Klinge, G. H. Schwabe, and H. Sioli (Editors). Biogeography and ecology in South America. Vol. I. In Monographiae biologicae Vol. 18. W. Junk N.V. The Hague.

MEGGERS, B. J. 1971. Amazonia—man and culture in a counterfeit paradise. Aldine, Atherton, Inc. Chicago.

MERTENS, R. 1948. Die Tierwelt des tropischen Regenwaldes. Kramer. Frankfurt.

MEYER, J., AND M. MALDAGUE. 1957. Observations simultanées sur la microflore et microfaune de certains sols du Congo Belge. Pédologie 7: 110–118.

MOORE, A. M., AND L. BURNS. 1970. Preliminary observations on the earthworm populations of the forest soils at El Verde. In H. T. Odum and R. F. Pigeon (Editors). A tropical rain forest. A study of irradiation and ecology at El Verde. Pp. I 283–I 284. Division of Technical Information. U.S. Atomic Energy Commission. Oak Ridge, Tennessee.

ODUM, H. T. 1970. Summary. An emerging view of the ecological system at El Verde. Pp. I 191–I 281. In H. T. Odum and R. F. Pigeon (Editors). A tropical rain forest. A study of irradiation and ecology at El Verde.

Division of Technical Information. U.S. Atomic Energy Commission. Oak Ridge, Tennessee.

————, W. ABBOTT, R. K. SELANDER, F. B. GOLLEY, AND R. F. WILSON. 1970. Estimates of chlorophyll and biomass of the Tabonuco forest of Puerto Rico. Pp. I 3–I 19. *In* H. T. Odum and R. F. Pigeon (Editors). A tropical rain forest. A study of irradiation and ecology at El Verde. Division of Technical Information. U.S. Atomic Energy Commission. Oak Ridge, Tennessee.

————, AND R. F. PIGEON (Editors). 1970. A tropical rain forest. A study of irradiation and ecology at El Verde. Division of Technical Information. U.S. Atomic Energy Commission. Oak Ridge, Tennessee.

————, AND J. RUIZ-REYES. 1970. Holes in leaves and the grazing control mechanism. Pp. I 69–I 80. *In* H. T. Odum and R. F. Pigeon (Editors). A tropical rain forest. A study of irradiation and ecology at El Verde. Division of Technical Information. U.S. Atomic Energy Commission. Oak Ridge, Tennessee.

OGAWA, H., K. YODA, AND T. KIRA. 1961. A preliminary survey on the vegetation of Thailand. Nature Life Southe. Asia 1: 21–157.

————, K. YODA, K. OGINO, AND T. KIRA. 1965. Comparative ecological studies on three main types of forest vegetation in Thailand. II. Plant biomass. Nature Life Southe. Asia 4: 49–80.

RODIN, L. E., AND N. I. BASILEVIC. 1964. The biological productivity of the main vegetation types in the northern hemisphere of the old world. Dokl. Akad. Nauk SSSR 157: 215–218.

————, AND N. I. BASILEVIC. 1968. World distribution of plant biomass. Pp. 45–52. *In* F. E. Eckhardt (Editor). Functioning of terrestrial ecosystems at the primary production level. Proc. Copenhagen Symposium on functioning of terrestrial ecosystems at the primary production level. UNESCO. Paris.

RODRIGUES, W. A. 1967. Inventario florestal pilôto ao longo da estrada Manaus-Itacoatiara, Estado do Amazonas; Dados preliminares. *In* Herman Lent (Editor). Atas do simpósio sôbre a biota amazônica 7 Botánica: 257–267. Conselho de Pesquisas. Rio de Janeiro.

SATTLER, W. 1963. Über den Körperbau, die Ökologie und Ethologie der Larve und Puppe von *Macronema* Pict. (Hydropsychidae), ein als Larve sich von "Mikro-Drift" ernährendes Trichopter aus dem Amazonasgebiet. Arch. Hydrobiol. 59: 26–60.

————. 1967. Über die Lebensweise, insbesondere das Bauverhalten, neotropischer Eintagsfliegen-Larven (Ephemeroptera, Polymitracidae). Beitr. Neotrop. Fauna 5: 89–110.

SCHALLER, F. 1960. Die tropische Bodenfauna und ihre produktions-biologische Bedeutung. Ber. Forsch. Hochschulleb. 1957–1960 (Technische Hochschule Braunschweig) 4: 102–108.

————. 1961. Die Tierwelt der tropischen Böden. Umschau 1961 (4): 97–100.

SCHNEIDER, F. 1939. Ein Vergleich von Urwald und Monokultur in bezug auf ihre Gefährdung durch phytophage Insekten, auf Grund einiger Beobachtungen an der Ostküste von Sumatra. Schweiz. Z. Forstwesen 90: 41–55; 82–89.

SCHULZE, E. D. 1967. Soil respiration of tropical vegetation types. Ecology 48: 652–653.

SMYTHE, N. 1970. Relationships between fruiting seasons and seed dispersal methods in a neotropical forest. Amer. Naturalist 104: 25–35.

STARK, N. 1971. Nutrient cycling II. Nutrient distribution in Amazonian vegetation. Trop. Ecol. 12: 177–201.

STRICKLAND, A. H. 1945. A survey of the arthropod soil and litter fauna of some forest reserves and cacao estates in Trinidad, British West Indies. J. Anim. Ecol. 14: 1–11.

TAKEUCHI, M. 1961. The structure of the Amazonian vegetation. II. Tropical rain forest. J. Fac. Sci. Univ. Tokyo. Section 3. Bot. 8: 1–26.

VOUTE, A. D. 1945–1946. Regulation of the density of the insect population in virgin forests and cultivated woods. Arch. Néerland. Zool. 7: 435–470.

WALTER, H., AND H. LIETH. 1960–1967. Klimadiagramm-Weltatlas. Volkseigener Betrieb Fischer. Jena.

WANNER, H. 1970. Soil respiration, litter fall and productivity of tropical rain forest. J. Ecol. 58: 543–547.

WENT, F. W., AND N. STARK. 1968. The biological and mechanical role of soil fungi. Proc. Natl. Acad. U.S.A. 60: 497–504.

WIEGERT, R. G. 1970. Energetics of the nest-building termite *Nasutitermes costalis* (Holgren), in a Puerto Rican forest. Pp. I 57–I 64. *In* H. T. Odum and R. F. Pigeon (Editors). A tropical rain forest. A study of irradiation and ecology at El Verde. Division of Technical Information. U.S. Atomic Energy Commission. Oak Ridge, Tennessee.

————, AND F. C. EVANS. 1967. Investigations of secondary productivity in grasslands. Pp. 499–518. *In* K. Petrusevicz (Editor). Secondary productivity of terrestrial ecosystems. Vol. 2. Institute of Ecology, Polish Academy of Sciences. International Biological Programme PT. Warsaw and Krakow.

24

Community architecture and organic matter dynamics in tropical lowland rain forests of Southeast Asia with special reference to Pasoh Forest, West Malaysia

TATUO KIRA

Department of Biology, Faculty of Science, Osaka City University, Osaka, Japan

Our knowledge of the floristics, physiognomy, and structure of humid tropical forests has been summarized by Richards (1952), but their properties as a peculiar type of ecosystem remain little investigated. Even after 10 years of International Biological Program (IBP, 1965–74), for instance, relatively few papers offer a reasonable estimate of primary productivity of humid tropical forests (e.g., Müller & Nielsen, 1965; Kira, Ogawa, Yoda, & Ogino, 1967; Ogino, Ratanawongse, Tsutsumi, & Shidei, 1967; Hozumi, Yoda, & Kira, 1969; Odum & Pigeon, 1970; Golley & Golley, 1972; see also the review by Murphy, 1975).

The integrated ecosystem research at Pasoh Forest Reserve, Negeri Sembilan, West Malaysia (1970–74), by Malaysian, Japanese, and British ecologists was one of the efforts to fill this gap (Soepadmo, 1973). Ten Japanese plant ecologists were responsible for the study of primary production and organic matter dynamics within this IBP project. This chapter is a preliminary summary of their studies, drafted on my own responsibility. Additional information on Southeast Asian rain forest ecosystems is also incorporated as far as possible from the experience of the Osaka City University group on tropical ecology.

Community architecture
Tree height
Tropical rain forests of Southeast Asia seem to include the tallest of all similar plant formations in the world. Richards (1974) stated that in African and Latin American tropics he had so far met with only a single tree taller than 60 m, whereas big trees of the same height class are not uncommon in Southeast Asia, especially in the rain forests of eastern Borneo. An example from eastern Kalimantan

562   *Tatuo Kira*

(Fig. 24.1) demonstrates that tall emergent trees in this forest are generally over 60 m in above-ground height. Big trees of *Koompassia excelsa, Shorea* spp., etc. are often taller than 70 m.

The above-ground structure of a forest stand can well be described by the hyperbolic relation between height and stem diameter (DBH) of trees characteristic of each stand (Ogawa, 1969; Kira & Ogawa, 1971; Fig. 24.1). Figures 24.2 and 24.3 relate diameter-height curves from several selected localities in Southeast Asia to differences in climate. Proceeding northward from eastern Kalimantan through the Malay Peninsula to northern Thailand, typical rain forests gradually give way to evergreen seasonal forests and then to deciduous seasonal forests. The transition is associated with a decrease in precipitation and increasing length of dry season and is accompanied by a decrease in tree height. The height of a tree with 1-m DBH is expected to be 61 m at Sebulu (*1*), 47 m at Pasoh (*2*), 46 m at Khao Chong (*3*), 39 m at Sakaerat (*4*), and 32 m at Ping Kong (*5*). The tree height in tropical forests seems to depend largely on the amount and seasonal distribution of rainfall, unless edaphic conditions are very unfavorable. The most luxuriant development of lowland rain forest in eastern Borneo may be ascribed to the abundant rainfall, which is extremely evenly distributed throughout the year.

Fig. 24.1. Hyperbolic relation between DBH and height of trees in equatorial rain forest, Sebulu, eastern Kalimantan, Indonesia.

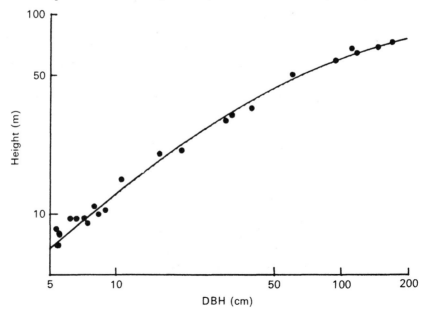

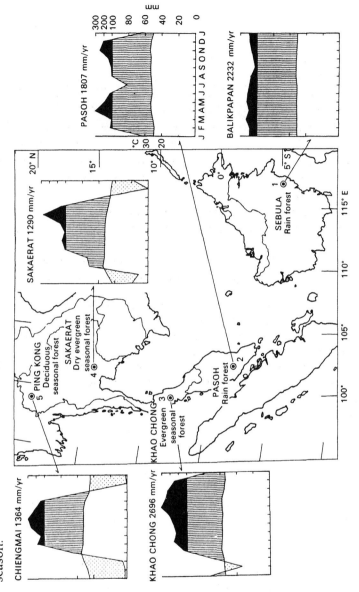

Fig. 24.2. Location and climate of five selected forests in Southeast Asia where tree DBH-height curves of Fig. 24.3 were obtained. Climate diagrams, drawn according to Walter's (1955) method, show annual distribution of monthly mean temperature and precipitation. Dotted areas indicate dry season.

Fig., 2   Location and climate of five selected forests in SE Asia where the DBH-tree height curves of Fig. 3 were obtained. The climate diagrams are drawn according to Walter's (1955) method, showing the annual march of monthly mean temperature and precipitation. Dotted areas indicate the dry season.

564   *Tatuo Kira*

Stratification and profile structure

Richards (1952) considered three stories to be the basic structure of tropical rain forests: (1) a layer of more or less isolated crowns of giant trees overtopping the forest; (2) a layer of the crowns of large trees, which may be dense and continuous in sufficiently humid districts but may be open and discontinuous where the climate is less moist; and (3) a layer of the crowns of small trees, which is not dense and discontinuous in the former case but may become a continuous main canopy in the latter case.

This general principle is applicable to any type of evergreen lowland forest of Southeast Asia except where the soil is very poor or is waterlogged.

Another aspect of forest structure is revealed by examination of the vertical distribution of foliage in a forest profile by means of destruc-

Fig. 24.3. DBH-height curves of trees in five tropical forests of Southeast Asia (see Fig. 24.2). *1*, tropical rain forest, Sebulu, eastern Kalimantan; *2*, tropical rain forest, Pasoh, western Malaysia; *3*, evergreen seasonal forest, Khao Chong, southern Thailand; *4*, dry seasonal evergreen forest, Sakaerat, central Thailand; *5*, deciduous seasonal forest, Ping Kong, northern Thailand.

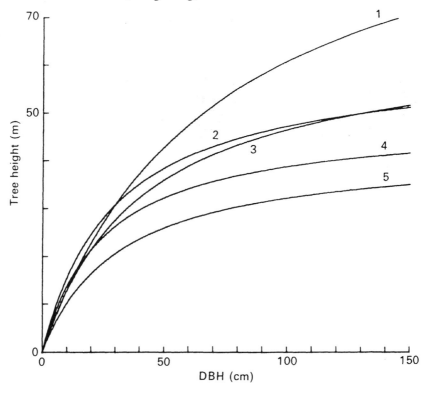

Organic matter dynamics   565

tive sampling (Kira, Shinozaki, & Hozumi, 1969). The profile diagram in Fig. 24.4, showing the vertical distribution of leaf area, leaf biomass, and woody organ biomass, was obtained by clear felling a 20-m by 100-m strip of undisturbed rain forest at Pasoh. All trees on the clear-felled plot were separated into main stem, branches, and leaves according to the so-called stratified clip technique (Monsi & Saeki, 1953) and weighed. The pattern of leaf distribution in Fig. 24.4 indicates the existence of a main canopy at 20–35 m above the ground formed by the dense assemblage of crowns of large trees, corresponding to the second layer of Richards. The leaf area density (LAD) decreases somewhat abruptly above 35 m, where big isolated crowns of giant emergent trees constitute the top layer. The transition from the main canopy to the third layer of small trees is gradual, showing that leaves are distributed more or less evenly between 35 and 10 m. High LAD in the ground layer below 1.3 m and in the overlying layer between 1.3 and 5 m are due, respectively, to the abundant occur-

Fig. 24.4. Profile structure of Pasoh Forest, based on clear felling of 20-m by 100-m strip. (From Kato et al., 1974)

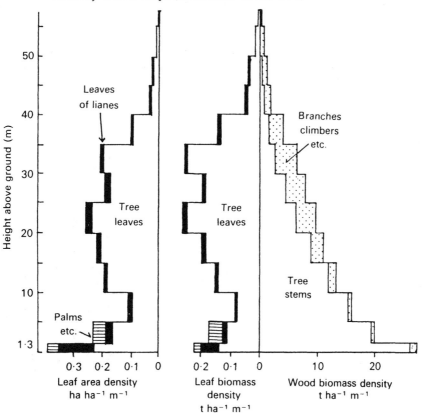

566   *Tatuo Kira*

rence of tree and liane seedlings and to the development of a shrub
layer including many small palms. A gap between shrub layer and
small tree layer does exist, but seems specifically exaggerated in this
destructive sampling plot.

Light profile

The three-dimensional distribution of light intensity and
photosynthetically active radiation was thoroughly investigated by
Yoda (1974c) in and near the destructive sampling plot. Figure 24.5 illustrates how light is successively intercepted by layers of leaf canopy. As the downward attenuation of light through a canopy space is
expected to be exponential if LAD remains uniform (Monsi & Saeki,
1953), a linear regression between log illuminance and above-ground
height in Fig. 24.5 suggests that LAD is almost homogeneous between 10- and 30-m levels. The wide space of the main canopy is
fairly evenly filled with leaves despite the apparent stratification
among component trees.

The mean relative illuminance on the ground surface was only
0.3%–0.4% of incident daylight over the forest, and that at breast
height was less than 0.5%. Such low levels of light at the bottom of

Fig. 24.5. Vertical distribution of mean relative illuminance in
Pasoh Forest. Black dots indicate observations in February 1973;
crosses, observations in July 1971. (From Yoda, 1974c)

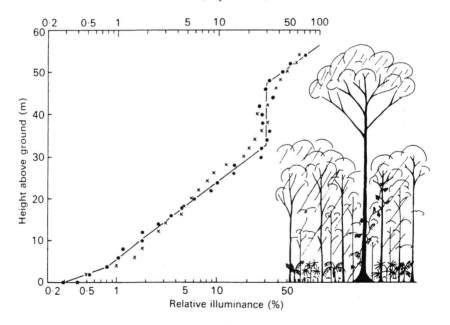

the canopy reflect a large leaf area index (LAI) of Pasoh Forest (about 7 ha/ha for all trees over 4.5 cm DBH).

Considering, however, the enormous height of the forest canopy, the mean LAD is exceedingly small: only 0.12–0.14 m^2/m^3. Even the maximum LAD in the 20- to 25-m layer barely reaches 0.25 m^2/m^3. These values are nearly half as small as the corresponding LAD's in temperate forests and almost 10 times smaller than those in herbaceous communities (Kira et al., 1969). Aoki, Yabuki, & Koyama (1975) pointed out that such a small LAD resulted in greater relative wind velocity inside the forest than in ordinary crop canopies with greater concentration of foliage. This may, in turn, favor the photosynthetic activity of the forest by preventing CO_2 starvation from which herbaceous communities tend to suffer in daylight on fine days.

Primary production rates
Methods

Rates of organic matter production by a plant community can be estimated on different principles. The methods described in the following section intend to estimate the total amount of CO_2 assimilated by the community, whereas the so-called summation method or harvest method arrives at the estimate of production rate by separately measuring the amounts of assimilated organic matter allotted to various community processes, such as community biomass increment, compensation of biomass losses due to animal grazing, death of plants, shedding of plant parts, and respiratory consumption by component plants (Kira et al., 1967; Newbould, 1967).

Plant biomass and biomass increment

The above-ground biomass of Pasoh Forest was estimated by two destructive samplings, in 1971 and 1973, including the clear felling of a 20-m by 100-m plot. Some 160 trees (DBH range from 4.5 cm to 102 cm) were felled and weighed using the stratified clip technique.

A series of allometric correlations among various dimensions of sample trees was empirically established, and a procedure was developed to estimate oven-dry weights of stem, branches, and leaves as well as total leaf area per tree from measured values of DBH. The steps of calculation were:

1. Estimating tree height (*H*) in meters from DBH (*D*) in centimeters

$$\frac{1}{H} = \frac{1}{2.0}\frac{1}{D} + \frac{1}{61}$$

568   *Tatuo Kira*

2. Estimating stem dry weight (w_S) in kilograms from D and H

$$w_S = 0.313(D^2H)^{0.9733} \qquad (D^2H \text{ in dm}^3)$$

3. Estimating branch dry weight (w_B) in kilograms from stem weight

$$w_B = 0.316\, w_S^{1.070}$$

4. Estimating leaf dry weight (w_L) in kilograms from stem weight

$$\frac{1}{w_L} = \frac{1}{0.124\, w_S^{0.794}} + \frac{1}{125}$$

5. Estimating total leaf area (u) in square meters from leaf weight

$$u = 11.4\, w_L^{0.900}$$

The total above-ground weight was calculated as the sum of w_S, w_B, and w_L.

.The total biomass and LAI in a given forest stand could thus be calculated if the DBH of all trees was measured. The biomass of all trees ($D \geqslant 4.5$ cm) on a 0.8-ha area including the clear-felled plot in Pasoh Forest consisted of 346 tons per hectare of stem, 77.9 t/ha of branch, and 7.77 t/ha of leaf, totaling 431 t/ha. The estimate of LAI was 6.87 ha/ha. The above-ground biomass and LAI of smaller undergrowth plants were very variable from place to place, ranging from 0.5 to 8.8 t/ha and 0.23 to 0.95 ha/ha, respectively. The comparison of actually harvested and calculated biomass on the clear-felled plot is shown in Table 24.1. The relative error of estimation was mostly within 10%.

The density of dry organic matter per unit space occupied by the forest is approximately 10.9 kg/m^3 if the average height of very uneven canopy surface is presumed to be 40 m. As the corresponding biomass density is known to range from 1 to 1.5 kg/m^3 in most closed forests (Kira & Shidei, 1967), the above-ground biomass stock in this rain forest seems moderate in proportion to its height.

No attempt was made to estimate total root biomass. Only the amount of fine roots less than 1 cm in diameter was measured by digging out soil cores (Yoda, 1974a). The fine root biomass was fairly evenly distributed everywhere in the forest, amounting to about 20 t/ha.

The LAI estimate of about 7 ha/ha (8 ha/ha on the clear-felled plot) was not as large as expected. The most reliable estimates of LAI, obtained in temperate forests of Japan, are as follows: larch plantation (39 years old), 6.7 ha/ha; secondary beech forest, 6.4 ha/ha; secondary evergreen oak forest, 6.6 ha/ha. All include the leaf area of undergrowth vegetation. The LAI estimate at Pasoh is no less accurate than these values, because all these figures were obtained by taking leaf area samples from every height level of forest canopy. If this is not done, estimates may be subject to a serious bias owing to the remarkable increase in ratio of leaf area to leaf weight from the surface to the bottom of the canopy (Kira et al., 1969; Kira, 1975). Ogawa, Yoda, Ogino, & Kira (1965) and Golley (pers. comm.; see also Golley, 1972) reported LAIs of 12.3 and 20 ha/ha, respectively, from the rain forests of southern Thailand and Panama; however, their method of leaf area sampling was obviously inadequate, so these extraordinarily large values are very doubtful.

The increment of biomass could be estimated by repeating DBH census on the same plot at certain time intervals. DBH increments during a 1.9-year period ranged from nearly zero to 1.3 cm and tended to be greatest in moderate-sized trees of 20–50 cm DBH (Fig. 24.6). Calculated biomass increment rates on the 0.8-ha plot are shown in Table 24.2. These are the result of balance between the growth of surviving trees and the death of a considerable number of small trees during the period.

The annual increment rate of above-ground tree biomass, 5.3 t ha^{-1}

Table 24.1. *Dry weight and leaf area of actually harvested above-ground biomass of trees (DBH ≥ 4.5 cm) and estimates calculated with allometric relations*

	Stem (kg)	Branch (kg)	Stem + branch (kg)	Leaf (kg)	Total (kg)	Leaf area (m²)
Harvested						
A. Trees	56,852	14,288	71,140	853	71,993	6,940
B. Lianes			1,285	45	1,330	463
C. A + B			72,425	898	73,323	7,403
Calculated						
D[a]	53,586	12,550	66,136	924	67,060	7,659
Relative error						
100 (D − A)/A	−5.7	−12.2	−7.0	+8.3	−6.9	+10.4
100 (D − C)/C			−8.7	+2.9	−8.5	+ 3.5

[a]The biomass of lianes was treated as part of their host trees' biomass in the analyses of allometric relation (see Kira & Ogawa, 1971).
Source: Kato, Tadaki, & Ogawa (1974).

570   *Tatuo Kira*

Fig. 24.6. DBH increments in relation to initial DBH in trees of clear-felled plot. Period of observation was 1.9 years, from April 1971 to March 1973. (From Kato et al., 1974)

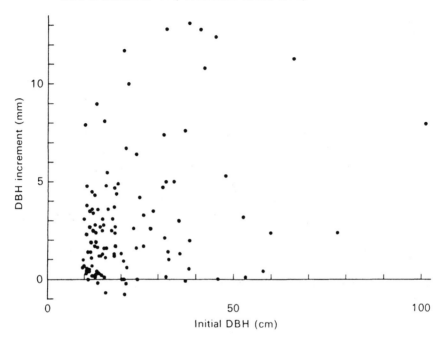

Table 24.2. *Above-ground biomass increment on 0.8-ha plot in Pasoh Forest, calculated from census of DBH of all trees (DBH ⩾ 4.5 cm) in April 1971 and March 1973 (time interval: 695 days)*

	Stem	Branch	Stem + branch	Leaf	Total	LAI (ha/ha)
Biomass in 1971 (t/ha^{-1})	337.74	75.98	413.7	7.61	421.3	6.73
Biomass in 1973 (t/ha^{-1})	345.81	77.85	423.7	7.77	431.4	6.87
Rate of increment (t ha^{-1} yr^{-1})	4.238	0.982	5.221	0.084	5.305	0.074
Relative increment rate (per yr)	0.0125	0.0129	0.0126	0.0110	0.0126	0.0109

yr^{-1}, was so small it could have been easily canceled by the additional death of a tree about 60 cm in DBH per hectare and per year. The plant biomass in this climax rain forest is apparently in an almost stationary state.

Litterfall
Leaves, small branches (diameter ≤ 10 cm), and other fine litter falling to the ground were collected with 30 round funnels (mouth area 1 m^2) placed regularly around a 2-ha plot (including the 0.8-ha plot mentioned above). The rates of fall of branch and bark did not show any appreciable seasonal trend, though the fluctuation from week to week was considerable. The rate of leaf fall tended to reach the maximum in February to April immediately after the minimum of monthly rainfall in January, and another less pronounced peak seemed to occur following a slight drought in midsummer. The fall of flowers, bract, and caterpillar frass was more or less synchronized with that of leaves. Statistical tests suggested that the number (30) of litter receptacles was barely enough to estimate the rate of total litterfall within the relative error of 10%.

The mean fall rates of fine litter are summarized in Table 24.3. The annual amount of total litterfall (11.1 t ha^{-1} yr^{-1}) was nearly twice or three times as large as the litterfall rates observed in temperate forests (Bray & Gorham, 1964; Tadaki & Kagawa, 1968), but was similar to the rates obtained so far in other tropical rain forests (Klinge,

Table 24.3. *Mean fall rates of fine litter on 2-ha plot, including clear-felled plot and 0.8-ha plot (Tables 24.2, 24.6), in Pasoh Forest*

Type of litter	Mean daily rate (gm m^{-2} day^{-1})	Mean annual rate (t ha^{-1} yr^{-1})
Leaf	1.927	7.03
Branch (diameter < 10 cm)	0.666	2.43
Flower	0.022	0.082
Fruit, seed	0.104	0.381
Bark	0.073	0.267
Bud scale, bract, etc.	0.082	0.298
Insect body	0.003	0.011
Insect frass	0.073	0.268
Others	0.090	0.327
Nonleaf litter total	1.114	4.07
Plant litter total	2.964	10.82
Total	3.041	11.10

572   *Tatuo Kira*

1974). More than 97% of this amount was of plant origin, and leaves accounted for about 63%. Dead branches tend to remain on trees for a certain period and are subject to decomposition before falling to the ground, so that the observed amount of branch fall has to be corrected for this prefall decomposition to know the real loss of biomass due to the death of branches.

As for big wood litter (diameter > 10 cm), all pieces of such big wood, either lying on the ground or standing dead, on five 2-ha areas were marked and numbered, the grade of decay recorded in terms of five arbitrary classes established visually, and their length and diameter measured to estimate their volume. The mean bulk density of wood of each decay class was also determined by appropriate sampling. The standing crop of big dead wood ranged between 42 and 65 t/ha and was much greater than the accumulation of other fine dead plant materials on the forest floor (3–5 t/ha). Similar observations repeated semiannually showed that the annual rate of supply of big dead wood to the ground amounted to 3.3–20.5 t ha^{-1} yr^{-1} with an average of 9.3 t ha^{-1} yr^{-1}. It is worthy of note that the rates of fall of fine litter and big wood litter are more or less similar in amount in such a fully mature forest community.

Table 24.4 illustrates the dynamics of big wood litter in the 2-ha plot, where the annual fall rate was the least among the five areas observed. The annual loss of biomass due to the death of big wood was estimated to be 3.7 t ha^{-1} yr^{-1}, considering the prefall decomposition.

Grazing consumption
Among the consumption of net plant production by heterotrophic organisms, only the consumption of leaves by caterpillars was estimated from the amount of frass caught by litter funnels (0.268 t ha^{-1} yr^{-1}; Table 24.3). As the mean efficiency of assimilation by forest caterpillars is around 13%, the rate of their leaf consumption is estimated at 0.31 t ha^{-1} yr^{-1}. Many other animals and heterotrophic plants may utilize live organic matter of plants, and a considerable amount of frass might have been lost without reaching litter funnels. Therefore, this amount, which equals 4% of leaf biomass or annual leaf production, is obviously a minimum estimate of biomass consumption by heterotrophs.

Net production rate
As summarized in Table 24.5, the sum of the rates of biomass increment, litterfall, and grazing consumption gives the first approximation of net production rate at 26.7 t ha^{-1} yr^{-1}. The mean turnover time of above-ground tree biomass is fairly long, amounting to

Table 24.4. *Dynamics of big wood litter (diameter > 10 cm) in same 2-ha plot in Pasoh Forest*

Grade of decay	Mean bulk density (gm/cm^3)	Accumulation on ground (t/ha)	Fall rate (t ha^{-1} yr^{-1})	CO_2 evolution[a] (mg m^{-2} hr^{-1})	Weight loss due to decomposition[a] (t ha^{-1} yr^{-1})
0	0.58	0.3	0.6	1	0.1
1	0.56	0.8	1.2	4	0.2
2	0.54	6.9	0.1	37	1.8
3	0.48	19.0	1.1	125	6.1
4	0.48	11.2	0.3	74	3.6
5	0.39	8.9		75	3.7
Total		47.1	3.3	316	15.5

[a]See text for explanation.
Source: Calculated from data of Yoneda, Yoda, & Kira (1974).

Table 24.5. *Estimation of net production (in t ha^{-1} yr^{-1}) on 0.8-ha plot in Pasoh Forest for 2-year period, April 1971 to March 1973, based on trees over 4.5 cm DBH*

	Stem	Big branch	Small branch	Other plant litter	Leaf	Above-ground total	Root	Total
Biomass increment (Δy)	4.238	0.982			0.084	5.305	0.530[a]	5.83
Litterfall (L')	3.30	2.43		1.36	7.03	14.12		
Estimated biomass loss (L)	3.67[b]	3.47[c]		1.36	7.03	15.53	5.0[d]	20.53
Grazing consumption (G)					0.31	0.31		0.31
Net production ($\Delta y + L + G$)		13.72			7.42	21.14	5.53	26.67

[a]Assumed to be 10% of above-ground biomass increase.
[b]Prefall loss of dry weight assumed to be 10%.
[c]Prefall loss of dry weight assumed to be 30%.
[d]Assumed to be 25% of fine root biomass.

574   *Tatuo Kira*

426/26.7 = 16 years. Kira (1976) obtained the following mean values of above-ground net production rate based on the studies at 316 forest stands in Japan: 11.15 ± 3.75 t ha^{-1} yr^{-1} in boreal conifer forests, 8.74 ± 3.47 t ha^{-1} yr^{-1} in cool temperate deciduous broadleaf forests, 14.25 ± 5.78 t ha^{-1} yr^{-1} in temperate conifer (except pine) forests, 13.64 ± 5.00 t ha^{-1} yr^{-1} in temperate pine forests, and 20.65 ± 7.21 t ha^{-1} yr^{-1} in warm temperate evergreen broadleaf forests. Pasoh Forest is thus considerably more productive than average temperate forests.

However, even temperate forests have been known to produce more than 30 tons of dry matter per hectare annually if the forests are dense enough and in early stages of development (Kira, 1975). Since the net productivity of a forest stand depends greatly on its age or tree size composition (Kira & Shidei, 1967; Kira, 1975), younger forests in the humid tropics may possibly be more productive than the mature forest at Pasoh, as already demonstrated with young plantations of rubber (Templeton, 1968) and oil palm (Ng, Thamboo, & de Souza, 1968).

Community respiration

Estimating the total respiration by a forest community involves serious technical difficulties. In the Pasoh Forest study, the estimate was made on essentially the same principle as first proposed by Yoda (Yoda et al., 1965; Yoda, 1967; Kira, 1968).

Leaf, branch, stem, and root samples of various component plants of Pasoh Forest, including a first-layer tree and 13 other tree species, were enclosed in plastic containers with KOH solution for a few hours under shade on the forest floor to determine the amount of absorbed CO_2 by titration with HCl. An effort was made to minimize (to within 30 minutes) the time from the felling of the sample tree to the start of measurement, because the detachment of samples from the felled tree enhanced their respiration rate to a considerable extent with the lapse of time. The negative effect of enclosing too much sample in a container, due to insufficient air circulation, was also carefully corrected for (Yoda, 1967).

The dark respiration rate of leaves decreased remarkably with the height from which samples were taken or with the mean intensity of light to which they were exposed at their original position in the canopy. As a result, the mean leaf respiration rate per tree increased with tree size or DBH (Fig. 24.7). The mean respiration rate (CO_2 production) in big trees (DBH > 20 cm) was 260–500 mg kg^{-1} hr^{-1} on a leaf fresh weight basis and 1.1–1.7 mg dm^{-2} hr^{-1} on a leaf area basis. These rates were consistent with the results of measurements with an infrared gas analyzer (Koyama, 1974).

Organic matter dynamics   575

Fig. 24.7. Dependence of mean dark respiration rate of leaves per tree on size of tree. Respiration rate expressed on fresh weight basis. (From Yoda, 1974b)

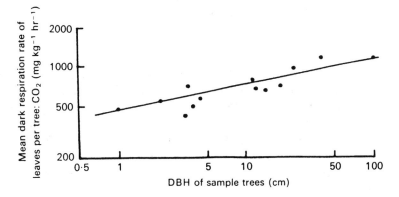

Fig. 24.8. Hyperbolic relations between wood respiration rate (fresh weight basis) and diameter of stem, branch, and root samples, corresponding to equations in text. A. *Shorea globifera*, DBH 32.4 cm. B. Mixed sample of small trees (DBH 3.1–4.2 cm) including *Hopea* sp., *Ochanostachys amentacea*, *Shorea pauciflora*, and *Shorea macroptera*. Cross, root samples. (From Yoda, 1974b)

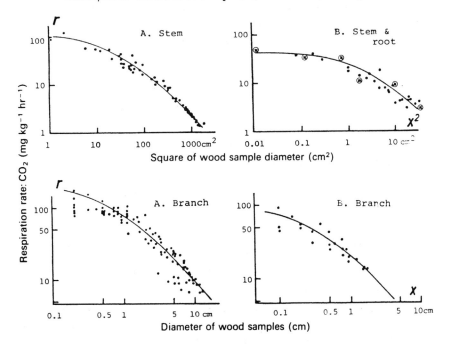

576   *Tatuo Kira*

Respiration rates of stem, branch, and root varied widely depending on their diameter, following the empiric formulation:

$1/r = Ax + B$ for branches
$1/r = Ax^2 + B$ for stem and roots

where r and x, respectively, refer to the respiration rate on a fresh weight basis and the diameter of woody organs (Fig. 24.8). Two coefficients, A and B, differed depending on the size (DBH) of the tree from which samples were collected. Yoda (1974b) calculated the total respiration in woody organs of a tree based on these formulations, considering the effect of tree size on A and B and the frequency distribution of x in the tree, which has been shown to follow a certain simple law (Shinozaki, Yoda, Hozumi, & Kira, 1964).

Combining all these results, the relation between DBH and total respiration per tree was worked out as shown in Fig. 24.9. The whole community respiration was then calculated for the same plot where the net production rate in Table 24.5 was obtained on the basis of DBH census and the relation of Figs. 24.7 and 24.9. The result given in Table 24.6 shows that leaves are responsible for about 53% of the total community respiration, although there is some evidence that the root biomass and root respiration were considerably underestimated because of the lack of actual biomass measurement.

Gross production rate

The gross production is here defined as the sum of net production and dark community respiration, disregarding the photorespiration, which is difficult to measure in situ. The gross produc-

Table 24.6. *Tentative estimates of community respiration and gross production rates in 0.8-ha plot in Pasoh Forest, given in* $t\ ha^{-1}\ yr^{-1}$

	Stem	Branch	Root	Leaf	Total
Respiration rate					
Trees (DBH > 4.5 cm)	5.2	13.1	6.1	26.1	50.5
Smaller trees and					
undergrowth		0.5	0.5	3.0	4.0
Total		18.8	6.6	29.1	54.5
Net production rate					
(trees only)		13.72	5.53	7.42	26.7
Gross production rate					
(trees only)		32.0	11.6	33.52	77.2

Respiration rates (at 25° C) were converted into corresponding rates of organic matter consumption, assuming a conversion factor, 0.61 gm dry matter/gm CO_2 respired.

Organic matter dynamics   577

Fig. 24.9. Respiration rates per tree of different organs in relation to tree size. (From Yoda, 1974b)

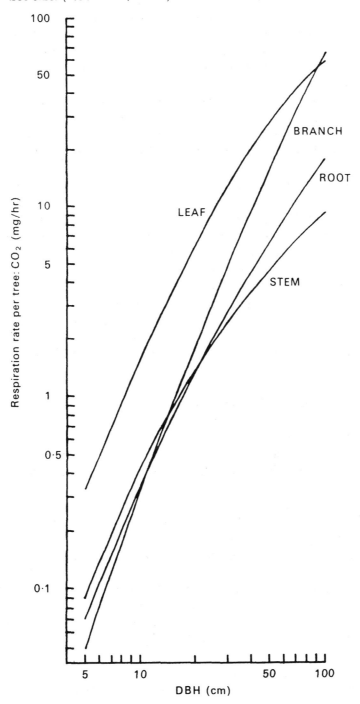

578   *Tatuo Kira*

tion rate in the tree components was estimated at 77.2 t ha^{-1} yr^{-1}. Although the gross production estimates so far reported are not so reliable, particularly with respect to the assessment of respiratory consumption, that of Pasoh Forest is greater than most of the estimates in warm temperate (40–80 t ha^{-1} yr^{-1}), cool temperate (20–40 t ha^{-1} yr^{-1}), and boreal forests (20–50 t ha^{-1} yr^{-1}) (Kira, 1975).

The ratio of net production to gross production was as small as 0.35. Even smaller ratios were reported from a subhumid forest in Ivory Coast (0.26) and an evergreen seasonal forest of southern Thailand by Müller & Nielsen (1965) and Kira et al. (1967), but it is highly probable that they overestimated respiration rates owing to the delay of measurement after the felling of sample trees.

As reviewed by Kira (Kira et al., 1969; Kira, 1975), the gross production rate as well as LAI tend to be greater in forests than in herbaceous communities growing under similar environmental conditions. However, the ratio of net production to gross production may be as large as 0.5–0.6 in the latter, resulting in more or less similar net productivity in both types of plant community. The age and size distribution of trees in a forest stand are additional important factors affecting this ratio, as pointed out above (Kira & Shidei, 1967).

The very small net production/gross production ratio is not inherent in tropical rain forests, but is a common property of forest communities in general, in particular of mature climax forests dominated by a number of big, old trees.

Gross canopy photosynthesis
Net photosynthesis in detached leaves
Koyama (1974) obtained light-photosynthesis curves with detached sun leaves of several tree species at Pasoh. One of the tallest layer species, *Shorea leprosula*, showed a very high rate of net photosynthesis (CO$_2$: 20–30 mg dm^{-2} hr^{-1}) at light saturation. This species is known as a light-demanding pioneer in secondary succession, but is also common in undisturbed rain forests. It is interesting to find that other typical secondary forest species such as *Mallotus, Macaranga,* and *Glochidion* also exhibited fairly high photosynthetic rates ranging from 20 to 25 mg dm^{-2} hr^{-1} of CO$_2$. Shade-tolerant species growing up to the emergent layer (e.g., *Shorea macroptera, Shorea pauciflora, Dipterocarpus crinitus, Dipterocarpus sublamellatus*) were not different from temperate hardwoods in their photosynthetic capacity (CO$_2$: 10–15 mg dm^{-2} hr^{-1}).

Canopy photosynthesis model
Of various canopy photosynthesis models that aim at calculating total canopy photosynthesis from the rate of photosynthesis of

single leaves, Monsi-Saeki's original model (Monsi & Saeki, 1953) was chosen because of its simplicity. It is based on two assumptions:

1. The vertical distribution of light flux density inside a leaf canopy is expressed by an exponential equation
2. All leaves have the same light-response curve given by a hyperbolic equation

The light distribution curve derived from Yoda's (1974c) observation is:

$$I = I_0 e^{-0.696F}$$

where I is light flux density at a given height in the canopy
I_0 is light flux density over the canopy surface
F is cumulative LAI between the height and the canopy surface

The light photosynthesis curve for *Dipterocarpus crinitus*

$$p = 7.422 \times 10^{-4} I'/(1 + 2.412 \times 10^{-5} I')$$

where p is rate of gross photosynthesis on a leaf area basis (mg dm^{-2} hr^{-1} of CO_2)
I' is light flux density on the leaf surface (lux)

is tentatively adopted as the basic equation of item 2. Then, Monsi-Saeki's model gives the rate of gross canopy photosynthesis (P) as:

$$P = \frac{7.422 \times 10^{-4}}{1.679 \times 10^{-5}} \ln \frac{1 + 1.679 \times 10^{-5} I_0}{1 + 1.679 \times 10^{-5} I_0 \exp[-0.696F^*]}$$

where F^* is the total LAI of the forest and assumed to be 8.0 ha ha^{-1}, including undergrowth leaves. A daily curve of I_0 obtained on a fine day in February 1973 (Yoda, 1974c) is utilized to estimate hourly means of I_0, which is then put into the equation to obtain hourly averages of canopy photosynthesis rate.

Assuming a dry matter/CO_2 conversion factor of 0.614, the daily gross photosynthesis on this particular day is estimated at 0.237 t ha^{-1} day^{-1}, which is equivalent to 86.5 t ha^{-1} yr^{-1}. More elaborate calculations would be possible, if more data on photosynthetic rates of leaves from various parts of forest canopy were available, using modified forms of Monsi-Saeki's original model proposed by Saeki (1960), Hozumi, Kirita, & Nishioka (1972), etc. For the moment, however, I can point out that this value is close to the estimate of gross production rate by the summation method, which would be something over 80 t ha^{-1} yr^{-1} if the production rates by smaller trees and undergrowth vegetation were taken into consideration (see Table 24.6).

Micrometeorologic methods

Aoki et al. (1975) made continuous 24-hour observations of micrometeorologic conditions in Pasoh Forest on November 7–8, 14–15, and 21–22, 1973. Anemometer, dry and wet bulb thermometer, and solarimeter were installed at six to eight height levels (0–53 m above the ground) on a walk-up tower constructed near the center of the IBP Research Area at a distance of about 800 m from the primary production study site. Air samples were also led from respective height levels into an infrared gas analyzer on the ground through a system of plastic tubes. The uppermost position of the instruments and air inlet (53 m) was well above the crown of the emergent tree (47 m tall) around which the tower was built. The net flux of CO_2 from the free air to the forest canopy was computed based on the energy balance method.

The authors obtained a CO_2 flux–incident radiation curve from the result of observations and thereby estimated the net daytime flux of CO_2 from the air to the canopy on a day receiving an average amount of radiation (347 cal cm^{-2} day^{-1}, annual mean for 1973 at Pasoh) at 36 kg ha^{-1} day^{-1}, assuming a sine curve for the daily change of solar radiation. This is equivalent to CO_2 flux of about 13 t ha^{-1} yr^{-1}. The negative flux of CO_2 during the night was 15 kg ha^{-1} hr^{-1}. In addition, there is another flux from ground surface to the air as soil respiration, which consisted of the CO_2 flux from the ground covered by fine litter (6.0 kg ha^{-1} hr^{-1}) and that from decaying big wood litter (2.4 kg ha^{-1} hr^{-1}) as stated later. The total annual soil respiration thus amounts to about 74 t ha of CO_2.

Considering the CO_2 budget of the forest, in which the horizontal flux due to advection was neglected because of the sufficient length of fetch (about 1 km), the rate of net canopy photosynthesis is expected to be the sum of the net daytime CO_2 flux and the soil respiration flux: $13 + 74 = 87$ t ha^{-1} yr^{-1} of CO_2. As the mean carbon content of wood was $49.1 \pm 1.0\%$, the dry matter/CO_2 conversion factor is 0.56 gm/gm. The net production rate in terms of dry matter is therefore estimated at 49 t ha^{-1} yr^{-1}.

The dark respiration rate of the above-ground parts of the forest is equal to the difference (CO_2 flux from the canopy to the air at night) minus (soil respiration), i.e., $15 - 6.0 - 2.4 = 6.6$ kg ha^{-1} hr^{-1} of CO_2. The annual rate becomes $6.6 \times 24 \times 365 \times 10^{-3} = 58$ t ha^{-1} yr^{-1} of CO_2. If the top/root ratio in respiration rate is assumed to be 7.3, according to Table 24.6, the total community respiration rate may amount to 66 t ha^{-1} yr^{-1} of CO_2, or to 40 t ha^{-1} yr^{-1} of dry matter consumption if the conversion factor 0.61 gm dry matter/gm CO_2 is applied to this case.

This community respiration rate is considerably smaller than the estimate of Table 24.6 (54.5 t ha^{-1} yr^{-1}), whereas the micrometeorologically estimated net production rate (49 t ha^{-1} yr^{-1}) is nearly twice as large as the result of the summation method (Table 24.5: 24.7 t ha^{-1} yr^{-1}). An overestimate of soil respiration rate might be a possible cause for this inconsistency. If the mean soil respiration rate were smaller by one-third, the calculated rates of net production and community respiration would be about 35 and 57 t ha^{-1} yr^{-1} in dry matter. Further examination and improvement of the methodology of soil respiration measurement seem necessary in this connection.

Decomposition and carbon cycling
Accumulation of dead organic matter
The accumulation of dead organic matter as litter layer on the ground surface (A_0 layer) and in the mineral soil layer down to 1 m depth is shown in Table 24.7. The accumulation of big wood litter

Table 24.7. *Accumulation (tons per hectare) of dead organic matter on forest floor (A_0 layer) and in mineral soil of Pasoh Forest*

	Primary production study site (2 ha)	Mean of four 2-ha plots
Dry matter in A_0 layer		
Leaf litter	1.72	1.65
Small branch litter	2.18	1.90
Big wood litter	47.1	49.0
Other components	0.58	0.79
Total	51.6	53.3
Carbon in A_0 layer		
Leaf litter	0.79	0.76
Small branch litter	1.04	0.91
Big wood litter	23.7	24.6
Other components	0.14	0.19
Total	25.7	26.5
Carbon in mineral soil (1 m depth)	66.2	68.7
Total	91.9	95.2

Source: Yoda (1974a).

(diameter > 10 cm) either lying on the ground or standing dead was vast (about 50 t ha^{-1} on average), whereas the amount of A$_0$ layer, consisting of fine litter only, was small (4.3 t ha^{-1}). The amount of organic matter in the mineral soil layer was about 69 t/ha^{-1} in terms of carbon, being 2.6 times as large as the carbon content of the A$_0$ layer.

If the linear reaction model proposed by Ogawa, Yoda, & Kira (1961) and Olson (1963) is applied to the dynamics of ground surface organic matter, the relative rate of disappearance of fine litter from the A$_0$ layer is calculated as (11.1 t ha^{-1} yr^{-1}) ÷ (4.34 t ha^{-1}) = 2.56 yr^{-1} and that of big wood litter as (9.3 t ha^{-1} yr^{-1}) ÷ (49.0 t ha^{-1}) = 0.190 yr^{-1}. The corresponding 95% disappearance time amounts to 3/2.56 = 1.2 years for fine litter and 3/0.190 = 15.8 years for big wood litter. Fresh, fine litter is expected to disappear almost completely from the ground surface within 14–15 months; newly fallen big wood litter may remain on the ground for 15–16 years before it disappears.

Soil respiration

Weekly observations of soil respiration were made with 30 pairs of Kirita's (1971) apparatus placed along the outer border of the 2-ha plot for primary production study. One of the pairs (an inverted cylindric tin container) was used for measuring the CO_2 output from undisturbed forest floor covered with fine litter; the other was used for determining the output from bare ground surface, where the A$_0$ layer had been completely removed. The difference between the two paired cylinders gave the amount of CO_2 evolved from the A$_0$ layer.

The method employed is a modification of Walter's (1952) apparatus, which consisted of an inverted box containing a certain amount of KOH solution placed on the ground surface. The original method was found to be subject to large error owing to the size of the box, the size of the KOH container, and the concentration of KOH used. The modified method used a piece of plastic sponge as the KOH holder to assure efficient absorption of CO_2. The apparatus was laid both on the undisturbed ground surface covered by litter and on the bare mineral soil surface after removal of all organic materials, in order to assess the CO_2 evolution from the ground surface litter layer. Removal of litter could increase the diffusion rate to and from the mineral soil, but no attempt was made to compensate for this.

The mean soil respiration rate of undisturbed ground surface based on 30 repetitions fluctuated mostly between CO_2 values of 500 and 700 mg m^{-2} hr^{-1} with a mean value of 595 mg m^{-2} hr^{-1} (Fig. 24.10). No apparent seasonal trend was recognized either in soil respiration rate or in soil surface temperature (24°–26° C), but there was some evidence that the moisture content of the A$_0$ layer and soil affected the rate of soil respiration.

On an average, about 76% of the total soil respiration was evolved from the surface of mineral soil. The annual totals were therefore, 52 t $ha^{-1} yr^{-1}$ of CO_2 for total soil respiration and 39.5 t $ha^{-1} yr^{-1}$ of CO_2 for mineral soil.

Beside this CO_2 flux from the open forest floor, an additional flux is supplied to the air by the decomposition of big wood litter. Yoneda (1975a,b) recently found that the rate of CO_2 evolution from decaying wood litter under natural conditions on the forest floor was more or less linearly correlated with the bulk density of the sample wood. Determining this relation experimentally and combining it with the amounts of accumulation of big wood litter of different grades of decay (see Table 24.4), Yoneda, Yuda, & Kira (1974) calculated the dynamics of big wood litter in Pasoh Forest as shown in Table 24.4 and Fig. 24.11.

The estimated mean rate of CO_2 evolution from big wood litter amounted to 317 mg $m^{-2} hr^{-1}$ or 28 t $ha^{-1} yr^{-1}$, which corresponded to the decomposition of dead wood of 15.5 t $ha^{-1} yr^{-1}$. The actually observed rate of supply of dead big wood to the ground (9.3 t $ha^{-1} yr^{-1}$) was much smaller than the estimated rate of decomposition. However, it is probable that the supply and decomposition are more or less balanced if the observation is made on a sufficiently wide area and over a sufficiently long period. The latter may have been too short in this study. In addition, our measurements may have overestimated the CO_2 flux from big wood litter to a certain extent, as only smaller branch wood (diameter 3–4 cm) was used for the measurements for technical reasons. Therefore, it was tentatively assumed that the real rate of decomposition of accumulating big wood litter

Fig. 24.10. Fluctuation of soil respiration rate in Pasoh Forest over period of 1 year. (From Ogawa, 1974)

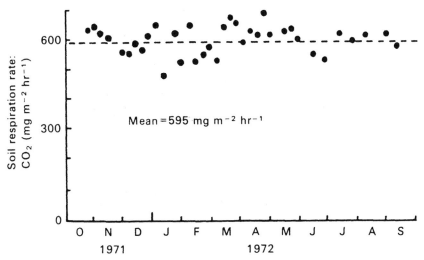

584   *Tatuo Kira*

was about 12 t ha^{-1} yr^{-1}, a rate equivalent to a mean CO_2 evolution rate of 240 mg m^{-2} hr^{-1}.

The sum total of CO_2 supply from decomposing dead organic matter to the air is thus estimated at $595 + 240 = 835$ mg m^{-2} hr^{-1} or 74 t ha^{-1} yr^{-1}.

Carbon cycling in the soil

The dynamics of organic matter in the soil system in terms of carbon pools and flows can be approximated by the model shown in Fig. 24.12. Of the pools and flows that make up the model, the pools in the A_0 layer (M_0) and as humus in mineral soil (M) as well as the fluxes as fine litterfall (L), soil respiration (SR), and CO_2 evolution from mineral soil (SR_M) were actually determined at Pasoh. In the primary production study plot, these were:

fine litterfall (L) = 5.5 t C ha^{-1} yr^{-1}
soil respiration rate (SR) = 14.2 t C ha^{-1} yr^{-1}
CO_2 flux from mineral soil (SR_M) = 10.8 t C ha^{-1} yr^{-1}
carbon pool in A_0 layer (M_0) = 2.0 t C ha^{-1}
carbon pool in mineral soil (M) = 66.2 t C ha^{-1}

Fig. 24.11. Accumulation, rate of supply, and calculated rate of decomposition of big wood litter (diameter > 10 cm) in Pasoh Forest. Figures are averages of five 2-ha plots. (Recalculated from data of Yoneda et al., 1974)

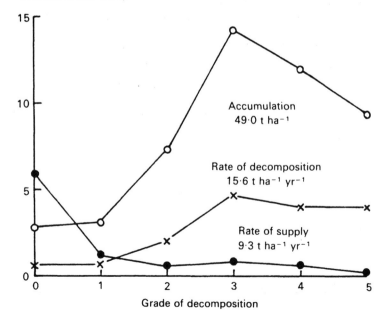

Accumulation
49.0 t ha^{-1}

Rate of decomposition
15.6 t ha^{-1} yr^{-1}

Rate of supply
9.3 t ha^{-1} yr^{-1}

Grade of decomposition

Organic matter dynamics   585

If a completely stationary state is assumed for this forest stand,

CO_2 flux from A_0 layer $(SR_A) = SR - SR_M$
$$= 14.2 - 10.8 = 3.4 \text{ t C ha}^{-1} \text{ yr}^{-1}$$

Downward transport of organic matter from A_0 layer to mineral soil $(V) = L - SR_A = 5.5 - 3.4$
$$= 2.1 \text{ t C ha}^{-1} \text{ yr}^{-1}$$

$k = V/M_0 = 2.1/2.0 = 1.050 \text{ yr}^{-1}$

Since $SR = L + L_R + R$,

$L_R + R = SR - L = 14.2 - 5.5 = 8.7 \text{ t C ha}^{-1} \text{ yr}^{-1}$

Fig. 24.12. A carbon cycling model in forest soils. (From Nakane, 1975)

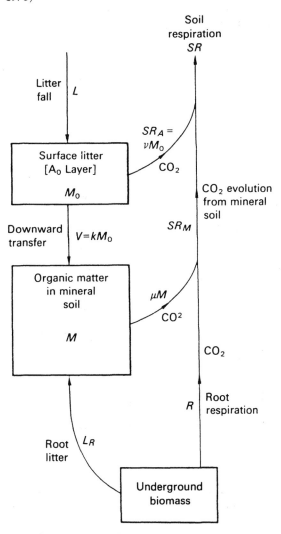

586   *Tatuo Kira*

If one of the two terms, L_R and R, is known, all parts of the model can be described quantitatively.

According to Tables 24.5 and 24.6, however, the carbon equivalents of root respiration (R) and root litter (L_R) are 2.9 t C ha^{-1} yr^{-1} and 2.5 t C ha^{-1} yr^{-1}, respectively, so that the sum (5.4 t C ha^{-1} yr^{-1}) is much smaller than the above figure. Some previous studies (Kucera & Kirkham, 1971; Edwards & Sollins, 1973) estimated the relative share of root respiration in the total soil respiration at 35%–40%. It is, therefore, tentatively assumed in the following treatments that the estimates of R and L_R were both underestimated and that the R/SR ratio equals 0.4.

Fig. 24.13. Carbon cycling in soils of Pasoh Forest and in warm temperate evergreen oak forest at Nara, central Japan. (Data for Nara Forest from Nakane, 1975)

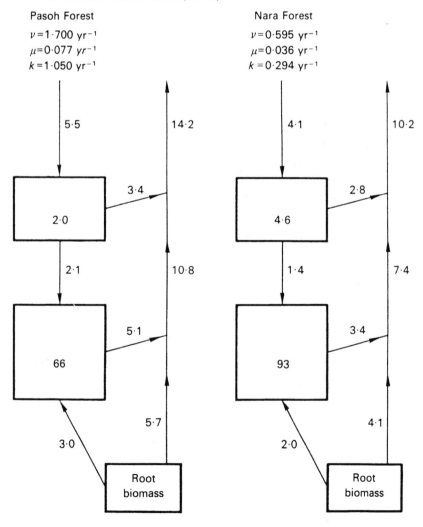

Pasoh Forest

$\nu = 1\cdot700$ yr^{-1}
$\mu = 0\cdot077$ yr^{-1}
$k = 1\cdot050$ yr^{-1}

Nara Forest

$\nu = 0\cdot595$ yr^{-1}
$\mu = 0\cdot036$ yr^{-1}
$k = 0\cdot294$ yr^{-1}

Figure 24.13 illustrates the carbon cycling system in Pasoh Forest soils and in soils of a warm temperate evergreen oak forest at Nara, central Japan. Both forests receive sufficient rainfall, but the annual mean temperature is higher at Pasoh (25° C) than at Nara (13.5° C). With the rise of temperature, the flows increase and the pools diminish in size. (Table 24.8). It is noteworthy that, in response to the temperature rise, all the pools and flows change at more or less the same ratio (1.2–1.5) except for the A_0 pool, which is apparently more sensitive than other parts of the system (2.3 in ratio). Nakane (1975) also found the same relation in the comparison of carbon cycling in the soils on different parts of a slope covered by evergreeen oak forest.

The 95% disappearance time in the A_0 layer, $3/(v+k)$, is 1.1 years at Pasoh and 3.4 years at Nara on a carbon basis, while the 95% decomposition time, $3/v$, is 1.8 years (Pasoh) and 5.0 years (Nara), respectively. That for humus in the mineral soil, $3/\mu$, is much longer, amounting to 39 years at Pasoh and 83 years at Nara.

The decomposition of big wood litter was neglected in the above analyses, because its influence on soil organic matter content seemed very local. However, considerable amounts of dead wood and leaf litter are carried by termites into their mounds (Abe, 1974; Matsumoto, 1974, 1976) and may result in another local cycling of carbon and nutrients characteristic of tropical ecosystems.

Table 24.8. *Effect of temperature on carbon cycling system in terms of ratios in carbon flux and carbon pools in Pasoh Forest (annual mean temperature 25° C) and Nara Forest (annual mean temperature 13.5° C)*

	Pasoh/Nara ratio in flux	Nara/Pasoh ratio in pool
Fine litterfall (L)	1.34	
Soil respiration rate (SR)	1.39	
CO_2 flux from A_0 layer (SR_A)	1.21	
CO_2 flux from mineral soil layer (SR_M)	1.46	
Transport from A_0 to mineral soil layer (V)	1.50	
CO_2 flux from organic matter in mineral soil (μM)	1.50	
Root litter (L_R)	1.50	
Root respiration (R)	1.39	
Carbon pool in A_0 layer (M_o)		2.30
Carbon pool in mineral soil layer (M)		1.41

Source: Data for Nara Forest from Nakane (1975).

588   *Tatuo Kira*

Acknowledgments

This paper is Japanese Contribution No. 10 to the IBP Pasoh Forest Project, supported by the Japan Society for the Promotion of Science, involving the following team members: T. Kira (project leader), H. Ogawa, K. Hozumi, K. Yabuki, K. Yoda, R. Kato, Y. Tadaki, H. Sato, H. Kirita, H. Koyama, M. Aoki, and T. Yoneda. I am grateful to the other members of the Pasoh Forest Project for free use of their original data and for useful discussions.

References

Abe, T. (1974). The role of termites in the breakdown of dead wood on the forest floor of Pasoh Study Area. Malaysian IBP Synthesis Meeting, Kuala Lumpur, August 1974 (unpublished).

Aoki, M., Yabuki, K., & Koyama, H. (1975). Micrometeorology and assessment of primary production of a tropical rain forest in West Malaysia. *J. Agric. Meteor. (Tokyo), 31*, 115–24.

Bray, J. R., & Gorham, E. (1964). Litter production in forests of the world. *Adv. Ecol. Res., 2*, 101–57.

Edwards, N. T., & Sollins, P. (1973). Continuous measurement of carbon dioxide evolution from partitioned forest floor components. *Ecology, 54,* 406–12.

Golley, F. B. (1972). Energy flux in ecosystems. In *Ecosystem Structure and Function,* ed. J. A. Wiens, pp. 69–90. Corvallis: Oregon State University Press.

Golley, P. M., & Golley, F. B. (eds.) (1972). *Tropical Ecology with an Emphasis on Organic Production.* Athens: Institute of Ecology, University of Georgia.

Hozumi, K., Kirita, H., & Nishioka, M. (1972). Estimation of canopy photosynthesis and its seasonal change in a warm-temperate evergreen oak forest at Minamata (Japan). *Photosynthetica, 6,* 158–68.

Hozumi, K., Yoda, K., & Kira, T. (1969). Production ecology of tropical rain forests in southwestern Cambodia. II. Photosynthetic production in an evergreen seasonal forest. *Nat. Life S.E. Asia, Tokyo, 6,* 57–81.

Kato, R., Tadaki, Y., & Ogawa, H. (1974). Plant biomass and growth increment studies in Pasoh Forest. Malaysian IBP Synthesis Meeting, Kuala Lumpur, August 1974 (unpublished).

Kira, T. (1968). A rational method for estimating total respiration of trees and forest stands. In *Functioning of Terrestrial Ecosystems at the Primary Production Level,* ed. F. E. Eckardt, pp. 399–407. Paris: UNESCO.

– (1975). Primary production of forests. In *Photosynthesis and Productivity in Different Environments,* ed. J. P. Cooper, pp. 5–40. Cambridge: Cambridge University Press.

– (1976).*Introduction to Terrestrial Ecosystems, Handbook of Ecology,* vol. 2. Tokyo: Kyoritsu Shuppan. In Japanese.

Kira, T., & Ogawa, H. (1971). Assessment of primary production in tropical and equatorial forests. In *Productivity of Forest Ecosystems, Proceedings of the Brussels Symposium, 1969,* ed. P. Duvigneaud, pp. 309–21. Paris: UNESCO.

Kira, T., Ogawa, H., Yoda, K., & Ogino, K. (1967). Comparative ecological studies on three main types of forest vegetation in Thailand. IV. Dry matter production, with special reference to the Khao Chong rain forest. *Nat. Life S.E. Asia, Kyoto, 6,* 149–74.

Kira, T., & Shidei, T. (1967). Primary production and turnover of organic matter in different forest ecosystems of the Western Pacific. *Jap. J. Ecol.*, *17*, 70–87.

Kira, T., Shinozaki, K., & Hozumi, K. (1969). Structure of forest canopies as related to their primary productivity. *Plant & Cell Physiol.*, *10*, 129–42.

Kirita, H. (1971). Re-examination of the absorption method of measuring soil respiration under field conditions. IV. An improved absorption method using a disc of plastic sponge as absorbent holder. *Jap. J. Ecol.*, *21*, 119–27. In Japanese with English summary.

Klinge, H. (1974). Litter production of tropical ecosystems. Malaysian IBP Synthesis Meeting, Kuala Lumpur, August 1974 (unpublished).

Koyama, H. (1974). Photosynthesis studies in Pasoh Forest. Malaysian IBP Synthesis Meeting, Kuala Lumpur, August 1974 (unpublished).

Kucera, C. L., & Kirkham, D. R. (1971). Soil respiration studies in tallgrass prairie in Missouri. *Ecology*, *52*, 912–15.

Matsumoto, T. (1974). The role of termites in the decomposition of leaf litter on the forest floor of Pasoh Study Area. Malaysian IBP Synthesis Meeting, Kuala Lumpur, August 1974 (unpublished).

– (1976). The role of termites in an equatorial rain forest ecosystem of West Malaysia. I. Population density, biomass, carbon, nitrogen and calorific content and respiration rate. *Oecologia (Berlin)*, *22*, 153–78.

Monsi, M., & Saeki, T. (1953). Ueber den Lichtfaktor in den Pflanzengesellschaften und ihre Bedeutung für die Stoffproduktion. *Jap. J. Bot.*, *14*, 22–52.

Müller, D., & Nielsen, J. (1965). Production brute, pertes par respiration et production nette dans la forêt ombrophile tropicale. *Det Forst. Fors. Danmark*, *29*, 69–110.

Murphy, P. G. (1975). Net primary productivity in tropical terrestrial ecosystems. In *Primary Productivity of the Biosphere*, eds. H. Lieth & R. H. Whittaker, pp. 217–31. New York: Springer-Verlag.

Nakane, K. (1975). Dynamics of soil organic matter in different parts of a slope under evergreen oak forest. *Jap. J. Ecol.*, *25*, 206–16. In Japanese with English summary.

Newbould, P. J. (1967). *Methods for Estimating the Primary Production of Forests: IBP Handbook 2*. Oxford: Blackwell.

Ng, S. K., Thamboo, S., & de Souza, P. (1968). Nutrient contents of oil palms in Malaya. II. Nutrients in vegetative tissues. *Malaysian Agric. J.*, *46*, 332.

Odum, T. T., & Pigeon, R. F. (eds.) (1970). *A Tropical Rain Forest: A Study of Irradiation and Ecology at El Verde*. Oak Ridge, Tenn.: U.S. Atomic Energy Commission. 3 vols.

Ogawa, H. (1969). An attempt at classifying forest types based on the tree height-DBH relationship. In Interim Report of JIBP-PT-F for 1968, ed. T. Kira, pp. 3–17. In Japanese, mimeographed.

– (1974). Litter production and carbon cycling in Pasoh forest. Malaysian IBP Synthesis Meeting, Kuala Lumpur, August 1974 (unpublished).

Ogawa, H., Yoda, K., & Kira, T. (1961). A preliminary survey on the vegetation of Thailand. *Nat. Life S.E. Asia, Kyoto*, *1*, 21–157.

Ogawa, H., Yoda, K., Ogino, K., & Kira, T. (1965). Comparative ecological studies on three main types of forest vegetation in Thailand. II. Plant biomass. *Nat. Life S.E. Asia, Kyoto*, *4*, 49–80.

Ogino, K., Ratanawongse, D., Tsutsumi, T., & Shidei, T. (1967). The primary production of tropical forests in Thailand. *Southeast Asian Studies, Kyoto*, *5*, 121–54. In Japanese.

590   *Tatuo Kira*

Olson, J. S. (1963). Energy storage and the balance of producers and decomposers in ecological systems. *Ecology, 44,* 322–31.

Richards, P. W. (1952). *The Tropical Rain Forest.* Cambridge: Cambridge University Press.

– (1974). Pasoh rainforest in perspective. Malaysian IBP Synthesis Meeting, Kuala Lumpur, August 1974 (unpublished).

Saeki, T. (1960). Relationship between leaf amount, light distribution and total photosynthesis in a plant community. *Bot. Mag. (Tokyo), 73,* 55–63.

Shinozaki, K., Yoda, K., Hozumi, K., & Kira, T. (1964). A quantitative analysis of plant form: The pipe model theory. *Jap. J. Ecol., 14,* 97–105, 133–39.

Soepadmo, E. (1973). Progress report (1970–1972) on IBP-PT Project at Pasoh, Negri Sembilan, Malaysia. In *Proceedings of the East Asian Regional Seminar for the I.B.P., Kyoto,* ed. S. Mori & T. Kira, pp. 29–39. Kyoto: Japanese Natl. Committee for the IBP.

Tadaki, Y., & Kagawa, T. (1968). Studies on the production structure of forest. XIII: Seasonal change of litterfall in some evergreen stands. *J. Jap. For. Soc., 50,* 7–13.

Templeton, J. K. (1968). Growth studies in *Hevea brasiliensis.* I. Growth analysis up to seven years after bud-grafting. *J. Rubber Res. Inst. Malaya, 20,* 136.

Walter, H. (1952). Eine einfache Methode zur ökologischen Erfassung des CO_2-Faktors am Standort. *Ber. Dtsch. Bot. Ges., 65,* 175–82.

– (1955). Klimagramme als Mittel zur Beurteilung der Klimaverhältnisse für ökologische, vegetationskundliche und landwirtschaftliche Zwecke. *Ber. Dtsch. Bot. Ges., 68,* 331–44.

Yoda, K. (1967). Comparative ecological studies on three main types of forest vegetation in Thailand. III. Community respiration. *Nat. Life S.E. Asia, Kyoto, 5,* 83–148.

– (1974a). Carbon, nitrogen and mineral nutrients stock in the soils of Pasoh Forest area. Malaysian IBP Synthesis Meeting, Kuala Lumpur, August 1974 (unpublished).

– (1974b). Respiration studies in Pasoh Forest plants. Malaysian IBP Synthesis Meeting, Kuala Lumpur, August 1974 (unpublished).

– (1974c). Three-dimensional distribution of light intensity in a tropical rain forest of West Malaysia. *Jap. J. Ecol., 24,* 247–54.

Yoda, K., Shinozaki, K., Ogawa, H., Hozumi, K., & Kira, T. (1965). Estimation of the total amount of respiration in woody organs of trees and forest communities. *J. Biol., Osaka City Univ., 16,* 15–26.

Yoneda, T. (1975a). Studies on the rate of decay of wood litter on the forest floor. I. Some physical properties of decaying wood. *Jap. J. Ecol., 25,* 40–6.

– (1975b). Studies on the rate of decay of wood litter on the forest floor. II. Dry weight loss and CO_2 evolution of decaying wood. *Jap. J. Ecol., 25,* 132–40.

Yoneda, T., Yoda, K., & Kira, T. (1974). Accumulation and decomposition of wood litter in Pasoh Forest. Malaysian IBP Synthesis Meeting, Kuala Lumpur, August 1974 (unpublished).

11

Human Impact and Species Extinction

Rodolfo Dirzo and Robert W. Sussman

The sense of crisis implied in the term conservation biology (Soulé 1986) acquires a special significance in the case of the tropics. There are two reasons for this urgency: the disproportionate concentration of biological diversity in the tropics, and the observed and expected magnitude and pace of threats to their survival due to human activities. The papers reprinted in this part were fundamental contributions to a growing literature that raised global concern about human impacts and extinction in tropical regions. These papers served as alarm calls and as conceptual foundations for a developing focus on conservation biology in the tropics.

Tropical Forest Biodiversity: What Is at Stake?

The biological wealth of the tropics is widely recognized (see part 3), particularly in terms of species richness. About two-thirds of the global species diversity of several major groups of organisms is concentrated in tropical ecosystems (Wilson 1992) and the world's most species-rich terrestrial ecosystems are tropical rain forests (Wilson 1988; Gentry 1988a, 1988b; Ashton 1993; Groombridge 1992; Valencia, Balslev, and Paz y Miño 1994; see also part 3). Other facets of tropical biodiversity, although not so widely appreciated, are also noteworthy, including the diversity of plant life forms—trees, shrubs, herbs, arborescent and understory palms, woody and nonwoody epiphytes, lianas, herbaceous vines, and the spectacular semiepiphytic and strangling trees (see part 8). The impressive life form diversity of tropical vegetation signals the wide variety of evolutionary solutions that plants have found to deal with tropical environments (see Ewel and Bigelow 1996 for a splendid discussion of the ecological significance of life form diversity in tropical ecosystems).

A closely related aspect of tropical biodiversity is the diversity of life histories and functional groups that enable plants to adapt and respond to the disturbances tropical forests typically experience under natural conditions (e.g., tree falls or landslides; see part 9). The simplest and most widely recognized classification system of functional groups coadapted to tree fall incidence is that of pioneer and shade-tolerant species (Swaine and Whitmore 1988; see also part 9), but this dichotomy encompasses a variety of functional groups. Denslow (1996) proposed a classification including ten functional groups of plants and five functional groups of fungi, microbes, and animals associated with the response and dynamics of the vegetation to natural disturbances.

Raquet-tailed Kingfisher. From Wallace (1869)

Another obvious facet of tropical biodiversity is the diversity of populations within species, a virtually unexplored aspect in tropical organisms. With the exception of some species of extreme geographic restriction and habitat specialization, such as the plant *Lacandonia schismatica* (Lacandoniaceae), only known from one population in tropical Mexico (Martínez and Ramos 1989), most species are composed of a conglomerate of local populations, many of which may have significant levels of genetic differentiation. Quantitative evidence of this level of tropical biodiversity is largely unavailable, but observations, particularly in species of wide distribution, reveal that in many cases this must be significant. For example, just within Mexico, local populations of the tree *Brosimum alicastrum* (Moraceae) display a surprising variation in height, maximum girth, phenology, bark morphology, seed size, and latex density (R. Dirzo, personal observation). Such intraspecific geographic variation makes it challenging to define the populations as all belonging to the same species without the confirmation of expert taxonomists.

Most of the concerns among scientists, and society in general, regarding the threats to tropical ecosystems emphasize the risk of extinction of species, but consideration should be given also to the risks of extinction of components of other facets of biodiversity. In addition, the loss or major perturbation of tropical forests is likely to bring about significant dislocations or outright loss of indigenous human populations, pharmacopoeias of a plethora of natural products, the loss or disruption of ecosystem services and disruption of regional climates, and a significant contribution to the anthropogenic emissions of greenhouse gases [see a review of these consequences by Laurance (1999); see also part 10]. Finally, conservation is not simply a problem of biology and the natural sciences. It also is a problem that involves the human population and its resources and the distribution of those resources. Thus, conservation programs must address the needs of the people of the countries on which they focus

(see for example Sponsel, Headland, and Bailey 1996).

Habitat Loss and Fragmentation

The second component of the conservation biology crisis in the tropics, namely the magnitude, pace, and pattern of tropical habitat loss and disruption, is receiving considerable public attention and has raised the interest of the scientific community. We may refer to a family of processes because, even though the general notion is that tropical forests are being affected by deforestation, this term conceals many different processes. These forests are being cleared, burned, logged, fragmented, and defaunated, and at levels that greatly surpass historical precedent. The papers of this part provided early warnings on the problem; our perceptions have changed considerably since the 1970s and 1980s. Numerous regional technical accounts (Green and Sussman 1990; Sussman, Green, and Sussman 1996), several global assessments (Lanly 1982; FAO 1993), and some major edited volumes (Sponsel, Headland, and Bailey 1996; Goldsmith 1998) have provided an increasingly comprehensive and multifaceted perspective on tropical deforestation, extinction, and related ecological processes (Whitmore and Sayer 1992; Laurance and Bierregaard 1997). These studies provide valuable insights into how fast tropical forests are disappearing. For example, using satellite imagery, Green and Sussman (1990) found that over a thirty-five-year period (1950–85) 50 percent of the eastern rain forests of Madagascar had been cleared, a rate of 1.5 percent of the original amount per year. Forest loss in different regions was correlated with human population density and to topography, with steep slopes being cleared more slowly.

A net global estimate of tropical deforestation (Whitmore 1997, 5, based on FAO 1993) reports a rate of 15.4 million ha per year. An additional 5.6 million ha is estimated to be logged per year, totaling 21 million ha per year. This implies that roughly 1.2 percent of all remaining tropical forests are cleared or logged annually. A regional dissection of this overall figure shows that, in relative terms (i.e., percent per year), Asia is the most threatened region due to its smaller remaining coverage and high rates. Asia is followed by the Americas and Africa, which are very similar. However, in absolute terms, the Neotropics have the highest rate of conversion (10 million ha/year), followed by Asia (6 million ha/year) and Africa (5 million ha/year). Within continents, rates of conversion are extremely variable among countries, localities, and types of forest. The most threatened areas are those with good access, productive, well-drained soils, and moderate topography—in general, where farming and ranching are feasible (Laurance 1999).

Although most attention has been given to the conversion of tropical rain forests, seasonally dry forests deserve special consideration. Janzen (1988) claimed that "the rain forest is not the most threatened of the major tropical forest types. The tropical dry forests hold this honor" (130) This statement is borne out by the FAO statistics (see Whitmore 1997). Janzen calculated that by the late 1980s out of the original 550,000 km^2 of dry forest on the Pacific coast of Mesoamerica, less than 2 percent was relatively intact. Kramer (1997) provides similar estimates for the region, and Smith (1997) reports an equally dramatic figure (98 percent forest loss) for this type of forest in Madagascar. In fact, satellite images reveal that there are less than 4,500 ha of rich gallery forest remaining in all of southern Madagascar, a type of forest that once bordered all of the rivers of the area (Sussman, Green, and Sussman 1996). In Mexico, seasonally dry tropical forest is particularly rich in plant species and endemism, and this forest type once had an extensive coverage in the country. It is estimated that by 1990 about 27 percent of the original 27 million ha of dry forest remained relatively intact. This forest is presently restricted to protected areas or to areas of difficult access, particularly in terrains with slopes of more than 45° (Trejo and Dirzo 2000).

Conversion to cattle pasture and to agricultural lands and logging are the major proximal

causes of alteration of tropical forest, but these activities vary from region to region and with time. While logging and conversion to agricultural lands have been the predominant drivers in Asia, extensive conversion to cattle ranching has been the predominant factor in many parts of the Neotropics. However, a recent review by Laurance (1998) indicates that logging is increasing aggressively in the Amazon. The author reports that multinational companies now own or control about 4.5 million ha of the Brazilian Amazon, and that the number increases to 12 million ha if Asian timber leases in Guyana, Suriname, and Bolivia are included. Projection of the patterns of land use indicates that a vast proportion of the African tropics will be converted to agricultural lands in the present century (Alcamo, Leemans, and Kreileman 1998).

Several authors advocate logging as a form of land use with considerable potential for wildlife conservation and provision of ecosystem services (Johns 1997), and some argue that selective logging may mimic natural disturbance processes (Hartshorn 1989; Chazdon 1998; see also part 12). In contrast, other authors (e.g., Bowles et al. 1998) emphasize that logging facilitates forest destruction. Overall, the history of logging has shown it to be a destructive force, but the successful cases indicate that if appropriate management principles are applied and an appropriate socioeconomic context is provided, logging may constitute a type of land use with potential to conserve tropical forests (part 12).

In addition to land use, habitat destruction is inextricably linked to the spatial configuration of the remaining habitat, as a mosaic of forest fragments is immersed in a matrix of converted land. Relevant statistics about the global magnitude of tropical forest fragmentation are not available, but satellite images and other remote sensing tools make it readily obvious that fragmentation is a distinctive feature of current tropical landscapes. Some estimates at local to regional scales highlight the magnitude of this phenomenon. For example, in the Brazilian Amazon, the area of forest that is fragmented (forest < 100 km^2 in area) or potentially susceptible to edge effects is more than 150 percent greater than that actually deforested (Skole and Tucker 1993). These figures are even more alarming in smaller regions such as Madagascar, where there are few large areas of forest remaining (Green and Sussman 1990)

Finally, in conjunction with the patterns of land use and cover change, a major surge of overexploitation of many species of plants and animals is presently taking place in many tropical ecosystems. Some logging operations constitute a readily obvious case of plant overexploitation, but a significant spasm of defaunation, particularly of medium to large vertebrates, is also taking place. Although defaunation is not nearly as visible as deforestation or timber exploitation and is therefore very difficult to quantify, the limited available evidence underscores its magnitude. For example, it has been estimated that subsistence hunting in the Brazilian Amazon may eliminate about 9.6 to 23.5 million mammals, birds, and reptiles per year (Redford 1992; Robinson, Redford, and Bennett 1999). Additional defaunation takes place due to commercial hunting and, above all, as an indirect effect of land use patterns. For instance, deforestation and forest fragmentation have contributed significantly to the local loss of several terrestrial vertebrates in the region of Los Tuxtlas, Mexico (Dirzo and Miranda 1991).

The fact that coincidence of exuberant tropical biological diversity with current patterns of land use and overhunting has the potential to trigger a major pulse of extinction of species or populations in tropical ecosystems has captured the attention of scientists and the general public. This situation requires a major international effort to be deployed if we are to preserve this most critical reservoir of planetary biological diversity. All of these issues, which at present constitute a vigorous field of basic and applied research, were addressed with different emphases and with perspectives sometimes appropriate to their times of publication, and sometimes with a remarkable forward-looking vision, by the five papers reprinted here. Our current knowledge of interconnections is still

very limited, but the papers in this part have been an important incentive and source of inspiration for present research in tropical conservation biology.

Foundations of Tropical Conservation Biology

One of the most compelling early alarm calls to the threats to tropical rain forests was given in a classic paper by Gómez-Pompa, Vázquez-Yanes, and Guevara (1972; paper 47). Their central argument is that the rain forests, throughout their range, are incapable of regenerating under present land use practices and thus constitute a nonrenewable resource. The authors, authorities on rain forest succession, described the regeneration process of the rain forest under natural conditions, with the aim of showing how the natural dynamics of regeneration were compatible with the activities of "primitive man" (see parts 9 and 12). In contrast, under modern, predominantly intensive and extensive use of land, sources of seeds for regeneration of primary tree species become increasingly less available due to their limited dispersal capabilities and the usually low densities of individuals (part 8). They predicted that, apart from cattle pastures and agricultural fields, tropical landscapes of the future would consist of secondary species mixed with species from drier environments. They also argued that some of the present tropical vegetation types with those characteristics, such as semievergreen forests and savannas, may have been the result of historical disturbance, highlighting the role of history in forming contemporary landscapes. The authors' conclusion, that the consequences of a mass extinction of species associated with tropical forest destruction are nonpredictable and that a major international effort is needed to preserve tropical forests and to understand those connections, was as valid then as it is today.

Following this initial warning, case studies were undertaken to assess the loss of species associated with forest destruction. Two of the papers reprinted in this part, those by Diamond (1973; paper 49) and Willis (1974; paper 50), are representative of these efforts. An important framework for these studies was the application of island biogeography theory (MacArthur and Wilson 1967, chap. 2). This theory proposed that at equilibrium, that is, when the immigration rate equals the extinction rate, there will be more species on a large island than on a small one. In addition, there should be more species on islands located closer to other land than on remote islands. Rates of extinction increase with decrease in size of the islands, presumably because of lower population sizes. In the case of supersaturated islands, certain species are particularly susceptible to extinction and they tend to disappear first. Also, the species that arrive first to an initially empty island tend to be those with superior dispersal ability (the taxon cycle; see part 6). Diamond (1973) applied several paradigms of island biogeography theory to address issues related to the variation in bird species diversity on true islands (New Guinea and satellites), as well as on the ecological "island archipelago" constituted by the isolated mountain ranges surrounded by a sea of uninhabitable lowlands in New Guinea. This paper is full of erudite analytical insights and discusses several issues of potential relevance to conservation biology. In his island-based study, Diamond (1973) provided a critical framework for assessing the effects of reduction, fragmentation, and isolation of formerly continuous tropical forests on species distributions and rates of extinction.

An unwitting "experiment" that permitted an assessment of the validity of some of the previous conclusions was that of the creation of Barro Colorado Island, Panama, a hilltop of 15.6 km² of lowland tropical forest. This island was created when Gatun Lake rose behind a dam on the Chagras River, forming the central section of the Panama Canal in 1910–14. Willis (1974), in a paper reprinted here, describes the population dynamics and local extinctions of ant-following birds after this isolation event. Willis found that a selective process of defaunation took place. Small species maintained stable populations, medium-sized species decreased in abundance, and large species of low

initial abundance declined to near extinction. Willis referred to this pattern of selective extinction as "truncation"—a phenomenon we see frequently today. Two important lessons can be learned from these two studies with birds. First, the loss of species caused by the small size and isolation of the remaining forests poses problems not only for the conservation of species but for studies aimed at understanding the ecology of tropical ecosystems. Second, at least in the case of birds, future forest reserves should have, whenever possible, corridor zones to reduce the impacts of isolation.

In a subsequent stage, studies began to focus on estimating and projecting rates and patterns of extinction and on linking the pace and patterns of tropical land use with biodiversity loss. Simberloff (1986; paper 52) addressed the question of whether we are on the verge of a mass extinction in tropical rain forests due to deforestation leading to habitat loss. Set against a background of the history of mass extinctions, Simberloff used species-area and rarefaction models to estimate species extinction rates for Neotropical plants and birds due to estimated loss of tropical forest cover. The projected numbers of species of plants and birds at equilibrium suggested quite dramatic potential losses of species of these two important groups of tropical organisms. Later projections of species extinction based on the species-area paradigm, but considering varying scenarios of deforestation and slopes of the species-area relationship, yielded equally dramatic predictions. For example, Reid (1992) forecast for year 2040 that extinction of tropical closed-forest species at equilibrium would range from 4–8 percent to 17–35 percent under optimistic and pessimistic scenarios of deforestation, respectively. Depending on the assumed number of global species, such estimates translate into dramatic numbers of species extinction. For example, with roughly ten million species on Earth, under an intermediate scenario of deforestation (10 million ha/year), estimates would amount to between eight thousand and twenty-eight thousand species per year, or twenty to seventy-five species per day. These estimates have encountered considerable skepticism (e.g., Heywood and Stuart 1992), yet most of the researchers who have made such forecasts argue that those numbers correspond to equilibrium points and that the figures refer to species committed to extinction. In addition to several statistical problems (reviewed by Simberloff 1992), an important limitation to this argument is that there is no reliable theory or empirical evidence to assess when equilibrium has been reached (Simberloff 1992).

Aside from the problems mentioned above, two additional assumptions limit the use of the species-area relationship in predicting the effects of deforestation (habitat loss) on species extinction (Simberloff 1992). One limitation is that the model assumes uniform habitat and species distributions. Tropical forests, however, are heterogeneous mosaics of habitat and some areas are particularly diverse or contain higher numbers of endemics (part 8). Given that some areas of high species richness seem to be particularly threatened by deforestation (see Raven 1988), more species are likely to be lost via deforestation than reductions in area would predict. Furthermore, the remaining area after a given pulse of deforestation generally does not consist of continuous forest but rather of forest fragments. An important source of information necessary to assess species extinction associated with land use is the distribution and rarity of species at several scales (see part 8). In a remarkable study on the distribution of a large number of tree species from upper Amazonian forests, Pitman et al. (1999) unraveled some unexpected patterns. The majority of the tree species are geographically widespread, a low proportion is restricted to a single forest type (habitat type), and most can be found *somewhere* in relative abundance, although 88 percent of the species had less than one individual per hectare overall. Such patterns of rarity are far from the commonly predicted worst-case scenario of tropical plant conservation. However, the fact that most species were scarce at small spatial scales underscores the importance of protection of tropical trees in very large reserves. These patterns also emphasize that even

if very extensive deforestation is necessary to drive global extinction of these trees, forest loss and fragmentation at a local scale are likely to lead to local population extinction and genetic erosion, as Heywood and Stuart (1992) pointed out.

Simberloff (1992) argued that habitat fragmentation threatens the survival of species quite independently from the loss predicted by the species-area relationships. This situation has stimulated work on areas such as the dichotomy of a single large or several small refuges (SLOSS) to investigate whether conservation efforts should aim at establishing a single large or several small refuges of equivalent area. Another fruitful line of research derived from the observation of the spatial configuration of the remaining forest is the observational or experimental evaluation of the ecological consequences of fragmentation. A recent review on the local loss of species in fragments of tropical rain forests (Turner 1996) yielded several conclusions. First, isolated fragments suffered species reductions with time after separation from continuous forest. The mechanisms of local extinction associated with fragmentation include the direct negative effects of human disturbance during and after habitat destruction, reductions in population size and immigration rates, edge effects, and alterations of biotic interactions leading to disturbances of community structure and higher-order effects. Another important conclusion of this review relates to the truncation effect illustrated in Willis's 1974 paper. Turner concluded that animals that are large, sparsely distributed, or very specialized in their diet are particularly susceptible to local extinction. The same conclusion applies to animals that are intolerant of the vegetation surrounding fragments.

Of particular relevance in this context is a megaproject on the biological dynamics of tropical forest fragments (BDFF) (formerly known as the Minimum Critical Size of Ecosystems Project), in Central Amazonia, Brazil (Bierregaard et al. 1992). This experiment, which established replicated forest fragments of varying sizes in land being converted to pasture, has yielded a significant proportion of our knowledge on the consequences of forest fragmentation in tropical ecosystems. Thus, our knowledge of this theme may be idiosyncratic and Turner (1996) makes a plea for studies to be undertaken in other tropical ecosystems.

It is significant that Simberloff's paper, reprinted here, not only cited studies addressing the role of fragmentation on potential species loss in, but also referred to the need for studies on the disruption of linkages between species (part 4). As he mentions, such linkages "are complex and numerous in the tropics, so that extinction of one species will likely have cascading effects that lead to other extinctions" (Simberloff 1986, 176). A recent review by Pace et al. (1999) also illustrates the occurrence of cascading effects in tropical ecosystems (see part 4). Tropical conservation biology now needs to incorporate the study of the conservation of ecological and evolutionary processes and to accommodate such study into the documentation of patterns and causes of local extinction.

One early step in this direction is Johns's (1986; paper 51) study, reprinted here, on the behavioral ecology of a group of six species of primates before and after selective logging operations in a lowland rain forest in Peninsular Malaysia. Interestingly, although the paper reports on just the first twelve months after the onset of logging, all the species of primates studied persisted without showing significant declines in their populations. It appears that the main effects of the logging operation were reductions and modifications of the degree of patchiness of the feeding resources. Primates displayed a variety of behavioral and foraging responses that allowed them to adjust to the modifications of the habitat and feeding resources. Johns was cautious in stressing that the remarkable degree of flexibility that allowed these species to persist in the logged forest is not necessarily shared by other primate species. The study continues, and Johns (1997) reports that the primates continue to recover. Possible subsequent consequences of the behavioral responses observed were not investigated in this study, and may have shown

additional direct and indirect effects. For example, the shifts in diet displayed by some of the species may lead to alterations of the patterns of seed dispersal or changes in the herbivory regimes of some plant species, which in turn may affect arthropod communities (part 4). Recent studies on the ecological role of other canopy primates (e.g., Chapman and Onderdonk 1988; Julliot 1999) suggest that these effects are possible. In raising these critical questions, Johns's study was an important step in addressing some potential consequences of forest disturbance on ecological processes involving animals and their food plants. The impact of forest disturbances on biotic interactions and trophic cascades is presently a vigorous area of research that may advance our understanding and management of tropical forests.

Conclusion

This collection of papers offered an important background to our understanding of the major threats tropical forests are facing currently and to the sorts of research and actions that may be needed to address the conservation of tropical ecosystems. However, conservation is not just a problem of biology and the natural sciences. It is also a problem that concerns resources available to human populations and the distribution of these resources. For example, it is possible that the ecological carrying capacity of humans already may be exceeded in several regions of tropical Africa (Myers 1993; Butynski 1996/97). Cooperation among biological and social scientists, government and nongovernment agencies, and local peoples will be necessary to save the vital resources of tropical forests for future generations.

We still have much to understand about the effects of human impacts on species extinction in tropical forests. It is worth noting that the massive extinctions predicted to occur in Mexico due to large-scale deforestation (Gómez-Pompa, Vázquez-Yanes, and Guevara 1972) have not yet occurred (Gómez-Pompa and Kaus 1999). Brown and Brown (1992) noted that little or no species extinction has yet occurred in the Atlantic rain forests of Brazil, despite massive deforestation, degradation, and fragmentation. A substantial number of species considered to be extinct from Atlantic rain forest twenty years ago have been rediscovered in isolated patches of habitat (Brown 1991). Over time, large-scale destruction and fragmentation of tropical forests will likely cause genetic erosion within populations and will increase vulnerability to extinction, particularly for small populations (Heywood and Stuart 1992). Perhaps we have underestimated the resilience of many populations that are currently finding refuge in patches of degraded forests, in secondary forests, in traditional agroforestry systems, or in other human-dominated systems (Brown and Brown 1992; Turner and Corlett 1996; Sosa and Platas 1998). The outcome may well depend upon the extent to which this resilience can compensate for our human failures to manage sustainably and conserve tropical forests (part 12).

Reprinted Selections

A. Gómez-Pompa, C. Vázquez-Yanes, and S. Guevara. 1972. Tropical rain forest: A nonrenewable resource. *Science* 177:762–65

J. M. Diamond. 1973. Distributional ecology of New Guinea birds. *Science* 179:759–69

E. O. Willis. 1974. Population and local extinctions of birds on Barro Colorado Island, Panamá. *Ecological Monographs* 44:153–69

A. D. Johns. 1986. Effects of selective logging on the behavioral ecology of West Malaysian primates. *Ecology* 67:684–94

D. Simberloff. 1986. Are we on the verge of a mass extinction in tropical rain forests? In *Dynamics of Extinctions*, edited by D. K. Elliot, 165–80. New York: Wiley. Reprinted by permission of John Wiley & Sons, Inc.

ment needs to be nearly instantaneous in order to make the neural quantum, the NQ, maximally visible.

When the increment is added to a steady background stimulus, the observer adopts a 2-quantum criterion. The NQ theory then predicts a rectilinear function whose location determines the slope: the smallest increment that is always detected is two times the largest increment that is never detected. Thus, the slope is inversely proportional to the size of the NQ.

Data fulfilling the NQ prediction have been obtained in a dozen different investigations over a span of four decades. Poikilitic functions having the predicted form have been obtained under a variety of procedures, often by experimenters who did not subscribe to the NQ theory. Some 140 NQ functions are presented, illustrating steplike functions for auditory loudness and pitch, and for

three types of visual patterns. The gating mechanism that produces the NQ function is probably central rather than peripheral.

References and Notes

1. E. G. Boring, *Amer. J. Psychol.* **37**, 157 (1926).
2. C. S. Peirce and J. Jastrow, *Nat. Acad. Sci. Mem.* 3, 11 pp. (1884).
3. A. D. Whalen, *Detection of Signals in Noise* (Academic Press, New York, 1971).
4. D. M. Green and J. A. Swets, *Signal Detection Theory and Psychophysics* (Wiley, New York, 1965); J. A. Swets, *Science* 134, 168 (1961).
5. G. v. Békésy, *Ann. Physik* 7, 329 (1930); English summary in *Experiments in Hearing* (McGraw-Hill, New York, 1960), p. 238.
6. S. S. Stevens, *Science* 118, 576 (1953); *ibid.* 170, 1043 (1970).
7. ——— and J. Volkmann, *ibid.* 92, 583 (1940).
8. S. S. Stevens, C. T. Morgan, J. Volkmann, *Amer. J. Psychol.* 54, 315 (1941).
9. G. A. Miller, *J. Acoust. Soc. Amer.* 19, 609 (1947).
10. J. Markowitz, *Investigation of the Dynamic Properties of the Neural Quantal Model* (Bolt Beranek & Newman, Cambridge, Mass., 1966).
11. U. Neisser, *Amer. J. Psychol.* **70**, 512 (1957).
12. G. A. Miller and W. R. Garner, *ibid.* 57, 451 (1944).
13. C. J. Duncan and P. M. Sheppard, *Proc. Roy. Soc. London Ser. B* 158, 343 (1963).
14. W. R. Garner and G. A. Miller, *J. Exp. Psychol.* 34, 450 (1944).
15. B. M. Flynn, *Arch. Psychol.*, No. 280 (1943).
16. J. F. Corso, *Amer. J. Psychol.* 64, 350 (1951).
17. W. D. Larkin and D. A. Norman, "An extension and experimental analysis of the neural quantum theory," in *Studies in Mathematical Psychology*, R. C. Atkinson, Ed. (Stanford Univ. Press, Stanford, Calif., 1964), p. 188.
18. R. D. Luce, *Psychol. Rev.* 70, 61 (1963).
19. D. A. Norman, *J. Math. Psychol.* 1, 88 (1964).
20. L. T. Troland, *The Principles of Psychophysiology*, vol. 2, *Sensation* (Van Nostrand, New York, 1930); C. H. Graham, Ed., *Vision and Visual Perception* (Wiley, New York, 1965).
21. C. G. Mueller, *J. Gen. Physiol.* 34, 463 (1951).
22. H. R. Blackwell, *Psychophysical Thresholds* (Engineering Research Institute, Univ. of Michigan, Ann Arbor, 1953), Bull. No. 36.
23. M. B. Sachs, J. Nachmias, J. G. Robson, *J. Opt. Soc. Amer.* 61, 1176 (1971).
24. S. S. Stevens and J. Volkmann, *Amer. J. Psychol.* 53, 329 (1940).
25. This research was supported by the National Institutes of Health, grant NS-02974 Laboratory of Psychophysics report PPR-372-137).

The Tropical Rain Forest: A Nonrenewable Resource

A. Gómez-Pompa, C. Vázquez-Yanes, S. Guevara

There is a popular opinion that the tropical rain forests because of their exuberant growth, their great number of species, and their wide distribution will never disappear from the face of the earth.

On the other hand, it has often been stated that the tropical rain forests (tall evergreen forests in tropical warm and humid regions) around the world must be protected and conserved for the future generations (1). It has also been stated that it is most important that knowledge about the structure, diversity, and function of these ecosystems has priority in future biological research (2). Unfortunately, either these voices have not been heard or their arguments have not been convincing enough

The authors are in the department of botany at the Institute of Biology, National University of Mexico, Mexico 20, D.F.

to promote action in this direction.

It is the purpose of this article to provide a new argument that we think is of utmost importance: the incapacity of the rain forest throughout most of its extent to regenerate under present land-use practices.

Even though the scientific evidence to prove this assertion is incomplete, we think that it is important enough to state and that if we wait for a generation to provide abundant evidence, there probably will not be rain forests left to prove it.

During the last few million years of their evolution, the rain forests of the world have produced their own regeneration system through the process of secondary forest succession. This regeneration system evolved in the many clearings that occurred naturally as a result of river floods, storms, trees

that die of age, and the like. The genetic pool available for recolonization was great, and a number of populations and species with characteristics that were advantageous in the rapid colonization of such breaks in the continuity of the primary rain forest were selected. These plants were fast-growing heliophytes, with seeds that have dormancy and long viability, and efficient dispersal mechanisms (3, 4). These sets of species played a fundamental role in the complex process of regeneration of the rain forest, and it is astonishing that very little is known about their biology, their behavior in the succession, and their evolution, even though they are the key to understanding the process of secondary succession, which is one of the most important ecological phenomena. The few works on the subject point out that there are certain repetitive patterns that can be predicted and that the species involved are fundamentally different from the primary species (5–7).

It is still uncertain how most of the primary species of the rain forest reproduce themselves and how the forest is regenerated, but from the evidence available it seems that there is a very complex system working at different times and in different directions, depending on the local situation and the plants involved (3).

One of the most important aspects

of natural regeneration is that on the floor of the primary rain forest there are always seedlings of young plants of many of the primary tree species. Under the effects of disturbance these seedlings will continue growing at an increased rate (8), and, at the same time, the secondary species start growth from dormant seeds in the soil. After several years the primary species will have grown taller than the secondary ones, and the major step in the regeneration has been accomplished.

There are taking place at the same time other processes, such as the colonization of trees and shrubs by epiphytic plants, about which even less is known, as well as the growth and establishment of climbing plants that has occurred probably since the early stages and of which many species will grow to the upper canopy of the rain forest. In all these cases the key plants are the seedlings of tall primary trees that will take over the upper canopy of the old successional series.

The regeneration of these primary species by the seedlings or young plants inside the forest is not the only possible way. Another important means of regeneration comes from seeds in the soil (9). In tropical rain forests this type of regeneration seems to be very effective mainly for species that happen to be in fruit during the disturbance of the area, because apparently there is a very short dormancy of the seeds of most of the primary species and the entire life of seeds of tropical tree species is in many cases very short (8, 10–12).

It seems appropriate to mention that we realize, of course, that the many, and quite different, primary tree species in the rain forests of the world may behave very differently in their germination responses and life-span. The available evidence indicates, nevertheless, that many primary tree species have large seeds (8, 13) with either short dormancy or none at all (10). The biological implications of this phenomenon are barely known (14), but it seems that the general trend is toward rapid germination, which is usually advantageous to the survival of the species. If one considers the predators of all types (fungi, bacteria, animals of various types) that are present in tropical warm and humid conditions, it seems reasonable to attribute survival power to the species, the seeds of which can germinate quickly and the seedlings of which can remain

alive for a long time in a slow-growing condition (8). The scarcity of seeds of primary trees stored in soils from rain forests has been demonstrated in one area in Mexico (9), but many more studies in this direction are needed, even though this fact has been noted earlier (8, 11).

Another possibility for the establishment of primary tree species in the early stages of regeneration is by long-distance dispersal by birds and by other animals such as monkeys, rodents, and others.

Very little is known about fruit and seed dispersal of tropical forest species (12, 15), but it seems that long-distance dispersal has played, and is playing, an important role in areas where human disturbance has not reached a critical level. The phenomenon of long-distance dispersal of tropical trees has almost never attracted the attention of researchers, but it may be extremely important in understanding the evolution of local populations and the adaptation to local ecological conditions (16), even though, from the point of view of regeneration, it may have little importance. Still another means of reestablishment of primary species in the early stages of succession is vegetative reproduction by means of rhizomes, bulbs, and roots that may remain alive after the destruction of the original forest and become active soon after the disruption.

Man and the Tropical Rain Forest

All that has been considered to this point concerns natural regeneration caused by natural catastrophes. The regenerative system of the rain forest seems to be very well adapted to the activities of primitive man. The use of small pieces of land for agriculture and their abandonment after the decrease of crop production (shifting agriculture) is similar to the occasional destruction of the forest by natural causes (17, 18). This type of activity can still be seen in many tropical areas where a mosaic pattern can be found, with large pieces of primary rain forest and patches of disturbed forest of different ages from the time of their abandonment. Several studies of these successional series are available (9, 17, 19–21), and in most cases they tend to agree that shifting agriculture has been a natural way to use the regenerative properties of the rain forest

for the benefit of man. How this operates is not well known, but we can extrapolate our knowledge of the natural regeneration of the rain forests and compare it with the data available. After the abandonment of the land by the primitive farmer, regeneration starts with the available seeds and other propagules in the soil. At present the seeds known to remain viable in the soil are mainly those of secondary species (9). After cultivation of an area, the possibility of any seedlings or young plants of the trees of the closest primary forest persisting is almost nil, and, because of the time involved in crop production, most of the future propagules of primary trees have to come in by natural dispersal (such as animals, water, gravity, or air).

There are several problems involved in connection with the speed of regeneration under these circumstances, but, in general, one can say that under the shifting cultivation system, the genetic pool of primary trees is retained, and from this pool comes the raw material for the successional processes. Of course, this is true in all cases where demographic pressure has not forced an intensive shifting agriculture with short periods of recovery, as in some tropical regions (20, 22).

We think that it is evident that the importance of retaining pieces of the original forest as the only way to reconstruct future forests cannot be overstressed. Whether the system of shifting agriculture is responsible for the extinction or simplification of some of the present tropical ecosystems is not completely certain, but it does seem clear that it prevents a mass extinction of species.

We cannot overstress the importance of the space factor in these considerations, because it makes an enormous difference if we use or destroy thousands of square kilometers or if we destroy one or two.

The Tropical Rain Forest in the Green Revolution Era

In recent times the trend in many tropical areas has been to look for ways to make permanent use of the land, in contrast with the old way of shifting cultivation. Permanent use can be accomplished with the help of the new technology and chemicals that have proved to be successful in many tropical areas.

Fig. 1. This destruction of a rain forest in southern Mexico is an example of what is occurring in large areas throughout the world.

These methods have opened greater possibilities for making available large extents of land for agricultural crops; the new trends can be seen in almost any tropical area today (Fig. 1). We shall not consider the problems of such methods and their possible consequences (*21, 23, 24*). Instead, we analyze this trend in relation to the natural regeneration process.

Under an intensive and extensive use of the land, sources of seeds of primary tree species for regeneration becomes less and less available because of the dispersal characteristics of those species and because of the scarcity of individuals of most of the tree species (*25*). The only species available that are preadapted for continuous disturbance are secondary species or primary species with some of the characteristics of the secondary ones (*26*). This group of species has characteristics that enable them to thrive in such conditions; they produce large numbers of seeds, which have means of long-distance dispersal and dormancy; these seeds accumulate and stay alive in the soil (that is, they have a long life-span). The process often called "savannization" and "desertization" (*27, 28*) of the tropical humid regions can very well be explained by these characteristics.

Also, plants preadapted for disturbance such as ones from drier environments with built-in adaptations to remain alive in a dormant condition for long periods of time may invade these areas and allow them to regenerate a forest vegetation.

An ecosystem consisting of secondary species mixed with species from drier environments will become established. Since these species are generally lower in stature at maturity, the vegetation will also be lower in stature than the one the climate can allow. According to this view, some of the vegetation types that have these characteristics—for example, some low semievergreen selvas, savanna woodlands, and savannas in Mexico (*29*), as well as some in Asia (*28*), Africa (*30*), and South America (*27, 31*)—may be the product of an extensive and intensive shifting agriculture of old cultures. Some of the old arguments on the effects of fire for the explanation of many of the anthropogenous savannas and savanna woodlands can be explained better with the idea that we propose of the mass extinction of many tall tree species.

Thus there may be a possibility of bringing back some of these areas to a tall forest condition by introduction of the proper trees. There is, however, a great lack of information about population differentiation in tropical tree species, and research in this field is urgently needed for making basic recommendations in tropical rain forest management (*16, 18*).

An example of this problem is the failure of a project of one of us (A. G.-P.) for study of population differentiation in a tropical rain forest species, *Terminalia amazonia.* Seed populations were collected from Central America and Mexico, and, after germination, the young plants were transplanted to an introduction station at the Mexican site of the collections. The study had to be discontinued, for all the seedlings from the populations from Central America were exterminated by predators, especially ants, and comparisons could not be made. It is interesting that in this case probably there has been evolution in connection with the chemical protection against local predators which is not reflected in the morphology because morphological differences can hardly be distinguished. This study needs to be repeated with other species, but it shows that there is a potential problem in induced regeneration by the introduction of seeds from distant populations. This idea has also been developed from the problem of biological control of tropical pests (*24*).

Other Implications

All the facts and ideas mentioned lead us to the conclusion that, with the present rate of destruction of the tropical rain forests throughout the world, there is great danger of mass extinction of thousands of species. This is due to the simple fact that primary tree species from the tropical rain forests are incapable of recolonizing large areas opened to intensive and extensive agriculture. There has been a long controversy among persons responsible for the intensive use of land in the tropics, and it seems that the most important argument has been that countries like those of Europe, the United States, and some temperate Asiatic ones (Japan) have used the land intensively and extensively and there is not much evidence of mass disappearance of species. In view of the successional processes already discussed and with respect to the understanding of some biological properties of the species of northern temperate and cold areas, the explanation seems evident. In temperate areas the primary tree species are in many cases represented by a great number of individuals, and the distribution of many of the temperate species is large, and, in addition, many of them possess seeds adapted to long periods of inactivity, thereby conserving their vitality (dormancy and long life-span) (*32*) for periods of time while buried in the soil. Even though there are no reliable records of the life-span of seeds of trees buried in the soil of temperate regions, the available data known to us (*33*) suggest strongly the possibility that seeds stored in soils long retain their potential for growth. All these aspects yield a very different general behavior of the land cleared for agriculture and its possible future regeneration. It is also important to note that an isolated tree from a primary temperate forest has greater probability of survival than an isolated tree from a tropical rain forest (*18*); this is due to the complex and delicate net of relationships of each individual with the environment. This means that a gene pool of primary trees can be maintained along roads, near houses, and the like, for temperate areas but not for the tropical rain forest. If we add to these ideas the great difference in number of national parks, arboreta, botanic gardens, and storage facilities in many temperate areas in contrast with the virtual absence of such resources in the tropics, the problem grows to an even larger and more critical dimension.

All that we have said is applicable to tropical evergreen rain forests in the warm and humid areas of the world. In drier tropical areas with a definite long dry season the problem is very different, and the plants behave in connection with the problems of regeneration under intensive exploitation, in a manner more similar to those of temperate areas. The reason for this is that these plants are in some ways preadapted to great disturbances since they possess better characteristics for survival during periods of adverse conditions (drought, fire).

Conclusions

All the evidence available supports the idea that, under present intensive use of the land in tropical rain forest regions, the ecosystems are in danger of a mass extinction of most of their species. This has already happened in several areas of the tropical world, and in the near future it may be of even greater intensity. The consequences are nonpredictable, but the sole fact that thousands of species will disappear before any aspect of their biology has been investigated is frightening. This would mean the loss of millions and millions of years of evolution, not only of plant and animal species, but also of the most complex biotic communities in the world.

We urgently suggest that, internationally, massive action be taken to preserve this gigantic pool of germplasm by the establishment of biological gene pool reserves from the different tropical rain forest environments of the world.

References and Notes

1. C. G. G. J. van Steenis, *Micronesica* 2, 65 (1965); E. J. H. Corner, *New Phytol.* 45, 192 (1946).
2. P. W. Richards, *Atas Simp. Biota Amazonica* 7, 49 (1967).
3. A. Gómez-Pompa, *Biotropica* 3, 125 (1971).
4. C. Vázquez-Yanes and A. Gómez-Pompa, in *Simp. Latinoam. Fisiol. Vegetal. Qua. Lima, Perú, 20 to 26 Sept.* (1971), pp. 79–80; C. G. J. van Steenis, in *Study of Tropical Vegetation. Proc. Kandy Symp., Kandy, Ceylon, 19 to 21 March 1956* (1958), pp. 212–218.
5. G. Budowski, *Turrialba* 15, 40 (1965).
6. C. F. Symington, *Malayan Forest.* 2, 107 (1933); A. Gómez-Pompa, J. Vázquez-Soto, J. Sarukhán, *Publ. Especial Inst. Nacl. Invest. Forest.* (*México*) 3, 20 (1964).
7. J. Sarukhán, *Publ. Especial. Inst. Nacl. Invest. Forest.* (*México*) 3, 107 (1964).
8. P. W. Richards, *The Tropical Rain Forest* (Cambridge Univ. Press, London, 1952).
9. S. Guevara and A. Gómez-Pompa, *J. Arnold Arboretum Harvard Univ.* 53, 312 (1972).
10. W. Croker, *Botan. Rev.* 4, 235 (1938); R. C. Barnard, *Malayan Forest Res. Inst. Res. Pamphlet*, No. 14 (1954); T. B. McClelland, *Proc. Fla. State Hort. Soc.* 57, 161 (1944); J. Marrero, *Caribbean Forest.* 4, 99 (1942).
11. J. P. Schulz, *Ecological Studies on Rain Forest in Northern Surinam* (Noord-Hollandsche Uitgevers Maatschappij, Amsterdam, 1960), p. 226.
12. L. van der Pijl, *Proc. Kon. Ned. Akad. Wetensch.* 69, 597 (1966); *Principles of Dispersal in Higher Plants* (Springer-Verlag, Berlin, 1969), p. 87.
13. ———, *Biol. J. Linnean Soc.* 1, 85 (1969).
14. D. H. Janzen, *Evolution* 23, 1 (1969).
15. N. Smythe, *Amer. Natur.* 104, 23 (1970).
16. A. Gómez-Pompa, *J. Arnold Arboretum Harvard Univ.* 48, 106 (1967).
17. ———, *Bol. Divulgación Soc. Mex. Hist. Nat.* 6, 5 (1971).
18. G. N. Baur, *The Ecological Basis of Rainforest Management* (Blight Government Printer, New South Wales, 1968).
19. H. C. Conklin, *FAO Forest. Develop. Pap.* 1 (1962); M. A. Martínez, *Bol. Especial Inst. Nacl. Invest. Forest.* (*México*) 7, 1 (1970); P. H. Nye and D. J. Greenland, *The Soil under Shifting Cultivation* (Commonwealth Bureau of Soils, Harpenden, 1960); M. Sousa, *Publ. Especial Inst. Nacl. Invest. Forest.* (*México*) 3, 91 (1964).
20. J. M. Blaut, in *Symposium on the Impact of Man on Humid Tropics Vegetation, Goroka* (1960), pp. 185–198.
21. J. Kadlec, Coordinator, *Man and the Living Environment, Workshop on Global Ecological Problems* (Univ. of Wisconsin Press, Madison, 1972), p. 176.
22. W. R. Geddes, in *Symposium on the Impact of Man on Humid Tropics Vegetation, Goroka* (1960), pp. 42–56; A. Dilmy, *ibid.*, pp. 119–122; H. Sioli and H. Klinge, in *Int. Symp. Stalzenau, The Hague* (1961), pp. 357–363.
23. F. Tamesis, in *Proc. Pacif. Forest. Congr. 5th Seattle* (1960), pp. 2025–2032; H. C. Conklin, *Trans. N.Y. Acad. Sci.* 17, 133 (1954).
24. D. H. Janzen, *Bull. Ecol. Soc. Amer.* 54, 4 (1970).
25. G. A. Black, Th. Dobzhansky, C. Pavan, *Botan. Gaz.* 111, 413 (1950); M. E. D. Poore, *J. Ecol.* (*Jubilee Symposium*) 52, 213 (1964); F. R. Fosberg, *Trop. Ecol.* 11, 162 (1970); V. M. Toledo and M. Sousa, *Bol. Soc. Botán. Méx.*, in press; other papers on the same subject appear in *Speciation in Tropical Environments*, R. H. Lowe-McConnell, Ed. (Academic Press, New York, 1969).
26. A. Gómez-Pompa, *Estudios Botánicos en la Región de Misantla, Veracruz* (Ediciones del Instituto Mexicano de Recursos Naturales Renovables, A. C., Mexico, D.F., 1966), p. 104.
27. G. Budowski, *Turrialba* 6, 22 (1956); F. W. Went and N. Stark, *BioSci.* 18, 1035 (1968).
28. M. Schmid, in "Study of tropical vegetation," *Proc. Kandy Symp., Kandy, Ceylon, 19 to 21 March 1956* (1958), pp. 183–192.
29. F. Miranda and E. Hernández X., *Bol. Soc. Botán. Méx.* 28, 29 (1963); A. Gómez-Pompa, *ibid.* 29, 76 (1964).
30. R. Sillans, thesis, Faculté des Sciences de l'Université de Montpellier (1958), p. 176.
31. M. G. Ferri, *Simposio o Cerrado* (Edit. Univ. de São Paulo, São Paulo, 1963).
32. L. V. Barton, *Seed Preservation and Longevity* (Hill, London, 1961); Anon., *Misc. Publ. U.S. Dept. Agri.* 654, 290, 361 (1948).
33. N. W. Olmstead and J. D. Curtis, *Ecology* 28, 49 (1946); H. J. Oosting and M. E. Humphreys, *Bull. Torrey Bot. Club* 67, 253 (1940).
34. *Flora of Veracruz*, contribution number 12. A joint project of the Institute of Biology of the National University of Mexico and the Arnold Arboretum and Gray Herbarium of Harvard University, to prepare an ecological floristic study of the state of Veracruz, Mexico. Information about this project was published in *Anal. Inst. Biol. Univ. Nacl. Mex. Ser. Bot.* 41, 1–2. Partially supported by NSF grant GB-20267X.

Distributional Ecology
of New Guinea Birds

Recent ecological and biogeographical theories can
be tested on the bird communities of New Guinea.

Jared M. Diamond

As indicated by frequent references in the syntheses of zoogeography by Wallace (*1*), of evolution by Mayr (*2*), and of ecology by MacArthur (*3*), the tropical island-continent of New Guinea and its birds have played a special role in advancing our understanding of animal populations. This role developed partly because birds are the best known, most easily observed and identified animals, and partly because of unique advantages of New Guinea itself. New Guinea provides a range of habitats from tropical rain forest to glaciers within distances of less than 16 kilometers, a range of elevations of over 5000 meters, and an equatorial position that minimizes seasonal migration with its associated complications. The rugged topography, which isolates populations in adjacent valleys or on adjacent mountains, has promoted speciation within small areas of a single land mass by essentially the same mechanisms that underlie speciation on large continents. In New Guinea's expanses of forest undisturbed by man, niche interrelations retain a simplicity and beauty lost in altered environments, and distributional patterns illustrating many intermediate stages in evolution and in niche displacement are readily identified. The number of breeding bird species, 513, is large enough to give rise to the complex interactions characteristic of continental faunas, but not so large as to be overwhelming. In spite of the physical difficulties of exploration in New Guinea, the distribution and taxonomy of its bird species are by now fairly well

The author is professor of physiology at the School of Medicine, University of California, Los Angeles 90024.

understood. New Guinea has served as the bird colonization source for the thousands of islands of the southwest Pacific; and New Guinea itself behaves as an "island archipelago" for montane birds, since its mountain ranges are isolated from each other by a "sea" of uninhabitable lowlands. The number of bird species on these oceanic islands and mountain islands varies with area and isolation, providing innumerable "experiments of nature" whereby the niche of a given species can be studied as a function of the competing species pool.

Within the past decade, new paradigms introduced by MacArthur and Wilson and their co-workers (*3–7*) have revolutionized our understanding of some central questions of ecology, such as: Why do different localities support very different numbers of animal or plant species? What determines the distribution of a given species? How do related species manage to coexist? These questions are not only of basic scientific interest but are also of practical importance in formulating conservation policies. Furthermore, the concepts of MacArthur and Wilson are proving increasingly helpful in understanding human populations. In this article I discuss these questions in the light of my studies of New Guinea birds, conducted during six expeditions to New Guinea and other islands of the southwest Pacific (*8–15*). A recent book discusses in detail many of the examples summarized here (*15*). Many patterns observed in New Guinea birds are relevant to other groups of animals in other parts of the world, especially in the tropics.

Species Diversity on Islands

If one were to count all the animal or plant species occurring within an area of 1 hectare, the result would vary greatly depending on the location of the census area. The species total would generally be much higher in the tropics than in the temperate zones, higher at the base of a mountain than at the summit, higher on a large island than on a small island, and higher on an island near a continent than on a remote island. It is important to understand this variation if, for example, one is establishing a system of national parks to ensure survival of as many native species as possible. Islands such as those of the southwest Pacific lend themselves well as test areas for a quantitative theory of species diversity, because each island represents a separate experiment, and because most insular variation in species diversity can be predicted from values of only two or three readily measured variables. We shall see that the diversity of bird species on most Pacific islands is in a state of dynamic equilibrium—that is, the diversity is determined by the island's present physical characteristics and is independent of the island's history. However, on some islands, the species diversity may also reflect the island's recent history.

The number of land and freshwater bird species coexisting on each tropical island of the southwest Pacific varies from 1 for some isolated atolls up to 513 for New Guinea itself. This variation is due partly to the greater variety of habitats present on the larger islands. However, even within a given habitat type (for example, in tropical lowland rain forest) there are great differences among islands in the number of bird species to be found. These differences are largely predictable from an island's area, its distance from New Guinea, and its elevation (*13*).

Figure 1 shows the number of bird species S occurring at sea level on islands between 8 and 500 km from New Guinea, as a function of island area A (expressed as square kilometers). Over a 3-millionfold range of areas the results fit the power function

$$S = 12.3 \, A^{0.22} \quad (1)$$

with an average error of 19 percent. Thus, a tenfold increase in area increases species diversity by somewhat less than a factor of 2. The numbered deviant points represent islands in various stages of "relaxation," as will be explained.

In Fig. 2 I have plotted, as a function of island distance D from New Guinea, the ratio of an island's actual S at sea level to the S value predicted from the island's area and Eq. 1. This ratio decreases exponentially with distance, by a factor of 2 for each 2600 km from New Guinea. Thus, the most remote islands of the southwest Pacific (Mangareva and the islands of the Pitcairn group, 8000 to 9200 km from New Guinea) have a bird species diversity only 12 percent that of islands of similar size near New Guinea.

The mountains of the higher southwest Pacific islands harbor additional bird species not occurring at sea level. On the average, each 1000 m of elevation L enriches an island's avifauna by a number of montane species equal to 8.9 percent of its avifauna at sea level. Thus, bird species diversity on the New Guinea satellite islands may be summarized by the empirical formula

$$S = (12.3) \ (1 + 0.089 \ L/1000) \times$$
$$(e^{-D/2600}) \ (A^{0.22}) \quad (2)$$

Similarly, species diversity in other plant and animal groups on other islands increases with island area and decreases with distance from the colonization source. These two trends constitute the fundamental law of island biogeography. The exponent of area is generally in the range 0.20 to 0.34 (4, 16).

To explain this law, MacArthur and Wilson (4), and Preston (16), suggested that insular species diversity represents a dynamic equilibrium between immigration and extinction. Islands constantly receive immigrants due to random dispersal of individuals from mainlands, and the immigration rate should increase with island area and proximity to the colonization source. On the other hand, island populations risk extinction due to competition and random fluctuations in population size, and extinction rates should be highest for the smallest islands with the smallest populations. Thus, at equilibrium, when the species immigration rate I on an island equals the species extinction rate E, there should be more species on a large island than on a small island, and more on an island near to other land than on a remote island. Furthermore, species turnover rates at equilibrium should decrease with increasing island area and remoteness.

As a test of the equilibrium theory, in 1968 and 1969 I resurveyed the land and freshwater birds of a temperate archipelago and of a tropical island whose birds had been surveyed 50 years previously: the nine Channel Islands off southern California (9), and Karkar Island off northern New Guinea (12). On each island I found that between 17 and 62 percent of the species present 50 years ago had disappeared, and an approximately equal number of species absent 50 years ago had immigrated. Thus, the species diversity had remained in dynamic equilibrium; Terborgh and Faaborg (17) obtained similar results for the birds of Mona Island in the West Indies. While a few of the extinctions and immigrations in these studies were related to effects of man, most of the changes were of the random kind expected in the absence of a human role. As predicted from colonization theory (4), most of the extinctions involved populations that were rare 50 years ago because of such factors as recency of colonization, small island size, presence of well-established competing species or small area or marginal suitability of island habitat. Among the Channel Islands the calculated minimum turnover rates, expressed as the percentage of island species immigrating or becoming extinct per year, range from 1.2 percent per year for the smallest or most barren islands down to 0.3 percent per year for the largest island.

Since the S and A values for Karkar fit Eq. 1 and lie on the general pattern of Fig. 1, it is probable that bird species diversity is near equilibrium on most southwest Pacific islands. However, there are some points in Fig. 1 that deviate conspicuously from the general pattern. These prove to be associated with islands on which natural processes (such as volcanic explosions or changing sea level) have displaced S from its equilibrium value at some approximately known recent time. On such islands S must be gradually returning to equilibrium as a result of a temporary imbalance between immigration and extinction; this process may be termed "relaxation." Analysis of the islands on which species diversity is undergoing relaxation provides further insight into immigration, extinction, and effects of island history (13).

The respective rates of immigration and extinction, I and E (expressed as species per year), depend on the instantaneous species diversity $S(t)$, where

t represents time. Let us assume constant coefficients K_1 and K_e (expressed as year^{-1}), respectively:

$$E = K_e \ S(t) \quad (3)$$
$$I = K_i \ [S^* - S(t)] \quad (4)$$
$$dS/dt = I - E = K_i S^* - (K_i + K_e) \ S(t) \quad (5)$$

where S^* is the mainland species pool. At equilibrium $(dS/dt = 0)$, the species diversity S_{eq} is given by

$$S_{eq} = K_i S^*/(K_i + K_e) \quad (6)$$

Relaxation to equilibrium from an initial species diversity $S(0)$ that differs from S_{eq} is described by:

$$[S(t) - S_{eq}]/[S(0) - S_{eq}] = e^{-t/t_r} \quad (7)$$

where "relaxation time" t_r is given by

$$t_r = (K_i + K_e)^{-1} \quad (8)$$

The relaxation time is the length of time required for the departure of species diversity from equilibrium, $|S(t) - S_{eq}|$, to relax to $1/e$ (or 36.8 percent) of the initial departure, $|S(0) - S_{eq}|$, where e is the base of natural logarithms. Actually, this treatment is only a crude approximation of the real situation, because K_e and K_i prove to be functions of $S(t)$. However, by applying Eqs. 3 to 8 to island faunas we can deduce the form of these functions, stipulate some conditions for an improved model, and come to some conclusions about the distribution of bird species.

As an example of an "experiment of nature" that permits estimation of $S(0)$, S_{eq}, one pair of values of $S(t)$ and t, and hence calculation of t_r, I will describe the situation on a land-bridge island, Misol. During the most recent Pleistocene glaciation, when much water was sequestered in glaciers and sea level was about 100 m below its present stand (18), Misol was part of the New Guinea mainland and must have supported virtually the full New Guinea lowland avifauna of 325 species. Since the severing of the New Guinea–to–Misol land bridge by rising sea level about 10,000 years ago, $S(t)$ on Misol must have been relaxing toward the value expected for an "oceanic island" of the same area, as a result of extinction exceeding immigration. Figure 1 (points marked +) shows that Misol and other large land-bridge islands are still supersaturated—that is, their present $S(t)$ values are still considerably in excess of the equilibrium value for oceanic islands, although considerably less than the initial value of 325. Misol has an area of 2040 km^2 and should have 65 lowland species at equilibrium (from Eq. 1) but actually has 135. If we take Eq. 7 and substitute $S(0) = 325$, $S(t) = 135$, $S_{eq} = 65$, and $t = 10,000$ years, we obtain a relaxation time of 7,600 years for the avifauna of Misol.

Relaxation times can also be estimated from four other types of "experiments of nature." These are: the fission of a large island into two smaller islands because of rising sea levels flooding a low isthmus; contraction in an island's area because of rising sea levels; gradual extinction, from land-bridge islands, of relict populations of those New Guinea lowland species that never cross water gaps of more than 8 km or even 50 m (such species must have reached the islands at the time of the land bridge, and were isolated without possibility of recolonization after submergence of the land bridge) (13); and recolonization of volcanic islands such as Krakatau, Long, and Ritter, after cataclysmic eruptions totally destroyed the fauna.

From calculated relaxation times obtained by these methods for 19 New Guinea satellite islands, the following conclusions can be drawn (13). (i) With decreasing island area, extinction rates increase (yielding shorter calculated t_r values) because of smaller population sizes. Thus, among land-bridge islands the calculated t_r for the relict populations decreases from 9000 years for an island of area 7800 km² (Aru), to 6100 years for 450 km² (Batanta), and to 2630 years for 145 km² (Pulu Adi). Species diversities on small land-bridge islands do not show an excess over equilibrium values (Fig. 1) because relaxation times for these islands are much shorter than the 10,000 years that have elapsed since severing of the land bridges. (ii) On supersaturated islands certain species are especially prone to extinction and tend consistently to disappear first. The resulting release of the remaining species from competition tends to increase their population densities and to decrease their risk of extinction. Expressed mathematically, K_e on a given island is an increasing function of $S(t)$. (iii) The species that arrive first at an initially empty island tend to be certain species with consistently superior dispersal ability, such as those that characteristically colonize mainland "second-growth" habitats (transient vegetational stages during regrowth of a forest clearing). Subsequent immigrants are drawn from a mainland species pool comprised of progressively poorer colonists. Expressed mathematically, K_i on a given island is a decreasing function of $S(t)$. (iv) The probability of extinction is much higher for recently arrived immigrants that still have a low population density, than for established species that have saturated available island habitats.

Patchiness of Species Distributions

Among the characteristics of tropical species that distinguish them from their high-latitude counterparts are the lesser tendency of tropical species to disperse, their subjection to greater niche compression by interspecific competition, and their lower extinction and higher speciation rates. All these characteristics contribute to the striking tropical phenomenon called "patchiness" (3, 7, 15). Whereas the local presence or

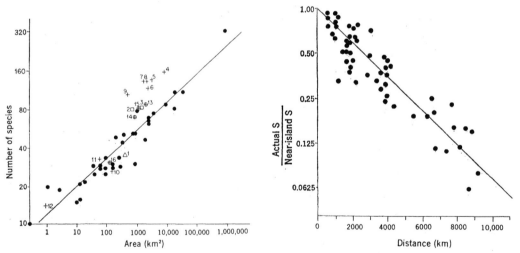

Fig. 1 (left). Number of resident land and freshwater bird species on New Guinea satellite islands, plotted as a function of island area on a double logarithmic scale. Symbols: ●, islands on which species diversity is presumed to be at equilibrium (the remaining, numbered islands are in various stages of "relaxation" after displacement of species diversity from an equilibrium value); △, exploded volcanic islands (1, Long); □, contracted islands (2, Goodenough; 3, Fergusson); +, land-bridge islands (4, Aru; 5, Waigeu; 6, Japen; 7, Salawati; 8, Misol; 9, Batanta; 10, Pulu Adi; 11, Ron; 12, Schildpad); ⊕, island fragments split off from a larger island by flooding of an isthmus (13, Batjan; 14, Amboina; 15, New Hanover; 16, Tidore). The straight line was fitted by least mean squares through points for all islands except the land-bridge islands. Note that the number of species increases with area; and that deviations for relaxing islands are more marked for large islands than for small islands, because of high extinction rates and short relaxation times on the latter. [After Diamond (13)] Fig. 2 (right). Ordinate (logarithmic scale), number of resident land and freshwater bird species (S) on tropical southwest Pacific islands more than 500 km from New Guinea, divided by number of species expected on an island of equivalent area less than 500 km from New Guinea (calculated from Eq. 1). Abscissa, island distance from New Guinea. The graph shows that species diversity decreases by a factor of 2 per 2600 km. [After Diamond (13)]

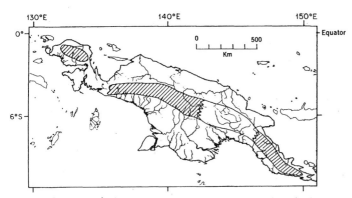

Fig. 3. Distribution of the Papuan tree creeper, *Climacteris leucophaea*, in the mountains of New Guinea. Although mountains and forests with similar tree bark extend uninterrupted for 1600 km, and although there is no other New Guinea bird in the same family, this bark-feeding species has a distribution gap (unshaded area) of 400 km in the middle of its range (hatched area). [After Diamond (*15*)]

absence of temperate-zone species can generally be predicted from knowledge of their particular habitat requirements, many tropical species are patchily distributed with respect to the available habitat—that is, they may be absent at a considerable fraction of the localities offering a suitable habitat for them. Temperate-zone biologists, because they are rarely confronted with examples of such patterns, often assume that the evidence for patchiness in the tropics can be dismissed as an artifact of inadequate exploration or insufficiently understood habitat requirements. To prove that a species actually is locally absent rather than just overlooked is certainly more difficult than to prove that it is present. Fortunately, the documentation of patchy distributions in New Guinea has been facilitated by many New Guinea natives who possess a detailed knowledge of local birds. Some natives were able to name (in their native languages) and accurately describe in advance all bird species that I eventually located in their areas; they could distinguish at a distance obscure sibling species in such taxonomically difficult genera as *Sericornis*; and could accurately describe other species known to them only from single individuals observed up to 10 years previously (*14, 15*). When such "walking encyclopedias" of bird lore confirm the permanent local absence of a species that is regularly encountered in other areas, one can have confidence that the species is actually absent and not merely overlooked. It is even more difficult to prove that a locality really does meet all of a bird's

habitat requirements, since a skeptic can always claim that some unspecified factor has been overlooked. However, many of the examples of patchy distribution that I describe briefly below and in detail elsewhere (*15*) involve well-studied species which appear to have distinct and readily defined requirements, and which are ubiquitous in habitats meeting these requirements in many geographical areas of New Guinea. Since there do seem to be some generalizations emerging about patchiness, it is becoming increasingly unnecessary to invoke unspecified factors as an explanation.

There are four main types of patchy distribution.

1) *Distributional gaps in a continuous habitat.* The Central Dividing Range of New Guinea provides an uninterrupted expanse of montane forest for 1600 km. Nevertheless, 18 montane bird species that would otherwise be uniformly distributed have a distributional gap of several hundred kilometers somewhere along the Central Range (Fig. 3). For instance, the finch *Lonchura montana* occurs commonly in large flocks throughout the alpine grasslands of western and eastern New Guinea, where it is the only specialized seed-eating bird, yet it is absent in the alpine grassland of central New Guinea, which has similar grass and an otherwise similar avifauna (*15*). Large distributional gaps in a continuous habitat also occur in the New Guinea lowlands. The interpretation of these remarkable patterns is discussed below.

2) *Very local distributions.* The distributions of many species are patchy to

an extreme degree, such that they occur at a few widely separated localities but are absent in similar habitats over most of New Guinea (*15*). For instance, the flycatcher *Poecilodryas placens* is known from six scattered areas, where it inhabits rain forests with a well-shaded understory of small saplings in locally flat terrain up to 1000 m above sea level. The species is absent from hundreds of well-explored localities with similar habitat elsewhere in New Guinea. Most of these very local species in New Guinea fall into one of two categories: distinctive "monotypic genera" with no close relatives (that is, genera consisting only of a single isolated species), or members of large genera consisting of many ecologically similar species. The highly fragmented distributions of these species suggest that they are slowly becoming extinct, either because they are the last survivors of unsuccessful evolutionary lines (monotypic genera), or because they cannot compete with several ecologically similar relatives in the same genus.

3) *Complementary checkerboard ranges.* Some local absences of species are correlated with the presence of ecologically similar congeners, indicating that one-to-one competitive exclusion occurs in New Guinea mainland habitats as on oceanic islands. For example, the extensive midmontane grasslands, which are a by-product of human agriculture during the last few centuries, have been colonized in irregular checkerboard fashion by eight *Lonchura* finch species native to other habitats. Each midmontane area supports only one finch species over a considerable local range of grass types and heights, altitudes, and rainfall conditions, but the areas inhabited by a given species are often scattered hundreds of kilometers apart. Evidence indicates that in each instance the first arrival became established over a local area and was able to exclude potential subsequent colonists of the seven other species, but the identity of each locally successful colonist depended partly on chance (*15*). In the slightly more complex situation illustrated in Fig. 4 ("compound checkerboard exclusion"), each local area can support coexisting populations of any two species out of three potential colonists, and the identity of the locally missing third species varies irregularly.

4) *Distributional islands on a mainland.* Comparison of mountains several kilometers apart within the same range invariably reveals faunal differences

that cannot be explained by differences in habitat (*15*). For example, species characteristic of lower montane forest at 800 to 1100 m were compared on four peaks of the North Coastal Range. In order of decreasing area and summit elevation, the mountains and their *number of lower montane species were:* Menawa (1890 m high), 45 lower montane species at 800 to 1100 m; Nibo (1560 m), 36 species; Somoro (1420 m), 34 species; and Turu (1140 m), 26 species. The four mountains had structurally similar forest at 800 to 1100 m, but the smaller mountains had less area of such forest and, correlated with this, fewer bird species characteristic of this forest. Similar findings have been described for Andean birds and North American mammals (*19*). These patterns are reminiscent of the fundamental species: area relation of island biogeography (see page 760). Evidently, *dispersal rates of birds between New Guinea mountains separated from each other by valleys a few kilometers wide are so low that the peaks behave as islands.*

Significance of Patchiness

While much remains baffling about patchy distributions in the tropics, such distributions appear to be caused by the synergistic effects of two characteristics of tropical species compared to temperate-zone species. These are the lower dispersal rates of tropical species, *which prolong the existence of distri-butional gaps as temporary or non-equilibrium phenomena;* and the greater pressure from interspecific competition, which stabilizes gaps as indefinitely maintained or equilibrium phenomena.

That the mean dispersal distances of many New Guinea bird species are less *than several kilometers is indicated (i)* by the absences of montane species on mountains separated by several kilometers from populations of the same species on other mountains; (ii) by the numerous species absent on oceanic islands a few kilometers or even only a few meters from the New Guinea mainland (*13*); and (iii) by the presence of distinct subspecies or even semispecies on mountains separated by valleys several kilometers wide or on islands separated by straits several kilometers wide. Once a species has become locally extinct for whatever reason, immigration from populations in immediately contiguous areas is so slow that distribu-

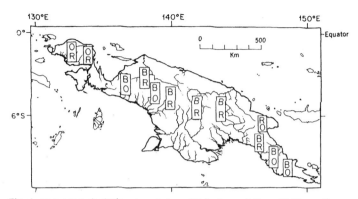

Fig. 4. Compound checkerboard exclusion: distributions of three *Melidectes* honey-eaters. O, *Melidectes ochromelas*; B, *M. belfordi*; R, *M. rufocrissalis* superspecies. Most mountainous areas of New Guinea support two species with mutually exclusive altitudinal ranges. At each locality depicted on the map of New Guinea, the letters above and below indicate the species present at higher and lower altitudes, respectively. The identity of the locally missing third species is subject to irregular geographical variation.

tional gaps in a continuous habitat may persist for long periods of time, albeit as nonequilibrium phenomena. For example, the finch *Lonchura montana* (discussed above) may have disappeared from the alpine grassland of central New Guinea several millennia ago, when the area of this habitat was reduced by *encroachment of forest; and this finch* may disperse too slowly to have refilled the whole gap since then. In the more seasonal temperate latitudes, by contrast, the annual north-south migrations, and the postbreeding wanderings of many nonmigratory species, flood suitable habitats with potential colonists of *most species each year. Mortality due* to climatic fluctuations in temperate latitudes places a premium on dispersal ability to recolonize vacated territories, whereas the greater stability of the tropics selects against dispersal.

Effects of interspecific competition on local distribution are easiest to rec-*ognize in the one-to-one situation of* simple checkerboard exclusion, where species A, for example, occurs only in the absence of species B and vice versa, or in compound checkerboard exclusion, where species A occurs only in absence of either species B or species C. The competitors in these situations are *usually, though not always, close rela-*tives within the same genus. It is more difficult to determine the connections in so-called diffuse competition, where absence of a species is due to the combined effects of many species, each somewhat distantly related to the absent species and potentially overlapping it *ecologically only in part (3, 10). A*

decline in species B following an invasion of its close competitor A may permit B's other close competitor C to increase, depressing the population of C's competitor D and ultimately affecting species ecologically far removed from A. Correlated with the greater diversity of species in the tropics than at higher latitudes is the fact that tropical species have more closely packed niches than their temperate counterparts, such that the local survival of a given species may be critically dependent on the mix of competitors as well as on the suitability of the habitat (*3*, pp. 231 ff). Thus, competition may stabilize *some distributional gaps indefinitely.*

These considerations help us to understand the differing numbers of species on different continents. Low dispersal may allow localized populations of disappearing species to linger, relatively undisturbed by influx of competitors, for long periods of time before *final extinction. Conversely, low disper-*sal favors high rates of speciation, since the first stage of speciation depends on the effectiveness of geographical barriers or distributional gaps (Fig. 8). Because the number of species at equilibrium on a continent depends on a balance between speciation rates and *extinction rates, tropical habitats should* be expected to have a greater number of species at equilibrium than habitats at higher latitudes (Fig. 5). Furthermore, with increasing continental area, extinction rates should decrease (because of larger population sizes and more local refuges), and speciation rates *should increase (because of more popu-*

764

Fig. 5. Speciation rates (solid curves) and extinction rates (dashed curves) on a single land mass, as a function of the number of species (abscissa). The ordinate is the total number of species produced through speciation or lost through extinction, per 10,000 years. The intersection of the curves ($N1$, $N2$) determines the number of species at equilibrium. The speciation curve is approximately linear, because the probability of speciation of a given species is approximately independent of the presence of other species, but extinction rates increase sharply as more species are packed together. On a large tropical land mass, high speciation rates (curve $S1$) and low extinction rates ($E1$) yield a high number of species at equilibrium ($N1$). On a similar-sized temperate land mass or a smaller tropical land mass, lower speciation rates ($S2$) and higher extinction rates ($E2$) yield fewer species at equilibrium ($N2$).

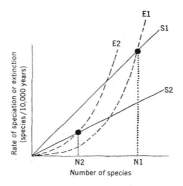

lations isolated over greater distances). Thus, one should also expect more species at equilibrium in a large center of speciation, such as the Amazon Basin, than in a small center, such as New Guinea (Fig. 5).

Ecological Segregation of Species

A central problem of ecology concerns community organization: How are resources divided among the species of an ecological community, and what mutual arrangements permit the coexistence of closely related species (20)?

The best understood segregating mechanism among New Guinea birds depends on altitude and involves an interesting behavioral response.

Altitudinal segregation. On New Guinea mountains not disturbed by man, forest extends uninterrupted from sea level to timberline at around 3800 m. Many bird species, especially those with no closely related species in the area, exhibit gradual changes in abundance with altitude. However, in many other instances one finds sequences of two, three, or even four closely related species replacing each other abruptly with altitude (15). For example, *Crateroscelis murina* and *Crateroscelis robusta*, two abundant and very similar warblers that glean for insects near the ground, differ ecologically mainly in

their altitudinal range (Fig. 6). With increasing elevation *C. murina* becomes increasingly abundant until it suddenly disappears at 1643 m, an altitude not far above its altitude of maximum abundance. At this elevation *C. robusta* suddenly appears near its maximum abundance and becomes progressively less common toward Mt. Karimui's summit. Prolonged observations at the transition altitude showed that the two species are interspecifically territorial at 1643 m, and no individual of either species was ever found transgressing the range of the other. There is no change in vegetation at this altitude; the nearest "ecotone" (a border between forest types) lies 338 m higher. In all, the New Guinea avifauna contains about 45 pairs, 13 trios, and 3 quartets of related species which replace each other altitudinally with similar abruptness. For a given species pair the transition altitude shows minor local variation correlated with local conditions of rainfall, exposure, and slope, but no systematic geographical variation over New Guinea. Altitudinal sequences with sharp transitions also occur among birds in the Peruvian Andes (21) and on all large mountainous islands of Indonesia and the southwest Pacific.

Strict transitions may be violated by young birds: when one finds an individual outside the normal altitudinal range of its species, it generally proves to be a juvenile or an immature bird.

Fig. 6. Altitudinal ranges of the warblers *Crateroscelis robusta* (●) and *C. murina* (○) on the west ridge of Mt. Karimui, New Guinea. On the left, each mark represents one individual heard, seen, or collected at the given altitude (the paucity of records at 650 to 1050 m results from my having spent little time at this altitude). The right-hand side gives the relative abundance in the whole avifauna—that is, the percentage of bird individuals of all species estimated as being *C. robusta* or *C. murina*. The two species replace each other abruptly at 1643 m, and each species reaches its maximum abundance near this altitude. Many other species show equally sharp transitions, although the altitude of maximum abundance frequently differs from the altitude at which the species transition occurs.

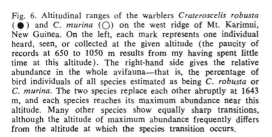

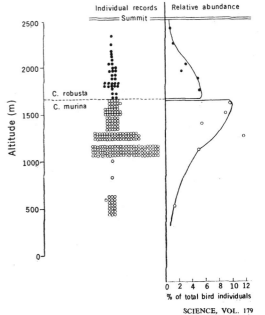

Among New Guinea birds generally, there is a characteristic altitudinal dependence of population structure. Typically, immature birds are found in a fringe at the bottom of the altitudinal range; somewhat higher, one finds immature birds plus nonbreeding adults, with females usually appearing at lower altitudes than males; next comes the optimal part of the species' range, with breeding adults of both sexes; and, finally, another fringe of immature birds but few adults appears at the upper altitudinal limit of some but not all species. This population structure is manifested to an extreme degree by some birds of paradise, whose displaying adult males may be compressed into the top 180 m of the altitudinal range, with adult females and especially immature birds being found up to 1000 m below the lowest adult male.

Ultimately the altitudinal sequences are related to differential adaptations that are continuous functions of altitude, one species being preferentially adapted to higher altitudes, cooler temperatures, and more montane vegetation than the other species. But the very sharpness of the transitions implies that competition superimposes a special behavior pattern on these differential adaptations, since the transitions do not coincide with sharp changes in temperature or vegetation. That is, each species must be capable of surviving over a wider altitudinal range than it actually inhabits and must be excluding related species from the range in which it is competitively superior to them. To confirm this interpretation, the local population of one member of a sequence would have to be removed in order to ascertain whether the adjacent species would expand their altitudinal ranges. This test of competition arises in New Guinea under two types of naturally occurring conditions.

The first test of niche expansion associated with relief of competition occurs on small or isolated mountains or islands (8, 10, 15). Because of the dependence of species diversity on area and isolation and because of the random element in colonization, one or another member of an altitudinal sequence may be missing on such a "mountain island." As shown in Fig. 7, under these circumstances a low-altitude species may expand into the range of a missing high-altitude relative, a high-altitude species may expand into the range of a missing low-altitude relative, and a high-altitude species and a low-altitude species may expand simultaneously into the range of a missing middle-altitude relative.

Reconstruction of the process of speciation provides the other test for competition and clearly demonstrates the origin of altitudinal sequences (15). Speciation occurs when an initially continuous population breaks up into geographical isolates, the isolates diverge, reestablish geographical contact and perfect their reproductive isolating mechanisms, and finally reinvade each other's geographical ranges if there are sufficient ecological differences to permit coexistence (2). While the slowness of evolution rarely permits following a given species through this process with time, the distribution patterns of different New Guinea montane species represent "snapshots" of seven different stages in a continuous speciation process (Fig. 8):

1) A single montane species extends from the western to the eastern end of New Guinea, occupying the same altitudinal range at all longitudes.

2) The local population in one area dies out, so that the east-west distribution becomes discontinuous.

3) The eastern and western populations, now isolated, diverge sufficiently that they would probably not interbreed if contact were established; hence,

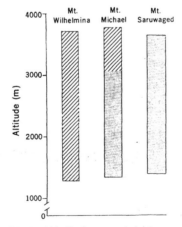

Fig. 7. Altitudinal ranges of the honey-eaters *Ptiloprora perstriata* (diagonally hatched bar) and *P. guisei* (solid bar) on three New Guinea mountains. On Mt. Michael, where both species are present, their altitudinal ranges are mutually exclusive. On Mt. Wilhelmina, where *P. guisei* is absent, and on Mt. Saruwaged, where *P. perstriata* is absent, the remaining species takes over most or all of the altitudinal range of its missing relative.

they are assumed to be distinct species. They may also develop slightly different altitudinal ranges.

4) Both populations reexpand geographically until their geographical ranges abut but do not overlap. There is no or little interbreeding, proving that the populations are in fact distinct species.

5) Each species begins to expand geographically into the range of the other, so that there is geographical overlap ("sympatric" distribution) for a short distance. Within the zone of sympatry the two species segregate altitudinally, each being confined to the altitudinal range in which it is competitively superior to the other. The narrower altitudinal range inside than outside the zone of sympatry is a clear demonstration of niche compression due to competition.

6) Expansion continues, and the western species reaches the eastern end of New Guinea and overruns the entire geographical range of its eastern sibling species. The eastern species has given up the upper (or lower) part of its altitudinal range throughout its whole geographical range, and there is no altitudinal overlap.

7) The eastern species continues to expand until it has reached the western end of New Guinea. The two species are now sympatric over the entire length of New Guinea, with mutually exclusive altitudinal ranges. Evolution may then continue in the direction of either stage 8a, 8b, or 8c.

8a) Stages 1 through 7 may be repeated one or two more times to yield series of three or four closely related species sympatric over the whole of New Guinea but occupying mutually exclusive altitudinal ranges.

8b) Two species that have become sympatric with mutually exclusive altitudinal ranges may diverge in other niche parameters besides altitudinal preference (for example, they may develop different diets or foraging techniques), so that partial altitudinal overlap as well as complete geographical overlap becomes possible.

8c) Each species becomes genetically molded to its compressed altitudinal range to a degree such that the range now reflects innate survival ability rather than competitive compression, a gap between the ranges of the two species develops, and neither species expands altitudinally on removal of the other.

This process seems to be the principal mechanism by which the rich diversity of bird species in the mountains of New Guinea evolved out of the lowlands (15).

What is the significance of sharp altitudinal transistions? If there were no special behavioral mechanism producing such transitions, one would expect two competing, territorial species with different altitudinal adaptations to replace each other in an overlap band which would consist of a mosaic of territories of the two species (22). In this overlap band the neighbor of a given individual would as likely belong to the other species as to the same species, whereas in the distributions of Fig. 6 each individual is surrounded by individuals of the same species. In fact, altitudinal segregation of congeneric species on mountainous Pacific islands with fewer than 66 species always involves broad overlap bands, and sharp transitions occur only on the more species-rich islands. This contrast suggests two selective pressures underlying sharp transitions. First, in species-poor areas the niche of a given species is nearly as broad as permitted by its intrinsic adaptations and is little compressed by interspecific competition. Under these conditions the success of a dispersing juvenile in colonizing a new territory will depend mainly on visible features of the environment. In species-rich areas, however, the task of identifying a territory that offers a high probability of breeding success for a given species becomes much more difficult, since success now depends critically on the presence and abundance of many other competing species. This in effect would require a dispersing juvenile to perform a faunal survey in addition to merely judging the appearance of the habitat. Second, a selective pressure may arise from the difficulty of finding mates in a species-rich community where many species are rare. Thus, I postulate that, on species-rich islands but not on species-poor islands, dispersing young birds are programmed genetically, or they learn by early experience, to seek out habitats where their species is already established, rather than habitats where they will be surrounded by individuals of other species. The presence of individuals of their own species becomes the only reliable indicator that the habitat is suitable for them. By waiting in the juvenile fringe or "kindergarten" at the lower or upper limit of the altitudinal range, the juveniles are in a ringside position from which they can eventually seize an optimal territory vacated by an adult.

Other spatial segregating mechanisms. Two further ecological segregating mechanisms, vertical stratification and habitat segregation, resemble altitudinal segregation in that closely related species become sorted out spatially.

Bird species are more stratified vertically in the New Guinea forest than in forests with fewer bird species but similar vegetational structure. Thus, standard bird nets 2 m in height and

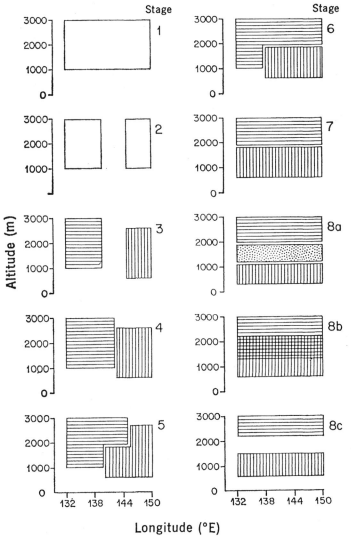

Stage 1
Stage 2
Stage 3
Stage 4
Stage 5
Stage 6
Stage 7
Stage 8a
Stage 8b
Stage 8c

Altitude (m)

Longitude (°E)

Fig. 8. Stages in the evolutionary transformation of one species into two species with mutually exclusive altitudinal ranges. See text for details. In each diagram altitudinal range is plotted as a function of longitude for some species or pairs of species in the mountains of New Guinea. Thus, in stages 1 through 4 there is neither geographical nor altitudinal overlap, in stages 5 through 8a and 8c there is geographical but not altitudinal overlap, and in stage 8b both geographical and altitudinal overlap. Each such distributional pattern represents a "snapshot" of a different stage in speciation and permits reconstruction of the whole process. Examples of species in each stage are: 1, *Ifrita kowaldi*; 2, *Climacteris leucophaea*; 3, *Melidectes nouhuysi* and *M. princeps*; 4, *Parotia lawesi* and *P. carolae*; 5, *Pachycephalopsis poliosoma* and *P. hattamensis*; 6, *Amblyornis macgregoriae* and *A. subalaris*; 7, *Ducula rufigaster* and *D. chalconota*; 8a, *Eupetes caerulescens*, *E. castanonotus*, and *E. leucostictus*; 8b, *Neopsittacus musschenbroekii* and *N. pullicauda*; 8c, *Meliphaga analoga* and *M. orientalis*.

resting on the ground catch only about half of the forest species locally present in New Guinea montane rain forest but all species in the species-poor rain forest of New Zealand. Some of the species in New Guinea forage only in the canopy; others forage regularly at 4 to 15 m above the ground but never descend to 2 m and hence are never caught in nets; and others forage only on the ground or up to a height of 2 m. As in the case of altitudinal ranges, vertical foraging ranges expand on species-poor mountains or islands where vertically abutting competitors are absent (*10*).

Some congeners become sorted by occupying different habitat types, often to the mutual exclusion of each other. For example, whereas there is only one species of barn owl (genus *Tyto*) in most parts of the world, New Guinea has three species: *Tyto capensis* in grassland, *T. alba* in partly wooded areas, and *T. tenebricosa* in forest. Among species sorting by habitat, spatial expansion is a frequent response to the absence of competing congeners on islands (*10, 11*). Expansion of New Guinea second-growth species into forest on islands is especially common, since New Guinea forest species are frequently absent on islands because of their poor dispersal ability.

Nonspatial Segregating Mechanisms

Spatial overlap of closely related species is possible if they separate on the basis of time, diet, or foraging techniques.

Infrequently, closely related bird species segregate by occupying the same space at different times of day or of the year. The kingfisher *Melidora macrorhina* is nocturnal. The other kingfishers are diurnal. The south New Guinea savanna near Merauke is alternately occupied by two marsh hawks, *Circus approximans* in the dry season and *C. spilonotus* in the wet season. Differences in body size provide the commonest means by which closely related species can take the same type of food in the same space at the same time (*15*). Larger birds can take larger food items than can smaller birds, but smaller birds can perch on more slender branches than can larger birds. One can frequently see a bird foraging out along a branch up to the point where the branch begins to bend under its weight. In a tree occupied by birds of many species the larger birds are often

concentrated toward the main branches, the smaller birds toward the periphery (Fig. 9). Among congeners sorting by size in New Guinea, the ratio between the weights of the larger bird and the smaller bird is on the average 1.90; it is never less than 1.33 and never more than 2.73. Species with similar habits and with a weight ratio less than 1.33 are too similar to coexist locally (that is, to share territories) and must segregate spatially. For instance, the cuckoo-shrikes *Coracina tenuirostris* and *C. papuensis* segregate by habitat on New Guinea, where their average weights are 73 grams and 74 grams, respectively, but they often occur together in the same tree on New Britain, where their respective weights are 61 g and 101 g. New Guinea has no locally coexisting pairs of species with similar habits and with a weight ratio exceeding 2.73, presumably because a

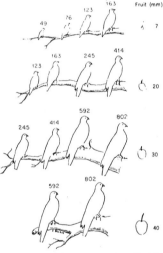

Fig. 9. Schematic representation of niche relations among the eight species of *Ptilinopus* and *Ducula* fruit pigeons in New Guinea lowland rain forest. On the right is a fruit of a certain diameter (in millimeters), and on the left are pigeons of different weights (in grams) arranged along a branch. Each pigeon weighs approximately 1.5 times the next pigeon. Each fruit tree attracts up to four consecutive members of this size sequence. Trees with increasingly large fruits attract increasingly large pigeons. In a given tree the smaller pigeons are preferentially distributed on the smaller, more peripheral branches. The pigeons having the weights indicated are: 49 g, *Ptilinopus nanus*; 76 g, *P. pulchellus*; 123 g, *P. superbus*; 163 g, *P. ornatus*; 245 g, *P. perlatus*; 414 g, *Ducula rufigaster*; 592 g, *D. zoeae*; 802 g, *D. pinon*.

medium-sized bird of relative weight $\sqrt{2.73} = 1.65$ can coexist successfully with both the large species and with the small species. Thus one finds a sequence of three or more species rather than just two species of such different sizes. For example, the eight fruit pigeons of the genera *Ptilinopus* and *Ducula* coexisting in the lowland forests of New Guinea form a graded size sequence over a 16-fold range in weight (Fig. 9).

May and MacArthur (*6*) predicted on theoretical grounds that species segregating along a single niche dimension in a fluctuating environment must maintain a certain minimum niche difference. This minimum spacing seems in fact to have been reached in nature by those bird species that segregate according to size. Thus, on Pacific islands with 30 to 50 bird species, the ratio between the weights of pairs of birds segregating by size is approximately 4, but this ratio has already been compressed to 2 on islands with 100 species. On New Guinea (513 species) the average value of this ratio is compressed no further, and the extra species are accommodated by expanding the size sequences to smaller or larger birds or else by finer subdivision of space or foraging techniques.

Similarly sized species that take the same food may overlap spatially if they harvest the food in different ways. For instance, small insectivorous birds differ in tactics according to whether insects are caught in midair by sallying, are pounced on and plucked off surfaces, are gleaned off surfaces, pried out of bark, taken from flowers, or are extracted from epiphytes and accumulations of dead leaves. Species with a given type of strategy further differ in the ratio between traveling time and stationary time, in the frequency of movements, and in their average rate of travel (*23*). Thus, the montane flycatchers *Pachycephala modesta* and *Poecilodryas albonotata* differ in that the former remains perched for an average of 2 seconds, the latter for an average of 30 seconds between moves; and in that the former travels 1 m, and the latter 12 m, per move. *Pachycephala modesta* could be described as a quick and cursory searcher, *Poecilodryas albonotata* as a slow and selective searcher.

Finally, related species may segregate by different diets. For example, the whistler *Pachycephala leucostigma* eats mainly fruit while other whistlers eat mainly insects.

Some General Features of Competition

Despite the abundant distributional evidence for competition between New Guinea bird species, one rarely sees a member of one territorial species fighting a member of another territorial species. Once territories are established, fighting simply does not pay: the winner as well as the loser may be injured, or both combatants may attract the attention of a predator. Even among migrant North American thrushes that must reestablish their territories each spring, interspecific chases and aggressive behavior disappear within a week after arrival on the breeding grounds (24). In tropical rain forest, where many bird species are permanently resident and are relatively long-lived, and where visibility inside the forest is poor, neighboring individuals may confine their aggressive behavior for years to songs and calls and simply learn to avoid each other's foraging space.

Species that colonize species-poor islands, where they are freed of competition from close relatives, often broaden the spatial parameters of the niche by immediately occupying a wider range of habitats, altitudes, or vertical foraging positions. However, the colonists rarely expand their diets or range of foraging techniques until after relatively long periods of time on an evolutionary scale (11). This combination of spatial elasticity with tactical and dietary conservatism reflects partly the degree of genetic programming underlying the stereotyped foraging strategies of birds, and partly the economics of feeding. Given a certain set of inflexible tactics, the economics of energy yield and energy expenditure in foraging dictate the diet but leave to the individual the decision about the space in which the tactics can be applied profitably (3, chap. 3).

How does the combined population density of all bird species on an island compare with the combined population density on a mainland? That is, islands have fewer species than mainlands, but the types of competitive release we have examined mean that the island colonists frequently have broader niches and higher population densities than on the mainland. How well does competitive release compensate on islands for the population densities of missing mainland species? Studies on this problem of density compensation have provided conflicting results. In the New Guinea area, total population densities in similar habitats on different islands

increase linearly or even more rapidly with species diversity, so that an island with few species also has a low density of individuals (11). However, on the Pearl Islands off Panama, total population densities of birds are even higher than on the Panama mainland (25). Part of the difference between these two sets of results may depend on whether the island colonists are as well adapted to the available habitat as are the mainland species they replace. Also, the low population densities on the New Guinea satellite islands, and on old isolated islands such as Madagascar (26) and New Zealand, may reflect genetic deterioration in their isolated populations, because of small gene pools, reduced intraspecific and interspecific competition, and (frequently) short population survival times to extinction (11).

Conclusions

The concepts by which MacArthur and Wilson have transformed the science of ecology in the past decade, and the results of ecological studies such as mine on New Guinea bird communities, have implications for conservation policies. For example, primary tropical rain forest, the most species-rich and ecologically complex habitat on earth, has for millions of years served as the ultimate evolutionary source of the world's dominant plant and animal groups. Throughout the tropics today, the rain forests are being destroyed at a rate such that little will be left in a few decades. When the rain forests have been reduced to isolated tracts separated by open country, the distribution of obligate rain forest species will come to resemble bird distributions on New Guinea land-bridge islands after severing of the land bridges. The smaller the tract, the more rapidly will forest species tend to disappear and be replaced by the widespread secondgrowth species that least need protection (13). This ominous process is illustrated by Barro Colorado Island, a former hill in Panama that became an island when construction of the Panama Canal flooded surrounding valleys to create Gatun Lake. In the succeeding 60 years several forest bird species have already disappeared from Barro Colorado and been unable to recolonize across the short intervening water gap from the forest on the nearby shore of Gatun Lake.

The consequences of the speciesarea relation (Fig. 1) should be taken into consideration during the planning of tropical rain forest parks (13). In a geographical area that is relatively homogeneous with regard to the fauna, one large park would be preferable to an equivalent area in the form of several smaller parks. Continuous nonforest strips through the park (for example, wide highway swaths) would convert one rain forest "island" into two half-size islands and should be avoided. If other considerations require that an area be divided into several small parks, connecting them by forest corridors might significantly improve their conservation function at little further cost in land withdrawn from development.

Modern ecological studies may also be relevant to the understanding of human populations. For instance, during a long period of human evolution there appear to have been not one but two coexistent hominid lines in Africa, the *Australopithecus robustus–A. boisei* ("*Zinjanthropus*") line, which became extinct, and the *Australopithecus africanus–A. habilis* line, which led to *Homo sapiens* (27). The need to maintain niche differences between these lines must have provided one of the most important selective pressures on the ancestors of modern man in the late Pliocene and early Pleistocene. Thus, any attempt to understand human evolution must confront the problem of what these ecological segregating mechanisms were. To what extent were contemporaneous species of the two lines separated by habitat, by diet, by size difference, or by foraging technique, and were their local spatial distributions broadly overlapping or else sharpened by behavioral interactions as in the case of the *Crateroscelis* warblers of Fig. 6? To take another example, there are striking parallels between the present distributions of human populations and of bird populations on the islands of Vitiaz and Dampier straits between New Guinea and New Britain. Some of these islands were sterilized by cataclysmic volcanic explosions within the last several centuries. The birds that recolonized these islands have been characterized as coastal and smallisland specialists of high reproductive potential, high dispersal powers, and low competitive ability, unlike the geographically closer, competitively superior, slowly dispersing, and breeding birds of mainland New Guinea (10, 11, 13). It remains to be seen whether the people of the Vitiaz-Dampier islands, the Polynesians, and other human populations that colonize insular or unstable habitats also have distinctive population ecologies.

References and Notes

1. A. R. Wallace, *The Geographical Distribution of Animals* (Macmillan, London, 1876).
2. E. Mayr, *Systematics and the Origin of Species* (Columbia Univ. Press, New York, 1942); *Animal Species and Evolution* (Harvard Univ. Press, Cambridge, Mass., 1963).
3. R. H. MacArthur, *Geographical Ecology* (Harper & Row, New York, 1972).
4. —— and E. O. Wilson, *The Theory of Island Biogeography* (Princeton Univ. Press, Princeton, N.J., 1967).
5. ——, *Evolution* **17**, 373 (1963); R. H. MacArthur and R. Levins, *Proc. Nat. Acad. Sci. U.S.A.* **51**, 1207 (1964); R. H. MacArthur, *Biol. Rev. Cambridge* **40**, 510 (1965); ——, H. Recher, M. Cody, *Amer. Natur.* **100**, 319 (1966); R. H. MacArthur and E. Pianka,

ibid., p. 603; E. O. Wilson, *Evolution* **13**, 122 (1959); *Amer. Natur.* **95**, 169 (1961); —— and D. S. Simberloff, *Ecology* **50**, 267 (1969).
6. R. M. May and R. H. MacArthur, *Proc. Nat. Acad. Sci. U.S.A.* **69**, 1109 (1972).
7. E. O. Wilson, *Psyche* **65**, 26 (1958).
8. J. M. Diamond, *Amer. Mus. Nov. No. 2284* (1967); *Explorers J.* **46**, 210 (1968); —— and J. W. Terborgh, *Auk* **85**, 62 (1968); J. M. Diamond, *Amer. Mus. Nov. No. 2362* (1969); J. Terborgh and J. M. Diamond, *Wilson Bull.* **82**, 29 (1970).
9. J. M. Diamond, *Proc. Nat. Acad. Sci. U.S.A.* **64**, 57 (1969).
10. ——, *ibid.* **67**, 529 (1970).
11. ——, *ibid.*, p. 1715.
12. ——, *ibid.* **68**, 2742 (1971).
13. ——, *ibid.* **69**, 3199 (1972).
14. ——, *Science* **151**, 1102 (1966).
15. ——, *Avifauna of the Eastern Highlands of New Guinea* (Nuttall Ornithological Club, Cambridge, Mass., 1972).
16. F. W. Preston, *Ecology* **43**, 185 (1962).
17. J. Terborgh and J. Faaborg, *Auk*, in press.
18. R. F. Flint, *Glacial and Pleistocene Geology* (Wiley, New York, 1957).
19. F. Vuilleumier, *Amer. Natur.* **104**, 373 (1970); J. H. Brown, *ibid.* **105**, 467 (1971).

20. D. Lack, *Ecological Isolation in Birds* (Harvard Univ. Press, Cambridge, Mass., 1971).
21. J. W. Terborgh, *Ecology* **52**, 23 (1971).
22. M. L. Cody, *ibid.* **51**, 455 (1970).
23. ——, *Amer. Natur.* **102**, 107 (1968).
24. D. H. Morse, *Wilson Bull.* **83**, 57 (1971).
25. R. H. MacArthur, J. M. Diamond, J. R. Karr, *Ecology* **53**, 330 (1972).
26. J. R. Karr, personal communication.
27. D. Pilbeam, *The Ascent of Man* (Macmillan, New York, 1972); L. S. B. Leakey, *Nature* **209**, 1279 (1966); F. C. Howell, *ibid.* **223**, 1234 (1969); W. Schaffer, *Amer. Natur.* **102**, 559 (1968).
28. I thank R. H. MacArthur and J. W. Terborgh, for stimulating discussions; the National Geographic Society, Explorers Club, American Philosophical Society, Chapman Fund, and Sanford Trust of the American Museum of Natural History, and Alpha Helix New Guinea Program of the National Science Foundation, for support; M. Cody, A. Grinnell, S. Kaufman-Diamond, S. Krasne, and G. Szabo, for criticism of the manuscript; D. Amador, for permission to use facilities of the American Museum of Natural History; and more residents of New Guinea than can be mentioned by name, for making fieldwork possible.

Humanizing the Earth

René J. Dubos

How gray and drab, unappealing and unsignificant, our planet would be without the radiance of life. If it were not covered with living organisms the surface of the earth would resemble that of the moon. Its colorful and diversified appearance is largely the creation of microbes, plants, and animals which endlessly transform its inanimate rocks and gases into an immense variety of organic substances. Man augments still further this diversification by altering the physical characteristics of the land, changing the distribution of living things, and adding human order and fantasy to the ecological determinism of nature.

Many of man's interventions into nature have, of course, been catastrophic. History is replete with ecological disasters caused by agricultural and industrial mismanagement. The countries

The author is a professor emeritus of the Rockefeller University, New York 10021. This article is the text of the B. Y. Morrison Memorial lecture, sponsored by the Agricultural Research Service of the U.S. Department of Agriculture. The lecture was delivered at the annual meeting of the AAAS, 29 December 1972, in Washington, D.C. Reprints may be obtained from Dr. Robert Nelson, Public Information Office, Agricultural Research Service, U.S. Department of Agriculture, Washington, D.C. 20250.

which were most flourishing in antiquity are now among the poorest in the world. Some of their most famous cities have been abandoned; lands which were once fertile are now barren deserts.

Disease, warfare, and civil strife have certainly played important roles in the collapse of ancient civilizations; but the primary cause was probably the damage caused to the quality of the soil and to water supplies by poor ecological practices. Similarly today, the environment is being spoiled in many parts of the world by agricultural misuse or overuse, by industrial poisoning, and of course by wars.

The primary purpose of the recent United Nations Conference on the Human Environment, held in Stockholm in June 1972, was to formulate global approaches to the correction and prevention of the environmental defects resulting from man's mismanagement of the earth. I shall not discuss the technical aspects of these problems, but rather shall try to look beyond them and present facts suggesting that man can actually improve on nature. In my opinion, the human use of natural resources and of technology is compatible with

ecological health, and can indeed bring out potentialities of the earth which remain unexpressed in the state of wilderness.

The disastrous ecological consequences of many past and present human activities point to the need for greater knowledge and respect of natural laws. This view is succinctly expressed by Barry Commoner in his fourth law of ecology: "Nature knows best." I shall first discuss the limitations of this law.

When left undisturbed, all environments tend toward an equilibrium state, called the climax or mature state by ecologists. Under equilibrium conditions, the wastes of nature are constantly being recycled in the ecosystem, which becomes thereby more or less self-perpetuating. In a natural forest, for example, acorns fall to the ground and are eaten by squirrels, which in turn may be eaten by foxes or other predators; the dead leaves and branches, the excrements of animals, are utilized by microbes, which return their constituents to the soil in the form of humus and mineral nutrients. More vegetation grows out of the recycled materials, thus assuring the maintenance of the ecosystem.

When applied to such equilibrated systems, the phrase "Nature knows best" is justified, but is in fact little more than a tautology. As used in this phrase, the word *nature* simply denotes a state of affairs spontaneously brought about by evolutionary adaptation resulting from feedbacks which generate a coherent system. There are no problems in undisturbed nature; there are only solutions, precisely because the equilibrium state is an adaptive state.

Ecological Monographs (1974) **44**:153–169

POPULATIONS AND LOCAL EXTINCTIONS OF BIRDS ON BARRO COLORADO ISLAND, PANAMÁ[1]

EDWIN O. WILLIS

Department of Biology, Princton University
Princeton, New Jersey 08540

Abstract. A 1960–71 study of populations of color-banded ant-following antbirds of three species on a tropical-forested lowland reserve, Barro Colorado Island, showed that the small species (Spotted Antbird, *Hylophylax naevioides*) remained stable at about 20 pairs/km². A medium-sized species, the Bicolored Antbird (*Gymnopithys bicolor*), decreased from about 3 pairs to 1.5 pairs/km². A large species, the Ocellated Antbird (*Phaenostictus mcleannani*), declined from 1.5 pairs/km² to near extinction—only one female remained in early 1971. Two of three other species that regularly follow army ants showed relatively stable populations, but a third large species (Barred Woodcreeper, *Dendrocolaptes certhia*) declined from two pairs to local extinction. Prior to 1960 a very large ground-cuckoo that follows ants had already become extinct there. Thus, the three largest of the seven original species that regularly followed ants were gone or nearly gone by 1970. The decrease in numbers of regular ant-following birds was not made up by increases in occasional followers.

Detailed studies of antbirds showed no clear reasons for declines, except that annual mortalities of adults were high in Ocellated Antbirds (about 30%) compared to Spotted Antbirds (15%–17%) and nest losses perhaps higher in the former (96% compared to 91%). Nest mortalities were slightly lower (88%) and adult mortalities intermediate (about 25%) in Bicolored Antbirds. Female Ocellated Antbirds had higher mortalities than males. The antbirds renest repeatedly during long nesting seasons, up to 14 times per year for Ocellated Antbirds. However, to replace females of this species under Barro Colorado conditions 19 nestings per year would be needed.

Concurrent listing of all birds of the island showed that 45 species of breeding birds, 22% of the avifauna present when the island was made a reserve, had disappeared by 1970. No new species replaced them. Of the lost species 13 are forest birds, in danger if forests are cut elsewhere. The other species, second-growth and forest-edge birds, have been crowded out by growth of the forest.

Loss of species from this tropical reserve, especially the part apparently caused by the small size and isolation of the reserve, poses problems for conservation and ecological studies of tropical biotas. It is suggested that large future reserves have corridor zones to each other, that is, that intensive human use not preempt too much area nor interrupt immigration of animals or plants from one refuge to another.

Key words: Antbirds; conservation; dispersal; extinctions; forests; islands; mortality; natality; parks; populations; tropics.

INTRODUCTION

The dynamics of bird populations of tropical forests are of considerable theoretical and practical interest. High nest-mortality rates (Ricklefs 1969) suggest high adult survival, which could mean emphasis on "*K*-selection," the perfection of adult longevity even at the expense of low reproductive rates. Sensitivity of birds to human or other disturbance of the tropical ecosystem also depends on population characteristics. The dynamics of bird populations also help determine persistence and rates of spread of arboviruses like Venezuelan equine encephalomyelitis (M. Gochfeld, *pers. comm.*).

The population dynamics of tropical birds are little known. Snow (1962*a*) found in Trinidad a low mortality rate, about 11% per year, in 38 adult male White-bearded Manakins (*Manacus manacus*), a spe-

cies of second growth. He estimated indirectly a similar mortality rate for the Golden-headed Manakin (*Pipra erythrocephala*), a Trinidadian forest bird. By contrast, Morel (1964) found high adult mortality in the Firefinch (*Lagonosticta senegala*), a bird of open country. Fogden (1972) estimated 10% mortality per year for a few individuals of many forest species on Sarawak, an island with few predators on adult birds.

Local extinctions of tropical birds have also had little study. The disastrous extinctions of native Hawaiian birds (Berger 1970) have started studies by the U.S. Fish and Wildlife Service, but detailed population studies have not yet been made. MacArthur and Wilson (1967) suggest that patterns of species diversity on islands are explainable as equilibria between immigration and extinction rates. Diamond (1971) found a loss and gain of at least one species per 3 yr on Karkar, an island off New Guinea; the rate was roughly the same as on Santa Cruz Island

[1] Manuscript received October 8, 1972; accepted August 15, 1973.

154   EDWIN O. WILLIS   Ecological Monographs
                                                                   Vol. 44, No. 2

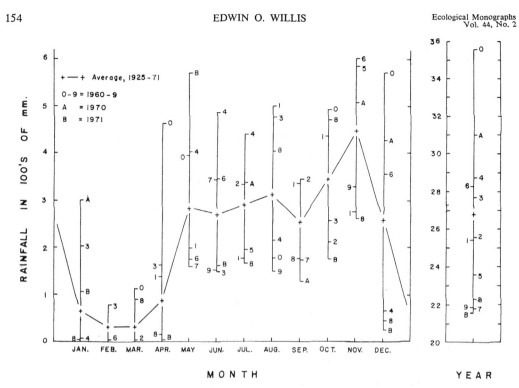

Fig. 1. Average rainfall on Barro Colorado Island, 1925–71, and variability 1960–71. Monthly rainfall is indicated only for extreme years. Absolute variability of rainfall is highest in rainy months, but especially in April–May and December–January; the rainy season can thus vary in length from 9 months (1960, 1970–71) to 7 months (1968, 1971). The only year with 6 months well below normal is 1968; 1969 is the only year with no month well above normal.

off California. He also suggests (Diamond, *pers. comm.*) high losses of "land-bridge" birds on other islands near New Guinea in the millennia since they were connected to it in the last glacial period.

Three species of birds that follow army ants (*Eciton burchelli* and *Labidus praedator*) in the lowland forest reserve of Barro Colorado Island, Panamá Canal Zone, are easily captured, marked, and resighted (Willis 1967, 1972a, 1973a): Spotted Antbirds (*Hylophylax naevioides*), Bicolored Antbirds (*Gymnopithys bicolor*), and Ocellated Antbirds (*Phaenostictus mcleannani*). Three other species regularly follow army ants, but are less easily captured: Gray-headed Tanagers (*Eucometis penicillata*), Plain-brown Woodcreepers (*Dendrocincla fuliginosa*), and Barred Woodcreepers (*Dendrocolaptes certhia*). In 1960–61 I studied the annual cycles of these birds. From 1961 to 1970 I returned for a few months each year to do a 10-yr study of their population dynamics. I concentrated on the three species of antbirds in a study area at the center of the island. In December, January, 1970–71, five college students helped search all of Barro Colorado for birds. During each study period I listed birds of other species seen. Other ornithologists visiting

the island also recorded presence or absence of birds. This report gives the results of the 10-yr study and the final census.

METHODS OF STUDY

Birds captured in mist nets were marked with individual combinations of colored celluloid legbands. The bands were read through binoculars thereafter, except for occasional individuals recaptured in nets. I tried to avoid recapturing birds, for about one bird in 200 breaks its leg or wing in nets. Even though most of these few birds recovered rapidly and survived well, a few were not seen again. These individuals are not counted in the analyses of population dynamics. Band loss was rare, and birds were marked with two or four bands so that loss of a band or two was easily detected. The birds pecked at bands for a few minutes after being released, but seemed undisturbed by them thereafter. I saw no evidence that any birds developed foot trouble because of bands, although there were a few cases of loss of foot or broken leg for unknown reasons; foot, leg, and also wing problems have occurred in unbanded birds. Such birds, banded or not, sometimes survived years afterward.

TABLE 1. Professional ant-followers of Barro Colorado Island

Species	Weight in grams	Dominance	Foraging height	Habitat
Rufous-vented Ground-Cuckoo	350(?)	1	Ground	[a]
Barred Woodcreeper	65	2	High[b]	Escarpment
Ocellated Antbird	50	3	Low	Escarpment
Plain-brown Woodcreeper	40	4	High[b]	General
Bicolored Antbird	32	4	Low	General
Gray-headed Tanager	30	5	High[b]	Flats
Spotted Antbird	18	6	Low	General

[a] Extirpated by 1960.
[b] These species move down at times, especially if larger birds are not present (Willis 1966).

STUDY AREA AND CLIMATE

The main study area on Barro Colorado Island included approximately the central 4 km² of the island (Willis 1967: Fig. 3) and sampled most of the vegetational and geological zones. Barro Colorado (9° 09′ N, 79° 51′ W) is a 15.6-km² hilltop of lowland evergreen forest. It was separated from nearby forests in 1910–14, when Gatun Lake rose behind a dam on the Chagres River to form the central part of the nearby Panamá Canal. Before 1923, when the island became a biological reserve, a few settlers cut down patches of forest. Much of the eastern half of the island is medium-height forest, probably under 100 yr old; much of the western half is tall forest, probably mature but almost certainly not virgin (Bennett 1963). Kenoyer (1929) and Standley (1933) discuss the vegetation and successional stages on the island.

Elevations range from 164 m to 26 m at lake level. A flat basalt cap slopes westward from the summit, surrounded except on the west by a steep escarpment zone of Bohio conglomerate, which extends onto peninsulas near the laboratory clearing. A flat main eastern peninsula (Barbour Point) is Caimito formation (Woodring 1958). The escarpment and flat areas differ in birds, as noted below.

In a strong dry season (January to April) only 7.9% of the average annual rainfall of 2,678 mm falls. There is great annual and monthly variability (Fig. 1). Some dry seasons have periods of high rainfall, and nearly always dry periods occur in the rainy season. Allee (1926) notes that temperature near the ground, where ant-following birds work, is very stable; there is little wind, even in the dry season. Some areas of undergrowth, particularly ridges and shores facing the strong northeast trade winds of the dry season, are rather windy. The leaf litter and forest floor dry out especially rapidly in these areas, but all areas eventually dry out in prolonged dry periods at any time of year.

Windstorms and landslides periodically fell trees in the forest. A major windstorm on October 1, 1961, felled scattered groups of trees all over the island, creating treefalls in which Chestnut-backed Antbirds became very common by about 1966 (Willis and

Oniki 1972). Local residents (fide D. H. Knight) report a storm in 1919 that felled much of the forest on Barbour Point and may account for the low forest there today. Several landslides in November 1959 created small zones of second growth in escarpment areas on the island. However, most of the forest is maturing gradually.

PROFESSIONAL ANT-FOLLOWERS

In the region of Barro Colorado Island there were originally 11 or more species of birds that follow army ants for most of their food. One of these "professional" ant-followers, the Ruddy Woodcreeper (*Dendrocincla homochroa*), is a casual visitant from the Pacific foothills. Two others, the Immaculate Antbird (*Myrmeciza immaculata*) and the Black-crowned Antpitta (*Pittasoma michleri*), were local in the wetter Caribbean foothills. A fourth, the Bare-crowned Antbird (*Gymnocichla nudiceps*), occurred in Caribbean second growth. None of the four was recorded from Barro Colorado in the 1920's and 1930's in the earliest ornithological studies (Chapman 1938, Eisenmann 1952); none has been recorded subsequently.

Of the remaining seven species (Table 1) the very large ground-cuckoo *Neomorphus geoffroyi* was collected and later observed on Barro Colorado Island to 1935. It is never numerous anywhere; probably the total population on Barro Colorado was a few pairs. Elsewhere from Nicaragua to Brazil these birds are often in riverine or slope forests, usually in areas crowded with treefalls and vines. Perhaps mature forest is unsuitable for them. The remaining six species (Table 1) were still present when I began work on Barro Colorado in 1960.

On Barro Colorado, Barred Woodcreepers and Ocellated Antbirds stayed mainly in escarpment zones toward the center of the island. All or nearly all individuals were on the study area. Gray-headed Tanagers were mainly in lighter woodland on the eastern half of the island. The other species were generally distributed, except that Spotted Antbirds were rare in the most precipitous canyons.

The three antbirds seldom cross open areas and

TABLE 2. Pairs of antbirds per square kilometer on 2- to 5-km² study areas, Barro Colorado Island, 1961–70

Year	Spotted Antbird	Bicolored Antbird	Ocellated Antbird
1961	22.2	3.16	1.92
1962	20.1	2.92	—
1963	18.7	2.48	1.79
1964	18.3	2.72	1.42
1965	18.6	2.47	1.11
1966	20.2	1.63	0.84
1967	19.9	1.56	0.72
1968	21.5	1.18	0.90
1969	19.3	1.42	0.40
1970	21.6	1.46	0.13

TABLE 3. Nest and fledgling success in three species of Antbirds on Barro Colorado Island

Item	Spotted	Bicolored	Ocellated
Minimum nest success (%)	9	12	(4)[a]
Number of nests with one fledgling (A)	8	1	(6)
Number of nests with two fledglings (B)	11	2	(4)
Number of fledglings/successful nest	1.6	1.7	(1.4)
Average days out of nest at discovery (t')	22	18	23
Number of broods of one at discovery (A')	38	7	10
Number of broods of two at discovery (B')	44	10	6
Average brood size at discovery	1.5	1.6	1.4
Percentage of fledglings surviving $(1-p)$	95	93	(90)
Complete brood loss by discovery $(C, \%)$	2.2	2.6	(6.4)
Average days out of nest at banding	20	19	32
Percentage of fledglings surviving to banding	(95)	(93)	(88)

[a] Records in parentheses are estimates. See Appendix 1 for calculations and symbols.

probably never cross Gatun Lake to or from Barro Colorado. The other species fly strongly across open areas and may cross the lake. No bird banded on Barro Colorado has yet been seen on the mainland or vice versa, but there has been little study on neighboring areas. Barro Colorado is 500 m or more from mainland forests. Diamond (*pers. comm.*) found most forest birds, even strongly flying ones, absent on a forested island only 55 m off the coast of New Guinea. Tropical birds of the undergrowth disperse across barriers extremely poorly compared to birds of northern or open habitats.

GENERAL POPULATION TRENDS

Gray-headed Tanager populations remained near one pair per square kilometer from 1961 to 1971. Banded individuals rarely persisted more than 2 or 3 yr, although one female banded in 1961 was still alive in 1971. Turnover of pairs was high, and many new birds appeared each year.

Plain-brown Woodcreeper populations were stable at about six to seven individuals per square kilometer (Willis 1972b). Settled individuals often survived many years; three of four females banded in 1961 were still alive in 1970. There was a large population of wandering birds, which usually disappeared within a year or two after banding. Turnover was high except in the settled birds.

Two pairs of Barred Woodcreepers were in the escarpment zone on the study area in 1960; another bird appeared in 1962. Probably there were no other birds on the island, and previous records of the species were few (Eisenmann 1952). One pair and the lone bird disappeared between 1964 and early 1965. The other pair separated, one bird to the south escarpment until 1966 and the other to the north escarpment (a kilometer or so distant) until 1969. The 1971 census found none on the island.

The populations of the three species of antbirds in the study area from 1961 to 1970 are shown in Table 2. Spotted Antbirds were common and had stable populations. Bicolored Antbirds decreased to half

the original density by 1968 and rose slightly by 1970. The 1971 census found 11 pairs, two male-male pairs, and several unmated males. Probably there were about 60 birds on the island, including some 20 pairs. Ocellated Antbirds were at this population level in 1961, for there were some 12 pairs on the study area. The 1971 census showed one pair and four unmated males on the island, all in escarpment zones on or near the study area.

In summary, of six professional ant-followers the largest disappeared between 1961 and 1970, and the next largest was nearly gone by 1970. The fourth declined to half the original density in this period. The third, fifth, and sixth seemed to have stable populations. Numbers of ant swarms remained about the same, so in 1970 there were fewer professional ant-followers per swarm than in 1960.

Many other species of birds take less than half their food—usually less than a tenth—by following army ants. There were no spectacular increases in ant-following by most of these birds. One large lake-shore species, the Greater Ani (*Crotophaga major*), turned up at several swarms at the center of the island in 1971. The large Rufous Motmots (*Baryphthengus ruficapillus*) also turned up more frequently in January 1971 than in January 1961. However, these increases did not fill gaps very well—there were similar numbers of "nonprofessional" birds in 1971 and 1961.

These changes apparently did not occur on the mainland, across Gatun Lake. In extensive humid forests of the Navy Pipeline Road, numbers of Barred Woodcreepers, Bicolored Antbirds, and Ocellated Antbirds per swarm from 1965 to 1971 were as high

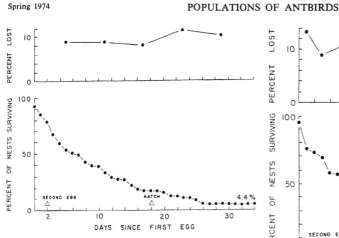

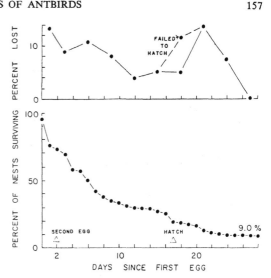

FIG. 2. Survivorship of 74 unvisited nests of Ocellated Antbirds (below); same data shown as mortalities per day for 6-day periods (above). Status of nests inferred by watching the parents at swarms of ants, by methods explained in Willis (1973b). Mortalities estimated at 8% on day 0 (the day the first egg is laid) and day 1 (the day between the laying of the two eggs), or nearly the average daily loss for day 2 (the day the last egg is laid) to day 7; survivorship of these antbird nests cannot be determined directly at unvisited nests until regular incubation begins on day 2.

FIG. 4. Survivorship of 102 visited nests of Spotted Antbirds (below); same data shown as mortalities per day for 3-day periods (above). The dotted line shows mortality when five nests that never hatched are counted as lost on day 17; the solid line nearby omits these five nests for comparison.

or higher than on Barro Colorado in 1961. Numbers of Plain-brown Woodcreepers, Spotted Antbirds, and Gray-headed Tanagers per swarm were always lower than on Barro Colorado. These three species were more common in dryer forests toward the Pacific side of the Canal Zone.

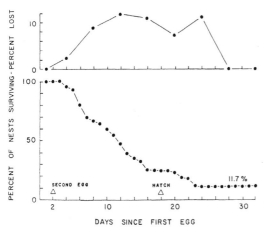

FIG. 3. Survivorship of nests of Bicolored Antbirds (below); same data shown as average daily mortalities for 4-day periods (above). Sixteen visited nests tabulated before day 2; 61 unvisited nests tabulated as well after day 2 (see Willis 1973b for a comparison of unvisited and visited nests).

POPULATION DYNAMICS OF ANTBIRDS

More detailed data are available on the changes in populations of the three species of antbirds. Three factors determining population dynamics—mortality, natality, and movements—will be discussed.

Mortality

Losses of antbirds are divisible into four categories: losses of nests and nestlings, losses of fledglings before banding, losses of first-year birds, and losses of adults. In some species losses differ in the last two categories between males and females or between breeding and nonreproductive birds.

Losses of nests.—As is usual for forest birds in and outside the tropics (Snow and Snow 1963), nest success is very low in all three antbirds (Table 3). Success seems unusually low in Ocellated Antbirds, if the rough estimates are correct. Details of survivorship for the three species, based on a modification (Appendix I) of the method of Ricklefs (1969), are shown in Fig. 2–4.

A few eggs and sets of eggs of Spotted Antbirds did not hatch; in some cases one egg instead of two was in the nest. In most cases these sets were predated. Two eggs in each of five nests of Spotted Antbirds failed to hatch on day 17 or thereafter and were eaten later by predators (Fig. 4). The failure of these nests may have been due to infertility, etc., or to a predator scaring the female off the nest at night; they could be considered "predated" nests if the last were true. Occasionally an antbird nest loses an egg

158   EDWIN O. WILLIS   Ecological Monographs
                                                                                Vol. 44, No. 2

TABLE 4.   Losses of three species of yearling antbirds

	Spotted				
Item	Male	Female	Both	Bicolored[a]	Ocellated[b]
Average age at banding (days)			20	19	32
Maximum age at banding (days)			53	65	85
Number banded	43	49	92	36	30
Percentage lost by April 15	52	75	64	58	47

[a] Females and males not distinguishable externally until about 6 months old. Three of seven known young females and one of 10 known young males were lost from January to August following the year of hatching.
[b] Males and females alike externally until breeding. Female survivorship probably about the same as male, for young stay with parents until the next breeding season (females and some males) or later (other males) and are protected by them. Parents not hostile to independently foraging young as in Spotted and Bicolored Antbirds.

or nestling, so that average brood size at fledging is less than 2.0 (Table 3). Possibly some of the lost young starved, as Ricklefs (1969) suggests, but genetic failures and capture by predators are among the other possibilities.

Losses of fledglings.—Fledglings seldom disappeared after they were flying well and easily located, but losses must have been moderately high in the first few days after they left nests. At that age the young were very well concealed, usually with separate parents. They were too difficult to detect to get daily observations of survivorship without inordinate time and increased risk of attracting the attention of predators. Losses of fledglings to time of discovery and time of banding are therefore estimated in Table 3 by the methods in Appendix I. Survival from fledging to time of discovery, probably not less than 90%, suggests that many Ocellated Antbird nests fledge only one young (57%, if survival to discovery is 90%).

Losses of first-year birds.—Many young birds are lost between the time of banding and the next April 15, at the start of their first complete breeding season (Table 4). "Loss" includes emigration of individuals from the study area as well as actual mortality. It is only possible to estimate roughly how many young birds wandered off the study area and survived. Very few of these young birds were de-

tected in later years, even though they must stay on the island. The 1971 census showed a very steep decrease in banded birds at increasing distances away from the study area for Spotted Antbirds (a few birds last seen as fledglings were detected off the study area, but no others), a moderate decrease for Bicolors, and no Ocellated Antbirds off the study area (even though they had sometimes been off the study area in 1960–61).

. If 7%–10% of the yearling antbirds moved off the study area to places where they were not detected again, true mortality rates in the 1st yr would be about 55% for Spotted Antbirds, 50% for Bicolored Antbirds, and 40% for Ocellated Antbirds. In this case, rates for females should be about 60% in Spotteds, 60% in Bicolors, and 40% in Ocellateds; rates for males should be about 50% in Spotteds, 45% in Bicolors, and 40% in Ocellateds.

Losses of adult birds.—Losses of birds that have already passed April 15 in their first breeding season are lower than in yearling birds (Table 5). The emigration of these birds from the study area is small, mostly of peripheral birds, so that loss rates are fairly close to true mortalities.

Territorial and unmated adult male Spotted Antbirds seem to have a mortality rate twice as high as mated males. Unmated males sing and wander

TABLE 5.   Losses of adult antbirds[a] per year

	Spotted			Bicolored			Ocellated		
Item	Male	Female	Both	Male	Female	Both	Male	Female	Both
Mated, territorial birds									
Number present at start year	534	469	1,032[b]	93	82	280[b]	68	67	160[b]
Number lost by next year	96	91	195	28	28	80	14	25	48
Percentage lost per year	17.6	19.4	18.8	30	34	29	21	37	30
Unmated, territorial birds									
Number present at start year	29	—	—	8	—	—	7	—	—
Number lost by next year	10	—	—	2	—	—	3	—	—
Percentage lost per year	34	—	—	25	—	—	42	—	—
Unmated, nonterritorial birds									
Number present at start year	—	—	—	83	—	—	18	1	19
Number lost by next year	—	—	—	20	—	—	6	0	6
Percentage lost per year	—	—	—	24	—	—	33	0	32

[a] Excluding a few peripheral banded birds that could not be checked a year later.
[b] Grand totals, including unmated, homosexual, or father-son associations as well.

around their territories and nearby territories, and their lower survival may be the price paid for advertising and for not having a mate to help keep the lookout. The loss rate is intermediate between that for settled adults and that for 1st-yr birds. The fairly high rate for adult unmated males eventually brings numbers of males into balance with numbers of females, offsetting high losses of 1st-yr females. Unmated males on territories ranged from two or three in most years (2%–5% of censused territories) to seven in 1964 (9.2%) and eight in 1970 (8.3%).

Unmated male Bicolored Antbirds had, by contrast, lower losses than mated ones (Table 5). Males that stayed on territories and formed a homosexual bond with a wandering male had especially low losses, 8% (1 of 12). Such males feed each other back and forth, dominate the ant swarm in their own area, and help each other look out for predators. All these advantages except feeding of the male accrue to mated birds, too, but the latter must travel to nests to build, incubate eggs, and feed young and thus lose in food, energy, and safety. Unmated birds can stay at swarms and need not lose in these ways, but are sometimes at the bottom of dominance hierarchies and are not as well fed and safe as homosexual and territorial birds (Willis 1967). Territorial females should survive better than their mates, for they do less work at nests or in care of young and incubate only in the rainy afternoon and evening, whereas males must incubate in the morning, when ants flush most food. Moreover, females often dominate their mates, waste less time chasing trespassers, etc. However, the territorial females do have to lay eggs and to incubate at night and may be predated by mammals more often (Willis 1973b). Table 5 suggests higher rather than lower losses for females.

Loss rates of Bicolored Antbirds varied from year to year. Male losses were unusually high in 1963 (13 of 24), female losses in 1963 (5 of 10), 1964 (4 of 7), 1966 (4 of 7), and 1968 (3 of 6). In 1969 female losses were low (zero of 6). Total losses of adults were low in 1962 (5 of 34) and 1969 (3 of 22), high in 1963 (18 of 34).

Possibly high losses in 1963 were due to high rainfall in January (Fig. 1). In 1970 a high January rainfall caused failure of flowering, then failure of November fruiting, and mass starvation in ground mammals (R. Foster, *pers. comm.*). The mammals tore up palms, in which Bicolored Antbirds often nest. Mortality and starvation of mammals also led ground omnivores and rodent-eating owls and hawks to seek new sources of food. Unfortunately, no naturalist was watching in late 1963. If approximately 10% of the "lost" Bicolors were wandering off the study area, as seems likely, true mortalities were about 20% for males and 25% for females.

TABLE 6. Nestings per month of study and percentages of successful nests (in parentheses) at different months

Month	Months of study (1960–71)	Species		
		Ocellated	Bicolor	Spotted
March	0.8	—	a	—
April	1.0	1.0 (0)[a]	3.0 (0)	1.0 (0)[a]
May	1.3	7.7 (10)	6.2 (12)	4.6 (33)
June	4.0	4.2 (38)	4.5 (29)	5.5 (27)
July	8.1	3.3 (12)	3.1 (0)	5.7 (9)
August	6.5	2.9 (15)	2.6 (23)	4.2 (7)
September	1.8	3.9 (25)	3.9 (20)	4.4 (50)
October	2.2	2.7 (20)	2.7 (33)	0.5 (0)[a]
November	1.7	1.2 (0)[a]	a	—
December	1.1	a	a	—

[a] Successful nests are known from these months, based on observation of known-age young out of the nest later. A nest is counted in a given month if the second and last egg were laid in that month, and if I was actually studying the birds on the day of laying that egg.

Mated male Ocellated Antbirds had lower losses than did unmated but territorial widowers (Table 5), perhaps because the latter sing loudly and wander widely around ant swarms looking for mates, and also have no mate to help keep the lookout. The few widowers that had accompanying sons had normal loss rates (1 of 3). Females had higher losses than males; perhaps some were lost because they incubate at night. They are often subordinate to trespassers when their mates are incubating and must forage peripherally or look for other ants; more might starve or be predated at such times.

If 5%–10% of the lost birds were wandering off the study area each year, true mortalities would be about 30% for adult females and unmated territorial males, 15% for mated males, and 25% for unmated wandering males.

Natality

Losses among these antbirds are made up by repetition of nesting, two eggs each time, over the course of long breeding seasons each year (Willis 1967, 1972a, 1973a).

Breeding seasons.—Table 6 indicates the total number of nests discovered or nestings detected per month of observations. Numbers in parentheses give the percentages of discovered nests that were successful for that month, omitting nests that were still occupied when I left. Midseason nests seemed less successful, in part because I usually visited in June to August and often left nests that may have been successful later. Broods of fledglings out of the nest seemed less frequent from midseason nests of Spotted Antbirds (Table 7). Fledglings in Table 7 come, in each case, from eggs laid 60 days previously.

No nesting has been detected in January and February, the early months of the dry season on Barro Colorado Island. Leaf litter is abundant, but probably only impedes capture of the few invertebrates present

160   EDWIN O. WILLIS   Ecological Monographs
                                                                                        Vol. 44, No. 2

TABLE 7. Broods of fledglings observed per month of study at different months

Month	Species		
	Ocellated (26)[a]	Bicolored (30)[a]	Spotted (35)[a]
May	—	[b]	—
June	0.2	—	2.7
July	1.1	0.6	3.5
August	0.8	0.9	4.6
September	1.1	—	2.8
October	0.9	1.8	2.3
November	0.6	0.6	5.3
December	0.9	0.9	[b]
January	0.4	0.8	—
February	0.5	—	—

[a] Age of young in days.
[b] Broods of fledglings of the indicated ages must have occurred in these months, based on observations of younger fledglings before or older young afterward. Observations are counted only if I was actually studying the birds on the day when fledglings reached the indicated age.

TABLE 8. Average number of days required for nesting by three species of antbirds

Item	Species		
	Spotted	Bicolored	Ocellated
Interval[a]	4	8	(4)[b]
Building	7	4	(3)
Laying	3	3	(3)
Incubation	15	15.5	(17)
Nestlings	10.5	13	(15)
Fledglings[c]	40	55 (45?)	28
Nest unsuccessful[d]	15	17	(13)

[a] From loss of previous nest to start of building.
[b] Data in parentheses are estimated.
[c] From fledging of young to start of building a new nest.
[d] From start of building to loss. See Appendix I, Part C, for calculations.

(Willis 1974). Invertebrates are few in the dry month of March, and only one Bicolored fledgling (in 1966) came from a nest started that month.

Rains normally start at the end of April, starting a "vernal bloom" of leaf-litter invertebrates that crests in June (Willis 1974). Regular nesting starts in all three species in April. The earliest clutch for Ocellateds was completed about April 14, 1961, the earliest for Bicolors (except the 1966 record) April 15, 1961, and the earliest for Spotteds about April 17, 1961. All pairs of antbirds are breeding May to September. As some pairs fledge early young and take care of them, the number of nests but not of breeding pairs goes down in June to September except in Spotteds. There an increase in unsuccessful nestings at midseason meant that each pair without fledglings was nesting more often. Leaf litter and invertebrates are becoming rare on the forest floor in August (Willis 1974), perhaps leading to low nest success and lowered numbers of nests.

Leaf fall increases gradually from August on (R. Foster, *pers. comm.*), leading to a weak "autumnal bloom" of invertebrates (Willis 1974). Spotted Antbirds stop nesting in early October (last clutch completed October 11, 1961). Some Ocellateds and Bicolors start clutches even in the heavy rains of November and 1st wk of December. Young out of the nest in January 1965 came from clutches completed about December 2, 1964, for Bicolors and December 4, 1964, for Ocellateds. In an average year the season of laying eggs must be about April 18 to October 10 (175 days) for Spotteds and April 15 to December 1 (230 days) for Bicolors and Ocellateds.

The heavy rains (Fig. 1) of early December 1960 and of December to early January 1970–71 did not induce any antbirds to extend their breeding seasons. Since little litter falls until a sharp peak after 2 wk of dry season (Foster, *pers. comm.*), there is little food

for antbirds even if rains last late. It is uncertain whether the antbirds start breeding early when the rainy season starts early, as in 1960, but in that year unusual numbers of yearling antbirds were out of the nest. Perhaps, as in other birds, a refractory period occurs late in the annual cycle, but breeding can begin early in the cycle if conditions are favorable. Fogden (1972) proposes that breeding can start in Sarawak birds at any time when they reach a state of good nutrition, but does not mention refractory periods.

Nesting periods.—A successful nesting requires about 75 days for Spotted Antbirds, 80 or 90 days for Bicolored Antbirds, and 70 days for Ocellated Antbirds (Table 8). In extreme cases these periods were 10 days shorter or longer; then new nests were started a week or so before or after fledglings of the preceding brood were independent. Intervals between an unsuccessful nest and the start of a new one probably add to the requirement for a complete nesting (except the first of the year) by 4–8 days.

Intervals between a successful nest and the start of a new one are short in Ocellated Antbirds. They are dominant, and young birds are foraging for themselves with the simple techniques required at 28 days out of the nest. Moreover, young often associate in clans with young of previous nestings or years and need not have their parents about to give the alarm.

Spotted and Bicolored Antbird young are foraging for themselves only at about 35–42 days out of the nest, perhaps because these are small and subordinate antbirds that must develop a variety of foraging techniques whenever domineering larger antbirds are present. Some Spotted young were still following their parents when the latter started a new nesting, but others were independent for 1–2 wk. The average period between successful nests (Table 8) is thus about the average time to independence of the earlier brood. The period of 55 days for Bicolors is based on one case, and that pair may have had an unsuccessful nest that was not detected. Young are normally feeding independently at 42 days out of the nest, even though they usually stay with their parents 1–2 wk longer.

Nestings per season.—Knowing the average lengths of time for successful and unsuccessful nestings, the intervals between them, and the breeding season, one can calculate the possible number of nests during a season if pairs breed without stopping.

If a pair of Bicolored or Spotted Antbirds has only unsuccessful nests, or only one successful nest at the end of the season, it will have on the average 10 nests per year, but an Ocellated pair will have an average of 14 nests. Detected nests for single pairs have not ranged above 6 or 7 per season, but I have not watched a single pair carefully for more than about three-quarters of a season. Oniki[2] found a pair of Slaty Antshrikes that had 3 unsuccessful nests in 60 days, so there could be 12 in 240 days. I found some Bicolored and Ocellated pairs nesting at this rate.

If a Spotted or Bicolored Antbird has one successful nest in the early or middle season, it can have 7 nests that year. An Ocellated pair can have 10 or 11 nests. The maximum number of successful nests per season is 3 for Spotted and Bicolored Antbirds, 4 for Ocellated Antbirds. Chances of the last are only 1 in 390,625 (1 chance in 25 to the power 4), even if some local or experienced pairs are unusually good at producing successful nests.

Age and location.—In some species, particularly birds that forage off their territories, old birds are better at rearing young than are young ones. The greater success of late nests in my study could suggest that birds gain experience during a year, but it is more likely that predators are less active then; May nests are also more often successful. Morton (1971) found that predation on nests of Clay-colored Robins (*Turdus grayi*) in the Canal Zone was higher in June and July than earlier in the year (that species does not nest after June or July), even though food supplies and weights of young were highest in June and July. In general, I found little evidence that old antbirds were more successful than young ones. A few old males seemed to find the key to repeated successes, but most never did.

Young female Ocellated Antbirds sometimes have fledglings their 1st yr but are unsuccessful in later years. The few males that mate their 1st yr have not been known to produce young then. Some old males at the island center were repeatedly successful in breeding; perhaps they were able to build up their clans because they found safe foraging and nesting areas. Other males up to 9 or more years old, mostly

nesting toward the edges of the island, were never very successful.

Spotted Antbird males and females sometimes produced fledglings in their 1st yr of breeding. Others seldom or never produced offspring, even over several years. Two males that were unusually successful (five, perhaps more, broods out in as many years) lived in areas where later pairs were generally unsuccessful, but in another case two successive pairs in one area were relatively successful. Most of the successful birds lived along small ridges with numerous small gullies where nests were often concealed. Some birds renested successfully in one or two small areas in their territories, but not all nests in these areas were successful. However, the evidence for greater success with age and area is not very strong.

Nesting success of Bicolored Antbirds does not seem to be be correlated with age or area. Possibly pairs toward the periphery of the island, away from the main escarpment zones occupied by Ocellated Antbirds, succeed better; six broods came from the center of the island out of 52 known nests and three from the periphery from 15 known nests. Young females and 2nd-yr males sometimes raise fledglings their 1st yr of nesting.

Movements

Few territorial adult antbirds moved off their territories to other areas (Table 9, part C6). A few peripheral birds probably wandered off the study area and were recorded as "lost" birds. Even adding to part C6 an estimate for these moving but lost birds, I doubt that total movements would surpass the following: 10% for male Spotteds, 15% for females; 15% for male Bicolors, 25% for females; and 10% for male Ocellateds, 20% for females.

Birds that stayed with the same mate usually stayed in much the same area (Table 9, part D1). Birds that were "divorced" (part D2), "widowed" (part D3), or "bachelors" (part D4) moved more commonly. Divorces and rematings were especially likely to be connected with movement. Females went to a new mate and a new area more commonly than did males. Often the female went to a neighboring male after he lost his mate, leaving her own mate without a female for the time being; perhaps some females or their nests get more food or survive better if a new area or male is available. In Bicolored Antbirds two males that had poor dominance over neighbors (i.e., small territories) accounted for four of the seven divorces.

Widowed birds moved fairly frequently, especially female Ocellateds. The female of this species is smaller than and subordinate to males and must quickly find a new mate if she is not to lose in foraging. Since local males of this clan-forming species are

---

[2] Y. Oniki. MS. The ecology and behavior of Slaty Antshrikes (*Thamnophilus punctatus*) on Barro Colorado Island, Panamá Canal Zone.

162 EDWIN O. WILLIS Ecological Monographs
Vol. 44, No. 2

TABLE 9. Movements of individual territorial antbirds

Item	Spotted			Bicolored			Ocellated		
	Male	Female	Both	Male	Female	Both	Male	Female	Both
A. Total number of birds	376	331	707	69	54	123	57	42	99
B. Stayed at home (numbers)									
1. Same mate next year (S_1)	249	249	498	36	36	72	36	36	72
2. Different mate (D_1)[a]	19	8	27	4	1	5	0	0	0
3. Lost mate (W_1)	64	34	98	12	7	19	15	1	16
4. No mate (B_1)	11	0	11	9[b]	0	9	4	0	4
5. Total staying (M_1)	343	291	634	61	44	105	55	37	92
C. Moved off home area (numbers)									
1. Same mate next year (S_2)	3	3	6	0	0	0	1[c]	1[c]	2
2. Different mate (D_2)[a]	11	22	33	3	6	9	0	0	0
3. Lost mate (W_2)	10	15	25	5	4	9	1	3	4
4. No mate (B_2)	5	0	5	0	0	0	0	1	1
5. Status unknown	4	0	4	0	0	0	0	0	0
6. Total moving (M_2)	33	40	73	8	10	18	2	5	7
D. Percentages									
1. Moving if same mate (S)	1.2	1.2		0	0		3	3	
2. Moving if new mate (D)	37	73		43	86		–	–	
3. Moving if lost mate (W)	14	31		29	36		6	75	
4. Moving if no mate (B)	31	—		0	–		0	100	
5. Moving (M)	8.8	12.4		12	18		4	12	

[a] Old mate still alive ("divorce and remating").
[b] Includes four with male partners (two "pairs").
[c] Moved closer to center of island (the favored zone for Ocellateds) when pair in that direction disappeared.

likely to be mated, related to her, or young, she is more likely to find an unrelated single male with a good territory if she moves. The female Spotted Antbird is also subordinate to the male, although no smaller, and loses to trespassing neighbors if she has no mate. However, Spotteds need not forage over army ants all the time, so the widow can often hide in remote corners of her home area until a suitor appears. Bicolored Antbird females, by contrast, often dominate their mates and trespassers, and widows can often pick up a new mate from the many old bachelor males about. Movements of widows and widowers are similar, about as frequent as in widow Spotteds. Both sexes of Ocellateds and Bicolors normally travel widely off the home area and are quite likely to gain a mate on a neighboring area. Since moving off a familiar home area must increase danger from predators and problems in finding food, it is perhaps still to be expected that many widows and widowers stay at home.

Bachelor adult females are rare in these antbirds, for only in 1 yr (1961) was there a surplus of 1 out of 12 females in one species (Ocellateds). Bachelor

adult males are usually fairly numerous, especially in Bicolors. Bachelor males of Ocellateds and Bicolors never moved off their home areas. They range so widely that they can pick up any widow from several neighboring home ranges, and in addition Ocellated widows move exceptionally and quickly home on the songs of an unmated male. If a bachelor male moves peripherally in his area or off it, he quickly goes to the bottom of the peck order and confronts more danger and difficulty in finding food. The male Spotted must confront more of these problems if he moves off his area, for prior to loss of mate he has little experience off his area. He also may not find the sedentary widows. Some bachelor Spotteds were males on territory for the 1st yr and may have picked relatively poor sites where they could not hold a female long enough. In such cases, moving to a new area would help.

Distances of movement were mostly short. Territories of Spotted Antbirds are about 200 m in diameter, of Bicolors about 400 m, and of Ocellateds about 500 m. Birds almost never moved the center of their activity more than one or two territorial diameters away, except in the case of widowed female Spotteds,

TABLE 10. Territorial turnover rates for antbirds

Item	Spotted			Bicolored			Ocellated		
	Male	Female	Both	Male	Female	Both	Male	Female	Both
Movements (%)[a]	8.8	12.4	10.3	11.6	18.5	14.6	3.5	11.9	7.1
Losses (%)[a]	18.8	19.4	19.1	27.4	34.1	30.3	22.7	37.3	29.6
Total	27	32	29	39	53	45	26	49	37

[a] Includes homosexual birds and birds without mates as long as on territory.

which sometimes moved a kilometer away. Young and other nonterritorial birds wandered more widely at times, but were "reflected back" by the water edge of Barro Colorado (details in Willis 1967, 1972*a*, 1973*a*).

Population changes

Territorial turnover rates.—Annual turnover rates of territorial or settled birds are the probabilities that given birds will not be on their territories a year later (Table 10). They thus include movements and losses, the latter caused by deaths and an unknown number of movements to areas where birds were not detected again.

Turnover rates for all these antbirds were high, especially for male and female Bicolors and female Ocellateds (Table 10). To some extent these rates reflect the declining populations of these two species. The turnover rates, none less than one in four, show that even tropical forest birds can have rather changeable populations. Annual turnover rates for Spotted Antbirds varied considerably (Fig. 5), as did those for Bicolors and Ocellateds. The seeming decline in turnover for Spotteds during the 10 yr may represent relaxation of competitive pressure from the declining Ocellated and Bicolored Antbirds, but the density of Spotteds did not increase (Table 2).

Population fluctuations.—Turnover is only one part of population dynamics; losses or gains of pairs are another, for these determine the fluctuations of populations (Table 11).

Most antbird areas with a mated pair were occupied by a pair the next year, especially in the stable population of Spotted Antbirds. In that species many

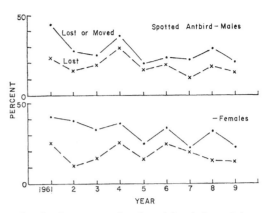

FIG. 5. Percentages of male and female Spotted Antbirds lost or lost plus moved each year from 1961 to 1969. Loss is probably too high in 1961 and too low in 1962; in 1962 peripheral birds were not censused as effectively as in other years.

areas that had only a male were occupied by a pair the next year. Few empty areas of any species gained a pair the next year; probably most such areas, either from small size or from some defect in food or safety, were not very suitable for nesting by a new pair. In declining populations, however, many areas became unoccupied, and swarms of ants wandered without resident birds or pairs. Even in Spotted Antbirds, sudden lack of a pair at a moving swarm of ants was often a result of temporary local vacancy; the neighbors only moved in at times.

The idea of "empty areas" surprises many ecologists familiar only with birds of northern or open

TABLE 11. Population losses in antbirds

| | Spotted | | Bicolored | | Ocellated | |
Item	Number	Percentage	Number	Percentage	Number	Percentage
A. Areas with male and female						
1. Total	506	100.0	86	100	72	100
2. Pair following year	465	91.8	64	74	57	79
3. Male alone next year	14	2.8	5	6	5	7
4. Became empty	27	5.4	17	20	10	14
B. Areas with male only						
1. Total	17	100	12	100	7	100
2. Pair following year	14	82	4	33	2	29
3. Male alone next year	2	12	7	58	2	28
4. Became empty	1	6	1	9	3	43
C. Empty areas						
1. Total	119	100	46	100	34	100
2. Pair following year	22	18.5	8	17	3	9
3. Male alone next year	5	4.2	1	2	0	0
4. Remained empty	92	77.3	37	81	31	91
D. Total areas						
1. Starting with birds	523	100.0	98	100	79	100
2. Lost the birds	28	5.3	18	18	13	16
3. Ending with birds	522	100.0	88	100	69	100
4. Started empty	27	5.2	9	10	3	4

TABLE 12. Mortality versus natality for female antbirds

| | Species | | |
Item	Ocellated	Bicolored	Spotted
(a) Fraction of nests pro- ducing fledglings[a]	(0.041)[b]	0.115	0.085
(b) Number of fledglings per nest	(1.4)	1.7	1.6
(c) Fraction of females	(0.5)	(0.5)	(0.5)
(d) Fraction of fledgling females surviving	(0.9)	(0.93)	0.95
(e) Fraction of immature females surviving	0.6	0.4	0.4
(f) Number of nests per year	19.4	6.9	6.2
(g) Adult female mortality	0.30	0.25	0.16

[a] See Appendix I, part C, for estimates of losses during building.
[b] Records in parentheses are estimates.

country. To a degree, an empty area for these birds is split up by neighbors. If the neighbors visit the empty area, they ordinarily set up dominance systems or chase trespassers and thus incorporate it into their own territories. However, an animal can efficiently eat or dominate only so much. A new antbird or pair usually occupies the area with little argument from neighbors. Tropical birds like these tend to approach the barnacle type of site use because "basal space" is held much or all of the year and because neighbors tend to live many years and to center activity in their own spaces. There is not the change in year-to-year distribution of birds that one often finds in birds that occupy an area seasonally. Looking at "empty spaces" helps in discussing declines and increases in populations, as well as in determining what sites are marginal for a species. Since tropical birds often have patchy distributions (Karr 1971), trying to detect why areas stay empty different lengths of time may eventually be useful.

If a Bicolored Antbird or Ocellated Antbird area had only a male, it was likely to retain only the male or to become empty the next year. Few females of these species were hatched each year, and these mostly filled vacancies in areas with pairs the preceding year. Empty areas rarely picked up a single male of any species, even more rarely than they picked up a mated pair. Probably the empty areas are more marginal in food or in other respects when a male has to defend and keep the lookout alone than when he has a mate.

The balance between areas that ended empty and ones that began empty is broken for Bicolored and Ocellated Antbirds (Table 11, D). The detailed data illustrate but do not suggest reasons for the general decline in these species noted in Table 2. It is possible to present data documenting the decline in several other ways. However, little additional information is to be gained, especially since the mathematics of de-

cline to extinction quickly make data "not significant" except for the decline.

Mortality and survival for females

Mortality and survival for females of the three species of antbirds are summarized in Table 12. The survival of young females must equal the loss of adult females if the species is to survive, so abcdef = g. The unknown is f, the number of nests per year for the average female to replace herself. Spotted and Bicolored Antbirds require only 6 to 7 nests per year to replace female losses; this is well within the limit of 7 to 10 possible nestings per female calculated earlier. Bicolored and Spotted Antbirds should be able to nest enough in areas where the rainy (nesting) season is shorter than on Barro Colorado, even in areas with 6 mo of rain, as long as mortalities are no higher than on Barro Colorado.

The average Ocellated Antbird female would require some 19 nests per year to replace herself. As noted earlier, only 10–14 nests per year seem possible. In areas with rain all year, the possible number of nests (assuming one success and no refractory period) would be 24, which would create a surplus. Apparently Ocellateds with the mortalities on Barro Colorado have to nest much of the year. Wherever they could not do this, they would decrease over time or be restocked by immigrants from better areas. If nest survival were 6.1% rather than 4.1%, only 13 nests per year would be required. However, possibly Ocellated Antbirds have nest and adult mortalities in many areas near the maximum, and they manage to survive because they are dominant and live mostly in rain forests, making nesting possible nearly all year.

DISCUSSION

Given the low nest and adult survival rates for Ocellated Antbirds, it is no surprise that Ocellateds declined on Barro Colorado during the 1960's; it is surprising they lasted so long there. Possibly nest and adult mortalities were unusually high in the 1960's. Could the study itself have had this effect? Since no nests were located, it seems unlikely that nests were affected directly. The only possible way would be if nest success were lowered because birds were disturbed by my watching them over ants. This could also have increased mortality. If so, one would expect lower natalities and higher mortalities in years when I watched the birds for long periods—1961 and 1965. Actually, however, adult mortalities were highest between 1968 and 1969, and natalities did not seem low in 1961 or 1965.

High mortality in 1968 could have resulted from low rainfall from 1967 to 1969, if low rainfall led to low arthropod numbers. There may have been less nesting and more traveling looking for suitable ant colonies in 1968. As it was more difficult for me to find ant colonies in June 1968, ants may have survived poorly that year. During the study period 1968 was also the only year when the rainy season was only 7 mo long and truncate at both start and close, and it was the only year with 6 mo of well below normal rainfall (Fig. 1). Out-of-season rains can also have disastrous effects, like the previously mentioned rain of January 1970; perhaps the early rain of March 1968 started breeding that stressed adults in the dry month of April. Possibly predation increased in 1968 also, as generalized predators scrambled for any available prey.

Bicolored Antbirds should not have decreased in the 1960's, according to Table 12. Perhaps the calculations, based mainly on 1961 data, overestimate nest success and underestimate adult mortality for the other years. Also, adult mortality may be higher at the edges of Barro Colorado, siphoning birds off the study area. A decrease of 50% did occur, but it is difficult to know why. Removing a percentage point here and there, especially on nest survival, could have disastrous effects difficult to detect without a huge sample size.

Spotted Antbirds fit the available data fairly well, although it is possible that they nest more than 6.2 times per year and that they have greater mortalities than estimated. If the mortality of young females is as "low" as indicated in Table 4, the species would have some leeway to take care of occasional bad years or to export a surplus to less prolific or more dangerous corners of the island.

All three antbirds have higher adult mortalities than the 11% Snow (1962a) found for males of a second-growth manakin in Trinidad. His data on a forest manakin (1962b) are from such a patchy forest (at Simla) and so indirect (111 of 200 netted birds were in female plumage, suggesting 11 were 1st-yr males) that I wonder if mortalities were 11%. Fogden's (1972) composite data for Sarawak suggest mortalities about 10%, but that island has few predators on adult birds. Since Bicolored and Ocellated Antbirds did not maintain their populations on Barro Colorado with adult mortalities above 25%, it may be that normal mortalities of forest birds are 15%–25%, and that some unusually safe birds like male manakins on leks or birds on predator-free islands keep mortalities below 15%. However, because some tropical birds have high nest mortalities is no reason to assume that they have low adult mortalities, or differ greatly from northern birds with respect to K- or r-selection. They may, like these antbirds, nest many times each year in a fecund race with death.

It is distressing that many birds on Barro Colorado Island, despite its protected status, seem to be losing their races. Appendix II lists breeding birds

that have disappeared from the island since it was set aside as a reserve in 1923. Other birds may have disappeared, but were not recorded by the early visitors to the island. Some species now present were not recorded by Chapman (1938) and other early explorers, but they are mostly small flycatchers that probably were overlooked. (One such small flycatcher, *Myiornis atricapillus*, is noisy and common, but has not been reported by any visitor other than Paul Slud and me; experience with calls of tropical birds can change recorded species diversities in censuses.) Since these birds were probably present, there were originally some 209 breeding species on Barro Colorado (Eisenmann 1952). Of these species 45, or 22%, have disappeared without replacement; several others, like Ocellated Antbirds, seem on the way out. A few species have invaded from time to time, but no successful colonizations have taken place so far (except among lake birds).

Thirty-two of the vanished species, about 71%, are birds of second growth. Such birds wander widely and probably would reappear on the island if part of it were cleared. Most of them are common in second growth elsewhere in Panamá and are in little danger of extinction. Thirteen species, however, are birds of woodland or forest. Their disappearance from nature reserves like Barro Colorado may presage their extinction if Latin Americans ever cut down tropical forests and leave only isolated forest reserves.

Eight of the 13 vanished forest species nest or forage mostly on or near the ground (John Terborgh, *pers. comm.*). These species may have disappeared because the monkey, coatimundi, and opossum populations of Barro Colorado are unusually high. Apparently not enough natural predators of mammals survive on this small island to keep numbers low in the absence of human predation. However, despite the monkeys some arboreal birds like Slaty Antshrikes[3] are doing well. The ground-living birds also might have the most difficulty flying to Barro Colorado across Gatun Lake, and that, rather than ground predators, could be the reason why their populations are not replenished. Black-faced Antthrushes, for instance, are common on Buenavista Point across the Panamá Canal, but have disappeared from Barro Colorado.

Two classes of causes could have led to the decline or disappearance of bird species on Barro Colorado: the growth of the forest, or the isolation and small size of the island. Horn (1971) has shown that monolayer trees take over from multilayer ones as a forest grows. The frequent observation of foresters that productivity slows in the mature forest thus has an evolutionary basis. Monolayers produce less leaf lit-

---

[3] See footnote 2.

166   EDWIN O. WILLIS   Ecological Monographs
                                                                                      Vol. 44, No. 2

ter, reducing productivity of leaf-litter arthropods, so fewer birds could survive near the ground in an old than in a new forest. However, on Barro Colorado frequent treefalls mean that monolayers never dominate in most areas (Robin Foster, *pers. comm.*). Certainly, the loss of birds of second-growth and forest edge seems to be attributable to growth of the forest. Possibly the growth of the forest also has led to opening the undergrowth and providing less food and cover for birds there. However, one wonders why birds restricted to forest, like Barred Woodcreepers and Ocellated Antbirds, should disappear during forest maturation.

The "island effect," the fact that islands have a small fraction of the species found in a larger or less isolated area, is well known (Preston 1962, MacArthur and Wilson 1967). To a certain extent, it is caused by lack of habitats on small areas—particularly a riverless, exposed hilltop like Barro Colorado. It is impossible to have a big river or an alpine habitat on a small island, for instance. It is also due to the lack of a range of habitats on small areas, so birds cannot move back and forth in extreme years. Barro Colorado lacks the range of rainfalls found in an area like the Canal Zone; in an unusually dry year Ocellated Antbirds could disappear and never be replaced by the offspring of birds that had survived on the wetter Caribbean side of the Zone. Other species could be eliminated from Barro Colorado by an unusually wet year, and not be able to reinvade from the dryer side of the Isthmus. There are few refugia in a small place in a difficult year.

Preston (1962) shows that the exponential decrease in species in decreasing fractions of a mainland area is about the 0.15 power of area, whereas islands of the same absolute sizes show decreases as the 0.30 power of area and are well below mainland fractions. Presumably an island has a lower immigration rate because species cannot get there easily and a higher extinction rate because the animals that do get there die off in local fluctuations from which they could escape or find refugia on the mainland (MacArthur and Wilson 1967).

The antbirds are clearly unable to immigrate to Barro Colorado or escape from it. They simply do not cross water gaps, even of a few hundred meters. Different species occur on different banks of the major rivers of the Amazon (Willis 1969). Antbirds are missing on oceanic islands around South America and are nearly gone from "land-bridge" islands formerly connected to the mainland, such as Margarita and Trinidad off Venezuela and the Pearl Islands (R. MacArthur, *pers. comm.*) and Coiba (Wetmore 1957) off Panamá. They are like the forest-dwelling "land-bridge" birds that Diamond (1971) has found do not cross water gaps in New Guinea. Birds like these

disperse poorly even overland, for no professional ant-following antbird has made the passage to the mountains of northern Venezuela; in that region, as on Trinidad, woodcreepers are the main ant-following birds. In such regions the "peninsula effect" (Simpson 1964) clearly lowers numbers of ant-following species the way the island effect does.

Extinction rates of forest-dwelling birds are low on Barro Colorado, about 0.3 forest species per year. This is about the same rate as on Karkar, a much larger island off New Guinea, for all species. However, the extirpated birds on Barro Colorado are not being replaced. This is a documented example of what happens when a "park" or "nature reserve" is separated from surrounding natural vegetation, even if not subjected to human interference significantly. Skutch (1971) documents a similar loss of species from the forest on his farm in Costa Rica.

"Ecological truncation," as in many other island situations, adds to the seriousness of the island effect. Large or specialized species go first—Ground-Cuckoos, then Barred Woodcreepers, then Ocellated Antbirds. Perhaps truncation occurs because large birds or specialists tend to have large territories with few individuals per unit area, and chance dry years or predators or genetic defects can wipe out most of a population. Where birds are limited to certain areas on the island, the limitation of Ocellateds to the escarpment zone for example, they are even more at the mercy of local events.

Even an occasional successful year helps little if it puts populations up over the normal level. Emigration cannot occur; the young stay around and encourage K-selection for adult longevity rather than r-selection for reproductive rates. The next time a catastrophe occurs, there are no rapidly breeding birds about. Moreover, the crowded birds or other animals cannot emigrate and must turn to alternate foods—which they may drive to extinction, destroy, or trample, or reduce to such a level that neither they nor species that normally feed on such food can survive. Specialized species disappear from parks, and only the "sparrows" are left—small, generalized birds that are jacks-of-all-trades.

A number of other problems are possible with islands—for instance, pests can occupy edge zones and reduce the total area available to birds, as mosquitoes did in carrying disease to lowland forest birds in Hawaii (Warner 1968). The Hawaiian events suggest the possibility that unusually high numbers of the lakeshore *Anopheles albimanus* kept Ocellated Antbirds from breeding near the lake shores after 1965. Apparently the mosquitoes increased after 1965 when the Panama Canal Company started to maintain the lake at a high level even in the dry season and *Hydrella* lake weeds, where these mosquitoes breed, increased. Certainly, the *Anopheles* concentrated in the daytime between the buttresses of trees in just the places where these antbirds probably nest (Willis 1973*a*). This kind of "edge effect" is the only known factor besides a low-rainfall cycle that changed at about the time of the main decrease in Ocellateds.

To determine if forest growth or the island effect is the cause of extirpation on Barro Colorado, birds of an extirpated species could be reintroduced. If they do not disappear quickly, forest growth and related factors are unlikely to have caused extirpation. If they disappear quickly, the experiment could be repeated a few times to see if the first time just happened to be a bad year. There is always the remote possibility that a species can survive before and after some critical stage of forest growth but not in the interim. However, this should also be observable on mainland areas.

Possibly the true causes of the decline of the Ocellated Antbird have not and will never be understood. Failure to detect causes in a 10-yr study suggests that causes can be difficult to detect in a tropical forest even with much effort. However, perhaps it matters less why animals in tropical parks disappear than it does that animals do disappear for practically undetectable reasons. We then realize that conservation theorems of general validity are needed rather than, or in addition to, specific techniques. Specific techniques, or "managements," can work well for a few species but are likely to have different effects on other species. These effects may be desirable in some cases, but not for an ecological study rather than an ecological experiment. Cutting half the forest on Barro Colorado would preserve many birds of second growth, for instance, but would probably have traumatic effects on the rest of the avifauna—the forest area would be even smaller and might lose even more species. The resulting truncation would probably make it difficult to learn why certain forest animals or plants behave as they do—their major competitors and predators might be gone.

One conservation theorem that seems generally valid is the Malthusian theorem, that food supplies grow arithmetically but populations geometrically. Translated into human terms, this has led to the suggestion of stable and limited numbers of people in time. The Barro Colorado observations suggest to me that the "island effect" points to another important theorem: arithmetic loss of space leads to geometric decline in the value of the remaining space. Translated into human terms, the "island effect" suggests that stable and limited human use of space will be necessary if we are not to lose many possibly valuable species of animals or plants or many important biological discoveries in a sea of humans, "rats, cockroaches, and sparrows." It matters little in conserva-

tion if we limit numbers of people in time, but do not also limit their intensive use of space. Limitation of human use of space will be most effective in preserving natural biotas if natural areas are not isolated islands in lakes or seas of humanity but instead are linked by corridor zones. Production of Ocellated Antbirds could then shift temporarily to the favorable end of a gradient if their usual reserve was subjected to temporarily unfavorable conditions. In a sense, the animals could then manage their populations while we manage our own.

ACKNOWLEDGMENTS

I appreciate the help especially of the staff of the Smithsonian Tropical Research Institute. Five students from Oberlin College, Steve Anderson, Ronn Kistler, Steve Kistler, Jeff Strassenger, and Douglas Wechsler, helped with the 1970 and 1971 census. Robin B. Foster's information on plant and litter cycles was invaluable. Yoshika Oniki, my wife, helped in many ways. Support was lacking in 1967 and 1968, but in other years the National Science Foundation, Woodrow Wilson Foundation, Frank M. Chapman Fund of the American Museum of Natural History, Sigma Xi, and Oberlin College contributed to a study no one foundation would have supported.

LITERATURE CITED

Allee, W. C. 1926. Measurement of environmental factors in the rain-forest of Panama. Ecology 7:273–302.

Bennett, C. F., Jr. 1963. A phytophysiognomic reconnaissance of Barro Colorado Island, Canal Zone. Smithson. Misc. Collect. 145:1–8.

Berger, A. J. 1970. The present status of the birds of Hawaii. Pac. Sci. 24:29–42.

Chapman, F. M. 1938. Life in an air castle. New York.

Diamond, J. M. 1971. Comparison of faunal equilibrium turnover rates on a tropical island and a temperate island. Proc. Natl. Acad. Sci. 68:2742–2745.

Eisenmann, E. 1952. Annotated list of birds of Barro Colorado Island, Panamá Canal Zone. Smithson. Misc. Collect. 117:1–62.

Fogden, M. P. L. 1972. The seasonality and population dynamics of equatorial forest birds in Sarawak. Ibis 114:307–343.

Horn, H. S. 1971. The adaptive geometry of trees. Princeton Univ. Press, Princeton, N. J. 144 p.

Karr, J. R. 1971. Structure of avian communities in selected Panamá and Illinois habitats. Ecol. Monogr. 41:207–233.

Kenoyer, L. A. 1929. General and successional ecology of the lower tropical rain forest of Barro Colorado Island, Panama. Ecology 10:201–222.

MacArthur, R. H., and E. O. Wilson. 1967. The theory of island biogeography. Princeton Univ. Press, Princeton, N. J. 203 p.

Morel, M. Y. 1964. Natalité et mortalité dans une population naturelle d'un passereau tropical, le *Lagonosticta senegala*. Terre Vie 3:436–451.

Morton, E. S. 1971. Nest predation affecting the breeding season of the Clay-colored Robin. Science 171:920–921.

Preston, F. W. 1962. The canonical distribution of

commonness and rarity. Ecology 43:185–215, 410–432.

Ricklefs, R. E. 1969. An analysis of nesting mortality in birds. Smithson. Contrib. Zool. 9:1–48.

Simpson, G. G. 1964. Species density of North American recent mammals. Syst. Zool. 13:57–73.

Skutch, A. F. 1971. A naturalist in Costa Rica. Univ. Florida Press, Gainesville. 378 p.

Snow, D. W. 1962a. A field study of the Black and White Manakin, *Manacus manacus*, in Trinidad. West Indies Zoologica 47:65–104.

———. 1962b. A field study of the Golden-headed Manakin, *Pipra erythrocephala*, in Trinidad. West Indies Zoologica 47:183–198.

Snow, D. W., and B. K. Snow. 1963. Breeding and the annual cycle in three Trinidad thrushes. Wilson Bull. 75:27–41.

Standley, P. C. 1933. The flora of Barro Colorado Island, Panama. Contrib. Arnold Arbor., Harv. 5:1–178.

Warner, R. E. 1968. The role of introduced diseases in the extinction of the endemic Hawaiian avifauna. Condor 70:101–120.

Wetmore, A. 1957. The birds of Isla Coiba, Panamá. Smithson. Misc. Collect. 134:1–105.

Willis, E. O. 1966. Competitive exclusion and the foraging behavior of Plain-brown Woodcreepers. Ecology 47:667–672.

———. 1967. The behavior of Bicolored Antbirds. Univ. Calif. Publ. Zool. 79:1–132.

———. 1969. On the behavior of five species of *Rhegmatorhina*, ant-following antbirds of the Amazon basin. Wilson Bull. 81:363–395.

———. 1972a. The behavior of Spotted Antbirds. AOU Monogr. 10.

———. 1972b. The behavior of Plain-brown Woodcreepers. Wilson Bull. 84:377–420.

———. 1973a. The behavior of Ocellated Antbirds. Smithson. Contr. Zool.

———. 1973b. Survival rates for visited and unvisited nests of Bicolored Antbirds. Auk 90:263–267.

———. 1974. Seasonal changes in the litter fauna on Barro Colorado Island, Panamá. Ecology (in press).

Willis, E. O., and Y. Oniki. 1972. Ecology and nesting behavior of the Chestnut-backed Antbird (*Myrmeciza exsul*). Condor 74:87–101.

Woodring, W. P. 1958. Geology of Barro Colorado Island, Canal Zone. Smithson. Misc. Collect. 135:1–39.

Appendix I.

Calculations of Nest Survival, Fledgling Mortality, and Unsuccessful Nesting

A. Nest survival

Nests that survive to the next day and those that do not are tallied separately for each day. Surviving nests are divided by the total number to find the fraction surviving that day. The fraction for the 1st day is multiplied by the fraction for the 2nd day to get the graphed fraction of survival or percentage (Fig. 2–4) for the 2nd day; the graphed fraction is multiplied by the fraction surviving on each day thereafter. Nests are not counted before detection even when certainly occupied earlier.

Since survivorship of nests is somewhat lower at the center of the breeding season (Table 6) in these antbirds, and since many of my visits to Barro Colorado were near the middle of the breeding season, I have weighted data for Fig. 2–4: all tallies are divided by the number of the same months I studied the birds from 1960 to 1971. A

tally for a July nest is divided by 8.1, for an April nest by 1.0, etc. Otherwise I would estimate survivorship too low, because I was most often present at a time of year when nests are least successful. (Unweighted data change final survivorships downward 1% or less in these cases.) Nests in 1961 tended also to be unsuccessful early in the year, perhaps abnormally so, but correction for a possible downward bias here does not seem warranted. Figures 2–4 probably represent minimum estimates of survivorship.

B. Fledgling mortality from brood sizes

Let A be the number of broods with one fledgling and B the number of broods with two at time t, say fledging. Let A' be the number of broods with one fledgling and B' the number with two at time t' (see Table 3). If p is the probability of a fledgling dying in the interval between t and t', then $1 - p$ is the probability that it survives that interval. The number of broods of one reduced to none is Ap, the number of broods of two reduced to none is Bp^2. By the binomial theorem the number of broods of two reduced to one is $2B(p)(1-p)$. Then

$$\frac{A'}{B'} = \frac{A - Ap + 2Bp - 2Bp^2}{B - 2Bp + Bp^2}$$

The method assumes that each young in a brood of two survives as well as each young of a brood of one. For these antbirds this seems fairly likely. One fledgling goes with one parent, the other with the other parent. If there is only one young, the other parent often does not feed or care for it. Usually, therefore, one fledgling gets no more care or little more care than does each of two. Where fledgling survival differs with brood size, p is an average of the separate probabilities of loss.

C. Average time for an unsuccessful nesting

If the percentage of nests lost on a day i from the start of building is p_i, if i ranges from 1 to N (the day a new nest is started, on the average), and M is the total percentage loss from day 0 to day N, the average number of days preempted by an unsuccessful nesting is

$$\frac{\sum\limits_{i=1}^{N} ip_i}{M}.$$

For antbirds, original data from Fig. 2–4 and Appendix I,A are used, but losses of nests before egg laying and complete loss of broods thereafter must be incorporated. Desertion of nests has never been noted, but some 5% seems possible; this would be 0.7% per day for Spotteds and 1.3% per day for Ocellateds and Bicolors. Complete loss (C) of fledglings to time t' (as in B) is

$$C = \frac{Ap + Bp^2}{A + B}.$$

Complete loss of fledglings for these antbirds is in Table 3. No complete loss was noted between day of discovery and day of independence of fledglings, but a small amount may be expected, so that the complete loss for Spotteds and Bicolors would be about 2.5%–3%, for Ocellateds 7–8%. If so, M for Ocellateds would be about 96%, for Bicolors about 89%, and for Spotteds about 92%. If one then assumes that most of the complete losses of broods took place in the first few days out of the nest, the average numbers of days per unsuccessful nesting are those given in Table 8.

APPENDIX II.

BREEDING BIRDS THAT HAVE DISAPPEARED
FROM BARRO COLORADO ISLAND

(g = nests or forages on or near the ground;
s = low second growth or edges of woodland;
* = disappeared as breeder between 1960 and 1970.)

*Little Tinamou (*Crypturellus soui*) gs
Roadside Hawk (*Buteo magnirostris*) s
Harpy Eagle (*Harpia harpyja*)
*Barred Forest-Falcon (*Micrastur ruficollis*)
*Red-throated Caracara (*Daptrius americanus*)
*Bat Falcon (*Falco rufigularis*) s
Great Curassow (*Crax rubra*) g
Marbled Wood-Quail (*Odontophorus gujanensis*) g
*Blue Ground-Dove (*Claravis pretiosa*) gs
Rufous-vented Ground-Cuckoo (*Neomorphus geoffroyi*) g
Tropical Screech-Owl (*Otus choliba*) s
Common Potoo (*Nyctibeus griseus*) s
Rufous-breasted Hermit (*Glaucis hirsuta*) s
White-vented Plumeleteer (*Chalybura urochrysia*) s
Blue-crowned Motmot (*Momotus momota*) gs
*White-necked Puffbird (*Notharchus macrorhynchus*) s
Cinnamon Woodpecker (*Celeus loricatus*) s
Red-crowned Woodpecker (*Centurus rubricapillus*) s

*Barred Woodcreeper (*Dendrocolaptes certhia*)
Buff-throated Automolus (*Automolus ochrolaemus*) g
Barred Antshrike (*Thamnophilus doliatus*) s
Streaked Antwren (*Myrmotherula surinamensis*) s
Black-faced Antthrush (*Formicarius analis*) g
*Thrushlike Manakin (*Schiffornis turdinus*) gs
Gray-capped Flycatcher (*Myiozetetes granadensis*) s
*Short-crested Flycatcher (*Myiarchus ferox*) s
Sulphur-rumped Flycatcher (*Myiobius sulphureipygeus*)
Black-tailed Flycatcher (*M. atricaudus*) s
N. Royal Flycatcher (*Onychorhynchus coronatus*)
Brownish Flycatcher (*Cnipodectes subbrunneus*)
Bay Wren (*Thryothorus castaneus*) s
Buff-breasted Wren (*Thryothorus leucotis*) s
*Black-bellied Wren (*Thryothorus fasciatoventris*) s
*Southern House Wren (*Troglodytes musculus*) s
White-breasted Wood-Wren (*Henicorhina leucosticta*) g
*Song Wren (*Leucolepis phaeocephalus*) g
Nightingale Wren (*Microcerculus philomela*) g
*Clay-colored Robin (*Turdus grayi*) gs
Chestnut-capped Warbler (*Basileuterus delattrei*) s
Thick-billed Euphonia (*Euphonia laniirostris*) s
*Crimson-backed Tanager (*Ramphocelus dimidiatus*) s
*Yellow-rumped Tanager (*Ramphocelus icteronotus*) s
White-lined Tanager (*Tachyphonus rufus*) s
Buff-throated Saltator (*Saltator maximus*) s
*Black-striped Sparrow (*Arremonops conirostris*) gs

Ecology, 67(3), 1986, pp. 684–694
© 1986 by the Ecological Society of America

EFFECTS OF SELECTIVE LOGGING ON THE BEHAVIORAL
ECOLOGY OF WEST MALAYSIAN PRIMATES[1]

ANDREW D. JOHNS
*Sub-Department of Veterinary Anatomy, University of Cambridge,
Cambridge, United Kingdom*

Abstract. This study documents changes within a community of one nocturnal and five diurnal primate species in response to selective logging of their tropical rain-forest habitat. Groups of two diurnal primate species, *Hylobates lar* and *Presbytis melalophos,* were observed in the wild for 14 mo before and 12 mo after the onset of logging. Both species showed alterations in activity budgets following logging, spending more time resting and less time feeding and travelling. These changes may be attributable to the reduction in the availability of their preferred, more nutritious foods. Both *H. lar* and *P. melalophos* were territorial in primary forest in the study area, and there was remarkably little change in their home ranges following logging. Changes that were apparent were generally to conform to changes in habitat topography. The extent of range overlap between *P. melalophos* groups appeared to increase in older logged forest, however, as food resources changed from an even to a clumped distribution.

The overall response of the studied primate community to selective logging appeared to be a reaction to reduced food availability and to fragmentation or other alterations of the habitat. An ability to adjust foraging strategies to cope with variation in habitat and food supply probably accounts for the continued survival of these primate populations in logged forest.

Key words: activity budgets; feeding behavior; habitat use; Hylobates lar; Presbytis melalophos; primate ecology; selective logging; social organization; tropical rain forest; West Malaysia.

INTRODUCTION

Primates are among the most conspicuous components of a tropical forest fauna, and may be a predominant component of the biomass (Eisenberg et al. 1972, Eisenberg 1980). Consequently, studies of the effects of selective logging (the selective removal of a certain proportion of the total trees present), or of other forms of habitat disturbance within tropical rain forest have largely concentrated on primates (see Johns 1983, Marsh et al., *in press*). Reductions in the density of primate populations following logging have been viewed as reflecting a reduction in the availability of food resources (Struhsaker 1973, 1976, Altmann et al. 1977, Dittus 1977).

Chivers (1974) has suggested that the initial loss of food trees through logging may be compensated for, in the short term, by fruiting and increased leaf flush of the remaining trees in response to conditions of physiological drought and by the rapid growth of colonizing tree species. In the longer term, establishment of colonizing species can cause shifts in the relative abundance of food types, and this may be reflected by shifts in the relative abundance of primate species. For example, *Colobus guereza* is one of the least common primate species in East African primary rain forest, but the most common in logged areas, while *C. badius* is common in primary forest but less abundant following logging (Struhsaker 1972). This pattern has been attributed to a preference shown by *C. guereza* for the

leaves of colonizing deciduous tree species (Oates 1977). For a primate species with low dietary diversity that selects tree species typical of primary and not of secondary forest, food resources may be critically reduced following logging (e.g., *Nasalis larvatus*; Salter and MacKenzie 1981).

In addition to influencing the relative abundance of different food types, logging will affect the dispersion of food resources, which inevitably affects ranging behavior and activity budgets of primates. Different species will respond in different ways, reflecting particular ecological idiosyncrasies. If habitat becomes fragmented and resources consequently become more clumped, then primates may either travel long distances between resource patches (e.g., Neville 1972, Homewood 1975), or range less far and feed less selectively, as seen commonly in response to seasonal food shortages (e.g., Waser 1975, Raemaekers 1980).

This paper considers the effects of a selective logging operation on a community of West Malaysian primates and examines the extent and the direction of changes in behavior and feeding ecology that enable species to persist in areas of logged forest.

THE FOREST AND THE PRIMATE COMMUNITY
AT SUNGAI TEKAM

Most lowland rain forest in West Malaysia has already been logged; it is thus the more difficult hill forest areas that are currently the main focus of timber exploitation (Johns 1983). The study was located within the Sungai Tekam Forestry Concession, Pahang, West Malaysia (4°10′ N, 102°40′ E). The concession has an

[1] Manuscript received 23 January 1984; revised 23 July 1984; accepted 4 September 1984; final version received 20 November 1985.

TABLE 1. Ranked basal area of predominant tree families in primary forest at the study site, Sungai Tekam, Malaysia.*

Family	Basal area (% of total)	No. trees (% of total)
Dipterocarpaceae	30.6	7.7
Leguminosae	25.3	7.7
Euphorbiaceae	8.4	27.0
Anacardiaceae	6.0	3.1
Moraceae	5.9	1.1
Burseraceae	3.0	4.1
Myrtaceae	2.8	2.7
Olacaceae	2.7	2.0
Annonaceae	2.6	6.1
Apocynaceae	2.1	0.4
Sapindaceae	1.8	5.2
Flacourtiaceae	1.3	2.9
Lauraceae	0.9	4.8
Meliaceae	0.8	5.4
Bombacaceae	0.7	0.1
No. trees		1140

* Basal area is obtained from a simple conversion of measured girth at breast height. The remaining tree families in the sample all ranked below 0.5% of the total basal area.

area of ≈315 km², and is composed primarily of hill dipterocarp forest (for a description of this forest type, see Whitmore 1984). The main study area was chosen to provide a site on which selective logging occurred halfway through the 26-mo study period. Additional study sites were established in other parts of the concession in previously logged forest. Details of study area location, topography, and climate are given elsewhere (Johns 1983).

The forest at the main study site at Sungai Tekam was not especially rich in timber trees, lacking the extensive stands of valuable dipterocarp *Shorea curtisii*

that were characteristic of much of the concession. The forest was dominated by emergent trees of other *Shorea* species, and legumes such as *Koompassia* spp. and *Intsia palembanica*. Lower canopy levels were dominated by species of the Euphorbiaceae (notably *Mallotus leucodermis* and *Elateriospermum tapos*), with Annonaceae, Meliaceae, and Sapindaceae well represented (Table 1).

Logging in the main study area began 14 mo after the onset of data collection. The extraction level was 18.3 stems/ha, a total of 3.3% of the total trees of ≥30 cm girth (at breast height) that were present. The main timber trees extracted were *Shorea* spp. (Dipterocarpaceae), *Koompassia malaccensis* and *Intsia palembanica* (Leguminosae), and *Dyera costulata* (Apocynaceae). Incidental damage during felling and transportation of logs caused a total loss of 50.9% of the total trees of ≥30 cm girth formerly present. Incidental loss appeared to be random among both tree height-classes and tree species (see Johns 1983), but damage was concentrated along ridgetops where access roads and log-loading areas were built.

Felling operations ceased after ≈5 mo, and all logs were removed after a further 2 mo. There was little or no further disturbance during the final 5 mo of the study.

A total of one nocturnal and nine diurnal primate species occur in West Malaysia (see Chivers 1980); six of these occur within the Sungai Tekam Concession (Table 2). These species show considerable overlap in diet and use of the canopy, although some differences in foraging strategy exist (MacKinnon and MacKinnon 1980).

TABLE 2. Selected socioecological characteristics of primate species occurring at Sungai Tekam, Malaysia.

	Hylobates lar (lar gibbon)	*Presbytis melalophos* (banded leaf monkey)	*Presbytis obscura* (dusky leaf monkey)	*Macaca fascicularis* (long-tailed macaque)	*Macaca nemestrina* (pig-tailed macaque)	*Nycticebus coucang* (slow loris)
Adult body mass (kg)*	5.0	6.0	6.0	3.0	7.0	0.7
Feeding strategy:						
Trophic group	frugivore	frugivore/ folivore	frugivore/ folivore	frugivore	frugivore	frugivore/ insectivore
Speciality	diverse diet	superabundant seeds	diverse diet	opportunisitic	opportunistic	mobile insects
Mean group size†	3.3	14.0	14.0	23	40	1.0
Range	2–5	13–15	12–16	...	...	...
No. groups	4	3	2	1	1	>12
Social structure†	monogamous pairs	uni-male groups	multi-male‡ groups	multi-male groups	multi-male groups	solitary
Intergroup relations†	territorial	territorial	?	mutual avoidance with much overlap	mutual avoidance with much overlap	males occupy territories, females occupy overlapping home ranges

* After MacKinnon and MacKinnon 1980.
† Data from Sungai Tekam (may differ between sites).
‡ After Curtin 1980.

686   ANDREW D. JOHNS   Ecology, Vol. 67, No. 3

Hylobates lar is a highly territorial species (Gittins and Raemaekers 1980). It feeds mainly at small, dispersed food sources (MacKinnon 1977), but is well adapted to exploit the sporadically fruiting fig trees, *Ficus* spp. (Raemaekers 1978).

Presbytis obscura and *P. melalophos* are anatomically specialized folivores, although *P. melalophos* feeds extensively on fruit (Curtin 1980). *P. obscura* is adapted to use large branches as pathways within the canopy; *P. melalophos* typically uses smaller supports and is more terrestrial (Fleagle 1978). The latter species is also reported to show a greater variety of diet, although at any one time it may feed predominantly on a very few species (Curtin 1980).

Macaca fascicularis is typically a species of riverine and secondary forests, occurring at low density in primary forest (Kurland 1973). It was infrequently observed at Sungai Tekam. *M. nemestrina* travels long distances along the ground between scattered food sources, and is well suited to a hill forest environment (Caldecott 1980, MacKinnon and MacKinnon 1980). It is primarily frugivorous, consuming little foliage but some plant stems and animal material (Crockett and Wilson 1980).

Nycticebus coucang overlaps very little with other primate species. It is nocturnal and feeds on both insects and fruit, spending the greater part of its foraging time searching for the former (E. Barrett, *personal communication*). It appears to show a social organization typical of many prosimian species, males occupying territories that overlap the home ranges of several females (e.g., Charles-Dominique 1977, 1978).

METHODS

Of the diurnal primates, only *Hylobates lar* and *Presbytis melalophos* were common in the main study area, and most observations were of these species. After initial contact, primate groups or individuals were observed for as long as possible, but long periods of contact were rare throughout the study. During contact periods, the behavior of each visible member of the group was noted every 10th min (recording of data followed the format of previous studies in Malaysia; e.g., Chivers 1974). For diurnal primates, data entries were eliminated that recorded animals fleeing (which was unambiguous and usually accompanied by loud calls) or staring directly and fixedly at the observer prior to fleeing (or engaging in short-distance movements directed towards gaining a better view of the observer). Animals sitting quietly among thick vegetation ("hiding") subsequent to fleeing from the observer were rarely observed; animals were not normally observed again until they resumed normal travel or other conspicuous activities. Where such observations were made, records recommenced an arbitrary 30 min after the cessation of fleeing, or when the animals resumed normal travel or feeding behavior (if this oc-

curred after <30 min). Data were also collected for the nocturnal slow loris, *Nycticebus coucang,* but since they were necessarily observed with the aid of lights, they must have been continuously aware of some form of disturbance. The extent to which the presence of lights affected their normal behavior pattern is unknown.

Logging creates a more open forest canopy, with the result that primates were more easily observed by a researcher, and vice versa. This meant that it was more difficult to approach primates undetected, but since they were visible from a greater distance this had little effect on the quantity or quality of data collected.

Records based on scanning observation are not necessarily independent, since successive scans may include the same groups of animals. For statistical analysis, however, it was assumed that the level of interdependence between scans did not bias the data significantly.

A source of further bias was that primates were only rarely followed throughout their entire active period; for example, observations of diurnal primates were more frequent during the early morning and late afternoon, when the primates were more often engaged in conspicuous activities such as travelling and feeding. At least for the analysis of activity budgets, this bias was eliminated by examining the data in terms of the proportion of time spent in each activity per hour of the day.

Home range areas of diurnal primates were calculated from the number of ¼-ha quadrats entered by groups. Although cumulative home range curves had not, in most cases, reached an asymptote either before or after logging, the rate of increase was very small.

Feeding observations were scored according to the number of individuals seen feeding on a particular food item in any scanning observation, relative to the total number of individuals seen (i.e., if all individuals in a scan were seen feeding on particular like items, a score of 1.0 would be recorded, and if only one individual of four seen was feeding a score of 0.25 would be recorded; see Clutton-Brock 1977).

The proportion of time spent feeding on a particular item does not necessarily reflect the volume or importance of that item ingested (Hladik and Hladik 1969, Hladik 1977), but changes in the proportional representation of different food types probably reflect changes in foraging strategy.

Different subcommunities within the primary forest vegetation at the study site were shown to possess different tree-height characteristics (Johns 1983). Consequently, height distribution of activity was recorded for canopy level rather than for absolute height above the ground. The following canopy levels were defined:

1) ground, including the herb and lower shrub level, generally no more than 2 m in height,
2) lower canopy, the discontinuous layer below the middle canopy,

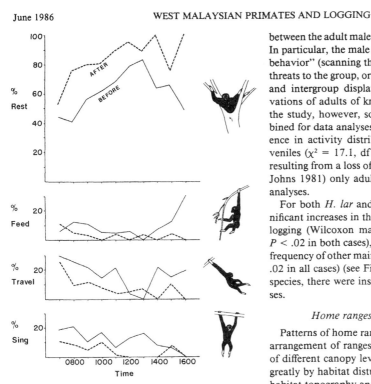

FIG. 1. Changes in activity pattern of *Hylobates lar* before and after logging (numbers of observations: 389 before logging, 429 after).

between the adult male and the females (Bennett 1983). In particular, the male spends more time in "vigilance behavior" (scanning the surrounding area for possible threats to the group, or for food sources), and in calling and intergroup display behavior. Insufficient observations of adults of known sex were collected during the study, however, so data for all adults were combined for data analyses. There was a significant difference in activity distribution between adults and juveniles ($\chi^2 = 17.1$, df = 2, $P < .001$); to avoid bias resulting from a loss of juveniles following logging (see Johns 1981) only adults were considered in the data analyses.

For both *H. lar* and *P. melalophos* there were significant increases in the frequency of resting following logging (Wilcoxon matched-pairs signed-ranks tests: $P < .02$ in both cases), and significant decreases in the frequency of other main activities (Wilcoxon tests: $P < .02$ in all cases) (see Figs. 1 and 2). For other primate species, there were insufficient data for similar analyses.

Home ranges and ranging behavior

Patterns of home range use, both in terms of spatial arrangement of ranges and use of area (including use of different canopy levels), are likely to be influenced greatly by habitat disturbance, particularly changes in habitat topography and in the form or distribution of food resources.

Hylobates lar.—Home ranges of *H. lar* groups showed

3) middle canopy, the continuous layer composed of the majority of trees,
4) upper canopy, the discontinuous layer above the layer of continuous vegetation but encompassing the upper regions of most large trees, and
5) emergents, the fragmented layer of trees whose crowns are almost wholly isolated from the surrounding upper canopy.

RESULTS

Activity budgets

The proportions of time spent in different activities reflect broad ecological features of a species and would be expected to change in response to major habitat disturbance, such as selective logging.

The activity budgets of male and female *Hylobates lar* at Sungai Tekam did not differ significantly, either before or after logging ($\chi^2 = 2.42$, 2.72, respectively; df = 3, $P > .05$), so observations of adult group members were combined for subsequent analyses. (Both of the two main study groups contained infants at various stages of the study, observations of which were excluded from the data analysis, but neither group contained juvenile or subadult animals.)

The specialized role of harem males in *Presbytis melalophos* tends to cause a divergence in activity patterns

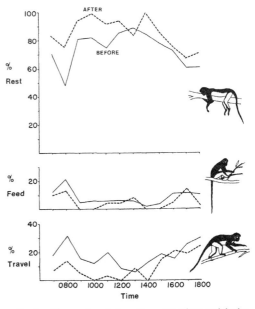

FIG. 2. Changes in activity pattern of *Presbytis melalophos* before and after logging (numbers of observations: 391 before logging, 293 after).

688   ANDREW D. JOHNS   Ecology, Vol. 67, No. 3

TABLE 3. Home range sizes and overlap between *Hylobates lar* groups before and after logging.

	Group JL1		Group JL2	
	Before	After	Before	After
Home range area (ha)	17	11	19	15
% home range overlap*	28	14	21	8
% old home range still used		54		75

* Percentage of the group's home range overlapped by home ranges of other groups.

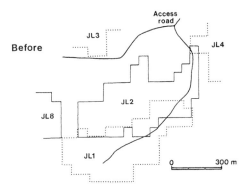

a relatively high degree of overlap (Table 3) in comparison to other studies (Carpenter 1940, Gittins and Raemaekers 1980). This was largely due to two groups sharing a routeway over a main access road; the routeway was the only suitable arboreal crossing point. That different groups may use the same travel routes has also been found for *H. klossii* (Whitten 1982).

The size of home ranges before logging appears small in comparison to the mean home range size of 54 ha recorded at another site in West Malaysia (Gittins and Raemaekers 1980). This probably reflects the fact that a second gibbon species, *H. syndactylus,* occurred sympatrically at the latter site and to a certain extent competed with *H. lar* for available food. Much smaller mean home range sizes were reported for two other sites where *H. syndactylus* was absent (25 ha [Carpenter 1940] and 39 ha [Ellefson 1974]).

Changes in the home ranges of both main study groups (JL1 and JL2) were observed immediately after logging began. During logging, groups tended to restrict their activity to those parts of their home range that had not yet been logged, or to move behind the logging front to logged portions of their former ranges, at all times keeping as far from the foci of logging activity as possible. Their home ranges in logged forest were somewhat different from their home ranges before the onset of logging (Fig. 3).

Presbytis melalophos.—Home range size (Table 4) again appears small in comparison with results from other areas; Bennett (1983) found a mean home range size of 32 ha. A factor to consider may be the relative scarcity of the sympatric *P. obscura* at the main study site (although not elsewhere in the Sungai Tekam Concession). However, although these two species share a high proportion of food sources, competition is probably avoided because the shared resources are superabundant (Curtin 1980). Thus, variability in *P. melalophos* populations is likely to be independent of the population density of *P. obscura* (see also Marsh and Wilson 1981).

During logging, *P. melalophos* groups shifted their home ranges to avoid centers of logging activity, limiting movement to former parts of their range and adjacent unoccupied areas. Groups adjacent to the logging area continued to maintain exclusive areas, the boundaries of which were not crossed by displaced groups. If unoccupied areas did not exist, home range

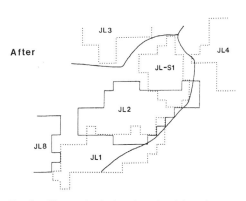

FIG. 3. Changes in the location of *Hylobates lar* home ranges following logging. JL-S1 represents a solitary maturing male gibbon that was present in the area following logging.

extension would not have been expected to occur without an increase in aggressive interactions between groups.

Following logging, *P. melalophos* groups showed considerable shifts in home range location (Fig. 4). The home range of group JM2 extended down precipitous slopes to the east of the study area, and the full extent of their home range was not mapped.

P. obscura.—There were no resident groups of this

TABLE 4. Home range sizes and overlap between *Presbytis melalophos* groups before and after logging.

	Group JM1		Group JM3	
	Before	After	Before	After
Home range area (ha)	14	17	15	20
% home range overlap*	15	2	32†	4
% old home range still used		56		86

* Percentage of the group's home range overlapped by home ranges of other groups.

† The large observed overlap is the result of a range shift: a section of forest was used exclusively by JM2 for several months, but was subsequently used exclusively by JM3; at no time was the area shared between groups.

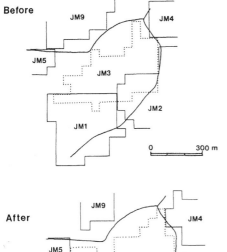

FIG. 4. Changes in the location of *Presbytis melalophos* home ranges following logging.

degree of terrestriality may result in an ability to exploit logged forest habitat efficiently.

Nycticebus coucang. — The slow loris was common at Sungai Tekam, but patchily distributed (Johns, *in press*). Little was discovered of its ranging patterns due to difficulties of recognizing and following individuals. *N. coucang* appears to use forest-edge habitat preferentially. It was seen significantly more frequently in edge habitat than in the forest interior on a survey route that included equal areas of each habitat type (Wilcoxon matched-pairs signed-ranks test; $T = 0$, $n = 6$, $P = .05$). Edge habitat characteristically has a larger number of supports per unit volume of vegetation, which may increase the efficiency of foraging, particularly for insect prey.

This species was infrequently seen in active logging areas, but reappeared once logging had ceased. It appears that animals concentrated in stretches of forest adjacent to logging areas. While the southern part of the study area was being logged, significantly fewer animals were seen in the same area before logging began (Mann-Whitney U test; $z = 3.13$, $n_1 = 17$, $n_2 = 16$, $P < .05$), whereas significantly more animals were seen in the northern part of the study area at this time than were seen before logging began ($z = 3.28$, $n_1 = 17$, $n_2 = 16$, $P < .05$). Insufficient data were collected to indicate significant changes in ranging patterns fol-

species within the study area, but at least two groups ranged through the area occasionally. Wide-ranging behavior has not previously been reported for this species (Curtin 1980), although very low densities have been reported in some forest areas (Marsh and Wilson 1981).

Groups avoided centers of logging activity; this species was not seen in the study area during logging. It is not known if home ranges or ranging behavior were significantly altered in logged forest.

Macaca fascicularis. — This species approached the study area prior to logging, but was not observed within it. Following logging, two groups appeared occasionally. This species is wide-ranging, but appearance of groups only after logging may indicate an alteration of ranging patterns.

M. nemestrina. — This macaque is extremely wide-ranging in primary forest (Crockett and Wilson 1980). The study area at Sungai Tekam was within the range of one group numbering 40 individuals.

Although avoiding direct contact with humans, this species spent more time in the study area during and following logging than before. An ability to exploit a variety of food resources opportunistically and a high

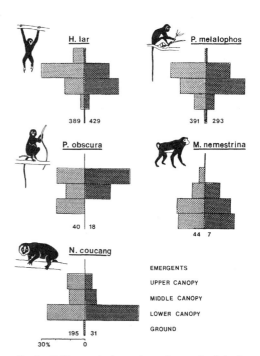

FIG. 5. Differences in the total use of canopy levels by five primate species before and after logging. Unlogged forest shown on the left and logged forest on the right of the central axis. For each species the number of observations is indicated.

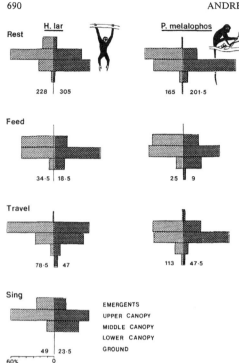

FIG. 6. Differences in the use of canopy levels by *Hylobates lar* and *Presbytis melalophos* before and after logging, analyzed by major activity and category. Unlogged forest shown on the left and logged forest on the right of the central axis. For each species and activity, the number of observations is indicated.

lowing logging, but it is likely that major changes do occur to adjust to changes in habitat topography.

Habitat use

The distributions before logging of four representative taxa of food species (*Ficus* spp., Moraceae; *Parkia* spp., *Sindora* spp., and *Intsia palembanica*, Leguminosae) were found not to differ significantly from a random distribution (Kolmogorov-Smirnov two-sample tests: $D = 0.21, 0.40, 0.28, 0.25$, respectively; $n_1 = n_2 = 10$, $P > .05$ in all cases). Many of these trees also serve as sleeping or calling sites, and it is likely that these resources were also randomly distributed. Following logging the habitat became a mosaic of cleared patches and areas of varying damage levels.

Data collected during six dawn-to-dusk follows achieved after logging revealed that for *H. lar* group JL1 there was a distinct localization of activity in areas less affected by logging; the distribution of activity differed significantly from a random one ($\chi^2 = 14.7$, df = 3, $P < .01$).

For *P. melalophos* groups, insufficient dawn-to-dusk follows were achieved to provide enough data for a similar analysis. When data from all partial follows in

addition in dawn-to-dusk follows were pooled, there was no apparent selection of areas less affected by logging; the distributon of activity did not differ significantly from a random one ($\chi^2 = 7.65$, df = 3, $P > .05$).

Significant changes in height distribution of activity were recorded for two of the five primate species for which data are available (see Fig. 5); insufficient observations were made of *M. fascicularis* to include this species in the analysis. For both *H. lar* and *P. melalophos* there was a marked increase in the use of the lower to middle canopy over the upper canopy ($\chi^2 = 89.4, 55.5$, respectively; df = 4, $P < .001$ in both cases). This was expected due to the loss of many large trees during logging. Sample sizes for *P. obscura* and *M. nemestrina* are probably inadequate to show significant changes, although it is expected that *M. nemestrina*, which spends a large proportion of its time close to or on the ground even in primary forest, is likely to be little affected by the changed habitat structure. *N. coucang* also spends much of its time in the lower canopy in primary forest, such that a lack of change in height distribution would be expected ($\chi^2 = 5.03$, df = 4, $P > .05$).

For *H. lar* and *P. melalophos* it is possible to compare details of activity distribution relative to the canopy levels at which the different activities took place (Fig. 6). In general, activities shifted from the upper canopy to the middle canopy after logging; the shift in resting was particularly significant for both species ($\chi^2 = 75.7, 53.4$, respectively; df = 4, $P < .001$ in both cases).

Feeding ecology

H. lar and *P. melalophos.* — For these species, there appears to have been a shift towards increased folivory in logged forest (Table 5). Following logging, fewer fruit were available, but there was an increase in the proportion of trees bearing new leaves (Johns 1983), so

TABLE 5. Changes in the proportional representation of food types in the diets of *H. lar* and *P. melalophos* occurring as a result of logging.*

	H. lar		*P. melalophos*	
	Primary forest	Logged forest	Primary forest	Logged forest
Food source				
	% of sample			
Termites/ants	2	4	0	0
Other animal material	0	0	1	0
Liana shoots	8	4	17	11
Young leaves	4	32	13	47
Petioles	0	0	4	0
Flowers	8	0	4	0
Fig tree fruit (*Ficus* spp.)	27	8	1	0
Liana fruit	17	0	1	0
Other fruit/seeds	33	52	58	42
No. feeding observations	58	29	73	28

* Figures represent a matched monthly sample, so that the effects of seasonality can be discounted.

that although many trees were destroyed the overall availability of new leaves remained the same. The extent of folivory was probably underestimated because leaf-eating was less detectable than fruit-eating, which frequently involves dropping pieces of fruit or peel to the forest floor.

Other species. — *Presbytis obscura* is essentially folivorous and, given that the overall abundance of new leaves is little changed by selective logging, would not be expected to alter its foraging behavior to a great extent after logging.

Macaca nemestrina is primarily frugivorous, but has an extremely variable diet. During and after logging, animals were frequently observed sifting through logging debris, presumably in search of fallen fruit and animal material.

Little is known of the feeding ecology of *Nycticebus coucang,* but animals were observed to spend long periods of time searching for arthropods in the lower story and in thick tangles of lianas and climbers, or in tangled logging debris. It appears that both fruit and gums are eaten opportunistically, a fact which probably aids this species to survive in logged forest.

Group structure and organization

The effects of logging on group structure have been documented elsewhere (Johns 1981). Logging causes a high level of infant mortality in all species, with the exception of *M. nemestrina.*

The heterogeneous structure of logged forest tends to force primates to search more intensively through the remaining patches of vegetation, resulting in more dispersed foraging. In *P. melalophos,* subgroups (associations of animals whose movements are dependent on those of each other, but not on those of other members of the group) were observed frequently after logging, but not beforehand. Following logging, of 33 contacts in which the number of animals present was reliably counted, 39% involved subgroups of less than five animals. Groups appeared to adopt fission rather than an increase in group spread; there was no significant difference in the spread of individual groups before and after logging ($n_1 = 22$, $n_2 = 12$, $\chi^2 = 1.16$, df = 1, $P > .05$).

DISCUSSION

Feeding and ranging behavior

The dispersion of food resources is of primary importance in determining ranging behavior of primate groups, and hence foraging strategy (Milton 1980, Marsh 1981). Theoretically, an efficient foraging strategy maximizes the net return of energy relative to that expended in foraging (Schoener 1971). The two main factors influencing foraging strategies are food "quality" (i.e., net energy gained from or nutrient value of a particular food) and the dispersion of that food. Changes in ranging patterns occurring as a result of logging will, to a

certain extent, be consistent with changes in the "cost efficiency" of feeding on certain foods, although animals may need to balance their diets by eating appropriate combinations of different food types (Gaulin and Gaulin 1982).

Both *H. lar* and *P. melalophos* decreased their level of activity following logging, spending less time feeding and travelling, and more time resting. Resting may be a necessary measure to conserve energy in the face of a reduction in the availability of preferred foods (e.g., Milton 1980). Such preferred foods are mostly fruits and seeds, specifically fruits rich in free sugars in the case of *H. lar* (Raemaekers 1978). In these foods the proportion of digestible material per volume of food swallowed is higher than in leaf material (Hladik et al. 1971, Raemaekers 1978); digestion of leaf material might be expected to be both slower and energetically more expensive (Waterman and Choo 1981). A reduction in the energy available to the primate would cause a reduction in the amount of time spent travelling, with a subsequent reduction in day range length.

Hylobates lar ate a wide variety of foods opportunistically, but although certain fruits were available after logging, animals included a far higher proportion of leaf material in their diet. This species has a limited ability to digest leaf material (Vellayan 1981), and day range length has been positively correlated with the amount of fruit and flowers eaten (Raemaekers 1980). This may reflect the energetic costs of digesting leaf material, particularly for species which have a high metabolic requirement relative to gut capacity (Waterman and Choo 1981).

Patterns of ranging behavior among colobine monkeys have recently been reviewed by McKey and Waterman (1982). Because of an inherent ability to digest leaf material, colobines need not exhibit energy conservation measures in response to decreased availability of more nutritious foods. Ranging patterns are most easily correlated with seasonal variation in the distribution and abundance of food sources. Ranging of *Colobus satanas,* for example, is adapted to exploit a seasonal procession of major food items, scarcity of which necessitates an increase in dietary diversity and increased day range length (McKey and Waterman 1982). Among other species, however, seasonal abundance of preferred foods has been positively correlated with day range length. It has been reported that when mature leaves form a high proportion of their diet, *Colobus badius* reduce day range length considerably (Clutton-Brock 1975). This difference is probably due to the fact that *C. badius* were exploiting the leaves of common trees, whereas *C. satanas* were selecting leaves from rare species (McKey and Waterman 1982).

Presbytis melalophos appeared to respond in the same way as *C. badius,* feeding on the leaves of common plant species in the absence of preferred seeds. This may reflect a lower degree of toxicity (lower concentrations of secondary compounds) in the vegetation in

692   ANDREW D. JOHNS   Ecology, Vol. 67, No. 3

West Malaysia compared to that in the forest occupied by *C. satanas* (Bennett 1983), although it may also reflect a greater plant species diversity, or a better detoxifying ability of *P. melalophos*. In this case, reduced day range length in conditions of a shortage of preferred foods reflects changes in the distribution of food sources exploited by the individual groups and is not indicative of energy conservation.

The system of land tenure adopted by *P. melalophos* at Sungai Tekam differs from that reported elsewhere. Home ranges appeared to be largely exclusive at Sungai Tekam, but overlap is extensive or complete at Kuala Lompat, another study site in Pahang (MacKinnon and MacKinnon 1980). Maintenance of an exclusive area (territory) requires that all essential resources are present in an area small enough to be defensible. An uneven distribution of resources at Kuala Lompat may not permit the division of the habitat into exclusive areas, since no area small enough to be defensible may contain sufficient food resources. The value, *D*, of the "index of defendability" proposed by Mitani and Rodman (1979) is 3.4 for *P. melalophos* at Sungai Tekam, which implies a potential for territoriality. However, Bennett (1983) gives a minimum monthly value of *D* = 1.4 for *P. melalophos* at Kuala Lompat, which implies that they, too, have the potential to defend their much larger home ranges against conspecifics. That they do not appear to do so is attributable to the superabundance of food resources at Kuala Lompat (Curtin 1980). This leads to the suggestion that in conditions of suddenly reduced food availability at Kuala Lompat, either groups would have to range more widely to obtain sufficient food (which, because of energetic considerations, they may not be able to do), or they would be forced to defend much larger territories than at Sungai Tekam. Since the population density is sufficiently high (7.2 groups/km²; Marsh and Wilson 1981) that all groups could not maintain territories of sufficient size, a sudden food shortage would be expected to cause increased intergroup conflict and a severe lowering of population density. A parallel is reported for *Alouatta palliata*, whose population on Barro Colorado Island increased steadily over a number of years, but was suddenly drastically reduced by starvation after a failed fruiting season (Foster 1983, Milton 1983). Logging operations in forest close to Kuala Lompat, which would be expected to cause a drastic reduction in food availability, caused "fierce fighting" among resident groups of *Presbytis* spp. (MacKinnon and MacKinnon 1978).

P. melalophos groups are territorial at Sungai Tekam probably because food supplies are not normally superabundant; most food patches are small and randomly distributed. Logging at Sungai Tekam altered the distribution of food resources, making it more clumped. This inevitably resulted in *P. melalophos* groups being forced to range more widely, and, because the available resources became small, clumped, and of reduced quality (many of the larger, more nutritious

food sources were removed during logging), energetic constraints on the groups may have prevented them from maintaining exclusive areas. Such a change in organization was not observed over the short period following logging at the main study site, but observations made in a nearby area logged 3–4 yr prior to the study indicated that such a change in group ranging patterns might indeed have occurred there. Sharing of food resources was observed; this was a common occurrence at Kuala Lompat (Bennett 1983) but was never observed in primary forest at Sungai Tekam.

Changes in food-source dispersion may also cause changes in group organization. In conditions of an initial reduction in the availability of preferred foods, *P. melalophos* groups began fissioning into smaller subgroups foraging independently (see also Waser and Floody 1974, Klein and Klein 1977).

Structural alteration of the habitat with logging causes changes in the distribution of activity through the canopy; animals spend a higher proportion of their time in the lower levels of the forest. Upper levels of the forest become more open following logging, and remaining in the lower levels thus reduces exposure to sun and rain. Also, seeking the dense cover of lower levels for resting reduces the groups' susceptibility to avian predation (Gautier-Hion et al. 1981).

Logging destroyed many travel routes through the upper canopy. This resulted in the more arboreal primates being forced to descend to lower levels, or even to the ground, in order to cross gaps. This is likely to have affected *H. lar* and perhaps *P. obscura* to the greatest extent, and since these species avoid terrestrial travel they may have been excluded from trees inaccessible by arboreal pathways.

Long-term survival of primate populations

Reduction of food resources to a critical point has been reported to cause mortality within a primate population, but such mortality is normally age/sex specific (Dittus 1977). Specifically, group size has been related to overall density of food resources acting on juvenile mortality (Marsh 1979). Mortality of infants occurred at Sungai Tekam during logging, and may be attributed to effects of the initial disturbance (Johns 1981). It was apparent, however, that the numbers of infants rapidly returned to normal in older logged forest; there was no evidence of a reduced level of viability of the population (Johns, *in press*). For no species was there a consistent population decrease in older logged forests at Sungai Tekam (Johns, *in press*). Data were limited to observations in forests logged up to 6 yr beforehand, however, and some populations, particularly the adult segment, have been shown to respond very slowly to even major environmental disturbance (Struhsaker 1976). Longer-term data are needed before definite conclusions can be drawn.

The absence of any consistent reduction in group density following logging at Sungai Tekam is inconsistent with results from surveys elsewhere (e.g., Wilson and Wilson 1975; Payne and Davies 1982). There is no reason to assume that primate density in the main study area at Sungai Tekam was low; it compared closely with results from a second primary forest site on the concession. Similarly, the relatively high densities at the logged forest sites cannot be attributed to compression (i.e., densities being inflated by immigration from adjacent areas) for two reasons. First, unlike those of certain species (e.g., *Pongo pygmaeus* [MacKinnon 1971], *Indri indri* [Petter and Peyriéras 1974]), primates at Sungai Tekam do not appear to move away from logging areas. Secondly, none of the logged forest sites investigated were directly adjacent to active felling areas; rather, they occupied central positions in blocks of forest logged at approximately the same time.

Evidence suggests that the primates studied at Sungai Tekam are able to persist in logged forest, and the reasons why *H. lar* and *P. melalophos* are able to do so have been indicated. These species show a remarkable degree of flexibility that is certainly not shared by all primate species.

ACKNOWLEDGMENTS

This study was supported primarily through contract number NO1-CO-85409, United States National Institutes of Health, with the University of Cambridge, United Kingdom. It was sponsored locally by the Dean and Faculty of Veterinary Medicine and Animal Sciences, Universiti Pertanian Malaysia, to whom I extend my thanks. Permission to work at Sungai Tekam was kindly given by Syarikat Jengka Sendirian Berhad. Planning and execution of the study were aided by many, in particular Drs. D. J. Chivers and M. Kavanagh. I am grateful to the following for comments on various drafts of this manuscript: E. Barrett, E. L. Bennett, J. O. Caldecott, D. J. Chivers, A. G. Davies, M. Kavanagh, J. P. Skorupa, and T. T. Struhsaker.

LITERATURE CITED

Altmann, J., S. A. Altmann, G. Hausfater, and S. McCluskey. 1977. Life history of yellow baboons: physical development, reproductive parameters, and infant mortality. Primates 18:315–330.

Bennett, E. L. 1983. The ecology and behaviour of the banded langur, *Presbytis melalophos,* in West Malaysia. Dissertation. University of Cambridge, Cambridge, England.

Caldecott, J. O. 1980. Habitat quality and populations of two sympatric gibbons (Hylobatidae) on a mountain in Malaya. Folia Primatologica 33:291–309.

Carpenter, C. R. 1940. A field study in Siam of the behavior and social relations of the gibbon, *Hylobates lar.* Comparative Psychology Monographs 16:1–212.

Charles-Dominique, P. 1977. Ecology and behaviour of nocturnal primates. Duckworth, London, England.

———. 1978. Solitary and gregarious prosimians: evolution of social structure in primates. Pages 139–149 *in* D. J. Chivers and K. Joysey, editors. Recent advances in primatology, volume 3. Academic Press, London, England.

Chivers, D. J. 1974. The siamang in Malaya: a field-study of a primate in tropical rain forest. Contributions to Primatology 4:1–335.

———, editor. 1980. Malayan forest primates. Plenum, New York, New York, USA.

Clutton-Brock, T. H. 1975. Ranging behaviour of the red colobus (*Colobus bandius tephrosceles*) in the Gombe National Park. Animal Behaviour 23:706–722.

———. 1977. Methodology and measurement. Pages 585–590 *in* T. H. Clutton-Brock, editor. Primate ecology. Academic Press, London, England.

Crockett, C., and W. L. Wilson. 1980. Ecological separation of Sumatran macaques. Pages 148–181 *in* D. G. Lindburg, editor. The macaques: studies in ecology, behavior and evolution. Van Nostrand-Reinhold, New York, New York, USA.

Curtin, S. H. 1980. Dusky and banded leaf monkeys. Pages 107–145 *in* D. J. Chivers, editor. Malayan forest primates. Plenum, New York, New York, USA.

Dittus, W. P. J. 1977. The social regulation of population density and age-sex distribution in the toque monkey. Behaviour 63:281–322.

Eisenberg, J. F. 1980. The density and biomass of tropical mammals. Pages 35–55 *in* M. E. Soulé and B. A. Wilcox, editors. Conservation biology. Sinauer, Sunderland, Massachusetts, USA.

Eisenberg, J. F., N. A. Muckenhirn, and R. Rudran. 1972. The relation between ecology and social structure in primates. Science 176:863–874.

Ellefson, J. O. 1974. A natural history of gibbons in the Malay Peninsula. Pages 1–136 *in* D. Rumbaugh, editor. Gibbon and siamang, volume 3. Karger, Basel, Switzerland.

Fleagle, J. G. 1978. Locomotion, posture and habitat utilization in two sympatric Malaysian leaf monkeys (*Presbytis obscura* and *Presbytis melalophos*). Pages 243–251 *in* G. G. Montgomery, editor. The ecology of arboreal folivores. Smithsonian Institution Press, Washington, D.C., USA.

Foster, R. B. 1983. Famine on Barro Colorado Island. Pages 201–212 *in* E. G. Leigh, Jr., A. S. Rand, and D. M. Windsor, editors. The ecology of a tropical forest. Oxford University Press, Oxford, England.

Gaulin, S. J. C., and C. K. Gaulin. 1982. Behavioral ecology of *Alouatta seniculus* in Andean cloud forest. International Journal of Primatology 3:1–32.

Gautier-Hion, A., J. P. Gautier, and R. Quris. 1981. Forest structure and fruit availability as complementary factors influencing habitat use by a troop of monkeys (*Cercopithecus cephus*). Terre et la Vie 35:511–536.

Gittins, S. P., and J. J. Raemaekers. 1980. Siamang, lar and agile gibbons. Pages 63–105 *in* D. J. Chivers, editor. Malayan forest primates. Plenum, New York, New York, USA.

Hladik, A., and C. M. Hladik. 1969. Rapports trophiques entre végétation et primates dans la forêt de Barro Colorado (Panama). Terre et la Vie 23:25–117.

Hladik, C. M. 1977. A comparative study of the feeding strategies of two sympatric species of leaf monkeys: *Presbytis senex* and *P. entellus.* Pages 323–353 *in* T. H. Clutton-Brock, editor. Primate ecology. Academic Press, London, England.

Hladik, C. M., A. Hladik, J. Bousset, P. Valderbouze, G. Viroben, and J. Delort-Lavel. 1971. Le régime alimentaire des primates de l'île de Barro Colorado (Panama): résultats des analyses quantitatives. Folia Primatologica 16:85–122.

Homewood, K. 1975. Can the Tana mangabey survive? Oryx 13:53–59.

Johns, A. D. 1981. The effects of selective logging on the social structure of resident primates. Malaysian Applied Biology 10:221–226.

———. 1983. Ecological effects of selective logging in a West Malaysian rain-forest. Dissertation. University of Cambridge, Cambridge, England.

———. *In press.* Effects of commercial logging in a West Malaysian primate community. *In* F. A. King and D. M. Taub, editors. Proceedings of the IXth Congress of the In-

694   ANDREW D. JOHNS   Ecology, Vol. 67, No. 3

ternational Primatological Society, Atlanta, Georgia, USA. Van Nostrand-Reinhold, New York, New York, USA.

Klein, L. L., and D. B. Klein. 1977. Feeding behaviour of the Columbian spider monkey. Pages 153–181 *in* T. H. Clutton-Brock, editor. Primate ecology. Academic Press, London, England.

Kurland, J. A. 1973. A natural history of Kra macaques (*Macaca fascicularis* Raffles 1821) at the Kutai Reserve, Kalimantan Timur, Indonesia. Primates 14:245–262.

MacKinnon, J. R. 1971. The orang-utan in Sabah today. Oryx 11:141–191.

———. 1977. A comparative ecology of Asian apes. Primates 18:747–772.

MacKinnon, J. R., and K. S. MacKinnon. 1978. Comparative feeding ecology of six sympatric primates in West Malaysia. Pages 305–321 *in* D. J. Chivers and J. Herbert, editors. Recent advances in primatology, volume 1. Academic Press, London, England.

MacKinnon, J. R., and K. S. MacKinnon. 1980. Niche differentiation in a primate community. Pages 167–190 *in* D. J. Chivers, editor. Malayan forest primates. Plenum, New York, New York, USA.

Marsh, C. W. 1979. Comparative aspects of social organisation in the Tana River red colobus, *Colobus badius rufomitratus*. Zeitschrift für Tierpsychologie 51:337–362.

———. 1981. Ranging behaviour and its relation to diet selection in Tana River red colobus (*Colobus badius rufomitratus*). Journal of Zoology (London) 195:473–492.

Marsh, C. W., A. D. Johns, and J. M. Ayres. *In press.* The effects of habitat disturbance. *In* J. S. Gartlan, C. W. Marsh, and R. A. Mittermeier, editors. The conservation of primates in tropical rainforest. Alan Liss, New York, New York, USA.

Marsh, C. W., and W. L. Wilson. 1981. A survey of primates in Peninsular Malaysian forests. Universiti Kebangsaan Malaysia, Kuala Lumpur, Malaysia.

McKey, D. B., and P. G. Waterman. 1982. Ranging behaviour of a group of black colobus (*Colobus satanas*) in the Douala-Edea Reserve, Cameroon. Folia Primatologica 39: 264–304.

Milton, K. 1980. The foraging strategy of howler monkeys: a study in primate economics. Columbia University Press, New York, New York, USA.

———. 1983. Dietary quality and population regulation in a howler monkey population. Pages 273–289 *in* E. G. Leigh, Jr., A. S. Rand, and D. M. Windsor, editors. The ecology of a tropical forest. Oxford University Press, Oxford, England.

Mitani, J. C., and P. S. Rodman. 1979. Territoriality: the relation of ranging pattern and home range size to defendability, with an analysis of territoriality among primate species. Behavioural Ecology and Sociobiology 5:241–251.

Neville, M. K. 1972. The population structure of red howler

monkeys (*Alouatta seniculus*) in Trinidad and Venezuela. Folia Primatologica 17:56–86.

Oates, J. F. 1977. The guereza and its food. Pages 275–321 *in* T. H. Clutton-Brock, editor. Primate ecology. Academic Press, London, England.

Payne, J. B., and A. G. Davies. 1982. A faunal survey of Sabah. World Wildlife Fund Malaysia, Kuala Lumpur, Malaysia.

Petter, J.-J., and A. Peyriéras. 1974. A study of the population density and home range of *Indri indri* in Madagascar. Pages 39–48 *in* R. D. Martin, G. A. Doyle, and A. C. Walker, editors. Prosimian biology. Duckworth, London, England.

Raemaekers, J. J. 1978. Changes through the day in the food choice of wild gibbons. Folia Primatologica 30:194–205.

———. 1980. Causes of variation between months in the distance travelled daily by gibbons. Folia Primatologica 34: 46–60.

Salter, R. E., and N. A. MacKenzie. 1981. Habitat-use behaviour of the proboscis monkey (*Nasalis larvatus*) in Sarawak. National Parks and Wildlife Office, Forest Department, Kuching, Sarawak.

Schoener, T. W. 1971. Theory of feeding strategies. Annual Review of Ecology and Systematics 2:369–403.

Struhsaker, T. T. 1972. Rainforest conservation in Africa. Primates 13:103–109.

———. 1973. A recensus of vervet monkeys in the Masai-Amboseli Game Reserve, Kenya. Ecology 54:930–932.

———. 1976. a further decline in numbers of Amboseli vervet monkeys. Biotropica 8:211–214.

Vellayan, S. 1981. Chemical composition and digestibility of natural and domestic food of the lar gibbon (*Hylobates lar*) in Malaysia. Dissertation. Universiti Pertanian Malaysia, Serdang, Selangor, Malaysia.

Waser, P. M. 1975. Monthly variations in feeding and activity patterns of the mangabey, *Cercocebus albigena* (Lydekker). East African Wildlife Journal 13:249–263.

Waser, P. M., and O. Floody. 1974. Ranging patterns of the mangabey, *Cercocebus albigena*, in the Kibale Forest, Uganda. Zeitschrift für Tierpsychologie 35:85–101.

Waterman, P. G., and G. M. Choo. 1981. The effects of digestibility-reducing compounds in leaves on food selection by some colobines. Malaysian Applied Biology 10: 147–162.

Whitmore, T. C. 1984. Tropical rain forests of the Far East. Second edition. Clarendon, Oxford, England.

Whitten, A. J. 1982. Home range use by Kloss gibbons (*Hylobates klossii*) on Siberut Island, Indonesia. Animal Behaviour 30:182–198.

Wilson, C. C., and W. L. Wilson. 1975. The influence of selective logging on primates and some other animals in East Kalimantan. Folia Primatologica 23:245–274.

9

ARE WE ON THE VERGE OF A MASS EXTINCTION IN TROPICAL RAIN FORESTS?

DANIEL SIMBERLOFF

Department of Biological Science
Florida State University
Tallahassee, Florida

INTRODUCTION

According to Myers (1981), destruction of moist tropical forests is proceeding so fast that they "may be reduced to degraded remnants by the end of the century, if they are not eliminated altogether. This will represent a biological debacle to surpass all others that have occurred since life first emerged 3.6 billion years ago." Is the situation really so dire?

I hope to bring to bear on this question recent approaches to biogeography (MacArthur and Wilson, 1967; Haffer, 1969) and to use real data. This is no mean task, as data on both the present tropical crisis and the mass extinctions of the geologic past are much less complete than those that ecologists are accustomed to using and render credible predictions extraordinarily difficult. This problem has been noted, and the contention advanced that we must act now even without strong evidence, since catastrophe is so imminent that conservation will be impossible by the time we have adequate evidence. "With the present rate of destruction of the tropical rain forests there is great danger of mass extinction . . . . Thousands of species could disappear before any aspect of their biology has been studied . . . . There is incomplete scientific evidence to prove this assertion, but if we wait for a generation to provide abundant evidence there will not be any rain forests left to prove it" (Gómez-Pompa et al., 1972). Soulé (1980) considers statistical confidence limits "luxuries that conservation biologists cannot now afford," but to me the urgency of the problem does not obviate statistical analysis.

HISTORICAL MASS EXTINCTIONS

Past mass extinctions (Newell, 1962, 1967) have been the most controversial phenomena to challenge paleobiologists (Schopf, 1974). During several relatively brief intervals, large fractions of the earth's biota have been eliminated (Table 1). No mass extinctions of plants are known, however (Newell, 1962, 1967). Taxonomic and stratigraphic uncertainty has beclouded identification of such episodes, but a recent systematic examination of fossil data confirms and focuses five marine mass extinctions (Raup and Sepkoski, 1982), while a spate of work on the Great American Interchange (Marshall et al., 1982) has elucidated a mass extinction of terrestrial mammals. A plethora of explanations have been proposed for mass extinctions. For marine mass extinctions, for example, meteorites, volcanic and metal poisons, extraterrestrial radiation, changes in temperature, salinity, and oxygen, and shortage of various resources or habitats have all been suggested causes (Valentine, 1973; Schopf, 1974).

Two related nomothetic principles, however, may explain at least part of many mass extinctions: area and provinciality effects (Moore, 1954; Flessa and Imbrie, 1973; Schopf, 1979). By *provinciality*, I mean how total area is divided into spatially separate units. In the evolutionary and paleontologic literature, this phenomenon is often called *endemism*, and ecologists sometimes term it *insularization*.

Perhaps ecology's oldest generalization is the species–area relationship (Watson, 1835; Connor and McCoy, 1979), that is, that large sites tend to have more species than small sites do, all other things being equal. This principle suggests that a decrease of area should be followed, with a time lag to be discussed below, by a decrease in biotic diversity. Of the six mass extinctions in Table 1, certainly four and perhaps five are accompanied by major marine areal decrease. The decrease was most severe for the most dramatic mass extinction, the Late Permian. Shallow seas decreased by 68%, and 52% of all families of marine animals disappeared.

New interest accrued to the relationship between area and biotic diversity in the wake of the equilibrium theory of island biogeography (MacArthur and Wilson, 1963, 1967), since the theory readily explains the relationship: larger sites have lower extinction rates and possibly higher immigration rates as well. However, there are other explanations for the species–area relationship (Simberloff, 1974a; Connor and McCoy, 1979), and most naturalists would agree that one of them— that larger areas tend to have more habitats, each with its own species complement— accounts for a large fraction of species–area relationships. Direct support for the equilibrium theory explanation is provided only by an experiment on arboreal arthropods of small mangrove islands (Simberloff, 1976). Although the deductive basis of the equilibrium theory area effect seems unexceptionable, the *speed* with

Table 1. Mass Extinctions of the Geological Past[a,b]

Period	Taxa	Area Change (%)	Maximum Length of Extinction (m.y.)	Provinciality	Extinction
Late Ordovician	Marine Animals	-38	5		-12% of families
Late Devonian	Marine animals	-11 to -21	25		-14% of families
	Amphibians		20		-99% of families
Late Permian	Marine animals	-68	22	14 down to 8	-52% of families
					-96% of species
	Amphibians		25		-78% of families
	Reptiles		25		-81% of families
Late Triassic	Marine animals	+10 to -27	5		-12% of families
	Amphibians		16.6		-99% of families
	Reptiles		16.6		-89% of families
Late Cretaceous	Marine animals	-27 to -43	6		-11% of families
	Reptiles		35		-57% of families
	Mammals		35		-32% of families
Pleistocene (Great American Interchange)	Mammals	0	3	2 down to 1	-27% of families
					-23% of genera

[a]Area change is for shallow seas.
[b]Data from Marshall et al. (1982), Newell (1967), Raup and Sepkoski (1982), Sepkoski (1976), Simberloff (1974), and D. Webb (personal communication, 1983).

which an areal decrease would be followed by a species diversity decrease by this route or any other is an empirical matter and might turn out to be so slow that conservationists would not concern themselves with species loss from this source.

Certainly, area changes cannot account for *all* mass extinctions. In Table 1, one can see that a number of mass extinctions of marine animals, accompanied by decrease in area of shallow seas, are contemporaneous, to the level of resolution afforded by the fossil record, with mass extinctions of terrestrial animals. As area of seas shrinks, area of land probably increases, so the terrestrial extinctions cannot be directly attributed to area decrease.

Part of this paradox may be resolved by a consideration of provinciality. That provinciality increases biotic diversity is another venerable rule. There appear to be two effects of provinciality on diversity. The first is evolutionary, the principle of "ecological vicars"—species that have evolved in different regions to perform similar ecological functions and that would not likely coexist in the same region. The same principle predicts a decrease in diversity when geological events decrease provinciality (Flessa and Imbrie, 1973; Schopf, 1979). The Late Permian marine extinction was accompanied not only by an areal decrease of 68% for shallow seas (Simberloff, 1974b) but by a decrease in number of marine provinces from 14 to 8 (Schopf, 1979). Theory provides no exact prediction of how much and how quickly diversity will decrease for a given decrease in provinciality. It is an empirical matter. For the Late Permian extinction, Schopf (1979) suggests that decrease in number of provinces was far more important than decrease in area, while the extinction of New World mammals in the Pleistocene Interchange was not accompanied by an areal decrease, but two provinces partially coalesced into one.

The second effect of provinciality on biotic diversity is much shorter term, and its study was inspired by the equilibrium theory. The conservation literature is confused about what the equilibrium theory predicts for the effect of number of provinces on biotic diversity. It is frequently asserted (references in Simberloff and Abele, 1976a) that single large refuges will, by the theory of island biogeography, preserve more species than will two or more small ones of equal total area. In fact, the theory makes no prediction (Simberloff and Abele, 1976a, 1982). This is an empirical matter and depends on the overlap of species sets in the separate refuges and the statistical form and parameters of the species–area relationship. For a variety of taxa and size ranges of sites, groups of small sites contain as many species as do single large ones and often more (Simberloff and Abele, 1982; Simberloff and Gotelli, 1984). A plausible explanation for these observations is that, on average, a single site embraces fewer habitats than does a group of distinct sites of equal total area, but there is no direct evidence that this is in fact the cause of the reported observations. In any event, no one claims that a single large site will contain fewer species than will a group of small ones of *smaller* total area, and this is the situation facing the tropics. If the group of small sites is but a subset of the single large one, it is also difficult to see how they would contain more habitats.

A final point must be noted about the historical mass extinctions. They may have occurred much more rapidly than Table 1 would suggest. As has often been noted (e.g., Newell, 1967; Hallam, 1973), the resolution of the fossil record is such that one can only place an upper bound on how long an extinction took, normally a matter of some few million years. The actual extinction, however, may have been much quicker. Recent interest in the impact hypothesis (Lewin, 1983) emphasizes the possibility that some historical mass extinctions may have been nearly instantaneous.

STATISTICAL PROTOCOLS

Any prediction of an imminent mass extinction in the tropics and comparison of what is likely to happen there with what happened during crises of the geological past must rest fundamentally on the species–area relationship, canonized as

$$S = cA^z \tag{1}$$

where S = number of species, A = area, and c and z are constants. Two other relationships between S and A fit many literature examples better than equation (1) does (Connor and McCoy, 1979). However, the qualitative results described below are valid if species and area are related by any of the relationships proposed by Connor and McCoy (1979). Similarly, $z = 0.25$; for real data, the exponent is usually around 0.25. Results are not substantially altered when the exponent to any value is set between 0.15 and 0.50.

Just as ecologists know that, on average, larger sites have more species than smaller ones do, so do they recognize that area is a very crude predictor of diversity. For a collection of 100 data sets studied by Connor and McCoy (1979), the average correlation coefficient between log area and log number of species [the transformation that linearizes equation (1)] is only 0.669. That is, only 44.8% of the variation in log S can be attributed to variation in log A. For three data sets, the correlation is negative. We will return to this problem.

The mass extinctions are almost all documented in terms of numbers of families. For purely statistical reasons, incompleteness of the fossil record is not nearly as debilitating at higher taxonomic levels as at the species level (Raup, 1972). This is a sampling problem. One is much less likely to miss all species in a genus or family than to miss any one of them. Ecological observations and theory, however, are at the species level. Empirically, one sees that family–area curves follow a similar form to species–area curves (Flessa, 1975), but with higher variance (personal observation). However, one can use rarefaction (Simberloff, 1978) to estimate how many families will be present if fewer species are present after an area reduction. One can estimate the new number of species from equation (1) and the new number of families by

$$E(F_B) = F_{\text{orig}} - \left(\frac{S_{\text{orig}}}{S_{\text{new}}}\right)^{-1} \cdot \sum_{i=1}^{F_{\text{orig}}} \left(\frac{S_{\text{orig}} - S_i}{S_{\text{new}}}\right) \tag{2}$$

A variance is easily calculated as well (Heck et al., 1975; Simberloff, 1978). Using the distribution of family sizes for living echinoids, Raup (1979) used equation (2) to estimate that 96% of all species went extinct in the Late Permian, given the observed extinction of 52% of all families.

A word is in order about rarefaction. It is used below because it seems the best statistical technique available for the questions raised, but it gives a *very* conservative estimate of decrease in number of families. This is because it assumes surviving species are a random sample with respect to family affiliation. However, confamilial species tend to be clumped both ecologically (with respect to both habitat and niche) and geographically. If a given species is extinguished by whatever means, the probability is increased that the *next* species to go extinct is in the same family. This is because the same forces that caused the extinction are more likely to affect confamilial than heterofamilial species. The effect of this nonrandomness on the rarefaction estimate of how many families will be left is to cause it to be too high; more families will be eliminated than estimated. Exactly how many more cannot be guessed without vastly more data on geography and ecology of tropical species of various taxa. But it will be the contention of this author that such data would allow a much more accurate assessment of the threat to the tropics than rarefaction permits. For now, the observation of the effects of this sort of contagion on random draws from a few distributions shows that the effect might well double the rarefaction estimate.

THE MODEL

I will attempt to fit tropical moist forest data to a model of increasing insularization. As tropical moist forest is destroyed or degraded, area decreases and insularization increases: a few large, continuous areas are converted into an archipelago of numerous, much smaller "islands." By the principles enunciated above, the area decrease should generate, with some lag time, a decrease in number of species. Conversely, if the component islands are large enough and last long enough, the increasing insularization might generate, also with some lag, an increase in number of species. We wish to predict the magnitude and speed of these two processes, and also how the change in number of species translates into change in number of families, for comparison to previous mass extinctions.

This model resembles the Pleistocene refuge theory of tropical diversity enunciated most explicitly by Haffer (1969) for neotropical birds, but even earlier in essence by Moreau (1963) for African birds. Haffer's model has also been adopted as an explanation for the great diversity of neotropical plants, butterflies, and several groups of vertebrates (references in Simpson and Haffer, 1978). His idea is that the Amazon rain forest, despite drastic recent anthropogenous insults, is near maximum extent, and that, as many as four times in the last 50,000 yr, moist forest has contracted to much smaller, isolated refugia during cooler, drier times. Intervening area became savanna, inhospitable to biota of moist forest. Populations of species of this biota are thus isolated and undergo allopatric speciation, increasing total number of species. Eventually, the climate becomes warmer and wetter again, the refugia expand, coalesce, and reconstitute a vast, continuous forest, and the new sister species invade one another's ranges or perhaps remain parapatric.

This model has been vigorously questioned by Benson (1982), Endler (1982), Strong (1982), and Beven et al. (1984). Much criticism centers around whether the posited Pleistocene climatic changes actually occurred and whether present biogeographic distributional data uniquely support the model. Its position seems established for now, however, by virtue of an approving review (Simpson and Haffer, 1978) and a massive symposium volume (Prance, 1982). Without arguing the merits of this debate, all parties would likely agree that severe insularization of a habitat, if maintained for long enough, would generate both a species loss from area decrease and a species gain from insularization if islands are sufficiently large and persistent. So I will assume that such insularization is now occurring and will be maintained and will proceed with my model.

Although different refuge theorists working with different taxa propose different numbers, sizes, and locations for refugia (cf. Simpson and Haffer, 1978), they agree that retrenchment in cooler times was severe. As an example (Figure 1), Pielou's rendition (1979) of Haffer's refugia (1969) will be used. The results do not change qualitatively when I use different schemes. Four regions of moist forest today are hypothesized to have been reduced to 10 refugia with total area just 16% of present (areas determined by planimetry). It is striking that few adherents of this view have suggested that this drastic areal decrease will cause extinctions; Fitzpatrick (1976) and Simpson and Haffer (1978) are exceptions. Rather, most have focused on opportunities for speciation that the increase in provinciality affords. Similarly, no refuge theorist proposes massive extinction once the refuges expand and coalesce. Instead, new sister species either coexist or remain parapatric.

One can easily rationalize these emphases in terms of time scales. For animals, at least, if the climatic change requires centuries or millennia, one would expect not immediate extinction, but movement to remain in the appropriate climatic regime (e.g., Coope, 1978). If the new climate does not persist long, one could hypothesize that extinction does not have time to occur, and the community trapped in the refuge never comes to a new equilibrium before area expands again. Of course, for diversity to increase, one must hypothesize that sufficient evolution occurs to generate new species in the same time span that is not long enough to allow extinctions.

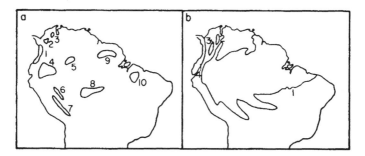

FIGURE 1. (a) The probable sites of patches of tropical rain forest that served as refugia for forest birds in dry periods in the Pleistocene (after Haffer, 1969). (b) The current extent of tropical rain forest in northern South America.

WHAT IS HAPPENING IN THE TROPICS

Biological data on tropical moist forest are almost nonexistent, and data on gross attributes like land cover are marginal. Myers (1980) made a heroic effort to collate, evaluate, and summarize the literature on how much forest there is and what is happening to it. The climatic range of tropical moist forest is ca. 16×10^6 km^2, of which the extent covered when Myers wrote was 9–11×10^6 km^2. The major previous statement (Sommer, 1976) had estimated 9.35×10^6 km^2 remaining. Sommer felt that, by 1976, 37% of Latin American forests, 41.6% of Asian forests, and 51.6% of African forests had already been destroyed, but since he had not considered edaphic or topographic factors, these estimates were likely inflated (Myers, 1980).

How quickly forest is being destroyed, where the process will be at the end of the century, and what the end point will be are even more matters for guesswork. Sommer (1976), using data from 13 nations encompassing 18% of all tropical moist forest, estimated a worldwide regression rate of 110,000 km^2/yr, which equals an astounding 21 ha/min. Other estimates (Myers, 1980) range from about half to about twice Sommer's estimate. Lanly (1982), using improved remote-sensing data on 76 nations comprising 97% of the tropics, estimates a current regression rate of 71,000 km^2/yr, while Myers (personal communication, 1983) suggests 92,000 km^2/ yr. However, these figures refer only to deforestation, or complete removal of tree cover. If one includes other forms of conversion, like logging, that constitute sufficiently severe habitat change that one might expect extinction to result, a more likely estimate of regression rate is 119,000 km^2/yr (Lanly, 1982) to 200,000 km^2/ yr (Myers, personal communication, 1983). For now I will use Sommer's estimate and err on the side of conservatism.

There is every reason to believe that this rate will increase, at least into the early years of the twenty-first century. The main reason for conversion is shifting agriculture (Lanly, 1982), which is very sensitive to population increase. The population of Africa is predicted to double in 23 yr, that of Latin America in 30 yr, and that of Asia in 36 yr (Kent, 1983). Pressure for food entailed by these increases is likely to be reflected in greatly increased shifting agriculture, with corresponding increased forest degradation. Indeed, the main brake on this degradation will probably be the increasing number of nations, like El Salvador, Madagascar, the Philippines, and Indonesia, in which forest conversion will be virtually complete within a decade if it is not already complete.

Where this destruction will end no one can say. Myers (1980) summarizes progress by various nations in setting aside refuges. Although some nations have made substantial commitments in this direction (particularly in light of the fact that most tropical moist forest resides in relatively underdeveloped countries), the total effort is woefully inadequate, with total area very small, protection limited, entire habitats not included, and so on. With rapid population increase, one cannot expect tropical nations to be willing to set aside land and to commit economic resources to long-term conservation.

From here on the discussion will be restricted to tropical moist forests of the neotropics. They comprise well over half of all tropical moist forest (Lanly, 1982). Neotropical forests are much less degraded than those of other regions. In Southeast Asia, for example, destruction is proceeding so quickly and there is so little forest left that primary lowland forest will be virtually extirpated by the year 2000. So focusing on American forests probably leads to an unduly optimistic picture. Nevertheless, availability of key biological data led this author to do so. Two taxa will be considered, land birds and flowering plants, for three reasons. First, these are the taxa for which most literature on neotropical conservation exists. Second, these taxa dominate Pleistocene refuge theory literature. Third, and most important, there is comprehensive data for these taxa on what species presently exist from massive compilations by Alwin Gentry for plants and J. V. Remsen for birds.

For plants, Raven (1976), in a seminal paper on the threat to the tropics, hazarded the guess that about 90,000 of the world's 240,000 species of flowering plants are found in tropical America. Gentry set out to compile all tropical American plants and found that Raven was remarkably accurate. From Gentry's list I find approximately 92,128 species in 239 families, although Gentry included nontropical species since his sources treated the neotropical biogeographic province as one entity. It is likely that fewer than 10,000 species are restricted to temperate parts of the province, so no great error will be introduced by using Gentry's list to represent tropical forest plants.

For area, Sommer (1976) suggests there has already been regression of 37%, but this is likely an overestimate since much that is in the climatic range of tropical moist forest probably was not tropical moist forest (see above). From that estimate, 10% was arbitrarily deducted, and it was assumed that in the recent past there has been regression of 27%, so that originally there were 6.93×10^6 km^2 of forest. It was also assumed that no plant species have yet been extinguished because of regression. Between now and the end of the century, Sommer's estimate of regression rate (1976) suggests 59,000 km^2 of forest destroyed per year in tropical America, or 952,470 km^2 by the end of the century. Myers's estimates (1980) are similar; he finds 5.6×10^6 km^2 now and, on a country-by-country basis, predicts a decrease of ca. 1,400,000 km^2 by the year 2000. Similarly, Lanly (1982) predicts a decrease in forested area of ca. 12.5% by the end of the century, but only for complete deforestation. He expects 3.9×10^6 km^2 of undisturbed productive forest to remain in the year 2000. In short, we are dealing with a projected areal decrease of 12–25% between now and the end of the century and ca. 40% between the Recent past and the end of the century. Finally, Gentry (1979) lists established national parks and equivalents for tropical America totaling ca. 96,700 km^2 of forest. This may be construed as a worst-case outcome of tropical forest destruction at some undefined future time.

Using Myers's predictions for amount of forest left at the end of the century and the worst-case estimate and assuming no extinction yet caused by recent regression, equilibrium numbers of species for those areas were calculated using equation (1) with $z = 0.25$ (Table 2). No substantial theory predicts how long it will take for these equilibria to be achieved. For plants, it may even take centuries because of their longevity. Indeed, since destruction will continue well beyond the end of

Table 2. Projected Plant Extinctions in New World Tropical Moist Forest

	Fraction of Original Area	Equilibrium Number of Species (N = 9)	Expected Number of Families E(F)
Originally	1.000	92,128	239
End of century	0.528	78,534	236.35
Worst-case end point	0.013	31,662	221.89

the century, the first equilibrium will never be achieved. Equation (2) gives rarefaction estimates of numbers of families expected for the predicted numbers of species. Confidence limits around these estimates are very small, but there is another reason, contagion, addressed above, why these predictions of decrease in numbers of families are likely gross underestimates. It is impossible to know just how low these estimates are, but they are almost certainly off by a factor of at least 2. It is also possible that predictions of numbers of species lost are low (see below).

Remsen's list of Amazon birds includes 704 species in 327 genera and 40 families. Consequences of three area reductions are considered: (1) If Amazonia were reduced by the end of the century exactly proportionally to Sommer's estimate for tropical forests generally (that is, to 0.593 of its extent before recent regression); (2) if Amazonia were reduced to refugia outlined by Haffer (Figure 1), a reduction to 0.160 of the original area; and (3) if Amazonia were reduced to national parks in Gentry's list in or near Amazonia, a reduction to 0.009 of the original area. For each reduction, number of species *at equilibrium* is computed by equation (1), and then the expected number of families and genera by equation (2). Results are in Table 3. The same caveats hold for rarefaction estimates of birds as for plants; it would not be surprising if actual decrease in generic and familial diversity turned out to be twice that predicted.

For neither taxon has provinciality been considered: not only will area be reduced, but it will be divided into a large number of mostly very small islands. To some

Table 3. Projected Extinctions of Land Birds of Amazonia

	Fraction of Original Area	Equilibrium Number of Species (N=9)	Expected Number of Genera E(G)	Expected Number of Families E(F)
Originally	1.000	704	327	40
End of century	0.593	618	304.63	39.72
Pleistocene refugia	0.160	445	251.80	38.73
Worst-case end point	0.009	217	155.26	34.77

extent, this is already true, and the effect will become even more extreme by the end of the century. Over the very long run, or maybe not so very long run, if refuge theorists are correct, increased provinciality would perhaps lead to new species. For example, the 84% decrease in area from the present to hypothesized Pleistocene refugia suggests, at equilibrium, a 37% decrease in number of species. The accompanying increase in provinciality from 4 to 10, given measured areas cited above, predicts an ultimate increase of 70% in number of species. This would be achieved once all allopatric populations had speciated.

I cannot be sanguine about this prospect for two reasons. First, though two species can arise from one very quickly if the right mutations occur, especially if selective pressures on two allopatric populations are very different, it does not seem plausible that this will happen often. Most newly allopatric populations will require at least a millennium or two to achieve species status, and I am not cheered by the thought of a thousand years of impoverishment.

Second, at some point, increases in provinciality without increases in area produce islands too small for long-term survival of some or all of the species initially stranded on them (Simberloff and Abele, 1976a, 1982; Simberloff and Gotelli, 1984). At exactly what point islands become so small that a substantial fraction of their biota will be extinguished must be determined empirically for each group, and this sort of research has just begun.

Shaffer (1981) contends that each species has a "critical population size" such that when populations fall below this point various stochastic forces, both genetic and ecological, are likely to extinguish it quickly. Above this point, extinction will be much slower. For tropical plants, there is no data that allow us to say anything about critical population sizes (and their associated critical areas). For birds, there are two hints that, at least for some species, they are quite large (the species require large areas). Barro Colorado Island in Lake Gatun was formed when the Chagres River was dammed during construction of the Panama Canal (Karr, 1982). Several bird species have since gone extinct. Since the area that is now the island was partly farmed and has since undergone secondary succession, habitat change alone would likely have produced some extinction (Simberloff and Abele, 1976a,b). But some extinctions are of forest species (Willis and Eisenmann, 1979) and cannot easily be attributed to succession. Several of these may be due to populations being reduced below their critical sizes. For example, some obligate army-ant-following species have disappeared, perhaps because a small (17-km^2) island simply does not have enough army ants to support them (Willis and Eisenmann, 1979).

Lovejoy and co-workers (1983) have recently begun an experiment in Brazil that should shed light on minimum population sizes and areas. They created islands of different size by felling surrounding forest and are monitoring avifaunal change. The two obligate ant followers have already disappeared from the smallest islands (1 and 10 ha). If many species have critical population sizes as large as the ant birds do, then the refuges set aside, even if guarded, may undergo substantial species loss before evolutionary changes occur. The data do not exist, but such problems will be greater for birds than for plants. Further, because of the longevity of plants, the time to extinction even after area becomes too small may be centuries.

Another problem, in addition to lack of data, pervades this effort to assess minimum areas. Area alone cannot adequately predict suitability for any particular species, just as it is an insufficient predictor of species richness (Boecklen and Gotelli, 1984). Predictions of faunal collapse based on species-area relationships alone typically have confidence intervals so large as to render them ludicrous. For example, the 95% simultaneous prediction interval for the estimate by Soulé et al. (1979) of the extinction coefficient for the Nairobi National Park spans 10 orders of magnitude (Boecklen and Gotelli, 1984). Their forecast in effect is that the Nairobi reserve will lose between 0.5 and 99.5% of its species in 5000 yr with a 95% level of confidence!

We surely can do better by looking carefully at habitats and biogeographic ranges of species. Kitchener et al. (1980), Game and Peterken (1983), and Simberloff and Abele (1982), among others, have all emphasized that by judiciously selecting sites to encompass a large variety of habitats, it may be possible to conserve as many species in a smaller total area as might have been predicted from species–area relationships to require a very large single area. Ashton (1981) has noted that many tropical tree species have very specialized edaphic requirements, but if these requirements are met, they may persist in small populations, sometimes fewer than 100 individuals.

Just as a detailed assessment of habitats should aid conservation prospects, so might ecological considerations enable us to predict more accurately the outcome of any particular action. Two sorts of studies are particularly needed. First, obligatory linkages between species are complex and numerous in the tropics, so that extinction of one species will likely have cascading effects that lead to other extinctions (Janzen, 1974). For example, Lovejoy (1973) notes that a single bee species cross-pollinates the Brazil nut tree, and the tree, while in flower, is the bee's major food. Similarly, Howe (1977) has shown that some frugivorous birds are seasonally each restricted to fruits of a single tree species, which in turn is dispersed almost exclusively by the bird that feeds on it.

Second, felling the forest over large areas will likely affect hydrology and other climatic factors (Myers, 1980, 1981; Ashton, 1981), which in turn could lead to extinctions as habitat changes. For example, Myers (1980) sketches a scenario in which reduced evapotranspiration of a reduced Amazonia leads to a drier forest in the entire region, and Salati (cited in Webster, 1983) suggests in addition major increases in flooding and river flow rates. On a small scale, Lovejoy et al. (1983) have observed increased wind-caused tree falls in their isolated 10-ha Brazilian forest and suspect a number of other tree deaths are caused by microhabitat change. They suggest that replacements for such deaths caused by habitat change are likely to be by different species, so that eventually proportions of different species in the forest will change. Local extinctions may result from such habitat modification.

Finally, sites set aside for conservation in Amazonia might not contain as many species as species–area relationships would have predicted. Prance (1977) and Gentry (1979) have argued that these sites do not encompass some major centers of plant diversity (Pleistocene refugia?) nor some edaphic and other ecologic conditions that make Amazonia so species-rich.

A MASS EXTINCTION?

Are we, then, on the verge of a mass extinction in the tropics? This author knows of no data to show that any plant or bird species has yet gone extinct in the New World tropics, but because these two taxa fossilize so poorly, we know of few such extinctions from the late Pleistocene, even though we are sure that extinctions occurred then. Perhaps the best circumstantial evidence that neotropical bird species are already extinct from forest destruction is provided by Hilty (1984), who has examined biogeographic ranges of Colombian birds. Several forest species' known ranges are completely obliterated and the birds have not been seen since, even though some are large, obvious birds that could be used for food. For example, the Cauca Guan, *Penelope perspicax*, is the size of a turkey and was restricted to the upper reaches of the Cauca Valley, an area in which forest is virtually all gone. For plants, range data are not nearly as reliable, so such inferences are more difficult.

Comparing data from Tables 2 and 3 to those of Table 1, we find that, at least in the New World, even with an increase in the rate of destruction, there is not likely to be a mass extinction by the end of the century comparable to those of the geological past. Doubling the rarefaction prediction of numbers of families lost (for reasons stated above), a loss of about 15% of all plant species and 2% of all plant families would be expected if forest regression proceeded as predicted until 2000 and then stopped completely (Table 2). How long it would take after that for these new equilibria to be achieved I cannot guess. For Amazon birds, the comparable figures are a 12% species loss and a 1% family loss (Table 3). As horrible as it is to contemplate losses of 15,000 plant species and 100 bird species, they are not comparable to the major geological mass extinctions.

However, sometime in the *next* century, and probably sooner rather than later if Myers's summary (1980) of forest regression rates is accurate and if there are no major changes in the way forests are treated, things may get much worse. If tropical forests in the New World were reduced to those currently projected as parks and refuges, by the end of the century about 66% of all plant species and 14% of families would disappear, after equilibration occurs (a few families may persist outside the New World). For the Amazon birds, 69% of all species and 26% of families would disappear before a new equilibrium was reached (a few families may persist outside Amazonia). Perhaps captive propagation, habitat manipulation, and other conservation techniques will ameliorate this situation somewhat, and it may be that the extinctions that establish the new equilibrium will be spread out over several millennia. However, the estimates throughout this chapter have been conservative, and the region (the neotropics) that is in the best condition now and is likely to persist longer has been treated. All told, then, it is clear that Myers was remarkably close to the mark. The imminent catastrophe in tropical forests *is* commensurate with all the great mass extinctions except for that at the end of the Permian.

ACKNOWLEDGMENTS

I thank Alwin Gentry, J. V. Remsen, Gary Graves, Steve Hilty, Norman Myers, Peter Raven, Dave Raup, and Dave Webb for laboriously gathered data and thoughtful advice.

REFERENCES

Ashton, P. S., 1981, Techniques for the identification and conservation of threatened species in tropical forests, in Synge, H., ed., *The Biological Aspects of Rare Plant Conservation*, New York, Wiley, pp. 155–164.

Benson, W. W., 1982, Alternative models for infrageneric diversification in the humid tropics: Tests with passion vine butterflies, in Prance, G. T., ed., *Biological Diversification in the Tropics*, New York, Columbia University Press, pp. 608–640.

Beven, S., Connor, E. F., and Beven, K., 1984, Avian biogeography in the Amazon Basin and the biological model of diversification, *J. Biogeogr*, **11**, 383–399.

Boecklen, W. J., and Gotelli, N., 1984, Island biogeographic theory and conservation practice: Species–area or specious–area relationships, *Biol. Conserv.*, **29**, 63–80.

Connor, E. F., and McCoy, E. D., 1979, The statistics and biology of the species–area relationship, *Am. Nat.*, **113**, 791–833.

Coope, G. R., 1978, Constancy of insect species versus inconstancy of Quaternary environments, in Mound, L. A., and Waloff, N., eds., *Diversity of Insect Faunas*, Oxford, Blackwell, pp. 176–187.

Endler, J. A., 1982, Pleistocene forest refuges: Fact or fancy? in Prance, G. T., ed., *Biological Diversification in the Tropics*, New York, Columbia University Press, pp. 179–200.

Fitzpatrick, J. W., 1976, Systematics and biogeography of the tyrannid genus *Todirostrum* and related genera (Aves), *Bull. Mus. Compar. Zool.*, **147**, 435–463.

Flessa, K. W., 1975, Area, continental drift and mammalian diversity, *Paleobiology*, **1**, 189–194.

Flessa, K. W., and Imbrie, J., 1973, Evolutionary pulsations: Evidence from Phanerozoic diversity patterns, in Tarling, D. H., and Runcorn S. K., eds., *Implications of Continental Drift for the Earth Sciences*, Vol. 1, London, Academic Press, pp. 247–285.

Game, M., and Peterken, G. F., 1983, Nature reserve selection in central Lincolnshire woodlands.

Gentry, A., 1979, Extinction and conservation of plant species in tropical America: A phytogeographical perspective, in Hedberg, I., ed., *Systematic Botany, Plant Utilization and Biosphere Conservation*, Uppsala, Sweden, Almqvist and Wiksell, pp. 115–126.

Gómez-Pompa, A., Vazquez-Yanes, C., and Guevara, S., 1972, The tropical rainforest: A nonrenewable resource, *Science*, **177**, 762–765.

Haffer, J., 1969, Speciation in Amazonian forest birds, *Science*, **165**, 131–137.

Hallam, A., 1973, Provinciality, diversity, and extinction of Mesozoic marine invertebrates in relation to plate movements, in Tarling, D. H., and Runcorn, S. K., eds., *Implications of Continental Drift for the Earth Sciences*, Vol. 1, London, Academic Press, pp. 287–294.

REFERENCES 179

Heck, K. L, Jr., van Belle, G., and Simberloff, D., 1975, Explicit calculation of the rarefaction diversity measurement and the determination of sufficient sample size, *Ecology,* **56,** 1459–1461.

Hilty, S. L., 1985, Zoogeographic changes in Colombian avifauna: A preliminary blue list.

Howe, H. F., 1977, Bird activity and seed dispersal of a tropical wet forest tree, *Ecology,* **58,** 539–550.

Janzen, D. H., 1974, The deflowering of Central America, *Nat. Hist.,* **4,** 48–53.

Karr, J. R., 1982, Avian extinction on Barro Colorado Island, Panama: A reassessment, *Am. Nat.,* **119,** 220–234.

Kent, M. M., 1983, 1983 world population data sheet of the Population Reference Bureau, Inc., Washington, D.C., Population Reference Bureau.

Kitchener, D. J., Chapman, A., Dell, J., Muir, B. G., and Palmer, M., 1980, Lizard assemblage and reserve size and structure in the Western Australian wheatbelt: Some implications for conservation, *Biol. Conserv.,* **17,** 25–62.

Lanly, J.-P., 1982, *Tropical Forest Resources (F.A.O. Forestry Paper 30),* Rome, Food and Agriculture Organization of the United Nations, 106 pp.

Lewin, R., 1983, Extinctions and the history of life, *Science,* **221,** 935–937.

Lovejoy, T. E., 1973, The Transamazonica: Highway to extinction?, *Frontiers,* **38,** 18–23.

Lovejoy, T. E., Bierregaard, R. O., Rankin, J. M., and Schubart, H. O. R., 1983, Ecological dynamics of forest fragments, in Sutton, S. L., Whitmore, T. C., and Chadwick, A. C., eds., *Tropical Rain Forest: Ecology and Management,* Oxford, Blackwell, pp. 377–384.

MacArthur, R. H., and Wilson, E. O., 1963, An equilibrium theory of insular zoogeography, *Evolution,* **17,** 373–387.

MacArthur, R. H., and Wilson, E. O., 1967, *The Theory of Island Biogeography,* Princeton, New Jersey, Princeton University Press, 203 pp.

Marshall, L. G., Webb, S. D., Sepkoski, J. J., Jr., and Raup, D. M., 1982, Mammalian evolution and the Great American Interchange, *Science,* **215,** 1351–1357.

Moore, R. C., 1954, Evolution of late Paleozoic invertebrates in response to major oscillations of shallow seas, *Bull. Mus. Compar. Zool.,* **112,** 259–286.

Moreau, R. E., 1963, Vicissitudes of the African biomes in the late Pleistocene, *Proc. Zool. Soc. Lond.,* **141,** 395–421.

Myers, M., 1980, *Conversion of Moist Tropical Forests,* Washington, D.C., National Academy of Sciences, 205 pp.

Myers, N., 1981, Conservation needs and opportunities in tropical moist forests, in Synge, H., ed., *The Biological Aspects of Rare Plant Conservation,* New York, Wiley, pp. 141–154.

Newell, N. D., 1962, Paleontological gaps and geochronology, *J. Paleontol.,* **36,** 592–610.

Newell, N. D., 1967, Revolutions in the history of life, *Geol. Soc. Am. Spec. Pap.,* **89,** 63–91.

Pielou, E. C., 1979, *Biogeography,* New York, Wiley, 351 pp.

Prance, G. T., 1977, The phytogeographic subdivisions of Amazonia and their influence on the selection of biological reserves, in Prance, G. T., and Elias, T. S., eds., *Extinction is Forever,* New York, New York Botanical Garden, pp. 195–213.

Prance, G. T., 1982, Forest refuges: Evidence from woody angiosperms, in Prance, G. T., ed., *Biological Diversification in the Tropics,* New York, Columbia University Press, pp. 137–159.

Raup, D. M., 1972, Taxonomic diversity during the Phanerozoic, *Science,* **177,** 1065–1071.

Raup, D. M., 1979, Size of the Permo-Triassic bottleneck and its evolutionary implications, *Science,* **206,** 217–218.

Raup, D. M., and Sepkoski, J. J., Jr., 1982, Mass extinctions in the marine fossil record, *Science,* **215,** 1501–1503.

Raven, P. H., 1976, Ethics and attitudes, in Simmons, J. B., et al., eds., *Conservation of Threatened Plants*, New York and London, Plenum Press, pp. 155–179.

Schopf, T. J. M., 1974, Permo-Triassic extinctions: Relation to sea-floor spreading, *J. Geol.*, 82, 129–143.

Schopf, T. J. M., 1979, The role of biogeographic provinces in regulating marine faunal diversity through geologic time, in Gray, J., and Boucot, A. J., eds., *Historical Biogeography, Plate Tectonics, and the Changing Environment*, Corvallis, Oregon, Oregon State University Press, pp. 449–457.

Sepkoski, J. J., Jr., 1976, Species diversity in the Phanerozoic: Species–area effects, *Paleobiology*, 2, 298–303.

Shaffer, M. L., 1981, Minimum population sizes for species conservation, *BioSci.*, 31, 131–134.

Simberloff, D., 1974a, Equilibrium theory of island biogeography and ecology, *Ann. Rev. Ecol. System.*, 5, 161–182.

Simberloff, D., 1974b, Permo-Triassic extinctions: Effects of area on biotic equilibrium, *J. Geol.*, 82, 267–274.

Simberloff, D., 1976, Experimental zoogeography of islands: Effects of island size, *Ecology*, 57, 629–648.

Simberloff, D., 1978, Use of rarefaction and related methods in ecology, in Cairns, J., Jr., Dickson, K. L., and Livingston, R. J., eds., *Biological Data in Water Pollution Assessment: Quantitative and Statistical Analyses*, ASTM STP 652, Philadelphia, American Society for Testing and Materials, pp. 150–165.

Simberloff, D., and Abele, L. G., 1976a, Island biogeography theory and conservation practice, *Science*, 191, 285–286.

Simberloff, D., and Abele, L. G., 1976b, Island biogeography and conservation: Strategy and limitations, *Science*, 193, 1032.

Simberloff, D., and Abele, L. G., 1982, Refuge design and island biogeographic theory: Effects of fragmentation, *Am. Nat.*, 120, 41–50.

Simberloff, D., and Gotelli, N., 1984, Effects of insularisation on plant species richness in the prairie-forest ecotone, *Biol. Conserv.*, 29, 27–46.

Simpson, B. B., and Haffer, J., 1978, Speciation patterns in the Amazonian forest biota, *Ann. Rev. Ecol. System.*, 9, 497–518.

Sommer, A., 1976, Attempt at an assessment of the world's tropical moist forests, *Unasylva*, 28, 5–24.

Soulé, M. E., 1980, Thresholds for survival: Maintaining fitness and evolutionary potential, in Soulé, M. E., and Wilcox, B. A., eds., *Conservation Biology: An Evolutionary-Ecological Perspective*, Sunderland, Massachusetts, Sinauer, pp. 151–169.

Soulé, M. E., Wilcox, B. A., and Holtby, C., 1979, Benign neglect: A model of faunal collapse in the game reserves of East Africa, *Biol. Conserv.*, 15, 259–272.

Strong, D. R., Jr., 1982, Comment, in Prance, G. T., ed., *Biological Diversification in the Tropics*, New York, Columbia University Press, pp. 157–158.

Valentine, J. W., 1973, *Evolutionary Paleoecology of the Marine Biosphere*, Englewood Cliffs, New Jersey, Prentice-Hall, 511 pp.

Watson, H. C., 1835, Remarks on the geographical distribution of British plants: n.p., London.

Webster, B., 1983, Forest's role in weather documented in Amazon, *New York Times*, July 5, p. 13.

Willis, E. O., and Eisenmann, E., 1979, A revised list of birds on Barro Colorado Island, Panama, *Smithson. Contrib. Zool.*, 291, 1–31.

12 Securing a Sustainable Future for Tropical Moist Forests

D. Lamb and T. C. Whitmore

The world's tropical forests hold most of the planet's biodiversity (see part 3), but large areas of these forests have been lost or altered over the last fifty years because of agricultural clearing, logging activities, and fire (see part 11). The rate of loss shows few signs of abating. Indeed, the rate at which remaining undisturbed tropical forest is being degraded may actually be increasing in many areas (Dudley, Jeanrenaud, and Sullivan 1995). Although we clearly know more now about the ecology of these forests than we did a hundred years ago, it is also evident that our knowledge of how to manage them and ensure their sustainability is still inadequate. Recent literature suggests that a lack of ecological knowledge is no longer the impediment to achieving sustainability that it once was, even though our ecological knowledge is imperfect and fragmentary. Rather, the inability to devise social and economic structures that complement this ecological knowledge now constitutes the major limitation preventing achievement of some form of sustainable management of tropical forests.

In this part we review the ways humans have sought to use tropical forests and the various attempts in recent years to make these uses sustainable. We start with agriculture, focusing on shifting cultivation systems and the harvesting of nontimber forest products. Forest management is our second main topic. We briefly review silvicultural systems that have been developed to allow the harvesting of tropical timbers. The literature shows that these systems have generally been unsuccessful for social and political, rather than technical, reasons. We also briefly consider in this part some of the early attempts to conserve tropical forests. This leads to our third theme, the contemporary interest in multiple use of these forests, efforts to involve rural communities in their management, and attempts at restoration of degraded landscapes. For each of these topics a classic paper is reprinted and subsequent developments are traced by reference to more recent publications.

Traditional Uses of Tropical Forests

Agriculture. Humans have occupied and used tropical forests for millennia. Today some communities still live in more or less traditional ways in rain forests throughout the tropics. A few live as hunter-gatherers, but most forest dwellers adopt some form of shifting cultivation. (See also the discussion in part 11). Shifting-cultivation systems are ecologically attractive because they enable the long-term

Assai palm (*Euterpe oleracea*). From Bates (1864)

production of food while maintaining soil fertility and biological productivity (part 10). They also permit the maintenance of forest cover across much of the landscape, although much of this is secondary forest and different in structure and composition from that initially present. Boserup (1965) published a model that continues to influence the analysis of past and present traditional agricultural systems (e.g., Leach 1997). She demonstrated the economic rationality of shifting-cultivation systems that give good returns per unit of labor and therefore are unlikely to be replaced by settled agriculture unless forced by population growth. Shifting-cultivation systems are multicrop, species-rich forms of agriculture that have proved sustainable over centuries (Rappaport 1971). The bush fallow is often artificially augmented with plants that provide useful products beyond the agricultural phase of the cycle (e.g., fruit and cordage trees). On most soils, shifting cultivation is sustainable only when human population density remains low enough for the fallow stage of the cycle to last eight or more years. The tree fallow periods commonly shorten once human density increases. Over time, soil fertility then declines and the fallow degrades to grassland (in Asia commonly dominated by *Imperata*). Shifting cultivation may also break down if contact with the outside world introduces pressures to plant cash crops (Bayliss-Smith 1982). Many accounts describe the range of shifting-cultivation practices found around the world. The account for northern Thailand by Kunstadter and Chapman (1978; paper 53) is an excellent overview. Schmidt-Vogt (1999) provides a more recent update of events in this region. In some localities shifting cultivators may also have some land under permanent agriculture or orchards. A recent description of such a situation in Vietnam is given by Fox et al. (2000). Hladik et al. (1993) give a comprehensive account of food gathering and human ecology in tropical forests generally.

In many places, low-yielding shifting-agricultural systems have been replaced by more productive forms of permanent agriculture that can absorb more labor, such as the monoculture paddy-rice systems of Asia (Geertz 1963), the agricultural systems of the Mayans in Mexico (Gómez-Pompa and Kaus 1990), and the terraced agriculture of parts of the Amazon (Mann 2000). However, there are also numerous examples throughout the tropics where large areas of primary rain forests have been converted to secondary forests or to anthropogenic grasslands. That is, human use of the forests has caused degradation. Many of these changes occurred in the distant past, and there has been recovery to some degree. However, more and more tropical forests are now being discovered that still bear signs of past human impact (Whitmore and Burslem 1998). The romantic notion of simple forest dwellers living in perfect harmony with the pristine rain forest environment is a fallacy, unpalatable to many of today's green evangelists (Hviding and Bayliss-Smith 2000). Insofar as this was ever true, forest recovery from past human impacts is more likely to have been a consequence of small human population densities. Alternatively, Gómez-Pompa and Kaus (1999) attribute the persistence of the Mayan lowland flora over five to six thousand years of dense human settlement to a managed mosaic of habitats including patches of selectively exploited forests, complex agroforestry systems, abandoned agricultural land, and secondary vegetation.

Nontimber Forest Products

Traditional forest societies all used nearby forests for hunting and for gathering various forest products. These products included foods, medicinal plants, building materials, and plants for religious or magical purposes (Powell 1976). Many societies had regulations governing harvesting. In some places these regulations simply defined forest ownership and limited access to a particular person or group. In other areas the rules could define the timing and extent of harvesting. In many cases these resources were used exclusively by the communities themselves, but in places fruits, nuts, and resins were traded, some of them passing through many hands. For example, Dunn (1975) describes the extensive trade between forest dwellers in south east Asia, China, India, and the Arabian peninsula. As external markets increase, traditional controls often disintegrate (Peluso 1983) and other groups become involved and begin to control the trade (Dove 1993).

External trade increased during the period of European colonization of the tropics (see part 1). Spices from Maluku in eastern Indonesia in the sixteenth century are perhaps the earliest and best-known example, although this trade came to be based on plantations rather than natural forest. The same happened with rubber *(Hevea brasiliensis)* from the Amazon basin. By the late nineteenth century there were numerous tropical forest products being regularly harvested from natural forests and a smaller number being cultivated in various ways (e.g., *Anacardium occidentale* [cashew], *Cinchona* [quinine], *Coffea, Elaeis guineensis* [oil palm], *Vanilla planifolia*). While most of the plantations were organized by Europeans and were simple monoculture cropping systems, some were developed by traditional communities and retained a high degree of biological diversity, for example the damar *(Shorea javanica)* forests of Sumatra (de Foresta and Michon 1993), and the fruit and drug-plant rich forests of the Amazon (Balée 1987).

Trade with Europe stimulated a research effort that sought to identify and describe the biological resources of the tropical world. Colonial powers created botanic gardens to introduce exotic plants for trial; the most famous success is probably the introduction of rubber to Asia, and the most notorious Captain Bligh's introduction of breadfruit *(Artocarpus altilis)* to the Caribbean. Economic activity facilitated the scientific studies of naturalists and researchers, already described in part 1, undertaken across the tropics and capturing some of the traditional knowledge concerning food and medicinal plants (Dunn 1975; Powell 1976), as well as seeking to describe the range of biological diversity. Among the various dictionaries of economic products that recorded this information perhaps the greatest is that of Burkill (1935; paper 54) for Peninsular Malaysia. We reprint one short entry. Other compendia from the colonial period are Heyne (1922) for the Dutch East Indies and Brown (1920–21, 1941–43) for the Philippines. Modern accounts are Burkill

(1985–97), an update of the classic dictionary for West Africa, and, most recently, *Plant Resources of South East Asia* (Jansen, Westphal, and Wulijarni-Soetjipto 1989–2000), an ambitious multivolume, multiauthor comprehensive work now almost complete. Besides these accounts of useful plants, numerous floras were published. A comprehensive account of the geographic origins of many of the world's natural genetic resources (including those outside the tropics), the history of their utilization, and of some of the current threats to their persistence in natural systems is given by Oldfield (1984).

Interestingly, timber was not a major component of traditional trade except for a few species, among them teak *(Tectona grandis)* from Asian seasonal forests and mahogany *(Swietenia mahagoni)* from the Caribbean. During the twentieth century nontimber commodities became known as "minor forest products" as the harvest of timber became vastly more important. From about the mid-1980s there has been renewed interest in nontimber products, driven by a perception that tropical forests might be better protected if the financial value of economic products other than timber could be demonstrated, and also by a desire to ensure that traditional forest dwellers benefit in some way from any harvesting operation (Bawa 1992; Panayatou and Ashton 1992). Various surveys have sought to show potential yields per hectare and just how valuable these products might be. Some have been misleadingly optimistic (Peters, Gentry, and Mendelsohn 1989) and others more realistic (Phillips 1993; Godoy, Lubowski, and Markandya 1993). There remain considerable problems in devising harvesting and marketing schemes that link these products with the international cash economy, that benefit traditional forest communities, and that are ecologically sustainable (Peluso 1983; Dove 1993).

Forest Management

Although certain timbers had been harvested for many years the first attempts to develop formal silvicultural management systems for timber production in tropical forests took place in Burma and India in the nineteenth century, based on German silvicultural systems of the time (Dawkins and Philip 1998). The broad objective of these early systems was to harvest timber at a rate that matched its growth rate. That is, silviculturists were probably the first explicitly to seek sustainability in their interactions with tropical forests, although their focus was on timber yields rather than biological diversity. Indeed, many silvicultural systems explicitly sought to increase the proportion of commercially desired species at the expense of competitive noncommercial species. This was seldom achieved.

The species-rich tropical forests were much more difficult to manage than the simple ecosystems of Europe. The problems included:

- The large numbers of tree species present and a lack of knowledge of the ecology, timber properties, and silviculture of most of these.
- Low tree density of marketable timber species and their irregular flowering and fruiting.
- The rapid growth of competing noncommercial ("weed") species compared to the rather slower growth of the more commercially important species.
- The potential for damage (including to seedlings or residual trees of commercial species) during harvesting.
- Problems of accessibility and markets.

Baur (1968) and Dawkins and Philip (1998) describe early approaches to resolving silvicultural problems. In Baur's view the most significant initial attempts at rain forest silviculture took place in Malaya. Experiences there were subsequently followed up in Trinidad and Nigeria and, subsequently, at a variety of locations in Africa and the Americas.

The end result of the initial work in Malaysia was the Malayan Uniform System (MUS), which was developed in Peninsular Malaysia after the Second World War. The MUS is probably the best known of all rain forest silvicultural systems. A good summary of the main elements by Wyatt-Smith (1959; paper 55), one of its main proponents, is reprinted here (see also Walton, Barnard, and Wyatt-Smith 1952).

The MUS regulated harvesting to coincide with the presence of seedlings of commercially desired species on the forest floor. Felling could take place only after surveys verified that sufficient seedlings were present. Follow-up surveys were carried out to check on subsequent growth. All the evidence suggests that the MUS achieved its objective of consistently regenerating the original crop species after harvesting, and with a planned increase in proportion of fast-growing species with low-density timber. Unfortunately the successful development of perhaps the best tropical silvicultural system to be routinely applied over large areas was overtaken by external events. In the early 1970s a decision was made on financial grounds to replace most of the lowland rain forest with rubber and oil palm plantations, restricting the remaining forest estate to hill forest areas occupied by different timber species. The MUS was not appropriate for these forests and a new Selective Management System (SMS) was developed (Whitmore 1984b). Wyatt-Smith (1995) gives a detailed account of silviculture in Peninsular Malaysia.

In other parts of the world, various silvicultural systems were developed that sought to reconcile ecological constraints with the prevailing social and economic circumstances (de Graaf 1986; Hardcastle 2001; Schmidt 1987; Parren and de Graaf 1995; Wadsworth 1997). These have had varying degrees of success, although the degree of logging damage has probably been greater in the dipterocarp forests of Asia where commercial timber volumes are higher than in the New World tropics. Significant efforts have been made in many tropical regions to develop low-impact forms of logging (de Graaf 1986; Hartshorn 1990; Parren and de Graaf 1995; Pinard and Putz 1996; Poore et al. 1999). Unfortunately, most of these systems have often been compromised by political, social, or economic problems rather than silvicultural or ecological difficulties (Poore et al. 1999; Lamb 1990). Now, at the turn of the millennium, there is a strong surge of interest in low-impact logging driven by demand in Europe and North America for timber certified to have come from well-managed forests (see below).

A common problem has been that many governments have regarded tropical forests as being a source of capital to fund economic development. Indeed Westoby, an influential member of the forestry division of the Food and Agriculture Organization (FAO) of the UN, argued in the early 1960s that forests and forestry were an ideal vehicle for economic development for two reasons: first, that forests are a potentially renewable and sustainable resource; and second, that logging and sawmilling are a means of promoting industrialization as well as a source of rural employment and skill development. Hence, forest utilization is a way of promoting economic and social development in developing societies. Westoby's ideas have been repeated by many subsequent commentators and governments (and are still being used, although perhaps rather wistfully now).

But over time Westoby changed his mind. The evidence was that tropical forests were not being used as he had thought. They were not being silviculturally managed; rather they were being overexploited and degraded. There was no social development or economic multiplier; instead the economic benefits were being captured by small political and economic elites. In fact, tropical forest utilization was helping social and economic inequities to increase in many tropical countries. His landmark address to the 1978 World Forestry Congress in Indonesia (Westoby 1979; paper 57) was a bitter call to arms and a repudiation of his earlier optimistic views.

Part of the reason for the failure of sustainable forest management is the long-term nature of all forestry operations. The slow growth of trees compared to agricultural crops means that harvests are infrequent and immobilize large amounts of land and capital. The direct financial returns to landowners or governments from timber harvesting inevitably seem less than those from competing land uses. The uncertainties of future timber markets and harvesting costs, together with the effects of compound interest, not least on the costs of silvicultural operations many years before harvest, require an act of faith in the value of forests perhaps unmatched by any other resource.

Leslie (1977) wrote a seminal paper discussing many of these issues. He was struck by the fact that economic theory suggested it would be preferable to abandon natural forest management and replace all natural forests by tree plantations or agriculture. Nonetheless, forest policy decisions were being made that seemed to ignore these economic "realities" (hence his title, "Where Contradictory Theory and Practice Co-exist"). Part of the reason was that the economic analyses were clearly imperfect. For example, they usually ignored nonmarket values such as social costs and benefits and the value of biodiversity or of watershed protection. Leslie concluded that "the best reason for not completely abandoning natural management of moist tropical forests lies therefore in the insurance it provides against the distinct possibility that decisions based on it being an uneconomic proposition could be mistaken." Ten years later, like Westoby, he changed his mind and admitted that his earlier analyses had been unduly pessimistic and that there was a much stronger case in favor of retaining tropical forests and managing them for timber production than he had previously thought (Leslie 1987). This paper, reprinted here as paper 56, is a powerful critique of mainstream economics.

Despite Leslie's views, the future of tropical forests remains uncertain. Nearly a century of research has failed to provide any management system able to reconcile ecological requirements with social and political forces that also yields some form of sustainability. A number of silvicultural systems have been developed (e.g., in both anglophone and francophone West Africa, in Asia, and in Neotropical countries such as Peru, Surinam, Trinidad, and Belize), but few have been implemented extensively in the Neotropics (Hartshorn 1995). Sadly, many of these projects have since been abandoned for social, economic or political reasons.

Conservation Forests

In the closing decades of the century attempts were made to retain at least some tropical forests by developing a comprehensive network of representative conservation areas. The objective was to protect these unique ecosystems from any form of exploitation rather than to use them. These attempts were primarily driven by nongovernment organizations, based mostly (but not exclusively) in nontropical countries. By the turn of the millennium, tropical countries had set aside 5–10 percent of their forests as national parks (summarized in Collins, Sayer, and Whitmore 1991; Sayer, Harcourt, and Collins 1992; Harcourt and Sayer 1996). The systems to manage these forests, where they exist at all, have frequently been no more successful than some of the earlier silvicultural management systems and many (though by no means all) of these parks have become degraded (but see Bruner et al. 2001). Where degradation has occurred the reasons have been remarkably similar to those encountered by tropical silviculturists (illegal fellings, traditional owners or landless migrants clearing forests for food production, etc.) The view as we write is that tropical forests will survive only if the people living in and near them and using them see natural forest to be more valuable than alternative uses of the land (Poffenberger 1990).

Multiple Use

The ongoing search for some form of sustainability has led to a flurry of international initiatives in recent years (Poore 1995, Mayers and Bass 1998) and has given rise to three new approaches. One approach has been to seek to devise improved management systems that are ecologically sustainable and able to produce not only timber, but also deliver other goods and services, such as biodiversity protection, socially valued forest products, and watershed protection. This new direction has come from debates within the International Tropical Timber Organisation (ITTO) and from the nongovernmental movement. A coalition of nongovernment organizations formed to sponsor the Forest Stewardship Council, which accredits (i.e., licenses) bodies to inspect production forests and certify, for the benefit of the consumer, whether management is socially, economically, and ecologically sustainable. Some governments and regional bodies have been spurred by FSC to set up their own certification schemes (e.g., Lembaga Ecolabel in Indonesia). The situation by 2000 was that it had become very difficult to sell uncertified tropical hardwoods into the European market, and North America was fast reaching the same state.

A second approach to attempt to achieve sustainability has been to seek to increase the benefits rural people receive from forest management. These benefits can take several forms. One is to try to protect the property rights traditional owners have over genetic resources, such as plants collected by Western pharmaceutical companies (Swanson 1995). Another has been to involve traditional landowners or land users in the management of their forests and to seek ways to increase the benefits they can achieve from doing so (Hartshorn 1990, Poffenberger 1990). Increased community or regional involvement might be achieved through some form of cooperative management with government agencies. Alternatively, day-to-day management responsibility might be handed over to the traditional owners. The approach has come from the recognition that most government-controlled schemes aimed at simply producing timber have failed to prevent deforestation and that success is more likely when those with a vested interest in forested lands are more deeply involved in decision making. The proposal is still too radical for many governments that are reluctant to accept that humble villagers are more able to successfully manage forest resources than a government bureaucracy. However, the idea is spreading and seems to be achieving some surprisingly good outcomes (Fisher 1995). Many of the lands available for use and management by local communities are likely to be the degraded forests left after logging and secondary forests, most of which are usually regarded as biologically impoverished and economically worthless, although this is not always the case (Lugo 1999). Little has been done to develop forms of management that might be used by village communities (Finegan 1992). What is not clear is whether control by local landowners will permit the maintenance of large areas of contiguous forest or whether it will encourage the development of anthropogenic landscapes consisting of a mosaic of crops and small forest patches (Fox et al. 2000; Poore et al. 1999; Whitmore 1999). Nor is it evident what proportion of the original biodiversity these schemes will retain (Laurance and Bierregaard 1997; see also part 11). Proposals for management by the local communities may be politically possible only when population pressure has become fairly high and most of the original forest (and biodiversity) has been degraded.

A third approach to secure a future for tropical moist forests has been to attempt restoration of degraded tropical forest landscapes, prompted by the realization that, in many regions, degraded or deforested areas now exceed the areas of intact, undisturbed forest. The methods being used range from ambitious attempts to "ecologically restore" the original forest and reinstate the original complement of plants and wildlife, to more modest goals of increasing landscape biodiversity by devising more complex agricultural systems (Ewel 1986), enriching secondary forests with economically useful or biologically important species, fostering diverse understories under monoculture plantations (Lugo, Parrotta, and Brown 1997), or using mixtures of high-value native species in plantations (Parrotta and Turnbull 1997).

Conclusion

The ecological uncertainties involved in reassembling a tropical rain forest, as well as the high cost of doing so, mean that most "restoration" efforts to date have been limited to small areas within nature reserves or in surrounding buffer strips. Enrichment planting has been carried out over some large areas, but its biological or commercial effectiveness has yet to be proved. Mixed-species plantation development using native species has been carried out over comparatively small areas to date, but it is attracting increasing interest in many countries. Such plantations do not restore the biological complexity of natural rain forests, but

they do offer the possibility of increasing landscape heterogeneity and an improvement in ecological services over comparatively large areas because they provide a commercial benefit to land managers. The extent to which any of these ways of overcoming tropical forest degradation can be implemented in any particular region depends, of course, on social and economic circumstances as much as on biological or ecological knowledge. Ways have yet to be found to integrate these social, economic, and ecological constraints.

The big question today is whether the enormous damage and deforestation that has occurred primarily during the past fifty years will continue, or whether recent initiatives to achieve sustainable use and curb forest loss will stem the tide. Will the mistakes made largely in the forests of Asia be repeated in central Africa and Amazonia? Despite the biological riches these forests contain, current rates of degradation and deforestation remain tragically high. Biologists should no longer indulge in the luxury of research that is largely disengaged from these unfolding events.

Reprinted Selections

P. Kunstadter, and E. C. Chapman. 1978. Problems of shifting cultivation and economic development in northern Thailand. In *Farmers in the Forest*, edited by P. Kunstadter, E. C. Chapman, and S. Sabhasri, 3–23. Honolulu: University of Hawaii Press

I. H. Burkill. 1935. Daemonorhops. In *A Dictionary of the Economic Products of the Malay Peninsula*, 747–49. 2 vols with sequential pagination. London: Crown Agents for the Colonies

J. Wyatt-Smith. 1959. Development of a silvicultural system for the conversion of natural inland lowland evergreen rain forest of Malaya. *Malayan Forester* 22:133–42

A. J. Leslie. 1987. A second look at the economics of natural management system in tropical mixed forests. *Unasylva* 39, no. 155:46–58

J. C. Westoby. 1979. Forest industries for socio-economic development. *Commonwealth Forestry Review* 58:107–16

1

Problems of Shifting Cultivation and Economic Development in Northern Thailand

Peter Kunstadter
E. C. Chapman

Rapid population growth in the tropics makes it essential to examine and evaluate the allocation of natural resources and the distribution of costs and benefits of these resources. In Thailand one of the primary resources is the forest-covered land of the hills and foothills of the North (chapter 2). Thai and "tribal" people have practiced unirrigated farming for centuries on this land using methods variously referred to as slash and burn, bush or forest fallow, swidden, *rai*, or shifting cultivation.[1] This book considers four kinds of social and economic problems in these marginal agricultural areas of northern Thailand: problems arising from sustained population growth; problems resulting from socio-economic inequalities of the marginal agricultural areas; problems of relatively low productivity per unit area of swidden cultivation; and problems of conserving soil, watershed, and forest resources. All of these are problems of the whole region of northern Thailand; they are not confined to remote foothill and upland villages.

"Shifting" cultivation does not necessarily imply that the cultivators themselves are nomadic. Some swiddeners live in villages that have been settled for hundreds of years and make repeated cyclical use of the same fields; others live in temporary villages which are abandoned as the fields become exhausted after a few years or a few cycles of cultivation and fallow; some farmers combine or supplement their use of permanent irrigated fields with shifting cultivation, especially where irrigable land is scarce.

Swidden cultivation is a marginal system in several respects. Yields per unit area (including fallow land), per unit of labor, or per unit of seed are often lower than in irrigated fields; swidden fields are usually located at some distance from markets, generally on land that is considered marginal or submarginal for annual or multi-crop farming. Swiddening is often carried out primarily as a subsistence operation, or even a supplementary subsistence operation, rather than as a source of cash crops, and swidden cultivators are often socially and economically marginal to the nation within which they live.

All of the northern provinces of Thailand are mountainous, with relatively small areas of valley land, as compared with the central plains provinces. They have a monsoonal climate, with a rainy season beginning in May or June and lasting until October or November. Almost no rain falls during the cold season, in December and January, and the hot season, beginning in mid-February and lasting until the rains start in May or June. The swidden growing season is strictly limited by the availability of water from rainfall and the small amount of moisture retained during the dry season. Production may be further limited because upland soils are generally well drained, and crops may suffer when monsoon rains are irregular.

The rural lowland people in the North are generally speakers of the Northern Thai dialect, while the hills are occupied by a variety of upland minority peoples ("hill tribes") including the Karen, Lua', Hmong (Meo),[2] Yao (Iu Mien), Akha (Ikaw), and Lahu (Musser). Swiddening is often thought of as a "hill-tribe" characteristic, but in fact both Thai and non-Thai people may engage in it in both the hills and the lowlands (see part IV).

The problems considered in this book are characteristic of much of Southeast Asia, and similar problems exist on the margins of intensively irrigated regions throughout the tropical world. In a comprehensive study, Spencer emphasized that shifting cultivation is the most widespread cropping system in South and Southeast Asia, although it dominates now only in Borneo and the hills of Thailand, Burma, Laos, Viet Nam, Cambodia, and southwestern China (Spencer 1966:4). Throughout these areas swidden farming is gradually giving way to more productive permanent systems of land use under the stress of economic necessity as populations grow, but there is also a countervailing tendency to force more people into this marginal form of agriculture as land:people ratios decline.

The problems of economic development of shifting cultivators in northern Thailand are *regional* in nature, that is *they are not limited to the plight of the individual subsistence farmer, nor to the condition of an isolated village, nor to any single ethnic group or ecological position.* The contributors to this book show clearly that shifting cultivation is practiced by both Thai and non-Thai peoples in northern Thailand, and by valley dwellers as well as hill villagers. The succeeding chapters also show clearly that the practitioners of shifting cultivation participate in many phases of the economy of the North beyond the confines of their own villages—in marketing their agricultural products, trading for supplies, and most notably, in the wage labor market of the region.

The forest fallow farmers of Northern Thailand participate both in the rapid population growth which is characteristic of all parts of Thailand, and in the complex pattern of internal population movements in recent years. In many instances hill people (e.g., Lua' and Karen; see chapters 6–9) work in the lowlands and, very commonly, Thai lowland swidden farmers move in fairly large numbers to seasonal jobs in other provinces for two to four months each year. Population growth throughout Thailand and the rapid occupation of remaining forested lowlands in the 1950s and 1960s, when the largest irrigation projects were completed, makes further absorption of population surpluses from marginal areas more difficult than in the past. In the absence of some basic economic changes, relief from mounting population pressure is often not readily available. This demographic consideration alone is sufficient to make it obvious that the economic problems of shifting cultivators are regional, and not limited to isolated villages.

HISTORICAL BACKGROUND

Contemporary relationships between population, natural resources, and the variety of agricultural technologies in northern Thailand are products of a long history of intensification of food production and population expansion. Two theories have been proposed regarding the origins of agriculture in Southeast Asia. In chapter 15 Pelzer discusses some of the basic ecological effects of the extensive use of fire in the development of forest farming. He outlines the view that root and tree crops, planted along watercourses in the lowlands and coastal regions, preceded the development of seed and grain crops on the hill slopes and in irrigated fields. A second theory, suggested by archaeological evidence which is beginning to accumulate from northern and northeastern Thailand, is that the tending of seed plants may have been practiced as early there as anywhere in the world, and may have preceded the domestication of root and tree crops (Gorman 1969, 1971b). Whichever sequence is correct, it is clear that some form of hill farming has been practiced in Southeast Asia for a very long time, and has resulted in extensive modification of vegetation in many areas. The demographic conditions accompanying this pattern of agriculture are as yet unknown. There is no evidence that would allow us to judge in detail the interaction of technological innovations (improved tools and crop plants) with population size, but it is evident that traditional technology could not have supported the current level of population.

The development or introduction of the metal knife, ax, hoe, and weeding tool blades allowed human populations to spread in space and expand in numbers, by making heavily forested lands available for more intensive agricultural use. The domestication of grain plants and the eventual development of irrigation technology must have allowed further increase of population and also resulted in concentration of population in the lowlands. This led to social differentiation: sizeable towns, formal governments, and other attributes of civilization developed in the valleys while swiddeners remained in marginal areas, living in relatively small and dispersed villages, affected more slowly and less directly by the development of valley-based civilizations.

New World crop plants have had major effects both in the subsistence economy and in the development of cash crops and plantation systems. Maize, manioc, and potatoes were introduced throughout Southeast Asia probably by the sixteenth and seventeenth centuries and had a profound effect on upland population size and distribution. Some groups, such as the Hmong (chapter 11), have a domestic economy based largely on maize, and their style of life must have been radically different before this crop became available. Other groups, such as the Lua' and Karen (part III), who are primarily rice growers, now depend heavily on maize as the earliest ripening starchy food, to tide them over for several months in the rainy season after their previous year's rice supply is exhausted and before the new rice ripens. Such alternative or supplemental food crops have allowed swidden populations to increase in numbers and expand in territory, a tendency which has also been supported by increasing opportunities for wage labor and by the spread of a cash economy.

Rapid population growth, urbanization, and the application of science and technology to agriculture are having profound effects on relationships between shifting cultivators and their natural and social environments. Thailand's population has grown rapidly, especially since the second world war, reaching a rate of over 3 percent per year in the early 1960s. The national growth rate has declined slightly in the 1970s but apparently remains high in the hill areas and the parts of the North where shifting cultivation is most widespread. The exact causes of the growth are not completely understood. They probably include a general rise in the level of public health and sanitation in areas where people are concentrated, control of a few important diseases (cholera, smallpox, and perhaps malaria), and absence of major political disruptions, all combined with general improvements in communication, transportation, and marketing.

The recent development of improved high-yield strains of rice will make great changes in Thailand's economy. The national agricultural economy has depended for many years on the production of rice for local subsistence as well as for export. The rice "premium" is the difference between the price of rice in Thailand and the price on the world market; it has been a primary source of government income while allowing local prices to remain low. This strategy worked well during the 1950s and early 1960s, when international rice prices were high. With the advent in the 1960s of the technology-intensive "green revolution," prices fell rapidly in Thailand's traditional markets, though exports remained high. Rapidly rising fertilizer costs, associated with the worldwide energy crisis in the early 1970s imply rising costs and rice prices (cf. Hirst 1974; Pimentel et al. 1973; Steinhart and Steinhart 1974). The total effect in the past few years has been increased uncertainty and rapid agricultural price fluctuations. The situation brings into question all plans for the economic development of Thailand based on intensification of rice agriculture for international exchange. This, along with sustained population growth and a rapid increase in landlessness among lowland farmers, diminishes the hope that surplus upland populations will be absorbed in the expanding intensive commercial rice agriculture in the lowlands.

Meanwhile, modernization and urbanization are proceeding rapidly and economic opportunities increasingly require formal education and nonrural skills. The result is a widening gap between the people of modernizing urban areas and those of rural areas, especially subsistence swidden farmers.

Unlike the earlier innovations (new tools, new crop plants), few if any of the modern innovations are directly applied to shifting cultivators. Except for malaria control and sporadic smallpox vaccination, these people are unlikely to have received much modern medical attention, though they may have been protected from contagious diseases by epidemic controls applied to the more accessible segments of the populations. Nor have they benefited much from the improved strains of crop plants or improved methods of cultivation, since these have been developed for lowland environments where purchase of fertilizer and pesticides and control of water are possible. Although starting in the early 1960s public schools were beginning to be made available in the upland areas, few if any of the children of shifting cultivators have yet progressed through high school. Despite the lack of direct modernization, the populations of the more marginal areas of shifting cultivation seem to be growing just as fast as, or faster than, those in the irrigated lowlands and in the cities (Kunstadter 1971).

VARIETIES OF UPLAND CULTIVATION SYSTEMS IN NORTHERN THAILAND

Assumptions concerning ethnic categories and their relationship to environment, economy, and social structure have important implications for public policy. Incorrect assumptions concerning ethnic categories include the ideas that only hill tribes practice swiddening and only Thais practice irrigated cultivation. Leach (1954) demonstrated that ethnic categories, environment, economic type, and social structure are not bound into an inevitable permanent pattern in mainland Southeast Asia. Nonetheless, land use in northern Thailand has usually been classified by ethnic group (cf. Van Roy 1971, especially chapters 2 and 3). When we look carefully at land use and ethnic distributions in northern Thailand we find almost as much variation in land use *within* some ethnic categories as between them. We find variations of land use within ecological zones, and we also find people from one ethnic category moving from one type of ecological zone and land use to another, sometimes without changing their ethnic identity (fig. 1.1; photos 14–19, 39, 118, 125).

Thus we have preferred to classify types of forest farming on the basis of relationships between cultivation and fallow periods. We have attached ethnic labels to these types only as aids to memory and they should be understood as such. It is evident from the descriptions of cultivation systems in the chapters which follow that variations in patterns of land use are associated with variations in physical and social environment, population density, major crop plants, and balance between subsistence and cash operations, as well as cultural traditions. The farmers alter their patterns of land use in response to these variations.

It is useful to think in terms of three types of swidden cultivation land use and one type of permanent upland cultivation: (1) short cultivation–short fallow (often used by Northern Thai); (2) short cultivation–long fallow, or "forest fallow" (often used by upland Karen and Lua'); (3) long cultivation–very long fallow or abandonment (often used by Hmong and other opium growing hill groups); (4) permanent field tree crops, associated with use of forest for swidden rice and fuel. Table 1.1 outlines the relationships between important variables and these land-use types.[3]

SHORT CULTIVATION–SHORT FALLOW ("NORTHERN THAI")

The Northern Thai system is one of short periods of cultivation, with short fallow periods (chapter 12). Secondary growth tends to be of the low tree and scrub type rather than a return to forest cover. Under primitive clearing and cultivating techniques the soil tends to lose fertility under this system, because the regrowth period is not long enough to allow the plants to bring sufficient nutrients above the soil surface, where they can be made available for agriculture by cutting and burning. In some cases the clearing and burning that precedes the planting of an unirrigated crop is preparatory to leveling and irrigating the field for annual cultivation. Use of these fields is often considered only supplementary to the "normal" irrigated form of agriculture in areas of high population: cultivable land ratio where there is insufficient irrigated or irrigable land, such as the foothill and terrace lands near Sa, Nan Province (chapter 12), or in the hills around Mae Sariang town.

The land that is swiddened may or may not be claimed by a village unit as a whole; individuals may retain use-rights for several periods of cultivation, or they may simply abandon their fields after using them temporarily. Fields are made wherever suitable land is available, usually in areas where the characteristic vegetation is of the Mixed Deciduous or Dry Dipterocarp type on relatively sandy or rocky soil. This is a very widespread pattern in the transitional zones between valley and hill lands, at elevations between 300 and 600 meters.

The principal crop is upland glutinous and nonglutinous rice, supplemented by various cash or catch crops (vegetables, cotton, maize, beans, chilies, etc.) planted after cultivation of the main crop. Because of the transitory and

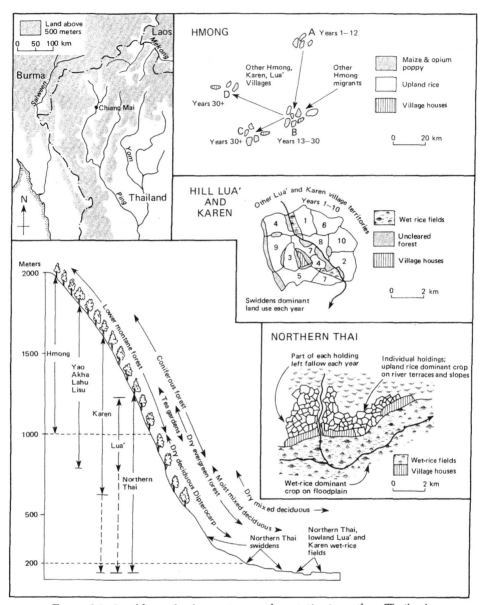

FIGURE 1.1   Land forms, land-use systems, and vegetation in northern Thailand.

marginal nature of much of this activity it is impossible to estimate the numbers of people involved. The number must be substantial; Judd estimated that more than a million people in northern Thailand were engaged in one or another type of shifting cultivation (1964:5).

SHORT CULTIVATION–LONG FALLOW ("HILL LUA' AND KAREN")

Upper terraces and foothills are often separated by relatively steep slopes from the rolling hills of the middle elevations, which range from 700 or 750 meters to well above 1,000 meters. In this zone the Lua' and Karen practice a forest fallow system of cultivation, with cultivation periods of only one year, and relatively long fallow periods of at least 6 or 7 years, up to 12 or 15 years in areas where land is plentiful (chapters 6–9). During the fallow period the forest cover and the soil normally rejuvenate to approximately the same condition as before the period of cultivation.

Native vegetation in these areas is often Dry Evergreen or Mixed Deciduous Forest on red clay or lateritic soils. Where swiddens have been cut, the primary climax forest is replaced with a secondary forest composed of fire-resistant species. Where population pressure is not already too great, this can be a stable system for an indefinite period of time, limited only by population growth or changes external to the system (such as changes in land laws, invasions by other populations, or changes in the aspirations of the villagers as a result of contact with new external conditions). These people live in permanent villages, some of which have been settled for generations or even hundreds of years.

The major crop is nonglutinous, slow ripening rice, which is raised primarily for subsistence. Numerous other crops (maize, sorghum, millet, chilies, beans, herbs, manioc, taro, sesame, etc.) are planted in the same fields. The people earn cash by selling small quantities of rice, garden or jungle products, or domestic animals, and by wage labor.

Characteristically the Lua' and Karen believe that the swidden land they cultivate belongs to the community, with individual household claims to use-rights. Community claims to the land usually go back several generations, and some were formally granted by the northern Thai princes (Nimmanahaeminda 1965), but these claims are no longer recognized by the Thai government. The land is worked by individual households, with cooperative (exchange) labor during times of heaviest work. Cooperation in agriculture is based primarily on kinship ties; within the village there is little or no work for wages in cash, and only small amounts of work for payment in rice. Almost all individuals and all families in the villages are directly involved in agriculture, but many of them supplement their incomes with wage labor away from the villages, especially during the slack agricultural seasons. Many upland Lua' and Karen villages also have irrigated fields, but because of the terrain the bulk of their land is used for hill farming. There are probably at least 100,000 Lua' and Karen participating in this type of system in northern Thailand (United Nations Survey Team 1967:56).

When unoccupied land was plentiful, Karen villages often split if their populations grew too large for convenient access to swidden fields. The upland Karen population has expanded very rapidly during the past century, and most of the suitable land has been occupied. The population continues to grow, and hard-pressed individuals or families who choose to remain as subsistence farmers must seek land in established villages where they have relatives, or accept a lowered standard of living. Others move temporarily or permanently to the lowlands, where wage work may be available.

TABLE 1.1   Characteristics of Four Types of Upland Cultivation

Type	Settlement Pattern and Migration	Location, Elevation (meters)	Major Crop Plants: Subsistence/Cash	Cultivation/ Fallow Cycle (years)
Short cultivation, short fallow ("N. Thai")	Permanent lowland villages; individuals move between lowland villages	Uncleared valley terraces, foothills (300–600 meters)	Rice/peanuts, soy beans, mung beans	1/2+
Short cultivation, long fallow ("Hill Lua' and Karen")	Permanent villages; individuals move between hill villages and to lowlands	Middle elevations in hills (500–1000 meters)	Rice/rice	1/7–1/12
Long cultivation, very long fallow ("Hmong")	Temporary agglomerations split and move when soil is exhausted	Higher elevations in hills (1000+ meters)	Maize/opium	3–4/40+
Permanent field tree crops ("Tea gardens" of N. Thai and others)	Permanent villages; individuals move in from upland and lowland	Hillsides (600–1300 meters)	Rice/tea, fermented tea	Rice on variable swidden cycle, tea continuous, firewood considered "free good"

LONG CULTIVATION–VERY LONG FALLOW ("HMONG")

There is no sharp upper elevation boundary to the system just discussed, but there is a general tendency for elevations above 1,200 to 1,500 meters to be unused or to be occupied by Hmong (Meo), Yao (Iu Mien), Lahu (Musser), Lisu (Lisaw), Akha (Ikaw), and Yunnanese Chinese (Haw), most of whom are relative newcomers to the areas they now occupy. The system of shifting cultivation used by many Hmong farmers is one of long periods of use of a single field (up to five years or more), followed by abandonment when the soil fertility is exhausted or when secondary growth of grasses makes further cultivation impossible. Limestone-based soils are often deliberately selected and highly prized for their ability to sustain intensive cultivation for several years. The Hmong system is the most notorious in Thailand, both because the principal cash crop is opium, and because of the apparent destructiveness of the method to forest and watershed resources. As we have indicated, it is not typical of swidden systems in northern Thailand. Including Hmong, Lahu, Lisu, Akha, and Haw, more than 100,000 people practice shifting cultivation of this type (United Nations

TABLE 1.1 *(continued)*

Cultivation Techniques	Effects on Soil Fertility	Land Acquisition	Individual Land Tenure	Wage Labor
Clearing and weeding by hand tool (rice), hoeing (peanut)	Gradual decline with inadequate fallow	Squatting	Use-rights recognized within community	Wage work common to supplement farm income
Clearing and weeding by hand tool, no hoeing	Stable with adequate fallow	Ancestral claims recognized by prince, no legal claim now	Use-rights heritable within communally held area	Wage work common to supplement farm income
Deep hoe cultivation, clean weeding, crop rotation (corn-opium)	Long term decline, grass replaces forest	Purchase from previous owners, if any, squatting	Individual ownership until field is abandoned	Consumers, not sellers of wage labor
Rice weeded by hand tool; tea, selective thinning, grazing to clear underbrush	Under rice, dependent on fallow cycle; under tea, stable if not overgrazed	Squatting, purchase, government lease, tenant farming	Use-rights recognized within community, some fee simple, some tenant farming	Individual entrepreneurs, wage labor, share cropping

Survey Team 1967:9; Young 1962:89), but this is probably only about 10 percent of the total number of shifting cultivators in the region.

These people are relative newcomers in Thailand, most of whom have arrived only since the turn of the century. Because they have had no access to the more fertile lands suited for permanent field cultivation, and because they are often involved in the illegal cultivation of opium, they have generally farmed in remote areas at higher elevations.

In areas that have been cultivated in this fashion, the forest cover almost never returns within a human lifetime. The secondary growth is usually some semipermanent or permanent form of grass which is less easily cleared (see chapter 2). It follows that land tenure in this system is not permanent. Evidently land is viewed by these farmers as a relatively free consumable good over which only temporary use-rights are appropriate. These people tend to live in less permanently settled villages, or villages that split or move from time to time. Land claims are not recognized after the fields are fallowed or abandoned (see Kickert 1969:36 for an example of land concepts of the Akha).

The main subsistence crop is maize or rice, and the primary cash crop has been opium, though Hmong in the Mae Tho area on the eastern border of Mae Sariang District, Mae Hong Son Province, have experimented with potatoes and other truck garden products as supplements or substitutes for opium, and in the 1970s coffee has also been tried on an increasing scale. Hmong farmers in northern Thailand are often not self-sufficient for their subsistence and must buy rice in large quantities from nearby Lua' and Karen villages. The opium and maize fields are usually on slopes, ridges, or peaks at relatively high elevations (1,000 meters or more).

Hmong have been in the far north of Thailand (Chiang Rai Province) for at least 80 years and have gradually spread south; there are now settlements in central Tak Province and Phitsanulok Province. The numbers of Hmong in Thailand have expanded due both to very rapid natural increase and, especially since mid-1975, to extensive migration from Laos. Hmong have had to obtain land from previous owners in many of the areas to which they have moved recently, and, according to Karen and Lua' informants, they have done so by purchase or by threat, or by a combination of the two. Lua' and Karen landowners are afraid to let the Hmong into their area because they fear the effect of Hmong cultivation practices on their watershed, and also because they do not want to become involved in the opium business.

In some areas the Hmong are reported to base their choice of new settlement sites on the availability of Lua' or Karen labor, as well as on the quality of the soil required to grow maize and opium. In the Mae Tho area and other parts of Mae Chaem District it is clear that Hmong settlements depend heavily on labor from other ethnic groups to assist in raising and marketing their opium crops. They also depend on these other ethnic groups as consumers of opium. The Hmong evidently prefer to pay wages in opium

rather than cash. In recent years some Hmong in the Mae Tho area also have tried to finance their opium cultivation by mortgaging their opium crops to Lua' villagers.

The Hmong system of cultivation is more complex and more labor intensive than that of the Lua' and Karen or Northern Thai. The soil is much more thoroughly prepared, by hoeing twice before the crops are planted. In the agricultural system around Mae Tho, maize is planted in May and harvested by August. The opium, planted in the maize fields late in August, matures in December and January. This pattern of cropping may be repeated for several years until the soil is exhausted or the grasses invade the field and make it impossible to cultivate. The relatively deep, clean cultivation with hoes makes it possible to continue planting for several years, but also contributes to soil erosion (photo 124). By contrast, the Lua' and Karen weed their fields using a sickle-like tool, which disturbs only the top centimeter or so of the soil (photo 41) and would have little or no effect in making subsurface soil nutrients available at the surface. The Northern Thai use a narrow-bladed spade (siem) for chopping weeds and roots on their rice swiddens, but they use hoes in cultivating peanuts.

Ultimately the soil fertility is lost under the Hmong system, and the fields are abandoned by their owners. Individual household heads then look for new fields, and if the fields of most of the area near the village have been exhausted or are otherwise unsuitable, the village may break up, or move as a whole to other favorable spots.[4]

PERMANENT TREE CROPS ("TEA GARDENS")

A fourth system of upland cultivation is practiced on hill slopes in the middle elevations (chapter 14). Fermented and cured tea are produced for the local market under several different land tenure and labor arrangements, primarily by people who identify themselves as Northern Thai. Their tea orchards usually start through selection of native tea plants growing wild in the area. Often the people cultivate subsistence rice swiddens to supplement cash income from tea, and raise cattle which they use to transport fermented tea to market or to a roadhead. They must cut substantial amounts of firewood, which is needed in tea processing; so their total land-use pattern includes cultivation of plantations and swiddens, maintaining grazing lands, and cutting firewood from the forest.

The communities are usually composed of people (or their descendants) who have moved out of the valleys, usually because of limited irrigable land and shortage of wage work opportunities in the lowlands. No comprehensive population figures exist for this type of population, but substantial numbers of people are involved, perhaps equaling the number of non-Thai "hill tribesmen" whose environment they share.

The effects of these systems on the environment, and their relationship to the lives and the livelihood of their practitioners are quite variable, and any generalization with respect to the upland cultivators in northern Thailand must take into consideration these variations. Nonetheless, we can say that in general the upland farmers are marginal to the national economy, are relatively poor, and have few sources of capital to promote their own economic development.

PRODUCTIVITY OF SHIFTING AGRICULTURE

Upland cultivation is probably inherently more variable in productivity than is irrigated agriculture because of variations in slope, aspect, and orientation of the hill fields, as well

as the uncertainty of rainfall. The accumulated data on swidden cultivation reveal tremendous variability in reported production. Climatic factors, soil type, state of soil fertility as related to vegetation type and length of time since previous cultivation, seed quality, cultivation techniques, insects and other pests have been offered as explanations, but available data do not yet allow a quantitative evaluation of the variability (table 1.2).

In Southeast Asia the reported range of rice production is from a low of 500–700 kg/ha among the Ma of South Viet Nam (Champsoloix 1960:50–53), or about 800 kg/ha among the Iban of Borneo (Freeman 1955), to a high of 4,500 kg/ha among the Rhade of Buon Kmrong Prong, on red soils in South Viet Nam (Maurice and Proux 1954), and up to 7,500 kg/ha projected from a small sample in Houei Khong, Laos (Bordsen 1968). Average yields in irrigated fields in Thailand are between 1,900 and 2,200 kg/ha, while in nonirrigated, rainfed fields, the average is between 630 and 940 kg/ha (Asian Development Bank 1969:160). The nonirrigated fields referred to here are probably mainly rainfed paddy fields, not hill fields. Our search of the literature, as well as the research reported in this book, indicated a range of from 814 kg/ha for Northern Thai farmers on frequently used soils in Nan Province (chapter 12) to 1,849 kg/ha for Yao farmers on good soil in Chiang Rai Province (Miles 1967).

Comparisons of production statistics from swidden farming and between swidden and irrigated agriculture are somewhat uncertain because so little effort has been devoted to standardized, repeated, large-scale measurements in swidden fields. Studies of production of shifting cultivation have used many different methods and a wide variety of units. In computing the entries of table 1.2, we have converted all pro-

Table 1.2 Productivity of Upland Agriculture*

Ethnic Group	Location	Rice Yield (kg/ha)				Source and Comments
		1st yr	2d yr	3d yr	4th yr	
BORNEO						
Iban		810				Freeman (1955:94–99)
Land Dyak		1,085				Geddes (1954:68)
LAOS						
Lamet	North Laos	1,335				Izikowitz (1951:287)
not stated	Houei Kong	3,550				Bordsen (1968:table 2) Mean of 10 locations; range: 1,000–7,500.
not stated	Sedone Province	4,340				Bordsen (1968:table 3) Mean of 7 locations; range: 2,620–6,820.
THAILAND						
N. Thai	Nan Province	814				Chapman (ch. 12)
Akha	Chiang Rai Province	840				Scholz (1969:96)
Skaw Karen	Mae Hong Son Province	959				Kunstadter (ch. 6)
Lua'	Mae Hong Son Province	1,032				Kunstadter (ch. 6)
Lahu Nyi	Chiang Mai and Chiang Rai Provinces	1,293				Walker (1970:494; 1976:181–182)
Pwo Karen	Mae Hong Son Province	1,464				Hinton (ch. 9)
Yao	Chiang Rai Province	1,849				Miles (1967:15)
SOUTH VIET NAM						
Jarai	Pleiku, Phu Bon	2,000–2,300	1,500	500–800		Lafont (1959:56, 1967:45–46) From forest.
		1,200–1,500	500–750			After 5–7 years fallow.

Group	Location		Yields (kg/ha)			Source and notes
Koho (Ma and Cil)	Haut Donnai, Djiring Valley	over 1,500				Bertrand (1952:270). Ranges: 3,000 on good earth well cleared to 500 on poor earth sown late.
Ma	Bao Loc Plateau	1,500	800–1,000			Lafont (1967:45). From forest. From shrubbery (first and only year).
Ma	Blao Plateau	1,500				Boulbet (1966:87)
	Basaltic area	800–2,400				
	Alluvial plains	600–3,000	1,000–3,500			
Ma	South Tuyen Duc Province	500–750	600–700			Champsoloix (1960:50–53)
Rhade	Ban Me Thuot area	2,300	1,500–1,700			Lafont (1967:45). From forest, on basaltic, red earth soils.
Rhade	Ban Me Thuot area	1,500	1,000			From secondary growth, black, sandy soils, rarely used 3 years.
Rhade	Buon Emap village, N of Ban Me Thuot	2,400–3,000	1,700	600		Maurice and Proux (1954:195–196). Good year, average year, poor year.
	near Ban Me Thuot	900–1,200	1,000			
		1,500–2,250				
Rhade	Buon Aring, Buon Brieng, Buon Pok 25 km NE of Ban Me Thuot	2,500	1,700	1,000		
	Buon Puan, Buon Dang Kang, Buon Hang	2,500	1,667	833		Maurice and Proux (1954). Black and sandy soil.
	Red earth areas	2,783	3,333	2,500		
	Buon Kmrong Prong	4,500	2,250	1,500		Red earth.
	Buon Kmrong Prong	3,000	2,250	1,500		Black, sandy soil.
	Buon Ko M'Leo	880	920	840		Champsoloix (1960:58). From savanna.
	Buon Ko M'Leo	900	970	850	800	From secondary forest.

* Literature on agricultural production from South Viet Nam and Laos cited in this table was reviewed by Ms. N.D. Volk. See also Kalland (1976).

duction figures to kilograms per hectare. In Kunstadter's study of Karen and Lua' rice production (chapter 6 in this volume), rice production was measured by volume and converted to weight using 12.4 kilograms/*tang* as the average field weight of upland rice.[5] This figure was derived empirically and has been used in converting to weight the figures given by other researchers in bushels, gallons, and *tang*. The mean weight of rice varies with moisture content (wetter rice weighs more) and the variety and shape of the grain. Relatively short grained rice, such as that commonly grown by the Lua', weighs more per unit volume than does long-grained rice. Weight per *tang* will increase with packing. Weight also varies with the cleanliness and care with which empty grains have been winnowed out. Because of these variables it would be preferable to determine production in terms of weight, rather than volume, and to convert *field* weight to *standard* weight by determining moisture content of the rice as measured in the field.

In some cases, notably Yao (Miles 1967), Ma (Boulbet 1966), Rhade (Lafont 1967; Maurice and Proux 1954), and in Laos (Bordsen 1968), upland rice cultivation may be as productive per unit of cultivated land per crop as in many irrigated areas. In other cases (Lahu, as reported by Walker; Lua' and Karen, as reported by Kunstadter; Northern Thai in Nan, as reported by Chapman) shifting cultivation may yield only 35 to 40 percent as much rice per unit of cultivated land. When the fallow period is taken into calculation, annual productivity per unit of land may fall by as much as a factor of ten.

In general, upland cultivation requires more labor in a given year than does irrigated agriculture because of the difficulties involved in clearing and weeding, but irrigated agriculture requires a much higher initial investment in labor per unit of land because of the necessity to clear, level, dike, and develop dams and ditches. Productivity of shifting cultivation per unit of labor probably goes down very rapidly as the quality of the land declines, since weeding is the task that consumes the greatest amount of labor, and the amount of weeding that must be done is proportional both to the number of weeds per unit area, and to the total area covered. This helps to explain why there is an upper limit on the amount of land used by any one family group for swiddening in a given year: with a given amount of labor, farming a larger area will not increase the total yield.

POPULATION AND ECONOMIC DEVELOPMENT

Two contrasting theories describe the relationship between population growth and economic development. Both assume the socioeconomic and demographic systems are closed. One of these theories states that population growth is a requisite for economic development and that pressure on the land forces development of more productive economic systems (Boserup 1965). The other, sometimes spoken of as the neo-Malthusian theory, holds that population grows as a result of economic development and that population growth and population pressure may hamper economic development, because gains in productivity are continually offset by demands of the expanding population and because expanding populations contain a larger share of dependents, since their age distribution contains a much higher proportion of very young people than does a nongrowing population. The theories in fact may not be contradictory. We find some support for both. For example, among the Lua' and Karen the development of small irrigation systems in the hills (learned from lowlanders) has apparently enabled these people to support larger hill populations than does an economy based exclusively on shifting cultivation. On balance, however, there is evidence that the standard of living of the upland people is declining as a result of population growth and that many hill villagers are forced out of the hills to seek wage work because of the poor economic conditions. Conversely, Keen (chapter 14) reports lowlanders are forced into the hills because of shortage of irrigated land. Evidently neither the socio-economic nor the demographic system is closed.

Economic conditions are deteriorating in many parts of the hills, both in subsistence and cash cropping areas, and in areas using all different types of swidden cycles. Scholz (1969), for example, in discussing the economy of an Akha village in Mae Chan District, Chiang Rai Province, indicates that upland rice is the villagers' main staple and has become their main cash crop as well. They have abandoned opium production in recent years because of the large amount of labor required for its production, the relatively low yield, and the poor quality of soil in the area where they live. They are unable to produce enough rice for subsistence, but nevertheless must sell a portion of their crop to purchase tools and other necessities—as well as opium. Meanwhile their population continues to grow. Oughton and Niwat (1971) discuss the increasing economic problems among *miang* (tea) growers in the Chiang Dao area of Chiang Mai Province, as indicated by the low return for labor, decreasing availability of land in the hills, and high land rents in the hills. In later chapters of this book Kunstadter and Hinton document increasing populations and declining productivity among Lua' and Karen hill swidden farmers in Mae Sariang District of Mae Hong Son Province, and Chapman describes the effects of and potential remedies for increased pressure on the land among lowland Northern Thai swiddeners in Sa District of Nan Province. Economic change has not kept pace with population growth in these areas of northern Thailand.

The prospects for control of population growth depend in part on the motivations for reducing family size. Under conditions of shifting cultivation it appears that some household heads desire to maximize their economic productivity by maximizing the amount of land they can appropriate and use. The chief limiting factor on the amount of land they can use is in the labor supply they can organize for such tasks as weeding. Therefore, they may desire to have the largest possible number of children as a potential labor force, or they may seek to enlarge the size of their households by adoption or the formation of extended families. Farmers with higher capital investment and limited land resources (as in intensive irrigated agriculture) may not feel the same need for large numbers of children. This might suggest that motivation for large families will persist in shifting cultivation communities as long as this form of agriculture is labor intensive (as contrasted with capital or energy intensive), and as long as land is treated as a somewhat free good, to be allocated among members of the community in proportion to need as determined by family size.

Land, of course, is not a free good, and even if it were an unlimited resource, use of the uplands would affect (through loss of watershed and soil erosion) the land resources at lower elevations. Thus the population planning motives of individual swiddening families may not be in harmony with the needs of people living in other ecological zones, or even with their own needs or the needs of their descendants.

POPULATION DYNAMICS OF SHIFTING CULTIVATORS

Settlements of shifting cultivators range in size from two or three households with 10 to 20 persons in a tiny Karen hamlet up to 200 to 300 households with a population of 1,000 to 1,500 persons in large Lua' villages, such as Baw Luang. The upper limit of size is apparently set by the distance to the fields, an especially important consideration when no transportation or pack animals are available.

In the hill areas that have been studied to date, the populations are characteristically young (median age between 16 and 17 years), with relatively high birth and death rates, and with rapid population growth or potential for it. Reproductive performance in a number of upland Lua' and Karen villages in Mae Sariang District was between 3 and 4.4 *surviving* children born to each woman of completed fertility, for an average doubling of population size each generation. These rates have evidently been sustained for several generations, even in the absence of modern medical care. Now that some of the major diseases (smallpox, cholera, malaria) are somewhat under control, the rate of population growth can be expected to increase (Kunstadter 1971).

MIGRATION OF SHIFTING CULTIVATORS

The traditional method of handling the problem of surplus population in villages of shifting cultivators has been village or household fission and migration. Migration has been of two sorts: temporary migration for wage work, and permanent resettlement. Resettlement has been in two directions: into relatively sparsely settled hill areas, and into valley communities. Migration within the hills has required no modification of existing technologies or social organizations. In the past most upland and foothill areas of Thailand have not been heavily populated, and relatively unused areas were available for new settlements. As a result of population increase, this is evidently no longer true in some areas (for example eastern Mae Sariang Dis-

trict), and some hill areas can no longer absorb the surplus populations they are producing. One "escape route," especially for Lua' hill people in the past, has been to the lowlands, but the rapid rate of lowland population increase may make it increasingly difficult to absorb migrants from the hills. When Lua' and other similar migrants have moved from the hills they have changed culture and rapidly assimilated themselves into Northern Thai society. Thus upland population growth is contributing directly to the growth of the lowland Thai population.

The problems of population in relation to technology and social organization are evidently quite different among the different upland groups. The upland Lua' and Karen have developed a relatively nondestructive balance between their subsistence technology and the land, but they have failed to solve the problem of population growth within their own village socio-economic system. In the absence of technological change, upland subsistence agricultural systems such as those of Lua' and Karen appear to be unable to accommodate and respond to labor surpluses with a comparable increase in productivity. The upland Lua' and Karen are already heavily engaged in wage labor for lowland employers. Some of the wage labor is actually done in the hills (lumbering, mining), but in these cases it involves nonrenewed or nonrenewable resources, and at this point it cannot be considered as a long-range economic solution to the problem of population surplus.

By contrast, the Hmong agricultural system, with its emphasis on cash cropping, evidently requires a larger labor supply than most Hmong families can produce. They attempt to make up for the deficit in labor by various devices calculated to increase the size of their families (extended families, plural marriage, and adoption),[6] and the systematic recruitment of labor. The Hmong system, with its dependence on opium as a major cash crop, even if it were morally or politically acceptable, is not balanced with respect to its use of land resources (chapters 10, 11). In the absence of technological improvements, it leads to persistent changes in soil or vegetation which make long term, permanent settlement impossible. Hmong settlements are forced to relocate periodically, leaving behind them areas which for a generation or more are no longer suitable for cultivation or forest regrowth.

ECONOMIC DEVELOPMENT IN THE NORTH

The expansion of population implies a need for the expansion of economic opportunities for those who have traditionally been engaged in swidden cultivation. Expanding the areas under cultivation does not seem to be the answer, since population increase will ultimately lead to degradation of soil resources as the length of the fallow period is shortened. Likewise, more labor-intensive shifting cultivation of the Hmong type does not seem to be the answer, for similar reasons. These considerations imply the necessity for technological and social change.

A number of schemes for economic development have been tried in northern Thailand and elsewhere, with varying degrees of success. Numerous attempts have been made to improve subsistence farming techniques through the introduction of improved strains of livestock, vegetables, and crop plants. The remarkable development of high yielding varieties of rice ("miracle rice") has had little direct effect on shifting cultivators for two reasons: no strains have been developed which are suitable for dry cultivation,[7] and those strains which have been developed for irrigated fields require technical knowledge and heavy investment in fertilizers and pesticides, which has not been practical for the vast majority of the impoverished shifting cultivators. High yielding varieties of maize have been introduced in some upland areas (e.g., Chiang Rai Province), but transportation and marketing difficulties limit the commercial success of these operations. Uncertainties of land tenure, the absence of cash for investment, the absence of credit, and the lack of transportation and marketing facilities will probably limit the effectiveness of any program designed to introduce improved strains of grain plants as cash crops into the shifting cultivation areas.

Cash cropping in the irrigated lowland areas has had spectacular success in many parts of the North, especially since the early 1960s. This has chiefly involved garlic, fruit trees, truck crops, peanuts, and tobacco. This has happened particularly in the area near Chiang Mai, and to some extent in all the northern provinces where tobacco has been fostered as a dry-season crop. The usual pattern has been for the tobacco companies to furnish seed, fertilizer, and instructions to the farmer and to guarantee to buy the crop at a fixed price. As a result, second-cropping of this "upland" (nonirrigated) cash crop has expanded rapidly, probably with an improvement in soil quality because of the fertilizer which the tobacco companies have provided in order to control the quality of the product. Because most tobacco is grown during the dry season, the expansion of this crop has helped to absorb the seasonal surplus of unemployed agricultural labor.[8]

Similar methods have not yet been tried with rice and have not been very successful when tried with maize. It seems unlikely that the success of the tobacco scheme could serve as a model for improving the production of subsistence crops, even in the lowland areas where marketing and transportation networks are available. To do so would require reorganization and reorientation of the rice marketing system in this area, which seems unlikely until the farm price of rice rises, or until the cost of improved rice production falls low enough to compete successfully in world markets which have already been affected by the "green revolution" (see Staub and Blase 1971). It seems even less likely that the model can be applied to the hill areas because of difficulties in transportation.

The major emphasis and the major expenditures in the public sector for agricultural development in Thailand in recent years have been for enlarged irrigation systems. These have been designed to subjugate larger areas and to make double- and triple-cropping possible in areas which previously could be irrigated only in the rainy season. These projects might be able to absorb some of the surplus population from the shifting cultivation areas, but to date they seem to have had little effect in this regard. Some of the dams that were built have actually made necessary the relocation of significant numbers of people from previously irrigated land which is now flooded, and forced some of them into shifting cultivation in the hills or into nonagricultural occupations in other areas. Unless they are designed specifically for relocation of upland cultivators, and unless steps are taken to see that people from marginal agricultural areas actually receive the newly irrigated land, the large-scale irrigation projects will have no beneficial effect for the forest farmers. Failure to consider the entire population of the watershed and drainage system which is being dammed is undoubtedly a shortcoming in the planning of these projects. Increased and unrelieved population pressure in the shifting cultivation areas will lead to increased erosion and increased silting problems behind the dams. Dams may have other ecological consequences for those living downstream: by removing silt before it reaches the fields, dams may be responsible for reducing the fertility of irrigated fields; the characteristics of the ecologically important

wetlands may be detrimentally affected; if fish ladders are not provided various species of fish may become extinct (already reported for several species in the Chao Phraya drainage); and the greatly reduced flow of rivers in the dry season may increase pollution problems.

Projects are now underway in Nan and Lampang provinces directed at the clearing, improvement, and assignment of permanent title of land used by lowland Thai shifting cultivators. The results of these projects are reported by Chapman and by Charley and McGarity elsewhere in this book. The techniques used have wide applicability on flat or gently sloping terrace lands which have been used by Northern Thai for slash-and-burn farming. Because permanent use of the land implies more intensive use, this system of clearing may offer temporary relief from the problems of expanding populations in the valley and foothill zones. Hill-tribe resettlement centers (e.g., Ban Pa Klang near Pua in Changwat Nan) have recently been established on such terrace land. On steeper slopes, however, development of this kind is much more costly and difficult to implement. On steeper slopes in areas of high-intensity rainfall (such as all northern Thailand), the risk of soil erosion necessitates close spacing of contour channels or absorption banks, or the construction of agricultural terraces. To the problem of the substantial cost involved can be added problems of unclear land titles and of administrative jurisdiction. Steeper land usually must be reclassified for legal cultivation (see chapter 3).

Nonagricultural economic development that has clear implications for shifting cultivators includes work in forestry and industrial development, especially mining. The lumbering industry in Thailand has traditionally been entirely extractive; only recently has attention been paid to development of superior strains of trees, to reforestation of cut-over areas, and to deliberate planting of lumber and pulp "crops." Chapter 16 discusses the success of some of these efforts, their implications as regards removal of land from swidden cultivation, and the ability (or inability) of these forestry industries to support equivalent populations through wage labor.

Observations in the Samoeng area of Chiang Mai Province[9] indicate some of the effects of mining on upland farmers. In the area of the Baw Keo mines, population density has been increased by the presence of wage labor opportunities, and much of the local irrigated or irrigable land has been spoiled for cultivation by deposition of the waste from hydraulic mining. This has increased the pressure on swidden lands by local farmers. The pressure on swidden lands is further increased by the high local price of rice, especially during the rainy season, as a result of poor transportation and marketing facilities. Thus local economic development and wage labor opportunities have brought, unintentionally, an accelerated rate of destruction of soil resources. When the mineral resources of the Baw Keo mines are exhausted in a few years' time, the agricultural resources probably will also have been completely devastated.

The development of agricultural processing and manufacturing industries in northern Thailand is only beginning. Although this has had some effect on the wage labor picture, we have few data on the effect of industrialization on the surplus population of forest farmers. Such anecdotal information as is available suggests that industries in the North may rely on labor recruited from Bangkok, the Central Plain, or other areas outside the North, especially for the more skilled jobs. Few forest farmers have the skills or the education to qualify them for industrial jobs, even if the recruitment networks were available to them.

Road building has often been considered a primary means of bringing development to remote areas. The building of roads into upland areas of the North has been followed rapidly by a series of changes, including the proliferation of local transportation systems, changes in settlement patterns, increases in land values along the roads, and movement into the hills by lowlanders able to capitalize on the improved access to upland resources. On balance, it is probably the lowlanders who have benefited the most from these changes, although improved transportation has aided upland farmers located close to a road in getting their products to market.

KNOWLEDGE NEEDED FOR DEVELOPMENT

One crucial dimension of the economic problems of upland cultivators is that of population. At present we have no adequate measure of the total population involved in swiddening and only a sketchy idea of its geographical distribution in northern Thailand. Studies done to date indicate that the population of forest farmers is multiethnic, large, and growing at least as fast as the urban or lowland rural population dependent on irrigated agriculture. Better estimates of the total population of forest farmers and their population dynamics (birth, death, and migration directions and rates) are needed for rational planning. Research is also needed to develop and test hypotheses, such as those mentioned above, regarding the relationships between household size, economic productivity, and motivations for family planning.

The total area under swidden cultivation is not known, nor is the average length of the cultivation cycle. This information, as well as knowledge of the trends in total area and cultivation cycles in the recent past, are vital for rational planning. Assessment of population and land areas affected is probably most rapidly and inexpensively estimated by examination of existing aerial photographs, perhaps supplemented by new photographs of selected areas, combined with sample surveys made on the ground to determine length of fallow cycle and size of households. The basic methodology for such a study has been worked out by the National Statistical Office in the study of opium production undertaken for the UNESCO Division of Narcotics between 1964 and 1967 (United Nations Survey Team 1967:54–55), and has been used successfully in some upland areas of Laos for estimating population size and agricultural potential.

PROBLEMS OF SWIDDEN LAND TITLE

Control of land is basic to any agricultural system. Secure title to land is essential for any agricultural development which requires external financial assistance. The Northern Region contains almost 90,000 sq km of land, of which only 0.33 percent (300 sq km) had land certificates in 1967, while 11 percent had "land possession" registration (see chapter 3 for definition of these types of titles), and the remaining 89 percent was considered "forest, wasteland and other." The Northern Region figures for land certificate and land possession are the lowest for any region of Thailand (Royal Thai Survey Department 1969:8.2), and reflect both the mountainous nature of the area and the fact that much of the agriculture there is swidden cultivation. The large portion of the North which is customarily used for swidden cultivation is not recognized in the land registration system. Thus, under ordinary circumstances upland cultivators cannot proceed through the several stages of application, registration, and survey to insure their title to the land which they use.

Judge Sophon Ratanakhon has done invaluable service in describing the legal obstacles facing forest farmers if they should desire to stabilize their system of land tenure and land use

(chapter 3). Thai land law assumes as "normal" the individually held, annually cultivated, irrigated or fixed field agriculture in lowland areas not covered by forests. Apparently the authors of the law wanted to discourage what they assumed to be the destructive features of upland cultivation. Perhaps they were thinking only of the type we have described as "long cultivation–very long fallow," and did not recognize the legal rights, or even the existence in large numbers, of settled swiddeners who use a regular rotation system of cultivation and fallow.

Thus land law conflicts at many points with the traditional land-use and land-tenure systems associated with various kinds of shifting cultivation. When the current land law was passed in 1954, holders of untitled land had the opportunity to register their possessions, but few if any swidden cultivators did so. Villagers might have the legal right to organize themselves as "self-help" or "cooperative" communities, and seek title to their communally held lands, but apparently this was not done except in the case of government-sponsored settlements *(nikhom).* The overall effect of the land laws (chapter 3), together with the forestry laws (chapters 4, 5), is to place virtually all swidden cultivators in violation of the law and subject to punishment, with little legal recourse to protect their traditional claims vis-à-vis other claimants or the government. Their rights are limited by the fact that their occupation of the land is probably illegal and not under protection of the government.

It is unlikely that any capital-intensive developments in shifting cultivation areas can become widespread until the question of land titles is clarified. The lack of clarity of title combined with increased population pressure is likely to increase instability of the shifting cultivators and to increase the frequency and violence of conflicts over land claims. Any capital-intensive developments will also depend on the development of agricultural credit and marketing systems appropriate to the upland environment.

Agricultural developments in the shifting cultivation areas must combine readily marketed cash crops with higher yielding subsistence crops, land-intensive cropping systems, and marketing and transportation facilities. Any one of these by itself will not solve the problems of increased population and relative decline in standard of living of the shifting cultivators. Even with extensive agricultural development, it is unlikely that this growth alone will be able to handle the economic and demographic problems of the region in the near future. The area will also need expanded wage-labor opportunities and recruitment networks coordinated with educational and training programs (cf. Staub and Blase 1971:122).

NOTES

1. This type of farming is now commonly designated in scientific literature as "swidden cultivation" (swidden: a cleared and burned field). The term "shifting cultivation" has the connotation, often untrue, of nomadism, for which reason the term "forest fallow," or the more neutral term "swidden," may be preferable. The Thai term *rai* and its Northern Thai cognate, *hai*, refer to unirrigated fields. In this book *rai* is reserved to designate the Thai unit of land measurement, equivalent to 0.16 hectare.

2. Throughout this book, the people referred to in popular and some earlier scientific literature as "Meo" and "Miao" are designated "Hmong," the term now becoming standard in scientific usage, and which is also the term the people prefer to use for themselves.

3. Conklin's distinction between "partial" and "integral" swidden systems and their subtypes is not followed here because people of any one community or ethnic group may engage in several different types, depending on availability of resources. The emphasis in our classification is on method of use of resources.

4. This description of the "Hmong system" is based largely on Kunstadter's observations and discussions with Karen, Lua', and Hmong informants in Mae Sariang and Mae Chaem districts. For other views of the Hmong see Geddes (1970, 1976) and chapter 11 in this book. For a description of the similar Lahu Nyi cultivation system see Walker (1970; 1976).

5. Lua' rice was well cleaned and dried when weighed. It was poured into a standard Thai *tang* measure (20 liters) and smoothed off at the top with a section of bamboo, according to the standard practice.

6. Methods of expanding household size among the Yao, especially through adoption of outsiders, are detailed by Kandre (1971) and Miles (1973).

7. The potential for developing high yield strains of upland rice may be limited since rice is apparently very dependent on adequate water supply for maximum yield.

8. Since large amounts of wood are required as fuel for drying the tobacco, the total ecological impact of tobacco growing is not clear.

9. Made by David H. Marlowe in 1967 (personal communication).

References

Asian Development Bank. 1969. *Asian Agricultural Survey.* Seattle: University of Washington Press.

Bertrand, P. 1952. "Le conditions de la culture du riz dans le Haut Donnai (Viet Nam)." *L'Agronomie Tropicale* 7(3):266–275.

Bordsen, Marcus C. 1968. "Report on the 1967 meter square measurements of rice yields to Mr. Keopraseuth Meksvanh, provincial agriculture chief, southern region, Pakse." 24 January 1968. Typescript. Pakse, Laos: IVS/AGR.

Boserup, Ester. 1965. *The Conditions of Agricultural Growth.* Chicago: Aldine Publishing Co.

Boulbet, Jean. 1966. "Le Miir, culture itinérante avec jachere forestière en pays Maa', région de Blao-Bassin de Fleuve Daa' Döông (Dông Nai)." *Bulletin de l'École Français d'Extrême Orient* 53(1):77–98.

Champsoloix, R. 1960. "Le ray dans quelques villages des Hauts Plateau du Viet Nam." In *Raports du Sol et de la Vegetation,* G. Viennot Bourgin, ed., pp. 46–62. Paris: Masson et Cie.

Freeman, J. D. 1955. *Iban Agriculture.* Colonial Office Research Studies No. 18. London: Her Majesty's Stationery Office.

Geddes, William R. 1954. *The Land Dyaks of Sarawak.* Colonial Office Research Studies No. 14. London: Her Majesty's Stationery Office.

———. 1970. "Opium and the Miao: A study in ecological adjustment." *Oceania* 41(1):1–11.

———. 1976. *Migrants of the Mountains: The Cultural Ecology of the Blue Miao (Hmong Njua) of Thailand.* Oxford: Oxford University Press, Clarendon Press.

Gorman, Chester F. 1969. "Hoabinhian: A pebble-tool complex with early plant associations in Southeast Asia." *Science* 163:671–673.

———. 1971a. "The Hoabinhian and after: Subsistence patterns in Southeast Asia during the late Pleistocene and early Recent periods." *World Archaeology* 2(3):300–320.

———. 1971b. "*A priori* models and Thai prehistory: A reconsideration of the beginnings of agriculture in Southeast Asia." Unpublished manuscript. Dunedin, New Zealand: University of Otago, Department of Anthropology.

Hirst, Eric. 1974. "Food-related energy requirements." *Science* 184:134–138.

Izikowitz, K. G. 1951. *Lamet: Hill Peasants in French Indo-China.* etnologiska Studier 17. Goteborg: Etnografiska Museet.

Kalland, Arne. 1976. *Carrying Capacity of Shifting Cultivation of Northern Thailand and Some Implications.* The Lampang Field Station, a Scandinavian Research Center in Thailand, 1969–1974, Reports, edited by Søren Egerod and Per Sørensen. The Scandinavian Institute of Asian Studies, Special Publication No. 5, pp. 289–297.

Kandre, Peter K. 1971. "Alternative modes of recruitment of viable households among the Yao of Mae Chan." *South-East Asian Journal of sociology* 4:43–52.

Kickert, Robert W. 1969. "Akha village structure." In *Tribesmen and Peasants in North Thailand,* Proceedings of the First Symposium of the Tribal Research Centre (1967), Chiang Mai, Thailand, Peter Hinton, ed., pp. 35–40. Chiang Mai: Tribal Research Centre.

Kunstadter, Peter. 1971. "Natality, mortality and migration of upland and lowland populations in northwestern Thailand." In *Culture and Population: A Collection of Current Studies,* Steven Polgar, ed., pp. 46–60. Carolina Population Center, Monograph 9, University of North Carolina at Chapel Hill. Cambridge, Mass.: Schenkman Publishing Co.

Lafont, Pierre-Bernard. 1959. "The 'slash-and-burn' (ray) agriculture system of the mountain populations of central Vietnam." Proceedings of the ninth Pacific Science Congress, vol. 7, pp. 56–59. Bangkok.

———. 1967. "L'agriculture sur brulis chez les Proto-Indochinois des hauts plateaux du Centre Viet Nam." Les cahiers d'Outre-mer, *Revue du Geographie* 20(77):37–48.

Leach, E. R. 1954. *Political Systems of Highland Burma.* Cambridge, Mass.: Harvard University Press.

Maurice, Albert, and Georges Marie Proux. 1954. "L'âme du riz." *Bulletin de la Societé des Études Indochinoises* 29(1–2):129–259.

Miles, Douglas. 1967. "Report on fieldwork in the village of Pulangka." Mimeographed. Chiang Mai: Tribal Research Centre.

———. 1973. "Some demographic implications of regional commerce: The case of North Thailand's Yao minority." In *Studies of Contemporary Thailand,* R. Ho and E. C. Chapman, eds. Canberra: Australian National University, Monograph HG/8, Department of Human Geography.

Nimmanahaeminda, Kraisri. 1965. "An inscribed silver-plate grant to the Lawa of Boh Luang." In *Felicitation Volumes in Southeast Asia Studies Presented to His Highness Prince Dhanivat Kromamum Bidyalabh Bridyakorn,* vol. 2, pp. 233–238. Bangkok: The Siam Society.

Oughton, G. A., and Niwat Imong. 1971. "Nikhom Doi Chiang Dao: Resources and development-potential survey." Supplement to report 3: "Further data on the native tea *(miang)* economy." Mimeographed. Chiang Mai: Tribal Research Centre.

Pimentel, David, L. E. Hurd, A. C. Bellotti, M. J. Forster, I. N. Oka, O. D. Sholes, and R. J. Whitman. 1973. "Food production and the energy crisis." *Science* 182:443–449.

Royal Thai Survey Department. 1969. Thailand national resources atlas. Supreme Command Headquarters. Bangkok.

Scholz, Friedhelm. 1969. "Zum Feldbau des Akha-Dorfes Alum, Thailand." [Contribution to the shifting-cultivation of the Akha village alum, Thailand]. *Yearbook of the South Asia Institute,* Heidelberg University, 1968/69, Band 3, pp. 88–99. Wiesbaden: Otto Harrassowitz.

Spencer, J. E. 1966. *Shifting Cultivation in Southeastern Asia.* University of California Publications in Geography, vol. 19. Berkeley and Los Angeles: University of California Press.

Staub, William J., and Melvin G. Blase. 1971. "Genetic technology and agricultural development." *Science* 173:119–123.

Steinhart, John S., and Carol E. Steinhart. 1974. "Energy use in the U.S. food system." *Science* 184:307–316.

United Nations Survey Team. 1967. "Report of the United Nations survey team on the economic and social needs of the opium-producing areas in Thailand." Bangkok: Government Printing House.

Van Roy, Edward. 1971. *Economic Systems of Northern Thailand.* Ithaca, N.Y.: Cornell University Press.

Walker, Anthony R. 1970. "Lahu Nyi (Red Lahu) village society and economy in northern Thailand." Terminal report to the Royal Thai Government. 2 vols., mimeographed. Chiang Mai: Tribal Research Centre.

———. 1976. "The swidden economy of a Lahu Nyi (Red Lahu) village community in North Thailand." *Folk* 18:145–188.

Young, O. Gordon. 1962. *The Hill Tribes of Northern Thailand.* 2nd ed., Monograph no. 1. Bangkok: The Siam Society.

A Dictionary of the Economic Products of the Malay Peninsula
I. H. Burkill

DACRYDIUM—(3) elatum

An oil can be distilled from the wood, consisting largely of cedrene Volatile oil. and cedrol (see Gildemeister, Aether. Oele, 2, ed. of 1929 p. 11), thus resembling commercial cedar-wood oil. [F. W. F.]

DACTYLIS, Linn. A genus of the family Gramineae, the only species being *D. glomerata*, Linn., the cock's-foot grass. It is a fodder Fodder-grass. grass of the first rank for the temperate regions of Europe and Asia; and it has been naturalized in many countries. In some of the mountains of Java it has run wild, but when tried on the Taiping hills it failed.

DACTYLOCTENIUM, Willd. A small genus of the family Grami- Grass of neae, one of its species, *D. aegyptiacum*, Willd. (Eleusine aegyptiaca, rather dry *Desf.*) being pantropic. This grass is chiefly found in dry countries places. or on sandy coasts. In the Malay Peninsula it occurs near the ports, and seems to be a recent introduction.

In parts of India and Africa which are liable to famines, its seeds Seeds as may be collected in times of need and turned into a meal used as famine food. food; but it is unpleasant in taste and produces internal disorders (Paton and Dunlop in Agric. Ledger, 1904 pp. 42 and 51).

The vegetative parts are eaten when young by animals, but all Fodder. writers seem to agree that its value is below the average.

Petrie (Proc. Linn. Soc. N.S. Wales, 38, 1913 p. 633) says that he Develops found it very rich in cyanogenetic glucosides, all parts giving strong poisonous reactions, except in the winter. properties, when growing.

DAEDALACANTHUS, T. Anders., see *Eranthemum*.

DAEMONORHOPS, Blume. A genus of upwards of one hundred species of palms—family Palmae—found in moist tropical Asia and Malaysia; with very few exceptions, climbers.

The canes, as Rattans (q.v.), are almost as useful as those of Rattans. *Calamus*. The fruits often contain a little edible flesh. The buds are Fruits and usually bitter, but some are edible. buds of some edible.

The fruits of a little group of closely allied species give Dragon's Kino, or blood—a kind of kino. Any one of these may be called 'rotan Dragon's jĕrnang' (dragon's-blood rattan). blood.

Another group of species has peculiar rings of prickles on the leaf- Vernacular sheaths: from the rings they are appropriately called 'rotan chin-chin' names. (finger-ring rattan), and because ants nest in the channels between the rings, they are called 'rotan sĕmut' (ants' rattan).

Because of the bitterness of the buds the name 'rotan sĕpat' arises.

Additional to the vernacular names recorded below are 'rotan chichit' for *D. oblongus*, Mart., 'rotan sĕpal' for *D. sepal*, Becc., and 'rotan anak lĕbah' for an unidentified species of the 'jĕrnang' group. For further remarks on the Malay names, see Rattans. Uses of

The chief use in Europe of Dragon's blood is for colouring Dragon's varnishes. In the East rattans and bamboos are dyed with it. In blood, as a varnish, and the Dindings, formerly, dish-covers of *Pandanus* matting were dyed dye.

DAEMONORHOPS

with it, and mats made, perhaps, of other material (Wray in Notes on Perak, Col. and Ind. Exhib. 1886).

Formerly in European medicine. In European medicine Dragon's blood was formerly used against dysentery and diarrhoea, and as an astringent in tooth-powders. It consists of a resin-alcohol—draco-resinotannol—to the extent of 56 per cent., associated with benzoic and benzolactic acids, &c. When heated, Dragon's blood gives off the benzoic acid, the scent of which accounts for the application to it of the vernacular name 'kĕmĕnyan merah (red benzoin). The Semang call it 'hadlud' or 'hanlid'. In *In Malaysian medicine.* Malaysia it is still used medicinally a little, not in the ways in which Europe has used it, but for indigestion, among the Benua (Skeat and Blagden, Pagan Races, 2, 1906 p. 354), and for passing blood in urine (Notes Sarawak Trade, Brit. Emp. Exhib. 1924 p. 56): for sprue and pains in the stomach (Med. Book Mal. Med. in Gard. Bull. S.S. 6, 1930 pp. 356, 361, and 363). It is prescribed, also (p. 359), for painting round the eye, for 'spots and specks' on the eye.

History in trade. A kino, of the nature of Dragon's blood, reached the ancient Greeks, apparently from Egypt, being doubtless the produce of the *Kinos used before Dragon's blood came from Malaysia.* Socotran *Dracaena cinnabari*, Balf. f., and fabulous tales were told of the way in which it was obtained. It was used as an eye medicine. In the later Middle Ages a similar resin from the Canary Islands, derived from *Dracaena draco*, Linn., came into the markets in competition with it. Only in the sixteenth century Sumatran Dragon's blood appeared, brought westwards in Arab trade, being something *Kinos from Malaysia came late.* that the Arabs had met with, not in India, but in Malaysia: for though nowadays it is used in India in Mohammedan medicine, it seems to have been a late adoption from Arabian medicine, and no part of Indian medicine until the Arabs introduced it.

It was mentioned by Acosta in 1578; and by various writers during the next hundred years. Morison and Ray showed familiarity with it. *Sources of Malaysian Dragon's blood.* Rumpf, in the seventeenth century, wrote, as the result of much labour, the first account of the plants which give it, saying that it was obtained in Palembang and Jambi from a certain rattan plant, and *Rumpf's knowledge of them.* that it might be got from other species as he had indications of its occurrence in some found in western Java and southern Borneo.

In the first part of the nineteenth century, botanists made endeavours to obtain a more exact knowledge of these palms, and Blume described, under the name of *Daemonorhops draco*, materials which he had assembled as the source of Dragon's blood, unfortunately uniting together more than one species. Beccari (Ann. Roy. Bot. Gard. Calcutta, 12, 1911 p. 106) says, that on examining the *Blume confused three sources under the name D. draco.* material which Blume left, he found in it a great mixture. He considers that Blume, embodying the information derived from Rumpf, had associated with Rumpf's species portions of leaves of *D. melanochaetes*, or perhaps *D. palembanica*, leaf-sheaths of *D. ruber*, fruits of *D. ruber*, and perhaps of *D. draconellus* and fragments not at all closely related. Beccari declares that the only plant which can bear the name, *D. draco*, is that part of Blume's complex which is also Rumpf's. Beccari goes back, then, to Rumpf's figure (plate 132, in

DAEMONORHOPS

vol. 5 of the *Herbarium Amboinense*) and states that he recognizes it as equal to certain materials collected by Teijsmann in the Palembang Residency of Sumatra and by Diepenhorst in Priaman. This material, therefore, in Beccari's opinion illustrates *D. draco*. It represents one of two rattans, which in Palembang, are recognized locally as giving Dragon's blood, and are called 'rotan jĕrnang bĕsar' and 'rotan jĕrnang kĕchil' (i.e. big and little). Beccari believes that the first is *D. draco*, while the second is *D. didymophyllus*, Becc.; but it remains possible that the fruits called 'buah rotan jĕrnang bĕsar' have actually two sources and part of them only, come from *D. draco*. A third Sumatran species, said to give Dragon's blood, is *D. ruber*, Blume, regarding which there are divergent statements, for Beccari (op. cit. p. 117) says that the secretion is very scanty and not worth collecting, while others claim it to be the chief source in Sumatra of Dragon's blood. It occurs in Java as well. *(What two of these three are: and a third source.)*

Rumpf had mentioned Banjermassin in southern Borneo as an additional centre of supply. The rattan which still gives the resin in that part of Borneo is said to be *D. motleyi*, Becc. *(Sources of, in S. Borneo,)*

Northern Borneo has a newer industry in Dragon's blood, two species there yielding it, being *D. draconellus*, Becc., and *D. mattanensis*, Becc. Beccari says that the first gives the best quality of Sarawak, and that the second gives very little. *(and in N. Borneo,)*

Lastly, in the Malay Peninsula there are three species known to yield it. *D. didymophyllus* occurs, as in Palembang, and yields a little: *D. propinquus*, Becc., a source mentioned below, has been found in Penang and may be met with again; and *D. micracanthus*, Becc., also occurs. *(and in Malaya.)*

In all, eight species are mentioned thus as sources.

In order to prepare Dragon's blood the fruits are collected and when quite dry are put into a basket with cockle-shells and shaken. The friction thus caused detaches the resin, which falls through the basket into a cloth placed below, as a gritty powder. This powder after being pounded into dust, is softened by means of hot water, and then moulded into cakes, sticks, &c. *(Extraction from the fruits.)*

Inferior grades may contain as much as 40 per cent. of fragments of the fruit-wall, and other debris.

Koenig (see Journ. Roy. As. Soc. Straits Branch, 27, 1894 p. 77) described the adulteration of it with dammar: and collectors are said to use the latex of *Garcinia parvifolia* to cement the dust together. *(Adulteration.)*

Koenig said that much Dragon's blood was prepared in the Dindings at the end of the eighteenth century. Krian seems also to have yielded a fair quantity. Low (Soil and Agric. Penang, 1836 p. 212) said that there were two kinds, the marsh and the hill—the latter the better. Since Low wrote, the forests have become much poorer in rattan plants. *(Destruction of supplies in Malaya.)*

Several rattans, the sap of which serves the Pagan tribes as an adjunct in dart-poison, have been recognized; but there is one which the Pangan use, reported under the name 'rotan riong', or 'rotan riang' (Ridley in Agric. Bull. Mal. Penins. 8, 1898 p. 200), which has not been identified. *(Sap in dart-poison.)*

749

Papers presented to the UNESCO Symposium on 'The Vegetation of
the Humid Tropics', Bogor, Indonesia, December 1958.

1. DEVELOPMENT OF A SILVICULTURAL SYSTEM FOR THE CONVERSION OF NATURAL INLAND LOWLAND EVERGREEN RAIN FOREST OF MALAYA

by

J. WYATT-SMITH

(Silvicultural Research Officer, Forest Research Institute, Malaya)

Introduction

SILVICULTURE is the art of cultivating forests to produce the maximum benefit to man. In the humid tropics, however, where the components of the forests are still largely unknown and where large tracts of original forest still cover vast areas in under-developed countries, countries with rapidly increasing populations and whose standards of living are rapidly improving, man's requirements are also changing fast and 'maximum benefit' is an uncertain and variable factor. Although silviculture should be founded on natural laws and should not be dictated by nor be subservient to forest management, it is obvious that prescriptions of sound management will not run contrary to sound silvicultural principles; it is equally certain, however, that in the humid tropics the problems of management will be changing to a far greater extent than in a developed country with a relatively stable population, and that silvicultural prescriptions may perforce have to change also, and without the necessary ecological background.

The first problem facing Forest Departments of any country is to have a forest estate, and efforts are usually initially directed to this end. Although in the humid tropics with large areas of original forest this might be thought to be a simple problem, this is often far from the case—the future development of the country cannot be forecast; nomadic tribes with traditional rights and practising shifting cultivation may exist; land use, soil, geological, and often even topographical maps, are not available; and the composition of the forest and potential value of the myriad of species are not known. In consequence, the sequence of events usually starts with highly selective logging or creaming of the forest for export purposes on land which is required for agricultural purposes, and the search for areas rich in these relatively few economic species for making into the permanent forest estate. These species are generally those with a high-class cabinet or naturally durable grade of timber. At the same time research into the botanical composition of the forest and in many cases into the timber properties and qualities of the species is undertaken. Any silvicultural practice carried out at this stage is generally directed at improving in the forest estate the proportion and stocking of the few known economic species, and this has in most countries been undertaken by line planting often with far from successful or economic returns.

Schimper (1903) describes rain forest as 'Evergreen, hygrophilous in character, at least 30 m. high, but usually much taller, rich in thick-stemmed lianes and in woody as well as herbaceous epiphytes'. To this, I consider, should be added a richness in woody species which far exceeds that of the forest cover of regions outside the humid tropics (Table 1). In Malaya with a flora of about 8,000 flowering plants it is estimated that there are at least 2,000 trees and of these about 800 are known to reach one metre in girth or commercial plants is a conservative estimate for the flora of Malaysia and that the number of different species of trees is about 3,000. It is probable, however, that the size. Van Steenis (1949) considers that 25,000 to 30,000 species of flowering latter is also a very conservative estimate in view of the estimated number of trees in Malaya, where the flora is probably best known for the region. At the time he wrote he considered that only about 5,000 out of these 25,000 to 30,000 species were critically known, and it is probably true to say that the herbaceous species and those of the shrub and lower storeys are better known than the larger trees. These tree species, apart from varying greatly in height, size, rate of growth, length of life, periodicity of flowering and fruiting, and properties of shade tolerance and light demands at different stages of their life form, differ greatly in their timber qualities. Nevertheless, species of one genera, or on occasions even of one family, are often found to be sufficiently alike in timber qualities for the timber to be marketed as a single grade under one group-name. This is extremely fortunate, since it would be impossible in most cases to obtain sufficient quantities of timber of a single botanical species from one locality and at a particular time in natural tropical evergreen rain forest. This great variation or range in timber quality, and in particular in natural durability of the numerous species, is one of the principal causes for changes in management and consequent silvicultural prescriptions throughout the years. The initial trend is to enrich the few desirable economic species in the natural forest at the expense of the many uneconomic ones—a step which carried to an extreme would possibly destroy nature's biological balance in the heterogeneous tropical community. This warning was stressed both at the Sixth British Commonwealth Forestry Conference in Ottawa 1952 and at the Second Session of the F.A.O. Asia Pacific Forestry Commission in Singapore in the same year, and cannot be overemphasised. This is especially so because our knowledge of the ecology of tropical evergreen rain forest is still extremely limited, and the preference of the forest industry is without doubt for a raw material of comparative uniformity. There is, therefore, a possibility of economic pressure for a more uniform crop, and the questions of economics and of the voting of money by governments for silvicultural operations in such a long term project as forestry are not those that can be dismissed lightly.

Exploitation and Utilisation Developments

Forest exploitation and utilisation in Malaya have gone through the usual historical sequence, from the stage of highly selective logging of a few valuable species in the initial stages to that of almost full utilisation of a far greater

TABLE I

Composition of Mixed Tropical Rain Forest   (a) (Taken *in toto* from Wyatt-Smith (1949) Table 6)

LOCALITY	ASIA			S. AMERICA	AFRICA	
	Bukit Lagong F.R., Malaya	Sungei Menyala F.R., Malaya	Mt. Dulit, Sarawak	Moraballi Creek, British Guiana	Okomu Forest Reserve, Nigeria	Messa Me Forest Reserve, Ivory Coast
Source of data	Wyatt-Smith (1949)	Wyatt-Smith (1949)	Richards (1936)	Davis and Richards (1933-34)	Richards (1939)	Aubréville (1938)
Size of plot (hectares)	1.6	1.6	1.5	1.5	1.5	1.4
Number of trees per hectare: Diameter:						
4 in. (10 cm.) and over ...	559 (b)	480	—	432	390	530
8 in. (20 cm.) and over ...	277 (b)	193	184	223	223	214
16 in. (40 cm.) and over ...	83 (b)	61	44	60	47	38
Number of species: Diameter:						
4 in. (10 cm.) and over ...	227	197	—	91	70	74
8 in. (20 cm.) and over ...	152	109	98	57	51	58
16 in. (40 cm.) and over ...	65	34	32	31	31	23
Individuals/species: Diameter:						
4 in. (10 cm.) and over ...	4.0	4.0	—	7.1	8.3	10.0
8 in. (20 cm.) and over ...	2.9	2.9	2.7	5.8	6.2	3.7
16 in. (40 cm.) and over ...	2.1	2.9	1.9	2.3	2.3	1.7
Percentage of most abundant species: Diameter:						
4 in. (10 cm.) and over ...	*Hydnocarpus filipes* 6.9 (b)	*Santiria laevigata* 5.3	—	*Pentaclethra macroloba* 11	*Strombosia retivenia* 30	*Pachylobus deliciosus* 15
8 in. (20 cm.) and over ...	*Hydnocarpus filipes* 5.4 (b)	*Santiria laevigata* 7.1	'Medang lit' 5	*Pentaclethra macroloba* 13	*Strombosia retivenia* 35	*Pachylobus deliciosus* 17
16 in. (40 cm.) and over ...	*Shora curtisii*	*Koompassia malaccensis*	'Marakah batu' & 'Meranti daging'	*Eschweilera sagotiana*	*Pausinystalia* sp. (or spp.)	*Piptadenia africana*
	8.9 (b)	11.2	10	16	14 (or less)	13

(a) The figures for the non-Malayan plots have been taken *in toto* from Table 1 in the paper by P. W. Richards—"Composition of primary tropical rain forest". Figures for the plot in Mauritius have not been included as the forest was considered by Vaughan and Wiehe to be not Tropical Lowland Evergreen Rain-Forest but probably akin to the Tropical Lower-Montane Evergreen Rain-Forest of Burtt Davy.

(b) Taken from plot of 5 acres (2.02 hectares).

number of species as is taking place today. It is known that there was Chinese interest in Malaya as early as the eighth century for *Dryobalanops aromatica* (kapur) from which crystalline camphor was obtained (Burkhill 1935), and for the timber of *Balanocarpus heimii* (chengal) for a century or more ago; there was also an early demand for Malacca cane. At the beginning of this century the demand of timber for all purposes was almost entirely for that of *Balanocarpus heimii* and of *Intsia palembanica* (merbau), which are both naturally durable; in addition the Forest Department was interested in the species *Palaquium gutta* (taban merah) because of the valuable product gutta percha obtained from its exudate. In the mid-twenties the demand was still mainly for naturally durable timbers, mostly for railway sleepers for which the species *Balanocarpus heimii, Intsia palembanica, Vatica* sp. (resak) and those species of the genera *Hopea* (giam) and *Shorea* (balau) with heavy hardwood timber were utilised. Various other species, and principally those *Shorea* spp. (meranti) with light timber, were being exploited but the emphasis was out of all proportion to their percentage representation in the forest. The demand for timber increased annually during the thirties and with medium powered sawmills replacing the hand sawyer in increasing numbers in many districts, the utilisation for timber of many species previously converted into firewood or girdled during improvement fellings was taking place. The proportion felled of non-naturally durable timber to naturally durable timber or heavy hard wood was still low. After the 1939-45 World War there was brisk demand for timber of all categories, both world-wide and local, and there was a continued increase in output and decided increase in species utilised as sawmill production improved. With the increased costs of labour, more modern methods of extraction, namely that of winch lorries and forest roads instead of hauling by buffalo, were also introduced and accordingly it became economically necessary to remove all utilisable trees in one operation. The number of economic species and utilisable trees removed was, however, still dependent on the distance of the forest operation from the market. Today in Malaya, exploitation still tends to be selective on the thinly populated and distant East Coast and even in Pahang where there is a long rail haul to Singapore or long road haul to the sawmills and consuming centre in Kuala Lumpur. In Kedah in the north west, however, where the population is high and area of good forest relatively scarce, exploitation is very nearly complete. Table 2 not only illustrates clearly the increased demand for timber during the past thirty years but the increased proportion of the non-durable timbers utilised.

The above development in forest utilisation has, apart from the introduction of sawmills and the more modern methods of extraction, been brought about by an increased botanical and wood technological knowledge of the species, extensive research into the timber qualities of a wide range of species and in particular to the research and modern developments of wood preservation, and last, but by no means least, the general education of the Malayan public into a rational use of the various types of timber. Important Malayan

TABLE 2

Volume of timber exploited in tons of 50 cu. ft. solid†

(taken from Annual Reports of the Malayan Forest Department)

Year	Class of Species for Royalty Rates				
	Mainly Balanocarpus heimii, Intsia palembanica, Vatica spp., heavy Hopea and Shorea spp., Mesua ferrea.	Mainly Dipterocarpus spp., Dryobalanops spp., Hopea spp., Ochanostachys amentacea, Scorodocarpus borneensis, some Shorea spp., Tetramerista glabra.	Mainly Anisoptera spp., Calophyllum spp., Cratoxylon arborescens, Dilenia spp., Dyera costulata, Sapotaceae, some Shorea spp., Sindora spp.	Others	Ratio of Heavy Hardwoods to remainder.
	(Heavy Hardwoods or naturally durable timbers)	(Lighter Hardwoods and not naturally durable timbers)			
1925	35,561	18,198	50,850	2,997	1 : 2.0
1935	56,262	141,828			1 : 2.5
1939	125,449	369,393			1 : 2.9
1950	95,151	638,246			1 : 6.7
1955	86,090	1,021,154			1 : 11.8

examples of the improved utilisation of the forest are *Koompassia malaccensis* (kempas), an extremely common large emergent tree of the jungle and which was left in the forest until post-war when it was found to be extremely suitable for railway sleepers when treated with a preservative, and *Dipterocarpus* spp. (keruing) which are now not only one of Malaya's most important 'species' for treated sleepers but produce the most preferred timber for export to the United Kingdom where it is used also in railway wagon construction. Formerly, owing to the siliceous timber of the former and resinous timber of the latter, hand sawing was difficult and species producing both these timbers were not, or only rarely, exploited. The introduction of sawmills and preservatives have completely changed the situation.

Silvicultural Developments

It might be asked at this stage why the emphasis has been on forest exploitation, extraction and utilisation in a paper on tropical silviculture, and especially when it was stated in the first paragraph that silviculture should not be dictated by nor be subservient to forest management. In dealing, however, with tropical vegetation, and in particular with natural vegetation, this is to a certain extent unavoidable. It is not possible initially to base silvicultural prescriptions upon ecological studies as these have probably not yet yielded final results, even if they have been initiated, and further, as has been shown, the degree of forest utilisation and exploitation changes enormously. Malaya is a good country to take as an example of silvicultural development in the

---

† Figures include volume of timber exploited in peat swamp forest.

humid tropics since forestry in its truest sense, namely that of the art of cultivating trees, has probably been practised here longer in the original forest than elsewhere. The rate of development also has probably been faster due to the extremely rapid opening up of the whole country with excellent lines of communications, and to the large local market for timber, a demand which is far greater than in most tropical, and greater than in many non-tropical, countries.

In Malaya the early interest was mainly with *Palaquium gutta, Balanocarpus heimii* and *Intsia palembanica,* and silviculture was concerned with improvement fellings in favour of the former, wherever this species occurred, and with the enrichment of the forest with the latter two species, species with naturally durable timber and which are fairly slow growing and to a certain extent shade tolerant. Regeneration was often very difficult and enrichment planting along lines was often resorted to. This was not only expensive but in general proved entirely unsuccessful.

Subsequently fellings, called Regeneration Improvement Fellings, were carried out departmentally or by contractors where there was a demand for firewood with the object of favouring the saplings and immature trees of the more valuable species, most of which were members of the family *Dipterocarpaceae* and which generally are light demanding. These were carried out prior to the removal of the economic crop and were directed not only at breaking up the canopy but at freeing the favoured saplings and regeneration through the cutting of unwanted competing undergrowth. The fellings were spread over 5 to 8 years, and in brief usually consisted of the following: —

YEAR	OPERATION
n − 1	Unmarked pole felling of unwanted species.
n	First marked seeding felling of unwanted species.
n + 1 to 3	First cleaning.
n + 2 to 4	Second marked seeding felling of unwanted species.
n + 4 to 6	Marked final felling of economic species.
n + 5 to 7	Cleaning after final felling.

Prior to 1926 the felling period was usually about five years, being subsequently extended to seven years. In the latter case the cleaning after the first seeding felling was only done if necessary, but a cleaning after the second seeding felling was always carried out with final felling only taking place if successful regeneration had been shown to be present during the cleaning. The cleaning in the early stages was usually complete and was done whether regeneration was present or not in the mistaken belief that this would assist seedling regeneration to develop in a fruit year. It was also generally believed that most regeneration originated from seedlings arising after the opening of the canopy and not from 'suppressed' regeneration already on the ground. Research results and general observations, however, were gradually casting doubt on this hypothesis and also on the need for so many cleanings, which it was felt continually set back the succession and encouraged creeper tangles which were worse for the regeneration than most of the woody saplings of equal size of the unwanted species.

The forced absence of cleanings during the war years of 1942-45 and the rapid development of sawmill conversion and mechanical extraction revolutionised the silvicultural operations carried out post-war.   Observations were widespread that regeneration, principally of the *Shorea* species producing a light weight grade of timber (meranti), had not suffered in the least for want of cleanings, in fact looked better for the competition undergone (Walton 1948). In addition, sawmill conversion, a big increase in the demand for timber and developments in wood preservation resulted in the exploitation of many more species.   Mechanical extraction, the cost of making roads and their high cost of maintenance under tropical conditions and the lack of demand for inland firewood made it an economic necessity to exploit the forest in one operation. All these reasons, both ecological and economic, resulted in a shift of silvicultural operations from pre-treatment and a series of fellings to one of a single felling and post-treatment: and the present Malayan Uniform System was born.   The post-treatment consists of poison-girdling of all trees greater than two inches in diameter of uneconomic species and of all commercial trees greater than the minimum felling girth or which are damaged and of bad form. It is certainly a moot point what the decision would have been if it had been found ecologically unsound to remove the economic timber in one operation, since it is probably true to say that it was entirely management problems rather than ecological grounds which forced the change and that it was just fortunate that ecological information did not run contrary to it but supported it.   It was equally fortunate that the silvicultural system in force was elastic enough for the forests to take the change without dire results, and that the present system which favours the quick growing light demanders with light weight non-durable timber and not the slower growing, more shade tolerant, heavier and durable timbers, fitted into the present economic trend.   This has to a certain extent spelled the doom of the formerly preferred heavy hardwooded species with naturally durable timber, but it is expected that some of them will survive in open competition; it is further laid down that more frequent cleaning must be carried out in the early stages in areas with very rich heavy hardwood regeneration and which management has laid down should be developed as heavy hardwood areas.   The present silvicultural system is elastic enough to cater for this.   Some forest officers consider that it has not proved entirely successful for some areas rich in *Dryobalanops aromatica*, a species which is shade tolerant in comparison with the quick growing *Shorea* species, and some method of reducing the sudden change from closed forest conditions to those of full light after final felling and poison girdling may have to be found.   The system, however, is again sufficiently elastic to allow for this, should it be found necessary, by either delaying the poison-girdling after final felling for a few years or by raising the minimum girth of unwanted trees girdled from the standard two inches to one of four or six inches diameter, the poles left being removed in a subsequent cleaning, possibly ten years later during the cleaning after the half chain square sampling stage.

Systematic linear sampling at all stages has been introduced as a guide to treatment, rather than the earlier sampling which was little more than a survey of results obtained.   Milliacre sampling of seedling regeneration less than five feet in height has been introduced to assess the amount of regeneration on the ground prior to an area being opened for felling.   In practice it is unfortunate to have to record that management problems frequently force an area to be opened for felling when sampling has shown that seedling regeneration of the desirable species is probably inadequate and when a delay of a few years might remedy the deficiency.   Quarter chain square and half chain square sampling was introduced for sampling the stocking and dominance classification of desirable species in the regenerated crop about five and ten years respectively after the end of final felling with a view to deciding on treatment.

Extensive sampling of this nature naturally presupposes a knowledge of the economic species in all stages of development, and adequate funds and staff, both subordinate and supervisory, to carry out the sampling and the treatment.   The first problem has largely been overcome in Malaya though is possibly still the major stumbling block in some countries, and funds have generally been adequate; however, the number of senior staff to supervise the annually increasing acreage of regeneration operations is becoming inadequate, especially so now that more and more of the annual feiling is taking place in the forest estate and the full annual coupe under sustained yield management is being taken up.   Some simplification of supervisory measures or reduction in the number of cleanings may be unavoidable.

The current silvicultural and ecological problems of interest to this Symposium are: (i) to devise a satisfactory sampling system for the study of the development of the regenerated forest in its later stages and the treatment if any that will be necessary, practical and economic, and (ii) to determine the existence in lowland evergreen rain forest of any distinct associations, since these may require modified treatment as may be the case with the recognised *Dryobalanops aromatica* consociation.   It must not be forgotten that the Malayan Uniform System was evolved primarily for those areas rich in the species of *Shorea* which produce a light weight grade of timber, species which are fast growing, light demanding and able to withstand considerable competition in the early stages.

Conclusion

Malayan forestry, in the short span of forty or so years, has thus gone a long way to tackling the problem of converting natural forest of what was thought to be poorly stocked in the few economic species of the day to one which it is expected will carry a more uniform crop and with a volume at

140

least four times as great and with fewer unwanted species on a rotation of about seventy years.   Malaya has been extremely fortunate that most of the economic species of today regenerate fairly freely, which is not the case in West Africa with a few exceptions nor in tropical America, and further, that the natural forests in this region have a one-family-predominance of large trees of which the majority of species have valuable timber which can be grouped for marketing into relatively few grades.

In conclusion, the various stages of development and problems arising which have led to the present stage of silvicultural progress in Malaya have in brief been as follows, and though it is doubtful, I consider, whether other countries in the region will be able to by-pass any of them, the time they take to develop a satisfactory silvicultural system may certainly be shorter.

1. Selective logging and creaming of the forest for a few naturally durable timbers.

2. Establishment of a Forest Department and appointment of senior staff.

3. Recruitment and initial training of junior staff.

4. Enactment of a Forest Law, adoption by Government of a Forest Policy and assurance of funds to implement it.

5. Initiation of botanical research to increase knowledge at all stages of plant development (taxonomic and autecological studies).

6. Exploration, timber cruising and forest reservation.

7. Initiation of timber research on the timber properties and qualities of the numerous species.

8. Establishment of rate of growth and silvicultural treatment plots and proper assessment of field observations.

9. Establishment of simple silvicultural system for the regeneration of the forest and implemented by simple Management Plans.

10. Sawmill research is started to introduce modern or to improve existing sawmill designs and to improve methods of exploitation and extraction.   The number of species utilised are greatly increased.

11. Research into timber preservation to increase and improve use of naturally non-durable timbers.

12. Development of local demand for timber and overseas markets.

13. The training of junior and intermediate staff is expanded and improved, and the number of staff enlarged.

14. The laying down of treatment plots in the regenerated crop.

From the Malayan example it appears that the essential quality of a silvicultural 'system' during the conversion period of natural forest is that it should be sufficiently elastic to enable the unavoidable and unforeseen changes to take place as necessary, changes brought about by management, economics, ecological studies or timber research and which are likely to be far greater in effect and more frequent than when a stable forest estate has been attained and the second rotation has been reached.

References

BURKHILL, I. H. 1935—'A Dictionary of the Economic Products of the Malay Peninsula'. London.

RICHARDS, P. W. 1952—'Tropical Rain Forest'. University Press, Cambridge.

SCHIMPER, A. F. W. 1903—'Plant geography upon a physiological basis'. Translated by W. R. Fisher. Oxford.

STEENIS, C. G. G. J. VAN 1949—'Flora Malesiana'. Series I, Vol. 4, x.

WALTON, A. B. 1948—'Some considerations for the future management and silvicultural treatment of Malayan forests'. Malay. Forester XI; 68-74.

WYATT-SMITH, J. 1949—'A note on tropical lowland evergreen rain-forest in Malaya'. Malay. Forester XII; 58-64.

2. METHODS USED FOR THE ECOLOGICAL STUDY OF MALAYAN FOREST VEGETATION

by

J. WYATT-SMITH

THIS subject was not only discussed at the 1956 UNESCO sponsored symposium on 'Study of Tropical Vegetation' in Ceylon after the delivery of an excellent paper on the subject by van Steenis (1958), but on various other occasions in connection with many of the papers during the three days that the symposium was held. Unfortunately no recommendations of standardisation or modifications of existing methods for the humid tropics was made other than that the method should depend on the purpose of the survey (UNESCO 1958), and it is extremely fortunate that the subject is one of the main topics of discussion at this second symposium sponsored by UNESCO in Indonesia.

Greig-Smith (1957) in his excellent book, 'Quantitative Plant Ecology' makes several pertinent statements which it would be well to ponder over in any discussion on this subject. He opens his preface with the words:

'Change from a qualitative to quantitative approach is characteristic of the development of any branch of science.'

He continues later in the same opening paragraph that:

'Plant ecology is at present in a transitional stage, and great advances can be expected from the quantitative techniques now being developed.'

A.J. Leslie s a former Director of FAO's
Forest Industries Division.

A second look at the economics of natural management systems in tropical mixed forests

A.J. Leslie

INTEGRATED WATERSHED MANAGEMENT IN THAILAND
the economics are better than they appear

R SCHMIDT

Unasylva 155, Vol.39, 1987/1

● Some years ago I attempted an assessment of the economic possibilities of natural management in the tropical moist forests (Leslie, 1977). It was, I now realize, unduly pessimistic on at least two counts.

First, it exaggerated the extent to which ecological complexity caused natural management to fail and enthusiasm for it to evaporate. There is no doubt that the most common and prominent feature of tropical forest management is the limited success of natural management systems. More often than not, this lack of success is the result of no management at all, rather than the failure of natural management. However, there are enough examples of success with natural management systems for it to be quite clear that technical difficulties are rarely the principal or even significant factors in the failure of management. Enough is known of the ecology of many different tropical forest types for them to be kept in permanent timber production management without destroying their natural structure. Indeed, as Jabil (1983) has pointed out, the lowland dipterocarp forests of Peninsular Malaysia, managed under the Malaysian Uniform System, would by now be providing second rotation yields had they not been cleared for agricultural development.

Second, my conclusion of about a decade ago was incomplete. Natural management is worth pursuing not simply, as I then felt, because of what might be lost if the economic case against it were wrong. At the same time, I suspected that there was something wrong with the economic argument by which natural management was so easily dismissed, and that this something was more than its reliance on the doubtful economics of timber production and other revenue-earning outputs. I now realize that the missing something is a combination of many serious flaws in both the underlying economic theory (Leslie, 1983) and its application in practice. More important, there is now increasing certainty that there is a much stronger economic case in *favour* of natural forest management.

The main purpose of this article, therefore, is to outline the argument through which I have come to that near reversal of a conclusion. Since it is an extension of the 1977 and 1983 papers referred to, I will not repeat their arguments. Rather I will concentrate on the broader and deeper aspects of economic analysis which another ten years have revealed.

Conservation of the tropical forests by management

The conservation of the tropical moist forests could well be, as many conservationists argue, the crucial conservation issue of our time. Mere concern, however, will not lead to conservation. Whatever cures a superficial examination of the visible causes of tropical deforestation might suggest, the underlying reason, as Westoby (1982) so clearly shows, is the extent and depth of poverty in the Third World. Unless that poverty is overcome, the chances of conserving much of the tropical moist forest — by talk, by exhortation, by research or even by directives — are negligible. Unfortunately, present attitudes are not disposed to acknowledge any international responsibility for Third World poverty, and present methods for distributing the trivial amounts of conscience money now devoted to the problem combine with the vested interests opposed to any real change to guarantee Third World poverty a permanent place in the world economy.

Given that, the tropical moist forest can survive only if the land itself is seen by the people concerned to be more valuable retained as forest than converted to any other form of land use. The key to convincing people that forests are worth preserving is industrial utilization of the tropical moist forest under sustained yield management. Contradictory though this may sound to those who see logging as the principal cause of deforestation, there is, under present conditions, no other way.

The conservation of the tropical mixed forest depends largely on the possibility and feasibility of managing it as a sustainable system, maintaining, for the most part,

There is now increasing certainty that there is a much stronger economic case in *favour* of natural forest management.

The key to convincing people that forests are worth preserving is industrial utilization of the tropical moist forest under sustained yield management.

the components of the original ecosystem (Catinot, 1974) through natural regeneration, while providing, at the same time, the raw material supply for a large-scale, rurally located, viable forest products industry.

It is a very tall order. After all, the conditions which have to be met for natural management to be effective (FAO, 1985a) are quite demanding. It must be:
• ecologically and technically possible;
• economically feasible and attractive; and
• socially and politically practicable.

This article is concerned with the second of those conditions: economic feasibility and attractiveness. This presupposes, of course, that the first condition can be met. In the Asian-Pacific region at least, it *is* generally being met with several forest types. Undoubtedly natural management is not so widely nor so well practised as it ought to be, but the reasons for that are more economic than ecological. And they are probably as exaggerated as the ecological difficulties once were.

The economic case against natural management

It is deceptively simple to show that natural management of the tropical mixed forest is not economic. According to the information summarized and evaluated by Masson (1983), tropical mixed forest under natural management seems to require a rotation of 60 years or more to produce a final commercial mean annual increment (M.A.I.) of 0.5 to 2.0 m^3/ha. The silvicultural costs associated with establishing the naturally managed forest range from US$20 to $100/ha. Although not reported by Masson, recurring costs of administration and management would appear to run between $0.5 and $1.5/ha annually.

Judging from the range of stumpage prices for tropical non-coniferous timbers reported in FAO (1985a), $20/$m^3$ would be a generous estimate of the average rate, with perhaps $6/$m^3$ as a realistic lower bound.

From those estimates, the extremes of revenue and cost on a 60-year rotation would be:

Highest revenue:
   M.A.I. 2.0 m^3/ha
   Stumpage $20/$m^3$
Lowest revenue:
   M.A.I. 0.5 m^3/ha
   Stumpage $6/$m^3$
Highest cost:
   Establishment cost $100/ha
   Recurrent costs $1.5/ha/yr
Lowest cost:
   Establishment cost $20/ha
   Recurrent costs $0.5/ha/yr

The corresponding benefit-cost ratios at various discount rates are summarized in Table 1.

From this Table it can be seen that the expected returns, or benefits, from natural management in the tropical moist forest are likely to cover the costs involved only when:
• growth rates and stumpage prices are close to the maximum possible;
• silvicultural and management costs are close to the minimum possible; or
• the discount rate is well below those that are commonly applied, recommended or required in investment appraisals.

It is no wonder then that natural management is so often dismissed on economic grounds. Rarely could it be realistically expected that the peak performance levels needed to make it economic would be achieved and maintained in practice.

This example is, of course, an extremely simplified version of the standard demonstration, but even more sophisticated treatments differ little in principle. The produc-

Glossary of terms used in this article

Benefit-cost ratio: the total economic returns, or benefits, likely to accrue from the implementation of a given project or activity as compared to the costs for undertaking that same activity. A ratio of benefits divided by costs of greater than 1.0 indicates that benefits outweigh costs; a ratio below 1.0 means that costs exceed benefits; a ratio of 1.0 indicates that they are equal.

Discount rate: the rate of interest at which the values of benefits and costs occurring at various future dates are transferred to present value equivalents.

Faustmann formula: a formula for calculating the present (discounted) net value per hectare of the stream of costs incurred and revenues accrued over an infinite series of timber rotations.

Shadow (accounting) prices: non-market prices applied to labour, capital, imported goods, etc. to achieve a more rational valuation and allocation of scarce resources: in a developing country, for instance, a vast shortage of tractors might cause the market price of tractors to be astronomically high, but the application of shadow prices can bring it within reach of potential consumers. The goal of applying shadow, or "accounting", prices is often to spur economic growth.

of view of an individual or corporate forest-owner whose sole interest or responsibility is the financial profitability of timber. But very little of the tropical moist forest fits into this category. Most of it, in fact, is under some form of public or communal ownership. The inadequacies of purely financial appraisals of public investments are so well documented (Gregerson and Contreras, 1979) that further comment would be superfluous. The distinction between a financial appraisal which excludes non-revenue producing benefits and external effects, and the true economic appraisal which includes them is now well-recognized. Moreover, in social benefit-cost analysis, a well-established and quite advanced technique exists for making the step from financial to economic appraisal.

Economic appraisal does more than correct for the omissions. It also substitutes social values for market values where there are grounds for believing the two are substantially different. Moreover, it widens the scope of the analysis well beyond the view of the agency directly responsible. These extensions, however, involve very great theoretical and practical difficulties. In spite of the advances that have been made in the techniques of social valuation (Sinden and Worrell, 1979) some of the difficulties can still be resolved only in quite arbitrary ways. One of these — the discount rate — is alone almost enough to undermine the standard economic formulation applied to forestry.

Before turning to that issue, I should mention two points of theory on which the standard evaluation, even in its most comprehensive form, is on rather weak ground. One is the awkward fact in temperate forestry management that, despite all the economic analysis and preaching over the century or more since the "Faustmann Formula" was finalized, it has had

tivity of the tropical mixed forest under natural management would seem therefore to be too low to be economically viable. This conclusion does indeed have an air of plausibility. Since natural management is very intensive in both its land and capital requirements (Masson, 1983); and since both of these are, almost by definition, in short supply in developing countries, it would seem uneconomic and even irresponsible to lock up large amounts in such a low output activity.

This economic case against natural management, as made above, would therefore be almost unanswerable but for one thing: it is almost entirely wrong.

The weakness of the economic case against natural management

One respect in which the case against natural management is wrong is self-evident: it is far too incomplete. It omits many benefits either because they do not earn revenue or are external to the administering agency for forestry. Evaluation in terms of commercial timber production alone may be a legitimate procedure from the point

Table 1. **Indicative benefit-cost ratios for tropical moist forest under natural management over a range of discount rates**

	Discount rate (%)											
	0	2	4	6	8	10	0	2	4	6	8	10
	Highest revenue						Lowest revenue					
Highest cost	12.6	4.9	1.7	0.6	0.2	0.1	0.95	0.36	0.13	0.04	0.02	0.01
Lowest cost	30.5	19.5	7.0	2.5	0.8	0.4	2.25	0.82	0.28	0.10	0.03	0.01

Source: Estimates above from Masson (1983) and FAO (1985)

very little influence on forest management and policy in practice. Similarly, in tropical forestry, natural management systems are still attempted despite their alleged economic non-viability.

That alone should raise doubts. Economics, at its best, is supposed to explain economic activity. To say that something should *not* be done when it so clearly *is* being done — and, in fact, is preferred — is hardly an explanation. Something must be wrong when the facts do not fit the theory. Normally the theory would be suspect, but in economics, as many critics have pointed out (Seligman, 1962; Karmack, 1983), it is more often the facts that are judged to be wrong.

In practice, non-revenue considerations are in fact taken into account, so that the social benefit-cost ratio is accepted as being greater than 1. In principle, a formal benefit-cost appraisal should be able to confirm this. In practice it cannot. Too much arbitrary quantification of generalized concepts is still needed. It is perhaps better than nothing, but it is far from definitive. All the same, the fact that natural management is supported in practice may be better explained, in part at least, by the inclusion of the non-revenue-producing benefits and externalities associated with it than by disposing of it as an error.

To that can be added a second doubt, on theoretical grounds. This is the implied assumption that a Western individualistic view of rationality is universally valid. In fact, the assumption is almost entirely without foundation. As Myrdal (1972) puts it: "There isn't much point in analysing the economics of tropical forestry in terms of economic theory that may apply in developed countries but may not apply in developing countries." The trouble is that the economic system and the institutional and cultural systems are interdependent.

Unfortunately its weaknesses have not dislodged the neoclassical

Table 2. **Average annual value in US$ per ha of non-revenue-producing services required for benefit-cost ratio:**[1]

	Discount rate (%)					
	0	2	4	6	8	10
Highest revenue/ lowest cost	−39.2	−62.7	−77.6	−30.0	265.9	1 439.2
Highest revenue/ highest cost	−36.9	−54.7	−43.9	105.2	776.3	3 271.4
Lowest revenue/ lowest cost	0.2	-9.2	54.4	242.5	955.7	3 494.1
	−2.2	1.2	20.6	107.5	445.2	1 661.9

Source: Table 1. *Note:* negative values indicate benefit-cost ratios > 1 and positive values indicate ratios < 1.

version from its implicit, self-professed standing as the only true economics. It retains this image by a powerful combination of:

• developing a body of theory whose cumulative intellectual brilliance and logical elegance divert attention from its irrelevance;

• ignoring criticisms or disarming them through subterfuges that twist contradictory evidence into confirmation, or dismissing dissenting views as belonging to special cases;

• monopolizing the teaching of economics and the staffing of economic policy institutions with people schooled in that tradition.

The possibility of an economic appraisal of natural management

It is clearly not enough to demonstrate that the standard economic analysis is almost meaningless. The failure of the case against natural management in the tropical mixed forest does not establish the case *for* it. It has to be shown that natural management systems are:

• economically feasible in themselves; and/or
• they are better than any alternative use for the land and other resources involved.

The first step is to move from the basically financial appraisal underlying the standard evaluation to an appraisal of the economic one. This means bringing into the analysis all the non-revenue aspects and external effects, as Myers (1980) urges, plus looking at the results from a wider point of view than that of the administering agency. In addition, all inputs and outputs should be expressed in monetary units at their social value.

Conceptually each step is logical and simple. In practice the operational difficulties are formidable. Three problems of special significance are worth mentioning: 1) the generality problem; 2) the boundary problem; and 3) the pricing problem.

The generality problem The expected financial results of forest management can be assessed in a general way, independently of forest type or location, without being entirely meaningless. The main financial effect of forest type and location is on stumpage prices. A range of likely average stumpage prices, such as that underlying the estimates summarized in Table 1, can be set wide enough to accommodate nearly all variations.

Such a generalized approach is much less tenable with an economic appraisal. Not only does the unpriced nature of the additional items preclude any sort of averaging, but many of them are also much more specifically related to forest type and location. For instance, the downstream importance of the hydrology of forested catchments will vary with topography and soils. The social value of forests on steep catchments with erodible soils is likely therefore to be higher than that of forests on easier topography with more stable

soils. At the same time, however, the social value of a forested catchment depends on the nature, the extent and the value of the downstream interests which could be affected by the way the forest is managed. Both aspects have to be taken into account in an economic appraisal, and they are so type- and site-specific that any generalized approach must have only limited validity.

Similar difficulties arise with considering wildlife as an output of forest management. The type of forest and the wildlife for which it provides a habitat are closely linked, so that the social value of a tropical mixed forest is extremely type-specific. But the location of the forest relative to population centres and different socio-economic groups also governs the social value of its wildlife. People working agricultural land adjacent to a forest that harbours predatory or crop-destroying wildlife are likely to have a different view of its value than are people living in cities some distance away or hunter communities living in the forest. The forest ecosystem and its location could thus interact in too complex and too specific a way for any generalized economic appraisal to have much meaning.

These qualifications do not necessarily mean, however, that absolutely nothing can be gained from extending the generalized financial appraisal of Table 1 to an economic perspective. One thing which can usefully be done is to demonstrate what increases in returns would be needed to transform the benefit-cost ratios to ratios greater than 1. The values recalculated in this form are presented in Table 2. They indicate the amounts that would have to be credited annually for non-revenue-producing services to make the difference.

Since these are simply transformed versions of the benefit-cost calculations, negative values

correspond to benefit-cost ratios greater than 1 in the financial appraisal and positive values to ratios less than 1. The lowest revenue/highest cost regime would thus be economically feasible if it were generally accepted that, at a discount rate of 4 percent, the total annual value of any relevant combination of services such as watershed protection, landscape, wildlife, gene pools, or yet to be discovered medicinal resources or conservation *per se*, is equivalent to about US$54/ha. At 10 percent the recognized and accepted annual value would have to be about US$3 490/ha.

Again, no great reliance can be placed upon these actual figures, but they do bring out several important principles. The first is that, the higher the revenue from timber production and the lower the cost of management, the more easily the management system will be able to satisfy multiple objectives.

The second is the valuation of the relevant non-revenue services by a form of the consumers' surplus criterion. This means that if a natural management regime delivers a given combination of revenue and non-revenue services accepted as satisfactory, then the value placed on the non-revenue services must be at least equal to any loss incurred on the revenue-earning side. The criterion is not quite so simple as it suggests (Blaug, 1978) and it has had its ups and downs in economic theory. But these are of less concern to the economics of tropical forestry than are two awkward questions that its use raises or dodges: who accepts them and on what basis?

The boundary problem Both of these questions are derived from and compounded by the third principle, summarized in Table 2, which is that the net value to be assigned to or accepted for the non-revenue items depends very largely on the discount rate used in

This economic case against natural management would therefore be almost unanswerable but for one thing: it is almost entirely wrong.

Unfortunately its weaknesses have not dislodged the neo-classical version from its implicit, self-professed standing as the only true economics.

the benefit-cost calculations. It is here that the boundary problem comes in. For instance, there may be wide acceptance in Malaysia or Indonesia that management which protects the habitat of the orang-utan or the white rhinoceros or other significant wildlife, together with watershed services, is worth an implied annual cost of $54/ha. That it is worth an implied cost of $3 500/ha annually would be almost unanimously rejected. Yet conservationists and others in developed countries especially might well feel that protecting such species from extinction is well worth such a price.

From a global point of view the latter valuation could in fact be nearer to the truth. The trouble is that it involves extending the boundaries of the appraisal to cover the world. The near futility of this is obvious. Calls for the conservation of the tropical forests imply that specific developing countries should carry the management costs necessary to satisfy people, mainly in developed countries, for whom costs will occur only if and when species become extinct or ecosystems disappear. Such an unfair distribution of costs to the poor and benefits to the wealthy would have to be backed by an effective and adequate international system of transfer payments. There is no such system at present, nor is there any apparent intention to develop one. Without it, calls for the conservation of the world's tropical forests will, justifiably, continue to go unheeded. And without it, economic appraisal on a world scale is pointless.

However, economic appraisal of natural management in tropical mixed forests has to be extended at least to the national level. Despite technical difficulties, that is feasible. Extension beyond that boundary, although desirable and involving no greater technical difficulty, would, with a few regional exceptions, have no practical significance.

Social values which are of primarily global concern would therefore be taken into account only to the extent that they would have an identifiable national impact.

This unfortunate fact of life simply confirms the point made at the outset. Under present conditions, the conservation of the tropical mixed forests in the interest of mankind as a whole depends on natural management as being an economic proposition for each country which has forests. In that respect, the pricing problem, especially as it relates to the discount rate, is crucial.

The pricing problem The third problem involved in the transition from financial to economic appraisal is that of expressing all the benefits and costs in social values. There are two aspects to this: first, the assessment of a social value for each revenue-affecting item wherever there are reasons for believing that it is not adequately represented by the market price; and second, the assignment of social values to the unpriced, hence non-revenue-affecting items.

The techniques of shadow or accounting prices for establishing social values usually concentrate on the first aspect: the adjustment of market prices. Logically the second aspect is no more than a special case of the accounting price problem with non-existent market prices. The point, however, is of little significance in a generalized appraisal of the economics of tropical forest management since it is only the total social value of an unspecified group of non-revenue items which, as argued earlier, has any relevance.

The idea behind accounting prices is that equilibrium market price in a perfectly competitive market and social value coincide. Therefore, in markets which depart widely from the perfectly competitive structure, it should be possible to estimate social value by calculating the price which would prevail if the market imperfections and distortions were removed. The substitution of accounting prices for actual prices would therefore be appropriate where wage rates were out of line with the actual labour supply or where the domestic prices for outputs or other inputs were held artificially high or low by protectionist policies or subsidies.

Imperfect markets with these and other similar distortions are as common in developing countries as they are in developed ones. An appraisal of the economics of tropical forest management calculated in accounting prices could be very different from one based on actual domestic prices. By how much it does can be gauged from recalculating the benefit-cost ratios of Table 1 in accounting prices. Suppose, for instance, the shadow wage rate is 75 percent of the legal rates paid by government and industrial forestry organizations, while labour accounts for two-thirds of the establishment and annual costs, and the accounting prices for timber are sufficiently higher to give socially valued stumpage rates 20 percent higher. The social costs and revenues would then have the following ranges:

* establishment from $17 to $83/ha
* annual maintenance and management from $0.40 to $1.25/ha/yr
* stumpage prices from $7 to $24/m^3.

Substituting these social values gives benefit-cost ratios running from 70.2 to 0.5 for the best possible outcome compared with 30.0 to 0.4 as the discount rate increases from 0 to 10 percent. For the worst possible case, the corresponding range of benefit-cost ratios is from 5.3 to 0.03, compared with 2.3 to 0.01. That is, the fact of substituting accounting prices for market prices lifts the benefit-cost ratios by a factor of two to three.

Similar substantial improve-

RAIN FOREST IN TAMIL NADU
management is a means of saving it

ments are naturally effected in the social values which would have to be accredited to non-revenue items for natural management to break even. With the highest revenue/lowest cost combination, a positive value would have to be credited: if the discount rate were 10 percent, that would only be 25 percent of the amount needed under the financial appraisal with market prices. For the worst combination, positive social values would have to be credited for all positive discount rates, but at levels of 20 to 25 percent less than under the financial appraisal. Thus, at a 4 percent discount rate where the financial appraisal indicated that the social value of the non-revenue items would need to be about $54/ha/yr for natural management to break even, the corresponding figure under the economic appraisal would be about $42.

Correcting for market imperfections and distortions can clearly make a substantial improvement in the economics of natural management when imperfections keep market prices for inputs higher and output prices lower than their social values. Even so, it is still the discount rate which has the greatest influence in economic feasibility. Since it is the key variable in the economic — or even the financial — analysis of tropical forest management, it is worth a special section (if not a book) to itself.

Time and the rate of interest in natural management

As a general rule, fairly long, if not very long, rotations are required to grow forests to a state of maturity corresponding to the specifications of the goods and services expected of them. Time, therefore, is a major — and often *the* major — input in the forestry production process. During a rotation, a stream of recurrent and intermittent costs and receipts occurs; in anticipatory evaluations, many of these have to be taken for granted for years in advance. Forestry economics has to deal with three aspects of time in the production process:
• the *cost* of time as an input in the production process;
• the *differences* in times of occurrence of the various other inputs and outputs; and
• the increasing *uncertainty* associated with events the further into the future that their occurrence, magnitude and timing have to be anticipated.

Consequently the economics of forestry is dominated by the cost of time and the uncertainties associated with it. The beauty of the Faustmann solution to the problem of time is that it accommodates all three of these aspects in a single figure and a single operation. Time, as an input, is accounted for by compounding interest on a cost or a revenue item from the date it occurs until the end of the rotation (or series of rotations), or by discounting it to the start of the rotations. Differences in the time distribution of costs and receipts are eliminated by compounding or discounting them to the same point in time; the interest rate at which this is done can be selected to incorporate the uncertainty.

Much of forest economics is therefore concerned with pre-investment assessments of the expected economic performance of options in forest policy and management. In that, the Faustmann approach is not only theoretically correct (Gaffney, 1957), but is indispensable. From that, it is clear that the rate of interest at which the appraisals are made is the most important factor in determining the performance of a given option or the comparative performance of a set of alternative options.

How powerful the interest rate can be is evident from the example whose results are summarized in Tables 1 and 2. Doubling the interest (discount) rate from 4 percent to 8 percent reduces the benefit-cost ratio by as much as it is increased by a fourfold reduction in establishment costs. Or, to put it another way, it is increased by five to 20 times the value which has to be credited to non-revenue services for natural management to break even in an economic appraisal.

Fourfold increases in productivity or fourfold reductions in costs are not easy to achieve, so it is not hard to see why compound interest has earned the reputation in forestry as a tyrant. It seems, as tyrants do, to dictate and to denounce. It dictates the adoption of plantation systems of high-yielding species on short rotations, and denounces those who persist with natural management systems for an irresponsible disregard of economic reality (Clawson, 1983). But, in reality, it does not necessarily lead to such conclusions. Everything, in fact, depends on the rate of interest. Relatively high rates of interest certainly favour short rotations and plantations, but at low rates the reverse could just as easily apply. Treloar and Morison (1962) showed this switchover effect quite strikingly in their comparison of the financial performance of forestry and agriculture in western Australia. If the same sort of switch applies with natural management as against plantations, then there is less justification for the supine acceptance of compound interest as the Achilles heel of natural management.

To test the possibility, the simplified example used earlier to illustrate the economies of natural management was taken as the basis for a comparison with a representative plantation regime. Benefit-cost ratios for both under a range of discount rates are summarized in Table 3.

A switch clearly occurs. Up to a discount rate of around 6 percent the natural management regime offers a better financial return than the plantation regime. Above 6 percent the position is reversed. Tests with other combinations of cost and revenue values suggest that the switchover rate is in the 5-6 percent range.

This, it is worth noting, occurs in a purely financial context. If non-revenue considerations — which affect natural management regimes much more than plantations — are included, the switchover rate would move higher. That, however, does not matter. The point is that, up to a certain discount rate, the chances are that natural management is a better option in tropical forestry on financial grounds alone. Up to that point, there is no need to invoke the non-revenue advantages of natural

Table 3. **Benefit-cost ratios for tropical mixed forest under natural management and for tropical forest plantation over a range of discount rates**

Regime	Discount rate (%)					
	0	2	4	6	8	10
Natural management	12.3	4.8	1.8	0.6	0.2	0.1
Plantation	1.3	0.9	0.7	0.5	0.3	0.2

	Natural	Plantation
Mean annual increment (m³/ha/yr)	1.8	18
Rotation (yrs)	60	20
Stumpage price (US$/ha)	15	5
Establishment costs (US$/ha)	—	—
Initial	50	1 000
2nd rotation	—	50
3rd rotation	—	100
Annual costs (US$/ha/yr)	1	1

systems or to resort to shadow-pricing to improve the standing of natural management relative to other forms of forest or land use. It all depends on the discount rate.

That raises, of course, the question of what is the correct discount rate to use in the evaluation of options in forestry. So crucial is the question that one would expect it to have been settled long ago, decisively and conclusively. But the fact is that it has not — neither for forestry nor for any other time-intensive form of economic activity. Actually, there is barely any agreement, let alone unanimity, on what is even an *appropriate* rate. Authoritative support can be found for almost any plausible rate from zero upwards.

Solow (1974), for instance, tends toward the zero-interest implication of Ramsey's argument that it is "ethically indefensible for society to discount future utilities" (Ramsey, 1928). The underlying idea that the interests of future generations are not any less significant than those of the present generation is further developed at some length in Rawls (1971). It is a view of intergenerational relationships, consistent with the attitudes of Melanesian and Polynesian societies, confirming that the conventional Western economic philosophy is by no means of universal vaῑdity. With that sort of support, the forest rent doctrine and the conservation view, both of which imply zero interest, are not quite so irrational as many forest economists have assumed.

The zero interest view has not convinced many economists, but there are certainly some who feel that any discounting of the future should be at relatively low rates. Böhm-Bawerk (1929), for instance, argued that we "systematically undervalue our future wants and the means which serve to satisfy them". Much the same point was made by Eckstein, quoted by Peterson (1977): "You cannot really determine your responsibility to unborn generations by using a discount rate which gives priority to current consumption." Such views are quite consistent with the position long held by silviculturists. If compound interest has to be applied in forestry, then the appropriate rate is a relatively low one.

The validity of a special low rate of interest for forestry, together with the extreme of zero interest, is rejected by most economists. That does not prove that the idea is wrong. Indeed it gets some interesting support from Marglin's (1967) investigations of the appropriate discount rate for public investment. His formulation of a synthetic discount rate led, to his evident surprise, to the finding that the appropriate rate decreases with the increasing length of the economic life of the project.

This striking confirmation of the silvicultural case for a special low rate of interest for forestry seems to have gone unnoticed in economic commentary. It is not hard to see why. By far the majority of economists believe that, if there is a social discount rate, then it is very closely related to interest rates applying in the private sector. To admit time-intensive projects as exceptions would weaken that position, so the Marglin paradox is best ignored.

The majority opinion thus favours some form of opportunity cost of capital as the appropriate rate for forestry as a public investment (Walker, 1983). The opportunity cost is then derived from the investment or consumption in the private sector displaced by the diversion of the funds to public investment. The general implication seems to be that the correct rate is thus much higher than what other views would lead to (Baumol, 1983; Fraser, 1985). In effect, this view rejects the Ramsey ethic regarding the rights of one generation relative to succeeding generations.

What is important about these widely differing verdicts on the vital question of the interest rate is that, in the final analysis, they are opinions only. The high interest rates which act against natural management systems in forestry, and against forestry in general, have no more basis than somebody's opinion. Repeated assertion, majority opinion or officially set, they are still no more than opinion.

Another remarkable feature of the discussion over the appropriate rate of interest is that, apart from zero, an actual rate is rarely specified. Occasionally a range is quoted (Fedkiw, 1960; Fraser, 1985), or an absolute lower level is implied (Baumol, 1983), or an arbitrary formula for calculating the rate is offered (Marglin, 1967; Little and Mirlees, 1968). Some treasury departments and institutions such as the World Bank do set quite specific rates to be used for the appraisal of public investment options, and they seem to range from 7 to 11 percent. But that still reflects only an opinion, and is therefore debatable, as Sugden and Williams (1978) point out.

More often, however, and especially in forestry, the problem is disposed of in phrases such as "at an acceptable rate of interest" (Worrell, 1956), or "the landowner's opportunity cost of capital" (Hyde, 1980), or it is dodged altogether because of the lack of any generally agreed way of choosing the rate (Gregerson and Contreras, 1979). On the face of it, this is a much less satisfactory way than the treasury or bank-set rate. Actually, however, that is not so; it is much more honest and realistic in that it

highlights the purely subjective nature of the choice.

All the same, it could be argued that there must be some limits to the range within which the rate must lie. At the lower end there could well be: zero. But that does not resolve the problem at all. It leaves the way wide open, as Hiley (1930) noted, for choosing the rate of interest to produce whatever predetermined result is wanted. If there is to be any point in bringing economic considerations into forest policy and management, there has to be a less permissive basis for the interest rate than that.

The problem is what basis to choose. If zero interest is rejected as a general rate for all intergenerational choice, then how far above zero is a generationally neutral or fair rate? The clue may lie in the opportunity cost of capital to the present generation. This is usually — although not altogether justifiably — established from the consumption of investment displaced from the private sector by the social investment. This rate, incidentally, is visualized as a marginal rate, not the average or the highest rates in the private sector. There is, naturally enough, little agreement, except in algebraic terms, on what the rate is or how it might be determined. Algebraic values are, of course, useless for appraisals in practice, so empirical evidence is needed if this approach is to provide the base for the social discount rate.

Some such studies dispel any notion that the opportunity cost of capital, established in this way, would be quite high. Anderson (1983) refers to a study of private sector bond yields in the United States over the period 1960 to 1978, which showed a real rate of return over the long run of around 2.5 percent. Risvand (1984) found that the real rate of interest in Denmark over the 160 years from 1819 to 1979 averaged 2 to 4 percent with no sustained tendency to move up

or down over that period. He also found, incidentally, that forestry gave a better long-term real rate of return than the rates earned on bonds or from bank interest. Since these are average rates, the marginal opportunity cost could be expected to be somewhat lower. In the light of such evidence, treasury or bank set rates of 7 to 11 percent must either be unrealistically high, or inclusive of inflation. Adjusting them for inflation puts them in the same 2 to 4 percent category.

One way out of the maze might be to follow what Prest and Turvey (1965) describe as the standard procedure and simply select a rate from those ruling at the time. It is an attractive approach, not least because it seems to dodge the theoretical difficulties. But there are catches in it. For a start, it is still entirely subjective. All that the procedure does is to restrict the range of rates from which the choice can be made. Then the ruling rates still have an inflationary content. The range of real rates, corrected for such distortions, could easily include the switchover rate, leaving the way wide open to choosing a rate on either side of it, which gives whatever result happens to be wanted.

Conclusion

Three points of considerable significance to tropical forest management emerge from this review. They are:
* the economic prospects of natural management are greatly, and perhaps primarily, governed by the rate of interest projected over time;
* the choice of the rate to use is almost entirely subjective;
* there is little in economic theory or practice to guide or constrain that choice, but the indications are that the appropriate rate is more likely to be at the lower end of any plausible range of real rates than at the upper end.

These findings go a long way toward resolving doubts about the economic feasibility of natural management in the tropical moist forest. It is almost undeniable that natural systems on the whole cannot compete at high rates of interest with alternatives in forestry such as industrial plantations or with alternative forms of land use. The improvements in growth rates and yields, or the increases in average stumpage values needed to overcome the effects of compounding costs or discounting revenues at high rates are unattainable or highly improbable. The extension of the appraisal to a purely economic basis hardly helps either. Even assuming that the net social return from the non-revenue services will be higher under natural management than under alternative forms of forest or land management, the extra value which has to be credited to natural management at high interest rates goes well beyond the credible.

This verdict seems to have been accepted too easily, both by those inclined to natural management and by those who advocate the plantation and agricultural alternatives. The way that acceptance has been won has all the marks of a confidence trick. High rates are needed to demonstrate the uneconomic basis of natural management. At low rates, the reverse could well apply. This important point is rarely referred to in the appraisals which show the economic inefficiency of natural management, while the dubious validity of high rates is never mentioned. Such concealment of vital information is not exactly honest.

It is not, therefore, necessary to defend natural management on the grounds, as I did in 1977, that the economic case against it could be wrong. The case *is* wrong, and not simply because of its inherent theoretical and practical weaknesses. It is wrong because, at the interest

rates which theoretical considerations and empirical studies suggest should be used in forest economics, natural management of the tropical mixed forest is likely to be a better economic and financial proposition than alternative land uses or management systems.

It is actually not quite so straightforward as that, for two reasons. The first is that if long-term, real rates of interest are expected to be several times higher in the future than they have been in the past, and that if they can also be decisively linked to higher social rates, then the economic efficiency of natural management would be greatly reduced. The onus of proof for that lies, however, with those who question natural management on economic grounds. There are few signs as yet to suggest that changes of such a magnitude are coming.

The second is that a demonstration of the efficiency of natural management in capital utilization does not necessarily confirm a similar efficiency in terms of land use. In other words, natural management could still be relatively expensive in its use of land. The point is debatable: the distinction between land and capital virtually disappears when long periods of time are involved. But even if this factor is allowed some validity, any such disparity would tend to be corrected by the longer-term advantages that natural management has over alternative land-use systems. For instance, some timbers and some non-revenue services are unique to the natural tropical mixed forests. They cannot be produced elsewhere or other than by natural management and they cannot be adequately replaced by substitutes.

The market outlook for them is, therefore, the direct opposite of the weak prospects for most of the products of the agricultural and plantation alternatives (Malaysia, 1986). In such circumstances, the relative economic prospects for

natural management, no matter how they are measured, can only improve.

In effect, these reservations act to strengthen the conclusion that natural management of the tropical mixed forest, wherever it is ecologically feasible, is also, on its own merits, economically preferable. ■

ANDERSON. D.A. Comments on
1983 J.L. Walker, National forest planning: an economic critique. *In* R.A. Sedjo, ed. *Governmental intervention, social needs and the management of US forests,* pp. 247-300. Baltimore, Resources for the Future, Johns Hopkins Univ. Press.

BAUMOL. W.J. As quoted by
1983 J.L. Walker. *In* R.A. Sedjo, ed. *Governmental intervention, social needs and the management of US forests.* (Chapter 7). Baltimore, Resources for the Future, Johns Hopkins Univ. Press.

BLAUG, M. *Economic theory in*
1978 *retrospect.* Cambridge, UK, Cambridge Univ. Press.

BÖHM-BAWERK, E. VON
1959 *Capital and interest.* Vol. 2. (Translation of 1929 ed.) Illinois, USA, South Holland Publ.

CATINOT. R. Le présent et
1974 l'avenir des forêts tropicales humides. *Bois et forêts des tropiques,* (154): 3-16.

CLAWSON, M. Problems of
1983 public investment in forestry. *In* R.A. Sedjo, ed. *Governmental intervention, social needs and the management of US forests.* (Chapter 7). Baltimore, Resources for the Future, Johns Hopkins Univ. Press.

FAO. *Forest product prices,*
1985a *1965-1984.* FAO Forestry Paper No. 61. Rome, FAO.

FAO. *Tropical Forestry Action*
1985b *Plan*. Rome, FAO.

FEDKIW, J. Financial manage-
1960 ment of large forest
ownerships. *Yale Univ.
School of Forestry Bull.*,
66: 1-45.

FRASER, G.A. *Benefit-cost*
1985 *analysis of forestry
investments*. Victoria, BC,
Canadian For. Serv.,
Pacific For. Centre.

GAFFNEY, M.M. *Concepts of*
1957 *financial maturity of
timber and other assets*.
Raleigh, N.C., A.F. Info.
Series No. 62. Dept
Agric. Economics, North
Carolina State Coll.

GREGERSON, H.M. &
1979 CONTRERAS, A.H.
*Economic analysis of
forestry products*. FAO
Forestry Paper No. 17.
Rome, FAO.

HILEY, W.F. *The economics of*
1930 *forestry*. Oxford, Oxford
Univ. Press.

HYDE, W.F. *Timber supply,*
1980 *land allocation and
economic efficiency*.
Baltimore, Johns Hopkins
Univ. Press.

JABIL, M. Problems and
1983 prospects in tropical rain
forest management for
sustained yield. *Mal. For.*,
46 (4): 398-408.

KARMACK, A.M. *Economics*
1983 *and the real world*.
Oxford, Blackwell.

LESLIE, A.J. Where contradic-
1977 tory theory and practice
co-exist. *Unasylva*, 29
(115): 2-17.

LESLIE, A.J. *The economic*
1983 *evaluation of tropical
forestry*. Gympie,
Queensland, Australia,
Workshop on Tropical
Forest Management,
ADAB/Dev. Studies
Centre, A.N.U.

LITTLE, I.M.D. & MIRLEES,
1968 J.A. *Manual of industrial
project analysis in
developing countries. Vol.
II. Social cost-benefit
analysis*. Paris, Development Centre, OECD.

MALAYSIA, Ministry of Primary
1986 Industries. International
Seminar on Commodities.
Kuala Lumpur.

MARGLIN, S.A. *Public invest-*
1967 *ment criteria*. London,
George Allen & Unwin.

MASSON, J.A. *Management of*
1983 *tropical mixed forests:*

*preliminary assessment of
present status*. FO:
Misc./83/17. Rome, FAO.

MYERS, N. The present status
1980 and future prospects of
tropical moist forests.
Env. Cons., 7 (2):
101-114.

MYRDAL, G.K. *Against the*
1972 *stream*. London, Macmillan.

PETERSON, R.M. The role of
1977 interest groups in policy
formulation. *In* F.J.
Convery & J.E. Davis,
eds. *Centres of influence
and US forest policy*.
Durham, North Carolina,
Duke Univ. School of
For. and Env. Studies.

PREST, A.R. & TURVEY, R.
1965 Cost-benefit analysis: a
survey. *Econ. J.*: re-
printed in *Surveys of
economic theory. Vol. III*
as Chapter XIII. London,
American Economic
Association & Royal
Econ. Soc., Macmillan.

RAMSEY, F.P. A mathematical
theory of saving. *Econ.
J.*, 38.

RAWLS, J. *A theory of justice*.
1971 Boston, Harvard Univ.
Press.

RISVAND, J. Rente Inflation og
1984 Skat I Skovbrugrt.
Skoven, 8: 215-7.

SELIGMAN, B.B. *Main
1962, currents in modern
1971 economics*. Chicago, Free
Press of Glencoe,
Quadrangle Books
Edition.

SINDEN, J.A. & WORRELL,
1979 A.C. *Unpriced values*.
New York, Wiley.

SOLOW, R.M. The economics
1974 of resources or the
resources of economics.
Am. Econ. Rev., 64 (2):
1-14.

SUGDEN, R. & WILLIAMS, A.
1978 *The principles of practical
cost-benefit analysis*.
Oxford, Oxford Univ.
Press.

TRELOAR, D.W.G. &
1962 MORISON, I.C. *Economic
comparisons of forestry
and agriculture*. Perth,
Ag. Econ. Res. Report
No. 3, Inst. of Agric.,
Univ. Western Australia.

WALKER, J.L. National forest
1983 planning: an economic
critique. *In* R.A. Sedjo,
ed. *Governmental
interventions, social needs
and the management of*

US forests. (Chapter 8).
Baltimore, Resources for
the Future, Johns
Hopkins Univ. Press.

WESTOBY, J.C. *Halting tropical
1982 deforestation: the role of
technology*. Draft for
Office of Tech. Assess-
ment, Congress of the
United States, Wash-
ington, D.C.

WORRELL, A.C. Optimum
1956 intensity of forest land
use on a regional basis.
For. Sci., 2 (3): 199-240.

Commonw. For. Rev. **58**, 2. (1979)

FOREST INDUSTRIES FOR
SOCIO-ECONOMIC DEVELOPMENT†

By JACK C. WESTOBY*

The Congress is about to start on the discussion of *Forests for Industrial Development*. I have been invited to open the proceedings in this discussion area by speaking to you about *Forest Industries for Socio-Economic Development*. Those of you who were with us six years ago in Buenos Aires will recognize that this Congress starts where the last one left off. The central theme six years ago was *Forests and Socio-Economic Development*. The central theme here in Jakarta is: *Forests for People*.

Are these not one and the same thing? – forests for socio-economic development and forests for people. Are we not in danger of treading again the ground we trod in Buenos Aires six years ago?

There would certainly seem to be some kind of relationship between the two. But how close that relationship is depends on what we mean by socio-economic development, and who we mean by the people.

If this were a Congress of economists or sociologists, I am sure it would be very difficult for us to agree about what constitutes socio-economic development. But we are neither. Nor are we a Congress of politicians. We are simply foresters, but sensible foresters. And because we are simply sensible foresters, I think we shall have no difficulty in reaching agreement on one or two simple propositions.

A nation can be said to be developing economically if its capacity to produce goods and services is expanding. We can go further and say that a nation is developing socio-economically if the goods and services which it is producing correspond to the real needs of its people, and if the expanded output of goods and services is so distributed that the most urgent of those needs are satisfied first, and in an equitable manner.

In other words, socio-economic development has three elements: productive forces which are expanding, output which matches real needs, distribution which ensures that real needs are met.

Does this sound reasonable to you? I hope so.

Some of you may wonder what I mean by 'real needs'. Since we are neither economists, sociologists nor politicians, we do not have to spend a long time arguing about this, either. Real needs are, first and foremost, food: next, clothing and shelter: then, elementary health and education services. I would not argue that this is a comprehensive list of real needs. But these are the basic ones. Only when we can see that more and more people are getting more and more of these basic needs satisfied can we talk about socio-economic development. The fact is that socio-economic development, like the giraffe, is hard to describe and hard to measure, but easy to recognise. Conventional measuring rods serve not at all. Per capita gross domestic product tells you very little about socio-economic development. Nor, for that matter, do most of the ingenious parameters contrived in an attempt to measure welfare. For what use is it to double the number of hospital beds per million if all those extra beds are in the capital and are accommodating only expatriates and the indigenous elite?

Indeed, one of the reasons why yardsticks like per capita GDP have fallen recently into disrepute (though not into disuse) is precisely because it has become obvious to all observers that, in a number of countries where this yardstick has risen, the number, and the

† Guest Speaker's address. Session for Industrial Development, Eighth World Forestry Congress, Jakarta, Indonesia, 1978.
* Formerly Director, Programme Coordination and Operations, Foresty Department, FAO.

proportion, of people whose basic needs remain unsatisfied has not diminished but has risen.

While it is true that, for most countries in the underdeveloped world, the post-war decades have brought a disappointing degree of economic growth, with but little of that growth translated into social progress, this is not because the development theorists have never revised their ideas, have all along clung grimly to outworn formulae. On the contrary, the development theorists have frequently been able to recognise failure when they saw it. They have shown themselves more than willing, like good family doctors, to change the prescription when the old medicine was plainly not doing any good. On the other hand, they have always been reluctant to admit that their earlier medicine had served only to make the sick patient sicker, and to increase his vulnerability to a whole range of new diseases.

Yes, development fashions have changed over the last three decades, and that is why gradually the files, the archives, the case-books of the development establishment – which consists of the multi- and bi-lateral development and financing agencies, with their supporting theorists in the universities and the foundations, never forgetting their protégés in the planning ministries of the underdeveloped world – the files of the development establishment have come to resemble the private cemetery of a fantastic zoo, a cemetery stuffed with the corpses of wild geese, lame ducks, red herrings, white elephants and dead horses.

It would be instructive to follow, step by step, the many changes in development fashions over the last three decades. But even if I had the time, I do not think that you would have the patience. Even so, one or two backward glances may not be out of place.

The multilateral agencies, which form the core of the development establishment, were in the first post-war years staffed by a very odd mixture: the usual quota of nominees of foreign offices, planted to make sure that the new agencies did not get out of line; a sprinkling of cosmopolitan floaters, survivors from the wreckage of pre-war international institutions; and an enthusiastic leaven of liberal humanists, convinced that more international cooperation was one way of making the world safer and better for all. They firmly believed in human progress: temporary setbacks there might be, but overall the march of man was upward and onward. Indeed, their vision of the world was of underdeveloped countries struggling to emerge from the swamps of backwardness on to the dry land of takeoff, and then up the slopes towards affluence. Thus all the nations, rich and poor, were straggled across the countryside, like a cross-country race. But they were all running essentially the same race. How did those in front come to be in front? Because they had what the others lacked: capital, skills, know-how. Only transmit some of these from those in front to those behind and the stragglers would start to catch up. The rich countries were parsimonious with their money, but they were prodigal with advice. So experts started to flood into the underdeveloped countries, and the era of development by exhortation was under way.

The development literature grew exponentially. The fatuity of disembodied advice, advice not backed up by concrete help, became obvious. The international assistance effort was stepped up, and development aid moved from exhortation to demonstration: from the 'tell me' phase to the 'show me' phase. The walking know-how of experts was supplemented by increasing amounts of hardware, while a reverse flow of young and serious Third World students trekked north and west to assimilate irrelevant knowledge and master inappropriate technologies.

We had entered the era of projects, projects that would remove the impediments to investment, for investment was the key to development: the era of pre-investment surveys, feasibility studies, leading to 'bankable' projects and actual investment. To sustain the flow of development assistance funds, articles appeared in the business weeklies showing how aid not only soothed the donor's conscience but lined his pockets too. It was possible to do well by doing good. Anyone who has ever worked in a development agency for any length of time, be it multi- or bi-lateral, can testify that this lesson at least was speedily learned by the business communities.

Ah, the debates of those bygone days! Do you remember some of them? Do you remember, for example, how the scarce ingredient in the development pantry was capital? Ergo, not a cent must be wasted. Every single project must be screened, gone over with a fine toothcomb;

each pay-out time calculated, each internal rate of return checked, re-checked, cross-checked and compared. No matter if the screening took 3, 4 or 5 years. Only the utmost rigour in screening could avert the catastrophe of misinvestment.

Thus spake the pundits. We waited eagerly for their next pronouncement. It was not long in coming.

There is no lack of resources, they said, no shortage of investment funds, public or private. There is only one obstacle standing in the way of development: the scarcity of sound projects. All this was said with a perfectly straight face, for the development establishment, besides having a short memory, has absolutely no sense of humour.

Down the years, the international apparatus for dealing with development problems grew by leaps and bounds, as attention concentrated on this or that piece of the development jigsaw.

Non-industrialised nations are poor. Industrialised nations are prosperous. Therefore prosperity lies in industrialisation. Thus, after a struggle, UNIDO was born, in the teeth of the opposition of the already industrialised nations.

Worsening terms of trade more than wiped out the flow of aid. Came the new cry, 'Trade, not aid'. The rich nations braced themselves behind their trade barriers and turned a deaf ear as long as they could, but eventually UNCTAD was born, in recognition of the intimate connection between trade and development.

The poor nations' efforts to develop were being frustrated by their propensity to breed too fast, so the UN Population Fund was set up. And so on and so forth.

Meanwhile, the picture entertained by the early visionaries – the cross-country race of development -- was steadily fading. Few nations succeeded in clambering out of the swamp on to the dry land. Some even fell back into the swamp. Hopes that some system of judicious handicapping would help to even up the race grew dim. Nor was this surprising. What kind of a race is it where the horses in front constitute the handicapping committee?

Little by little the horrid truth began to dawn, even in the ranks of some of the development establishments. The underdeveloped countries are not underdeveloped because they started late in the development race. They are not underdeveloped because they lack adequate resources. They are not underdeveloped because they lack know-how. They are not underdeveloped because they are overpopulated. They are underdeveloped as a consequence of the development of the rich nations. The development of the latter is founded on the underdevelopment of the former, and is sustained by it. The ties between the affluent, industrialised countries and the backward, low-income countries are intimate and compelling. Their nature is such that the objective impact of most of the so-called development effort to date has been to promote underdevelopment.

It was this growing realisation that eventually led to the demand, on the part of the poor nations, for a wholesale revision of the rules of the game, for 'a new world economic order', and that notion is now enshrined in the resolutions and decisions of the constellations of United Nations agencies and is providing the justification for innumerable north-south dialogues. So far, the poor nations have had but little success in getting the rules of the game changed in their favour.

I spoke earlier of remedies that made the sick patient sicker. Nowhere has this become more clear than in the realm of food and agriculture. What kinds of projects did the developers favour? Those where foreign partners stood ready to invest, where profitable overseas markets were waiting, where there was valuable foreign exchange to be earned. These were the kind of projects that could pass through the eye of the World Bank's needle into the heaven of implementation. This is how more and more of the best lands in Central and South America, in north, east and west Africa, in parts of Asia, came to produce strawberries, carnations, peppers, egg-plants, pineapples, bananas and cucumbers for the Global Super-market, destined for the tables and sitting rooms of North America, Europe and Japan; more tea, coffee and sugar for thirsty foreigners; more ground nuts, palm kernels, cotton and rubber for other countries' industries.

But what about the men and women whom this 'development' had enlisted in the service of the rich countries' tables? Neither they nor the land they worked were any longer producing food for themselves or for their immediate neighbours. Indeed, many of them, instead of eating rice, maize, millet, etc., learned for the first time to eat bread, bread which had to be made from imported wheat or flour. This was the kind of 'development' that paid off its loans promptly, yielded good profits on investments, but left millions vulnerable to the vagaries of climate and international trade. In the statistics, it appeared as economic growth, but it was not socio-economic development. It was, in fact, active underdevelopment.

Or take the famed green revolution, which achieved the bizarre paradox of simultaneously producing more food and making more people hungry. With the new wizard varieties, production soared. It soared on the lands of the bigger and better-off farmers, those with access to credit and hence to improved seed, pesticides, irrigation systems, mechanisation, those strong enough to dispense with middlemen and moneylenders. As production soared, so prices fell, and so did the incomes of the small and marginal farmers. Choked by the debt burden, thousand upon thousand of small farmers sold or forfeited their land to join the swelling ranks of the landless rural poor. The statistics showed economic growth. They even show rising agricultural output. What they failed to show was active socio-economic development.

I could go on giving examples, but there is no need. What has happened is that many low-income countries have become increasingly dependent on alien technologies, foreign experts, imported fertilizers and pesticides, wayward and cutthroat overseas markets, and production decisions taken thousands of miles away. What is worse, countries which once could feed themselves have become dependent on imports of basic foods, while more and more of their people go hungry.

A few years ago the plight of the forgotten millions of poor farmers began to receive the attention of the development establishment. No less an authority than Mr. MacNamara (1973), President of the World Bank, said:

"Of the two billion persons living in our developing member countries, nearly two-thirds, or some 1.3 billion, are members of farm families, and of these there are some 900 million whose annual incomes average less than $100 . . .

. . . for hundreds of millions of these subsistence farmers, life is neither satisfying nor decent. Hunger and malnutrition menace their families. Illiteracy forecloses their futures. Disease and death visit their villages too often, stay too long, and return too soon.

The miracle of the Green Revolution may have arrived, but, for the most part, the poor farmer has not been able to participate in it. He simply cannot afford to pay for the irrigation, the pesticide, the fertilizer, or perhaps for the land itself, on which his title may be vulnerable and his tenancy uncertain."

These were strong words. They were an admission on the part of the number one development doctor that the time had come for a change of medicine. Mr. MacNamara was, of course, right to be concerned about the plight of the poor farmer, though he might have said more about the plight of the landless rural poor, whose numbers are increasing everywhere, and who now make up a third or a half of the population in some parts of the world (Mellor, 1978).

The new concern is by now reflected in the words of all the development agencies and, though to a lesser extent, in their deeds. And within the last year there has come into existence the International Fund for Agricultural Development, prepared to lend up to $350 million a year for projects 'that have a strong food production orientation, foster the use of appropriate technology, have as target groups the poorest and the landless, generate considerable employment, and have a direct impact on the nutrition of the poorest'.*

I hope you are not losing patience with these random ruminations on development problems. They are not completely random. I have tried to show that one of the main lessons

* Statement by IFAD's first President, Ambassador Abdulmuhsim Al-Sudeary of Saudi Arabia, reported in *Ceres* No. 62, March-April 1978.

learned by the development establishment since the last World Forestry Congress is that economic growth does not necessarily mean socio-economic development. But I was also gently preparing you to face up to the unpalatable fact that, as yet, forest industries have made little or no contribution to socio-economic development in the underdeveloped world – certainly not the significant contribution that was envisaged for them a couple of decades ago. Indeed, the probability is that such forest industries as have been established have, like parallel developments in food and agriculture, served but to deflect attention from real needs, diverted resources from what should have been the true priorities, and served to promote socio-economic *under*development.

The arguments that were advanced for giving a certain priority to forest industries seemed valid enough at the time. Here was a group of industries based on a renewable resource, a resource which all underdeveloped countries possessed or could create; industries with considerable flexibility both as to scale of operations and technology; industries with pronounced backward and forward linkages, ensuring that their growth would exercise a multiplier effect on the whole economy; industries which, located near the wood resource, offered the prospect of creating new poles of development, checking the squalid centrifugal development that has scarred so many underdeveloped countries; industries producing a wide range of products, many of which correspond to basic needs; products, moreover, with a high income elasticity, enhancing prospects of industry viability once under way; products which could substitute expensive imports and, exported, earn valuable foreign exchange (Westoby, 1962).

I am sure you have all heard these arguments before: you may even have used them. Certain it is that, as foresters began to use them, the development institutions, financing agencies and planning ministries began to listen to the foresters. Forestry yielded its time-honoured place as the Cinderella sector, the sector commanding absolute posteriority. A stream of forestry projects began to be approved. The forestry sector was in business. Our efforts to convert the development agencies to forestry were doubtless helped by the fact that FAO's global studies had shown beyond a shadow of doubt that rising affluence in Europe, North America and Japan would require an increasing flow of timber from the underdeveloped world, and that the foreign exchange these exports would generate could not but help the credit-worthiness of the underdeveloped exporting countries.

We flattered ourselves that our arguments had been well-founded, and that reason had prevailed.

How naive we were!

The growing interest in, and acceptance of, forestry projects had little or nothing to do with the conversion of the development establishment to the idea that forestry and forest industries had a significant and many-sided contribution to make to overall economic and social development. It had everything to do with the fact that many of the rich, industrialised countries needed and needed badly, new wood material resources, and their forest industries, their equipment manufacturers, together with miscellaneous agents and operators, scented golden opportunities for profit in those underdeveloped countries with forest resources. This was the dominant consideration which determined the location, shape and direction of forest and forest industry development projects. The forest and forest industry pre-investment survey became the archetypal project. The international financing agencies knew what foreign investors wanted, and the multilateral and bilateral agencies fell into line. They helped the underdeveloped countries to bear the expense and drudgery of resource data collection, including mapping and wood testing, thereby relieving potential investors of these tasks and charges. Likewise, they bore the cost of initial feasibility studies. They supported forestry colleges, schools and training courses, building up the ranks of local trained people, enabling eventual operators to economise on the import of more costly, expatriate, personnel.

Thus did the development establishment help to contract, in the course of the last two decades, over 100 million hectares – probably nearer 150 million hectares – of tropical forest land to industry for harvesting (Schmidthüsen, 1976). Thus did the removals of tropical hardwood logs quadruple between 1950 and 1976, while exports, nearly all destined for the wood-hungry, affluent, industrialised nations, rose from under 3 to well over 40 million cubic metres. Meanwhile, the proportion of tropical logs processed in the source countries declined. Pringle (1976) has pointed out that had the 49 million cubic metres exported unprocessed in 1973 been processed where it was grown, this would have brought another $2,000 million or more to the source countries, as well as providing several hundred thousand man-years of employment. Though every underdeveloped country now has a forest service, these forest services are nearly all woefully understaffed, and miserably underpaid. Because they exist, exploitation is facilitated; because they are weak, exploitation is not controlled. Because exploitation has been uncontrolled, and management non-existent, marginal farmers, shifting cultivators, and landless poor have followed in the wake of the loggers, completing the forest destruction. Of the original moist forest area, over half has disappeared in Africa, over one-third in Latin America, and over two-fifths in Asia. And the tropical forest continues to shrink (Sommer, 1976).

Because nearly all the forest and forest industry development which has taken place in the underdeveloped world over the last decades has been externally oriented, aimed at satisfying the rocketing demands of the rich, industrialised nations, the basic forest products needs of the peoples of the underdeveloped world are further from being satisfied than ever: their need for fuel, building materials, low-cost housing, cheap furniture, industrial and cultural papers. The famous multiplier effects are missing. Few new poles of development have been created. The weak forest services in the underdeveloped world are largely concerned with assuring and facilitating a steady outflow of wood raw material to the rich countries. Of the new revenues generated, woefully little has been ploughed back into forestry, either into management, into regeneration or new planting, or into research.

But this is not the worst of it. Just because the principal preoccupation of the forest services in the underdeveloped world has been to help promote this miscalled forest and forest industry development, the much more important role which forestry could play in supporting agriculture and raising rural welfare has been either badly neglected or completely ignored. In precious few countries have the energies of the foresters been bent upon helping the peasant to develop the kind of forestry that would serve his material welfare. This is why there are so few village woodlots and fuel plantations. This is why so little work has been done on forage trees, fruit and nut orchards. This is why so few shelterbelts have been created. This is why more and more watersheds have become denuded, so that the flood and drought oscillations which spell calamity for the peasant take on ever greater amplitude. This is why forestry has been invoked so rarely to reclaim or rehabilitate land. This is why so few of the many possible agro-forestry combinations have been actively explored and developed. This is why so few industries have been established which are specifically geared to meeting real local needs.

But perhaps things are beginning to change? In the last year or two we have heard much more about forestry in rural development. FAO has prepared a basic study on forestry for local community development. A whole area of this present Congress is being devoted to 'Forestry for Rural Communities'. The World Bank is actively exploring the possibility of supporting nationally oriented rural forestry programmes, and its new Forestry Sector Policy paper is replete with good intentions. Other Development Banks will almost certainly follow by adopting some of the new language. A new International Council for Research in Agro-Forestry has come into existence, directed by an international forestry personality in whom we cannot but have every confidence (Dr. King).

Does not all this show that the tide has turned, that the development establishment has repented its past errors, and now has its feet firmly set upon the true path?

I think it would be prudent to wait a while before we set the victory bells ringing. At most, we should give but two cheers for this tardy change of heart. The truth is that it is much easier to acknowledge that there is a problem than it is to get something done about it. It is not simply a matter of gearing the development establishment towards new objectives.

Here it is only fair to mention that some of the non-governmental agencies, dependent on unofficial sources for funds, have for some time concerned themselves with the plight of the forgotten millions, though often in a clumsy and ineffectual way. Moreover, some of the more altruistic bilateral aid programmes, those less directly tied to their national business interests, have sought ways and means of helping the millions whom traditional development aid has passed by. They have not met with conspicuous success.

Nor does the problem lie in the reluctance of agency staffs to depart from time-honoured practice and respond to the new precepts which are now beginning to rain on them from above.

The real problem lies elsewhere. The fact is that in many of the underdeveloped countries neither government nor officialdom display any great enthusiasm for mitigating the lot of their poorer people.

The present Congress is not an intergovernmental Conference, nor am I an international bureaucrat. I therefore do not have to pay lip-service to the polite fiction that there is invariably an identity of interest between governments and the people whom they are supposed to represent. In most underdeveloped countries today the interests of those monopolizing political power and the interests of the disinherited masses are not identical: they are diametrically opposed. That is why the demand for a 'new economic order', with its attendant scenario of poor nations versus rich nations, is the biggest, brightest and most convenient red herring yet devised.

This scenario has today come to dominate the world political stage. Every international forum now presents an opportunity for Ministers from underdeveloped countries − be they Ministers of Finance, of Health, of Industry, of Agriculture, of Planning, or whatever − to ascend the rostrum in turn to inveigh against imperialism and neo-colonialism. Their co-delegates do not even bother to listen: they have heard it all before a hundred times. And they accept it tolerantly, knowing that the speech is not intended for them; it is intended for the record, and for subsequent dissemination back home. For it is a great convenience for rulers if the dispossessed in their own countries can be persuaded that the source of their misery lies not at all in their own rulers but in the alien rapacity of rich countries and the far-off machinations of transnational corporations. Their attention is thereby diverted. It is diverted from the fact that those who inveigh most demagogically against imperialism are often *de facto* the outstationed agents of imperialism, and that the contrast of affluence within many underdeveloped countries, between the small ruling elite and the mass of the population, exceeds even the inequalities between rich and poor nations.

But this latest red herring, big and shiny as it is, is also beginning to smell. It, too, is destined for the cemetery. For the world is beginning to change. It is beginning to change not because the development establishment has had a change of mind or a change of heart. It is beginning to change because, in the underdeveloped world, more and more governments are coming to power which are genuinely concerned about inequalities within their countries, and which are striving to do something about it. These are governments for whom the words 'social justice' are not a parrot cry but an emblem of faith and a guide to action. These are countries where the people have drawn the correct lessons from the failure of the past decades. The number of such countries is destined to grow.

How can such countries ensure that the forest industries they create truly contribute to socio-economic development? What kind of forest and forest industry priorities should they set?

One thing is clear. All their forest and forest industry priorities will be subordinated to, and carefully geared to, their national development priorities. And among these the most imperative is to ensure that their people are adequately fed. This is not simply a matter of switching investment from industry to agriculture. It is a matter of facilitating and encouraging those structural changes which will enable the rural masses, at all levels, to feed themselves, and to move progressively beyond that to the production of an agricultural surplus which will ensure that the urban population, too, is fed and no longer dependent either on food aid or on costly food imports. This is the only basis for sound industrialisation. Such governments will therefore closely scrutinise all present and possible future forestry activities from the standpoint of how best they can protect, support, promote and diversify the agricultural economy. It is to this aspect they will give pride of place in their forestry planning and in the forestry goals they establish. I do not need to reiterate here the hundred and one ways in which forestry can promote food production and enrich the rural economy. Other discussion areas of this Congress are being devoted precisely to the discussion of this problem. However, I should perhaps emphasise, in case it might be overlooked, that agriculture-supportive forestry does not by any means exclude forest industries. Small rural industries are an integral part of agriculture-supportive forestry: fuelwood, charcoal, poles, stakes, fencing, hurdles, screens, farm tools and implements, building materials, simple furniture. But these activities, like all other agriculture-supportive activities, are activities that cannot be carried out on the required scale and in the required manner by a conventionally oriented and conventionally organised forest service. They will only be effective, and will only make sense, if they are carried out by the peasants themselves, for themselves. The role of the forester, wherever he may sit in the organisational structure, can only be to stimulate, offer guidance and suggestions, impart techniques and carry out training.

Moreover, although there are various forestry activities which an individual peasant can carry out, those activities which can contribute most to supporting agriculture and promoting rural welfare call for cooperative or communal endeavour. Since it is now becoming evident that the only way forward for agriculture in most underdeveloped countries lies through the promotion of mutual aid and cooperation, it is logical that agriculture and forestry should be soundly integrated at the village level.

The second priority in these countries will be the use of the existing forest resource base, and the creation, where necessary, of new wood resources, for industrialisation directed towards the satisfaction of the most basic domestic needs. Insofar as measures aimed at reducing inequalities in income distribution are successful, this in itself will bring about a changed pattern of demand. However, this may not be sufficient to ensure that existing and new forest industries are geared to the satisfaction of basic needs, and market intervention or market manipulation may be necessary. Moreover, since in the underdeveloped countries a substantial proportion of needs for processed wood arises in the public sector, governments are in a strong position to pursue policies which can assure the viability of the domestic oriented wood industries they bring into existence.

Have export-oriented forest industries any place in the forestry programmes of such countries? Yes, they have a place. If the forest resource is sufficiently rich to offer the opportunity of expanding or creating export-oriented forestry activities, such opportunities will not be neglected. However, any such developments will be subordinated to the first two priorities I have outlined. Moreover, wise governments will digest and apply the lessons of the last two decades of bitter experience. They will refuse to be dazzled by the prospects of quick and easy export earnings. They will take a cool and calm look at the seductive proposals of would-be concessionaires and private foreign capital. They will be swift to denounce and punish all attempts at bribes. For while it is true that the sums involved in forest exploitation and forest industries are trivial compared with, say, military aircraft or oil, we are all painfully aware that the accounts of timber concessionnaires and equipment salesmen are tarnished with obscure miscellaneous items no less than the accounts of Lockheed and Exxon.

These governments will be careful not to sign away their resource heritage. if they decide they can afford to consume forest capital, this will be a conscious choice, accompanied by specific plans for changed land-use. Most important of all they will temper the pace of such export-oriented developments to their own rising capacity to supervise and control them. All programmes and projects, from whatever source they arise, which can introduce serious distortions and jeopardise their own national objectives will be firmly rejected.

If these prescriptions are adhered to, then it is possible that economic growth, as measured by conventional criteria, may be slower. But development will be accelerated, and socioeconomic development will become a reality. Growth is a necessary condition for development, but it is not sufficient condition. The kind of growth we have seen in the past, growth which widens social inequalities, marginalizing the many, is the antithesis of socio-economic development. In far too many underdeveloped countries we have so far seen come into existence only forest industries which have negated development.

FOREST INDUSTRIES FOR SOCIO-ECONOMIC DEVELOPMENT 115

A policy of self-reliance does not mean a policy of complete self-sufficiency, of national autarchy. But it does mean aiming at a degree of self-sufficiency that will provide protection against external market fluctuations and the capacity to withstand external political pressures. It means getting the social priorities right and sticking to them.

I fear that what I have had to say to you today will have disappointed some of you and annoyed others. It would have been more in line with the tradition of Congresses of this kind had I reiterated those many aspects of forest industries which make them particularly suited to promoting socio-economic development, if I had brought those arguments up-to-date, if I had then gone on to talk about the most suitable scale of operations, the most appropriate technology, the needs for training and for technology transfer, problems of location, the industry viability/environment dilemma, the need to reorient research. All these are doubtless fascinating subjects, and we could go on discussing them for hours. We do little good thereby, but equally we do little harm.

But it was impossible for me to give you that kind of address. I have been a close observer of the international forestry scene for close on three decades. For most of that time I have been particularly concerned with and about the underdeveloped world. It has become obvious to me, as it must be becoming obvious to you, that very, very few of the forest industries that have been established in the underdeveloped countries have made any contribution whatever to raising the welfare of the urban and rural masses, have in any way promoted socio-economic development. The fundamental reason is that those industries have been set up to earn a certain rate of profit, not to satisfy a range of basic popular needs.

But the choice between need-oriented industry and profit-oriented industry is neither a technical choice nor an economic choice. It is not a matter of choosing prescription A or prescription B of the development establishment. It is not a matter of opting for the Alpha school of economists or the Beta school. It is a political choice. It is a matter of who holds power in a given society, and on whose behalf that power is exercised. Once power is exercised by or on behalf of the broad popular masses, then, and then only, will the contribution of forest industries to socio-economic development start to be realised.

That is why we as foresters deceive ourselves if we think that our debates here will provide us with the key to the contribution of forestry and forest industries to socio-economic development. Whether or not that contribution will be secured will be decided elsewhere. It will be decided by the struggles which are being conducted, on every continent, by the dispossessed and hungry millions, struggles to win a fair and decent life, to break out of the power of landlords, of moneylenders, of the agents of foreign capital. The fancy packages of comprehensive, integrated, rural development which the development agencies now serve up are so much window-dressing until that power is broken.

Between now and the next World Forestry Congress thousands of foresters will have the opportunity, may have the obligation, to decide which side they are on in that struggle. Whether they stand on the side of power, landed property, the status quo. This is where, historically, most foresters stood. For centuries much of the work of foresters went into creating and protecting royal and princely estates, extinguishing every kind of common right in the forest and enforcing exclusive property. The folk lore and oral tradition of many countries still makes the forester the people's enemy, the gendarme of the landed proprietor.

Or whether they share the aspirations of the common people, and are prepared to work for the day when the rich and many-sided contribution of forestry is harnessed to the service of all, not to that of a privileged few.

Forests for people: that is the theme of this Congress. Is it to be an empty catchphrase? Is it to be an objective, a rallying point, a guide to action? Every forester must decide and, having decided, bear witness in word and deed.

116   COMMONWEALTH FORESTRY REVIEW

                              REFERENCES

Dr. KING, K. F. S., Formerly Guyana's Minister of Economic Development, and from late
    1974 to mid-1978 Assistant Director-General in charge of FAO's Department of
    Forestry.

MELLOR, John W. (1978) (Chief Economist, AID), 'The Landed and the Landless', *Ceres*
    61, January-February 1978.

MACNAMARA, Robert S. (1973) *One Hundred Countries, Two Billion People.* Pub. Praeger,
    New York.

PRINGLE, S. L. (1976) 'Tropical Moist Forests in World Demand, Supply and Trade',
    Unasylva **28** (112-113), 106-118.

SCHMIDTHÜSEN, Franz (1976) 'Forest Utilization Contracts on Public Land in the Tropics',
    Unasylva **28** (112-113), 52-73.

SOMMER, Adrian (1976) 'Attempt at an Assessment of the World's Tropical Moist Forests',
    Unasylva **28** (112-113), 5-25.

WESTOBY, Jack C. (1962) *The Role of Forest Industries in the Attack on Economic Under-
    development*, FAO.

Bibliography

Abrams, P. A. 1983. The theory of limiting similarity. *Annu Rev Ecol Syst* 14:359–76.

Acosta, J. de. 1598. *Historia natural y moral de las Indias, en que se tratan las cosas notables del cielo, elementos, metales, plantas y animales de ellas; y los rítos, ceremonias, leyes, gobierno y guerras de los Indios.* Madrid.

Acosta-Solis, M. 1968. *Naturalistas y viajeros científicos que han contribuido al conocimiento florístico y fitogeográfico del Ecuador.* Quito, Ecuador: Instituto Ecuatoriano de Ciencias Naturales.

Adis, J. 1984. Vertical distribution of arthropods on trees in black water inundation forests (Central Amazonia, Brazil). In *Tropical Rain-Forest: The Leeds Symposium,* ed. A. C. Chadwick and S. L. Sutton, 123–26. Leeds: Leeds Philosophical and Literary Society.

Alcamo, J., R. Leemans, and E. Kreileman. 1998. *Global Change Scenarios of the 21st Century.* Oxford: Elsevier.

Allee, W. C. 1926. Distribution of animals in a tropical rain forest with relation to environmental factors. *Ecology* 7:445–68.

Allen, G. M., and H. J. Coolidge. 1930. *Mammals of Liberia.* African Republic of Liberia Contributions to the Department of Tropical Medicine Institute for Tropical Biology and Medicine, no. 5. Cambridge: Harvard University Press, Cambridge.

Alvarez-Buylla, E. R., and M. Martinez-Ramos. 1992. Demography and allometry of *Cecropia obtusifolia,* a Neotropical pioneer tree: An evaluation of the climax-pioneer paradigm for tropical rain forests. *J Ecol* 80:275–90.

Amedegnato, C. 1997. Diversity of an Amazonian canopy grasshopper community in relation to resource partitioning and phylogeny. In *Canopy Arthropods,* ed. N. E. Stork, J. Adis and R. K. Didham, 281–319. London: Chapman and Hall.

Anderson, J. A. R. 1961. The destruction of *Shorea albida* forest by an unidentified insect. *Emp For Rev* 40:19–29.

André, H. M., P. Lebrun, and M.-I. Noti. 1992. Biodiversity in Africa: A plea for more data. *J Afr Zool* 106:3–15.

Appanah, S., A. H. Gentry, and J. V. LaFrankie. 1993. Liana diversity and species richness of Malaysian rainforests. *J Trop For Sci* 6:116–23.

Armbruster, W. S. 1997. Exaptations link evolution of plant-herbivore and plant-pollinator interactions: A phylogenetic approach. *Ecology* 78:1661–72.

Ashton, P. S. 1964. Ecological studies in the mixed dipterocarp forests of Brunei State. *Oxf For Mem* 25:1–75.

———. 1969. Speciation among tropical forest trees: Some deductions in the light of recent evidence. *Biol J Linn Soc* 1:155–96.

———. 1976. Mixed dipterocarp forest and its variation with habitat in the Malayan lowlands: A re-evaluation at Pasoh. *Malay For* 39:56–72.

———. 1977. A contribution of rain forest research to evolutionary theory. *Ann Missouri Bot Gard* 64:694–705.

———. 1988. Dipterocarp biology as a window to the understanding of tropical forest structure. *Annu Rev Ecol Syst* 19:347–70.

———. 1989. Species richness in tropical forests. In *Tropical Forests: Botanical Dynamics, Speciation, and Diversity,* ed. L. Holm-Nielsen, I. Nielsen, and H. Balslev, 239–51. New York: Academic Press.

———. 1993. Species richness in plant communities. In *Conservation Biology,* ed. P. L. Fiedler and S. K. Jain, 4–22. New York: Chapman and Hall.

———. 1998. Niche specificity among tropical trees: A question of scales. In *Dynamics of Tropical Forest Communities,* ed. D. M. Newbery, H. H. T. Prins, and N. D. Brown, 491–514. Oxford: Blackwell.

Ashton, P. S., T. J. Givnish, and S. Appanah. 1988. Staggered flowering in the Dipterocarpaceae: New insights into floral induction and the evolution of mast fruiting in the aseasonal tropics. *Am Nat* 132:44–66.

Aubréville, A. 1933. La forêt de la Côte d'Ivoire. *Bull Com Afr Occid Franç* 15:205–61.

———. 1936. *La flora forestiere de la Côte d'Ivoire, 1.* Paris.

———. 1938. La forêt coloniale: Les forêts de l'Afrique occidentale française. *Acad Sci Coloniales Ann* 9:1–245.

Augspurger, C. K. 1982. A cue for synchronous flowering. In *Ecology of a Tropical Forest: Seasonal Rhythms and Long-Term Changes,* ed. E. G. Leigh, A. S. Rand, and

D. M. Windsor, 133–50. Washington: Smithsonian Institution Press.

———. 1983a. Seed dispersal of the tropical tree, *Platypodium elegans,* and the escape of its seedlings from fungal pathogens. *J Ecol* 71:759–71.

———. 1983b. Offspring recruitment around tropical trees: Changes in cohort distance with time. *Oikos* 40:189–96.

Austin, M. P., P. S. Ashton, and P. Greig-Smith. 1972. The application of quantitative methods to vegetation survey. III. A re-examination of rain forest data from Brunei. *J Ecol* 60:309–24.

Austin, M. P., and P. Greig-Smith. 1968. The application of quantitative methods to vegetation survey. II. Some methodological problems of data from rain forest. *J Ecol* 56:827–44.

Baillie, D. A., P. S. Ashton, M. N. Court, J. A. R. Anderson, E. A. Fitzpatrick, and J. Tinsley. 1987. Site characteristics and the distribution of tree species in mixed dipterocarp forests on Tertiary sediments in Central Sarawak, Malaysia. *J Trop Ecol* 3:201–20.

Baker, H. G. 1970. Evolution in the tropics. *Biotropica* 2:101–11.

Baker, H. G., and I. Baker. 1983. Floral nectar sugar constituents in relation to pollinator types. In *Handbook of Experimental Pollination Biology,* ed. C. E. Jones and R. J. Little, 117–41. New York: Van Nostrand Reinhold.

Balée, W. 1987. Cultural forests of the Amazon. *Garden* 116:12–14, 32.

Ball, G. E., ed. 1985. *Taxonomy, Phylogeny, and Zoogeography of Beetles and Ants: A Volume Dedicated to the Memory of Philip Jackson Darlington, Jr. (1904–83).* Series Entomologica, no. 33. Dordrecht: Dr W. Junk Publishers.

Balslev, H., R, Valencia, G. Paz y Miño, H. Christensen, and I. Nielsen. 1998. Species count of vascular plants in one hectare of humid lowland forest in Amazonian Ecuador. In *Forest Biodiversity in North, Central, and South America, and the Caribbean,* ed. F. Dallmeier and J. A. Comiskey, 585–94. Paris: UNESCO; New York: Parthenon.

Barraclough, T. G., and A. P. Vogler. 2000. Detecting the geographical pattern of speciation from species-level phylogenies. *Am Nat* 155:419–34.

Barton, N. 1998. The geometry of adaptation. *Nature* 395:751–52.

Basset, Y. 1992. Host specifity of arboreal and free-living insect herbivores in rain forests. *Biol J Linn Soc* 47:115–33.

———. 1999. Diversity and abundance of insect herbivores collected on *Castanopsis acuminatissima* (Fagaceae) in New Guinea: Relationships with leaf production and surrounding vegetation. *Eur J Entomol* 96:381–91.

———. 2001. Invertebrates in the canopy of tropical rain forests: How much do we really know? *Plant Ecol* 153:87–107.

Basset, Y., H.-P. Aberlenc, H. Barrios, G. Curletti, J.-M. Béranger, J.-P. Vesco, P. Causse, A. Haug, A.-S. Hennion, L. Lesobre, F. Marquès, and R. O'Meara. 2001. Stratification and diel activity of arthropods in a lowland rain forest in Gabon. *Biol J Linn Soc* 74:585–607.

Basset, Y., H.-P. Aberlenc, and G. Delvare. 1992. Abundance and stratification of foliage arthropods in a lowland rain forest of Cameroon. *Ecol Entomol* 17:310–18.

Basset, Y., E. Charles, and V. Novotny. 1999. Insect herbivores on parent trees and conspecific seedlings in a Guyana rain forest. *Selbyana* 20:146–58.

Basset, Y., S. E. Miller, G. A. Samuelson, and A. Allison. 1996. How many host-specific insect species feed on a species of tropical tree? *Biol J Linn Soc* 59:201–16.

Basset, Y., V. Novotny, S. E. Miller, and R. Pyle. 2000. Quantifying biodiversity: Experience with parataxonomists and digital photography in New Guinea and Guyana. *BioScience* 50:899–908.

Basset, Y., and G. A. Samuelson. 1996. Ecological characteristics of an arboreal community of Chrysomelidae in Papua New Guinea. In *Chrysomelidae Biology,* ed. P. H. A. Jolivet and M. L. Cox, 243–62. Vol. 2. *Ecological Studies.* Amsterdam: SPB Academic Publishing.

Bates, H. W. 1862. Contributions to an insect fauna of the Amazon Valley. Lepidoptera: Heliconidae. *Trans Linn Soc London* 23:495–567.

———. 1864. *The Naturalist on the River Amazons.* London: John Murray. Reprint of 2d ed., Berkeley: University of California Press, 1962.

Bates, M. 1944. Observations on the distribution of diurnal mosquitos in a tropical forest. *Ecology* 25:159–70.

Baur, G. N. 1968. *The Ecological Basis of Rain Forest Management.* Sydney: Forestry Commission of New South Wales.

Bawa, K. S. 1974. Breeding systems of trees in a lowland tropical forest. *Evolution* 28:85–92.

———. 1990. Plant-pollinator interactions in tropical rain forests. *Annu Rev Ecol Syst* 21:399–422.

———. 1992. The riches of tropical forests: Non-timber products. *Trends Ecol Evol* 7:361–63.

Bayliss-Smith, T. P. 1982. Pre-industrial systems. 1: New Guinea. In *The Ecology of Agricultural Systems,* ed. T. P. Bayliss-Smith, 24–36. Cambridge: Cambridge University Press.

Beard, J. S. 1944. Climax vegetation in tropical America. *Ecology* 25:127–58.

———. 1946. The natural vegetation of Trinidad. *Oxf For Mem* 20:1–152.

Beccari, O. 1904. *Wanderings in the Great Forests of Borneo.* Trans. E. H. Giglioli, ed. F. H. H. Guillemard. London: A. Constable, London. Reprint with an Introduction by the Earl of Cranbrook, Singapore: Oxford University Press, 1986.

Becerra, J. X. 1997. Insects on plants: Macroevolutionary chemical trends in host use. *Science* 276:253–56.

Becker, P., L. W. Lee, E. D. Rothman, and W. D. Hamilton. 1985. Seed predation and the coexistence of tree species: Hubbell's model revisited. *Oikos* 44:382–90.

Beddall, B. G. 1969. *Wallace and Bates in the Tropics.* London: Macmillan.

Beebe, W. 1918. *Jungle Peace.* New York: H. Holt.

———. 1921. *The Edge of the Jungle.* New York: H. Holt.

———. 1925. *Jungle Days.* New York: G. P. Putnam's Sons.

———, ed. 1944. *The Book of Naturalists.* Princeton: Princeton University Press.

Bellingham, P. J., E. V. J. Tanner, and J. R. Healey. 1994. Sprouting of trees in Jamaican montane forests, after a hurricane. *J Ecol* 82:747–58.

———. 1995. Damage and responsiveness of Jamaican montane tree species after disturbance by a hurricane. *Ecology* 76:2562–80.

Belt, T. 1874. *The Naturalist in Nicaragua.* London: John Murray. Reprint of 2d ed., Chicago: University of Chicago Press, 1985.

Benson, W. W. 1972. Natural selection for Müllerian mimicry in *Heliconius erato* in Costa Rica. *Science* 176: 936–39.

Bierregaard, R. O., T. E. Lovejoy, V. Kapos, A. A. dos Santos, and R. W. Hutchins. 1992. The biological dynamics of tropical rainforest fragments. *BioScience* 42:859–66.

Black, G. A., T. Dobzhansky, and C. Pavan. 1950. Some attempts to estimate species diversity and population density of trees in Amazonian forests. *Bot Gazette* 111:413–25.

Booth, A. H. 1956. The distribution of primates in the Gold Coast. *J West Afr Sci Assoc* 2:122–33.

Boserup, E. 1965. *The Conditions of Agricultural Growth.* London: Allen and Unwin.

Boucher, D. H., J. H. Vandermeer, M. A. Mallona, N. Zamora, and I. Perfecto. 1994. Resistance and resilience in a directly regenerating rainforest: Nicaraguan trees of the Vochysiaceae after Hurricane Joan. *For Ecol Management* 68:127–36.

Bowles, I. A., R. E. Rice, R. A. Mittermeier, and G. A. B. da Fonseca. 1998. Logging and tropical forest conservation. *Science* 280:1899–900.

Braker, E. 2000. The changing face of tropical biology? *Tropinet* 11 (1): 1–2.

Brandani, A., G. S. Hartshorn, and G. H. Orians. 1988. Internal heterogeneity of gaps and species richness in Costa Rican tropical wet forest. *J Trop Ecol* 4:99–119.

Bray, J. R., and J. T. Curtis. 1957. The ordination of upland forest communities in southern Wisconsin. *Ecol Monogr* 27:325–49.

Brokaw, N. V. L. 1982. The definition of treefall gap and its effects on measures of forest dynamics. *Biotropica* 14:158–60.

———. 1985. Gap-phase regeneration in a tropical forest. *Ecology* 66:682–87.

Brokaw, N. V. L., and R. T. Busing. 2000. Niche versus chance and tree diversity in forest gaps. *Trends Ecol Evol* 15:183–88.

Bronstein, J. L. 1994. Our current understanding of mutualism. *Quarterly Rev Biol* 69:31–51.

Bronstein, J. L., P. H. Guyon, C. Gliddon, F. Kjellberg, and G. Michaloud. 1990. The ecological consequences of flowering asynchrony in monoecious figs: A simulation study. *Ecology* 71:2145–56.

Brower, A. V. Z. 1996. Parallel race formation and the evolution of mimicry in *Heliconius* butterflies: A phylogenetic hypothesis from mitochondrial DNA sequences. *Evolution* 50:195–221.

Brown, J. H., and A. Kodric-Brown. 1977. Turnover rates in insular biogeography: Effect of immigration on extinction. *Ecology* 58:445–49.

Brown, J. H., and M. V. Lomolino. 1998. *Biogeography.* 2d ed. Sunderland, Mass.: Sinauer Associates.

Brown, K. S. 1991. Conservation of Neotropical environments: Insects as indicators. In *Conservation of Insects and Their Habitats,* ed. N. M. Collins and J. A. Thomas, 499–504. London: Academic Press.

Brown, K. S., and W. W. Benson. 1974. Adaptive polymorphism associated with multiple Müllerian mimicry in *Helcionius numata. Biotropica* 6:205–28.

Brown, K. S., and G. G. Brown. 1992. Habitat alteration and species loss in Brazilian forests. In *Tropical Deforestation and Species Extinction,* ed. T. C. Whitmore and J. A. Sayer, 119–42. London: Chapman and Hall.

Brown, N. D. 1993. The implications of climate and gap microclimate for seedling growth conditions in a Bornean lowland rain forest. *J Trop Ecol* 9:153–68.

Brown, N. D., and S. Jennings. 1998. Gap-size differentiation by tropical rainforest trees: A testable hypothesis or a broken-down bandwagon? In *Dynamics of Tropical Communities,* ed. D. M. Newbery, H. H. T. Prins, and N. Brown, 79–94. Oxford: Blackwell.

Brown, N. D., and T. C. Whitmore. 1992. Do dipterocarp seedlings really partition tropical rain forest gaps? *Philosophical Trans Royal Soc London,* ser. B, 335: 369–78.

Brown, S., A. J. R. Gillespie, and A. E. Lugo. 1989. Biomass estimation methods for tropical forests with applications to forest inventory data. *For Sci* 35:881–902.

Brown, S., and A. E. Lugo. 1982. The storage and production of organic matter in tropical forests and their role in the global cycle. *Biotropica* 14:161–87.

Brown, W. H. 1920–21. *Minor Forest Products of Philippine Forests.* 3 vols. Manila: Bureau of Printing.

———. 1941–43. *Useful Plants of the Philippines.* 3 vols. Manila: Department of Agriculture and Natural Resources.

Brown, W. L. 1960. Ants, acacias, and browsing mammals. *Ecology* 41:587–92.

Bryant, J. P., F. S. Chapin III, and D. R. Klein. 1983. Carbon/nutrient balance of boreal plants in relation to vertebrate herbivory. *Oikos* 40:357–68.

Bryant, J. P., and P. J. Kuropat. 1980. Selection of winter

forage by subarctic browsing vertebrates: The role of plant chemistry. *Annu Rev Ecol Syst* 11:261–85.

Budowski, G. 1965. Distribution of tropical American rain forest species in the light of successional processes. *Turrialba* 15:40–42.

Burkill, H. M. 1985–97. *The Useful Plants of West Tropical Africa.* 4 vols. Kew: Royal Botanic Gardens.

Burkill, I. H. 1935. *A Dictionary of the Economic Products of the Malay Peninsula,* vols. 1 and 2. London: Crown Agents for the Colonies, London. Reprint, 1966, published on behalf of the Governments of Malaysia and Singapore by the Ministry of Cooperatives.

———. 1965. *Chapters on the History of Botany in India.* Delhi: Manager Government of India Press.

Burslem, D. F. R. P., and T. C. Whitmore. 1999. Species diversity, susceptibility to disturbance, and tree population dynamics in tropical rain forest. *J Veget Sci* 10: 767–76.

Bush, M. B. 1994. Amazonian speciation: A necessarily complex model. *J Biogeogr* 21:5–17.

Butynski, T. M. 1996/97. African primate conservation: The Species and the IUCN/SSC Primate Specialist Group Network. *Primate Conservation* 17:87–100.

Buxton, A. P. 1952. Observations on the diurnal behaviour of the redtail monkey (*Cercopithecus ascanius schmidti* Matschie) in a small forest in Uganda. *J Animal Ecol* 21:25–58.

Byrne, M. M., and D. J. Levey. 1993. Removal of seeds from frugivore defecations by ants in a Costa Rican rain forest. *Vegetatio* 107/108:363–74.

Carpenter, C. R. 1940. A field study in Siam of the behavior and social relations of the gibbon, *Hylobates lar. Comp Psychol Monogr* 16:1–212.

Castroviejo, S. 1989. Spanish floristic exploration in America: Past and present. In *Tropical Forests,* ed. L. Holm-Nielsen, I. Nielsen, and H. Balslev, 347–53. New York: Academic Press.

Chapin, F. S., III, E. S. Zavaleta, V. T. Eviners, R. L. Naylor, P. M. Vitousek, H. L. Reynolds, D. U. Hooper, S. Lavorel, O. E. Sala, S. E. Hobbie, M. C. Mack, and S. Diaz. 2000. Consequences of changing biodiversity. *Nature* 405:234–41.

Chapin, J. P. 1932–54. The birds of the Belgian Congo. *Bull Am Mus Nat Hist* 65, 75, 75A, 75B.

Chapman, C. A., and D. A. Onderdonk 1988. Forests without primates: Primate/plant codependency. *Am J Primatol* 45:127–41.

Chapman, F. M. 1917. The distribution of bird-life in Colombia: A contribution to the biological survey of South America. *Bull Am Mus Nat Hist* 36:1–729.

———. 1926. The distribution of bird life in Ecuador. *Bull Am Mus Nat Hist* 55:1–784.

Charles-Dominique, P. 1971. Eco-ethologie des prosimiens de Gabon. *Biol Gabonica* 7:121–228.

———. 1977. *Ecology and Behavior of Nocturnal Primates.* London: Duckworth.

Charles-Dominique, P., M. Atramentowicz, M. Charles-Dominique, H. Gérard, A. Hladik, C. M. Hladik, and M. F. Prévost. 1981. Les mammiferes frugivores arboricoles nocturnes d'une forêt Guyanaise: Interelations plantes-animaux. *Rev Ecol (Terre Vie)* 35:341–435.

Chazdon, R. L. 1988. Sunflecks and their importance to forest understorey plants. *Adv Ecol Res* 18:1–63.

———. 1998. Tropical forests: Log 'em or leave 'em? *Science* 281:1295–96.

Chazdon, R. L., R. K. Colwell, J. S. Denslow, and M. R. Guariguata. 1998. Statistical methods for estimating species richness of woody regeneration in primary and secondary rain forests of NE Costa Rica. In *Forest Biodiversity Research, Monitoring, and Modeling: Conceptual Background and Old World Case Studies,* ed. F. Dallmeier and J. Comiskey, 285–309. Counforth: Parthenon Publishing; Paris: UNESCO.

Clark, D. A., and D. B. Clark. 1984. Spacing dynamics of a tropical rain forest tree: Evaluation of the Janzen-Connell model. *Am Nat* 124:769–88.

———. 1992. Life history diversity of canopy and emergent trees in a Neotropical rain forest. *Ecol Monogr* 62:315–44.

Clark, D. B., D. A. Clark, and J. M. Read. 1998. Edaphic variation and the mesoscale distribution of tree species in a Neotropical rain forest. *J Ecol* 86:101–12.

Clark, D. A., D. B. Clark, R. Sandoval M., and M. V. Castro C. 1995. Edaphic and human effects on landscape-scale distributions of tropical rain forest palms. *Ecology* 76:2581–94.

Clark, D. B., M. W. Palmer, and D. A. Clark. 1999. Edaphic factors and the landscape-scale distributions of tropical rain forest trees. *Ecology* 80:2662–75.

Clinebell, R. R., O. L. Phillips, A. H. Gentry, N. Stark, and H. Zuuring. 1995. Prediction of Neotropical tree and liana species richness from soil and climatic data. *Biodiversity Conserv* 4:56–90.

Cody, M. L. 1975. Trends toward a theory of continental species diversities: Bird distributions over Mediterranean habitat gradients. In *Ecology and Evolution of Communities,* ed. M. L. Cody and J. M. Diamond, 214–57. Cambridge, Mass.: Belknap.

Coley, P. D. 1980. Effects of leaf age and plant life history patterns on herbivory. *Nature* 284:545–46.

———. 1982. Rates of herbivory on different tropical trees. In *Ecology of a Tropical Forest: Seasonal Rhythms and Long-Term Changes,* ed. E. G. Leigh, A. S. Rand, and D. M. Windson, 123–32. Washington: Smithsonian Institution Press.

———. 1983. Herbivory and defense characteristics of tree species in a lowland tropical forest. *Ecol Monogr* 53:209–33.

Coley, P. D., and J. A. Barone. 1996. Herbivory and plant defenses in tropical forests. *Annu Rev Ecol Syst* 27:305–35.

Coley, P. D., J. P. Bryant, and F. S. Chapin III. 1985. Resource availability and plant herbivore defense. *Science* 230:895–99.

Colinvaux, P. A. 1987. Amazon diversity in the light of the paleoecological record. *Quaternary Sci Rev* 6:93–114.

Collins, N. M., J. A. Sayer, and T. C. Whitmore, eds. 1991. *The Conservation Atlas of Tropical Forests: Asia and the Pacific.* Gland: IUCN; London: Macmillan.

Colwell, R. K., and J. A. Coddington. 1994. Estimating terrestrial biodiversity through extrapolation. *Philosophical Trans Royal Soc London,* ser. B, 345:101–18.

Colwell, R. K., and G. C. Hurtt. 1994. Nonbiological gradients in species richness and a spurious Rapoport effect. *Am Nat* 144:570–95.

Colwell, R. K., and D. C. Lees. 2000. The mid-domain effect: Geometric constraints on the geography of species richness. *Trends Ecol Evol* 15:70–76.

Condit, R. 1995. Research in large, long-term tropical forest plots. *Trends Ecol Evol* 10:18–22.

———. 1997. *Tropical Forest Census Plots: Methods and Results from Barro Colorado Island, Panama, and a Comparison with Other Plots.* New York: Springer-Verlag.

Condit, R., P. S. Ashton, P. Baker, S. Bunyavejchewin, S. Gunatilleke, N. Gunatilleke, S. P. Hubbell, R. B. Foster, A. Itoh, J. V. LaFrankie, H. S. Lee, E. Losos, N. Manokaran, R. Sukamar, and T. Yamakura. 2000. Spatial patterns in the distribution of tropical tree species. *Science* 288:1414–18.

Condit, R., R. B. Foster, S. P. Hubbell, R. Sukumar, E. G. Leigh, N. Manokaran, S. Loo de Lao, J. V. LaFrankie, and P. S. Ashton. 1998. Assessing forest diversity from small plots: Calibration using species-individual curves from 50 ha plots. In *Forest Biodiversity Research, Monitoring, and Modeling: Conceptual Background and Old World Case Studies,* ed. F. Dallmeier and J. Comiskey, 247–68. Paris: Parthenon Publishing.

Condit, R., S. P. Hubbell, and R. B. Foster. 1996. Changes in a tropical forest with a shifting climate: Results from a 50-ha permanent census plot in Panama. *J Trop Ecol* 12:231–56.

Condit, R., S. P. Hubbell, J. V. LaFrankie, R. Sukumar, N. Manokaran, R. B. Foster, and P. S. Ashton. 1996. Species-area and species-individual relationships for tropical trees: A comparison of three 50-ha plots. *J Ecol* 84:549–62.

Connell, J. H. 1971. On the role of natural enemies in preventing competitive exclusion in some marine animals and rain forest trees. In *Dynamics of Populations,* ed. P. J. den Boer and G. R. Gradwell, 298–312. Wageningen, Netherlands: Centre for Agricultural Publishing and Documentation.

———. 1978. Diversity in tropical rain forests and coral reefs. *Science* 199:1302–10.

Connell, J. H., and M. D. Lowman. 1989. Low-diversity tropical rain forests: Some possible mechanisms for their existence. *Am Nat* 134:88–119.

Connell, J. H., and E. Orias. 1964. The ecological regulation of species diversity. *Am Nat* 98:399–414.

Connell, J. H., J. G. Tracey, and L. J. Webb. 1984. Compensatory recruitment, growth, and mortality as factors maintaining rain forest tree diversity. *Ecol Monogr* 54:141–64.

Cook, R. E. 1969. Variation in species density of North American birds. *Syst Zool* 18:63–84.

Coomes, D. A., and P. J. Grubb. 1998. Responses of juvenile trees to above- and belowground competition in nutrient-starved Amazonian rain forest. *Ecology* 79:768–82.

Corbet, P. S. 1966. The role of rhythms in insect behaviour. In *Insect Behaviour,* ed. P. T. Haskell, 13–28. London: Royal Entomological Society.

Corner, E. J. H. 1949. The Durian Theory or the origin of the modern tree. *Ann Bot* n.s. 13:367–414.

———. 1954. The evolution of tropical forest. In *Evolution as a Process,* ed. J. Huxley, A. C. Hardy, and E. B. Ford, 34–46. London: G. Allen and Unwin.

Cox, P. A., T. Elmqvist, E. D. Pierson, and W. E. Rainey. 1991. Flying foxes as strong interactors in South Pacific island ecosystems: A conservation hypothesis. *Conserv Biol* 5:448–54.

Cranbrook, Gathorne Earl. 1986. Introduction. In O. Beccari, *Wanderings in the Great Forests of Borneo.* Singapore: Oxford University Press.

———. 1988. Introduction. In H. Forbes, *A Naturalists's Wanderings in the Eastern Archipelago.* Singapore: Oxford University Press.

Crook, J. H., and J. S. Gartlan. 1966. Evolution of primate societies. *Nature* 210:1200–1203.

Crump, M. L. 1974. Reproductive strategies in a tropical anuran community. *Misc Publ Mus Nat Hist Univ Kansas* 61:1–68.

Curran, L. M., I. Caniago, G. Č. Paoli, D. Astianti, M. Kusneti, M. Leighton, C. E. Nirarita, and H. Haeruman. 1999. Impact of El Niño and logging on canopy tree recruitment in Borneo. *Science* 286:2184–88.

Currie, D. J. 1991. Energy and large-scale patterns of animal- and plant-species richness. *Am Nat* 137:27–49.

Currie, D. J., and V. Paquin. 1987. Large-scale biogeographical patterns of species richness in trees. *Nature* 329:326–27.

Cushman, J. H., and A. J. Beattie. 1991. Mutualisms: Assessing the benefits to hosts and visitors. *Trends Ecol Evol* 6:193–95.

Dalling, J. W., S. P. Hubbell, and K. Silvera. 1998. Seed dispersal, seedling establishment, and gap partitioning among tropical pioneer trees. *J Ecol* 86:674–89.

Dallmeier, F., and J. A. Comiskey, eds. 1998. *Forest Biodiversity Research, Monitoring, and Modeling: Conceptual Background and Old World Case Studies.* Counforth: Parthenon Publishing; Paris: UNESCO.

———, eds. 1999. *Forest Biodiversity in North, Central, and South America, and the Caribean: Research and*

Monitoring. Counforth: Parthenon Publishing; Paris: UNESCO.

Dallmeier, F., M. Kabel, and R. Rice. 1992. Methods for long-term biodiversity plots in protected tropical forest. In *Long-term Monitoring of Biological Diversity in Tropical Forest Areas,* ed. F. Dallmeier, 11–46. MAB Digest 11. Paris: UNESCO.

Darlington, P. J., Jr. 1957. *Zoogeography: The Geographical Distribution of Animals.* New York: John Wiley and Sons.

———. 1959. Area, climate, and evolution. *Evolution* 13:488–510.

———. 1971. Interconnected patterns of biogeography and evolution. *Proc Nat Acad Sci USA* 68:1254–58.

Darwin, C. 1839. *Journal of Researches into the Geology and Natural History of the Various Countries Visited by H.M.S. Beagle, Under the Command of Captain Fitzroy, R. N. from 1832–1836.* London: Henry Colburn.

———. 1859. *On the Origin of Species by Means of Natural Selection, or the Preservation of Favoured Races in the Struggle for Life.* London: J. Murray.

Davenport, T. R. B., P. C. Howard, and C. Dickinson. 1996. *Mpanga, Zika, and Other Mpigi District Forest Reserves.* Forest biodiversity report 24. Kampala: Uganda Forest Department.

Davis, D. E. 1945a. The annual cycle of plants, mosquitos, birds, and mammals in two Brazilian forests. *Ecol Monogr* 15:243–95.

———. 1945b. The occurrence of the incubation-patch in some Brazilian birds. *Wilson Bull* 57:188–90.

Davis, T. A. W., and P. W. Richards. 1934. The vegetation of Moraballi Creek, British Guiana: An ecological study of a limited area of tropical rain forest. Part II. *J Ecol* 22:106–55.

Dawkins, H. C., and M. S. Philip. 1998. *Tropical Moist Forest Silviculture and Management: A History of Success and Failure.* Wallingford: CABI.

de Foresta, H., and G. Michon. 1993. Creation and management of rural agroforests in Indonesia: Potential applications in Africa. In *Tropical Forests, People, and Food,* ed. C. M. Hladik, A. Hladik, O. F. Linares, H. Pagezy, A. Semple, and M. Hadley, 709–24. Paris: UNESCO; Carnforth: Parthenon.

de Graaf, N. R. 1986. *A Silvicultural System for Natural Regeneration of Tropical Rain Forest in Suriname.* Wageningen, Netherlands: Agricultural University.

Dejean, A., D. McKey, M. Gibernau, and M. Belin. 2000. The arboreal ant mosaic in a Cameroonian rainforest (Hymenoptera: Formicidae). *Sociobiology* 35:403–23.

de la Fuente, M. A. S., and R. J. Marquis. 1999. The role of ant-tended extrafloral nectaries in the protection and benefit of a Neotropical rainforest tree. *Oecologia* 118:192–202.

DeLucia, E. H., and R. B. Thomas. 2000. Photosynthetic responses to CO_2 enrichment of four hardwood species in a forest understory. *Oecologia* 122:11–19.

Denslow, J. S. 1980. Gap partitioning among tropical rain forest trees. *Biotropica* 12:47–55.

———. 1984. Influence of disturbance on species diversity: Reply to T. C. Whitmore. *Biotropica* 16:240.

———. 1987. Tropical rain forest gaps and tree species diversity. *Annu Rev Ecol Syst* 18:431–51.

———. 1995. Disturbance and diversity in tropical rain forests: The density effect. *Ecol Applic* 5:962–68.

———. 1996. Functional group diversity and responses to disturbance. In *Biodiversity and Ecosystem Processes in Tropical Forests,* ed. G. H. Orians, R. Dirzo, and J. H. Cushman, 127–51. Berlin: Springer.

Denslow, J. S., A. Ellison, and R. E. Sanford, Jr. 1998. Treefall gap size effects on above- and below-ground processes in a tropical wet forest. *J Ecol* 86:597–609.

Desmond, A. 1994. *Huxley: The Devil's Disciple.* London: Michael Joseph.

Desmond, A., and J. Moore. 1991. *Darwin.* London: Michael Joseph.

Detwiler, R. P., and C. A. S. Hall. 1988. Tropical forests and the global carbon cycle. *Science* 239:42–47.

Diamond, J. M. 1973. Distributional ecology of New Guinea birds. *Science* 179:759–69.

Dirzo, R., and A. Miranda. 1991. Altered patterns of herbivory and diversity in the forest understory: A case study of the possible consequences of contemporary defaunation. In *Plant-Animal Interactions: Evolutionary Ecology in Tropical and Temperate Regions,* ed. P. W. Price, T. M. Lewinsohn, G. W. Fernandes, and W. W. Benson, 273–87. New York: Wiley and Sons.

Dobzhansky, T. 1950. Evolution in the tropics. *Am Sci* 38: 209–21.

Docters van Leeuwen, W. M. 1954. On the biology of some Javanese Loranthaceae and the role birds play in their life-history. *Beaufortia* 4:105–205.

Dodson, C. H. 1975. Coevolution of orchids and bees. In *Coevolution of Animals and Plants,* ed. L. E. Gilbert and P. H. Raven, 91–99. Austin: University of Texas Press.

Dodson, C. H., R. L. Dressler, H. G. Hills, R. M. Adams, and N. H. Williams. 1969. Biologically active compounds in orchid fragrances. *Science* 164:1243–49.

Dolphin, K., and D. L. J. Quicke. 2001. Estimating the global species richness of an incompletely described taxon: An example using parasitoid wasps (Hymenoptera: Braconidae). *Biol J Linn Soc* 47:279–86.

Dove, M. 1993. A revisionist view of tropical deforestation and development. *Environ Conserv* 20:17–24.

Dressler, R. L. 1968. Pollination by euglossine bees. *Evolution* 22:202–10.

———. 1981. *The Orchids: Natural History and Classification.* Cambridge: Harvard University Press.

Du Chaillu, P. 1861. *Explorations and Adventures in Equatorial Africa.* London: J. Murray.

Dudley, N, J.-P. Jeanrenaud, and F. Sullivan. 1995. *Bad Harvest: The Timber Trade and the Degradation of the World's Forests.* London: Earthscan Publications.

Duivenvoorden, J. F. 1996. Patterns of tree species richness in rain forests of the middle Caquetá area, Colombia, NW Amazonia. *Biotropica* 28:142–58.

Dunn, F. L. 1975. *Rain Forest Collectors and Traders.* Malayan Branch Royal Asiatic Society Monograph 5.

Edwards, P. J., and P. J. Grubb. 1977. Studies of mineral cycling in a montane rain forest in New Guinea I. The distribution of organic matter in the vegetation and soil *J Ecol* 65:943–69.

Edwards, W. H. 1847. *A Voyage up the River Amazon: Including a Residence at Para.* New York: D. Appleton and Company.

Eggeling, W. J. 1947. Observations of the ecology of the Budongo rain forest, Uganda. *J Ecol* 34:20–87.

Ehrlich, P. R., and P. H. Raven. 1964. Butterflies and plants: A study in coevolution. *Evolution* 18:586–608.

Eltringham, H. 1916. On specific and mimetic relationships in the genus *Heliconius*. *Trans Entomol Soc London* 1916:101–55.

Emmons, L. H. 1980. Ecology resource partitioning among 9 species of African rain forest. *Ecol Monogr* 50:31–54.

Engler, A. 1892. Uber die Hochgebirgsflora des tropischen Afrika. *Abh Preuss Akad Wiss* 1–461.

Erwin, T. L. 1979. Thoughts on the evolutionary history of ground beetles: Hypotheses generated from comparative faunal analyses of lowland forest sites in temperate and tropical regions. In *Carabid Beetles: Their Evolution, Natural History, and Classification,* ed. T. L. Erwin, G. E. Ball, D. R. Whitehead, and A. Halpern, 539–92. The Hague: Dr. W. Junk.

———. 1982. Tropical forests: Their richness in Coleoptera and other arthropod species. *Coleopterists' Bull* 36:74–75.

———. 1988. The tropical rain forest canopy: The heart of biotic diversity. In *Biodiversity,* ed. E. O. Wilson, 123–29. Washington: National Academy Press.

———. 1995. Measuring arthropod biodiversity in the tropical forest canopy. In *Forest Canopies,* ed. M. D. Lowman and N. M. Nadkarni, 109–27. San Diego: Academic Press.

———. 1998. Evolution at the equator: Arboreal and alticolous beetles and their taxon pulses with descriptions of a new *Agra* subclade and its species (Coleoptera: Carabidae: Lebinii). In *Phylogeny and Classification of Caraboidea (Coleoptera: Adephaga): Proceedings of a Symposium, 28 August 1996, Florence, Italy,* ed. G. E. Ball, A. Casale, and A. V. Taglianti, 491–510. Torino: Museo Regionale di Scienze Naturali.

Erwin, T. L., and J. C. Scott. 1980. Seasonal and size patterns, trophic structure, and richness of Coleoptera in the tropical arboreal ecosystem: The fauna of the tree *Leuhea seemannii* Triana and Planch in the Canal Zone of Panama. *Coleopterists' Bull* 34:305–22.

Evans, G. C. 1972. *The Quantitative Analysis of Plant Growth.* Oxford: Blackwell.

Ewel, J. J. 1986. Designing agricultural systems for the humid tropics. *Annu Rev Ecol Syst* 17:245–71.

Ewel, J. J., and S. W. Bigelow. 1996. Plant life forms and tropical ecosystem functioning. In *Biodiversity and Ecosystem Processes in Tropical Forests,* ed. G. H. Orians, R. Dirzo, and J. H. Cushman, 101–26. Berlin: Springer.

Eyre, S. R., ed. 1971. *World Vegetation Types.* London: Macmillan.

FAO 1993. *Forest Resources Assessment. 1990: Tropical Countries.* FAO Forestry Paper 112. Rome: United Nations Food and Agriculture Organization.

Farrell, B. D. 1998. "Inordinate fondness" explained: Why are there so many beetles? *Science* 281:555–59.

Farrell, B. D., and T. L. Erwin. 1988. Leaf-beetle community structure in an Amazonian rainforest canopy. In *Biology of Chrysomelidae,* ed. P. Jolivet, E. Petitpierre, and T. H. Hsiao, 73–90. Dordrecht: Kluwer.

Fearnside, P. M., and W. M. Guimarães. 1996. Carbon uptake by secondary forests in Brazilian Amazonia. *For Ecol Management* 80:35–46.

Fedorov, A. A. 1966. The structure of the tropical rain forest and speciation in the humid tropics. *J Ecol* 54:1–11.

Feeny, P. P. 1976. Plant apparency and chemical defense. In *Biochemical Interactions between Plants and Insects,* ed. J. Wallace and R. S. Mansell, 1–40. Vol. 10 of *Recent Advances in Phytochemistry.* New York: Plenum Press.

Fernandez de Oviedo y Valdes, G. [1526] 1950. *Sumario de la natural historia de las Indias.* Edited with introduction and notes by Jose Miranda. Mexico City: Fondo de Cultura Economica.

Ferreira, A. R. [1783–92] 1971. *Viagem filosófica pelas capitanias do Grao Para, Rio Negro, MatoGrosso e Cuiaba.* With a preface by Arthur Cezar Ferreira Reis. Rio de Janeiro: Conselho federal de cultura.

Fiala, B., Grunsky, H., Maschwitz, U., and Linsenmair, K. E. 1994. Diversity of ant-plant interactions: Protective efficacy in *Macaranga* species with different degrees of ant association. *Oecologia* 97:186–92.

Fiala, B., Maschwitz, U., Pont, T. Y. and Helbig, A. J. 1989. Studies of a South East Asian ant-plant association: Protection of *Macaranga* trees by *Crematogaster borneensis*. *Oecologia* 79:463–70.

Finegan, B. 1992. The management potential of Neotropical secondary lowland rain forest. *For Ecol Management* 47:295–321.

Fischer, A. G. 1960. Latitudinal variations in organic diversity. *Evolution* 14:64–81.

Fisher, R. A. 1930. *The Genetical Theory of Natural Selection.* Oxford: Oxford University Press.

Fisher, R. A., A. S. Corbet, and C. B. Williams. 1943. The relation between the number of species and the number of individuals in a random sample of an animal population. *J Ecol* 12:42–58.

Fisher, R. J. 1995. *Collaborative Management of Forests for Conservation and Development*. Gland: IUCN/WWF.

Fittkau, E. J., and H. Klinge. 1973. On biomass and trophic structure of the Central Amazonian rain forest ecosystem *Biotropica* 5:2–14.

Fleming, T. H. 1973. The number of mammal species in several North and Central American forests. *Ecology* 54:555–63.

Fleming, T. H., R. Breitwisch, and G. H. Whitesides. 1987. Patterns of tropical vertebrate frugivore diversity. *Annu Rev Ecol Syst* 18:91–109.

Flenley, J. R. 1979. *The Equatorial Rain Forest: A Geological History*. London: Butterworth.

Floren, A., and K. E. Linsenmair. 2000. Do ant mosaics exist in pristine lowland rain forests? *Oecologia* 123:129–37.

Fogden, M. P. L. 1972. The seasonality and population dynamics of equatorial forest birds in Sarawak. *Ibis* 114:307–42.

Forbes, E. L. 1888. Relations of ants and aphids. *Am Nat* 21:579.

Forbes, H. O. 1885. *A Naturalist's Wanderings in the Eastern Archipelago*. New York: Harper and Brothers. Reprint, with an introduction by the Earl of Cranbrook, Singapore: Oxford University Press, 1989.

Foster, R. B. 1990. The floristic composition of the Rio Manu floodplain forest. In *Four Neotropical Rainforests*, ed. A. H. Gentry, 99–111. New Haven: Yale University Press.

Fox, J., D. M. Truong, A. T. Rambo, N. P. Tuyen, L. T. Cuc, and S. Leisz. 2000. Shifting cultivation: A new old paradigm for managing tropical forests. *BioScience* 50:521–28.

Fox, J. E. D. 1973. Dipterocarp seedling behaviour in Sabah. *Malay For* 36:205–14.

Frankie, G. W., H. G. Baker, and P. A. Opler. 1973. Comparative phenological studies of trees in tropical wet and dry forests in the lowlands of Costa Rica. *J Ecol* 62:881–919.

Freese, C. H. 1977. Food habits of white-faced capuchins (*Cebus capucinus*) in Santa Rosa National Park, Costa Rica. *Brenesia* 10/11:43–56.

Frost, S. W. 1942. *General Entomology*. New York: McGraw-Hill. Reprint (as *Insect Life and Insect Natural History*) New York: Dover, 1959.

Futuyma, D. J., and M. Slatkin, eds. 1983. *Coevolution*. Sunderland, Mass.: Sinauer.

Galil, J., and D. Eisikowitch. 1968. On the pollination ecology of *Ficus sycomorus* in East Africa. *Ecology* 49:259–69.

Gálvez, A., M. Maqueda, M. Martínez-Bueno, and E. Valdivia. 2000. Scientific publishing trends and the developing world. *Am Sci* 88:526–33.

Gaston, K. J. 1991. The magnitude of global insect species richness. *Conserv Biol* 5:283–96.

———, ed. 1996. *Biodiversity: A Biology of Number and Difference*. Oxford: Blackwell Science.

———. 2000. Global patterns in biodiversity. *Nature* 405: 220–27.

Gaston, K. J., T. M. Blackburn, and J. I. Spicer. 1998. Rapoport's rule: Time for an epitaph? *Trends Ecol Evol* 13:70–74.

Gates, B. T. 1998. *Kindred Nature*. Chicago: University of Chicago Press.

Gautier, J. P., and A. Gautier-Hion. 1969. Les associations polyspecifiques chez les Cercopithecidae du Gabon. *Terre Vie* 23:164–201.

Gautier-Hion, A. 1971. L'écologique du Talapoin du Gabon. *Terre Vie* 25:427–90.

———. 1978. Food niches and coexistence in sympatric primates in Gabon. In *Feeding Behavior in Relation to Food Availability and Composition*, ed. C. M. Hladik and D. J. Chivers, 269–86. New York: Academic Press.

Gautier-Hion, A., J. M. Duplantier, R. Quris, F. Feer, C. Sourd, J. P. Decoux, G. Dubost, L. Emmons, C. Erard, P. Hecketsweiler, A. Moungazi, C. Roussilhon, and J. M. Thiollay. 1985. Fruit characters as a basis of fruit choice and seed dispersal in a tropical forest vertebrate community. *Oecologia* 65:324–37.

Gautier-Hion, A., and G. Michaloud. 1989. Are figs always keystone resources for tropical frugivorous vertebrates? A test in Gabon. *Ecology* 70:1826–33.

Geertz, H. C. 1963. *Agricultural Involution*. Berkeley: University of California Press.

Gentry, A. H. 1974. Flowering phenology and diversity in tropical Bignoniaceae. *Biotropica* 6:64–68.

———. 1982. Patterns of Neotropical plant species diversity. *Evol Biol* 15:1–84.

———. 1988a. Changes in plant community diversity and floristic composition on environmental and geographical gradients. *Ann Missouri Bot Gard* 75:1–34

———. 1988b. Tree species richness of upper Amazon forests. *Proc Nat Acad Sci USA* 85:156–59

———. 1989. Speciation in tropical forests. In *Tropical Forests: Botanical Dynamics, Speciation, and Diversity*, ed. L. B. Holm-Nielsen, I. C. Nielsen, and H. Balslev, 113–34. London: Academic Press.

———. 1990a. Floristic similarities and differences between southern Central America and upper and central Amazonia. In *Four Neotropical Rainforests*, ed. A. Gentry, 141–57. New Haven: Yale University Press.

———, ed. 1990b. *Four Neotropical Rainforests*. New Haven: Yale University Press.

———. 1992. Tropical forest biodiversity: distributional patterns and their conservational significance. *Oikos* 63:19–28.

Gentry, A. H., and C. Dodson. 1987a. The contribution of non-trees to species richness of a tropical rain forest. *Biotropica* 19:149–56.

———. 1987b. Diversity and phytogeography of Neotropical vascular epiphytes. *Ann Missouri Bot Gard* 74:205–33.

Gentry, A. H., and L. H. Emmons. 1987. Geographical variation in fertility, phenology, and composition of the understory of Neotropical forests. *Biotropica* 29:216–27.

Gilbert, G. S., S. P. Hubbell, and R. B. Foster. 1994. Density and distance-to-adult effects of a canker disease of trees in a moist tropical forest. *Oecologia* 98:100–108.

Gilbert, L. E. 1975. Ecological consequences of a coevolved mutualism between butterflies and plants. In *Coevolution of Animals and Plants,* ed. L. E. Gilbert and P. H. Raven, 210–40. Austin: University of Texas Press.

———. 1980. Food web organization and conservation of Neotropical diversity. In *Conservation Biology: An Evolutionary-Ecological Perspective,* ed. M. E. Soulé and B. A. Wilcox, 11–34. Sunderland, Mass.: Sinauer.

———. 1983. Coevolution and mimicry. In *Coevolution,* ed. D. J. Futuyma and M. Slatkin, 282–310. Chicago: University of Chicago Press.

Gillett, J. B. 1962. Pest pressure: An underestimated factor in evolution. In *Taxonomy and Geography,* Systematics Association Publication no. 4, 37–46.

Givnish, T. J. 1999. On the causes of gradients in tropical tree diversity. *J Ecol* 87:193–210.

Gleason, H. A. 1926. The individualistic concept of the plant association. *Bull Torrey Bot Club* 53:7–26.

Godoy, R., Lubowski, R., and Markandya, A. 1993. A method for the economic valuation of non-timber tropical forest products. *Economic Bot* 47, 220–33.

Goldsmith, F. B., Ed. 1998. *Tropical Rain Forest: A Wider Perspective.* London: Chapman & Hall.

Gómez-Pompa, A., and A. Kaus. 1990. Traditional management of tropical forests in Mexico. In *Alternatives to Deforestation,* ed. A. B. Anderson, 45–64. New York: Columbia University Press.

———. 1999. From pre-Hispanic to future conservation alternatives: Lessons from Mexico. *Proc Nat Acad Sci USA* 96:5982–86.

Gómez-Pompa, A., C. Vázquez-Yanes, and S. Guevara. 1972. Tropical rain forest: A nonrenewable resource. *Science* 177:762–65

Goodland, R. J. 1975. The tropical origin of ecology: Eugen Warming's jubilee. *Oikos* 26:240–45.

Grace, J., J. Lloyd, J. McIntyre, A. Miranda, P. Meir, H. Miranda, J. Moncrieff, J. Massheder, I. Wright, and J. Gash. 1995. Fluxes of carbon dioxide and water vapour over an undisturbed tropical forest in south-west Amazonia. *Global Change Biol* 1:1–12.

Graham, A. 1997. Neotropical plant dynamics during the Cenozoic-diversification, and the ordering of evolutionary and speciation processes. *Syst Bot* 22:139–50.

Green, G. M., and R. W. Sussman 1990 Deforestation history of the eastern rain forests of Madagascar from satellite images. *Science* 248:212–15.

Greenslade, P. J. M. 1971. Interspecific competition and frequency changes among ants in Solomon Islands coconut plantations. *J Applied Ecol* 8:323–53.

———. 1972a. Distribution patterns of *Priochirus* species

(Coleoptera: Staphylinidae) in the Solomon Islands. *Evolution* 26:130–42.

———. 1972b. Evolution in the staphylinid genus *Priochirus* (Coleoptera). *Evolution* 26:203–20.

———. 1983. Adversity selection and the habitat templet. *Am Nat* 122:352–65.

Greig-Smith, P., M. P. Austin, and T. C. Whitmore. 1967. The application of quantitative methods of vegetation survey. I. Association analysis and principal component ordination of rain forest. *J Ecol* 53:483–503.

Groombridge, R., ed. 1992. *Global Biodiversity Status of the Earth's Living Resources.* London: Chapman and Hall.

Grubb, P. J. 1977. The maintenance of species-richness in plant communities: The importance of the regeneration niche. *Biol Rev* 52:107–45.

———. 1996. Rainforest dynamics: The need for new paradigms. In *Tropical Rainforest Research: Current Issues,* ed. D. S. Edwards, S. C. Choy, and W. E. Booth, 215–33. Dordrecht: Kluwer Academic Publishers.

Grubb, P. J., J. R. Lloyd, T. D. Pennington, and T. C. Whitmore. 1963. A comparison of montane and lowland rain forest in Ecuador. I. The forest structure, physiognomy, and floristics. *J Ecol* 51:567–601.

Grubb, P. J., and D. J. Metcalfe. 1996. Adaptation and inertia in the Australian tropical lowland rain-forest flora: Contradictory trends in intergeneric and intrageneric comparisons of seed size in relation to light demand. *Functional Ecol* 10:512–20.

Grubb, P. J., and P. F. Stevens. 1985. The forest of the Fatima Basin and Mt. Kerigomna, Papua New Guinea. Res. Sch. Pacific Studies, Australian National University, Biogeography and Geomorphology Monograph no. 5.

Grubb, P. J., and T. C. Whitmore. 1966. A comparison of montane and lowland forest in Ecuador. II. The climate and its effects on the distribution and physiognomy of forests. *J Ecol* 54:303–33.

Haberlandt, G. 1893. Eine botanische Tropenreise. Leipzig.

Haddow, A. J., P. S. Corbet, and J. D. Gillett. 1961. Entomological studies from a high tower in Mpanga Forest, Uganda. I. Introduction. *Trans Royal Entomol Soc London* 113:249–56.

Haffer, J. 1969. Speciation in Amazonian forest birds. *Science* 165:131–37.

———. 1997. Alternative models of vertebrate speciation in Amazonia: An overview. *Biodiversity Conserv* 6: 451–76.

Hall, J. B., and M. D. Swaine. 1976. Classification and ecology of closed-canopy forest in Ghana. *J Ecol* 64:913–51.

Hall, R., and D. J. Blundell, eds. 1996. *Tectonic Evolution of Southeast Asia.* Special publication 106. London: Geological Society of London.

Hall, R., and J. D. Holloway, eds. 1998. *Biogeography and Geological Evolution of SE Asia.* Leiden: Backhuys.

Hallam, A. 1973. *A Revolution in the Earth Sciences: From Continental Drift to Plate Tectonics.* Oxford: Clarendon Press.

———. 1994. *An Outline of Phanerozoic Biogeography.* Oxford: Oxford University Press.

Hallé, F., and P. Blanc, eds. 1990. *Biologie d'une canopée de forêt équatoriale.* Report of Radeau des Cimes mission, October–November 1989, French Guyana. Paris: OPRDC.

Hammond, D. S., and V. K. Brown. 1998. Disturbance, phenology, and life-history characteristics: Factors influencing distance/density-dependent attack on tropical seeds and seedlings. In *Dynamics of Tropical Communities,* ed. D. M. Newberry, H. H. T. Prins, and N. Brown, 51–78. Oxford: Blackwell Science.

Hammond, P. M. 1992. Species inventory. In *Global Biodiversity: Status of the Earth's Living Resources,* ed. B. Groombridge, 17–39. London: Chapman and Hall.

Harcourt, C. S., and J. A. Sayer, eds. 1996. *The Conservation Atlas of Tropical Forests: The Americas.* New York: Simon and Schuster.

Hardcastle, P. D. 2001. *Silvicultural Options for the Rain Forest Zone of Cameroon.* London: DfID.

Hardy, F. 1936. Some aspects of tropical soils. *Trans 3rd Int Congr Soil Sci (Oxf)* 2:150–63.

Harms, K. E., S. J. Wright, O. Calderon, A. Hernandez, and E. A. Herre. 2000. Pervasive density-dependent recruitment enhances seedling diversity in a tropical forest. *Nature* 404:493–95.

Harrison, J. L. 1954. The natural food of some rats and other mammals. *Bull Raffles Mus* 25:157–65.

———. 1957. Habitat studies of some Malayan rats. *Proc Zool Soc London* 128:1–21.

———. 1962. The distribution of feeding habits among animals in a tropical rain forest. *J Anim Ecol* 31:53–64.

———. 1969. The abundance and population density of mammals in Malayan lowland forests. *Malay Nat J* 22:174–78.

Hart, T. B. 1995. Seed, seedling, and sub-canopy survival in monodominant and mixed forests of the Ituri Forest, Africa. *J Trop Ecol* 11:443–59.

Hart, T. B., Hart, J. A. and Murphy, P. G. 1989. Monodominant and species-rich forests of the humid tropics: Causes for their co-occurrence. *Am Nat* 133, 613–33.

Hartshorn, G. S. 1972. The ecological life history and population dynamics of *Pentaclethra macroloba,* a tropical wet forest dominant, and *Stryphonodendron excelson,* an occasional associate. Ph.D. diss., University of Washington.

———. 1978. Tree falls and tropical forest dynamics. In *Tropical Trees as Living Systems,* ed. P. B. Tomlinson and M. H. Zimmermann, 617–38. Cambridge: Cambridge University Press.

———. 1989. Application of gap theory to tropical forest management: Natural regeneration on strip clearcuts in the Peruvian Amazon. *Ecology* 70:567–69.

———. 1990. Natural forest management by the Yanesha Forestry Cooperative in Peruvian Amazonia. In *Alternatives to Deforestation: Steps toward Sustainable Use of the Amazon Rain Forest,* ed. A. Anderson, 128–38. New York: Columbia University Press.

———. 1995. Ecological basis for sustainable development in tropical forests. *Annu Rev Ecol Syst* 26:155–75.

Heinrich, B., and P. H. Raven. 1972. Energetics and pollination ecology. *Science* 176:597–602.

Hellmayr, C. E. 1918–38. *Catalogue of Birds of the Americas. Field Mus Nat Hist Publ Zool Ser,* vol. 13, parts 1 (nos. 1–4), 2 (nos. 1–2), 3–11.

Herre, E. A. 1985. Sex ratio adjustment in fig wasps. *Science* 228:896–98.

Herre, E. A., C. A. Machado, E. Bermingham, J. D. Nason, D. M. Windsor, S. S. McCafferty, van Houten, W., and K. Bachmann. 1996. Molecular phylogenies of figs and their pollinator wasps. *J Biogeogr* 23:521–30.

Herrera, C. M. 1984. A study of avian frugivores, bird-dispersed plants, and their interactions in Mediterranean scrublands. *Ecol Monogr* 54:1–24.

Heyne, K. 1922. Nuttige planten van Nederlandsch Indïe. 3 vols. Wageningen, Netherlands: Batavia, Ruygrok & Co.

Heywood, V. H., and S. N. Stuart. 1992. Species extinctions in tropical forests. In *Tropical Deforestation and Species Extinction,* ed. T. C. Whitmore and J. A. Sayer, 91–117. London: Chapman and Hall.

Hingston, R. W. G. 1930. The Oxford University expedition to British Guiana. *Geogr J* 76:1–24.

Hladik, A., and C. M. Hladik 1969. Rapports trophiques entre végétation et primates dans la forêt de Barro Colorado (Panama). *Terre Vie* 23:25–117.

Hladik, C. M., A. Hladik, O. F. Linares, H. Pagezy, A. Semple, and M. Hadley, eds. 1993. *Tropical Forests, People, and Food.* Paris: UNESCO; Carnforth: Parthenon.

Hocking, B. 1970. Insect associations with the swollen thorn acacias. *Trans Royal Entomol Soc London* 122: 211–55.

Hodkinson, I. D., and D. Casson. 1991. A lesser predilection for bugs: Hemiptera (Insecta) diversity in tropical rain forests. *Biol J Linn Soc* 43:101–9.

Hougen-Eitzman, D., and M. D. Rausher. 1994. Interactions between herbivorous insects and plant-insect coevolution. *Am Nat* 143:677–97.

Holdridge, L. R. 1947. Determination of world plant formations from simple climatic data. *Science* 105:367–68.

Holdridge, L. R., W. Grenke, W. Hatheway, T. Liang, and J. Tosi. 1971. *Forest Environments in Tropical Life Zones: A Pilot Study.* Oxford: Pergamon Press.

Holl, K., and M. Kappelle. 1999. Tropical forest recovery and restoration. *Trends Ecol Evol* 14:378–79.

Holland, J. N., and T. H. Fleming. 1999. Mutualistic interactions between *Upiga virescens* (Pyralidae), a pollinating seed-consumer, and *Lophocereus schottii* (Cactaceae). *Ecology* 80:2074–84.

Hooker, J. D., Sir. 1875–97. The flora of British India. London: L. Reeve [by J. D. Hooker assisted by botanists].

Horvitz, C. C., and D. W. Schemske. 1984. Effects of ants and an ant-tended herbivore on seed production of a Neotropical herb. *Ecology* 65:1369–78.

———. 1995. Spatiotemporal variation in demographic transitions of a tropical understory herb: Projection matrix analysis. *Ecol Monogr* 65:155–92.

Houghton, R. A., J. E. Hobbie, J. M. Melillo, B. Moore, B. J. Peterson, G. R. Shaver, and G. M. Woodwell. 1983. Changes in the carbon content of terrestrial biota and soils between 1860 and 1980: A net release of CO_2 to the atmosphere. *Ecol Monogr* 53:235–62.

Howe, H. F. 1977. Bird activity and seed dispersal of a tropical wet forest tree. *Ecology* 58:539–50.

———. 1980. Monkey dispersal and waste of a tropical wet forest tree. *Ecology* 61:944–59.

———. 1983. Annual variation in a Neotropical seed-dispersal system. In *Tropical Rain Forest: Ecology and Management*, ed. S. L. Sutton, T. C. Whitmore, and A. C. Chadwick, 221–27. Oxford: Blackwell Scientific.

———. 1986. Consequences of seed dispersal by birds: A case study from Central America. *J Bombay Nat Hist Soc* 83:19–42.

———. 1993. Specialized and generalized dispersal systems: Where does the "paradigm" stand? *Vegetatio* 107/108:3–14.

Howe, H. F., and G. F. Estabrook. 1977. On intraspecific competition for avian dispersers in tropical trees. *Am Nat* 111:817–32.

Howe, H. F., E. W. Schupp, and L. C. Westley. 1985. Early consequences of seed dispersal for a Neotropical tree (*Virola surinamensis*). *Ecology* 66:781–91.

Howe, H. F., and J. Smallwood. 1982. Ecology of seed dispersal. *Annu Rev Ecol Syst* 13:201–28.

Howe, H. F., and G. A. Vande Kerckhove. 1981. Removal of wild nutmeg (*Virola suranimensis*) crop by birds. *Ecology* 62:1093–106.

Howe, H. F., and L. C. Westley. 1988. *Ecological Relationships of Plants and Animals*. New York: Oxford University Press.

Hubbell, S. P. 1979. Tree dispersion, abundance, and diversity in a tropical dry forest. *Science* 203:1299–309.

———. 1980. Seed predation and the coexistence of tree species in tropical forests. *Oikos* 35:214–29.

———. 1998. The maintenance of diversity in a Neotropical tree community: Conceptual issues, current evidence, and challenges ahead. In *Forest Biodiversity Research, Monitoring, and Modeling: Conceptual Background and Old World Case Studies*, ed. F. Dallmeier and J. Comiskey, 17–44. Counforth: Parthenon Publishing; Paris: UNESCO.

Hubbell, S. P., and R. B. Foster. 1986a. Biology, chance, and the history and structure of tropical rain forest tree communities. In *Community Ecology*, ed. J. Diamond and T. J. Case, 314–29. New York: Harper and Row.

———. 1986b. Canopy gaps and the dynamics of a Neotropical forest. In *Plant Ecology*, ed. M. J. Crawley, 77–96. Oxford: Blackwell Scientific.

———. 1986c. Commonness and rarity in a Neotropical forest: Implications for tropical tree conservation. In *Conservation Biology: The Science of Scarcity and Diversity*, ed. M. E. Soulé, 205–32. Sunderland, Mass.: Sinauer Associates.

———. 1987. The spatial context of regeneration in a Neotropical forest. In *Colonization, Succession, and Stability*, ed. A. J. Gray, M. J. Crawley, and P. J. Edwards, 395–412. Oxford: Blackwell Scientific Publications.

Hubbell, S. P., R. B. Foster, S. T. O'Brien, K. E. Harms, R. Condit, B. Wechsler, S. J. Wright, and S. L. de Lao. 1999. Light-gap disturbances, recruitment limitation, and tree diversity in a Neotropical forest. *Science* 283:554–57.

Hughes, R. F., J. B. Kauffman, and V. J. Jaramillo. 1999. Biomass, carbon, and nutrient dynamics of secondary forests in a humid tropical region of Mexico. *Ecology* 80:1892–907.

Humboldt, A. von, and A. Bonpland (1805–34). Voyage aux régions équinoxiales du nouveau continent, fait en 1799, 1800, 1801, 1802, 1803 et 1804. Paris: F. Schoell. First English edition published as *Personal narrative of travels to the equinoctial regions of the New Continent, during the years 1799–1804*, trans. H. M. Williams (London: Longman, Hurst, Rees, Orme, and Brown, 1814–29).

———. 1805. Essai sur la geographie des plantes: Accompagne d'un tableau physique des régions équinoxiales, fondé sur des mésures exécutées, depuis le dixieme degré de latitude boreale jusqu'au dixieme degré de latitude australe, pendant les années 1799, 1800, 1801, 1802 et 1803. Paris: Chez Levrault, Schoell.

Huston, M. A. 1979. A general hypothesis of species diversity. *Am Nat* 113:81–101.

———. 1994. *Biological Diversity: The Coexistence of Species on Changing Landscapes*. Cambridge: Cambridge University Press.

Hutchinson, G. E. 1959. Homage to Santa Rosalia, or why are there so many kinds of animals? *Am Nat* 93:145–59.

Huxley, C. R. 1978. The ant-plants *Myrmecodia* and *Hydnophytum* (Rubiaceae) and the relationships between their morphology, ant occupants, physiology, and ecology. *New Phytol* 80:231–68.

Huxley, J. 1935. *T. H. Huxley's Diary of the Voyage of the H. M. S. Rattlesnake*. Garden City, N.Y.: Doubleday, Doran and Co.

Hviding, E., and T. Bayliss-Smith. 2000. *Islands of Rainforest: Agroforestry, Logging, and Eco-tourism in Solomon Islands*. Burlington, Vt.: Ashgate Publishing.

Intachat, J., and J. D. Holloway. 2000. Is there stratification in diversity or preferred flight height of geometroid moths in Malaysian lowland tropical forest? *Biodiversity Conserv* 9:1417–39.

Iwao, K., and M. D. Rausher. 1997. Evolution of plant resistance to multiple herbivores: Quantifying diffuse coevolution. *Am Nat* 149:316–35.

Jacobs, M. 1988. *The Tropical Rain Forest: A First Encounter*. Berlin: Springer-Verlag.

Jansen, P. C. M., E. Westphal, and N. Wulijarni-Soetjipto, eds. 1989–2000. *Plant Resources of South East Asia*. Vols. 1–13, 16, 19. Leiden: Bogor and Backhuys.

Janzen, D. H. 1966. Coevolution of mutualism between ants and acacias in Central America. *Evolution* 20:249–75.

———. 1967. Why mountain passes are higher in the tropics. *Am Nat* 101:233–49.

———. 1970. Herbivores and the number of tree species in tropical forests. *Am Nat* 104:501–28.

———. 1971. Euglossine bees as long-distance pollinators of tropical plants. *Science* 171:203–5.

———. 1973a. Sweep samples of tropical foliage insects: Description of study sites, with data on species abundances and size distributions. *Ecology* 54:659–86.

———. 1973b. Sweep samples of tropical foliage insects: Effects of seasons, vegetation types, elevation, time of day, and insularity. *Ecology* 54:687–708.

———. 1974a. Tropical black water rivers, animals and mast-fruiting by Dipterocarpaceae. *Biotropica* 6:69–103.

———. 1974b. Epiphytic myrmecophytes in Sarawak: Mutualism through the feeding of plants by ants. *Biotropica* 6:237–59.

———. 1977. Why are there so many species of insects? *Proceedings of the XV International Congress of Entomology*, 84–94. College Park, Md.: Entomological Society of America.

———. 1979. How to be a fig. *Annu Rev Ecol Syst* 10:13–51.

———. 1980. When is it coevolution? *Evolution* 34:611–12.

———. 1988. Tropical dry forests. The most endangered major tropical ecosystem. In *Biodiversity*, ed. E. O. Wilson, 130–37. Washington: National Academy Press.

Janzen, D. H., G. A. Miller, J. Hackforth-Jones, C. M. Pond, K. Hooper, and D. P. Janos. 1976. Two Costa Rican bat-generated seed shadows of *Andira inermis* (Leguminosae). *Ecology* 57:1068–75.

Jerdon, T. T. C. 1862–64. The birds of India: Being a natural history of all the birds known to inhabit continental India, with descriptions of the species, genera, families, tribes, and orders, and a brief notice of such families as are not found in India, making it a manual of ornithology specially adapted for India. Calcutta: Printed for the Author by the Military Orphan Press.

———. 1867. The mammals of India; a natural history of all the animals known to inhabit continental India. Roorkee: Printed for the author by the Thomason College Press, Roorkee.

Johns, A. D. 1986. Effects of selective logging on the behavioral ecology of West Malaysia primates. *Ecology* 67:684–94.

Johns, A. G. 1997. *Timber Production and Biodiversity Conservation in Tropical Rainforests*. Cambridge: Cambridge University Press.

Jolivet, P. 1988. Food habits and food selection of Chrysomelidae: Bionomic and evolutionary perspectives. In *Biology of Chrysomelidae*, ed. P. Jolivet, E. Petitpierre, and T. H. Hsiao, 1–24. Dordrecht: Kluwer Academic Publishers.

Jones, E. W. 1955. Ecological studies on the rain forest of southern Nigeria. IV (part 1): The plateau forest of the Okomu forest reserve. *J Ecol* 43:564–94

———. 1956. Ecological studies on the rain forest of southern Nigeria IV (part 2): The reproduction and history of the forest. *J Ecol* 44:83–117.

Jordan, C. F. 1971. Productivity of a tropical forest and its relation to a world pattern of energy storage. *J Ecol* 59:127–42.

———, ed. 1981. *Tropical Ecology*. Stroudsburg, Pa.: Hutchinson Ross.

———. 1985. *Nutrient Cycling in Tropical Forest Ecosystems*. New York: Wiley.

Jordan, C. F., and R. Herrera. 1981. Tropical rain forests: Are nutrients really critical? *Am Nat* 117:167–80.

Jordan, C. F., and N. Stark. 1978. Retención de nutrientes en la estera de raíces de un bosque pluvial Amazónico. *Acta Cient Venez* 29:263–67.

Jordan, C. F., R. L. Todd, and G. Escalante. 1979. Nitrogen conservation in a tropical rain forest. *Oecologia* 39:123–28.

Jordano, P. 1995a. Angiosperm fleshy fruits and seed dispersers: A comparative analysis of adaptations and constraints in plant-animal interactions. *Am Nat* 145:163–91.

———. 1995b. Frugivore-mediated selection on fruit and seed size: Birds and St. Lucie's cherry, *Prunus mahaleb*. *Ecology* 76:2627–39.

Joron, J., and J. L. B. Mallet. 1998. Diversity in mimicry: Paradox or paradigm? *Trends Ecol Evol* 13:461–66.

Juenger, T., and J. Bergelson. 1998. Pairwise versus diffuse natural selection and the multiple herbivores of scarlet gilia, *Ipomopsis aggregata*. *Evolution* 52:1583–92.

Julliot, C. 1999. Impact of seed dispersal by red howler monkeys *Allouata seniculus* on the seedling population in the understorey of tropical rain forest. *J Ecol* 85:431–40.

Kahn, R., and A. de Castro. 1985. The palm community in a forest of Central Amazonia, Brazil. *Biotropica* 17:210–16.

Karr, J. R. 1971. Structure of avian communities in selected Panama and Illinois habitats. *Ecol Monogr* 41:207–33.

———. 1976. Within- and between-habitat diversity in

African and Neotropical lowland habitats. *Ecol Monogr* 46:457–81.

Karr, J. R., and K. E. Freemark. 1983. Habitat selection and environmental gradients: Dynamics in the "stable" tropics. *Ecology* 64:1481–94.

Kaspari, M., S. O'Donnell, and J. R. Kercher. 2000. Energy, density, and constraints to species richness: Ant assemblages along a productivity gradient. *Am Nat* 155:280–93.

Kaufman, D. M., and M. R. Willig. 1998. Latitudinal patterns of mammalian species richness in the New World: The effects of sampling method and faunal group. *J Biogeogr* 25:795–805.

Kaufman, L. S. 1997. Asynchronous taxon cycles in haplochromine fishes of the greater Lake Victoria region. *South Afr J Sci* 93:601–6.

Keeler-Wolf, T. 1988. Fruit and consumer differences in three spcies of trees shared by Trinidad and Tobago. *Biotropica* 20:38–48.

Keller, C. 1892. Neue Beobachtungen über Symbiose zwischen Ameisen und Akazien. *Zool Anz* 388:137–43.

Keller, M., D. A. Clark, D. B. Clark, A. M. Weitz, and E. Veldkamp. 1996. If a tree falls in the forest. . . . *Science* 273: 201.

Khadari, B., M. Gibernau, M.-C. Anstett, F. Kjellberg, and M. Hossaert-McKey. 1995. When figs wait for pollinators: The length of fig receptivity. *Am J Bot* 82:992–99.

Kiester, A. R. 1971. Species density of North American amphibians and reptiles. *Syst Zool* 20:127–37.

Kingsland, S. E. 1985. *Modeling Nature: Episodes in the History of Population Ecology*. Chicago: University of Chicago Press.

Kingsley, M. H. 1897. *Travels in West Africa*. Boston: Beacon.

Kinzey, W. G. 1977. Diet and feeding behaviour of *Callicebus torquatus*. In *Primate Ecology: Studies of Feeding and Ranging Behaviour in Lemurs, Monkeys, and Apes*, ed. T. H. Clutton-Brock, 127–51. London: Academic Press.

Kira, T. 1978. Community architecture and organic matter dynamics in tropical lowland rain forests of Southeast Asia with special reference to Pasoh Forest, West Malaysia. In *Tropical Trees as Living Systems*, ed. T. B. Tomlinson and M. H. Zimmerman, 561–90. New York: Cambridge University Press.

Kira, T., and T. Shidei. 1967. Primary production and turnover of organic matter in different forest ecosystems of the Western Pacific. *Japanese J Ecol* 17:70–87.

Kitajima, K., and C. K. Augspurger. 1989. Seed and seedling ecology of a monocarpic tropical tree, *Tachigalia versicolor*. *Ecology* 73:2129–44.

Klein, L. L., and D. J. Klein 1975. Social and ecological contrasts between four taxa of Neotropical primates. *Socioecology and Psychology of Primates*, ed. R. A. Tuttle, 59–85. The Hague: Mouton.

Kleinfeldt, S. 1978. Ant-gardens: The interaction of *Codo-*

nanthe carssifolia (Gesneriaceae) and *Crematogaster longispina* (Formicidae). *Ecology* 59:449–56.

Knapp, S. 1999. *Footsteps in the Forest: Alfred Russel Wallace in the Amazon*. London: Natural History Museum.

Kobe, R. K. 1999. Light gradient partitioning among tropical tree species through differential seedling mortality and growth. *Ecology* 80:187–201.

Kochummen, K. M., J. V. LaFrankie, and N. Manokaran. 1990. Floristic composition of Pasoh Forest Reserve, a lowland rain forest in Peninsular Malaysia. *J Trop For Sci* 3:1–13.

Kramer, E. A. 1997. Measuring landscape changes in remnant tropical dry forests. In *Tropical Forest Remnants: Ecology, Management, and Conservation of Fragmented Communities*, ed. W. F. Laurance and R. O. Bierregard, 400–409. Chicago: University of Chicago Press.

Kramer, K. 1933. Die natuurlijke verjonging in het Goenoeng Gedeh complex. *Tectona* 26:156–85.

Kress, W. J. 1986. The systematic distribution of vascular epiphytes: An update. *Selbyana* 9:2–22.

Krishtalka, L. 1986. Dancing in time. *Nature* 320:653.

Kunstadter, P., and E. C. Chapman. 1978. Problems of shifting agriculture and economic development in northern Thailand. In *Farmers in the Forest*, ed. P. Kunstadter, E. C. Chapman, and S. Sabhasri, 3–23. Honolulu: University of Hawaii Press.

Lack, D. 1944. Ecological aspects of species-formation in passerine birds. *Ibis* 86:260–86.

———. 1968. *Ecological Adaptations for Breeding in Birds*. London: Methuen.

La Condamine, C.-M. de. 1745. *Relation abregée d'un voyage fait dans l'interieur de l'Amerique meridionale, depuis la côte de la mer du Sud, jusques aux côtes du Bresil et de la Guiane, en descendant la rivière des Amazones*. Paris. Reprinted as *A Voyage through the Inner Parts of South America* (London, 1747).

Lamb, D. 1990. *Exploiting the Tropical Rain Forest: An Account of Pulpwood Logging in Papua New Guinea*. Paris: UNESCO; Carnforth: Parthenon.

Lambert, F. 1991. The conservation of fig-eating birds in Malaysia. *Biol Conserv* 58:31–40.

Lang, G. E., D. H. Knight, and D. A. Anderson. 1971. Sampling the density of tree species with quadrats in a species-rich tropical forest. *For Sci* 17:395–400.

Lanly, J. P. 1982. *Tropical Forest Resources*. FAO Forestry Paper no. 30. Rome: United Nations Food and Agriculture Organization.

Larsen, K. 1989. Danish botanists in the tropics—tropical botany in Denmark. In *Tropical Forests: Botanical Dynamics, Speciation, and Diversity*, ed. L. B. Holm-Nielsen, I. C. Nielsen, and H. Balslev, 339–46. London: Academic Press.

Latham, R. E., and R. E. Ricklefs. 1993. Global patterns of

tree species richness in moist forests: Energy-diversity theory does not account for variation in species richness. *Oikos* 67:325–33.

Laurance, W. F. 1998. A crisis in the making: Responses of Amazonian forests to land use and climate change. *Trends Ecol Evol* 10:411–15.

———. 1999. Reflexion on the tropical deforestation crisis. *Biol Conserv* 91:109–17.

Laurance, W. F., and R. O. Bierregaard Jr., eds. 1997. *Tropical Forest Remnants*. Chicago: University of Chicago Press.

Leach, H. M. 1997. Intensification in the Pacific: A critique of the archaeological criteria and their application. *Current Anthropol* 40:311–39.

Leigh, E. G., Jr. 1999. *Tropical Forest Ecology*. New York: Oxford University Press.

Leslie, A. J. 1977. Where contradictory theory and practice co-exist. *Unasylva* 29, no. 115: 2–17, 40.

———. 1987. A second look at the economics of natural management system in tropical mixed forests. *Unasylva* 39, no. 155: 46–58.

Leston, D. 1973. The ant mosaic: Tropical tree crops and the limiting of pests and diseases. *Pest Articles News Summary* 19:311–41.

Lewis, L., and E. V. J. Tanner. 2000. Effects of above- and belowground competition on growth and survival of rainforest tree seedlings. *Ecology* 81:2525–38.

Lieberman, M., and D. L. Lieberman. 1994. Patterns of density and dispersion of forest trees. In *La Selva: Ecology and Natural History of a Neotropical Rain Forest*, ed. L. A. McDade, K. S. Bawa, H. A. Hespenheide, and G. S. Hartshorn, 106–19. Chicago: University of Chicago Press.

Lieberman, M., D. L. Lieberman, G. S. Hartshorn, and R. Peralta. 1995. Small-scale altitudinal variation in lowland wet tropical forest vegetation. *J Ecol* 83:505–16.

Lieberman, M., D. L. Lieberman, and R. Peralta. 1989. Forests are not just Swiss cheese: Canopy stereogeometry of non-gaps in tropical forests. *Ecology* 70:550–52.

Liebherr, J. K., and A. E. Hajek. 1990. A cladistic test of the taxon cycle and taxon pulse hypotheses. *Cladistics* 6: 39–60.

Lieth, H., and R. H. Whittaker 1975. *Primary Productivity of the Biosphere*. New York: Springer-Verlag.

Lim, B. L. 1960. Abundance and distribution of Malaysian bats in different ecological habitats. *Fed Mus J* 11:61–76.

Longino, J. T., and R. K. Colwell. 1997. Biodiversity assessment using structured inventory: Capturing the ant fauna of a tropical forest. *Ecol Applic* 7:1263–77.

Longman, K. A., and J. Jenik. 1987. *Tropical Forest and Its Environment*. 2d ed. London: Longman.

Lott, R. H., G. N. Harrington, A. K. Irvine, and S. McIntyre. 1995. Density-dependent seed predation and plant dispersion of the tropical palm *Normanbya normanbyi*. *Biotropica* 27:87–95.

Lugo, A. E. 1995. A review of Dr. Howard T. Odum's early

publications: From bird migration studies to Scott Nixon's turtle rass model. In *Maximum Power: The Ideas and Applications of H. T. Odum*, ed. C. A. S. Hall, 3–10. Niwot: University Press of Colorado.

———. 1999. Will concern for biodiversity spell doom to tropical forest management? *Sci Total Environ* 240: 123–31

Lugo, A. E., J. A. Parrotta, and S. Brown. 1997. Loss in species caused by tropical deforestation and their recovery through management. *Ambio* 22:106–9.

Mabberly, D. J. 1992. *Tropical Rain Forest Ecology*. 2d ed. London: Blackie.

MacArthur, R. H. 1964. Environmental factors affecting bird species diversity. *Am Nat* 98:387–97.

———. 1965. Patterns of species diversity. *Biol Rev* 40: 510–33.

———. 1969. Patterns of communities in the tropics. *Biol J Linn Soc* 1:19–30.

———. 1972. *Geographical Ecology*. New York: Harper and Row.

MacArthur, R. H., and R. Levins. 1967. The limiting similarity, convergence and divergence of coexisting species. *Am Nat* 101:377–85.

MacArthur R. H., and J. MacArthur 1961. On bird species diversity. *Ecology* 42:594–98.

MacArthur, R. H., H. Recher, and M. L. Cody. 1966. On the relation between habitat selection and species diversity. *Am Nat* 100:319–32.

MacArthur, R. H., and E. O. Wilson. 1963. An equilibrium theory of insular biogeography. *Evolution* 17:373–87.

———. 1967. *The Theory of Island Biogeography*. Princeton: Princeton University Press.

Machado, C. A., E. A. Herre, S. McCafferty, and E. Birmingham. 1996. Molecular phylogenies of fig pollinating and non-pollinating wasps and the implications for the origin and evolution of the fig–fig wasp mutualism. *J Biogeogr* 23:531–42.

Majer, J. D. 1993. Comparison of the arboreal ant mosaic in Ghana, Brazil, Papua New Guinea, and Australia: Its structure and influence on arthropod diversity. In *Hymenoptera and Biodiversity*, ed. J. LaSalle and I. D. Gauld, 115–41. Wallingford, U.K.: CAB International.

Maley, J. 1987. Fragmentation de la forêt dense humide africaine et extension des biotopes montagnards au Quaternaire Récent: Nouvelles données polliniques et chronologiques; implications paléoclimatiques et biogéographiques. In *Palaeoecology of Africa and the Surrounding Islands* 18, ed. K. Heine and J. Runge, 307–32. Rotterdam: Balkema.

———. 1996. The African rain forest: Main characteristics of changes in vegetation and climate from the Upper Cretaceous to the Quaternary. *Royal Soc Edinburgh Proc*, ser. B, 104:31–76.

Mallet, J., and N. H. Barton. 1989. Strong natural selection in a warning-color hybrid zone. *Evolution* 43:421–31.

Mallet, J., and M. Joron. 1999. Evolution of diversity in

warning color and mimicry: Polymorphisms, shifting balance, and speciation. *Annu Rev Ecol Syst* 30:201–33.

Mann, C. C. 2000. Earthmovers of the Amazon. *Science* 287:786–88.

Marquis, R. J. 1984. Leaf herbivores decrease fitness of a tropical plant. *Science* 226:537–39.

———. 1991. Hervivore Fauna of *Piper* (Piperaceae) in a Costa Rican Wet Forest: Diversity, specificity, and impact. In *Plant-Animal Interactions: Evolutionary Ecology in Tropical and Temperate Regions,* ed. P. W. Price, T. M. Lewinsohn, G. W. Fernandes, and W. W. Benson, 179–208. New York: John Wiley and Sons.

Martin, T. E. 1992. Interaction of nest predation and food limitation in reproductive strategies. *Curr Ornithol* 9:163–97.

Martínez, S. E., and C. H. Ramos, 1989. *Lacandonia schismatica* (Triuridales): Una nueva familia de México. *Ann Missouri Bot Gard* 76:128–35.

Mattingly, P. F. 1949. Studies on West African forest mosquitoes. Part 1. The seasonal distribution, biting cycle, and vertical distribution of four of the principal species. *Bull Entomol Res* 40:149–68.

May, R. M. 1988. How many species are there on Earth? *Science* 241:1441–49.

———. 1990. How many species? *Philosophical Trans Royal Soc London,* ser. B, 330:293–304.

———. 1999. Unanswered questions in ecology. *Philosophical Trans Royal Soc London,* ser. B, 354:1951–59.

———. 2000. The dimensions of life on Earth. In *Nature and Human Society: The Quest for a Sustainable World,* ed. P. H. Raven and T. Williams, 30–45. Washington: National Academy Press.

May, R. M., and R. H. MacArthur. 1972. Niche overlap as a function of environmental variability. *Proc Nat Acad Sci USA* 69:1109–13.

Mayers, J., and Bass, S. 1998. The role of policy and institutions. In *Tropical Rain Forest: A Wider Perspective,* ed. F. B. Goldsmith, 269–302. London: Chapman and Hall.

Mayle, F. E., R. Burbridge, and T. J. Killeen. 2000. Millennial-scale dynamics of southern-Amazonian rain forests. *Science* 290:2291–94.

Mayr, E. 1963. *Animal Species and Evolution.* Cambridge: Belknap Press.

———. 1969. Bird speciation in the tropics. *Biol J Linn Soc* 1:1–17.

Mayr, E., and R. O'Hara. 1986. The biogeographic evidence supporting the Pleistocene refuge hypothesis. *Evolution* 40:55–67.

Mazer, S. J., and N. T. Wheelwright. 1993. Fruit size and shape: Allometry at different taxonomic levels in bird-dispersed plants. *Evol Ecol* 7:556–75.

McClure, H. E. 1966. Observations on fruiting and flowering seasons in a Malayan forest. *Malay For* 19:193–201.

———. 1974. *Migration and Survival of the Birds of Asia.* Bangkok: U.S. Army Medical Component, SEATO Medical Project.

McKey, D. B. 1975. The ecology of coevolved seed dispersal systems. In *Coevolution of Animals and Plants,* ed. L. E. Gilbert and P. H. Raven, 159–91. Austin: University of Texas Press.

———. 1984. Interaction of the ant-plant *Leonardoxa africana* (Caesalpinaceae) with its obligate inhabitants in a rainforest in Cameroon. *Biotropica* 16:81–99.

McKey, D. B., P. G. Waterman, C. N. Mbi, J. S. Gartlan, and T. H. Strushaker. 1978. Phenolic content of vegetation in two African rain forests: Ecological implications. *Science* 202:61–64.

Medway, Lord. 1972a. The Gunung Benom Expedition 1967:6. The distribution and altitudinal zonation of birds and mammals on Gunong Benom. *Bull Br. Mus (Nat Hist) Zoology* 23:105–54.

———. 1972b. Phenology of a tropical rain forest in Malaya. *Biol J Linn Soc* 4:117–46.

———. 1976. Reproductive cycles of the flat-headed bats, *Tylonycteris pachypus* and *T. robustulata* (Chiroptera: Vespertilioninae) in a humid equatorial environment. *Zool J Linn Soc* 51:33–61.

Medway, Lord, and D. R. Wells. 1976. *The Birds of the Malay Peninsula.* Vol. 5. London: H. F. and G. Witherby.

Michaloud, G., S. Carrière, and M. Kobbi. 1996. Exceptions to the one:one relationship between African fig trees and their fig wasp pollinators: Possible evolutionary scenarios. *J Biogeogr* 23:513–20.

Miles, D. B., and A. E. Dunham. 1996. The paradox of the phylogeny: Character displacement of analyses of body size in island *Anolis. Evolution* 50:594–603.

Miller, S. E. 1996. Biogeography of Pacific insects and other terrestrial invertebrates: A status report. In *The Origin and Evolution of Pacific Island Biotas, New Guinea to Eastern Polynesia: Patterns and Processes,* ed. A. Keast and S. E. Miller, 463–75. Amsterdam: SPB Academic Publishing.

Milne, G. 1937. Essays in applied pedology. 1. Soil type and soil management in relation to plantation agriculture in East Usambara. *East Afr Agric J* 3 (July): 7–20.

Misra, R., and B. Gopal, eds. 1968. *Proceedings of the Symposium on Recent Advances in Tropical Ecology.* Parts 1 and 2. Varanasi, India: International Society for Tropical Ecology.

Moermond, T. C., and J. S. Denslow. 1985. Neotropical avian frugivores: Patterns of behavior, morphology, and nutrition with consequences for fruit selection. In *Neotropical Ornithology,* ed. P. A. Buckley, M. S. Foster, E. S. Morton, R. S. Ridgely, and N. G. Smith, 865–97. American Ornithological Union Monographs, no. 36.

Molofsky, J., and Augspurger, C. K. 1992. The effect of litter on early seedling establishment in a tropical forest. *Ecology* 73:68–77.

Morales, M. A., and E. R. Heithaus. 1998. Food from seed-dispersal mutualism shifts sex ratios in colonies of the ant *Aphenogaster rudis. Ecology* 79:734–39.

Moreau, R. E. 1936a. A contribution to the ornithology of

Kilimanjaro and Mount Meru. *Proc Zool Soc London* 1935:843–91.

———. 1936b. Breeding seasons of birds in East African evergreen forest. *Proc Zool Soc London* 1936:631–53.

———. 1950. The breeding seasons of African birds. 1. Land birds. *Ibis* 92:223–67.

———. 1966. *The Bird Faunas of Africa and Its Islands.* New York: Academic Press.

Morley, R. J. 2000. *Origin and Evolution of Tropical Rain Forests.* Chichester: Wiley.

Morton, E. S. 1973. On the evolutionary advantages and disadvantages of fruit-eating in tropical birds. *Am Nat* 107:8–22.

Müller, F. 1879. *Ituna* and *Thyridis:* A remarkable case of mimicry in butterflies. *Proc Entomol Soc London* 1879:20–29.

Mutis, J. C. [1760–90] 1957–58. Diario de observaciones de Jose Celestino Mutis, 1760–1790. Edited with prologue and notes by Guillermo Hernandez de Alba. Bogotá: Editorial Minerva.

Myers, N. 1980. *Conversion of Tropical Moist Forests.* Washington: National Academy of Sciences.

———. 1993. Population, environment, and development. *Environ Conserv* 20:205–16.

Naskrecki, P., and R. K. Colwell. 1998. *Systematics and Host Plant Affiliations of Hummingbird Flower Mites of the Genera Tropicoseius Baker & Yunker and Rhinoseius Baker & Yunker (Acari: Mesostigmata: Ascidae).* Lanham, Md.: Entomological Society of America.

Nason, J. D., and J. L. Hamrick. 1997. Reproductive and genetic consequences of forest fragmentation: Two case studies of Neotropical canopy trees. *J Hered* 8:264–76.

Nason, J. D., E. A. Herre, and J. L. Hamrick. 1998. The breeding structure of a tropical keystone plant resource. *Nature* 391:685–87.

———. 1996. Paternity analysis of the breeding structure of strangler fig populations: Evidence for substantial long-distance wasp dispersal. *J Biogeogr* 23:501–12.

National Research Council (NRC). 1960. *Conference on Tropical Botany, Fairchild Tropical Garden, May 5–7.* Publication 822. Washington: National Academy Press.

Nelson, B. W., C. A. C. Ferreira, M. F. da Silva, and M. L. Kawasaki. 1990. Endemism centres, refugia, and botanical collection density in Brazilian Amazonia. *Nature* 345:714–16.

Newbery, D. M., and J. Proctor. 1984. Ecological studies in four contrasting lowland rain forests in Gunung Mulu National Park, Sarawak. *J Ecol* 72:475–93.

Nicholson, M. 1995. Historical introduction to *Personal Narrative of a Journey to the Equinoctial Regions of the New Continent,* by A. von Humboldt. Abridged and translated by Jason Wilson. London: Penguin Books.

Nielsen, E. S., and L. A. Mound. 2000. Global diversity of insects: The problems of estimating numbers. In *Na-*
ture and Human Society: The Quest for a Sustainable World, ed. P. H. Raven and T. Williams, 213–22. Washington: National Academy Press.

Nores, M. 1999. An alternative hypothesis for the origin of Amazonian bird diversity. *J Biogeogr* 26:475–85.

North, M. 1894. *Recollections of a Happy Life.* Ed. Mrs. John Addington Symonds. 3 vols. London: Macmillan.

Notman, E., D. L. Gorchov, and F. Cornejo. 1996. Effect of distance, aggregation, and habitat on levels of seed predation for two mammal-dispersed Neotropical rain forest tree species. *Oecologia* 106:221–27.

Novotny, V., and Y. Basset. 2000. Ecological characteristics of rare species in communities of tropical insect herbivores: Pondering the mystery of singletons. *Oikos* 89: 564–72.

Nye, P. H., and D. J. Greenland. 1960. *The Soil under Shifting Cultivation.* 5.

Odum, H. T., B. J. Copeland, and R. Z. Brown. 1968. Direct and optical assay of leaf mass of the lower montane rain forest of Puerto Rico. *Proc Nat Acad Sci USA* 49:429–84

Odum, H. T., and C. F. Jordan. 1970. Metabolism and evapotranspiration of the lower forest in a giant plastic cylinder. In *A Tropical Rain Forest,* ed. H. T. Odum and R. F. Pigeon, I165–I189. Washington: Office of Information Services, U.S. Atomic Energy Commission.

Odum, H. T., and R. F. Pigeon, eds. 1970. *A Tropical Rain Forest.* Washington: Office of Information Services, U.S. Atomic Energy Commission.

Odum, H. T., and J. Ruíz-Reyes. 1970. Holes in leaves and the grazing control mechanism. In *A Tropical Rain Forest,* ed. H. T. Odum and R. F. Pigeon, I69–I80. Washington: Office of Information Services, U.S. Atomic Energy Commission.

Ogawa, H., K. Yoda, K. Ogino, and T. Kira. 1965. Comparative ecological studies on three main types of forest vegetation in Thailand. 2. Plant biomass. *Nat Life Southeast Asia* 4:49–80.

Oldfield, M. L. 1984. *The Value of Conserving Genetic Resources.* Washington: U.S. Department of the Interior.

Oliviera, A. A. de, and S. A. Mori. 1999. A central Amazonian terra firme forest. 1. High tree species richness on poor soils. *Biodiversity Conserv* 8:1219–44.

Opler, P. A., G. W. Frankie, and H. G. Baker. 1976. Rainfall as a factor in the release, timing, and synchronization of anthesis by tropical trees and shrubs. *J Biogeogr* 3: 231–36.

Orians, G. H. 1969. The number of bird species in some tropical forests. *Ecology* 50:783–801.

———. 1982. The influence of tree-falls in tropical forests in tree species richness. *Trop Ecol* 23:256–79.

Orr, H. A. 1998. The population genetics of adaptation: The distribution of factors fixed during adaptive evolution. *Evolution* 52:935–49

Ostertag, R. 1998. Belowground effects of canopy gaps in a tropical wet forest. *Ecology* 79:1294–304.

Pace, M. L., J. J. Cole, S, R. Carpenter, and J. F. Kitchell. 1999. Trophic cascades revealed in diverse ecosystems. *Trends Ecol Evol* 14:483–88.

Paine, R. T. 1966. Food web complexity and species diversity. *Am Nat* 100:65–75.

Palmer, M. W. 1991. Estimating species richness: The second-order jackknife reconsidered. *Ecology* 72:1512–13.

———. 1994. Variation in species richness: Towards a unification of hypotheses. *Folia Geobot Phytotax Praha* 29:511–30.

Panayatou, T., and Ashton, P. S. 1992. *Not by Timber Alone*. Washington: Island Press.

Parker, G. G. 1995. Structure and microclimate of forest canopies. In *Forest Canopies*, ed. M. D. Lowman and N. M. Nadkarni, 431–55. San Diego: Academic Press.

Parren, M. P. E., and de Graaf, N. R. 1995. The quest for natural forest management in Ghana, Côte d'Ivoire, and Liberia. Tropenbos ser. 13. Wageningen, Netherlands: Tropenbos.

Parrotta, J., and J. Turnbull. 1997. *Catalysing Native Forest Regeneration on Degraded Tropical Lands*. Special issue of *For Ecol Management* 99:1–290.

Paulian, R. 1947. Observations ecologiques en forêt de Basse Côte d'Ivoire. *Encyclopedie Biogeogr Ecol* 2:1–147.

Pellmyr, O. 1989. The cost of a mutualism: Interactions between *Trollius europaeus* and its pollinating parasites. *Oecologia* 78:53–59.

Pellmyr, O., and J. N. Thompson. 1996. Sources of variation in pollinator contribution within a guild: The effects of plant and pollinator factors. *Oecologia* 107:595–604.

Pellmyr, O., J. N. Thompson, J. M. Brown, and R. G. Harrison. 1996. Evolution of pollination and mutualism in the yucca moth lineage. *Am Nat* 148:827–47.

Peluso, N. L. 1983. Networking in the commons: A tragedy for rattan. *Indonesia* 35:95–108.

Peters, C. M., A. H. Gentry, and R. O. Mendelsohn. 1989. Valuation of an Amazonian rain forest. *Nature* 399:655–56.

Petraitis, P. S., R. E. Latham, and R. A. Niesenbaum. 1989. The maintenance of species diversity by disturbance. *Quart Rev Biol* 64:393–418.

Phillips, O. 1993. The potential of harvesting fruits in tropical rain forests: New data from Amazonian Peru. *Biodiversity Conserv* 2:18–38.

Phillips, O. L., P. Hall, A. H. Gentry, S. A. Sawyer, and R. Vásquez. 1994. Dynamics and species richness of tropical rain forests. *Proc Nat Acad Sci USA* 91:2805–09.

Phillips, O. L., P. Hall, S. A. Sawyer, and R. Vásquez. 1997. Species richness, tropical forest dynamics, and sampling: Response to Sheil. *Oikos* 79:183–87.

Pianka, E. R. 1966. Latitudinal gradients in species diversity: A review of concepts. *Am Nat* 100:33–46.

———. 1967. On lizard species diversity: North American flatland deserts. *Ecology* 48:333–51.

Pichi Sermolli, R. E. G., and C. G. G. J. van Steenis. 1983. Dedication. *Flora Malesiana* ser. 1, vol. 9 (3): 19–29.

Pinard, M. A., and F. E. Putz 1996. Retaining forest biomass by reducing logging damage. *Biotropica* 28:278–95.

Pires, J. M., T. Dobzhansky, and G. A. Black. 1953. An estimate of the number of species of trees in an Amazonian forest community. *Bot Gazette* 114:467–77.

Pitman, N. C. A., J. Terborgh, M. R. Silman, and P. Núñez V. 1999. Tree species distributions in an upper Amazonian forest. *Ecology* 80:2651–61.

Plotkin, J. B., M. D. Potts, D. W. Yu, S. Bunyavejchewin, R. Condit, R. Foster, S. Hubbell, J. LaFrankie, N. Manokaran, H.-S. Lee, R. Sukumar, M. A. Nowak, and P. S. Ashton. 2000. Predicting species diversity in tropical forests. *Proc Nat Acad Sci USA* 97:10850–54.

Poffenburger, M. 1990. *Keepers of the Forest: Land Management Alternatives in Southeast Asia*. West Hartford: Kumarian Press.

Poore, M. E. D. 1963. Problems in the classification of tropical rain forest. *J Trop Geogr* 17:12–19.

———. 1968. Studies in Malaysian rain forest. 1. The forest on Triassic sediments in Jengka forest reserve. *J Ecol* 56:143–93.

———. 1995. Forestry and nature conservation: Changing perspectives. *Commonwealth For Rev* 74:5–19.

Poore, D., and 19 others. 1999. No forests without management. *Trop For Update* 84:10–12.

Poulsen, A., and H. Balslev. 1991. Abundance and cover of ground herbs in an Amazonian rain forest. *J Veget Sci* 2:315–22.

Powell, J. M. 1976. Ethnobotany. In *New Guinea Vegetation*, ed. K. Paijmans, 106–83. Amsterdam: Elsevier.

Prance, G. T. 1977. Floristic inventory of the tropics: Where do we stand? *Ann Missouri Bot Gard* 64:659–84.

———, ed. 1982. *Biological Diversification in the Tropics*. New York: Columbia University Press.

Preston, F. W. 1948. The commonness, and rarity, of species. *Ecology* 29:254–83.

Proctor, J. 1983. Mineral nutrients in tropical forests. *Prog Physical Geogr* 7:422–31.

———. 1987. Nutrient cycling in primary and old secondary rainforests. *Applied Geogr* 7:135–52.

Quammen, D. 1996. *The Song of the Dodo*. New York: Simon and Schuster.

Rabinowitz, D. 1981. Seven forms of rarity. In *The Biological Aspects of Rare Plant Conservation*, ed. H. Synge, 205–17. New York: Wiley.

Raby, P. 1997. *Bright Paradise: Victorian Scientific Travelers*. Princeton: Princeton University Press.

Raemaekers, J. J., and D. J. Chivers. 1980. Socio-ecology of Malayan forest primates. In *Malayan Forest Primates: Ten Years' Study in Tropical Rainforest*, ed. D. J. Chivers, 279–316. New York and London: Plenum Press.

Raffles, T. S. 1821. Descriptive Catalogue of a Zoological Collection, made on account of the Honourable East India Company, in the Island of Sumatra and its Vicinity. *Trans Linn Soc London* 13:239–74.

———. 1825. *Die Vulkane auf Java, von T. S. Raffles; Uber den Monte-Somma, von L. A. Necker; Und uber die Vulkane in der Auvergne von K. Daubeny*. Elberfeld: Schonian'sche Buchhandlung.

Rappaport, R. A. 1971. The flow of energy in an agricultural society. *Sci Am* 2253:116–32.

Rausher, M. D. 1992. Natural selection and the evolution of plant-insect interactions. In *Insect Chemical Ecology: An Evolutionary Approach*, ed. B. D. Roitberg and M. B. Isman, 20–88. New York: Chapman and Hall.

Raven, P. H. 1988. Our diminishing tropical forests. In *Biodiversity*, ed. E. O. Wilson, 119–22. Washington: National Academy Press.

Raven, P. H., and D. I. Axelrod. 1974. Angiosperm biogeography and past continental movements. *Ann Missouri Bot Gard* 61:539–673.

Ray, J. 1678. *The ornithology of Francis Willughby*. London: Printed by A. C. for John Martyn.

Real, L. A., and J. H. Brown, eds. 1991. *Foundations of Ecology: Classic Papers with Commentaries*. Chicago: University of Chicago Press.

Recher, H. F. 1969. Bird species diversity and habitat diversity in Australia and North America. *Am Nat* 103:75–80.

Redford, K. H. 1992. The empty forest. *BioScience* 42:412–22.

Reid, W. V. 1992. How many species will there be? In *Tropical Deforestation and Species Extinction*, ed. T. C. Whitmore and J. A. Sayer, 55–73. London: Chapman and Hall.

Renner, S. S. 1998. Effects of habitat fragmentation on plant pollinator interactions in the tropics. In *Dynamics of Tropical Communities*, ed. D. M. Newberry, H. H. T. Prins, and N. Brown, 339–60. Oxford: Blackwell Science.

Rhoades, D. F., and R. G. Cates. 1976. Toward a general theory of plant antiherbivore chemistry. In *Biochemical Interactions between Plants and Insects*, ed. J. Wallace and R. S. Mansell, 168–213. Vol. 10 of *Recent Advances in Phytochemistry*. New York: Plenum Press.

Richards, P. W. 1936. Ecological observations on the rain forest of Mount Dulit, Sarawak. *J Ecol* 24:1–37, 340–60.

———. 1952. *The Tropical Rain Forest: An Ecological Study*. Cambridge: Cambridge University Press.

———. 1963. What the tropics can contribute to ecology. *J Ecol* 51:231–41.

———. 1973. Africa, the "odd man out." In *Tropical Forest Ecosystems in Africa and South America: A Comparative Review*, ed. B. Meggars, E. S. Ayensu, and W. D.

Duckworth, 21–26. Washington: Smithsonian Institution Press.

———. 1996. *The Tropical Rain Forest: An Ecological Study*. 2d ed. Cambridge: Cambridge University Press.

Ricklefs, R. E. 1977. A note on the evolution of clutch size in altricial birds. In *Evolutionary Ecology*, ed. B. Stonehouse and C. Perrins, 193–214. London: Macmillan.

———. 1989. Nest predation and the species diversity of birds. *Trends Ecol Evol* 4:184–86.

———. 2000. Rarity and diversity in Amazonian forest trees. *Trends Ecol Evol* 15:83–84.

Ricklefs, R. E., and E. Bermingham. 1999. Taxon cycles in the Lesser Antillean avifauna. *Ostrich* 70:49–59.

Ricklefs, R. E., R. E. Latham, and H. Qian. 1999. Global patterns of tree species richness in moist forests: Distinguishing ecological influences and historical contingency. *Oikos* 86:369–73.

Ricklefs, R. E., and D. Schluter, eds. 1993. *Species Diversity in Ecological Communities: Historical and Geographical Perspectives*. Chicago: University of Chicago Press.

Ridley, H. N. 1930. *The Dispersal of Plants throughout the World*. Ashford, Kent: L. L. Reeve.

Riley, C. V. 1892. The yucca moth and yucca pollination. In *Missouri Botanical Garden Annual Report*, vol. 3: 99–159.

Robbins, R. K. 1993. Comparison of butterfly diversity in the Neotropical and Oriental regions. *J Lepidopterists Soc* 46:298–300.

Robertson, G. P. 1984. Nitrification and nitrogen mineralization in a lowland rainforest succession in Costa Rica, Central America. *Oecologia* 61:99–104.

Robertson, H. G. 2000. Afrotropical ants (Hymenoptera: Formicidae): Taxonomic progress and estimation of species richness. *J Hymenoptera Res* 9:71–84.

Robinson, J. G., K. H. Redford, and E. L. Bennett. 1999. Wildlife harvest in logged tropical forests. *Science* 284:595–96.

Robinson, M. H. 1978. Is tropical biology real? *Trop Ecol* 19:30–50.

———. 1992. The uniqueness of tropical natural history. *Malay Nat J* 45:273–309.

Rohde, K. 1992. Latitudinal gradients in species diversity: The search for the primary cause. *Oikos* 65:514–27.

———. 1997. The larger area of the tropics does not explain latitudinal gradients in species diversity. *Oikos* 79:169–72.

———. 1998. Latitudinal gradients in species diversity: Area matters, but how much? *Oikos* 82:184–90.

Room, P. M. 1975. Relative distributions of ant species in cocoa plantations in Papua New Guinea. *J Applied Ecol* 12:47–61.

Rosenzweig, M. L. 1995. *Species Diversity in Space and Time*. Cambridge: Cambridge University Press.

Rosenzweig, M. L., and E. A. Sandlin. 1997. Species diversity and latitudes: Listening to area's signal. *Oikos* 80:172–76.

Roubik, D. W., and J. D. Ackerman. 1987. Long-term ecology of euglossine orchid bees (Apidae: Euglossini) in Panama. *Oecologia* 73:321–33.

Roxburgh, W. 1820–24. *Flora Indica; or descriptions of Indian plants. Ed. by William Carey, to which are added descriptions of plants more recently discovered by Nathaniel Wallrich.* 8 vols. Serampore.

Roy, K., D. Jablonski, J. W. Valentine, and G. Rosenberg. 1998. Marine latitudinal diversity gradients: Tests of causal hypotheses. *Proc Nat Acad Sci USA* 95:3699–702.

Rumpf, G. E. 1705. *D'Amboinsche Rariteitkamer.* Amsterdam: F. Halma.

———. 1741–50. *Herbarium Amboinense.* 6 vols. Amsterdam.

———. *The Ambonese Curiosity Cabinet: Georgius Everhardus Rumphius* (translation of Rumpf 1705). Translated, edited, annotated, and with an introduction by E. M. Beekman. New Haven: Yale University Press.

Sabrosky, C. W. 1952. How many insects are there? In *Insects: The Yearbook of Agriculture 1952,* ed. A. Stefferud, 1–7. Washington: Government Printing Office.

Salo, J., R. Kalliola, I. Häkkinen, Y. Mäkinen, P. Niemelä, M. Puhakka, and P. D. Coley. 1986. River dynamics and the diversity of Amazon lowland forest. *Nature* 322: 254–58.

Sanderson, I. T. 1940. The mammals of the north Cameroons forest area. *Philosophical Trans Royal Soc London,* ser. B, 24:623–725.

Sayer, J. A., C. S. Harcourt, and N. M. Collins, eds. 1992. *The Conservation Atlas of Tropical Forests: Africa.* Gland: IUCN; Basingstoke: Macmillan.

Schemske, D. W., and H. D. Bradshaw Jr. 1999. Pollinator preference and the evolution of floral traits in monkeyflowers (*Mimulus*). *Proc Nat Acad Sci USA* 96:11910–15.

Schemske, D. W., and C. C. Horvitz. 1984. Effects of ants and an ant-tended herbivore on seed production of a Neotropical herb. *Ecology* 65:1369–78.

Schimper, A. F. W. 1884. *Ueber Bau und Lebensweise der Epiphyten Westindiens.* Vol. 17 of Botanisches Centralblatt. Cassel.

———. 1888. *Die epiphytische Vegetation Amerikas.* Vol. 2 of Botanische Mittheilungen aus den Tropen. Jena.

———. 1898. Pflanzengeographie auf physiologischer Grundlage. Jena: Gustav Fischer. Published in English as *Plant Geography upon a Physiological Basis,* trans. W. R. Fischer, ed. P. Groom and I. B. Balfour (Oxford: Clarendon Press, 1903).

Schlesinger, W. H. 1991. *Biogeochemistry: An Analysis of Global Change.* San Diego: Academic Press.

Schluter, D. R., and R. E. Ricklefs. 1993. Species diversity: An introduction to the problem. In *Species Diversity in Ecological Communities: Historical and Geographical Perspectives,* ed. R. E. Ricklefs and D. Schluter, 1–10. Chicago: University of Chicago Press.

Schmidt, R. 1987. Tropical rain forest management. *Unasylva* 39, no. 156: 2–17.

Schmidt-Vogt, D. 1999. *Swidden Farming and Fallow Vegetation in Northern Thailand.* Geoecological Research, no. 8.

Schneirla, T. C. 1971. *Army Ants: A Study in Social Organization.* San Francisco: W. H. Freeman and Co.

Scholtz, C. H., and S. L. Chown. 1995. Insects in Southern Africa: How many species are there? *South Afr J Sci* 91:124–26.

Schulz, J. P. 1960. Ecological studies on rain forest in northern Suriname. *Verh K Ned Akad Wet Afd Natuurk* 53: 1–267.

Schupp, E. W. 1992. The Janzen-Connell model for tropical tree diversity: Population implications and the importance of spatial scale. *Am Nat* 140:526–30.

Schupp, E. W., and D. H. Feener. 1991. Phylogeny, life form, and habitat dependence of ant-defended plants in a Panamanian forest. In *Ant-Plant Interactions,* ed. C. R. Huxley and D. F. Cutler, 175–97. Oxford: Oxford University Press.

Scott, N. J. 1976. The abundance and diversity of the herptofaunas of tropical forest litter. *Biotropica* 8:41–58.

Sharp, D. 1895. *Insects,* vol. 1. Cambridge Natural History, vol. 5. London and New York: Macmillan. Reprint New York: Dover, 1970.

Sheail, J. 1987. *Seventy-five Years in Ecology: The British Ecological Society.* Oxford: Blackwell Scientific.

Sheil, D. 1996. Species richness, tropical forest dynamics, and sampling: Questioning cause and effect. *Oikos* 76: 587–90.

———. 1997. Further notes on species richness, tropical forest dynamics, and sampling: A reply to Phillips et al. *Oikos* 79:188–90.

———. 1999. Tropical forest diversity, environmental change, and species augmentation: The intermediate disturbance hypothesis. *J Veget Sci* 10:851–60.

Sheppard, P. M., J. R. G. Turner, K. S. Brown, W. W. Benson, and M. C. Singer. 1985. Genetics and the evolution of Müllerian mimicry in *Heliconius* butterflies. *Philosophical Trans Royal Soc London,* ser. B, 308:433–613.

Simberloff, D. 1986. Are we on the verge of a mass extinction in tropical rain forests? In *Dynamics of Extinctions,* ed. D. K. Elliot, 165–80. New York: Wiley.

———. 1992. Do species-area curves predict extinction in fragmented forest? In *Tropical Deforestation and Species Extinction,* ed. T. C. Whitmore and J. A. Sayer, 75–89. London: Chapman and Hall.

Simms, E. L. 1990. Examining selection on the multivariate phenotype: Plant resistance to herbivores. *Evolution* 44:1177–88.

Simpson, G. G. 1950. History of the fauna of Latin America. *Am Sci* 38, 361–89.

———. 1964. Species density of North American recent mammals. *Syst Zool* 13:57–73.

———. 1980. *Splended Isolation: The Curious History of South American Mammals.* New Haven: Yale Univ. Press.

Sirks, M. J. 1945. Rumphius, the blind seer of Amboina. In

Science and Scientists in the Netherlands Indies. New York: Board for the Netherlands Indies, Surinam and Curaçao of New York City.

Skole, D., and C. J. Tucker. 1993. Tropical deforestation and habitat fragmentation in the Amazon: Satellite data from 1988 to 1998. *Science* 260:1905–10.

Skutch, A. F. 1950. The nesting seasons of Central American birds in relation to climate and food supply. *Ibis* 92:185–222.

———. 1954. *Life Histories of Central American Birds.* Pacific Coast Avifauna, vol. 34. Berkeley: Cooper Ornithological Society.

Smith, A. G., and Briden, J. C. 1977. *Mesozoic and Cenozoic Palaeocontinental Maps.* Cambridge: Cambridge University Press.

Smith, A. G., D. G. Smith, and B. M. Funnell. 1994. *Atlas of Mesozoic and Cenozoic Coastlines.* Cambridge: Cambridge University Press.

Smith, A. P. 1997. Deforestation, fragmentation, and reserve design in western Madagascar. In *Tropical Forest Remnants, Ecology, Management and Conservation of Fragmented Communities,* ed. W. F. Lawrence and R. O. Bierregaard Jr., 415–41. Chicago: University of Chicago Press.

Smith, C. M., and J. L. Bronstein. 1996. Site variation in reproductive synchrony in three Neotropical figs. *J Biogeogr* 23:477–86.

Smith, D. A. S. 1979. The significance of beak marks on the wings of an aposematic, distasteful, and polymorphic butterfly. *Nature* 281:215–16.

Snow, D. W. 1965. A possible selective factor in the evolution of fruiting seasons in tropical forest. *Oikos* 15:274–81.

———. 1971. Evolutionary aspects of fruit-eating by birds. *Ibis* 113:194–202.

Sobrado, M. A., and E. Medina. 1980. General morphology, anatomical structure, and nutrient content of sclerophyllous leaves of the "Bana" vegetation of Amazonas. *Oecologia* 45:341–45.

Sork, V. L. 1987. Effects of predation and light on seedling establishment of *Gustavia superba. Ecology* 68:1341–50.

Sosa, V., and T. Platas. 1998. Extinction and persistence of rare orchids in Veracruz, Mexico. *Conserv Biol* 12:451–55.

Soulé, M. E., ed. 1986. *Conservation Biology: The Science of Scarcity and Diversity.* Sunderland, Mass.: Sinauer Associates.

Spencer, H., G. Weiblen, and B. Flick. 1996. Phenology of *Ficus variegata* in a seasonal wet tropical forest at Cape Tribulation, Australia. *J Biogeogr* 23:467–76.

Sponsel, L. E., T. N. Headland, and R. C. Bailey, eds. 1996. *Tropical Deforestation: The Human Dimension.* New York: Columbia University Press.

Spruce, R. 1908. *Notes of a Botanist on the Amazon and Andes.* Vols. 1 and 2. Edited and condensed by A. R. Wallace. London: Macmillan.

Srivastava, D. S., and J. H. Lawton. 1998. Why more productive sites have more species: An experimental test of theory using tree-hole communities. *Am Nat* 152:510–29.

Stearn, W. T. 1968. Alexander von Humboldt and plant geography. In *Humboldt, Bonpland, Kunth, and Tropical American Botany,* ed. W. T. Stearn, 116–20. Lehre: Verlag von J. Cramer.

Steenis, C. G. G. J. van. 1936. On the origin of the Malaysia mountain flora. Part 3. Analysis of floristical relationships. *Bull Jard Bot Btzg* (ser. 3) 14:56–72.

———. 1958. Rejuvenation as a factor for judging the status of vegetation types: The biological nomad theory. In *Study of Tropical Vegetation* (Proceedings of the Kandy Symposium, UNESCO, Paris), 212–18.

———. 1962. The land-bridge theory in botany. *Blumea* 11:235–372.

Stehli, F. G., and D. S. Webb. 1985a. A kaleidoscope of plates, faunal and floral dispersals, and sea level changes. In *The Great American Biotic Interchange,* ed. F. G. Stehli and D. S. Webb, 3–16. New York: Plenum.

———, eds. 1985b. *The Great American Biotic Interchange.* New York: Plenum.

Sternberg, J. G., G. P. Waldbauer, and M. R. Jeffords. 1977. Batesian mimicry: Selective advantage of color pattern. *Science* 195:681–83.

Stevens, G. C. 1989. The latitudinal gradient in geographical range: How so many species coexist in the tropics. *Am Nat* 133:240–56.

Stiles, F. G. 1975. Ecology, flowering phenology, and hummingbird pollination of some Costa Rican *Heliconia* species. *Ecology* 56:285–301.

———. 1977. Coadapted competitors: The flowering seasons of hummingbird-pollinated plants in a tropical forest. *Science* 196:1177–78.

Stiles, F. G., and L. L. Wolf. 1970. Hummingbird territoriality at a tropical flowering tree. *Auk* 87:465–92.

Stone, D. E. 1988. The Organization for Tropical Studies (OTS): A success story in graduate training and research. In *Tropical Rainforests: Diversity and Conservation,* ed. F. Almeda and C. M. Pringle, 143–87. San Francisco: California Academy of Sciences and Pacific Division, AAAS.

Stork, N. E. 1988. Insect diversity: Facts, fiction, and speculation. *Biol J Linn Soc* 35:321–37.

———. 1991. The composition of the arthropod fauna of Bornean lowland rain forest trees. *J Trop Ecol* 7:161–80.

———. 1993. How many species are there? *Biodiversity Conserv* 2:215–32.

Stuart, L. C. 1950. A geographic study of the herptofauna of Alta Verapaz, Guatemala. *Contrib Lab Vertebr Biol Univ Michigan* 45:1–77.

———. 1951. The herptofauna of the Guatemala plateau, with special reference to its distribution on the southwestern highlands. *Contrib Lab Vertebr Biol Univ Michigan* 49:1–71.

Sussman, R. W. 1974. Ecological distinctions in sympatric species of lemur. In *Prosimian Biology,* ed. R. D. Martin, G. A. Doyle, and A. C. Walker, 75–108. London: Duckworth.

———. 1977. Socialization, social structure, and ecology of two sympatric species of lemur. In *Primate social Development: Biological, Social, and Ecological Determinants,* ed. S. Chevalier-Skolnikoff and F. Poirier, 515–29. New York: Garland Press.

Sussman, R. W., G. M. Green, and L. K. Sussman. 1996. The use of satellite imagery and anthropology to assess the causes of deforestation in Madagascar. In *Tropical Deforestation: The Human Dimension,* ed. L. E. Sponsel, T. N. Headland, and R. C. Bailey, 296–315. New York: Columbia University Press.

Sutton, S. L. 1989. The spatial distribution of flying insects. In *Tropical Rain Forest Ecosystems,* ed. H. Lieth and M. J. A. Werger, 427–36. Amsterdam: Elsevier.

Sutton, S. L., C. P. Ash, and A. Grundy. 1983. The vertical distribution of flying insects in the lowland rain forest of Panama, Papua New Guinea, and Brunei. *Zool J Linn Soc* 78:287–97.

Svenning, J.-C. 1999. Microhabitat specialization in a species-rich palm community in Amazonian Ecuador. *J Ecol* 87:55–65.

Swaine, M. D. 1996. Rainfall and soil fertility as factors limiting forest species distributions in Ghana. *J Ecol* 84:419–28.

Swaine, M. D., and J. B. Hall. 1988. The mosaic theory of forest regeneration and the determination of forest composition in Ghana. *J Trop Ecol,* 4, 253–69.

Swaine, M. D., and Whitmore, T. C. 1988. On the definition of ecological species groups in tropical rain forests. *Vegetatio* 75:81–86.

Swanson, T. ed. 1995. *Intellectual Property Right and Biodiversity Conservation: An Interdisciplinary Analysis of the Values of Medicinal Plants.* Cambridge: Cambridge University Press.

Symington, C. F. 1943. *Foresters' Manual of Dipterocarps. Malay For Rec* 16. Reprinted with plates and introduction, Penerbit UniversitiMalaya, Kuala Lumpur, 1974.

Tatersall, I. 1982. *The Primates of Madagascar.* New York: Columbia University Press.

Tavakilian, G., A. Berkov, B. Meurer-Grimes, and S. Mori. 1997. Neotropical tree species and their faunas of xylophagous longicorns (Coleoptera: Cerambycidae) in French Guiana. *Bot Rev* 63:303–55.

Taylor, P. H., and S. D. Gaines. 1999. Can Rapoport's rule be rescued? Modeling causes of the latitudinal gradient in species richness. *Ecology* 80:2474–82.

Temminck, C. J. 1839–44. *Verhandelingen over de Natuurlijke Geschiedenis der Nederlandsche Overzeesche Bezittingen.* Leiden: S. en J. Luchtmans and C. C. van der Hoek.

Terborgh, J. 1971. Distribution on environmental gradients: Theory and a preliminary interpretation of distributional patterns in the avifauna of the Cordillera Vilcabamba, Peru. *Ecology* 52:23–40.

———. 1973. On the notion of favorableness in plant ecology. *Am Nat* 107:481–501.

———. 1977. Bird species diversity on an Andean elevational gradient. *Ecology* 58:1007–19.

———. 1983. *Five New World Primates: A Study in Comparative Ecology.* Princeton: Princeton University Press.

———. 1985. The role of ecotones in the distribution of Andean birds. *Ecology* 66:1237–46.

———. 1986. Keystone plant resources in the tropical forest. In *Conservation Biology: The Science of Scarcity and Diversity,* M. E. Soulé, 330–44. Sunderland, Mass.: Sinauer Associates.

Terborgh, J., R. B. Foster, and P. Nuñez V. 1996. Tropical tree communities: A test of the nonequilibrium hypothesis. *Ecology* 77:561–67.

Terborgh, J., E. Losos, M. P. Riley, and M. Bolaños-Riley. 1993. Predation by vertebrates and invertebrates on the seeds of five canopy tree species of an Amazonian forest. *Vegetatio* 107/108:375–86.

Terborgh, J., and J. S. Weske. 1969. Colonization of secondary habitats by Peruvian birds. *Ecology* 50:765–82.

———. 1975. The role of competition in the distribution of Andean birds. *Ecology* 56:562–76.

Thomas, C. D. 1990a. Fewer species. *Nature* 347:237.

———. 1990b. Herbivore diets, herbivore colonization, and the escape hypothesis. *Ecology* 71:610–15.

Thompson, J. N. 1994. *The Coevolutionary Process.* Chicago: University of Chicago Press.

Thompson, W. A., G. C. Stocker, and P. E. Kriedemann. 1988. Growth and photosynthetic response to light and nutrients of *Flindersia brayleyana* F. Muell., a rainforest tree with broad tolerance to sun and shade. *Aust J Plant Physiol* 15:299–315.

Tilman, D., and S. Pacala. 1993. The maintenance of species richness in plant communities. In *Species Diversity in Ecological Communities,* eds R. E. Ricklefs and D. Schluter, 13–25. Chicago: University of Chicago Press.

Trejo, I., and R. Dirzo. 2000. Deforestation of seasonal dry forest: A national and local analysis in México. *Biodiversity Conserv* 94:133–42.

Treseder, K., D. W. Davidson, and J. R. Ehleringer. 1995. Absorption of ant-provided carbon dioxide and nitrogen by a tropical epiphyte. *Nature* 375:137–39.

Tuomisto, H., and K. Ruokolainen. 1994. Distribution of Pterodophyta and Melastomataceae along an edaphic gradient in an Amazonian rain forest. *J Veget Sci* 5:25–34.

———. 1997. The role of ecological knowledge in explaining biogeography and biodiversity in Amazonia. *Biodiversity Conserv* 6:347–57.

Tuomisto H., K. Ruokolainen, R. Kalliola, A. Linna, W. Danjoy, and Z. Rodriguez. 1995. Dissecting Amazonian biodiversity. *Science* 269:63–66.

Turner, I. M. 1996. Species loss in fragments of tropical

rain forest. A review of the evidence. *J Applied Ecol* 33: 200–209.

Turner, I. M., and R. T. Corlett. 1996. The conservation value of small, isolated fragments of lowland tropical rain forest. *Trends Ecol Evol* 11:330–33.

Turner, J. R. G. 1982. How do refuges produce biological diversity? Allopatry and parapatry, extinction and gene flow in mimetic butterflies. In *Biological Diversification in the Tropics,* ed. G. T. Prance, 309–35. New York: Columbia University Press.

———. 1984. Mimicry: The palatability spectrum and its consequences. In *The Biology of Butterflies,* ed. R. I. Vane-Wright and P. R. Ackery, 141–61. New York: Academic Press.

Uhl, C., K. Clark, N. Dezzeo, and P. Maquirino. 1988. Vegetation dynamics in Amazonian treefall gaps. *Ecology* 69:751–63.

Valencia, R., H. Balslev, and C. Paz y Miño. 1994. High tree alpha-diversity in Amazonian Ecuador. *Biodiversity Conserv* 3:21–28.

van der Hammen, T. 1974. The Pleistocene changes of vegetation and climate in tropical South America. *J Biogeogr* 1:3–26.

Vandermeer, J. H. 1977. Notes on density dependence in *Welfia georgii* Wendl. Ex Burret (Palmae) a lowland rainforest species in Costa Rica. *Brenesia* 10/11:9–15.

Vandermeer, J. H., I. Granzow de la Cerda, D. Boucher, I. Perfecto, and J. Ruiz. 2000. Hurricane disturbance and tropical tree species diversity. *Science* 290:788–91.

van der Pijl, L. 1972. *Principles of Dispersal in Higher Plants.* 2d ed. New York: Springer-Verlag.

Van Schaik, C. P., J. W. Terborgh, and S. J. Wright. 1993. The phenology of tropical forests: Adaptive significance and consequences for primary consumers. *Annu Rev Ecol Syst* 24:353–77

Vásquez, R. 1997. *Flórula de las reservas biológicas de Iquitos, Perú: Allpahuayo-Mishana, Explornapo Camp, Explorama Lodge.* Saint Louis: Missouri Botanical Garden Press.

Velasco, J. de. [1789] 1841–44. *Historia del reino de Quito en la America Meridional, escrita por el presbitero.* Quito: Impr. del Gobierno.

Vitousek, P. M. 1982. Nutrient cycling and nutrient efficiency. *Am Nat* 119:553–72.

———. 1984. Litterfall, nutrient cycling, and nutrient limitation in tropical forests. *Ecology* 65:285–98.

Vitousek, P. M., and R. L. Sanford, Jr. 1986. Nutrient cycling in moist tropical forest. *Annu Rev Ecol Syst* 17:137–67.

Von Hagen, V. W. 1945. *South America Called Them: Explorations of the Great Naturalists.* New York: Alfred A. Knopf.

———. 1951. *South America: The Green World of the Naturalists.* London: Eyre and Spottiswoode.

von Martius, K. F. P. 1829–33. Flora brasiliensis. 8 vols. Stuttgart.

Vrba, E. S., G. D. Denton, T. C. Partridge, and L. H. Burickle, eds. 1995. *Paleoclimate and Evolution.* New Haven: Yale University Press.

Vuilleumier, B. S. 1971. Pleistocene changes in the fauna and flora of South America. *Science* 173:771–80.

Wadsworth, F. 1997. *Forest Production for Tropical America.* Agriculture Handbook 710. Washington: U.S. Department of Agriculture, Forest Service.

Wadsworth, F. H., and G. H. Englerth. 1959. Effects of the 1956 hurricane on forests in Puerto Rico. *Caribbean For* 20:38–51.

Wagner, T. 1998. Influence of tree species and forest type on the chrysomelid community in the canopy of an Ugandan tropical forest. In *Proceedings of the Fourth International Symposium on the Chrysomelidae,* ed. M. Biondi, M. Daccordi, and D. G. Furth, 253–69. Torino: Museo Regionale di Scienze Naturali.

Walker, L. R., N. V. L. Brokaw, D. J. Lodge, and R. B. Waide, eds. 1991. *Ecosystem, Plant, and Animal Responses to Hurricanes in the Caribbean.* Special issue of *Biotropica* 23:313–521.

Wall, D. H., and J. C. Moore. 1999. Interactions underground. *Bioscience* 49:109–17.

Wallace, A. R. 1853. *A Narrative of Travels on the Amazon and Rio Negro, with an Account of the Native Tribes, and Observations on the Climate, Geology, and Natural History of the Amazon Valley.* London: Reeve. Rev. ed. London: Ward, Lock and Co., 1889.

———. 1858. On the tendency of varieties to depart indefinitely from the original type. *J Linn Soc (Zool)* 3 (August 20): 53–62.

———. 1869. *The Malay Archipelago.* London: Macmillan and Co.

———. 1876. *The Geographical Distribution of Animals.* Vols. 1 and 2. Reprint, New York: Hafner, 1962.

———. 1878. *Tropical Nature and Other Essays.* London: Macmillan.

———. 1895. *Natural Selection and Tropical Nature.* London: Macmillan.

Wallich, N. 1829. *Plantae Asiaticae Rariores.* London: Treuttel Junr. and Richter.

Walter, H. 1936. Nährstoffgehalt des Bodens und natürliche Waldbestände. *Forstl Wschr Silva* 24:201–5, 209–13.

Walton, A. B., R. C. Barnard, and J. Wyatt-Smith. 1952. The silviculture of lowland dipterocarp forest in Malaya. *Malay For* 15:181–97.

Ward, P. 1969. The annual cycle of the yellow-vented bulbul *Pycnonotus goiavier* in a humid equatorial environment. *J Zool London* 157:25–45.

Ward, P. S. 1991. Phylogenetic analysis of ant-plant associations involving pesudomyrmecine ants. In *Ant-Plant Interactions,* ed. C. R. Huxley and D. F. Cutler, 335–52. Oxford: Oxford University Press.

Warming, J. E. B. 1892. *Lagoa Santa*. Copenhagen.
———. 1895. *Plantesamfund. Grundtraek af den okolo-giske Plantegeografi*. Copenhagen: Philipsen. Published in English as *Oecology of Plants: An Introduction to the Study of Plant Communities* (Oxford: Clarendon Press, 1909).

Watt, A. S. 1947. Pattern and process in the plant community. *J Ecol* 35:1–22.

Webb, C. O., and D. R. Peart. 1999. Seedling density dependence promotes coexistence of Bornean rain forest trees. *Ecology* 80:2006–17.

———. 2000. Habitat associations of trees and seedlings in a Bornean rain forest. *J Ecol* 88:464–78.

Webb, L. J. 1958. Cyclones as an ecological factor in tropical lowland rain-forest, North Queensland. *Aust J Bot* 6:220–28.

Webb, L. J., J. G. Tracey, and W. T. Williams. 1972. Regeneration and pattern in the subtropical rain forest. *J Ecol* 60:675–95.

Webb, L. J., J. G. Tracey, W. T. Williams, and G. N. Lance. 1967. Studies in the numerical analysis of complex rain forest communities. *J Ecol* 55:171–91.

Webb, S. D. 1991. Ecogeography and the Great American Interchange. *Paleobiology* 17:266–80.

Wells, D. R., 1969. A preliminary survey of migration, body weight, and moult in Siberian blue robins, *Erithacus cyane*, wintering in Malaysia. *Malay For* 32:441–43.

Wenny, D. G., and D. J. Levey. 1998. Directed seed dispersal by bellbirds in a tropical cloud forest. *Proc Nat Acad Sci USA* 95:6204–7.

Went, F. A. F. C., and F. W. Went. 1945. A short history of general botany in the Netherlands Indies. In *Science and Scientists in the Netherlands Indies*, ed. P. Honig and F. Verhoon, 390–402. New York: Board for the Netherlands Indies, Surinam and Curaçao of New York City.

West, S. A., E. A. Herre, D. M. Windsor, and P. R. S. Green. 1996. The ecology and evolution of the New World non-pollinating fig wasp communities. *J Biogeogr* 23: 447–58.

Westoby, J. C. 1979. Forest industries for socio-economic development. *Commonwealth For Rev* 58:107–16.

Wetmore, A. 1926. Observations of the birds of Argentina, Paraguay, Uruguay, and Chile. *Bull U.S. Natl Mus* 133: 1–448.

Wheeler, W. M. 1910. *Ants: Their Structure, Development, and Behavior*. New York: Columbia University Press.

Wheelwright, N. T., and G. H. Orians. 1982. Seed dispersal by animals: Contrasts with pollen dispersal, problems of terminology, and constraints on coevolution. *Am Nat* 119:402–13.

White, F. 1979. The Guineo-Congolian region and its relationships to other phytochoria. *Bull Jard Bot Nat Belg* 49:11–55.

———. 1983. *The Vegetation of Africa*. Paris: UNESCO Press.

Whitmore, T. C. 1973. Frequency and habitat of tree species in the rain forests of Ulu Kelantan. *Garden's Bull Singapore* 26:195–210.

———. 1974. *Change with Time and the Role of Cyclones in Tropical Rain Forest on Kolombangara, Solomon Islands*. Commonwealth Forestry Institute Paper 46. Oxford: Commonwealth Forestry Institute.

———. 1975. *Tropical Rain Forests of the Far East*. 1st ed. Oxford: Clarendon Press.

———. 1978. Gaps in the forest canopy. In *Tropical Trees as Living Systems*, ed. P. B. Tomlinson and M. M. Zimmermann, 639–55. New York: Cambridge University Press.

———, ed. 1981. *Wallace's Line and Plate Tectonics*. Oxford: Clarendon Press.

———. 1984a. Gap size and species richness in tropical rain forests. *Biotropica* 16:139.

———. 1984b. *Tropical Rain Forests of the Far East*. 2d ed. Oxford: Clarendon Press.

———, ed. 1987. *Biogeographical Evolution of the Malay Archipelago*. Oxford: Clarendon Press.

———. 1989a. Forty years of rain forest ecology: 1948–1988 in perspective. *GeoJournal* 19:347–60.

———. 1989b. Tropical forest nutrients: Where do we stand? A tour de horizon. *Mineral Nutrients in Tropical Forest and Savanna Ecosystems*, ed. J. Proctor, 1–13. Oxford: Blackwell Scientific.

———. 1993. Changing scientific perceptions of the Eastern tropical rain forests: A personal view. *Global Ecol Biogeogr Letters* 3:115–21.

———. 1997. Tropical forest disturbance, disappearance, and species loss. In *Tropical Forest Remnants*, ed. W. F. Laurance and R. O. Bierregaard, 3–12. Chicago: University of Chicago Press.

———. 1998. *An Introduction to Tropical Rain Forests*. 2d ed. Oxford: Oxford University Press.

———. 1999. Arguments on the forest frontier. *Biodiversity Conserv* 8:865–68.

Whitmore, T. C., and N. D. Brown. 1996. Dipterocarp seedling growth in rain forest canopy gaps during six and a half years. *Philosophical Trans Royal Soc London*, ser. B 351:1195–203.

Whitmore, T. C., and D. F. R. P. Burslem. 1998. Major disturbances in tropical rain forests. In *Dynamics of Tropical Communities*, ed. D. M. Newbery, H. H. T. Prins, and N. Brown, 549–65. Oxford: Blackwell Science.

Whitmore, T. C., R. Peralta, and K. Brown. 1986. Total species count in a Costa Rican tropical rain forest. *J Trop Ecol* 1:375–78.

Whitmore, T. C. and G. T. Prance, eds. 1987. *Biogeography and Quaternary History in Tropical America*. Oxford: Clarendon Press.

Whitmore, T. C., and J. A. Sayer. 1992. *Tropical Deforestation and Species Extinction*. London: Chapman and Hall.

Whitmore, T. C., and K. Sidiyasa. 1986. Composition and structure of a lowland rain forest at Torant, northern Sulawesi. *Kew Bull* 41:747–56.

Whittaker, R. H. 1975. *Communities and Ecosystems.* 2d ed. New York: Macmillan.

Wiebes, J. T. 1979. Co-evolution of figs and their insect pollinators. *Annu Rev Ecol Syst* 10:1–12.

Wight, R., and G. A. Arnott. 1834. *Prodromus florae Indiae orientalis: Containing abridged descriptions of the plants found in the peninsula of British India, arranged according to the natural system.* 8 vols. London.

Wilkinson, G. 1939. Root competition and silviculture. *Malay For* 8:11–15.

Williams, W. T., G. N. Lance, L. J. Webb, J. G. Tracey, and M. B. Dale. 1969. Studies in the numerical analysis of complex rain forest communities. 3. The analysis of successional data. *J Ecol* 57:513–35.

Willis, E. O. 1974. Population and local extinctions of birds on Barro Colorado Island, Panama. *Ecol Monogr* 44: 153–69.

Willis, J. C. 1922. *Age and Area: A Study in Geographical Distribution and Origin of Species.* Cambridge: Cambridge University Press.

Wills, C., R. Condit, R. B. Foster, and S. P. Hubbell. 1997. Strong density- and diversity-related effects help maintain tree species diversity in a Neotropical forest. *Proc Nat Acad Sci USA* 94:1252–57.

Wilson, E. O. 1958. Patchy distributions of ant species in New Guinea rain forests. *Psyche* 65:26–38.

———. 1959a. Adaptive shift and dispersal in a tropical ant fauna. *Evolution* 13:122–44.

———. 1959b. Some ecological characteristics of ants in New Guinea rain forests. *Ecology* 40:437–47.

———. 1961. The nature of the taxon cycle in the Melanesian ant fauna. *Am Nat* 95:169–93.

———. 1985. The search for faunal dominance. In *Taxonomy, Phylogeny, and Zoogeography of Beetles and Ants,* ed. G. E. Ball, 489–93. Dordrecht: Dr. W. Junk Publishers.

———. 1976. Which are the most prevalent ant genera? *Studia Entomol* 19:187–200.

———. 1988. The current state of biological diversity. In *Biodiversity,* ed. E. O. Wilson and F. M. Peters, 3–18. Washington: National Academy Press.

———. 1990. *Success and Dominance in Ecosystems: The Case of the Social Insects.* Oldendorf/Luhe, Germany: Ecology Institute.

———. 1992. *The Diversity of Life.* Cambridge: Belknap Press.

Wilson, E. O., and R. W. Taylor. 1967a. An estimate of the potential evolutionary increase in species density in the Polynesian ant fauna. *Evolution* 21:1–10.

———. 1967b. The ants of Polynesia (Hymenoptera: Formicidae). *Pacific Insects Monogr* 14:1–109.

Wilson, J. 1995. Introduction to *Personal Narrative of a Journey to the Equinoctial Regions of the New Continent* by A. von Humboldt, abridged and translated by Jason Wilson (London: Penguin Books).

Wolda, H. 1978. Seasonal fluctuations in rainfall, food, and abundance of tropical insects. *J Anim Ecol* 36:643–57.

Wolda, H., C. W. O'Brien, and H. P. Stockwell. 1998. Weevil diversity and seasonality in tropical Panama as deduced from light-trap catches (Coleoptera: Curculionoidea). *Smithsonian Contrib Zool* 590:1–79.

Wolf, L. L., F. R. Hainsworth, and F. G. Stiles. 1972. Energetics of foraging: Rate and efficiency of nectar extraction by hummingbirds. *Science* 176:1351–52.

Wong, Y. K., and T. C. Whitmore. 1970. On the influence of soil properties on species distribution in a Malayan lowland dipterocarp rain forest. *Malay For* 33:42–54.

Worthington, E. B. 1938. *Science in Africa.* London: Oxford University Press.

Wright, D. H. 1983. Species-energy theory: An extension of species-area theory. *Oikos* 41:496–506.

Wright, S. J. 1983. The dispersion of eggs by a bruchid beetle among *Scheelea* palm seeds and the effect of distance to the parent. *Ecology* 64:1016–21.

Wright, S. J., and M. Colley, eds. 1994. *Accessing the Canopy: Assessment of Biological Diversity and Microclimate of the Tropical Forest Canopy. Phase I.* Nairobi: United Nations Environment Programme.

Wyatt-Smith, J. 1959. Development of a silvicultural system for the conversion of natural inland lowland evergreen rain forest of Malaya. *Malay For* 22:133–42.

———. 1995. *Manual of Malayan Silviculture for Inland Forests.* 2 vols. 2d ed. Malayan Forest Records 23.

Yih, K., D. H. Boucher, J. H. Vandermeer, and N. Zamora. 1991. Recovery of the rain forest of southeastern Nicaragua after destruction by Hurricane Joan. *Biotropica* 23:106–13.

Yu, D. W., and D. W. Davidson. 1997. Experimental studies of species-specificity in *Cecropia*-ant relationships. *Ecol Monogr* 67:273–94.

Zimmerman, J. K., E. M. Everham III, R. B. Waide, D. J. Lodge, C. M. Taylor, and N. V. L. Brokaw. 1994. Responses of tree species to hurricane winds in subtropical wet forest in Puerto Rico: Implications for tropical tree life histories. *J Ecol* 82:911–22.

Contributors

Yves Basset
Smithsonian Tropical Research Institute
Apartado 2072 Balboa
Ancon, Panama

David F. R .P. Burslem
Department of Plant and Soil Science
University of Aberdeen
Cruikshank Building
St. Machar Drive
Aberdeen AB24 3UU
United Kingdom

Robin L. Chazdon
Department of Ecology and
    Evolutionary Biology
University of Connecticut
Storrs, CT 06269-3043
USA

Earl of Cranbrook
Great Glemham House
Great Glemham, Saxmundham
Suffolk IP17 1LP
United Kingdom

Julie S. Denslow
USDA Forest Service
Institute of Pacific Islands Forestry
23 E. Kawili St.
Hilo, HI 96720
USA

Rodolfo Dirzo
Instituto de Ecologia, UNAM
Ap. Post. 70-275
México 04510 D.F.
Mexico

David Lamb
Department of Botany
University of Queensland
Brisbane, Queensland 4072
Australia

Bette A. Loiselle
Department of Biology and
Director, International Center
    for Tropical Ecology
University of Missouri–St. Louis
8001 Natural Bridge Road
St. Louis, MO 63121-4499
USA

Robert Marquis
Department of Biology
University of Missouri–St. Louis
8001 Natural Bridge Road
St. Louis, MO 63121-4499
USA

Scott E. Miller
National Museum of Natural History
Smithsonian Institution
Washington, DC 20560-0105
and
International Centre of Insect Physiology
and Ecology
Box 30772
Nairobi, Kenya

Vojtech Novotny
Institute of Entomology
Czech Academy of Sciences
  and Biological Faculty
University of South Bohemia
Branisovska 31, 370 05 Ceske
Budejovice, Czech Republic

Douglas W. Schemske
Department of Plant Biology
166 Plant Biology
Michigan State University
East Lansing, MI 48824-1312
and
W. K. Kellogg Biological Station
3700 E. Gull Lake Dr.
Hickory Corners, MI 49060-9516
USA

Robert W. Sussman
Anthropology Department
Box 114
Washington University
St. Louis, MO 63130
USA

Michael D. Swaine
Deptment of Plant and Soil Science
University of Aberdeen
Cruikshank Building
St. Machar Drive
Aberdeen AB24 3UU
United Kingdom

T. C. Whitmore
Department of Geography
University of Cambridge
Downing Place
Cambridge CB2 3EN
United Kingdom